Chris Payne

SAMS

Teach Yourself ASP.NET in 21 Days

SECOND EDITION

SAMS
201 West 103rd St., Indianapolis, Indiana, 46290 USA

Sams Teach Yourself ASP.NET in 21 Days, Second Edition

International Standard Book Number: 0-672-32445-8

Library of Congress Catalog Card Number: 2002105533

Printed in the United States of America

First Printing: August 2002

05 04 03 02 4 3 2 1

Acquisitions Editor
Neil Rowe

Development Editor
Kevin Howard

Managing Editor
Charlotte Clapp

Indexer
Erika Millen

Proofreader
Michael Henry

Technical Editors
Mike Diehl
Mike Nishazaki

Team Coordinator
Lynne Williams

Multimedia Developer
Dan Scherf

Interior Designer
Gary Adair

Cover Designer
Aren Howell

Page Layout
D&G Limited, LLC

Contents at a Glance

Table of Contents

Foreword

Active Server Pages.NET, or ASP.NET, is Microsoft's latest version of its popular dynamic Web programming technology, Active Server Pages (ASP). ASP.NET, however, is much more than a simple upgrade from classic ASP: A new programming model and a plethora of brand-new tools are just two of the many new features of ASP.NET. The numerous differences between classic ASP and ASP.NET create a bit of a steep learning curve for developers moving from classic ASP to ASP.NET—a learning curve that this book will surely help to flatten.

Although having experience with classic ASP or another dynamic Web programming technology will aid in learning ASP.NET, such prior experience is not required. Each lesson's concepts are explained assuming that the reader has no prior ASP experience. However, if you have created Web pages using classic ASP, you'll appreciate the "That's Not ASP!" section at the end of each chapter. These sections highlight the differences between classic ASP and ASP.NET and are ideal for developers coming from a classic ASP background.

The new features in ASP.NET make designing dynamic Web pages quicker and easier than ever before. For example, ASP.NET offers developers a number of powerful Web controls, which are HTML-like tags that provide useful functionality, such as displaying a calendar, showing a random banner advertisement, and displaying an HTML table whose rows and columns contain data from a database. These Web controls allow developers to provide rich, W3C-compliant HTML with a minimal amount of coding. To get started with Web controls, refer to Day 5, "Beginning Web Forms."

Sams Teach Yourself ASP.NET in 21 Days breaks down the many complexities of ASP.NET into 21 essential lessons (with a couple bonus lessons thrown in for good measure). Each lesson contains useful information that you will be able to start applying to your Web applications immediately. With the abundance of new features in ASP.NET, this incremental teaching style is beneficial for those new to ASP.NET to get a quick jump start on this exciting new technology.

ASP.NET is an exciting new Web development technology that is going to take the world by storm. This next generation of Web development technology makes designing impressive Web sites an easy and fun process. If you're ready to get started with ASP.NET, you'll find *Sams Teach Yourself ASP.NET in 21 Days* an invaluable resource.

Happy Programming!

Scott Mitchell

`mitchell@4guysfromrolla.com`

`http://www.4GuysFromRolla.com`

About the Author

Chris Payne has had a passion for computers and writing since a young age. He holds a bachelor of science degree in biomedical engineering from Boston University. Chris supported himself through college by working as an independent consultant and by writing technical articles focused on Web development. Currently making his home in Orlando, Florida with his wife, Chris is working as a Web developer and continuing his career as an author of both technical and fictional material.

Dedication

To Eva Saravia, my wife, for her beauty, love, and support, and my brother, Daniel, for being excited about this book. —Chris Payne

Acknowledgments

First, I would like to thank Shelley Kronzek for her faith in me. Without her support, this book would never have been started with me at the helm, and certainly would never have been completed properly. Her motivational skills are unsurpassed, and she truly is a great person.

I'd also like to thank Scott Mitchell, for his help in getting this thing together, and for providing me with no-holds-barred criticism. This book was made immensely stronger by his help.

I couldn't forget to thank my other friends at Sams: Jim Terral, Elizabeth Finney, and all my other editors. You all were unbelievably patient with me, and the experience of working with you has enriched me.

A big thanks goes to my friends and family, for being patient while I was holed up trying to hit deadlines. Chris Assenza, without whom my writing career wouldn't be existent; the Saravia family (Carlos, Anita, Carlos Jr., and even Walter!) for putting me up (and eating my leftovers); Angie, Daniel, Austin, and Kaylee Canary for being the best of friends; Liz and Doug Miller just because; and many, many others.

We Want to Hear from You!

As the reader of this book, *you* are our most important critic and commentator. We value your opinion and want to know what we're doing right, what we could do better, what areas you'd like to see us publish in, and any other words of wisdom you're willing to pass our way.

As an executive editor for Sams Publishing, I welcome your comments. You can e-mail or write me directly to let me know what you did or didn't like about this book—as well as what we can do to make our books better.

Please note that I cannot help you with technical problems related to the *topic* of this book. We do have a User Services group, however, where I will forward specific technical questions related to the book.

When you write, please be sure to include this book's title and author as well as your name, e-mail address, and phone number. I will carefully review your comments and share them with the author and editors who worked on the book.

Email: `feedback@samspublishing.com`

Mail: Michael Stephens
Executive Editor
Sams Publishing
201 West 103rd Street
Indianapolis, IN 46290 USA

For more information about this book or another Sams Publishing title, visit our Web site at `www.samspublishing.com`. Type the ISBN (0672324458) or the title of a book in the Search field to find the page you're looking for.

Introduction

Welcome to *Sams Teach Yourself ASP.NET in 21 Days, Second Edition*! You most likely picked up this book because you're curious about building robust Internet applications. You've come to the right place! Throughout the next 21 days (and two bonus days), you'll examine every major aspect of Active Server Pages.NET, the Web-based programming framework from Microsoft: from how these pages look to how they are tied into the operating system.

ASP.NET is a technology that allows you to build and control dynamic Web pages easily. It is the next generation of Microsoft's Active Server Pages (which I'll refer to as *classic ASP*), and provides many enhancements to take advantage of new technology. With it, you can interact with databases, personalize Web pages for visitors, display pages on mobile devices (such as cell phones), and even build an entire e-commerce shopping site from scratch.

As you move through the tutorial-style lessons in this book, you'll discover just how easily these tasks can be accomplished. Not only will you see examples and learn how to build these and other applications, but you'll also gain the understanding to be confident in any endeavor you choose to pursue in ASP.NET.

This second edition is updated with the latest changes to the .NET Framework, and is completely compatible with the RTM version of .NET (build 3705 and higher). The examples and exercises have been updated as well. In addition, this edition more fully embraces C# with examples, discussion, and code.

Who Is This Book's Intended Audience?

This book is intended to bring beginners of ASP.NET to advanced levels. That description covers a large group of people. To fully absorb the lessons in this book, you need to be familiar with computer technology and terms (for example, how to navigate your hard drive or browse pages on the Internet). Previous programming experience is not required, but will help immensely. Knowledge of basic HTML is also a must.

Classic ASP developers will also benefit greatly from this book. Not only do I show you how to do advanced tasks in ASP.NET, but each day also has a special section—"That's Not ASP!"—that caters specifically to those who have such prior experience. These sections discuss the changes in ASP.NET from classic ASP, and provide examples that will help your migration to ASP.NET move more smoothly.

Most importantly, this book is for people who have a desire to build a strong Web presence (or even a simple home page) using the power of ASP.NET. If you've never built anything other than an HTML page, ASP.NET is the perfect place to start. It gives you tremendous power, and is easy to get started in. You'll be amazed at what you can do with ASP.NET.

What Do You Need to Know Prior to Reading This Book?

The only must-have prerequisites are a basic knowledge of HTML and some familiarity with your operating system. Each lesson will present, define, and explain new topics, so that you can grasp them and quickly move on.

That said, a knowledge of programming concepts will help you move through the book. If you have experience developing traditional applications, or even Web applications, you will be familiar with many of the concepts in this book, allowing you to proceed easier.

Also, no experience with classic Active Server Pages is necessary. Concepts that stem from this older framework are explained as if they were completely new, so anyone can learn them or possibly gain a deeper understanding of them.

What Software Do You Need to Complete the Examples Provided with This Book?

You will need to use either Windows 2000, XP, or Windows NT with Service Pack 6 to take advantage of most of the examples for this book. Some components of ASP.NET will function on Windows Me, 98, or earlier versions of Windows, but support is problematic, and trying ASP.NET with these operating systems is not recommended.

A Web server is required. This can range from IIS 5 to Personal Web Server. I'll show you in the first lesson how to go about setting up the server properly. Also, you'll need to get the .NET Framework SDK from Microsoft to work the examples. Again, setup is examined in Day 1.

Finally, to take advantage of the database examples, you'll need some form of OLE DB–compliant database system, such as Microsoft Access or SQL Server. Without it, you won't be able to play around with the related examples.

How This Book Is Organized

This book is divided into five parts (encompassing 23 days of lessons). The first week will be spent learning the fundamentals of ASP.NET: how to get started in it, how to build ASP.NET pages, and how to use Visual Basic.NET and C# to enhance your pages. We'll also take an in-depth look at the Web forms framework—an integral part of ASP.NET that makes developers' lives much easier. This week presents the foundation you'll need to continue.

The entire second week is spent on data manipulation techniques (after all, most people get into Web programming because they are interested mainly in database interactions). You'll learn how to set up your databases, how to retrieve information and display it in your ASP.NET pages, and how to modify that data. You'll learn about traditional databases, interacting with regular files, XML, and caching.

The third week rounds out your journey through ASP.NET by focusing on larger, application-level topics, such as debugging, componentizing, and configuration. These topics are necessary to build complete Web based applications.

Next, you'll spend a couple days examining topics that aren't central to learning ASP.NET, but might help you after you're through with the book. These include a complete analysis of a Web-based application, and how to use ASP.NET for mobile devices such as cell phones or PDAs.

Finally, the appendices provide a complete reference section for the topics covered in the book, as well as tips on how to avoid problem areas.

The book is organized in a tutorial style. Each day's lesson will build on the lesson previous to it, so it might be helpful to proceed in a linear fashion, although it is certainly not required. In general, topics are discussed first, followed by some examples (which are accompanied by analyses). Each day's lesson concludes with answers to commonly asked questions, a short quiz to test your new knowledge (no cheating!), and a few exercises for you to play with on your own. All these are carefully chosen to further your knowledge and extend your experience with the technology, but are in no way required to be completed.

Conventions Used in This Book

The following typographic conventions are used in this book:

- Code lines, commands, statements, variables, and any text you type or see onscreen appears in a `mono` typeface. **`Bold mono`** typeface is often used to represent the user's input.
- Placeholders in syntax descriptions appear in an *`italic mono`* typeface. Replace the placeholder with the actual filename, parameter, or whatever element it represents.
- *Italics* highlight technical terms when they're being defined.
- The ➥ icon is used before a line of code that is really a continuation of the preceding line. Sometimes a line of code is too long to fit as a single line on the page. If you see ➥ before a line of code, remember that it's part of the line immediately above it.
- The book also contains Notes, Tips, and Cautions to help you spot important or useful information more quickly. Some of these are helpful shortcuts to help you work more efficiently.

Finally…

I hope you have a wonderful time learning this exciting technology. With it, you can do many amazing things over the Internet, many of which are in high demand in the technology market. Without further ado, let's get on with the lessons!

WEEK 1

At a Glance

ASP.NET is a very complex topic, and therefore requires a very solid foundation. The first week of this book covers the basics of ASP.NET: what it is and what you need to get started, as well as the fundamental concepts of building ASP.NET pages. These topics will provide you with the concepts necessary for every ASP.NET application; consequently, you will use them very often.

Day 1, "Getting Started with ASP.NET," will be an overview of ASP.NET, including its companion technologies in the .NET Framework. You'll examine installation issues and how you'll be setting up your projects for the rest of this book.

You then dive straight into your first ASP.NET program in Day 2, "Building ASP.NET Pages," to whet your appetite for things to come. You spend a lot of time in Day 2 looking behind the scenes of your ASP.NET pages, which is vitally important for building more complex applications.

Day 3, "Using Visual Basic.NET and C#," discusses everything you need to know about VB.NET and C# to build your ASP.NET pages. You'll learn about control structures, variables, looping logic, and more. With these tools, you'll be able to make your pages do nearly anything!

Day 4, "Using ASP.NET Objects with C# and VB.NET," will be spent introducing and dealing with examples on some of the most common ASP.NET objects. These objects will add tremendous power to your pages.

Day 5, “Beginning Web Forms,” introduces you to the Web forms framework, which allows you to easily build and control user interfaces in ASP.NET. This framework consists of server controls, which are the building blocks of your UIs. This framework is also extensible, as you’ll see in Day 6, “Learning More About Web Forms,” where you’ll learn how to build your own server controls. Finally, in Day 7, “Validating ASP.NET Pages,” you’ll examine another class of server controls, the validation controls, which allow you to validate the input that users enter into your ASP.NET pages easily.

By the end of the week, you will have a solid grip on ASP.NET fundamentals, and be ready to dive into more advanced topics in the following weeks. You’re in for a fun ride, so let’s get started!

WEEK 1

DAY 1

Getting Started with ASP.NET

Welcome to the first day of your journey through Active Server Pages.NET! Also known as ASP.NET, this is Microsoft's way to build powerful Web sites that go beyond regular HTML pages. If you want to create Internet applications, you've come to the right place.

ASP.NET is a robust, easy-to-use solution for developing complex Web sites. Rather than building simple pages that are only for display, you'll create Web pages that visitors can interact with in wonderful ways. ASP.NET pages allow you to add a new dimension to the Web experience.

Today, you'll learn about the following:

- How the Web works with the client/server model
- What Active Server Pages.NET is
- How ASP.NET ties the client and server together
- What the .NET Framework is and how it ties in with ASP.NET

- What you need to get started building ASP.NET pages, and how to install the required software
- How to create ASP.NET pages
- How ASP.NET is different from traditional Active Server Pages

The Way the Web Works

The Internet is a wonderful thing. It allows people from all over the world to communicate with each other via their computers. This technology has brought about many new possibilities, including e-mail, instant messaging, and the World Wide Web.

Originally, Web sites were very simple. There were HTML pages on any topic you could imagine. People could share whatever they liked, and there was always an audience for it. Those early pages were static—visitors couldn't interact with them in any way.

The Web quickly evolved and new levels of functionality were added, including images, tables, and forms. This finally allowed visitors to interact with Web sites, giving rise to guestbooks and user polls. Web site developers began to build other neat little tricks into their sites, such as image rollovers and dropdown menus.

This allowed interactivity, but true dynamic content was still lacking. Then server processing was introduced. You could now interact with databases, process content, and determine new types of visitor demographics over the Web.

ASP.NET is a server technology that brings together the different pieces of the Web to give Web site developers more power than ever. But before we get too far into ASP.NET, let's take a look at how dynamic processing works.

Dynamic Processing

NEW TERM The Internet works on the *client/server model*. Two computers work together, sending information back and forth, to perform a task. The most common scenario is communication between a *server* (a computer that holds information) and a *client* (a computer that wants the information).

NEW TERM The client computer sends a request for information to the server computer. The server then responds to the client with the information that was requested of it. This paradigm is the *request/response model*, and it's an integral part of the client/server model.

A Web server is a computer that holds information about a Web site—its HTML pages, images, and so on. The client is the visitor to the Web site (specifically, the visitor's Web browser). Figure 1.1 illustrates this concept.

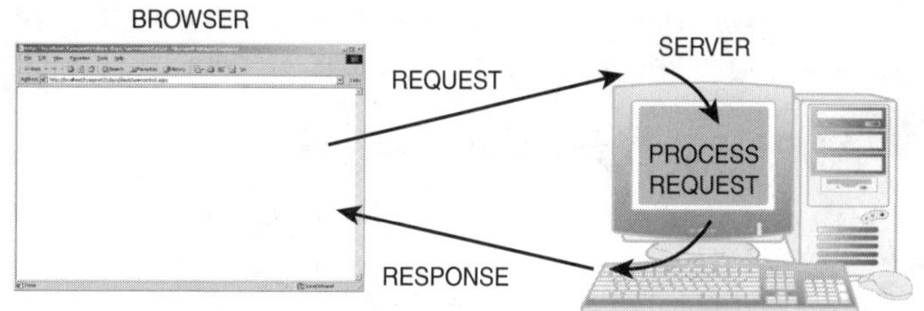

FIGURE 1.1
The request/response model.

Although this is a marvelous way to communicate and distribute information, it's rather simple and static. It can't provide any dynamic information or processing. The server simply waits around for someone to request information, and then it returns the data that's already stored on its hard drive without really looking at what it's sending. Generally, a static Web request follows these four steps:

1. The client (the Web browser) locates a Web server through its URL (such as `www.microsoft.com`).
2. The client requests a page (such as `index.html`).
3. The server sends the requested document.
4. The client receives the document and displays it.

Once the client has received the information, the process is finished. The server has no idea what's happening on the client. How could it, since the server and client are two separate computers? They only communicate with one another during the request response process. Once the page has been delivered, the server doesn't care what happens.

Enter server processing. This comes in many forms, including the common gateway interface (CGI) and Microsoft's Active Server Pages, which is now referred to as classic ASP. In this scenario, the server takes a look at what it sends before it sends it, and it can take orders from the client. The server can return dynamic data, such as that from a database, calculations it performs, and anything else the client may ask for. The modified work flow is as follows:

1. The client (the Web browser) locates a Web server through its URL (such as `www.microsoft.com`).
2. The client requests a page (such as `index.html`).
3. The server examines the requested file and processes any code it contains.
4. The server translates the results of the processing to HTML (if necessary) and sends the requested document to the client.
5. The client receives the document and displays it.

Even in this scenario, the process is over once the client receives the page. The server has no idea what the client is doing unless it makes another request.

The ASP.NET Difference

NEW TERM There's another model for communicating between servers and clients, known as the *event-driven model*. The server waits around for something to happen on the client. Once it does, the server takes action and performs some piece of functionality.

Imagine going to the library. If you followed the request/response model, you'd ask the librarian for information, and he would either give you the answer or point you in the right direction. In the event-driven model, the librarian already knows what you're doing. If you're writing a report and need information on Benjamin Franklin, the librarian brings you the correct items automatically. If you're thirsty, the librarian brings you a glass of water. If you trip and fall, the librarian brings you a bandage.

Of course, a Web server can't know what you're thinking, but it *can* respond to your actions. If you type some text on the Web page, the server responds to it. If you click an image, the server responds. This model is much easier for building applications than using a request/response scenario. ASP.NET works in this way—it detects actions and responds to them.

But wait a second! How can ASP.NET know what's going on in your computer? How can the server react to things happening on the client? ASP.NET relies on clever client-side processing to simulate an event-driven model.

Client-Side Processing

Client-side processing occurs when you place some programming code in an HTML page that the client can understand. This code is simply HTML that the browser executes. For example, take a look at Listing 1.1.

LISTING 1.1 Client-Side Code Is Executed with JavaScript

```
<html>
<head>
   <script language="JavaScript">
   <!--
      alert("Hello World!");
   // -->
   </script>
</head>
<body>
    Welcome to my page!
 </body>
 </html>
```

If you're familiar with client-side scripting or JavaScript, this may look familiar. When the browser receives this page, it treats the entire thing as HTML. The `<script>` tags denote a portion of the page that contains commands, known as script, for the client.

If your browser supports client-side scripting, it will understand that line 5 is telling it to display a message box to the user saying "Hello World!", as shown in Figure 1.2.

FIGURE 1.2
Client-side scripting allows you to interact with the client.

So now you have two places to execute code: on the server, where everything is returned to the client as HTML, and on the client. These two locations of code are distinct and cannot interact with each other. Table 1.1 outlines the differences between client-side and server-side code.

TABLE 1.1 The Differences Between Client-Side and Server-Side Code

Location	*Description*
Client side	This code isn't processed at all by the server. That's solely the client's responsibility.
	Code is written in scripts—plain-text commands that instruct the client to do something.
	Generally used for performing dynamic client effects, such as image rollovers or displaying message boxes.
Server side	This code is executed only on the server. Any content or information that this code produces must be converted to plain HTML before being sent to the client.
	Code can be written in scripts as well, but ASP.NET uses compiled languages (more on that later).
	Used for processing content and returning data.

How ASP.NET Ties It Together

So how does ASP.NET know what's going on with a client? Client-side script cannot interact with server-side code. However, ASP.NET cleverly skirts around this problem. The only way for a client to communicate with the server is during a request.

Using client-side script, ASP.NET supplies information about what the client is doing during requests. Going back to the library scenario, this is why the librarian seems to have magical powers that can detect whatever you need. He has a network of spies that observe you, even though you don't know it. When you do something, a spy quickly runs to the librarian to tell him what has happened. The librarian can then determine the correct course of action, such as bringing you a glass of water or a bandage.

ASP.NET's spies are client-side scripts. Whenever something happens on the client, a client-side script executes and sends information to the server, just as submitting a form sends information to a server. The browser is simply an unknowing accomplice. It thinks it's just doing its job displaying HTML. So, client-side scripts can't exactly interact with the server-side, but they can relay messages via posts to the server.

Thus, ASP.NET ties together the server and the client, which allows developers to do things in Web pages that weren't possible before. You don't have to focus on handling requests and responses, but are free to concentrate on building the logic. You can react to user events immediately instead of waiting until forms are submitted. And you can know the structure of the user interface (UI) and how to handle it ahead of time. ASP.NET truly makes developers' lives easier.

The .NET Framework

Where does the .NET in ASP.NET come from? It stands for the .NET Framework, a set of objects and blueprints from Microsoft for building applications. The .NET Framework provides the underlying functionality of ASP.NET.

All applications developed under the .NET Framework, including ASP.NET applications, have certain key features that ensure compatibility, security, and stability. Let's examine these features individually.

Common Language Runtime

The Common Language Runtime (CLR) is an environment that manages the execution of code. In other words, it runs and maintains any code that you write.

Traditionally, when you create an application, you write some code in a programming language (such as Visual Basic), compile it into a format that the computer can understand (1's and 0's), and then execute it. Note that different types of computers speak different languages (for instance, PCs and Macintoshes). This means that every time you want to use an application on a different type of computer, you have to recompile it to the new computer's language. In the .NET Framework, things work a little differently.

New Term With the .NET Framework and CLR, you still write code and compile it. However, instead of compiling it into something the computer understands, you compile it into a language called the Microsoft Intermediate Language (MSIL). This language is a shorthand way of representing all the code you've written. ASP.NET pages are compiled into MSIL as well. When you compile to MSIL, your application produces something called *metadata*. This is descriptive information about your application. It tells what the application can do, where it belongs, and so on.

> Along with MSIL and metadata, a new class of programming language compilers has been created—for C#, COBOL, Perl, and so on. These compilers are similar to existing ones, but now can output MSIL as well as compiled code.

Then, when you want to run your program, the Common Language Runtime takes over and compiles the code once more into the computer's native language. This way MSIL can go on any type of computer. The CLR can speak many different computer languages and does all the compiling for you. Once you compile your application, you can bring it to any other computer! Figure 1.3 illustrates the difference between the traditional process and the .NET Framework.

Figure 1.3

The traditional application framework versus the .NET Framework.

Traditional Method

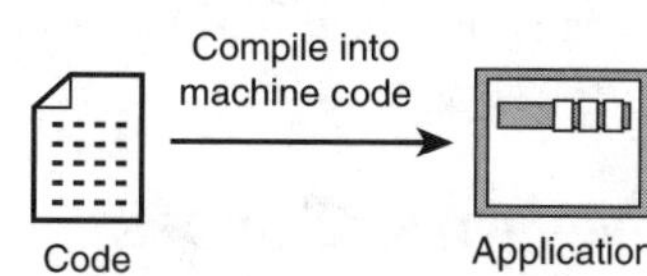

In the .NET Framework

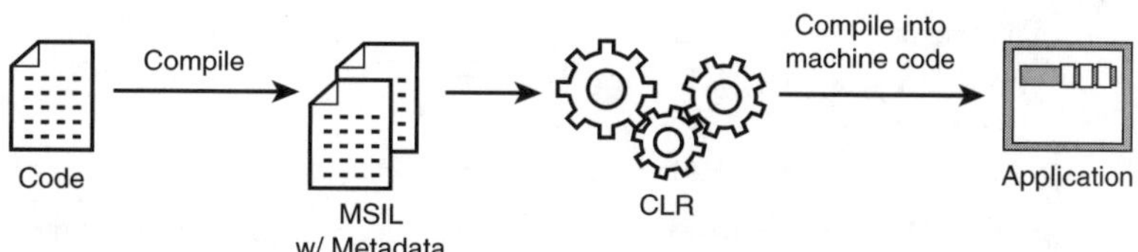

If you're familiar with the Java platform, you may see the similarities here. Java code is also translated and executed by a run-time environment called the Java Virtual Machine (JVM). This allows a developer to write code, compile once, and have the JVM handle any cross-platform issues.

The CLR uses the metadata to find out how to run the application, which makes it very easy to install programs. The traditional method required information about the application to be stored in a registry or a central depository for application information. Unfortunately, the registry would be invalidated whenever an aspect of your application changed (its directory was moved, a new component was installed, and so on), and the application wouldn't run properly. With metadata, there's no need for the registry. All necessary information is stored with the application files, so any changes you make are put into effect automatically. Imagine installing a new application just by copying some files!

NEW TERM Code that works with the CLR is called *managed code*. This is because the CLR manages its execution and provides benefits (such as resource management) without the developer having to build it manually. Code that's run outside of the CLR is known as *unmanaged code*.

That's not all the CLR does, however. It provides services such as error handling, security features, versioning and deployment support, as well as cross-language integration. That means you can choose any language you want to write your .NET applications, including ASP.NET applications!

.NET Framework Classes

NEW TERM The .NET Framework comes with blueprints that describe programming objects. Everything in the .NET Framework is treated as an object—ASP.NET pages, message boxes, and so on. These objects are placed into logical groups called *namespaces*. For example, all objects that deal with databases are in the `System.Data` namespace, all XML objects are in the `System.Xml` namespace, and so on. Grouping objects this way is a very useful way to build libraries of objects. You'll be using namespaces as you build your ASP.NET applications.

Again, you can see similarities to Java. The .NET namespaces are similar to Java packages.

Setting Up and Installing ASP.NET

To run ASP.NET pages, you need to have two things on your computer: Internet Information Server (IIS) and the .NET Framework Software Development Kit (SDK). These items are available for Windows 2000 and Windows NT 4 with Service Pack 6a.

Without these items, your computer won't know what to do with ASP.NET files. It will treat them as unknown items and ask you which application should be used to open them, as shown in Figure 1.4.

FIGURE 1.4

Without IIS and the .NET Framework SDK, your computer won't know how to handle ASP.NET files.

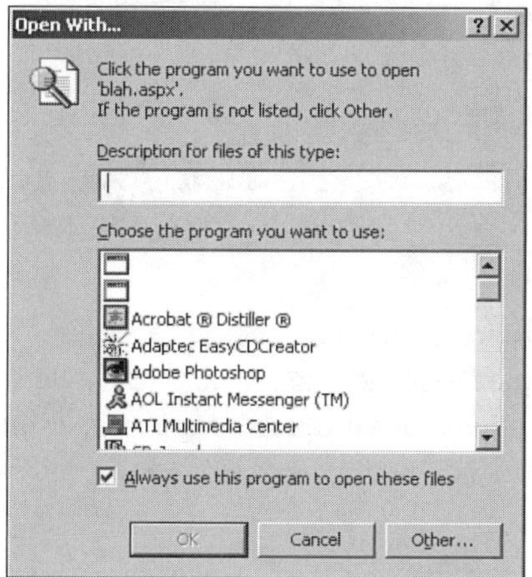

Recall that ASP.NET is a server-side technology, which implies that you need a Web server on your computer. Once you have one properly set up and running, visitors can request pages from your computer over the Internet.

ASP.NET pages require a bit more work to handle, however, because Web servers don't understand them. In addition, you need the .NET Framework SDK, which provides the functionality to run ASP.NET pages, as well as supplying the .NET objects and classes.

First, let's examine how to set up your Web server, and then we'll look at the .NET SDK.

Installing Internet Information Server

Internet Information Server is Microsoft's professional Web server that comes bundled with Windows 2000 and XP, or as a separate download for Windows NT Server. If you're running NT Server, download the NT Option Pack for free at `http://www.microsoft.com/msdownload/ntoptionpack/askwiz.asp`, and get started using IIS 4.0. If you have Windows 2000, you'll already have a copy of IIS 5.0, and for Windows XP, IIS 5.1.

To set IIS 5.0 or 5.1 up, go to Start, Settings, Control Panel, Add/Remove Programs, and then select Add/Remove Windows Components. You'll see a window that allows you to add optional Windows components (see Figure 1.5).

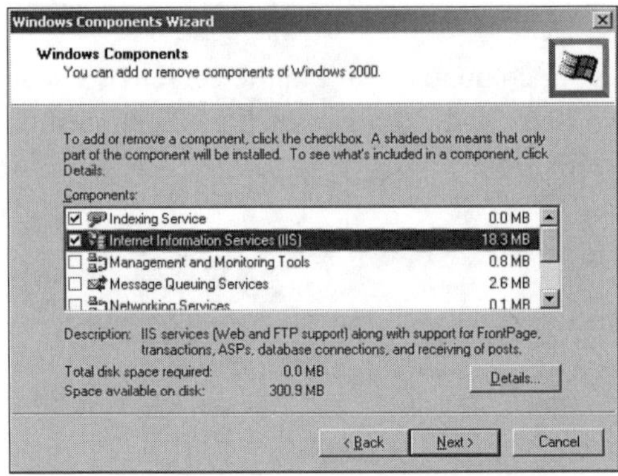

FIGURE 1.5

Installing and removing Windows 2000 components.

Select Internet Information Services (IIS) and click Next. Or you can click the Details button to install individual pieces of IIS, such as an FTP or SMTP service. You'd be fine just using the default options, but it doesn't hurt to install them all. Once you click Next, Windows 2000 (or XP) will gather some information and begin the installation process.

Congratulations, you now have a Web server installed on your computer! Open your browser and type `http://localhost`, and your Web site will open. The page that comes up is a default page created by IIS. You can also access your server by typing `http://computername`, where *`computername`* is the name of your computer. If you don't know the name of your computer, using `localhost` will work fine.

> Getting a domain name for your site, like `www.MySite.com`, is a completely separate process that is well beyond the scope of this book. Check out Network Solutions (`www.networksolutions.com`) for more information.

Let's access the Internet Services Manager (ISM), which allows you to configure IIS's settings. Go to Start, Settings, Control Panel, Administrative Tools, and then select Internet Services Manager. Figure 1.6 shows this application.

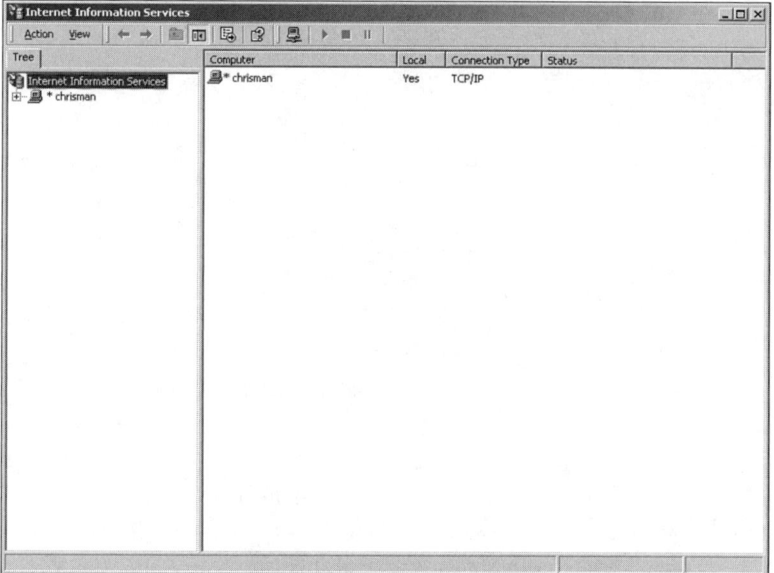

FIGURE 1.6
Configuring IIS with the ISM.

Tip

There *is* a shortcut to reach the ISM. Go to Start, Programs, Administrative Tools, and you should see it there as well. If you don't see Administrative Tools in this list, right-click somewhere on the taskbar and select Properties, Advanced. In the menu at the bottom of the window that pops up, you can choose to display the Administrative Tools.

This application shows the directory structure of your Web site, and the FTP and SMTP sites if you chose to install them. Expand the Default Web Site menu and you should see a few directories and files already there. Right-click on Default Web Site and select Properties.

There are a lot of options to play with, and you could spend a lot of time here. For now, you're only concerned with the Home Directory tab. Notice the Local Path box near the middle of this page, as shown in Figure 1.7. This defaults to `c:\inetpub\wwwroot`, also known as the *root folder*. When a visitor comes to your Web site, he's viewing the contents of this folder. Thus, if a visitor goes to `www.`*`yoursite`*`.com`, he's actually looking at whatever is in the `c:\inetpub\wwwroot` folder.

In fact, open My Computer from the desktop and go to your `C:` drive. You should see this directory now, if it wasn't there before. This is where you'll be placing all of your ASP.NET files.

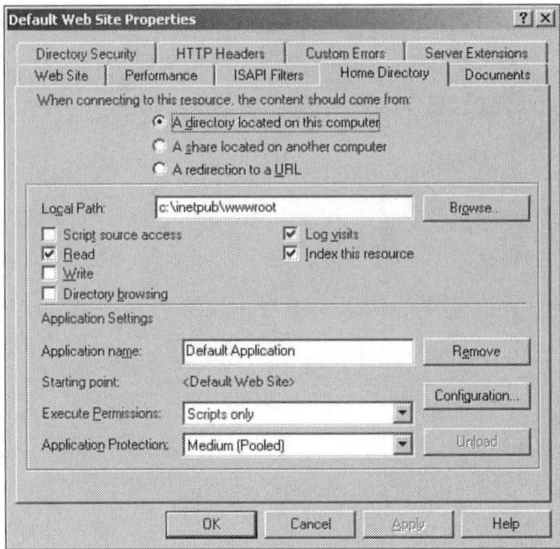

FIGURE 1.7

Viewing the Home Directory properties for the default Web site.

NEW TERM Click Cancel to go back to the ISM. All of the directories you see here are called *virtual directories*. (If you don't see any directories, don't worry because you'll create one in a moment.) A virtual directory is a folder on your computer that can be accessed through your Web site as though it were inside `c:\inetpub\wwwroot`.

To create a virtual directory, right-click on Default Web Site, go to the New menu, and select Virtual Directory. You'll see a wizard like the one in Figure 1.8. Click Next and type in an alias. This is the name of the folder that Web site visitors will type to access part of your Web site. Click Next once you've entered an alias. On the next page, choose the directory on your computer. This can be any directory, anywhere on your computer. The next page lets you choose some options, but for now, just click Next and then Finish.

FIGURE 1.8

The Virtual Directory Wizard lets you create virtual directories easily.

You should now see an item in the ISM with the alias that you created. If your directory name was `images`, you could now type `http://localhost/images` into your Web browser and view that directory's contents.

In most cases, virtual directories will be placed in the root folder—that is, at `c:\inetpub\wwwroot`. The interesting part is that the actual directory can be located anywhere on your computer, but visitors to your site can access it just as if it were at the root folder. Virtual directories are important for ASP.NET, as you'll see in the coming days.

Installing the .NET Framework SDK

The .NET Framework SDK contains the tools and applications that will allow ASP.NET pages to run. This includes the Common Language Runtime you learned about in "The .NET Framework" earlier today.

This SDK is free at `www.microsoft.com/NET`, but be aware that it's over 100MB and can take more than 6 hours to download on a 56KB modem. You can also order the SDK on CD-ROM for a nominal shipping charge.

Once you have a copy of the SDK, run the setup program. This process may take some time because Windows extracts files and gathers information (see Figure 1.9). Once Windows is done examining your computer, you should see a window similar to the one in Figure 1.10.

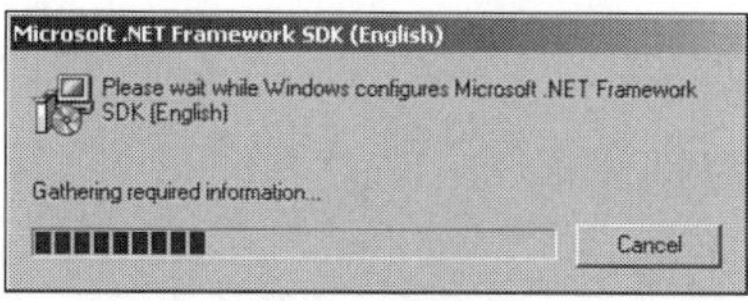

FIGURE 1.9
Setting up the .NET Framework SDK.

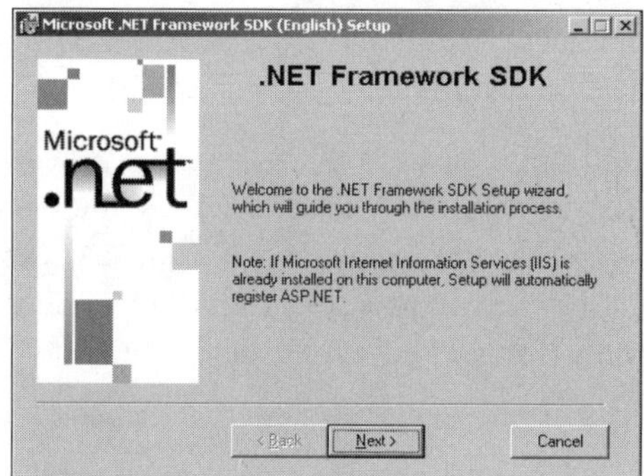

FIGURE 1.10
The .NET Framework SDK setup screen.

Click Next and accept the agreement, click Next again to select the components you want to install, click Next again to choose the directory to install to, and click Next one last time to install the .NET Framework. After it's done, a shortcut to the .NET Framework SDK Overview will appear on your desktop (if one doesn't appear, you can access the .NET Framework by selecting Start Menu, Programs). Click on this and go through it to find out more about the SDK. This shortcut also contains a link to the .NET Framework SDK Documentation, so be sure to check that out as well.

Create a text document called `MyPage.aspx` in your `c:\inetpub\wwwroot` folder. (`.aspx` means that this is an ASP.NET file. More on this in the next section.) Now try double-clicking on this file. You receive the window shown in Figure 1.4 again. What happened?

Recall that ASP.NET is a server technology, which means it requires a Web server in order to run. Therefore, ASP.NET files must go through a server to function (such as IIS). Now open your browser and type `http://localhost/MyPage.aspx`. You'll see the empty ASP.NET page.

Simply opening the ASP.NET page in your browser by clicking on the File menu, selecting Open, and navigating to the file won't work either. This merely tries to open the file in the browser without going through the Web server. You must go through the server by using `http://localhost`. This is a common mistake among beginners.

Now you're ready to begin running ASP.NET pages!

Creating ASP.NET Pages

ASP.NET pages are simply pure text, like HTML files. Once you have a Web server and the .NET Framework SDK up and running, you can easily create ASP.NET pages in any text editor you choose.

ASP.NET pages have the `.aspx` extension, so any files you want the server to interpret as ASP.NET pages must end in `.aspx`, such as `default.aspx`. Let's create a simple file to get started. Open Notepad (or your editor of choice) and type in the code in Listing 1.2. (Don't worry about understanding it yet. We'll get there soon enough.)

LISTING 1.2 Your First ASP.NET Page in VB.NET

```
<%@ Page Language="VB" %>

<script runat="server">
   sub Page_Load(obj as object, e as eventargs)
      lblMessage.Text = "Welcome to ASP.NET!"
   end sub
</script>

<html><body>
    <asp:Label id="lblMessage" runat="server"/>
 </body></html>
```

Listing 1.2 was written using VB.NET, but recall that you can use multiple programming languages to write ASP.NET pages. Listing 1.3 shows the exact same page using C#—we'll examine the differences in Day 4, "Using ASP.NET Objects with C# and VB.NET."

LISTING 1.3 Your First ASP.NET Page in C#

```
<%@ Page Language="C#" %>

<script runat="server">
   void Page_Load(Object obj, EventArgs e) {
      lblMessage.Text = "Welcome to ASP.NET!";
   }
</script>

<html><body>
    <asp:Label id="lblMessage" runat="server"/>
 </body></html>
```

Create a new directory named `day1` in your `c:\inetpub\wwwroot` folder and save this file as `listing0102.aspx` (or `listing0103.aspx` for the C# version). This page simply displays a welcome message to visitors. Open your Web browser and access this page with the URL `http://localhost/day1/listing0102.aspx`. You should see the window shown in Figure 1.11.

Throughout this book, you'll be creating a new directory for each lesson. Each directory will be placed in its own `c:\inetpub\wwwroot\tyaspnet21days` folder. For example, Day 2's ASP.NET pages will go into the `c:\inetpub\wwwroot\tyaspnet21days\day2` folder. This directory will then be accessible through the browser via `http://localhost/tyaspnet21days/day2`. This will make things easy to find.

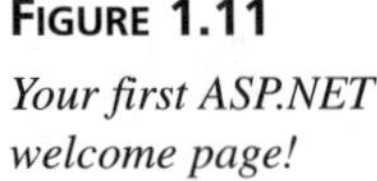

FIGURE 1.11
Your first ASP.NET welcome page!

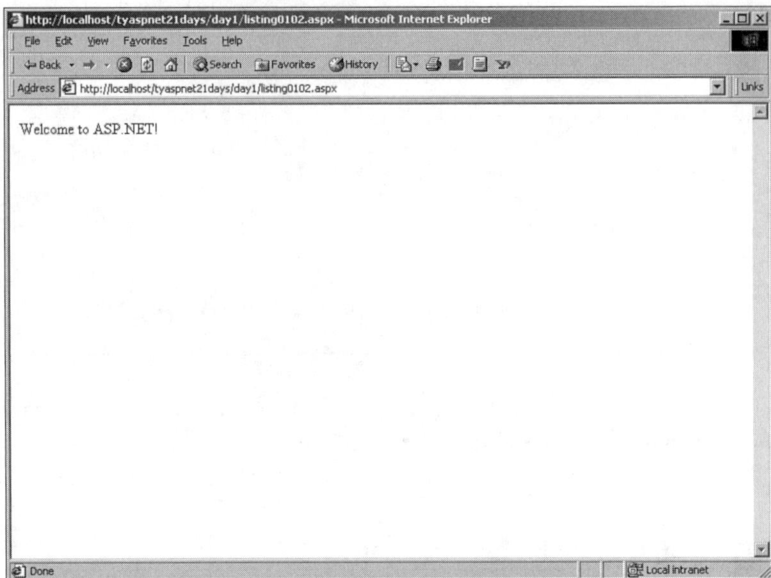

Remember that browsers can only understand HTML. Right-click on this output and select View source. You should see the code in Listing 1.4.

LISTING 1.4 The HTML from Your ASP.NET Page

```
<html><body>
   <span id="lblMessage">Welcome to ASP.NET!</span>
</body></html>
```

What happened to the rest of the code in `listing0102.aspx` (see Listing 1.2)? ASP.NET compiled it into MSIL, which was then compiled into machine language by the CLR and executed. The output from the execution is what you see in Listing 1.4. ASP.NET translated all of its output to HTML because it's the only language that browsers can read.

Development Environments

As much as you may like Notepad, it's not the ideal application for creating ASP.NET pages. It's easy and fast to use, but doesn't offer many features that would make ASP.NET development easier.

Microsoft Visual Studio.NET (VS.NET) is another commonly used editor. This powerful product allows you to manage entire Web sites, and it provides features such as creating and deleting virtual directories, working with databases, and dragging and dropping HTML components. It even color-codes your ASP.NET code to make it easier to read.

> **Note**
>
> Older versions of Visual Studio (6.0 and below) will work as well. However, they don't support the .NET Framework, so some features won't work correctly. For example, older versions won't color-code your ASP.NET code.

Another common environment is Microsoft FrontPage. This is a visual tool that allows you to create Web pages without having to write any HTML code. Unfortunately, it won't write ASP.NET code for you, so you'll have to do that yourself. For more information, check out *Sams Teach Yourself FrontPage in 21 Days*.

None of the pages you'll create in this book require more than Notepad, so the development environment is entirely up to you. The additional features provided by Visual Studio.NET and FrontPage may be of use, but these programs lack the sheer simplicity of Notepad. There are also quite a few non-Microsoft editors out there, such as HoTMetaL. Many of them don't yet support the .NET Framework, however, so they may not be as functional as the Microsoft editors.

Essentially, use what you are most comfortable with. This book will stick to Notepad because it is easy to use and is universally available. Visual Studio.NET and FrontPage are both commercial products that may be out of many people's budgets.

Elements of an ASP.NET Page

Let's examine a typical ASP.NET page, shown in Listing 1.5. This page displays a message to the user and a form that lets her enter her name. When she clicks the Submit button, she sees a customized welcome message.

LISTING 1.5 Interacting with the User

```
<%@ Page Language="VB" %>

<script runat="server">
   Sub tbMessage_Change(Sender As Object, E As EventArgs)
      lblMessage.Text = "Hello " + tbMessage.Text
   End Sub
</script>

<html><body>
    <font size="5">Sam's Teach Yourself ASP.NET in 21 Days:
```

LISTING 1.5 continued

```
      Day 2</font><hr><p>
      <% Response.Write("Our First Page<p>") %>

      <form runat="server">
         Please enter your name:
         <asp:textbox id="tbMessage"
            OnTextChanged="tbMessage_Change"
            runat=server/>
         <asp:button id="btSubmit" Text="Submit"
            runat=server/><p>
         <asp:label id="lblMessage" font-size="20pt"
            runat=server/>
      </form>
   </body></html>
```

Save this page as `listing0105.aspx` in the `c:\inetpub\wwwroot\tyaspnet21days\day1` directory. View it from a Web browser with the URL `http://localhost/tyaspnet21days/day1/listing0105.aspx`. Enter your name in the box and click Submit. You'll see a nice hello message, as shown in Figure 1.12.

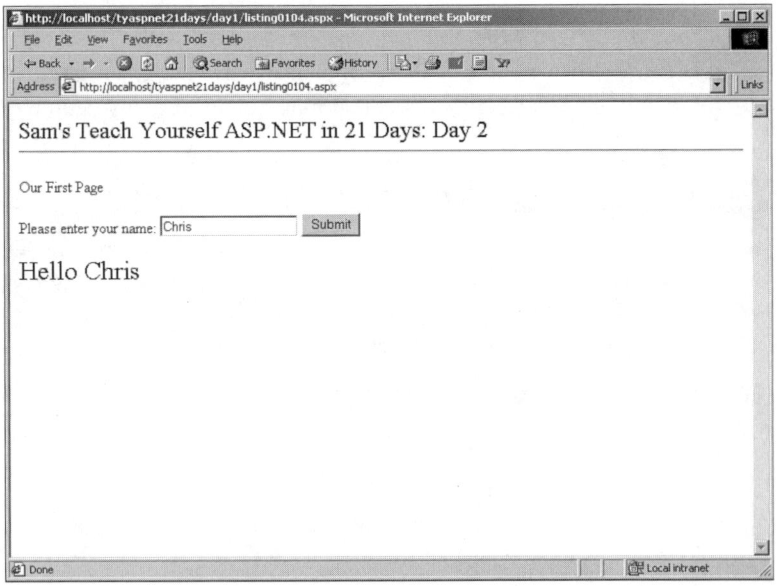

FIGURE 1.12

A simple ASP.NET page that displays a personalized welcome message.

ANALYSIS This page highlights the most common elements found in ASP.NET pages. On line 1 is the `<%@ Page %>` directive, which supplies the ASP.NET page with specific information that's used during the compiling process. In this case, you're telling ASP.NET that you're using the Visual Basic.NET programming language to write your code (you can use "C#" or "CS" to signify that you want to use C# for the programming language).

NEW TERM Lines 3–7 contain a block of code called a *code declaration block*. This looks similar to the client-side code that you learned about earlier today in "Client-Side Processing," but it includes a new tag, `runat="server"`. This is the code that ASP.NET uses to process its pages, and it's where you'll control all the functionality. This code is also compiled into MSIL.

> **Tip**
>
> If you're familiar with client-side programming, you know that typically a `<script>` block is placed in the `<head>...</head>` tags in HTML. These blocks, however, can be placed anywhere in the page, and placing them at the very top is a good way to keep your ASP.NET code separate from the HTML code.

NEW TERM Starting on line 9, you begin the HTML page. This is the content that will be sent to the browser (along with whatever your ASP.NET code spits out). Line 12 begins with `<%`. This is known as a *code render block*. It contains additional instructions that ASP.NET uses to produce output. In this case, it tells ASP.NET to write `"Our First Page"` to the browser. Code render blocks aren't compiled, and as such they're not as efficient as code declaration blocks. You'll be using them sparingly throughout this book.

NEW TERM On line 14 you have another traditional HTML element, but then there's that `runat="server"` again. When you specify this tag, the form becomes a *Web form*. Anything contained within a Web form can be watched over by ASP.NET. (Recall the analogy of the librarian and his spies.)

NEW TERM On lines 16, 19, and 21, you have a few new elements that look like HTML elements. These are known as *Web controls*. Often they perform very similarly to HTML elements, but with added functionality that ASP.NET can use. Notice that each of these items also has the `runat="server"` line.

That's your first look at an ASP.NET page. As you can see, the code is easy to read.

Comparison of ASP and ASP.NET

ASP.NET is a complete overhaul of traditional Active Server Pages. Therefore, it offers a very different methodology for building Web applications.

If you're familiar with classic ASP, you'll be glad to know that ASP.NET is much more powerful, offering developers a more efficient way to build Web applications. The following sections will discuss some of the general differences between ASP and ASP.NET.

Subsequent days will highlight these differences in sections titled "That's Not ASP!"

Note that although ASP and ASP.NET are completely different, they can operate side-by-side. That is, your Web server can serve both classic ASP and ASP.NET Web pages at the same time. Once you've installed the ASP.NET engine, you won't have to rewrite any of your old ASP pages (although you may want to do so and take advantage of ASP.NET's enhancements).

Fundamental Changes from ASP

Classic ASP was built on top of the Windows operating system and IIS. It was always a separate entity, and therefore its functionality was limited.

ASP.NET, on the other hand, is an integral part of the operating system under the .NET Framework. It shares many of the same objects that traditional applications would use, and all .NET objects are available for ASP.NET's consumption. Instead of being limited to the six inherent objects in ASP, ASP.NET has a plethora of useful components it can build from.

ASP also made it abundantly clear that client and server were two separate entities. Once ASP was finished with its work on the server, it passed the HTML to the client and forgot about it. ASP.NET ties together the client and the server through clever use of server-side and client-side code, all invisible to the developer. Web development is now much more like traditional application development than the disconnected request/response model that ASP development typified.

Furthermore, ASP.NET code is compiled, whereas classic ASP used interpreted scripting languages. Using compiled code means an automatic boost in performance over ASP applications. This makes ASP.NET pages much more like traditional applications, and they'll be treated that way throughout the book.

Because of these and other enhancements, ASP.NET puts a lot of power into the developer's hands. You'll see more of the differences as the book touches on specific topics.

Programmatic Enhancements Over ASP

Along with these fundamental changes, ASP.NET offers many programmatic enhancements, including caching, code compilation, and greater simplicity and security.

Perhaps one of the biggest enhancements in ASP.NET is its ease of deployment. As discussed earlier, metadata stores all necessary information for applications, so you no longer have to register Web applications or COM objects. When deploying classic ASP applications, you needed to copy appropriate DLLs and use `REGSVR32.EXE` to register the components. With ASP.NET, all you need to do is copy the DLL files. The .NET Framework handles everything else.

Session state was a very important concept in classic ASP. It's the ability to automatically determine if a sequence of requests is coming from the same client, mainly through the use of cookies. This session management made it easy to keep track of users and their actions. Easy-to-build shopping carts and data scrolling were born. However, as Web sites began moving to server farms (collections of servers all handling the same Web site) developers began to see the limitation of ASP-based session management. Namely, sessions weren't transferable across servers.

Session management has become much easier and more powerful with ASP.NET. ASP.NET addresses this issue by providing built-in session support that's scalable across Web farms. It also provides reliability that can even survive server crashes, and it can work with browsers that don't support cookies.

In classic ASP, nearly all of the code was executed in code render blocks (that is, inside `<%...%>` tags). In ASP.NET, this type of code isn't compiled and isn't recommended for frequent use. Instead, you use the code declaration blocks, which are compiled and provide better performance. Using these blocks also avoids having code and HTML interspersed throughout the page, which makes it very difficult to read through an ASP page. Code declaration blocks can be placed right at the top of the page, separated from the rest of the HTML, and they can still control the visual aspects of the page (see Listing 1.5).

There are many more programmatic enhancements that you'll learn about later in the book. You'll see that everything that was lacking in ASP is now fully implemented and easy to use in ASP.NET.

Differences in Programming Methodologies

Because ASP.NET ties the server and the client together in ways that weren't possible in classic ASP, developing ASP.NET applications requires a more intuitive approach. The developer no longer has to worry about remembering user state information or requesting input variables—it's all handled by ASP.NET. Instead, the developer can focus on responding to the user's actions without worrying about the details of the request/response model.

In addition, ASP.NET is now completely object-oriented. Classic ASP strove to introduce the concept of object-oriented programming (OOP), but was unable to because that was a fundamentally different programming paradigm. Developers who are comfortable with aspects of OOP will be happy working with ASP.NET, and those who aren't will find that it's easy to learn and intuitive to use.

ASP developers need not despair, though. Even though there are a lot of changes in ASP.NET, many of your hard-earned skills are still applicable. In fact, you'll see that ASP.NET makes things much easier for you most of the time. ASP.NET is a logical step forward in Internet programming.

Summary

Today you took a look at the fundamental concepts of the .NET framework and ASP.NET. After today, you should begin to see just how powerful ASP.NET is, and how it makes Web development much more efficient and robust.

To process ASP.NET pages, you need a Web server (such as Internet Information Server) and the .NET Framework SDK. These provide the tools and structure to execute ASP.NET pages. ASP.NET must be processed through a Web server or it won't work.

The .NET Framework is set of blueprints and objects. Applications developed within this framework are compiled into Microsoft Intermediate Language, and they produce metadata that describes them. The Common Language Runtime compiles the MSIL into machine code and uses the metadata to help execute the applications.

Today you examined some typical ASP.NET pages. You learned about the most common parts of an ASP.NET page, including the `<%@ Page %>` directive, code declaration and render blocks, and Web forms. These all provide the foundation for building complex ASP.NET pages.

Finally, you compared ASP.NET to its predecessor, Active Server Pages. ASP.NET provides a much better framework for building Web applications and is easier and more intuitive to use. It also provides many more programmatic enhancements. However, many classic ASP programming concepts still apply to ASP.NET, so ASP developers should have few problems moving to the ASP.NET.

The most important point to take away from today's lesson is that ASP.NET pages are a server technology that enables you to build dynamic Web pages.

Tomorrow, you'll develop your first ASP.NET application and learn why everything works the way it does. You'll also take a closer look at the .NET Framework and how it works together with ASP.NET.

But for now, get some sleep and have sweet dreams of ASP.NET pages!

Q&A

Q What's a .NET Framework class?

A A *class* is a blueprint that defines an object. It contains information on what an object should do, what its properties are, and so on. An *object* is something that you can manipulate—something tangible that can perform actions.

A .NET Framework class is simply any class that's part of .NET. For example, there's a class that defines how ASP.NET pages should act and look, and ASP.NET pages are objects that you can manipulate.

Q I thought ASP.NET was a programming language?

A Nope, ASP.NET is simply a framework for building interactive Web pages. This is a very common mistake among beginners. ASP.NET is like a book, which is simply a container for words. The writer uses English (or any other language) to create the book. Similarly, you use programming languages such as Visual Basic.NET and C# to write the code within an ASP.NET page. This code is what makes things happen, but ASP.NET provides the framework for the code to act upon and build from.

Workshop

This workshop will help reinforce the concepts covered in today's lesson. Answers can be found in Appendix A.

Quiz

1. What must ASP.NET do before it sends anything to the browser?
2. What does CLR stand for?

3. What is metadata?
4. What are three programmatic improvements of ASP.NET over ASP?
5. How does ASP.NET work with the client and server machines?
6. Why can't you simply double-click on an ASP.NET file to run it?
7. What is a virtual directory?
8. If you created a file called `hello.aspx` and placed it in the `c:\inetpub\wwwroot\tyaspnet21days\MyApplication` directory, how could you access it from the Web browser?
9. What's the difference between code declaration blocks and render blocks?

Exercises

What will be the output of the following ASP.NET page? Where would you save this file so users could access it?

```
<%@ Page Language="VB" %>

<script runat="server">
   sub Page_Load(Sender as Object, e as EventArgs)
      lblMessage.Text = "This is my first exercise!"
   end sub
</script>

<html><body>
    <asp:Label id="lblMessage" runat="server"/>
  </body></html>
```

WEEK 1

DAY 2

Building ASP.NET Pages

Yesterday set the stage for your adventures in ASP.NET. You looked at the new ASP.NET framework and how to get it running on your server. You also looked at ASP.NET's background and the history of the Web. Now that you know how to get ASP.NET up and running, it's time to dive right into development!

You've already learned about the parts of your first ASP.NET page. Today you're going to dissect that page and look under the hood. How exactly does ASP.NET work, and what does all the code mean? You'll also try your hand at creating some more code, which will give you the feel of developing ASP.NET pages.

Today's lesson will concentrate on a lot of the behind-the-scenes work of the .NET Framework to give you a full understanding of how this new architecture functions. This will make developing future ASP.NET applications much easier.

Don't worry if you're not already familiar with the programming concepts outlined today. Day 3, "Using Visual Basic.NET and C#," and Day 4, "Using ASP.NET Objects with C# and VB.NET," will cover these topics in depth. Today you'll just be getting your hands dirty!

Today's lesson will cover the following:

- The parts of your simple ASP.NET page
- How the page works
- How to distinguish between ASP.NET code and HTML
- Some ASP.NET coding syntax—comments and line breaks
- How the Common Language Runtime works with ASP.NET
- The different ASP.NET programming languages

A Simple ASP.NET Application

Let's take another look at a code listing from yesterday. Listing 2.1 shows a simple page that takes the user's input and prints out a message saying "Hello". This simple page has a lot of interesting features that won't be discussed in depth until later in this book, but today you'll look at the overall picture.

LISTING 2.1 Your First ASP.NET Page in VB.NET

```
<%@ Page Language="VB" %>

<script runat="server">
   Sub tbMessage_Change(Sender As Object, E As EventArgs)
      lblMessage.Text = "Hello " + tbMessage.Text
   End Sub
</script>

<html><body>
   <font size="5">Sam's Teach Yourself ASP.NET in 21 Days:
   Day 2</font><hr><p>
   <% Response.Write("Our First Page<p>") %>

   <form runat="server">
      Please enter your name:
      <asp:textbox id="tbMessage"
         OnTextChanged="tbMessage_Change"
         runat=server/>
      <asp:button id="btSubmit" Text="Submit"
         runat=server/><p>
      <asp:label id="lblMessage" font-size="20pt"
         runat=server/>
   </form>
</body></html>
```

Listing 2.2 shows the same page in C#.

LISTING 2.2 Your First ASP.NET Page in C#

```
1:  <%@ Page Language="C#" %>
2:
3:  <script runat="server">
4:     void tbMessage_Change(Object Sender, EventArgs e) {
5:        lblMessage.Text = "Hello " + tbMessage.Text;
6:     }
7:  </script>
8:
9:  <html><body>
10:     <font size="5">Sam's Teach Yourself ASP.NET in 21 Days:
11:     Day 2</font><hr><p>
12:     <% Response.Write("Our First Page<p>"); %>
13:
14:     <form runat="server">
15:        Please enter your name:
16:        <asp:textbox id="tbMessage"
17:           OnTextChanged="tbMessage_Change"
18:           runat=server/>
19:        <asp:button id="btSubmit" Text="Submit"
20:           runat=server/><p>
21:        <asp:label id="lblMessage" font-size="20pt"
22:           runat=server/>
23:     </form>
24:  </body></html>
```

Before examining the details of the page, let's take a test drive. Open either listing in your browser (`http://localhost/tyaspnet21days/day2/listing0201.aspx` or `listing0202.aspx`). Type your name into the text box and click the Submit button. You should see "Hello [your name]" in large letters under the text box, similar to Figure 2.1. (Notice that the text you entered is still in the text box after you click Submit. You'll learn about this later today in the "Viewstate" section.)

Web Forms

If you know regular HTML, this page should look pretty familiar. On line 9 of either listing is the opening `<html>` and `<body>` tags, and the corresponding closing tags are at the end of the listing. There are some new tags in the form, so let's take a look at that section, shown in Listing 2.3.

FIGURE 2.1

The page produced by Listing 2.1.

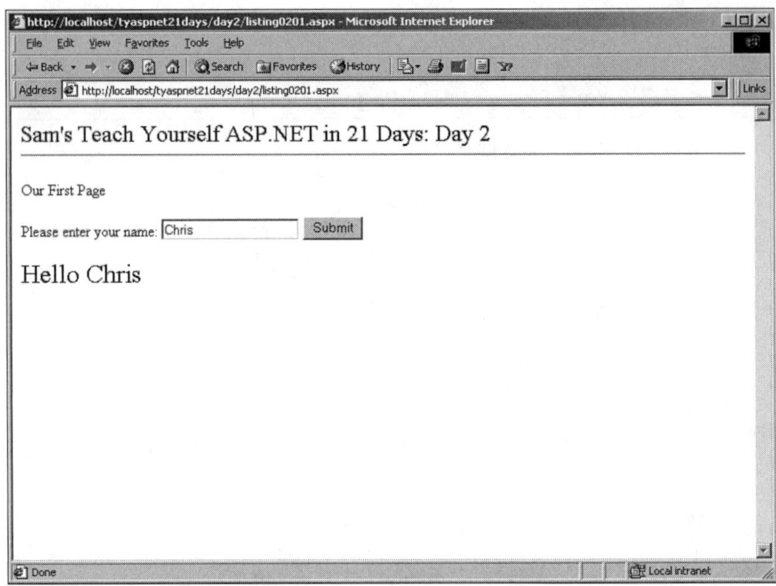

LISTING 2.3 The Form Section from Listing 2.1

```
<form runat="server">
   Please enter your name:
   <asp:textbox id="tbMessage"
      OnTextChanged="tbMessage_Change"
      runat=server/>
   <asp:button id="btSubmit" Text="Submit"
      runat=server/><p>
   <asp:label id="lblMessage" font-size="20pt"
      runat=server/>
</form>
```

NEW TERM Notice that you didn't specify an action for the form. Normally, you would specify an action to tell an HTML form where to go to take care of the user input—to process it or enter it into a database, for instance. If you don't specify the action, the form goes right back to itself. This is called a *postback form* because it *posts back* to itself. You can then include some ASP.NET code on this page to deal with the input.

ASP.NET uses postback forms extensively to process all of its user input. You'll become very familiar with this as you develop more pages.

The first new thing you'll notice is the `runat` keyword in the form tag. By specifying `"server"`, you're instructing ASP.NET that you want to keep track of this form on the server. Recall from yesterday that the server has spies that alert it to what's happening on the client. This keyword links the visitor's input to what the server thinks is going on. Without this attribute, the form will act as a normal HTML form. If you view the source of this file from the Web browser, you'll see something like Listing 2.4.

LISTING 2.4 Source from `index.aspx`

```
<form name="ctrl2" method="post" action="index.aspx"
   id="ctrl2">
<input type="hidden" name="__VIEWSTATE"
   value="YTB6LTEwNzAyOTU3NjJfX1949e1355cb" />
```

Not exactly what you typed in, is it? This will be explained further later today in "Viewstate." For now, just know that the ASP.NET engine inserts these HTML tags to help keep track of what's going on.

> **Caution**
>
> In case you're curious, specifying `runat="client"` in the `<form>` tag will not produce a normal HTML form. In fact, it will result in the error "Parser Error Message: The Runat attribute can only have the value 'Server'." If you want to create a regular HTML form, simply leave off the `runat` attribute.

Forms in ASP.NET that specify `runat="server"` are known as *Web forms* and are part of a framework that ASP.NET uses to provide much of the functionality for your applications. You'll learn more about these forms on Day 5, "Beginning Web Forms."

The next items of interest are the `<asp:textbox>`, `<asp:button>`, and `<asp:label>` tags. These are ASP.NET Web server controls, and each one has properties that you can use to provide functionality for your page. Again, if you view the source for this file from the Web browser, you'll see that the HTML equivalents of these ASP.NET controls are a text input, Submit button, and span tag, as shown in Listing 2.5.

LISTING 2.5 Source from `index.aspx`

```
Please enter your name:
<input name="tbMessage" type="text" value="Chris"
   id="tbMessage" />
<input type="submit" name="btSubmit" value="Submit"
   id="btSubmit" /><p>
<span id="lblMessage" style="font-size:20pt;">Hello
   Chris!</span>
```

Also notice the `id` attribute in each of the controls. This is a unique name that you provide for the control so that you can reference it from other places in the page. For example, the label has the ID `lblMessage`. Further down the page, you could create some code that asks, "What is the text inside `lblMessage`?" (In fact, you'll do something similar to that in the `<script>` block.)

Caution

> Don't forget to specify `runat="server"`! `runat="server"` is very important to ASP.NET pages. It tells ASP.NET that these items need to be processed on the server. Otherwise, ASP.NET would send the items straight to the client without any server interaction. And since browsers ignore any tags they don't understand, these items wouldn't be shown to the user. This is a very common mistake among ASP.NET beginners.

Tip

> ASP.NET is very insistent about making the developer write strict code. This means that all tags should have opening *and* closing tags, such as `<body>...</body>` and `<form>...</form>`. Therefore, you should also see `<asp:textbox>...</asp:textbox>` as well.
>
> However, here's a little shortcut. If you don't need to specify anything between the opening and closing tags, you can simply place a forward slash before the closing bracket, such as `<asp:textbox />`. Without the closing tag, ASP.NET will produce errors.

NEW TERM The text box you've built has another attribute, `OnTextChanged="tbMessage_Change"`. If you've worked with client-side scripting, this should look familiar. Your text box has an event called `TextChanged`. An *event* is something that occurs in your application, such as a mouse click or a selection change. The `TextChanged` event occurs when the content of the text box changes. By adding `OnTextChanged="tbMessage_Change"`, you're telling ASP.NET to execute the `tbMessage_Change` procedure on the occurrence of the `TextChanged` event. Unlike client-side scripting, however, these events are handled by the server.

This is the basis for the event-driven model. Generally, ASP.NET applications simply respond to user input. A lot of the code in an ASP.NET page will be dedicated to handling such events, and you'll see these types of procedures very often.

Code Declaration Blocks

Considering the `<script>` block next, you can see the procedure in Listing 2.6.

Listing 2.6 The Script Block for Your First ASP.NET Page

```
3:  <script runat="server">
4:     Sub tbMessage_Change(Sender As Object, E As EventArgs)
5:        lblMessage.Text = "Hello " + tbMessage.Text
6:     End Sub
7:  </script>
```


Again, if you're familiar with any form of scripting, you should recognize this section. The `<script>` tag is usually for client-side scripting. It delimits a section of the page that the application will process dynamically, called a *code declaration block* in ASP.NET. It isn't just rendered to the page like pure HTML, but contains programming code that should be executed by the computer. Don't forget to include `runat="server"`! Otherwise this code would be sent straight to the browser without being executed by ASP.NET.

Line 4 creates a Visual Basic subprocedure that performs some piece of functionality. From the analysis of Listing 2.3, you know that the text box uses this method when its `TextChanged` event occurs. There's a lot of syntax involved with this part, so we'll only cover the basics now. All you need to know is that whenever this procedure is called, it sets the `Text` property of the label named `lblMessage` to "Hello" plus the text of the text box, as shown on line 5. The result is that the page will now display "Hello [your name]!" The code `(Sender As Object, E As EventArgs)` on line 2 is a standard line that's required for most methods that handle events. This will be discussed in more detail on Days 5 and 6, and the Visual Basic code will be discussed tomorrow.

It's also important to use the `runat="server"` attribute to specify that the script block itself runs on the server. Otherwise, ASP.NET would treat it as client-side code, and it wouldn't produce the expected results. In this case ASP.NET would produce an error, as shown in Figure 2.2.

> You can actually place the `<script>` block anywhere in the page, but it's a good practice to separate it as much as possible from the presentation, or HTML, code. This makes it much easier to manage and debug your code if problems arise. Later you'll see how you can completely separate this code from this page altogether.

Code Render Blocks

Finally, let's look at line 12:

```
12:  <% Response.Write("Our First Page<p>") %>
```

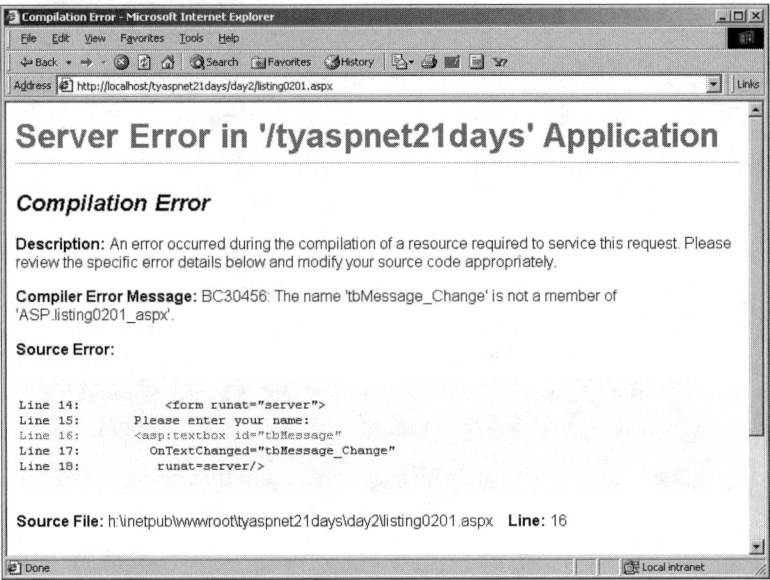

FIGURE 2.2

This error occurs if the `runat="server"` *attribute isn't used.*

This is a code render block. Between the `<%` and `%>` tags is VB code that the server processes before it sends the output to the browser. If you remove these tags, ASP.NET will treat the code as pure HTML and you'll get a page that looks like Figure 2.3.

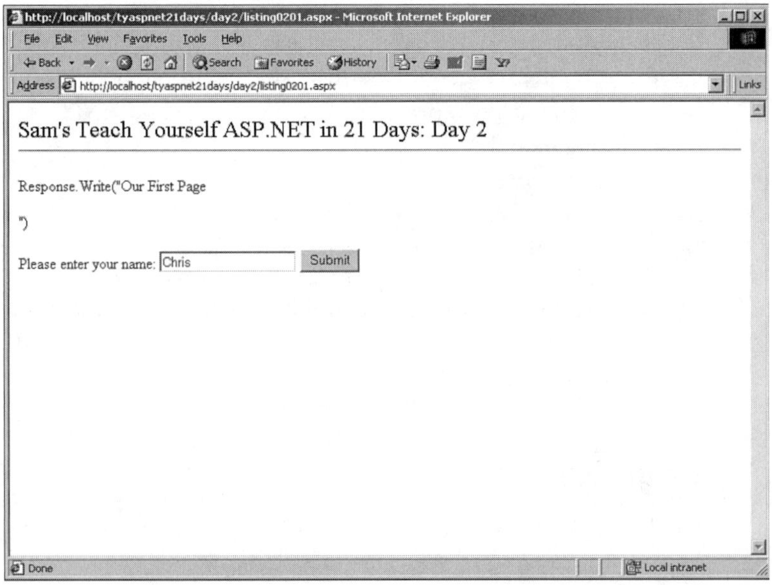

FIGURE 2.3

The page from Figure 2.1 without the `<%` *and* `%>` *tags.*

Line 12 uses the `Write` method of the `Response` object to print out some text to the browser. You'll examine this object and its methods on Day 4, but for now you just need to know that it provides an easy way to write text dynamically to the browser.

If the output of `Response.Write` contains any HTML tags, the browser will interpret them as if they were plain HTML. For example, if you used the following, "Our First Page" would be rendered in bold characters:

```
<% Response.Write("<b>Our First Page</b>") %>
```

Notice that all the characters to be rendered are enclosed in quotation marks. This is a simple example, but the method can produce some interesting output, as you'll see on Day 4.

Tip

There's a shortcut to using `Response.Write`—using the `<%=` tag. For example, the following two lines of code are equivalent:

```
<% Response.Write("Hello") %>
<% = "Hello" %>
```

You may see this syntax interspersed throughout ASP.NET pages, so you should be aware of its existence.

The code render block is very similar to the code declaration block. You could even place this line in the `<script>` tags and it would work similarly. There are a few differences between line 12 and the `<script>` block, however. The first is that the code declaration block is compiled into machine code (by way of MSIL), which makes it faster and more stable than the code render block. The second difference is that each of these blocks is processed in a different order. If you moved line 12 into the code declaration block, you might not receive exactly the same output as when it's separate.

For these reasons, you'll be using code declaration blocks much more often than code render blocks throughout your ASP.NET pages. The render blocks were the staple of traditional ASP, but they've been replaced with better mechanisms in ASP.NET.

Page Directives

Line 1 of Listing 2.1 specified the following:

```
1:  <%@ Page Language="VB" %>
```

This is called a *page directive*. It allows you to include special instructions to ASP.NET on how to handle your pages. This page directive in particular tells ASP.NET that you'll be using Visual Basic as the default programming language on your page. You'll learn how to use other page directives throughout this book. Later today, in "Importing Namespaces," you'll learn about the `import` directive.

If you wanted to use C# as the default language for an ASP.NET page, you could use the following page directive:

```
<%@ Page Language="C#" %>
```

Day 4 will look at C# in more detail.

The Flow

Now that you know what the code looks like, what happens when someone requests the page from his Web browser?

The first time you request a page, ASP.NET compiles the code in the page's code declaration blocks. If you noticed a slight delay before the browser displayed the page, this is probably the cause. If you request the page a second time without changing any of the code, there won't be any delay. If you change the code even slightly, however, ASP.NET must recompile the page. Even though this results in a slight delay initially, it provides a tremendous increase in performance after the first request. So how does the engine know when the code changes?

Remember reading about managed code on Day 1? This ASP.NET page is precisely that—some managed code that the Common Language Runtime is handling. The page is compiled into Microsoft Intermediate Language (MSIL), which is then compiled into native machine language when the page is requested. The actual source file that you created is stored separately, however, and the CLR keeps an eye on it. If it changes, the CLR recompiles the page.

Once the form is submitted and the code is compiled, ASP.NET starts to process all of the code you created and any events that have occurred. In this case, the `TextChanged` event occurred because you typed some text into the text box. The ASP.NET engine examines this event, determines what it should do, and does it.

ASP.NET then converts any server controls into HTML elements. For instance, it converts your `<asp:TextBox>` control into the HTML text input box. It then evaluates any of the code render blocks and outputs any HTML if necessary.

Finally, the resulting HTML is sent to the browser. The browser receives *only* standard, legal HTML—ASP.NET doesn't send any code or server controls to the browser. Therefore, *any* Web browser can visit and properly render an ASP.NET page. As far as the Web browser's concerned, an ASP.NET page is simply an HTML page with a slightly different extension. For instance, Figure 2.4 shows the HTML received by the browser.

FIGURE 2.4

The HTML source code received by the browser from Listing 2.1.

```
listing0201[1] - Notepad
File Edit Format Help

        <html><body>
            <font size="5">Sam's Teach Yourself ASP.NET in 21 Days:
            Day 2</font><hr><p>
            Our First Page<p><form name="ctrl0" method="post" action="listing0201.aspx"
id="ctrl0">
<input type="hidden" name="__VIEWSTATE"
value="dDwtMTA4MDU5NDMzODt0PDtsPDE8MD47PjtsPHQ8O2w8MTwxPjsxPDU+Oz47bDx0PHA8cDxsPFRleHQ7PjtsPENoc
mlzOz4+Oz47Oz47dDxwPHA8bDxUZXh0Oz47bDxIZWxsbyBDaHJpczs+Pjs+Ozs+Oz4+Oz4+Oz7pac6MWxbJoPM8WScFu7Scu
/868w==" />

      Please enter your name:
      <input name="tbMessage" type="text" value="Chris" id="tbMessage" />
      <input type="submit" name="btSubmit" value="Submit" id="btSubmit" /><p>
      <span id="lblMessage" style="font-size:20pt;">Hello Chris</span>
   </form>
</body></html>
```

This is an important concept to grasp. The browser is a dumb application, in a sense. It can only interpret HTML, and that's it. ASP.NET knows this, so anything that needs to be sent to the browser is converted into HTML. Luckily, ASP.NET is sneaky, and it knows ways to trick HTML into doing some processing as well. You'll learn more about this on Day 5.

Figure 2.5 outlines the workflow for a typical ASP.NET page.

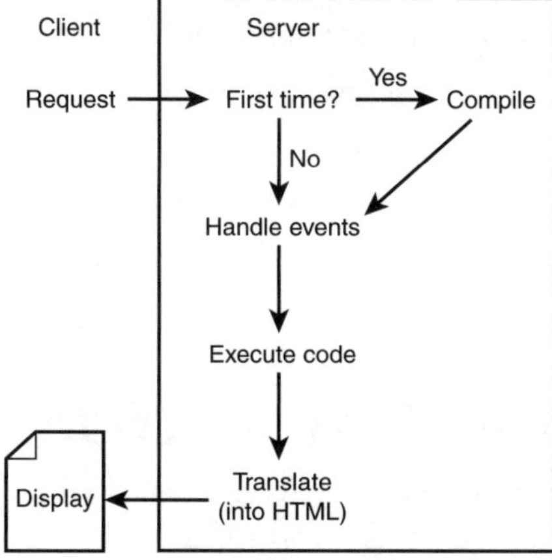

FIGURE 2.5

The ASP.NET workflow, from request to display.

This, in a nutshell, is how ASP.NET pages are processed and delivered.

Viewstate

The viewstate describes how an object looks at that particular moment. For example, the viewstate for the text box shown in Figure 2.1 contains the text "Chris", the viewstate for a button indicates whether or not it's being clicked, and so on. An application that keeps track of this information is said to *maintain state*.

If you fill out an HTML form and come back to it later, chances are the fields you've filled out will be empty. This is because the Web is a *stateless* medium—it doesn't allow you to keep track of viewstate or other such information. This was often a pain for traditional ASP developers because it required mechanisms to maintain and retrieve this information. ASP.NET makes this much easier.

ASP.NET automatically keeps track of the viewstate for you. This means that if you fill out an HTML form and click Submit, the values will still be there when the page comes back! This is an important part of ASP.NET and is integral to a number of different mechanisms.

ASP.NET does this by outputting hidden HTML form fields whenever you tell a form `runat="server"`. Remember the hidden field on line 3 of Listing 2.4? That string of seemingly random characters is ASP.NET's way of telling itself what each control looks like. When the form is submitted, ASP.NET automatically retrieves this string and uses it to fill out the form information again. ASP.NET uses the fact that browsers can only understand HTML and writes itself reminders in the pages that are sent to the client.

For example, look at the following line written on the server:

```
<form runat="server">
```

This sends the following HTML code to the browser:

```
<form name="ctrl2" method="post" action="listing0201.aspx"
   id="ctrl2">
<input type="hidden" name="__VIEWSTATE"
   value="YTB6LTEwNzAyOTU3NjJfX1949e1355cb" />
```

Viewstate management showcases ASP.NET's focus on making the Web a more traditional application environment.

Writing ASP.NET and HTML Code

With all this interspersed code and all these server controls, it may be difficult for you to figure out what's what in ASP.NET pages, and where to put it. This "spaghetti code" was one of the problems facing traditional ASP developers.

ASP.NET tries to simplify this as much as possible. There are two ways to write ASP.NET code: in code declaration blocks or in code render blocks. Thus, you should be able to pick out any ASP.NET code in a page easily. The first method is preferred for a number of reasons: It's compiled (unlike code render blocks), it eliminates the spaghetti code problem, and it's a better way to design your applications.

Everything else, then, is HTML. Even the server controls that you used in Listing 2.1 are written in the page as plain HTML. (True, these controls are objects on the server side, but their interface on the browser is described using HTML.) Even the event specifier, as shown on line 17 of Listing 2.3, is HTML. There are also a number of ways to write pure HTML using ASP.NET, such as `Response.Write` or the shortcut `<%=` tag.

Figure 2.6 shows the general way that you should try to structure your ASP.NET pages, with ASP.NET and HTML code grouped separately. If you use code render blocks in your HTML, it becomes much more difficult to maintain the ASP.NET code because it's all over the map.

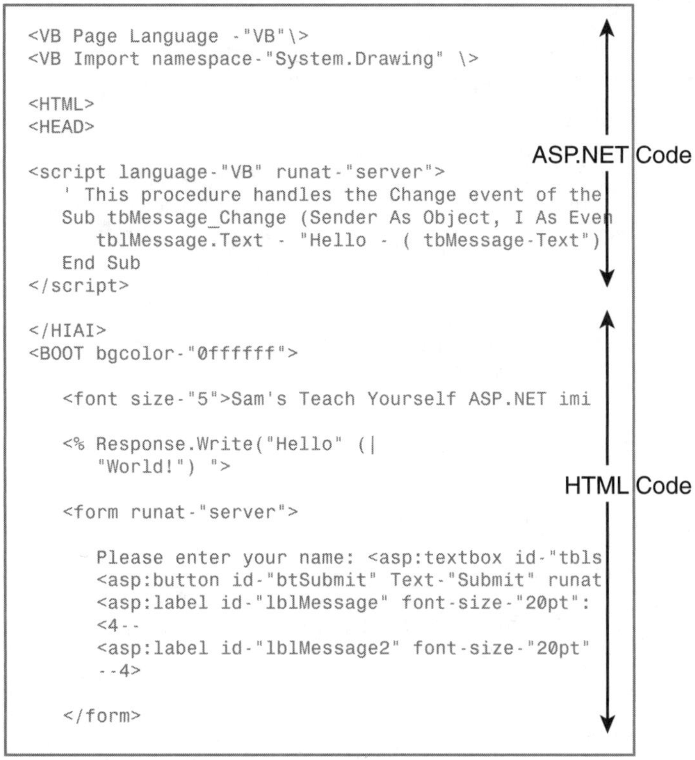

FIGURE 2.6

The ideal way to structure ASP.NET pages.

```
<VB Page Language -"VB"\>
<VB Import namespace-"System.Drawing" \>

<HTML>
<HEAD>

<script language-"VB" runat-"server">
   ' This procedure handles the Change event of the
   Sub tbMessage_Change (Sender As Object, I As Even
      tblMessage.Text - "Hello - ( tbMessage-Text")
   End Sub
</script>

</HIAI>
<BOOT bgcolor-"0ffffff">

   <font size-"5">Sam's Teach Yourself ASP.NET imi

   <% Response.Write("Hello" (|
      "World!") ">

   <form runat-"server">

      Please enter your name: <asp:textbox id-"tbls
      <asp:button id-"btSubmit" Text-"Submit" runat
      <asp:label id-"lblMessage" font-size-"20pt":
      <4--
      <asp:label id-"lblMessage2" font-size-"20pt"
      --4>

   </form>
```

ASP.NET Code

HTML Code

Do	Don't
Do separate your ASP.NET code from your HTML as much as possible by using code declaration blocks.	**Don't** use code render blocks to intersperse code or HTML output (using `Response.Write`) when another method may suffice. (And one often will!)

Commenting Your Code

Comments are lines in your code that don't affect its execution. These lines are inserted mainly for the benefit of the developer or anyone else who's trying to understand the code, although they can also be used to stop a piece of code from executing. The end user will never see the commented lines because they aren't sent to the browser.

Commenting your code will help you immensely when you develop more complex applications later on. They allow you to put the logic of your code into plain English, which is very helpful if you forget what it does.

In ASP.NET, there are three ways to comment your code. First, if you're familiar with HTML, you should know about the HTML commenting marks, `<!--` and `-->`. These can be used anywhere to comment out HTML only.

Within all ASP.NET code, you can use the commenting style of the programming language you're using. For example, with Visual Basic.NET, you can use a single quote to comment out one line at a time. Lines 3 and 4 of the following code snippet contain a comment.

```
1:    <script language="VB" runat="server">
2:       sub Page_Load(obj as object, e as eventargs)
3:          ' this method executes as soon as the ASP.NET page
4:          ' loads
5:          some code
6:       end sub
7:    </script>
```

C# uses two slashes:

```
<script language="C#" runat="server">
   function Page_Load(object obj, eventargs e) {
      // this method executes as soon as the ASP.NET page
      // loads
      ...
```

Finally, everywhere but in code declaration blocks, you can use the server-side comment marks `<%--` and `--%>`. Just as with HTML comment marks, these can be used to comment out multiple lines at once. Listing 2.7 shows all three commenting styles in action.

LISTING 2.7 Various Commenting Styles

```
<%
    ' this is a Visual Basic comment
    ' on multiple lines
%>
<!-- This is an HTML comment
on multiple lines -->
<%-- This is a server-side comment
on multiple lines --%>
```

> If you try to use the server-side comment marks (<%-- and --%>) in a code declaration block, you'll receive errors.

Code That Spans Multiple Lines

With HTML, it's easy to write code that spans multiple lines. For instance, the following two blocks of code are equivalent:

```
<b>Hello World!</b>

<b>Hello
World!</b>
```

With ASP.NET and Visual Basic.NET, however, it's not so simple. If you try to use the following, you'll receive an error:

```
<%
   Response.Write
      ("Hello World")
%>
```

This is shown in Figure 2.7.

Visual Basic.NET has introduced the line continuation character, denoted by an underscore (_). Let's modify the previous code a bit:

```
<%
   Response.Write _
      ("Hello World")
%>
```

This now produces the right output, without any errors. You'll be seeing plenty of these line continuation characters throughout this book!

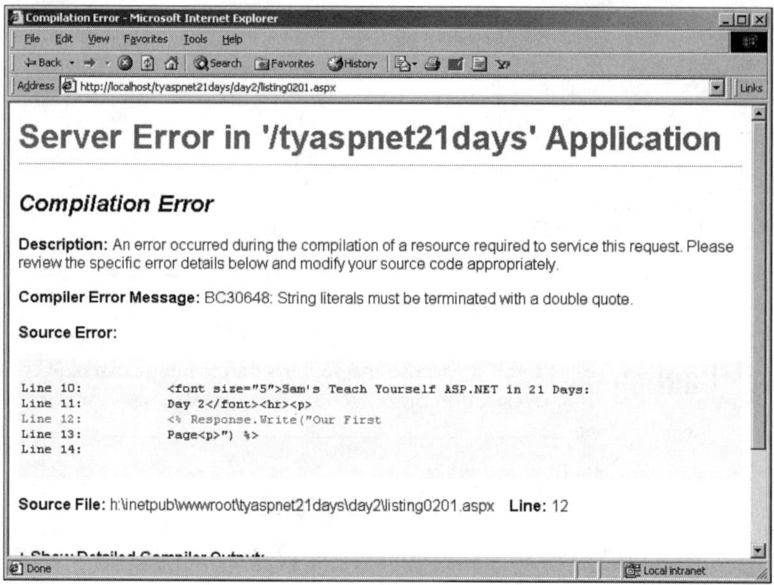

FIGURE 2.7
An error produced by spanning lines.

C# isn't limited by line breaks because each complete line in C# must be suffixed by a semicolon (;)—C# considers every line without a semicolon to be part of the following line. Thus, the following code snippets will work the same with C#:

```
<%
   Response.Write
("Hello World");

   Response.Write("Hello World");
%>
```

There's another thing to be wary about when you're using line continuation characters—they don't work in the middle of a string (even in C#). For example, the following will produce another error:

```
<%
   Response.Write("Hello _
      World")
%>
```

ASP.NET will interpret the character as an underscore in the text and will expect some more code. To break up a line containing a string, close the string first and then use the string concatenation character (the ampersand for VB.NET, or the plus symbol for C#) and the line continuation character:

```
<%
   'VB.NET
   Response.Write("Hello" & _
      "World")

   'C#
   Response.Write("Hello" +
      "World");
%>
```


The Impact of the Application

This small application may not seem like much, but it shows you the foundation upon which all other ASP.NET applications will be built. You've learned about the event-driven model, as well as Web controls, which are an integral part of ASP.NET. This application will teach you how ASP.NET and the rest of the .NET Framework interact, which will show you just how powerful this new Framework is.

Let's take a look at some more of the technical details, including where these items fall into the .NET framework. These details are important for developing ASP.NET applications and need to be covered early on.

More on ASP.NET Compilation

You can think of the .NET Framework as a set of blueprints for objects. For example, the `System.Web.UI.Page` object blueprint tells you the basics of what should be in an ASP.NET page and how it should function.

When you build and compile an ASP.NET page, then, it becomes an actual object based on the `System.Web.UI.Page` blueprint. It contains its own properties and methods, all derived from `System.Web.UI.Page`. Each ASP.NET page is simply another object based on this blueprint. In this way, each ASP.NET page extends the .NET Framework by providing some custom functionality. Your applications then become a defining part of the framework.

You're beginning to see just how powerful the hierarchical framework is and how it can be made much more powerful with your additions. If you find some feature lacking in the original framework, you can simply build it and add it as though it were always there!

There's also a blueprint for pure HTML called the `System.Web.UI.LiteralControl` class. Therefore, HTML is part of the .NET Framework as well. The objects based on the `System.Web.UI.LiteralControl` blueprint hold all literal values and are rendered to the Web browser as HTML text. This means that the HTML also has properties, methods, and events, just as other objects do.

Importing Namespaces

Each namespace in the .NET Framework is essentially a collection of blueprints. ASP.NET comes with its own blueprints, but sometimes this set is not enough. Therefore, you must reference other sets from your ASP.NET pages to build different types of objects. You can access these additional objects and methods by using the `Import` keyword:

```
<%@ Import Namespace="System.Drawing" %>
```

This line imports all of the classes of the `System.Drawing` namespace, such as the `font` and `image` classes. You can now use these blueprints for custom objects. You can also import your own user-defined namespaces. By default, the following namespaces are imported into every ASP.NET page automatically:

- `System`
- `System.Collections`
- `System.IO`
- `System.Web`
- `System.Web.UI`
- `System.Web.UI.HtmlControls`
- `System.Web.UI.WebControls`

These namespaces are part of ASP.NET. You don't have to import them explicitly, nor will you ever see the commands used to import them. ASP.NET knows that these namespaces are needed, so they're just there for you to use. Figure 2.8 shows a small sampling of the namespaces available in the .NET Framework.

Importing a namespace does *not* import the namespaces underneath it, however, as you can guess from Figure 2.8. Only classes that belong to that interface are imported.

You don't *need* to import a namespace to use its objects; it's just an easier way to do so. For instance, you can use the following in your ASP.NET page:

```
dim objFile as File
```

(Don't worry about the syntax just yet. The namespace portion is the important thing for now.)

The `File` is part of the `System.IO` namespace. Not importing this namespace wouldn't prevent you from using this object, however. You could use the following instead:

```
dim objFile as System.IO.File
```

In other words, you reference the object by using its entire namespace name. This tells ASP.NET exactly where to look to find this blueprint. Importing namespaces simply allows you to use the shorthand version for your blueprint names.

Occasionally, though, if there are two classes with the same name in two different namespaces, you will have to use the full namespace name anyway.

FIGURE 2.8

A small sampling of the .NET namespaces.

```
System
System.CodeDom
System.CodeDom.Compiler
System.Collections
System.Collections.Specialized
System.ComponentModel
System.ComponentModel.Design
System.ComponentModel.Design.Serialization
System.Configuration
System.Configuration.Assemblies
System.Configuration.Install
System.Data
System.Data.Common
System.Data.OleDb
System.Data.SqlClient
System.Data.SqlTypes
System.Diagnostics
System.Diagnostics.SymbolStore
System.DirectoryServices
System.Drawing
System.Drawing.Design
System.Drawing.Drawing2D
System.Drawing.Imaging
System.Drawing.Printing
System.Drawing.Text
System.EnterpriseServices
System.EnterpriseServices.CompensatingResourceManager
```

For a full listing of all the .NET namespaces and their properties, be sure to check out the extensive .NET Framework documentation that's bundled with the ASP.NET environment you're using.

Common Language Runtime and ASP.NET

Let's take a step back and quickly look at exactly how ASP.NET applications are handled by the CLR. You need to know what the CLR does so that you can anticipate any actions it will take on our code.

Intermediate Language

When an ASP.NET page is compiled, it's translated into the Microsoft Intermediate Language (MSIL). This is an efficient CPU-neutral set of instructions for controlling applications. Essentially, it's the programming code you wrote in a more compact form. You can't run or execute MSIL itself, but it can be easily converted to machine-native code for actual execution. This MSIL code is stored in a portable executable (PE) file.

Execution

When your application is ready to be executed, the MSIL is converted to machine-native language by a just-in-time (JIT) compiler that is part of the CLR. Machine-native code is much more efficient to run than uncompiled code. Because MSIL is CPU-independent, the JIT compiler must translate it into the language of the specific machine the user is on. Consequently, there must be many JIT compilers—one for each different type of machine.

NEW TERM When the PE file is compiled to native code, the JIT compiler verifies that it's *type-safe*. That is, it doesn't allow objects to reference memory locations that they aren't allowed to. In other words, if you create one object of type *X*, the JIT compiler prevents you from using that object as if it were of type *Y*. This ensures that each application is isolated and doesn't interfere with other applications, preventing memory corruption and crashes. The JIT compiler only allows type-safe code to pass the verification. You'll see many more examples of this as you develop ASP.NET pages. It's a very common situation.

Processing

NEW TERM The traditional method used by operating systems to handle applications involves *processes*. A process runs one application, and it determines the resources available to that application. The process boundaries make sure that applications are isolated from each other—if one process (or application) fails, the rest can continue without any hiccups. Figure 2.9 shows a typical list of processes running on Windows 2000.

Imagine that an operating system is a beehive. Each bee does its own thing and doesn't interfere with the others. If the bees did interfere with each other, they might crash or bump each other around. Each bee can be considered a process because it runs a honey-collecting "program" and knows where the boundaries of the flowerbed are. If one bee crashes and burns, the rest of the colony can continue without problems.

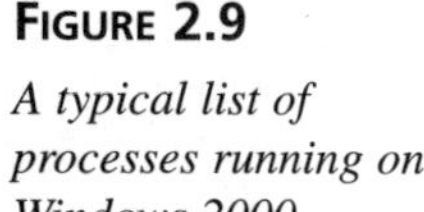

FIGURE 2.9

A typical list of processes running on Windows 2000.

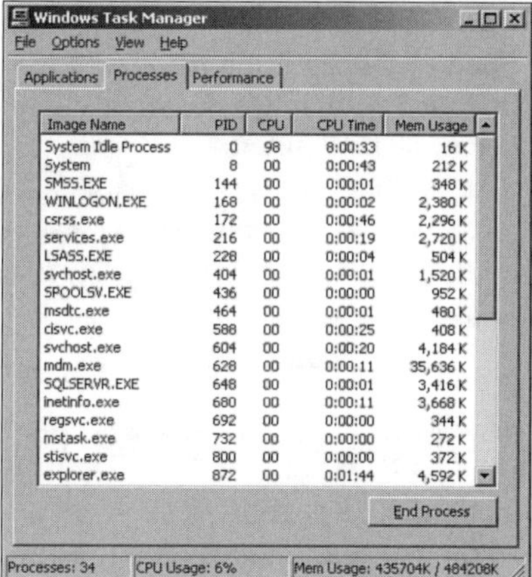

NEW TERM This method can still be rather costly in terms of performance and stability, however. The .NET Framework introduces *application domains*, which are new, smaller units of processing. Because the CLR knows that all of the code it will execute is type-safe, it can spend less time monitoring the processes. A single application can have multiple application domains if needed, which means even better fault-tolerance.

Imagine that beehive again, only now each honey-collecting program uses multiple bees. If one of these bees crashes, wanders off course, or gets eaten by another bug, the honey-collecting program can still go on and the failed bee will soon be replaced by another. This is the way .NET treats its applications.

2

Assemblies

NEW TERM The *assembly* is the basic unit of sharing and reusability in the CLR. Assemblies contain other files that represent a common unit, such as ASP.NET pages, PE files, images, or VB.NET source files. A similar object in the traditional Windows framework is a dynamic linked library (DLL). Assemblies, however, allow the .NET Framework to enforce much tighter security and versioning for applications, which in turn allow for much more stable code. The CLR can only execute code that's contained in an assembly. Therefore, even ASP.NET pages are placed in assemblies that are created dynamically when the page is requested.

Side-by-Side Execution

The CLR provides the ability to run multiple versions of the same assemblies at once. This is like running multiple versions of a DLL at once in the traditional framework—which was impossible but highly sought after. This topic will become important during Week 3 as you develop more sophisticated ASP.NET applications.

Before you ask, side-by-side execution is *not* why ASP and ASP.NET pages can run at the same time. Rather, the reason is that each type of page is handled by a different IIS ISAPI filter.

ISAPI (Internet Server Application Programming Interface) programs respond when the Web server receives an HTTP request. Filters can be used for any Web server event, such as a Read or Write event. These filters are very useful for Web applications.

What Does the CLR Mean for ASP.NET?

In terms of ASP.NET development, the CLR gives developers a lot less to worry about. It manages memory much better than the traditional method, and it offers ASP.NET applications much better performance and stability. With better fault isolation, you no longer need to restart IIS or even reboot the server when a Web application crashes. ASP.NET is much more stable and efficient than previous methods of Web development.

ASP.NET Programming Languages

You may be confused by this section and ask, "Aren't I learning a new programming language already?" ASP.NET is *not* a programming language. It's simply a framework that allows you to build applications over the Web.

Having said that, you can write your ASP.NET pages in just about any programming language you want—such as Visual Basic.NET or C# or JScript.NET. All of the code is compiled to MSIL anyway, and the compilers must emit metadata describing each application. Because of this intermediate compiler language, the JIT compiler only needs to understand MSIL. Days 3 and 4 will examine VB.NET and C#, the two most common languages for ASP.NET programming.

Because the CLR needs to ensure that all of its parts can work together, it defines a basic subset of features that every programming language must follow. Otherwise, objects developed in different languages wouldn't work together properly. This subset is called the Common Language Specification (CLS). As long as your applications only use features that are available in the CLS, they're guaranteed to work on all platforms and will be completely usable by objects compiled in other languages.

Another Look at the Code

Now that you have a better understanding of how ASP.NET works, let's take another look at the code from the beginning of today's lesson, as shown in Listing 2.8.

LISTING 2.8 Your First VB.NET ASP.NET Page Revisited

```
1:     <%@ Page Language="VB" %>
2:
3:     <script runat="server">
4:        Sub tbMessage_Change(Sender As Object, E As EventArgs)
5:           lblMessage.Text = "Hello " + tbMessage.Text
6:        End Sub
7:     </script>
8:
9:     <html><body>
10:       <font size="5">Sam's Teach Yourself ASP.NET in 21 Days:
11:       Day 2</font><hr><p>
12:       <% Response.Write("Our First Page<p>") %>
13:
14:       <form runat="server">
15:          Please enter your name:
16:          <asp:textbox id="tbMessage"
17:             OnTextChanged="tbMessage_Change"
18:             runat=server/>
19:          <asp:button id="btSubmit" Text="Submit"
20:             runat=server/><p>
21:          <asp:label id="lblMessage" font-size="20pt"
22:             runat=server/>
23:       </form>
24:    </body></html>
```

It's easy to spot the different sections of ASP.NET code here—in the code declaration block on lines 3–7, and in the code render block on line 12. You know what each section does as well. The first defines a method that the text box uses for its `TextChanged` event, and the second simply writes out "Our First Page<p>" to the browser.

Upon first request, the code declaration block is compiled into MSIL code, which is then translated into native machine code by the JIT compiler. However, the rest of the page, including the code render blocks, is evaluated at runtime—when the page is loaded into the browser.

You can also see the three server controls in the form. These act similarly to regular HTML controls, but they provide additional functionality for your application. Days 5 and 6 will examine these and other server controls.

You've also examined the importance of the `runat="server"` attribute. Without it, ASP.NET pages wouldn't function correctly. This attribute is the key to maintaining the viewstate, and to providing a link between what happens in the browser and the actions the server should take.

After today's lesson, you'll be able to give intricate details on this page's mechanisms, both within the .NET Framework and from a user's perspective. You've come a long way in two days!

That's Not ASP!

If you're familiar with traditional ASP, you'll notice a lot of differences between it and ASP.NET from today's lesson. A big change is the move from code render blocks to code declaration blocks. Code render blocks used to be the standard method of processing and were preferred over code declaration blocks.

Now code declaration blocks are much preferred because they're compiled and take advantage of the CLR's features. These blocks also make it much easier to separate ASP.NET code from HTML. In fact, code declaration blocks are absolutely required if you want to process events and form submissions. Code render blocks will now throw errors in many situations because the process model has changed.

Another major change is the move from scripting languages to compiled languages. Previously, everyone wrote ASP.NET pages in VBScript, and occasionally JScript. ASP.NET no longer supports these interpreted languages, but you can use any compiled language you want that can produce MSIL, such as VB.NET or C#. This allows you to use features such as early binding and strongly typed variables. The move to compiled languages was definitely worth it. And if you're familiar with VBScript, you can move to VB fairly easily because the two languages are very similar. For more information, check out `http://www.gotdotnet.com/languages.aspx`.

ASP.NET is now fully object-oriented as well. Every object fits nicely into the .NET Framework and fully supports OOP principles, such as inheritance, overloading, and interfaces.

One welcome similarity between the two is that `Response.Write` still works as before. It can be used throughout an ASP.NET page to produce output, or even to provide debugging capabilities (as many ASP developers will attest to). ASP.NET now has some nicer mechanisms to do the latter, as you'll see in Week 3.

Although `Response.Write` still works, be aware that now you must use it with parentheses. For example, the following will no longer work:

```
Response.Write "Hello World!"
```

You must enclose the string within parentheses. Appendix B highlights some more of these types of changes, which may cause common mistakes.

The biggest change, although perhaps not the easiest to see, is to the process model of ASP.NET. Code is now compiled into MSIL, and then into machine language with a JIT compiler. Applications are now divided into application domains instead of processes, and files are now organized into assemblies and namespaces. These changes won't mean much to a beginning ASP.NET developer, but they'll become readily apparent when you start to really dig into the .NET Framework.

Summary

Today's lesson taught you a lot about the ASP.NET framework. Although it may seem like overkill at the moment, you'll appreciate this information when you develop more complex ASP.NET applications.

ASP.NET processes events and code on the server. The browser only sees HTML, which means that clients don't need any additional applications or downloads. This is an important aspect of ASP.NET—it converts all code to HTML before sending it to the client.

The runat="server" attribute provides a lot of functionality for ASP.NET pages, allowing components to link to the server and maintain viewstate. This attribute is vital to ASP.NET pages.

ASP.NET code is separated from HTML by using <script>...</script> and <%...%> tags. Most code should be placed within the former tags because these sections are compiled and eliminate the "spaghetti code" problem.

Comments are delimited by one of three sets of tags: <!--...--> for HTML comments, ' for VB comments, and <%--...--%> for server-side comments. These comments are usually used to provide helpful explanations of the code, and they don't affect its execution at all.

Use the code continuation character (_) to break up long statements into multiple lines in VB.NET. When you use this character within a string, don't forget to close the string first and add an ampersand.

The .NET Framework and the CLR introduce a lot of new concepts for ASP.NET applications, including application domains (the new way of providing application boundaries), assemblies, and namespaces. ASP.NET is an integral part of the .NET Framework, and each page that you create extends this framework.

Finally, ASP.NET allows you to use compiled languages such as VB, C++, and C#. Interpreted languages such as VBScript are no longer supported.

In the next two days, you'll examine how to program ASP.NET pages. Today you learned what ASP.NET pages look like and how their different parts work, but now it's time to learn how to build code that handles these pages. Day 3 will focus on programming techniques with VB.NET and C#, and Day 4 will focus on C#. These are the two most common programming languages for use with ASP.NET.

See you tomorrow!

Q&A

Q Does importing namespaces cause additional overhead?

A Importing namespaces is similar to using include files or accessing references in other programming languages. There's no processing overhead, and unlike other languages, file sizes may not necessarily increase either. Also, the JIT compiler only compiles small portions of code that are in use at a time, so importing namespaces doesn't necessarily mean longer compiling and processing times.

Q Can ASP.NET pages really be built using any programming language?

A Theoretically, yes, although the language must be supported by the CLR and must be able to produce MSIL. Currently, support is limited to C#, VB.NET, JScript.NET, and the managed extensions for C++, but developers can add support for any language to the CLR relatively easily.

Workshop

This workshop will help reinforce the concepts covered in today's lesson. Answers can be found in Appendix A.

Quiz

1. How does ASP.NET maintain the state of server controls?
2. What namespace do the ASP.NET `Page` and `LiteralControl` classes belong to?
3. What are the seven namespaces automatically imported into every ASP.NET page?
4. What does "type-safe" mean?
5. What is the Common Language Specification?

Exercises

1. Create a simple ASP.NET page in VB.NET or C# that accepts two number inputs from the user and displays their product when the Submit button is clicked. Use two text box controls, a label control, and a Submit button control. Also use the standard event handler code defined in the "Code Declaration Blocks" section of today's lesson. Try using the `Cint()` function to convert the text in the text boxes to integers for multiplication, such as `Cint(tbNumber1.Text)`.

   Follow Listing 2.1 for guidance.
2. Build upon the previous exercise by providing multiple Submit buttons that perform the basic arithmetic operations, essentially creating a calculator.

WEEK 1

DAY 3

Using Visual Basic.NET and C#

In the past two days, you've learned what an ASP.NET page looks like and what its various parts do. You've also gained a solid foundation on the .NET Framework, and now you're going to start learning how to build your own ASP.NET pages using Visual Basic.NET and C#.

Using either of these languages will allow you to build dynamic pages that use all the power of ASP.NET. Today's lesson covers ASP.NET's syntax, general programming structures, and programming methodologies, with examples of each. This is by no means intended to be a complete guide to VB.NET or C#, but it's a good introduction to the concepts you'll need to know in later chapters.

Even if you're familiar with VB.NET or C#, you still need to read today's discussion. It is *not* simply a primer on the languages—it contains information on working with ASP.NET pages using VB.NET and C#.

Today's lesson will cover the following:

- An introduction to VB.NET and C#
- What variables and arrays are
- What conditional, looping, and branching logic are
- What functions and subroutines are
- How to write an event handler
- What classes are
- Some useful VB.NET functions for programmers with prior experience

Introduction to Visual Basic.NET and C#

Visual Basic (VB) is a programming language that has been in use for several years. At first VB was used only for building quick application prototypes, but it has grown tremendously throughout its lifetime. Now it's a powerful environment for building all types of full-blown standalone applications.

VB.NET is the latest incarnation of this language, and it's fully supported by the .NET Framework and the CLR. It's one of the most popular languages for ASP.NET development, and best of all, its learning curve isn't very steep. For these reasons, you'll be using VB.NET throughout this book for your ASP.NET pages.

C# (pronounced "see-sharp") is a new programming language from Microsoft that's fully supported by the .NET Framework. Since C# is derived from C++ and C, programmers who are familiar with those languages don't have to bother learning VB.NET to program their ASP.NET pages.

C# also bears a close resemblance to the Java programming language, so even Java developers should feel comfortable moving to this new language.

Many of the concepts covered today will be very similar to the VB.NET concepts. Both VB.NET and C# are powerful languages for ASP.NET development, so you can develop your pages with the language you're most comfortable with.

Variables

Variable is a generic term for some data in the computer's memory that has a name. For example, if you put the string "Hello World!" in a variable and called it x, it would be placed in memory and take up 10 (or so) bytes. This information can now be referenced by that name.

Since a variable is just a location in memory, you can manipulate it by changing it, deleting it, moving it, and so on. The important part of a variable, however, is what's inside the memory location.

Data Types

You can store many different types of information inside a variable, such as strings, numbers, and dates. Each type has a set of rules that govern its usage, which you'll discover as you develop your ASP.NET pages. There are 10 basic data types in Visual Basic.NET, called *primitive* types. These are the basic building blocks for using variables, hence the term *primitives*. These 10 are divided into five different categories: integers, floating-point numbers, strings, dates, and Booleans. Table 3.1 summarizes these types.

TABLE 3.1 VB.NET and C# Primitives

VB.NET Type	*C# Type*	*Category*	*Description*
`Byte`	`byte`	Integers	A 1-byte integral number (also known as `System.Int`)
`Short`	`short`	Integers	A 2-byte integral number (also known as `System.Int16`)
`Integer`	`int`	Integers	A 4-byte integral number (also known as `System.Int32`)
`Long`	`long`	Integers	An 8-byte integral number (also known as `System.Int64`)
`Single`	`float`	Floating-points	4-byte number with decimal point (also known as `System.Single`)
`Double`	`double`	Floating-points	8-byte number with decimal point (also known as `System.Double`)
`Decimal`	`decimal`	Floating-points	12-byte number with decimal point (also known as `System.Decimal`)
`Char`	`char`	Strings	A single Unicode character (also known as `System.Char`)
`Date`	-	Dates	A date and/or a time value (also known as `System.DateTime`)
`Boolean`	`bool`	Booleans	A true or false value (also known as `System.Boolean`)

In addition to these, C# has other data types that are similar. For example, `uint` has the same size and range as `int`, but doesn't cover negative numbers. Most of the time, though, you'll use the standard ones defined in Table 3.1.

Integers

An integer is a *whole number*—a number without a fraction or decimal part. For instance, 3, 6767, and –1 are all integers, whereas 3.4 and –3 1/2 are not.

Although integers are a general type of variable, there are also subtypes that you may use depending on how much memory you need. An `integer` (or `int`) technically uses 32 bits of memory—4 bytes. This means that it can store any number from –2,147,483,648 to 2,147,483,647. Usually this will be more than enough for your needs. There are also `bytes` (8 bits), `chars` (16 bits), `shorts` (16 bits), and `longs` (64 bits). You won't have to worry much about these, but they're there in case you need to use them.

Floating-Point Numbers

Floating-point numbers are numbers with a fractional part, such as 4.5, –1.956445, or even 3.0.

There are also subtypes for these, depending on how many decimal places you need: `single`, `double`, and `decimal`. Again, you won't have to worry much about these because the default memory size will usually work.

Strings

Strings are groups of characters, such as "hello", "my name is", "@$@#$!", and even "234". You've already used these in the first two lessons. They're among the most common data types that you'll be using in ASP.NET. Strings in VB.NET and C# are enclosed with double quotes, such as "hello".

Dates

Dates are, well, date and time values. The actual data type is called `DateTime`. (Note that VB.NET has its own `DateTime` data type, but C# doesn't—this means you'll have to use the built-in .NET `System.DateTime` data type instead. They work exactly the same.) It can be stored in many different forms, such as "1/2/2001", "Wednesday January 5th, 2001 8:09:30PM", and so on. These are all dates to VB.NET and C#, and it's easy to convert from one to the other.

You can represent dates as strings, but the `DateTime` data type allows these programming languages to perform special operations on dates that wouldn't be possible with a string, such as adding hours, minutes, or even days. The .NET Framework has a large number of date functions that you'll be using throughout your ASP.NET pages.

Booleans

A Boolean is a general term for a true/false values, such as 1/0, yes/no, and on/off. In VB.NET and C#, the `Boolean` data type can only be true or false.

Object

The `Object` data type is a general term for a variable that isn't specified as another type. It has a special purpose in the .NET Framework that you'll learn about later.

Declaring Variables

So how do you use a variable or a data type? First, you have to tell the system that you want to set aside a piece of memory, and you have to give it a name. This is done in VB.NET with the following line:


```
Dim MyVariable
```

The word `Dim` tells VB.NET to create a location in memory called `MyVariable`. You can now use this name in other places in your code. However, since you didn't tell VB.NET what kind of variable (data type) you want, it created an `Object` type. To declare the variable as a specific type, use the following:

```
Dim MyVariable As String
```

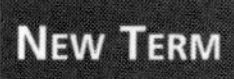

This is known as *explicit declaration*. Now VB.NET knows that you want to store a `String` in that memory location. The code in C# would look like the following:

```
string MyVariable;
```

The difference is that you put the data type *before* the name in C#, and don't require the `dim` keyword. Don't forget the semicolon at the end of the line!

It's strongly recommended that you *always* explicitly declare your variables. If you tell VB.NET or C# how much memory to set aside, it won't have to bother changing this amount later. It also allows you to perform operations on that variable that are inherent to that data type.

You can now assign values to this variable:

```
MyVariable = "Hello World!"
```

Or in C#:

```
MyVariable = "Hello World!";
```

You can even combine the declaration with the assignment or declare multiple variables on one line:

```
'VB.NET
Dim MyVariable As String = "Hello World!"
Dim MyIntA, MyIntB, MyIntC as Integer
Dim MyIntA as Integer = 9, MyIntB as Integer = 7

//C#
string MyVariable = "Hello World!";
int MyIntA, MyIntB, MyIntC;
int MyIntA = 9, MyIntB = 7;
```

The first line of either code snippet declares a variable named `MyVariable` as a `String` data type and assigns it the value "Hello World!" The second line declares three variables, `MyIntA`, `MyIntB`, and `MyIntC`, all as `Integer` (or `int`) data types. Finally, the third statement creates an `Integer` `MyIntA` and assigns it a value of 9, and it also creates an `Integer` named `MyIntB` with a value of 7. These are all valid ways to declare your variables.

Listing 3.1 shows an example.

LISTING 3.1 Declaring Variables in ASP.NET

```
<%@ Page Language="VB" %>

<script runat="server">
   dim MyIntA as integer = 8, MyIntB as Integer = 7

   sub Page_Load(Sender as object, e as eventargs)
      Response.Write(MyIntA * MyIntB)
   end sub
</script>

 <html><body>
 </body></html>
```

The C# version is slightly different. Listing 3.2 shows the code.

LISTING 3.2 Declaring Variables in ASP.NET Using C#

```
<%@ Page Language="C#" %>

<script runat="server">
   int MyIntA = 8, MyIntB = 7;

   void Page_Load(Object Sender, EventArgs e) {
```

LISTING 3.2 continued

```
7:         Response.Write(MyIntA * MyIntB);
8:     }
9:   </script>
10:
11:   <html><body>
12:   </body></html>
```

You'll learn about the syntax of these listings as you move through today's lesson. All you need to know now is that line 4 in the code declaration block declares two variables, `MyIntA` and `MyIntB`. Then you simply print out their product on line 7. This produces the output in Figure 3.1.

FIGURE 3.1
The page produced by Listing 3.1.

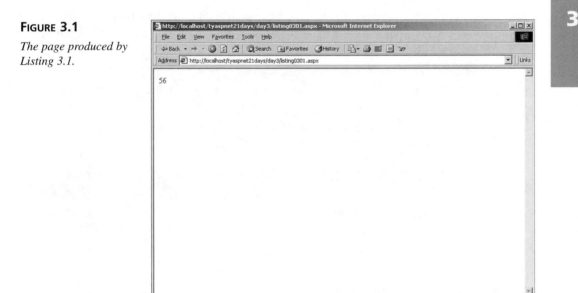

Naming Variables

Naming your variables properly is an important part of programming. If you've been experimenting, you may have noticed some restrictions on variable names. The following list summarizes the rules for naming variables:

- Do not use spaces, dashes, or periods, which will cause errors in your applications. Underscores are fine, however.
- Names must begin with a letter or underscore.

- Names cannot be existing VB.NET or C# keywords.
- Names should not be longer than 255 characters.

There are also some well-known styles that you should apply when creating names. These styles make it much easier to read your code:

- Use an abbreviation of the variable's data type as a prefix. This helps you keep track of which variable is used for which purpose:

  ```
  Dim intMyInteger as Integer 'int for integer
  Dim strName as String 'str for string
  bool blnGo 'bln for Boolean
  ```

  This doesn't take much effort, and it helps tremendously later on, by allowing you to easily see what kind of data you're dealing with.

- Use names that make sense. Giving variables names like `I` or `temp` may make sense to you now, but if you return to the code in a week, you'll have no idea what those variables were used for.

  Don't go overboard and use something like `intUsedToKeepTrackofMyLoopInThePage`. This is overkill and will only slow you down. Instead, use something like `intLoop` or `intIterator`.

- Try to declare all variables in one location, generally at the top of the page. This will save you a lot of hassle trying to find things later on.

Do	Don't
Do use names that are adequately descriptive!	**Don't** use temporary variable names, or reuse names—it only makes code confusing!

Data Type Conversions

Type conversions change a variable's type from one data type to another. This process is also known as *casting*. Both VB.NET and C# can convert some types automatically (implicit conversions), but others have to be specified explicitly (explicit conversions).

VB.NET provides you with several functions to cast one type to another, as shown in Table 3.2.

TABLE 3.2 Conversion Functions

Cbool	CByte	CChar	CDate
CDec	CDbl	CInt	CLng
CObj	CShort	CSng	CStr
CType	Asc		

For example, `CByte` transforms one data type into a `byte`, and `CStr` converts into a `String`. These functions are very helpful in ASP.NET pages, and you'll see them quite often. Listing 3.3 shows an example of converting data types.

LISTING 3.3 Converting Data Types Without Casting

```
1:    <%@ Page Language="VB" %>
2:
3:    <script runat="server">
4:       dim strName as String = "a"
5:       dim intNumber as integer = 4
6:
7:       sub Page_Load(Sender as object, e as eventargs)
8:          Response.Write("The value of strName is: ")
9:          Response.Write(strName & "<p>")
10:
11:          Response.Write("The value of intNumber is: ")
12:          Response.Write(intNumber & "<p>")
13:
14:          Response.Write("Their product is: ")
15:          Response.Write(intNumber * strName & "<p>")
16:       end sub
17:    </script>
18:
19:    <html><body>
20:
21:    </body></html>
```

ANALYSIS You declare two variables on lines 4 and 5, one with the value "a" and one with the value 4. The first is a `String` value and the second is an `Integer`. When you try to multiply them on line 15, you receive the error shown in Figure 3.2 because you cannot multiply a `String` and an `Integer`.

This is a very common situation in ASP.NET. Here, you must cast the `String` value to an `Integer` with `Asc`, which turns a character into its corresponding ASCII numeric value. Let's modify line 15:

```
Response.Write(intNumber * Asc(strName) & "<p>")
```

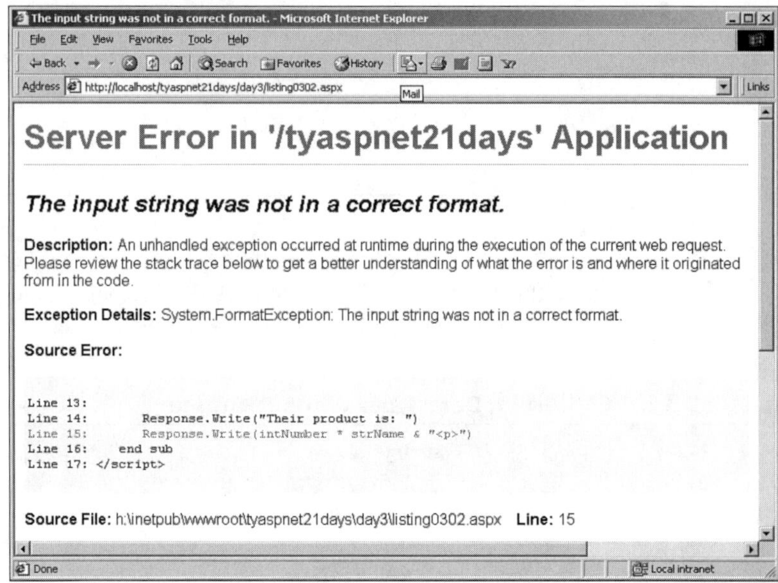
The input string was not in a correct format. - Microsoft Internet Explorer
File Edit View Favorites Tools Help
Back Search Favorites History
Address http://localhost/tyaspnet21days/day3/listing0302.aspx
Links
Server Error in '/tyaspnet21days' Application
The input string was not in a correct format.
Description: An unhandled exception occurred at runtime during the execution of the current web request. Please review the stack trace below to get a better understanding of what the error is and where it originated from in the code.
Exception Details: System.FormatException: The input string was not in a correct format.
Source Error:
Line 13:
Line 14: Response.Write("Their product is: ")
Line 15: Response.Write(intNumber * strName & "<p>")
Line 16: end sub
Line 17: </script>
Source File: h:\inetpub\wwwroot\tyaspnet21days\day3\listing0302.aspx Line: 15
Done
Local intranet

FIGURE 3.2
An error caused by incorrect data type manipulation.

Now your page will work as expected.

Caution

Be aware that some conversions will cause you to lose data. For instance, if you convert from a floating-point number to an integer, you'll lose all of the decimal values.

There's another way to convert data types in VB.NET. Many data types have a method that allows you to convert to another specified type. These methods always begin with `To` and end with the data type to convert to. (We'll discuss methods later in "Branching Logic.")

For example, to convert an `Integer` to a `String`, we can use `ToString`:

```
dim MyIntA as Integer = 4
dim MyString as String
MyString = MyIntA.ToString
```

Be careful with these functions, however, because some conversions aren't allowed. For instance, you can't convert from a `String` to an `Integer` with the `ToInt32` method. You'll see these methods throughout the code examples.

Casting in C# is a bit different than in VB.NET. Rather than having a method to do so, you use what is known as a casting operator. This operator is simply the type of data you want to convert to, surrounded by parentheses and placed in front of the variable to convert. For example, the following code snippet creates an integer, and then casts it to a double:

```
int intA = 10;
double dblA;

dblA = (double)intA;
```

This will work for simple conversions—those that cast one data type to a similar one. For example, an integer to a double. It will not work, however, for other casts like an integer to a string.

The final method to cast data types works in both C# and VB.NET, and involves the `Convert` class. This class has numerous methods that take one data type and convert it to another. To convert an integer to a string and then back again, for instance, use the following code:

```
int intA = 10;
string strA;

strA = Convert.ToString(intA);
intA = Convert.ToInt32(strA);
```

Arrays

Arrays are often the most useful types in any programming language—and the most frustrating to grasp. Different programming languages provide different rules for arrays, so it's easy to become confused. The .NET Framework simplifies this process and creates one set of rules for all arrays.

Arrays are groups of variables stored together that can be referenced individually by their indices. Imagine an egg carton. The carton itself is the container, and each egg is a variable. You can reference each egg by its index: egg 1, egg 2, and so on. (Figure 3.3 demonstrates this concept.) This allows you to store similar elements together.

Arrays in VB.NET and C# are zero-based, meaning that the first item in an array is stored at index 0. Thus, the last item's index array is always one minus the number of items in the array. All variables in an array must be of the same data type—you can't mix and match. Let's look at a simple declaration of an array in VB.NET:

```
Dim MyArray(6) As Integer
Dim MyArray2() As String = {"dog", "cat", "horse", _
   "elephant", "llama"}
```

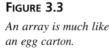

FIGURE 3.3
An array is much like an egg carton.

On the first line you simply declare an array with six total slots (that are empty) for `Integers`. This means the last item in the array will be at index 5. The number in parentheses on line 1 tells you how many elements should be in the array. This number is also referred to as the *length* of the array. If you want to explicitly declare the array, as on line 2, you must leave this number off and use curly brackets ({}) to set the values. The length of this second array is 5. "Dog" is at index 0 and you would refer to it as `MyArray2(0)`, while "llama" is `MyArray2(4)`.

The code in C# would be

```
int[] MyArray = new int[6];
string[] MyArray2 = new string[5] {"dog", "cat", "horse",
➥"elephant", "llama"};
```

There are a few differences here. First, instead of using parentheses for arrays, we use square brackers [...]. Next, the brackets must go after the data type rather than the variable name. Finally, to initialize the array you must use the `new` keyword, followed by the data type with brackets and the number of elements in the array.

Listing 3.4 shows an example of using arrays in VB.NET, and Listing 3.5 shows the same example in C#.

LISTING 3.4 Declaring and Referencing Array Elements

```
<%@ Page Language="VB" %>

<script runat="server">
   dim arrColors(5) as String

   sub Page_Load(obj as object, e as eventargs)
      arrColors(0) = "green"
      arrColors(1) = "red"
      arrColors(2) = "yellow"
      arrColors(3) = "blue"
      arrColors(4) = "violet"
```

LISTING 3.4 continued

```

        Response.Write("The first element is: ")
        Response.Write(arrColors(0) & "<p>")

        Response.Write("The third element is: ")
        Response.Write(arrColors(2) & "<p>")

        Response.Write("The 5-3 element is: ")
        Response.Write(arrColors(5-3) & "<p>")
    end sub
</script>

<html><body>

</body></html>
```


LISTING 3.5 Declaring and Referencing Array Elements in C#

```
<%@ Page Language="C#" %>

<script runat="server">
   string[] arrColors = new string[5];

   void Page_Load(Object Sender, EventArgs e) {
      arrColors[0] = "green";
      arrColors[1] = "red";
      arrColors[2] = "yellow";
      arrColors[3] = "blue";
      arrColors[4] = "violet";

      Response.Write("The first element is: ");
      Response.Write(arrColors[0] + "<p>");

      Response.Write("The third element is: ");
      Response.Write(arrColors[2] + "<p>");

      Response.Write("The 5-3 element is: ");
      Response.Write(arrColors[5-3] + "<p>");
   }
</script>

<html><body>

</body></html>
```

ANALYSIS On line 4 of either listing you create your array of strings, and you assign values to it on lines 7–11. Lines 14, 17, and 20 show various ways of referencing the elements. Figure 3.4 shows the output of this code.

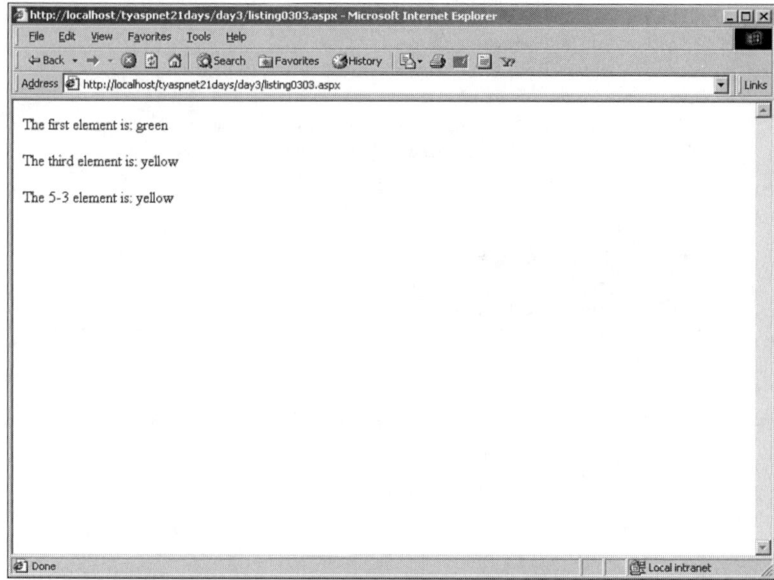

FIGURE 3.4
Different methods to access array elements.

There are two functions in VB.NET designed specifically to manipulate arrays: `Redim` and `Erase`.

Once you declare an array, you're limited to the size you've specified. However, `Redim` can be used to change the array size. For example:

```
Redim arrColors(6)
```

Your colors array now has a size of 6. The existing values are destroyed in the process, however. You can use the keyword `preserve` to save these values:

```
Redim Preserve arrColors(6)
```

If the new array size is smaller, the values that fall outside the array's dimensions are discarded. If the new size is larger, the extra indices are simply initialized to the default values.

NEW TERM The `Erase` statement sets each value in the array to `Nothing`, which is VB.NET's way of saying there's no value stored in the variable:

```
Erase arrColors
```

> The `Array` class in the .NET Framework provides more functions for array manipulation. See the .NET Framework SDK documentation for more information.

Operators

Operators are symbols that are used to perform some action. For instance, the = operator can be used to assign a value to something:

```
strName = "Hello"
```

You should be already familiar with many of the operators because you use them in everyday life. Table 3.3 lists all of VB.NET's operators, in order of precedence.

TABLE 3.3 VB.NET Operators, in Order of Precedence

Function	*Operator*
Exponentiation	^
Unary negation	+, -
Multiplication, division into (6 \ 2 = .3333)	*, \
Division by (6 / 2 = 3)	/
Modulus (6 mod 4 = 2)	Mod
Addition, subtraction	+, -
Bitwise NOT, AND, OR, and XOR	Not, And, Or, Xor
Concatenation	&, + (string)
Equal to, not equal to, less than, greater than	=, <>, <, >
Less than or equal to, greater than or equal to	<=, >=
Relational	TypeOf…Is, Is, Like
Assignment	=, ^=, *=, /=, \=, +=, -=, &=
Logical NOT, AND, OR, and XOR	AND, ANDALSO, OR, XOR, ORELSE

You can use parentheses to change the order of precedence as well. For example, 4+5*3 = 19, while (4+5)*3 = 27.

The C# operators are listed in Table 3.4.

TABLE 3.4 C# Operators, in Order of Precedence

Type	*Operators*
Primary	(x), x.y, f(x), a[x], x++, x--, new, typeof, sizeof, checked, unchecked
Unary	+, -, !, ~, ++x, --x, (T)x
Multiplicative	*, /, %
Additive	+, -
Shift	<<, >>
Relational	<, >, <=, >=, is
Equality	==, !=
Logical AND	&
Logical XOR	^
Logical OR	|
Conditional AND	&&
Conditional OR	||
Conditional	?:
Assignment	=, *=, /=, %=, +=, -=, <<=, >>=, &=, ^=, |=

Conditional Logic

Conditional logic allows you to specify which code should be executed depending on which conditions are met. It's a very powerful mechanism that's essential to all applications. This section will discuss several different methods of handling conditional logic: `if` statements and `case` (or `switch` in C#) statements.

`If` Statements

`If` statements are the simplest form of conditional logic. The process flow for an `if` statement is simple: If something happens or a certain condition is met, perform some action.

Here's a real-world example of an `if` statement: Imagine you work on an assembly line in a clock factory, and it's your job to put the clocks together. Your boss tells you, "If the hour hand is broken, throw the clock away."

Let's take a look at the syntax in VB.NET:

```
if (condition) Then
   some code
end if
```

In C#:

```
if (condition) {
   some code
}
```

If the condition is met, you execute the code between the `if` and `end if` lines (or `{` and `}`) . If it isn't met, you simply continue on after this section. Listing 3.6 shows some examples.

LISTING 3.6 Simple `If` Statements

```
1:     <%@ Page Language="VB" %>
2:
3:     <script runat="server">
4:        sub Page_Load(Sender as object, e as eventargs)
5:           dim MyMessage As String = "Hello"
6:           dim MyBool As Boolean = True
7:
8:           'if-statement 1
9:           if MyMessage = "Hello" then
10:              Response.Write("True")
11:           end if
12:
13:           'if-statement 2
14:           if MyBool then
15:              Response.Write("True")
16:           end if
17:        end sub
18:     </script>
19:
20:     <html><body>
21:
22:     </body></html>
```

ANALYSIS On lines 5 and 6, you declare two variables, `MyMessage` and `MyBool`. In `if` statement 1 (lines 9–11), you evaluate a simple expression: Does the string `MyMessage` contain the text "Hello"? If so, write "True" to the Web browser using `Response.Write`.

`If` statement 2 (lines 14–16) demonstrates a shortcut; when you simply want to see if a variable is true, you can write `if` *`variable`* `then` rather than `if` *`variable`* `= TRUE then`. Conversely, when you want to determine if a variable evaluates to false, use the not keyword, such as `if not` *`variable`* `then`.

Back to the clock factory. The boss thinks the factory is wasting too much money on broken clocks, so he decides to tighten the rules a bit: "If the hour hand is broken, throw the clock away. If the minute hand is broken, fix it. If anything else is wrong, just put it in a box."

The keyword `elseif` (or `else if` in C#) allows you to provide an "or" condition, such as "Or if the minute hand is broken." The `else` keyword allows you to handle any other condition, such as "If *anything* else is wrong…" Listing 3.7 shows some examples.

LISTING 3.7 `If...Then...Else` Statements in C#

```
1:    <%@ Page Language="C#" %>
2:
3:    <script runat="server">
4:       void Page_Load(Object Sender, EventArgs e) {
5:          string MyMessage = "Hello";
6:          bool MyBool = true;
7:
8:          //if-statement 3
9:          if (MyMessage == "Hi" & MyBool) {
10:             Response.Write(MyMessage);
11:          } else if (MyMessage == "Hello") {
12:             Response.Write("True");
13:          } else {
14:             Response.Write("False");
15:          }
16:
17:          //if-statement 4
18:          if (!MyBool) Response.Write("False");
19:       }
20:    </script>
21:
22:    <html><body>
23:
24:    </body></html>
```

ANALYSIS `If` statement 3 (lines 9–15) uses the `else if` and `else` keywords to evaluate other conditions. Line 9 asks if `MyMessage` is `"Hi"` and if `MyBool` is true by using the `&` operator (`AND` in VB. NET). If both conditions are met, write `MyMessage` out to the browser. Or, if `MyMessage` is `"Hello"`, write `"True"` out to the browsers, as shown on lines 11 and 12. Finally, if any other condition occurs, just write `"False"` to the browser. This allows you to provide some very complex conditional logic.

Notice how we use the double equal sign (==) in C# to evaluate equality, whereas the single equal sign would suffice in VB.NET. In C#, the single equal sign is only for assignment, not comparison.

`If` statement 4 (line 18) is another shorthand way of writing an `if` statement. You can combine the entire `if` statement on one line and completely omit the closing bracket or `end if`.

You can accomplish a lot with `If` statements, but there are times when it's awkward or won't accomplish exactly what you need. Enter `case` and `switch` statements.

Case and Switch Statements

`Case` statements, sometimes called `Select` statements, and `switch` statements are essentially the same as `if` statements with `elseif` clauses. A `case` statement examines one variable, and you specify the criteria of that variable with which something should occur. Let's examine the syntax in VB.NET:

```
Select Case variable
  Case option 1
     code
  Case Else
     code
End Select
```

You can specify as many *cases* as you want and simply use a `Case Else` to catch anything that doesn't meet your criteria. For example:

```
Select Case FirstName
   Case "Ringo"
      Response.Write("Drummer")
   Case "Paul"
      Response.Write("Not the drummer")
   Case Else
      Response.Write("Another Beetle")
End Select
```

You can also specify multiple cases on one line. In C#, the flow is the same, but the syntax is a bit different:

```
switch (FirstName) {
   case "Ringo":
      Response.Write("Drummer");
      break;
   case "Paul":
      Response.Write("Not the drummer");
      break;
   default:
      Response.Write("Another Beetle");
      break;
}
```

The break keyword in C# is very important. If it wasn't there, the execution would continue on to the next case statement. You have to use the break statement to stop execution for a particular case.

Let's look at the factory example again. The boss now tells you that if the clock's hour, minute, or second hand is broken, throw it away. If a spring is broken, just replace it. Otherwise, put the clock in the box. The code for this would look similar to Listing 3.8.

LISTING 3.8 The Clock case Statement

```
<%@ Page Language="VB" %>

<script runat="server">
   sub Page_Load(Sender as object, e as eventargs)
      dim strClockStatus As String
      strClockStatus = "MinuteHandBroken"

      select Case strClockStatus
         case "MinuteHandBroken", "HourHandBroken", _
            "SecondHandBroken"
             Response.Write("Throw clock away")
          case "SpringBroken"
             Response.Write("Replace spring")
          case else
             Response.Write("Put clock in box")
       end select
    end sub
 </script>

 <html><body>

 </body></html>
```

This listing prints out "Throw clock away." What does Listing 3.9 print out?

LISTING 3.9 Case Statement Execution Order

```
<%@ Page Language="VB" %>

<script runat="server">
   sub Page_Load(Sender as object, e as eventargs)
      dim intAge As integer = 7

      select Case intAge
         case "7"
            Response.Write("That's a string!")
          case 7
```

LISTING 3.9 continued

```
11:                Response.Write("You're 7 years old.")
12:             case <10
13:                Response.Write("Wow, you're young!")
14:          end select
15:       end sub
16:    </script>
17:
18:    <html><body>
19:
20:    </body></html>
```

ANALYSIS Listing 3.9 prints out only "That's a string!" Each one of these cases is valid, but only the first one will be executed. Therefore, make sure that your cases don't overlap, or put the most specific ones on top.

One difference between the `case` and `switch` statements is that `switch` can only evaluate equality conditions. In other words, the less than comparison on line 12 of Listing 3.9 would not work in C#.

Do	Don't
Do use `case` statements when you need to check a variable for multiple conditions.	**Don't** use many `if` statements just to check a single variable.

Looping Logic

Loops allow you to perform an action over and over again until some condition is met. There are three types of loops in VB.NET and C#: `While`, `Do`, and `For`.

`While` Loops

`While` loops are useful when you know don't know how many times you need to do something, such as when you want to loop through an unknown number of cars until you run into a Mercedes. These loops are based on conditional expressions, and they continue to run until the condition becomes false. The syntax for a `while` loop in VB.NET is as follows:

```
While condition
   code
End While
```

In C#:

```
while (condition) {
   code
}
```

For example, the following code counts from 1 to 10 and prints out the number to the browser:

```
int intCount = 1;
while (intCount < 10) {
   Response.Write(intCount + "<br>");
   intCount += 1;
}
```

On the second line, the program checks if `intCount` is greater than 10. It shouldn't be, because you just set it to be equal to 1. The program executes the code inside the `while` loop, writing the number to the browser and adding 1 to `intCount`. It then goes back to the second line and checks if `intCount` is now greater than 10. `intCount` is 2 now, so the loop continues. When it finishes, you'll see the numbers 1 through 9 displayed in the browser. Figure 3.5 illustrates this process.

FIGURE 3.5

The looping process.

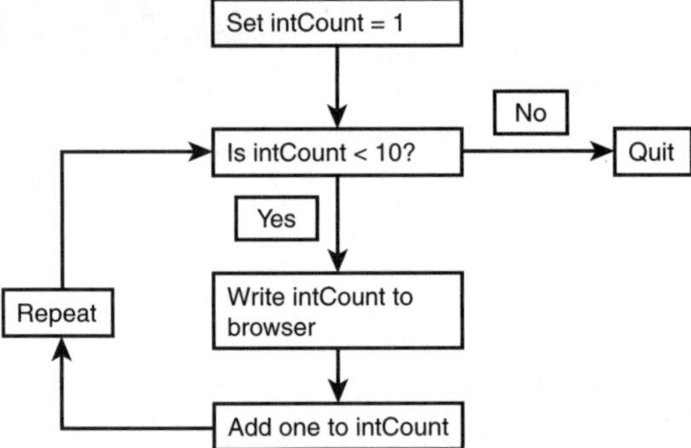

Why do we use 9 instead of 10? Once `intCount` hits 10, the statement on line 2 is no longer true—it evaluates to false—so the loop exits and continues after line 5.

The `do` loop is the same as the `while` loop; the syntax is just slightly different. The `do` loop comes in many forms, such as the following:

```
'VB.NET
Do
   code
Loop While condition
```

```
//C#
do {
   code
} while condition
```

Here's another one:

```
Do While condition
   code
Loop
```

The different forms produce different output depending on how many times you want them to execute. Let's look at an example of each:

```
dim intCount as Integer = 10
Do
   Response.Write(intCount & "<br>")
   intCount = intCount + 1
Loop While intCount < 10

Do While intCount < 10
   Response.Write(intCount & "<br>")
   intCount = intCount + 1
Loop
```


The first loop prints out the number 10, while the second loop prints out nothing. Why? The first loop evaluates the condition on the last line of the loop. Therefore, the code inside the loop will be executed once no matter what. The second loop evaluates the condition right up front, and in this case it stops the code from ever executing.

You should use a `Do` loop when you want the code inside the block to execute at least once. Conversely, you should use a `Do While` loop if you don't care whether the code is executed at all. In VB.NET, you can also use `until` in place of `while`:

```
dim intCount as Integer = 1
Do
   Response.Write(intCount & "<br>")
   intCount = intCount + 1
Loop Until intCount >= 10
```

This loop does exactly the same thing as the first loop in the previous listing. The difference is that using `until` will let the loop go until the condition is true, whereas using `while` stops when the condition is false. In this case, the loop stops when `intCount` is greater than or equal to 10.

For Loops

Use a `for` loop when you know how many times you want to execute your code. This loop increments a counter to tell itself when to stop executing. The `for` loop syntax is as follows:

```
'VB.NET
For variable = startvalue To stopvalue [Step step-size]
   code
Next [variable]

//C#
for (variable = startvalue; variable comparison stopvalue; step) {
   code
}
```

This loop uses the *`step-size`* to increment *`variable`* until it reaches the *`stopvalue`*, at which point the loop stops executing. (In VB.NET, you can leave the `step` parameter out if you want—it defaults to a value of 1.) For example:

```
For intCount = 1 to 10
   Response.Write(intCount & "<br>")
Next
```

or:

```
For intCount = 10 to 1 step -1
   Response.Write(intCount & "<br>")
Next
```

The first loop prints out the numbers 1 through 10, while the second prints them in reverse order.

In C#, the previous code snippet would be

```
for (intCount = 10; intCount == 1; intCount--) {
   Response.Write(intCount + "<br>");
}
```

Another form of the for loop is the for...each loop (foreach in C#). This loop iterates through all of the items in a collection, such as an array. For example:

```
dim arrWeekDays() as String = {"Monday", "Tuesday", _
   "Wednesday", "Thursday", "Friday"}

For Each strDay in arrWeekDays
   Response.Write(strDay & "<br>")
Next
```

On the first line, you create an array of strings containing the weekdays. On the fourth line, you loop through each item in the array. The variable `strDay` is simply a counter that the loop uses—you could specify any variable here. The loop assigns each variable in the array to `strDay`, and you print that value out on the fifth line. The result is that the days of the week are displayed in the browser, as shown in Figure 3.6.

FIGURE 3.6

Using a `for...each` loop to iterate over the items in an array.

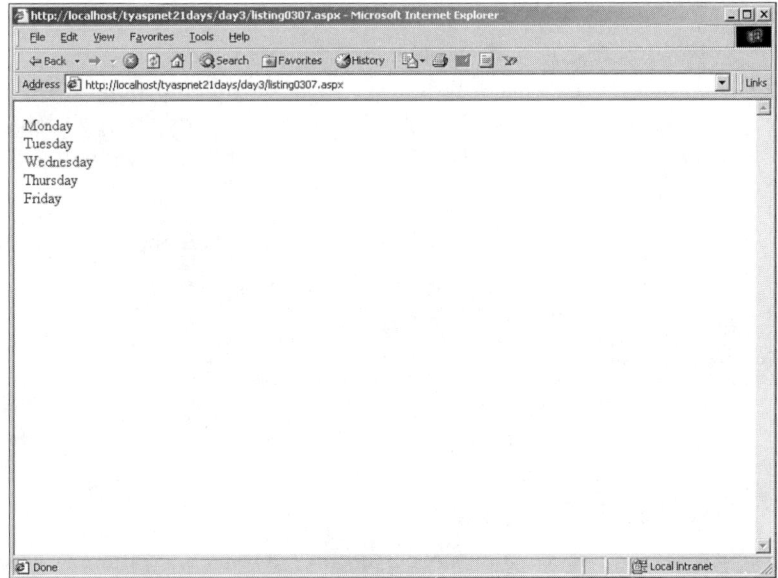

Infinite Loops

NEW TERM Notice that you had to manually increment the counter in your `while` and `do` loops, whereas the `for` loops did so automatically. It's very important to increment your counter in these loops. Otherwise, you'd end up with an *infinite loop*—a loop that never exits. Not only is this a pain for visitors to your site, but it also drains system resources very quickly and can cause the site to crash.

If you ever need to exit a loop before it finishes, you can use the `exit` (`break` in C#) keyword to stop the loop. The syntax for this keyword in VB.NET depends on where you use it. For example:

```
Do While intCount < 10
   Response.Write(intCount & "<br>")
   intCount = intCount + 1
   if intCount = 7 then
      exit do
   end if
Loop
```

```
For intCount = 1 to 10
   Response.Write(intCount & "<br>")
   if intCount = 7 then
      exit for
   end if
Next
```

The first loop iterates through the numbers 1 through 10, but if the number equals 7 (which it eventually will, in this case), you stop the loop by using `exit do` (note that it prints out only 1–6). The second loop does exactly the same thing, but using `exit for` (this one prints out 1–7). The `exit` statement that's used will depend on the type of loop you're in.

In C#, the syntax doesn't change no matter where the keyword is used:

```
for (intCount = 1; intCount == 10; intCount++) {
   Response.Write(intCount + "<br>");
   if (intCount == 7) {
      break;
   }
}
```

Branching Logic

Branching logic causes code execution to branch in different directions. Typically, this type of logic is used when some code needs to be used over and over again from different locations.

In the factory example, every time a clock is assembled, it needs to be put in a box. The boxing machine is in the basement. When you're through with a clock, you send it to the basement for a box, and then it comes right back up for you to apply the proper postage. The boxing machine is essentially branching logic—it can be used from any location in the factory, not just your assembly line. Putting a single boxing machine in the basement is much more efficient than putting one next to each assembly line.

There are two types of branching logic controls in VB.NET: functions and subroutines. The only difference between the two is that functions send information back to whatever called them, and subroutines don't. In other words, functions compute values, and subroutines perform actions. In C#, there is only a function, and it may or may not return values. These two controls are essential to ASP.NET development—without them, nothing would get done. Let's examine subroutines first.

Subroutines

Subroutines (sometimes called procedures) in VB.NET follow this format:

```
Sub name (parameters)
   code
End Sub
```

In C#:

```
void name (parameters) {
   code
}
```

In VB.NET you use the keyword `sub`, but there is no corresponding keyword in C#. The word that precedes the name of the function in C# describes the data type that is returned by the function. `void` means no value is returned (we'll see more on this in a moment).

You've been looking at this type of syntax already in all of your ASP.NET pages. Recall this line:

```
sub Page_Load(Sender as object, e as EventArgs)
   code
end sub
```

Listing 3.10 contains some code in VB.NET that multiplies numbers; Listing 3.11 shows the same code in C#.

LISTING 3.10 Multiplying Numbers in a Subroutine

```
<%@ Page Language="VB" %>

<script runat="server">
   sub Page_Load(obj as object, e as eventargs)
      MultiplyNumbers(8,9)

      MultiplyNumbers(4,12)

      MultiplyNumbers(348,23)
    end sub

    sub MultiplyNumbers(intA as integer, intB as integer)
       Response.Write(intA * intB & "<br>")
    end sub
 </script>

 <html><body>

 </body></html>
```

Listing 3.11 Multiplying Numbers in a Subroutine in C#

```
1:     <%@ Page Language="C#" %>
2:
3:     <script runat="server">
4:        void Page_Load(Object Sender, EventArgs e) {
5:           MultiplyNumbers(8,9);
6:
7:           MultiplyNumbers(4,12);
8:
9:           MultiplyNumbers(348,23);
10:        }
11:
12:        void MultiplyNumbers(int intA, int intB) {
13:           Response.Write(intA * intB + "<br>");
14:        }
15:     </script>
16:
17:     <html><body>
18:
19:     </body></html>***
```

Analysis

New Term

In the code declaration block on line 12, you create a subroutine named `MultiplyNumbers`. The variables in the parentheses are called *parameters* or *arguments*. These are values that are passed into the subroutine from the code that's using it. The subroutine can use these values to perform any actions it needs to. A group of parameters is called a *parameter list*. Specifying these parameters is very similar to declaring variables (note the differences between C# and VB.NET). The parameters you declare here must be passed in by the calling code that uses this subroutine, or else you'll receive errors.

On line 13, you write the product of these parameters to the browser using `Response.Write`, and you close the subroutine on line 14. Now that you've created the subroutine, you can use it from anywhere else on the page. This subroutine will never execute unless you tell it to explicitly—it won't execute just because you put it there.

New Term

On line 5 you *call* the subroutine. This tells the program to execute the code inside the subroutine and come back to line 5 when it's done (you can see the branching logic at work here). When you call `MultiplyNumbers`, you specify the two parameters that the subroutine defined—two `Integers`. `MultiplyNumbers` takes these integers and performs its actions.

Lines 7 and 9 do identical things but pass different parameters to the subroutine. This is part of the beauty of branching logic controls—you can call them from anywhere and give them different parameters to play with each time. This code will produce what's shown in Figure 3.7.

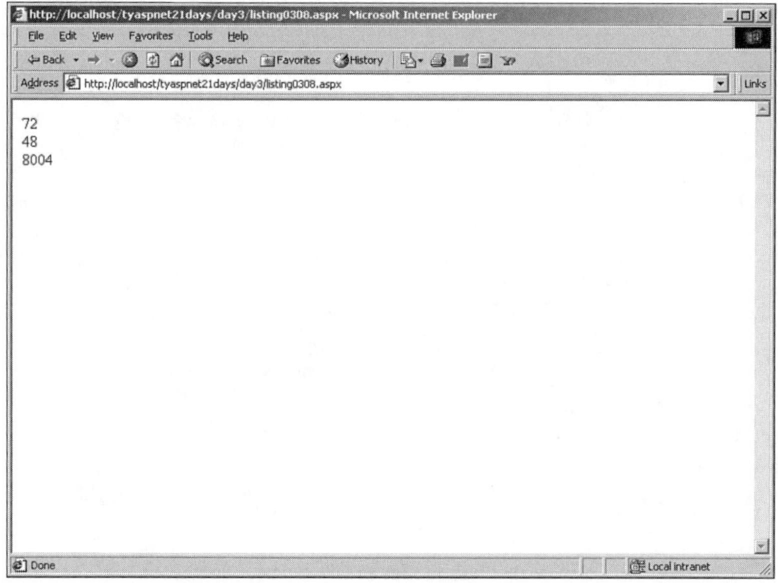

FIGURE 3.7
Using subroutines to perform encapsulated logic.

> **Caution**
>
> If you're familiar with VBScript and traditional ASP, you may remember calling subroutines and functions with the following syntax:
>
> `MultiplyNumbers 8, 9`
>
> That is, without parentheses. With C#, VB.NET, and ASP.NET, you must always include the parentheses when calling a function or there will be an error.

Functions

Functions are very similar to subroutines—their syntax is nearly identical, and they can both perform the same actions. Functions, however, return a value to the code that called it. Let's modify Listing 3.10 to use a function instead of a subroutine.

LISTING 3.12 Multiplying Numbers in a Function

```
<%@ Page Language="VB" %>

<script runat="server">
   sub Page_Load(obj as object, e as eventargs)
      Response.Write(MultiplyNumbers(8,9) & "<br>")
```

LISTING 3.12 continued

```
7:          Response.Write(MultiplyNumbers(4,12) & "<br>")
8:
9:          Response.Write(MultiplyNumbers(348,23) & "<br>")
10:      end sub
11:
12:      function MultiplyNumbers(intA as integer, intB as integer) _
13:         as Integer
14:         Return intA * intB
15:      end function
16:   </script>
17:
18:   <html><body>
19:
20:   </body></html>
```

ANALYSIS The `MultiplyNumbers` function would look like the following code snippet in C#:

```
12:      int MultiplyNumbers(int intA, int intB) {
13:         return(intA * intB);
14:      }
```

This code is slightly different from Listing 3.10. The first difference is that the function on line 12 doesn't write the product of the two parameters to the browser. Rather, it uses the `return` keyword to send the product back to the code that called it. Note that the function also specifies `As Integer` after the parameter list (or `int` in front of the function name in C#). This is used to tell the calling code what type of data to expect in return. This listing produces the same output as the previous listing. On line 5, you call `MultiplyNumbers` inside a `Response.Write`. This seems kind of odd at first glance, but let's examine it further. First, line 5 calls `MultiplyNumbers` with the parameters 8 and 9. Then this function takes over, multiplies the two parameters on line 14, and returns them to line 5. `Response.Write` on line 5 now only sees the product, 72. It's equivalent to writing `Response.Write(72)`.

This allows you to use function calls in many different places. For example, you could write any of the following:

```
MultiplyNumbers(8,9)
intCount = MultiplyNumbers(8,9) * 72
if MultiplyNumbers(8,9) < 80 then
   ...
```

These all work because the function executes first and the code will end up seeing only the returned value. There are two ways to return values in VB.NET. The first way you've already seen—using the keyword `return`. The second way is to assign the return value to the function itself. For example, the following works the same way as the function in Listing 3.12:

```
12:    function MultiplyNumbers(intA as integer, intB as integer) _
13:       as integer
14:       MultiplyNumbers = intA * intB
15:    end function
```

A function doesn't have to return a value, but it may if necessary. You could have included the `Response.Write` statement in the function, as you did for the subroutine in Listing 3.10, but this method works for the sake of demonstration,. Optionally, you can also specify the data type of the return value:

```
function MultiplyNumbers(intA as integer, intB as integer)_
   as integer
```


This tells the calling code that you're returning an `integer`.

> Always make sure to specify a return type when declaring a function. This includes readability of the code and also increases type safety.

There is an important thing to note with the `return` keyword. Once you call `return`, all execution in that particular method stops, and execution returns to the calling method. In other words, if you wrote `Response.Write("HI")` after line 14 in Listing 3.12, it would never be executed because `return` passed the control back to the `Page_Load` method.

Optional Parameters

What happens if you think you may use a parameter for your function or subroutine, but you don't need the code to tell you what it is? You want the parameter to be optional. Luckily, VB.NET allows you to do this with the `Optional` keyword. Let's look at an example:

```
function MultiplyNumbers(intA as integer, optional intB as__
   integer = 3) as Integer
   return intA * intB
end function
```

On the first line, you use the `optional` keyword to tell VB.NET that any code that calls this function isn't *required* to specify a value for `intB`, but that it may. You could then call this function with either of the following:

```
MultiplyNumbers(8)
MultiplyNumbers(8,9)
```

What happens if the code doesn't specify a value? On the third line, you multiply the two values together. If `intB` wasn't specified, this would produce an error.

When you specify that a parameter is optional, you must also specify a default value. On the first line, you have `optional intB as integer = 3`. This tells VB.NET what this value should be in case it isn't specified.

There is one caveat to using `optional`: Once you specify that one parameter is optional, all subsequent parameters must also be optional. The following code would produce an error:

```
function MultiplyNumber(intA as integer, optional intB as _
   integer = 3, intC as integer) as Integer
```

Instead, use this:

```
function MultiplyNumber(intA as integer, optional intB as _
   integer = 3, optional intC as integer = 4) as Integer
```

In C#, there is no equivalent `optional` keyword. The only way to provide optional parameters is to use method overloading—a concept of object-oriented programming that is out of the scope of this lesson. See the .NET Framework documentation for more details.

Event Handlers

Events, as discussed on Days 1, "Getting Started with ASP.NET," and 2, "Building ASP.NET Pages," are actions that may occur in your application—a mouse click or a button press, for instance. Usually, whenever an event occurs, you need to do some processing. For example, when a Submit button is clicked, you should enter form information into a database. Or if the user clicks a link, you want to send him to the appropriate page. This functionality doesn't happen by itself—you must tell the program what to do.

NEW TERM You do this by creating an *event handler*. The syntax is identical to that for a subroutine, so you should be familiar with it already. The difference lies in the parameter list. When an event is *raised*—meaning the event has occurred—it produces variables that describe the event. Your event handler can use these variables to figure out what to do.

Nearly all of the events in ASP.NET produce the same parameter list. Listing 3.13 shows an example.

LISTING 3.13 Handling Events in ASP.NET

```
<%@ Page Language="VB" %>
<script runat="server">
   Sub Button_Click(Sender As Object, e As EventArgs)
```

LISTING 3.13 continued

```
5:          Response.Write("You clicked the button!")
6:       End Sub
7:    </script>
8:
9:    <html><body>
10:      <form runat="server">
11:         <asp:button id="btSubmit" Text="Submit"
12:            runat=server
13:            OnClick="Button_Click"/><p>
14:      </form>
15:   </body></html>
```

ANALYSIS Line 4 contains what appears to be a normal subroutine. However, the parameter list distinguishes it as an event handler. The first parameter is an `Object` data type that represents the object that raised the event. The second parameter is a new type you haven't seen yet, `EventArgs`. This parameter contains any information specific to the event that occurred. Typically, this variable will be empty. This is the standard event handler parameter list, although in a few days you'll see some exceptions to the rule. In C#, this standard list looks like the following code snippet:

```
void event_handler_name(Object Sender, EventArgs e)
```

Remember that you can call your parameters whatever you like. You're using `Sender` and `e` here for simplicity and standardization.

On line 11, you create an ASP.NET button control. You may recall this control from Days 1 and 2, and it's explored further on Day 5, "Beginning Web Forms." For now, you just need to know that you set its ID—its unique name—to `btSubmit`, set the text it will display to `Submit`, and specify that it runs at the server. Whenever this button is clicked, it raises an event called `Click`. On line 13, you tell the button the following: "When the `Click` event occurs, execute the subroutine `Button_Click`." You just defined its event handler.

Now, whenever the button is clicked, it executes the subroutine on lines 4–6 and writes "You clicked the button!" to the browser. Save this code in a file called `listing0310.aspx` and view it from your browser. When you click the button, you'll see Figure 3.8.

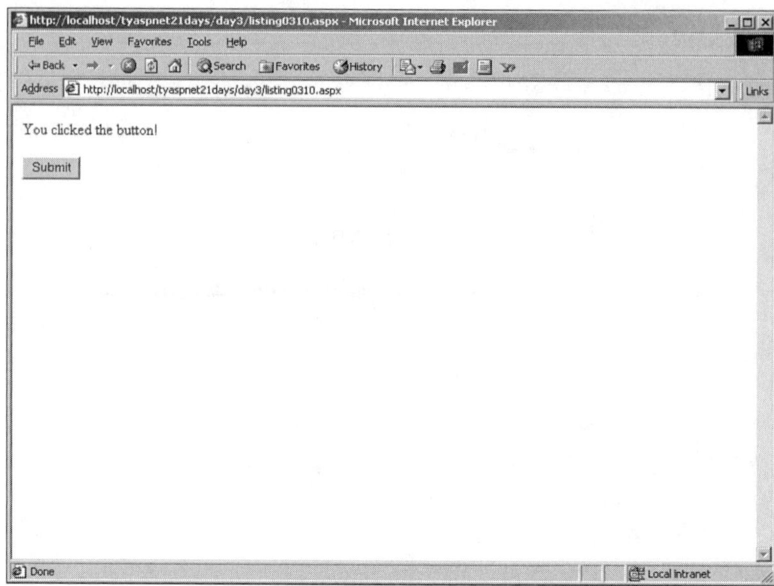

FIGURE 3.8
Handling events in ASP.NET.

This is the basis for handling all actions in ASP.NET pages. Once you learn how to handle events, ASP.NET becomes much more powerful. Let's modify Listing 3.13 a bit to use the parameters supplied to the event handler as shown in Listing 3.14.

LISTING 3.14 Using Event Parameters in ASP.NET

```
<%@ Page Language="VB" %>

<script runat="server">
   Sub Button_Click(Sender As Object, e As EventArgs)
      Response.Write(Sender.Text)
   End Sub
</script>

<html><body>
    <form runat="server">
       <asp:button id="btSubmit" Text="Submit"
          runat=server
          OnClick="Button_Click"/><p>
    </form>
 </body></html>
```

ANALYSIS When you view this page and click the button, you'll see the word "Submit" in place of "You clicked the button!" Let's examine line 5. Recall that the first parameter represents the object that raised the event. In this case, it happens to be the Submit button. Thus, `obj` is one name you can use to reference this button. The other name is the `id` value, `btSubmit`. Line 5 writes the `Text` property of the button to the browser. On line 11, the `Text` property is set to `"Submit"`. You could change line 5 to read as follows and it would produce the same output:

```
Response.Write(btSubmit.Text)
```

But we're getting ahead of ourselves. You'll examine this more thoroughly on Day 5.

Caution

Generally, events in ASP.NET can be handled only if the code that generates them lies within `<form>...</form>` tags. This is because the events must be posted to the server, which will be discussed in more detail on Day 5.

3

There's another event that you've been using quite a bit in today's examples: the `Page_Load` event. Recall Listing 3.12, for example. On line 4 is a method called `Page_Load`, with the standard event parameter list: `Sender as object, e as EventArgs`. When an ASP.NET page loads, the `Page_Load` event is raised and you can use it to do some processing. Typically, you'll use this event handler to display something to the user as soon as the page loads. Day 4, "Using ASP.NET Objects with C# and VB.NET," will take a closer look at this event.

Classes

Classes are programming definitions of an object. For example, the definition for a clock would be as follows: contains a second, minute, and hour hand; chimes on the hour, every hour; and can be set to different times. Similarly, classes define objects by telling other code what the object contains and what it can do.

Classes are essential in object-oriented programming (as well as ASP.NET). You define a class to wrap up some common code and properties, just like combining clock parts to build a clock. In fact, the .NET Framework consists of many, many classes that define objects, although you haven't learned about all of them yet. When you use `Response.Write`, you're calling the `Write` subroutine of the `Response` object, which is defined by the `Response` class. Even more remarkable is that when you create ASP.NET pages, you're actually creating objects based on the `Page` class in the .NET framework.

Note that classes are definitions, while objects are actual, usable items that are based on those definitions. It's very helpful to make this distinction, although sometimes the terms are used interchangeably.

Everything in the .NET Framework and VB.NET is represented by classes, so it's important that you get used to referring to things that way.

So how do you create your own classes? The syntax is simple:

```
'VB.NET
Class name
   subroutines, functions, and properties
End Class

//C#
class name {
   subroutines, functions, and properties
}
```

The key to creating classes is combining common code. Listing 3.15 contains a simple example in VB.NET, using your clock. Listing 3.16 shows the C# version.

LISTING 3.15 An ASP.NET Clock Class

```
<%@ Page Language="VB" %>

<script runat="server">
   Class Clock
      public Second as integer
      public Minute as integer
      public Hour as integer

      sub SetTime(intSec as integer, intMin as integer, _
          intHour as integer)
          Second = intSec
          Minute = intMin
          Hour = intHour
       end sub
    End Class

    sub Page_Load(Sender as object, e as EventArgs)
       dim objClock as new Clock

       objClock.Second = 60

    end sub
```

LISTING 3.15 continued

```

</script>

<html><body>

</body></html>
```

LISTING 3.16 An ASP.NET Clock Class in C#

```
1:  <%@ Page Language="C#" %>
2:
3:  <script runat="server">
4:     class Clock {
5:        public int Second;
6:        public int Minute;
7:        public int Hour;
8:
9:        void SetTime(int intSec, int intMin, int intHour) {
10:           Second = intSec;
11:           Minute = intMin;
12:           Hour = intHour;
13:        }
14:     }
15:
16:     void Page_Load(Object Sender, EventArgs e) {
17:        Clock objClock = new Clock();
18:
19:        objClock.Second = 60;
20:
21:     }
22:
23:  </script>
24:
25:  <html><body>
26:
27:  </body></html>
```

ANALYSIS

NEW TERM

Any variables declared in a class, as done on lines 5–7, are known as *properties* of the class. This class contains a `Second` property, a `Minute` property, and an `Hour` property, as well as a subroutine to set the time. On line 20, you set the `Second` property of the class to 60.

New Term The `public` keyword tells ASP.NET that this item can be seen and modified by any code, whether it's inside or outside the class. This is called a *global* variable. Conversely, if you use the keyword `private`, the variable or subroutine can be used only inside the class. This is useful for preventing other code from modifying variables that you depend on. That's beyond the scope of this lesson, however—see a guide to object-oriented programming for more details.

The `SetTime` method sets the second, minute, and hour properties of the class to the input parameters. In your ASP.NET page, you could do the following:

```
'VB.NET
Dim objClock as new Clock
objClock.SetTime(60,4,12)
objClock.Second = 59

//C#
Clock objClock = new Clock();
objClock.SetTime(60,4,12);
objClock.Second = 59;
```

The first line declares an `objClock` variable that is a data type based on the `Clock` class. Note that both versions use the `new` keyword, but the C# version uses an equal sign to initialize the object—we'll examine this more tomorrow. You can then set the properties or call the methods of that class by using the `objClock` variable, as shown on the second and third lines. By wrapping up common code such as you've done, you can think of programming as simply manipulating objects.

> **Note** You put your class inside the code declaration block here, but typically it would be in another file to make the code easier to read. For VB.NET classes, this file usually ends with the extension `.vb`, and for C#, `.cs`. You'll learn more on that on Day 15, "Using Business Objects."

What's with `New`?

The keyword `new` is very important—it's used to initialize a new object. For example, the following sets a variable to the `Clock` data type, but it doesn't initialize the variable (that is, it doesn't give the variable a value):

```
'VB.NET
dim objClock as Clock

//C#
Clock objClock
```

You can't yet use these variables because they don't have any values assigned to them. The new keyword gives a value to the variable. Using the new keyword is similar to saying this:

```
'VB.NET
dim intNumber as Integer = 7

//C#
int intNumber = 7
```

To initialize an object variable, you can also use the following in VB.NET, which more closely resembles the C# syntax:

```
dim objClock as Clock = New Clock
```

This is identical to simply using the new keyword.

Inheritance

Inheritance is an important part of classes and object-oriented programming. It won't be discussed thoroughly here, but you should know the basics for your ASP.NET pages.

NEW TERM Suppose you create a Clock class. Later on, you learn that you have two different types of clocks: analog and digital. Rather than throwing away your Clock class and creating two new ones, you can simply create the new classes based on the existing Clock. The original Clock contains properties and methods that are common to all clocks, so the new clocks can simply add any properties or methods they need. This is known as *inheritance*.

Inheritance saves a lot of headaches when you're developing. You don't have to create entirely new classes when there's a similar one that already does what you want. Let's look at an example that uses your original Clock:

```
'VB.NET
Class AnalogClock : Inherits Clock
   private ClockWound as Boolean = false
   sub WindClock()
      ClockWound = true
   end sub
End Class

//C#
class AnalogClock : Clock {
   private bool ClockWound = false;
   void WindClock() {
      ClockWound = true;
   }
}
```

You've created a new class, `AnalogClock`, that inherits from the original `Clock` class. This new class automatically inherits the `Second`, `Minute`, and `Hour` properties and the `SetTime` method, so you don't need to re-create them here. You only need to add the items that are specific to this class—a Boolean value, `ClockWound`, and a method to wind the clock. Your ASP.NET page could now look like this:

```
dim objAnalogClock as new AnalogClock
objAnalogClock.SetTime(60, 4, 12)

objAnalogClock.WindClock
```

Along with inheritance comes the ability to override the parent's methods. If the `SetTime` method should be different for the `AnalogClock` for some reason, you can just provide a different method with the same name:

```
Class AnalogClock : Inherits Clock
   private ClockWound as Boolean = false
   sub WindClock()
      ClockWound = true
   end sub
   sub SetTime(intSec as integer, intMin as integer, _
      intHour as integer)
      Second = intSec
      Minute = intMin
      Hour = intHour - 12
   end sub
End Class
```

`objAnalogClock.SetTime` will now use the modified subroutine.

Inheritance is a wonderful mechanism, but it's too complex to get into in this book. You'll use it in your ASP.NET pages, especially in code-behind forms, which are discussed on Day 19, "Separating Code from Content."

Useful VB.NET Functions

If you are familiar with prior versions of VB.NET, you may wonder where all of your favorite functions and subroutines have gone. Many have been incorporated in some way or another into the classes of the .NET Framework. Many, however, are still part of VB.NET. This section briefly describes many common and useful VB.NET functions that you'll be using throughout the book. This section is by no means a complete reference, but it will provide some general information.

(If you're wondering where these functions are in C#, you'll find most of them built into the .NET Framework classes. You'll see their usage as we progress through this book.)

Tables 3.5, 3.6, and 3.7 introduce many of these common functions.

TABLE 3.5 Date/Time Functions

Function	*Description*
`dateDiff(`*`dateinterval`*`,` *`date1`*`,` *`date2`*`[,` *`firstdayofweek`* `[,` *`firstdayofyear`*`]])`	Returns a number specifying the number of *`dateinterval`*s between date1 and date2. *`dateinterval`* can be yyyy (year), q (quarter), m (month), y (day of year), d (day), w (weekday), ww (week), h (hour), n (minute), s (second).
`day(`*`datetime`*`)`	Returns an integer from 1 to 31 specifying the day of the month.
`dayofweek`	Returns an integer specifying the day of the week (0 = Sunday, 6 = Saturday); this is a property of the `datetime` data type.
`hour(`*`time`*`)`	Returns an integer from 0 to 23 specifying the hour of the day.
`isdate(`*`datetime`*`)`	Returns a Boolean specifying if the supplied `datetime` is recognized as a valid date.
`minute(`*`time`*`)`	Returns an integer from 0 to 59 specifying the minute of the hour.
`month(`*`datetime`*`)`	Returns an integer from 1 to 12 specifying the month.
`now()`	Returns a `datetime` data type specifying the current date and time according to your computer.
`second(`*`time`*`)`	Returns an integer from 0 to 59 specifying the second of the minute.
`year(`*`datetime`*`)`	Returns an integer representing the year (from 1 to 9999).

TABLE 3.6 Math Functions

Function	*Description*
`abs(`*`value`*`)`	The absolute value of *`value`*
`atan(`*`value`*`)`	The arctangent of *`value`*
`cos(`*`value`*`)`	Cosine of *`value`*
`exp(`*`value`*`)`	e^*`value`*
`fix(`*`value`*`)`	Returns the integer portion of a number, rounding up for negative numbers
`hex(`*`value`*`)`	Changes base 10 to hexadecimal
`int(`*`value`*`)`	Returns the integer portion of a number, rounding down for negative numbers
`log(`*`value`*`)`	Returns the natural logarithm
`oct(`*`value`*`)`	Changes base 10 to octal

TABLE 3.6 continued

Function	*Description*
`rnd`	Returns a random number
`round(value [, dec])`	Rounds to integer, or with `dec` decimal places
`sin(value)`	Sine of `value`
`sqrt(value)`	Square root of `value`
`tan(value)`	Tangent of `value`

TABLE 3.7 String Functions

Function	*Description*
`instr([start, ]string1, string2[, compare])`	Returns a number specifying the first position of `string2` in `string1`, or 0 otherwise; `compare` can be 0 (`BinaryCompare`) or 1 (`TextCompare`)
`left(string, length)`	Returns a string containing a specified number of characters from the left side of a string
`len(string | variable)`	Returns a number containing the length of a string or number of bytes required to store a variable
`mid(string, start[, length])`	Returns a string containing a specified number of characters from another string: `Dim strstring as string = mid("hello", 3)` This returns "llo"
`replace(expression, find, replace[, start[, count [, compare]]])`	Replaces `find` in the expression with `replace`, starting at `start`; `count` is number of replacements to perform; default is –1 (all possible replacements); `compare` is similar to `instr`
`right(string, length)`	Returns a string containing a specified number of characters from the right side of a string

For Future VB.NET and C# Gurus: Where to Go

Visual Basic.NET is a powerful and developer-friendly programming language that will enable you to build complex, enterprise-level ASP.NET applications. Although we didn't delve too deeply into it today, you should be able to start pounding out those ASP.NET pages.

C# is a very complex and powerful language, and this lesson won't go into any more depth about it. You have a good head start, though, and soon you'll start applying your C# skills to more ASP.NET pages.

For further reference on VB.NET and C#, check out the following:

- MSDN Developer Reference (`msdn.Microsoft.com`)
- .NET Framework Online Reference (`www.Microsoft.com/net`)
- The VB.NET language specification and reference in the .NET SDK documentation

That's Not ASP!

The largest difference between ASP and ASP.NET that was discussed today is the move from VBScript to VB.NET or C#. Although much of the syntax is similar, there are a few syntax changes that can ambush a new ASP.NET programmer.

VB.NET itself introduces a lot of changes. It's now fully object-oriented, which may take some getting used to if you're a VBScript developer. Classes are used extensively throughout the .NET Framework, whereas they were seldom seen with traditional ASP. It pays to learn how to use them early on.

C# may be familiar to C++ developers, but it can be completely new for classic ASP coders. Hopefully you've seen today, though, that C# isn't really that much different than VB.NET—many of the concepts are the same, it's just the syntax that is different.

Another large change from ASP to ASP.NET is the use of the event-driven model. Although the underlying mechanism for this model relies on request/response machinery, there's a new layer of abstraction that allows developers to spend more time on building applications than on digging through posted data. You'll learn much more about this on Days 5 and 6.

Appendix B, "Common ASP.NET Mistakes," lists some common mistakes that may ensnare ASP developers as they migrate to ASP.NET.

Summary

Today you learned how to build your own ASP.NET pages using VB.NET and C#. After today's lesson, you should have a strong grasp of the programming fundamentals that will allow you to build more complex pages.

You began today's lesson by looking at variables in both VB.NET and C#. Variables are named locations in memory that you can manipulate by referencing their names. There are 10 basic data types for variables, divided into five categories: integers, floating-point numbers, Booleans, strings, and datetimes.

Arrays are collections of variables that can be referenced by indices. These are useful for storing similar information in one place. All arrays are indexed starting at 0. You cannot create an array that has an index starting at any value other than 0.

You learned about three types of logic today: conditional, looping, and branching. Conditional logic uses `if` statements and `case` (or `switch`) statements to evaluate conditions. Looping logic uses `while`, `do`, and `for` loops to execute a code block multiple times. Branching logic uses subroutines and functions that each perform some action, but functions can return values.

You also looked at events, which are things that may happen to your application, and event handlers, which are the methods that perform an action when an event occurs. These are very similar to subroutines but are distinguished by their parameter lists.

Finally, you were introduced to classes and inheritance. You examined classes, which are definitions of objects. They group common code together to represent an entity with properties and methods. Classes are an important part of the .NET Framework and ASP.NET. Inheritance allows you to extend existing classes to meet your needs and override methods that don't.

Today you learned about many of the most difficult tasks in ASP.NET programming. Once you can easily create methods, event handlers, and classes, you'll be ready to take on any ASP.NET page! While C# and VB.NET are two completely different languages, you'll learn that they both use the same set of common classes and objects; the functionality of each language is virtually identical, and only the syntax varies slightly. You should be able to switch from one language to another fairly easily (or at least understand both from a high level). We'll use both languages throughout this book, so you can choose to follow the one you prefer. You are encouraged, though, to try to learn and follow both—you'll be much better off in the long run.

Tomorrow you'll examine some of the most common objects used with ASP.NET, that can be used with both VB.NET and C#.

Q&A

Q Is VB.NET or C# case sensitive?

A VB.NET is not. For example, the class names `MyClass` and `myclass` are identical. However, C# is case insensitive, so `MyClass` and `myclass` are two different variables. Similarly, `Response.Write` and `Response.write` are two different methods; the latter would result in an error if used. The case sensitivity of C# confuses many classic ASP developers.

Q What happened to the `variant` type?

A If you're familiar with previous versions of VB, you'll remember that the `variant` type was a generic data type used to represent any variables not declared as a specific type. In VB.NET, `variant` has been replaced with the `Object` type.

Workshop

This workshop will help reinforce the concepts covered in today's lesson. The answers can be found in Appendix A.

Quiz

1. When should you use a `for` loop? A `while` loop?
2. What is the output of the following code snippet?

```
Dim I as integer = 5
Do
   Response.Write(I & " ")
   I = I + 2
Loop Until I > 10
```

3. What is the output of the following code snippet?

```
Dim I as integer = 5
Do
   I = I + 2
   Response.Write(I & " ")
Loop Until I > 10
```

4. What are the standard event handler parameters for ASP.NET pages?

Exercises

Create an ASP.NET page with a class that represents you, with properties that describe your hair color, eye color, and birth date. Use the `DayOfWeek` property of the `DateTime` data type to determine the day of the week of your birthday. The `DayOfWeek` property returns an value from the `DayOfWeek` enumeration—convert this into a string representing the day. Call this method whenever a user clicks the Submit button, and print the output to the browser.

Hint: You'll need to use the `new` keyword with the `DateTime` data type. Pass three parameters into the new `DateTime` data type: the year, month, and day of month, in that order. For example:

```
dim MyDate as new DateTime(2002,1,1)   'January 1, 2002
```

WEEK 1

DAY 4

Using ASP.NET Objects with C# and VB.NET

Yesterday you learned how to build your own ASP.NET pages using VB.NET and C#. You learned about the various structures for controlling your pages, including loops, conditional statements, functions, and events. Using these structures allows you to build powerful ASP.NET pages.

However, if that's all ASP.NET could do, it wouldn't be very great for Web development. As part of the .NET Framework, ASP.NET can take advantage of hundreds of built-in classes and objects that enhance and extend the functionality of your pages. Today you're going to study a few of the most common objects that will be used throughout this book.

Today's lesson will cover the following:

- What objects are and some of their properties
- How to take advantage of the most common ASP.NET objects
- How to work with sessions and cookies

A Recap of Objects

As discussed yesterday, objects are reusable pieces of code and classes are the definitions behind those objects. Yesterday you tried your hand at creating a simple `Clock` object.

The .NET Framework consists of many classes that define objects, and ASP.NET is free to use all of them. Of course, there are some objects that would never be used in a real-world ASP.NET page because they don't apply to ASP.NET, but you can use them nevertheless. Let's recap some concepts from yesterday.

Properties

Properties are variables that describe an object. Listing 4.1 shows the clock example from yesterday in C#.

LISTING 4.1 The `clock` Class in C#

```
1:    <script language="C#" runat="server">
2:       public class Clock {
3:          public int Second;
4:          public int Minute;
5:          public int Hour;
6:          public static int ClockCounter = 0;
7:
8:          public void SetTime(int intSec, int intMin,
9:             int intHour)
10:           {
11:              Second = intSec;
12:              Minute = intMin;
13:              Hour = intHour;
14:           }
15:        }
16:
17:    </script>
```

ANALYSIS Lines 3, 4, and 5 specify three properties for your class: `Second`, `Minute`, and `Hour`. If you were building a car class, the properties could be `Color`, `Make`, and `Model`.

Methods

Methods are things you can do with objects, such as winding a clock or setting the time. In Listing 4.1, the `SetTime` method on line 8 sets the properties for the class. Methods for a car would include `Accelerate` and `Stop`.

Object Instances

NEW TERM Before you can use an object, you must create an *instance* of it. That is, you must create a variable that holds the object in memory. It's important to understand the difference between an actual object and an object instance.

Using the clock example, you know that a clock is a generic object. My `Clock` object is an instance, however, and I can set its time. Your `Clock` object would be another instance, with its own set of properties. Figure 4.1 shows two instances of the clock, with different properties.

FIGURE 4.1
Two instances of the same `Clock` *object have different properties.*

Using this analogy, it doesn't make much sense to set the minute hand for a generic clock object. Would that affect all clocks? Which clock would it set? Generally, you can only set properties and call methods for *instances* of objects. Let's look at an example in C#:

```
Clock.Second = 41;  //would produce an error because we can't
                    //modify the properties of an object
```

```
Clock objClock = new Clock();
objClock.Second = 41;  //works because objClock is an instance
```

The second set of commands is the correct way to set properties. First create an instance of the object, and then set its properties. In VB.NET, these lines would be as follows:

```
dim objClock as New Clock
objClock.Second = 41
```

Static Members

Note that I said, "*Generally*, you can only set properties… for instances." There are ways to set properties or call methods directly from the object. For example, suppose you have a counter in your clock class that tells you how many clock instances have been created. This is a general property that doesn't belong with any specific instance—it's "just there." Properties and methods of classes that don't belong to any specific instance are called *static* members and are declared with the `static` keyword (the same in both C# and VB.NET):

```
public static int ClockCounter = 0;

public static int AddClock() {
   return ClockCounter + 1;
}
```

In your ASP.NET page, these could be referenced as follows:

```
<%
   Clock objClock = new Clock();
   objClock.SetTime(4,6,7);

   Clock.AddClock;
   Response.Write(int.ToString(Clock.ClockCounter));
%>
```

On the next-to-last line of the previous code snippet, you call the static method `AddClock`, which increments the total number of clocks. This method doesn't need to be called from an instance. On the next line, you've used two static members. `ToString` is a static method of the `int` object that converts an `int` into a string, and `ClockCounter` is your static property that tells you how many clocks there are.

You won't be creating static members very often in your own classes, but it's useful to know what they are because ASP.NET has a ton of them.

ASP.NET Objects

This section isn't going to cover all of the objects available to ASP.NET—that would take an encyclopedia! Instead, it covers a few of the most common ones that you'll be using often in your ASP.NET pages. You should already be somewhat familiar with the first one—the `Response` object.

> None of these objects are "built-in" to ASP.NET. That is, all of the following objects are part of the .NET Framework (not ASP.NET) and can be used by any application under that framework.

The `Response` Object

The `Response` object allows the server to communicate with the client. For example, you can use the `Write` method of the `Response` object to send HTTP output to the browser. You've already seen an example of this method:

```
Response.Write("Hello world!")
```


But what happens, exactly, when you use this object? When a user requests a page, ASP.NET creates an instance of the `HttpResponse` object, which contains information (properties and methods) needed to communicate with the client. This instance's name is `Response`, so you can use this name to access properties and methods of the `HttpResponse` object. As you may have guessed, one of these methods is `Write`, which writes a string out to the browser.

So, one way to think about it would be that once an ASP.NET application starts, ASP.NET automatically executes the following code:

```
dim Response as new HttpResponse
```

The variable `Response` can then be used throughout your pages.

The `Write` Method

Let's create an ASP.NET page that more closely examines the `Write` method. See Listing 4.2.

LISTING 4.2 Using `Response.Write`

```
<%@ Page Language="VB" %>

<script runat="server">
   sub Page_Load(obj as object, e as eventargs)
      dim i as integer
```

LISTING 4.2 continued

```
6:
7:          Response.Write("This is an example")
8:          Response.Write("<HR width=100%\>")
9:
10:          for i = 1 to 5
11:             Response.Write("<font size=" & i & ">Hi!<br></font>")
12:          next
13:       end sub
14:    </script>
15:
16:    <html><body>
17:
18:    </body></hhtml>
```

ANALYSIS The Write method expects a string for its parameter, so you enclose the input in quotes. See the caution later today for more detail. Let's examine line 8 more closely:

```
Response.Write("<HR width=100%\>")
```

NEW TERM Specifically, notice the seemingly out-of-place backslash character at the end of the line. Without this character, this line would contain the string %>, which tells ASP.NET that it has come to the end of the script block. It would stop execution in the middle of the string, which causes an error. This is a special character sequence that you have to set apart somehow so ASP.NET doesn't get confused. Therefore, you introduce the *escape character* (\).

The backslash isn't shown in the HTML output. If you wanted to output double quotes, you'd have to escape them with another set of quotes:

```
Response.Write("<HR width=""100%"">")
```

This listing should produce what's shown in Figure 4.2.

Caution

VB.NET performs some casting of data types automatically, if possible. Casting from an integer to a string would be one example. This is why you can use Response.Write(6) in a VB.NET ASP.NET page.

However, C# doesn't perform the same casting automatically. Therefore, using Response.Write(6) will produce an error in a C# ASP.NET page. Instead, use the following:

```
Response.Write(6.ToString());
```

Always remember to cast your variables appropriately!

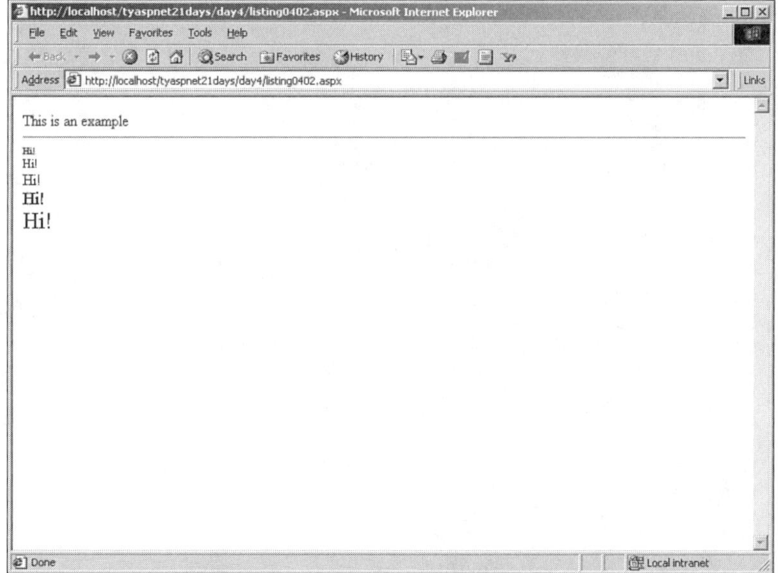

FIGURE 4.2
Writing output to the browser using `Response.Write`.

Buffering Pages

Buffering allows you to control when output is sent to the browser. You've probably experienced this when browsing Web pages but weren't aware of it.

When the output is buffered, nothing is sent to the browser until all code has been executed. This is the default method for ASP.NET. Unbuffered output, on the other hand, goes to the browser immediately.

For example, suppose you had two `Response.Write` methods in your page. With buffered output, the output of both methods would be stored in memory and sent to the browser all at once when all ASP.NET code had stopped executing. With unbuffered output, the output of each method is sent to the browser immediately. Figure 4.3 illustrates this concept.

Buffering provides a nice performance boost, so generally you should leave it on. However, to turn buffering off, simply specify `BufferOutput = false` before you send any output to the browser.

The following will cause an error because you've already sent output to the browser:

```
<html><body>
   <% Response.Buffer = False %>
</body></html>
```

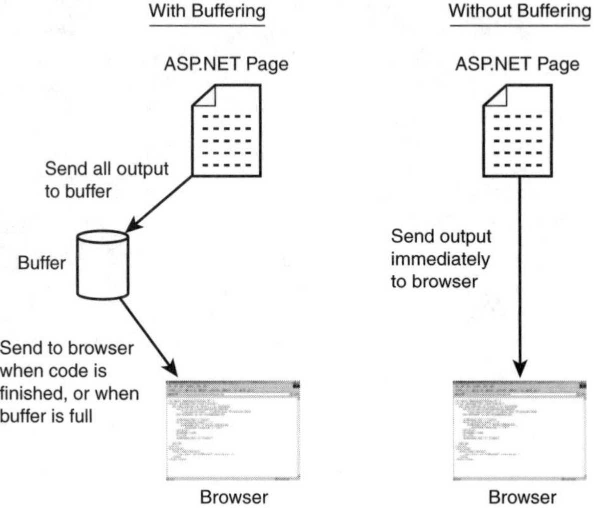

FIGURE 4.3
The difference between buffered and unbuffered output.

Instead, use the following:

```
<% Response.Buffer = False %>
<html><body>
   blah blah
</body></html>
```

You manipulate the buffer by using the `Clear`, `Flush`, and `End` methods. `Clear` empties the buffer, effectively losing anything you've stored, while `Flush` sends whatever is in the buffer to the browser immediately. The `End` method stops the `Response` object from sending any new output to the browser—any output that's currently in the buffer is sent. Listing 4.3 shows an example.

LISTING 4.3 Testing Output Buffering

```
<%@ Page Language="VB" %>

<script runat="server">
   sub Page_Load(obj as object, e as eventargs)
      dim i as integer

      Response.Write("Before flush<br>")
      Response.Flush()
      for i = 0 to 5000
          'just wasting time
       next

       Response.Write("After flush, before clear<br>")
```

LISTING 4.3 continued

```
14:         Response.Clear()
15:         for i = 0 to 5000
16:            'just wasting time
17:         next
18:
19:         Response.Write("After clear, before end<br>")
20:         Response.End()
21:         for i = 0 to 5000
22:            'just wasting time
23:         next
24:
25:         Response.Write("After end<br>")
26:      end sub
27:   </script>
28:
29:   <html><body>
30:
31:   </body></html>
```


ANALYSIS Buffering is on by default, so you don't have to specify it explicitly. On line 7, you store "Before flush" in the buffer, and on line 8 you send it to the browser immediately. You use a `for` loop simply to waste time (that is, insert a pause) so you can better see the effects of buffering. On line 13, you store another string in the buffer but clear it immediately after. On line 19, you store yet another string, and you call `End` on line 20. The result is that the buffer is sent to the browser, and all further output is not. Therefore, you should see only "After clear, before end."

This code produces what's shown in Figure 4.4.

Redirecting Users

The `Response` object also allows you to send users to other pages without their knowledge, using the `Redirect` method. For example:

```
<%@ Page Language="VB" %>
<script runat="server">
   sub Page_Load(obj as Object, e as EventArgs)
      Response.Redirect("http://www.microsoft.com")
   end sub
</script>
<html><body>
  Hello!
</body></html>
```

FIGURE 4.4
Manipulating the `Response` *buffer.*

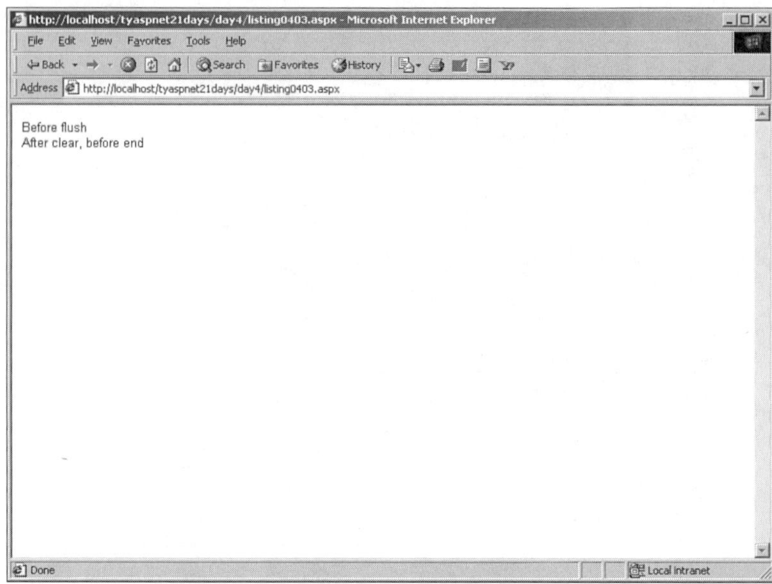

When a user requests this page, he'll be sent to `www.microsoft.com` immediately and will never see your Hello message. This is a useful method if you want to send a user someplace depending on the username and password he enters in your form, for example.

The `Request` Object

In contrast to the `Response` object, the `Request` object allows browser-to-server communication. The browser sends a lot of information to the server when requesting a page. Whenever this happens, an `HttpRequest` object is created to deal with all that information. This object variable is called `Request`. Thus, the `Request` object represents the client requesting a Web page, and the Web server sends it back as a response using the `Request` and `Response` objects.

This object's functionality isn't necessary for typical ASP.NET development because ASP .NET handles most of it for you. However, there are a few things you should know about.

Discovering Client Information

NEW TERM One of the main uses of this object is to gather custom information from the browser, such as user input into forms or *querystring* values. The querystring is any information tacked onto the end of the request URL. For instance:

```
http://www.Microsoft.com?id=Chris&sex=male
```

The querystring, `?id=Chris&sex=male`, presents data in key/value pairs. `id` is the first key and `Chris` is the first value, `sex` is the second key and `male` is the second value, and so on. The first key/value is always preceded by a question mark, and subsequent pairs are separated by ampersands, as shown.

The querystring is useful for passing information between pages. For example:

```
Response.Redirect("mypage.aspx?ID=Chris")
```

`myPage.aspx` could now use this querystring information as needed.

Caution

Be careful not to store too much information in the querystring. Older browsers had a limitation of only 255 characters in this string, and you never know when one of your visitors will use an old browser. Also, placing large amounts of text here can open up some bugs on older versions of IIS.

ASP.NET provides a layer of abstraction so that you don't need to use the `Request` object to gather form information (as you'll see on Day 5, "Beginning Web Forms"), but the object is still there for your use. Using the previous URL, you could type the following C# code to retrieve querystring values:

```
Request.Querystring;        //returns "id=Chris&sex=male"
Request.Querystring("id"); //returns "Chris"
```

If the user had submitted a form, you could use this:

```
Request.Form;         //returns all form values
Request.Form(name);   //returns a single value specified by name
```

Both the `Querystring` and `Form` properties represent collections of information. This information is typically supplied by user input and retrieved by ASP.NET using the `Request` object. You won't use this object much in this book because the Web forms framework handles many of the requests for you.

Two other common collections used with `Request` are `ServerVariables` and `Cookies`. The former returns miscellaneous information about the server, such as the IP address or HTTP protocol. The latter returns information about *cookies*, which are small files on the client's computer (see "The `HttpCookie` Object" later today).

Table 4.3 shows some of the common environment variables in the `ServerVariables` collection.

Table 4.3 Commonly Used Environment Variables

Variable	*Description*
`URL`	The URL of the ASP.NET page, starting after the server and domain name (that is, after `http://www.server.com/`)
`PATH_INFO`	The same as `URL`
`PATH_TRANSLATED`	The full physical path of the ASP.NET on the server
`SERVER_NAME`	The Web server's name
`SERVER_SOFTWARE`	The name of the Web server software, such as `Microsoft-IIS/5.0`

The `HttpCookie` Object

New Term A *cookie* is a small file on the user's computer that contains information specific to one Web site. This file can contain things such as usernames and passwords that will be used to customize a user's visit to the site. Cookies can contain any simple data type, such as `strings`, `integers`, `floats`, `booleans`, and so on. For example, many sites that display news headlines will allow users to select which types of news they want to see. This information can be stored in cookies so that the next time the user visits, the site can read those values and customize accordingly.

> **Tip**
>
> One common mistake beginners make with cookies is that they assume that the server sends cookies to the client. In other words, that a Web site writes information to your hard drive, and that somehow Web sites can read your hard drive. This is untrue.
>
> What actually happens is that the Web server, through HTTP, sends an instruction to the browser on your machine. The browser on your computer, then, is the one that writes cookies to your machine, not the Web server. When you disable cookies, you are instructing your browser to ignore the create cookie command from the server. In this way, cookies are actually safer than some people think.

The `HttpCookie` object provides methods for accessing and creating these cookies. You can use this object to examine the properties of a cookie. However, the most common way to manipulate cookies is through the `Request` and `Response` objects, which both have a `Cookies` property that returns a reference to an `HttpCookie` object.

Creating Cookies

The `Response` object allows you to create cookies easily. There are two ways to create cookies: You can create multiple cookies, each with a single value, or you can create a single cookie with multiple key/value pairs. The following code snippet demonstrates both methods:

```
'set up some cookie variables
Response.Cookies("MyCookie").Value = "Single Cookie"

Response.Cookies("21DaysCookie")("Username") = "Chris"
Response.Cookies("21DaysCookie")("Preference") = "800x640"
```

ANALYSIS The second line creates a cookie on the client's computer named `"MyCookie"` with the value `"Single Cookie"`. You can create as many cookies and key/value pairs as you like using this method—but it can add up to a lot of cookies! The second set of code creates a single cookie named `"21DaysCookie"` that has two key/value pairs. To specify key names, you simply add another name in parentheses (or brackets in C#), as in the following:

```
Response.Cookies[CookieName][KeyName];
```

On the second line, notice that you must use the `Value` property to assign a string to the cookie. Simply using `Response.Cookies("MyCookie")` returns an `HttpCookie`, and you can't write to that object. The `Value` property returns a string object that you can modify. In the second group of code, however, you don't need to specify `Value` because ASP.NET knows you need a string if you specify a key name.

4

Caution If you create a cookie with a value and then add keys to it, the initial value will be erased. You cannot create a cookie with both values and keys.

Suppose a visitor comes to your Web site and you create a cookie for her. If she never comes back to your site, there's no reason for her to keep the cookie. She can delete the cookie manually, of course, but there's an easier way. You can use the `Expires` property to render the cookie invalid at any time you choose. For example:

```
Response.Cookies("21DaysCookie").Expires = _
   DateTime.Parse("1/1/2002")
```

Or:

```
Response.Cookies("21DaysCookie").Expires = _
   DateTime.Now.AddMonths(1)
```

The first example tells the cookie to expire on January 1st, 2002. The second one tells the cookie to expire one month from the time the code executes. The default `Expires` value renders the information invalid after 1,000 minutes. This is great if you simply want to maintain information for the current session (see "The `Session` Object" later today). However, cookies are usually used to store information for much longer periods—weeks, months, or even years.

To delete a cookie from the client, you must set the cookie's `Expires` value to some time in the past, or to 0. The cookie will then be deleted as soon as the user closes her browser.

There are four other properties of the `HttpCookie` object that you should be aware of. `Domain` restricts the use of the cookie to whatever domain you specify, such as `www.myserver.com`. This provides greater access control for the cookie, but typically you can just leave it as the default value. `Path` is similar to `Domain`, but it restricts the ASP.NET pages that can access the cookie to a certain path on your server. `HasKeys` tells you if this cookie has keys or is simply a single-value cookie. Finally, `Secure` tells ASP.NET whether or not it should transmit the cookie securely—that is, only over the HTTPS protocol instead of HTTP. The default value is `false`.

Accessing Cookies

The browser sends all cookie information to the server when it makes a request. Therefore, you can use the `Request` object to gather that information. Accessing a cookie follows the exact same syntax as creating a cookie. In the following listing, you'll use `Response.Write` to write the cookie values to the browser:

```
'set up some cookie variables
Response.Write( _
   Request.Cookies("MyCookie").Value)

Response.Write( _
   Request.Cookies("21DaysCookie")("Username"))
Response.Write( _
   Request.Cookies("21DaysCookie")("Preference"));
```

Again, notice the difference between accessing a value and key/value pairs—specifically, the use of the `Value` property. Since key/value pairs are simply collections of data, you can iterate through them easily, as shown in Listing 4.4.

LISTING 4.4 Looping Through Cookie Keys

```
<%@ Page Language="VB" %>

<script runat="server">
   sub Page_Load(Sender as Object, e as EventArgs)
      dim strVariable as string

      'set up some cookie variables
      Response.Cookies("temp").Value = "HI"
```

LISTING 4.4 continued

```
9:          Response.Cookies("21DaysCookie")("Username") = "Chris"
10:          Response.Cookies("21DaysCookie")("Preference") = _
11:             "800x640"
12:          Response.Cookies("21DaysCookie")("Password") = _
13:             "CookiesRock"
14:          Response.Cookies("21DaysCookie")("LastVisit") = _
15:             DateTime.Now.ToString
16:          Response.Cookies("21DaysCookie")("UserAgent") = _
17:             Request.ServerVariables("HTTP_USER_AGENT")
18:
19:          for each strVariable in Response.Cookies _
20:             ("21DaysCookie").Values
21:             Label1.Text += "<b>" & strVariable & "</b>: " & _
22:                Request.Cookies("21DaysCookie")(strVariable) & "<br>"
23:          next
24:       end sub
25:    </script>
26:
27:    <html><body>
28:       <form runat="server">
29:          <asp:Label id="Label1" runat="server"/>
30:       </form>
31:    </body></html>
```


ANALYSIS On line 29, you've created an ASP.NET `Label` server control, which will be discussed on Day 5. For now, just know that it displays HTML text in a `<span>` element.

Note that most of this code is in the `Page_Load` event handler, which is discussed in the next section. On lines 8–17, you create your cookie and set up some keys and values. On line 17, you even use the `Request.ServerVariables` collection to return the `HTTP_USER_AGENT` setting.

Line 19 returns a collection of the cookie's keys. Using a `for...each` loop, you print the key names and values to the label. Recall that the `for...each` loop assigns the value returned from the collection, in this case the key name, to the counter `strVariable`. You access the key's value with this:

```
Request.Cookies("21DaysCookie")(strVariable)
```

You should see something similar to Figure 4.5.

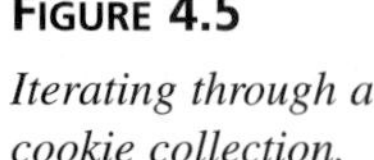

FIGURE 4.5
Iterating through a cookie collection.

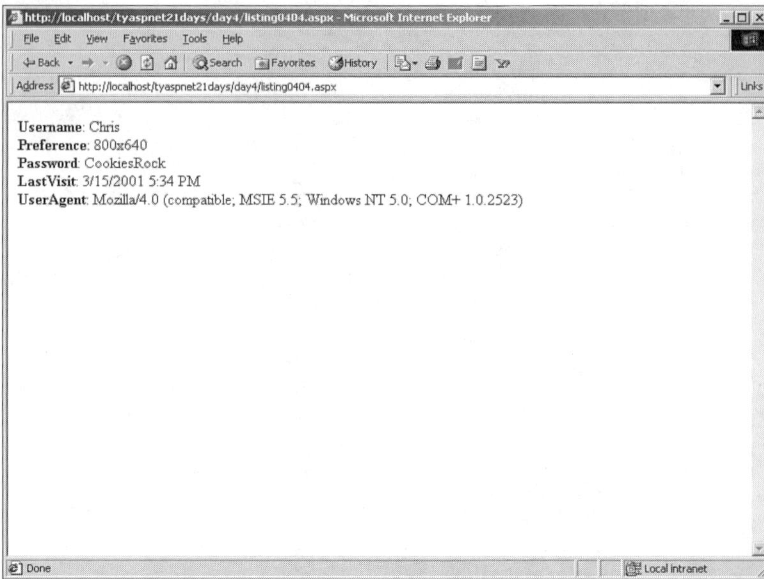

Cookies are a great tool for maintaining information about a user. Their only drawback is that they aren't supported on all browsers. You'll learn another method for maintaining information later today in "The `Session` Object."

The `Page` Object

The `Page` object contains all the properties and methods for every ASP.NET page that you build. When you execute an ASP.NET page, it inherits from the `Page` class in the .NET Framework.

Recall the discussion about inheritance yesterday. A class defines some parameters and methods for objects based on that class. When you create another class that inherits from that parent class, you also inherit its members. However, you can also create your own members for the child class.

ASP.NET pages are the child objects for the `Page` object, which is where the pages inherit the members from. Any methods or properties you define in the ASP.NET page become members of the object based on your page. This means that if you create another page, it can access the methods and properties of the first page! This is object-oriented programming at work.

This object only has a few useful built-in members. `IsPostBack` tells you if a form on this page posted to this same page. (For a discussion of postback forms, see Day 2,

"Building ASP.NET Pages.") You'll be using this property quite often after you learn about Web forms on Days 5 and 6, "Learning More About Web Forms."

`Databind` binds all data expressions to the controls on the page—we're getting way ahead of ourselves, though. This is discussed on Day 9, "Using Databases with ASP.NET."

Finally, this object has an event that you're very interested in—`Load`. This event fires whenever the page starts loading into the browser—a very useful time for ASP.NET developers. Listing 4.5 shows an example.

LISTING 4.5 Using the `Page_Load` Event

```
1:    <%@ Page Language="VB" %>
2:
3:    <script runat="server">
4:       sub Page_Load(Sender as Object, e as EventArgs)
5:          tbMyText.Value = "This is the page load event!"
6:       end sub
7:    </script>
8:    <html><body>
9:       <form runat="server">
10:          <input type="text" size="25"
11:             id="tbMyText" runat="server" />
12:       </form>
13:    </body></html>
```


ANALYSIS On line 10, you create a simple HTML form text input box named `tbMyText` and specify that it runs at the server. On line 4, you define the event handler for the `Load` event, `Page_Load` (note the standard event handler parameter list). When this event fires—that is, when the page loads into the browser—you set the `Value` property of `tbMyText` to `"This is the page load event!"` Figure 4.6 shows the output of this code.

In effect, you fill out the form field before the user even sees it.

Note

> Note the format of the event handler's name. ASP.NET requires event handlers to follow the naming convention of *object_event*. In this case, it's `Page_Load`.
>
> This is a necessary convention. Otherwise, how would ASP.NET know which event handler to use for its built-in events?
>
> You don't have to follow this naming convention for event handlers that you define. It only applies to the events that you don't have programmatic access to.

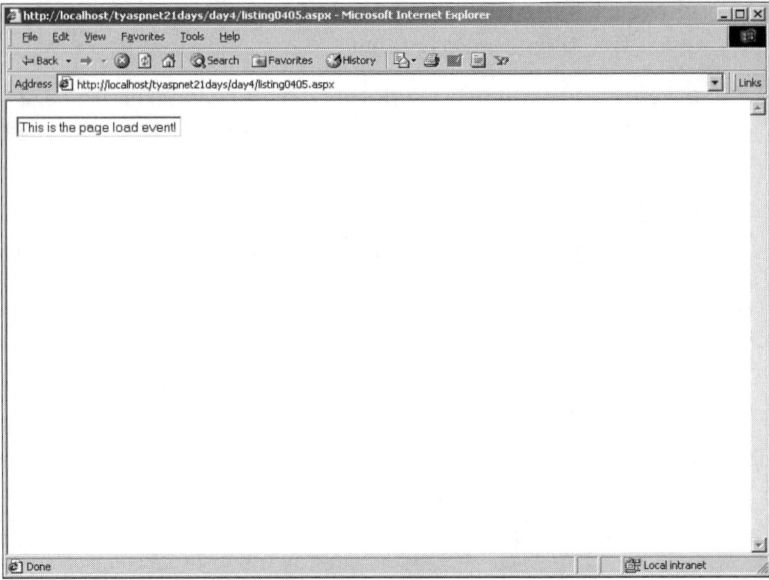

FIGURE 4.6
The `Page_Load` *event at work.*

The `Load` event is very important for ASP.NET developers. You can do a lot of things with this event, including verifying user identities, loading data from a database, and redirecting the user. In fact, nearly all of the ASP.NET pages that you'll see from now on will have a handler for this event.

Let's look at another example. Suppose you want to show the user different messages depending on what time he visits the page. You could implement this as shown in Listing 4.6.

LISTING 4.6 Displaying Different Messages with the `Load` Event

```
<%@Page Language="C#" %>

<script runat="server">
   void Page_Load(Object Sender, EventArgs e) {
      DateTime Now = DateTime.Now;
      int intHour = Now.Hour;

      Label1.Text = "The time is now " +
➥Now.ToString("T") + "<p>";

       if (intHour < 12) {
          Label1.Text +="Good morning!";
       } else if (intHour > 12 & intHour < 18) {
          Label1.Text +="Good afternoon!";
```

LISTING 4.6 continued

```
14:          } else {
15:             Label1.Text +="Good evening!";
16:          }
17:       }
18:    </script>
19:
20:    <html><body>
21:       <form runat="server">
22:          <asp:Label id="Label1" runat="server"/>
23:       </form>
24:    </body></html>
```

ANALYSIS On line 22, you create another `Label` control. In your `Load` event, you set the `Now` variable to the current time and use the `Hour` property of the `DateTime` object to return the hour.

Line 8 displays the current time in the `Label` control. The `ToString` method returns a string with the formatted date and takes one argument, a string that tells the object how to format the date. Table 4.4 lists the valid formatting strings.

TABLE 4.4 Valid `DateTime` `Format` Strings

String	*Example*
"d"	2/01/2001
"D"	Thursday, February 01, 2001
"f"	Thursday, February 01, 2001 4:32 PM
"F"	Thursday, February 01, 2001 4:32:30 PM
"g"	2/01/2001 4:32 PM
"G"	2/01/2001 4:32:30 PM
"m"	February 01
"r"	Thu, 01 February 2001 16:32:30 GMT
"s"	2001-01-01T16:32:30
"t"	4:32 PM
"T"	4:32:30 PM
"u"	2001-01-01 16:32:30Z
"U"	Thursday, February 01, 2001 16:32:30
"y"	February, 2001
"dddd, MMMM dd yyyy"	Thursday, February 01 2001

TABLE 4.4 continued

String	*Example*
"ddd, MMM d """yy	Thu, Feb 1 '01
"dddd, MMMM dd"	Thursday, February 01
"M/yy"	2/01
"dd-MM-yy"	01-02-01

Starting on line 11, you use a series of `if` statements to determine the proper message to display in the label. Figure 4.7 shows the output of this page at the time of this writing.

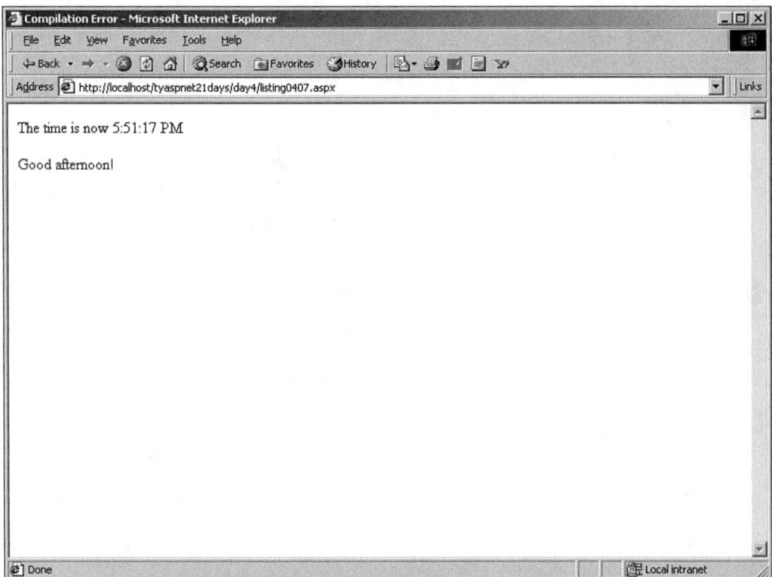

FIGURE 4.7
Displaying customized messages in the `Load` *event.*

You'll be using the `Load` event for more interesting things after you learn about Web forms in a few days.

The `Session` Object

The `Session` object presents a very interesting concept. Because the Web is a stateless medium (see Day 2), information about a particular user is hard to keep track of. There's no way to use HTTP to find out if a series of requests comes from one user or a bunch of different users. This makes it hard to tailor a Web site for one user.

The `Session` object combats this limitation. It allows you to store items (such as variables, objects, strings, or whatever) that are pertinent to a specific user in a single location on the server. Essentially, it acts as that user's personal storage locker of information. Imagine lockers in a school—you put your belongings in your locker to store while you're in class. When you leave for the day, the locker is emptied.

NEW TERM The `Session` object works by the same mechanism. When a user visits your site, he's allocated a "locker" into which the developer can put whatever information she likes. The user's time at the site is called a *session*. Once the user leaves the site, the locker is abandoned, the information is lost, and the session ends.

Imagine that a user comes to your site and enters his name in a form, which you would like to remember. You can put the name into the `Session` object and then recall it from anywhere you want, assuming the session hasn't ended. The syntax is as follows:

```
Session.Add(variablename, value)
```

Or:

```
Session(variablename) = value;
```

You can store as many variables in session for each user as your computer's memory will hold. Listing 4.7 is a page that implements the preceding example.

LISTING 4.7 Storing Variables in `Session`

```
<%@ Page Language="VB" %>

<script runat="server">
   sub Submit_Click(Sender as Object, e as EventArgs)
      if tbName.Value <> ""
         Session("Name") = tbName.Value
         Response.Write("Hi " & Session("Name") & "!")
      else
         Response.Write("You forgot to enter a name.")
       end if
    end sub
 </script>

 <html><body>
    <form runat="server">
       Please enter your name:
       <input type="text" id="tbName"
          runat="server"/>

       <p>
       <asp:Button id="btSubmit"
```

LISTING 4.7 continued

```
22:                 text="Submit"
23:                 runat="server"
24:                 OnClick="Submit_Click" />
25:         </form>
26:     </body></html>
```

ANALYSIS Let's examine the function in the code declaration block. First, on line 5 you check if the user did indeed enter a value in the text box. If she didn't, you use `Response.Write` to print an error message on line 9. If she did, however, you create a new `Session` variable called `"Name"` and assign it the value in the text box on line 6. Finally, on line 7, you write a Welcome message to the user using the variable you just put into the `Session` object. Figure 4.8 displays the output.

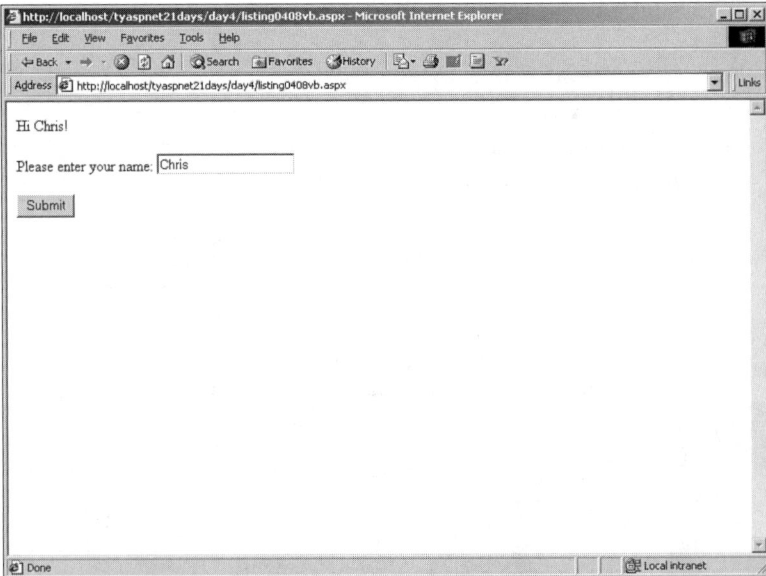

FIGURE 4.8
Storing and retrieving `Session` *variables.*

Note how the text you entered stays in the text box, even after you click the Submit button. This is the automatic viewstate management at work!

Using the `Session` object is very easy and very helpful. Let's create another page that uses the `Session` variable you just created. See Listing 4.8.

LISTING 4.8 Retrieving Variables in `Session`

```
<%@ Page Language="VB" %>

<script runat="server">
   sub Page_Load(Sender as Object, e as EventArgs)
     Label1.Text = "Welcome back " & Session("Name") & "!"
   end sub
</script>

<html><body>
    <form runat="server">
       <asp:Label id="Label1" runat="server"/>
    </form>
 </body></html>
```

Assuming you haven't closed the browser or let it sit there for an extended length of time, you should now see a Welcome message using the name you stored in Listing 4.7. You can even store objects and data stores in `Session`, just as with any other variable.

How does ASP.NET keep track of sessions? Normally, when a user visits the site and a session is started, the computer generates a unique ID for that user, which is then stored on the client computer as a cookie. As the user moves from page to page, ASP.NET reads this cookie value to determine which session this user belongs to. You can easily read this value with the following:

```
Response.Write(Session.SessionID)
```

The `Session` ID is a 120-bit string that is guaranteed to be unique for each user. Once the session expires, the cookie is deleted. (You can change this behavior, though, as you'll see on Day 18, "Configuring and Deploying ASP.NET Applications.")

Controlling `Session`

There are various ways to control how the `Session` object behaves in your ASP.NET applications. The first is the `Timeout` value, which sets how long a session can be idle before ASP.NET abandons it. In other words, if a user visits your site but doesn't click on anything, or leaves the site for an amount of time equal to this timeout value, the session and all its information will be lost. This value is 20 minutes by default in IIS 5.0, but you can easily change it as follows:

```
Session.Timeout = x 'x is the number of minutes
```

There are a number of reasons you may want to change this value. Let's examine a typical Web site: Each user that comes to the site gets a unique `Session` object, which means each user gets his own piece of the server's memory. Even if he leaves the site after only

30 seconds, his session is still alive for another 19 minutes and 30 seconds. After a while, this can add up to a lot of memory.

Table 4.5 shows the growth of sessions with the default timeout value, assuming 100 visitors come to your site every half hour and a timeout value of 120 minutes.

TABLE 4.5 The Growth of Sessions

Time	*Users*	*Sessions*	*Description*
0:00	100	100	100 sessions are created for the first 100 site visitors.
0:30	100	200	The first 100 sessions are still active whether or not the visitors are still on the site. 100 new visitors means 100 new sessions.
1:00	100	300	Another 100 visitors adds 100 new sessions, while the first two groups' sessions still haven't expired.
1:30	100	400	100 new visitors = 100 new sessions.
2:00	100	500	...
2:30	100	500	100 new visitors create 100 new sessions, but the first group's sessions finally expire after two hours.
3:00	100	500	It just keeps going and going...

You're obviously wasting a lot of memory—500 sessions for only 100 concurrent visitors—not always an efficient way to work. Setting the `Timeout` too low could also result in some problems, however. Imagine an e-commerce site where users can add items to a shopping cart. The `Session` object can easily hold such items, but if you set the `Timeout` too low, a user may lose all the items in the cart before she even gets a chance to check out!

Twenty minutes is ideal for many situations, but you may need to tweak this setting depending on your circumstances. A secure banking Web site may want a smaller value, while an online e-mail site may want a bigger one.

You can also cause a session to expire immediately by using the `Abandon` method. Imagine a Web site where users can check their e-mail. After a user is done, he wants to log out so that other people can't use his e-mail account when he's away from his computer. Abandoning the session is one way to accomplish this. Simply call the following:

```
Session.Abandon
```

The temporary cookie is deleted, as well as any session information.

Working with `Session`

The `Session` object can be manipulated just like an array. You can loop through all the variables and manipulate them as needed. Listing 4.9 uses the `for...each` statement in VB.NET to loop through and display the contents of the session.

LISTING 4.9 Iterating Through `Session` Variables

```
1:    <%@ Page Language="VB" %>
2:
3:    <script runat="server">
4:       sub Page_Load(obj as object, e as eventArgs)
5:         dim strVariable as string
6:
7:         'set up some session variables
8:         Session("Name") = "Chris"
9:         Session("FavoriteColor") = "Blue"
10:         Session("EyeColor") = "Brown"
11:         Session("AMessage") = "Welcome to my world"
12:         Session("ASPNET") = "rocks!"
13:
14:         for each strVariable in Session.Contents
15:            Label1.Text += "<b>" & strVariable & "</b>: " & _
16:               Session(strVariable) & "<br>"
17:         next
18:       end sub
19:    </script>
20:    <html><body>
21:       <form runat="server">
22:          <asp:Label id="Label1" runat="server"/>
23:       </form>
24:    </body></html>
```


ANALYSIS On lines 8–12, you set up some useless `Session` variables. On line 14, you set up your `for...each` loop. This iterates through all the items in a collection; in this case, it's all the `Strings` in your Session `Contents` collection. Each item in this collection represents a key value—a `Session` variable name—such as `"Name"`, `"FavoriteColor"`, and so on. You retrieve the actual value of the key by using `Session(strVariable)`. Then you simply display the key/value pairs in the `Label` control, as shown in Figure 4.9.

Sessions Without Cookies

By default, ASP.NET uses cookies to store `Session` IDs and keep track of users. What happens, however, if the user's browser doesn't support cookies or the user just isn't accepting any? Luckily, ASP.NET has another way to keep track of sessions.

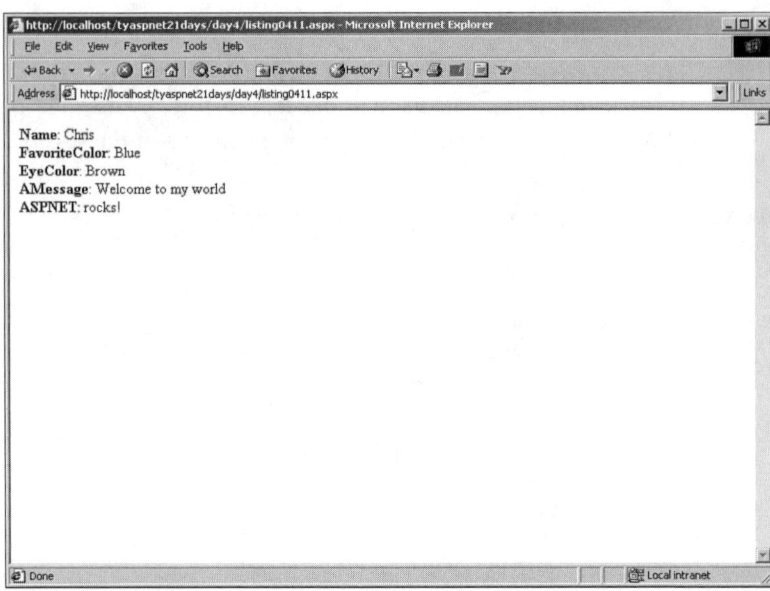

FIGURE 4.9
Using loops to display `Session` *keys and values.*

NEW TERM *Cookie munging* is the process that ASP.NET uses to keep track of sessions without cookies. Before a page is sent to the browser, ASP.NET scans the HTML code for any hyperlinks. At the end of each link, ASP.NET tacks on an encoded version of the `Session` ID. When the user clicks a link, ASP.NET grabs that string, decodes it, and passes it to the page the user is requesting. This page can now use that ID to set or retrieve any `Session` variables. ASP.NET also places the encoded `Session` ID in each link on this page as well. This all happens automatically if ASP.NET detects that the visitor doesn't support cookies. Figure 4.10 illustrates this concept.

You'll learn some more advanced ways to configure session on Day 18.

Session Recommendations

There once was a time where it was recommended to put as little information into session variables as possible. Limited memory resources, older versions of Web servers, and the situation outlined by Table 4.5 made storing loads of data in session detrimental to the performance of your Web site. Things, however, have changed.

Nowadays, servers are often equipped with 512 megabytes of memory and more. If your Web site architecture is set up properly, most of this memory is not doing anything; it's just sitting there going to waste. Why shouldn't we use it instead?

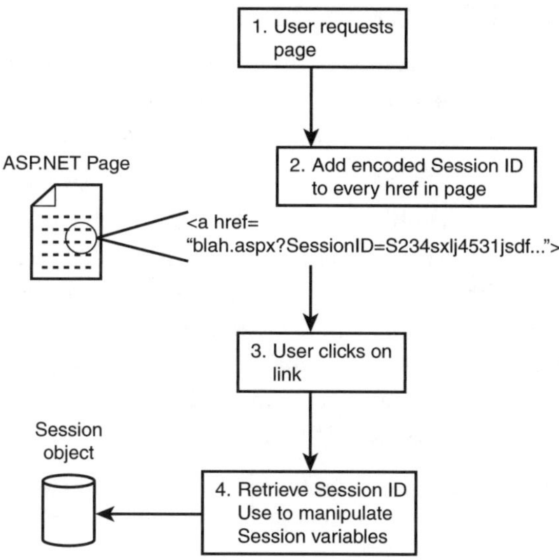

FIGURE 4.10
Cookie munging involves adding encoded `Session` *IDs to hrefs in the form of querystrings.*

4

Let's imagine that you store user infomration in a database. To retrieve this information, you need to work with ADO.NET and communicate back and forth to a database, not to mention the fact that the database has to search the hard drive for the requested information.

When you store this data in memory via session instead, you don't have to perform all of those steps. Accessing from memory can be as much as 100 times faster than retrieving from the database. You may be scared that you have too much data to store in memory, but you'll often find that your entire store of data doesn't add up to more than a few megabytes, and relative to the amount of memory on your server the performance benefits greatly outweigh the drawbacks—if you can call using your system resources as they were designed to be used a drawback.

You'll learn more about using your system memory to its full potential in Day 14, "Using ASP.NET's Improved Caching Capabilities."

Do	Don't
Do use `Session` variables to store as much user-specific information as you can. The performance of your site will be greatly enhanced.	**Don't** use `Session` variables when you have a limited amount of memory to spare, or you need to use your Web server for things other than serving a Web site (for instance, if your Web server is your home PC).

The `HttpApplication` Object

The `HttpApplication` object represents an ASP.NET application. (ASP.NET defines an *application* as all the files in a single virtual directory and below.) This object will be examined in much more detail on Day 18, but this section will cover some introductory topics.

New Term Like the `Response` object, ASP.NET creates an `HttpApplication` object named `Application` whenever your application starts—that is, as soon as someone requests any page from your site for the first time. Only one `Application` object is created for your entire application, unlike the `Session` object, where a new one was created for each new user. Like the `Session` object, however, the `Application` object can be used to store variables and objects in memory. These *application variables* are available across your entire application and don't apply to any specific user.

For example, suppose you have a footer or disclaimer that you need to place on every single page. You can store this in an application variable with the following:

```
Application("Disclaimer") = "Copyright 2001"
```

And then you simply call it from every page:

```
Response.Write(Application("Disclaimer"))
```

Imagine if you stored this string in a `Session` object. Each new user that visited your site would receive this string in his session. If you had 100 users, you'd have stored this string 100 different times. This is a waste of memory when storing it in `Application` will suffice.

Like the `Session` object, it's a good idea to store information in `Application` variables because you can access it faster than you could from other sources.

Do	Don't
Do use application variables when a variable isn't specific to any user. **Do** use `Session` variables when storing personalized information.	**Don't** use application variables to store personalized content, such as usernames, passwords, and so on. **Don't** store large amounts of HTML in the `Application` object when you can simply write it in an HTML page.

There are a few events that you can handle from the `Application` object, but let's leave those for Day 18.

The `HttpServerUtility` Object

The last object today is the `HttpServerUtility` object, which provides several helper methods that are used in processing requests. You can use the name `Server` to access this object's members.

Redirecting Users

You've examined one way to redirect users with the `Response` object, but there are two other ways. The `Response.Redirect` method sends HTTP information to the browser, instructing it to go to another page. This requires a round trip that may not be necessary. Therefore, ASP.NET can also use the `Execute` and `Transfer` methods of the `HttpServerUtility` object to send users off to different pages.

`Server.Transfer` simply transfers execution to another page. This doesn't require any information to be sent to the browser—it all occurs on the server without the user's knowledge. For instance, this code snippet examines a user's password (assuming he entered one in a form):

```
if (strPassword == "blahblah") _
   Server.Transfer("success.aspx")
```


If the password matches the string on line 1, you transfer him to another page. This is a valuable method for easily redirecting users.

`Server.Execute` transfers ASP.NET execution to another page, but it returns to the original page when it's done. This is useful if you need to execute some code on another page (such as data processing, for instance) but continue on the same page. It works much like the branching logic we described yesterday, and follows the same format as `Server.Transfer`.

Formatting Strings

Typically, when you send output to the browser, it's interpreted as HTML. For example, the following prints a line break in the browser:

```
Response.Write("<br>")
```

However, there are times when you want the actual word to be printed. Instead of a line break, you want `<br>` to actually appear on the visitor's screen. To do this, you can use the `HtmlEncode` method of the `HttpServerUtility` object. The following would output `<br>` and the user would see `<br>` in the browser:

```
Response.Write(Server.HTMLEncode("<br>"))
```

`<` is the HTML-encoded equivalent to `<`, while `>` translates to `>`. `HtmlEncode` makes these two substitutions to your text.

`UrlEncode` does something similar, but it formats a specified string using the rules for a URL. For example, the ampersand and question mark have special meanings in a URL, so `Server.UrlEncode` changes these characters to their URL-encoded versions. This is helpful if you ever need to place a string into the querystring.

`Server.HtmlDecode` and `Server.UrlDecode` perform these operations in reverse, translating encoded character sequences to the characters they represent (from `<` to <, for example).

The `MapPath` method doesn't exactly format a string, but it helps to determine the proper string you need. This method translates a virtual path to a physical path on the server. For example, the following:

```
Server.MapPath("/TYASPNET21Days/day4")
```

would translate to this:

```
c:\inetpub\wwwroot\TYASPNET21Days\day4
```

This is very helpful when you need to know a physical path, such as when you're writing files to the server (as you'll learn on Day 13, "Reading and Writing Files on the Web Server").

Controlling Scripts

The `HttpServerUtility` object provides one property to control the execution of ASP.NET scripts: `ScriptTimeout`. This value tells the server how long to wait before terminating a script or page. For example, the following tells ASP.NET that any code that has been executing for 90 seconds should be terminated:

```
Server.ScriptTimeout = 90
```

Occasionally, code you write may have a bug, such as an infinite loop, and may go on executing forever or until your server crashes. Using this property prevents that from happening. ASP.NET thinks any code that executes for longer than the `ScriptTimeout` period isn't working correctly and terminates it.

On the other hand, occasionally some code really does take that long to execute (if it's very complex, for instance) and the `ScriptTimeout` property may be too short. Thus, you can easily extend the time.

Creating Objects

Finally, the `CreateObject` method instantiates a COM object identified by `progid`. We'll skip this topic for now and return to it in more detail in Week 3.

That's Not ASP!

If you're familiar with classic ASP, you should notice a lot of changes in ASP.NET, but also a lot of similarities. Many of the objects you were familiar with in ASP are still available, but they've taken on slightly different forms in the .NET Framework. For instance, there's now a class called `HttpCookie` that provides the methods and properties used to manipulate your cookies. The `Request`, `Response`, and `Session` objects are still pretty much the same. The `HttpServerUtility` object replaces the old `Server` object, and you now have a new object called `Page` that represents the page itself.

These objects provide a lot of functionality, and many of the concepts and methodologies for implementing them in ASP.NET are the same as those in ASP. For example, the use of `Session` variables still follows the rules of memory limits applied in ASP. However, this and other objects work behind the scenes to provide a much more stable and powerful environment. The `Session` object can now store variables across server farms, and can even save data upon server crashes. You'll examine that in more detail on Day 18.

Moving to object-oriented programming may require some getting used to, but once you learn it, it will simplify the way you do things. It's vital that you learn how to use the built-in .NET objects because they're the key to developing strong ASP.NET applications.

Yesterday and today, you learned about two of the new ASP.NET programming languages, VB.NET and C#. Luckily, they don't require much of an adjustment on the part of VBScript developers. They open up a whole new world for C and C++ developers, who now can develop ASP.NET pages in a familiar language.

Although certain ASP.NET features seem to improve upon traditional ASP only cosmetically, their new framework provides much more power—and soon you'll begin to take advantage of it!

Summary

Objects have properties and methods to describe them. Many of these properties and methods require instances of the objects, but static members do not.

The `Response` object allows server-to-browser communication, while the `Request` object allows browser-to-server communication. The `Response` object is useful for displaying information to the user or redirecting her, while `Request` allows you to discover information about the client.

The `HttpCookie` object provides mechanisms for reading and writing cookies, mainly through the `Response` and `Request` objects. Remember that cookies are stored on the client's computer, so they don't use up valuable server resources.

The `Page` object represents the ASP.NET page. The `Load` event of this object is very useful, and you'll be using it quite often from now on.

The `Session` object stores information about a user's current session. You can keep personal information in `Session` variables, such as usernames or site preferences. `Session` variables can often speed up performance tremendously, so weigh this methods of maintaining user information versus your server resources wisely.

The `HttpApplication` object represents an ASP.NET application, which includes all files and pages in a virtual directory and the directories below it. This object has some useful events that you'll look into on Day 18. It can also be used to store application-wide variables.

Finally, the `HttpServerUtility` object provides additional methods that help developers process user requests. These include formatting strings, redirecting users, controlling script execution, and creating objects.

Today's lesson covered a lot of material about ASP.NET objects. Tomorrow you're going to look at Web forms, a new framework for building interactive user interfaces with ASP.NET. This framework provides a number of additional objects, such as HTML Server Controls and Validation Controls.

Q&A

Q Does ASP.NET support caching?

A You bet! Rather than using the `Response.Expires` method (as in traditional ASP), ASP.NET has a complex caching system that you'll learn about in Week 2.

Workshop

This workshop will help reinforce the concepts covered in today's lesson. Answers can be found in Appendix A.

Quiz

1. What are static members?
2. Will the following code snippet work?

```
<html><body>
   Hi there!
   <%
      Response.Redirect("page2.aspx")
   %>
</body></html>
```

3. What language is the following code snippet written in?

```
Response.Write("Hello there!")
```

Exercises

1. Create an ASP.NET page in C# that acts as a secure login page. Allow the user to enter a username and password in a text box. If they match a string you specify, redirect the user to a "success" page. Otherwise, display an error. If the user is valid, save her username in a `Session` variable.
2. Write the success page in VB.NET. Display a personalized Welcome message using the `Load` event of the `Page` object and a `Label` control. Also inform the user of the current time and his `Session` ID. Check the `IsPostback` property of the `Page` object to ensure that this message is only displayed the first time he arrives at the page. Provide a button for him to log out, with a confirmation message.

WEEK 1

DAY 5

Beginning Web Forms

Web forms are an interesting concept in Web development. They allow ASP.NET to provide programmatic control over the user interface by using objects that reside on the server. Indeed, they're an integral part of ASP.NET.

Today you're going to examine the Web forms framework and look at why you're using them in your ASP.NET pages. These controls can dramatically enhance the functionality of your pages, while allowing you to easily develop complex user interfaces.

Tomorrow's lesson will continue this discussion of Web forms with some more advanced topics.

Today's lesson will cover

- What HTML forms are and how they work
- What Web forms are, how they work, and why they're better than HTML forms
- How to use server controls
- How to react to control events

- How to use HTML server controls
- How to use Web server controls

Introduction to Forms

Let's take a look again at how the Web works. Recall from Day 1, "Getting Started with ASP.NET," that a client sends a request to a server for some information, and the server responds by sending the appropriate file. This is the basis of the request/response model.

The client can also send data to the server. HTML forms allow user interaction with Web pages—they provide communication between the client and server. For example, Listing 5.1 displays a typical HTML form that allows the user to enter his name and click a Submit button.

LISTING 5.1 A Typical HTML Form

```
<html><body>
   <form method="post">
      Please enter your name:
      <input type="text" size="20">
      <input type="Submit" value="Submit">
   </form>
</body></html>
```

When the user clicks the Submit button, the form *posts* to the server any data that the user has entered. This is similar to a client request, but the browser sends additional information along with the post that the server can use for its purposes. HTML forms consist of elements that make up a user interface. They're completely client-based. Users enter data into these elements and submit the form, which posts the data to the server. Figure 5.1 illustrates this concept.

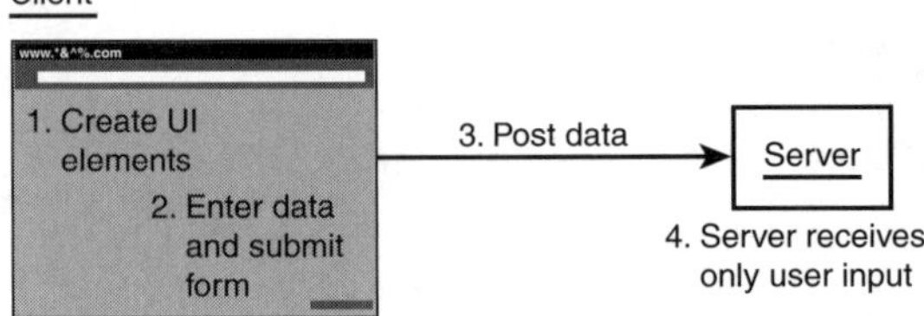

FIGURE 5.1
The server receives only the information that the user enters.

Other than a post and a request, there's no way for the server to communicate with the client. Thus, all Web-based applications must rely on this model, making programming sometimes difficult. With such sparse communication between client and server, it's difficult for either one to gather much information about the other. For instance, the server won't know the capabilities of the client browser or what it's trying to do, making the client's behavior completely unpredictable.

The server also has no idea what the user interface looks like or what kind of data it should expect once the form is posted. All the server knows is what the form tells it, which usually isn't very much. As soon as the post is finished, the server forgets everything the form told it and it loses track of what's going on.

Introduction to Web Forms

Web forms are very similar to traditional HTML forms. The difference is that Web forms are server-based, meaning you create the user elements on the server. The server has complete knowledge of what the interface looks like, what it can do, what data it expects, and so on.

NEW TERM On the server, you create objects known as *server controls* that represent pieces of the UI. Unlike HTML form elements, these objects are completely controllable—they have properties, events, and methods that you can manipulate. As soon as the client requests the page, ASP.NET converts these controls into HTML, which renders perfectly in the browser. Figure 5.2 illustrates the process.

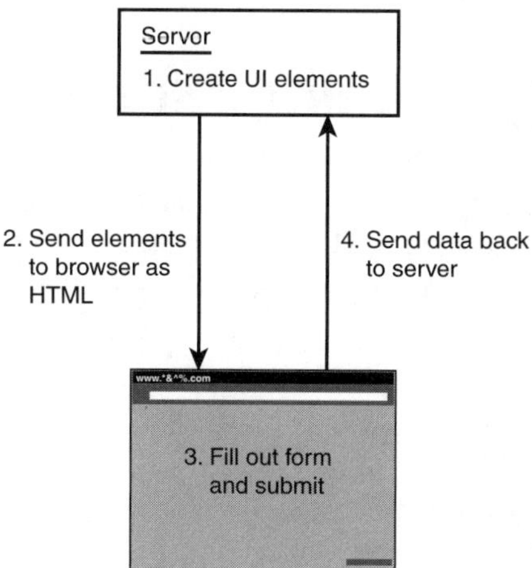

FIGURE 5.2
With Web forms, the server knows what the form looks like and what it can do.

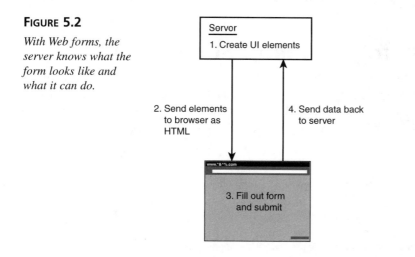

Through the client-side script that ASP.NET generates automatically, these controls alert the server whenever something happens, such as a button click. When an event does occur, the client-side script posts information to the server, often without the user's knowledge. Thus, the server is constantly notified of what's happening on the client, and the server and client are tied together.

> This showcases the event-driven model at work. However, remember that underneath it all, ASP.NET still relies on request/response to send information back and forth. Using the event-driven model on top of the request/response model provides a more intuitive environment for application development.

Also, since the server created the controls, it can remember what was entered in each control. Recall from Day 2, "Building ASP.NET Pages," that ASP.NET uses hidden form fields to remember the viewstate of each control and can update them accordingly.

Web forms make our lives much easier by telling the server what's going on in the user interface. Imagine trying to drive blindfolded while a passenger yelled out "Left!" or "Right!" at the appropriate times. Using traditional HTML forms was similar—they didn't tell the server what was going on, but they occasionally supplied data. How could the server control the application properly?

Web forms lift the "blindfold." The server can see everything that's going on and properly "drive" the program.

Web Forms Programming Model

Web forms pages are divided into two parts: the visual elements and the accompanying UI logic. These two components are completely separate from each other conceptually, and they can be physically located anywhere you want. Typically, both parts are contained within one `.aspx` file. Listing 5.2 shows an example Web form.

LISTING 5.2 A Typical Web Forms Page

```
<%@ Page Language="VB" %>

<script runat="server">
   Sub tbMessage_Change(Sender As Object, E As EventArgs)
      lblMessage.Text = "Hello " + tbMessage.Text
   End Sub
</script>

<html><body>
    <font size="5">Sam's Teach Yourself ASP.NET in 21 Days:
    Day 2</font><hr><p>
```

LISTING 5.2 continued

```
12:       <% Response.Write("Our First Page<p>") %>
13:
14:       <form runat="server">
15:          Please enter your name:
16:          <asp:textbox id="tbMessage"
17:             OnTextChanged="tbMessage_Change"
18:             runat=server/>
19:          <asp:button id="btSubmit" Text="Submit"
20:             runat=server/><p>
21:          <asp:label id="lblMessage" font-size="20pt"
22:             runat=server/>
23:       </form>
24:    </body></html>
```

ANALYSIS This should look familiar—it's the example you looked at on Day 2. The UI is contained within the HTML portion of the page, consisting of the server controls on lines 16, 19, and 21. These controls have properties, methods, and events that you can control. The UI logic—the code that controls the UI—is contained in the code declaration block on lines 3–7.

There's nothing exotic about creating Web forms. Any ASP.NET page that contains server controls and UI logic is a Web form. Let's take a look at some of the pieces that make up Web forms.

Server Controls

As discussed previously, server controls are the user interface elements of a Web form. There are four types of server controls in ASP.NET: HTML server controls, Web controls, validation controls, and user controls. HTML server controls represent the normal HTML form elements, such as text input boxes and buttons, but they're created on the server, where you can control them. Web controls are similar, but they provide more functionality and can represent more complex user interfaces. Validation controls are used to validate user input, and user controls are custom-built controls that perform some piece of functionality. All of these controls will be covered today and tomorrow, except for validation controls, which will be covered on Day 7, "Validating ASP.NET Pages."

All server controls have properties, methods, and events. They provide much more functionality than traditional HTML form elements, and they make it easier for the developer to build user interfaces.

When you build a server control, you don't have to worry about writing HTML. When the page is requested, server controls automatically spit out the HTML that will produce the proper display. For example, the following line creates a `Button` server control on the server:

```
<asp:Button text="Submit" runat="server" />
```

When this button is requested, it spits out the following HTML to the client:

```
<input type="submit" name="ctrl1" value="Submit" />
```

The two lines barely resemble each other. The first line is used only by the server—the client never sees it. (And if it did, the browser wouldn't know what to do because it only understands HTML.) The second line is what the client sees. By building controls this way, you can spend less time worrying about the HTML that will provide the UI layout, and more time thinking about what your UI should do.

NEW TERM

Also, ASP.NET knows the capabilities of each browser, so it sends the appropriate HTML to each one. For example, if a browser doesn't support Dynamic HTML (DHTML), ASP.NET won't send it any. This is known as *down-level support* because ASP.NET can tone down the HTML output for browsers that don't support higher-level functionality.

Ideally, down-level support will render everything properly for every control. In reality, you aren't so lucky. Some elements will have problems rendering on different browsers because not all browsers treat HTML the same. When you're developing for the major browser versions, though, down-level support will function properly. (Most of the time!)

Server Control Events

Server controls generate multitudes of events. In other words, there are a lot of things a user can do to a server control: click on a button, click a link, fill out a text box, select an item in a list box, and so on. All of these events must be handled by the server, so every time an event occurs, the client posts data to the server.

Note

It's important to distinguish passive user events from active events. An *active event* is one that requires an explicit user action—meaning the user must intentionally perform the action. This includes clicking a button or a link, filling out a text box, and so on. A *passive event* is one that can be performed without the user's direct intention, such as moving the mouse cursor over an image.

Only active events are handled on the server—there are too many passive ones to reliably post all that data back to the server. However, you can still handle these with client-side script.

There are two ways events are posted to the server: immediately as they occur, or collectively during a single post. The latter is a bit more efficient because you don't have to send as many posts, which means that less data is traveling back and forth between the client and server.

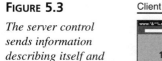

In many cases, you'll want to use the latter method. For example, imagine a user typing his name into a form. Every time he types a letter, an event occurs. You wouldn't want to post data every time a letter changes, but only when the user has finished entering the data or clicks the Submit button. Events like this are *cached*, meaning they're stored up on the client until the user decides to post the data. At that point the server can evaluate them one at a time.

Note

Actually, this event, known as the `TextChanged` event, only happens when the user enters some text and leaves that UI element (that is, uses the Tab key to move to another element). But the idea is the same.

You can force these events to be posted to the server immediately, as you'll see in "Posting Data Immediately" later today.

As discussed on Day 3, "Using Visual Basic.NET and C#," all server control events in ASP.NET send two pieces of data as parameters to the server: an object that represents the control that generated the event, and an object that describes any specific information about the event.

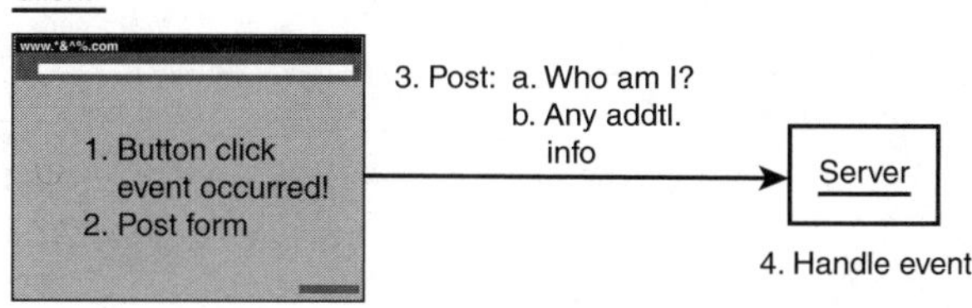

FIGURE 5.3

The server control sends information describing itself and any specific information about the event.

Controls automatically generate events whenever something happens. To handle the event on the server, you need to tell the control what method to use. For example, the following tells ASP.NET to execute the `ClickHandler` method on the server upon the occurrence of the `Click` event:

```
<asp:Button runat="server" OnClick="ClickHandler" />
```

This method could look like the following:

```
1:    sub ClickHandler(Sender as Object, e as Eventargs)
2:       do something...
3:    end sub
```

As mentioned on Day 3, line 1 shows the standard event parameter list for ASP.NET server controls. The second parameter can vary depending on the type of event that has occurred. Most of the time, you'll be using this standard parameter list.

For example, let's look at the example in Listing 5.3.

LISTING 5.3 An Event Handler

```
<%@ Page Language="VB" %>

<script runat="server">
   Sub Button1_Click(Sender as Object, e as EventArgs)
      Label1.Text="You clicked <b>" & Sender.Text & "</b>"
   end Sub
</script>

<html><body>
    <font size="5">Sam's Teach Yourself ASP.NET in 21
    Days: Day 5 </font><hr><p>

    <form runat="server">
       <asp:Button id=Button1 runat="server" Text="Button1"
          onClick="Button1_Click" />
       <p>
       <asp:Label id=Label1 runat=server />
    </form>
 </body></html>
```

When you click on the button, the code should produce the output shown in Figure 5.4.

OUTPUT

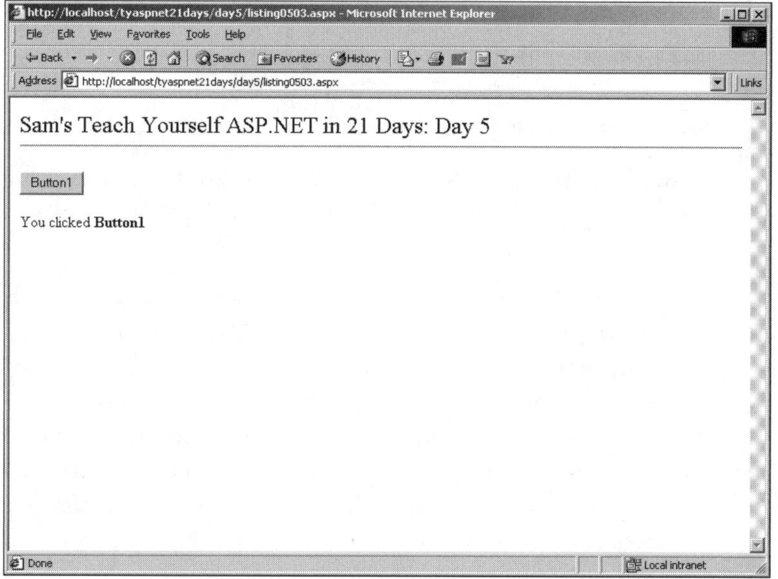

FIGURE 5.4
The page produced by Listing 5.3.

ANALYSIS Even though you haven't looked at the server controls yet, you can see that the `Button` control on line 14 has a `Click` event. This event posts information to the server and executes the `Button1_Click` method, which is defined in the code declaration block on lines 4–6.

> **Caution**
>
> Don't forget to include `runat="server` so that the server controls will work properly.
>
> Also, note that the `<form>` tag is required here. Without it, none of the data would be posted to the server and the page wouldn't work.

Let's take a look at line 5 in particular:

```
5:    Label1.Text = "You clicked <b>" & Sender.Text & "</b>"
```

This line sets the `Text` property of the control named `Label1` (the `Label` on line 17) to whatever is specified after the equal sign. `Sender` is the name of one of the parameters. Since you know it represents the `Button`, you can grab its `Text` property as well.

5

Looking down to line 14, you see that the `Button`'s text property is set to `Button1`. The following line could be used to produce the same output:

```
Label1.Text="You clicked <b>" & Button1.Text & "</b>"
```

But let's take a look at the C# version of line 5:

```
5:     Label1.Text = "You clicked <b>" +
➥((Button)Sender).Text + "</b>";
```

Aside from the regular syntactic changes, there is one other change you must make from VB.NET. Recall that VB.NET is forgiving in the way it casts variables—VB.NET automatically casts some data types for you. C# does not.

Note that the `Sender` variable is passed in as an `Object` data type rather than a `Button`. The `Object` data type does not have a property called `Text`, though the `Button` data type does. If you try to use `Sender.Text` in C#, you would get an error. VB.NET would automatically cast the `Object` to a `Button` so that you could access the `Text` property. C# won't do this for you, so you need to explicitly cast the `Sender` variable as a `Button`. This is done by prefixing the variable name with type of data you want to convert to (see Day 3 for more information on casting). As long as you remember to explicitly cast your variables (which you should do regardless of the language you use), you'll be fine.

The second parameter in your method, `e`, currently doesn't contain any information because the `Button` control had nothing else to send. However, you need to include it anyway because it's part of the standard event parameter list.

Thus, you can handle events however you want. Events will keep occurring, and you can easily provide the methods to handle them. You can just leave the event handler out for the events that you want to ignore. Also, this method allows you to have one method that can handle many different events. There's nothing stopping you from creating 20 `Button` controls that all reference the same method.

Caution

> Let's say you specify in the server control that a method should handle an event:
>
> ```
> <asp:Button runat="server" OnClick="SomeMethod" />
> ```
>
> If you don't create the `SomeMethod` method somewhere in your code declaration block, you'll receive an error.

Posting Web Forms

Let's imagine a typical ASP.NET scenario. When the page loads into the browser, you display a welcome message in a server control. This message becomes part of the control's viewstate, and ASP.NET automatically remembers it.

Then the user submits the form, or an event occurs that causes a post to the server. The server then processes any data or events it needs to, and then it sends the page back to the client for display.

Since ASP.NET remembers the viewstate for the control, it automatically fills in the welcome message again without any intervention from you! This is the same for user-entered information. If a user enters her name in a text box, she'll find that the text she entered stays in the text box even after the form is submitted. This is a welcome change from traditional HTML forms, where the values were lost upon every post.

Because of this, you don't need to refill the server controls' values after the form is posted. ASP.NET does it for you.

As mentioned on Day 4, "Using ASP.NET Objects with C# and VB.NET," the `Page` object has a property called `IsPostBack` that tells you whether or not the form has already been posted. You can check this property and decide whether or not to fill in server controls. For example, let's take a look at Listing 5.4.

LISTING 5.4 Checking the `IsPostBack` Property


```
<%@ Page Language="C#" %>

<script runat="server">
   void Page_Load(Object Sender, EventArgs e) {
      if (!Page.IsPostBack) {
         lblMessage.Text = "Hello world!!!!";
      }
   }

    void Submit(Object Sender, EventArgs e) {
       lblMessage2.Text = "Form posted";
    }
 </script>

 <html><body>
    <form runat="server">
       <asp:Button id="btSubmit" runat="server" Text="Submit"
          onClick="Submit" />
       <p>
       <asp:Label id="lblMessage" runat=server />
```

LISTING 5.4 continued

```
21:          <p>
22:          <asp:Label id="lblMessage2" runat=server />
23:       </form>
24:    </body></html>
```

ANALYSIS When this page loads, the words "`Hello World!!!!`" will be displayed in the label on line 20. When the user clicks the Submit button, "`Form posted`" will appear in the second label on line 22. The first label will still have the hello message because ASP.NET saves it in the viewstate and automatically fills it in for you.

On line 5, you check the `IsPostBack` property, and if it's true (meaning the form has been submitted), you don't execute line 6. You won't have to refill the label every time the form is posted because ASP.NET does it for you. Figure 5.5 shows the output from this code after the form has been posted.

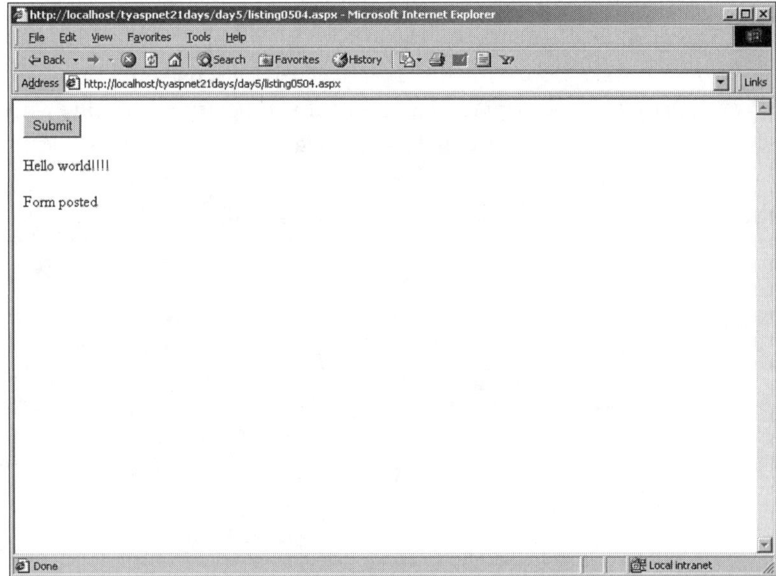

FIGURE 5.5
The text in the label stays there even though the form is submitted and you don't explicitly fill it yourself.

This was just a simple example, and not processing line 6 isn't going to save you a lot of time. But as the commands get more and more complex, checking `IsPostBack` will become very useful.

Saving State

As you know, Web forms save the viewstate of each control in the form through hidden form fields. This viewstate tells you what is entered in the control (if anything), whether the control is selected or not, which item is selected, and so on. The viewstate provides a lot of information that ASP.NET uses to maintain the state of each server control.

There *is* another way to save information in Web forms, though. You can use the *state bag*, an object that holds values when a form is posted. When you place something in the state bag and submit the form, the server saves the information and sends it back to the client after it's finished processing. This is an easy way to store custom information that a user didn't enter, such as a calculation. You can access the state bag through the `ViewState` variable.

Let's look at an example. Listing 5.5 saves the current time in the state bag as soon as the page is loaded. When the user clicks the Submit button, you compare the start time to the new time.

LISTING 5.5 Saving Values in the State Bag

```
<%@ Page Language="VB" %>

<script runat="server">
   Sub Page_Load(Sender as Object, e as EventArgs)
      if not Page.IsPostBack then
         ViewState("StartTime") = DateTime.Now
         lblMessage.Text = "The time is now: " & _
            ViewState("StartTime")
      end if
   end sub

   Sub Submit(obj as object, e as EventArgs)
      lblMessage.Text = "The time is now: " & _
         DateTime.Now & "<br>started at: " & _
         ViewState("StartTime")
   end Sub
</script>

<html><body>
   <font size="5">Sam's Teach Yourself ASP.NET in 21
   Days: Day 5 </font><hr><p>

   <form runat="server">
      <asp:Button id="btSubmit" runat="server" Text="Submit"
         onClick="Submit" />
```

LISTING 5.5 continued

```
26:         <p>
27:         <asp:Label id="lblMessage" runat=server />
28:      </form>
29:   </body></html>
```

ANALYSIS You want to store the time of the first viewing of the page, so you check the `IsPostBack` property on line 5 in the `Page_Load` event handler. If this is the first viewing, you store the current time (as denoted by `DateTime.Now`) in `ViewState`. `ViewState` is the name of the state bag that ASP.NET creates for you. Interacting with it is exactly the same as interacting with the `Session` object from yesterday. You then display this time in a label control.

Whenever the user clicks the Submit button, the `Submit` method is executed. This method, beginning on line 12, displays the current time and the time stored in the state bag in the label. Figure 5.6 shows the output from this listing. The value from the state bag is different from the current value.

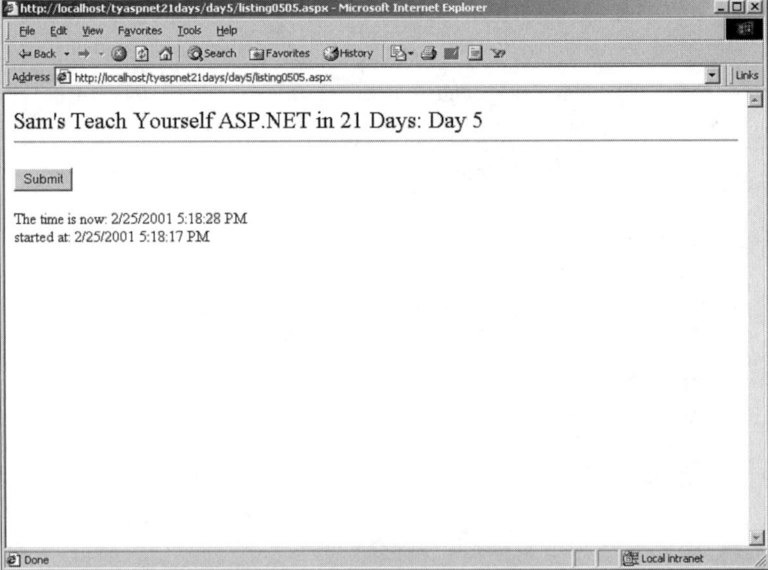

FIGURE 5.6
The state bag holds the time of the first viewing.

Unlike the `Session` or `Application` objects, the state bag is emptied as soon as the user leaves the page. The values are saved only as long as the same form is posted over again. Once a new page is loaded, the state bag is discarded.

Do	Don't
Do use the state bag when you need to save custom values for a particular form.	**Don't** use the state bag when you need to save information for an indefinite amount of time. Instead, use the `Session` or `Application` objects, a cookie, or a database.

Web Forms Processing Order

Occasionally, you'll need to process pages in a particular order. For instance, you may not want to display a message until after an event has been handled. This will become especially important as you examine databases in Week 2. Thus, it's helpful to know the order in which Web forms are processed:

1. The page is requested (or posted).
2. The viewstate is restored for any controls.
3. The `Page_Load` event occurs.
4. Events are handled (that is, the methods that handle events are called). Any events that were cached are handled first, followed by the event that posted the form. If multiple events are raised at once, they're processed in no particular order.
5. The `Page_Unload` event occurs.

The process is initiated by a user requesting the page. ASP.NET then restores the state of every control on the page and fires the `Page_Load` event, which may or may not be handled with an event handler. Any events that have occurred are then handled by developer-defined functions. Finally, the `Page_Unload` event fires and releases any memory that doesn't need to be tied up. You'll become very familiar with this process as you develop more Web forms.

HTML Server Controls

You're already familiar with HTML elements: input text boxes, select lists, buttons, images, tables, and so on. These are all elements that represent some visual aspect of a Web page. For example, you can create a text box using the following HTML tag:

```
<input type="text" id="MyTextBox" value="blah" />
```

HTML elements are completely client-based; the server has no knowledge of any of these controls. A browser knows what `<input type="text">` is supposed to look like and renders it accordingly.

As mentioned earlier today in "Introduction to Web Forms," HTML server controls are server-side elements. They're objects that are created on the server, with properties, methods, and events that you can handle. They generate HTML for the browser to display.

HTML server controls are very easy to create—simply add the `runat="server"` attribute to any HTML element. Every HTML element has a corresponding HTML server control. In fact, you've already used one control many times: the `HtmlForm` control, which looks like `<form runat="server">`. The following is an `HtmlInputText` control:

```
<input type="text" id="MyTextBox" runat="server" />
```

Don't forget that you write server controls completely using regular HTML, so it doesn't matter what programming language your page is in; HTML server controls will always have the same form.

In this case, the server creates an `HtmlInputText` control. When the client requests the page, ASP.NET generates the appropriate HTML code to display the control as a text input box. The code to create HTML server controls is exactly the same as the HTML elements they represent, with the addition of the `runat="server"` attribute.

Once you turn an HTML element into an HTML server control, every attribute of the element can be modified through code. For example, you could change the text inside the preceding `HtmlInputText` control with the following line:

```
MyTextBox.Value = "Text changed"
```

Let's take a look at an example. Listing 5.6 shows how you can manipulate the attributes of HTML server controls.

LISTING 5.6 Manipulating HTML Server Controls

```
1:     <%@ Page Language="VB" %>
2:
3:     <script runat="server">
4:        Sub Click(Sender as Object, e as EventArgs)
5:           select case Sender.Value
6:              case "Left"
7:                 word_image.align = "left"
8:              case "Right"
9:                 word_image.align = "right"
10:              case "Center"
11:                 word_image.align = "center"
12:           end select
13:
14:           Left.Style("Border-Style") = "notset"
15:           Right.Style("Border-Style") = "notset"
16:           Center.Style("Border-Style") = "notset"
17:
18:           Sender.Style("Border-Style") = "inset"
19:         end Sub
20:     </script>
21:
22:     <html><body>
23:         <font size="5">Sam's Teach Yourself ASP.NET in
24:         21 Days: Day 5 </font><hr><p>
25:
26:         <form runat="server">
27:            <input type="Button" id="Left" runat="server"
28:               Value="Left" OnServerClick="Click" />
29:            <input type="Button" id="Center" runat="server"
30:               Value="Center" OnServerClick="Click" />
31:            <input type="Button" id="Right" runat="server"
32:               Value="Right" OnServerClick="Click" />
33:         </form>
34:
35:         <img src="word.gif" id="word_image" runat="server">
36:         <div id="Label1" runat="server">This is an example
37:         of text. When the buttons above are clicked, the image
38:         will move around the text accordingly.<p> This example
39:         demonstrates the HtmlImage and HtmlInputButton controls.
40:         </div>
41:
42:     </body></html>
```

ANALYSIS Let's examine the HTML portion of the page first, beginning on line 22. You have six HTML elements here: a form, three input buttons, an image, and a `<div>` section. Notice that all of these elements have the `runat="server"` attribute, which makes them all HTML server controls.

The `HtmlInputButton` controls (which represent input buttons) all have an event called `ServerClick`, which occurs whenever they're clicked. When this event occurs, you execute the `Click` method on the server, as shown on lines 28, 30, and 32.

> **Note**
>
> If you're familiar with client-side scripting, you know that HTML buttons also have a `Click` event, which occurs on the client side. Make sure you use the correct event for your code: `ServerClick` for a server-side event, and `Click` for the client side (that is, for dynamic HTML functionality).

Let's go back and examine the code declaration block. The only method here is the `Click` event handler. This method uses a `case` statement to determine which button invoked it. You know that `Sender` represents a button server control (don't forget to cast it as such in C#), so you check its value to determine which button was clicked. Then you set the `align` property of the image accordingly.

On lines 14–16, you set the style of the button elements. (Note that these are all styles that you could specify on normal HTML elements.) Specifically, you want to make the button that was clicked appear to be pushed in. Therefore, you first have to "unpress" each button control by setting its style to `notset`. Then, on line 18, you set the style of the button represented by `obj` to `inset`. Figures 5.7 and 5.8 show two different buttons being clicked.

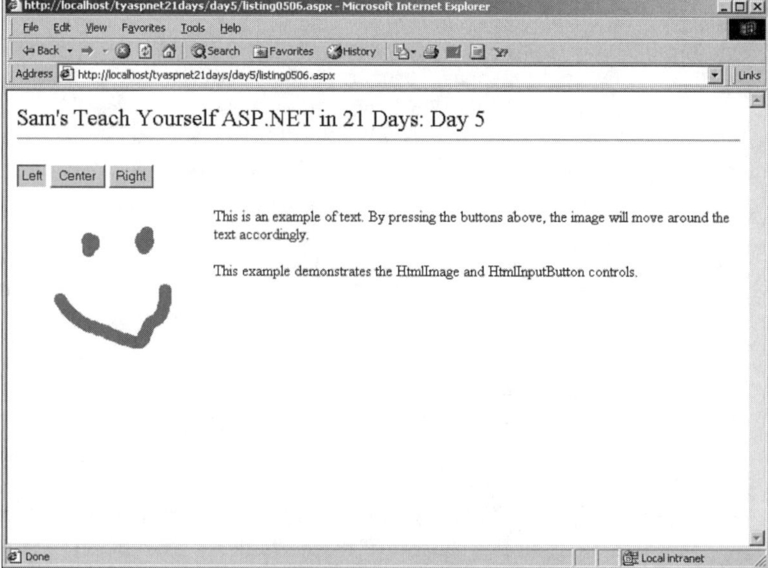

FIGURE 5.7

The left HTML server button when it's being clicked.

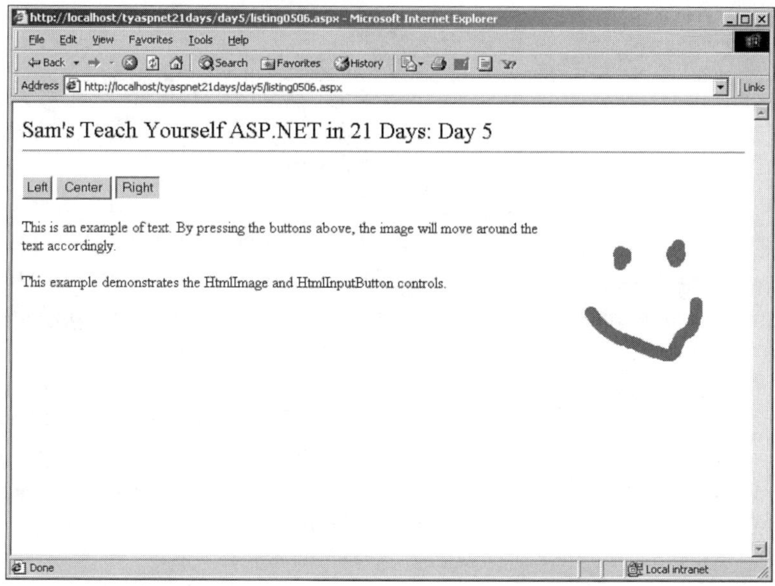

FIGURE 5.8

The right HTML server button when it's being clicked.

> Don't forget to change the image source to an actual image you have on your server.

Any attribute of an HTML element is easy to manipulate when it's transformed into an HTML server control.

Table 5.1 summarizes the predefined HTML server controls. You can also convert any HTML element not included in this list to an HTML server control simply by adding the `"runat="server"` attribute. Note that all of these controls belong to the `System.Web.UI.HtmlControls` namespace.

5

TABLE 5.1 HTML Server Controls

HTML Control	*Description*
`HtmlAnchor`	Creates a Web navigation link. Note that the `HtmlAnchor` control generates a post operation. HTML element: `<a>`
`HtmlButton`	Performs a task. This control can contain any arbitrary HTML, and therefore it's very flexible in look and feel. However, it isn't compatible with all browsers. HTML element: `<input type="button">`

TABLE 5.1 continued

HTML Control	*Description*
`HtmlForm`	Defines an HTML form. The values of controls within the form are posted to the server when the form is submitted. HTML element: `<form>`
`HtmlGenericControl`	Creates a basic object model (properties, methods, events) for any HTML element converted to a control.
`HtmlImage`	Displays an image. HTML element: `<img>`
`HtmlInputButton`	Performs a task. This button is supported on all browsers. HTML element: `<input type="button">`
`HtmlInputCheckBox`	Creates a box that users can click to turn it on and off. The `CheckBox` control includes a label. HTML element: `<input type="checkbox">`
`HtmlInputFile`	Allows users to specify files to be uploaded to a server. (The server must allow uploads.) HTML element: `<input type="file">`
`HtmlInputHidden`	Stores state information for a form (information that needs to be available with each round trip to the server). HTML element: `<input type="hidden">`
`HtmlInputImage`	Like a button, but displays a graphic. HTML element: `<input type="image">`
`HtmlInputRadioButton`	Displays a button that can be turned on or off. Radio buttons are typically used to allow the user to select one item from a short list of fixed options. HTML element: `<input type="radio">`
`HtmlInputText`	Displays text entered at design time that can be edited by users at runtime or changed programmatically. This control can also be used to create password boxes that display their values as asterisks. HTML element: `<input type="text">`
`HtmlSelect`	Displays a list of text and graphical icons. HTML element: `<select>`
`HtmlTable`	Creates a table. HTML element: `<table>`
`HtmlTableCell`	Creates an individual cell within a table row. HTML element: `<td>`
`HtmlTableRow`	Creates an individual row within a table. HTML element: `<tr>`
`HtmlTextArea`	Displays large quantities of text. Used for multi-line text entry and display. HTML element: `<textarea>`

Web Server Controls

Web server controls are similar to HTML server controls. They're created on the server and allow you to build complex user interfaces easily. They require the `runat="server"` attribute to work correctly. They also provide rich programmatic capabilities.

Unlike HTML server controls, however, Web controls don't necessarily map one-to-one to HTML elements and can represent more complex UI elements. For example, the `Calendar` Web control represents a complex HTML table with multiple rows and columns that displays a calendar.

You've already seen a few Web controls in action. The `Label` and `Button` controls used throughout today's lesson are two of them. To create a Web control, you use the following syntax:

```
<asp:Control id="name" runat="server">
```

For example, a `Label` control looks like this:

```
<asp:Label id="Label1" runat="server" />
```

This control displays a `<div>` section when rendered in the browser. Once you know the names of the controls, creating them is easy. Table 5.2 summarizes the list of ASP.NET controls.

TABLE 5.2 Web Server Controls

Web Control	*Description*
`AdRotator`	Displays a predefined or random sequence of images.
`Button`	Used to perform a task.
`Calendar`	Displays a graphic calendar that allows users to select a date.
`CheckBox`	Displays a box that users can click to turn something on or off.
`CheckBoxList`	Creates a grouping of check boxes. The list control makes it easy to create multiple check boxes that belong together.
`DataGrid`	Displays information, usually data-bound, in tabular form with columns. Provides mechanisms to allow editing and sorting.
`DataList`	Like the `Repeater` control, but with more formatting and layout options, including the ability to display information in a table. The `DataList` control also allows you to specify editing behavior.
`DropDownList`	Allows users to either select from a list or enter text.
`HyperLink`	Creates Web navigation links.
`Image`	Displays an image.

TABLE 5.2 continued

Web Control	*Description*
`ImageButton`	Like a `Button` control, but incorporates an image instead of text.
`Label`	Displays text that users can't edit directly.
`LinkButton`	Like a `Button` control, but has the appearance of a hyperlink.
`ListBox`	Displays a list of choices. Optionally, the list can allow multiple selections.
`Panel`	Creates a borderless division on the form that serves as a container for other controls.
`RadioButton`	Displays a single button that can be turned on or off.
`RadioButtonList`	Creates a grouping of radio buttons. Within the group, only one button can be selected.
`Repeater`	Displays information from a data set using HTML elements and controls you specify, repeating the elements once for each record in the data set.
`Table`	Creates a table.
`TableCell`	Creates an individual cell within a table row.
`TableRow`	Creates an individual row within a table.
`TextBox`	Displays text entered at design time that can be edited by users at runtime or changed programmatically.
	Note: Although other controls allow users to edit text (for example, `DropDownList`), their primary purpose isn't usually text editing.

Appendix C, "ASP.NET Controls: Properties and Methods," lists the properties, methods, and events for all of these controls. Also, the `DataList`, `DataGrid`, and `Repeater` controls will be saved for the discussion of data binding on Day 9, "Using Databases with ASP.NET."

Using Web Controls

Using Web controls is just like using HTML server controls. You create them on the server and specify properties and methods to handle their events. Many of them post data to the server. You've already seen how to work with the `Label` and `Button` controls, two of the most common Web controls.

Let's look at an example of some Web controls in action. Listing 5.7 shows a typical demographic form that asks for name, age, and income. Once it gets the user's input, it outputs some information dynamically.

LISTING 5.7 User Demographics with Web Controls

```
<%@ Page Language="VB" %>

<script runat="server">
   sub Submit(Sender as Object, e as EventArgs)
      dim strIncome as string = lbIncome.SelectedItem.Text
      dim strAge as string = rlAge.SelectedItem.Text

      lblMessage.Text = "Hello " & tbName.Text & "!<p>" & _
         "Your income is: " & strIncome & "<br>" & _
          "Your age is: " & strAge & "<br>"

       if rlAge.SelectedIndex < 3 then
          lblMessage.Text += "You're a young one!<p>"
       else
          lblMessage.Text += "You're a wise one!<p>"
       end if

       if cbNewsletter.Checked then
          lblMessage.Text += "You will be receiving our" & _
             " newsletter shortly."
       end if
    end sub
 </script>

 <html><body>
    <form runat="server">
       <asp:Label id="lblHeader" runat="server"
          Height="25px" Width="100%" BackColor="#ddaa66"
          ForeColor="white" Font-Bold="true"
          Text="A Web Controls Example" />
       <br>
       <asp:Label id="lblMessage" runat="server" /><p>

       Enter your name:
       <asp:TextBox id="tbName" runat="server" /><p>

       Choose your age:<br>
       <asp:RadioButtonList id="rlAge" runat="server"
          RepeatDirection="horizontal">
          <asp:ListItem><18</asp:ListItem>
          <asp:ListItem>19-24</asp:ListItem>
          <asp:ListItem>25-34</asp:ListItem>
          <asp:ListItem>35-49</asp:ListItem>
```

LISTING 5.7 continued

```
44:            <asp:ListItem>50-65</asp:ListItem>
45:         </asp:RadioButtonList><p>
46:
47:         Choose your income:<br>
48:         <asp:ListBox id="lbIncome" runat="server"
49:            size=1>
50:            <asp:ListItem>< $999/year</asp:ListItem>
51:            <asp:ListItem>$1000-$9999</asp:ListItem>
52:            <asp:ListItem>$10000-$49999</asp:ListItem>
53:            <asp:ListItem>> $50000</asp:ListItem>
54:         </asp:ListBox><p>
55:
56:         Do you want to receive our newsletter?<br>
57:         <asp:CheckBox id="cbNewsletter" runat="server"
58:             Text="Yes!" /><p>
59:
60:         <asp:Button id="btSubmit" runat="server"
61:            Text="Submit" OnClick="Submit" />
62:      </form>
63:   </body></html>
```

ANALYSIS First, let's examine the HTML portion of the page. This example uses several different Web controls. Lines 27–30 display a familiar `Label` control, but with some additional style attributes specified. These style attributes can be used with nearly any Web control, so feel free to customize your displays. Line 32 holds another `Label` that you'll use to display messages. Line 35 contains a `TextBox` control that allows the user to enter her name. Lines 38–45 display a `RadioButtonList`—a collective group of radio buttons—with five options, denoted by the `ListItem` control. Lines 48–54 display a `ListBox`, similar to a `select` HTML element. This control displays four different options. On line 57 is a simple `CheckBox` control, and line 59 has a familiar `Button` control. Figure 5.9 shows what this listing looks like in the browser.

Each Web control renders to an existing HTML element, and no controls are actually sent to the browser. If you view the source from this page, you'll see that there's nothing new—all of the HTML is perfectly satisfactory to the browser.

In the code declaration block, you perform some actions based on the user's input. Lines 5 and 6 retrieve the selected values from the `ListBox` and `RadioButtonList` controls, respectively. You can see that these two controls share the `SelectedItem` property, which returns the item selected. The `Text` property of the selected item returns any text that was contained in the item ("< $999/year," for example).

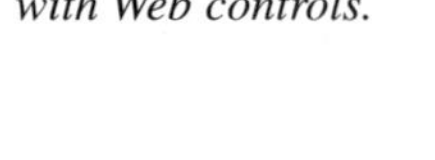

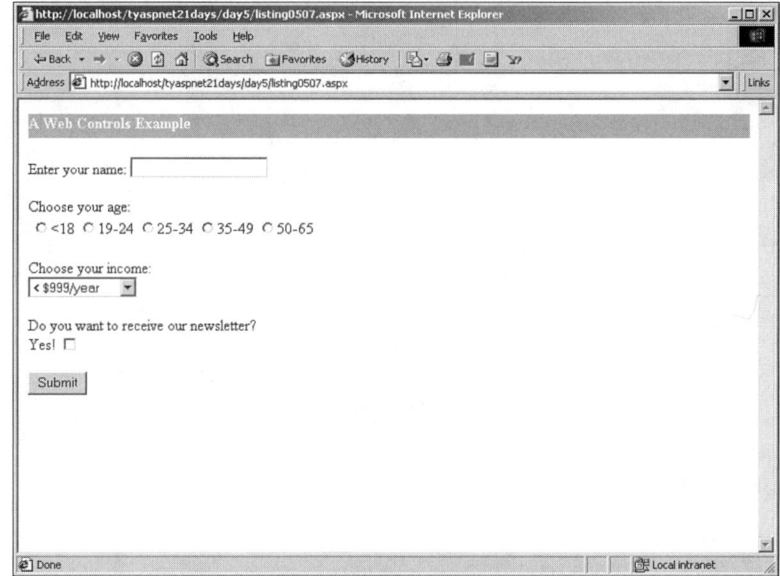

FIGURE 5.9

The demographic form with Web controls.

Lines 8–10 simply display the entered information back to the user. The `Text` property of the `tbName TextBox` control retrieves the user's name.

The `if` statement on lines 12–16 displays a message depending on the user's age. The `SelectedIndex` property returns the index of the selected item in the `rlAge RadioButtonList` control. For example, the first item has an index of 0, and the last item has an index of 4. If this index is less than 3, meaning the user's age is under 35, one message is displayed, while another message is displayed if he's older.

5

Finally, the `if` statement on line 18 checks the `CheckBox` control's `Checked` property to determine if the check box is checked. (Say that three times fast!) If it is, you display a message alerting the user that he'll be added to your newsletter list. Figure 5.10 shows the output after the user has entered some information and submitted the form.

Tip

> Most Web controls share a common set of properties. For example, the `TextBox`, `Label`, `LinkButton`, `Hyperlink`, `Button`, and `CheckBox` controls all share the `Text` property, which returns or sets the text in the control. The `ListBox`, `ComboBox`, `DataList`, and `DataGrid` controls all share the `SelectedItem` property. This standard interface makes it very easy for you to develop pages with Web controls.

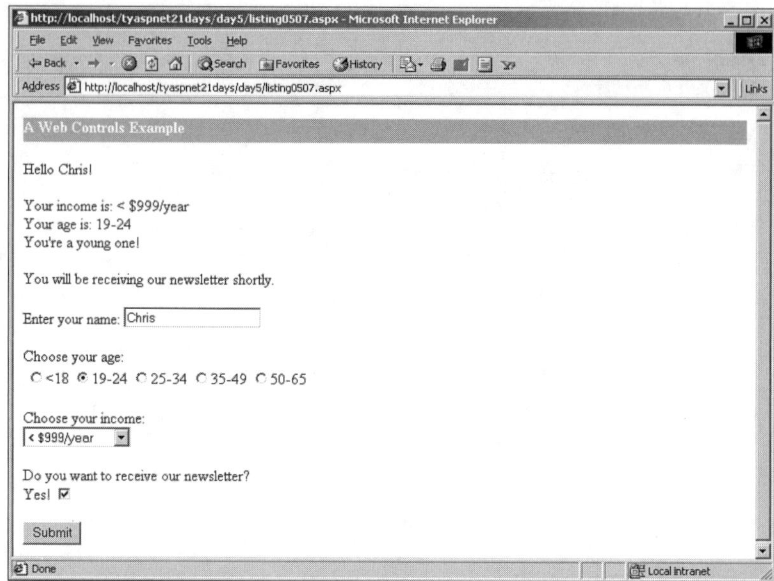

FIGURE 5.10
The submitted demographic form.

You'll be using Web controls extensively throughout this book, so it pays to get comfortable with them as soon as possible. Once you master a few controls, the rest will come easily.

Posting Data Immediately

As mentioned earlier today, you don't have to cache events and send them to the server all at once. In fact, sometimes you may not want to wait.

For example, imagine you've built a form that displays cities in a state. The two lists, cities and states, are provided in `ListBox` controls. Once a state is selected, you post the form, do some processing, and filter the list of cities to display only those in that particular state. In this case, you wouldn't want to wait until the user submits the form himself.

You can post data immediately with the `AutoPostBack` property of Web controls. Setting this property to `true` tells the Web control to post the data as soon as any event occurs. Let's look at Listing 5.8, which relies on two events to post data.

LISTING 5.8 Using `AutoPostBack`

```
<%@ Page Language="VB" %>
<%@ Import Namespace="System.Drawing" %>

<script runat="server">
```

LISTING 5.8 continued

```
5:       sub NameHandler(Sender as Object, e as EventArgs)
6:          lblMessage.Text = tbName.Text & ", select a color: "
7:       end sub
8:
9:       sub ListHandler(Sender as Object, e as EventArgs)
10:          lbColor.BackColor = Color.FromName _
11:             (Sender.SelectedItem.Text)
12:       end sub
13:    </script>
14:
15:    <html><body>
16:       <form runat="server">
17:          <asp:TextBox id="tbName" runat="server"
18:             OnTextChanged="NameHandler"
19:             AutoPostBack="true" /><p>
20:
21:          <asp:Label id="lblMessage" runat="server"
22:             Text="Select a color: " /><p>
23:          <asp:ListBox id="lbColor" runat="server"
24:             OnSelectedIndexChanged="ListHandler"
25:             AutoPostBack="true" >
26:             <asp:Listitem>Red</asp:Listitem>
27:             <asp:Listitem>blue</asp:Listitem>
28:             <asp:Listitem>green</asp:Listitem>
29:             <asp:Listitem>white</asp:Listitem>
30:          </asp:ListBox>
31:       </form>
32:    </body></html>
```


ANALYSIS On line 17, you declare your `TextBox` Web control. When the `TextChanged` occurs, you execute the `NameHandler` method on line 5. Notice that the `AutoPostBack` property of this control is set to `true`, which means that a post will occur as soon as the `TextChanged` event occurs.

> **Note**
>
> The form will be auto-posted only on the events that you specify handlers for. In the preceding `TextBox`, the form will be submitted on the `TextChanged` event and no other.

On line 21, a `Label` control displays an instruction to the user. On line 23 is a `ListBox` control with four items, again with the `AutoPostBack` property set to `true`. Whenever the user selects a different item in the list, a post will occur and the `ListHandler` method will be executed.

Notice that there's no Submit button, so the user cannot submit the form manually.

The `NameHandler` method simply takes the value of the text box and adds it to the `Label` for a customized message.

The `ListHandler` method sets the background color of `ListBox` depending on the item selected. The color can't be set by using just the color name (such as "red") by itself or by supplying a hexadecimal value (such as "#FF0000") alone. You have to use the .NET Framework's `Color` object to set the color.

The `Color.FromName` method creates a `Color` object based on the supplied color name. `Color.FromName("red")` creates a red object, and so on. You can use this object to set the color of your `ListBox`. (The `Color` object belongs to the `System.Drawing` namespace, hence the `Import` directive on line 2.) Figure 5.11 shows this page after the user selects a color and inputs a value in the text box.

For the color example to work, you need to be using a browser that supports cascading style sheets (IE or Netscape 4+). Older browsers don't support setting background colors for list boxes.

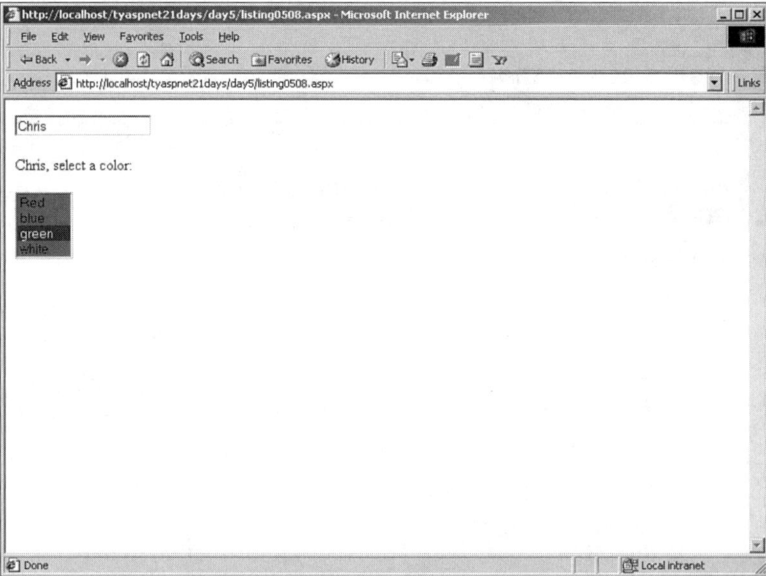

FIGURE 5.11
Using `AutoPostBack` *to submit a form.*

Web Server Controls Versus HTML Server Controls

A lot of the server controls seem to provide overlapping functionality. For example, the `HtmlAnchor` HTML server control and the `HyperLink` Web control both do the same thing. When should you use one instead of the other?

In general, HTML server controls make it easy to convert traditional HTML forms to Web forms. It's very simple to just add `runat="server"` to each HTML element and gain access to it programmatically. This makes converting old pages a snap and adds power to your applications.

One drawback of HTML server controls is that they don't provide a standard interface. HTML elements provide many different attributes and keywords to set properties, which may be confusing at times. Also, HTML server controls don't provide down-level support inherently, so ASP.NET won't generate different HTML for each browser version automatically. This gives you less automatic control, but it allows you to customize the pages manually.

Web controls should be used when you're building pages from scratch. They usually provide a more powerful mechanism than HTML server controls, and they support a standard interface. They also provide down-level support.

Do	Don't
Do use regular HTML elements when you don't need to manipulate them programmatically. For example, normally you wouldn't need to manipulate a link, so just use a standard `<a href>` tag instead of an `HtmlAnchor` or `HyperLink` control. **Do** use HTML server controls when you don't want to spend a lot of time converting existing pages to Web forms. **Do** use Web server controls when you're creating new Web forms that require programmatic access. **Do** convert existing elements to Web server controls instead of HTML server controls, if you have the time.	**Don't** create unnecessary server controls (that is, controls that you'll never access programmatically). The more objects the server needs to create, the more resources are required. The performance loss is very small, but it still isn't worth it.

That's Not ASP!

The Web forms model is unlike anything in traditional ASP. Back then, there was no way for the server to keep track of controls, or even to create UI controls to display to the client. A developer could build a system that performed similarly to Web forms, but it look a lot of time and expertise.

Traditional ASP relied on the request/response model for interacting with users. There was no event-driven model to provide a layer of abstraction between the user interface and the application logic. Developers had to process pages linearly (and all at once) when they were submitted, instead of reacting to user events.

Additionally, because the Web is stateless, all form information was lost once submitted. That is, unless the developer explicitly took action to prevent it by retrieving form variables. For example, the following code was a typical sight in classic ASP:

```
<input type="text" name="tbName"
   value="<% = Request.Form("tbName") %>">
```

Developers constantly had to repopulate the form elements if they wanted to provide the illusion of a persistent state. ASP.NET saves viewstate automatically for you, so you don't have to worry about that any more.

HTML and Web server controls are completely new in ASP.NET. The server's capability to create UI elements and keep track of their states is revolutionary. The best way to develop powerful applications is for the code to know what's going on in the UI—in other words, the server knows what the client is doing.

These controls also render properly for each browser, outputting the correct HTML for different versions—a far cry from classic ASP. Multiple versions of pages often had to be created for different browser versions, which was a nightmare.

The Web forms framework is a huge boon for Web developers, both in UI creation and in application logic. Once you've been developing with Web forms for a while, you'll wonder how you ever lived without them!

Summary

You've covered a lot of territory today. You've learned about ASP.NET Web forms, and you've looked at both HTML server controls and Web controls. Not bad for a beginning chapter on Web forms! After today, you should be able use the rich functionality of these controls to build intricate user interfaces.

Web forms provide many benefits for ASP.NET pages. They let the server keep track of the UI: what the user is doing, and what each element should do. Through clever use of client-side script, ASP.NET pages post information about events to the server, which can handle them accordingly.

Web forms are made up of four types of server controls: HTML server controls, Web server controls, validation controls, and user controls. These controls have properties, methods, and events that allow the developer to manage applications intimately. Web forms also save the state of each control automatically.

You can turn any existing HTML element into an HTML server control by adding the `runat="server"` attribute. These controls are created on the server, and the appropriate HTML output is sent to the browser. Using HTML server controls allows you to manipulate the attributes of the HTML elements.

Web server controls are more complex than HTML server controls, and often they represent more involved user interface elements. These controls are created on the server and provide a plethora of properties and methods for you to manipulate.

Tomorrow you'll examine another type of server controls: user controls. These are custom-built controls that can encapsulate any piece of functionality you want. You're well on your way to building complex ASP.NET pages!

Q&A

Q Does maintaining the viewstate slow down performance? Is there any way to turn it off?

A Maintaining viewstate decreases performance very slightly, if at all. There's an additional step that ASP.NET must accomplish when maintaining viewstate. In performance-critical situations, you can disable viewstate with the following:

```
EnableViewState=false
```

You can set this property for any individual control, or for the page as a whole, in the `<%@ Page %>` directive.

Q Some of the actions won't do anything on my Web form. What's wrong?

A Don't forget to enclose all the controls for which you want to handle events in an `HtmlForm` control: `<form runat="server">`. (This is a common mistake.)

Also, make sure that you're using the correct syntax to declare the event handler:

```
<asp:ControlName id="name" runat="server"
   OnEventName=eventHandler />
```

Finally, remember that events are handled in no particular order on the server. Occasionally, you may create an event handler that effectively stops another event from occurring.

For example, in the `Page_Load` event, you may clear the text from a `TextBox`. The method that handles the `TextChanged` event of the `TextBox` won't work properly because the `Page_Load` event has already cleared the text. In this case, check the `IsPostBack` property to make sure you aren't executing code that you don't need or don't want to execute.

Workshop

This workshop will help reinforce the concepts covered in today's lesson. Answers can be found in Appendix A.

Quiz

1. How do Web forms keep track of viewstate?
2. What does the state bag do, and how do you access it?
3. True or false: Events in Web forms are processed before the `Page_Load` event.
4. What is the standard event parameter list?
5. What is the importance of the `runat="server"` tag?
6. Why should you use HTML server controls?
7. What's wrong with the following code snippet?

```
<asp:Button id="btSubmit"
   Click="HandleThis" >
```

8. Which property can be used to make a control post immediately to the server upon an event?
9. When should you use Web controls instead of HTML server controls?

Exercises

1. Build an application for choosing a baby's name. The user will select the sex of the baby, and then a `ListBox` will display a few possible names. When the user selects a name, a message will be displayed using the selected name.
2. Build a standard user registration page with the following fields: name (required), address, phone (required), fax, and e-mail address (required). If any of the required values are missing, display an error message to the user.

DAY 6

Learning More About Web Forms

Yesterday you took a look at Web forms and the new capabilities they give the Web developer. You examined the mechanisms behind Web forms and studied HTML server controls and Web server controls. These are some great tools to add to your belt.

Today's lesson continues this look at Web forms. You'll examine the extensibility of Web forms and learn how you can easily build your own additions to this framework with user controls and custom controls. User controls allow you to package common UI functionality so you can use it over and over again. Custom controls contain UI functionality that you create from scratch. By combining yesterday's lesson with today's, you'll be able to program great ASP.NET pages before your first week is up!

Today you'll learn about the following:

- How Web forms are extensible
- What a user control is
- How to create and use user controls

- How to build and use custom controls
- How to make your custom controls behave more like regular server controls
- How to create server controls in your code during runtime

The Extensibility of Web Forms

Yesterday you learned that one of the Web form's primary purposes is to allow developers to create complex user interfaces and the logic associated with them. This includes extending the Web forms framework with your own custom mechanisms.

Web forms provide HTML server and Web server controls for building UIs. Each control wraps a piece of functionality into an easy-to-use module and provides properties, methods, and events to build your applications and react to user actions. Yesterday, you learned how to use these controls and build your user interfaces, but that's just the beginning. Web forms let you use these controls any way you want. You can even create your own custom controls based on them! This is a very powerful feature.

User Controls

User controls are wonderful features of Web forms. They allow you to package and reuse any UI functionality that you want. Do you need a combination `Calendar/DropDownList` control to use in your Web application? Simply combine those two controls and wrap them up into a user control. User controls work exactly like server controls, so you can place them wherever you want and you don't have to figure out how they work.

Let's examine a typical user control scenario. Imagine you've created a Web site that requires users to log in to access certain sections. Login forms are fairly standard; they contain two text boxes (for username and password information) and a Submit button, as shown in Figure 6.1. You could use two `TextBox` controls and a `Button` control, and then wire up the methods to handle those controls. But what if you need this form on several pages? Rather than creating these three controls and their event handlers over and over again, you can simply create a user control that does the exact same thing but only takes up one line of code.

A more complex example is a news portal Web site that displays news from around the Web in subelements on the main page. Since all of these subelements follow the same format but pull data from different sources, they could be implemented as user controls. Each user control wraps up the display functionality, and you can set up each one to retrieve different information. In fact, you can use a single user control and create multiple instances of it, much as you can create multiple instances of text box controls.

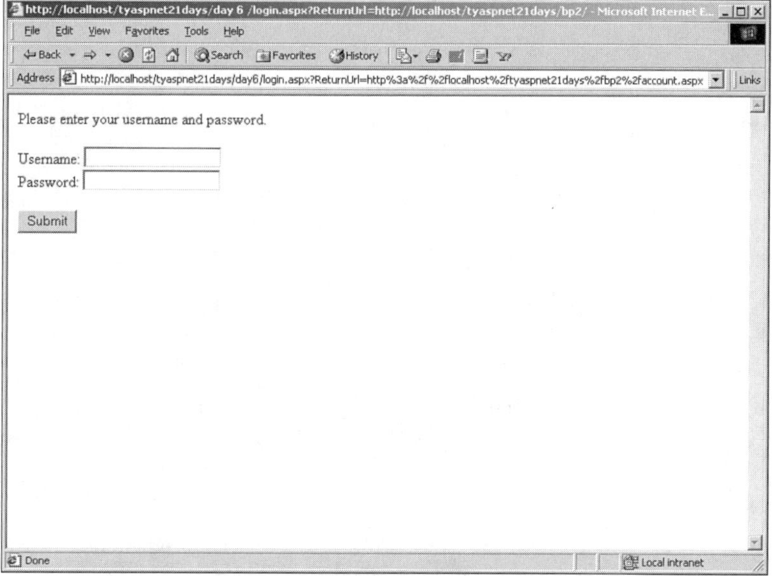

FIGURE 6.1

A typical login form with two text box controls and a Submit button.

Of course, user controls don't necessarily have to encapsulate any real functionality. You can build a user control that simply contains a navigation bar with links, or a standard header or footer for your pages. The possibilities are endless.

User controls fully support the Web forms framework, so your controls can have properties and events just as built-in controls do. Also, with the .NET Famework, you can author each individual user control in any programming language that supports MSIL (although you can only use one language per control).

And best of all, user controls are easy to make. By changing a few simple things, you can convert just about any ASP.NET page you've already built into a user control. Let's take a look at how to accomplish this.

Creating User Controls

Essentially, a user control is an ASP.NET file with a different extension: `.ascx`. It contains UI elements and code to control those elements. The difference is that user controls are embedded in other pages, rather than standing alone. Think of a server control—the `TextBox` control, for example. This control displays an HTML text box and provides built-in properties and methods, which it handles itself. It cannot stand alone and must be used within an ASP.NET page. User controls are exactly the same.

Let's take a look at a simple user control, shown in Listing 6.1. This control encapsulates the user login form described in the previous section.

LISTING 6.1 A Typical Login Form Wrapped in a User Control

```
1:    <table style="background-color:<%=BackColor%>;
2:       font: 10pt verdana; border-width:1;border-style:solid;
3:       border-color:black;" cellspacing=15>
4:       <tr>
5:          <td><b>Login: </b></td>
6:          <td><ASP:TextBox id="User" runat="server"/></td>
7:       </tr>
8:       <tr>
9:          <td><b>Password: </b></td>
10:          <td><ASP:TextBox id="Pass" TextMode="Password"
11:                 runat="server"/></td>
12:       </tr>
13:       <tr>
14:          <td></td>
15:          <td><ASP:Button Text="Submit" runat="server"
16:                 OnClick="Submit_Click" /></td>
17:       </tr>
18:    </table>
19:    <p>
20:    <ASP:Label id="lblMessage" runat="server"/>
```

ANALYSIS Save this listing as `LoginForm.ascx`. Notice that it looks very similar to the HTML portion of an ASP.NET page. It contains two text box controls, a button control, a label control, and a table to provide formatting. However, it doesn't include any `<html>`, `<form>`, or `<body>` tags. You can't see what this control will look like yet because first it needs to be placed in an ASP.NET page.

Also notice the `<%@=BackColor%>` on line 1. This looks like a code render block because that's what it is. It sets the background color of the table to the value contained in the variable named `BackColor`. More on this later. For now, let's examine how to create this user control from an ASP.NET page, shown in Listing 6.2.

LISTING 6.2 The ASP.NET Page That Your User Control Is Based On

```
<%@ Page Language="VB" %>

<script runat="server">
   dim Username as string
   dim Password as string
   dim BackColor as string
```

Listing 6.2 continued

```
 7:
 8:     sub Submit(Sender as Object, e as EventArgs)
 9:        lblMessage.Text = "Username: <b>" & User.Text & _
10:            "</b><br>" & "Password: <b>" & Pass.Text & _
11:            "</b><p>"
12:     end sub
13:  </script>
14:
15:  <html><body>
16:     <form runat="server">
17:        <table style="background-color:<%=BackColor%>;
18:           font: 10pt verdana;border-width:1;
19:           border-style:solid;border-color:black;"
20:           cellspacing=15>
21:           <tr>
22:              <td><b>Login: </b></td>
23:              <td><ASP:TextBox id="User" runat="server"/></td>
24:           </tr>
25:           <tr>
26:              <td><b>Password: </b></td>
27:              <td><ASP:TextBox id="Pass" TextMode="Password"
28:                     runat="server"/></td>
29:           </tr>
30:           <tr>
31:              <td></td>
32:              <td><ASP:Button Text="Submit" runat="server"
33:                     OnClick="Submit" /></td>
34:           </tr>
35:        </table>
36:        <p>
37:        <ASP:Label id="lblMessage" runat="server"/>
38:     </form>
39:  </body></html>
```

Analysis You declare the variables `Username`, `Password`, and `BackColor` on lines 4–6. These can be used to store the corresponding information. On line 8, you create the `Submit` method, which simply displays the supplied information in a label. The HTML portion of the page, beginning on line 15, should look familiar because it's similar to Listing 6.1. Figure 6.2 shows the results when viewed in a browser.

There are three steps to converting an ASP.NET page to a user control. The first step is to remove all `<html>`, `<form>`, and `<body>` tags. Keep all other HTML formatting tags, however. The ASP.NET page that contains the user control will already have these tags, so there's no reason to use them again in your user control. Adding these tags may cause formatting errors or may even cause your application to crash.

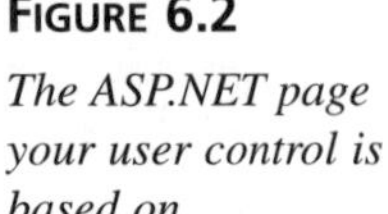

FIGURE 6.2
The ASP.NET page your user control is based on.

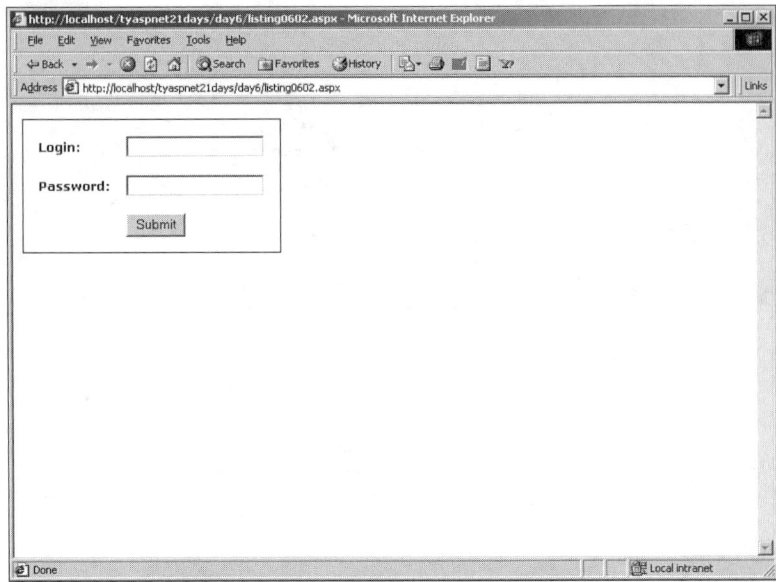

Secondly, you must rename your file to include an `.ascx` extension. For example, `listing0602.aspx` would become `listing0602.ascx`. The new extension is required in order for the file to be recognized as a user control and not a malformed ASP.NET page.

Finally, if the page you're converting includes an `@ Page` directive, you must change it to an `@ Control` directive. This directive supports all the same attributes as the `@ Page` directive, except for tracing. Take the following directive, for example:

```
<%@ Page Language="VB" %>
```

This would become the following:

```
<%@ Control Language="VB" %>
```

After applying these changes to Listing 6.2, you end up with the user control in Listing 6.1. You're nearly ready to use it in any ASP.NET page.

> **Note** You don't have to create a user control from an existing ASP.NET page. It was done that way here because it highlights the changes effectively. You can easily create user controls from scratch if you follow these guidelines.

So far, this user control encapsulates the UI elements of the login form. This already saves you time and energy if you want to implement this module in an ASP.NET page.

User controls can encompass much more functionality, however. They can contain the code to control the UI elements as well. Let's build a code declaration block that exposes all the properties, events, and methods you want this control to have. Listing 6.3 exposes the `Username`, `Password`, and `BackColor` properties from Listing 6.2 and defines a `Submit` method that handles the `OnClick` event of the button.

LISTING 6.3 The User Control Code Declaration

```
1:    <script language="VB" runat="server">
2:       public BackColor as String = "White"
3:       public UserName as string
4:       public Password as string
5:
6:       public sub Submit(Sender as Object, e as EventArgs)
7:          lblMessage.Text = "Username: <b>" & User.Text & _
8:             "</b><br>" & "Password: <b>" & Pass.Text & "</b><p>"
9:       end sub
10:   </script>
11:
12:   <table style="background-color:<%=BackColor%>;
13:      font: 10pt verdana;border-width:1;
14:      border-style:solid;border-color:black;"
15:      cellspacing=15>
16:      <tr>
17:         <td><b>Login: </b></td>
18:         <td><ASP:TextBox id="User" runat="server"/></td>
19:      </tr>
20:      <tr>
21:         <td><b>Password: </b></td>
22:         <td><ASP:TextBox id="Pass" TextMode="Password"
23:                runat="server"/></td>
24:      </tr>
25:      <tr>
26:         <td></td>
27:         <td><ASP:Button Text="Submit" runat="server"
28:                OnClick="Submit" /></td>
29:      </tr>
30:   </table>
31:   <p>
32:   <ASP:Label id="lblMessage" runat="server"/>
```

ANALYSIS Replace the previous `LoginForm.ascx` file with the code in this listing. The only addition is the code declaration block on lines 1–10. It's largely similar to the one from Listing 6.2, with a few modifications. On line 2, the `BackColor` property is initially set to `"White"`, and you define the `UserName` and `Password` properties for the user to manipulate. Notice the `public` keyword; another ASP.NET page can now use these properties programmatically to set or get the values in the UI.

The `Submit` method is exactly the same as it is in Listing 6.2. Since user controls are very similar to ASP.NET pages, you can simply copy and paste this code. Once this file is saved with an `.ascx` extension, you're ready to use it in your ASP.NET pages.

Using User Controls

User controls are used in ASP.NET pages just like other server controls. You create an instance in the UI portion of the page, and you control it programmatically in your code. Because these controls are custom built, however, you need to use some additional syntax. To place user controls onto other ASP.NET pages, you must first *register* the control on the page with the `@ Register` page directive. Registering a control effectively tells ASP.NET that you want to extend your Web form with a new server control. This is done so that the page has a valid path and defined name to use for the control. Let's look at the syntax for this directive:

```
<%@ Register TagPrefix="Prefix" TagName="ControlName"
➥src="filepath" Namespace="name" %>
```

The `TagPrefix` attribute defines the group that your control belongs to. All of the Web server controls you examined yesterday had a `TagPrefix` of `asp`. For example:

```
<asp:Button id="btOne" runat="server" />
```

User controls can have any `TagPrefix` you desire. Simply specify it in the `@ Register` directive. The `TagName` property then gives the user control a name so the page can reference it. For example, your login form user control could use the name `LoginForm`. The `src` property specifies the location of the source for the user control. The page must know this path so that it knows what the user control can do. Finally, the `Namespace` attribute is an optional element that specifies a namespace to associate with the `TagPrefix`. This helps to further group and classify your user controls.

Let's create an ASP.NET page to take advantage of your new login form user control. Listing 6.4 shows an ASP.NET page that includes an `@ Register` directive and creates an instance of the user control.

LISTING 6.4 Embedding a User Control in ASP.NET Is Easy

```
<%@ Page Language="VB" %>
<%@ Register TagPrefix="TYASPNET" TagName="LoginForm"
➥src="LoginForm.ascx" %>

<script runat="server">
```

LISTING 6.4 continued

```
5:      sub Page_Load(Sender as Object, e as EventArgs)
6:         lblMessage.Text = "Properties of the user " & _
7:            "control:<br> " & _
8:            "id: " & LoginForm1.id & "<br>" & _
9:            "BackColor: " & LoginForm1.BackColor & "<br>" & _
10:            "Username: " & LoginForm1.Username & "<br>" & _
11:            "Password: " & LoginForm1.Password
12:      end sub
13:   </script>
14:
15:   <html><body>
16:      <form runat="server">
17:         <TYASPNET:LoginForm id="LoginForm1" runat="server"
18:            Password="MyPassword"
19:            Username="Chris"
20:            BackColor="Beige" />
21:      </form>
22:      <p>
23:      <asp:Label id="lblMessage" runat="server" />
24:   </body></html>
```

ANALYSIS This page has quite a few interesting features. First, notice the `@ Register` directive on line 2. You set your prefix to `TYASPNET` and your control name to `LoginForm`. You can now reference this control elsewhere with the code, as shown on line 17:

```
<TYASPNET:LoginForm>
```

The `Page_Load` event simply displays the user control's properties in the label on line 23. Finally, you implement the control on lines 17–20. The syntax is exactly the same as it is for any other server control. The `runat="server"` is still required as well. The properties you set on lines 18–20 are the public variables you created on lines 2–4 of Listing 6.3.

Also notice the ID of the label on line 23: `lblMessage`. This is the same ID that you used for the label in the user control. Normally you'd get an error if you placed two controls with the same ID on one page, but this listing seems to work fine. The reason is that ASP.NET doesn't care which controls are used inside the user control or what their IDs are. It only cares that the user control presents a piece of UI functionality that will handle itself; it doesn't need to bother with the details. The public properties of the user control are also exposed to the page, but again, ASP.NET doesn't care what you do with them. It only knows that these properties are available, and the user control will take care of the rest.

Because ASP.NET doesn't care about the details, it's impossible to set properties of the controls inside the user control from the ASP.NET page. For example, placing the following code inside Listing 6.4 would result in an error:

```
User.Text = "clpayne"
Pass.Text = "helloworld!"
```

Recall that `User` and `Pass` refer to controls inside the user control, and ASP.NET doesn't know or care about them. Thus, you need to provide the code to handle your UI elements *inside* the user control.

Figure 6.3 shows this page when viewed in a browser.

FIGURE 6.3

The login form user control presents the appropriate UI display.

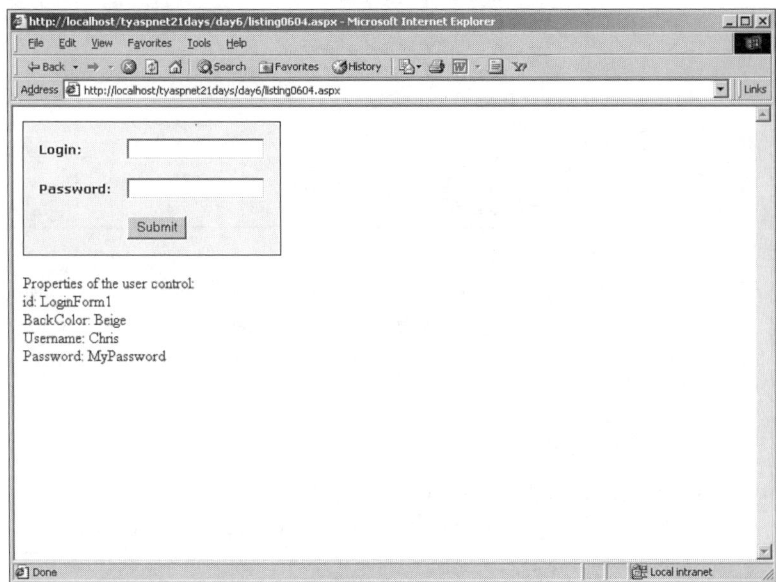

Enter some text into the login form and click the Submit button. The form post is handled, even though you didn't add any code to do so in Listing 6.4. This is because you put the functionality in the user control itself.

After you click the Submit button, the user will see what's shown in Figure 6.4.

Enhancing the User Control

So far, the `Username` and `Password` properties of your user control remain unused. When these properties are set, the login form should be prefilled with these values. You cannot use code render blocks as you did for the `BackColor` property. They are not allowed within server control tags, and an error will be produced. Instead, you'll have to convert the `Username` and `Password` public variables into actual VB.NET property elements. Replace lines 3 and 4 of `LoginForm.ascx` with the code in Listing 6.5.

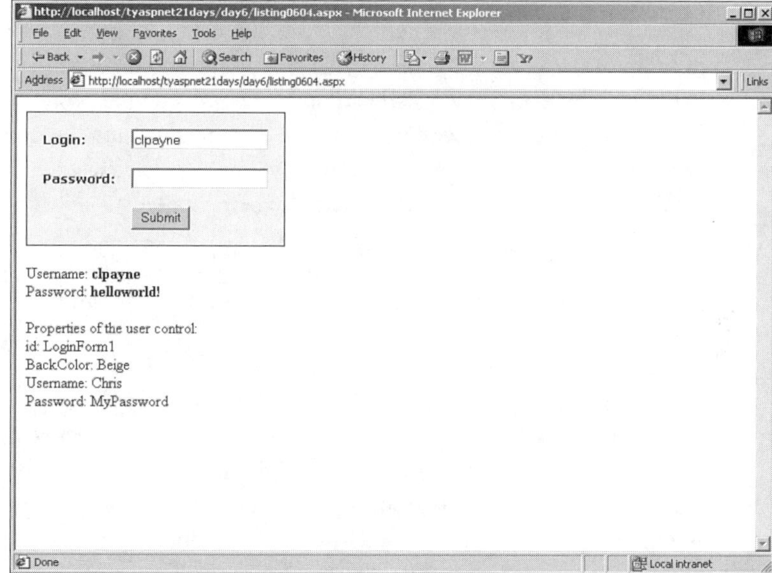

FIGURE 6.4

The user control handles its own form submissions.

LISTING 6.5 Using VB.NET Properties Instead of Public Variables

```
   public property UserName as string
      Get
         UserName = User.Text
      End Get
      Set
         User.Text = value
      End Set
    end property

    public property Password as string
      Get
         Password = Pass.Text
      End Get
      Set
         Pass.Text = value
      End Set
    end property
```

ANALYSIS This is new VB.NET syntax. Essentially, you've transformed public variables into properties of the user control. The difference is that public variables provide very limited functionality; you can only assign and retrieve values. The properties of the user control allow you to perform actions each time the value is set or accessed.

Line 3 looks a lot like what you saw previously: `public UserName as string`, with the addition of the keyword `property`. When you use this keyword, you must have a corresponding `end property`, as shown on line 10. Inside the property tags, you have two additional elements: `Get` and `Set`. These elements contain the code which will be used to retrieve and assign values to the property. For example, when a developer writes the following line, the `Get` statement is actually being called:

```
dim strName as string = LoginForm1.UserName
```

And inversely, the `Set` statement is called with the following:

```
LoginForm1.UserName = "Chris"
```

Inside these elements, you can add code to perform any functionality that you want to happen when the property is accessed. On line 5, which occurs when the user retrieves the value, you return the value contained in the `User` text box control by assigning the value to the property itself. On line 8, which occurs when the property value is set, you assign the incoming value to the `User` text box control. The `value` keyword refers to the value that the user has assigned to this property. For example, in the following line, `value` would refer to `"Chris"`:

```
LoginForm1.UserName = "Chris"
```

> **Tip**
>
> If you want to create a read or write-only property, simply leave out the `Set` or `Get` element and add the keyword `ReadOnly` or `WriteOnly`. For example, the following code snippet creates a `Username` property that can only be read from
>
> ```
> public ReadOnly property UserName as string
>    Get
>       UserName = User.Text
>    End Get
> end property
> ```

Lines 12–19 provide the exact same functionality for the `Password` property and the `Pass` text box control. The following code snippet shows the use of the property syntax in C#:

```
3:      public string UserName {
4:         get {
5:            return User.Text;
```

```
        }
        set {
           User.Text = value;
        }
     }

     public string Password {
        get {
           return Pass.Text;
        }
        set {
           Pass.Text = value;
        }
     }
```

Now request Listing 6.4 from the browser again. You should see the page shown in Figure 6.4.

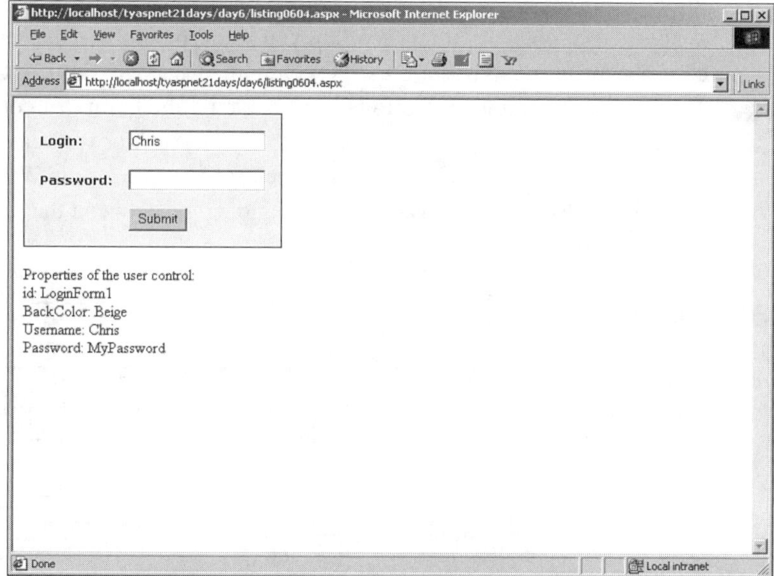

FIGURE 6.4

Using properties to prefill user control elements.

The username field is now prefilled because you set the corresponding property on line 19 of Listing 6.4. Notice that the password field is still empty. This is because that particular text box control has its `TextMode` property set to `Password`, and ASP.NET won't fill the text box for security reasons. However, note that the `Password` property is still assigned the value, as shown in the label below the user control. If you remove the `TextMode="Password"` code from this text box control, the value will appear.

Your user control is now fully functional, with properties that can be manipulated from an ASP.NET page and methods to handle its own events. This control can be placed in any ASP.NET page and will work the same as it does here.

Custom Controls

The ASP.NET framework also allows you to create custom controls. This is an advanced topic, but you should be comfortable learning about custom controls because you're familiar with the Web forms framework.

Custom controls are *not* user controls. Rather than encapsulating some prebuilt UI functionality, custom controls can define their own, completely original behavior. For instance, ASP.NET doesn't provide a built-in control for rendering line art. A developer could build a custom control to provide this functionality, and it could easily be reused and placed in any ASP.NET application.

Whereas user controls are used when you want to combine the functionality of existing controls, custom controls are used when none of the existing controls meet your needs. The Web forms framework allows you to extend the library of controls with your own controls. Custom controls can be completely original, or they can extend an existing control's behavior. At this point, it will be helpful to examine the Web forms framework in more detail. Figure 6.5 illustrates the relationships between the different concepts in the Web forms framework.

FIGURE 6.5

The hierarchy of objects in the Web forms framework.

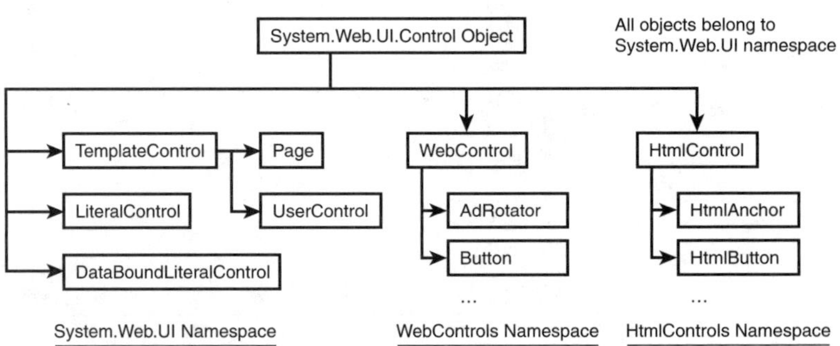

All objects in the Web forms framework are derived from the `System.Web.UI.Control` class, directly or indirectly. This class provides the basic methods and properties common to all controls, such as `ID`, `GetType`, and `ToString`. Each object under the `Control` object provides additional functionality.

The Web forms framework allows you to insert a custom control anywhere in this hierarchy, as long as it's derived from the `Control` class somehow. You can extend existing functionality, or simply create new mechanisms that reside in one of the namespaces shown in Figure 6.5. Typically, you'll derive from the `WebControl` or `HtmlControl` classes because they provide the most prebuilt functionality for displaying user interfaces.

Creating Custom Controls

Let's build a custom control. Listing 6.6 shows a class that's derived from the `Control` class and displays a simple message to the user. Listing 6.7 shows the C# version of the code.

LISTING 6.6 A Custom Control Is Nothing More Than a VB.NET Class

```
Imports System
Imports System.Web
Imports System.Web.UI

Namespace MyCustomControls
   Public Class CustomControl1 : Inherits Control
      Protected Overrides Sub Render(Output as
➥HtmlTextWriter)
         Output.Write("This is my custom control!
➥The time is now " & DateTime.Now.ToString)
      End Sub
   End Class
End Namespace
```

LISTING 6.7 Your Custom Control in C#

```
using System;
using System.Web;
using System.Web.UI;

namespace MyCustomControls {
   public class CustomControl1 : Control {
      protected override void Render(HtmlTextWriter Output) {
         Output.Write("This is my custom control!
➥The time is now " + DateTime.Now.ToString());
      }
   }
}
```

ANALYSIS Save this file as `CustomControl1.vb` (or `CustomControl1.cs` for the C# version). Notice that this is a VB.NET or C# source file, not an ASP.NET page. Therefore, you have to perform a few additional steps, such as importing namespaces that were automatically imported for `.aspx` files. On lines 1–3, you import these namespaces. The `Imports` keyword (`using` in C#) is similar to the `@ Import` directive for ASP.NET pages.

Next, on line 5, you declare the namespace that this control will belong to. This can be any made-up namespace you want. Just remember to include the `End Namespace` or closing bracket, as shown on line 11. On line 6, you create your class that's derived from the `Control` class. (See Day 3, "Using Visual Basic.NET and C#," for more information on creating classes.)

Lines 7–9 contain one of the most important parts of user controls. `Render` is the method that allows existing controls to display HTML in the browser. This method is inherited by all server controls from the `Control` class. In order to get your custom control to display HTML in the browser, you must provide an implementation for this method. However, since this method already exists in the `Control` class, you must override it using the `Overrides` keyword in VB.NET, or `override` in C#. (Built-in server controls do this as well.) Don't forget the `Protected` keyword!

The `Render` method takes one parameter, an `HtmlTextWriter` object named `Output`. This object provides all the methods needed to help the `Render` method produce HTML output. You'll use it to spit out the display for your custom control. On line 8, you use the `Write` method of the `Output` variable to send HTML to the browser. It's the current time and a welcome message in this case.

Finally, to use your custom control in another ASP.NET page, you must compile the code—ASP.NET cannot use VB.NET or C# source files directly. Open a command prompt, navigate to the directory containing `CustomControl1.vb`, and type the following:

```
vbc /t:library /out:..\..\bin\CustomControls.dll /r:System.dll
➥/r:System.Web.dll CustomControl1.vb
```

This will compile the `CustomControl1.vb` source file into an MSIL file named `CustomControls.dll` (as specified by the `/out` parameter) for ASP.NET to use. For the C# version, the command is nearly identical:

```
csc /t:library /out:..\..\bin\CustomControls.dll /r:System.dll
➥/r:System.Web.dll CustomControl1.cs
```

You should see something similar to the following output:

```
Microsoft (R) Visual Basic.NET Compiler version 7.00.9114
for Microsoft (R) .NET CLR version 1.00.2523
Copyright  Microsoft Corp 2000. All rights reserved.
```

Make sure the `c:\inetpub\wwwroot\bin` directory already exists, or you'll receive an error when you try to compile your code.

For more information on namespaces, classes, compilation commands, the `\bin` directory, and creating objects in general, see Day 15, "Using Business Objects."

Using Custom Controls

Once the custom control is built and compiled, you can implement it on any page, just as you would with a user control. Again, you must use the `@ Register` directive, but this time the syntax is slightly different:

```
<%@ Register TagPrefix="ACME" Namespace="MyCustomControls"
➥Assembly="CustomControls"%>
```

The `TagPrefix` attribute remains the same as with user controls. However, `TagName` and `src` have been replaced with the `Namespace` and `Assembly` attributes. `Namespace` is simply the namespace you created in your custom control on line 5 of Listing 6.6: `MyCustomControls`. The `Assembly` attribute specifies the compiled source file, `CustomControls`. (Notice there's no `.dll` extension. ASP.NET assumes this when you use the `Assembly` element.) You can then implement this control in your ASP.NET page just like any other control. Listing 6.8 shows a simple example of using this control.

LISTING 6.8 Implementing Your Custom Control Is Exactly Like Implementing User and Server Controls

```
<%@ Page Language="VB" %>
<%@ Register TagPrefix="ACME" Namespace="MyCustomControls"
➥Assembly="CustomControls"%>

<html><body>
   <form runat=server>
      The custom control produces the following output:<p>

      <ACME:CustomControl1 id="MyControl" runat=server/>
   </form>
</body></html>
```

Note that this code will work regardless of the language you built your custom control in. This listing produces the output in Figure 6.6 when viewed in a browser.

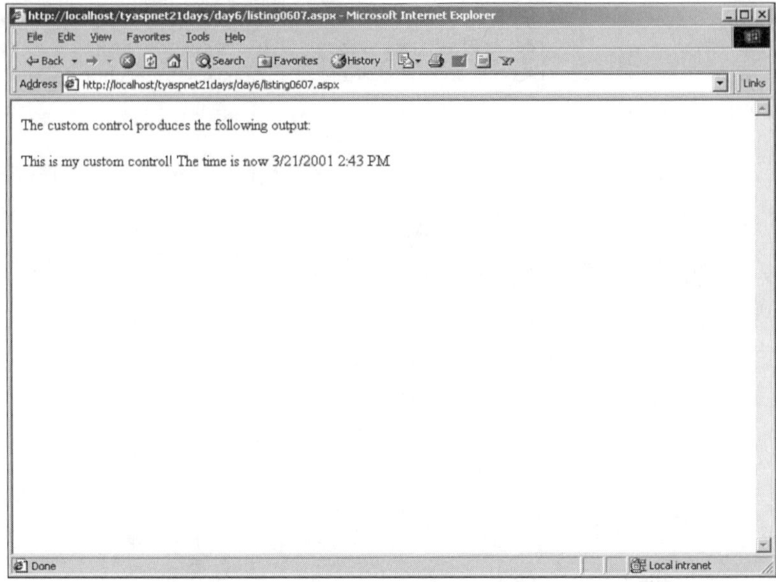

FIGURE 6.6

The custom control outputs the HTML specified in the `Write` *method of the* `HtmlTextWriter` *object.*

Using Properties and State

So far, you've only looked at using custom controls to write HTML to the browser. Just like other server controls, though, custom controls can have properties, methods, and events, can participate in form posts, and can even maintain state.

To add a property to your control, simply declare a public variable or a property element in your custom control class. For example, you could modify the class in Listing 6.6 so it looks like Listing 6.9.

LISTING 6.9 Adding Properties to Your Custom Control

```
   Public Class CustomControl1 : Inherits Control
      private strMessage as string = "This is my custom
➥control!"
      public property Message as string
         Get
             Message = strMessage
          End Get
          Set
             strMessage = value
          End Set
       end property

       Protected Overrides Sub Render(Output as HtmlTextWriter)
```

LISTING 6.9 continued

```
18:         Output.Write(strMessage & " The time is now " & _
19:            DateTime.Now.ToString)
20:      End Sub
21:   End Class
```

ANALYSIS On line 7, you create a private variable, `strMessage`, that holds the text to display to the user. On lines 8–15, you create a public property that can be used to set and retrieve the value from `strMessage`. (See "Enhancing the User Control" earlier today for information on how to create properties.) In the `Render` method, you've modified the code to display the text contained in `strMessage`, rather than the static text that was there originally.

Recompile this custom control with the command prompt command:

```
vbc /t:library /out:..\bin\CustomControls.dll /r:System.dll
➥/r:System.Web.dll CustomControl1.vb
```

Modify Listing 6.8 to utilize the new `Message` property:

```
<ACME:CustomControl1 id="MyControl" runat=server
   Message="Hello world!" />
```

Listing 6.8 will now display the new message, as shown in Figure 6.7.

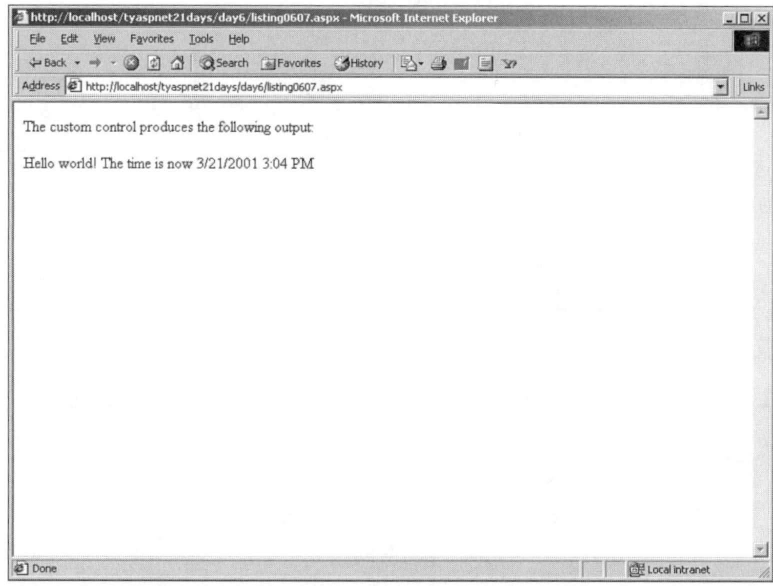

FIGURE 6.7
Adding a property to your custom control enhances its functionality.

If you want the control to maintain state, you simply have to add the items to the state bag (see Day 4, "Using ASP.NET Objects with C# and VB.NET"). Listings 6.10 and 6.11 show a new custom control that implements state management.

LISTING 6.10 Creating a Custom Control with State Management

```
Imports System
Imports System.Web
Imports System.Web.UI

Namespace MyCustomControls
   Public Class CustomControl2 : Inherits Control
      public property Message as string
         Get
            Message = ViewState("Message").ToString
          End Get
          Set
             ViewState("Message") = value
          End Set
       end property

       public property Size as integer
          Get
             Size = CType(ViewState("Size"), Integer)
          End Get
          Set
             ViewState("Size") = value
          End Set
       end property

       Protected Overrides Sub Render(Output as
➥HtmlTextWriter)
          Output.Write("<font size=" & Me.Size & ">" & _
             Me.Message & "</font>")
       End Sub
    End Class

 End Namespace
```

LISTING 6.11 Creating a Custom Control with State Management

```
using System;
using System.Web;
using System.Web.UI;

namespace MyCustomControls {
   public class CustomControl2 : Control {
```

LISTING 6.11 continued

```
7:          public string Message {
8:             get {
9:                return ViewState["Message"].ToString();
10:             }
11:             set {
12:                ViewState["Message"] = value;
13:             }
14:          }
15:
16:          public int Size {
17:             get {
18:                return (int)ViewState["Size"];
19:             }
20:             set {
21:                ViewState["Size"] = value;
22:             }
23:          }
24:
25:          protected override void Render(HtmlTextWriter
➥Output) {
26:             Output.Write("<font size=" + this.Size + ">" +
➥this.Message + "</font>");
27:          }
28:       }
29:
30:    }
```

ANALYSIS Save these files as `CustomControl2.vb` and `CustomControls2.cs`, respectively. This control displays a simple message to the user, specified by the `Message` property. As such, it's very similar to `CustomControl1.vb`. However, the `Message` property is now maintained in state. In the `Set` element on line 12, you persist the supplied value to a variable in the state bag named `Message`, rather than to a private variable as in Listing 6.9. The `Get` statement on line 9 then retrieves this value from the state bag. Remember to use the `ToString` method to convert the value returned from state to a string, because ASP.NET returns it as an object by default.

You've added a new property, `Size`, which specifies the font size to render the message in. This property element works very similarly to the `Message` property, except that it's an integer. Again, the `Get` and `Set` elements retrieve and assign the value to the state bag. The `CType` method (or the `int` casting operator) on line 18 converts the data returned from the state bag to an integer.

Compile this file with the following command:

```
vbc /t:library /out:..\ ..\bin\CustomControls.dll /r:System.dll
➥/r:System.Web.dll CustomControl2.vb
```

or for C#:

```
csc /t:library /out:..\ ..\bin\CustomControls.dll /r:System.dll
➥/r:System.Web.dll CustomControl2.cs
```

Listing 6.12 shows an ASP.NET page that uses this new control.

LISTING 6.12 Implementing the State Maintenance Custom Control on an ASP.NET Page

```
1:    <%@ Page Language="VB" %>
2:    <%@ Register TagPrefix="ACME" Namespace="MyCustomControls"
➥Assembly="CustomControls"%>
3:
4:    <script runat="server">
5:       sub Submit(Sender as Object, e as EventArgs)
6:          MyControl.Size = MyControl.Size + 1
7:       end sub
8:    </script>
9:
10:    <html><body>
11:       <form runat=server>
12:          The custom control produces the following output:<p>
13:
14:          <ACME:CustomControl2 id="MyControl" runat=server
15:             Message="Hello world!"
16:             Size=1 />
17:
18:          <asp:Button runat="server"
19:             Text="Increase size!"
20:             OnClick="Submit"/>
21:       </form>
22:    </body></html>
```

ANALYSIS Your custom control is implemented on line 14, with values specified for both the `Message` and `Size` properties. When a user submits the form by clicking on the button on line 18, the `Submit` method (line 5) increases the size of the displayed message by 1, using the `Size` property of the custom control.

Note that this can occur only if state management is enabled for the custom control. ASP.NET needs to know what the size was *before* the post to be able to increase it by 1. If state isn't maintained, `MyControl.Size` will always return 1; that is, the value set on line 16. But the size increases with every form post, indicating that the control is maintaining state. Figure 6.8 shows the output after you've clicked the button several times.

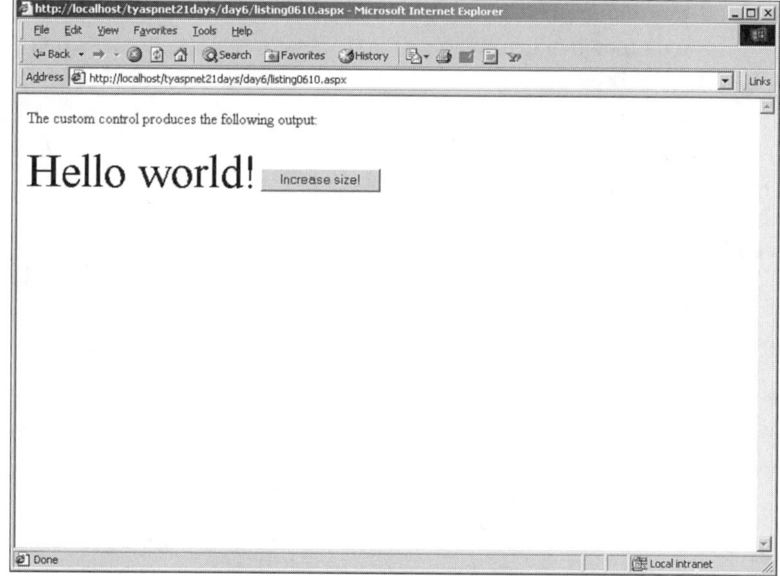

FIGURE 6.8

The increasing font size is evidence that state is maintained.

Wiring Up Events

One of the most important aspects of server controls is that they react to the user's actions. Building this functionality into custom controls isn't difficult, but you need to know how server controls function when they're requested by a client. All server controls follow the order of execution described here. Note that this doesn't list all of the steps, but only the most important ones:

1. Load state information.
2. Process postback data. The control examines any incoming data from a form post.
3. Load the control. This is similar to the `Page_Load` event.
4. If form data has changed, raise events to handle it.
5. Handle the event that caused the postback.
6. Save the state of the controls.
7. Render the output to the browser.

Notice that there are two separate steps to handle events related to postback data. First, you must detect the changes in data, as shown in step 2. Then you execute the methods that handle these changes, as shown in step 4. This two-step process translates directly to the methods that must be accomplished so your custom controls can handle events. You

6

determine if an event needs to be raised, and then you call a method to raise it. The event can then be handled by the ASP.NET page that implements this control. Figure 6.9 illustrates this procedure.

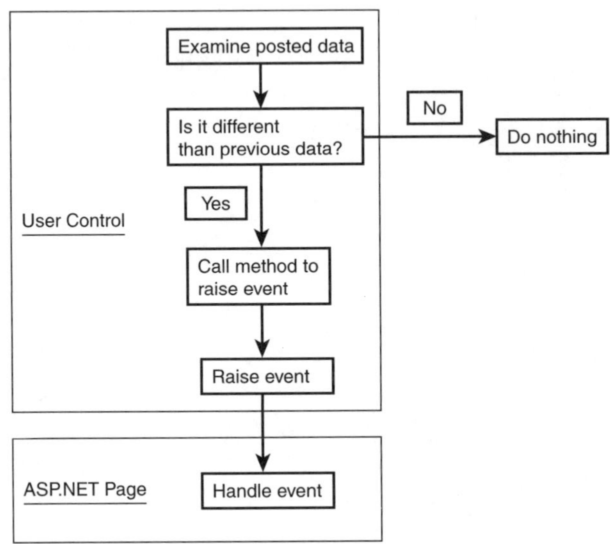

FIGURE 6.9
The steps required to handle events in custom controls.

To build an event for a custom control, first you must decide which event you want to handle. Do you want to react to changes in a text box? A button click? The type of data generated by the event plays a part in how you implement the functionality in the user control. You simply provide implementations for steps 2 and 4. Luckily, the work is very cut-and-dried, and you don't have to write much code yourself. Let's take a look at a new custom control that contains events, shown in Listings 6.13 and 6.14.

LISTING 6.13 An Event-Wary Custom Control

```
Imports System
Imports System.Web
Imports System.Web.UI
Imports System.Collections.Specialized

Namespace MyCustomControls
   Public Class CustomControl3 : Inherits Control :
➥Implements IPostBackDataHandler
      public Event TextChanged(obj as object, e as eventargs)
      protected sub OnTextChanged(e as EventArgs)
         RaiseEvent TextChanged(Me, e)
       end sub
```

LISTING 6.13 continued

```

         Public Function LoadPostData(PostDataKey As String,
➥Values As NameValueCollection) As Boolean Implements
➥IPostBackDataHandler.LoadPostData
            dim strOldValue as String = Me.Message
            dim strNewValue as String = Values(postDataKey)
            if not strOldValue = strNewValue
               Me.Message = strNewValue
               return true
            end if
            return false
         End Function

         Public Sub RaisePostDataChangedEvent() Implements
➥IPostBackDataHandler.RaisePostDataChangedEvent
            OnTextChanged(EventArgs.Empty)
         end sub

         public property Message as string
            Get
               Message = ViewState("Message").ToString
            End Get
            Set
               ViewState("Message") = value
            End Set
         end property

         Protected Overrides Sub Render(Output as
➥HtmlTextWriter)
            Output.Write("<input name=" & Me.UniqueID & _
               " type=text value=""" & Me.Message & """>")
         End Sub
      End Class

   End Namespace
```

6

LISTING 6.14 An Event-Wary Custom Control in C#

```
using System;
using System.Web;
using System.Web.UI;
using System.Collections.Specialized;

namespace MyCustomControls {
   public class CustomControl3 : Control,
➥IPostBackDataHandler {
```

LISTING 6.14 continued

```
8:          public event EventHandler TextChanged;
9:          protected virtual void OnTextChanged(EventArgs e) {
10:            TextChanged(this, e);
11:          }
12:
13:          public bool LoadPostData(String PostDataKey,
➥NameValueCollection Values) {
14:            string strOldValue = this.Message;
15:            string strNewValue = Values[PostDataKey];
16:            if (strOldValue != strNewValue) {
17:               this.Message = strNewValue;
18:               return true;
19:            }
20:            return false;
21:          }
22:
23:          public void RaisePostDataChangedEvent() {
24:            OnTextChanged(EventArgs.Empty);
25:          }
26:
27:          public string Message {
28:            get {
29:               return ViewState["Message"].ToString();
30:            }
31:            set {
32:               ViewState["Message"] = value;
33:            }
34:          }
35:
36:          protected override void Render(HtmlTextWriter Output) {
37:            Output.Write("<input name=" + this.UniqueID + "
➥type=text value=\"" + 38:    this.Message + "\">");
39:          }
40:       }
41:
42:    }
```

ANALYSIS Save these files as `CustomControl3.vb` and `CustomControl3.cs`. There appears to be a lot of complex functionality here, but don't worry! It's actually very simple once you dissect it. The first thing to notice is `Implements IPostBackDataHandler` on line 7 (the `Implements` keyword is represented by a comma in C#). `IPostBackDataHandler` is an interface that defines how controls interact with postback information; it provides a blueprint for how to write your code. This is a standard item that's required if you want to handle events, so don't worry about it too much. Once you learn the syntax, the rest is easy.

Next, on line 8, you declare an event. This is very similar to declaring a variable, except that you must use the `event` keyword. In this case, you're going to handle the text changing in your custom control, hence the event name `TextChanged`. Notice that you supply the standard event parameter list here as well for VB.NET; for C# it's not necessary.

On lines 9–11, you declare a subroutine, `OnTextChanged`, that raises the `TextChanged` event. Recall that in your ASP.NET pages, you use the syntax *`OnEventName`* to specify event handlers for your controls (for example, `OnTextChanged="HandleChange"`). On lines 9–11, you define this *On* event. For VB.NET you need to use the `RaiseEvent` method to raise an event, which causes the `TextChanged` event to fire with the specified parameters. In C#, you can simply call the event name. Again, this code is standard. All you need to do to customize it for your controls is change the names of the events.

Next is the `LoadPostData` method, which corresponds to step 2 of a control's order of execution. This method takes two parameters: the first specifies the name of the control whose data is being examined (this will always be the custom control), and the second specifies the data that the user submitted in the form post. The `LoadPostData` method returns true if you want the event to be handled, and false otherwise. The declaration of this method is pretty long, but it's standard.

Inside this method, on lines 14–20, you examine the posted data. You retrieve the old value of the control on line 14 by accessing the `Message` property of your control. You then retrieve the new data by accessing it from the second parameter in the `LoadPostData` method. On line 16, you compare these values to determine if the data has changed. If it has, you return true, which tells ASP.NET that a method must be executed to handle this event. Otherwise, you return false.

Finally, the `RaisePostDataChangedEvent` on line 23 calls the methods to handle the event. This is another long declaration, but again, it's standard. It simply calls the `OnTextChanged` method, which in turn raises the `TextChanged` event, which can then be handled in your ASP.NET page.

The rest of the listing is almost exactly the same as Listing 6.9. The only difference is that you now have to provide a `name` property for the control that will generate the event, as shown on line 37. Use the `UniqueID` property to return the name of the custom control. Without this step, your control won't generate any events.

Also, don't forget to import the `System.Collections.Specialized` namespace, as shown on line 4, and change the class's name to `CustomControl3`, as shown on line 7.

Let's take a brief moment to recap:

- You first created an event using the `event` keyword, and then you created a method using the *`OnEvent`* syntax that raises the event with the `RaiseEvent` method.
- Next, you used the standard `LoadPostData` method to determine if the data has changed and if it warrants raising an event.
- The `RaisePostDataChangedEvent` method is responsible for calling another method that raises the event you defined in step 1.

Much of the syntax used here is standard, and so is the procedure to implement it.

Now that the custom control is coded, let's compile the VB.NET version using the following command:

```
vbc /t:library /out:..\ ..\bin\CustomControls.dll /r:System.dll
➥/r:System.Web.dll CustomControl3.vb
```

And the C# version with

```
csc /t:library /out:..\..\bin\CustomControls.dll /r:System.dll
➥/r:System.Web.dll CustomControl3.cs
```

Listing 6.15 shows an ASP.NET page that implements this custom control.

LISTING 6.15 Handling the Custom Control's Events in an ASP.NET Page

```
<%@ Page Language="VB" %>
<%@ Register TagPrefix="ACME" Namespace="MyCustomControls"
➥Assembly="CustomControls"%>

<script runat="server">
   sub Submit(obj as object, e as eventargs)
      'do nothing
   end sub

   sub ChangeIt(obj as object, e as eventargs)
      Response.write("Event handled!")
    end sub
 </script>

 <html><body>
    <form runat=server>
       The custom control produces the following output:<p>
       <ACME:CustomControl3 id="MyControl" runat="server"
          Message="Hello world!"
          OnTextChanged="ChangeIt" />
       <asp:Button runat="server"
          Text="Submit"
```

LISTING 6.15 continued

```
22:             OnClick="Submit" />
23:       </form>
24:    </body></html>
```

ANALYSIS Now, it's time for some easy stuff! This page is just like any other ASP.NET page that you've developed, so it should be a breeze compared to Listing 6.12. Moving to line 17 first, you see the implementation of your custom control. This looks just like the implementation for the previous custom control you developed, but now it has `OnTextChanged="ChangeIt"` on line 19. According to Listing 6.12, this line will cause the `ChangeIt` method to execute whenever the data in the text box has changed (after the form is posted, that is). On line 20, you create a simple button control that will cause the form to be posted. It calls the `Submit` method on line 5, which is just a place holder. It doesn't actually do anything.

The `ChangeIt` method on line 9 writes a message to the browser that the event has fired and has been handled. View this page from the browser, and experiment by submitting the form and changing the text values. Notice that if you don't change the text in the text box, the `ChangeIt` method isn't executed, which means that the event didn't fire. Figure 6.10 shows the output after you change the text and click the button.

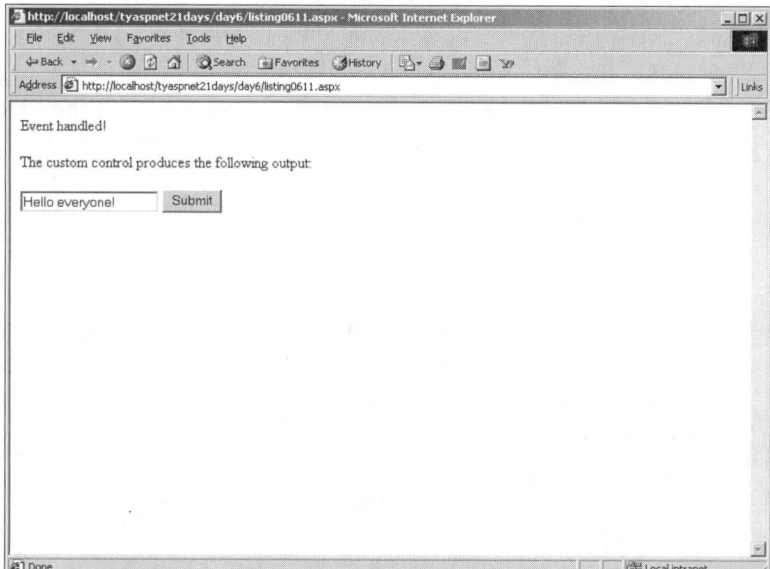

FIGURE 6.10
Handling the user control's events from an ASP.NET page.

There's a lot more you can do with custom controls. For instance, you can cause normally non-posting elements (such as text boxes or images) to post automatically during an event. You can create existing server controls inside your custom control, to do with as you want. You can even make your custom control generate JavaScript to perform client-side event handling.

This is just the tip of the iceberg, but now you know the basics of creating and using fully functional custom controls. For more information, see the .NET Framework documentation or the ASP.NET Quickstart samples supplied with the .NET SDK.

Creating Controls at Runtime

So far, you've been creating server controls at *design time*—that is, when you build the ASP.NET pages. You can also create them dynamically at *runtime*—when the page is requested from the browser.

What's the difference? Technically, all controls are created at runtime. They're loaded and rendered when the user requests a page. However, design time implementation allows you to set properties of the control before it's requested. When the page is requested, ASP.NET already knows that it must create the control and knows how to do so. With runtime creation, ASP.NET doesn't know that a control must be created until it comes across the code that tells it to do so.

So why would you want to create controls at runtime, when doing so at design-time provides just as much functionality without requiring you to learn any additional syntax? At times, you may not know ahead of time how many controls you need. A typical example is retrieving data from a database. Suppose you want to display the data in an HTML table. Each item will go in its own row. Chances are that you won't know how many items are in the database. Thus, you won't know how many table rows to create ahead of time. Runtime creation solves this problem, allowing you to create as many new rows as needed, when you need them.

Creating built-in controls is just like creating any other object. For example, the following code creates and some properties of a text box control and sets them when the page loads. You don't need to provide the implementation of the control in the HTML portion of the page:

```
<script language="VB" runat="server">
   sub Page_Load(Sender as Object, e as EventArgs)
      dim objTB as TextBox
      objTB.ID = "tbOne"
      objTB.Text = "Hello there!"
```

```
      Page.Controls.Add(objTB)
   end sub
</script>
```

The objTB text box control will appear in your page when it loads. You can create as many server controls as you want this way. Once a control has been created, it must be added to a container—either another control (such as a Panel) or the Page itself. Every control that can contain other controls has a Controls property, which in turn has an Add method that takes the control to add. The previous code snippet produces the output shown in Figure 6.11 when viewed in a browser.

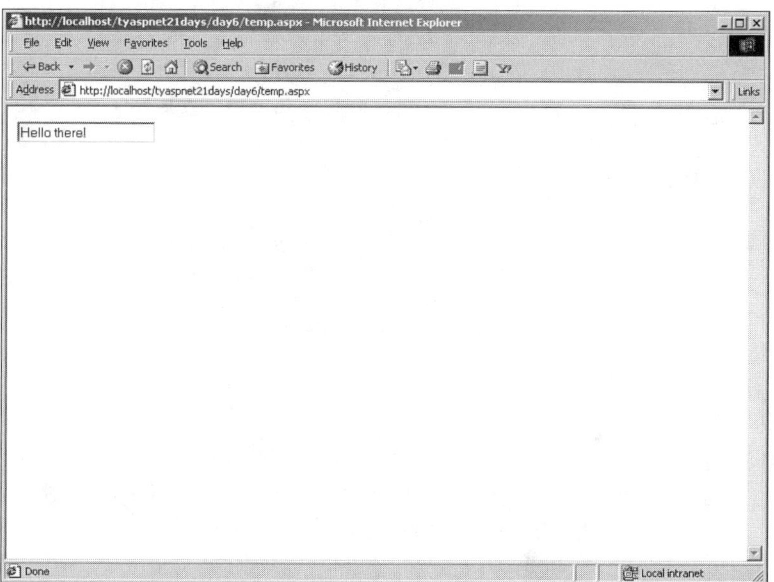

FIGURE 6.11
Server controls can be added to pages dynamically at runtime.

Note that you can't assign event handlers this way, however. The following will produce an error:

```
objTB.OnTextChanged = "HandleIt"
```

Instead, you must add an event handler to this control dynamically, using the AddHandler method in VB.NET:

```
AddHandler objTB.TextChanged, addressOf HandleIt
```

The AddHandler method takes two parameters: the event to handle (the TextChanged event in this case—*not* OnTextChanged) and the method that should handle the event. You must use the addressOf operator here. It provides a pointer to the appropriate

6

method. You can now create a `HandleIt` method that will be executed whenever the `TextChanged` event fires for this control.

In C#, use the following code:

```
objTB.TextChanged += new EventHandler(this.HandleIt);
```

> If you want your runtime-created controls to participate in state management, they must be added to a form inside your ASP.NET page. Using `Page.Controls.Add` won't do this for you. Instead, create a `Panel` inside `<form runat="server">` tags and use *`PanelID`*`.Controls.Add`.

You can use these methods to add custom controls to your pages dynamically as well. The following code snippet shows how to add your third custom control to an ASP.NET page at runtime:

```
<script runat="server">
   dim objCC as new MyCustomControls.CustomControl3
   sub Page_Load(Sender as Object, e as EventArgs)
      objCC.ID = "MyControl"
      objCC.Message = "Hello world!"
      Page.Controls.Add(objCC)
   end sub
</script>
```

Use the namespace name followed by the name of the control to create a new instance, as shown on the second line. (Don't forget to register the control!) The previously described methods won't work with user controls, however. After all, how would you refer to it without a namespace name? The `Page.LoadControl` method can be used to load a user control dynamically. This method loads your user control from the source file you specify, and it returns an object that reflects the filename. Listing 6.16 shows an example.

LISTING 6.16 The `LoadControl` Method Returns an Object Based on the Filename of the User Control

```
<%@ Page Language="VB" %>
<%@ Register TagPrefix="TYASPNET" TagName="LoginForm"
➥src="LoginForm.ascx" %>

<script runat="server">
   sub Page_Load(Sender as Object, e as EventArgs)
      dim objUC as LoginForm_ascx
```

LISTING 6.16 continued

```
7:          objUC = Page.LoadControl("LoginForm.ascx")
8:          objUC.ID = "Control1"
9:          objUC.BackColor = "Beige"
10:          Panel1.Controls.Add(objUC)
11:
12:          lblMessage.Text = "Properties of the user " & _
13:             "control:<br> " & _
14:             "id: " & objUC.id & "<br>" & _
15:             "BackColor: " & objUC.BackColor & "<br>" & _
16:             "Username: " & objUC.Username & "<br>" & _
17:             "Password: " & objUC.Password
18:       end sub
19:    </script>
20:
21:    <html><body>
22:       <form runat="server">
23:          <asp:Panel id="Panel1" runat="server"/>
24:       </form>
25:       <p>
26:       <asp:Label id="lblMessage" runat="server" />
27:    </body></html>
```

ANALYSIS On line 2, you register your user control. This syntax should be familiar by now. Let's examine line 6. You create a new variable `objUC` of type `LoginForm_ascx`. Where did this new data type come from? ASP.NET created it from the name of the source file of your user control (`LoginForm.ascx`) when you registered the control. It simply substituted an underscore for the period, because the period holds special meaning in .NET. This new data type contains all the properties and methods that were declared in your user control, so you can use it to set properties for the control.

On line 7, the `LoadControl` method creates an instance of your user control from the source file. This method returns an object of type `LoginForm_ascx`, so your variable `objUC` can be used to hold the data. On lines 8 and 9, you assign properties just as you did for the dynamically loaded controls you created previously (notice that you only assign the `ID` and `BackColor` properties), and on line 10 you add it to the `Panel` control on line 22. Lines 12–16 display the properties of your control in the label on line 25. When viewed from the browser, this listing will display the image shown in Figure 6.12.

You can assign event handlers to user controls just as you did with regular server controls.

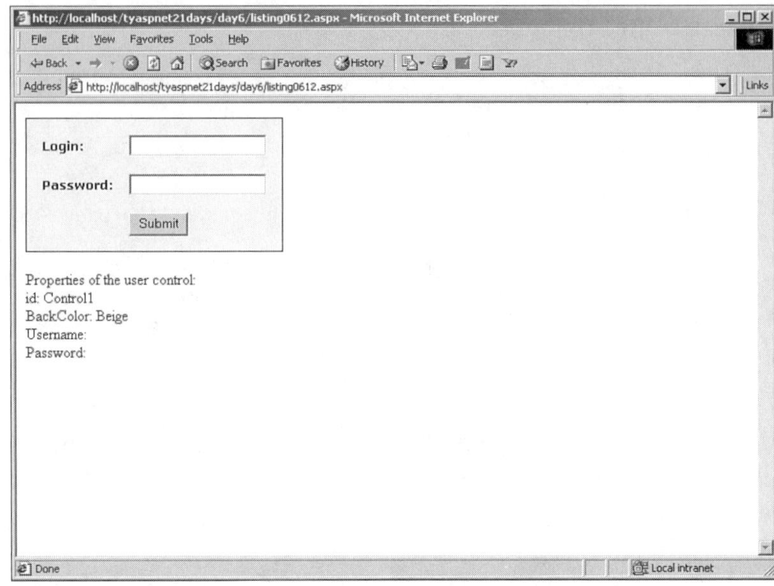

FIGURE 6.12

The runtime-created control functions just like the design-time control.

That's Not ASP!

There's not much comparison between today's lesson and classic ASP.NET. The Web forms framework is completely new, as are the custom and user controls. However, you can draw some parallels to the older technology.

User controls are similar to server-side includes, which were often used to encapsulate portions of the user interface for reuse on many pages. Although they could contain code to handle the UI, they weren't accessible programmatically from the containing ASP page. User controls greatly expand on server-side includes, providing ASP.NET with complete information about the encapsulated UI. ASP.NET can create and assign properties to user controls and doesn't need to worry about the implementation. All the unnecessary details are hidden. It's important to make the distinction that user controls are completely self-contained objects that can enhance your pages, while server-side includes merely allow you to divide code into separate pages for reuse.

The closest parallel to custom controls in classic ASP is COM objects. These objects were created from scratch by a developer to provide reusable functionality. However, COM objects didn't provide UI information (although they could if needed). Custom controls provide reusable functionality as it applies to the UI. You wouldn't normally create a custom control that doesn't contain UI information. The way ASP.NET interacts with COM objects and custom controls is completely different. For more information about how COM objects play a part in ASP.NET, see Day 15.

Summary

Whew, today was a long day! You learned a lot about the Web forms framework and how to extend it by creating your own server controls. You also learned the difference between creating controls at runtime and at design time, and now you should be familiar with both methods.

User controls are simply pieces of user interface code that are contained in files with the extension `.ascx`. Any existing ASP.NET page can be transformed into a user control by removing all `<html>`, `<body>`, and `<form>` tags, changing any `@ Page` directives to `@ Control`, and changing the file extension from `.aspx` to `.ascx`. User controls can and should contain the logic that controls the UI elements. This allows you to fully encapsulate a piece of UI functionality and easily implement it on any ASP.NET page. Custom controls allow you to create server controls that perform any type of functionality you want. These controls are used when no existing server controls fit your needs. They're created in VB.NET source files and must be compiled using the VB.NET compiler (see Day 15 for more information).

With custom controls, you can add state and event capabilities. The former is easy to implement. Simply use the state bag to store any properties of your control, instead of private variables. The latter is more complex, but luckily it's standard. You can write it once and simply copy-and-paste it to other controls.

You must register both user controls and custom controls with the `@ Register` directive before you can use them on your pages. The syntax is slightly different for each:

```
'user control
<%@ Register TagPrefix="Prefix" TagName="Name"
➥src="filepath" %>

'custom control
<%@ Register TagPrefix="Prefix" Namespace="Namespace"
➥Assembly="Assembly"%>
```

6

You can create server controls at runtime in addition to design time. This allows you to control the UI even in unforeseen circumstances, such as when you have too much data to fit in your existing UI. Regular server controls and custom controls can be created just like any other object in ASP.NET, with the `dim` statement. On the other hand, user controls must use the `Page.LoadControl` method to create new instances. This method returns a data type based on the filename of your user control's source file. Use a variable of this data type to assign properties to your control.

Tomorrow's lesson will complete this look at Web forms by examining the validation controls. These controls allow you to easily validate any user input before it can cause errors in your application. You'll be amazed at how easily you can force users to enter the information you want.

Q&A

Q How is user control processing different from ASP.NET page processing?

A Actually, user control processing is very similar to ASP.NET pages. Upon first request, they're compiled, just like `.aspx` files. They can also contain `Page_Load` event handlers! When a `Page_Load` event handler exists in both a user control and an ASP.NET page, the latter is handled first. All other events are handled in the same order as if they were contained within the ASP.NET page.

Q What's the difference between a user control and a code-behind form?

A If you've been experimenting with ASP.NET, you may have heard of code-behind forms. The distinction between the two is often confusing for beginners. A user control encapsulates a user interface and its functionality for reuse in other applications. A code-behind form is a class that declares objects and their methods for use in an `.aspx` file, without any user interface elements.

It may help to think of a user control as a puzzle piece—you can use it to build a larger picture of the UI. It already contains a piece of the picture, and it knows how to handle itself once it's put in place. A code-behind form, then, is the parent of an `.aspx` file (literally). It tells the `.aspx` file what it can do and how to do it, without telling it how it should look.

Workshop

This workshop will help reinforce the concepts covered in today's lesson. The answers can be found in Appendix A.

Quiz

1. True or False: A user control can be used on its own.
2. What are the three requirements to turn an `.aspx` file into a user control?
3. Build a `@ Register` directive for a user control with the tag prefix and the names `ACMEVBCustomControls` and `TextWriter`, located in the `shared.ascx` file in a subdirectory named `ucontrols`.
4. True or False: A custom control must be compiled to be used on an ASP.NET page.
5. True or False: A custom control must be derived from the `Object` class, directly or indirectly.

6. Using VB.NET's property element syntax, create a simple property for a custom control called `Color` that stores information in viewstate.
7. True or False: The `LoadControl` method can be used to load a custom control dynamically.

Exercises

1. Enhance the calculator exercise from Day 2 so that it resembles the Windows calculator. Include memory functions (using `Session` variables), clear and backspace buttons, and the additional operator buttons. Encapsulate it as a user control. This exercise can get fairly complex, but don't worry! You've learned all of the techniques you need to build it.

   Hint: Building the UI should be fairly easy. Just use an HTML table. Also note that much of the functionality is duplicated. For instance, each number button should do the same thing (display a number in a text box), so they can all reference the same event handler. Finally, hidden form fields will help when you're trying to determine which numbers are being manipulated. For instance, a user presses 6, then multiply, then 7. Store the 6 in a hidden field so it's not lost after subsequent form posts.
2. Create a meeting planner. It should include a calendar, a text box for user entries, and a label to display the current data. Use `AutoPostBack` and the `TextChanged` event when the user enters something in the text box. Store them in session variables so that the user can return to them at a later time. When a note is added, create a label dynamically to provide feedback. Consult Appendix C to learn about the Calendar control's events and methods.

DAY 7

Validating ASP.NET Pages

Validating user input in ASP.NET Web forms is one of the most important tasks for developers. Users are very unpredictable when it comes to supplying information, so you must take extra precautions to make sure they give you the correct data. For example, suppose you ask a user for a credit card number. What happens if he enters non-valid input, such as `dgffg934053`? Or what if he leaves off one digit of the number? Obviously, this will cause some problems in your application, especially when he tries to place an order.

In ASP.NET, these types of validation are easy to perform. You have a bevy of options for validating user input, including pattern matching and making sure the input is within a given range. The Validation controls provide a number of methods to alert users about errors, and they can do so dynamically without requiring a post to the server. And when one of the built-in options doesn't meet your needs, you can build your own!

Today you're going to look at various ways to validate user input easily with ASP.NET. Specifically, you'll look at the Validation server controls, which make data entry validation easier than ever. You'll also look at examples of creating your own validation routines.

Today's lesson will cover the following:

- Why and how to validate user input before ASP.NET
- What ASP.NET Validation controls are and how they work
- How to implement Validation controls in your pages
- How to customize error messages displayed to the user
- How to build custom Validation controls

Validation Scenarios

Imagine going to school to register for classes. The registrar asks you for your name. If you tell him that your name is "56," he's going to wonder if you're telling the truth. Most likely, he'll ask you for your name again. He must either verify that your name is indeed "56" or get your real name.

Any time that you ask people for information, you have to be prepared for the unexpected. You never know what they'll say when presented with a simple question. With computers, this kind of behavior can be disastrous. If an application is expecting one type of data, giving it another type of data may result in an error or even a crash (as you may have already experienced with your ASP.NET pages). Input validation is the process of making sure that the user provides the correct type of data.

Input validation is a must when you allow users to enter information manually into your ASP.NET pages. Most users will do their best to comply and enter the information you ask for in the proper format, but sometimes they make mistakes. Other users may like to try breaking applications by entering invalid information. In either case, getting data that you weren't expecting is a very common situation.

For example, imagine that you've created an e-commerce site that takes orders for office supplies. Eventually, you'll need to take personal information from the user, such as her name, e-mail, billing address, and so on. You must ensure that this information is accurate, or the order won't be processed correctly. For example, if the user enters a number for the shipping state, such as 45, and the application doesn't catch it immediately, the shipment may never be delivered and you'll end up with an irate customer.

So what happens if the user enters a number in place of her name? Or she enters a random string of characters for her e-mail address? Eventually, what you end up with is incorrect data being entered into your system. Detecting invalid input is vital for presenting a solid application.

Input validation also provides benefits for developers—specifically, coherent data. When you're designing your application, you should always be able to count on the data being in a specific format. For example, if you need to add two numbers, you need to make sure they are indeed numbers. Otherwise, the add operation won't work and your application will fail. When the input has been validated beforehand, you know that your add operation will succeed.

Let's examine a typical situation that requires user input validation. Listing 7.1 shows a simple user interface ASP.NET page that allows users to enter some personal information.

LISTING 7.1 A Typical Scenario for Validation

```
<html><body>
   <form runat="server">
      <asp:Label id="lblHeader" runat="server"
         Height="25px" Width="100%" BackColor="#ddaa66"
         ForeColor="white" Font-Bold="true"
         Text="A Validation Example" />
      <asp:Label id="lblMessage" runat="server" /><br>
      <asp:Panel id="Panel1" runat="server">
         <table>
          <tr>
             <td width="100" valign="top">
                First and last name:
             </td>
             <td width="300" valign="top">
                <asp:TextBox id="tbFName" runat="server" />
                <asp:TextBox id="tbLName" runat="server" />
             </td>
          </tr>
          <tr>
             <td valign="top">Email:</td>
             <td valign="top">
                <asp:TextBox id="tbEmail"
                   runat="server" />
             </td>
          </tr>
          <tr>
             <td valign="top">Address:</td>
             <td valign="top">
                <asp:TextBox id="tbAddress"
                   runat="server" />
             </td>
          </tr>
```

LISTING 7.1 continued

```
         <tr>
            <td valign="top">City, State, ZIP:</td>
            <td valign="top">
               <asp:TextBox id="tbCity"
                  runat="server" />,
               <asp:TextBox id="tbState" runat="server"
                  size=2 /> 
               <asp:TextBox id="tbZIP" runat="server"
                  size=5 />
            </td>
         </tr>
         <tr>
            <td valign="top">Phone:</td>
            <td valign="top">
               <asp:TextBox id="tbPhone" runat="server"
                  size=11 /><p>
            </td>
         </tr>
         <tr>
            <td colspan="2" valign="top" align="right">
               <asp:Button id="btSubmit" runat="server"
                  text="Add" />
            </td>
         </tr>
         </table>
      </asp:Panel>
   </form>
</body></html>
```

ANALYSIS This listing uses a few Web controls to display a user interface. The user interface prompts the user for first and last name, e-mail address, street address, city, state, ZIP code, and phone number (note, though, that the form won't actually do anything when submitted, yet). The result of Listing 7.1 is shown in Figure 7.1.

Once the form is submitted, you have to verify that each field contains a valid entry before entering the data in a database. A common way to do this is through a series of `if` statements, as shown in Listing 7.2. This series of `if` statements validates all of the server controls in Listing 7.1.

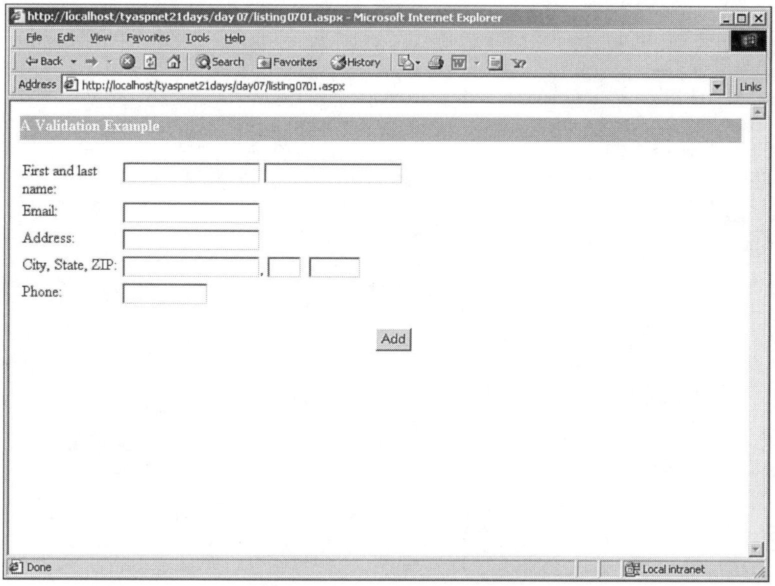

FIGURE 7.1

A typical user-entry page.

LISTING 7.2 Validating User Input from Listing 7.1 Through `if` Statements

```
<script runat="server">
   sub Submit(Sender as Object, e as EventArgs)
      if tbFName.Text <> "" and not IsNumeric(tbFName.Text)
➥then
         if tblName.Text <> "" and not IsNumeric
➥(tblName.Text) then
            if tbAddress.Text <> "" then
               if tbCity.Text <> "" and not IsNumeric(tbCity.
➥Text) then
                  if tbState.Text <> "" and not IsNumeric(
➥tbState.Text) then
                     if tbZIP.Text <> "" and IsNumeric(
➥tbZIP.Text) then
                        if tbPhone.Text <> "" then
                           lblMessage.Text = "Success!"
                        else
                           lblMessage.Text = "Phone is
➥incorrect!"
                        end if
                     else
                        lblMessage.Text = "ZIP is
➥incorrect!"
```

LISTING 7.2 continued

```
16:                         end if
17:                      else
18:                         lblMessage.Text = "State is incorrect!"
19:                      end if
20:                   else
21:                      lblMessage.Text = "City is incorrect!"
22:                   end if
23:                else
24:                   lblMessage.Text = "Address is incorrect!"
25:                end if
26:             else
27:                lblMessage.Text = "Last name is incorrect!"
28:             end if
29:          else
30:             lblMessage.Text = "First name is incorrect!"
31:          end if
32:       end sub
33:    </script>
```

ANALYSIS As you can see, validating all of the controls in this manner is rather long and tedious. The `if` statement on line 3 verfies that the user has filled in the first name field, and also that the supplied data is not a number. The second `if` statement on line 4 does the same for the last name field. You proceed this way until you've checked every control that contains user input. Don't forget the `else` statements, which display a message telling the user what the error is.

After checking all of the user inputs in this fashion, you can take one of two courses. If all of the information entered by the user is in the correct format, you can insert the data in the data source. If any of the information is formatted improperly, you need to alert the user to the errors in the input (done with the `else` statements) and allow her to fix them before inserting the results into the data store (by simply redisplaying the page).

However, this can get quite complex because you often have to check for multiple cases on each input. For example, for the first name, you have to check that the field isn't blank, doesn't contain any numbers, doesn't contain spaces, and so on. This makes for a lot of `if` statements. As tedious as this may be, it's a typical method of validating user input. The process boils down to the following steps:

1. Display the form to the user and allow her to enter data.
2. Upon form submission, use `if` statements to check every user input. This includes checking for blank entries, the proper format and data type, valid ranges of information (for dates), and so on.

3. If all `if` statements pass, perform your functionality.
4. If an `if` statement fails, redisplay the form, preferably with the fields prefilled with the previously entered user input. This allows the user to correct only the incorrect fields and leave the correct ones. Start over at step 2.

ASP.NET Validation

ASP.NET Validation server controls allow you to easily validate any data a user has entered in a Web form. These controls support such validations as required fields and pattern matching, and they also make it easy to build your own custom validations. In addition, Validation controls allow you to completely customize the way error messages are displayed to users when data values don't pass validation.

Validation controls are similar to Web controls (see Day 5, "Beginning Web Forms"). They're created on the server, they output HTML to the browser, and they're declared with the same syntax:

```
<asp:ValidatorName runat="server"
   ControlToValidate="ControlName"
   ErrorMessage="Descriptive Text"/>
```

The difference is that these controls don't display anything unless the input fails validation. Otherwise, they're invisible and the user can't interact with them. Thus, a Validation control's job is to watch over another server control and validate its content. The `ControlToValidate` property specifies which user input server control should be watched. When the user enters data into the watched control, the Validator control checks the data to make sure it follows all the rules you've specified (see "How Validation Controls Work" later today).

Table 7.1 summarizes the types of predefined validation controls offered by ASP.NET. You'll use all of these controls as you progress through today's lesson. They all belong to the `System.Web.UI.WebControls` namespace.

TABLE 7.1 ASP.NET Validation Control Types

Validation Control	*Description*
`RequiredFieldValidator`	Ensures that the user doesn't skip a field that is required.
`CompareValidator`	Compares a user's entry against a constant value, against a property value of another control, or against a database value using a comparison operator (less than, equal to, greater than, and so on).
`RangeValidator`	Checks that a user's entry is between specified lower and upper boundaries. You can check ranges within pairs of numbers,

TABLE 7.1 continued

Validation Control	*Description*
	alphabetic characters, and dates. Boundaries can be expressed as constants or as values derived from another control (from the .NET SDK documentation).
`RegularExpressionValidator`	Checks that the entry matches a pattern defined by a regular expression. This type of validation allows you to check for predictable sequences of characters, such as those in Social Security numbers, e-mail addresses, telephone numbers, postal codes, and so on (from the .NET SDK documentation).
`CustomValidator`	Checks the user's entry using validation logic that you code yourself. This type of validation allows you to check for values derived at runtime.

Unfortunately, Validation controls will only validate input with a subset of ASP.NET server controls. Most of the time, these controls will be more than enough to validate all user input. The controls that can have their input validated by ASP.NET's Validation controls are

- `HtmlInputText`
- `HtmlTextArea`
- `HtmlSelect`
- `HtmlInputFile`
- `TextBox`
- `ListBox`
- `DropDownList`
- `RadioButtonList`

Note that the Validation controls are supplements to the controls listed. They don't allow user input themselves.

How Validation Controls Work

To create a Validation control on an ASP.NET page, simply add the proper Validation control tag to your Web form. Each Validation control that you add has a specific job: watching over one other server control. When a user enters any information into that server control, its corresponding validator scrutinizes the input and determines if it passes the tests that you've specified. All this is accomplished without any intervention or extra code from the developer.

Validation controls work on both the client and server. When a user enters data into a Web control and it violates the validation rule you've specified, the user will be alerted immediately. In fact, ASP.NET won't allow a form to be posted that has invalid information! This means you don't have to send information back and forth from the server to provide validation—it occurs on the client side automatically. This provides a large boost in performance and a better experience for the users.

> **Note** Client-side validation only occurs on browsers that support DHTML and JavaScript.

When the form is finally posted to the server, ASP.NET validates the inputs again. This allows you to double-check the data against resources that may not have been available on the client side, such as a database. You don't need to validate on the server again if you trust the client-side validation, but it can often help in situations that require more complex validation routines.

Although much of this functionality comes automatically, there are a lot of things that must be accomplished behind the scenes in order for these controls to work. Listing 7.3 is a simple example.

LISTING 7.3 A Simple Validation Example

```
<%@ Page Language="VB" %>

<script runat="server">
   sub Submit(Sender as Object, e as EventArgs)
      if Page.IsValid then
         lblMessage.Text = "You passed validation!"
      end if
   end sub
</script>

 <html><body>
    <form runat="server">
       <asp:Label id="lblMessage" runat="server" /><p>

       Enter your name:
       <asp:TextBox id="tbFName" runat="server" /><br>
       <asp:RequiredFieldValidator runat="server"
          ControlToValidate="tbFName"
          ErrorMessage="First name required"/><p>

```

LISTING 7.3 continued

```
21:         <asp:Button id="tbSubmit" runat="server"
22:            Text="Submit"
23:            OnClick="Submit" />
24:      </form>
25:   </body></html>
```

ANALYSIS Save this file as `listing0703.aspx` and view it from your browser. Before looking at what goes on backstage, let's take a tour of the page itself.

In the HTML portion of the page, you see four server controls: `Label` (line 13), `TextBox` (line 16), `RequiredFieldValidator` Validation control (lines 17 through 19), and a `Button` control (lines 21 through 23). `RequiredFieldValidator` is declared just like any other control. It contains a control name and `runat="server"`. The `ControlToValidate` property specifies which server control this validator should watch over (`tbFName` in this case).

If any data is entered into the `tbFName` text box, the `RequiredFieldValidator` is satisfied. This control only checks to see if a field contains data. Every Validation control has an `IsValid` property that indicates if the validation has passed. In this case, if the user enters any data, this property is set to true. Otherwise, it's false. When the form is posted, the `Submit` method on line 4 is executed. The `Page.IsValid` property makes sure all Validation controls on the page are satisfied. You could also check each individual control's `IsValid` property, but this way is faster. Lines 5–7 display a message to the user if all of the Validation controls in the page are satisfied with the user input.

Try clicking Submit without entering anything in the text box. You should see what's shown in Figure 7.2.

What happened? The Validation control on line 17 checks if its dependent control has any data in it. Since you didn't enter any information, the validator stops the form from posting and displays the message you specified in the `ErrorMessage` property on line 19. The server doesn't get to see the user input at all.

Try entering some information into the text box and moving out of the element. The error message disappears automatically! Erase the text, and the error message appears again. Each element is validated as soon as the focus leaves it.

Note

> The dynamic appearance of the error message is only supported on browsers that support dynamic HTML (Internet Explorer and Netscape 4+).

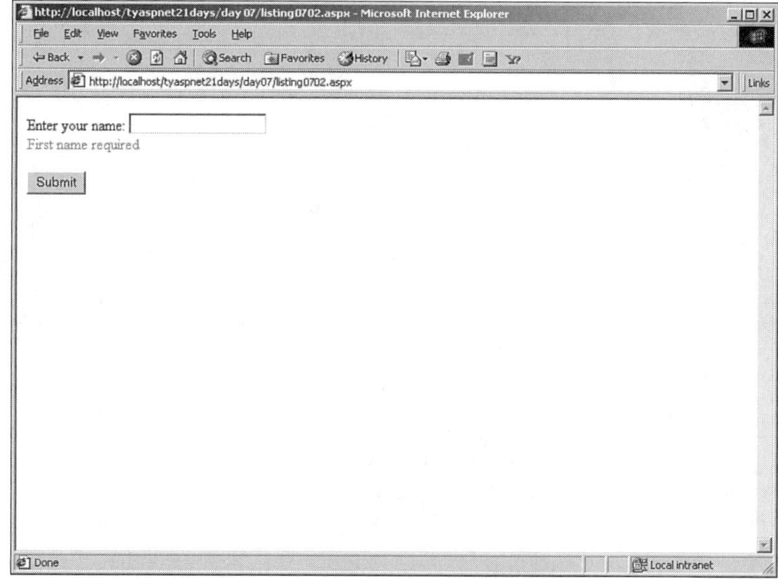

FIGURE 7.2

The Validation control displays an error message.

Let's take a look at the HTML produced by your ASP.NET page. Right-click on the page and select view source. Listing 7.4 shows a portion of the HTML source.

LISTING 7.4 The Condensed Source from Your Validation Page

```
...
   <form name="ctrl1" method="post" action="listing0702.aspx"
      language="javascript" onsubmit="ValidatorOnSubmit();"
      id="ctrl1">
...
...
   <script language="javascript"
      src="/_aspx/1.0.2523/script/WebUIValidation.js">
   </script>
...
...
   <span id="ctrl6" controltovalidate="tbFName"
      errormessage="First name required" evaluationfunction=
      "RequiredFieldValidatorEvaluateIsValid" initialvalue=""
      style="color:Red;visibility:hidden;">
   First name required</span><p>
...
...
   <script language="javascript">
   <!--
...
```

LISTING 7.4 continued

```
22:    ...
23:          function ValidatorOnSubmit() {
24:             if (Page_ValidationActive) {
25:                ValidatorCommonOnSubmit();
26:             }
27:          }
28:       // -->
29:       </script>
30:    ...
31:    ...
```

ANALYSIS This page has a lot of content, so let's just examine the important parts. On line 2, you see your standard form tag. However, notice that when this form is submitted (that is, when the `Submit` method is raised), the form executes the `ValidatorOnSubmit` function instead of posting directly to the server. This function, located on line 25, determines if validation is enabled for the page (which it is, by default) and executes another function that performs the validation processing (see "Disabling Validation" later today for more information).

On line 8, you see that your page includes a reference to the `WebUIValidation.js` JavaScript file, located on the server. This script, automatically generated by ASP.NET, contains all the necessary client-side DHTML functions to display dynamic error messages, validate the input, and post the data to the server. This file is quite large, so we won't examine it here—it's usually located at `c:\inetpub\wwwroot\_aspx\`*`version`*`\script`.

On line 12, you see the HTML output of the Validation server control—a `<span>` element. It contains a custom attribute, `evaluationfunction`, that tells `WebUIValidation.js` what type of validation to perform. Also, this span is set to "hidden," which means the user can't see it—that is, until the validator functions have their say.

This is a complicated process, but you don't have to build any of it because ASP.NET handles everything automatically.

When this client-side script executes and evaluates each Validation control on the page, it sets a parameter for each based on the outcome of the validation. These parameters are sent to the server for validation again. Figure 7.3 illustrates this process.

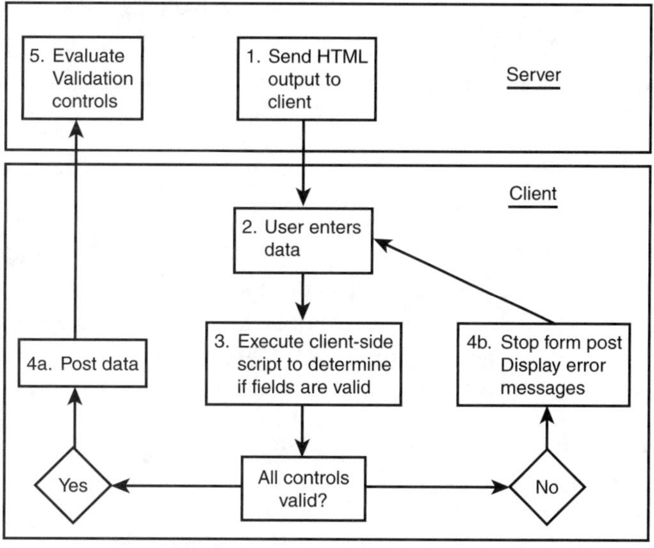

FIGURE 7.3
The validation process occurs on both the server and client sides.

Note

Recall that client-side validation only occurs on browsers that support DHTML. Additionally, if a client has JavaScript disabled, client-side validation won't occur.

Why does the server need to validate the information again? Suppose that you need to validate some of the information against a database that resides on the server. Or that you want to prevent a user from submitting a form more than once. Sometimes the extra validation might be necessary, and the added precaution can't hurt.

When the server receives the form data, it checks the state of each Validation control (through the `IsValid` property). If they've all been satisfied, ASP.NET sets the `IsValid` property for the `Page` object to true. Otherwise, it's set to false. Even if it's false, execution of your code will still continue. The code will be executed whether or not the input was validated. Therefore, it's up to you to stop your code from executing if the data is invalid. This is usually done with a simple check to the `Page.IsValid` property.

Using Validation Controls

All Validation controls share similar properties. At a minimum, each control should specify two properties (not including `runat="server"`). First, they all must contain the `ControlToValidate` property, which specifies the name of the server control that this validator should watch over. Second, each control must have an `ErrorMessage` property that tells ASP.NET what message to display to the user if the validation fails. There are a few additional properties as well, which will be covered later today in "Customizing Validation."

Let's go back to Listing 7.1 and revise it to use Validation controls. First, let's examine what types of validation you'll need.

For your first name and last name text boxes, you'll need to ensure that the user enters data—any data at all, just as long as there's text in the boxes. This validation calls for a `RequiredFieldValidator` control. For an added security step, you'll also make sure that the first and last names aren't the same. This prevents users from simply typing a string of characters (such as "asdf") into each box. You'll use a `CompareValidator` for this.

For the e-mail box, you'll need to ensure that the e-mail address is in a valid format, such as *somename@somesite.com*. Again, this is to prevent users from entering random strings of characters. The `RegularExpressionValidator` control will perform this functionality. The ZIP code and phone number text boxes will also need to be checked for valid formats. For instance, the ZIP code must be five digits, without letters, and the phone number (for our purposes) must be in the format *`xxx-xxxx`*.

Finally, let's assume that you want to allow only users from a certain region of the United States (a certain range of ZIP codes) to submit your form. This type of validation can be performed with the `RangeValidator` control. Listing 7.5 shows the UI portion of this page.

LISTING 7.5 The UI Portion of Your Enhanced User Form

```
<html><body>
   <form runat="server">
      <asp:Label id="lblHeader" runat="server"
         Height="25px" Width="100%" BackColor="#ddaa66"
         ForeColor="white" Font-Bold="true"
         Text="A Validation Example" />
      <asp:Label id="lblMessage" runat="server" /><br>
      <asp:Panel id="Panel1" runat="server">
         <table>
          <tr>
             <td width="100" valign="top">
                First and last name:
             </td>
             <td width="300" valign="top">
                <asp:TextBox id="tbFName" runat="server" />
                <asp:TextBox id="tbLName" runat="server" />
                <br>
```

LISTING 7.5 continued

```
            <asp:RequiredFieldValidator runat="server"
               ControlToValidate="tbFName"
               ErrorMessage="First name required"/><br>
            <asp:RequiredFieldValidator runat="server"
               ControlToValidate="tbLName"
               ErrorMessage="Last name required"/><br>
            <asp:CompareValidator runat="server"
               ControlToValidate="tbFName"
               ControlToCompare="tbLName"
               Type="String"
               Operator="NotEqual"
               ErrorMessage="First and last name
➥           cannot be the same" />
         </td>
      </tr>
      <tr>
         <td valign="top">Email (.com's only):</td>
         <td valign="top">
            <asp:TextBox id="tbEmail"
               runat="server" /><br>
            <asp:RegularExpressionValidator
               runat="server"
               ControlToValidate="tbEmail"
               ValidationExpression="\w+\@\w+\.com"
               ErrorMessage="That is not a valid email"
            />
         </td>
      </tr>
      <tr>
         <td valign="top">Address:</td>
         <td valign="top">
            <asp:TextBox id="tbAddress"
               runat="server" />
         </td>
      </tr>
      <tr>
         <td valign="top">City, State, ZIP (5-digit):</td>
         <td valign="top">
            <asp:TextBox id="tbCity"
               runat="server" />,
            <asp:TextBox id="tbState" runat="server"
               size=2 /> 
            <asp:TextBox id="tbZIP" runat="server"
               size=5 /><br>
            <asp:RegularExpressionValidator
               runat="server"
               ControlToValidate="tbZIP"
               ValidationExpression="[0-9]{5}"
```

LISTING 7.5 continued

```
                  ErrorMessage="That is not a valid ZIP" />
               <br>
               <asp:RangeValidator runat="server"
                  ControlToValidate="tbZIP"
                  MinimumValue="00000" MaximumValue="22222"
                  Type="String"
                  ErrorMessage="You don't live in the
➥              correct region" />
            </td>
         </tr>
         <tr>
            <td valign="top">Phone (<i>xxx-xxxx</i>):</td>
            <td valign="top">
               <asp:TextBox id="tbPhone" runat="server"
                  size=11 /><br>
               <asp:RegularExpressionValidator
                  runat="server"
                  ControlToValidate="tbPhone"
                  ValidationExpression="[0-9]{3}-[0-9]{4}"
                  ErrorMessage="That is not a valid phone"
               />
            </td>
         </tr>
         <tr>
            <td colspan="2" valign="top" align="right">
               <asp:Button id="btSubmit" runat="server"
                  text="Add" />
            </td>
         </tr>
         </table>
      </asp:Panel>
   </form>
</body></html>
```

ANALYSIS That's quite a bit of code, but there are only a few things you need to examine. The rest is plain HTML. First, let's take note of what this page *doesn't* do. The e-mail, city, state, ZIP, and phone controls do *not* have corresponding `RequiredFieldValidators`, essentially making them optional. If the user enters nothing in these fields, validation will pass because none of the other Validation controls care if a field is empty. Even if the field is blank, the control's `IsValid` property will return true. Next, note that the form only accepts certain types of e-mail addresses, ZIP codes, and phone numbers. The e-mail addresses can only end in `.com`. The ZIP code can only be five digits (some postal codes use nine digits, *`xxxxx-xxxx`*). And phone numbers can only contain seven digits, with a dash between the third and fourth digits. These validation rules can be quite limiting, but they're fine for the purposes of this lesson. In a real-world situation, you'd probably want to make your rules more general.

Let's look at lines 18–30. You have two instances of `RequiredFieldValidator`, on lines 18 and 22. These controls make sure that the user enters some data into the first name and last name text boxes, respectively. You've already seen this control used earlier today. These lines contain only the two required properties, `ControlToValidate` and `ErrorMessage`.

`CompareValidator` on line 24 can compare the value of one server control to a constant, or to another server control. Here, you're comparing `tbFName` and `tbLName` to make sure they aren't the same. The `Type` property tells ASP.NET what kind of values you're comparing, such as `String`, `Double`, `DateTime`, and so on. The `Operator` specifies what type of comparison should be made. In this case, you're comparing two strings from two text boxes, and you want to make sure the values aren't equal. Again, you have the standard `ControlToValidate` and `ErrorMessage` properties. Tables 7.2 and 7.3 list the valid operators and types used with the `CompareValidator`.

TABLE 7.2 Operators for Use with the `CompareValidator`'s `Operator` Property

Operator	*Description*
`DataTypeCheck`	Checks if the data is a certain data type (`string`, `integer`, and so on)
`Equal`	Checks for equality
`GreaterThan`	Checks for greater than
`GreaterThanEqual`	Checks for greater than or equal to
`LessThan`	Checks for less then
`LessThanEqual`	Checks for less than or equal to
`NotEqual`	Checks for inequality

TABLE 7.3 Types for Use with the `CompareValidator`'s `Type` Property

Type	*Description*
`Currency`	Currency values
`Date`	Date values
`Double`	Double values (floating point)
`Integer`	Integer values
`String`	String values

To compare against a constant value, change `ControlToCompare` to `ValueToCompare`. For example, the following `CompareValidator` checks if the value entered matches the string "Chris." If it does, validation fails and an error message is displayed:

```
<asp:CompareValidator runat="server"
   ControlToValidate="tbFName"
   ValueToCompare="Chris"
   Type="String"
   Operator="NotEqual"
   ErrorMessage="Your first name cannot be the same as mine"/>
```

If you just wanted to check if the user input is a valid data type, you could set the `Operator` property of the `CompareValidator` to `DataTypeCheck` and leave the `ControlToCompare` property out. Be careful with this operator, though. In a Web form, all inputs evaluate to strings, so you might not get the correct validation. For example, the following `CompareValidator` will be satisfied if the user enters `76.7878`:

```
<asp:CompareValidator runat="server"
   ControlToValidate="tbFName"
   Type="String"
   Operator="DataTypeCheck"
   ErrorMessage="You must enter a string value" />
```

Note that when you have two or more Validation controls referencing one server control, all conditions must be satisfied for the input to be valid. Therefore, the first name and last name boxes must both be filled out, *and* they cannot contain the same text.

On line 38, you declare a `RegularExpressionValidator` control, which checks if the user input matches a pattern of characters. The only new property in this control is `ValidationExpression` on line 41, which specifies the regular expression that should be used to validate the input. In this case, the string `\w+\@\w+\.com` means one or more word characters (in other words, a letter), followed by the `@` symbol, followed by one or more word characters, followed by `.com`. For more information, refer to the "Regular Expressions" section later today.

On line 62, you have another `RegularExpressionValidator` that checks if a proper ZIP code was entered. The string `[0-9]{5}` means five of any of the characters 0 through 9.

On line 68, you have a `RangeValidator` control, which checks if the specified server control's value falls between the limits you've specified. This is so you can limit the form to people in particular regions of the U.S. You can even compare dates and strings with this control! Line 70 specifies the `MinimumValue` and `MaximumValue` properties that set the boundaries for your ZIP codes. You set the `Type` property to `String` so that the ZIP codes will be evaluated properly. (If you used `Double` or `Integer`, the string `00001` would evaluate to `1`—for numbers, all preceding zeroes are stripped out—which is *not* what you want.)

Finally, on line 81, you have another `RegularExpressionValidator`. This control is used to validate the user's phone number. It ensures that the number is seven digits long. The `ValidationExpression` string `[0-9]{3}-[0-9]{4}` will match three of any of the characters 0 through 9, followed by a dash, followed by four of any of the characters 0 through 9. This can represent any U.S. 7-digit phone number.

Tip

You can specify multiple patterns to match in a `RegularExpressionValidator` by using the `|` symbol (meaning "or") in the `ValidationExpression` property. For example, the following string matches any phone number that has seven digits with dashes, 10 digits with dashes, or 10 digits with no dashes:

```
([0-9]{3}-[0-9]{4})|([0-9]{3}-[0-9]{3}-[0-9]{4})|([0-9]{10})
```

The user could enter any of the following and it would be valid:

```
458-9865
625-458-9865
6254589865
```

Experiment with the form to produce different outputs (note again that the form doesn't do anything when submitted except validate the controls). Test the `RegularExpressionValidator` controls by entering both values that match the pattern and values that don't. Also, try entering values in some fields but leaving others blank, and then submit the form. Figure 7.4 shows an attempt to enter some invalid data. Note the error messages next to the offending text boxes. Figure 7.5 shows the page when everything has been entered correctly.

Caution

Don't forget that only the `RequiredFieldValidator` control considers a blank field invalid. All of the other controls accept empty fields. This means that despite the e-mail address field being left blank, the check by the `RegularExpressionValidator` will pass and this control's `IsValid` property will return true. The validator won't stop the form from being processed even if there's no data in the field.

Therefore, you must use the `RequiredFieldValidator` control in addition to the other validators if you want to check for actual values.

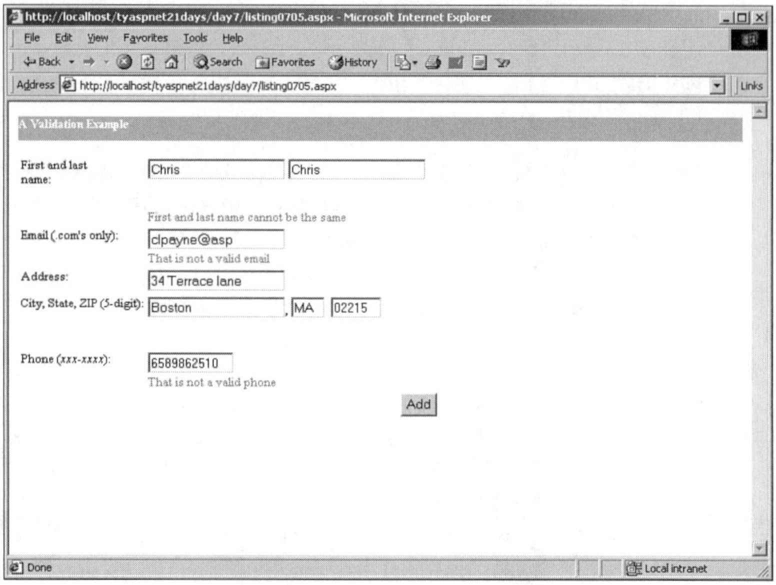

FIGURE 7.4

A test of the validation form, with errors.

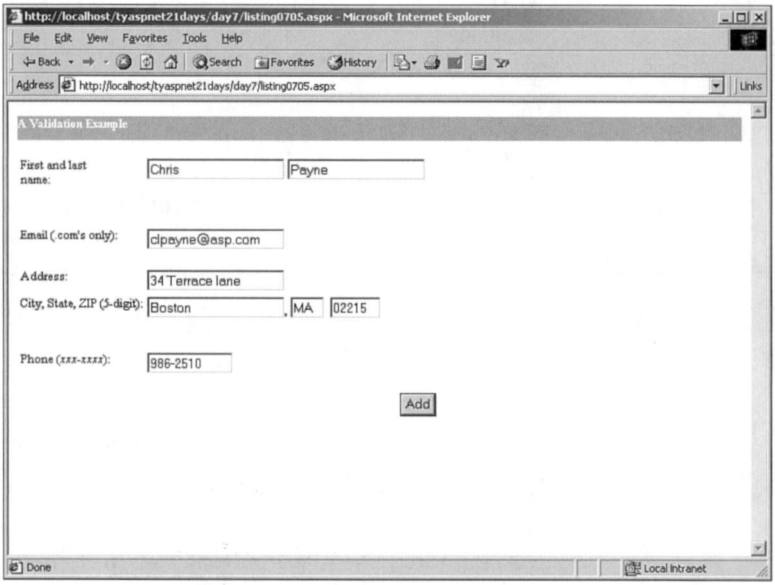

FIGURE 7.5

A test of the validation form, without errors.

Validating on the Server

Client-side validation is a wonderful tool that saves you a lot of headaches. But you still have to handle the validation yourself on the server side. Just because a form is invalid doesn't mean ASP.NET won't execute your code. Therefore, you have to add some checks to your methods.

The simplest way to check for validity in your form is to check the `Page` object's `IsValid` property. If all the Validation controls are satisfied with the input, this property is `true`; if *any* of the Validation controls are invalid, it's `false`. Thus, you could simply check this property and decide whether or not to execute your code. For example, Listing 7.6 shows a possible code declaration block used with Listing 7.5.

LISTING 7.6 Testing `Page` Validity

```
1:    <%@ Page Language="VB" %>
2:
3:    <script runat="server">
4:       sub Submit(Sender as Object, e as EventArgs)
5:          if Page.IsValid then
6:             lblMessage.Text = "Success!"
7:          else
8:             lblMessage.Text = "One of the fields is invalid"
9:          end if
10:      end sub
11:   </script>
12:   ...
13:   ...
14:            <tr>
15:               <td colspan="2" valign="top" align="right">
16:                  <asp:Button id="btSubmit" runat="server"
17:                     text="Add"
18:                     OnClick="Submit" />
19:               </td>
20:            </tr>
21:            </table>
22:         </asp:Panel>
23:      </form>
24:   </body></html>
```

ANALYSIS The `Submit` method on line 5 checks, with one property, if all of the Validation controls are valid. You can then execute your code or not, depending on your needs. If the controls are valid, you could insert the data into a database or e-mail the user—whatever you would normally do during a form submission. If the controls are invalid, you should display a message to the user explaining why the submission failed—why client-side validation passed but server-side didn't.

The `Validators` collection contains references to all of the Validation controls on the page. You can loop through this collection to determine individual control validity:

```
sub Submit(Sender as Object, e as EventArgs)
   if Page.IsValid then
      lblMessage.Text = "Success!"
   else
      dim objValidator as Ivalidator
      For Each objValidator in Validators
         if not objValidator.IsValid then
            lblMessage.Text += objValidator.ErrorMessage
         end if
       Next
    end if
 end sub
```

This code loops through each Validation control in `Validators` and displays the error messages for each invalid control. You can also check the `IsValid` property on any control in particular by referencing its name. To do this, you must assign the `id` property for each Validation control, which you haven't done so far. For example, if the `RegularExpressionValidator` for the e-mail text box had the `id valEmail`, the following code would display the error message if e-mail validation failed:

```
if not valEmail.IsValid then
   lblMessage.Text =+ valEmail.ErrorMessage
end if
```

Disabling Validation

There are several ways to disable validation without having to delete your Validation controls. The first method is to simply set the `Enabled` property of each validation control to false:

```
<asp:RegularExpressionValidator runat="server"
   ControlToValidate="tbZIP"
   Enabled="false" />
```

This prevents the control from sending any output to the client and thus validating the specified control.

You can also disable all validation on the client side by setting the `clienttarget` property of the `<%@ Page %>` directive to `downlevel`:

```
<%@ Page Language="VB" clienttarget="downlevel" %>
```

This command makes ASP.NET think that it's dealing with an older browser that doesn't support DHTML. In effect, all DHTML events are disabled, including client-side validation.

Only use this option as a last resort. Disabling all DHTML events means that there will be no dynamic client-side handling at all.

For example, ASP.NET will no longer use the <style> tag to change Web controls' appearance. All CSS attributes are disabled.

Regular Expressions

A *regular expression* is a string that contains special symbols (or sequences of symbols) that can be used to match patterns of characters. For example, you've probably seen an asterisk used when performing searches. The following string means "display all files in the current directory":

```
dir *.*
```

This is a form of regular expression. The asterisk is a wildcard that can be used to represent any other character. It matches a specified pattern of filenames—specifically, all files that contain a string, followed by a period, followed by another string. The key to learning regular expressions is finding out how to match patterns of text.

Regular expressions are difficult to master and their syntax is very complex, so today's lesson won't go into any depth. Creating or deciphering expressions involves learning which characters have special meaning in the language and how to specify normal characters. Deciphering a few examples may help you to understand expressions that you come across. Table 7.4 shows the most common characters used with regular expressions. These characters by themselves are useful. However, it's when they're combined that the true power of regular expressions shines through.

TABLE 7.4 Regular Expression Language Elements

<table>
<tr><th>Character(s)</th><th>Meaning</th></tr>
<tr><td>Regular characters</td><td>All characters other than ., $, ^, {, [, (, |,), *, +, ?, and \ are matched to themselves. In other words, the regular expression hello matches any string with the text hello. These exception characters all have special meanings.</td></tr>
<tr><td>.</td><td>Matches any one character.</td></tr>
<tr><td>$</td><td>Matches patterns at the end of a string. For example, $hello will match the string hello only when it's at the end of a string. It will match I said hello, but not Did you say hello?.</td></tr>
</table>

TABLE 7.4 continued

Character(s)	*Meaning*
^	Matches patterns at the beginning of a string. Similar to $. When used in square brackets, ^ means "not." For example, [^aeiou] means "match any one character that is *not* in the given list."
{}	Used to match a certain quantity of characters. For example, hello{2} matches the string hellohello. aye{2} matches ayeaye.
[]	Used to match any one of a group of characters. For example, [aeiou] matches any one of the letters a, e, i, o, or u. You can also use the dash to specify ranges. [a-z] matches any one of the lowercase letters a through z.
()	Used for grouping strings. Similar to using parentheses to change the order of precedence in operations.
|	Means logical or. (hello)|(HELLO) means "match either hello or HELLO."
*	Match zero or more matches. h*ello means "match zero or more occurrences of the letter h, followed by the letters ello."
+	Match one or more occurrences. h+ello would match hello and hhhhello, but not ello.
?	Match zero or one occurrences. h?ello matches ello and hello, but not hhello.
\	An escape character. When any of the previous special characters are preceded by the backslash, they're matched literally. For example, h*ello matches the string h*ello but not h\\\ello or hhhello. Additionally, certain normal characters have special meaning when preceded by a backslash.

When you're deciphering regular expressions, it helps to look for the special characters. Because they can be grouped, examine the characters *between* special characters as well. For example, the expression `href\s*=\s*(\"([^\"]*)\"|(\S+))` means `href` followed by zero or more white spaces (`\s*`), then by `=`, then by zero or more white spaces again. This is then followed by a double quote (`\"`), then by zero or more occurrences of anything that's not a double quote (`[^\"]*`), followed by a double quote *or* one or more non-white space characters (`\S+`). This string can be used to find anchors in an HTML page, such as `href = "blah:` and `href="hey"`.

Note that the escape character (`\`) is used in several places where it isn't necessary. For example, `"` has no special meaning for a regular expression. It matches the string `"`.

However, when in doubt, it's usually safe to use the escape character.

The regular expression `[0-9]{5}-[0-9]{4}|[0-9]{5}` means any five characters between 0–9, followed by a dash, followed by any four characters between 0–9, *or* any five characters between 0–9. Values like `90210` or `83647-1422` will pass, whereas values like `9021A` or `902` will not.

Regular expressions are commonly used throughout computing to match patterns of text. For more information, check out the .NET Framework SDK documentation, or the following online resources:

- `http://www.4guysfromrolla.com/webtech/regularexpressions.shtml`
- `http://www.asplists.com/asplists/aspregexp2.asp?tab=links`
- `http://www.amazon.com/exec/obidos/ASIN/1565922573/`

Customizing Validation

Validation controls are highly customizable. You can manipulate the way error messages are displayed, decide how users are alerted about errors, and even create custom Validation controls. ASP.NET gives developers a rich set of capabilities.

Error Messages

The examples you've been developing today all place the Validation controls immediately after the controls to validate. This isn't a requirement—Validation controls can be located anywhere on the page. You can place them all at the top of the page if you want to group error messages, for instance.

Let's take a look at Figure 7.4 again. There's a lot of white space between the UI elements on the page because of your Validation controls. Even though the validators may not display any message, they still take up space. You can remove the `<br>` after each control to eliminate the white space, but then the error messages are still placed as if something were in the way, as shown in Figure 7.6. This type of display is called *static*. You can easily combat this, however, by allowing dynamic display. Simply set the `Display` property to `Dynamic`. For example, the following code shows the first name and last name fields `RequireFieldValidators` as dynamically displayed objects:

```
<asp:RequiredFieldValidator runat="server"
   ControlToValidate="tbFName"
   ErrorMessage="First name required"
   Display="dynamic"/>
<asp:RequiredFieldValidator runat="server"
   ControlToValidate="tbLName"
```

7

```
    ErrorMessage="Last name required"
    Display="dynamic"/>
<asp:CompareValidator runat="server"
    ControlToValidate="tbFName"
    ControlToCompare="tblLName"
    Type="String"
    Operator="NotEqual"
    ErrorMessage="First and last name cannot be the same"
    Display="dynamic" />
```

The only addition is the `Display="dyanamic"` property. Adding this property to all of the controls in Listing 7.4 produces Figure 7.7.

FIGURE 7.6

The error message seems out-of-place because other Validation controls are in the way.

The white space problem is now eliminated. As the controls are validated, the page layout changes to make room for the error messages.

This method may cause some unexpected changes in the page layout, so don't use it if you depend on a certain look, or until you've completely tested the new layouts.

Also, the `Dynamic` property is only supported by browsers that support the `visible` CSS style attribute (IE 5+ and Netscape 4+). This attribute can be used to selectively hide UI elements from the user.

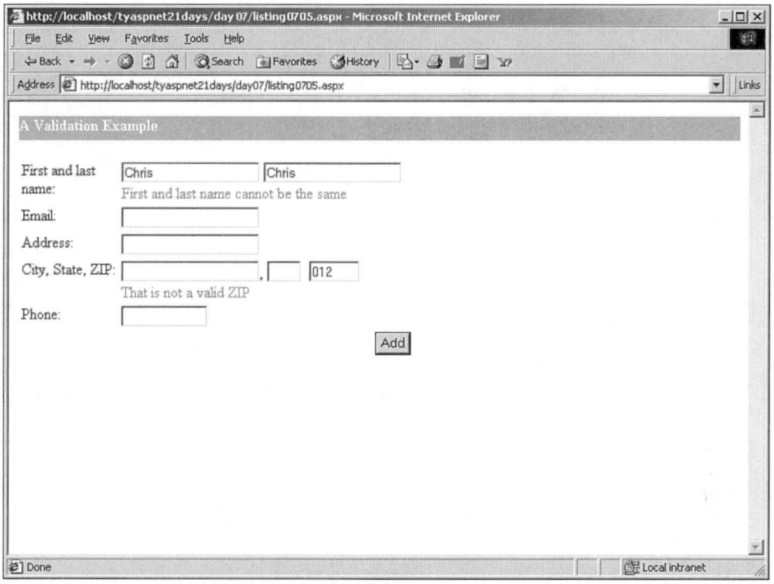

FIGURE 7.7
Dynamic display eliminates the white space problem.

Displaying Validation Summaries

So far, all of these examples have placed the error messages directly next to the server controls that are being validated. (Technically, the error messages are placed where the Validation control is located in the page.) This is very useful for telling users which controls have errors, especially with client-side validation. However, this isn't always the best place for error messages. You have a choice of where you place them:

- In-line—In the same place where the Validation control is located in the page layout.
- Summary—In a separate summary (can be a pop-up window on DHTML-capable browsers).
- Both in-line and summary—The respective error messages can be different.
- Customized.

The summary method is useful when you want to list all of the error messages in one location, such as at the top of the page. Depending on your application, users may prefer this method over an in-line display.

Rather than simply placing all of your Validation controls in one location, you can leave them where they are and use the `ValidationSummary` control. This control displays error messages with a specified format in a single location on the page. For example, add the following code near the top of Listing 7.5:

```
1:    <asp:ValidationSummary runat="server"
2:       DisplayMode="BulletList" />
```

After filling out the form information and clicking the Submit button, you should see what's shown in Figure 7.8.

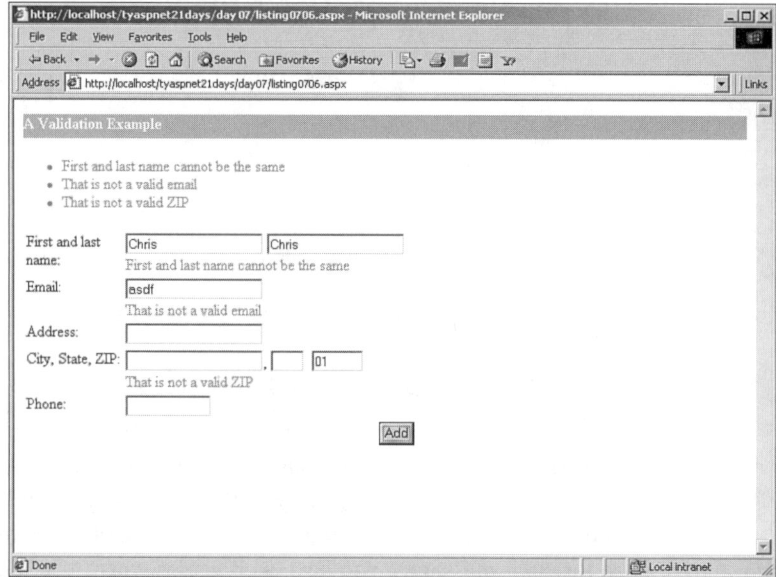

FIGURE 7.8
Displaying error message summaries.

This control is a bit different from the other Validation controls. It doesn't use the `ControlToValidate` or `ErrorMessage` properties. Rather, it takes the error messages from all the other controls in the page and displays them in one place. `DisplayMode` can be used to display the messages in a bulleted list (by specifying `BulletList`, as shown on line 2), or in paragraph format (with `SingleParagraph`).

The messages displayed in the `ValidationSummary` control are whatever you've specified in the `ErrorMessage` properties of the Validation controls. To change the in-line error message, use the `Text` property:

```
<asp:RequiredFieldValidator runat="server"
   ControlToValidate="tbFName"
   ErrorMessage="First name required"
   Text="Forgot first name!"
   Display="dynamic"/>
```

The first name validator will now display “Forgot first name!” beneath the first name text box and “First name required” in the `ValidationSummary` control. If you don’t want to display the in-line error messages, you can set each control’s `Display` property to `none`.

By adding the `ShowMessageBox` property, you can create a pop-up message box with the `ValidationSummary` control. For example, change the previous summary code snippet to read as follows:

```
<asp:ValidationSummary runat="server"
   ShowMessageBox="true"
   DisplayMode="BulletList" />
```

After entering invalid information and clicking Submit, you should see the dialog box in Figure 7.9.

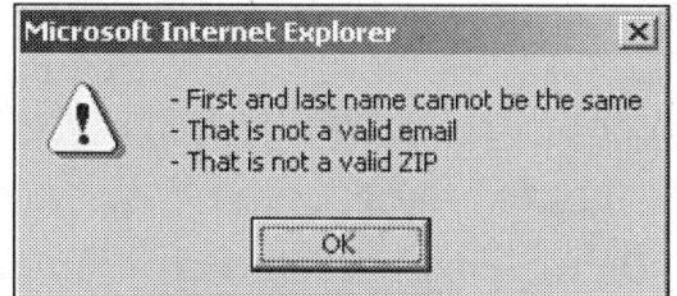

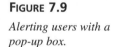

FIGURE 7.9
Alerting users with a pop-up box.

Table 7.5 summarizes the parameters required to display the Validation control error messages in a variety of formats and positions.

TABLE 7.5 Error Message Layout Parameters

Type	*ValidationSummary*	*Validation Control Settings*
In-line	Not required	`Display` = `Static` or `Dynamic`
		`ErrorMessage` = In-line error text
Summary	Required	`Display` = None
		`ErrorMessage` = Summary error text
Both	Required	`Display` = `Static` or `Dynamic`
		`ErrorMessage` = Summary error text
		`Text` = In-line error text

You can set the `Text` property of the Validation controls to any valid HTML tags. This means you can use images to display your error messages or provide links to further descriptions!

Finally, you can customize each error message with the typical style properties available to any server control. For example:

- `ForeColor`—The color of the error message text
- `BackColor`—The color behind the text
- `Font`—The font face, size, weight, and so on
- `BorderWidth`, `BorderColor`, and `BorderStyle`—The size and color of the border around the error message
- `CSSStyle` and `CSSClass`—Style settings pulled from cascading style sheets

For more information, see the common property list in Appendix C, "ASP.NET Controls: Properties and Methods."

Custom Validation Controls

If none of the predefined Validation controls suit your needs, you can easily create your own customized Validation controls. For example, some Web sites require you to choose a username when you register with them. This username often needs to be of a certain length. None of the existing Validation controls check the length of user input, so you have to do this manually.

With the `CustomValidator` control, you can easily define any type of validation you need by using the familiar Validation control syntax. This control only provides the framework for your custom validation; you must build the actual routine yourself. In other words, you can use this control to watch over another server control. When the user enters data, the `CustomValidator` will execute a method that you've built.

For example, Listing 7.7 shows a typical login form for a secure Web site.

LISTING 7.7 Using a Custom Validator

```
<%@ Page Language="VB" %>

<script runat="server">
   sub Submit(Sender as Object, e as EventArgs)
      'do something
   end sub

   sub ValidateThis(Sender as Object, args as _
      ServerValidateEventArgs)
       if len(args.Value) < 8 then
          args.IsValid = false
       else
          args.IsValid = true
```

LISTING 7.7 continued

```
14:          end if
15:       end function
16:    </script>
17:
18:    <html><body>
19:       <form runat="server">
20:          <asp:Label id="lblMessage" runat="server" />
21:          <table>
22:          <tr>
23:             <td valign="top">Username:</td>
24:             <td valign="top">
25:                <asp:Textbox id="tbUserName" runat="server" />
26:                <br>
27:                <asp:CustomValidator runat="server"
28:                   OnServerValidate="ValidateThis"
29:                   Display="Dynamic"
30:                   ControlToValidate="tbUserName"
31:                   ErrorMessage="The username must be 8
32:    ➥             characters or longer"/>
33:             </td>
34:          </tr>
35:          <tr>
36:             <td valign="top">Password:</td>
37:             <td valign="top">
38:                <asp:Textbox id="tbPassword" runat="server"
39:                   TextMode="password" />
40:             </td>
41:          </tr>
42:          <tr>
43:             <td align="right" colspan="2">
44:                <ASP:Button id="tbSubmit" runat="server"
45:                   OnClick="Submit"
46:                   text="Submit" />
47:             </td>
48:          </tr>
49:          </table>
50:       </form>
51:    </body></html>
```

ANALYSIS On line 27, you see the `CustomValidator` control. It's similar to all of the other Validation controls you've looked at so far, with the `ControlToValidate`, `ErrorMessage`, and `Display` properties. However, there's one new property: `OnServerValidate`. This property is used to specify the event handler that should handle the validation.

Let's look at the code declaration block. On line 4, you have your `Submit` method, which doesn't do anything yet. Recall from Day 5, "Beginning Web Forms," that Web form events are processed in no particular order. The `ServerValidate` event of the `CustomValidator` control is the only major exception to that rule. This event will always be processed first so that any other methods can check for validity on the `Page` object.

On line 8 is your event handler for the `ServerValidate` event. Notice that the parameter list is different from what you're used to. The second parameter, `args`, is a `ServerValidateEventArgs` object that contains the control that contains the user input in question.

In your function, you check if the length of the input is less than eight characters (using the `Len` function). If it is, the input is invalid and youset the `IsValid` property to false. When you fill out this form and click Submit, you should see what's shown in Figure 7.10.

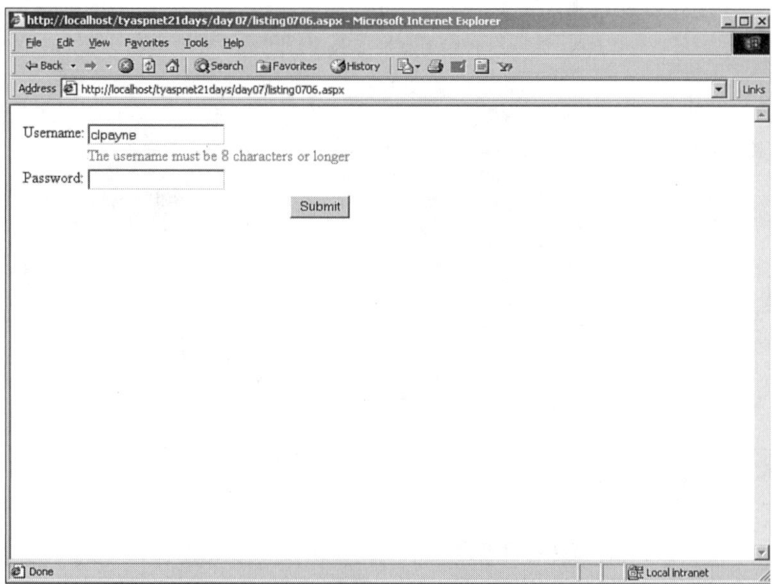

FIGURE 7.10

Your custom validator allows you to perform customized validation checks.

The custom validator event handler can be used to validate information however you want. You can even use custom validation to check values against a database on the server!

To test your validator, add the following code to the `Submit` method on line 4:

```
5:    if Page.IsValid then
6:       lblMessage.Text = "It's all good!"
```

```
        'do some other processing
    end if
```

This method will handle the form submission once all fields are valid. However, the validation handler will execute first and return a `Boolean` value specifying whether or not the input is valid. If it's valid, the `CustomValidator` control sets its `IsValid` property to true, and `Page.IsValid` evaluates to true as well.

The `CustomValidator` also allows you to validate on the client-side. To do this, you need to create a JavaScript event handler that resides on the client. For example, the following script block performs the same validation routine as Listing 7.7, only in JavaScript on the client side:

```
<script language="JavaScript">
   function validateLength( oSrc, txtValue ){
      var retValue = true; // assume ok
      if(txtValue.length < 8){
         retValue = false;}
      return retValue
   }
</script>
```

Add this script block to Listing 7.7, directly below the existing code declaration block. Then, in the `CustomValidator` control, you must set the `OnClientSideValidate` property to the JavaScript method:

```
<asp:CustomValidator runat="server"
   OnServerValidate="ValidateThis"
   OnClientValiate="validateLength"
   Display="Dynamic"
   ControlToValidate="tbUserName"
   ErrorMessage="The username must be 8 characters or longer"/>
```

When you view this page from the browser, you'll have the same dynamic error-display capabilities you had with the other Validation controls. When the user inputs invalid information and moves to another control, the JavaScript method executes and returns false, setting the `CustomValidator`'s `IsValid` property to false as well. The dynamic error message will be displayed automatically without having to post information to the server! Of course, you can still use your server validation routine as an additional check.

That's Not ASP!

With classic ASP, user input validation involved many separate checks, resulting in long, complex code. Listing 7.1 shows an example. The process often required many separate `if` statements to evaluate several conditions for each control. You had to make sure that users had entered items such as dates, names, and phone numbers in a valid format, and you had to find ways to make those values valid if they were not. This was tedious and error-prone.

With ASP.NET Validation controls, all your classic ASP validation worries fade away. You can validate user input automatically and provide feedback to the user dynamically. No more complex, nested `if` statements to debug!

Note that all of the functionality you learned about today was possible with classic ASP. However, it was up to the developer to build all of the client-side script and make sure that error messages were displayed properly. If you took a look at the `WebUIValidation.js` file from Listing 7.4, you'll see that this was not an easy task. There's quite a bit of functionality and code in this file. ASP.NET handles all of this for you, and even adjusts the script depending on the capabilities of the client browser.

Validation controls are one of the greatest improvements of ASP.NET over ASP, and you should take advantage of them thoroughly!

Summary

Today you learned about validating ASP.NET pages with the Validation server controls. These are powerful controls that make it easy to validate user input.

ASP.NET Validation controls are very similar to Web server controls. They're created on the server and render HTML to the browser. Each Validation control watches over the input from one other server control. They rely on client-side JavaScript code to provide client-side validation, and they can also be validated on the server.

Every Validation control should have two properties, at minimum: `ControlToValidate`, which specifies the server control that should be watched, and `ErrorMessage`, which contains the text that should be shown to the user if validation fails. You learned how to use each Validation control in your Web forms in "Using Validation Controls."

Validation controls also provide a lot of options for customization. You can use the `ValidationSummary` control to provide a summary of the error messages in one place, with various formatting options. This control also allows you to alert the user with a pop-up box using the `ShowMessageBox` property.

Finally, you learned about creating custom validation routines with the `CustomValidator` control. This control has a `OnServerValidate` property that specifies which server method should handle the validation. This method can validate the input any way you want, even by comparing against database values.

You've reached the end of the first week! By now, you should have a solid understanding of how ASP.NET and the Web forms framework operate. You've looked at all of the different server controls available to you, and you can even create a few of your own. Next week, you'll start on data access. You'll examine how to interact with databases, XML files, and other forms of data, adding immense power to your applications!

Q&A

Q Do I have to validate on the server side as well as the client side?

A No, you don't need to test for validity on the server once a form is submitted. Often, client-side validation will succeed in forcing all the correct user input. However, there are times when it pays to be safe, especially because the client-side validation relies on JavaScript, which has different mechanisms than ASP.NET.

Q The dynamic error messages aren't being displayed. What's wrong?

A Be sure that you've tried to submit the form at least once. The error messages will appear after the first attempt to submit (that is, if the input is invalid). After the first post, the dynamic messages should appear and disappear automatically when you move through the UI elements.

Also, make sure that you're using a newer browser version that supports DHTML (IE or Netscape 4+).

Q When should I use Validation controls?

A Whenever you need to! Validating input is a must for any serious application, and the Validation controls make it very easy in ASP.NET.

That said, Validation controls do add some overhead to your pages, increasing file sizes. Since increased file sizes take longer to send back and forth with the server, your users may notice a slight decrease in performance. Also, to get the full benefit of the Validation controls, the client must support JavaScript and DHTML.

If you're in a performance-critical situation where bandwidth is a precious commodity, or if you know that you'll have clients with older browsers, it may be wise to stick with the traditional form of validation. That is, stick with `if` and `case` statements on the server.

Workshop

This workshop will help reinforce the concepts covered in today's lesson. The answers can be found in Appendix A.

Quiz

1. What are the five Validation controls?
2. True or false: Validation controls are created on the client side.
3. What two properties should every Validation control have?
4. What does the `clienttarget=downlevel` parameter do?
5. Assuming you have two server controls, `tbName` and `tbAge`, will the following validator work?

   ```
   <asp:CompareValidator runat="server"
      ControlToValidate="tbName"
      ValueToCompare="tbAge"
      ErrorMessage="Error!"/>
   ```

6. What's the property you need to set for the `CustomValidator` control that specifies the event handler?

Exercises

Build a login page similar to Listing 7.7, but build it into a user control. Handle all validation inside the user control, as opposed to the containing ASP.NET page.

WEEK 1

In Review

Congratulations on completing your first week! So far, you've learned a lot about ASP.NET and the .NET framework. You've also learned how to build useful ASP.NET pages using Visual Basic, HTML, and ASP.NET server controls, and how to take advantage of the Web forms framework. You're ready to build your own applications!

Bonus Project 1

At the end of each week, you'll build an application using the skills you learned for that week. Each week will expand upon the same examples, so by the time you're through, you'll have a complex, fully functional application. You'll build the foundation of the application in this lesson; the bonus project at the end of Week 2 will add data capabilities; and bonus project 3 will add some more advanced features.

I highly recommend that you work through these bonus projects. They will better familiarize you with ASP.NET concepts because you'll be using real-world situations. Let's get started on your application!

A Banking Application

Your first bonus project is to build and set up a banking application that will be used online. This application will allow users to log in and check their account balances, pay bills, and so on. But for now, you're just going to use the server controls you've learned about to build the UI. Although this application will become fairly complex in the coming weeks, it relies on only a small number of pages that you'll sketch here.

Your banking application should do the following:

- Provide users secure access to their accounts
- Allow users to see their transaction histories and account balances
- Allow users to pay bills online

These bullets describe the scope of the application—what it *needs* to be able to do. Laying out these objectives beforehand will help you as you build your application.

Let's determine the pages you need. First, the users will need a login page that will serve to authenticate and direct them to their accounts. Second, you'll need an account summary page that lists transactions and balances. Finally, you'll need a page that users can utilize to pay bills online. Because you want to present a standard user interface for the site, you'll use a common header and navigation bar for every page, in the form of user controls.

- Login page—`login.aspx`
- Account summary page—`account.aspx`
- Bill paying page—`bills.aspx`
- Two user controls—`header.ascx` and `nav.ascx`

> Obviously, there can be more to the application than the pages listed here, but because you're just starting out, let's keep it fairly simple.
>
> However, you should feel free to play around with the application! You can add many features that you've already learned about, so don't be afraid to enhance the program.

User Controls

The menu, or navigation, control can be fairly simple for now. Let's first create a table with links to other pages, as shown in Listing BP1.1.

Listing BP1.1 Your User Control–Based Menu

```
<table align="left" width="150" height="350"
   bgcolor="#cccc99">
<tr>
   <td align="right" nowrap bgcolor="Black">
      <a href="account.aspx">Account Summary</a><p>
```

LISTING BP1.1 continued

```
        <a href="bills.aspx">Pay Bills</a><p>
        <a href="Logout.aspx">Sign Out</a><p>
      </td>
   </tr>
    </table>
```

Save this file as nav.ascx. Let's also create a user control to display a standard header, as shown in Listing BP1.2. This control will contain only an ASP.NET Label control to display a standard header.

LISTING BP1.2 Your User Control Header

```
<asp:Label id="Header" runat="server"
   text="ASP.NET Banking Center"
   Height="25px"
   Width="100%"
   BackColor="#cccccc"
   ForeColor="Black"
   Font-Size=20
   Font-Bold="False"
   Font-name="Arial"
    BorderStyle="outset" />
```

Save this file as header.ascx, and move on to the ASP.NET pages.

The Login Page

The login page is fairly simple. You'll need to provide users with a few text box controls to enter their user information, and then build a method to determine whether they are valid users.

The validation method can be accomplished easily using ASP.NET's security system, but because you haven't learned about that yet, you'll have to make do with another method. You'll revisit this section again after you learn about the ASP.NET security system.

You also want to make sure that you start developing this application with a consistent UI, so include your header user control. The menu user control will not be used because users should not have access to the pages it lists quite yet. Let's take a look at the code in Listing BP1.3.

LISTING BP1.3 `login.aspx`—Authenticating Users

```
<%@ Page Language="VB" %>
<%@ Register TagPrefix="ASPNETBank" TagName="Header"
➥src="header.ascx" %>

<script runat="server">

   '******************************************************
   '
   ' Login.aspx: Logs users in
   '
   '******************************************************

   '******************************************************
   'When user clicks submit button, verify that they are a
   'valid user. If they are, log them in, and set a cookie
   'with their user name, and redirect to account.aspx.
   'Otherwise display error message
   '******************************************************
   sub Submit(obj as Object, e as EventArgs)
      if tbUsername.text = "clpayne" and _
         tbPassword.text = "pass" then
         Response.Cookies("FirstName").Value =
➥tbUsername.text
         Response.redirect("account.aspx")
      else
         lblMessage.Text = "<font color=red>Sorry, " & _
            "invalid username or password!</font><p>"
      end if
   end sub
</script>

<html><body>
   <ASPNETBank:Header runat="server" />
   <font face="arial">
   <p>
   Welcome to the ASP.NET Banking Center. Please enter
   your username and password to gain access to your
   account information.<p>

   <form runat="server">
      <asp:Label id="lblMessage" runat="server" />
      <table>
      <tr>
         <td width="75" rowspan="3"> </td>
         <td width="50" valign="top">
            <font face="arial">Username:</font>
         </td>
         <td width="50" valign="top">
```

LISTING BP1.3 continued

```
47:             <font face="arial">
48:             <asp:Textbox id="tbUsername" runat="server" />
49:             </font>
50:          </td>
51:       </tr>
52:       <tr>
53:          <td valign="top">
54:             <font face="arial">Password:</font>
55:          </td>
56:          <td valign="top">
57:             <font face="arial">
58:             <asp:Textbox id="tbPassword"
59:                TextMode="password" runat="server" /><p>
60:             </font>
61:          </td>
62:       </tr>
63:       <tr>
64:          <td align="right" colspan="2">
65:             <font face="arial">
66:             <ASP:Button id="btSubmit" runat="server"
67:                onClick="Submit"
68:                Text="Submit" />
69:             </font>
70:          </td>
71:       </tr>
72:       </table>
73:    </form>
74:    </font>
75: </body></html>
```

ANALYSIS On line 2, you register your header user control—you should remember this procedure from Day 6, "Learning More About Web Forms." You can now use your header user control in your page just as you would a normal ASP.NET server control. There is one method for this page, `Submit`, which is called when the user clicks the submit button on line 66.

Because you aren't using a database here, you can be a bit sneaky and hard-code the username and password value on lines 19 and 20. *Don't* do this in your final application; in fact, you'll fix this next week after you learn how to use databases. For now, however, this will suffice.

The `if` statement on line 19 then verifies whether the user supplied the correct credentials. If he did, you set a cookie value with the username for reference later. Then the user is redirected to his account page, which you'll create next. If the user is *not* valid, you simply display a message using the `Label` control on lines 24 and 25.

This page serves as the gateway to your application. The user will always get this page before entering the guts of the bank center. Figure BP1.1 shows what this page should look like after a user enters the wrong credentials.

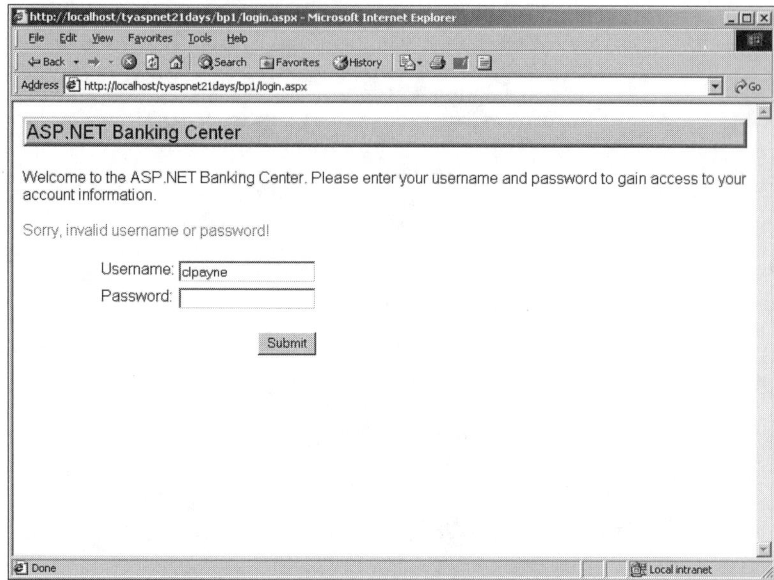

FIGURE BP1.1 *Validating user credentials.*

The Account Page

The account page will list a history of the user's transactions and his current balance. The transaction history will be handled through databases and data-bound server controls (also coming next week), so leave these out for now. That leaves pretty much just a few server controls for the UI, plus the standard header and menu user controls.

You'll want to present the user with a customized welcome message, so access the cookie you set on the login page:

```
Request.Cookies("FirstName").Value
```

This command retrieves the value (as a string) of whatever is contained in the user cookie variable `FirstName`. This is similar to using session variables for storage.

Listing BP1.4 shows the code for this page.

LISTING BP1.4 account.aspx—The User's Account Summary Information

```
<%@ Page Language="VB" %>
<%@ Register TagPrefix="ASPNETBank" TagName="Header"
➥src="header.ascx" %>
<%@ Register TagPrefix="ASPNETBank" TagName="Menu"
➥src="nav.ascx" %>

<script runat="server">
   '*******************************************************
   '
   ' Account.aspx: lists account summaries and current
   ' balances for the current user
   '
   '*******************************************************

   '*******************************************************
   ' When the page loads, display a welcome message in the
   ' "WelcomeMsg" label
   '*******************************************************
   sub Page_Load(obj as object, e as eventargs)
      If (Request.Cookies("FirstName") is Nothing) Then
         lblWelcomeMsg.Text = "Welcome <b>" & _
            Request.Cookies("FirstName").Value & "!</b>"
      End If
   end sub
</script>

<html><body>
   <ASPNETBank:Header runat="server" />
   <table>
   <tr>
      <td valign="top" width="150">
         <ASPNETBank:Menu runat="server" />
      </td>
      <td width="550" valign="top">
         <font face="arial">

         <form runat="server">
            <table>
            <tr>
               <td width="10">
                   
               </td>
               <td width="100%">
                  <font face="arial">
                   <p>
                  <asp:Label id="lblWelcomeMsg"
                     runat="server"/><p>
                  Your account balance is <b>$945.31</b>
```

LISTING BP1.4 continued

```
47:                         <p></font>
48:                       </td>
49:                   </tr>
50:                   </table>
51:                </form>
52:                </font>
53:             </td>
54:          </tr>
55:          </table>
56:          </font>
57:  </body></html>
```

ANALYSIS On lines 2 and 3, you register your two user controls. Then in the `Page_Load` event, you set the `Text` property of the label on line 44. You use the value in the cookie you set in `login.aspx`, which contains the user's login name. The user is then greeted with a personalized welcome message by the label. Figure BP1.2 shows the display of this page.

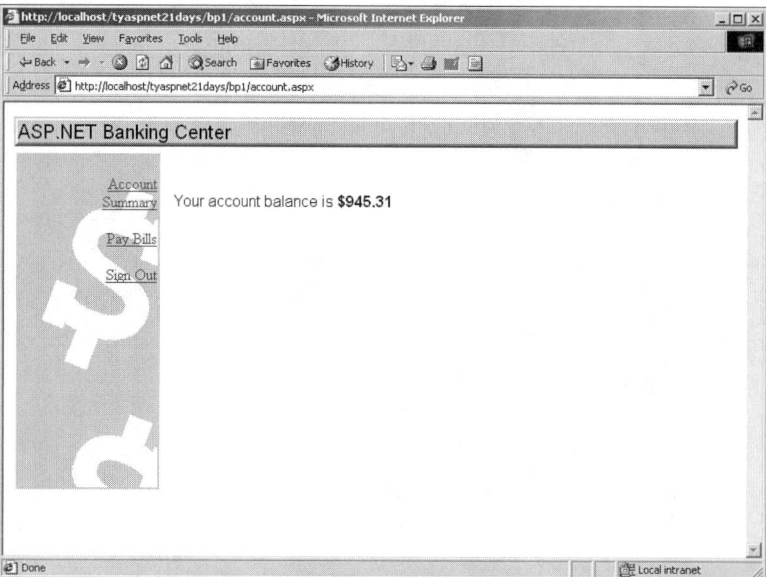

FIGURE BP1.2
The account summary page.

This page doesn't do much else yet. Line 46 places a temporary value, which will be replaced next time with a value from the database. The transaction history will also be displayed in this area with dynamic information.

Paying Bills

Your application will allow users to pay bills online (not really, of course, because this is all fake money). Users will supply appropriate information for a payee; your application will automatically transfer the funds. Eventually, you'll add functionality so that payees can post transactions from any location (in other words, debit their accounts)! But I'm getting ahead of myself. Let's take a look at the code for this page in Listing BP1.5.

LISTING BP1.5 `bills.aspx`—Online Bill Payment

```
<%@ Page Language="VB" %>
<%@ Register TagPrefix="ASPNETBank" TagName="Header"
➥src="header.ascx" %>
<%@ Register TagPrefix="ASPNETBank" TagName="Menu"
➥src="nav.ascx" %>

<script runat="server">
   '*******************************************************
   '
   ' Bills.aspx: Allows user to pay bills online
   '
   '*******************************************************
</script>

<html><body>
   <ASPNETBank:Header runat="server" />

   <table>
   <tr>
      <td valign="top" width="150">
         <ASPNETBank:Menu runat="server" />
      </td>
      <td width="550" valign="top">
         <font face="arial">
         <asp:Label id="lblMessage" runat="server"/>
         <form runat="server">
            <table>
            <tr>
               <td width="10"> </td>
               <td width="100%">
                  <font face="arial">
                   <p>
                  Welcome to the bill paying service!
                  Please fill out the information below
                  and hit "Pay that Bill!" to
                  automatically transfer funds.<p>

                  <table>
```

Listing BP1.5 continued

```
                  <tr>
                     <td width="150" valign="top">
                        <font face="arial">Payee:
                     </td>
                     <td width="100" valign="top">
                        <font face="arial">
                        <asp:textbox id="tbPayee"
                           runat="server"/>
                     </td>
                  </tr>
                  <tr>
                     <td valign="top">
                        <font face="arial">Amount:
                     </td>
                     <td valign="top">
                        <font face="arial">
                        <asp:textbox id="tbAmount"
                           runat="server"/>
                     </td>
                  </tr>
                  <tr>
                     <td valign="top" colspan="2"
➥align="right">
                        <font face="arial">
                        <asp:button id="btSubmit"
                           runat="server"
                           Text="Pay That Bill!"
                           />
                     </td>
                  </tr>
                  </table>
                  </font>
               </td>
            </tr>
            </table>
         </form>
         </font>
      </td>
   </tr>
   </table>
   </font>
</body></html>
```

Analysis This file is similar to `account.aspx` in Listing BP1.4. It has the same user controls and same basic layout. You simply added a few text boxes for the user to input data, and a Submit button to submit the data. Currently, the Submit button does nothing. This listing produces the output shown in Figure BP1.3.

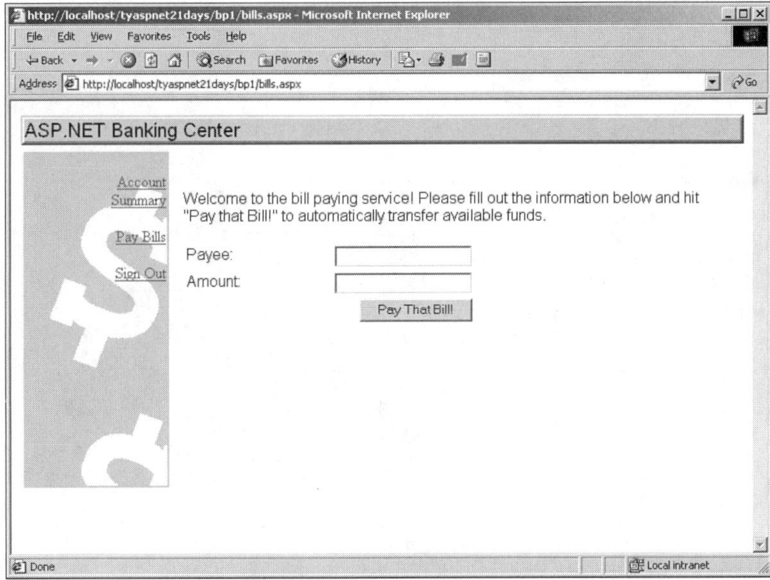

FIGURE BP1.3

Customers can pay bills online.

Summary

Congratulations on building your first complete ASP.NET application! With this project, you've seen how to apply the knowledge you've learned over the past week, and how to start the foundation for increasingly complex ASP.NET applications.

The purpose of the bonus projects is to approach an application at every stage of development. In this lesson, you started with a simple design phase, followed by page and function layout. This project will also help to develop your ASP.NET skills so that you will be comfortable in your other projects.

Future bonus projects will enhance this application further. Next time, you'll add database capabilities to your application, making it truly dynamic. After that you'll learn about using "componentizing" and Web services to build a powerful, robust, real-world application. But first, you've got to get through Week 2!

WEEK 2

At a Glance

Last week, you set up the foundations for ASP.NET programming. You built pages, server controls, and several sample applications, and you validated your pages—which will be the groundwork for the next two weeks.

This week you'll learn about more advanced topics, starting with data access. The entire week will focus on learning different methods of data access, from databases to XML. The first few days this week will be spent introducing you to databases and teaching you how to use them in your ASP.NET pages to produce dynamic data. You'll also learn about the very exciting new ASP.NET concept, data binding, that allows you to automatically display data in your pages without having to build complex UI elements.

In Day 10, "Communicating with ADO.NET," you'll learn about ADO.NET, a very useful tool for accessing databases. ADO.NET provides many of the objects and functionality you'll use in ASP.NET from now on.

Then you'll spend a day learning about how to use XML in ASP.NET in Day 11, "Using XML in ASP.NET." Coupled with ADO.NET, XML allows you to use any type of data, anywhere in your pages. XML is used extensively throughout ASP.NET, and you'll learn about where that occurs as well.

In Day 12, "Employing Advanced Data Techniques," you'll examine methods to access file contents. Using .NET Framework objects, you'll read, write, edit, move, and delete files and more! In Day 13, "Reading and Writing Files on the Web Server," you'll learn how ASP.NET can place data in a cache for quick and easy access in your applications.

Finally, you'll wrap up the week with a discussion on ASP.NET's caching mechanism, which can greatly increase the performance of your pages. This final lesson wraps up your data access week, and by the end, you'll be an expert at developing data-driven ASP.NET applications.

This week is going to be a busy one, so let's get underway!

WEEK 2

DAY 8

Beginning to Build Databases

Today's lesson discusses database fundamentals—what they are, how to create them, and how to use them. This lesson won't be a thorough reference on databases, but it will give you a good background to help build your applications in later lessons.

Databases are incredibly useful tools for storing large amounts of data in efficient ways, and they allow you to view, modify, and work with all types of information. They make ASP.NET applications immensely more useful, as you'll see in the coming few days.

Today's lesson will cover the following:

- What databases are
- The difference between relational and flat-file databases
- How to create your own databases using Access 2000 and SQL Server 2000
- How to select, insert, update, and delete data using the Structured Query Language (SQL)
- Interacting with databases using ASP.NET

What Are Databases?

NEW TERM Databases are stores of data. That's it. We won't dissect it further because a database can be *any* store of data, from a simple text file to a complex product inventory system spanning multiple computers. Databases are among the most important aspects of computing, which explains their importance to Web development.

Interacting with databases is one of the most useful things you can do with ASP.NET. Microsoft recognizes this and has made it very easy for you to interact with databases using ASP.NET.

Many commercial database applications are available today, including Microsoft Access, Oracle, Informix, and DB2. These all provide different mechanisms for storing data, but they all share common database concepts.

NEW TERM In database terminology, a *table* is a two-dimensional representation of data. Again, databases come in a wide variety of shapes and sizes, so tables can be nearly anything. Figure 8.1 shows a simple database table created in Microsoft Notepad.

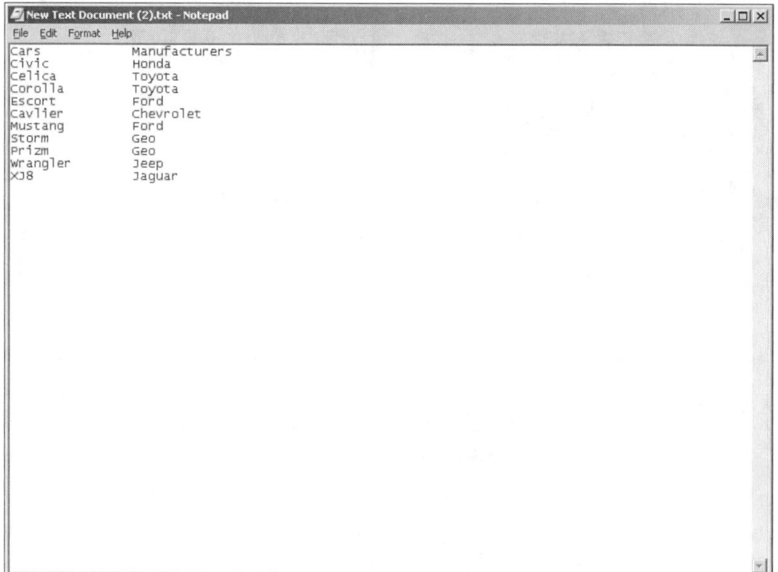

New Text Document (2).txt - Notepad

File Edit Format Help

Cars	Manufacturers
Civic	Honda
Celica	Toyota
Corolla	Toyota
Escort	Ford
Cavlier	Chevrolet
Mustang	Ford
Storm	Geo
Prizm	Geo
Wrangler	Jeep
XJ8	Jaguar

FIGURE 8.1

A database table can come in many forms, including a simple text file created in Notepad.

The table in Figure 8.1 shows two columns: `Cars`, which contains the model names; and `Manufacturers`, which contains the names of the manufacturers. A column, therefore, describes one property of information. A row contains actual data from one or more columns—it describes one item in detail, and is often called a data *record*. A column in a row is called a *field*. For example, Figure 8.1 has 11 rows (or records), and each row has two fields: `Cars` and `Manufacturers`.

Tip

> It may be helpful to think of a field as the intersection of a row and a column.

Each record is a unique item, and you can have as many fields to describe that item as you wish. For example, you could add columns for the number of miles, the year, and the last oil change.

Figure 8.1 shows a database consisting of a single table. However, databases usually consist of many tables, each of which is a type of object. Multiple tables help you to relate information more logically and efficiently. For example, let's assume you want to store the following information about cars and manufacturers in your table:

- Make
- Model
- Mileage
- Manufacturer
- Manufacturer's address
- Manufacturer's phone number

Although you could store all this information in a single table, you'd be repeating a lot of information over and over again. For instance, Geo only has one address and phone number, so why repeat that information for every car, as shown in Figure 8.2?

FIGURE 8.2
Redundant information in a table.

Cars

Make	Year	Mileage	Manufacturer	ManufacturerAddress
Prizm	1993	193,000	Geo	Dayton, OH
Metro	1995	34,005	Geo	Dayton, OH
Metro	1990	340,507	Geo	Dayton, OH

NEW TERM Typically, this type of data storage is called a *flat-file database*, in which information corresponding to multiple tables is stored in one giant file. A lot of information is repeated, taking up a lot of space and time. Flat-file databases are also error-prone. Imagine having to enter the same address over and over again manually. Chances are, you'll make a mistake. A much more efficient way to store this data would be in two separate tables, as shown in Figure 8.3.

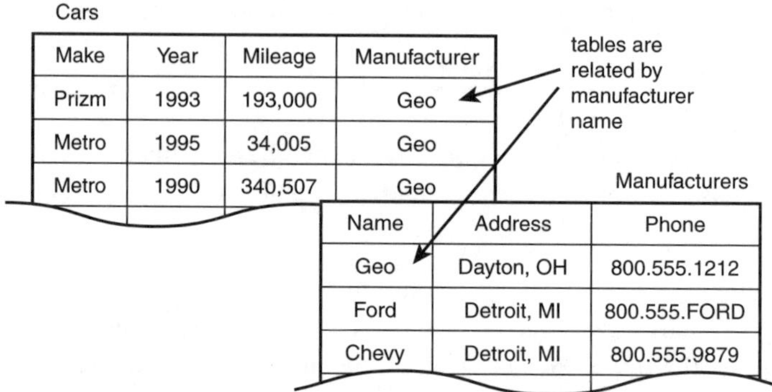

FIGURE 8.3
Moving redundant information into a separate table.

NEW TERM In this manner, the `Cars` table now only has to keep track of the manufacturer's name. The `name` field is then *related* to the `name` field in the `Manufacturers` table, which stores all pertinent information about the manufacturers. This type of database, in which tables are linked by relationships, is called a *relational database*.

NEW TERM Relational databases offer many benefits over flat-file databases, including more efficient storage, faster searching, and more logical grouping. This book won't go into detailed design methods for relational databases, but there's a whole study of these techniques called *normalization* that dictates how to properly separate database tables into distinct objects. In general, if you see data that's repeated more than a few times in a table, it may be helpful to move it into its own table and create a relationship between the two tables.

For more information on database design, check out *Sams Teach Yourself Database Design in 24 Hours*.

Keys and Constraints

NEW TERM As discussed previously, it's important to keep repetitive information in a database to a minimum. Most importantly, you don't want to have duplicate records because that's the ultimate waste of space. Therefore, *primary keys* have been introduced to prevent such an occurrence. Let's assume that you have a database of family members, with the columns `name`, `address`, and `birthdate`. You could declare the `name` column as the primary key, and then no two records could have the same name.

This is very helpful for keeping your database under control, but it's not a very realistic solution because many people can have the same names. As you'll see later today in "Creating Databases," you can also define primary keys over multiple columns as well. In this case, if the primary key included the `name`, `address`, *and* `birthdate` columns, the database would disallow entering records in which all three columns contain the same information as another record in the table.

NEW TERM This is more helpful than the previous example, but it's still not foolproof. Perhaps you discover a long-lost second cousin with the same name and birth date as your sister, who just happens to move in with you. This would give you two records in your database with the same name, address, and birth date. An even better way to ensure that your database contains no duplicate records is to introduce another column that has nothing to do with your other columns, and for which you can guarantee uniqueness. Such a column is called an *identity column* because it can be used to uniquely and accurately identify a record in your database. The most common identity column is simply an incrementing number—every new record would get a number that's one higher than the record before.

NEW TERM Now that you've ensured that each record in your table is unique, you need to create a link to another table. You do this by building a relationship between columns in different tables. Each column should contain the same information. In Figure 8.3, you can see that the tables are linked by the `Manufacturer` column in the `Cars` table, and by the `Name` column in the `Manufacturers` table. Although the columns have different names, they both contain the same information—the manufacturers' names. Columns that are used to link two tables are called *foreign keys*.

The `Cars` table has a foreign key to the `Manufacturers` table, and it's a many-to-one relationship. This means that there can be many records in the first table that correlate to one record in the second table. For example, there are many cars made by Geo, but there's only one company named Geo. Similarly, there can also be one-to-many and one-to-one relationships.

Database Communication Standards

NEW TERM There are many different database systems out there, such as Microsoft Access, Oracle, and Informix. If each one required a unique protocol to access the database information, developers would have a difficult time creating data-driven applications that weren't specifically tied to a particular database system. Fortunately, most commercial database systems adhere to the Open DataBase Connectivity standard, or ODBC. This standard was developed by Microsoft to provide a common interface for databases so that developers don't have to write different code to access different databases. Databases that adhere to this standard are *ODBC-compliant*.

Unfortunately, ODBC has its limitations. Developers have criticized it for being difficult to work with because it requires low-level application code that varies depending on the database being used.

In response to this, Microsoft next developed OLE DB, a Windows COM-based data access object that provides access to all types of different data. OLE DB is now the standard for database connectivity. It includes ODBC as well, so virtually every commercial database is supported.

When Should I Use a Database?

Databases are an efficient way to store large amounts of persistent data. Managing such information comes at a performance cost, though. Although databases are extremely efficient at storing large amounts of complex, interrelated data, you may want to simply use a cookie or session variable if you only want to store temporary or miniscule amounts of information such as a site visitor's name or e-mail.

Databases are the optimal choice when you need to store information that forms complex relationships between different types of data. Another advantage of databases is that they provide a central storage location for large amounts of data. Most large software applications that require data storage use a database of some sort.

Working with databases through an ASP.NET Web page is an easy and natural process. In a little while, you'll see how easy it is to access any database from your ASP.NET pages.

Creating Databases

Now that you have a grasp of the database fundamentals, let's get started building your first database. First, you'll develop one in Microsoft Access 2000, and then you'll move to Microsoft SQL Server 2000, where you'll see the many similarities (and differences!) between these two database systems. You'll be using Access for most of these examples because it's easier to learn. SQL Server is much more common in real-world situations that require database systems, though, so there's a short discussion on it.

You'll use the database you build here in subsequent lessons, so let's design something useful. For starters, create a user table for storing the following information:

- First name
- Last name

- Address
- City
- State
- ZIP code
- Phone number

This is a typical user database and can be applied to many different applications. To start your database in Access, run Access and select New from the File menu. You should see something similar to Figure 8.4. Select Blank Database, name it `banking.mdb`, and save it in the `c:\ASPNET\data` directory. (You can use any directory you choose—just be aware that the examples in this book will refer to this directory.)

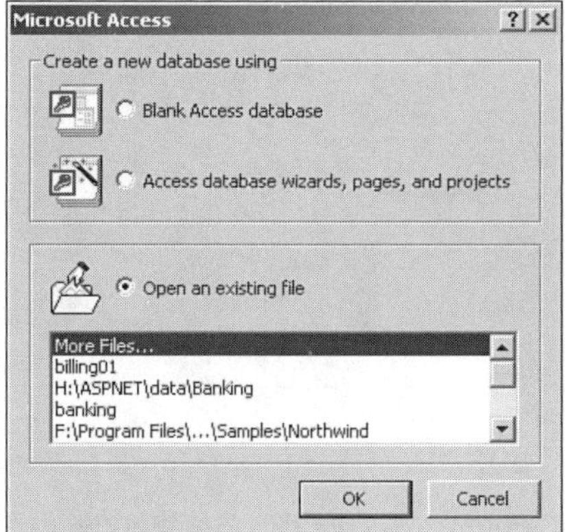

FIGURE 8.4
Creating a new, blank database.

You should see the following options: Create table in Design view, Create table by using wizard, and Create table by entering data. Choose Design view and start entering your columns. Enter `FirstName` in the `Field Name` column, and select Text in the `Data Type` column. Optionally, you can enter a description for this field, such as "User's first name." Enter the other fields described in the previous listing, and you should end up with something similar to Figure 8.5.

> Note that the available options may be different depending on the version of Access you're using.

Finally, add one more column named `UserID`, which will be your identity column. Assign it the data type `Autonumber` and right-click on the black arrow next to its name.

Select Primary Key from the menu and notice how the key symbol appears next to the name. Next, simply save the table by choosing File, Save from the menu. Save the table as `tblUsers`. Choose File, Close from menus to close `tblUsers`.

FIGURE 8.5

Enter the field information for the table.

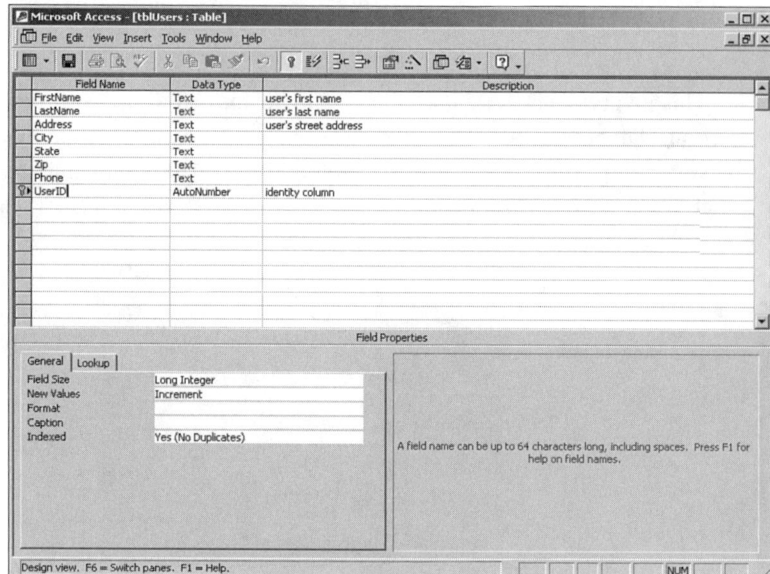

> **Tip**
>
> If you want to define a primary key over more than one column, select each column by holding down the `Ctrl` key, and right-click to select Primary Key from the menu.

That's all there is to it! You can now add data simply by double-clicking on the `tblUsers` option that appears on your menu. Notice that when you input data, you don't need to enter a value for the `UserID` column. It inserts and increments a number automatically, as shown in Figure 8.6.

Table 8.1 lists the various data types provided in Access 2000. Similar data types are present in all database systems, although the exact names may be different.

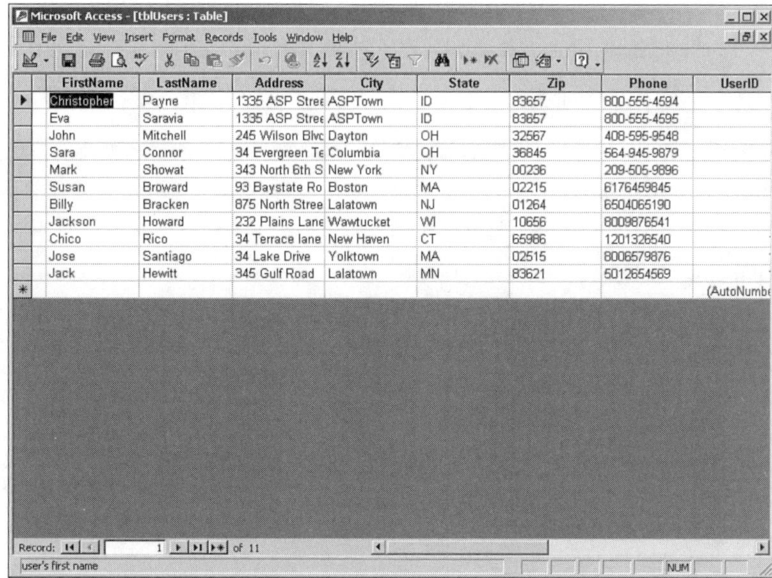

FIGURE 8.6
Enter data into your new table.

TABLE 8.1 Access 2000 Data Types

Data Type	*Description*
`Autonumber`	An automatically incremented integer used to uniquely identify rows in a table.
`Currency`	Used to store monetary data.
`Date/Time`	Used to store date and time values. Access 2000 can store dates between the years 100 and 9999.
`Memo`	Used to store up to 65,535 alphanumeric characters.
`Number`	Used to store numeric values.
`Text`	Used to store up to 255 alphanumeric characters.
`Yes/No`	Used for columns that can only have one of two values (similar to bit or boolean types).

Things are a bit more complicated in SQL Server 2000, but the procedure is essentially the same. Access will be appropriate for your needs, but typically, SQL Server is used for larger databases that require more security and stability.

Now let's create `tblUser` in Microsoft SQL Server 2000. Start by opening up Enterprise Manager from the SQL Server 2000 menu group in your Start menu. If everything is set up properly, you should see a Windows Explorer–like navigation system, with Microsoft

SQL Servers at the top and the name of your server a couple levels below. Expand the databases folder, as shown in Figure 8.7, and select New Database from the Action menu.

FIGURE 8.7

Expand the databases folder and select New Database from the Action menu.

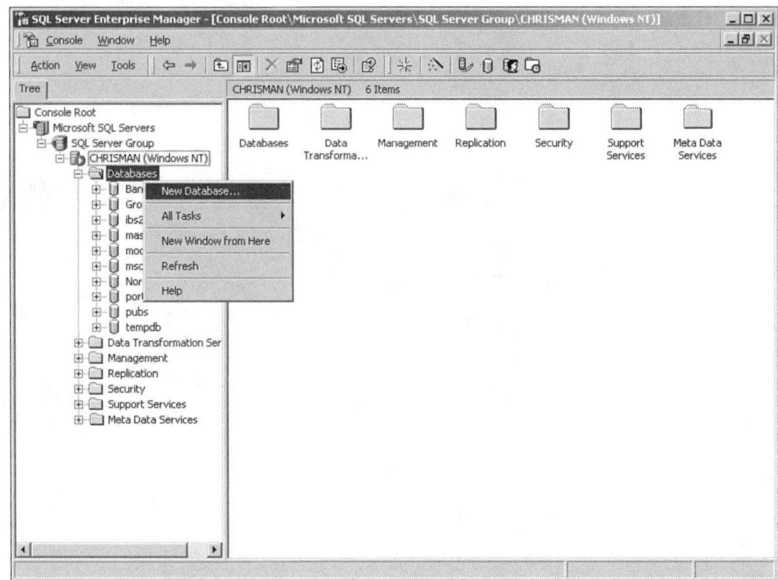

Enter the name Banking in the dialog box that pops up. For now, simply accept the default options under the General tab and click OK. SQL Server will create the database and transaction log for you. You should now see Banking under the Databases folder—expand this tab and select the Tables node.

You'll see that SQL Server has already inserted quite a few tables for you. These are system tables used by SQL Server to keep track of the items you place in your database. Ignore these for now and select New Table from the Action menu. You get a matrix similar to that in Access. Enter the information again, as shown in Figure 8.8, except use the `varchar` data type instead of `Text` (which has a different meaning in SQL Server).

Notice that SQL Server provides many more data types than Access did. SQL Server is simply a more powerful application and allows developers to specify the database options with much greater granularity. SQL Server doesn't require you to initially set up a primary key—but let's define one now. Create a new column with the name `UserID` and set it to a data type of `int`. In the Columns panel below, select Yes for the `Identity` property (see Figure 8.9). Then right-click this field and select Set Primary Key. Next, save this table as `tblUsers` and close this design view by clicking the x in the upper-right corner.

FIGURE 8.8

Enter field names and data types.

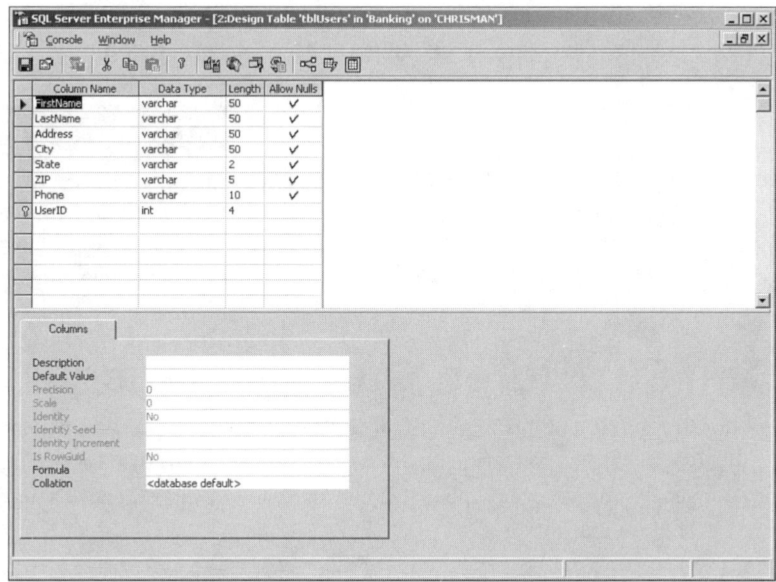

FIGURE 8.9

Set the identity field and primary key.

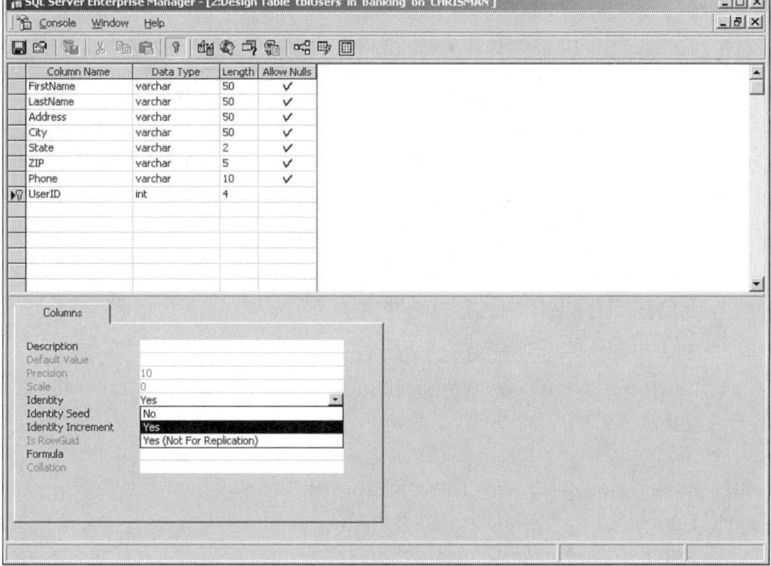

To enter data into your new table, right-click the table and select Open Table, Return All Rows. This will present you with a tabular data entry mechanism similar to that of Access. Enter a few names and addresses for fun. (Don't enter anything in the `UserID`

field.) Click the exclamation point (Run) on the menu to autoincrement the UserIDs. Close the new table by clicking x in the upper-right corner.

Do	Don't
Do use SQL Server if you're developing a large, performance-critical database solution that requires advanced database functionality.	**Don't** use SQL Server for very simple databases with only a few tables. It introduces complications that might not be necessary.

The Structured Query Language

Structured Query Language, or SQL (pronounced *sequel*), is an efficient language used by developers to retrieve, add, delete, or modify information in a relational database. Nearly all modern databases communicate via this standard language, so it's essential that you learn the basics of SQL.

For a more detailed treatment, try *Sams Teach Yourself SQL in 21 Days.*

There are a few easy ways to test out the SQL statements in the following sections. If you're using Access, open your database and click on the Query tab, create new queries in design view, close the box that pops up, and select SQL View from the View menu (see Figure 8.10). You can enter these queries directly and save or execute them here.

In SQL Server, open the Query Analyzer from the Start menu.

The SELECT Statement

The SELECT statement is probably the most common SQL statement. Its basic purpose is to grab a set of data from a database table. The syntax for the SELECT statement is as follows:

```
SELECT selectlist
FROM tablename
[WHERE searchCondition]
[ORDER BY orderbyExpression [ASC | DESC ]}
```

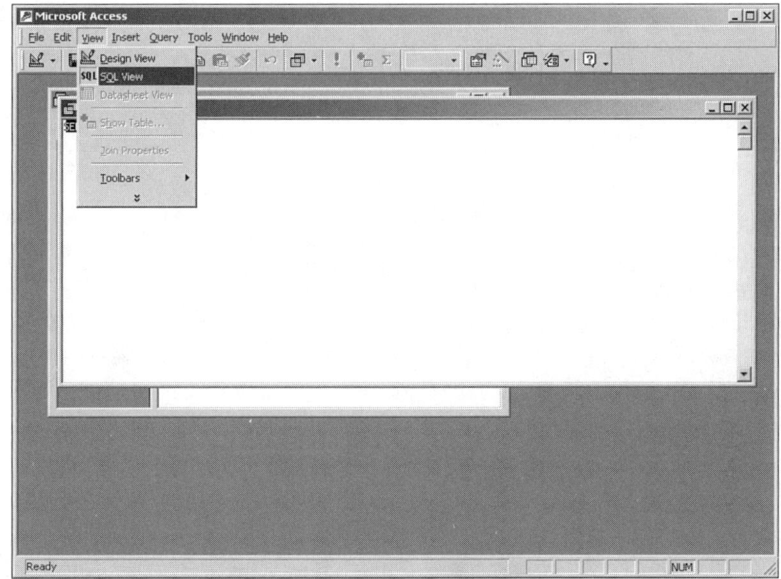

FIGURE 8.10
Entering SQL queries in Access.

The structure follows basic English patterns. *`selectlist`* is generally a comma-delimited list of the columns you want to return. `FirstName, LastName` would return the values in those two columns, for instance. Additionally, an asterisk can be used to return all of the columns from a particular table. *`tablename`* is the name of the table to grab the data from. Here's a simple `SELECT` statement that you could use for the databases you've created:

```
SELECT * FROM tblUsers
```

This statement returns all the rows from all the columns in the `tblUsers` table, and you can do whatever you like with them.

The following statement is functionally identical to the one you just built:

```
SELECT FirstName, LastName, Address, City, State, ZIP,
Phone FROM tblUsers
```

> You shouldn't use `SELECT *` because often it returns more information than you need. This can result in decreased performance. Instead, explicitly specify the columns you need to return. This will take a bit longer when coding, but your code will enjoy performance benefits.

SELECT statements always return all the rows in your database (unless qualified with a WHERE clause, as discussed in the next section). Figures 8.11 and 8.12 show the data returned from your Access database when used with the following SELECT statements:

```
SELECT * FROM tblUsers
SELECT FirstName, Phone FROM tblUsers
```

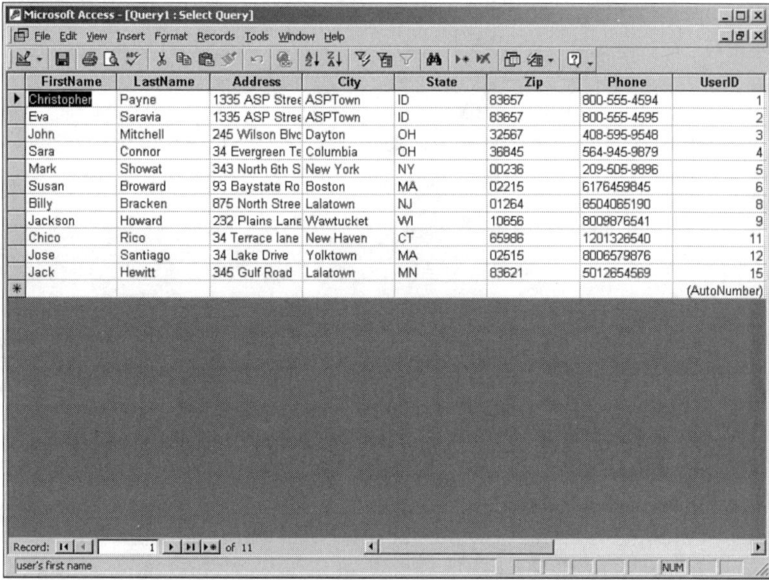

FirstName	LastName	Address	City	State	Zip	Phone	UserID
Christopher	Payne	1335 ASP Stree	ASPTown	ID	83657	800-555-4594	1
Eva	Saravia	1335 ASP Stree	ASPTown	ID	83657	800-555-4595	2
John	Mitchell	245 Wilson Blvc	Dayton	OH	32567	408-595-9548	3
Sara	Connor	34 Evergreen Te	Columbia	OH	36845	564-945-9879	4
Mark	Showat	343 North 6th S	New York	NY	00236	209-505-9896	5
Susan	Broward	93 Baystate Ro	Boston	MA	02215	6176459845	6
Billy	Bracken	875 North Stree	Lalatown	NJ	01264	6504065190	8
Jackson	Howard	232 Plains Lane	Wawtucket	WI	10656	8009876541	9
Chico	Rico	34 Terrace lane	New Haven	CT	65986	1201326540	11
Jose	Santiago	34 Lake Drive	Yolktown	MA	02515	8006579876	12
Jack	Hewitt	345 Gulf Road	Lalatown	MN	83621	5012654569	15
*							(AutoNumber)

FIGURE 8.11
Returning all rows with the SELECT *statement.*

You can use the WHERE clause to specify additional criteria for the returned data. A WHERE clause can generally be any logical statement, similar to an if statement in regular programming languages. For example:

```
SELECT * FROM tblUsers WHERE FirstName = 'Chris'
SELECT * FROM tblUsers WHERE City = 'ASP Town' AND LastName = 'Mitchell'
```

The first statement returns only records where the FirstName field value is "Chris." The second statement returns only the records where City is "ASP Town" and the LastName field is equal to "Mitchell".

To use wildcards for your SQL WHERE clause criteria, you can use the LIKE keyword followed by wildcard operators. Table 8.2 lists the operators that the LIKE keyword accepts.

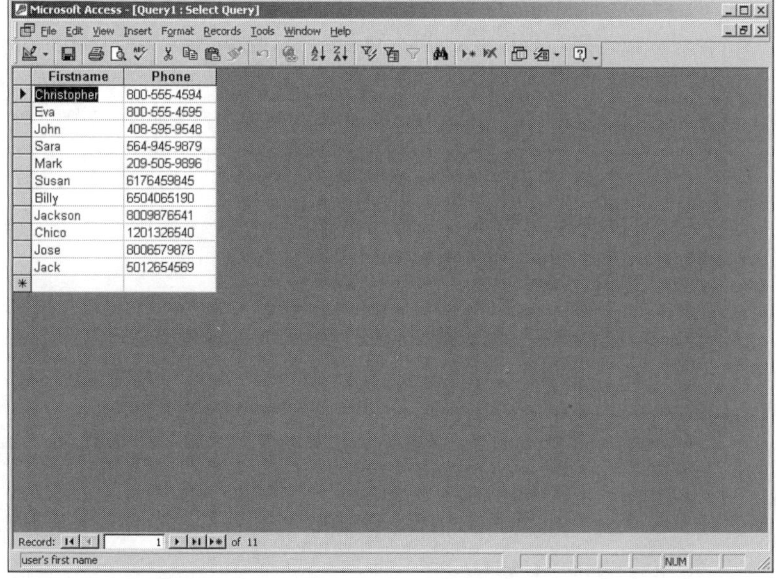

FIGURE 8.12
Returning specific columns for all rows with the `SELECT` *statement.*

TABLE 8.2 Access `LIKE` Operator Wildcards

Operator	*Translation*
`*`	A string of zero or more characters; in SQL Server, this wildcard is represented by `%`
`_`	Exactly one character
`[]`	A specific character in the given set

The following statements show a few examples of using `LIKE`:

```
1  SELECT * FROM tblUsers WHERE FirstName LIKE '*s*'
2  SELECT * FROM tblUsers WHERE FirstName LIKE '_hris'
3  SELECT * FROM tblUsers WHERE FirstName LIKE '[abcd]hris'
```

The SQL statement on line 1 returns any rows where the `FirstName` contains an `s` somewhere in the value. The `*` operator works the same in SQL as it does in Windows, meaning zero or more characters.

The SQL statement on line 2 returns any records where the first name contains any one letter, followed by the string "hris". With the given data, this only returns one record, but you get the point. Finally, the SQL statement on line 3 returns any records where the first name contains a string that begins with any of the letters a, b, c, or d, followed by the string "hris".

The ORDER BY clause specifies the order in which the data is returned, such as alphabetical order. Without this clause, there's no way to know in what order the database will return records. Even though they may have been entered alphabetically during data entry, that doesn't mean the records will be returned the same way. The ORDER BY clause lets you specify which columns to order the data by, and how. If used with columns containing string characters, it converts those characters into their ASCII equivalents and sorts based on those numbers. For example

```
SELECT * FROM tblUsers
ORDER BY FirstName ASC
```

This statement returns all records sorted alphabetically by first name. Likewise, specifying DESC sort order instead of ASC returns reverse-alphabetic order. You can specify multiple columns delimited by commas in the ORDER BY clause as well, each with its own sort order. SQL will use the additional columns if the first one contains any duplicate data. Just don't specify any columns that aren't in the table!

For example, the following statement returns what's shown in Figure 8.12:

```
SELECT * FROM tblUsers
ORDER BY FirstName, Phone ASC
```

Notice that when the first names are the same (the two Jacks), the records are sorted by the phone numbers.

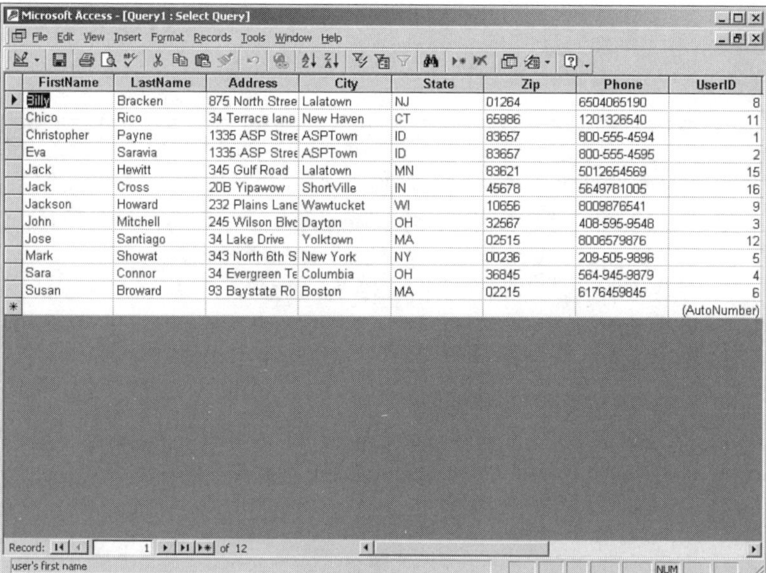

FirstName	LastName	Address	City	State	Zip	Phone	UserID
Billy	Bracken	875 North Stree	Lalatown	NJ	01264	6504065190	8
Chico	Rico	34 Terrace lane	New Haven	CT	65986	1201326540	11
Christopher	Payne	1335 ASP Stree	ASPTown	ID	83657	800-555-4594	1
Eva	Saravia	1335 ASP Stree	ASPTown	ID	83657	800-555-4595	2
Jack	Hewitt	345 Gulf Road	Lalatown	MN	83621	5012654569	15
Jack	Cross	20B Yipawow	ShortVille	IN	45678	5649781005	16
Jackson	Howard	232 Plains Lane	Wawtucket	WI	10656	8009876541	9
John	Mitchell	245 Wilson Blvc	Dayton	OH	32567	408-595-9548	3
Jose	Santiago	34 Lake Drive	Yolktown	MA	02515	8006579876	12
Mark	Showat	343 North 6th S	New York	NY	00236	209-505-9896	5
Sara	Connor	34 Evergreen Te	Columbia	OH	36845	564-945-9879	4
Susan	Broward	93 Baystate Ro	Boston	MA	02215	6176459845	6
							(AutoNumber)

FIGURE 8.13

Ordering columns in a SELECT *statement.*

You can also use SELECT statements to return data from more than one table at once. This is done with a comma-delimited list of table names for the *tablename* argument. Typically, you would have to relate the tables somehow, but we'll discuss that further tomorrow.

All of the other SQL statements that you'll examine today follow the same basic form as the SELECT query. Consequently, we won't spend much time on the next three statements.

The INSERT Statement

Another common SQL statement is the INSERT statement, which is used to insert new rows (new data) into a database table. Its basic syntax is as follows:

```
INSERT [INTO] tablename
[(column list)]
VALUES (DEFAULT | NULL | expression)
```

This is a straightforward statement and is similar in syntax to SELECT. Let's build an example using your user database:

```
INSERT INTO tblUsers (FirstName, LastName, Address, City _
   State, Zip, Phone)
VALUES ('Chris', 'Payne', '135 ASP Street', 'ASPTown', 'FL', _
   '36844', '8006596598')
```

This statement inserts a new row with the field values specified in the VALUES clause. The data type you supply in VALUES must match the data type in the corresponding column or you'll receive an error. Also, if you specify a column, you must specify a value or you'll get another error.

The UPDATE Statement

The UPDATE statement updates existing rows in a database table. You can specify a WHERE clause with this statement to update only a subset of the values in a database table. The syntax is as follows:

```
UPDATE tablename
SET column name = (DEFAULT | NULL | expression)
[WHERE searchCondition]
```

If you leave off the WHERE clause, the specified column(s) are updated in every row in the database. Be very careful with this statement, because it's easy to ruin your data! Again, using your tblUser database table as an example:

```
UPDATE tblUsers
SET Address = '136 ASP Street', Town = 'ASPVille'
WHERE FirstName = 'Chris' AND LastName = 'Payne'
```

This statement changes the `Address` and `Town` values for the record where the `FirstName` is "Chris" and the `LastName` is "Payne," which currently is only one record. You can specify only the columns you need in the *`column name`* list, and the `WHERE` clause is exactly the same as the `SELECT` statement—you can use wildcards as well.

The `DELETE` Statement

The last SQL statement you're going to look at today is the `DELETE` statement, which deletes rows from a database. Let's look at the syntax:

```
DELETE FROM tablename
[WHERE searchCondition]
```

This one is pretty simple. The only thing to remember is the `WHERE` clause, which is very important. If you don't specify this clause, the `DELETE` statement will delete all the rows in the entire table—normally a disastrous occurrence. Again, the `WHERE` clause is exactly the same as for the `SELECT` statement. For example, the following deletes only records with the first name "Chris":

```
DELETE FROM tblUsers
WHERE FirstName = 'Chris'
```

Accessing Data with ASP.NET

The rest of today will be spent on the basics of accessing databases from ASP.NET pages. Tomorrow you'll put this knowledge to use and access the actual data from your pages.

In general, there are five steps to accessing data through an ASP.NET Web page:

1. Set up a database connection.
2. Open the database connection.
3. Fill a `DataSet` with the desired data.
4. Set up a `DataView` to display data.
5. Bind a server control to the `DataView` via data binding.

Imagine accessing data as going to a buffet line. Setting up and opening a database connection are equivalent to finding and walking up to the buffet. As you're selecting the food you want, you fill up your plate by placing mashed potatoes on one side, meatloaf on the other, and so on. The `DataSet` is your plate—it holds any type of food… or data. Earlier you looked at the SQL `SELECT` statement, which returned a set of rows from a database table. In ASP.NET, a `DataSet` can be used to hold these results.

When you group your food/data this way, you're using *food views*. `DataViews` provide a view of the data that you can show users.

Data binding is a bit more complex, but imagine it as creating a magical link from the food on your plate to the food at the buffet. If you add some more macaroni to your plate, the buffet also gets some more macaroni.

Let's Access Data!

Listing 8.1 shows a simple ASP.NET page that accesses the database you've created. Specifically, all of the columns and rows of the `tblUser` table are accessed and displayed. Let's take a look at the code!

LISTING 8.1 Accessing Data with ASP.NET

```
<%@ Import Namespace="System.Data" %>
<%@ Import Namespace="System.Data.OleDb" %>

<script language="VB" runat="server">
   sub Page_Load(Sender as Object, e as EventArgs)
      'set up connection
      dim objConn as new OleDbConnection _
         ("Provider=Microsoft.Jet.OLEDB.4.0;" & _
         "Data Source=c:\ASPNET\data\banking.mdb")

       'open connection
       dim objCmd as new OleDbDataAdapter _
          ("select * from tblUsers", objConn)

      'fill dataset
       dim ds as DataSet = new DataSet()
       objCmd.Fill(ds, "tblUsers")

       'select data view and bind to server control
       MyDataList.DataSource = ds.Tables("tblUsers"). _
     DefaultView
       MyDataList.DataBind()
     end sub
 </script>

 <html><body>
   <ASP:DataList id="MyDataList" RepeatColumns="2"
      RepeatDirection="Vertical" runat="server">
      <ItemTemplate>
         <div style="padding:15,15,15,15;font-size:10pt;
            font-family:Verdana">
         <div style="font:12pt verdana;color:darkred">
            <i><b><%# DataBinder.Eval(Container. _
```

LISTING 8.1 continued

```
34:                DataItem, "FirstName")%> 
35:                <%# DataBinder.Eval(Container. _
36:                DataItem, "LastName")%>
37:                </i></b>
38:             </div>
39:             <br>
40:             <b>Address: </b><%# DataBinder.Eval(Container. _
41:                DataItem, "Address") %><br>
42:             <b>City: </b><%# DataBinder.Eval(Container. _
43:                DataItem, "City")%><br>
44:             <b>State: </b><%# DataBinder.Eval _
45:                (Container.DataItem, "State") %><br>
46:             <b>ZIP: </b><%# DataBinder.Eval _
47:                (Container.DataItem, "Zip") %><br>
48:             <b>Phone: </b><%# DataBinder.Eval _
49:                (Container.DataItem, "Phone") %><br>
50:                </div>
51:           </ItemTemplate>
52:       </ASP:DataList>
53:     </body></html>
```

ANALYSIS Before you can do any data access, you need to import the data namespaces, as shown on lines 1 and 2. (If you were using Microsoft's SQL Server for your database, you'd be using `System.Data.SqlClient`—we'll cover this more tomorrow.)

Lines 7–9 contains the code that sets up the connection to the database. `Data Source` is set to the Access data file you created earlier today. On lines 12 and 13, you open the connection to the database and execute a familiar SQL statement that returns all of the data from the table. These lines correspond to the first and second steps in your data access procedure.

Lines 16 and 17 create and fill a `DataSet` object with the returned data. This represents step three.

Lines 20–22 represent steps four and five. You bind the data to a `DataList` Web control, which automatically displays the data. The only thing left to do is to create the `DataList` control.

The `DataList` server control uses templates to format the data as you want it, and it automatically loops through your database records. It also learns the size and shape of the browser and creates columns so all of the data fits in one window. This saves you a lot of hassle. You can see that most of the syntax in the templates is simply HTML formatting tags.

However, there are those odd `<%#` and `%>` tags, which look kind of like code render blocks. These are data binding expressions. Data binding allows you to explicitly link a data source to a server control. Whatever happens to the data source also happens to the control, which allows for easy data manipulation. (Don't worry if this is a bit fuzzy now; we'll spend a lot of time on it tomorrow.)

Figure 8.14 shows the output of the `DataList` control.

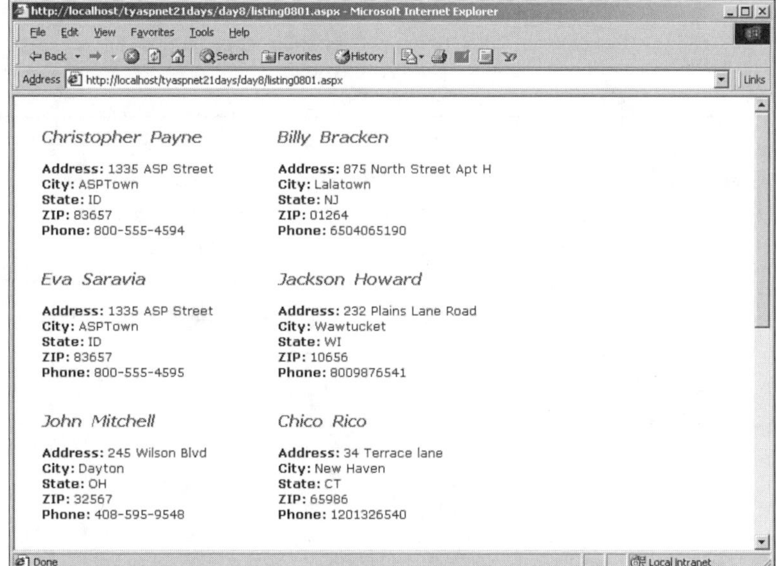

FIGURE 8.14
The contents of the `tblUsers` *table.*

That's Not ASP!

If you're familiar with traditional ASP, you'll see quite a difference from what you're used to. (Even if you're not familiar with classic ASP, you should still read this section!) Setting up and opening a connection to the database will look familiar—the syntax has changed a bit, but the format is the same. The first major difference, aside from having to import namespaces, is that you're filling a `DataSet` instead of returning a `recordset`. Listing 8.2 shows the typical process of grabbing data from a database using traditional ASP and VBScript.

LISTING 8.2 Accessing Data with Traditional ASP

```
<%
   Dim objConn
   Set objConn = Server.CreateObject("ADODB.Connection")
```

LISTING 8.2 continued

```
4:          objConn.ConnectionString = "Provider=" & _
5:          "Microsoft.Jet.OLEDB.4.0;Data Source=" & _
6:          "C:\ASPNET\data\banking.mdb"
7:       objConn.Open
8:
9:       Dim strSQL
10:       strSQL = "SELECT * FROM tblUsers"
11:
12:       Dim objRS
13:       Set objRS = Server.CreateObject("ADODB.Recordset")
14:       objRS.Open strSQL, objConn
15:    %>
```

ANALYSIS Lines 2–7 are the equivalent of lines 7–9 in Listing 8.1. You create an ADO connection, specify the connection string, and open the connection to your database. In lines 9–14 of Listing 8.2, you set up your SQL statement and fill a new `recordset` object with data returned from that statement. This `recordset` object contains many different properties and collections that can be used to display the data, as shown in Listing 8.3.

LISTING 8.3 Displaying Data with Traditional ASP

```
<%
   Do While Not objRS.EOF
      Response.write "<B>" & objRS("FirstName") & " " & _
         objRS("LastName") & "</B><BR>" & _
         objRS("Address")  & "<BR>" & objRS("City") & _
         "<BR>" & objRS("State") &"<BR>"& objRS("Zip") & _
         objRS("Phone") & "<P><HR><P>"
          objRS.Movenext
   Loop

    objRS.Close
    Set objRS = Nothing

    objConn.Close
    Set objConn = Nothing
 %>
```

In this listing, you loop through the records returned in the `recordset` and use `Response.Write` to print out the fields. You use `objRS.Movenext` to move to the next record; otherwise, you'd end up with an infinite loop. Finally, you close and destroy your `recordset` and `connection` objects.

Back in Listing 8.1, much of this was unnecessary. On line 17 of that listing, you filled up your `DataSet`, which held a generic set of data. You then bound the `DataSet` to a control on line 22, and that was it. The data binding expression automatically looped through the records and displayed the fields. The Common Language Runtime automatically cleaned up and destroyed our objects when you were done with them.

The ASP.NET method is more powerful, yet much easier to implement, and it runs faster and more efficiently as well. With ASP.NET, you no longer have to worry about looping through data, and you can spend much more time figuring out exactly how the data should be displayed. The `DataSet` also provides many more capabilities than the `recordset`, including full XML support and the capability to resync with a data source.

Luckily, many of the concepts behind data access are still the same, which means that your existing skills are still useful. As you explore these mechanisms today and tomorrow, you'll see how much more powerful the new framework is.

Summary

Databases are very important to all applications, especially Web-based programs. Accessing data over the Internet is invaluable, and ASP.NET has made it simple to interface with any database.

Today you learned about database fundamentals—the differences between flat-file and relational databases, and ways to constrain and link your database tables. You then used Access 2000 to create a database that you'll use in your applications later.

Next you took a brief look at SQL and the very important `SELECT`, `INSERT`, `UPDATE`, and `DELETE` statements, and you examined how to use them in your database tables. Finally, you looked at how to access data through a simple ASP.NET page, and you compared and contrasted data access with ASP.NET and traditional ASP.

Tomorrow you're going to examine how to access and modify databases from ASP.NET, and you'll look at the data-centric server controls you skipped on Day 6. So far, you've only seen a tiny portion of ASP.NET's powerful database capabilities. As the week progresses, you'll start to use databases like an expert!

Q&A

Q Should I use relational database designs?

A Absolutely! It may be awkward at first, but nearly all of today's database applications are built for relational databases. You'll need a lot of practice to design databases effectively, but you'll never learn if you don't jump in!

Today you only designed a single-table database (which makes it hard to see relational designs), but in a few days you'll start adding more tables and creating complex relationships. Trust us, it only gets more fun from here!

Q What type of data is XML?

A XML itself is a specification that allows you to create a well-defined structure for your data. That said, you can store any type of data with XML.

The beauty part of XML is threefold: 1) It's text-based, which makes it easy for users to read and modify; 2) it's a standard; and 3) it can be transferred easily over the Web. Thus, you can store the database you created as XML and anyone can access it easily. Try allowing others to access your SQL Server 2000 database—you'll see that it's a *much* more complicated task.

(Of course, ASP.NET allows others to access your databases easily, but imagine what your life would be like without ASP.NET. You'll examine XML and ASP.NET in Day 11, "Using XML in ASP.NET.")

Q Are there any drawbacks to using a database with ASP.NET?

A The main drawback of using databases over the Web is that it takes a long time (relatively speaking) to connect to them. ASP.NET is better than traditional ASP in this regard, but there are still performance hits.

Generally, databases can be a good way to go if you have large amounts of data that you may need indefinitely. The performance issues can be relatively minor if your system configuration is set up well, and databases provide benefits, such as easy manipulation of data, that set them apart from other methods of data storage.

Workshop

This workshop will help reinforce the concepts covered in today's lesson. The answers can be found in Appendix A.

Quiz

1. What is a relational database?
2. What does SQL stand for, and what does it do?
3. What does ODBC stand for?
4. True or False: You can access any ODBC-compliant database through ASP.NET.
5. What are the five steps to accessing a database from ASP.NET?

Exercises

1. Create your own database from scratch and use it to store information on pets that you've owned. (If you've never owned any, make some up!) What fields do you need?
2. Play with Listing 8.1—specifically, the `DataList` control. Modify the formatting tags in the template to see how you can change the display, and use what you know about ASP.NET server controls to change the properties of the `DataList` control.

WEEK 2

DAY 9

Using Databases with ASP.NET

Yesterday you learned all about databases—when to use them, how to build them, and best of all, how to access their data from ASP.NET Web pages. However, yesterday's lesson was only a very brief overview of this process. Today, you'll examine using databases with ASP.NET in much greater detail.

You'll also take a look at data binding and the server controls that were skipped over on Day 6, "Learning More About Web Forms." These additional features make ASP.NET very well suited for database-driven applications.

Today's lesson will cover the following:

- The new `DataSet` object
- What data binding is and how it works with ASP.NET
- Three more ASP.NET server controls: `Repeater`, `DataList`, and `DataGrid`
- A data binding example

Introduction to Accessing Data from ASP.NET

Data access over the Web has made some major advances in recent years. It's moved from accessing simple text files for small guestbooks to moving large corporations' entire data systems online—some consisting of several terabytes of data. (One terabyte equals approximately 1,000 gigabytes, or 1,000,000 megabytes.) Even stockbrokers and order execution systems have moved online, generating massive amounts of data daily. Luckily, you have ASP.NET to help you with all that!

Classic ASP pages used ActiveX Data Objects (ADO) to access and modify databases. ADO is a programming interface used to access data. This method was efficient and fairly easy for developers to learn and implement. However, ADO suffered from a dated model for data access with many limitations, such as the inability to transmit data so it is easily and universally accessible. Coupled with the move from standard SQL databases to more distributed types of data (such as XML), Microsoft introduced ADO.NET—the next evolution of ADO.

ADO.NET is a major revision of ADO that enables ASP.NET pages to present data in much more efficient and different ways. For example, it fully embraces XML and is easily able to communicate with any XML-compliant application. ADO.NET offers a lot of exciting new features that will make your life (as a developer) much easier.

ADO.NET is a very large topic, which is why tomorrow's lesson is devoted to it. For now, you just need to know that ASP.NET pages use ADO.NET to communicate with any type of data store. Figure 9.1 depicts the model of data access with ADO.NET and ASP.NET. ADO.NET is completely compatible with OLE DB-compliant data sources, such as SQL or Jet (Microsoft Access's database engine).

FIGURE 9.1

Data access model with ADO.NET and ASP.NET.

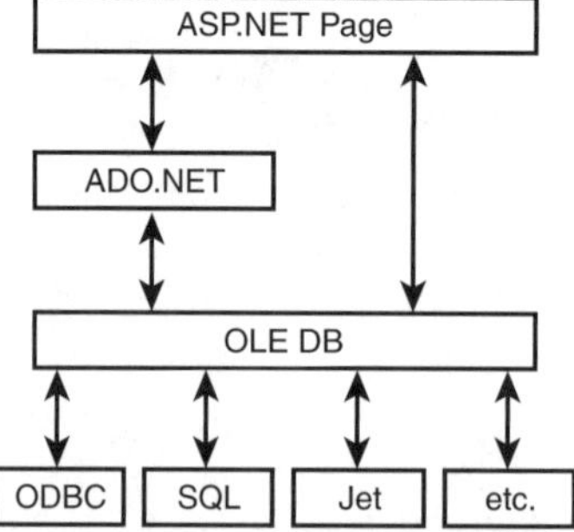

The DataSet

ADO.NET revolves around the `DataSet`. This object is a completely new concept that replaces the traditional `Recordset` in ADO. A `Recordset` provided methods that allowed you to retrieve and display database rows, or records. A `Recordset` was very helpful when you needed to return data, but suffered from some limitations. Specifically, its representation of the data was fairly simple: It couldn't contain more than one set of data, and didn't contain information on the relationships between data.

The `DataSet` is a simple, memory-resident data store that provides a consistent programming model for accessing data, no matter what type of data it contains. Unlike a `Recordset`, the `DataSet` contains complete sets of data, including constraints, relationships, and even multiple tables at once. Figure 9.2 shows a high-level view of the `DataSet` object model.

FIGURE 9.2

The `DataSet` object model.

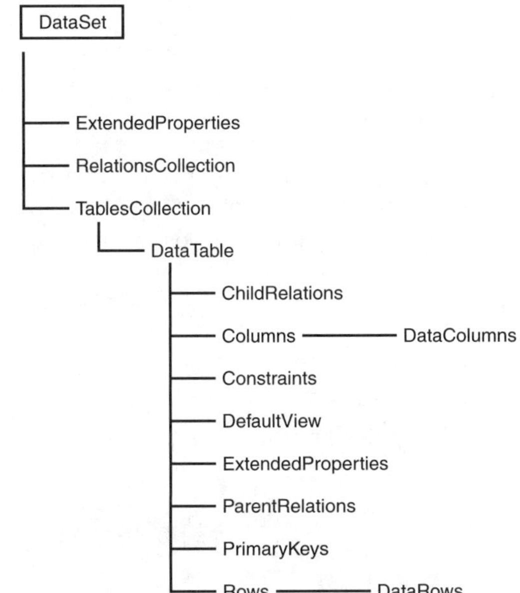

Imagine a box with several compartments. In each compartment, you can put any object you like as long as it fits in the box. You can see and manipulate each object in the box—take it out, add more, just look at it, and so on. That's what the `DataSet` is, essentially. When you establish a connection to the database, you hand it a box and tell the data store to fill it with some stuff. You can fill it with tables of data, your own data from elsewhere, other objects—any data you like. No matter what objects you put inside, the box will allow you to do the same things with each object, such as view, add, delete, and so on. Oh, and your box is dynamic, so it will expand or shrink depending on how many objects are in it!

Figure 9.2 includes a `DataTable` object, which represents a single database table. (The `DataSet` maintains a collection of these tables in the `TablesCollection` object.) The `DataTable` completely represents the corresponding table, including its relationships and key constraints. It contains two other collections, `Rows` and `Columns`, which represent the data and schema of the tables, respectively.

Now imagine your box again. Each compartment is a `DataTable`. The box now has an LCD panel on the outside that automatically lists the objects inside it. (Wouldn't that be great for a refrigerator?) Your box is becoming pretty functional! Figure 9.3 illustrates this box object.

The `RelationsCollection` object allows you to navigate between tables by the relationships defined on them. It's no longer necessary to use complex joins and unions (the old way of relating tables) in your SQL queries because ADO.NET makes it much easier. The actual relationships are represented by `DataRelation` objects, which contain information on the two tables being joined, the primary and foreign key relationships, and the name of the relationships.

You can also *add* relationships using the `DataRelation` object. ADO.NET automatically enforces key constraints as well—it won't allow you to change one table in a way that would violate the relationship to the other table.

FIGURE 9.3
Your `DataSet` *box model.*

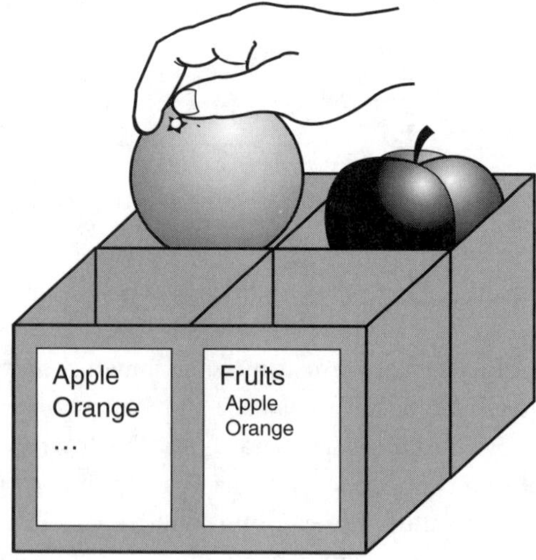

Once again, your box is enhanced. You can now tell it which objects are related and *how* they're related. For example, let's say you have an apple and an orange, and you tell the box that the two are related because they're both fruit. The next time you see the box, you can say, "Show me fruit," and it will list the apple and the orange. Then suppose you try to add a carrot, and you tell the box that the carrot is also related to apples and oranges. The box will reject this because a carrot is a vegetable—it violates the rules of the relationship.

The `ExtendedProperties` object contains any additional information, such as user names and passwords.

The example of fruit in a box is a bit simplistic, but it explains the concepts of the `DataSet`. It cares nothing about where the data came from or where it's going—it's completely separate from any data store. Therefore, you can use the `DataSet` as a standalone entity. The next section will explain in more detail how your `DataSet` actually functions.

Using the `DataSet`

There are two ways to use a `DataSet`: fill it with data from an existing data store, or create your own empty `DataSet` from scratch. First, let's take a look at creating your own `DataSet`.

Since the `DataSet` is a data store that resides in memory, you can create your own programmatically and add tables to it. This can be a very helpful feature if you just want to use dynamic data in your ASP.NET applications without having to deal with databases directly. Listing 9.1 shows an example.

LISTING 9.1 Creating a `DataSet` Programmatically

```
'create an empty dataset
dim ds as new DataSet("MyDataSet")

'create a new table and columns
dim dTable as New DataTable("Users")
dTable.Columns.Add("FirstName", System.Type. _
   GetType("System.String"))
dTable.Columns.Add("LastName", System.Type. _
   GetType("System.String"))
dTable.Columns.Add("UserID", System.Type. _
   GetType("System.Int32"))
dTable.Columns("UserID").AutoIncrement = true

'add table
ds.Tables.Add(dTable)

```

LISTING 9.1 continued

```
17:  'define primary key
18:  dim keys() as DataColumn = {ds.Tables("Users"). _
19:     Columns("UserID")}
20:  ds.Tables("Users").PrimaryKey = keys
21:
22:  'add a sample row
23:  dim dr as DataRow = dTable.NewRow()
24:  dr(0) = "Chris"
25:  dr(1) = "Payne"
26:  dTable.Rows.Add(dr)
```

ANALYSIS Listing 9.1 creates a `DataSet`, adds to it a single table, and fills it with some data. You don't even need an actual database—you can use this `DataSet` anywhere in your ASP.NET pages now. (Note that the `System.Data` namespace is required for the objects used in this listing.)

Line 2 instantiates a new `DataSet` named "`MyDataSet`". You then create a new table, `"Users"`, on line 5, and add three columns: `"FirstName"`, `"LastName"`, and `"UserID"`. The `Add` method takes two parameters—the name of the new column and the type of the column. Use the `GetType` method to return a type representing the object in question, as shown on lines 7, 9, and 11. Line 12 sets the `AutoIncrement` property of the `"UserID"` field to true so that this column will automatically set values when a new column is added. This guarantees you a unique identifier for each row. Line 15 adds the new table to the `DataSet`'s tables collection.

The `PrimaryKey` property on line 20 takes an array of `DataColumn` objects so that you can define keys over multiple columns to specify a unique record. For instance, in the user database example, a first name might not be unique but a first name/last name combination might be. You can define an array of these two `DataColumn` objects and set the primary key. Luckily, you already have a unique identity field—`"UserID"`—so you set up an array consisting of only this column on line 18 and set the primary key to this array.

You can now use this `DataSet` to store data. You can even write this data to an actual file or insert it into a database if you want. Line 23 creates a new row to hold values, while lines 24–25 assign the value `"Chris"` to the `"FirstName"` field and the value `"Payne"` to the `"LastName"` field. You don't need to set a value for the `"UserID"` column because the `DataSet` will do that automatically. Finally, you simply add this row to your table on line 26. The method for adding each item in a `DataSet` is generally one of the two shown in Table 9.1.

TABLE 9.1 Processes for Adding Objects to a DataSet

Method 1:	*Method 2:*
1. Instantiate a new item.	1. Add a new item to the DataSet.
2. Set the item's properties.	2. Access the item through the DataSet object model to set its properties.
	3. Add the item to the DataSet.

Here's an example of method 1:

```
dim dTable as New DataTable("Users")

'set properties for dTable
' or add columns to dTable
dTable.MinimumCapacity = 25
...

ds.Tables.Add(dTable)
```

Here's an example of method 2:

```
ds.Tables.Add(new DataTable("Users")

'set properties for dTable
' or add columns to dTable
ds.Tables("Users").MinimumCapacity = 25
```

Neither method results in a distinct performance benefit. The first method has better readability, while the second is more compact.

You can then access each of the DataSet's properties and values by using the familiar "dot" syntax. To refer to a specific column or row, you can use the following:

```
ds.Tables(tablename).Columns(column index or name)
ds.Tables(tablename).Rows(row index)
```

This provides a very powerful mechanism for interacting with the DataSet. Similarly, you can access or change a particular field value with the following:

```
strValue = ds.Tables(tablename).Rows(row index)(field name).
➥ToString:
ds.Tables(tablename).Rows(row index)(field name) = strValue
```

Relationships

Now let's assume you've created two tables in this manner and you want to relate them. The first table is your user table, and the second table, "Books", holds lists of books that each person has read. These tables are related by the `"UserID"` of each user. Assuming both tables have a `"UserID"` field, Listing 9.2 shows some more code.

LISTING 9.2 Creating Relationships with a `DataSet`

```
'create a new relation
dim dr as DataRelation = New DataRelation("UserBooks", _
   ds.Tables("Users").Columns("UserID"), _
   ds.Tables("Books").Columns("UserID"))

'add the relation
ds.Relations.Add(dr)
```

ANALYSIS You create a new relation by specifying the relation name—`"UserBooks"` in this case—and the column from each table that should make up the relation. This relation allows you to navigate between the two tables via the linked columns.

You can also create relations over more than one column in each table. Simply pass arrays of `DataColumn` objects for the second two parameters. For example, the following code creates relations between the `UserID` and `FirstName` fields in both `Users` and `Books` tables:

```
dim dcUsers(2) as DataColumn
dcUsers(0) = ds.Tables("Users").Columns("UserID")
dcUsers(1) = ds.Tables("Users").Columns("FirstName")

dim dcBooks(2) as DataColumn
dcBooks(0) = ds.Tables("Books").Columns("UserID")
dcBooks(1) = ds.Tables("Books").Columns("FirstName")

dim dr as DataRelation = New DataRelation("UserBooks", _
   dcUsers, dcBooks)
ds.Relations.Add(dr)
```

Note, however, that when you specify arrays of `DataColumns`, both of the second parameters must be arrays of the same size.

Filling `DataSets`

Now that you know what a `DataSet` is and what you can do with it, let's fill it with some data from the database you created yesterday. There are a lot of new objects introduced here that I won't get to until tomorrow, so don't worry if you don't understand all the code.

Listing 9.3 shows an example of filling a `DataSet` in an ASP.NET page with the results returned from an SQL query.

LISTING 9.3 Retrieving Database Rows with a `DataSet`

```
1:  <%@ Page Language="VB" %>
2:  <%@ Import Namespace="System.Data" %>
3:  <%@ Import Namespace="System.Data.OleDB" %>
4:
5:  <script runat="server">
6:     sub Page_Load(Sender as Object, e as EventArgs)
7:        'set up connection
8:        dim myConnection as new OleDbConnection _
9:           ("Provider=Microsoft.Jet.OLEDB.4.0;" & _
10:           "Data Source=c:\ASPNET\data\banking.mdb")
11:
12:        'open connection
13:        dim myCommand as new OleDbDataAdapter _
14:           ("select * from tblUsers", myConnection)
15:
16:        'fill dataset
17:         dim ds as DataSet = new DataSet()
18:         myCommand.Fill(ds, "tblUsers")
19:     end sub
20:  </script>
21:
22:  <html><body>
23:  </body></html>
```

ANALYSIS On lines 2 and 3, you see the two new namespaces that you have to import when filling `DataSet`s this way. (Actually, only `System.Data` is required for the `DataSet`, but `System.Data.OleDb` provides some additional helper objects.) All the action happens in the `Page_Load` event here. Again, don't worry if you don't recognize the objects or commands—I'll discuss them in detail tomorrow.

On lines 8–10, you set up a connection to the database with an `OleDbConnection` object. This object tells ASP.NET where to go to get the data it needs; specifically, the banking database you created yesterday. On line 13, you create a new `OleDbDataAdapter` object, which is used to execute SQL statements in ASP.NET. This object takes as parameters a SQL statement, and the `OleDbConnection` object you created on line 8. The SQL statement here simply retrieves all the data stored in the `tblUsers` table.

On line 17, you create a new `DataSet`, which should look familiar. On line 18, you use the `Fill` method of the `OleDbDataAdapter` object to fill the `DataSet` with the data retrieved by the SQL query. The second parameter specifies in which table in the

DataSet the data adapter should place the results. Note that you didn't explicitly create this table—the Fill method does it for you automatically!

You can now manipulate the data in this DataSet, as well as all of the other properties we learned about earlier today. In addition, you can now bind the data in the DataSet to controls in your ASP.NET page. Data binding is discussed in the next section.

Filling a DataSet with data from a database is even easier than creating the DataSet yourself. You needed only four lines of code here to retrieve the data, and only a couple more to display it, as you'll see in the next section.

Data Binding

Data binding gives you extensive control over your data. You can bind nearly any type of data to any control or property of a control on an ASP.NET page. This gives you complete control over how data moves from the data store to the page and back again. You can simply display the data to the user, use it to set the style properties on a control, or even allow the user to modify the data directly and update the data store.

There are two ways to bind data to an ASP.NET page: use a control's DataSource property, or use a data-binding expression. The first method is most commonly used for more complex ASP.NET server controls and will be covered in a minute. The second method can be used anywhere. The syntax for a data-binding expression is as follows:

```
<%# property or collection %>
```

> Although this syntax looks very similar to code render blocks used with traditional ASP, it's not. Code render blocks are always evaluated at page runtime. Data-binding expressions are only evaluated using the DataBind() method.

It's that simple. This expression will do different things depending on where it's used. Take Listing 9.4, for example, which declares a few variables and then binds them to various place in the page.

LISTING 9.4 Binding Data to Different Places in a Page

```
<script runat="server">
   dim strName as String = "Chris"
   dim myArray() as String = {"Hello", "World"}
   dim myString as String = "Chris"
```

LISTING 9.4 continued

```
5:
6:     sub Page_Load(Sender as Object, e as EventArgs)
7:        Page.DataBind()
8:     end sub
9:  </script>
10:
11:  <html>
12:  <form runat="server">
13:  ...
14:  My Name is <%# strName %>
15:
16:  <asp:Listbox datasource='<%# myArray %>' runat="server" />
17:
18:  <asp:Textbox text='<%# myString %>' runat="server" />
19:  ...
20:  </form>
21:  </html>
```

Line 14 displays the value of `strName` next to the HTML output `"My Name is"`. On line 16, the `ListBox` takes a collection and automatically loops through it to properly display the values of `myArray` as list items. Line 18 produces a text box that displays whatever is in `myString`. Thus, you can see that data binding offers a lot of flexibility.

In lines 14 and 18, data binding doesn't provide you much benefit; after all, you could just write the text in the variables' places. However, the `ListBox` on line 16 is a different case. Data binding allows the `ListBox` to iterate over the items in the array, and fill itself up with strings. Without data binding, you'd have to manually fill up the `ListBox` with some kind of loop.

> **Caution**
>
> Be aware that your data-binding expressions must return types that are expected by your controls. For example, the text box control on line 18 expects a string value. If the data-binding expression doesn't produce one, you'll receive an error. It's often helpful to cast your data-binding expressions. For example, even though it might not be necessary here, changing line 18 to
>
> ```
> <asp:Textbox text='<%# myString.ToString %>' runat="server" />
> ```
>
> ensures that the data is in the proper format.

Data-binding expressions are only evaluated when the `DataBind` method is called—ASP.NET doesn't process them for you automatically. You have a lot of choices about when and where to call this method. If you call `DataBind` at the page level, every data-binding expression on the page will be evaluated. This is typically accomplished in the `Page_Load` event:

```
sub Page_Load(Sender as Object, e as EventArgs)
   DataBind()
end sub
```

You can also call `DataBind` for each control individually, which gives you greater control over how your application uses data. For instance, imagine that you allow users to view and modify their personal information on your Web site. You could display all of their information on one page but let them update only one field at a time. This would save you the hassle of collecting and verifying every single field on the page again. Listing 9.5 shows an example.

LISTING 9.5 Different Ways to Use `DataBind`

```
1:  Sub Page_Load(Sender as object, e as EventArgs)
2:     'do some stuff
3:     DataBind()
4:  End Sub
5:
6:  Sub Submit_Click(Sender as object, e as EventArgs)
7:     if Text1.TextChanged then
8:        Label1.DataBind()
9:     end if
10:  end sub
```

ANALYSIS The first `Sub` on lines 1–4 binds all the data on the page as soon as the page is loaded. This is a very typical situation, and often that's what you'll want to do. The second `Sub`, on lines 6–10, is the event handler for the `Click` event of a Submit button. If this subprocedure determines that the text in the `Text1` control has changed, it evaluates the data-binding expression for the `Label1` control *only*. This is very helpful when users modify data fields.

Using Data Binding

This flexible syntax gives you a lot of freedom about how you use data in your pages. However, how do you create and use the data sources?

The simplest way is to create a *page-level variable*. This is a variable that isn't contained within a method. You can then use this value anywhere within your page in a data-binding expression:

```
<script language="VB" runat="server">
    dim strName as string = "My Name"

    sub Page_Load(Sender as Object, e as EventArgs)
        DataBind()
    end sub

</script>
...
...
<asp:Label id="lblName" runat="server" text='<%# strName %>' />
<%# strName %>
```


The last two lines show two examples of binding this page property. It's as simple as that. This doesn't do a lot for you, however. You could actually, in the `Page_Load` event, simply use the following command to fill the label:

```
lblName.Text = "My Name"
```

The true power of data binding comes from using dynamic values in server controls.

Let's take a look at an example in Listing 9.6.

LISTING 9.6 Binding One Server Control to Another

```
<script language="VB" runat="server">
   sub Index_Changed(Sender as Object, e as EventArgs)
      DataBind()
   end sub
</script>

<html><body>
   <form runat="server">

      <asp:Listbox runat="server" id="lbColors"
         width="150"
         AutoPostBack=true
         rows="1"
         SelectionMode="Single"
         OnSelectedIndexChanged="Index_Changed" >
         <asp:Listitem value="1">Red</asp:Listitem>
         <asp:Listitem value=" 2">Blue</asp:Listitem>
         <asp:Listitem value=" 3">Green</asp:Listitem>
         <asp:Listitem value=" 4">Yellow</asp:Listitem>
      </asp:Listbox><p>

      <asp:Label id="lblMessage" runat="server"
         Text='<%# List1.selectedItem.Text %>' />
    </form>
 </body></html>
```

The `Label` on line 22 uses a data-binding expression that binds to the `SelectedItem` property of the `ListBox`. Whenever the selected index changes, you call `DataBind` again to bind the new value to the `Label`. The effect is that the `Label` will show whatever is selected. This is just an example of how you can bind to any public property of the page. Figure 9.4 shows the output of this page.

FIGURE 9.4

Displaying selected data with data binding.

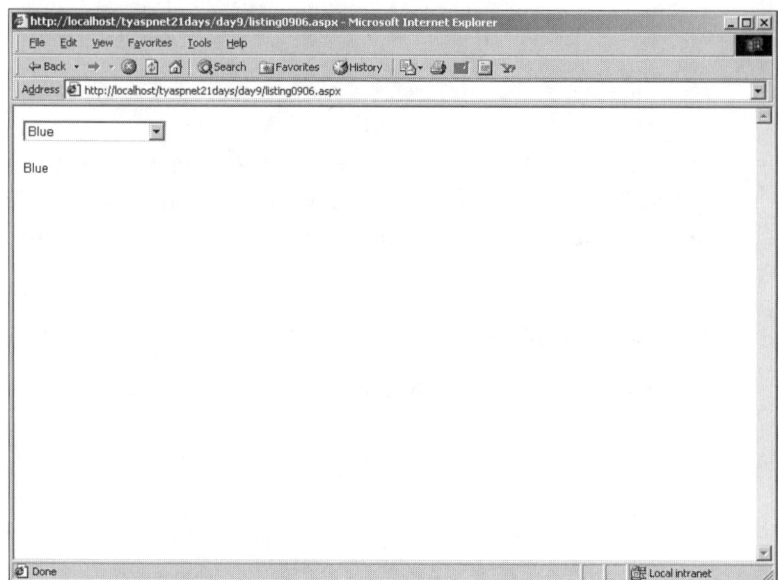

Some server controls can also bind to data classes, rather than simple properties, for more elaborate data manipulation. These controls have a `DataSource` property that's accessible only at design time. Simply set this property to a data class (such as an array or data view) and call `DataBind`, and these controls handle much of the work for you. Listing 9.7 expands on the previous example.

LISTING 9.7 Using the `DataSource` Property

```
<script runat="server">
   sub Page_Load(Sender as Object, e as EventArgs)
      if not Page.IsPostBack then
         'create an array of colors
         dim arrColors() as string = _
            {"red", "orange", "yellow", "green", _
             "blue", "indigo", "violet"}
         lbColors.SelectedIndex = 0
         lbColors.DataSource = arrColors
      end if
      DataBind()
```

LISTING 9.7 continued

```
12:     end sub
13:  </script>
14:
15:  <html><body>
16:     <form runat="server">
17:        <asp:Listbox runat="server" id="lbColors"
18:           width="150"
19:           AutoPostBack="true"
20:           SelectionMode="Single" >
21:        </asp:Listbox><p>
22:
23:        <asp:Label id="lblMessage" runat="server"
24:           Text='<%# lbColors.SelectedItem.Text %>' />
25:     </form>
26:  </body></html>
```


ANALYSIS You create a data class (an array in this case) on line 5 and set the listbox's `DataSource` property on line 9. Now the listbox populates itself *automatically* using the array. The label works exactly as it did before—when the selection changes, it updates itself. There is one difference here, however. When you first load the page, the `ListBox` doesn't have an item selected, and therefore, lines 23–24 will cause an error; you can't bind to the `SelectedItem` property if nothing is selected. Therefore, on line 8, you select the first item in the `ListBox`.

Figure 9.5 shows this page in action.

Notice the addition of the `Postback` check on line 2. You only need to create your array the first time the page is viewed. After that, the listbox fills itself automatically using the built-in viewstate management. Therefore, you add a check to determine if the form has been submitted. If it has, you don't need to repopulate the listbox.

This check also serves another purpose—if you take it out, you receive an `Object reference not set to an instance of an object.` error from the label. Let's examine the flow of the page to figure this one out. See Figure 9.6.

Let's assume that your page has been submitted. In your `Page_Load` event, you set the `DataSource` property of the listbox and bind it. Essentially, this reinitializes the listbox and destroys the state information. Then the `Index_Changed` event fires, which evaluates all data-binding expressions on the page. The data-binding expression for the label tries to use the `SelectedItem` property of the listbox. Because you eliminated the state information, the reference to `SelectedItem` returns a null object, which throws an error. Thus, you add the postback check, which prevents the page from reinitializing the listbox when the form is submitted.

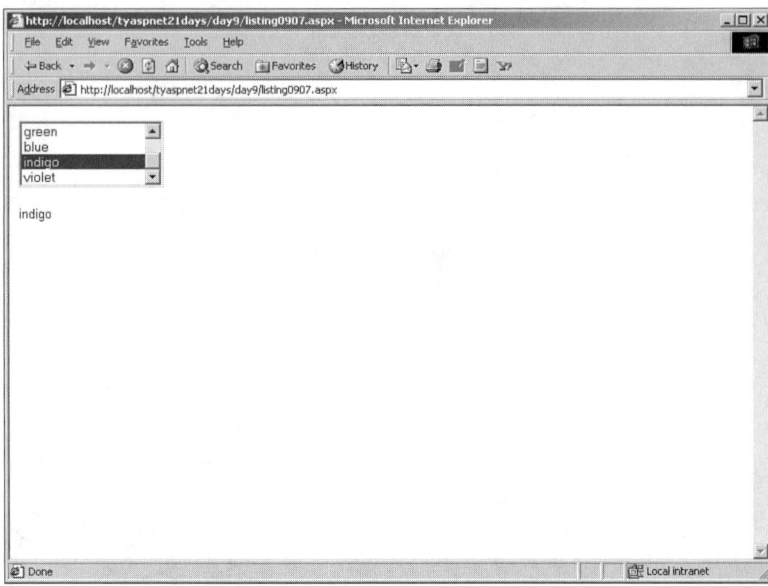

FIGURE 9.5

Binding data at design time.

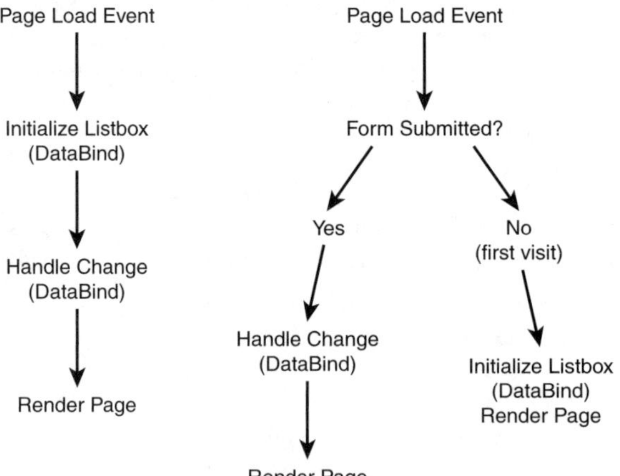

FIGURE 9.6

On the left is the workflow without a `Postback` *check. On the right is the workflow with a* `Postback` *check.*

Beware of little things like these. Because of the way the event-driven model works, you must be careful when binding data on a page.

Now that you know how data binding works, you might wonder how it benefits users of your ASP.NET pages. The answer is that it doesn't do much at all for your users, unless you count the fact that it cuts development time for you and speeds site delivery for them. The biggest benefit of data binding is the features it provides you, as the developer: decreased development time, ease of use, standardized methods, and so on.

Now you're ready to take a look at some of the more complex ASP.NET server controls that use data binding.

Data Binding Controls

On Day 5, you examined the various ASP.NET server controls, but not the three complex list controls: the `Repeater`, `DataList`, and `DataGrid` server controls. These are called *list controls* because they take collections of data and loop through them automatically. They're similar to other controls, such as `DropDownList` and `ListBox`, but they offer much more complex functionality. They act as containers for other controls that actually display the data, such as labels. These controls are very powerful and save developers a lot of manual work.

Each of the server controls in the next few sections has its advantages and disadvantages, as you'll see when we examine the controls. Essentially, the trade-offs are functionality and complexity; one control gives you more features, but is also more complex to use. The controls are presented in order of complexity.

`Repeater` Server Control

The `Repeater` ASP.NET server control is a container that loops through data. It doesn't have a predefined display—you must specify its layout using template controls. It provides a highly customizable interface. If you don't specify a layout, the control won't be rendered.

Templates are controls that allow you to use HTML tags and text, as well as other controls, to control the display of data in rich Web controls. You must use templates with a `Repeater` control, which supports the following types of templates:

- `ItemTemplate`—This template is required by the `Repeater` control. It produces one row of output for each data row. You use other server controls to display the actual data by binding them to the appropriate fields.
- `AlternatingItemTemplate`—This is the same as the `ItemTemplate`, but it renders for every other data row. This allows you to specify different style settings, such as alternating row colors.
- `HeaderTemplate` and `FooterTemplate`—These templates render HTML immediately before and after all the data rows have been rendered. A typical use would be to open and close tables with `<table>` and `</table>` tags.
- `SeparatorTemplate`—These templates render items between each data row—for example, the HTML tags `<br>`, `<p>`, or `<HR>`.

These templates have no particular format or syntax—you simply use them as containers for your display. Let's take a look at a typical example, shown in Listing 9.8. You'll use `tblUser`, the same database table you created for yesterday's lesson.

LISTING 9.8 A Typical `Repeater` Control

```
<%@ Page Language="VB" %>
<%@ Import Namespace="System.Data" %>
<%@ Import Namespace="System.Data.OleDb" %>

<script runat="server">
   sub Page_Load(Sender as Object, e as EventArgs)

      'set up connection
      dim myConnection as new OleDbConnection _
         ("Provider=Microsoft.Jet.OLEDB.4.0;" & _
         "Data Source=c:\ASPNET\data\banking.mdb")

       'open connection
       dim myCommand as new OleDbDataAdapter _
          ("select * from tblUsers", myConnection)

       'fill dataset
       dim ds as DataSet = new DataSet()
       myCommand.Fill(ds, "tblUsers")

       'select data view and bind to server control
       Repeater1.DataSource = ds.Tables("tblUsers"). _
          DefaultView
       DataBind()
    end sub
</script>

<html><body>
   <ASP:Repeater id="Repeater1" runat="server" >
      <HeaderTemplate>
         <table>
         <tr>
            <td bgcolor="#cccc99" width=200><b>Name</b></td>
            <td bgcolor="#cccc99" width=200><b>Phone</b></td>
         </tr>
      </HeaderTemplate>

      <ItemTemplate>
         <tr>
            <td> <%# Container.DataItem("FirstName") %> 
                 <%# Container.DataItem("LastName") %>
            </td>
            <td> <%# Container.DataItem("Phone") %> </td>
```

LISTING 9.8 continued

```
44:          </tr>
45:       </ItemTemplate>
46:
47:       <AlternatingItemTemplate>
48:          <tr>
49:             <td bgcolor="#cccc99"">
50:                <%# Container.DataItem("FirstName") %> 
51:                <%# Container.DataItem("LastName") %>
52:             </td>
53:             <td bgcolor="#cccc99">
54:                <%# Container.DataItem("Phone") %>
55:             </td>
56:          </tr>
57:       </AlternatingItemtemplate>
58:
59:       <SeparatorTemplate>
60:          <tr>
61:             <td colspan="2" align="center">
62:                - - -
63:             </td>
64:          </tr>
65:       </SeparatorTemplate>
66:
67:       <FooterTemplate>
68:          </table>
69:       </FooterTemplate>
70:    </ASP:Repeater>
71: </body></html>
```

Figure 9.7 contains the output for Listing 9.8 when viewed through a browser.

ANALYSIS The `Page_Load` event handler has been copied directly from yesterday's lesson (Listing 8.1). Again, it contains a few objects that I won't cover until tomorrow. You set up and open your database connection on lines 8–15, fill a `DataSet` on line 19, and bind a `DataView` to your `Repeater` on line 22.

Note that there are two ways you can bind data to the `Repeater` control (as well as the `DataList` and `DataGrid` controls that you'll see later today). The first method is the one shown here: You assign the `DataSource` property of the control to a `DataView`, which tells the control the table and data to display. Another method is simply to assign the `DataSet` to the control, and use the `DataMember` property to tell it what data to display. For example, you could replace lines 22–23 with the following:

```
Repeater1.DataSource = ds
Repeater1.DataMember = "tblUsers"
```

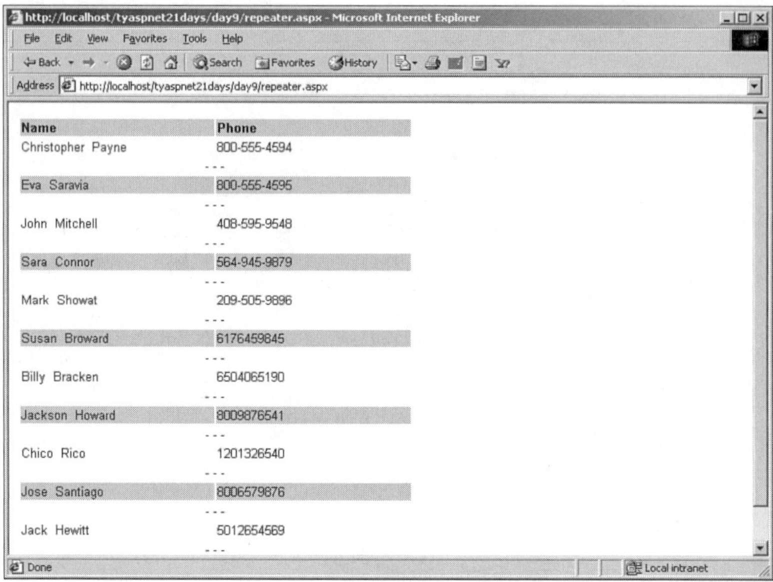

FIGURE 9.7

The `Repeater` *control (with templates) in action.*

Then you would simply call `DataBind`. Both examples are functionally equivalent; both methods will work, and you'll be using them interchangeably throughout today's lesson. The reason for having two methods is that the second allows you to easily use a `DataSet` to bind data, rather than having to worry about creating a `DataView`. The first method lets you bind data with different types of objects.

Next, in the body of your page, you declare the `Repeater` control on line 29. Your header template simply creates an HTML table and prints out headers for the columns `"Name"` and `"Phone"`. Next, your item template binds three data fields to the page. `Container.DataItem` is the collection of data fields for the current control's parent—the `Repeater`, in this case. You bind the `"FirstName"`, `"LastName"`, and `"Phone"` fields to this template, and the `Repeater` control will automatically loop through the records and render these fields on the page. Your alternating item template does exactly the same thing, except it specifies a different background color for the table rows.

Your separator template on line 59 simply creates a new HTML row with a few dash marks to introduce separations between the rows (if alternating colors weren't enough). And finally, your footer template simply closes the HTML table. This is followed by the closing `</asp:Repeater>` tag.

That's it! You can see how the `Repeater` control allows you to display data easily, while giving you complete control over the way it's presented.

The Repeater control also has two events that you can respond to: ItemCreated and ItemCommand. ItemCreated is raised immediately *before* a new item or template is created. You could use this to set the style properties programmatically at run-time, for example. Its syntax is as follows:

```
sub_name_ItemCreated(Sender as Object, e as _
   RepeaterItemEventArgs)
```


The RepeaterItemEventArgs contains one property, Item, which is the item that was just created. For example, Listing 9.9 shows a code snippet that handles this event.

LISTING 9.9 Handling the Repeater's Events

```
sub Repeater1_ItemCreated(Sender as Object, e as _
   RepeaterItemEventArgs)
   dim type as String
   select case (e.Item.ItemType)
      case ListItemType.Item
         type = "Item"
      case ListItemType.AlternatingItem
         type = "AlternatingItem"
      case ListItemType.Header
          type = "Header"
       case ListItemType.Footer
          type = "Footer"
       case ListItemType.Separator
          type = "Separator"
    end select

...
    Label1.Text = Label1.Text & "A Repeater " & type & _
       " has been created <br>"
end sub
...
<asp:Repeater id="Repeater1" runat="server"
OnItemCreated="Repeater1_ItemCreated">
...
</asp:Repeater>
<asp:ListBox id="Label1" runat="server"/>
```

The label would then list, in order, the types of templates that were created.

The ItemCommand event is raised whenever a server control inside the Repeater control fires an event. The contained control "bubbles" the command up to the Repeater. For example, if you place a button or link control inside one of the templates, you can detect when a user has clicked it and react accordingly. In each control, you can set a Command property that contains a string that will be bubbled up so your handler can determine a course of action.

Note that you can also simply respond to that control's event directly, without having to go through the Repeater's ItemCommand event. However, the Repeater generates these controls dynamically, so you'll have to discover their individual names somehow or reference them through a collection.

> The Repeater control only *presents* data—it doesn't allow users to edit or modify the actual data source. If you want to allow users to do this, you can use the DataList or DataGrid Web controls. They'll be examined in the next two sections.

DataList Server Control

The DataList control is very similar to the Repeater control, except that it allows user interaction and data modification. You can use this control with templates to list items just as you would with the Repeater. However, the DataList supports two additional types of templates:

- SelectedItemTemplate—This template contains additional elements that will be rendered only when the user selects an item in the Datalist control. Typical uses would be to change style properties to reflect a row selection, or to expand the item like a hierarchical listing (parent-child).
- EditItemTemplate—This template specifies the layout of an item when it's in edit mode.

Let's take a look at an example. Again, you'll be using the same Page_Load event you used yesterday and in Listing 9.8, so that code is omitted. Listing 9.10 shows the DataList control itself (note that you'll have to change line 22 to reference the new of the DataList control instead of the Repeater).

LISTING 9.10 A Typical DataList Control

```
<asp:DataList id="DataList1" runat="server"
   SelectedItemStyle-BackColor="#cccc99"
   repeatlayout="table"
   repeatdirection="horizontal"
   DataKeyField="UserID">

   <ItemTemplate>
      <asp:LinkButton id="button1" runat="server"
```

LISTING 9.10 continued

```
 9:          Text='<%# Container.DataItem("FirstName") & " " & _
10:             Container.DataItem("LastName") %>'
11:          CommandName="Select" />
12:       <p>
13:    </ItemTemplate>
14:
15:    <SelectedItemTemplate>
16:       <%# Container.DataItem("FirstName") & " " & _
17:          Container.DataItem("LastName") %><br>
18:       Phone:
19:       <%# Container.DataItem("Phone") %>
20:       <br>
21:       Address:
22:       <%# Container.DataItem("Address") %>
23:       <br>
24:       <%# Container.DataItem("City") %>,
25:       <%# Container.DataItem("State") %>
26:        <%# Container.DataItem("ZIP") %>
27:       <br>
28:    </SelectedItemTemplate>
29: </asp:DataList>
```

Note

Don't forget to enclose the `DataList` in `<form>` tags! Otherwise, the events you define for it won't do anything.

ANALYSIS On lines 1–5, you declare your `DataList` control using many of the properties for server controls that were discussed on Day 5. `SelectedItemStyle-BackColor` defines the background color for the `SelectedItemTemplate`, when it's visible. `DataKeyField` is the name of the field to use as the primary key of the data. This key will serve as a unique identifier and is helpful when you're identifying rows in your list.

In the item template beginning on line 7, you simply create a `LinkButton` control (line 8) that's bound to the `"FirstName"` and `"LastName"` data columns. When this link is clicked, it generates and passes the command `"Select"` to the `DataList`.

Finally, the selected item template simply displays some data-bound information. Whenever an item (or data row) is selected in the `DataList`, this template will be shown for that particular row. But first, you have to define the method to handle the link-clicks (see Listing 9.11).

LISTING 9.11 Handling Click Events for a `DataList`

```
sub DataList1_ItemCommand(Sender as object, e as _
   DataListCommandEventArgs)
   DataList1.SelectedIndex = e.Item.ItemIndex
   DataList1.DataBind()
end sub
```

Add this procedure to the code declaration block of Listing 9.10, and add the following property to the `DataList`:

```
OnItemCommand="DataList1_ItemCommand"
```

This procedure handles any events that are bubbled up to the `DataList` container control, including the `Click` event of the `LinkButton`. It takes a special type for the event arguments, `DataListCommandEventArgs`, which contains the following properties:

- `CommandArgument`—The argument property of the command
- `CommandName`—The name of the command
- `CommandSource`—Gets the source of the command
- `Item`—Gets the item selected in the `DataList`

The method you defined sets the `SelectedIndex` property of the `DataList` control to the item the user selected and calls the `Databind` method. When you click on one of the items in the `DataList`, the result is that the `SelectedItemTemplate` for the selected item is displayed, as shown in Figure 9.8.

Note that the `SelectedItemTemplate` will take the place of whatever is displayed for an item. In this case, you display the first and last names of your users. This is covered up when the preceding template is shown, so you simply repeat this information in the template, as shown on lines 16–17.

Editing Items

The `DataList` control also allows you to edit displayed items. It contains special commands that you can use to signal ASP.NET to put an item into edit mode. Listing 9.12 is a modification of Listing 9.10 that shows all the special commands available.

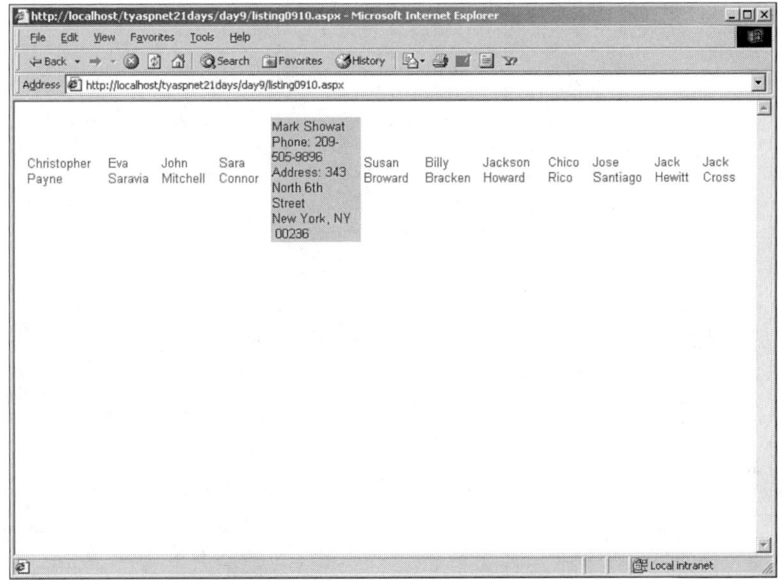

FIGURE 9.8
The results of the `DataList` *control.*

LISTING 9.12 Editing Selections in a `DataList`

```
<asp:DataList id="DataList1" runat="server"
   SelectedItemStyle-BackColor="#cccc99"
   repeatlayout="table"
   repeatdirection="horizontal"
   OnItemCommand="DataList1_ItemCommand"
   OnEditCommand="DataList1_EditCommand"
   OnCancelCommand="DataList1_CancelCommand"
   OnUpdateCommand="DataList1_UpdateCommand"
   OnDeleteCommand="DataList1_DeleteCommand"
    DataKeyField="UserID">

    <ItemTemplate>
       <asp:LinkButton id="button1" runat="server"
          Text='<%# Container.DataItem("FirstName") & _
             " " & Container.DataItem("LastName") %>'
          CommandName="Edit" />
       <p>
    </ItemTemplate>

    <EditItemTemplate>
       <asp:LinkButton id="lbtCancel" runat="server"
          CommandName="Cancel"
          Text="Cancel" />
```

LISTING 9.12 continued

```
24:         <asp:LinkButton id="lbtUpdate" runat="server"
25:            CommandName="Update"
26:            Text="Update" />
27:         <asp:LinkButton id="lbtDelete" runat="server"
28:            CommandName="Delete"
29:            Text="Delete" />
30:      </EditItemTemplate>
31:   </asp:DataList>
```

ANALYSIS This listing won't work yet. You have to define the methods to handle its events first—you'll get to that in a moment. When users click each item, a menu of choices will be displayed, thanks to the `EditItemTemplate` on line 20. Let's first examine the code in this listing.

On line 16, you change the `"Select"` command of the `Linkbutton` to `"Edit"`. This is a special command reserved by ASP.NET that automatically raises the `DataList`'s `EditCommand` event. You must then declare the handler for this event as follows:

```
sub DataList1_EditCommand(Sender as object, e as _
   DataListCommandEventArgs)
   DataList1.EditItemIndex = e.Item.ItemIndex
   DataList1.DataBind()
end sub
```

Add this method to the code declaration block. You simply set the `EditItemIndex` property of the `DataList` to the selected item, which then displays the `EditItemTemplate`, beginning on line 20, and turns on edit mode for that item. Typically, you allow an item to be put in edit mode to enable the user to edit fields, which in turn updates the data store. You'll examine this in more detail tomorrow. You built three new link buttons that contain three more special commands: `Cancel`, `Update`, and `Delete`. These link buttons are shown on lines 21–29. When these commands are bubbled up, they raise the `DataList`'s `CancelCommand`, `UpdateCommand`, and `DeleteCommand` commands, respectively. You build these handlers just as you did for `EditCommand`:

```
sub DataList1_CancelCommand(Sender as Object, e as _
   DataListCommandEventArgs)
   DataList1.EditItemIndex = -1
   DataList1.DataBind()
end sub

sub DataList1_UpdateCommand(Sender as Object, e as _
   DataListCommandEventArgs)
   ' update data store
   DataList1.DataBind()
end sub
```

```
sub DataList1_DeleteCommand(Sender as Object, e as _
   DataListCommandEventArgs)
   ' delete from data store
   DataList1.DataBind()
end sub
```

Add these methods to your code declaration block as well. To take an item out of edit mode, you simply set the `EditItemIndex` to `-1`. To actually update or delete data from the data store, you have to build methods manually. Remember to always call the `DataBind` method again, or else the `DataList` won't be updated to reflect any events or changes. Finally, you can view this listing from the browser now that all your event handlers are defined. Figure 9.9 shows what happens when you click on an item and turn on edit mode.

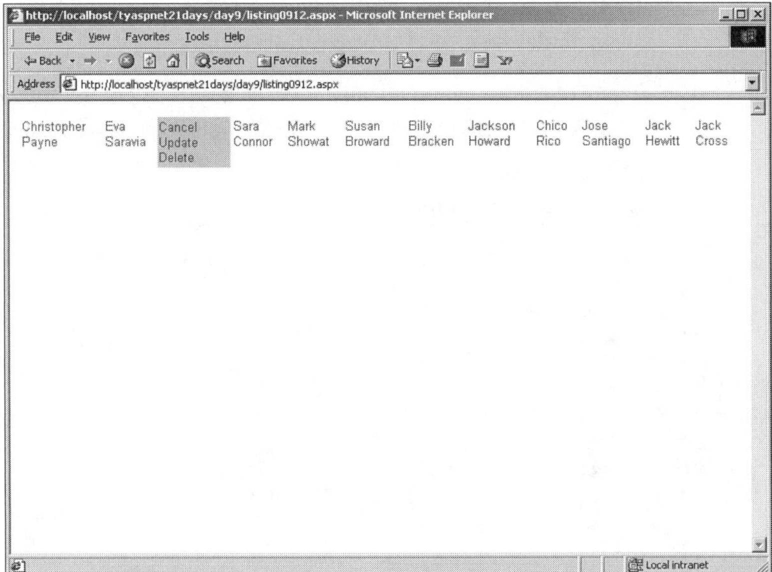

FIGURE 9.9
Placing an item in edit mode.

Clicking on the `Update` and `Delete` buttons currently doesn't do anything, but clicking on `Cancel` takes the item out of edit mode and places it in select mode. This produces a figure similar to Figure 9.8.

`DataGrid` Server Control

The `DataGrid` control is similar to both the `DataList` and `Repeater` controls, except that it provides even more functionality. This control uses columns to display data in a grid layout. By default, the `DataGrid` generates a column for every field in the data store.

However, you can specify the fields to display manually, as well as how to display them. You can define the following types of columns:

- Bound columns—These allow you to specify which columns to display and in what order, and allow you to format style attributes. These columns are the default used by the `DataGrid`.
- Button columns—These columns display buttons for all the items on the grid, for which you may define custom functionality. A typical example is an Add to Shopping Cart button.
- Edit command columns—Allow you to edit items. Replace all bound columns with modifiable fields.
- Hyperlink columns—Display data as hyperlinks.
- Templated columns—You can use templates, as with `Repeater` and `DataList` controls, to define custom formats for the columns.

The `DataGrid` control automatically chooses a type of column based on the data being presented, but it's easy enough to change the default behavior. Listing 9.13 shows an example.

LISTING 9.13 `DataGrid` Example

```
<asp:DataGrid id="DataGrid1" runat="server"
   BorderColor="black"
   GridLines="Vertical"
   cellpadding="4"
   cellspacing="0"
   width="450"
   Font-Names="Arial"
   Font-Size="8pt"
   ShowFooter="True"
    HeaderStyle-BackColor="#cccc99"
    FooterStyle-BackColor="#cccc99"
    ItemStyle-BackColor="#ffffff"
    AlternatingItemStyle-Backcolor="#cccccc"
    AutoGenerateColumns="False">

    < Columns>

       <asp:TemplateColumn HeaderText="Name">
          <template name="ItemTemplate">
             <asp:Label id="Name" runat="server"
                Text='<%# Container.DataItem("FirstName")& _
                " " & Container.DataItem("LastName") %>'/>
          </template>
       </asp:TemplateColumn>

       <asp:BoundColumn HeaderText="Address"
```

LISTING 9.13 continued

```
            DataField="Address"/>

        <asp:BoundColumn HeaderText="City" DataField="City"/>

        <asp:BoundColumn HeaderText="State"
            DataField="State" />

        <asp:BoundColumn HeaderText="Zip" DataField="Zip" />

        <asp:HyperlinkColumn HeaderText="Edit" text="Edit"
            NavigateURL="edit.aspx"/>

        <asp:ButtonColumn HeaderText="Delete?" text="X"
            CommandName="delete"
            ButtonType="PushButton"/>

    </Column>

</asp:DataGrid>
```

Listing 9.13 demonstrates the various properties of the `DataGrid` and how to create your own columns for the data. Using the same `Page_Load` event as Listing 9.10 (with the name changed from the `ListBox` to the `DataGrid`) produces the result shown in Figure 9.10.

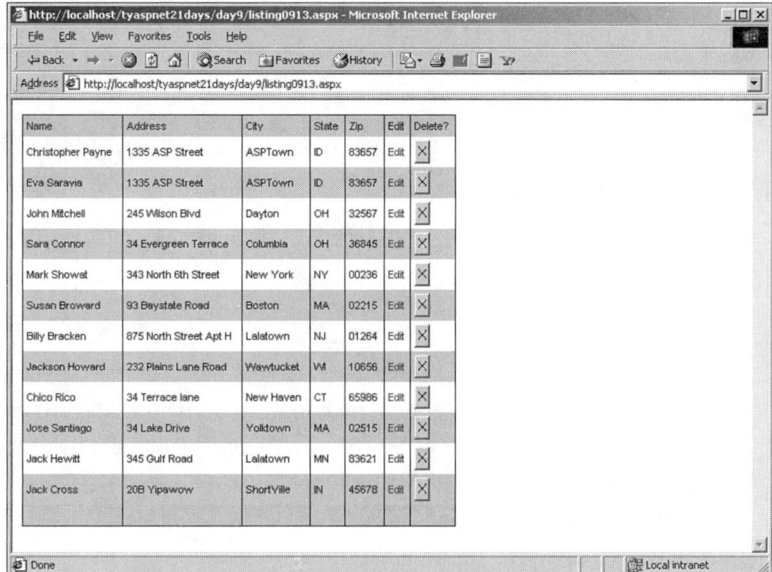

FIGURE 9.10

The `DataGrid` *control in action.*

ANALYSIS This control has a lot of properties you can manipulate. Lines 2–13 simply set up properties that you should already be familiar with. Line 14 tells this `DataGrid` that you want to set up your own columns, which you'll proceed to do in the next section. If you set `AutoGenerateColumns=True`, the `DataGrid` would generate its own columns and you wouldn't have to specify custom ones. `AutoGenerateColumns` causes the `DataGrid` to use all data source columns available, so you might prefer to define your own columns; by doing so, you can limit what the user sees.

> **Note**
>
> If you set `AutoGenerateColumns=True` and still provide custom column definitions, the `DataGrid` will render both. It will display all columns plus the additional ones you define. This means you could end up with multiple copies of the same column. For example, using Listing 9.13 but changing `AutoGenerateColumns` to `true` on line 14 generates Figure 9.11.

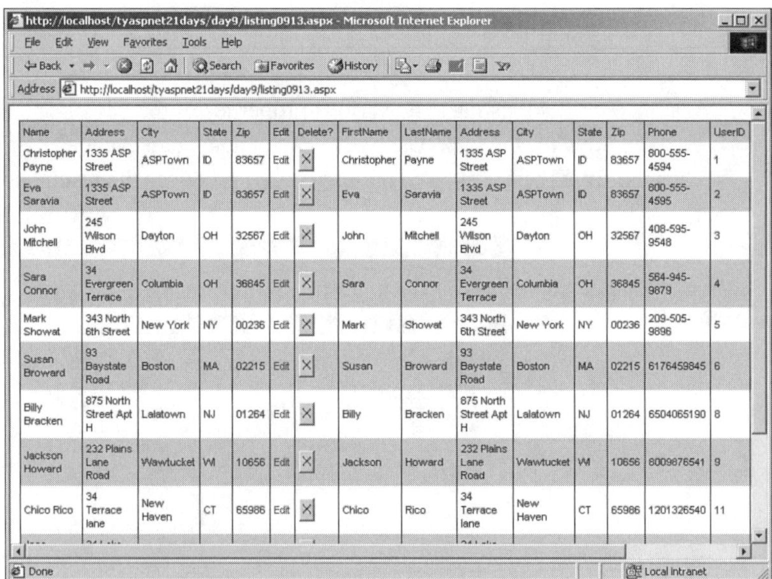

Name	Address	City	State	Zip	Edit	Delete?	FirstName	LastName	Address	City	State	Zip	Phone	UserID
Christopher Payne	1335 ASP Street	ASPTown	ID	83657	Edit	X	Christopher	Payne	1335 ASP Street	ASPTown	ID	83657	800-555-4594	1
Eva Saravia	1335 ASP Street	ASPTown	ID	83657	Edit	X	Eva	Saravia	1335 ASP Street	ASPTown	ID	83657	800-555-4595	2
John Mitchell	245 Wilson Blvd	Dayton	OH	32567	Edit	X	John	Mitchell	245 Wilson Blvd	Dayton	OH	32567	408-595-9548	3
Sara Connor	34 Evergreen Terrace	Columbia	OH	36845	Edit	X	Sara	Connor	34 Evergreen Terrace	Columbia	OH	36845	564-945-9879	4
Mark Showat	343 North 6th Street	New York	NY	00236	Edit	X	Mark	Showat	343 North 6th Street	New York	NY	00236	209-505-9896	5
Susan Broward	93 Baystate Road	Boston	MA	02215	Edit	X	Susan	Broward	93 Baystate Road	Boston	MA	02215	6176459845	6
Billy Bracken	875 North Street Apt H	Lalatown	NJ	01264	Edit	X	Billy	Bracken	875 North Street Apt H	Lalatown	NJ	01264	6504065190	8
Jackson Howard	232 Plains Lane Road	Wawtucket	WI	10656	Edit	X	Jackson	Howard	232 Plains Lane Road	Wawtucket	WI	10656	8009876541	9
Chico Rico	34 Terrace lane	New Haven	CT	65986	Edit	X	Chico	Rico	34 Terrace lane	New Haven	CT	65986	1201326540	11

FIGURE 9.11
`AutoGenerateColumns=True` *causes all columns to be displayed, plus the custom columns you've defined.*

To define your custom columns, you must add them to the `Columns` collection of the `DataGrid` control. This can be done either programmatically at run-time or at design time, as you've done here. Using the `<Columns>` tag, you start defining the custom columns on line 16.

`TemplateColumn`, `HyperlinkColumn`, `BoundColumn`, and `ButtonColumn` are all ASP.NET controls used specifically for the `DataGrid` control. In Figure 9.10, you saw the output of the different types of columns. These columns are fairly simple and only contain a few properties you haven't seen yet. The `BoundColumn` control uses the `DataField` property to bind to a column in your data store. The `ButtonColumn` control displays a `LinkButton` control by default, but you can use the `ButtonType` property to specify a different type, as shown on line 41. The `HyperLink` column on line 36 simply redirects to a different page (note that unless you've created the file `edit.aspx`, this link won't work).

Feel free to play with the settings on the `DataGrid`. You'll find that this control is very useful for displaying data from databases, and it allows you to customize nearly every aspect of its display.

Editing Items

The `DataGrid` control also makes it easy to allow users to edit entries. Simply create an `EditCommandColumn`, and ASP.NET handles much of the display mechanism on its own. Let's modify Listing 9.13 a bit to include an edit command column. See Listing 9.14.

LISTING 9.14 `DataGrid` Example with Editable Columns

```
<asp:DataGrid id="DataGrid1" runat="server"
   ...
   ...
   AutoGenerateColumns="False"
   OnEditCommand="DataGrid1_Edit"
   OnCancelCommand="DataGrid1_Cancel"
   OnUpdateCommand="DataGrid1_Update" >

   <Columns>

    ...
    ...

    <asp:EditCommandColumn
       EditText="Edit"
       CancelText="Cancel"
       UpdateText="Update"
       ItemStyle-Wrap="false"
       HeaderText="Edit" />

    </property>

</asp:DataGrid>
```

ANALYSIS Because you've created a new `EditCommandColumn`, you can delete the previous `HyperlinkColumn` on line 36 of Listing 9.13. You can also remove the delete `ButtonColumn` on line 39 because the `EditCommandColumn` will add one for you. Leaving everything else the same, you tell the `DataGrid` which methods will handle its `Edit`, `Cancel`, and `Update` events on lines 5–7. On line 14, you declare your `EditCommandColumn`, which will display a `LinkButton` with the text "Edit". When the user clicks this link, you enter edit mode for the selected item, and each bound column changes to a text box that the user can modify. Figure 9.12 shows what happens when you click this new Edit button.

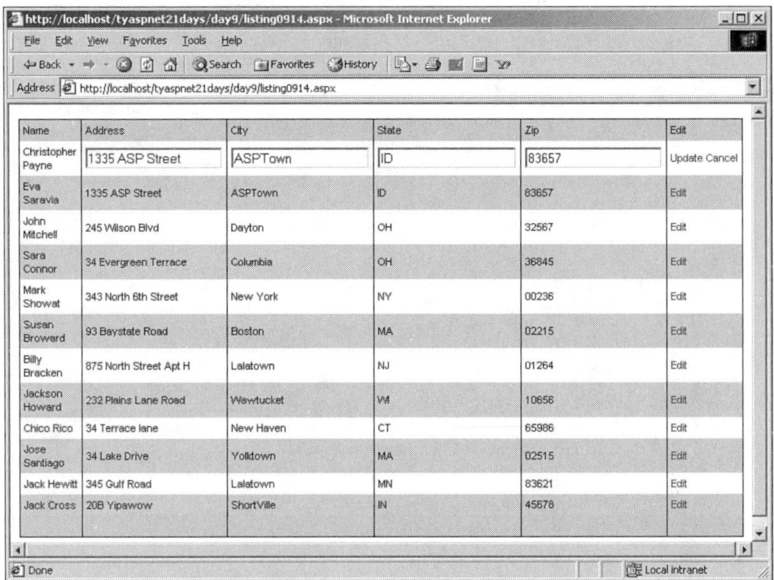

FIGURE 9.12

The `EditCommandColumn` *allows you to modify bound columns in a* `DataGrid`.

> **Note** Only `BoundColumns` change into modifiable fields! The rest, such as `TemplateColumns`, retain their original interface. Make sure that any columns you want the user to edit either are `BoundColumns` or contain textboxes for editing.

`EditCommandColumn` also automatically displays the Update and Cancel links. You can define methods to handle these events as well:

```
sub DataGrid1_Edit(Sender as object, e as DataGridCommandEventArgs)
   DataGrid1.EditItemIndex = e.Item.ItemIndex
   DataGrid1.DataBind()
end sub
```

```
sub DataGrid1_Update(Sender as object, e as DataGridCommandEventArgs)
   'do updates
   DataGrid1.DataBind()
end sub

sub DataGrid1_Cancel(Sender as object, e as DataGridCommandEventArgs)
   DataGrid1.EditItemIndex = -1
   DataGrid1.DataBind()
end sub
```


These methods are similar to those for the `DataList` control.

Sorting

The `DataGrid` control doesn't have intrinsic support for sorting data rows, but it enables you to build such functionality by providing built-in events and displays. When you turn sorting on, by default the `DataGrid` turns every column header into a `LinkButton` that users may click to sort by that column. You'll have to build your own sorting mechanism, but at least ASP.NET provides you with the basics. You can also specify custom sorting, in which you define the columns that the user can sort by, and even provide custom sorting links.

To turn sorting on, simply add `AllowSorting="true"` to the declaration of the `DataGrid`. Then build a method named `SortCommand` to handle the sorting events:

```
sub DataGrid1_SortCommand(Sender as Object, _
                 e as DataGridSortCommandEventArgs)
   ' sort the data using the SortField property
   '  of the eventargs
   DataGrid1.DataBind()
End Sub
```

The `SortField` property of the `DataGridSortCommandEventArgs` parameter tells you which column was clicked. You can use this information to sort your data accordingly, whether by sorting a `DataView` (which will be covered tomorrow) or by changing your SQL command. You'll look at sorting data programmatically in much more detail tomorrow.

> If you want to use the default sorting mechanism, you must allow the `DataGrid` to generate its columns automatically—set `AutoGenerateColumns=True`. Otherwise, sorting won't work as expected. Figure 9.13 shows an example of turning on sorting with `AutoGenerateColumns=True`.

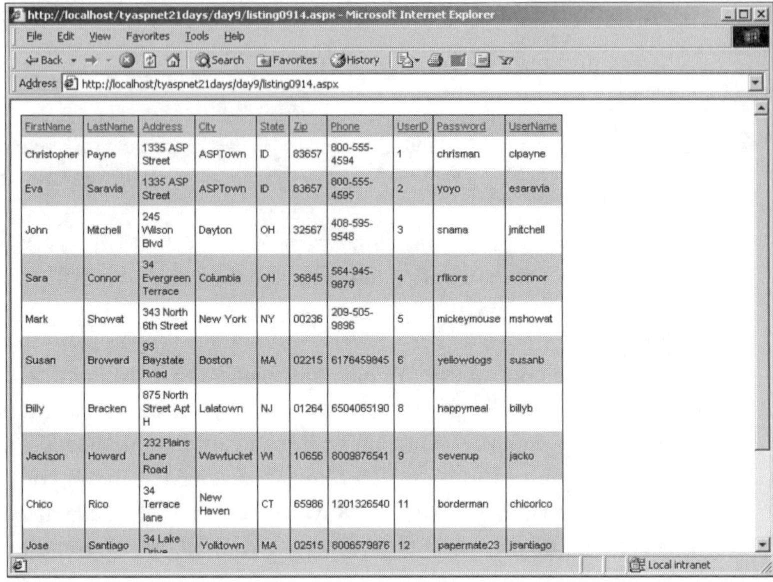

FIGURE 9.13

When `AllowSorting=True`, *all headers turn into links to sort by.*

To use custom sorting, turn on sorting and specify a `SortField` for each column that you want to make sortable. For example, if you want to allow users to sort the list by address, you could use the following code:

```
<asp:BoundColumn HeaderText="Address" DataField="Address"
   sortField="Address" />
```

Paging

Paging is the capability of the `DataGrid` to divide the data into multiple pages if there are too many records to display on one page. This was once a complex task that developers had to build themselves, but ASP.NET now handles it for you.

When paging is set up, ASP.NET divides the returned results into the number of pages you specify and provides buttons for the user to navigate the list. It then uses the `CurrentPageIndex` property of the `DataGrid` to determine which page should be displayed currently. When the user clicks on a button to go to the next page, the entire data set is re-created and the process starts over. This can result in long load times for your pages if you have large amounts of data. Therefore, the `DataGrid` control allows you to define custom paging procedures, which may not suffer from such conditions.

To turn paging on, set `AllowPaging=True` (this is true by default), and set the `PageSize` property to the number of records you want to display at once. You can also specify the style of the paging buttons to display by using the `PagerStyle` property. The two built-in styles are the Next and Previous buttons and the numeric page numbers. Let's modify the previous listing to include paging, shown in Listing 9.15.

LISTING 9.15 Adding Paging Capabilities to the `DataGrid`

```
1:  sub DataGrid1_PageIndexChanged(Sender as Object,
➥e as DataGridPageChangedEventArgs)
2:     DataGrid1.CurrentPageIndex = e.NewPageIndex
3:     DataGrid1.DataBind()
4:  end sub
5:  ...
6:  ...
7:  <asp:DataGrid id="DataGrid1" runat="server"
8:     ...
9:     AllowPaging="true"
10:     PageSize=2
11:     PagerStyle-Mode=NumericPages
12:     PagerStyle-PageButtonCount = 2
13:     OnPageIndexChanged="DataGrid1_PageIndexChanged" >
```

You first define a new method, `DataGrid1_PageIndexChanged`, to handle the paging events. The `DataGrid` won't automatically change the page for you, so you have to do so yourself as shown on line 2. The `DataGridPageChangedEventArgs` contains the property `NewPageIndex`, which tells you the page number the user has clicked on. Simply set the `DataGrid`'s `CurrentPageIndex` to this value, rebind the data to the control, and ASP.NET handles the rest.

In your `DataGrid` control, you add five new properties. Line 9 turns paging on (this is the default), and line 10 specifies that you want to display two records per page. Line 11 sets the paging mode to display numeric page numbers. This property can be either `"NumericPages"` or `"NextPrev"`, which display the next and previous buttons. On line 12, you tell the grid to only display two page-navigation numbers at once—this property is only valid if the mode is `NumericPages`. If there are more pages than this value, the user will see a clickable ellipsis. Finally, you declare the handler for the `PageIndexChanged` event. Figure 9.14 shows the paging features in action.

If you don't want to use the built-in paging buttons, you can create custom ones. Simply set the `PagerStyle-Visible` property to false and place your own buttons where you like (for instance, in the header or footer). You'll have to create your own navigation methods to handle these events as well—move between pages by changing the `CurrentPageIndex` property in your code.

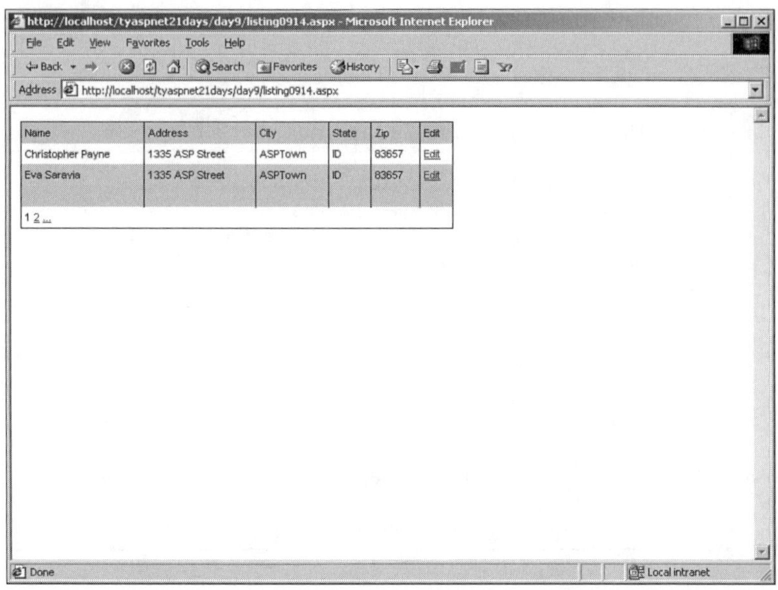

FIGURE 9.14 *Paging with the* `DataGrid` *control.*

The `DataGrid` also allows you to use manual paging for tighter control over the process. This involves getting deeper into the mechanisms of ADO.NET, so we'll leave this topic for tomorrow.

Summary of Data Binding Controls

Now you know why you skipped over these three controls on Day 5—they're quite complex! These controls make it very easy to display dynamic data using any type of data source, which was once one of the greatest difficulties facing ASP developers.

With so many options, and with all the controls sharing a lot of the same features, it may be confusing to decide which one to use and where. Table 9.2 summarizes the options and provides suggestions on which controls to use in your situation.

TABLE 9.2 Summary of Data Binding ASP.NET Server Controls

Control	*Features/When to Use*
`Repeater`	Simple, read-only output with no inherent support for selecting or editing.
	No inherent look; must be defined manually using templates.
	No inherent paging mechanism.

TABLE 9.2 continued

Control	*Features/When to Use*
	You should use this control when you only have very simple data to display. This control is very helpful for use with one-dimensional arrays and collections, and it's highly efficient and lightweight for use just about anywhere.
`DataList`	Provides a default, customizable table display.
	Editable content.
	Single and multiple selections.
	Optional multiple columns.
	Paging not inherent.
	A more advanced version of the `Repeater`, this control provides more functionality, allowing you to select and edit items. Use this control if you need to display simple data that may require user interaction, or for any two-dimensional data in general. A typical use would be to display a Windows Explorer–type file hierarchy.
`DataGrid`	Provides a default, extensively customizable grid display.
	Editable content, including deletion.
	Single and multiple selections.
	Paging supported inherently.
	Support for customized functionality.
	This control is the powerhouse of the list controls. It provides a full-featured set of display capabilities, complete customization capabilities, and powerful paging, sorting, and editing functionality. Use this control when you want to allow user interaction with the data, or when you need its data organizing power. Usually recommended for data from complex databases. A typical use for this control would be as part of a shopping cart in an e-commerce application where users can update, remove, and add items directly.
	It might seem like a good idea to use this control all the time, but it carries a lot of overhead and might not be ideal for situations requiring small, fast display.

Let's build an example to solidify your understanding of data binding and these controls. You'll build a simple `DataGrid` application that sets its background colors to values stored in a `DataSet`—a “row colorizer,” if you will. This may not sound like much, but it encapsulates a lot of what you learned today. Figure 9.15 shows you what this sample should look like.

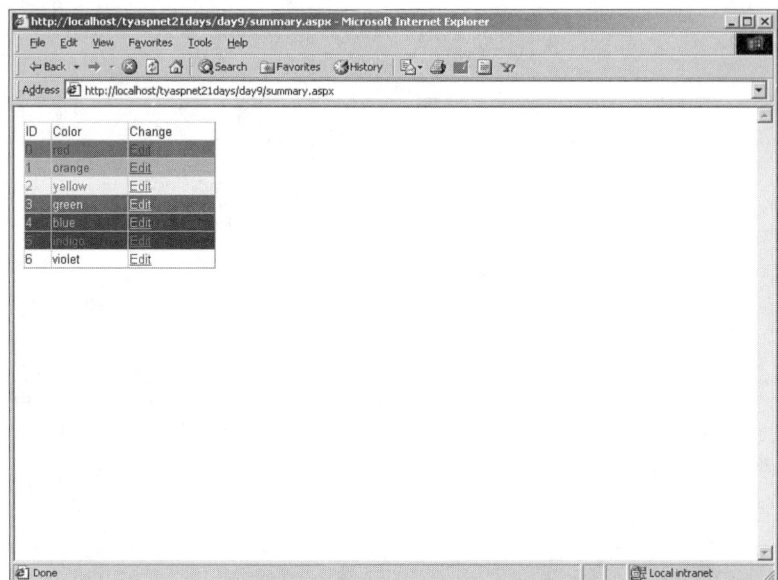

FIGURE 9.15

Your completed Row Colorizer application.

The first step is figuring out how you’re going to get your data. Let’s use a custom `DataSet` so you don’t have to deal with any databases just yet. You can use this `DataSet` to fill your `DataGrid`. Let’s examine the code that creates the `DataSet`. Listing 9.16 shows a method that you’ll be adding to in a moment.

LISTING 9.16 Creating Your `DataSet` with the Colors of the Rainbow

```
function CreateDataSet as DataSet
   'create an array of colors
   dim i as integer
   dim arrColors() as String
   if ViewState("Colors") is nothing then
      arrColors = new String(7) {"red", "orange", _
         "yellow", "green", "blue", "indigo", "violet"}
      ViewState("Colors") = arrColors
   else
       arrColors = ViewState("Colors")
    end if

    'create an empty dataset
```

LISTING 9.16 continued

```
14:      ds = new DataSet("MyDataSet")
15:
16:      'create a new table and columns
17:      dim dTable as New DataTable("Colors")
18:      dTable.Columns.Add("Color", GetType(String))
19:      dTable.Columns.Add("ID", GetType(Int32))
20:      'add table
21:      ds.Tables.Add(dTable)
22:
23:      'add rows
24:      for i = 0 to 6
25:         dim dr as DataRow = dTable.NewRow()
26:         dr(0) = arrColors(i).ToString
27:         dr(1) = i
28:         dTable.Rows.Add(dr)
29:      next
30:
31:      return ds
32:   end function
```

Save this listing in the file `summary.aspx`, in the code declaration block (you'll be adding other methods and UI elements to this file shortly). This should look similar to Listing 9.1—the first `DataSet` you built today. You're using the colors of the rainbow (red, orange, yellow, green, blue, indigo, violet) for your data.

Look at lines 5–11. It might look scary, but don't worry: It's not! Imagine a typical situation with the row colorizer. A user visits the page and sees several rows in a `DataGrid`, all different colors. These colors are stored in an array you've created. Each time the page loads, the array is created anew and the `DataGrid` uses it to set the colors. Then the user tries to edit the colors in the grid, and changes the first row to blue instead of red. However, the result won't be as expected. When the user submits the form again, the array will be created anew, and the `DataGrid` will use it instead of the new value. This is because the `Page_Load` event, which is responsible for creating the array, executes *before* the method that handles the `DataGrid`'s update event. Therefore, your update method doesn't add new data; it only reinserts the old. Figure 9.16 illustrates this process.

You might be wondering whether you could just *not* bind the data in step 4. Wouldn't that solve the problem? Unfortunately, no. If the data is not bound, the `DataGrid` won't contain any data, and subsequent methods won't be able to access the values. Consequently, not binding the data in step 4 would cause an error to occur.

FIGURE 9.16

Your update event won't receive the correct data.

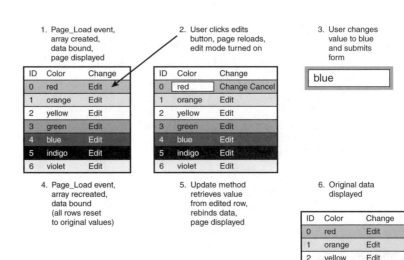

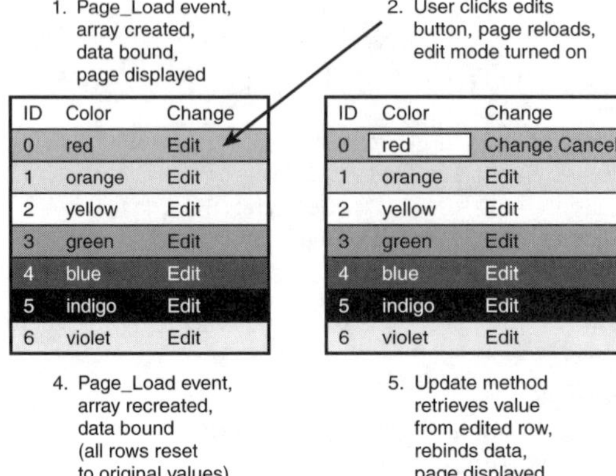

Therefore, you need to store your color array in a place where it won't be reinitialized to the original values each time the page is submitted. The state bag is the answer (see Day 5, "Beginning Web Forms," for more information). The first time you create your array, you store it in the state bag. Subsequent page loads and method calls will now refer to this array, which is initialized only once. Your update method can modify values in the array in the state bag, and everything will work beautifully. Let's look at the code, and this will make more sense.

Line 5 checks whether there is already an array in the state bag. If there isn't—as should be the case upon first viewing of the page—you instantiate your array on lines 6 and 7. If the state bag already contains an array, meaning that the array was already created (and perhaps modified), you simply retrieve it. On lines 13–29, you create a `DataSet` and add `DataTables` and the information from the array to it. You should be familiar with this task by now. Rather than creating seven rows manually, you instantiate an array with the values on line 2 and use a `for` loop to add them to the `DataSet`, as shown on lines 24–29.

Finally, you return the `DataSet` to whatever method called this function. Presumably, this calling method will bind the `DataSet` to the `DataGrid`.

Let's take a look at the declaration for the `DataGrid`, shown in Listing 9.17.

Listing 9.17 Your Rainbow `DataGrid`

```
<html><body>
   <form runat="server">
      <ASP:DataGrid id="dgColors" runat="server"
         AutogenerateColumns="false"
         width="200"
         OnEditCommand="dgColors_Edit"
         OnCancelCommand="dgColors_Cancel"
         OnUpdateCommand="dgColors_Update"
         OnItemCreated="ChangeColor" >

          <Columns>
             <asp:templateColumn headertext="ID">
                <ItemTemplate>
                   <asp:Label id="lblID" runat="server"
                     Text='<%# Container.DataItem("ID") %>'/>
                </ItemTemplate>
             </asp:templatecolumn>

             <asp:BoundColumn datafield="Color"
                headertext="Color" />

             <asp:EditCommandColumn headertext="Change"
                EditText="Edit"
                UpdateText="Change"
                CancelText="Cancel" />
           </Columns>
       </ASP:DataGrid>
    </form>
 </body></html>
```

Add this listing to the end of `summary.aspx`. This is a standard `DataGrid` with handlers defined for the `Edit`, `Cancel`, `Update`, and `ItemCreated` events. Note that the second column, the `BoundColumn`, contains the color from the `DataSet` that will be editable. The `EditCommandColumn` will automatically display all the links to allow the user to edit, update, and cancel. Listing 9.18 shows the rest of the code declaration block for this page.

Listing 9.18 The Completed `summary.aspx`

```
<%@ Page Language="VB" %>
<%@ Import Namespace="System.Data" %>
<%@ Import Namespace="System.Data.OleDb" %>

<script runat="server">
   dim ds as DataSet
```

LISTING 9.18 continued

```
dim blnSet as Boolean = false

sub Page_Load(Semder as Object, e as EventArgs)
   ds = CreateDataSet
   blnSet = true
   if not Page.IsPostBack then
      BindGrid
   end if
end sub

sub BindGrid()
   dgColors.DataSource = ds
   dgColors.DataMember = "Colors"
   DataBind()
end sub

sub ChangeColor(Sender as object, e as DataGridItemEventargs)
   dim intIndex as Integer = e.Item.ItemIndex

   if blnSet then
      if intIndex > -1 then
         e.Item.BackColor = Drawing.Color.FromName _
            (ds.Tables("Colors"). _
            Rows(intIndex)("Color"))
         e.Item.ForeColor = Drawing.Color.FromName _
            (ds.Tables("Colors"). _
            Rows(6-intIndex)("Color"))
      end if
   end if
end sub

sub dgColors_Edit(Sender as object, e as DataGridCommandEventargs)
   dgColors.EditItemIndex = e.Item.ItemIndex
   BindGrid
end sub

sub dgColors_Cancel(Sender as object, e as DataGridCommandEventargs)
   dgColors.EditItemIndex = -1
   BindGrid()
end sub

sub dgColors_Update(Sender as object, e as DataGridCommandEventargs)
   dim strColor as String = Ctype(e.Item.Cells(1). _
      Controls(0), TextBox).Text

   ds.Tables("Colors").Rows(e.Item.ItemIndex) _
      ("Color") = strColor
   ViewState("Colors")(e.Item.ItemIndex) = strColor
```

LISTING 9.18 continued

```
55:
56:         dgColors.EditItemIndex = -1
57:         BindGrid
58:     end sub
59: </script>
```


This listing contains all the code for `summary.aspx` except the HTML and `CreateDataSet` function. On lines 6–7, you declare two variables that will be used throughout your page: a `DataSet` and a Boolean value, which you'll get to in a moment. The `Page_Load` method, beginning on line 9, fills the `DataGrid` from line 6 with data from the `CreateDataSet` function. If the page has not been posted back on itself, the controls on the page are bound with a custom function, `BindGrid`, which you'll examine soon.

This method also does one more thing: It sets the `blnSet` variable to `true`. This variable tells you when the data has been created—it is initially set to `false` on line 7 because the `CreateDataSet` method hasn't been executed. After this method executes, you set this variable to `true`. You'll come back to it in a moment.

Next, on line 17, is the `BindGrid` method, which simply assigns the `DataSource` and `DataMember` properties of the `DataGrid` and calls `DataBind`.

Let's examine the methods on lines 38, 43, and 48 before returning to the `ChangeColor` method on line 23. The first two methods, `dgColors_Edit` and `dbColors_Cancel`, simply set the turn on and off edit mode, and rebind the data. The first method sets the `EditItemIndex` property to the item the user selected, whereas the second method sets it to `-1` to turn off edit mode. The data is then rebound so that the changes will take effect.

The `dgColors_Update` method on line 48 is a bit more complex. First, you grab the changed value from the event arguments of the `DataGrid` on line 49. The value is stored in the first control, in the second cell of each row, written as `Item.Cells(1).Controls(0)`. Because this returns a generic object, you must cast it as a text box and then use the `Text` property to grab the value. On line 52, you update the value stored in the corresponding row of the `DataSet`. Literally, `ds.Tables("Colors").Rows(e.Item.ItemIndex)("Color")` means the value stored in the `"Color"` field at the data row corresponding to the row the user selected on the `DataGrid`, in the table `"Colors"`, in the variable `ds`, which happens to be your `DataSet`. (That's long-winded, but it proceeds in a logical manner.) You set this value to the changed value from the `DataGrid`, and do the same thing for the array of colors you've stored in the state bag on line 54. This is so that the next time the `DataGrid` is created, it will use the updated value instead of the original one. Then you take the item out of edit mode, and finally rebind the `DataGrid`.

Now the changes that users make to the values will be persisted, but you're not done yet! You have to color each row according to the corresponding value in the `DataSet`. To do this, you'll use the `Item_Created` event of the `DataGrid`, which fires immediately before every item on the grid is created. The event handler for this method is described next.

The `ChangeColor` method on line 23 is executed every time a new row is created in the `DataGrid`. Therefore, with seven items in the colors array, this method will be executed at least seven times each time the page is requested. Line 24 retrieves the index number of the row in the `DataGrid` in question, for easier access later. Lines 26–35 are responsible for changing the color of each row to the corresponding value in the `DataSet`. There are a few caveats to this section, so let's examine it more closely.

On line 26, you examine the `blnSet` variable again. The reason is simple: Recall that this variable indicates whether or not the `DataSet` has been created. The code on lines 27–34 accesses rows in the `DataSet`, and if the `DataSet` hasn't been created yet, you'll have some problems. Therefore, you must check whether the data is ready for access.

Wait a second. Doesn't the `Page_Load` method *always* execute before this event? And isn't the `Page_Load` method responsible for creating the data? In that case, theoretically, the data should always be created before the `ChangeColor` method executes, so why the check? Normally, this would be true, but `DataGrids` aren't average server controls—they do things a bit differently.

When you first view a `DataGrid`, or when you click on the Edit button, things work the same as with other server controls: The `Page_Load` method executes first, followed by event handlers in no particular order, including the handler for the `ItemCreated` event. At this stage, you won't have any problems. However, when you click the Update, Cancel, or Delete button, the data in the `DataGrid` is bound again *before* the `Page_Load` method executes. This means that, in this case, the `ChangeColor` method executes seven times before the `Page_Load` method executes and creates the `DataSet`. During these seven executions, you can't access the data because it hasn't been created yet. Thus, the check on `blnSet` on line 26 is to handle just this scenario. Using some well-placed `Response.Write` methods, Figures 9.17 and 9.18 show the order of execution when the edit and cancel command buttons have been clicked, respectively.

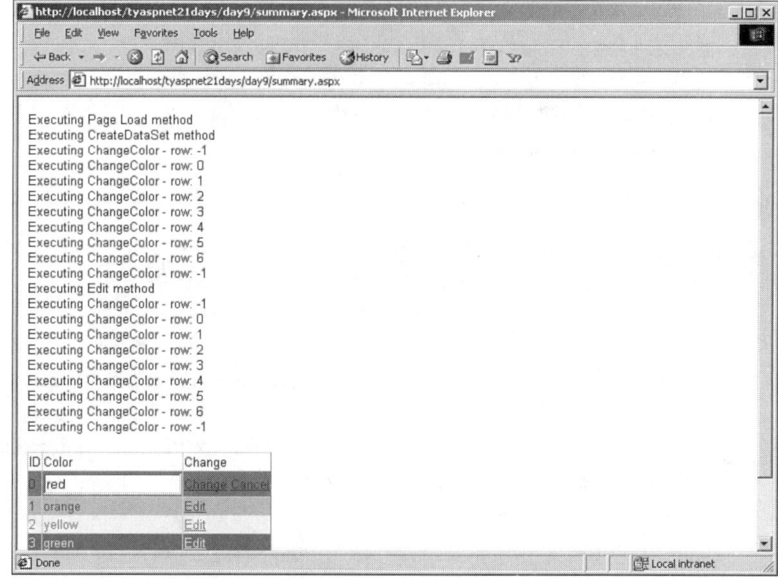

FIGURE 9.17 *With the edit method, the* `Page_Load` *method executes first.*

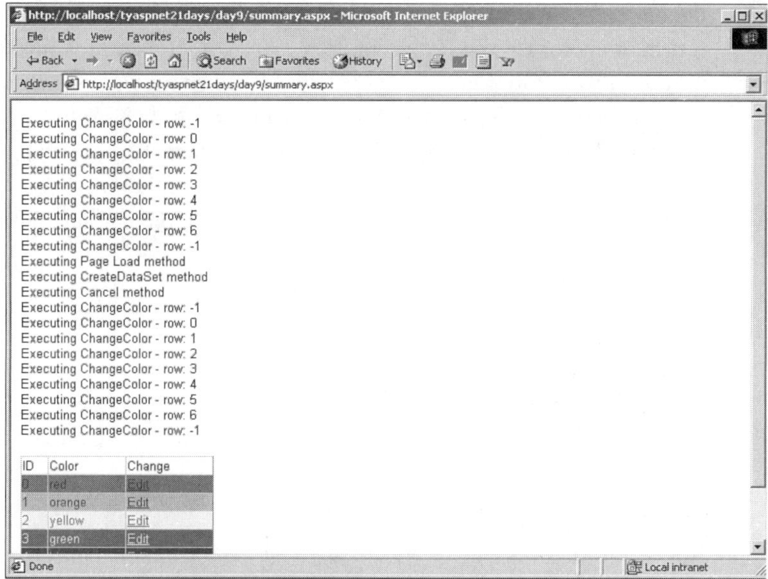

FIGURE 9.18 *With the cancel, update, and delete commands, the data is rebound before the* `Page_Load` *event.*

Let's move onto line 27. This check ensures that you are manipulating valid items in the `DataGrid`—you'll examine this in more detail later. Line 28 sets the background color for each row in the `DataGrid` using the `BackColor` property. Essentially, what you want to do is grab the color stored in the row that the user has selected. Unfortunately, the process isn't as simple as it sounds because the `BackColor` property accepts only a `System.Drawing.Color` object, and the value in the data store is a string. Therefore, you must cast appropriately. Unfortunately, you cannot cast directly from a string to a color—you have to go about it in a different way.

> **Note**
>
> `e.Item.ItemIndex` will return `-1` for headers and footers, and the corresponding index number for all other rows.

The `Color` object has a method, `FromName`, that takes a string that represents a valid color name, such as `"Red"` or `"Green"`. It will convert this string into a `Color` object for you. Therefore, on line 29, you pass the `FromName` method the color name stored in your `DataSet`, and get back a valid `Color` object. Now you have your color for the row that the user selected. On line 28, you set the `BackColor` property of the current row (represented by the `DataGridItemEventArgs.Item` property) to that color.

When you view this output, the words tend to blend into this colored background, so you decide to change the foreground color as well. On lines 31–33, you do the same thing to return the color for the foreground. You know that a contrasting color will show up well, so you use the formula `6 - ItemIndex` to return the composite color. (Note that you also could have used `e.Item.Count - e.Item.ItemIndex`, but because you know the count and it will never change, you hard-code the value.) You set the foreground color on line 31, and you're done! You now have a beautiful rainbow-colored `DataGrid` (shown in Figure 9.12) that users can manipulate. They can change the values in the data store, and the corresponding row's color change as well.

> **Note**
>
> If you specify a color not contained in the `Color` object, such as `"bluegreen-violet"` or `"reddd"`, the application will throw an error. Later, you might want to add a routine to verify that the user's entry is an actual color by using the `IsKnownColor` method of the `Color` object.

Let's examine this code a bit further. The `ItemCreated` event fires *before* an item is actually created. You can verify this by examining `DataGrid1.Items.Count` during the `ChangeColor` method. This property returns the actual number of items in the grid. The first value it returns, which is when the `ItemCreated` event fires for the first time, is 0.

Therefore, you can't actually set the color of the row during the `ItemCreated` event because it hasn't been created yet. Trying to do so using the following syntax will produce an error:

```
dgColors.Items(intIndex).BackColor = whatever
```

Going strictly by the index value to determine which row was created won't be accurate—especially because it returns `-1` twice in this example. This is the reason for the `if` statement on line 27 in Listing 9.18: You want to make sure that you don't try to set the color for a row that isn't even there.

However, the `ChangeColor` method knows which row we're currently working on, whether or not it has actually been created. That's why the code on lines 28–33 works; ASP.NET is smart enough to give you a reference to the row even though the event fired before the row is created. This bit of information isn't critical to know, but it may help if you ever come across this situation.

That's Not ASP!

Today's lesson illustrates two of the greatest improvements of ASP.NET over classic ASP: the `DataSet` and data binding. The first is somewhat similar to the older `Recordset` object, but provides much more functionality. It can represent complete sets of data, including relationships between tables and hierarchical data sets.

Data binding allows you to easily display content in your pages. In classic ASP, you had to manually loop through any data store, such as the `Recordset` shown in the following code snippet:

```
<%
   Do While Not objRS.EOF
      Response.write "<B>" & objRS("FirstName") & " " & _
         objRS("LastName") & "</B><BR>" & _
         objRS("Address")  & "<BR>" & objRS("City") & _
         "<BR>" & objRS("State") &"<BR>"& objRS("Zip") & _
         objRS("Phone") & "<P><HR><P>"
      objRS.Movenext
   Loop
%>
```

Developers had to build the code to handle the display as well as the HTML for it. Thus, code and UI elements were interspersed together throughout a page, which was prone to error and often led to confusion (this problem was known as *spaghetti code*).

With data binding and server controls, that is no longer necessary. These controls will automatically loop through any object that can be iterated, such as a `DataSet`, array, or even other listing server controls! In addition, they provide a plethora of capabilities to control the display of the data.

After you've experienced data binding and the listing server controls, you'll wonder how you ever got by without them! They can easily cut you development time in half, at the same time providing more functionality than with classic ASP.

Summary

Yesterday you looked at the fundamentals of databases and how to use them in your ASP.NET Web pages. Today's lesson expanded on that topic immensely and showed you complex new ways of adding, editing, sorting, and paging data on your pages. Specifically, you learned about data binding and three new server controls, which provide tremendous functionality, and shorten the work of developers.

First you examined the `DataSet`, an integral part of ADO.NET's new architecture. You learned how the `DataSet` is used to represent heterogeneous data while maintaining a consistent interface. Tomorrow you'll learn about the entire ADO.NET toolset and how it works within the new distributed data paradigm.

You spent a lot of time today on the three primary data-binding controls—the `Repeater`, `DataList`, and `DataGrid` ASP.NET server controls—and how easily they promote data presentation and manipulation. These controls provide a lot of complex functionality for very little work on the developer's part. Each of these controls provide similar functionality, and they share a lot of common properties, methods, and events. After you learn how to use one, you can easily apply your knowledge to the others. Learning these controls is a big step toward becoming an ASP.NET database expert—and you're almost there!

So far, you've been lightly skimming over ADO.NET and its mechanisms for accessing and modifying data. Tomorrow, you'll make up for that by taking an in-depth look at how ADO.NET functions with ASP.NET. You'll also learn how to allow users to update your data stores using ADO.NET—a very important topic. In the meantime, start playing with these data binding server controls!

Q&A

Q Can a `DataSet` hold XML data?

A Absolutely. In fact, when the `DataSet` is traveling from the server to the client and back, it's first transformed into XML. This allows it to move data into places that normally wouldn't be accessible, such as behind restricted firewalls, which are designed to stop unauthorized data. Because XML is plain text, firewalls ignore it and allow it through.

Q What does the `MinimumCapacity` property in Table 9.1 do?

A This property sets the minimum number of rows that you expect will reside within this table. Setting this property in no way restricts you from adding more rows. Instead, it sets aside memory resources ahead of time so that access to these rows will be faster during runtime. You'll get to this and other specific ADO.NET properties tomorrow.

Workshop

This workshop will help reinforce the concepts covered in today's lesson. Answers can be found in Appendix A.

Quiz

1. What namespaces must you import to use data mechanisms in your ASP.NET pages?
2. True or False: The `DataSet` can contain multiple tables.
3. What are the three collections of the `DataSet`, and what do they do?
4. What is the syntax for data-binding expressions?
5. Does the `DataList` control support paging?
6. What are the two properties of a `DataGrid` that you must specify to turn on sorting and paging, respectively?

Exercises

Enhance the planner application from exercise 2 in Day 6 to use data binding. Bind the `DayLabel` to the Calendar's `selectedDate`, and format it properly.

WEEK 2

DAY 10

Communicating with ADO.NET

After only two days, you're well on your way to becoming a database expert! Two days ago, you were introduced to databases and took a quick look at how to use them with ASP.NET. Yesterday, you dug deep and got into the `DataSet` and data binding controls in Web forms. Up until now, however, you haven't taken an in-depth look at the intrinsic objects of ADO.NET.

Today you'll learn about ADO.NET, its framework, and how it works with ASP.NET. There's going to be a lot of theory in today's lesson, but it will be spiced up with a lot of examples. By the end of today, you should be able to access any type of data store from your ASP.NET pages and use them to produce dynamic, data-enabled pages.

Today's lesson will cover the following:

- How to modify data in a `DataSet`
- How to manipulate `DataRows` and `DataTables`
- How to make changes in a `DataSet` be automatically reflected in the data source, using an `OleDbCommandBuilder` object

- How to use an `OleDbConnection` object
- How to use an `OleDbCommand` object
- How to use an `OleDbDataReader` object
- How to use an `OleDbDataAdapter` object

An Introduction to ADO.NET

ADO.NET is the next generation of ActiveX Data Objects (ADO). It's a model for data access that was built with scalability, the statelessness of the Web, and XML at its core. ADO.NET provides an interface to all OLE DB–compliant data sources and lets you connect to, retrieve, manipulate, and update them. You can use it whether you're in a remote environment, using a distributed application, or using disconnected data.

In terms of ASP.NET development, ADO.NET provides the framework for accessing any type of data for use with ASP.NET pages. This allows users to view or change information stored in any kind of data warehouse, including databases, text files, and XML data stores. You should become very familiar with ADO.NET because it's important for dynamic application development. Knowing its intricacies will save you a lot of headaches down the road.

ADO.NET Versus ADO

Although Microsoft has touted ADO.NET as the next evolution of ADO, and though it has some of the same objects, it's really very different than its predecessor. Whereas ADO was connection-based, ADO.NET relies on short, XML message-based interactions with data sources. This makes ADO.NET much more efficient for Internet-based applications.

A fundamental change from ADO to ADO.NET was the adoption of XML for data exchanges. XML is a text-based markup language, similar to HTML, that presents an efficient way to represent data (we'll discuss XML more later today and in Day 11, "XML and ASP.NET"). ADO.NET is intimately familiar with XML and uses it in all transactions. This allows ADO.NET to reach, exchange, and persist data stores much more easily than ADO. It also gives ADO.NET much better performance because XML data is easily converted to and from any type of data. It doesn't require the complex conversions that wasted processor time with classic ADO.

Another major change is the way ADO.NET interacts with databases. ADO requires "locking" of database resources and lengthy connections for its applications, but ADO.NET doesn't; it uses disconnected data sets (with the `DataSet` object), which eliminates lengthy connections and database locks. This makes ADO.NET much more scalable because users aren't in contention for database resources.

Table 10.1 summarizes the major changes from ADO to ADO.NET.

TABLE 10.1 Changes from ADO to ADO.NET

In ADO	*In ADO.NET*
Data represented by:	
`Recordset`, resembling a single table or query result	`DataSet`, which can contain multiple tables from any data source
Data access:	
Accessing rows in a `RecordSet` sequentially	Allows complete non-sequential access of data in `DataSet` through collection-based hierarchy
Relationships between multiple tables:	
Requires SQL `JOINs` and `UNIONs` to combine data from multiple tables into one recordset	Uses `DataRelation` objects, which can be used to navigate between related tables
Sharing data:	
Requires data to be converted to data types supported by the receiving system, which degrades performance	Uses XML, so no conversions are necessary
Programmability:	
Uses a `Connection` object to transmit commands to a data source's underlying constructs	Uses strongly typed characteristics of XML; does not require use of data constructs; can reference everything by name
Scalability:	
Database locks and connections resulted in contention for data resources	No locks or lengthy active connections, so contentions are eliminated
Firewalls:	
Problematic because firewalls prohibit many types of requests	Not a problem because XML is completely firewall-proof

ADO.NET and XML

XML is a very useful tool for data distribution. It's completely text-based, which means that it's easy for people to write and read, and it can be transported around the security measures put in place on the Internet.

XML stores data by providing a hierarchical representation of fields and their data. For instance, if you had a database named `Users` with the fields `Name`, `UserID`, and `Birthdate`, it would be represented in text form as

```
<Users>
<User>
   <Name />
   <UserID />
   <Birthdate />
<User>
</Users>
```

This basic structure is known as an XML *schema*. (Actually, it's a bit more complicated than that, but that's beyond the scope of this book.) You can then use this schema to represent all the data in your tables:

```
<Users>
<User>
   <name>Chris Payne</name>
   <UserID>1</UserID>
   <birthdate>June 27</birthdate>
</User>
<User>
   <name>Eva Saravia</name>
   <UserID>2</UserID>
   <birthdate>July 15</birthdate>
</User>
</Users>
...
...
```

This can be read by anyone with a text editor (such as Notepad), whereas the corresponding database table could only be read by someone using that particular database application or converting it to another database application. XML is an efficient, implementation-independent way of storing and sending data, which is why it has become such a phenomenon on the Web.

Thus, it's only logical for databases and their interfaces to adopt this method of communication. It makes life much easier for everyone. ADO.NET uses XML in all data exchanges and for internal representations of data. As soon as data comes out of a database, it's represented in XML and is sent wherever you need it to be. Because any application can easily understand XML (as you'll see tomorrow), this approach ensures broad compatibility for your data; your data can be sent anywhere, to any type of system, and you'll be guaranteed that that the receiver will be able to comprehend it.

The adoption of XML by ADO.NET is a big step toward delivering applications as services across the Internet, which is the ideology behind the .NET Framework. This is just touching on the basics, but in the next few days you'll see the benefits your applications will reap as you develop more distributed programs.

The ADO.NET Object Model

ADO.NET consists of two key parts: the `DataSet`, which was discussed thoroughly yesterday, and the managed providers. A `DataSet` is the representation of data that's passed between ADO.NET components, such as from a data store to an ASP.NET page. It's the mechanism that data is represented outside of the data store.

NEW TERM *Managed providers* serve as a communication layer between a `DataSet` and a data store. They provide all the mechanisms for connecting to, accessing, manipulating, and retrieving information from any OLE DB–compliant data store, such as Microsoft Access or SQL Server.

Microsoft provides two managed providers with ADO.NET: the SQL managed provider and the OLE DB managed provider. The first is used solely for interacting with Microsoft SQL Server, and it provides all the methods for communication between the SQL Server and the `DataSet`. The second provider, OLE DB, mediates communication between a `DataSet` and any OLE DB–compliant data source. Both providers offer the same basic functionality for interacting with data stores, so what's the difference?

The SQL managed provider uses a protocol called *tabular data stream* to talk to SQL Server. This is a very efficient way to communicate with SQL Server, and it doesn't rely on OLE DB, ADO, or ODBC. This protocol is completely managed by the CLR, so it benefits from all the features you learned about in Week 1. This is why Microsoft recommends using SQL Server data stores for use with ADO.NET and ASP.NET.

Note The SQL provider in ADO.NET works only with SQL Server versions 7.0 and greater. If you are using an earlier version, use the OLE DB provider instead.

The OLE DB provider, on the other hand, allows communication with all other data stores efficiently—and it can even be used to access SQL Server if need be.

From a developer standpoint, there is almost no difference between the two. They are both used in the same way, have the same objects, and use the same syntax. The only real difference is what happens behind the scenes (you'll learn how to switch between the two in a moment), and that they belong in different namespaces.

Each managed provider has three components:

- Interfaces for connecting and commanding data stores and interacting with the `DataSet`.
- A data stream for fast, efficient access to data (similar to the `DataSet`, but faster and with less functionality).
- Objects that connect to a database and execute low-level database system-specific commands.

Throughout the rest of the book, you'll be using the OLE DB provider because it allows access to the types of data that you'll be using. Much of the syntax is similar in both providers, so converting to the SQL provider shouldn't be difficult.

In fact, all the objects for the ADO provider are prefixed with `OleDb`. In most cases, simply substituting this with `Sql` and importing the `System.Data.SqlClient` namespace allows you to use the SQL provider instead of the OLE DB provider.

The DataSet Revisited

Even though you learned about the `DataSet` yesterday, the lesson skipped over some of its concepts and properties.

NEW TERM Now that you know what the `DataSet` is and what it does, it's important to remember that it's a completely separate entity from the data source. There are no ties at all. Because of this, the `DataSet` is said to be *disconnected*. In this way, each user receives his own copy of the data to do with as he wishes. Changes made to the `DataSet` are *not* reflected in the data source. Any changes must be explicitly pushed back to the data source with methods that you'll see later today.

Table 10.2 shows the properties of the `DataSet`.

TABLE 10.2 DataSet Properties

Property	*Description*
`CaseSensitive`	Indicates whether string comparisons in the `DataTable` objects are case sensitive.
`DataSetName`	Gets or sets the name of the current `DataSet`.
`EnforceConstraints`	Indicates whether existing database constraints should be observed when performing updates.
`ExtendedProperties`	Gets the collection of custom user information.
`HasErrors`	Indicates whether there are errors in any of the rows in any of the tables of the `DataSet`.
`Relations`	Gets the collection of table relations for the `DataSet`.
`Tables`	Gets the collection of tables for the `DataSet`.

Table 10.3 shows the methods of the `DataSet`.

TABLE 10.3 DataSet Methods

Method	*Description*
`AcceptChanges`	Commits all changes made to the `DataSet`, either since it was loaded or since `AcceptChanges` was last called.
`Clear`	Removes all rows in all tables in the `DataSet`. Does *not* delete actual database content.
`Clone`	Clones the structure of the `DataSet`, including `DataTables`, relations, and constraints.
`Copy`	Copies the structure and data of the `DataSet`.
`GetChanges`	Returns a copy of the `DataSet` that contains all changes made to underlying data since the last load.
`HasChanges`	Indicates whether the `DataSet` contains any changes.
`Merge`	Merges this `DataSet` with another.
`ReadXML`	Reads XML schema and data into the `DataSet`.
`ReadXMLSchema`	Reads XML schema information into the `DataSet`.
`RejectChanges`	Rolls back any changes made to this `DataSet`.
`WriteXML`	Writes the XML that represents the `DataSet` to an XML file, including data and schema.
`WriteXMLSchema`	Writes the XML that represents the `DataSet` to an XML file, including schema information.

The preceding tables didn't list all the properties and methods of the `DataSet` object. They skipped over some of the generic inherited items. See either the .NET Framework SDK Documentation or Appendix D, "ADO.NET Controls: Properties and Methods," for more complete information.

As you can see, the `DataSet` provides a lot of features that you haven't seen before, such as reading and writing XML data. Don't be afraid to experiment with any of these properties. The `DataTable` and `DataRow` objects also provide many of the same properties and methods as the `DataSet`, so they aren't all listed here. Figure 10.1 illustrates the object model of the `DataSet`.

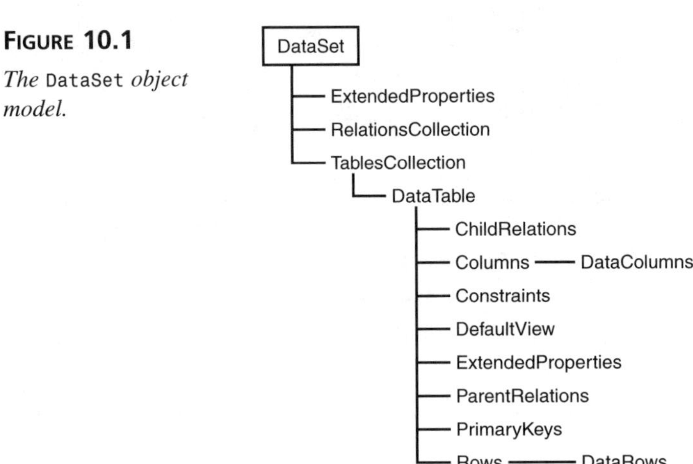

FIGURE 10.1
The `DataSet` *object model.*

Modifying Data in a `DataRow`

Because you should be familiar with the workings of the `DataSet`, let's examine modifying the data within one. The `DataSet` stores data in a form similar to a database; it contains tables, columns, and rows. Often, you'll manipulate the data contained in a `DataSet` with SQL statements that modify more than one record at a time, but there are times when you need to have more direct control over each row. The `DataRow` object represents a row of data in the `DataTable`, and as you learned yesterday, you can directly edit the content in each `DataRow`.

There are some more features of the `DataRow` and `DataTable` that you should know about. The first is the `RowState` property, which indicates the condition of the current row. Possible values include `Detached`, `Unchanged`, `New`, `Deleted`, and `Modified`.

`Detached` means that the row has been created but currently isn't part of any `RowsCollection` in a `DataSet`. The last four are self-explanatory.

As part of the `RowState`, a `DataTable` maintains three versions of every row: original, current, and proposed. The `DataTable` uses these versions to determine the `RowState`. The original version is the row when it was first added to the `DataTable`. Usually this value will be the same as the value in the data source. The current version is the row after you've made any changes. The proposed version exists in one special condition—when the `BeginEdit` method is called on the row.

The `BeginEdit` method is used to make multiple changes to rows without having to apply validation rules. For example, if you have a group of rows that must add up to a certain value, you can put them in edit mode and manipulate the values without having to worry about what they add up to. The row moves out of edit mode and the validation rules are applied when the `EndEdit` or `AcceptChanges` method is called. You can also use edit mode to cancel any proposed changes. Figure 10.2 shows the process for modifying a row.

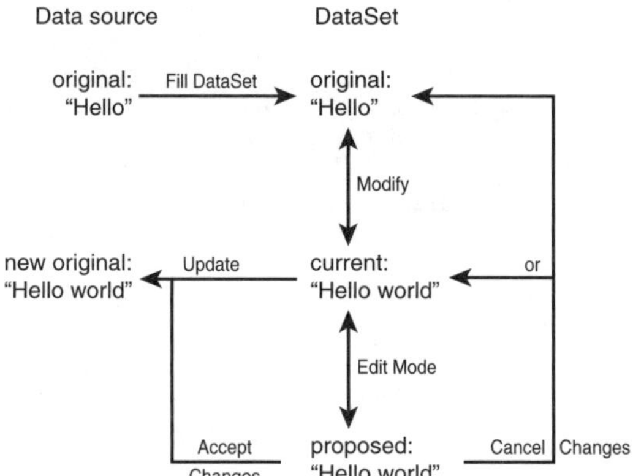

FIGURE 10.2
Modifying a row.

The original value (from the data source) is moved into the `DataSet` when the `Fill` method is called. If you make any changes to the value, it becomes the current value. You can now either revert to the original value, update the data store with the current value, or move into edit mode. In edit mode, you can accept the changes and update the data store, or cancel the changes and revert to either the original or current versions. In fact, you can revert to either of these versions and then update the data store from edit mode, if you like. Each of the versions is accessible through the `DataRowVersion.Original`, `DataRowVersion.Current`, and `DataRowVersion.Proposed` properties.

As the data in a DataRow is modified, errors may arise for one reason or another. Each error is stored in the RowError property of the DataRow as a string. You can manually insert an error in this property as well. You can retrieve all errors at once by calling the GetErrors method, which returns an array of DataRows. If any errors are present, merges and updates to the data source will not occur; first the errors must be reconciled. Don't worry if this doesn't make much sense; after you start developing examples, it will become clearer.

The DataRow provides two methods that seem very similar, Delete and Remove, but there is an important difference between the two. Delete completely destroys the row and the data it contains. Once this happens, the data can no longer be accessed. Remove, however, simply removes a row from the DataTable so that it can't be accessed programmatically. The actual data source isn't changed, so the data is still there. You just can't see it. This is helpful if you don't want to use every row of a DataTable.

Finally, RejectChanges gets rid of all changes that were made since the row was loaded, or since the last time AcceptChanges was called. For example, the following code snippet loads data into a DataSet, modifies a value in the first row, and then rejects the changes:

```
dim objConn as new OleDbConnection _
   ("Provider=Microsoft.Jet.OLEDB.4.0;" & _
   "Data Source=c:\ASPNET\data\banking.mdb")

dim objCmd as new OleDbDataAdapter _
   ("select * from tblUsers", objConn)

dim ds as DataSet = new DataSet()
objCmd.Fill(ds, "tblUsers")

ds.Tables("tblUsers").Rows(0)("FirstName") = "Chris"

'do some other stuff

ds.Tables("tblUsers").Rows(0).RejectChanges
```

Viewing Data in a DataTable

The DataTable has a Select method that allows you to filter and sort the data in your table. The method returns an array of DataRows and is invoked as follows:

```
Tablename.Select(filter expression, sort order, _
   DataRowViewState)
```

For example:

```
dim ds as new DataSet("MyDataSet")
dim dTable as new DataTable("MyTable")
' fill data set and datatable here
Dim MyRows() as DataRow = ds.Tables("MyTable").Select _
   (Nothing, "UserName", DataViewRowState. _
    CurrentRows)
```

This listing returns an array of all modified `DataRows` sorted by the `"UserName"` field. You can specify `Nothing` for any of the parameters you don't need. Thus, you can return any or all versions of a row, and they can be sorted or filtered, or both. Let's look at another example, shown in Listing 10.1.

LISTING 10.1 Retrieving Rows Using the `Select` Method

```
<%@ Page Language="VB" %>
<%@ Import Namespace="System.Data" %>
<%@ Import Namespace="System.Data.OleDb" %>

<script runat="server">
   sub Page_Load(Sender as object, e as eventargs)
      dim objConn as new OleDbConnection _
         ("Provider=Microsoft.Jet.OLEDB.4.0;" & _
         "Data Source=c:\ASPNET\data\banking.mdb")

       dim objCmd as new OleDbDataAdapter _
          ("select * from tblUsers", objConn)

       dim ds as DataSet = new DataSet()
       objCmd.Fill(ds, "tblUsers")

       dim dTable as DataTable = ds.Tables("tblUsers")
       Dim CurrRows() as DataRow = dTable.Select(Nothing, _
          Nothing, DataViewRowState.CurrentRows)
       Dim I, J as integer
       Dim strOutput as string

       For I = 0 to CurrRows.Length - 1
          For J = 0 to dTable.Columns.Count - 1
             strOutput = strOutput & dTable.Columns(J). _
                ColumnName & " = " & _
                CurrRows(I)(J).ToString & "<br>"
          next
       next

       Response.write(strOutput)
    end sub
 </script>
```

LISTING 10.1 continued

```
34:
35:  <html><body>
36:
37:  </body></html>
```

ANALYSIS

This listing retrieves all current rows from a `DataSet`, and displays their fields and values in the browser. In the `Page_Load` method, you set up `OleDbConnection` and `OleDbDataAdapter` objects on lines 7–12. After yesterday's lesson, this should look familiar. You then create a `DataSet` and fill it with data using the `Fill` method on lines 14 and 15. Then, on line 17, you retrieve the only table in the `DataSet` and store it in the variable `dTable` for easier access later in the code.

> **Tip**
>
> In Listing 10.1, if you wanted to access the data from a SQL database instead of Access, you would simply change the `OleDbName objects to SqlName` objects.

On line 18, you use the `Select` method to grab all the rows that have changed in the `DataTable`—the current rows—and place them in an array. You use a `for` loop to iterate through the array rows on line 23, and another nested `for` loop to go through the columns for each row on line 24. You collect each field name and its value in a string, and then print out the string on line 31. This listing produces the output shown in Figure 10.3.

Another way to sort and filter data is by using `DataViews`. A `DataView` is an object that represents a `DataTable`, but unlike a `DataTable`, the `DataView` is bindable to Web controls. You can create multiple `DataViews` for a single `DataTable`.

In an ASP.NET page, this allows you to have two different controls that are bound to the same `DataTable` but display different data. For example, the following code snippet shows how to create and set properties for a `DataView`:

```
dim MyView as new DataView(dTable)
MyView.RowStateFilter = DataViewRowState.ModifiedOriginal
MyView.Sort = "UserID ASC"
MyView.RowFilter = "City = ASPTown"
```

On the first line, you create a new `DataView` from the `dTable` variable. (`dTable` is a previously created `DataTable`, filled with data.) On the second line, you set the `DataView` to filter out all row versions except the original versions. The third line specifies a sort order, and the last line specifies a criterion by which to return rows. You can see that the

`DataView` contains many of the same properties the `Select` method uses to retrieve rows. Knowing these properties will help you immensely when you're actually modifying data sources.

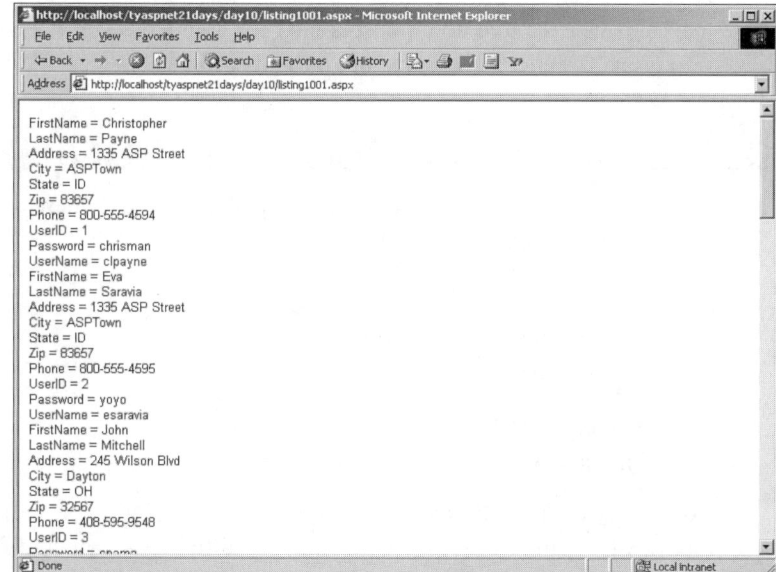

FIGURE 10.3

`For` *loops and the* `Select` *method are able to loop through each row in the* `DataSet`.

Concurrency

NEW TERM Since each user has his own view of the `DataSet`, he's free to do with it as he pleases and update the data source whenever he's ready. What happens, though, when two or more people try to update the same data in a table at the same time? *Concurrency* is a system that monitors this scenario to make sure no problems arise. There are two types of concurrency: *pessimistic* and *optimistic*.

Whenever a user accesses or tries to change data with pessimistic concurrency, a lock is placed on the data so that no other user can modify it and interfere with the first user. As soon as the first user is done, the second user can try again.

Optimistic concurrency, on the other hand, does *not* place any locks on data. Rather, it monitors the rows to determine whether the original data has been modified, and then applies the change. Let's say two users grab the data on a boat named *U.S.S. Enterprise*—both users start with the same data. The first user changes the name to *U.S.S. Enterprise A*. If the second user tries to change it again later, his changes won't be applied because he no longer has a valid copy of the data. He'll have to grab a current version of the data and try again. In database terms, if two users retrieve the same set of data, only the first user's changes will be applied. The second user's data will no longer be valid because the data source has changed, and his attempt will fail.

ADO.NET can work with either type of concurrency, and luckily, it provides built-in mechanisms to handle both transparently for you. However, it's helpful to know how the process works in case you ever run into this problem.

Database Interaction with ADO.NET

As mentioned on Day 8, "Beginning to Build Databases," there are five general steps to interacting with data in ASP.NET pages:

1. Create a database connection object.
2. Open the database connection.
3. Populate a `DataSet` with the desired data.
4. Set up a `DataView` to display data.
5. Bind a server control to the `DataView`.

You examined the fifth item in detail yesterday, so you'll concentrate on the first four today. A few of these steps can be done in multiple ways (with different objects), so all of them will be covered in turn. Before you move on, though, you need to examine the information needed to connect to a database.

Connection Information

Before you can use ADO.NET in your ASP.NET pages to talk to databases, you have to provide specific information about the database you're interested in accessing. This important information includes where the database is located, what type of database it is (for example, MS Access, SQL Server, or Oracle), what version it is, and so on. This information is supplied to ADO.NET using a *connection string* that you build manually. (Don't worry, it's not as bad as it sounds.)

NEW TERM Once upon a time, the easiest way to provide this information for your database was to build a System Data Source Name (DSN) file. You should already have one of these files, which provides default information for some data stores installed by your operating system. These files contained all the information required by a connection string for your applications to use. While they were convenient, they weren't very efficient. There are better mechanisms to connect to databases in ASP.NET, but you may still occasionally hear the term DSN connection, so it's good to know.

A very common way to connect to a database nowadays is to specify your connection string via a DSN-less connection. This requires you to specify all the necessary information in the connection string in your application. Using your banking user database as an example, the connection string would look similar to this:

```
"Provider=Microsoft.Jet.OLEDB.4.0;Data Source=
➥C:\ASPNET\data\banking.mdb"
```

For a SQL database, the connection string would look something like the following:

```
"Provider=SQLOLEDB.1;Initial Catalog=Northwind;
➥Data Source=MyServer;User ID=sa;"
```

This string tells ADO.NET which provider to use and the location of the database. There are a number of other parameters you may specify as well, such as `UID` and `PWD` for a username and password used to connect to the database. The ones specified here are the most common, however, so we won't go into the others yet.

The `OleDbConnection` Object

Now that you've seen how to set up the connection with the connection string, let's try opening your database. The `System.Data.OleDb.OleDbConnection` object (or `System.Data.SqlClient.SqlConnection` object for SQL databases) does just this. Listing 10.2 shows an example.

Listing 10.2 Opening a Database Connection with the `OleDbConnection` Object

```
1:  Dim strConnectionString as string = _
2:     "Provider=Microsoft.Jet.OLEDB.4.0;" & _
3:     "Data Source=c:\ASPNET\data\banking.mdb" "
4:  Dim Conn as New OleDbConnection( _
5:     strConnectionString)
6:  Conn.Open()
7:  ...
8:  Conn.Close()
```

And that's it! You now have an open connection to your database. The connection string is declared on line 1, and the `OleDbConnection` object on line 4 uses it to connect to the database. Line 6 uses the `Open` method to open the connection to the database, and line 7 uses `Close` to close it. Always remember to close the connection when you're through with it.

Most of the time, this is all you will ever need to do with an `OleDbConnection` object: open and close a database connection. You'll learn a few more tricks in Day 12, "Employing Advanced Data Techniques."

The `OleDbCommand` Object

Now that you've connected to the database, you can issue commands against the database, such as filling a `DataSet` or updating records. Figure 10.4 shows a partial object model for the `OleDbCommand` object.

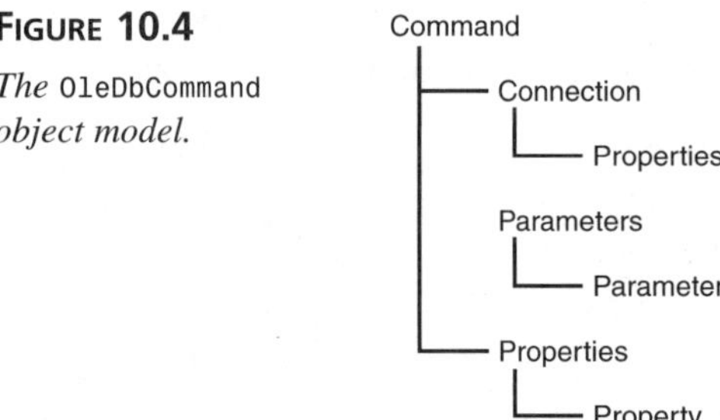

FIGURE 10.4
The `OleDbCommand` *object model.*

Commands to databases are in the form of SQL statements, so you should be familiar with them already. All you have to do is assign a SQL statement to your `OleDbCommand` object, as shown Listing 10.3.

LISTING 10.3 Creating and Initializing an `OleDbCommand` Object

```
1:  'set up SQL statement
2:  Dim strSQL as string = "SELECT * FROM tblUsers"
3:
4:  'create object and set properties
5:  Dim objCmd as New OleDbCommand()
6:  objCmd.Connection = Conn
7:  objCmd.CommandText = strSQL
8:
9:  'or
10:  'Dim objCmd as New OleDbCommand(strSQL, Conn)
11:
12:  'or
13:  'Dim objCmd as New OleDbCommand(strSQL, _
14:  strConnectionString)
```

ANALYSIS The `OleDbCommand` object provides a number of ways for you to initialize it by specifying different parameters. The parameters it will accept are the SQL statement and the `OleDbConnection` object (shown on line 10), *or* the connection string that will build the `OleDbConnection` object (shown on line 13). Simply specifying the command won't do much, however. You must execute the command with one of the `Execute` methods. The one you'll use depends on what you plan on doing with the returned data. For example, to fill an `OleDbDataReader` (see the next section for information on this object), use

```
'create a DataReader
dim objReader as OleDbDataReader
objReader = objCmd.ExecuteReader
```

To execute a query that doesn't return any data, use

```
objCmd.ExecuteNonQuery
```

You'll examine more `Execute` methods as we progress through the book.

The `OleDbDataReader` Object

The `OleDbDataReader` is a lightweight object that allows simple access to a data store. Essentially, it's a streaming `DataSet`. So why use the `OleDbDataReader` when you have the `DataSet`?

When you retrieve data from a database, a `DataSet` grabs all the information and holds it in memory until you tell it otherwise. This allows you to do some pretty neat things with this disconnected data store. For instance, you can modify it without worrying about other users messing up the data, and you can transform it into different formats. However, after you start returning large amounts of data from a database, you run into memory limitations because the entire `DataSet` is stored in memory. Couple that with thousands of users accessing the database at the same time (with each user having his own `DataSet`), and you run into major problems. (Note that such an example is an extreme case, but it helps to illustrate the need for a smaller object than the `DataSet`.)

The `OleDbDataReader` puts only one row into memory at a time. It *streams* the data from the data store as you request it. This can prevent a lot of memory problems, and consequently, it results in increased performance as well. Unfortunately, because the data is streamed, the `OleDbDataReader` doesn't provide as much functionality as a `DataSet`. It's read-only, and you can't go back to records you've already passed.

After you've filled your `OleDbDataReader`, it's very easy to loop through the records. Simply call the `Read` method. Listing 10.4 shows an example.

LISTING 10.4 Looping Through Records in an `OleDbDataReader` Object

```
<%@ Page Language="C#" %>
<%@ Import Namespace="System.Data" %>
<%@ Import Namespace="System.Data.OleDb" %>

```

LISTING 10.4 continued

```
5:    <script runat="server">
6:       void Page_Load(Object Sender, EventArgs e) {
7:          OleDbConnection objConn = new OleDbConnection
➥("Provider=Microsoft.Jet.OLEDB.4.0;Data Source=
➥c:\\ASPNET\\data\\banking.mdb");
8:
9:          OleDbCommand objCmd = new OleDbCommand
➥("select * from tblUsers", objConn);
10:
11:         OleDbDataReader objReader;
12:
13:         objConn.Open();
14:         objReader = objCmd.ExecuteReader();
15:
16:         while (objReader.Read()) {
17:            Response.Write(objReader.GetString(0) + "<br>");
18:         }
19:         objConn.Close();
20:      }
21:   </script>
22:
23:   <html><body>
24:
25:   </body></html>
```

ANALYSIS Lines 7–9 should look familiar; you create an `OleDbConnection` and an `OleDbCommand` and execute a SQL statement. (Note that the connection string uses two backslashes in the file path; this is because a single backslash in C# has special meaning, so we need to escape it with another.) These few steps will become very familiar to you very quickly. Line 11 creates a new `OleDbDataReader` object. The `Fill` method of the `OleDbDataAdapter` object automatically opened and closed a database connection for you, but when working with an `OleDbDataReader`, you must perform this step manually, as shown on lines 13 and 19. Line 14 executes the SQL statement and streams the returned data through the `OleDbDataReader` object. Lines 16–18 loop through each record of the `OleDbDataReader`.

The `Read` method automatically advances to the next record, stopping when there are no more. Line 17 retrieves the first field from each record using the `GetString` method, which appropriately returns a string value (I'll discuss this method more in a moment). This string is then displayed using `Response.Write`. The output is shown in Figure 10.5.

FIGURE 10.5
The `Read` *method allows you to loop through an* `OleDbDataReader`*'s records.*

You can test if there are any more records programmatically by examining the `HasMoreRows` property, which will return true if there are more records and false otherwise.

Caution

> It's very important that you also close the `OleDbDataReader` when you're through with it. Closing the associated `OleDbConnection` object will also do this for you.

The `OleDbDataReader` also has a series of `Get` methods that return data from the fields as their native type (`GetByte`, `GetInt32`, `GetString`, and so on). Use these commands to avoid having to cast your data when it comes out of the `OleDbDataReader`.

Do	Don't
Do use an `OleDbDataReader` when performance is critical and you only need to display database information.	**Don't** use a `OleDbDataReader` if you need to manipulate or modify the data before or after displaying it to a user.

Update, Insert, and Delete

Because the OleDbDataReader is read-only, you cannot use it to modify data. Rather, you have to use appropriate SQL statements with the OleDbCommand object: Update, Insert and Delete.

None of these statements returns any records like the Select statement, however. Therefore, you should use the ExecuteNonQuery method, which returns an integer that tells you how many records were affected by the statement Listing 10.5 shows an example.

LISTING 10.5 Executing Non-Select Statements with the OleDbCommand Object

```
dim I as integer

'set up SQL statement
Dim strSQL as string = "DELETE FROM tblUsers" & _
" WHERE UserID = 5"
'create object and set properties
Dim objCmd as New OleDbCommand(strSQL, Conn)

I = objCmd.ExecuteNonQuery()
```

Because UserID is your identity field, this statement should affect zero records or one record, depending on whether there was a row with that ID. You can examine the variable I to see whether your statement was effective. The Update and Insert statements will perform similarly (see Day 8 for more discussion about these SQL statements).

The OleDbDataAdapter Object

Just as the OleDbCommand object dealt with OleDbDataReaders, the OleDbDataAdapter deals with DataSets. The OleDbDataAdapter's main function is to pull data from a data store into a DataSet, and to push DataSet data back into the data store. The model for this object is outlined in Figure 10.6. The four command methods are used to delete, insert, select, and update data in a DataSet. The TableMappings collection defines how tables and columns from data sources are matched to DataSets.

The OleDbDataAdapter object is very powerful. Although its main purpose is simply to retrieve data, it can also create entirely new tables from existing data or spit data out as XML. We'll get to the more advanced features later, but first let's examine the basics.

Creating an OleDbDataAdapter object is similar to creating an ADOCommand object, as shown in Listing 10.6.

FIGURE 10.6

The `OleDbDataAdapter` *object model.*

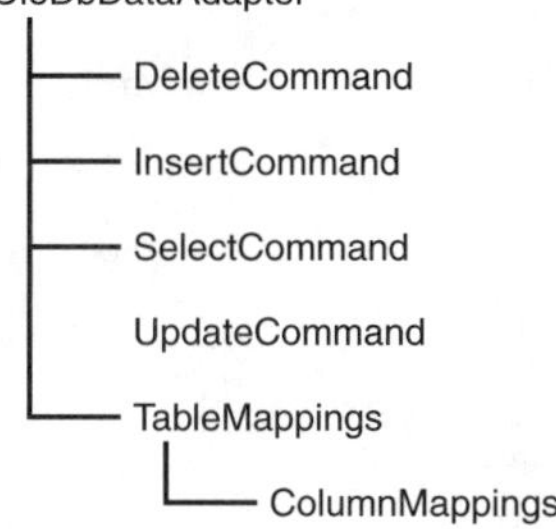

LISTING 10.6 Creating an `OleDbDataAdapter` Object

```
1:  'set up SQL statement
2:  Dim strSQL as string = "SELECT * FROM tblUsers"
3:
4:  'create object and set properties
5:  Dim objCmd as  New OleDbDataAdapter()
6:  objCmd.SelectCommand.Connection = Conn
7:  objCmd.SelectCommand.CommandText = strSQL
8:
9:  'or
10:  'Dim objCmd as New OleDbDataAdapter _
11:  '    (strSQL, Conn)
12:
13:  'or
14:  'Dim objCmd as New OleDbDataAdapter( _
15:  '    strSQL, strConnectionString)
```

ANALYSIS As shown in Figure 10.6, the `OleDbDataAdapter` has four command methods. Each of these command methods is actually an `OleDbCommand` object, with its own `Connection` and `CommandText` properties, as shown on lines 6 and 7. The command object method that's set when you provide an SQL statement during the initialization of the object (lines 10 and 14) is the `SelectCommand` method. If you want to specify other command methods, such as an `Insert`, you must do so manually.

Note

Remember that when you use the `Update`, `Insert`, and `Delete` command methods, you're not actually altering the underlying data store, but rather the `DataSet`, which is disconnected from the data store. The changes are reflected on the data source only after the `OleDbDataAdapter.Update` method is called.

Populating DataSets

Let's take a look at an example of populating a `DataSet`, and then you'll explore the various methods. See Listing 10.7.

LISTING 10.7 Filling a `DataSet`

```
1:  dim strConnectionString as String = _
2:  "Provider=Microsoft.Jet.OLEDB.4.0;" & _
3:  "Data Source=c:\ASPNET\data\banking.mdb"
4:  Dim ds as DataSet = New DataSet("MyDataSet")
5:  Dim strSQL as String = "SELECT * FROM tblUsers"
6:
7:  Dim objCmd as new OleDbDataAdapter(strSQL, _
8:  strConnectionString)
9:
10:  objCmd.Fill(ds, "Users")
```

ANALYSIS On line 4, you create an empty `DataSet` named `"MyDataSet"`, and on line 7, you create a new `OleDbDataAdapter` object with its `Select` command initialized to the SQL string you created on line 5. The result of this code snippet is a `DataSet` that contains a `DataTable` called `"Users"`, which in turn contains all the records from the `tblUsers` table.

How is this possible, since you only created an empty `DataSet`? The `Fill` method of the `OleDbDataAdapter` object takes any schema information (tables, columns, primary key definitions, and so on) from the data source that doesn't already exist in the `DataSet` and creates it automatically. Thus, it fills the `"Users"` `DataTable` with all the columns from the data source. Similarly, if you've already created a `DataTable` with some of the columns, the `FillDataSet` method will create the rest. If you create all the columns, this method will only fill the table with data. This is a very powerful feature of `OleDbDataAdapter`, and as you'll see in the next section, it only gets better.

Updating Data Sources

Yesterday you learned how to manipulate the data in a `DataSet` by accessing its fields and values through its collections. What happens, though, after you modify data in this way?

After you change the data, you can use the `OleDbDataAdapter`'s associated `OleDbCommand` objects to push those changes back to the data store. These commands concern only the data you've *already* changed. For instance, you can't simply specify an `Insert` statement and expect a new record to appear in the data source. The `Insert` statement must reference a new row you've already created in the `DataSet`. Listing 10.8 shows an example of setting the `OleDbDataAdapter`'s `UpdateCommand` property.

LISTING 10.8 Manipulating a `DataSet` with the `OleDbDataAdapter` Object

```
sub Page_Load(Sender as Object, e as EventArgs)
   'create connection
   dim Conn as new OleDbConnection( _
      "Provider=Microsoft.Jet.OLEDB.4.0;" & _
      "Data Source=c:\ASPNET\data\banking.mdb")

   'create DataSet and OleDbDataAdapter
   Dim ds as new DataSet("MyDataSet")
   Dim objCmd as new OleDbDataAdapter("SELECT * FROM " & _
       "tblUsers WHERE UserID < 10", Conn)

    'fill DataSet
    objCmd.Fill(ds, "tblUsers")

    'change some data
    ds.Tables("tblUsers").Rows(2)(3) = "ASPVille"

    dim dr as DataRow = ds.Tables("tblUsers").NewRow()
    dr(0) = "Greg"
    dr(1) = "Smith"
    dr(2) = "434 Maple Apt B"
    dr(3) = "Minneapolis"
    dr(4) = "MN"
    dr(5) = "12588"
    dr(6) = "5189876259"
    ds.Tables("tblUsers").Rows.Add(dr)

    'provide SQL command and active connection
    objCmd.UpdateCommand = new OleDbCommand
    objCmd.UpdateCommand.CommandText = "Update tblUsers " & _
       "SET City='ASPVille' WHERE UserID=3"
    objCmd.UpdateCommand.Connection = Conn

    'provide another SQL command and active connection
    objCmd.InsertCommand = new OleDbCommand
    objCmd.InsertCommand.CommandText = "Insert INTO " & _
       "tblUsers (FirstName, LastName, Address, City, " & _
       "State, ZIP, Phone) VALUES ('Greg', 'Smith', " & _
       "'434 Maple Apt B', 'Minneapolis', 'MN', '12588', " & _
       "'5189876259'"
    objCmd.InsertCommand.Connection = Conn

end sub
```

ANALYSIS In this listing, you first create your `OleDbConnection` and `OleDbDataAdapter` on lines 3–10, and fill your `DataSet` using the SQL `select` statement on line 13. This is similar to the process when using an `OleDbCommand` object. You make some changes to the `DataSet` on lines 16–26: You edit a single value on line 16, and add a completely new row on lines 18–26. On line 29, you create a new `OldDbCommand` object to use with the `OleDbDataAdapter`'s `Update` command. On line 30, you specify an update statement to use when you update the data source. Similarly on line 36, you specify an `Insert` statement. Notice how the `Insert` and `Update` commands reference the data in the modified rows only. These statements don't actually do anything yet. They will be executed against the data source when you call the `Update` method.

> **Note**
>
> Note that these commands don't really alter any data. They merely provide commands to instruct ADO.NET how you want to push the data that you've already changed. For example, if you hadn't made any changes on lines 16–26, the command methods would do nothing, regardless of the SQL statements you specified.

The `Update` method of `OleDbDataAdapter` pushes changes in a `DataSet` back to the data source. It uses the `Insert`, `Update`, and `Delete` commands that you've specified to alter the data source. Let's modify Listing 10.8 to include the `Update` command. Add the following code after line 41:

```
objCmd.Update(ds, "tblUsers")
```

The method's parameters are the `DataSet` object variable, which contains the modified data, and the table from which you want to pull data. You can leave out the table parameter, but that requires a table mapping—which we'll discuss in the next section.

This might seem like a real pain—having to change the data manually, and then building a SQL statement showing that you've changed it. Luckily, ADO.NET can help. If these commands aren't specified, and if any rows are actually changed in the `DataSet`, the `OleDbDataAdapter` object can generate the commands for you *automatically*, using an `OleDbCommandBuilder` object. For example, let's examine the following code snippet:

```
dim ds as new DataSet("MyDataSet")
dim objCmd as new OleDbDataAdapter _
   ("select * from tblUsers", Conn)
dim objAutoGen as New OleDbCommandBuilder(objCmd)
...
'retrieve and
'modify some data
...
objCmd.Update(ds, "tblUsers")
```

The first three lines are the same as usual. On the fourth line, however, you create a new `OleDbCommandBuilder` object specifying the `OleDbDataAdapter` as a parameter. This object, after the `Update` method is called, examines the differences between the `DataSet` and the data source, and generates SQL statements to make the former match the latter, taking a lot of headache out of the process.

Look at the following line:

```
ds.Tables("tblUsers").Rows(3).Delete
```

When coupled with the `OleDbCommandBuilder` object and the `Update` method, this will generate the delete SQL statement:

```
DELETE FROM tblUsers WHERE UserID = 4
```

The `OleDbDataAdapter` uses the primary key values to determine which row should be deleted. In this case, the fourth row's primary key `"UserID"` (indicated by `Rows(3)`) is 4. The auto-generate feature will work only if a primary key or unique column is present.

You might be wondering why you need to specify a `select` statement if the command builder will build the statements for you. This is because your command builder needs an initial statement to tell it what kind of data and what fields to expect. Without the initial statement, the builder wouldn't know how to form the proper SQL statements. In other words, the statement you use to retrieve data from the data source will affect the rows you can update. If your initial SQL statement uses "`select * ...`" as shown in the previous code snippet, the `DataSet` that you are working with must also have all of the columns from the data source. The following code snippet demonstrates this, and will cause an error:

```
'global variables
dim ds as new DataSet("MyDataSet")

sub CreateData()
   'create connection object here
   'fill dataset
   dim objCmd as new OleDbDataAdapter _
      ("select UserID, FirstName, LastName from tblUsers", Conn)
      objCmd.Fill(ds, "tblUsers")

   'add new row to users table
   'do some other modifications
end sub

sub UpdateData()
   dim objCmd as new OleDbDataAdapter _
```

```
        ("select * from tblUsers", Conn)
    dim objAutoGen as New OleDbCommandBuilder(objCmd)

    objCmd.Update(ds, "tblUsers")
end sub
```

Assume you call the `CreateData` method first to populate your `DataSet`, for example, to display in a `DataGrid`. Then after the data has been modified, you call the `UpdateData` method to insert the data into the database from your `DataSet`. In this situation, you'll receive an error. The `OleDbCommandBuilder` will try to update every field in the table because the `select *` statement in the `UpdateData` method says so. However, the `DataSet` only has three fields, as shown in the `CreateData` method; you can't update columns that aren't there in the `DataSet`. Instead, match the two SQL statements together; so, in `UpdateData`, the statement should read:

```
select UserID, FirstName, LastName from tblUsers
```

The `OleDbCommandBuilder` must make a trip to the data source to figure out how to build the commands; it needs table schema information—this is the reason for the initial `select` statement. If bandwidth is a critical factor, or you don't want to make extraneous trips to the data source (to improve performance, for instance), don't use an `OleDbCommandBuilder` object; build your SQL statements by hand instead.

Mappings

Table and column mappings allow you to *map* one table or column in the data store to one in the `DataSet`. This mapping will be used by ADO.NET when data is moved from one data source to another. This allows you to use columns or tables with different names in each location, or even to map two completely different columns or tables to each other. Figure 10.7 illustrates this concept.

These mappings are stored in the `TableMappings` collection of the `OleDbDataAdapter` object. Let's take a look at an example, shown in Listing 10.9.

LISTING 10.9 Creating Table Mappings for the `banking` Database

```
Dim ds As DataSet = New DataSet()
Dim Conn as New OleDbConnection _
   "Provider=Microsoft.Jet.OLEDB.4.0;" & _
   "Data Source=c:\ASPNET\data\banking.mdb"))
Dim objCmd As New OleDbDataAdapter _
   ("SELECT * FROM tblUsers", Conn)

'add mappings
objCmd.TableMappings.Add("Table", "Users")
 With objCmd.TableMappings(0).ColumnMappings
```

LISTING 10.9 continued

```
11:     .Add("UserID", "ID")
12:     .Add("LastName", "Lastname")
13:     .Add("FirstName", "Firstname")
14:     .Add("Phone", "Phone")
15:     .Add("Address", "StreetAddress")
16:     .Add("City", "City")
17:     .Add("State", "State")
18:     .Add("Zip", "Zip")
19: End With
20: objCmd.FillDataSet(ds)
```

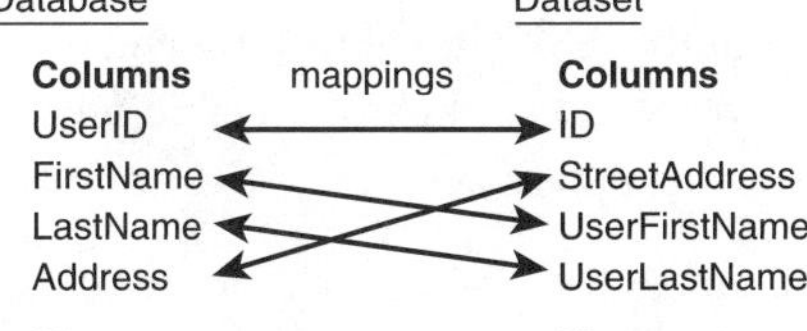

FIGURE 10.7
Mappings allow you to link seemingly unrelated columns.

ANALYSIS This example uses the `banking` database you created on Day 8, and maps the columns in the `tblUsers` table to columns in a `DataSet`.

Lines 1–6 should be pretty familiar by now. You create and initialize your `DataSet`, connection, and `OleDbDataAdapter` objects. On line 9, you add a new mapping from the table in the data store to a `Users` table in your `DataSet`. The first parameter is the source table (where you're pulling the data from), and the second parameter is the destination table (where the data is going to). Since you supplied a select statement with the `OleDbDataAdapter` declaration, ADO.NET knows that you want to use the results of that statement as the source table.

The name `Table` that you specify on line 9 is a special name used by ADO.NET. When the `Fill` or `Update` command is issued without specifying a `DataSet` table parameter, ADO.NET looks for a mapping called `Table` to determine where the data should come from. For example, let's say you're using the mapping from Listing 10.9 and call the following:

```
objCmd.Update(ds)
```

ADO.NET will pull the data from the `Users` table in your `DataSet` because the `Table` mapping instructs it to. Normally, you would need to use the following to perform the update:

```
objCmd.Update(ds, "Users")
```

On lines 10–20, you simply add `ColumnMappings` to the `TableMapping` that you just defined. These mappings provide easier-to-use column names for a few of the columns and map the others as they are.

Mappings serve purposes other than simply providing friendlier column names. When you start getting more familiar with SQL statements, you'll notice that some of them don't return fields or named columns—some simply return a value. These situations aren't very likely to come up during ASP.NET development, though. We'll examine them more in Day 12.

Using ADO.NET with ASP.NET

Enough theory, let's get on with the ASP.NET development. You're going to build your first full-featured (but simple) database application, which will allow users to view and modify data. You need to put these newly acquired skills to the test.

You're only going to need one page for this application. It will display data from your users table in a `DataGrid` control. You'll use the editing features of the `DataGrid` to make changes to the data, and then you'll push everything back to the data source using an `OleDbCommand` object.

First, let's build the user interface. Listing 10.10 shows a standard `DataGrid` with bound columns for each of the fields in your database, plus an `EditCommandColumn` and a `ButtonCommandColumn` to allow deletions of data. You also use a panel to display additional input fields for inserting new rows into the database. You also build a label control to display any messages to the user.

LISTING 10.10 The UI for Your Database Application

```
<html><body>
   <asp:Label id="lblMessage" runat="server"/>

   <form runat="server">
      <asp:DataGrid id="dgData" runat="server"
         BorderColor="black" GridLines="Vertical"
         cellpadding="4" cellspacing="0" width="100%"
         AutoGenerateColumns="False"
         OnDeleteCommand="dgData_Delete"
         OnEditCommand="dgData_Edit"
         OnCancelCommand="dgData_Cancel"
         OnUpdateCommand="dgData_Update"
         OnPageIndexChanged="dgData_PageIndexChanged" >

         <Columns>
```

LISTING 10.10 continued

```
            <asp:TemplateColumn HeaderText="ID">
               <ItemTemplate>
                  <asp:Label id="Name" runat="server"
                     Text='<%# Container.DataItem
                     ➥("UserID") %>'/>
               </ItemTemplate>
            </asp:TemplateColumn>

            <asp:BoundColumn HeaderText="FirstName"
               DataField="FirstName" />
            <asp:BoundColumn HeaderText="LastName"
               DataField="LastName" />
            <asp:BoundColumn HeaderText="Address"
               DataField="Address" />
            <asp:BoundColumn HeaderText="City"
               DataField="City"/>
            <asp:BoundColumn HeaderText="State"
               DataField="State" />
            <asp:BoundColumn HeaderText="Zip"
               DataField="Zip" />
            <asp:BoundColumn HeaderText="Phone"
               DataField="Phone"/>

            <asp:EditCommandColumn
               EditText="Edit"
               CancelText="Cancel"
               UpdateText="Update"
               HeaderText="Edit"/>

            <asp:ButtonColumn HeaderText="" text="Delete"
               CommandName="delete" />
         </Columns>
      </asp:DataGrid><p>

      <asp:Panel id="AddPanel" runat="server">
         <table>
         <tr>
            <td width="100" valign="top">
               First and last name:
            </td>
            <td width="300" valign="top">
               <asp:TextBox id="tbFName" runat="server"/>
               <asp:TextBox id="tbLName" runat="server"/>
            </td>
         </tr>
         <tr>
            <td valign="top">Address:</td>
            <td valign="top">
```

LISTING 10.10 continued

```
63:                 <asp:TextBox id="tbAddress" runat="server" />
64:              </td>
65:           </tr>
66:           <tr>
67:              <td valign="top">City, State, ZIP:</td>
68:              <td valign="top">
69:                  <asp:TextBox id="tbCity"
70:                    runat="server" />,
71:                 <asp:TextBox id="tbState" runat="server"
72:                    size=2 /> 
73:                 <asp:TextBox id="tbZIP" runat="server"
74:                    size=5 />
75:              </td>
76:           </tr>
77:           <tr>
78:              <td valign="top">Phone:</td>
79:              <td valign="top">
80:                 <asp:TextBox id="tbPhone" runat="server"
81:                    size=11 /><p>
82:              </td>
83:           </tr>
84:           <tr>
85:              <td colspan="2" valign="top" align="right">
86:                 <asp:Button id="btSubmit" runat="server"
87:                    text="Add" OnClick="Submit" />
88:              </td>
89:           </tr>
90:           </table>
91:        </asp:Panel>
92:     </form>
93:  </body></html>
```

ANALYSIS There's really not much to do on this page. You're just displaying server controls with a number of different properties. The real work will come in the code declaration block, which you'll see in a moment. The `DataGrid` and its event handlers (lines 9–13) are the most important part of this listing. Each of the server controls in the panel allows the user to add new data to the database, after the user clicks the Add button on line 86.

If you're writing this in C#, you'll need to change line 19 to read as follows:

```
Text='<%# DataBinder.Eval(Container, "DataItem.UserID") %>'/>
```

Let's examine your code declaration block next. You'll have to handle several things in this section, including loading data into the `DataGrid`, handling the `DataGrid`'s events, and updating the data source when the user fills out the form and clicks the Submit button. Listing 10.11 shows the code in VB.NET, and Listing 10.12 shows the code in C# (be prepared—it's long).

LISTING 10.11 The ASP.NET Code for Listing 10.10

```
<%@ Page Language="VB" %>
<%@ Import Namespace="System.Data" %>
<%@ Import Namespace="System.Data.OleDb" %>

<script runat="server">
   'declare connection
   dim Conn as new OleDbConnection( _
      "Provider=Microsoft.Jet.OLEDB.4.0;" & _
      "Data Source=c:\ASPNET\data\banking.mdb")

    sub Page_Load(Sender as Object, e as EventArgs)
       if Not Page.IsPostBack then
          FillDataGrid()
       end if
    end sub

    sub Submit(Sender as object, e as eventargs)
       'insert new data
       dim i, j as integer
       dim params(7) as string
       dim strText as string
       dim blnGo as boolean = true

       j = 0

       for i = 0 to AddPanel.Controls.Count - 1
          if AddPanel.controls(i).GetType Is _
             GetType(TextBox) then
             strText = Ctype(AddPanel.Controls(i), _
                TextBox).Text
             if strText <> "" then
                params(j) = strText
             else
                blnGo = false
                lblMessage.Text = lblMessage.Text & _
                   "You forgot to enter a value for " & _
                   AddPanel.Controls(i).ID & "<p>"
                lblMessage.Style("ForeColor") = "Red"
             end if
             j = j + 1
          end if
       next

       if not blnGo then
```

LISTING 10.11 continued

```
         exit sub
      end if

      dim strSQL as string = "INSERT INTO tblUsers " & _
         "(FirstName, LastName, Address, City, State, " & _
          "Zip, Phone) VALUES (" & _
         "'" & params(0) & "'," & _
         "'" & params(1) & "'," & _
         "'" & params(2) & "'," & _
         "'" & params(3) & "'," & _
         "'" & params(4) & "'," & _
         "'" & params(5) & "'," & _
         "'" & params(6) & "')"

      ExecuteStatement(strSQL)

      FillDataGrid()
   end sub

   sub dgData_Edit(Sender as object, e as
   ➥DataGridCommandEventArgs)
      FillDataGrid(e.Item.ItemIndex)
   end sub

   sub dgData_Delete(Sender as object, e as
   ➥DataGridCommandEventArgs)
      dim strSQL as string = "DELETE FROM tblUsers " & _
         "WHERE UserID = " & e.Item.ItemIndex + 1

      ExecuteStatement(strSQL)

      FillDataGrid()
   end sub

   sub dgData_Update(Sender as object, e as
   ➥DataGridCommandEventArgs)
      if UpdateDataStore then
         FillDataGrid(-1)
      end if
   end sub

   sub dgData_Cancel(Sender as object, e as
   ➥DataGridCommandEventArgs)
      FillDataGrid(-1)
   end sub

   sub dgData_PageIndexChanged(Sender as Object, e as
   ➥DataGridPageChangedEventArgs)
```

LISTING 10.11 continued

```
      dgData.DataBind()
   end sub

   function UpdateDataStore(e as
   ➥DataGridCommandEventArgs) as boolean

      dim i,j as integer
      dim params(7) as string
      dim strText as string
      dim blnGo as boolean = true

      j = 0

       for i = 1 to e.Item.Cells.Count - 3
          strText = Ctype(e.Item.Cells(i).Controls(0), _
             TextBox).Text
          if strText <> "" then
             params(j) = strText
             j = j + 1
          else
             blnGo = false
             lblMessage.Text = lblMessage.Text & _
                "You forgot to enter a value<p>"
          end if
       next

       if not blnGo then
          return false
          exit function
       end if

       dim strSQL as string = "UPDATE tblUsers SET " & _
          "FirstName = '" & params(0) & "'," & _
          "LastName = '" & params(1) & "'," & _
          "Address = '" & params(2) & "'," & _
          "City = '" & params(3) & "'," & _
          "State = '" & params(4) & "'," & _
          "Zip = '" & params(5) & "'," & _
          "Phone = '" & params(6) & "'" & _
          " WHERE UserID = " & Ctype(e.Item.Cells(0). _
             Controls(1), Label).text

       ExecuteStatement(strSQL)
       return blnGo
    end function

    sub FillDataGrid(Optional EditIndex as integer=-1)
       'open connection
       dim objCmd as new OleDbCommand _
```

LISTING 10.11 continued

```
         ("select * from tblUsers", Conn)
      dim objReader as OleDbDataReader

      try
         objCmd.Connection.Open()
         objReader = objCmd.ExecuteReader()
      catch ex as Exception
         lblMessage.Text = "Error retrieving from the " & _
            database."
      end try

      dgData.DataSource = objReader
      if not EditIndex.Equals(Nothing) then
         dgData.EditItemIndex = EditIndex
      end if

      dgData.DataBind()

      objReader.Close
      objCmd.Connection.Close()

   end sub

   function ExecuteStatement(strSQL)
      dim objCmd as new OleDbCommand(strSQL, Conn)

      try
         objCmd.Connection.Open()
         objCmd.ExecuteNonQuery()
      catch ex as Exception
         lblMessage.Text = "Error updating the database."
      end try

      objCmd.Connection.Close()
   end function
</script>
```

LISTING 10.12 The ASP.NET Code for Listing 10.1 in C#

```
<%@ Page Language="C#" %>
<%@ Import Namespace="System.Data" %>
<%@ Import Namespace="System.Data.OleDb" %>

<script runat="server">
   OleDbConnection Conn = new OleDbConnection
➥("Provider=Microsoft.Jet.OLEDB.4.0;Data Source=
➥c:\\ASPNET\\data\\banking.mdb");
```

LISTING 10.12 continued

```
      void Page_Load(Object Sender, EventArgs e) {
         if (!Page.IsPostBack) {
            FillDataGrid();
         }
      }

      void Submit(Object Sender, EventArgs e) {
         int i, j;
         string[] paramso = new string[7];
         string strText;
         bool blnGo = true;

         j = 0;

         for (i = 0; i <= AddPanel.Controls.Count - 1; i++) {
            if (AddPanel.Controls[i].GetType() ==
➥typeof(TextBox)) {
               strText = ((TextBox)AddPanel.Controls[i]).Text;
               if (strText != "") {
                  paramso[j] = strText;
               } else {
                  blnGo = false;
                  lblMessage.Text += "You forgot to enter
➥a value for " + AddPanel.Controls[i].ID.ToString() + "<p>";
                  lblMessage.Style["ForeColor"] = "Red";
               }
               j++;
            }
         }

         if (!blnGo) {
            return;
         }

         string strSQL = "INSERT INTO tblUsers (FirstName,
➥LastName, Address, City, State, Zip, Phone) VALUES (" +
            "'" + paramso[0] + "'," +
            "'" + paramso[1] + "'," +
            "'" + paramso[2] + "'," +
            "'" + paramso[3] + "'," +
            "'" + paramso[4] + "'," +
            "'" + paramso[5] + "'," +
            "'" + paramso[6] + "')";

         ExecuteStatement(strSQL);

         FillDataGrid();
      }
```

LISTING 10.12 continued

```

void dgData_Edit(Object Sender,
➥DataGridCommandEventArgs e) {
   FillDataGrid(e.Item.ItemIndex);
}

void dgData_Delete(Object Sender,
➥DataGridCommandEventArgs e) {
   string strSQL = "DELETE FROM tblUsers " +
      "WHERE UserID = " + (e.Item.ItemIndex + 1).
➥ToString();

   ExecuteStatement(strSQL);

   FillDataGrid();
}

void dgData_Update(Object Sender,
➥DataGridCommandEventArgs e) {
   if (UpdateDataStore) {
      FillDataGrid(-1);
   }
}

void dgData_Cancel(Object Sender,
➥DataGridCommandEventArgs e) {
   FillDataGrid(-1);
}

void dgData_PageIndexChanged(Object Sender,
➥DataGridPageChangedEventArgs e) {
   dgData.DataBind();
}

bool UpdateDataStore(DataGridCommandEventArgs e) {
   int i,j;
   string[] paramso = new string[7];
   string strText;
   bool blnGo = true;

   j = 0;

   for (i = 1; i <= e.Item.Cells.Count - 3; i++) {
      strText = ((TextBox)e.Item.Cells[i].Controls[0]).
➥Text;
      if (strText != "") {
         paramso[j] = strText;
         j++;
```

LISTING 10.12 continued

```
           } else {
              blnGo = false;
              lblMessage.Text += "You forgot to enter " +
                 "a value<p>";
           }
        }

         if (!blnGo) {
            return false;
         }

         string strSQL = "UPDATE tblUsers SET " +
            "FirstName = '" + paramso[0] + "'," +
            "LastName = '" + paramso[1] + "'," +
            "Address = '" + paramso[2] + "'," +
            "City = '" + paramso[3] + "'," +
            "State = '" + paramso[4] + "'," +
            "Zip = '" + paramso[5] + "'," +
            "Phone = '" + paramso[6] + "'" +
            " WHERE UserID = " + ((Label)e.Item.Cells[0].
➥Controls[1]).Text;

         ExecuteStatement(strSQL);
         return blnGo;
      }

      void FillDataGrid() {
         FillDataGrid(-1);
      }

      void FillDataGrid(int EditIndex) {
         OleDbCommand objCmd = new OleDbCommand
➥ ("select * from tblUsers", Conn);
         OleDbDataReader objReader;

         try {
            objCmd.Connection.Open();
            objReader = objCmd.ExecuteReader();

            dgData.DataSource = objReader;
            if (!EditIndex.Equals(null)) {
               dgData.EditItemIndex = EditIndex;
            }

            dgData.DataBind();

            objReader.Close();
            objCmd.Connection.Close();
```

LISTING 10.12 continued

```
140:
141:          } catch(Exception ex) {
142:             lblMessage.Text = "Error retrieving from the
➥database. Please" +
143:                " make sure all values are correctly input";
144:          }
145:       }
146:
147:       void ExecuteStatement(String strSQL) {
148:          OleDbCommand objCmd = new OleDbCommand(strSQL, Conn);
149:
150:          try {
151:             objCmd.Connection.Open();
152:             objCmd.ExecuteNonQuery();
153:          } catch(Exception ex) {
154:             lblMessage.Text = "Error updating the database.
➥Please" +
155:                " make sure all values are correctly input";
156:          }
157:
158:          objCmd.Connection.Close();
159:       }
160:    </script>
```

ANALYSIS That's quite a bit of code, but it's not as bad as it looks. First, let's look at the methods used to retrieve data and fill the `DataGrid`, and then we'll return to the methods to update the database (the following discussion will refer to the VB.NET version of the previous listing).

On line 7, outside of any methods, you declare an `OleDbConnection` object. Because this object doesn't belong to any particular method (rather, it belongs to the page), it can be used by every method. The first method that executes (as always), is the `Page_Load` method, shown on lines 11–15. This method checks whether the form has been posted back; if not, it calls another method, `FillDataGrid`, which is responsible for retrieving data from the database and binding it to the `DataGrid`. This method is shown on lines 133–157, and it should look familiar to you. Note the optional parameter `EditIndex` in the declaration of the method; I'll explain this in a moment. On lines 135–137, you create `OleDbCommand` and `OleDbDataReader` objects, using the `OleDbConnection` object declared on line 7.

The next step is wrapping your calls to the database in a `try` statement. This statement tentatively executes a block of code, upon the condition that no errors occur. If an error *does* occur, you can use a `catch` statement, shown on line 142, to handle the error and continue execution. Otherwise, your application would simply crash. You haven't done this so far because your applications have only been simple examples. However, there are a number of things that could go wrong when you're connecting to a system outside of your ASP.NET environment, which in this case is the database. When you start to develop professional applications, you'll need to prevent such errors from crashing your application, or even worse, letting the users see an error happen.

Do	Don't
Do use `try...catch...finally` statements when connecting to any object or system outside your ASP.NET environment. This includes databases, managed components, COM objects, and so on.	**Don't** expect that nothing will go wrong, or that you've dealt with all possible problems.

Don't worry if this doesn't make complete sense yet. You'll look at the `try` statement in detail next week in the discussion of debugging (see Day 20, "Debugging ASP.NET Pages").

Inside the `try` block, you connect to the database and try to fill your `OleDbDataReader`. If that doesn't work, you send a message to the user with your label. You set the data source of the `DataGrid` to the `DataReader` on line 147. Before you bind the data, however, let's examine that optional parameter, `EditIndex`, again. Every time the user tries to edit an item, you have to set the `EditItemIndex` property of the `DataGrid` appropriately, and then bind the data. This method allows you to set the `EditItemIndex` property here, which saves you the hassle of setting the edit mode and rebinding later on. Therefore, you include an `if` statement on line 148 to see if this `EditIndex` parameter was specified. If so, you set the `EditItemIndex` property of the `DataGrid`.

(To create an optional parameter in C#, you simply create the same method twice: once with the parameter as normal, and once without. The method without the parameter can then simply call the one with the parameter supplying a valid value for the parameter. This way, the user can choose which version she wants to use; this is known as method overloading, and is a part of object-oriented programming. See the `FillDataGrid` methods of Listing 10.12 on lines 119 and 123 to see it in action.)

Finally, you close the `DataReader` and connection objects on lines 154 and 155. When you request this page from the browser, you should see something similar to Figure 10.8, depending on the data you have in your database.

FIGURE 10.8

The UI for your database application.

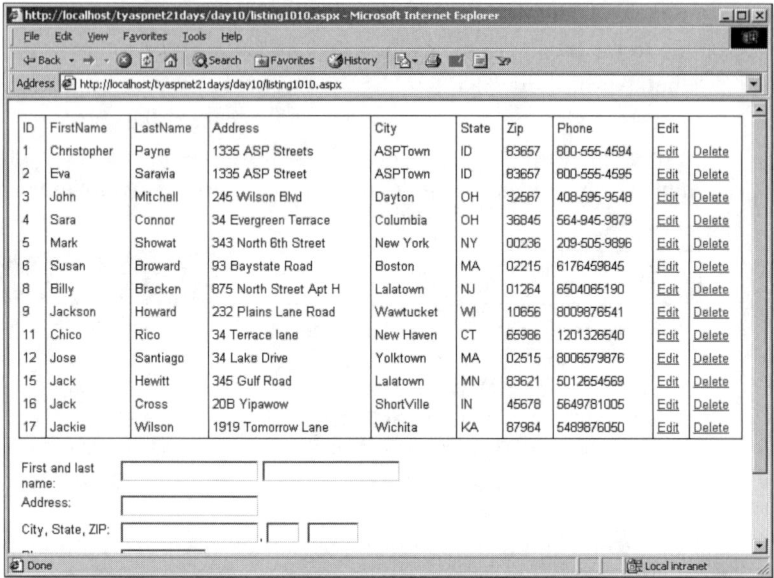

Now that your data is viewable, you need to add the methods to allow the user to edit the items in the `DataGrid`. Lines 64, 68, 77, 83, and 91 show the methods that will execute on the `Edit`, `Delete`, `Update`, `Cancel`, and `Update` events of the `DataGrid`.

For the `Edit` and `Cancel` commands of your `DataGrid`, you can simply call the `FillDataGrid` method with an optional edit index parameter, like so:

```
sub dgData_Edit(Sender as object, e as _
   DataGridCommandEventArgs)
   FillDataGrid(e.Item.ItemIndex)
end sub

sub dgData_Cancel(Sender as object, e as _
   DataGridCommandEventArgs)
   FillDataGrid(-1)
end sub
```

The `Edit` method sets the `EditItemIndex` property of the `DataGrid` to the item the user selected, and `Cancel` sets it to `-1`, which turns off edit mode.

For the `Update` command, you're going to have to be creative. You need to collect all the data from the text boxes that will be generated dynamically when the user clicks the edit link. Therefore, you need a `for` loop, shown on line 100. This loop iterates through all but the last three cells for the selected item in the `DataGrid` (remember the last three don't contain any data—they are the Update, Cancel, and Delete buttons), and stores the value in the variable `strText`, shown on line 101. If this value is not an empty string, you store it in an array that will be used later to update the database. If it is empty, you need to stop the procedure and alert the user, as shown on lines 106–108.

Notice the different looping variables, `i` and `j`. `i` is used for iterating through the row's cells, while `j` is used for the indices in the parameter array. The reason you need both is that the cells' indices don't match up to your array indices. For example, the `"FirstName"` cell is at index 1, but you need to store it at index 0 in your array. Otherwise, you'll get "index out of bounds" errors. You use `j` to keep track of what array index you're at. Figure 10.9 illustrates this concept.

FIGURE 10.9

The cell indices and array indices don't match.

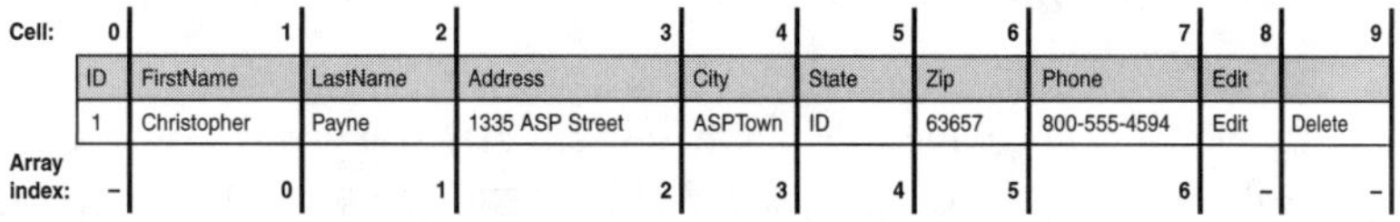

Cell:	0	1	2	3	4	5	6	7	8	9
	ID	FirstName	LastName	Address	City	State	Zip	Phone	Edit	
	1	Christopher	Payne	1335 ASP Street	ASPTown	ID	63657	800-555-4594	Edit	Delete
Array index:	-	0	1	2	3	4	5	6	-	-

If any of the text boxes were empty, on line 106 you set a Boolean (`blnGo`) parameter to remind yourself. If this value is false, meaning one of the text boxes is blank, you want to stop the update. Otherwise, you'll end up with invalid data. You don't want blanks for your user database. This is done with the check on lines 113–116:

```
if not blnGo then
   return false
   exit function
end if
```

Next, you want to construct your SQL update statement. Because all your values are stored in the `param` array (or `paramso` in Listing 10.12), you can do this easily, as shown on lines 118–127.

On lines 126–127, you set the `WHERE` clause of the insert. You only want to update the item that was edited, so you need to determine the identity field of that item. Luckily, the identity field is `"UserID"`, which is already on your `DataGrid`, in cell 1 of each row. You grab the control from this cell, cast it as a label, and grab the text. Then, according to Figure 10.10, if you edit the first row, the corresponding SQL statement will be

```
UPDATE tblUsers SET FirstName = 'Christopher',LastName =
➥'Payne',Address = '1335 ASP Street',City = 'ASPTown',
➥State = 'ID',Zip = '83657',Phone = '800-555-4594'
➥WHERE UserID = 1
```

Finally, you simply need to execute the update statement. This is done by calling another method, `ExecuteStatement`, which is shown on lines 159–170. This method simply encapsulates the steps of creating an `OleDbCommand` object and executing the SQL statement.

Again, you use a `try...catch` statement here to ensure there are no unhandled errors, and you use the `ExecuteNonQuery()` method to perform your update.

Next, let's look at the `Delete` command method, shown on lines 68–75:

```
sub dgData_Delete(Sender as object, e as _
   DataGridCommandEventArgs)
   dim strSQL as string = "DELETE FROM tblUsers " & _
            "WHERE UserID = " & Ctype(e.Item.Cells(0). _
             Controls(1), Label).text

   ExecuteStatement(strSQL)

   FillDataGrid()
end sub
```

Relatively speaking, this method is simple. You create your SQL delete statement using the `UserID` field of the row for your `WHERE` clause, and then you simply execute the statement and refill your `DataGrid`. Note, however, that this method is not foolproof. When you delete an identity field in a database, the field is typically not reseeded; meaning if the current user ID is 19, and you delete that user, the next user will be 20, not 19 again. Thus, the calculation used in the previous code snippet won't work once you start adding and deleting records. Instead, you'll need to go with another method—I'll leave that as an exercise for you.

The only thing left to do is add new records to the database when a user fills out the form fields and clicks the Add button. The `Submit` method (lines 17–62) is similar to the `Update` method you just examined, except that you're executing an `insert` command instead of an `update`.

Let's take a quick overview of the `Submit` method. Remember placing all the user input controls in a panel? The reason you did that was so that you could loop through them, just as you did with the cells in the `DataGrid`. This time, instead of looping through a `DataGridCommandEventArgs`'s `Cells` collection, you're looping the panel's `Controls` collection. Now you see the reason for the panel. Also, the SQL statement varies in syntax slightly. Other than that, everything is exactly the same as the `Update` method.

Congratulations, that's it! You should now have a complete application that allows users to update, add, and delete records from your database. There was a lot of code, but much of it was fairly straightforward.

You also got to practice some good coding design methods by separating things into separate functions as much as you could. Modularizing your applications is great for readability and code reuse. It would be very simple to just copy and paste much of this code into another application, and it should work fine with few modifications.

As you might have noticed, you lose a little control over how the fields are rendered when you use the `EditCommand` for the `DataGrid`. The text boxes were longer than they needed to be, for example. In the future, when you're using a `DataGrid` control, it may be easier to use `TemplateColumns` and text boxes instead of `BoundColumns` and the `EditCommand`. There are fewer events to handle, and you have more control over the rendering. But that's a stylistic issue that you can handle as you please.

That's Not ASP!

If you're familiar with classic ASP or ADO, you might be wondering how your good old `Recordset` fits into all this.

Although the actual ADODB `Recordset` is a thing of the past, the concept is still there. In essence, a `DataReader` is simply a `Recordset` that uses a forward-only cursor, whereas the `DataSet` is a `Recordset` that uses a scrollable or dynamic cursor. The new ADO.NET objects are a bit more functional, of course, but the basic functionality is similar.

When working with a `Recordset`, regardless of the cursor type, you are continuously connected to the database, which requires locks on the data. This can be rather inefficient, especially if you have many concurrent users. The `DataSet` is a completely disconnected data store, which means you simply grab the data from the database and you're off and running; no need to maintain a connection to the database, no need to lock the data. In addition, the `DataSet` can represent much more about a data store than simply its data. As you learned today, `DataSets` can contain multiple tables (which is impossible with `Recordsets`), relationships, and mappings. This is a powerful new model for dealing with data, and might eliminate some database woes that were present with traditional ADO. All that functionality can come at a price, however. Therefore, you also have the `OleDbDataReader`, which more closely resembles the `Recordset`. The difference is that the former is completely object-oriented, and deals with type-safe data.

The `OleDbConnection` and `OleDbCommand` objects are very similar to the `ADODB Connection` and `Command` objects from traditional ADO, so you should feel fairly comfortable transitioning to them. Concepts that existed in classic ASP, such as transactions and parameter objects, still exist in ASP.NET. In fact, in Day 12, we'll examine these in more detail.

Although there are many differences between classic ADO and ADO.NET, there are also many similarities that will aid developers familiar with classic ADO. A large number of the changes in ADO.NET are simply to make the data model more coherent, flexible, and powerful.

Summary

Today was another long day, but you learned a great deal. You're becoming familiar with database-driven ASP.NET applications now, and you should be comfortable using data binding and list controls. You've rapidly progressed from beginner to an advanced-intermediate level.

Today you examined ADO.NET and its fundamentals. ADO.NET consists of two main components: the `DataSet` and managed providers. You spent yesterday examining the `DataSet`, and today you learned a bit more about the technical aspects of its data model, including `RowState` and concurrency. You also explored the OLE DB managed provider and its various objects, including the `OleDbCommand` and `OleDbDataAdapter` objects, which provide tremendous functionality for interacting with databases.

The `OleDbDataReader` is a lightweight cousin of the `DataSet` and is useful for high-performance applications. However, the `DataSet` provides more functionality. Generally, if you simply want to display data, use an `OleDbDataReader`.

Finally, you combined all the aspects of ADO.NET and ASP.NET to produce a full-service, data-driven application. Putting it all together was a very useful exercise and showed you the additional considerations that come into play when you're developing an entire application.

Tomorrow, you're going to open up XML and figure out how it can be used with ASP.NET. XML will allow you to develop a truly distributed application, which is essential for developing Web Services.

Q&A

Q Refresh my memory. How can I switch from the SQL managed provider to the OLE DB provider?

A At the simplest, all you need to do is replace all `OleDb` prefixes with `Sql`, making sure you import the `System.Data.SqlClient` namespace, and possibly updating your connection string to work with SQL. Other than that, there are some slight differences in the two providers, but in everyday situations, these changes will suffice.

Q Are the `OleDbDataAdapter` and `OleDbCommand` objects completely different? Why are there two different objects?

A The `OleDbDataAdapter` is a more abstract version of the `OleDbCommand` object. When you set the `SelectCommand`, `UpdateCommand`, `InsertCommand`, and `DeleteCommand` methods, ADO.NET is actually creating new `OleDbCommand` objects. These objects are used to interface with the data store to execute SQL commands. Using an `OleDbDataAdapter` simply allows you to place the results in a `DataSet` (as well as use `TableMappings`).

You can think of the `OleDbDataAdapter` object as a high-level object, while the `OleDbCommand` object is a low-level object that interacts directly with databases.

Workshop

This workshop will help reinforce the concepts covered in today's lesson. The answers can be found in Appendix A.

Quiz

1. What are the two major parts of ADO.NET?
2. What do managed providers do?
3. What is disconnected data?
4. Which of the following constructors isn't valid for the `OleDbCommand` object (line 4, 5, 6, 8, or 9)?

```
dim strSQL as string = "SELECT * FROM tblUsers")
dim Conn as new OleDbConnection("DSN=21DaysBanking")

dim objCmd as new OleDbCommand()
dim objCmd as new OleDbCommand(strSQL)
dim objCmd as new OleDbCommand(strSQL, _Conn)
dim objCmd as new OleDbCommand(Conn)
dim objCmd as new OleDbCommand(strSQL, _
   "DSN=21DaysBanking")
```

5. What type of data model does an `OleDbCommand` object fill?
6. Does an `OleDbCommand` object need to be closed?
7. What are the five members of the `OleDbDataAdapter` object?
8. Which of the following constructors isn't valid for the `OleDbDataAdapter` object (line 5, 6, 7, 9, or 10)?

```
dim strSQL as string = "SELECT * FROM tblUsers")
dim Conn as new OleDbConnection("DSN=21DaysBanking")
dim objADOCmd as new OleDbCommand(strSQL, Conn)

dim objCmd as new OleDbDataAdapter()
dim objCmd as new OleDbDataAdapter(objADOCmd)
dim objCmd as new OleDbDataAdapter(strSQL, _
   Conn)
```

```
dim objCmd as new OleDbDataAdapter(Conn)
dim objCmd as new OleDbDataAdapter(strSQL, _
   "DSN=21DaysBanking")
```

Exercises

Modify the example application you built today to use the `OleDbDataAdapter` and `DataSet` objects instead of `OleDbCommand` and `OleDbDataReader`. If you use the `OleDbCommandBuilder` as well, don't forget the limitation about the initial `select` statement matching the columns in the `DataSet` that was described earlier today.

WEEK 2

DAY 11

Using XML in ASP.NET

By now, you should have a strong grasp of data access with ASP.NET. You know how to access and display data, as well as how to modify it with ADO.NET—several different ways, in fact. However, any discussion of databases and the Internet isn't complete without mentioning the Extensible Markup Language, or XML.

XML is the new universal language for representing data on the Web. It has received a lot of attention because it eliminates many of the problems typically associated with data access and distribution, such as security, understandability, readability, and data conversions.

ASP.NET and the .NET Framework were designed with a strong focus on XML, which not only increases their strengths but makes them simpler to use. You'll spend today learning about XML and its place in the ASP.NET framework, with plenty of discussion on reading, writing, and converting XML.

Today's lesson will cover the following:

- What is XML?
- How to read, write, and validate XML with the `XmlTextReader` and `XmlTextWriter` objects

- How to use the XML Document Object Model
- How the XML .NET Framework works with relational data

An Introduction to XML

XML is a text-based format for describing data. It brings with it new ways to deliver data to Web-enabled applications, allowing nearly any type of data to be sent and used anywhere. This sounds like some type of magic wand, but XML's usefulness stems from two simple features. First, XML is extensible (hence the name, Extensible Markup Language), meaning you can easily extend it by adding your own custom tags and structure. Second, it's text-based, meaning you can create or read XML with any text editor, such as Notepad.

Like HTML, XML uses simple markup tags to describe its contents. Unlike HTML, however, there are no standard tags—you make up your own. This is the power of XML—you can create any tags you want, so you can represent any type of data. This also means that XML is easy to read and modify.

For example, you could make up the following tags and XML would understand them, even though HTML browsers wouldn't:

```
<Name>...</Name>
<Occupation>...</Occupation>
<FavRestaurant>...</FavRestaurant>
```

XML is represented as plain text—you can create XML data in Notepad if you want. Thus, it's an easy way to transport data to various sources. With most database applications, the internal data is stored in a database-specific format. When you're working with different data stores (or different computer platforms) in the same project, complex conversions from one format to the other commonly are needed. With XML, on the other hand, the data is presented in a structured, textual format, removing the need for any archaic conversions. Due to its textual nature, XML is easy for users to read and understand. Also, XML can bypass sophisticated security measures that often prevent other types of communication from occurring, or that need complex workarounds. These security measures often allow plain text to pass through, so XML is perfect for transporting data anywhere.

Internet applications often involve working with multiple data sources residing on different platforms. XML is an ideal way to represent data in such an Internet application.

The XML Data Model

Listing 11.1 contains an example XML file representing the inventory of a bookstore.

LISTING 11.1 A Bookstore's Inventory in XML Form

```
<bookstore>
  <book genre="novel" style="hardcover">
    <title>The Handmaid's Tale</title>
    <price>19.95</price>
    <author>
      <first-name>Margaret</first-name>
      <last-name>Atwood</last-name>
    </author>
  </book>
  <book genre="novel" style="paperback">
    <title>The Poisonwood Bible</title>
    <price>11.99</price>
    <author>
      <first-name>Barbara</first-name>
      <last-name>Kingsolver</last-name>
    </author>
  </book>
  <book genre="novel" style="hardcover">
    <title>Hannibal</title>
    <price>27.95</price>
    <author>
      <first-name>Richard</first-name>
      <last-name>Harris</last-name>
    </author>
  </book>
  <book genre="novel" style="hardcover">
    <title>Focault's Pendulum</title>
    <price>22.95</price>
    <author>
      <first-name>Umberto</first-name>
      <last-name>Eco</last-name>
    </author>
  </book>
</bookstore>
```


NEW TERM Save this file as `books.xml`. You'll learn about the specifics later today in the section on XML schemas. For now, notice that XML is made up of structured, hierarchical tags. There are two `<book>` tags, each with its own attributes (`genre` and `style`), and several subelements (`title`, `author`, `price`). The actual data is represented within these sub-element tags. The entire set is wrapped in `<bookstore>` tags that describe this data set. This type of data representation is often called a *document tree* or *data tree*.

In a traditional database, such as Access, the data will look something like Figure 11.1.

FIGURE 11.1

The XML data from Listing 11.1, viewed in Microsoft Access.

Bookstore

Genre	Style	Title	AuFirstName	AuLastName	Price
novel	hardcover	The Handmaid's Tale	Margaret	Atwood	19.95
novel	paperback	The Poisonwood Bible	Barbara	Kingsolver	11.99

The XML version is more portable, it's easier for others to read and use, and it doesn't need any complex mechanisms to set up. Let's save this listing in a text file called `books.xml` for use later. Save it in the `c:\inetpub\wwwroot\tyaspnet21days\day11` folder (or somewhere else you'll remember easily). Now try viewing this file from your browser. If you're using a newer browser (IE 5.0 and above), you should see something similar to Figure 11.2.

FIGURE 11.2

XML viewed from the browser.

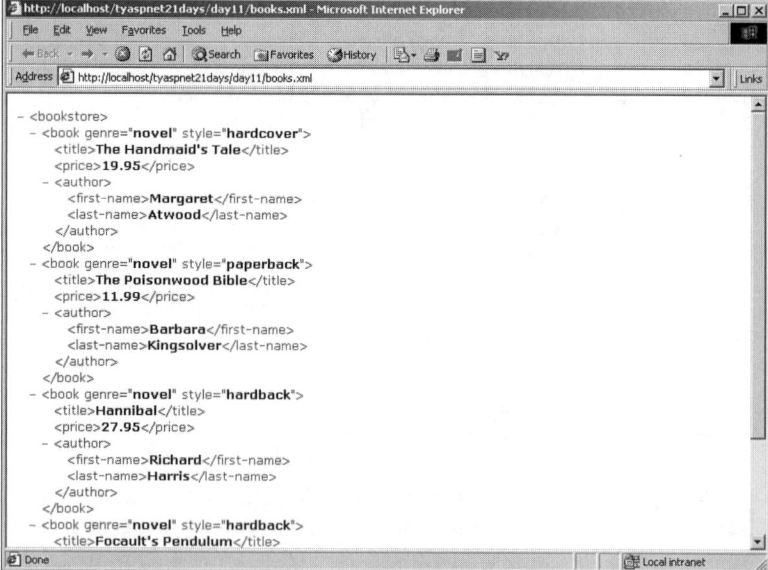
http://localhost/tyaspnet21days/day11/books.xml - Microsoft Internet Explorer
File Edit View Favorites Tools Help
Back Search Favorites History
Address http://localhost/tyaspnet21days/day11/books.xml
Links
- <bookstore>
- <book genre="novel" style="hardcover">
<title>The Handmaid's Tale</title>
<price>19.95</price>
- <author>
<first-name>Margaret</first-name>
<last-name>Atwood</last-name>
</author>
</book>
- <book genre="novel" style="paperback">
<title>The Poisonwood Bible</title>
<price>11.99</price>
- <author>
<first-name>Barbara</first-name>
<last-name>Kingsolver</last-name>
</author>
</book>
- <book genre="novel" style="hardback">
<title>Hannibal</title>
<price>27.95</price>
- <author>
<first-name>Richard</first-name>
<last-name>Harris</last-name>
</author>
</book>
- <book genre="novel" style="hardback">
<title>Focault's Pendulum</title>
Done
Local intranet

Internet Explorer can parse the XML automatically and display it as a hierarchy for you. You can click on the - sign to collapse a branch, or click the + sign to expand it. XML provides a wonderful mechanism for representing data.

XML Schemas

If you define your own tags, how will others know what kind of data you're talking about? *XML schemas* define this format. They describe what types of data to expect, how fields should be formatted, their sizes, and so on. It isn't necessary for an XML document to have a schema, but it helps tremendously; after all, if you want to speak the same language with someone else, it helps that you both know the language.

There are three major types of schemas: the document type definition (DTD), the Microsoft XML-Data Reduced schema (XDR), and the XML Schema Definition Language (XSD). The actual schemas are simply plain text files that have the appropriate extension (`.dtd`, `.xdr`, or `.xsd`). Any of these can be used with your XML files, but for applications in the .NET Framework, the XDR is the preferred one.

Let's look at the XDR schema that defines Listing 11.1.

LISTING 11.2 The XML Schema of Listing 11.1

```
<?xml version="1.0"?>
<Schema xmlns="urn:schemas-microsoft-com:xml-data"
   xmlns:dt="urn:schemas-microsoft-com:datatypes">
   <ElementType name="first-name" content="textOnly"/>
   <ElementType name="last-name" content="textOnly"/>
   <ElementType name="name" content="textOnly"/>
   <ElementType name="price" content="textOnly"
      dt:type="fixed.14.4"/>
   <ElementType name="author" content="eltOnly" order="one">
       <group order="seq">
          <element type="name"/>
       </group>
       <group order="seq">
          <element type="first-name"/>
          <element type="last-name"/>
       </group>
    </ElementType>
    <ElementType name="title" content="textOnly"/>
       <AttributeType name="genre" dt:type="string"/>
       <AttributeType name="style" dt:type="enumeration"
          dt:values="paperback hardcover"/>
    <ElementType name="book" content="eltOnly">
       <attribute type="genre" required="yes"/>
       <attribute type="style" required="yes"/>
       <element type="title"/>
```

LISTING 11.2 continued

```
26:            <element type="price"/>
27:            <element type="author"/>
28:         </ElementType>
29:         <ElementType name="bookstore" content="eltOnly">
30:            <element type="book"/>
31:         </ElementType>
32:      </Schema>
```

ANALYSIS Save this listing as `books.xdr` in the same folder as `books.xml`. This also looks like plain HTML, but it's much more. Let's examine it more closely. On line 1, you simply specify the type of XML you're creating—version 1.0 in this case. This line is required for these examples to work properly. On line 2, you open your `<Schema>` tag. `xmlns` stands for XML namespace, which is a standard group of XML tags that someone has put together to promote further standardization—sort of like providing a standard dictionary to use for XML terms. Typically, if you specify a namespace at all, you'll use a standard one such as `schemas-microsoft-com:xml-data`, as done here, or use a custom schema, which we'll talk about later today.

There is, however, one important thing to note about the namespace, which will come in very handy in tomorrow's lesson. The namespace in XML is used to categorize elements in the schema, just like namespaces in .NET categorize .NET classes. The difference in XML is that XML uses a colon to separate the namespace name from the element, whereas .NET uses a period. The syntax to define a namespace then is as follows:

```
xmlns:prefix="value"
```

The *`prefix`* is the optional name you'll use to refer to the namespace, and its actual value is arbitrary. So, for example, if you had the following declaration:

```
xmlns:xs="blahblah.org"
```

Then each of the elements on lines 4–31 could be prefixed by `"xs:`":

```
<xs:ElementType ...>
<xs:AttributeType ...>
...
```

As you can see, there are no prefixes on lines 4–31. Why? Because, and this is important, an `xmlns` attribute with a blank prefix signifies the default namespace. (If you don't specify an `xmlns` attribute at all, you don't have any namespace at all.) Anytime you specify a value for the *`prefix`* in the `xmlns` attribute, you are providing a non-default namespace. If you leave the prefix out, XML assumes that all elements in the schema that are not otherwise specified belong to this default namespace.

Which brings up another point: You can have as many namespaces as you want in an XML file or schema. Each will follow the same syntax as `xmlns` did here, but using a different prefix. Make sure that you prefix your elements accordingly when you have more than the default namespace.

The key thing to note about XML namespaces is that they group elements in the XML file. When you learn about searching XML files tomorrow, this will become important.

The `<ElementType>` tags are where you define the format of data. Lines 4–7 define the `first-name`, `last-name`, `name`, and `price` elements, which you'll use later in the schema. Placing these definitions here is similar to declaring variables at the top of your pages. The `content` attribute defines what type of data may go in this tag, and `dt:type` defines a few more attributes, such as the data type and how it's formatted.

Lines 9–17 define another element, `author`. This element also has a few other tags inside it, defined by the elements described on lines 4–7. Lines 18–21 define a few more elements and attributes that you may use in your schema.

Finally, line 22 defines the `book` element, which contains all the other elements defined so far. This section should match the format of the XML file; in other words, the title, followed by the price, followed by the author. On line 29, you define another element that in turn contains the `book` element.

11

Note

> You didn't have to define the elements before you used them—you could have defined them all in the `book` element. However, doing it this way is a better method for building schemas, just like it's a good idea to define your variables before you use them in ASP.NET.

The schema, `books.xdr`, defines the columns in a database table. The `books.xml` XML file defines the rows. In this way, these two files can represent nearly any type of data. Now if you want your `books.xml` file to use the new schema, you need to alter it slightly. Change the first two lines to read:

```
<?xml version="1.0"?>
<bookstore xmlns="x-schema:books.xdr">
```

In other words, you need to specify the version of XML you're using, and then just add a reference to your new schema file. You only need to do so for the top element in your XML file; all subelements will follow suit.

We'll skip over the other two types of schemas for now—we'll touch on them briefly again later today. Much of the syntax is similar for all three schema types, so it really depends on what you're comfortable with.

NEW TERM An XML file that follows a schema and whose tags are properly expressed (meaning they adhere to the XML standards set forth by the World Wide Web Consortium, W3C) is known as a *well-formed* XML document. Creating well-formed XML files ensures that your data will be readable from any XML-compliant application. In general, a well-formed XML file must follow these guidelines:

- It must contain at least one element.
- It must contain a unique opening and closing tag that contains the entire document, forming the root element.
- All other tags must be nested, with opening and closing tags, and cannot overlap.

For more information on W3C standards documentation, check out `http://webreference.com/xml/reference/standards.html`.

Accessing XML with ASP.NET

Accessing XML is very similar to accessing a database with ADO.NET. The .NET Framework provides a lot of objects that give you varying degrees of control over the data, each with its own advantages and drawbacks. This section will look at the two simplest objects: the `XmlTextReader` and the `XmlTextWriter` in the `System.XML` namespace.

Reading XML

The `XmlTextReader` provides a simple, fast mechanism for accessing the raw contents of an XML file. This object is similar to an `OleDbDataReader` in that it provides forward-only access, without a lot of the overhead that the `DataSet` requires.

To open an XML file, simply create a new `XmlTextReader` and pass it the filename of the XML file. If you create the ASP.NET file `XMLReader.aspx` and put it in the same directory as your XML file, you could simply use the following:

```
'VB.NET
Dim reader As new XmlTextReader(file name with path)

//C#
XmlTextReader reader = new XmlTextReader(file name with path);
```

There are no connection strings to worry about. The full pathname is necessary, however. This can be produced by the `Server.MapPath` method. (See Day 4, "Using ASP.NET

Objects with C# and VB.NET.") To access the data, you use the `Read` method, which is similar to the `OleDbDataReader`. For example:

```
Do While (reader.Read())
   ' Do some work on the data
Loop
```

The `Read` method advances through the XML file automatically whenever it's called. Listing 11.3 presents an ASP.NET Web page that reads and displays the contents of the `books.xml` file using the `XmlTextReader` class.

LISTING 11.3 Accessing XML Data with `XmlTextReader`

```
1:    <%@ Page Language="VB" %>
2:    <%@ Import Namespace="System.Xml" %>
3:
4:    <script runat=server>
5:       sub Page_Load(Sender as Object, e as EventArgs)
6:          dim reader as XmlTextReader
7:
8:          try
9:             reader = new XmlTextReader(Server.MapPath _
10:               ("books.xml"))
11:            While reader.Read()
12:               Response.Write("<b>" & reader.Name & "</b> " & _
13:                  reader.Value & "<br>")
14:            End While
15:         catch ex as Exception
16:            Response.Write("Error accessing XML file")
17:         finally
18:            reader.Close
19:         end try
20:   end sub
21:   </script>
22:
23:   <html><body>
24:
25:   </body></html>
```

ANALYSIS The first new thing to note is the `Import` statement on line 2, which imports the `System.Xml` namespace. This `Import` statement allows you to work with the XML-related classes, such as `XmlTextReader`.

Next, you declare your `XmlTextReader` on line 6. You then wrap the code that will access the XML in a `try` block. (Remember that whenever you access resources outside ASP.NET, you should use a `try` statement.) On line 9, you open the reader with your XML file. This syntax requires that you specify the entire path to the XML file, so use

`Server.MapPath` to return that information. Specifically, `Server.MapPath` will return `c:\inetpub\wwwroot\tyaspnet21days\day11\books.xml`.

Finally, use the `Read` method to loop through the XML contents automatically and display each item's `Name` and `Value` in the browser. Don't forget to close the reader, as shown in the `finally` block on lines 17 and 18. Figure 11.3 contains a screenshot of Listing 11.3 when viewed through a browser.

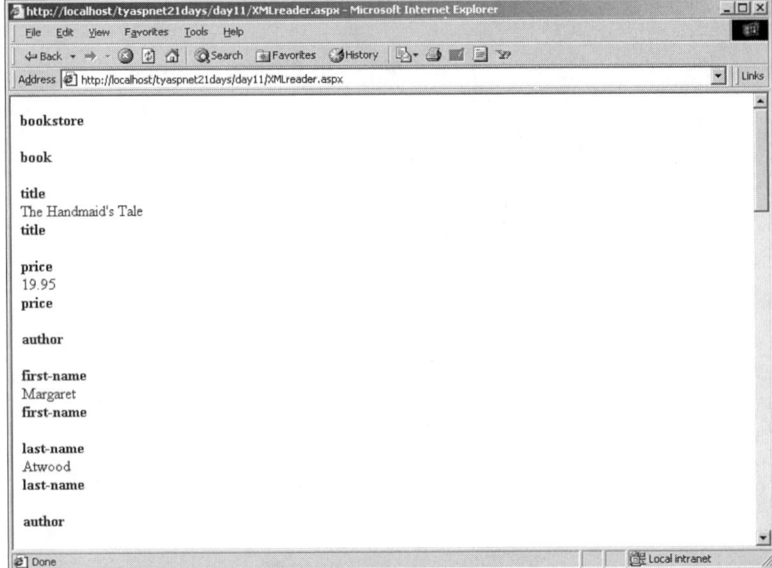

FIGURE 11.3
Displaying the contents of `books.xml`.

Figure 11.3 shows all of the tags in your XML file, including opening and closing tags—not exactly what you wanted. Unfortunately, the `XmlTextReader` object provides very limited functionality. It doesn't care what tags it returns, so it just returns all of them!

To combat this, the `XmlTextReader` has a `NodeType` property that tells you what kind of data you're looking at. Table 11.1 lists some of the most common node types available.

TABLE 11.1 `NodeTypes` for the `XmlTextReader`

Type	*Description*
`Attribute`	An attribute
`CDATA`	This section escapes text that would otherwise be recognized as a markup language, such as HTML
`Comment`	Comments delimited by `<!--` and `-->` tags

TABLE 11.1 continued

Type	*Description*
`Document`	The root of the XML data tree
`Element`	An element, typically the actual data in an XML file
`None`	You're not examining a node
`Text`	Returns the text content of an element
`XMLDeclaration`	The XML declaration node, such as `<?XML version='1.0'?>`

Let's use these `NodeTypes` and modify Listing 11.3 to return only the data you're interested in.

LISTING 11.4 Using `NodeTypes` to Return Data

```
<%@ Page Language="VB" %>
<%@ Import Namespace="System.Xml" %>

<script runat=server>
   sub Page_Load(Sender as Object, e as EventArgs)
      dim reader as XmlTextReader
      dim i as integer

      try
         reader = new XmlTextReader(Server.MapPath _
            ("books.xml"))
         While reader.Read()
            Select Case reader.NodeType
               Case XMLNodeType.Element
                  if reader.HasAttributes then
                     for i = 0 to reader.AttributeCount - 1
                        Response.Write(reader.GetAttribute _
                           & " ")
                     next
                     Response.Write("<br>")
                  end if
               Case XMLNodeType.Text
                  Response.Write(reader.Value & "<br>")
            End Select
         End While
      catch ex as Exception
         Response.Write("Error accessing XML file")
      finally
         reader.Close
      end try
   end sub
</script>
```

LISTING 11.4 continued

```
33:
34:     <html><body>
35:
36:     </body></html>
```

ANALYSIS You inserted a `case` statement on line 13 to evaluate the type of node before you output anything. The first case, on line 14, executes if the reader object's `NodeType` is an `Element`. If the node has any attributes, you loop through them and use the `GetAttribute` method to return the corresponding value. On line 23, you simply output the value if the node is a text item. Figure 11.4 shows the output of this new code listing.

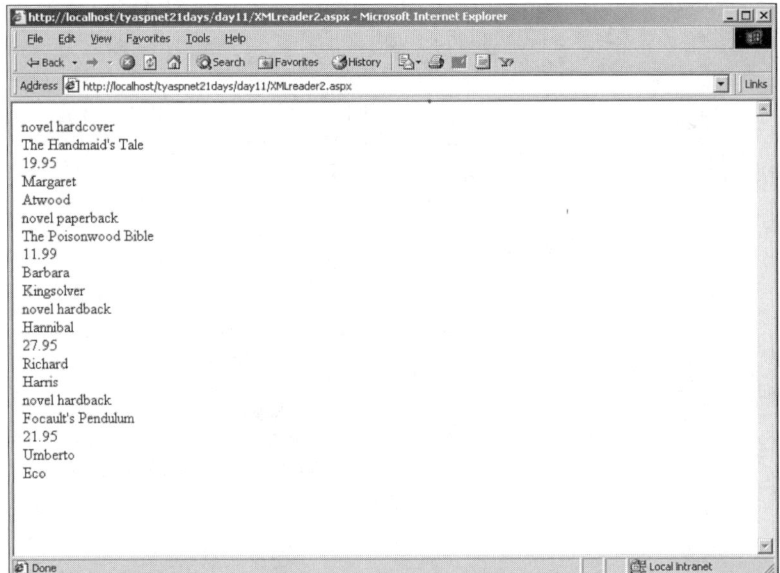

FIGURE 11.4
Displaying the contents of `books.xml` *using* `NodeTypes`.

This produces a better representation of the data.

If you know the specific structure of the XML file, such as the names of the elements and their attributes, you can customize your code further so that only the items you're interested in are displayed. For example, if you only want to see the genre attribute, you can write the following in place of the attribute loop on lines 13–24:

```
Response.Write(reader.Item("genre") & "<br>")
```

Writing XML

The `XmlTextWriter` object makes it just as easy to write XML files as `XmlTextReader` makes it to read them. This object provides `Write` methods that produce the appropriate output.

For example, Listing 11.5 creates a new XML file and places an entry in it.

LISTING 11.5 Writing XML Files Using `XmlTextWriter`

```
<%@ Page Language="VB" %>
<%@ Import Namespace="System.Xml" %>

<script runat=server>
   sub Page_Load(Sender as Object, e as EventArgs)
      dim writer as XmlTextWriter

      try
         writer = new XmlTextWriter(Server.MapPath _
             ("books2.xml"), nothing)

          writer.WriteStartDocument
          writer.Formatting = Formatting.Indented
          writer.Indentation = 3
          writer.WriteStartElement("bookstore")
             writer.WriteStartElement("book")
                writer.WriteAttributeString("genre", "history")
                writer.WriteAttributeString("style", "hardcover")

                writer.WriteElementString("title", "Vietnam")

                writer.WriteElementString("price", _
                   "6.99")

                writer.WriteStartElement("author")
                   writer.WriteElementString("first-name", _
                      "Michael")
                   writer.WriteElementString("last-name", _
                      "Avery")
                writer.WriteEndElement()
             writer.WriteEndElement()
          writer.WriteEndElement()

          writer.Flush
       catch ex as Exception
          Response.Write("Error accessing XML file")
       finally
          writer.Close
          Response.Write("Finished processing")
```

LISTING 11.5 continued

```
40:         end try
41:      end sub
42:   </script>
43:
44:   <html><body>
45:
46:   </body></html>
```

ANALYSIS The structure of this listing is similar to that for the `XmlTextReader`. You declare your writer on line 6 and wrap everything else in a `try` block. You then instantiate your writer on line 9. The first parameter is the name of the XML file to write to, the second parameter is the encoding (the default is UTF-8). If there's no file with this name, ASP.NET will create one. Otherwise, it uses the existing file.

> **Caution**
>
> Creating an XML file in this way will overwrite any file with the same name. In this case, existing content in `books2.xml` will be lost. So make sure you're not overwriting anything important!

Line 12 writes the XML declaration tag to the file, `<?XML version='1.0'?>`. This is part of a well-formed XML document. Lines 13 and 14 specify how you want the outputted XML to look. On line 13, you tell ASP.NET to indent the file, and on line 14, you tell it to use three spaces to do so. This makes reading the file later much easier on the eyes. The `Formatting` property can be set to `Indented` or `None`. You can use the `IndentChar` property to set the character used for indenting.

Line 15 starts the data generation. You use the `WriteStartElement` and `WriteEndElement` methods to open and close element tags. Line 15 produces the tag `<bookstore>`, and line 32 produces the corresponding closing tag, `</bookstore>`. Line 16 opens the `<book>` tag, and line 31 closes it.

On lines 17 and 18, you create the attributes for the `<book>` tag, `genre` and `style`, and assign the values accordingly. `WriteElementString` encapsulates the start and end element functionality for simple elements. Here's line 20:

```
writer.WriteElementString("title", "Vietnam")
```

It produces the following output:

```
<title>Vietnam</title>
```

In essence, `WriteElementString` produces the opening and closing tags specified by the first parameter, and it inserts the string value specified by the second parameter.

After closing all the opened tags, you flush the content on line 34. This is similar to flushing the response buffer (see Day 5, "Beginning Web Forms"), except that the content is written to a file instead of the browser. Finally, you close the writer on line 38.

Normally, calling the `Close` method will output the XML. Calling `Flush` isn't necessary unless the writer needs to be reused for other output.

Calling the `Close` method also closes any open element and attribute tags, although it's highly recommended that you remember to do so manually.

Figure 11.5 shows the XML output file.

FIGURE 11.5

The `books2.xml` *output from Listing 11.5.*

```
books2.xml - Notepad
File Edit Format Help
<?xml version="1.0"?>
<bookstore>
    <book genre="history" style="hardcover">
        <title>Vietnam</title>
        <author>
            <first-name>Michael</first-name>
            <last-name>Avery</last-name>
        </author>
        <price>6.99</price>
    </book>
</bookstore>
```


Validating XML

XML *must* be well-formed—after all, it's supposed to be a universal data representation language. If XML is *not* well-formed, achieving this standard becomes very difficult. Imagine two companies trying to share an XML data file. A file that's not well-formed leaves data open to interpretation, which could lead to disastrous results if both companies interpret it differently.

ASP.NET allows you to validate XML against a schema. To do so, you create a new object, the `XmlValidatingReader`, and specify the type of validation you want to use:

```
'create reader here
dim validator as new XMLValidatingReader(reader)

'DTD schema
validator.ValidationType = ValidationType.DTD
'XDR schema
validator.ValidationType = ValidationType.XDR

'XSD schema
validator.ValidationType = ValidationType.Schema
'let ASP.NET choose automatically
validator.ValidationType = ValidationType.Auto
```

Then you add an event handler for the validation routine, which will use the schema specified in the XML document. You'll be using XDR validation here. Like you did with `books.xml`, modify the `bookstore` element in `books2.xml` to read as follows:

```
<bookstore xmlns="x-schema:books.xdr">
```

This tells ASP.NET that you'll use the schema described in `books.xdr` (in Listing 11.2) to validate your file. If the XML file is valid and follows the schema, you shouldn't notice any difference and the output should be the same as before.

Listing 11.6 shows the beginning of an example (continued in Listing 11.7).

LISTING 11.6 Validating XML in C#

```
<%@ Page Language="C#" %>
<%@ Import Namespace="System.Xml" %>
<%@ Import Namespace="System.Xml.Schema" %>

<script runat="server">
   private XmlTextReader reader;
   private XmlValidatingReader validator;

   void Page_Load(Object Sender, EventArgs e) {
      try {
         reader = new XmlTextReader(Server.MapPath
➥("books2.xml"));
         validator = new XmlValidatingReader(reader);
         validator.ValidationType = ValidationType.XDR;

         validator.ValidationEventHandler += new
➥ValidationEventHandler(this.ShowError);

```

LISTING 11.6 continued

```
17:             while (validator.Read()) {
18:                //do nothing;
19:             }
20:          } catch (Exception ex) {
21:             Response.Write("Error accessing XML file");
22:          } finally {
23:             reader.Close();
24:          }
25:    }
```

ANALYSIS This listing looks somewhat similar to all your other listings. Note the additional namespace `System.Xml.Schema` on line 3. You'll need this to validate against your schema information. You start validating by creating an `XmlTextReader` (line 6) and opening your XML file, `books2.xml` (line 11). Next you instantiate your `XmlValidatingReader` on line 12 by supplying it the `XmlTextReader` object. This is so your validating reader will know which XML data file to validate. On line 13, you specify that you want to use the XDR schema defined in your XML file to validate the data.

Most built-in events in ASP.NET have a predefined event handler (the `Page_Load` method for the `Page` object's `Load` event, for instance). The validation event doesn't, however, so you have to define one using the syntax on line 15 (or the `AddHandler` method for VB.NET):

```
AddHandler validator.ValidationEventHandler, new
➥ValidationEventHandler(addressof ShowError)
```

Essentially, this code assigns an event handler to the event in question—`ValidationEventHandler` in this case. The `ShowError` method will be executed whenever this event fires. This method can be named anything you want. You don't need to worry too much about the details behind this mechanism, but it's useful to know the syntax if you ever need to use it.

Also note the empty `while` loop on lines 17–19. Normally you could read the data and output whatever you like here, but for our purposes of validation here, you don't need to. You only want to read the data to verify it, not to display it.

The `ShowError` function, which makes up the remainder of your ASP.NET Web page, can be found in Listing 11.7.

LISTING 11.7 The `ShowError` Function

```
26:      void ShowError(Object Sender, ValidationEventArgs e) {
27:         Response.Write("<font color=\"red\">" + e.Message +
➥"<br>");
28:
29:         if (reader.LineNumber > 0) {
30:            Response.Write("Line: " + reader.LineNumber +
➥" Position: " + reader.LinePosition + "</font><p>");
31:         }
32:      }
33:   </script>
34:
35:   <html><body>
36:
37:   </body></html>
```

ANALYSIS Here you define the `ShowError` function that's called whenever something in the XML file fails the validation. Note the `ValidationEventArgs` parameter in the method decla-ration. This parameter contains a `Message` property that contains a user-friendly description of any errors that occur. Thus, on line 30, you output this description to the browser in a red font. You use the `LineNumber` and `LinePosition` properties of the `XmlValidatingReader` to display the location of the error in the XML file. This is very useful for tracking down problems.

> **Note** You may have noticed in Listing 11.6 that you moved the declaration of the `XmlTextReader` outside the `Load` event. This allows you to use this object from any method within the page, rather than simply within the `Page Load` event. This is why you can use it from the `ShowError` method.
>
> Had you left the declaration in the `PageLoad` event, accessing the reader from the `ShowError` function would produce an error.

If the format of your `books2.xml` file looks exactly like `books.xml` (and it should), you shouldn't receive any errors and everything should work as planned. However, let's modify the XML a bit so you can see validation at work. See Listing 11.8.

LISTING 11.8 `Books2.xml`—A Non-Valid XML File

```
<?xml version="1.0"?>
<bookstore xmlns="x-schema:books.xdr">
   <book genre="history">
      <title>Vietnam</title>
```

LISTING 11.8 continued

```
          <price>hello!</price>
          <author>
             <first-name>Michael</first-name>
             <last-name>Avery</last-name>
          </author>
       </book>
    </bookstore>
```

According to your schema, `books.xdr`, this file has two errors—it omits the `style` attribute in the `book` element, and it uses a string in the `price` attribute. Figure 11.6 shows the error messages you get when viewing the output of the validation code (Listings 11.6 and 11.7) through a Web browser.

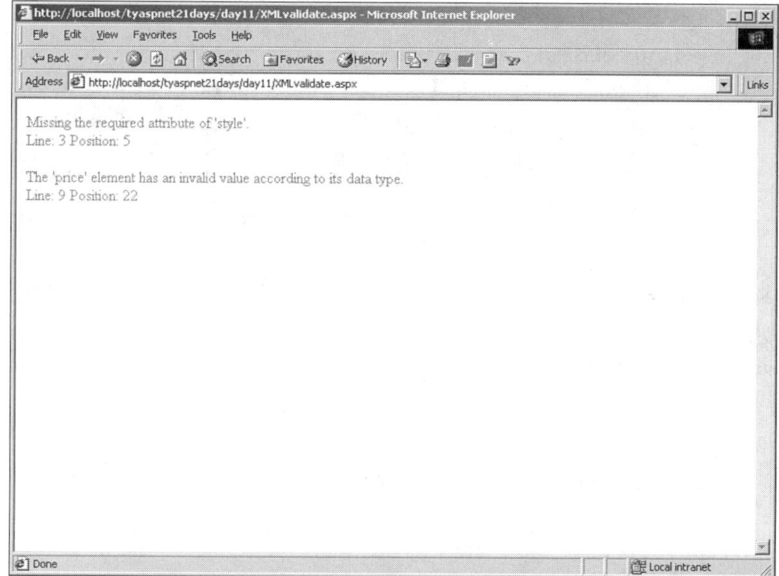

FIGURE 11.6
Errors in validation.

If you had used the `while` loop in Listing 11.6 to output any data, that data would have appeared in Figure 11.6 along with the error messages.

The XML Document Object Model

The XML Document Object Model (DOM) is a specification, developed by the W3C, that details how applications that access XML should behave. This includes the classes these applications should create, how they should read and write XML, and the features the classes should have. For the actual specifications, check out these pages at W3C's Web site:

`http://www.w3.org/TR/REC-DOM-Level-1`

`http://www.w3.org/TR/DOM-Level-2-Core/`

Up until now, you haven't been paying any attention to the XML DOM. The `XmlTextReader` and `XmlTextWriter` don't implement the DOM because it introduces too much overhead. These two objects are built for fast, lightweight XML access. However, there are times when you need the full functionality of the DOM to edit, navigate, and otherwise modify your XML files, just like you need the `DataSet` to provide more functionality than a data reader.

The `XmlNode` class provides the basic functionality described by the XML DOM. It represents an element in the XML document tree, and it can be used to navigate child and parent nodes, as well as to edit and delete data. The `XmlDocument` class extends the `XmlNode` class and allows you to perform operations on the XML file as a whole, such as loading and saving files. There are numerous other classes in the DOM that are derivations of the `XmlNode` class, such as `XmlElement` and `XmlAttribute`, but you won't learn about these here. Figure 11.7 details the interaction of the XML DOM classes.

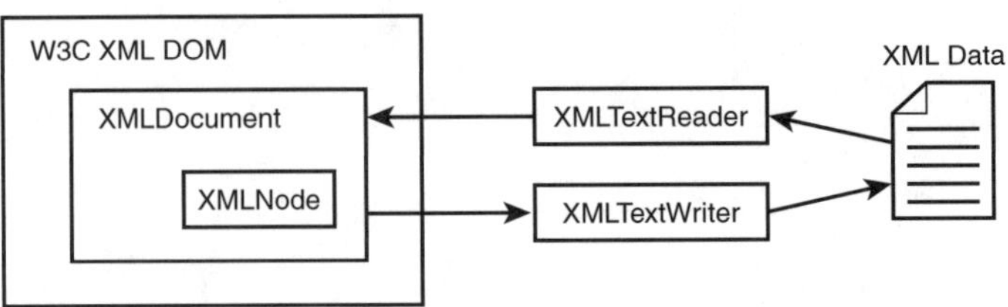

FIGURE 11.7 *The interaction of the Microsoft XML classes.*

The `XmlNode` represents one *branch* of the XML file, which includes all attributes, child elements, and both opening and closing tags. For example, the `<title>...</title>` tags in `books.xml` represent two elements, but only one node. Each node can have multiple child nodes, and each represents another branch. Thus, when you interact with XML using the DOM, you're viewing it as you would a traditional data store.

For example, when viewing data in Microsoft Access, you don't consider the start of one field and the end of the same field as two different objects—they're part of one field. The `XmlTextReader` and `Writer` treated each object as an individual entity, but the DOM considers them one field. Figure 11.8 illustrates the concept of nodes in an XML file.

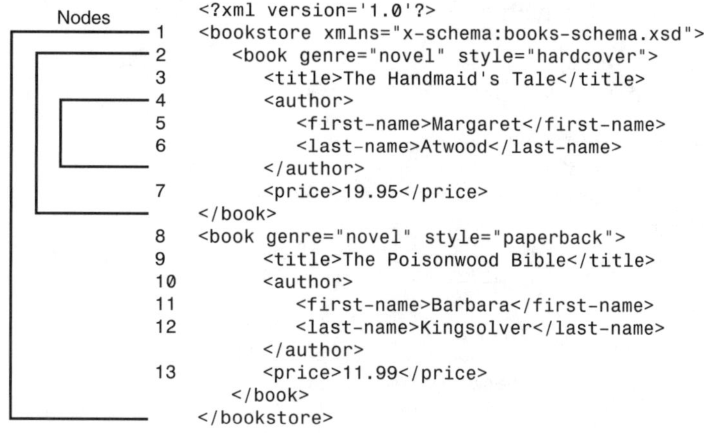
Nodes
<?xml version='1.0'?>
1 <bookstore xmlns="x-schema:books-schema.xsd">
2 <book genre="novel" style="hardcover">
3 <title>The Handmaid's Tale</title>
4 <author>
5 <first-name>Margaret</first-name>
6 <last-name>Atwood</last-name>
</author>
7 <price>19.95</price>
</book>
8 <book genre="novel" style="paperback">
9 <title>The Poisonwood Bible</title>
10 <author>
11 <first-name>Barbara</first-name>
12 <last-name>Kingsolver</last-name>
</author>
13 <price>11.99</price>
</book>
</bookstore>

FIGURE 11.8
Nodes in an XML file.

Loading XML Data

You can load data into an `XmlDocument` in a number of different ways. The two most common methods are to load the data from an `XmlTextReader` or directly from the original XML file, both shown in the following code snippet:

```
dim xmldocument as XmlDocument = new XmlDocument()

'loading from an XmlTextReader
dim reader as new XmlTextReader(server.MapPath("books.xml"))
xmldocument.Load(reader)

'loading directly from a file
xmldocument.Load(server.MapPath("books.xml"))
```

Why would you load it from an `XmlTextReader` if you could skip this step and go directly to the file? Often it may not be necessary to use the `XmlDocument`, so an `XmlTextReader` will suffice. However, if you ever need the functionality of the `XmlDocument`, you don't need to retrieve the data from the XML file all over again. Rather, you can just load it from the `Reader` object you're already using.

Once the data is loaded, you can use the `XmlNode` object to view the data in the file. For example, you can iterate through the nodes to display the data, just as you used the `Read` method of the `XmlTextReader` to iterate through elements. Listings 11.9 and 11.10 show an example.

LISTING 11.9 Opening an XML File with `XmlDocument`

```
1:   <%@ Page Language="VB" %>
2:   <%@ Import Namespace="System.Xml" %>
3:
4:   <script runat=server>
5:      private i as integer
6:      private strOutput as string = ""
7:
8:      sub Page_Load(Sender as Object, e as EventArgs)
9:         dim xmldoc as new XMLDocument()
10:
11:          try
12:             xmldoc.Load(Server.MapPath("books.xml"))
13:             ShowTree(xmldoc.DocumentElement)
14:
15:             catch ex as Exception
16:                strOutput = "Error accessing XML file"
17:          end try
18:
19:          output.Text = strOutput
20:    end sub
```

ANALYSIS The first part of this file is simple. You create a new `XmlDocument` named `xmldoc` on line 9, and you load the data from your XML file on line 12. The `ShowTree` method, shown in Listing 11.10, loops through the nodes and displays the data. The `DocumentElement` property of the `XmlDocument` returns the first, or base, element in the file (the XML version declaration, in this case). You supply the `ShowTree` method with this starting point so it loops through the entire file.

LISTING 11.10 Iterating Through an XML File with `XMLNodes`

```
sub ShowTree(node as XMLNode)
   Dim attrnode As XmlNode
   Dim map As XmlNamedNodeMap

   If Not(node.HasChildNodes)
      strOutput += "  <b>" & node.Name & _
         "</b> &lt;" & _
         node.Value & "&gt;<br>" & vbcrlf
   Else
      strOutput += "<b>" & node.Name & "</b>"
      If node.NodeType = XmlNodeType.Element Then
         map = node.Attributes
         For Each attrnode In map
            strOutput += " <b>" & attrnode.Name & _
               "</b> &lt;" & _
```

Listing 11.10 continued

```
36:                         attrnode.Value & "&gt; " & vbcrlf
37:                     Next
38:                  End If
39:                  strOutput += "<br>"
40:               End If
41:
42:               If node.HasChildNodes then
43:                  node = node.FirstChild
44:                  While not IsNothing(node)
45:                     ShowTree(node)
46:                     node = node.NextSibling
47:                  end while
48:               end if
49:            end sub
50:         </script>
51:
52:         <html><body>
53:            <asp:Label id="output" runat="server" />
54:         </body></html>
```


New Term The `ShowTree` method uses a programming concept called *recursion*. A recursive function will call itself over and over again until some condition is exhausted, like a loop. In this case, the `ShowTree` method will display the information for a node, and if there are any children for that node, it will call itself for each child. If there are no more children, it simply moves to the next node in the file. In this way, this method works its way down the XML hierarchy to display all the child nodes. Figure 11.9 illustrates this concept.

Analysis On line 25, if the node doesn't have any children, you simply want to display its name and value. `strOutput` is a string that you're using to collect the output; it will be displayed in the label (`output`) on line 53 once you're through. If there *are* children and the node is an element type, you display all the attributes belonging to that node. The `XmlNamedNodeMap` object, declared on line 23 and used on line 32, represents a collection of attributes for each node. You can then iterate through this collection to retrieve the values (lines 33–37).

If this node has any children, you want to start the recursive function. This is accomplished by the block of code on lines 42–48. First you assign your node variable to the first child node of the current node. You then call `ShowTree` starting from this child node, which will display any data associated with the node. If this node has children, you get its first child and repeat the process again. The `while` loop on line 44 and the `NextSibling` property on line 46 iterate through all the children of each node.

FIGURE 11.9

Using recursion to loop through your nodes.

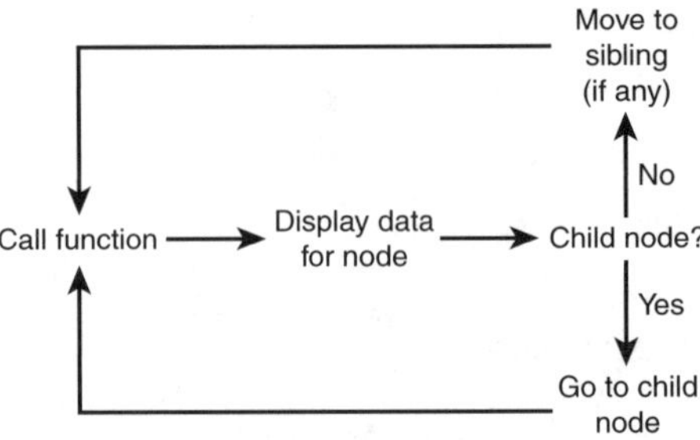

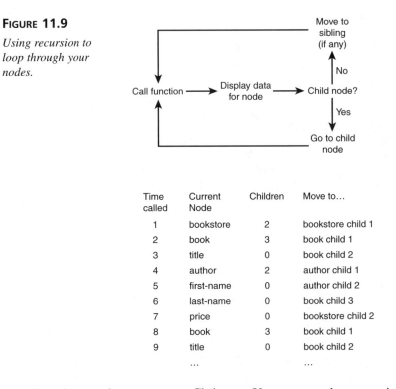

Time called	Current Node	Children	Move to…
1	bookstore	2	bookstore child 1
2	book	3	book child 1
3	title	0	book child 2
4	author	2	author child 1
5	first-name	0	author child 2
6	last-name	0	book child 3
7	price	0	bookstore child 2
8	book	3	book child 1
9	title	0	book child 2
	…		…

Imagine opening presents on Christmas. You open one box, examine its contents, and move on to the next box. But one of your relatives tries to be sneaky and gives you a very large box. Once you open it, you find another, smaller, box. In this box, you find another box, and so on, until you eventually find your present. The process comes down to this: You open one present, and if it doesn't have any smaller boxes inside, you move on to the next present. If it does, you have to open all the boxes inside before moving on to the next present. Recursion is a similar process—you open all the XML branches, and if there are children, you open them up before moving on to the next branch.

The `ShowTree` method runs through the entire XML document to produce the output shown in Figure 11.10.

Do	Don't
Do use `XmlDocument` and `XmlNode` when you need to modify or create XML data.	**Don't** use `XmlDocument` and `XmlNode` when you only need to examine the data—these objects introduce overhead that may slow down your application unnecessarily.

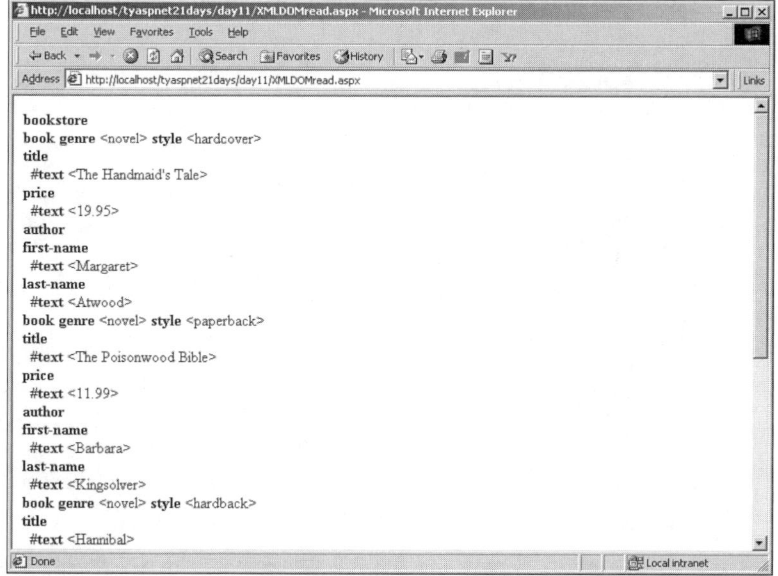

FIGURE 11.10
The output of Listings 11.8 and 11.9 when viewed through a browser.

Modifying XML Data

The `XmlDocument` object also provides many methods to create and modify XML documents. To add new elements, you can use the series of `Create` methods—`CreateComment`, `CreateAttribute`, `CreateNode`, and so on. You can create virtually any type of element you need with these methods. For example:

```
'load data into xmldoc here
dim eleBook as XmlElement = xmldoc.CreateElement _
("Book")
dim attStyle as XmlAttribute = xmldoc.CreateAttribute _
("style")

eleBook.SetAttributeNode(attStyle)
eleBook.SetAttribute("style", "hardcover")

dim root as XmlElement = xmldoc.Item("bookstore")
root.AppendChild(eleBook)
```

You create a new `XmlElement` and `XmlAttribute` on lines 2 and 4, respectively. You then add the attribute to the element with the `SetAttributeNode` method, and you set a value for that attribute with the `SetAttribute` method. Finally, you add the new element to the `book` element of the XML document.

Modifying data is even easier. All you have to do is set the values that you want. For example:

```
if node.Name = "price" then
   node.Value = "8.99"
end if
```

That's all there is to it! If you need to modify all of the values in a file, you can simply use recursion to loop through each element. Table 11.2 lists some of the methods used to create or modify values in the `XmlDocument`.

TABLE 11.2 Methods to Modify an `XmlDocument`

Method	*Description*
`AppendChild`	Adds the specified node to the end of the list of children for the current node
`CreateAttribute`	Creates an `XmlAttribute` with the specified name
`CreateCDataSection`	Creates a `CData` section with the specified data
`CreateComment`	Creates an `XmlComment` with the specified data
`CreateElement`	Creates an `XmlElement` with the specified name
`CreateNode`	Creates an `XmlNode` with the specified type, name, and namespace URI (to ensure unique naming schemes)
`CreateTextNode`	Creates an `XmlText` with the specified data
`CreateXmlDeclaration`	Creates an `XmlDeclaration` section with the specified version, encoding, and string specifying whether attributes are standalone; version must be "1.0"
`GetElementById`	Returns the `XmlElement` with the specified ID
`GetElementsByTagName`	Returns an `XmlNodeList` collection with all the elements that match the specified name
`ImportNode`	Imports the specified node from another document; the `Boolean` value specifies whether or not to import all child nodes as well
`InsertAfter`	Inserts the first `XmlNode` after the second `XmlNode`
`InsertBefore`	Inserts the first `XmlNode` before the second `XmlNode`
`PrependChild`	Adds the specified node to the beginning of the list of children for the current node
`RemoveAll`	Removes all children and attributes of the current node
`RemoveChild`	Removes the specified child node
`ReplaceChild`	Replaces the second `XmlNode` with the first

TABLE 11.2 continued

Method	*Description*
`WriteContentTo`	Saves all children of the current node to the specified `XmlWriter` (such as an `XmlTextWriter`)
`WriteTo`	Saves the current node to the specified `XmlWriter` (such as an `XmlTextWriter`)

Note

Note that some of these methods also have overloaded versions that allow different parameters to be used. Please see the .NET Framework SDK documentation for more information.

The `XmlElement` and `XmlNode` objects share many of the same methods as the `XmlDocument`.

Use the `Save` method to write any changes back to a file:

```
xmldoc.Save("books2.xml")
```


Tip

If you want to append to an existing XML file, simply load all the data into an `XmlDocument`, make your changes, and save it to a file with the same name. The old file will be overwritten, but since the data was loaded into the `XmlDocument`, you'll have lost nothing.

Listing 11.11 loads an XML file and appends a new book node.

LISTING 11.11 Using the DOM to Append Data

```
<%@ Page Language="VB" %>
<%@ Import Namespace="System.Xml" %>

<script runat=server>
   sub Page_Load(Sender as Object, e as EventArgs)
      dim xmldoc as new XMLDocument()
      dim strOutput as string = ""
      try
         xmldoc.Load(Server.MapPath("books.xml"))
          dim eleBook as XmlElement = xmldoc.CreateElement _
             ("book")
          dim attStyle as XmlAttribute = xmldoc. _
```

LISTING 11.11 continued

```
13:             CreateAttribute _
14:             ("style")
15:
16:          eleBook.SetAttributeNode(attStyle)
17:          eleBook.SetAttribute("style", "hardcover")
18:
19:          dim root as XmlElement = xmldoc.Item("bookstore")
20:          root.AppendChild(eleBook)
21:
22:          xmldoc.Save(Server.MapPath("books.xml"))
23:
24:       catch ex as Exception
25:          strOutput = "Error accessing XML file"
26:       end try
27:
28:       output.Text = "Append operation successful"
29:    end sub
30: </script>
31:
32: <html><body>
33:    <asp:Label id="output" runat="server" />
34: </body></html>
```

ANALYSIS Lines 1–9 are typical—create an `XmlDocument` and fill it with the contents of `books.xml`. On line 10 and 14 you create a new `XmlElement` named `book` and a new `XmlAttribute` to hold information about the book. Note that you create these new items from the existing `XmlDocument` `xmldoc`. This ensures that the new items follow the same format as the existing data.

On lines 16 and 17, you declare the attribute as part of the `book` element and set a value for the attribute. On line 19 you retrieve the root element, `bookstore`, so that you can append your new book element to it, as shown on line 20. Finally, you use the `Save` method to write the changes back to the `books.xml` file. No data has been lost.

XML and the `DataSet`

XML in the .NET Framework is very closely related to ADO.NET. The `DataSet` internally represents its data as XML. This means that the `DataSet` in the computer's memory is stored as XML and not some abstract data model. So you're viewing XML data in either situation: directly with the XML classes, or indirectly through ADO.NET. The `DataSet` simply provides a different view than XML.

Let's examine the current situation. On one hand, you have ADO.NET and its objects. There are simple objects that provide quick and easy access to data, such as the `OleDbDataReader`. Then there are the more complex objects, like the `DataSet`, which contains relational information and provides more functionality than the `OleDbDataReader`.

Next you have the XML .NET Framework, which also has simple and complex objects. The `XmlTextReader` provides simple, lightweight access to reading XML data, and the `XmlDocument` provides more functionality. The latter doesn't do well representing relational data, however, so the `XmlDataDocument` was introduced.

The `XmlDataDocument` is to XML as the `DataSet` is to ADO.NET. These two objects are very similar to each other, and you can easily convert from one to another. In a way, these two objects are the bridge between ADO.NET and XML.

The `XmlDataDocument` is similar to the `XmlDocument`, but it provides a relational data representation that's analogous to the `DataSet`. The `XmlDataDocument` can be used anywhere the `XmlDocument` can, in fact, with the same methods and properties.

Whenever you load data into an `XmlDataDocument`, the .NET Framework automatically creates a `DataSet` for you, accessed via the `XmlDataDocument.DataSet` property. The XML schema is used to build the columns and their data types in the `DataSet`. If a schema isn't provided, ASP.NET will infer the structure accordingly.

This allows you to modify data however you want. You can open an XML file using the XML objects and then move them into a `DataSet` for binding with a server control, for instance. Or retrieve data from a database with the `DataSet` and save it to an XML file. Any changes made to the `DataSet` will be reflected in the `XmlDataDocument`. Changes to the `XmlDataDocument` may or may not result in changes to the `DataSet`, however. If the new data corresponds to the fields in the `DataSet`, the row will be added.

Figure 11.11 shows the relationship between the two objects.

Let's take a look at the relationship between these two objects. Using your `books.xml` file, you'll load the data into a `DataSet` from an `XmlDataDocument` and output the data in two different ways. Let's look at Listing 11.12, which shows the code declaration block using a `DataSet` and `XmlDataDocument` (the HTML portion of the page simply shows a `Label` and two `DataGrids`).

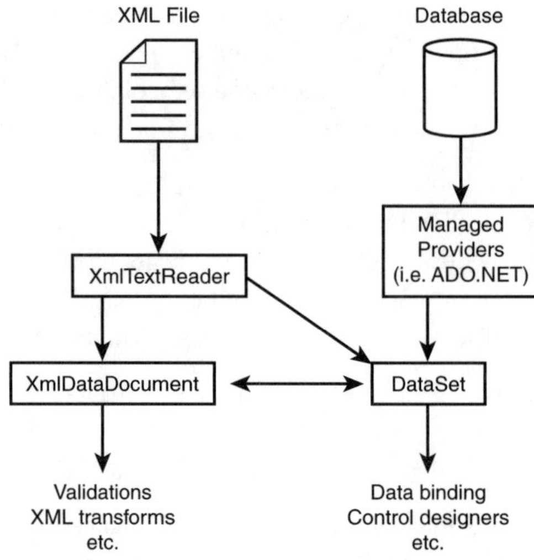

FIGURE 11.11

The relationship between the `DataSet` *and the* `XmlDataDocument`.

LISTING 11.12 Using `DataSets` and `XmlDataDocuments` to Display Data

```
<%@ Page Language="VB" %>
<%@ Import Namespace="System.Xml" %>
<%@ Import Namespace="System.Data" %>
<%@ Import Namespace="System.Data.OleDb" %>

<script runat=server>
   private i, j as integer
   private strOutput as string = ""

    sub Page_Load(Sender as Object, e as EventArgs)
       dim xmldoc as new XMLDataDocument()

       try
          xmldoc.DataSet.ReadXml(Server.MapPath("books.xml"))

          'select data view and bind to server control
          DataGrid1.DataSource = xmldoc.DataSet
          DataGrid1.DataMember = xmldoc.DataSet.Tables(0). _
             TableName
          DataGrid2.DataSource = xmldoc.DataSet
          DataGrid2.DataMember = xmldoc.DataSet.Tables(1). _
             TableName

          DataGrid1.DataBind()
          DataGrid2.DataBind()

          For i = 0 To xmldoc.DataSet.Tables.Count - 1
             strOutput += "TableName = """ & _
                xmldoc.DataSet.Tables(i).TableName & """<br>"
```

LISTING 11.12 continued

```
        strOutput += "  " & "Columns " & _
          "count = " & xmldoc.DataSet.Tables(i). _
          Columns.Count.ToString() & "<br>"

        For j = 0 To xmldoc.DataSet.Tables(i). _
          Columns.Count-1
          strOutput += "    " & _
               "ColumnName = """ & xmldoc.DataSet. _
               Tables(i).Columns(j).ColumnName & """, & _
               type = " & xmldoc.DataSet.Tables(i). & _
               Columns(j).DataType.ToString() & "<br>"
        Next
      Next

      strOutput += "<p>"

      catch ex as Exception
        strOutput = "Error accessing XML file"
    end try

    output.Text = strOutput
  end sub
   </script>
<html><body>
  <asp:Label id="output" runat="server" />

  <asp:DataGrid id="DataGrid1" runat="server"
      BorderColor="black"
      GridLines="Vertical"
      cellpadding="4"
      cellspacing="0"
      width="450"
      Font-Name="Arial"
      Font-Size="8pt"
      HeaderStyle-BackColor="#cccc99"
      FooterStyle-BackColor="#cccc99"
      ItemStyle-BackColor="#ffffff"
      AlternatingItemStyle-Backcolor="#cccccc" />
  <p>
  <asp:DataGrid id="DataGrid2" runat="server"
      BorderColor="black"
      GridLines="Vertical"
      cellpadding="4"
      cellspacing="0"
      width="450"
      Font-Name="Arial"
      Font-Size="8pt"
      HeaderStyle-BackColor="#cccc99"
      FooterStyle-BackColor="#cccc99"
```

LISTING 11.12 continued

```
79:             ItemStyle-BackColor="#ffffff"
80:             AlternatingItemStyle-Backcolor="#cccccc" />
81:    </body></html>
```

ANALYSIS This listing starts off by creating an `XmlDataDocument`. Rather than loading this object directly with data, you use the `ReadXml` method of the `DataSet` property to read in the data, as shown on line 14. This method creates a relational view of the data automatically, as you'll see in a moment.

> **Note**
>
> The code in Listing 11.12 will only work if the elements in your XML file follow the same formats. For example, if you ran Listing 11.11 as is, you would see a new `<book>` element near the bottom of `books.xml`:
>
> ```
> <book style="hardcover" xmlns="" />
> ```
>
> Even though this element is well-formed by our previous definition (it will even pass validation), it doesn't follow the same format as the other `<book>` elements in `books.xml`. Listing 11.12 will get confused, thinking this is a new element with the same name, and the created `DataSet` will error out.
>
> To remedy this problem, simply remove the offending `<book>` element.

Let's skip to line 27 for a moment. You'll loop through the tables in the `DataSet`, outputting the names of each table and the column count with lines 27–32. Your second `for` loop on lines 34–41 outputs the names of the columns and their data types, as represented in the `DataSet`. The `DataSet` knows which kind of data each field represents because it infers the schema from the data structure. These two loops will print a representation of the relational XML data.

However, since you're using a `DataSet`, there's an easier way to do this. On lines 17–22, you simply bind the data to two different `DataGrid` controls defined in your page (you'll find out why you're using two `DataGrids` in a moment). Figure 11.12 shows the output of this listing.

Wait a minute… this figure shows two tables, but you only have a single XML file. What happened?

The .NET Framework read the XML schema and saw that the data could be represented relationally. Specifically, it separated the author information and placed it into another table. It also automatically generated a foreign key column to link the two tables! In the two `DataGrids`, you can see the data represented in a more traditional format.

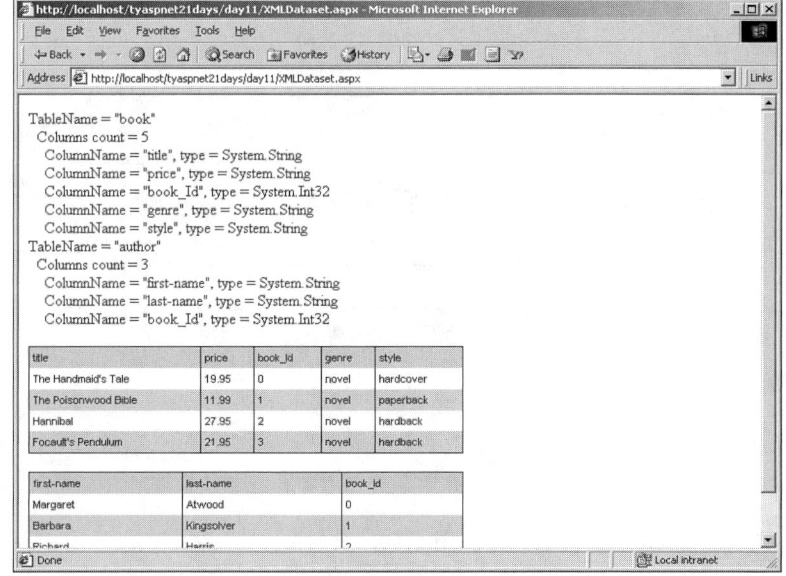

FIGURE 11.12

Viewing relational XML data with an `XmlDataDocument` *and* `DataSet`.

How exactly did the `DataSet` determine the data structure without a schema? It's very simple, actually:

- Any elements with attributes become tables.
- Any elements that contain other elements become tables.
- If there are two or more elements with the same name, they become a table.
- All direct children of the root node become tables.

Everything else becomes a column. Then, if any data in the XML file matches the columns, it's added as a row to the `DataSet`.

These reasons are why Listing 11.12 would generate an error, as mentioned in the previous note. The `DataSet` will try to make two different tables—one for the regular `<book>` elements and one for the new, offending element—and because they both have the same name, you'll receive an error.

Is this truly relational? What happens when you add another `book` node in the XML file with the same author as an existing node? Figure 11.13 shows this situation using the `DataGrids`.

Uh-oh, that didn't turn out right. ASP.NET failed to detect that you already have an author named Barbara Kingsolver, and it added a new entry to the `author` table. Trying to create a primary key over the first name and last name columns will result in an error.

Unfortunately, there's no easy way to resolve this. You'd have to manually update the foreign key and delete the extra row in the `author` table.

FIGURE 11.13

Adding more relational data.

genre	style	title	book_Id	price
novel	hardcover	The Handmaid's Tale	0	19.95
novel	paperback	The Poisonwood Bible	1	11.99
novel	paperback	The Poisonwood Book	2	13.99

first-name	last-name	book_Id
Margaret	Atwood	0
Barbara	Kingsolver	1
Barbara	Kingsolver	2

Regardless of this limitation, being able to represent data in a `DataSet` or with XML is a powerful feature. Relational information can be created in XML and transferred to a `DataSet` for storage in a database, or the other way around for transportation as an XML file.

As you've been learning over the past few days, relational data is a very common and efficient manner for representing data, and XML is certainly no slouch in this area. The `XmlDataDocument`, coupled with the `DataSet`, can access and manipulate relational data from any source.

That's Not ASP!

If you're familiar with traditional ASP, this whole lesson may be very new to you. XML support was nearly nonexistent with ASP. There were no built-in objects to handle this type of data, and implementing the full XML DOM was often the only choice (and a painful one).

Thankfully, the .NET Framework (and thus ASP.NET) integrates fully with XML. You also have two different ways to interact with XML: ADO.NET or the XML .NET architecture.

Unfortunately, this new architecture shares little with any previous methods for XML access, which means many of these methodologies are new and will take some time to learn. Luckily, ASP.NET makes it relatively easy for you by providing well-defined classes and objects that present a consistent programming model.

Summary

Today's lesson covered XML access from ASP.NET. Because XML is so tightly integrated with the .NET Framework, it's easy to make the most of XML data from within your ASP.NET pages.

Use the `XmlTextReader` for simple, fast access to an XML data source. This object provides access to the raw data, which means each element (such as opening and closing tags) is treated individually. The `Read` method will allow you to loop through the elements.

The `XmlTextWriter` object is similar to the `XmlTextReader`, except it's used to write XML documents. It uses a series of `Write` methods to create each XML element.

The `XmlValidatingReader` provides validation capabilities. You can use this object to validate an XML source against any type of schema, and to add methods in cases where validation fails.

The `XmlDocument` and `XmlNode` objects provide access to XML data with full DOM support. This means the XML file is treated more like a traditional data model, versus a simple text file. You can load data with the `XmlDocument.Load` method and manipulate the data with the `XmlNode` object and the functions listed in Table 11.2.

11

The XML .NET Framework also supports relational XML data with the `XmlDataDocument`, which is analogous to the `DataSet` object in ADO.NET. This allows you to build UI support for XML data by using the data binding features of ASP.NET.

Tomorrow you're going to look at file input and output through ASP.NET. Reading from and writing to files on the server can be a great help to ASP.NET, providing additional information that can be used for configuration or data stores.

Q&A

Q How does using different types of schemas affect the exercises in today's lesson?

A Actually, the examples are affected very little. The different schemas only provide different types of definitions for an XML file, but the XML files themselves don't change. It's like having a Merriam-Webster dictionary versus an Oxford dictionary; both have the same set of words, they just define them differently.

For an example of using the different schemas with validation, check out the following Microsoft URL:

`http://support.microsoft.com/default.aspx?scid=kb;en-us;Q307379`

For general information on the three different schemas mentioned today, plus a few other, less-well-known ones, check out this URL:

`http://www.xml.com/pub/q/all_schema`

Q Which method of accessing XML is better, through ADO.NET or through the .NET Framework XML classes?

A The answer to this question is highly subjective. Many people find the objects of ADO.NET easier to manipulate. Others may prefer to manipulate the XML more directly. Luckily, you're not stuck either way. If you start off using one way, you can easily convert to the other. There's no real performance advantage either way.

Workshop

This workshop will help reinforce the concepts covered in today's lesson. The answers can be found in Appendix A.

Quiz

1. When should you use an `XmlTextReader` versus an `XmlDocument`?
2. What does XML DOM stand for?
3. What's the difference between a node and an element?
4. Will the following code snippet work?

```
dim xmldoc as new XMLDataDocument()

xmldoc.DataSet.ReadXml("books.xml")
```

Exercises

1. Create a new XML file that uses the `books.xdr` schema. Make sure your format is correct by using ASP.NET to validate it.
2. Build an interface that allows users to edit XML data from a `DataGrid`. Be sure to write the changes back to the file.

WEEK 2

DAY 12

Employing Advanced Data Techniques

You've been rapidly learning different methods of data access. Now that you have a strong foundation, it's time to move to a more advanced level. Today's lesson will focus on more complex techniques than the ones you've been using up till now. You'll examine new database and XML I/O techniques that will help you develop master-level applications.

First, you'll look at a few new ways to retrieve data by using parameters and stored procedures. Parameters allow you to create your queries more efficiently. Stored procedures are prebuilt SQL statements that provide many benefits to your application, including speed and readability. You'll also learn how to use transactions to ensure that SQL commands are executed properly.

Next, you'll learn more about XML. Today's lesson will introduce the `XmlNavigator` object, which can be used to read an XML file, similar to the `XmlDocument` object. With this new object, you'll be able to use XPath queries and XSL transforms. The former is a query language used with XML (like SQL is to databases), and the latter allows you to transform XML files into other types of structured documents, such as HTML files. An important part of becoming an expert in ASP.NET is learning many different ways to do one thing. After today's lesson, you'll know several different ways to access data from both databases and XML files.

Today's lesson will cover the following:

- What a parameterized query is and how to use it
- What stored procedures are and how to use them
- How to use transactions
- Another way to read XML documents
- How to query XML files
- How to transform XML files

Advanced Database Techniques

So far, you've been using the `OleDbDataAdapter`, `OleDbCommand`, and `DataSet` objects to handle your database needs (along with a few other supporting objects). These objects provide all the functionality you need for your applications, but they also provide some things you haven't yet learned about, including parameters, stored procedures, and transactions.

Parameters are a new way to build dynamic SQL statements. Rather than assembling a statement from a hodgepodge of different sources, you can use parameters to tell databases which data you're requesting. It's easier and more elegant. Stored procedures are prebuilt SQL statements that can enhance the performance of your applications. When coupled with parameters, stored procedures are an excellent way to query databases. Transactions allow you to prevent data corruption by using an all-or-none paradigm of database manipulation—either all of the changes are made or none of them are. You'll learn about several common places to use transactions.

These advanced database techniques will help you build much stronger applications and increase their performance as well.

Parameterized Queries

Imagine building a house. You need detailed information about the sizes of materials and where they belong. One way would be to assemble all your pieces and then write this information directly on them. Each two-by-four would have the length and location written on it, as would each window, door frame, pipe, and so on. This method may work, but it's very imprecise and can lead to problems. Instead, you use a blueprint, a sheet of paper that tells you where things should go and how they fit together.

Data access is similar. When you create SQL statements to access data, you can pull together all the pieces of your query and concatenate them together, while making notes as to which item does what. Or, you can use a more organized method to properly determine which information goes where. The second method uses *parameters*, pieces of information that are created separately from the SQL query, to supply data. Databases can deal with parameters in much the same way as builders use blueprints.

We use parameters with the `OleDbCommand` object to specify additional information, such as the data to return or how to insert it into a `DataSet`. Recall the discussion of SQL statements from Day 10, "ADO.NET." To build dynamic queries, you often had to build statements that pulled information from various Web controls on your ASP.NET Web page. For example, imagine the following SQL statement:

```
strSQL = "select * from tblUsers where UserID = 1"
```

The `UserID` value might be pulled from a text box on the page. You could use the following, where `tbId` is the name of the text box:

```
strSQL = "select * from tblUsers where UserID = " & tbId.Text
```

This serves your purpose of building a dynamic query, but it's unorganized. What if you have three different text boxes? It becomes difficult to know which box should contain which information, especially to another developer who's trying to read your code.

NEW TERM However, a more efficient method is to use parameters. A *parameter* is a value that's either passed in to or returned from a query. Using parameters helps you keep your information straight and makes your queries easy to read. Let's replace the previous query with a parameterized one:


```
strSQL = "select * from tblUsers where UserID = @ID"
```

You replace the dynamic portion of the string with a query parameter, denoted by the `@` symbol. Note that it's a part of the SQL statement. You now have to supply a value for this parameter somewhere. You can specify this parameter with the `Parameters` collection of `OleDbCommand` object (see Day 10 for more info on the `OleDbCommand` object). Listing 12.1 shows an example.

LISTING 12.1 Specifying Parameters for SQL Statements—Partial Sample

```
dim objCmd as OleDbCommand = new OleDbCommand _
   ("select * from tblUsers where UserID = @ID", Conn)

dim objParam as OleDbParameter
```

LISTING 12.1 continued

```
5:    objParam = objCmd.Parameters.Add("@ID", OleDbType.Integer)
6:    objParam.Direction = ParameterDirection.Input
7:    objParam.Value = tbId.Text
```

ANALYSIS On lines 1 and 2, you create your `OleDbCommand` object as normal (assuming that you've already created an `OleDbConnection` object named `Conn`). Notice the parameterized query on line 2. On line 4, you create your `OleDbParameter` object, which will be used to pass in the parameter value. On line 5, you add this parameter to your `OleDbCommand` object, specifying the name and type. The name must match the parameter in the query (`@ID` in this case). The type is an `OleDbType` value that represents the data type of the value you're passing in. Table 12.1 lists the most common possible values.

TABLE 12.1 Common `OleDbType` Values

Type	*Description*
`Binary`	Stream of bytes (maps to an array of bytes)
`Boolean`	Boolean value
`BSTR`	A character string (maps to `String`)
`Char`	A character string (maps to `String`)
`Currency`	A currency value (maps to `Decimal`)
`Date`	A date (maps to `DateTime`)
`Decimal`	A `Decimal` value
`Double`	A `Double` value
`Empty`	No value
`Error`	32-bit error code (maps to `Exception`)
`Integer`	32-bit integer (maps to `Integer`)
`LongVarChar`	A long string value (maps to `String`)
`VarChar`	String value (maps to `String`)
`Variant`	A special data type that can represent any data type if none is specified (maps to `Object`)

On line 6, you specify the parameter direction. Since this parameter will be used for part of a `select` query, you're passing in the value. Thus, the direction is `Input`. If you were expecting a value to be returned and placed in this parameter, the direction would be `Output`. You'll learn about these directions more in the section on stored procedures later today.

Finally, you set the value of the parameter to the text in the text box on line 7 (`tbId`). Whatever is entered into the text box will be passed as the parameter into the `select` query. Let's look at a full example of this in Listing 12.2.

LISTING 12.2 Using Parameters to Return Values

```
1:   <%@ Page Language="VB" %>
2:   <%@ Import Namespace="System.Data" %>
3:   <%@ Import Namespace="System.Data.OleDb" %>
4:
5:   <script runat="server">
6:      dim Conn as new OleDbConnection("Provider=" & _
7:               "Microsoft.Jet.OLEDB.4.0;" & _
8:               "Data Source=c:\ASPNET\data\banking.mdb")
9:
10:      sub GetData(Sender as Object, e as EventArgs)
11:         dim objCmd as OleDbCommand = new OleDbCommand _
12:            ("select * from tblUsers where UserID = @ID", Conn)
13:         dim objReader as OleDbDataReader
14:         dim objParam as OleDbParameter
15:
16:         objParam = objCmd.Parameters.Add("@ID", _
17:            OleDbType.Integer)
18:         objParam.Direction = ParameterDirection.Input
19:         objParam.Value = tbID.Text
20:
21:         try
22:            objCmd.Connection.Open()
23:            objReader = objCmd.ExecuteReader
24:         catch ex as OleDbException
25:            Label1.Text = "Error retrieving from the database."
26:         end try
27:
28:         DataGrid1.DataSource = objReader
29:         DataGrid1.DataBind()
30:
31:         objReader.Close
32:         objCmd.Connection.Close()
33:      end sub
34:   </script>
35:
36:   <html><body>
37:      <form runat="server">
38:         <asp:Label id="Label1" runat="server" /><br>
39:         Enter an ID: <asp:TextBox id="tbID" runat="server"
40:            AutoPostBack=True
41:            OnTextChanged=GetData /><p>
42:         <asp:DataGrid id="DataGrid1" runat="server"
43:            BorderColor="black" GridLines="Vertical"
```

LISTING 12.2 continued

```
44:             cellpadding="4" cellspacing="0" width="100%"
45:             Font-Name="Arial" Font-Size="8pt"
46:             HeaderStyle-BackColor="#cccc99"
47:             ItemStyle-BackColor="#ffffff"
48:             AlternatingItemStyle-Backcolor="#cccccc"
49:             AutoGenerateColumns="true" />
50:       </form>
51:    </body></html>
```

ANALYSIS This listing should look familiar—it's very similar to the database examples you developed on Day 10. In your HTML section, you've created three server controls: a `DataGrid` (lines 42 through 49), a `Label` (line 38), and a `TextBox` (lines 39 through 41). When the user enters a value in the text box, you'll fire the `TextChanged` event, which will display the filtered data in the `DataGrid` (note the `AutoPostBack=True` on line 40). On line 6, you declare an `OleDbConnection` object for use with your page methods.

The `GetData` method is fired on the `TextChanged` event of the text box and displays the appropriate data. Your parameterized query is on lines 11 and 12. On lines 16–18, you create your parameter, assign its direction, and set its value to the text in the `tbID` text box. The rest of the method retrieves the data and binds it to the `DataGrid`. Figure 12.1 shows the output of this listing after you enter a value in the text box.

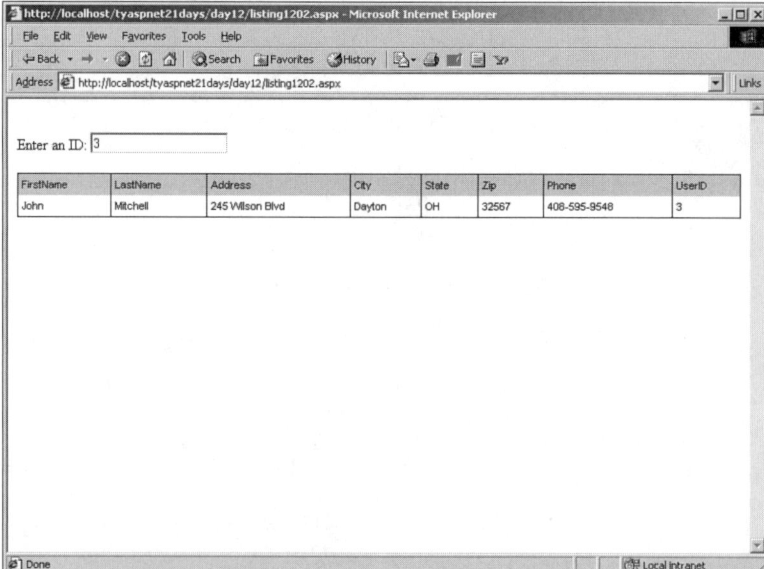

FIGURE 12.1
The parameterized query uses a value from the text box to return data.

You can use multiple parameters for each query as well. For instance:

```
strSQL = "SELECT * FROM tblUsers WHERE UserID=@ID AND
   FirstName=@Name"
```

You can even place returned values in a parameter:

```
strSQL = "SELECT @Phone=Phone FROM tblUsers WHERE UserID=@ID
   AND FirstName=@Name"
```

Parameters that return information are known as *output parameters*. When this query is executed, the value returned by the statement `SELECT Phone FROM tblUsers WHERE UserID=@ID AND FirstName=@Name` (which should be a single phone number) is stored in the parameter `@Phone`. You can use the parameters collection to obtain the value of `@Phone` after the query has been executed. For example, the following code snippet creates an output parameter for the previous SQL statement:

```
dim objParam as OleDbParameter
objParam = objCmd.Parameters.Add("@Phone", OleDbType.BSTR)
objParam.Direction = ParameterDirection.Output
```

You can retrieve this value by accessing its `Value` property after the query has been executed:

```
dim strPhone as string = objParam.Value
```

Parameters are very useful for building dynamic queries, but their true power becomes more apparent when they're used with stored procedures.

Stored Procedures

A *stored procedure* is a set of commands (usually SQL statements combined with other DB-specific language) that a database can execute. What's the difference between a stored procedure and a normal SQL statement?

First, a stored procedure is compiled. You already know how compiling ASP.NET code benefits your pages. Compiling stored procedures provides many of the same benefits, including an increase in pure speed.

New Term When a stored procedure is executed in a database, an *execution plan* is created, allowing the database to retrieve the information faster in subsequent executions. The database looks at the data and the query and determines the most efficient way to return the data. Then it saves this method in an execution plan. Thus, not only do stored procedures benefit from being compiled, but also from being aided by execution plans.

Creating stored procedures allows another layer of abstraction between your ASP.NET pages and the data. Remember that modularity is one of the goals of object-oriented programming. When you separate the SQL queries from the ASP.NET pages, you're doing three things:

- Allowing those queries to be reused
- Making your code easier to read
- Saving time

If you have a very long SQL statement, placing it in your ASP.NET page will result in a lot of code that simply doesn't need to be there. It clutters up the code that does the actual work. Also, since these statements must be sent from your ASP.NET pages to the database, you're using up valuable bandwidth. Finally, imagine you've used a SQL statement in several different ASP.NET pages. If something in your database has changed and your SQL statement needs to be updated, you have to change it in every single page. This can be a very tedious task. With stored procedures, you only need to update once and the change will be reflected throughout your application.

Moving your SQL statements into stored procedures eliminates all of these problems and provides other benefits. Even very simple one-line SQL statements will benefit from being moved into a stored procedure.

Enough discussion. Let's create some stored procedures!

Creating Stored Procedures in SQL Server 2000

Stored procedures are used in many different database systems. For example, both SQL Server and Access use them, although each one provides a distinct method of creating them. This section will show you how to create a stored procedure in SQL Server 2000. You'll create one in Access in the next section.

Open Enterprise Manager as you did on Day 8, "Beginning to Build Databases." Expand the Microsoft SQL Servers and SQL Server Group nodes, as well as the node indicating the name of your server and the Databases node. Open the Banking database you created on Day 8 by clicking on the + symbol, as shown in Figure 12.2.

SQL Server comes with quite a few built-in stored procedures. Take a quick look at these by clicking on the Stored Procedures node and double-clicking one of the names in the right-hand window. Most of these are more complex than the one you'll develop now, but they'll give you an idea of what your procedure should look like. Right-click on the stored procedure icon and select New Stored Procedure. You should see a new box, similar to the one in Figure 12.3.

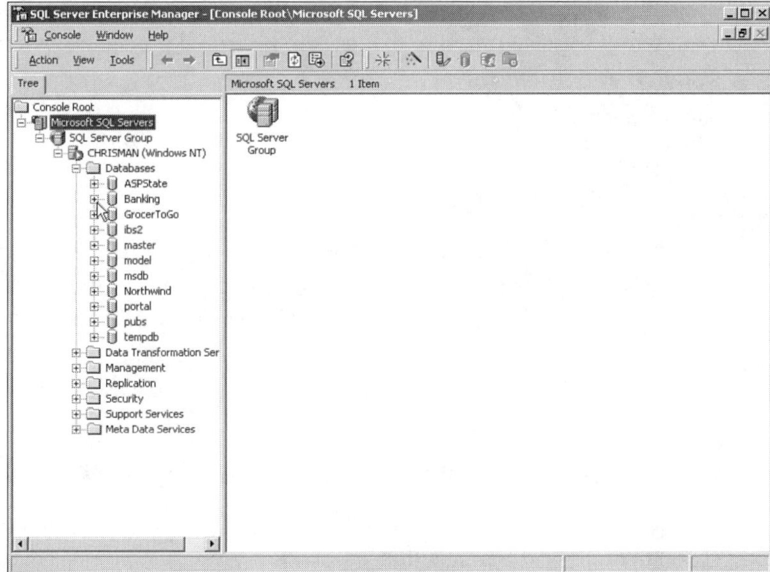

FIGURE 12.2

Expand the Banking database from Day 8.

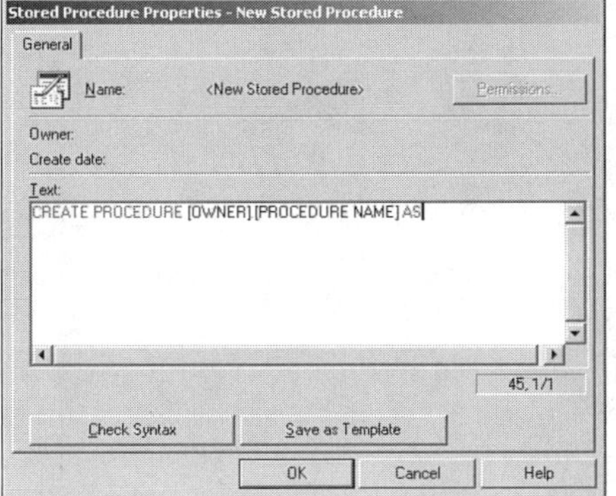

FIGURE 12.3

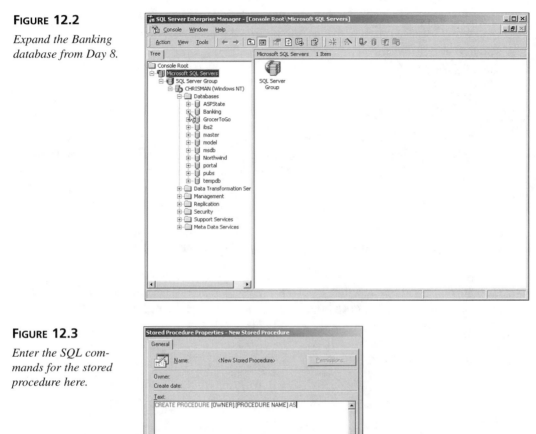

Enter the SQL commands for the stored procedure here.

Replace `[OWNER].[PROCEDURE NAME]` with the name of the stored procedure, such as `SelectIDFromName`. (You don't need to be concerned with the `OWNER` attribute for now. For more information, see the SQL Server 2000 online documentation.) Since you're going to be using a parameterized query, you also have to define the parameters immediately after the name and in front of the `AS` keyword:

```
CREATE PROCEDURE SelectIDFromName
   @FirstName varchar,
   @LastName varchar,
   @ID int OUTPUT
AS
```

The `OUTPUT` keyword tells SQL Server that you want to store a value in this parameter and return it to the program that called the stored procedure. After the `AS` keyword, you enter your SQL statement:

```
SELECT @ID = UserID
FROM tblUsers
WHERE FirstName = @FirstName
   AND LastName = @LastName
```

Your `select` statement retrieves the `UserID` value for the first and last names you enter and sets the `@ID` parameter equal to that value. You can use this as an output parameter later on. Optionally, you can click the Check Syntax button to ensure that you've input the proper syntax. SQL Server will examine the code and let you know if you've made a mistake. Click OK to save the stored procedure. You should now see it in the list along with the other procedures.

Creating Stored Procedures in Access 2000

Since you've been using Access throughout this book, you should also learn how to create stored procedures with this application. Access supports stored procedures but refers to them as *queries*. Let's open your banking database you created in Day 8. Click on the Queries tab on the left side, as shown in Figure 12.4.

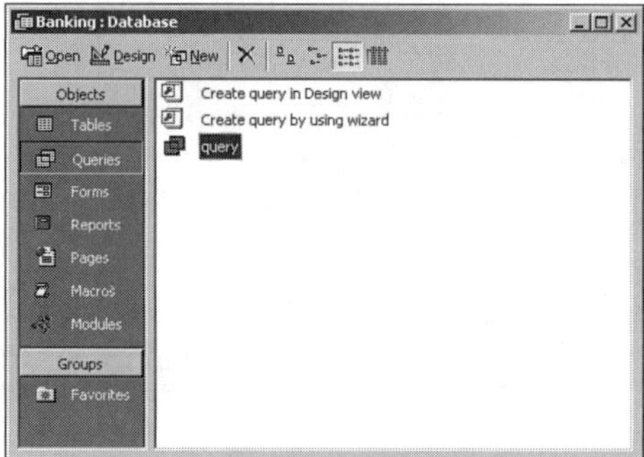

FIGURE 12.4

In Access, stored procedures are called queries.

Since you're familiar with SQL statements, you don't need to bother with the wizards. Click Create query in Design view. A box labeled Show Tables pops up, asking you which tables to include. Click Close to get rid of this box, and then look to the upper-left corner of the Access menu. You should see a drop-down menu item called View. Select this menu and then select SQL View, as shown in Figure 12.5. Now you can enter your SQL statement straight into the query:

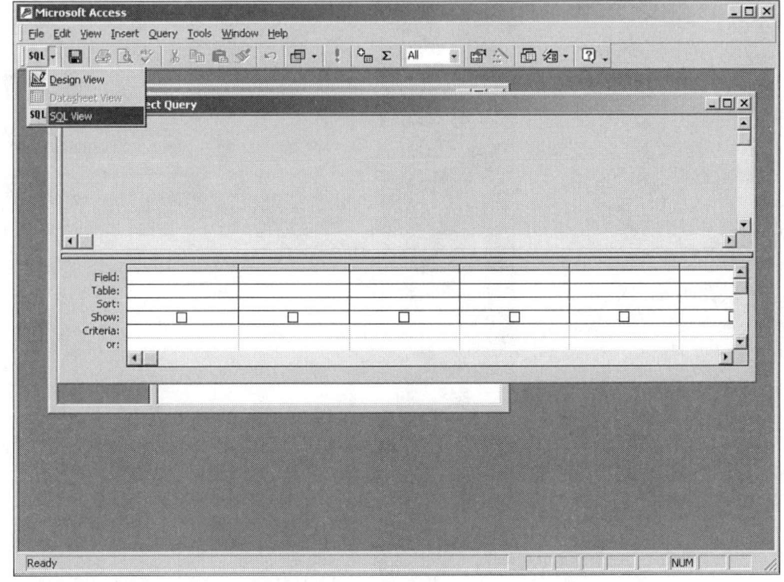

FIGURE 12.5
Access SQL mode by clicking on the drop-down menu in the upper-left corner of Access.

```
SELECT UserID FROM tblUsers
WHERE FirstName = @FirstName
   AND LastName = @LastName
```

Enter the SQL statement into the window, as shown in Figure 12.6. Close the window by clicking on the x in the upper-right corner, and click Yes at the Save prompt. Save this query as `SelectIDFromName`. It should now appear in your list of queries.

> **Note** The Access database engine doesn't support output parameters from queries, which explains why there's no `@ID` parameter in your query. You'll learn how to get around this later.

Using Stored Procedures from ASP.NET

Calling a stored procedure from an ASP.NET Web page is simple. You only need to set one additional property that you haven't seen yet, called `CommandType`:

```
dim objCmd as OleDbCommand = new OleDbCommand _
   ("SelectIDFromName", Conn)
objCmd.CommandType = CommandType.StoredProcedure
```

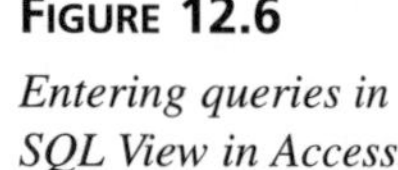

FIGURE 12.6

Entering queries in SQL View in Access.

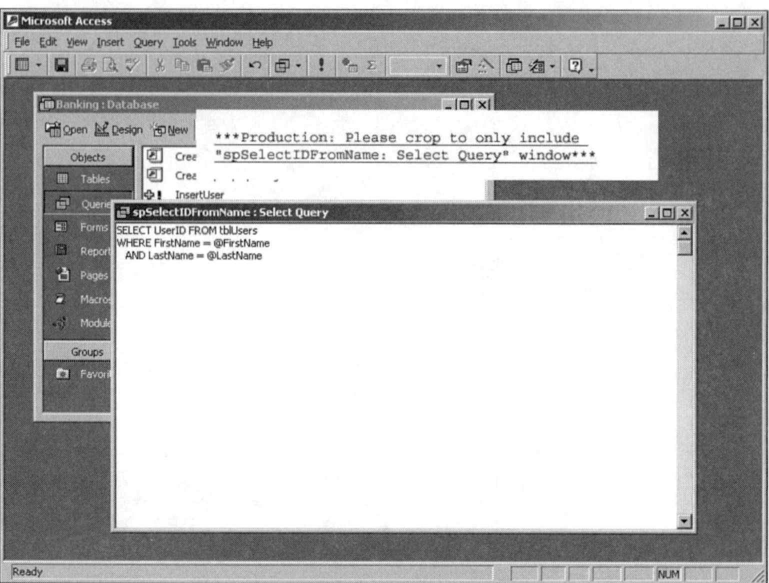

On line 1, you create an `OleDbCommand` object as usual. However, instead of specifying a SQL query, you specify the name of the stored procedure you just created. On line 3, you tell ASP.NET that you're dealing with a stored procedure by setting the `CommandType` property to `StoredProcedure`. ADO.NET takes this information, looks for a stored procedure saved in the database, and executes it, returning any data as necessary.

This won't quite work yet, however. Recall that you created a few parameters. In order for your stored procedure to return any data, you need to specify values for the `@FirstName` and `@LastName` parameters. You can do this in two ways: in-line or through the `OleDbParameters` collection. The first method is very simple. Change line 1 in the previous listing to read as follows, where the *`values`* are the parameters to pass in:

```
dim objCmd as OleDbCommand = new OleDbCommand _
   ("SelectIDFromName value, value", Conn)
```

For instance:

```
dim objCmd as OleDbCommand = new OleDbCommand _
   ("SelectIDFromName 'Chris', 'Payne'", Conn)
```

This is easy to do but isn't very efficient, especially if you have to collect the values from form objects and such. Using the parameters collection, you could define the preceding parameters with the following code:

```
dim objParam as OleDbParameter
objParam = objCmd.Parameters.Add("@FirstName", _
```

```
   OleDbType.Char)
objParam.Direction = ParameterDirection.Input
objParam.Value = tbFirst.Text

objParam = objCmd.Parameters.Add("@LastName", _
   OleDbType.Char)
objParam.Direction = ParameterDirection.Input
objParam.Value = tbLast.Text
```

This should look familiar. You did the same thing in "Parameterized Queries" earlier today. You can now fill a `DataReader` as usual by using the `ExecuteReader` method of the command object, and you can bind it to a control if you wish:

```
try
   objCmd.Connection.Open()
   objReader = objCmd.ExecuteReader
catch ex as OleDbException
   Label1.Text = "Error retrieving from the database."
end try

DataGrid1.DataSource = objReader
DataGrid1.DataBind()

objReader.Close
objCmd.Connection.Close()
```

What happened to your output parameter? With Access, you weren't able to retrieve the `@ID` as an output parameter. However, your command object returned the value as the result of the SQL `SELECT` statement. In the previous listing, you can access this value through the `DataReader`. Listing 12.3 shows a complete example of using parameters by combining the previous code snippets, and Figure 12.7 shows the output of this data in a `DataGrid`.

LISTING 12.3 Parameters Aid in Data Retrieval

```
<%@ Page Language="VB" %>
<%@ Import Namespace="System.Data" %>
<%@ Import Namespace="System.Data.OleDb" %>

<script runat="server">
   dim Conn as new OleDbConnection("Provider=" & _
            "Microsoft.Jet.OLEDB.4.0;" & _
            "Data Source=c:\ASPNET\data\banking.mdb")

    sub Submit(Sender as Object, e as EventArgs)
       dim objCmd as OleDbCommand = new OleDbCommand _
          ("SelectIDFromName", Conn)
       dim objReader as OleDbDataReader
```

LISTING 12.3 continued

```
      objCmd.CommandType = CommandType.StoredProcedure

      dim objParam as OleDbParameter
      objParam = objCmd.Parameters.Add("@FirstName", _
         OleDbType.Char)
      objParam.Direction = ParameterDirection.Input
      objParam.Value = tbFirst.Text

      objParam = objCmd.Parameters.Add("@LastName", _
         OleDbType.Char)
      objParam.Direction = ParameterDirection.Input
      objParam.Value = tbLast.Text

      try
         objCmd.Connection.Open()
         objReader = objCmd.ExecuteReader
      catch ex as OleDbException
         Response.Write("Error retrieving data.")
      end try

      DataGrid1.DataSource = objReader
      DataGrid1.DataBind()

      objCmd.Connection.Close()
   End Sub
</script>

<html><body>
   <form runat="server">
      Enter a first name:
      <asp:TextBox id="tbFirst" runat="server"/><br>
      Enter a last name:
      <asp:TextBox id="tbLast" runat="server"/><p>

      <asp:Button id="btSubmit" runat="server"
         Text="Submit"
         OnClick="Submit"/><p>

      <asp:DataGrid id="DataGrid1" runat="server"
         BorderColor="black"
         GridLines="Vertical"
         cellpadding="4"
         cellspacing="0"
         width="100%"
         Font-Name="Arial"
         Font-Size="8pt"
         HeaderStyle-BackColor="#cccc99"
         ItemStyle-BackColor="#ffffff"
```

LISTING 12.3 continued

```
            AlternatingItemStyle-Backcolor="#cccccc"
            AutoGenerateColumns="true" />
      </form>
   </body></html>
```

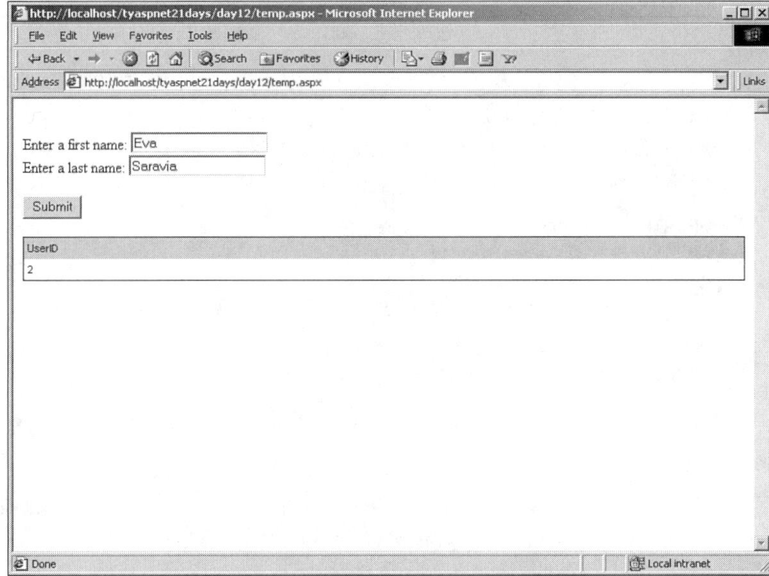

FIGURE 12.7

Returning values from a parameterized stored procedure.

The `DataReader` contains one row and one column that holds the value that your stored procedure returned.

> SQL Server loves to use output parameters, so you can take advantage of them and get by without needing a `DataReader`. See "Parameterized Queries" earlier today for information on how to do so.

Input and output parameters are very useful for supplying data to stored procedures. There are a few other types of parameters you haven't looked at yet, such as the `InputOutput` and `ReturnValue` parameters. Table 12.2 describes all of the possible parameter directions.

TABLE 12.2 Parameter Directions

Direction	*Description*
`Input`	Represents a value passed into a query
`InputOutput`	A value that can both be passed in and returned from a query
`Output`	A value returned from a query
`ReturnValue`	Represents a returned value, but not a parameter

You've already examined `Input` and `Output` parameters. The `InputOutput` parameter is useful when the data passed into a query is expected to change (when updating a database, for example). The following query is an example of such a situation. You need to update the `FirstName` field based on a value passed into the `FirstName` field:

```
UPDATE tblUsers SET FirstName = "Christopher"
WHERE FirstName = "Chris"
```

You could parameterize this by modifying it as follows:

```
UPDATE tblUsers SET @FirstName = "Christopher"
WHERE @FirstName = "Chris"
```

Now `@FirstName` is both the input and output parameter; its value changes after the query executes. The `InputOutput` parameter is ideal for this situation.

The `ReturnValue` type is very useful for queries that don't return data from columns. For example, the following SQL statement would return an integer specifying the number of rows in the table:

```
SELECT Count(*) from tblUsers
```

This information doesn't come from any single column, so it isn't represented by any field name. The value is simply returned from the query without any name or parameter. This type of data is perfect for the `ReturnValue` parameter type. To access this data, you could use the following:

```
objParam = objCmd.Parameters.Add("RETURN VALUE", _
   OleDbType.Integer)
objParam.Direction = ParameterDirection.ReturnValue
```

Stored procedures are very useful tools that can increase the performance of your ASP.NET applications. They also open a new realm of possibilities for interacting with databases, allowing very complex queries, and using more advanced database controls.

Transactions

How many times have you been performing a long task and realized halfway through that your work is all wrong? Doesn't it make you wish you could roll back time and start over?

Databases can do this by using *transactions*. A transaction is a set of tasks that must all either complete successfully or fail. For example, imagine that you've created a complex stored procedure that executes 50 SQL statements. Without a transaction, if any one of these statements fails—number 50, for example—the stored procedure will stop execution and you'll be left with one statement that didn't execute. If you want to execute that one statement, you'll be stuck executing all of the preceding 49 statements once again.

There are many cases where this would be highly undesirable. Imagine a banking application. A user wants to transfer some money from his checking account to a savings account. First you'd deduct the amount from his checking account (stored in a database) and then add that amount to the savings account (also stored in a database). Let's assume the first step is accomplished without a hitch. But when you try to add the money to the other account, you're alerted that the account has a block on it and can't have anything deposited in it at that time. Uh-oh, now you have a problem. The balances shown in the database are different from what they should be because you already took some money out.

This is exactly the type of situation that transactions are designed for. If you use a transaction for this procedure, you don't need to worry about failing somewhere in the middle of the operation. If anything happens, you can just roll back the changes.

You may recall the `AcceptChanges` and `RejectChanges` methods for the `DataSet` from Day 10. These methods allow you to perform actions similar to transactions, but they work only on disconnected data. Transactions work on an entire database over an active connection, assuming that the database application you're using supports transactions (most major commercial ones do).

There are three basic operations in a transaction: begin, rollback, and commit. Begin starts the transaction. Any operations that follow are executed and then stored in a special log so the database can examine them later. Rollback allows you to undo any changes that have occurred. The database refers back to the log and can determine the state of the data before the operation occurred. Commit makes any changes final, meaning they can't be undone or rolled back. Essentially, it removes the operations from the log.

Let's look at a typical example, shown in Listing 12.4.

LISTING 12.4 Using Database Transactions

```
<%@ Page Language="VB" %>
<%@ Import Namespace="System.Data" %>
<%@ Import Namespace="System.Data.OleDb" %>

<script runat="server">
   'declare connection
   dim Conn as new OleDbConnection("Provider=" & _
            "Microsoft.Jet.OLEDB.4.0;" & _
            "Data Source=c:\ASPNET\data\banking.mdb")

   sub Page_Load(Sender as Object, e as EventArgs)
      dim objTrans as OleDbTransaction
      dim objCmd as OleDbCommand = new OleDbCommand _
         ("DELETE from tblUsers where UserID = 32", Conn)

      Conn.Open()
      objTrans = Conn.BeginTransaction()
      objCmd.Transaction = objTrans

      try
         objCmd.ExecuteNonQuery

         objCmd.CommandText = "INSERT INTO tblUsers " & _
            "(FirstName, LastName, Address, City, State, " & _
            "Zip, Phone) VALUES " & _
            "('Jose', 'Santiago', '34 Lake Drive', " & _
            "'Yolktown', 'MA', '02515', '8006579876')"
         objCmd.ExecuteNonQuery()
         objTrans.Commit()
         Label1.Text = "Both operations performed successfully"
      catch ex as OleDbException
         objTrans.RollBack()
         Label1.Text = ex.Message & "<p>"
         Label1.Text = "Both operations failed"
      finally
         objCmd.Connection.Close()
      end try
   end sub
</script>

<html><body>
   <form runat="server">
      <asp:Label id="Label1" runat="server"
         maintainstate=false /><br>
   </form>
</body></html>
```

ANALYSIS This page executes two SQL statements. However, if there's some unforeseen error during the execution, none of the changes will be applied to the database. For example, if the second SQL statement had a syntax error, the execution would stop halfway through. Since you began your transaction before any statements were executed (on line 17), the changes made by the first statement would be rolled back.

On line 7, you create your `OleDbConnection` object as usual. You create an `OleDbTransaction` object on line 12, and you specify a SQL statement for your command object on line 14. Transactions require a valid, open connection, so you open your connection object on line 16 and then start the transaction by calling `BeginTransaction`. Note that this method is a member of the `OleDbConnection` object. The connection object must initiate the transaction. This is so you don't try to use transactions if your database doesn't support them. The connection object detects this and would stop you if necessary. Then all other commands (rollback, commit) are executed on the `OleDbTransaction` object.

On line 18, you tell your `OleDbCommand` object which `OleDbTransaction` object you're using through the `Transaction` property. In the `try` block, you execute the `DELETE` SQL statement, build a SQL `INSERT` statement, and try to execute it as well. If nothing has gone wrong so far, you call the `Commit` method to make the changes final.

If something does go wrong, you want to roll back all changes. Your `try` block catches the exception and sends the execution to the `catch` statement, where you call the `RollBack` method and print out a message to the user. No matter whether or not an error occurs in the `try` block, the `finally` block is called, which closes your connection.

The result of this is that all of the statements are executed, or none of them are.

Advanced XML Techniques

In Day 11's lesson on XML, you looked at how XML can be used to represent nearly any type of data. You also learned how to open, read, and write to XML files through ASP.NET. There's a lot more you can do with XML, though.

The next few sections will introduce some advanced techniques for manipulating XML. You'll learn how to navigate XML documents using the `XPathNavigator` object, which allows you to use the concepts in the following two sections: XPath queries and XSL transforms. XPath is a query language used to retrieve information from XML files, much as SQL is used to return data from databases. XSL transforms make it possible to transform an XML document into any other type of structured document, such as an HTML page. With these methods, you'll be able to control XML in any way you want.

XPathNavigator

NEW TERM Earlier this week, you learned how to navigate XML text documents with the `XmlNode` and `XmlDocument` objects. When you're accessing XML data, these objects create a *node tree*. That is, they take a look at the whole XML file and build an object-oriented, hierarchical representation of the data. Basically, the `XmlDocument` collects an entire XML file's contents before it lets you view the data. The `XPathNavigator`, on the other hand, doesn't build a node tree. Rather, it only looks at one node at a time. It builds the nodes when you move to them—a dynamic `XmlDocument`, if you will.

`XPathNavigator` provides cursor-style access to an XML document. Imagine looking at an XML file on a chalkboard. You can use a pointer to point to each item in succession until you reach the end of the file. The pointer always has a position on the board, and you can always move forward or back to another element. A cursor in the `XPathNavigator` is similar. This cursor keeps track of where you are in the XML document, and you can use it to move through the file by calling various `MoveTo` methods.

The `XPathNavigator` navigates around an `XPathDocument` object. This object does little other than work with an `XPathNavigator`, so we won't get into too much detail with it.

Let's look at an example of using these new objects, as shown in Listings 12.5–12.7. Listing 12.5 shows how to create an `XPathNavigator` and `XPathDocument`. Listing 12.6 uses the various `MoveTo` methods to get around in the XML file, and Listing 12.7 displays the data to the user.

LISTING 12.5 Creating an `XPathNavigator`

```
<%@ Page Language="VB" %>
<%@ Import Namespace="System.Xml" %>
<%@ Import Namespace="System.Xml.XPath" %>

<script runat="server">
   sub Page_Load(Sender as object, e as EventArgs)
      ' Create a XPathDocument
      Dim objReader as New XmlTextReader(Server.MapPath
➥("../day11/books.xml"))

      Dim objDoc as XPathDocument = new _
         XPathDocument(objReader)
      Dim objNav as XPathNavigator = objDoc.CreateNavigator()

      DisplayNode(objNav)
   end sub
```

ANALYSIS You create an XmlTextReader (line 8) and open the books.xml file from Day 11. Then you create an XPathDocument from the XmlTextReader on line 10, and then simply create your XPathNavigator on line 12. The CreateNavigator method is pretty much the only interesting feature of the XPathDocument object; it simply creates your XPathNavigator so you can move around the XML file. Finally, you call a custom DisplayNode method, shown in Listing 12.6. This method is responsible for looping through each element of the XML file and calling an appropriate method for displaying the data.

LISTING 12.6 Looping Through with the DocumentNavigator

```
16:    sub DisplayNode(objNav as XPathNavigator)
17:       If objNav.HasChildren then
18:          objNav.MoveToFirstChild()
19:          Format(objNav)
20:          DisplayNode(objNav)
21:          objNav.MoveToParent()
22:       End If
23:
24:       While objNav.MoveToNext()
25:          Format(objNav)
26:          DisplayNode(objNav)
27:       end While
28:    end sub
```


ANALYSIS This is a recursive procedure. First, you determine if this node has any children. If it does, you want to display the data for each child. MovetoFirstChild moves the cursor to the first child of the current node. Format is a custom function that does the actual writing of data to the page. On line 20, you call DisplayNode again to repeat the process for this child node. This occurs over and over again until there are no more children. After you've looped through all of the children, the MoveToParent method is called, which moves the cursor up a level in the XML hierarchy.

The second part of this method is also recursive—it's responsible for moving across levels in the hierarchy that are on the same level. The MoveToNext method moves the cursor to the next node until there are no more. At that point it returns false, causing your While loop to end. Again, you call your Format method on line 25 to display the data and call DisplayMode. This process repeats until there are no more nodes in the XML document.

Finally, Listing 12.7 shows the Format method, which presents the data to the user.

Listing 12.7 Displaying Data with the `DocumentNavigator`

```
29:     Private Sub Format(objNav As XPathNavigator)
30:        If Not objNav.HasChildren then
31:           if objNav.NodeType <> XmlNodeType.Text then
32:              lblMessage.Text += "&lt;<b>" & _
33:                 objNav.Name & "</b>&gt;"
34:           end if
35:           lblMessage.Text += " - " & objNav.Value & _
36:                 "<br>" & vbCrLf
37:        Else
38:           Dim i As Integer
39:           lblMessage.Text += "&lt;<b>" & objNav.Name & _
40:              "</b>&gt;" & vbCrLf
41:
42:           If objNav.HasAttributes then
43:              lblMessage.Text += "<br>Attributes of &lt;" & _
44:                 objNav.Name & "&gt;<br>" & vbCrLf
45:           End If
46:
47:           while objNav.MoveToNextAttribute()
48:
49:
50:              lblMessage.Text += "&lt;<b>" & objNav.Name & _
51:                 "</b>&gt; " & objNav.Value & " "
52:
53:           end while
54:           lblMessage.Text += "<br>" & vbCrLf
55:        End If
56:     end sub
57:     </script>
58:
59:     <html><body>
60:        <ASP:Label id="lblMessage" runat="server"/>
61:     </body></html>
```

Analysis Don't be intimidated by this method. Much of it simply writes HTML formatting tags to the browser. The `if` statement on line 30 determines if this node has any children. If it doesn't, you simply want to display the name and value of the node if it's not a text node. If the mode does have children, you display the name and value. The `if` statement on line 42 determines if there are any attributes, and it prints out a message if there are. Finally, the `while` loop on line 47 loops through these attributes and displays them. The `MoveToNextAttribute` method simply moves to the next attribute in the current element. If there are no more attributes, this method returns false, and your `while` loop will exit.

Figure 12.8 shows the output of this listing.

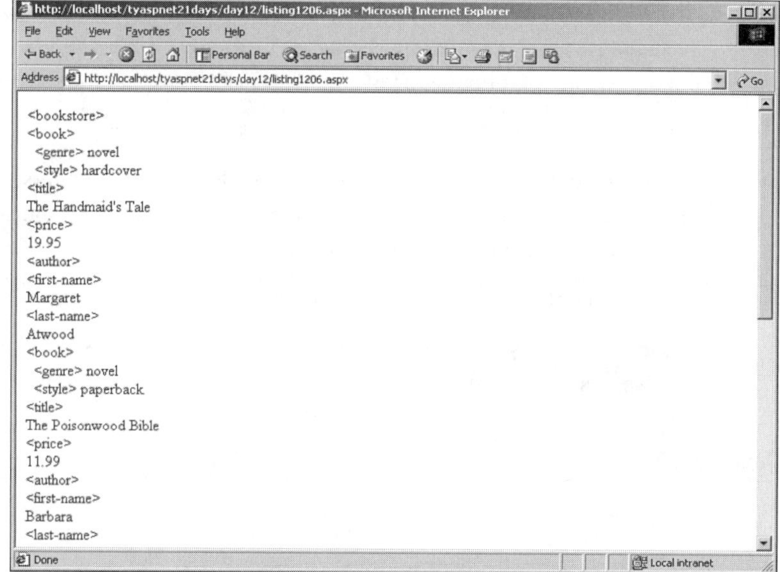
http://localhost/tyaspnet21days/day12/listing1206.aspx - Microsoft Internet Explorer
<bookstore>
<book>
<genre> novel
<style> hardcover
<title>
The Handmaid's Tale
<price>
19.95
<author>
<first-name>
Margaret
<last-name>
Atwood
<book>
<genre> novel
<style> paperback
<title>
The Poisonwood Bible
<price>
11.99
<author>
<first-name>
Barbara
<last-name>

FIGURE 12.8 *Using* `DocumentNavigator` *to display XML data.*

If you remember yesterday's lesson, "Using XML in ASP.NET," you'll see that most of the methods you've used here are exactly the same as the ones you used for the `XmlDocument` object. The `XPathNavigator` and `XmlDocument` are similar because they both inherit from the same place—the XML Document Object Model. This means you can use the same series of `Insert` and `Create` methods to build and edit your XML documents.

Then why should you use `XPathNavigator` instead of `XmlDocument`? For one thing, `XPathNavigator` doesn't use as much memory because it doesn't create the entire node tree in the beginning. It creates the tree dynamically as you move through the file. `XPathNavigator` also supports two things the `XmlDocument` doesn't: XPath queries and `XslTransforms`.

12

XPath

XPath is the World Wide Web Consortium's (W3C) language specification for accessing parts of an XML file. It allows you to query XML data just as you would query a traditional database with SQL statements. This language can get fairly complex, so you won't learn its syntax today. Instead, you'll learn how to use these queries for actual XML documents.

XPath queries are strings consisting of keywords that represent parts of an XML file. These queries are executed by the `Select` method of `XPathNavigator`. Using your `books.xml` file, you could specify the following:

```
objNav.Select("descendant::*")
```

This query returns all of the child elements, their child elements, and so on. Literally, it means select all of the descendants (children, their children, and so on). The following query returns just the price of the last book in the list:

```
objNav.Select("//book[last()]/price/text()")
```

Listing 12.8 shows how to create a simple page that takes an XPath query from the user and displays the returned data.

LISTING 12.8 Using XPath Queries to Return XML Data

```
<%@ Page Language="VB" %>
<%@ Import Namespace="System.Xml" %>
<%@ Import Namespace="System.Xml.XPath" %>

<script runat="server">
   sub SelectData(Sender as Object, e as EventArgs)
      Dim objReader as New XmlTextReader(Server.MapPath
➥("../day11/books.xml"))

      Dim objDoc as XPathDocument = new _
         XPathDocument(objReader)
      Dim objNav as XPathNavigator = objDoc.CreateNavigator()

      lblMessage.Text = ""

      try
         dim objIterator as XPathNodeIterator =
➥objNav.Select(tbQuery.Text)

         While objIterator.MoveNext()
            Format(objIterator.Current)
         end while
      catch ex As Exception
         lblMessage.Text = ex.Message
      end try

      objReader.Close()
   end sub

   Private Sub Format(objNav As XPathNavigator)
      Dim strValue As String
      Dim strName As String
```

LISTING 12.8 continued

```
31:
32:         If objNav.HasChildren then
33:            strName = objNav.Name
34:            objNav.MoveToFirstChild()
35:
36:            strValue = objNav.Value
37:         Else
38:            strValue = objNav.Value
39:            strName = objNav.Name
40:         End If
41:
42:         lblMessage.Text += "&lt;<b>" & strName & _
43:            "</b>&gt;" & strValue & "<br>"
44:      End Sub
45:   </script>
46:
47:   <html><body>
48:      <form runat=server>
49:         <asp:Textbox id="tbQuery" runat=server/>
50:         <asp:Button id="btnSubmit" text="Submit"
51:            runat=server OnClick="SelectData"/><BR>
52:         <asp:Label id="lblMessage" runat=server/>
53:      </form>
54:   </body></html>
```

ANALYSIS Much of the work happens in the `SelectData` method, which is the event handler for the button control shown on line 50. Lines 7–11 should look familiar—here's where you create your `XmlDocument` and `XPathNavigator` objects. Your `try` block on line 15 is where the real fun begins. You use the `Select` method supplied with the query entered in the text box to return the XML data. The `Select` method returns an object of type `XPathNodeIterator`, which simply provides a recordset-type collection of elements that meet your query conditions. The only members of the `XPathNodeIterator` that we're interested in are `MoveNext`, which moves to the next node returned from the query, and `Current`, which returns an `XPathNavigator` object that represents an individual node returned from your query (remember that nodes can have children). The code on lines 18–20 essentially loops through the returned results from your XPath query until there are no more, and then passes each individual node from the results to the `Format` method.

The `Format` method, beginning on line 28, is similar to the same method in Listing 12.6—just toned down a bit.

Try this page out by viewing it in your browser and entering the following XPath query:

`descendant::*`

If the listing worked correctly, no results should have been returned. What happened? This is where XML namespaces come into play.

Assuming that you are using the well-formatted `books.xml` file we created yesterday, you'll have the `xmlns` namespace value specified. Because of this, all elements in `books.xml` belong to the `xmlns` namespace, but your XPath query doesn't know that. By default, it searches for elements that don't belong in any namespace, and in our case, there are none.

There are two ways to solve this. First, you can simply remove the `xmlns` definition from your XML file, but this is obviously not desirable. The better way to do this is to let your XPath query know which namespaces to expect. For that we'll need to introduce a couple of new classes.

An `XPathExpression` class is to an XPath query as a stored procedure is to a SQL statement. This class takes an XPath query and compiles it for faster execution. It also allows namespaces to be specified, which is exactly what we want. In general, you'll want to use the `XPathExpression` object when querying your XML files.

The second object is the `XmlNamespaceManager`, which does exactly what its name implies: manages XML namespaces. Using this object, you'll specify any namespaces used in your XML file. Add the following code to Listing 12.8 immediately after line 15:

```
Dim expr as XPathExpression = objNav.Compile(tbQuery.Text)
Dim mngr as XmlNamespaceManager = new XmlNamespaceManager
➥(objReader.NameTable)
mngr.AddNamespace("","x-schema:books.xdr")
expr.SetContext(mngr)
```

The first line simply creates your new `XPathExpression` object from the query specified in the text box. The `XPathNavigator.Compile` object does this for you. The second line creates your namespace manager, using the `XmlTextReader` you created earlier as a guide. The `NameTable` property lets the manager know ahead of time what type of data to expect—for our discussion that's all we need to know.

The third line is where the namespace is added. The `XmlNamespaceManager` class has a method called `AddNamespace` that takes two parameters: the name of the namespace and its value. The first parameter here is blank, which symbolizes the default namespace. Otherwise you'd place the namespace name here.

On the last line you use the `SetContext` method of the `XPathExpression` object to make your XPath query aware of the new namespace. Essentially, you are telling the query that you have some namespaces to use. Without this line, your query wouldn't know to use the appropriate namespace.

Next, change the old line 16 to use your new `XPathExpression` object and its namespaces instead of the textbox directly:

```
dim objIterator as XPathNodeIterator = objNav.Select(expr)
```

Now enter your query again. This listing produces what's shown in Figure 12.9.

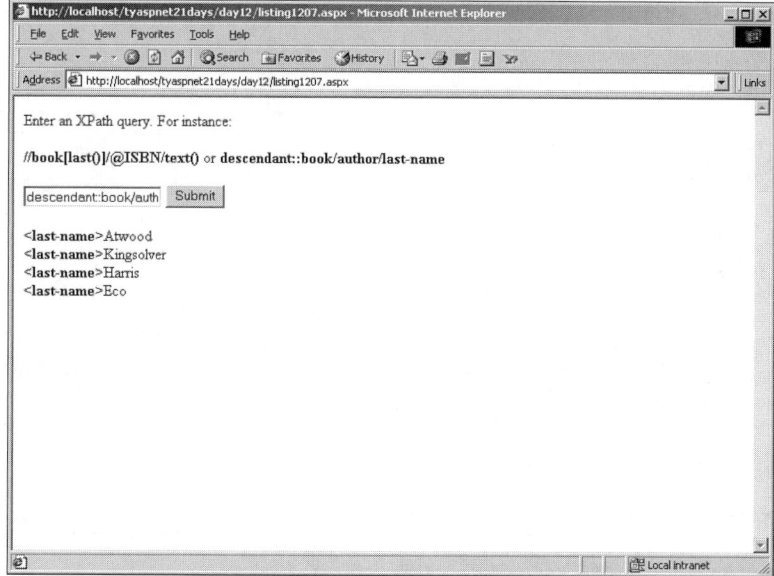

FIGURE 12.9
Querying XML data with XPath.

That seemed like a lot of work, but once you understand the concepts behind it, it makes a lot of sense. The XPath language provides a very robust and wonderful mechanism for retrieving XML data. Now you don't have to use a `DataSet` to perform these queries. For more information on XPath queries, see the W3C's online resources at `http://www.w3c.org/TR/xpath`.

XslTransforms

The Extensible Stylesheet Language (XSL) is another modeling language developed for use with XML. It works similarly to any programming language, with keywords and functions. This language allows you to convert any XML document into any other structured document, such as another XML file or an HTML file. This allows you to change your XML files into something more useful, especially for display purposes. Note that the data contained in the XML files isn't actually converted. It's simply presented in a different way.

All XSL instructions are handled by an XSL transform (XslT) processor. You use XSL to create a style sheet that tells the XslT how to transform the data. Just as you use style sheets to tell HTML how to format parts of a page, you use XSL to tell the XslT how to format the XML data once it's been transformed. Figure 12.10 illustrates the process of converting one XML document into another.

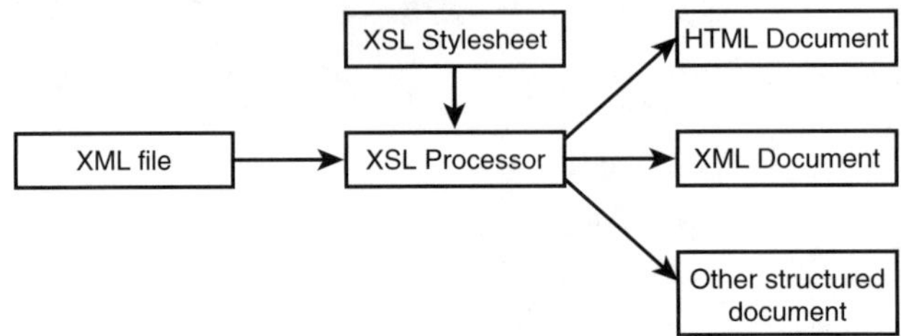

FIGURE 12.10
An XSL processor uses an XSL style sheet to transform an XML file into another structured document.

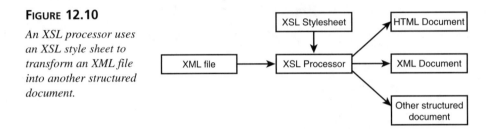

The XSL processor relies on XPath queries to return parts of an XML file, which it then formats according to the XSL style sheet. Performing a transformation is very simple in ASP.NET—you only need to supply an XSL stylesheet. The XSL stylesheet uses XPath syntax to search for specific elements, and then transforms them accordingly. Listing 12.9 shows the `books.xsl` stylesheet.

LISTING 12.9 An XSL Stylesheet

```
<?xml version="1.0"?>
<xsl:stylesheet xmlns:xsl="http://www.w3.org/1999/XSL/Transform"
   xmlns:op="x-schema:books.xdr"
   version="1.0" >
   <xsl:template match="op:bookstore">
      <HTML><BODY>
      <TABLE width="450">
      <TR>
         <TD><b>Title</b></TD>
          <TD><b>Price</b></TD>
       </TR>
       <xsl:apply-templates select="op:book"/>
       </TABLE>
       </BODY></HTML>
    </xsl:template>
    <xsl:template match="op:book">
       <TR>
          <TD><xsl:value-of select="op:title"/></TD>
          <TD><xsl:value-of select="op:price"/></TD>
       </TR>
    </xsl:template>
 </xsl:stylesheet>t
```

ANALYSIS This stylesheet transforms an XML document into an HTML document. There are a couple of things to note. First, remember that in our `books.xml` file we declared a default namespace. This XSL stylesheet must be made aware of that namespace, or it will assume that the elements you are searching for belong to no namespace, and your transformation won't work. So, on line 3, you reference the default namespace used in your `books.xml` file. Note that here, however, we specify a prefix for the default namespace. Let's take a step back and examine why.

There are three files we are concerned about here: the source XML file, the XSL stylesheet file, and the output file (which in this case will be an HTML file). If you specify a default namespace in the XSL file, it will be used for the output file as well. However, the XSL and output files have no way of knowing what the default namespace in the source file is. Therefore, you have to define it, as shown on line 3.

The catch is that you cannot define the default namespace from the source file as the default namespace in the XSL file. If you try to, then the XSL file will assume the namespace belongs to the output file, and not the source file. The XPath queries will similarly assume that the elements they are searching for belong to no namespace at all, and your transformation won't work.

It boils down to this: If you want your output file to have a default namespace, specify it in the XSL stylesheet as the default namespace. If, however, you want to use your default namespace from your source file, you'll have to use a prefix in the XSL file (we used "`op`" in this case).

One more thing to note is that if you reference a schema file in your XSL stylesheet, it must be in the same directory as the stylesheet. Thus, you must copy the `books.xdr` file from yesterday into the `/day12` directory as well.

12

The `xsl:template` tags specify how to format a particular section of the XML document. For instance, line 20 formats any nodes that are named `op:book` (here we see the prefix of the source file's default namespace). `xsl:apply-templates` essentially means, "Insert this `xsl:template` element here." The `xsl:value-of` tags insert the specified element values (again, notice the `op` prefix on lines 18–19. Finally, in our file, anything other than these three tags are considered literal values.

You've chosen to format the XML file as an HTML file here, which explains the `HTML` and `Table` tags. You could easily transform into another XML file—it's only a matter of the tags you supply.

Listing 12.10 uses this stylesheet to produce the HTML document from the `books.xml` file you created in Day 11.

LISTING 12.10 Using an XSL Stylesheet and XslT to Produce an HTML Document from an XML File

```
1:     <%@ Page Language="VB" %>
2:     <%@ Import Namespace="System.Xml" %>
3:     <%@ Import Namespace="System.Xml.XPath" %>
4:     <%@ Import Namespace="System.Xml.Xsl" %>
5:
6:     <script runat="server">
7:        sub Page_Load(Sender as Object, e as EventArgs)
8:           Dim objReader as New XmlTextReader(Server.MapPath
➥("../day11/books.xml"))
9:
10:          Dim objDoc as XPathDocument = new _
11:             XPathDocument(objReader)
12:
13:          Dim objXSLT As XslTransform = New XslTransform()
14:          dim objWriter as XmlTextWriter = new XmlTextWriter _
15:             (Server.MapPath("output.html"), nothing)
16:
17:          try
18:             objXSLT.Load(Server.MapPath("books.xsl"))
19:             objXSLT.Transform(objDoc, nothing, objWriter)
20:
21:             lblMessage.Text = "File written successfully"
22:          catch ex As Exception
23:             lblMessage.Text = ex.Message
24:          finally
25:             objReader.Close
26:             objWriter.Close
27:          end try
28:       end sub
29:    </script>
30:
31:    <html><body>
32:       <asp:Label id="lblMessage" runat="server"
33:          maintainstate=false/>
34:    </body></html>
```

ANALYSIS The first thing you should notice is the additional namespace, `System.Xml.Xsl`. Lines 8–11 again perform standard procedures: creating an `XmlDocument` and `XPathNavigator`. On line 13, you create your `XslTransform` object, and on line 14, you create an `XmlTextWriter` object to write the transformed document into an HTML file named `output.html`.

Inside your `try` block, you load the XSL file into your `XslTransform` object, which will use the style sheet as the schema to format your new HTML document. You then call the `Transform` method on the `XslTransform` object to convert your document according to the XSL stylesheet. The first parameter is the content of the XML file you want to transform (represented by the `XPathDocument`), the second parameter represents any additional parameters you want to supply to the XSL file (none in this case), and the final parameter is the `XmlTextWriter` to place the transformed contents.

Finally, you close your writer and write a simple message to the user. You should now have an `output.html` file in the same directory as this listing. It contains the content from the XML file, as shown in Figure 12.11.

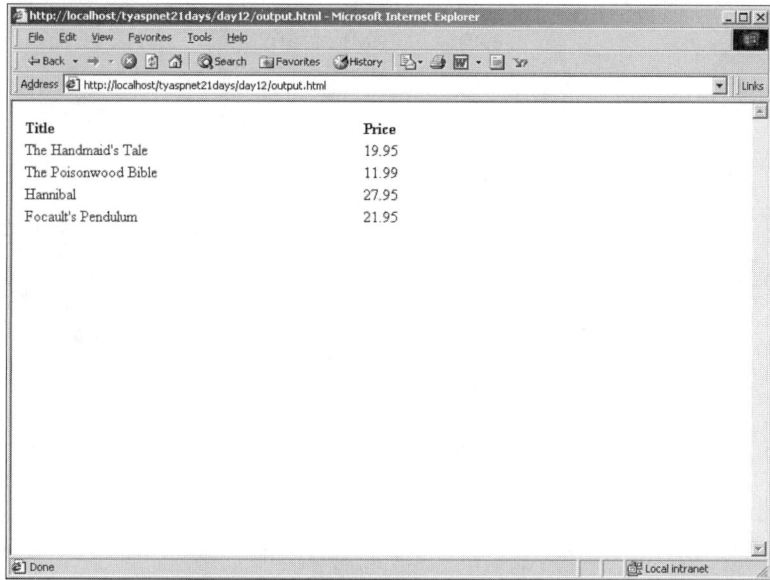

FIGURE 12.11
The HTML output from your XSL transform.

You also could have loaded the transformed contents into an `XmlReader` to display immediately by replacing line 19 with the following:

```
objReader = objXslT.Transform(objNav, nothing)
```

Here, `objReader` is the `XmlReader`. That's all there is to it. Listing 12.11 shows a full example of using an `XmlReader` instead of an `XmlTextWriter`.

LISTING 12.11 Displaying Transformed XML Data with an `XmlReader`

```
<%@ Page Language="VB" %>
<%@ Import Namespace="System.Xml" %>
<%@ Import Namespace="System.Xml.XPath" %>
<%@ Import Namespace="System.Xml.Xsl" %>

```

LISTING 12.11 continued

```
6:     <script runat="server">
7:        sub Page_Load(Sender as Object, e as EventArgs)
8:           Dim objReader as New XmlTextReader(Server.MapPath
➥("../day11/books.xml"))
9:
10:          Dim objDoc as XPathDocument = new _
11:             XPathDocument(objReader)
12:
13:          Dim objXSLT As XslTransform = New XslTransform()
14:          dim objWriter as XmlTextWriter = new XmlTextWriter _
15:             (Server.MapPath("output.html"), nothing)
16:
17:          try
18:             objXSLT.Load(Server.MapPath("books.xsl"))
19:             dim objReader2 as XmlReader = objXslT.Transform
➥(objDoc, nothing)
20:             While objReader2.Read()
21:                Response.Write("<b>" & objReader2.Name & "</b> " & _
22:                   objReader2.Value & "<br>")
23:             End While
24:
25:             lblMessage.Text = "File written successfully"
26:          catch ex As Exception
27:             lblMessage.Text = ex.Message
28:          finally
29:             objReader.Close
30:             objWriter.Close
31:          end try
32:       end sub
33:    </script>
34:
35:    <html><body>
36:       <asp:Label id="lblMessage" runat="server"
37:          maintainstate=false/>
38:    </body></html>
```

This listing is exactly the same as Listing 12.10, except that you're using an `XmlReader` instead of an `XmlTextWriter`. Therefore, content isn't sent to an output file. On lines 18–21, you use a `while` loop and the `Read` method to loop through and display the data.

The `XmlTransform` object only has two methods, `Load` and `Transform`, so it's fairly easy to use.

As you'll recall, XslTs rely on XPath queries. The XSL file specifies node names that need to be transformed. The `XmlTransform` object uses XPath queries to retrieve these named nodes without you ever knowing it. You could have used these queries to retrieve data and format them yourself, but why bother when you have the `XmlTransform` object to do it for you?

For more information on XSL, see the W3C's online resources at `http://www.w3c.org/TR/xsl` and `http://www.w3c.org/TR/xslt`.

That's Not ASP!

Many of the techniques covered today are also available in classic ASP. For instance, parameterized stored procedures were once a very common way to execute database queries. XML manipulation was also possible through an ASP add-on component. ASP.NET provides much easier ways to perform these techniques because all of the necessary functionality is built-in and fully object-oriented.

These concepts are familiar to many ASP developers, so moving to ASP.NET shouldn't be too difficult. Only the implementation has changed. Existing stored procedures, XSL stylesheets, and XPath queries can still be used. You just need to use different objects to access them.

Summary

There are many ways to accomplish any given task in ASP.NET. For example, on Day 10, you learned how to use the `OleDbCommand` and `OleDbDataAdapter` objects to retrieve data from a database using SQL statements. Today you learned how to parameterize those statements and retrieve the same data. On Day 11, you learned how to use the `XmlDocument` object to manipulate XML files. The `XPathNavigator` object used today can accomplish the same tasks, as well as a few others. The more of these methods you learn, the stronger a programmer you'll become. However, even if you learn every available method, generally it's a good idea to select a particular method and stick with it. This makes it easier for you to understand your code later on, as well as for other developers to read your code.

Parameterized queries allow you to pass in variable data to SQL statements, both for input and output. You use parameters by substituting the variable part of your queries with variables prefixed by the `@` symbol. For example:

```
SELECT FirstName FROM tblUsers WHERE UserID = @ID
```

Parameters can be created in ASP.NET with the `OleDbParameter` object. You can specify the parameter name, value, type, and direction, such as input or output. For example:

```
dim objParam as OleDbParameter
objParam = objCmd.Parameters.Add("@ID", OleDbType.Integer)
```

```
objParam.Direction = ParameterDirection.Input
objParam.Value = 1
```

Stored procedures are compiled SQL statements that allow database applications to execute queries much more efficiently than regular statements. There are a number of benefits to using stored procedures, including increased performance and more modularity in your applications.

You create stored procedures using regular SQL statements within a database application, such as MS SQL Server 2000 or Access. You can then execute these procedures from ASP.NET with the `OleDbCommand` object by setting the `CommandType` property to `StoredProcedure`. You can also create parameters for stored procedures, just as you would with normal parameterized queries. Returned values can be placed in output parameters. They can also return value parameters or a data control such as a `DataReader`.

Transactions allow databases to undo changes. Any commands executed within a transaction are logged. The database can then revert to a state before the commands were executed to undo the changes. In effect, transactions allow you to build an all-or-none execution. You start a transaction by calling `BeginTransaction` on the connection object, and then all subsequent statements are protected—they can be rolled back. The `Commit` method makes changes final, and the `RollBack` method undoes any changes.

`XPathNavigator` allows cursor-style access to an XML document, dynamically loading nodes as necessary. This object is similar to the `XmlDocument` object and supports many of the same methods. In addition, `XPathNavigator` supports XPath queries and XSL transforms.

XPath queries are statements that gather specific parts of an XML file, much as SQL statements gather parts of a data store. You execute XPath queries with the `XPathNavigator.Select` method.

XSL transforms allow you to convert one XML file into another structured document, such as an HTML page. The `XmlTransform` class uses XSL stylesheets to determine the format of the converted document. It supports two methods: `Load` and `Transform`. The former loads the XSL stylesheet, while the latter transforms an XML document, placing the result in either `XmlReader` or `XmlTextWriter`.

Tomorrow you're going to look at another important part of data access: file I/O. ASP.NET uses many different files to execute your applications, and you'll examine them tomorrow. You'll also learn how to read and write files, as well as examine and modify their properties.

Q&A

Q How do transactions roll back data?

A A database maintains what is known as a *transaction log*. This log keeps track of all the statements that are executed and the data that has changed. The database refers to this log to determine the state of the data before the statements were executed, and moves back to that state if necessary. If necessary, a transaction log can even be used to regenerate an entire database.

Q How much of a performance benefit do stored procedures actually provide?

A That's difficult to say. It depends on the database application you're using and the commands being executed, among other things. Studies have shown, however, that using stored procedures can result in up to a 25% decrease in processing time. For more information, check out the article at
`http://www.4guysfromrolla.com/webtech/sqlguru/q120899-2.shtml`.

Workshop

This workshop will help reinforce the concepts you've learned in today's lesson. Answers can be found in Appendix A.

Quiz

1. Specify a SQL statement to create an empty stored procedure (one that doesn't execute any SQL statement) that accepts one input parameter and one output parameter of your choice.
2. What are the four parameter directions?
3. True or false: You use output parameters if you want to return multiple rows of data.
4. Will the following code work?

```
Response.Write("ID = " & objCmd.Parameters("@ID"). _
   Value.ToString())
objReader.Close()
```

5. What's the difference between `XPathNavigator` and `XmlDocument`?
6. What is an XSL stylesheet used for, and how is it related to XPath queries?
7. How do you return data from an XSL transform with `XmlReader`? With `XmlTextWriter`?

Exercises

Create a stored procedure that inserts a new row into your `tblUsers` table using parameters. Build an ASP.NET page that allows users to enter this data, and execute this procedure with parameters.

WEEK 2

DAY 13

Reading and Writing Files on the Web Server

File input/output (I/O) is a very important topic to ASP.NET. You've already been using outside files in your ASP.NET pages (such as XML data files, databases, and so on), but today you're going to learn more about how other types of files can help extend your ASP.NET applications.

There are many uses for external files other than simply providing a place to store extra data. Today's lesson will cover the following:

- How ASP.NET uses files and where we'll see them
- How to include files in your ASP.NET pages
- How to access file and directory properties
- How to open, read from, and write to files
- How to provide custom file storage (isolated storage) for each user

Using Files with ASP.NET

Through the .NET Framework, ASP.NET makes it very easy to access external files (files other than the actual `.aspx` files). External files are, in fact, necessary for ASP.NET to function correctly. Such files include the `web.config` and `global.asax` files, which control the way the applications behave.

External files can also be used to extend ASP.NET. You've seen a few types of these already, such as user and custom controls, and namespaces compiled into DLLs. These all allow you to provide more functionality for your applications, while keeping your pages relatively simple.

Finally, ASP.NET also allows you to access files that might not be native parts of your application at all, but might be useful anyway. These include text data stores, imported news headline files, readme files for applications, résumés, or whatever else you find useful. ASP.NET allows you to access the entire file system of the server, so you have a lot of flexibility.

Including External Files

One method ASP.NET can use to access files is called *file inclusion*. This method simulates taking the content of one file and inserting it into another; luckily, you don't have to actually do that. The methods I'll talk about in the following sections show you different methods to include files.

Server-Side Includes

A server-side include file is a way to separate code from a page. This is helpful if you ever need to reuse that code, or simply want to make it easier to edit your pages.

The syntax for using server-side includes is as follows:

```
<!--#include file="FileName"-->
```

or:

```
<!--#include virtual="FileName"-->
```

The keyword `virtual` is used to specify a file by virtual directory, whereas `file` specifies a file path in the local directory structure. For example, if you want to include the contents of the file in `http://www.yourserver.com/includes/file1.aspx` in an ASP.NET Web page running from `http://www.yourserver.com/someDir1/someDir2/someFile.aspx`, you could use either one of these `#include` statements:

```
<!--#include file="../../includes/file1.aspx"-->
<!--#include virtual="/includes/file1.aspx"-->
```

Note that the `#include file` statement must be changed depending on the directory in which the ASP.NET page making the server-side include call is located, relative to the include file. These type of includes are called relative file paths. This can get frustrating as files move around, so ASP.NET allows you to also specify includes with absolute directories as well, using the `#include virtual` syntax, as shown in the second statement in the previous code snippet. This allows you to specify the path for a server-side include, regardless of where the calling ASP.NET pages are located.

Let's encapsulate a commonly used header in a server-side include that you can reference from your ASP.NET pages. Start by creating a file named `header.aspx` and placing the following code inside it:

```
<a href="index.aspx"><img src="header.gif" alt="Home"></a><hr>
<a href="index.aspx">Home</a> <a href="logout.aspx">Log out</a>
```

Don't encapsulate any other tags, such as `<form>` elements; these will be contained in the calling ASP.NET page. Now let's create the following ASP.NET page in the same directory, and include the header:

```
<script language="VB" runat="server">
   Sub Page_Load(obj as Object, e as EventArgs)
      'do something
   End Sub
</script>

<html><body>
   <!--#include file="header.aspx"-->
   Hi there!
</body></html>
```

ASP.NET inserts the content from `header.aspx` into our file *before* it processes any ASP.NET commands. Therefore, when the page is ready to be executed, ASP.NET thinks it looks like this:

```
<script language="VB" runat="server">
   Sub Page_Load(obj as Object, e as EventArgs)
      'do something
   End Sub
</script>

<html><body>
   <a href="index.aspx"><img src="header.gif" alt="Home"></a><hr>
   <a href="index.aspx">Home</a> <a href="logout.aspx">Log out</a>
   Hi there!
</body></html>
```

This listing will produce the page shown in Figure 13.1.

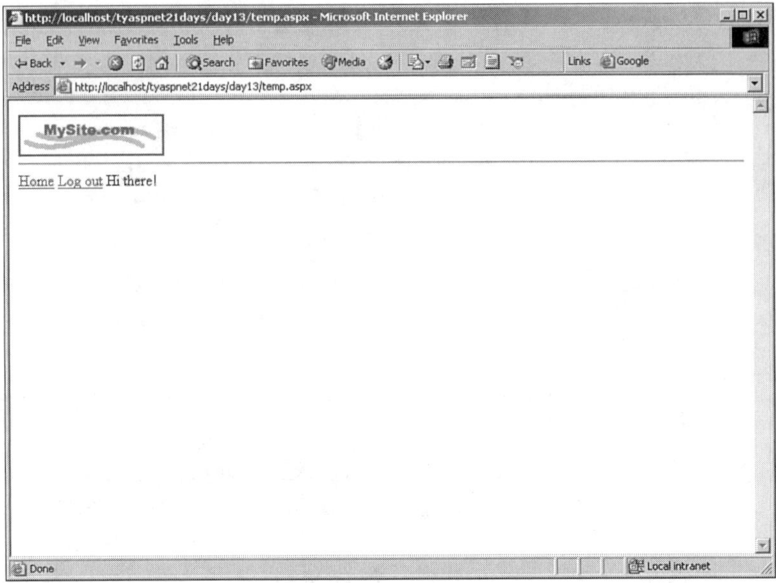

FIGURE 13.1
Server-side includes are treated as if they were part of the calling ASP.NET page.

Note

Remember that all this happens on the server, before anything is sent to the browser. The files are merged on the server, before any code is executed, and before anything is sent to the client. Therefore, a `Response.Redirect` would still work.

We can use a server-side include anywhere in the page, so this header could have just as easily been a footer. It can even include tags such as `<html>` and `<body>`, or ASP.NET server controls.

By default, server-side includes can be used only from files with the extensions `.shtml`, `.shtm`, `.stm`, `.asp`, `.asa`, `.asax`, and `.aspx`. When used in an `.html` file, for example, the include will not be processed. You can change these extensions with the Internet Services Manager in IIS 5.0.

Server-Side Includes Versus Other Includes

You might be wondering about the difference between a server-side include and a user control. Both can be used for identical reasons: to encapsulate portions of UI. The difference is that user controls are for displaying UI, whereas server-side includes can be used for any purpose, including encapsulating commonly used functions or constants.

Typically, if you want to encapsulate a UI element, it is a better idea to do it in a user control because it can have programmatic elements that you may manipulate, whereas you can't do this using a server-side include.

Do	Don't
Do use server-side includes when you want to include commonly used programmatic elements, such as classes or functions, in your pages.	**Don't** use server-side includes when you are only encapsulating UI—use a user control instead.

Other Includes

There are other methods to include files in ASP.NET—most of which we have already covered. For code-behind forms, see Day 19, "Separating Code from Content." For the `import` keyword, see Day 2, "Building ASP.NET Pages." Finally, for user controls, see Day 5, "Beginning Web Forms."

These methods vary in their implementations, but each allows ASP.NET pages to access the contents of another file.

Accessing Files

The `System.IO` namespace provides a lot of functionality that you can take advantage of from your ASP.NET pages, including reading and writing files, creating and deleting directories, and examining file and directory attributes. This namespace also allows you to react to events that occur on the file system, such as a directory being deleted or created by another user.

Files, Streams, Readers, and Writers

Before you begin examining the `System.IO` classes and accessing files, you should learn the differences between files and streams because they are very distinct in ASP.NET.

New Term Technically, a *file* is a collection of data with a name that is located in a distinct place, and is stored for an indefinite period of time. For example, a file exists on your computer's hard drive, has a filename and path, and can be accessed whenever you need it. Think of a file as a box with stuff inside it—a tangible object.

New Term A *stream*, on the other hand, is not concerned with filenames, paths, or storage locations. A stream can be used to read and write data from any location, such as a hard disk, a network, or memory. Therefore, a stream is a way to access any data, including files. When you open and read files, you're actually using streams to do so. The `Stream` class is a base object that many other classes inherit from.

Streams are used for binary access: They read raw data from files as 1s and 0s. This method of access has its place, but in ASP.NET, we're mostly concerned with Unicode access; that is, reading characters and strings as opposed to 1s and 0s.

The .NET Framework provides two other objects for just this purpose: `TextReader` and `TextWriter`. I won't talk much about these base objects here, but know that many classes inherit from these two as well. The `XmlTextReader` and `XmlTextWriter` from Day 11, "Using XML in ASP.NET," were two. You'll learn a few more today.

Here we have arrived with two separate branches of entities: `Stream` and its subclasses for binary access; `TextReader` and `TextWriter` and their subclasses for Unicode access. When exploring the .NET Framework, you'll be able to tell the difference immediately: Classes and objects that inherit from `Stream` generally have the word `stream` in their name (`FileStream`, `MemoryStream`, and so on). Classes that inherit from `TextReader` and `TextWriter` generally have the word `reader` or `writer` in their name (`XmlTextReader`, `BinaryWriter`, and so on).

Thankfully, there are classes that can convert between the binary and Unicode data. You'll be examining two important ones for ASP.NET file I/O—`StreamReader` and `StreamWriter`—later today. Figure 13.2 depicts the relationship between all these objects.

Note

Don't get `Streams` and *streaming* confused. `Streams` allow access to data stores, whereas streaming provides dynamic access to data, piece by piece, when you request it; the former is a noun, the latter is a verb. `Streams` can be *streamed*, but don't have to be.

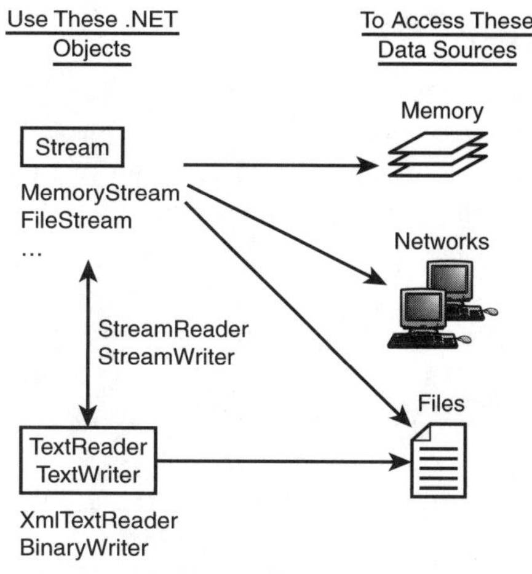

FIGURE 13.2
The relationship between `Streams`*,* `TextReaders`*, and* `TextWriters`*.*

NEW TERM The `Stream` object allows *asynchronous access*. This means that while you are performing operations on the file, you can continue to execute other code at the same time. For example, if you are writing information into a very large file, and you expect it to take a minute of processing time, you can open the file asynchronously and perform the write operation in the background, while running the code to redirect users around your site.

The opposite of this is *synchronous* execution. With this mode, you must wait for the code to finish executing before continuing on with something else, which might result in some performance penalties. Figure 13.3 shows the order of operation differences between the two modes. I focus on only synchronous access here because it is easier to use and is more common, but for more information, see the .NET Framework SDK documentation.

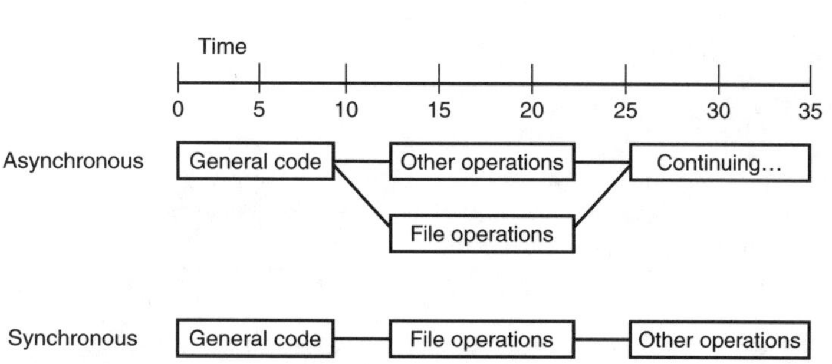

FIGURE 13.3
Asynchronous operation often results in better performance.

13

Examining Files and Directories

There are four main objects that we will focus on: the `File` and `Directory` objects, and the `FileInfo` and `DirectoryInfo` objects. The first two objects provide methods to create, modify, and delete files and directories, and the latter two provide properties to examine their attributes. Listing 13.1 shows an example.

LISTING 13.1 Viewing File and Directory Information

```
1:<%@ Import Namespace="System.IO" %>
2:<script language="VB" runat="server">
3:
4:   sub Page_Load(Sender as Object, e as EventArgs)
5:      dim f as new FileInfo(Server.MapPath("listing1301.aspx"))
6:
7:      lblMessage.Text = "File information<br>" & _
8:         "<b>Name: </b>" & f.Name & "<br>" & _
9:         "<b>Path: </b>" & f.DirectoryName & "<br>" & _
10:         "<b>Last access time: </b>" & f.LastAccessTime & _
11:            "<br>" & _
12:         "<b>Last write time: </b>" & f.LastWriteTime & _
13:            "<br>" & _
14:         "<b>Length: </b>" & f.Length & " bytes<p>"
15:
16:       'return parent directory
17:       dim dir as DirectoryInfo = f.Directory
18:
19:       lblMessage.Text += "Directory information<br>" & _
20:          "<b>Name: </b>" & dir.Name & "<br>" & _
21:          "<b>Full name: </b>" & dir.FullName & "<br>" & _
22:          "<b>Last access time: </b>" & dir.LastAccessTime & _
23:             "<br>" & _
24:          "<b>Last write time: </b>" & dir.LastWriteTime & _
25:             "<br>" & _
26:          "<b>Parent: </b>" & dir.Parent.Name & "<br>"
27:
28:    end sub
29:
30:</script>
31:
32:<html><body>
33:    <asp:label id="lblMessage" runat=server/>
34:</body></html>
```

ANALYSIS Save this listing as `Listing1301.aspx`. On line 1, you import the additional namespace, `System.IO`. On line 5, you instantiate a new `FileInfo` object with the file containing the code from this listing (this way you guarantee that the file exists).

Recall from Day 4, "Using ASP.NET Objects with C# and VB.NET," that the `Server.MapPath` method maps a virtual directory to its physical path. Lines 8–14 list all the properties of this file. Figure 13.4 illustrates the values returned for each property.

On line 17, you use the `Directory` property to return a `DirectoryInfo` object based on the file's parent directory. Then, on lines 20–26, you display the properties for this directory. Many of the properties of the `FileInfo` and `DirectoryInfo` objects are similar.

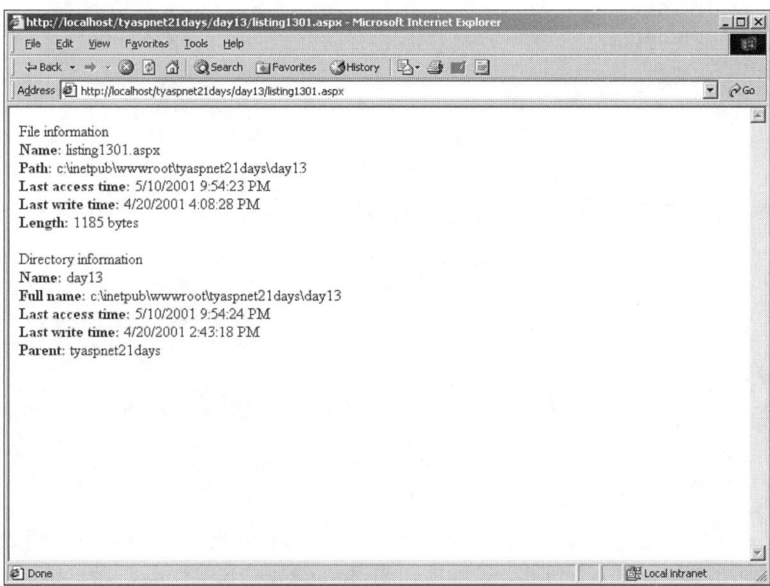

FIGURE 13.4
Viewing file and directory properties.

Caution

> If the specified file does not exist, you will receive an error. Use the `FileExists` method of the `File` object to determine whether a file exists.
>
> Similarly, use the `DirectoryExists` method of the `Directory` object to determine whether a directory is valid.

13

The `File` and `Directory` objects also have an `Attributes` collection that provides additional information, such as whether the file is read-only or hidden. These attributes are listed in Table 13.1.

TABLE 13.1 File and Directory Attributes and Values

Attribute	*Value*
`Readonly`	1
`Hidden`	2
`System`	4
`Directory`	16
`Archive`	32
`Encrypted`	64
`Normal`	128
`Temporary`	256
`SparseFile`	512
`ReparsePoint`	1024
`Compressed`	2048
`Offline`	4096
`NotContentIndexed`	8192

These values are accumulated per file. For example, for the file `listing1301.aspx` in Listing 13.1, the line

```
Response.Write(f.Attributes)
```

produces the string `"32"`, which means that this file is archived. To change the attributes for the file, simply sum the values and set the `Attributes` property. For example, to make the file hidden, compressed, encrypted, and not indexed, use

```
f.Attributes = 10306
```

You cannot assign attribute values directly. For instance, this line

```
f.Attributes.Hidden = 2
```

will result in an error. The `Hidden` attribute is a constant and cannot be modified. You must change the attributes directly, like so:

```
f.Attributes = 2
```

These attribute values can be a pain to memorize, so you can use their names instead, separating each attribute with an `Or` operator (the `|` operator in C#):

```
f.Attributes = FileAttributes.Hidden Or _
   FileAttributes.Compressed Or _
   FileAttributes.NotContentIndexed
```

This code snippet does the same as setting the attribute value to `10306`. The `Or` operator is part of VB.NET's bitwise operators, which allow you to compare bit values. Other operators include `And`, `Not`, and `Xor`. To determine whether a file has a certain attribute set, use the `And` operator:

```
if f.Attributes And FileAttributes.Hidden > 0 then
   Response.write("Hidden")
end if
```

This is great for displaying information on one file or directory. However, what happens when you need to view more information, such as for all the files in a directory? The `DirectoryInfo` object provides two methods that return collections of files and directories: `GetFiles` and `GetDirectories`. Listing 13.2 shows an example of iterating over these collections.

LISTING 13.2 Iterating over Files and Directories Within a Directory

```
<%@ Import Namespace="System.IO" %>
<script language="C#" runat="server">

   void Page_Load(Object Sender, EventArgs e) {
      DirectoryInfo dir = new DirectoryInfo
➥(Server.MapPath("/tyaspnet21days"));

      DataGrid1.DataSource = dir.GetFiles("*.*");
      DataGrid1.DataBind();

       DataGrid2.DataSource = dir.GetDirectories();
       DataGrid2.DataBind();

   }

 </script>

 <html><body>
    <b>File information</b><br>
    <asp:DataGrid id="DataGrid1" runat="server"
       width="100%"
       Font-Name="Arial"
       Font-Size="10pt"
       AlternatingItemStyle-Backcolor="#cccccc"
       AutogenerateColumns="true" />

    <p>
```

LISTING 13.2 continued

```
27:       <b>Directory information</b><br>
28:       <asp:DataGrid id="DataGrid2" runat="server"
29:          width="100%"
30:          Font-Name="Arial"
31:          Font-Size="10pt"
32:          AlternatingItemStyle-Backcolor="#cccccc"
33:          AutogenerateColumns="true" />
34:    </body></html>
```

ANALYSIS On line 7, you specify `GetFiles("*.*")` to return all files in the current directory; `"*.*"` means any string, followed by a period, followed by any string (for example, `Listing1301.aspx`). Because this method returns a collection, you can easily use a `DataGrid` to display the items in the way you want. You use `GetDirectories` on line 10 to return a collection of the directories in the current directory, and likewise, display the information in a `DataGrid`. Figure 13.5 shows the output of this listing.

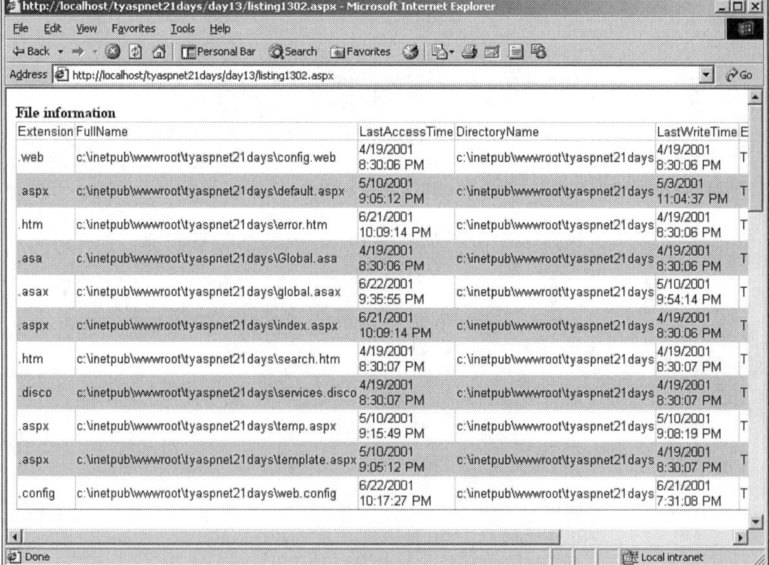

FIGURE 13.5
Looping through the files and directories collection.

You could have also used a `for each` loop to iterate through the collections, but the `DataGrid` provides a much easier mechanism for display. To loop through and display all the subfolders and their files, you could use a recursive function.

Let's develop a slightly more useful example. You'll create a file browser that can be used to view the contents of your hard drive, much like Windows Explorer. This page should allow users to view files by navigating through directories (as in Windows), and also allow users to enter a directory name manually for quicker navigation. Listing 13.3 shows the ASP.NET code for this page.

LISTING 13.3 Building a File Navigation System—`Listing1303.aspx`

```
<%@ Import Namespace="System.IO" %>
<script language="VB" runat="server">
   private dir as DirectoryInfo
   private f as FileInfo
   private strDir as string

   sub Page_Load(Sender as Object, e as EventArgs)
      if not Page.IsPostBack then
         strDir = Request.Params("dir")

         if strDir = "" then
            strDir = "c:\"
         end if

         tbDir.Text = strDir
         dir = new DirectoryInfo(strDir)
         ListFiles()
      end if
   end sub

   sub tbDir_Handle(Sender as Object, e as EventArgs)
      strDir = Sender.Text
      if Directory.Exists(strDir) then
         dir = new DirectoryInfo(strDir)
         ListFiles()
      else
         lblMessage.Text = "Invalid directory"
      end if
   end sub

   sub ListFiles()
      dim hl as HyperLink
      dim d as DirectoryInfo
      if not dir.Root.FullName = dir.FullName then
         hl = new HyperLink
         hl.Text = ".."
         hl.NavigateURL = "listing1303.aspx?dir=" & _
            Server.URLEncode(dir.Parent.FullName)
         Panel1.Controls.Add(hl)

```

LISTING 13.3 continued

```
41:         Panel1.Controls.Add(new LiteralControl("<br>"))
42:      end if
43:
44:      for each d in dir.GetDirectories
45:         hl = new Hyperlink
46:         hl.Text = d.Name
47:         hl.NavigateURL = "listing1303.aspx?dir=" & _
48:            Server.URLEncode(d.FullName)
49:         Panel1.Controls.Add(hl)
50:
51:         Panel1.Controls.Add(new LiteralControl("<br>"))
52:      next
53:
54:      for each f in dir.GetFiles("*.*")
55:         lblMessage.Text += f.Name & "<br>"
56:      next
57:   end sub
58:</script>
```

ANALYSIS Save this file as `listing1303.aspx`. The first time the user visits this page, he will see the directory listing for the root drive (`C:\`, in this case). The `Request` parameter `dir` is checked on line 9—its value is used to find out what the current directory should be. If this parameter is blank (as it should be on first viewing), you use the default directory `C:\`. You then create a new `DirectoryInfo` object for this directory on line 16, set a text box's `Text` property to the same directory on line 15 (for UI purposes), and call the `ListFiles` method on line 17.

The `ListFiles` function, beginning on line 31, iterates over the collection of directories within the current directory, as you have done previously. First, however, you perform a check to determine whether you're at the root directory on line 34. If not, you want to display the `..` marker, which allows users to move up one directory. You create a new `Hyperlink` control to display the `..`, and append the path of the current directory's parent folder on the querystring. When the user clicks on this link, this same page is brought up, with an additional querystring parameter named `dir` that specifies the new directory path—the next highest directory, in this case. The `Page Load` event uses this parameter to create a new directory object. On line 41, you create a new `LiteralControl` that introduces a line break after the `..` marker.

You do a similar task for each directory: You create a `Hyperlink` control that directs the user back to this page. The `Hyperlink` displays the short name of the directory (shown on line 46), and you append the full name to the querystring (shown on line 47). This page uses this parameter to display a new directory. On line 51, you again add a `LiteralControl` to provide a line break between directory links.

On lines 54–56, you iterate over the files in the directory and add their names to a label control. Before you examine the final method, `tbDir_Handle`, take a look at the UI portion of this page in Listing 13.4.

LISTING 13.4 UI Portion of the Directory Listing Page —`Listing1303.aspx`

```
<html><body>
   <form runat="server">
      <b>Directory:</b>
      <asp:Textbox id="tbDir" runat="server"
         OnTextChanged="tbDir_Handle"
         AutoPostBack=true /><p>
      <asp:Panel id="Panel1" runat="server"
         MaintainState="true" />
      <asp:label id="lblMessage" runat=server
         maintainstate=false />
   </form>
</body></html>
```

ANALYSIS There are three elements on this page: a `TextBox` control that displays the current directory path; a `Panel` that holds the `Hyperlink` controls; and a `Label` that holds the filenames and any miscellaneous messages. When the text in the text box has changed (presumably when the user changes a directory manually), the `tbDir_Handle` event takes control.

This handler, as shown on lines 21–29 of Listing 13.3, retrieves the text from the text box and uses it to set the new directory. Note the `if` statement on line 21. Any time you allow the user to enter information manually, you want to make sure that it is valid information. The `DirectoryExists` method is used here to determine whether the specified path is an existing directory. If the directory isn't valid, an error message is sent to the user. This is a very important check, especially with this type of application.

Finally, if the directory is valid, the `ListFiles` method is called again to list the directories. Figure 13.6 shows a sample output.

There are two items about this application I haven't yet discussed. The first is the use of `Server.URLEncode`. Every time you create a `Hyperlink` and specify a querystring, `Server.URLEncode` is used to ensure that any special characters are converted to strings that won't mess up the URL. For example, if the path name were `c:\Program`

`Files\temp.txt`, you might receive an error when dealing with the space between `Program` and `Files`. Using `Server.URLEncode` replaces this string with

```
c%3a%5cprogram+files%5ctemp.txt
```

FIGURE 13.6

A sample directory listing using your directory browsing application.

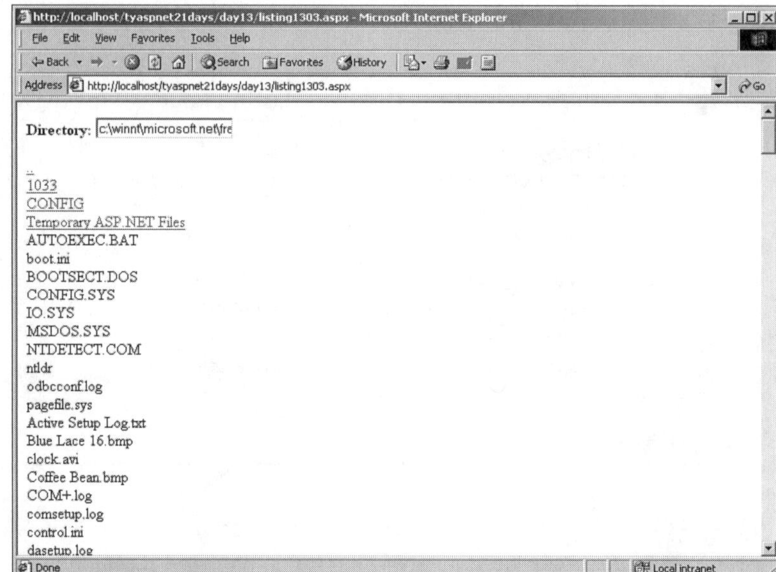

All offending characters are replaced with other characters that HTML understands as substitutes.

The second item I haven't discussed is the different methods of calling this page. In the `Page_Load` event, you check to make sure that the page wasn't just posted back on itself. If it wasn't, it means that the user has changed the current directory by clicking on a `Hyperlink` control (which doesn't post a form, it only redirects), and you want to use the `Page_Load` event handler to list the directories and files. If the page was posted back on itself, you want to use the `tbDir_Handle` method to list the directories and files. The check for postback is very important: without it, the directories might be listed twice on the page.

Opening Files

There are several different methods to open a file with ASP.NET depending on your circumstances. As I discussed earlier, ASP.NET allows you to open files for both binary and Unicode access. Binary access allows you to read the bits (ones and zeroes) that make up a computer file directly. Unicode is a scheme that translates these bits into something we can read, such as letters and numbers. Because binary access isn't that important for your needs, we'll concentrate on the Unicode methods.

Using the `File` Object

One method to open files is by using the `File` object. After you have instantiated the object with a file, you can use several different methods to open the file, depending on what you plan to do with the data. Table 13.2 summarizes these methods.

TABLE 13.2 The `File` Object's `Open` Methods

Method	*Description*
`Open`	Opens a file with specified privileges and returns a `Stream` object.
`OpenRead()`	Returns a read-only stream for the file.
`OpenText()`	Returns a `StreamReader` from an existing file.
`OpenWrite()`	Returns a read-write `Stream`.

There are several things to know about these methods. First, let's examine the types of privileges available.

The `Open` method takes three parameters: *`FileMode`*, *`FileAccess`*, and *`FileShare`*, in that order. The *`FileMode`* privilege tells the operating system how to open the file; for example, whether an existing file should be overwritten or appended to. Table 13.3 summarizes the modes available.

TABLE 13.3 `FileMode` Values

Mode	*Description*
`Append`	Opens the file if it exists, and moves to the end of the file. Or, if the file doesn't exist, creates a new one. This mode can be used only with the `Write` file access privilege (you'll get to that in a moment).
`Create`	Creates a new file or overwrites an existing one.
`CreateNew`	Creates a new file.
`Open`	Opens an existing file.
`OpenOrCreate`	Opens a file if it exists; otherwise, creates a new one.
`Truncate`	Opens an existing file, and then truncates it so that its size is zero bytes, effectively erasing its contents.

`FileAccess` specifies the access privileges on a file. The possible values are `Read`, `ReadWrite`, and `Write`, which create read-only, read-write, and write-only access, respectively.

Finally, `FileShare` specifies what should happen if two processes try to access the file at the same time; for instance, if two visitors come to your Web site and try to change a file's contents at the same time. The values specified affect the second process that accesses the file. The values are the same as those for `FileAccess`, with one additional value: `None`, which specifies that another process cannot access the file at the same time as another process.

One thing you might have noticed is that these methods of the `File` class, with the exception of `OpenText`, all return `Stream` objects, which allow only binary access—not ideal for us. I'll discuss how to get around that when we talk about reading files.

The following code shows an example of using the `File` object to open a file.

```
'create a File object and StreamReader
dim objFile as new File(Server.MapPath("log.txt"))
dim objReader as StreamReader

'open the file
objReader = objFile.OpenText

'do some stuff

'close the StreamReader
objReader.close
```

Or, you could use the `Open` method:

```
dim objFile as new File(Server.MapPath("log.txt"))
dim objStream as Stream
objStream = objFile.Open(FileMode.OpenOrCreate, FileAccess.Read)
```

Using the `FileStream` Object

The `FileStream` object allows you to create a `Stream` to access a file. One benefit of using the `FileStream` object is that you do not have to use a `File` object first. However, you must make sure that the file you are accessing exists. This was not necessary when opening files with the `File` object because if you successfully created a `File` object, you know that the file does exist. The following code demonstrates how to open a file:

```
dim fs as new FileStream(Server.MapPath("log.txt"), _
   FileMode.OpenOrCreate)
```

This opens a file with the `OpenOrCreate` instruction. The `FileStream` object uses the same parameters as the `File.Open` method, with the addition of the path to the file.

The `FileStream` object also provides a method, `Seek`, that allows you to move to any position in the stream (such as to the end or beginning). The syntax for this method is as follows:

```
Seek(offset, origin)
```

The *`offset`* parameter specifies how far from the *`origin`* you want to move. *`origin`* can be one of the following `SeekOrigin` enumeration values: `SeekOrigin.Begin`, which specifies the beginning of the stream; `SeekOrigin.Current`, which specifies from the current position; or `SeekOrigin.End`, which specifies the end of the file. For example, the following code snippet moves to the beginning and end of a file:

```
'Seek to the beginning of a file
objFile.Seek(0, SeekOrigin.Begin)
'Seek to the end of a file
objFile.Seek(0, SeekOrigin.End)
```

Reading Files

Now that you have an open file, you are ready to read its content. For ASP.NET, this is done mainly with the `StreamReader` object. As discussed earlier, this object converts from binary to Unicode, which gives you the characters and strings you need to use in your pages. Instantiating a `StreamReader` object is simple:

```
dim objReader as new StreamReader(object)
```

The *`object`* parameter can be either a `Stream` object (such as the `FileStream` created in the last snippet) or a path to a specific file. Let's create a simple file to use for our examples. Place the following in `log.txt` text file in the `/TYASPNET21Days/Day13` directory:

```
The Quick Foxes
Jumped Over
The Lazy
Brown Dog
```

`StreamReader` provides several methods to read characters from a file. The first, `Read`, returns a single character from the stream as an integer, and moves ahead by one. For example:

13

```
dim f as new File(Server.MapPath("log.txt"))
objReader = f.OpenText
Response.Write(objReader.Read & "<br>")
objReader.Close
```

The preceding code would return `84`, which is the ASCII representation of the uppercase letter T. Calling `Read` again would return `104`, which is the ASCII representation of the lowercase letter h, and so on. These numbers aren't very useful as is, so you should convert them to actual Unicode characters with the `Chr` method of the `Strings` class:

```
Response.Write(Strings.Chr(objReader.Read) & "<br>")
```

This would return `T` for the first call, `h` for the second, and so on.

Reading single characters at a time might be a bit tedious, so the `StreamReader` provides two other methods that return more characters: `ReadLine`, which reads characters until it reaches a line break, and `ReadToEnd`, which reads until it reaches the end of the stream. For example:

```
objReader = new StreamReader(Server.MapPath("log.txt"))
Response.Write(objReader.ReadToEnd)
objReader.Close
```

would return

```
The Quick Foxes Jumped Over The Lazy Brown Dog
```

What happened to the line breaks? If you view the HTML source of this output, you'll see that the line breaks are still there. Unfortunately, HTML doesn't interpret actual line breaks as HTML breaks (that is, as `<br>`). You can use the `ReadLine` method to insert those:

```
Response.Write(objReader.ReadLine & "<br>")
```

This method, however, only reads one line at a time, so you'll have to use a loop to iterate through the entire file. If you hit the end of the file using `ReadLine` or `Read` and you try to read the next character, you'll receive an error. Luckily, the `StreamReader` object provides a method, `Peek`, that helps you avoid this.

The `Peek` method reads the next character, but doesn't actually return it. This allows you a sneak peek of the next character in the stream. If that next character happens to be the end of the stream, the `Peek` method returns `-1`. Now you can read through the stream without any worries:

```
dim objReader as new StreamReader(Server.MapPath("log.txt"))
while objReader.Peek() > -1
   Response.Write(objReader.ReadLine & "<br>")
end while
objReader.Close
```

Figure 13.7 shows the output of this code.

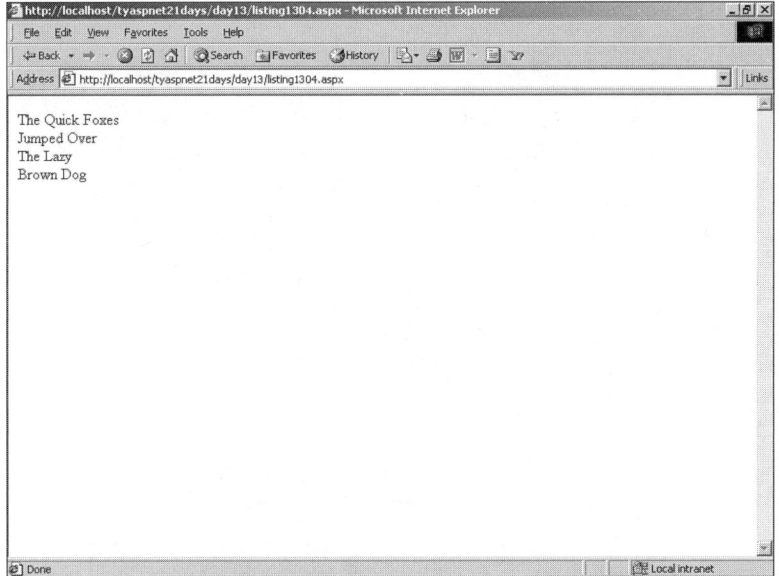

FIGURE 13.7
Reading a stream with the `ReadLine` *method.*

Caution

Because the `Peek` method does not actually read from the stream, it does not advance the `StreamReader`. Make sure to use a method of the `StreamReader` that advances the position, or you'll end up with an infinite loop. For instance:

```
while objReader.Peek() > -1
   Response.Write("<br>")
end while
```

would result in an infinite loop because the position in the stream is never advanced.

The `Read` method can also be used to return a specified number of characters from a stream. The syntax for this method is

```
objReader.Read(char(), start, count)
```

This method reads *`count`* number of characters from the stream, beginning at the position indicated by *`start`*, and places the output into the array of `Chars`, *`char()`*. For example:

```
objReader = new StreamReader(Server.MapPath("log.txt"))
dim arrString() as Char = new Char(10)

objReader.Read(arrString, 0, 10)
for i = 0 to Ubound(arrString) - 1
```

```
   Response.Write(arrString(i))
next
objReader.Close
```

On line 2, you create an array of `Chars`, `arrString`. On line 4, you use the `Read` method to read 10 characters from the stream, starting at position 0 (the beginning of the stream), and place them into `arrString`. This output returns:

```
The Quick
```

Eight characters, plus one space (`k` is the end).

Imagine that for educational purposes, you want to show the source code for one of your ASP.NET Web pages to a Web site visitor; for instance, to teach a particular method. When the visitor tries to view the source of an ASP.NET file from the browser, he'll see only HTML—all ASP.NET commands have been processed and removed. Thus, it is up to you to show your visitor the file *before* it is processed. You can do this with the `System.IO` classes, and Listing 13.5 shows how.

LISTING 13.5 Viewing ASP.NET Source Code in the Browser

```
<%@ Import Namespace="System.IO" %>
<script language="VB" runat="server">
   sub Page_Load(Sender as Object, e as EventArgs)
      dim fs as new FileStream(Server.MapPath _
         ("listing1305.aspx"), FileMode.Open, _
         FileAccess.Read)
      dim objReader as new StreamReader(fs)

      lblMessage.Text = "<pre>"
      while objReader.Peek() > -1
         lblMessage.Text += Server.HTMLEncode _
            (objReader.ReadLine) & "<br>"
      end while
      objReader.Close
      fs.close
      lblMessage.Text += "</pre>"
   end sub
</script>

<html><body>
   <form runat="server">
      <asp:label id="lblMessage" runat=server />
   </form>
</body></html>
```

ANALYSIS In the `Page_Load` event handler, you create a new `FileStream` based on the file you want to view. On line 7, you create a `StreamReader` to read that stream's content. The `<pre>` tag allows the formatting to remain the same as it is in the source file. You then use the `Peek` and `ReadLine` methods to loop through the lines of the file, making sure to call `Server.HTMLEncode` so that the HTML tags are not interpreted. Finally, you close your `StreamReader` and `FileStream` objects, and write the closing `</pre>` tag in the label. Figure 13.8 shows the output for this listing.

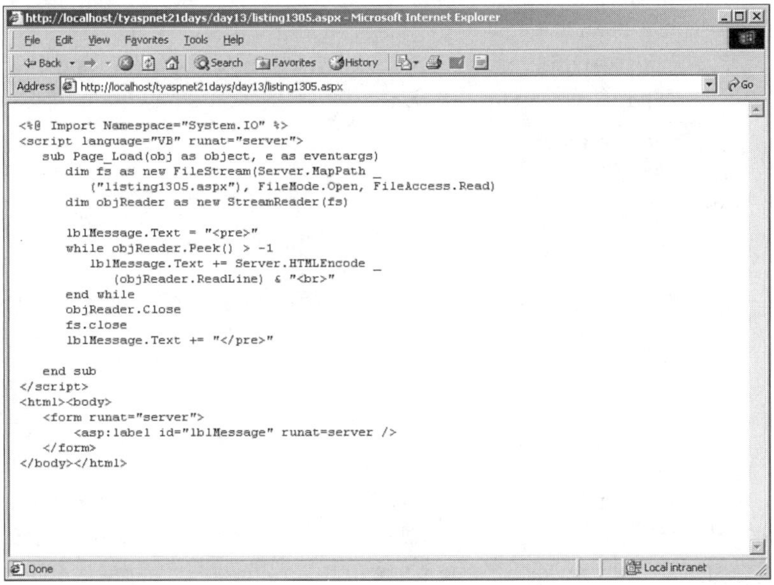

FIGURE 13.8
Viewing ASP.NET source code from the browser.

```
<%@ Import Namespace="System.IO" %>
<script language="VB" runat="server">
   sub Page_Load(obj as object, e as eventargs)
      dim fs as new FileStream(Server.MapPath _
         ("listing1305.aspx"), FileMode.Open, FileAccess.Read)
      dim objReader as new StreamReader(fs)

      lblMessage.Text = "<pre>"
      while objReader.Peek() > -1
         lblMessage.Text += Server.HTMLEncode _
            (objReader.ReadLine) & "<br>"
      end while
      objReader.Close
      fs.close
      lblMessage.Text += "</pre>"

   end sub
</script>
<html><body>
   <form runat="server">
       <asp:label id="lblMessage" runat=server />
   </form>
</body></html>
```

Writing Files

The `StreamWriter` object allows you to write data to streams. The syntax for a `StreamWriter` is very simple. As with the `StreamReader` object, `StreamWriter` can be built around a `Stream` object or from a path that specifies a file.

```
dim objWriter as new StreamWriter(FileStream Or Path, Append)
```

The *Append* parameter is a Boolean that specifies whether a file should be appended to. If this value is false, an existing file will be overwritten. If the file does not exist, it will be created. If *Append* is true, anything you write to the file will be added to the end of what is already there.

The `StreamWriter` object provides two methods to write data: `Write` and `WriteLine`. For example:

```
dim objWriter as new StreamWriter(Server.MapPath
➥("log.txt"), true)

objWriter.WriteLine("And I care because?")
objWriter.Write("because I say so.")

objWriter.Close
```

Line 1 creates a new `StreamWriter` on the `log.txt` file, for appending. Lines 4 and 5 use the two different methods to write strings to the file, and you close the writer on line 7. After executing this code, the `log.txt` should now look like:

```
The Quick Foxes
Jumped Over
The Lazy
Brown DogAnd I care because?
because I say so.
```

There is a line break after the call to `WriteLine`. However, there is no line break between the new text we added and the old. To introduce a line break, simply call the `WriteLine` method without any parameters:

```
objWriter.WriteLine()
```

The `StreamWriter` object provides buffered output. Recall the discussion about buffered page output on Day 4. By default, when you write data using either the `Write` or `WriteLine` method, `StreamWriter` buffers the output before sending it to the stream. You can set the `AutoFlush` property to true to force `StreamWriter` to flush its buffer after every call to `Write` or `WriteLine`.

You can also call the `Flush` method to flush the buffer manually. Setting `AutoFlush` to false will result in slightly better performance. An example of a situation in which you would want to set `AutoFlush` to `true` is if your users expect immediate feedback; for example, if you are adding a large amount of content to a file, and want the user to be able to see the changes in the file before processing is finished.

Other File and Directory Operations

Both the `File` and `Directory` objects provide methods for copying, creating, moving, and deleting files and directories. These methods are straightforward. Table 13.4 summarizes them. The methods not otherwise specified apply to both objects.

TABLE 13.4 Miscellaneous `File` and `Directory` Methods

Method	*Description*
`Directory.CreateDirectory`	Creates a directory with the specified path. If a nonexistent directory is specified in any part of the path, ASP.NET will generate an error.
`Directory.Delete`	Deletes a directory. *`Recursive`* is a Boolean value that specifies whether to delete subdirectories and files as well.
`File.Copy`	Copies an existing file to a new file. *`Overwrite`* specifies whether any existing files should be overwritten.
`File.Create`	Creates a file in the specified path.
`File.CreateText`	Creates a `StreamWriter` object that writes to a new text file.
`File.Delete`	Deletes a file.
`FileSystemInfo.Extension`	This function returns a file extension.
`Move`	Moves the specified file or directory from the *`oldpath`* to the *`newpath`*.

To rename a file or path, you can use the `File.Move` method. You can also use `Copy` to rename a file, but remember to delete the old filename after you've made the copy.

Summary of File Objects

With so many ways to access the file system in ASP.NET, choosing which object to use and when may be confusing. Table 13.5 summarizes the objects and their uses.

TABLE 13.5 Summary of `System.IO` Objects and Enumerations

Object	*When to Use*
`BinaryReader` and `BinaryWriter`	Reading and writing binary data from streams (for example, data types and objects)
`Directory`	Creating, deleting, and manipulating directories
`File`	Creating, deleting, and manipulating files on disk
`FileInfo` and `DirectoryInfo`	Viewing and manipulating properties of files and directories
`FileAttributes` and `DirectoryAttributes`	Determining file and directory attributes
`FileMode`, `FileAccess`, and `FileShare`	Specifying the privileges and behavior for opening files
`FileStream`	Accessing files, with the ability to seek randomly to any point in the file

TABLE 13.5 continued

Object	*When to Use*
`MemoryStream`	Accessing streams in memory
`SeekOrigin`	Specifying an origin for the `FileStream.Seek` method
`StreamReader` and `StreamWriter`	Reading and writing bytes to and from streams
	Reading and writing Unicode characters to and from streams
`StringReader` and `StringWriter`	Reading and writing to and from strings; provides the same functionality as `StreamReader` and `StreamWriter`

Isolated Storage

With the methods described throughout today's lesson, you can store data in a file in a unique path, such as `c:\inetpub\wwwroot\tyaspnet21days\day13\log.txt`. This is a very powerful and useful method for storage, but suffers from some drawbacks.

First, you have to know or create a unique path for every file. This isn't too much of a problem in the scenarios you've examined today, but imagine what happens when you create an ASP.NET application that must be distributed to different servers, each with its own file system structure. It can be a real pain to maintain all these different file locations.

Second, when you create files, they are vulnerable to access by other users or applications that have access to the file (anyone from a Web visitor to someone physically located at the computer). This is great for a file that keeps track of a page counter, for instance, when every person should have access to the contents, but what if you want to store personal information? It is difficult to keep track of whose information is whose.

ASP.NET's isolated storage mechanism is a way to combat all of this. Isolated storage is similar to cookies in that data is isolated by user. Each user gets her own isolated storage area. It also allows you to forget about storage locations. You don't have to worry about unique pathnames anymore. Isolated storage saves data to stores that can reside anywhere, even on the client computer like a cookie.

You need to learn a few new things before you can use isolated storage, but after that, much of this mechanism works the same as the other file access methods.

Creating Isolated Storage Locations

There are two objects you should be concerned with for isolated storage: the `IsolatedStorageFile` object and the `IsolatedStorageFileStream` object, which are similar to the `File` and `FileStream` objects I talked about earlier today. In fact, the `IsolatedStorageFileStream` object has the same methods and properties as the `FileStream` object.

Unlike the `File` object, however, the `IsolatedStorageFile` object does not represent files, but rather a storage location. Files within the storage location are represented by `IsolatedStorageFileStream` objects. This can be a little confusing at first, so it is important to get the objects straight in your mind.

Examine Listing 13.6, which shows you how to create a file in isolated storage.

LISTING 13.6 Creating an Isolated Storage File

```
 1:<%@ Page Language="VB" %>
 2:<%@ Import Namespace="System.IO" %>
 3:<%@ Import Namespace="System.IO.IsolatedStorage" %>
 4:
 5:<script runat="server">
 6:   sub Page_Load(obj as object, e as eventargs)
 7:      dim stream as IsolatedStorageFileStream
 8:      dim writer as StreamWriter
 9:      dim data as string = "blue"
10:
11:      stream = new IsolatedStorageFileStream("colors.txt", _
12:         FileMode.OpenOrCreate)
13:      writer = new StreamWriter(stream)
14:      writer.WriteLine(data)
15:      writer.Close()
16:   end sub
17:</script>
18:
19:<html><body>
20:</body></html>
```


ANALYSIS Notice the addition of the `System.IO.IsolatedStorage` namespace on line 3. Don't forget to include this in your pages. On lines 7–9, you declare your variables, which include the new `IsolatedStorageFileStream` object. You should already be familiar with the `StreamWriter` object on line 8.

The next block of code should also look familiar—the only new item is the use of the `IsolatedStorageFileStream` object. The syntax for creating this object is the same as that for creating the `FileStream` object. You then perform familiar operations with the `StreamWriter` on lines 13 and 14, and close the writer on line 15, which also closes the `IsolatedStorageFileStream`. That's all there is to it.

This code creates a file called `colors.txt` in an isolated storage location particular to the current user. If another user were to try to access this file, he wouldn't be able to, just as a user can't access another person's cookies. The locations of the saved files vary according to the operating system used, as described in Table 13.6.

TABLE 13.6 The Default Isolated File Storage Locations

Operating System	*Location*
Windows 95, 98, or Me	`c:\Windows\Local Settings\Application Data`
Windows NT 4.0	`c:\WinNT\Profiles\<user>\Application Data`
Windows NT 4.0 (Service Pack 4) and Windows 2000 (upgrade from NT 4.0)	`c:\WinNT\Profiles\<user>\Local Settings\Application Data`
Windows 2000 (clean install and upgrades from Windows 95, 98, Me, and Windows NT 3.51)	`c:\Documents and Settings\<user>\Local Settings\Application Data\Microsoft`

For example, after executing Listing 13.6 on Windows 2000 (a clean install), navigate to the directory `C:\Documents and Settings\Default User\Local Settings\Application Data`. You should see a new folder named `IsolatedStorage`. Within this folder are several other folders that ASP.NET uses to keep track of what's going on, as well as the file created on line 11. Often, you won't care what occurs in these directories, but it is helpful to know where the files are physically located.

Accessing Isolated Storage

Isolated storage data is isolated by two different methods: by user and assembly, or by user, assembly, and domain. The first method means that a store will be created for each application a user uses. For example, a storage file created by user A in application A will not be accessible by the same user in application B. The second method also adds the application domain into the equation. For ASP.NET, this is the URL for your application.

Recall from Day 2 that every ASP.NET page is compiled into a dynamically generated assembly. This means that under normal circumstances, no two separate ASP.NET pages will use the same assembly, which in turn means that no two separate ASP.NET pages can access the same isolated storage location. Figure 13.9 illustrates this concept.

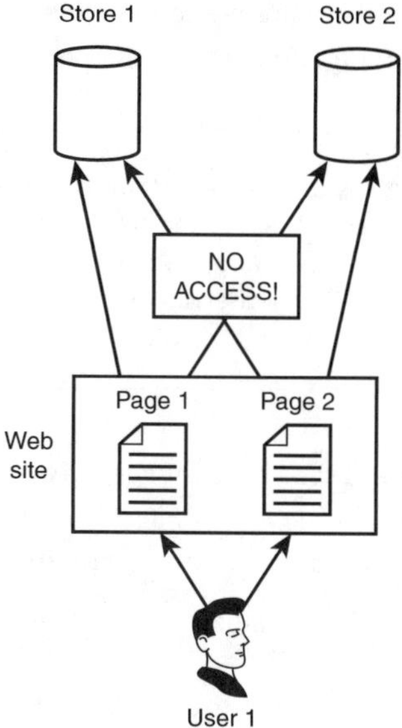

FIGURE 13.9
The same user, accessing two different ASP.NET pages in the same application, will not be able to access the same store.

You can use the `IsolatedStorageFileStream` to easily read from isolated storage. Listing 13.7 demonstrates this.

LISTING 13.7 Reading from Isolated Storage with the `IsolatedStorageFileStream`

```
<%@ Page Language="VB" %>
<%@ Import Namespace="System.IO" %>
<%@ Import Namespace="System.IO.IsolatedStorage" %>

<script runat="server">
   sub Page_Load(Sender as Object, e as EventArgs)
      dim stream as new IsolatedStorageFileStream _
         ("colors.txt", FileMode.OpenOrCreate)
      dim objReader as new StreamReader(stream)

      while objReader.Peek() > -1
         Response.Write(Server.HTMLEncode _
            (objReader.ReadLine) & "<br>")
     end while
      objReader.Close
   end sub
</script>

<html><body>
   <asp:Label id="lblMessage" runat="server" />
</body></html>
```

This listing will look familiar because there are no new methods. It should print out the word blue, which you stored in your storage location in the previous listing.

Note that you might not see any output from this listing. Recall that two different ASP.NET pages cannot access the same isolated store. Therefore, Listing 13.7 should not be able to access the store from Listing 13.6. Placing Listings 13.6 and 13.7 together solves the problem (the same goes for Listings 13.6 and 13.8).

Reading from isolated storage with the `IsolatedStorageFile` object is a bit different. You must first obtain the reference to the files in isolated storage, and then you can use the `IsolatedStorageFileStream` object to do as you want with the files. Listing 13.8 shows this procedure.

LISTING 13.8 Reading from Isolated Storage with the `IsolatedStorageFile Object`

```
<%@ Page Language="VB" %>
<%@ Import Namespace="System.IO" %>
<%@ Import Namespace="System.IO.IsolatedStorage" %>

<script runat="server">
   sub Page_Load(Sender as Object, e as EventArgs)
      dim objISOFile as IsolatedStorageFile = _
         IsolatedStorageFile.GetUserStoreForDomain()

      lblMessage.Text = "<b>Files:</b> "
      dim intCount = Ubound(objISOFile.GetFileNames("*.*"))
      for i = 0 to intCount
         lblMessage.Text += objISOFile.GetFileNames _
            ("*.*")(i) & "<br>"
      next

      lblMessage.Text += "<b>Assembly: </b>" & _
         objISOFile.AssemblyIdentity.ToString & "<br>"
      lblMessage.Text += "<b>Domain: </b>" & _
         objISOFile.DomainIdentity.ToString & "<br>"
      lblMessage.Text += "<b>Current Size: </b>" & _
         objISOFile.CurrentSize.ToString & "<br>"
      lblMessage.Text += "<b>Max Size: </b>" & _
```

LISTING 13.8 continued

```
24:         objISOFile.MaximumSize.ToString & "<br>"
25:   end sub
26:</script>
27:
28:<html><body>
29:   <asp:Label id="lblMessage" runat="server" />
30:</body></html>
```

ANALYSIS On line 7, you instantiate an `IsolatedStorageFile` object. The `IsolatedStorageFile.GetUserStoreForDomain` method returns the `IsolatedStorageFile` that is particular for the current user, assembly, and domain. The `IsolatedStorageFile.GetUserStoreForAssembly` method returns only the storage location for a particular user and assembly.

The `GetFileNames` method returns an array of filenames that matches a specified search string; `"*.*"`, in this case. Lines 12–15 loop through this array and print out the names to a label control. The `GetDirectoryNames` method performs a similar operation, and also uses a search string to filter the results.

Finally, lines 17–24 print out the properties of the isolated storage area. The `AssemblyIdentity` property returns a URL that specifies the assembly that this storage location is particular to (this is a dynamic assembly .NET generates for your Web application). `DomainIdentity` specifies the domain associated with this storage location—similar to the domain property for cookies. The `CurrentSize` and `MaxSize` properties specify the size dimensions of the current user's data store in bytes. Figure 13.10 shows the output of this code.

Figure 13.10 shows the dynamic assembly generated by ASP.NET for your application, the domain (which reflects the Web site domain), and the current and max sizes of the storage area.

You can create an `IsolatedStorageFileStream` around the `IsolatedStorageFile` and use a `StreamReader` to access the contents, as was done earlier:

```
dim objISOFile as IsolatedStorageFile = _
   IsolatedStorageFile.GetUserStoreForDomain()
dim stream as new IsolatedStorageFileStream _
   ("options.txt", FileMode.OpenOrCreate, objISOFile)
```

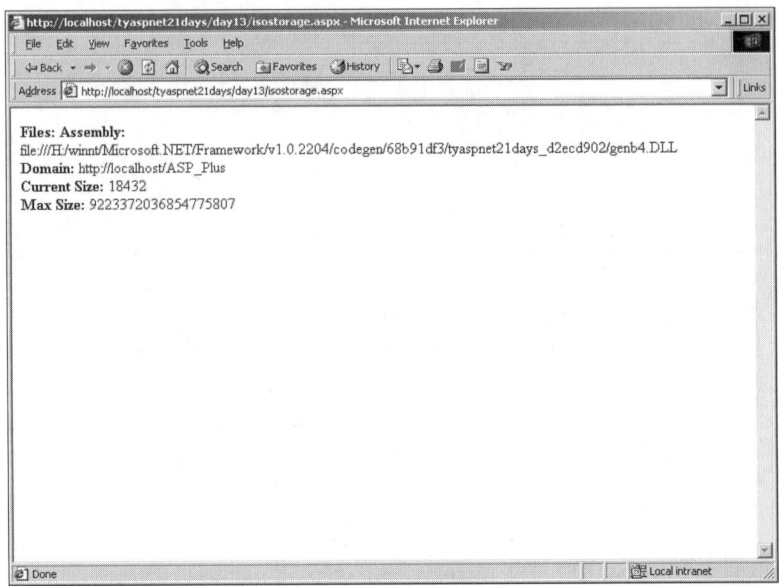

FIGURE 13.10 *Viewing isolated storage information with the* `IsolatedStorageFile` *object.*

That's Not ASP!

File I/O with traditional ASP was accomplished via the `FileSystem` object. This object provided a lot of the same functionality I described today. ASP.NET comes with access to all the .NET Framework classes, which means that unlike traditional ASP, ASP.NET can perform the same file I/O operations as any standalone application.

Luckily, many of the concepts and even syntax are the same in ASP.NET as they were in traditional ASP. A few of the object names have changed, and some of the behind-the-scenes functionality is different, but developers familiar with the `FileSystemObject` shouldn't have many problems moving to the new paradigm.

Among the most significant changes is the move to a completely object-oriented design. Each file and directory can be represented with an object in the .NET Framework, and each of these objects provides its own methods, properties, and collections of additional objects. It might take some time to get used to using these tightly related objects as opposed to the loosely structured menagerie that was the `FileSystemObject`.

Including files is also a bit different in ASP.NET. Because of the way ASP.NET interacts with the .NET Framework, it is essential to include information from other files in your applications. The traditional method of server-side includes is still provided, but there are now many other ways to include files to extend your ASP.NET pages.

Finally, isolated storage is a completely new mechanism for data storage and file access. It eliminates many of the problems that developers faced when building customized user storage solutions. Traditional ASP provided no built-in methods—other than those with cookies or databases—to maintain persistent data for individual users. Why not still use cookies? You can store a lot more information with isolated storage than with cookies, which allows for much greater customization of your Web sites. Also, isolated storage is easier to deploy, can reside on either server or client, and provides much stronger security measures.

The argument for using isolated storage versus databases is a bit more indistinct. The mechanism you use will often depend on the situation and server configurations. Nevertheless, both methods are useful mechanisms for persistent data storage.

Summary

Today you learned all about how ASP.NET handles file access. ASP.NET allows you to include other files in your pages, to extend functionality using other files in your pages, and to read and write files to the server.

Use the server-side include syntax to include other files in your ASP.NET page:

```
<!--#include file="filename"-->
'or
<!--#include virtual="filename"-->
```

This is often useful in places that don't require user controls.

Files are physical objects on the hard drive, consisting of binary data. Streams are objects that allow access to these files, and other types of data stores, such as memory locations and network computers. The `System.IO` namespace provides all the objects described here.

The `File` and `Directory` objects provide access to file and directory attributes, as well as the ability to manipulate them; that is, copy them, delete them, move them, and so on. The `Attributes` collection of each object enumerates the attributes such as archived, hidden, or indexed properties.

`FileShare`, `FileAccess`, and `FileMode` specify the privileges used to open files, such as read-write access, whether to create a new file or open an old one, and how other applications can access the files once opened.

The `StreamReader` and `StreamWriter` objects allow you to write Unicode characters to streams by converting them into binary data. The `Read`, `ReadLine`, `ReadToEnd`, and `Peek` methods allow you to read through the contents of a stream, whereas the `Write` and `WriteLine` methods allow you to create output to streams.

Isolated storage provides a mechanism to store data in files that are particular for a user, assembly, or domain, without having to determine unique pathnames. This allows for highly customized user data storage, similar to cookies. The `IsolatedStorageFile` object represents a virtual storage location for the particular user, and the `IsolatedStorageFileStream` object represents files within the storage location. The latter object can be used with `StreamReader` or `StreamWriter` objects to read and write data to the files.

Tomorrow you're going to take a look at a concept often used with database and file I/O design: caching. ASP.NET provides a robust caching mechanism that is very interesting to play with. See you tomorrow!

Q&A

Q Does including files increase my file size?

A The only increase in file size you will see (on the server) is due to any `include` commands you've used. For example, the following:

```
<!--#include file="log.txt"-->
```

will result in a few more bytes because you had to type in more characters. Because the file is not actually included until ASP.NET begins its processing, you will not notice any large file size increases.

However, when the page is requested by a client, all the includes are parsed into the calling page, and the file size is then increased. This might or might not affect the download times of the client, depending on the code you've included.

Q How do file permissions affect file I/O?

A To access files from ASP.NET, you must first have the correct permissions for those files. For example, assuming that the computer you worked on today is your own and that you were accessing the files directly (for example, not over the Internet), you should have had the correct permissions because the files were your own.

If you access files on another server over the Internet, chances are that you would not have access to many files. I'll discuss this topic further when I talk about security in Week 3.

Workshop

This workshop will help reinforce the concepts I've covered in today's lesson. It is very helpful to understand fully the answers before moving on. Answers can be found in Appendix A.

Quiz

1. What is the difference between a file and a stream?
2. What are the six `FileMode` values?
3. What does the `Peek` method do, and why is it helpful?
4. How do you verify the existence of a file or directory on a server?
5. Use the `File` object to open a file called `userdata.txt` in the root directory of your `c:` drive, for appending. If this file doesn't exist, use the `File` object to create it, and make sure that no other applications can access this file while you are using it.

Exercises

1. Create an ASP.NET page that will open a file specified by a user in a text box, and display the contents in a label. Make sure to check whether the file exists. Note that the user must be required to enter the full path to the file as well.
2. Modify Exercise 1 so that the content of the file is displayed in an editable text box. Allow the user to make changes, and when the user clicks a submit button, write the changes back to the file.

WEEK 2

DAY 14

Using ASP.NET's Improved Caching Capabilities

You've spent this week learning different methods for accessing data. You looked at using databases on Days 8, 9, 10, and 12, at XML on Day 11, and at files on Day 13. Today's lesson will continue this discussion of data access, talking about what you can do with this data once you've retrieved it.

Caching is a technique that's commonly used in computing to improve performance by storing commonly accessed data in memory. ASP.NET provides a number of mechanisms for caching data. Today you'll learn the following:

- What caching is and why it's used
- How ASP.NET uses caching without you knowing it
- How to cache pages and objects
- How to use caching dependencies
- Ways to manipulate the cache
- How to use caching effectively

What Is Caching?

Caching is a computer's way of recalling things quickly. Frequently accessed data (or even data that isn't accessed so frequently) is stored in a place where the computer can retrieve it more quickly and easily than it can from the data's original location. A cache acts as a pocket of information that allows easy access. Figure 14.1 illustrates the benefits a cache provides.

FIGURE 14.1
A cache is an easy-access storage location.

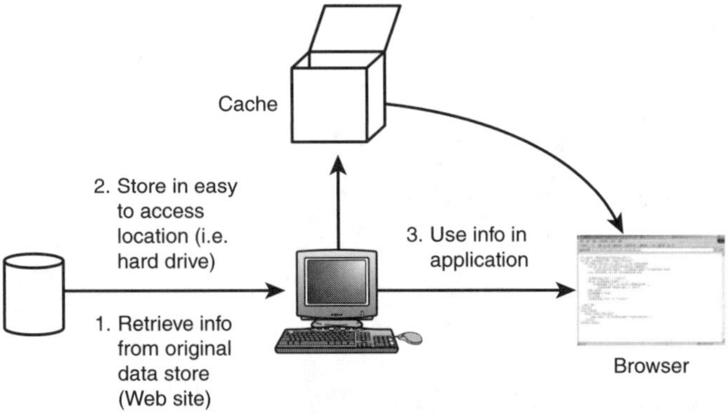

If you've ever used a Web browser, you should be familiar with caching already. When you visit a page, the browser caches that page (and any images) in a special location on your hard drive. This does two things for you. First, the next time you visit that page, instead of having to download the page (or images) all over again, the browser simply loads it from your hard drive. Second, it allows you to view that page (or images) again without having to revisit the page at all. This showcases the two most important aspects of caching: fast access, and access when it normally wouldn't be possible.

NEW TERM This brings up an interesting point: What happens if data you've cached gets too old? If the Web server replaces the page or image with a more up-to-date version? Since the cache is the first place your computer will look, you'll end up with the old version. When this happens, the cache needs to be invalidated—its period of usefulness has *expired*.

In general, caching is a *good thing.* (Don't let anyone tell you otherwise!) Anytime you can cache something, you receive a performance benefit; after all, that's the whole reason for caching. As mentioned in Day 4, "Using ASP.NET Objects with C# and VB.NET," the `Session` object that computers nowadays have plenty of RAM to spare for holding data. Most of the time only a small fraction of a server's resources are fully utilized; it only makes sense to put that to use by using caching. Throughout today's lesson I'll give you recommendations on the when and where of caching, and just how good of a thing it is.

How ASP.NET Uses Caching

ASP.NET comes with many caching mechanisms built-in. Caching is very important to Web applications because data transfer over the Internet can be painfully slow. By caching data, ASP.NET gives its applications a much-needed performance boost. ASP.NET also allows developers to modify cache settings as needed.

There are two caching locations for data in ASP.NET: client-side and server-side. Caching performed by a browser is client-side—all data is stored on the user's computer and is initiated and managed by the browser. Server-side caching is managed by the server using the server's resources, and the browser has no control over it whatsoever.

Server-side caching is the focus of today's lesson. You'll see that this method allows much greater flexibility and benefits than client-side caching. Figure 14.2 illustrates the differences between the two methods.

FIGURE 14.2

The differences between server-side and client-side caching.

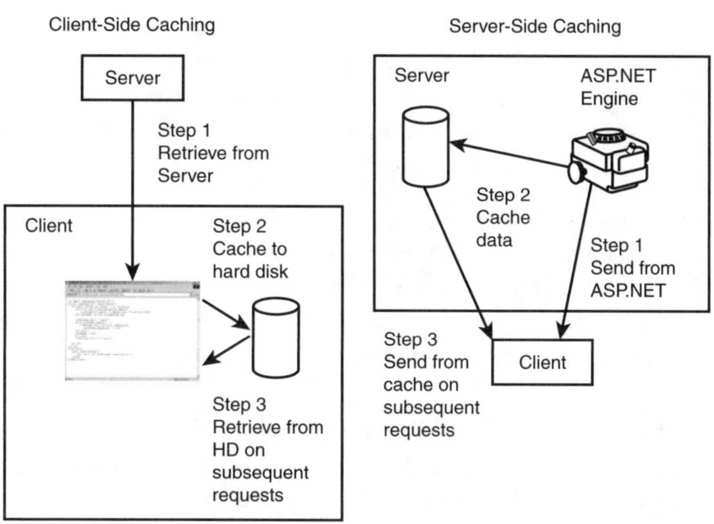

You'll also see that caching isn't limited to images or Web pages. It spans a wide range of data types. The next few sections take a look at a few of the caching mechanisms of ASP.NET.

14

Page Caching

All ASP.NET pages are compiled when they're requested. If you've ever developed applications in any compiled programming language, you'll know that compiling a program takes some time and computing power. If an ASP.NET Web page had to be recompiled each time it was requested, the performance of ASP.NET applications would suffer tremendously.

Luckily, once ASP.NET pages are compiled, they're cached on the server. It's these compiled pages that are served to clients. The user will experience some sluggishness in performance on the first request to the file due to compilation, but subsequent requests will be faster.

The Common Language Runtime monitors the source files for changes. If you modify the original `.aspx` file, the change will be detected, and ASP.NET will then render the existing cached page invalid and will compile and cache the new page.

Thus, ASP.NET provides improved performance by caching the compiled pages instead of recompiling them every time.

Configuration Caching

If you've been developing ASP.NET applications along with this book, you might have noticed another performance setback. The first time an application is started—that is, the first time any page is requested from a virtual directory—ASP.NET must load all configuration settings from `web.config` (see Day 18, "Configuring and Deploying ASP.NET Applications"). This can take some time, depending on the complexity of your application.

Take a look at the system `web.config` file (typically located at `C:\WINNT\Microsoft.NET\Framework\`*`version`*`\CONFIG\machine.config`). You'll see that it can get pretty complex. Typically, this file is more than 450 lines long! These configuration settings are cached the first time an application is started, allowing ASP.NET to apply configuration information to its files much faster than it could without caching.

Output and Data Caching

Page output caching is the process of caching any content generated by dynamic pages, such as calculated values or even controls such as `DataGrids`. Output caching doesn't happen automatically, but it's easy to use. You'll learn more in "How to Use Caching" later today.

Don't confuse caching with buffering. You use a buffer to store output temporarily until execution is finished, at which point the buffer is emptied. You use caching to store data for an extended amount of time so that it's available to you later. These two methods of data storage sometimes confuse beginners.

Data caching allows you to store any type of data in cache, from database records to user controls. It's similar to output caching, but you're not limited to content generated by a page. This method doesn't happen automatically, so what needs to be cached is up to you.

How to Use Caching

ASP.NET allows you to control output and data caching to suit your application's needs. Each method gives you slightly different mechanisms for caching, so it's important to understand all of them.

The next few sections will examine three different methods for caching data in ASP.NET. Each of these methods has advantages and disadvantages. Luckily, implementing them is a snap, so you'll be caching data in no time!

Caching Page Output

Enabling output caching is very simple. All you need is the `OutputCache` page directive:

```
<%@ OutputCache Duration="time" Location="where" VaryByParam="how" %>
```

This causes the output to be cached in the location specified by the *`where`* parameter for the number of seconds specified by the *`time`* parameter. The `Location` parameter can be set to any of the values in Table 14.1. (Note that `Location` is an optional parameter.) The `VaryByParam` attribute allows you to cache different versions of the page based on querystring values; we'll discuss `VaryByParam` a bit more once you've created your first cached page.

TABLE 14.1 Valid `Location` Parameter Values

Value	*Description*
`Any`	The output cache can be stored in any of the following locations. This is the default value.
`Client`	The output cache will be located on the client.

14

TABLE 14.1 continued

Value	*Description*
`Downstream`	The cache will be stored on a server "downstream" from the server that originally processed the request. This is used in the case of proxy servers.
`None`	Output caching is not enabled for the requested page.
`Server`	The cache is located on the server that processed the request.

When you're using output caching, all information is stored on the hard disk of the computer specified by `Location` instead of in memory. This has a greater negative impact on performance, but it also means that output caching provides a virtually free method of caching; it doesn't use up any valuable resources.

Let's take a look at an example. Listing 14.1 displays a simple welcome message and the current time.

LISTING 14.1 Using the Output Cache

```
<%@ Page Language="C#" %>
<%@ OutputCache Duration="30" VaryByParam="none" %>

<script runat="server">
   void Page_Load(Object Sender, EventArgs e) {
      lblMessage.Text = "Welcome! The time is now " +
➥DateTime.Now.ToString("T");
   }
</script>

 <html><body>
    <font size="5">Using the Output Cache</font><hr>

    <asp:Label id="lblMessage" runat="server"/>
 </body></html>
```

ANALYSIS This looks like a normal ASP.NET page with an additional `OutputCache` directive. It causes the contents generated by the ASP.NET page to be cached for 30 seconds. After that, the cache will be invalidated (in other words, it will expire) and the next request will cause this page to be cached again. The `VaryByParam` attribute is set to `none`, which means that we're ignoring any querystring values (again, more on this in a moment). Figure 14.3 shows the output of this code.

FIGURE 14.3

The results of caching the current time.

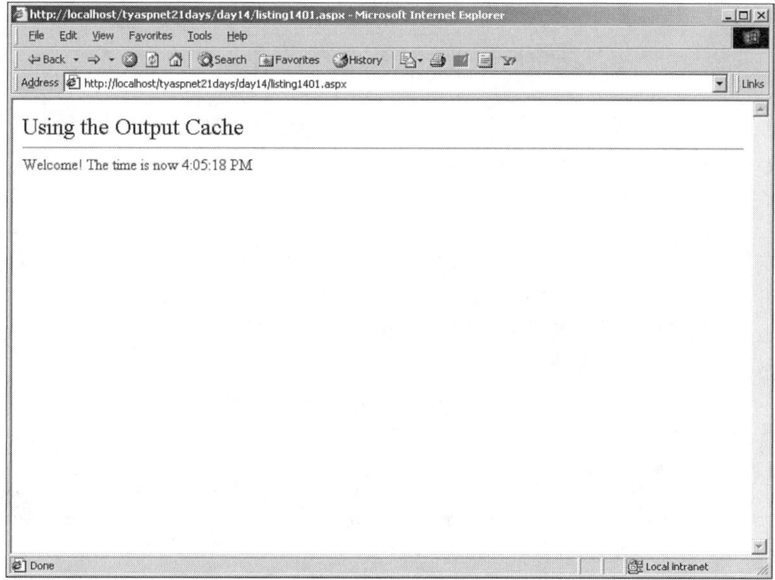

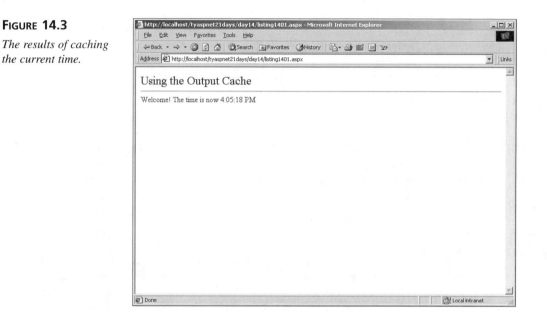

Notice the time in the output. If you click Refresh, the page will keep displaying the same time. This is because the page is retrieved from the server cache, and the code inside the page isn't executed. If you revisit this page after 30 seconds, the time will be updated because the cache has expired.

The caching mechanism is a lot more powerful than this simple example shows. As mentioned earlier, the output cache can compare the querystrings supplied to a page to determine what to cache. Let's modify Listing 14.1 slightly to show this effect (see Listing 14.2).

LISTING 14.2 Supporting Querystring Caching

```
<%@ Page Language="C#" %>
<%@ OutputCache Duration="30" VaryByParam="true" %>

<script runat="server">
   void Page_Load(Object Sender, EventArgs e) {
      lblMessage.Text = "Welcome " + Request.Params["id"] +
➥"! The time is now " + DateTime.Now.ToString("T");
   }
</script>

 <html><body>
```

Listing 14.2 continued

```
11:        <font size="5">Using the Output Cache</font><hr>
12:
13:        <asp:Label id="lblMessage" runat="server"/>
14:    </body></html>
```

Analysis Listing 14.2 added a method to retrieve a querystring parameter `id` on line 6. Notice also that the `VaryByParam` attribute is now set to true, instructing ASP.NET to take notice of the querystring. Save this page as `listing1402.aspx` and request it from the browser, giving your name to the page in the querystring (such as `http://localhost/TYASPNET21Days/Day14/listing1402.aspx?id=Chris`). You should now see a customized welcome message. Also note the time—if you click the Refresh button, you should still see the same time.

Now modify the URL slightly: `listing1402.aspx?id=Sammy`. You should see a new welcome message, with a more current time. Refresh this page a few times to ensure the page is cached.

Finally, type in the original URL and request the page again: `listing1402.aspx?id=Chris`. You'll see the original welcome message, as well as the original time! You're not moving backward through time, but rather requesting a page that was already cached. Figure 14.4 shows the progression of three separate requests to the page.

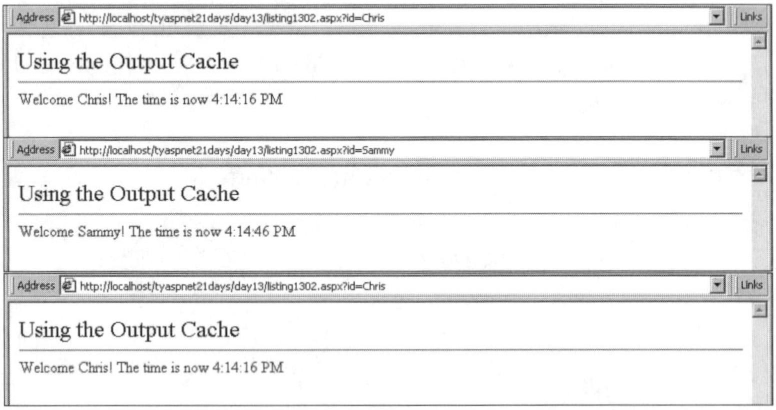

Figure 14.4

ASP.NET reads the querystring parameters to determine the caching procedure.

Because you set `VaryByParam` to true, ASP.NET reads the querystring to determine if the requested page is in the cache. If the querystring is different, ASP.NET registers a *cache miss*, which means that it didn't find the page in cache. It then reexecutes the page and caches the new version. (Note that a cache miss is also generated when the cache expires and a request is made, causing the page to be executed again.)

> **Note**
>
> This means that requests with the same querystring parameters, but in a different order, will generate two different cached pages. For example:
>
> `page.aspx?first=Chris&last=Payne`
>
> This will generate a different cache than the following:
>
> `page.aspx?last=Payne&first=Chris`

You can control this functionality by setting additional attributes (other than `VaryByParam`) in the `<%@ OutputCache %>` directive: `VaryByHeader` and `VaryByCustom`. `VaryByHeader` is used to cache pages based on the HTTP headers in the page. For example, you can use the following directive to vary caching by the language the user is using to browse the Web site:

```
<%@ OutputCache Duration="60" VaryByParam="None"
➥VaryByHeader="Accept-Language" %>
```

We won't cover the various HTTP headers here, so let's move to the next varying mechanism.

`VaryByCustom` takes a comma-delimited list of variables that ASP.NET should use to distinguish cached items. For example, the following directive tells ASP.NET to cache page outputs as separate items only if the `firstname` querystring value differs. Any other querystring values will not cause new items to be cached:

```
<%@ OutputCache Duration="600" VaryByParam="true"
➥VaryByCustom="firstname" %>
```

Add this directive to Listing 14.2 and request it from the browser using the following URL: `http://localhost/tyaspnet21days/day14/listing1402.aspx?firstname=Chris&lastname=Payne`. Note the time that's displayed. Now change the URL to read `listing1402.aspx?firstname=Chris&lastname=Saravia` and refresh the page. Note that the time doesn't change because the page with the `firstname` querystring value `Chris` has already been cached. The `lastname` querystring value is ignored. You can add the `lastname` parameter to the directive so the page is cached based on both querystring values:

```
<%@ OutputCache Duration="600" VaryByParam="true"
➥VaryByCustom="firstname,lastname" %>
```

Note that if you leave the `VaryByCustom` parameter out, the default is to vary caching by all supplied parameters.

For example, this could be used on a Web site that sells concert tickets. First the user selects the state that the concert will take place in and the price she's willing to pay for tickets. The selected state and price are stored in the querystring. The next page pulls a list of concert events from a database, sorted by state, and caches the page output. The page should be cached based only on the selected state. The price that the user is willing to pay has no bearing on this page; it's only "tagging along" on the querystring. By setting `VaryByCustom="state"` and not `price`, you limit the number of pages that will be cached and limit the resources you're using.

You can also use `VaryByCustom` to vary caching by other variables, such as the browser version. For example, the following string will create a different set of cached pages for each different major browser version:

```
<%@ OutputCache Duration="30" VaryByParam="None"
➥VaryByCustom="majorversion" %>
```

User Controls

Caching can be extended to user controls. For example, if you only wanted to cache part of a page—a `DataGrid`, for instance—you could wrap that part in a user control and set its cache options with the `OutputCache` directive. This is known as *fragment caching*.

Fragment caching is very useful when only parts of your page should be cached. For example, let's say you've created a simple user control that displays text boxes for the user to enter username and password information. This control doesn't need to be regenerated upon every request to the page because it never changes. Therefore, it can be cached. However, the page containing the user control may contain sensitive information, such as the time or personalized content. In that case, you wouldn't want to cache the entire page because the user will continue seeing old information. Only non-changing elements should be cached, such as the user control.

Listing 14.3 shows the definition for a simple user control. (See Day 6, "Learning More About Web Forms," for information on how to create user controls.)

LISTING 14.3 A Cached User Control

```
<%@ Control Language="VB" %>
<%@ OutputCache Duration="30" %>

<script runat="server">
   sub Page_Load(Sender as Object, e as EventArgs)
      lblMessage.Text = "Control last viewed at " & _
```

LISTING 14.3 continued

```
7:             DateTime.Now.ToString("T")
8:       end sub
9:    </script>
10:
11:    <font size="5">Using the Output Cache</font><hr>
12:    <asp:Label id="lblMessage" runat="server"/>
```

ANALYSIS This control simply displays a label showing the last time that this control was accessed. Notice that the cache duration is set to 30 seconds on line 2. Save this control as `control.ascx`. Listing 14.4 shows an ASP.NET page using this control.

LISTING 14.4 Implementing the User Control

```
1:    <%@ Page Language="C#" %>
2:    <%@ Register TagPrefix="MyControl" TagName="View"
➥Src="control.ascx" %>
3:
4:    <script runat="server">
5:       void Page_Load(Object Sender, EventArgs e) {
6:          lblMessage.Text = "Page last viewed at " +
➥DateTime.Now.ToString("T");
7:       }
8:    </script>
9:
10:    <html><body>
11:       <MyControl:View runat="server" /><p>
12:       <asp:Label id="lblMessage" runat="server"/>
13:    </body></html>
```

ANALYSIS Again, this page is very simple. The user control is registered on line 2. The `Page Load` event displays the time when the page is accessed. The user control is implemented on line 11. Note that Listing 14.4 doesn't contain the `OutputCache` directive. That's only contained in the user control.

When you request this page from the browser, you should see that the access times for the control and page are the same. Refresh the page, however, and you'll see the difference. The control is cached, so you still see an old version of it. However, the page isn't cached, so its access time keeps getting updated. Figure 14.5 shows the discrepancy in time after the page is refreshed.

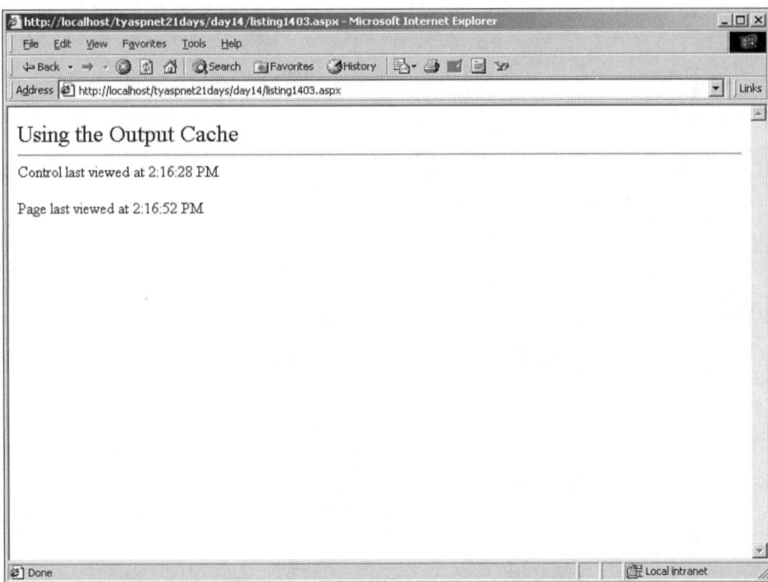

FIGURE 14.5
Fragment caching in action.

> **Caution**
>
> Because the user control is cached, any attempts to modify it programmatically in the ASP.NET page will result in errors. For instance, trying to assign the user control an `id` value or giving it other properties will result in errors. Since the control is cached, its code isn't evaluated when requested and attempts to modify it will fail.
>
> This may seem like a huge drawback to caching, but you should never experience problems if you use it correctly. Only the items that won't change should be cached. Typically, these items don't need to be manipulated in code at all. If you find that you do need to manipulate a cached control, perhaps it shouldn't have been cached in the first place.

This is a great way to cache only certain parts of pages. As you'll see in the next section, however, the `Cache` object provides an even more useful method.

Caching Objects

You can use the `Cache` class to add objects to the cache programmatically, which can also greatly improve performance. Imagine creating a large `DataGrid` object—a process that takes time. You must connect to the data, retrieve it, and then create and populate the `DataGrid`. What if you could do all that just one time and cache the results? In fact, caching data returned from databases is one of the most common uses of the `Cache` class.

The `Cache` class provides three advantages over output caching. First, you can cache any object you want; you don't need to cache an entire page or user control. Rather, you can cache items with more granularity, such as data returned from a database or an individual server control. Second, the `Cache` class allows you to use sliding expiration. Finally, you can set dependencies on the items placed in the `Cache` class. This means that you can set cached data to be dependent on another item. A cached `DataGrid` can be dependent on the underlying data. When the data source changes, the cached `DataGrid` will be rendered invalid and created anew. See "Cache Dependencies" later today for more information.

Listing 14.5 shows an example of using the `Cache` class to cache data returned from a database. When this page is loaded for the first time, you retrieve the data from the database and bind it to a `DataGrid`. You'll also store it in cache so that the next time the page is requested, you can simply pull the data from the cache. This results in faster execution.

LISTING 14.5 Caching Database Results with the `Cache` Class

```
<%@ Page Language="C#" %>
<%@ Import Namespace="System.Data" %>
<%@ Import Namespace="System.Data.OleDb" %>

<script runat="server">
   void Page_Load(Object Sender, EventArgs e) {
      if (!Page.IsPostBack) {
         CreateData();
      }
   }

   void CreateData() {
      DataView source;

      source = (DataView)Cache["DataSet"];

      if (source == null) {
         string strConnString =
➥"Provider=Microsoft.Jet.OLEDB.4.0;Data Source=
➥C:\\ASPNET\\data\\banking.mdb";

         OleDbDataAdapter objCmd = new
➥OleDbDataAdapter("select * from tblUsers", strConnString);

         DataSet ds = new DataSet();
         objCmd.Fill(ds, "tblUsers");

         source = new DataView(ds.Tables["tblUsers"]);
         Cache["DataSet"] = source;
```

LISTING 14.5 continued

```
27:
28:             lblMessage.Text = "Data set created explicitly";
29:          } else {
30:             lblMessage.Text = "Data set retrieved from cache";
31:          }
32:
33:          dgData.DataSource = source;
34:          dgData.DataBind();
35:       }
36:
37:       void ExpireCache(Object Sender, EventArgs e) {
38:          Cache.Remove("DataSet");
39:          CreateData();
40:       }
41:    </script>
42:
43:    <html><body>
44:       <form runat="server">
45:          <asp:Label id="lblMessage" runat="server"
46:             maintainState=false/><p>
47:          <asp:Button id="btSubmit" runat="server"
48:             text="Expire Cache"
49:             OnClick="ExpireCache"/><p>
50:          <asp:DataGrid id="dgData" runat="server"
51:             BorderColor="black"
52:             GridLines="Vertical"
53:             cellpadding="4"
54:             cellspacing="0"
55:             width="450"
56:             Font-Name="Arial"
57:             Font-Size="8pt"
58:             HeaderStyle-BackColor="#cccc99"
59:             ItemStyle-BackColor="#ffffff"
60:             AlternatingItemStyle-Backcolor="#cccccc" />
61:       </form>
62:    </body></html>
```

ANALYSIS The `Page Load` event on lines 6–10 is fairly standard. The `CreateData` method on line 12 is where the real action takes place.

You want to store a `DataView` of the data returned from the database for easier access later. Therefore, on line 13 you create a new `DataView`. On line 15, you try to retrieve this `DataView` from the `Cache` object. If there is no `DataView` with the specified name in cache (as it should be upon first viewing), your variable `source` is set to `null` (or `nothing` in VB.NET). Note that the items stored in cache are of the `Object` data type, which is why you must cast your variables accordingly as on line 15.

The `if` statement on line 17 checks this condition. If `source` is equal to `null`, meaning there was nothing in cache, you want to retrieve the data from the database. Lines 18–24 perform this retrieval—you should be fairly familiar with this process by now. On line 25, you set your `source` variable to a `DataView` on the `DataSet`, and you store it in cache on line 26. The result is that this particular view of your returned data is now in cache, which in turn means that the returned data is in cache. Lines 28 and 30 simply display a text message telling you where the data came from.

In order to test your application, you also want to be able to clear the cache manually. The `ExpireCache` method on line 37 does this. Whenever the user clicks the button on line 47, this event handler executes. The `Remove` method of the `Cache` object removes the specified item from cache. In this case, you want to remove your `DataView`. Finally, you call your `CreateData` method again to display the `DataGrid` once more.

Note

The `Remove` method returns an object of the type that you want to delete. This allows you to perform additional operations on the object if necessary. For example, you could replace line 40 with the following:

```
DataView dv = (DataView)Cache.Remove("DataView");
```

This allows you to perform any final operations on the object before it's finally expunged from cache, such as retrieving the information one last time.

If you specify the name of an object that doesn't exist in cache, this method returns `null`.

After you call the `Remove` method on your `DataView`, you have to retrieve the data from the database once again. This means the `if` statement on line 17 tries to execute the code block within. Figure 14.6 shows an example output from this listing upon first viewing, and Figure 14.7 shows the output after Refresh has been clicked.

The first time you view this page, you should see "Data set created explicitly." Clicking Refresh will cause "Data set retrieved from cache" to appear. Finally, clicking the Expire Cache button will cause the original message to reappear. Depending on your computer setup, you may see an obvious change in performance when retrieving the information from the cache. Even though it may not seem like much of a difference here, imagine thousands of users trying to access the same page at once. The benefits of caching increase exponentially with the load.

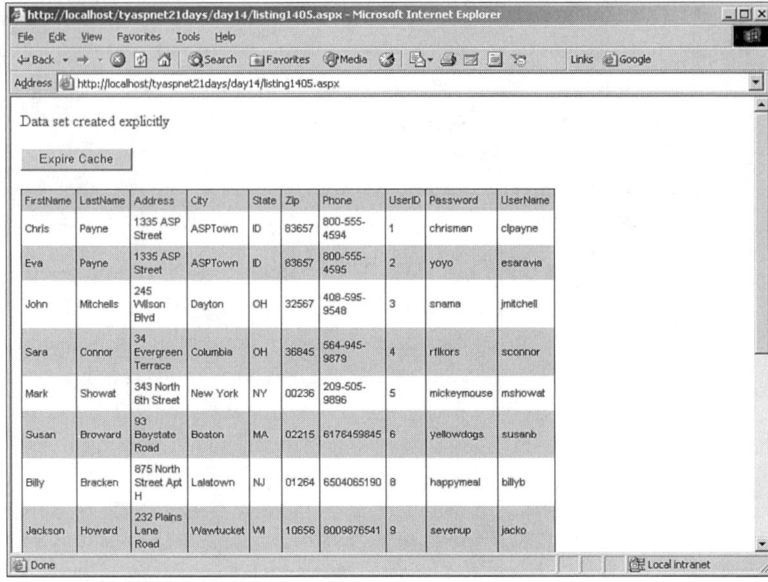

FIGURE 14.6

Caching data returned from a database.

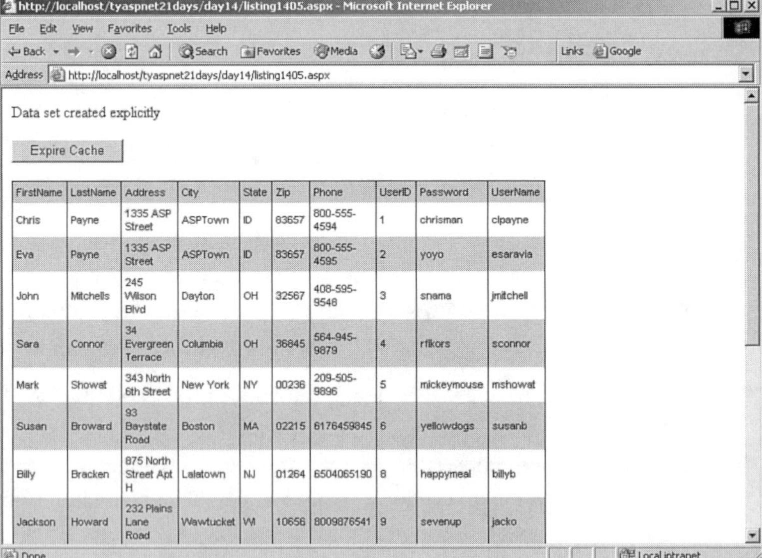

FIGURE 14.7

Upon subsequent views, the `DataSet` *is retrieved from cache.*

Note

> Note that if you click the Refresh button *after* clicking the Expire Cache button, your browser will ask if you want to resubmit the form data. Answering Yes will resubmit the button click, causing the cache to be expunged again and leaving unwary users wondering why they're getting a "Data set created explicitly" message rather than "Data set retrieved from cache."
>
> If you want to refresh the page after clicking the Expire Cache button, you'll have to retype the URL into the browser. Or you can simply add a hyperlink to the page, setting it to the same URL as this page. Essentially, this will cause a refresh.

There are three different ways to place items in the cache. The first one was examined in the previous listing. The next two ways are with the `Add` and `Insert` methods. The two methods are similar, but the `Insert` method provides you with more choices. Let's look at the syntax for the `Add` method first:

```
Cache.Add(key, value, dependencies, absoluteExpiration, _
   slidingExpiration, priority, _
   onRemoveCallBack)
```

There are a lot of parameters with this method, so let's examine each one in detail. The first two, *`key`* and *`value`*, are what you used in previous listings. *`key`* is the name of the object you want to store in cache, and *`value`* is the actual item or object to store. *`dependencies`* will be covered in a moment. *`absoluteExpiration`* is the absolute date that you want the cache to expire, such as "June 6, 2001."

`slidingExpiration` is similar to *`absoluteExpiration`*, but it refreshes the expiration date each time the page is requested. For example, if you set the expiration date to five hours from now with *`absoluteExpiration`*, the cache will expire in five hours no matter what. With *`slidingExpiration`*, the cache will expire five hours *after* the last request. This means that if someone requests the page four hours from now, the cache will expire five hours after that, which is nine hours from now, and so on. Thus, the expiration date *slides* as requests come in. You specify this sliding time with a `TimeSpan` object.

The *`priority`* parameter determines how the cache will throw away the object in certain situations, such as when memory is low. Generally, items with a higher priority will remain in the cache longer than those with a lower priority. This is roughly analogous to the *cost* of keeping the item in memory. If an item has a higher cost to create in terms of time or system resources, you should keep it in cache longer, and vice versa.

Finally, *`onRemoveCallBack`* is the method that should be called when this item is removed from cache.

Let's add your DataView to the cache with the Add method, replacing line 28 in Listing 14.5:

```
Cache.Add("DataSet", source, null, DateTime.Now.
➥AddMinutes(1), TimeSpan.Zero,
➥CacheItemPriority.High, _
ic:ccc]OnRemove);
```

ANALYSIS Here you add the source variable, which contains the DataView you want to store. You set the dependency to null for now, set the expiration date to one minute from now, and set sliding expiration to 0, which effectively turns sliding off. You use the High and Slow values of the CacheItemPriority object to set the priority parameter (see Table 14.2 for descriptions of these values). Finally, the last parameter specifies the delegate that will be executed when this item is removed from cache. (Note that you could set this value to null if you didn't want to handle the event.) If you specify a method name that doesn't exist, you'll receive an error.

Delegates are a special type of object that we haven't yet discussed thoroughly, and we're only going to briefly cover them here. A delegate is essentially a pointer to a method. Events use delegates to determine what event handler should be executed when the event is raised. So OnRemove in this case needs to point to a method to handle the removal of a cache item. In C#, this is a three-step process.

First, you need to create the delegate itself, just like you would any other variable. Immediately after line 5 of Listing 14.5 (before the Page_Load method), insert the following code:

```
private static CacheItemRemovedCallback OnRemove;
```

We now have a delegate named OnRemove that is of type CacheItemRemovedCallback. This type dictates how our event handler will look—creating this method is the next step. The following code snippet shows the HandleRemove method:

```
void HandleRemove(String key, Object value,
➥CacheItemRemovedReason reason)
   [code]
}
```

This method receives the key and object that was removed, as well as the reason for its removal. The reason parameter can be one of the following:

- DependencyChanged—An object that this item depended on (such as a database) has changed.
- Expired—This object is past its expiration date.

- `Removed`—You used the `Remove` method.
- `Underused`—The system removed it from cache because the computer was running low on memory.

The third step is to assign your event handler to your delegate. In the `Page_Load` method, add the following code:

```
OnRemove = new CacheItemRemovedCallback(this.HandleRemove);
```

Now, whenever an item is removed from cache, the `HandleRemove` method will be executed. In VB.NET, this process is a bit easier; you don't need to worry about delegates because VB.NET handles them for you. All you need to do is change the `Cache.Add` method to read as follows:

```
Cache.Add("DataSet", source, nothing, DateTime.Now.AddMinutes(1),
➥TimeSpan.Zero, CacheItemPriority.High,
➥addressof HandleRemove)
```

The `addressof` operator provides the same function as a delegate.

Table 14.2 lists the different values for the `CacheItemPriorities` parameter.

TABLE 14.2 `CacheItemPriorities` Values

Priority Values	*Description*
`AboveNormal`	These items are less likely to be removed from cache than items with a `Normal` priority.
`BelowNormal`	More likely to be removed than items with a `Normal` priority.
`Default`	This value evaluates to `Normal`.
`High`	Items with this value are least likely to be removed from cache.
`Low`	The most likely to be removed from cache.
`Normal`	The base level of priority.
`NotRemovable`	These items will not be removed from cache.

Note that the descriptions in Table 14.2 only apply when the cache automatically removes items due to memory limit restrictions, and not when manually removing items.

14

The `Insert` method provides the exact same syntax but allows some parameters to be optional. You can call the `Insert` method in any of the following ways:

```
Cache.Insert(key, value)

Cache.Insert(key, value, dependencies)

Cache.Insert(key, value, dependencies, absoluteExpiration, _
   slidingExpiration)

Cache.Insert(key, value, dependencies, absoluteExpiration, _
   slidingExpiration, priority, _
   onRemoveCallBack)
```

Caution If you insert or add an item with the same name as an object already in cache, the existing item will be removed in favor of the new one.

With this mechanism, you can cache nearly any part of a page, from `DataViews` to `DataGrids` to user controls.

Cache Dependencies

The caching mechanism of ASP.NET allows you to specify that items stored in cache via the `Cache` class are dependent on other items. For example, suppose you've created a cached `DataView` object from the data in an XML file. If the XML file has changed, you want the `DataView` to change as well. Figure 14.8 illustrates the connection between cache and external sources.

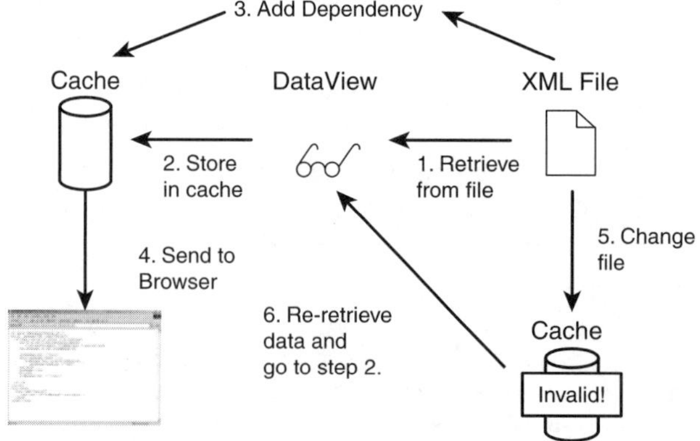

FIGURE 14.8
Dependencies allow the cache to depend on another source.

Without the dependency shown in Figure 14.7, the cache would have no idea that the data has changed and users would keep receiving old, out-of-date data.

Cache dependencies can be created on files, directories, or other items in cache. Let's modify Listing 14.5 a bit more to retrieve the data from the XML file you created on Day 11, "Using XML in ASP.NET," and to add a dependency to your object (see Listing 14.6). This time we'll use VB.NET instead of C#.

LISTING 14.6 Using Cache Dependencies

```
<%@ Page Language="VB" %>
<%@ Import Namespace="System.Data" %>
<%@ Import Namespace="System.Data.OleDb" %>
<%@ Import Namespace="System.IO" %>

<script language="VB" runat="server">
   sub Page_Load(Sender as Object, e as EventArgs)
      if not Page.IsPostBack then
         CreateData()
      end if
   end sub

   sub CreateData()
      dim source as DataView
      dim objFs as FileStream
      dim objReader as StreamReader
      dim ds as new DataSet()

      source = Cache("DataView")

      if source is nothing then
         objFs = New FileStream(Server.MapPath _
            ("../day11/books.xml"), FileMode.Open, _
            FileAccess.Read)
         objReader = New StreamReader(objFs)
         ds.ReadXml(objReader)
         objFs.Close()

         dim objDepend as new _
            CacheDependency(Server.MapPath
➥("../day11/books.xml"))

         source = new DataView(ds.Tables(0))
         Cache.Insert("DataView", source, objDepend,
➥DateTime.Now.AddMinutes(1), TimeSpan.Zero)

         lblMessage.Text = "Data set created explicitly"
      else
         lblMessage.Text = "Data set retrieved from cache"
      end if

      dgData.DataSource = source
```

Listing 14.6 continued

```
41:         dgData.DataBind()
42:      end sub
43:
44:   </script>
45:
46:   <html><body>
47:      <form runat="server">
48:         <asp:Label id="lblMessage" runat="server"
49:            maintainState=false/><p>
50:         <asp:DataGrid id="dgData" runat="server"
51:            BorderColor="black"
52:            GridLines="Vertical"
53:            cellpadding="4"
54:            cellspacing="0"
55:            width="450"
56:            Font-Name="Arial"
57:            Font-Size="8pt"
58:            HeaderStyle-BackColor="#cccc99"
59:            ItemStyle-BackColor="#ffffff"
60:            AlternatingItemStyle-Backcolor="#cccccc" />
61:      </form>
62:   </body></html>
```

Analysis The HTML portion of the listing hasn't changed (with the exception of removing the Expire Cache button). Most of this listing is the same as Listing 14.5, but let's look at the differences.

On lines 22–27, you retrieve data from an XML file instead of your database. However, you place the data in a `DataSet` as before. (Don't forget to include the `System.IO` namespace.) On line 29, you create a new `CacheDependency` object in the `books.xml` XML file you created on Day 11. Finally, you display a message telling the user where the data came from, and you bind the data to the `DataGrid`.

This page should work as before. The first time you view it, the `DataView` will be created explicitly. Subsequent requests will retrieve the data from cache. Now open the XML file in Notepad or a similar word processor, and add a new record. Request the page again and you'll notice that the data is created explicitly once again. Without the dependency, ASP.NET would have no way to know the data has changed and would keep delivering the old data from cache. Figure 14.9 shows the output after you've added some records to the XML file.

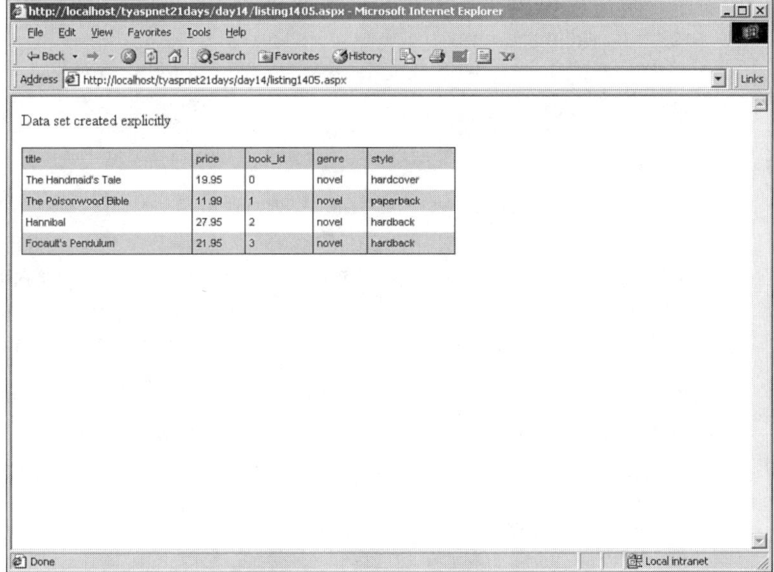

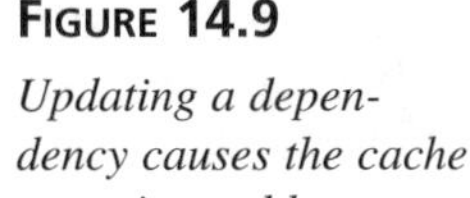

FIGURE 14.9

Updating a dependency causes the cache to expire and be recreated.

Using the `HttpCachePolicy` Class

The previous sections showed the basics of how to use page caching. This may be enough to suit your needs, but ASP.NET provides another class that gives you greater control over the caching mechanism—the `HttpCachePolicy` class. You can access this class through the `HttpResponse` object's `Cache` member (`Response.Cache`). It contains advanced methods for manipulating how the cache is handled. The `HttpCachePolicy` object uses HTTP headers to control caching, thereby controlling page output caching. The difference between the `HttpCachePolicy` and page output caching is that the former allows much greater control over the caching mechanism.

Manipulating the Cache

The `Response.Cache` object offers a few different methods to manipulate the expiration dates. Using these methods allows you to replace the `OutputCache` directive.

The first method, `SetExpires`, sets the absolute expiration time for the cache. For example, the following tells the cache to expire 30 seconds from now:

```
Response.Cache.SetExpires(DateTime.Now.AddSeconds(30))
```

The following code snippet tells the cache to expire at 3 p.m. today, local time:

```
Response.Cache.SetExpires(DateTime.Parse("3:00:00PM"))
```

14

Another way to set the absolute expiration time is with the `SetMaxAge` method. This tells the cache the maximum age the cache can be before it must be invalidated. For example, the following line tells the cache that it must expire after 0 hours, 30 minutes, and 0 seconds:

```
Response.Cache.SetMaxAge(new TimeSpan(0,30,0))
```

These two methods are very similar. Use the `SetExpires` method if you know the exact time you want the cache to expire (even if it's relative to the current time). Use the `SetMaxAge` method if you don't know or don't care the exact time the cache expires, but you do know that it must expire after a certain amount of time. Also note that `SetExpires` takes a `DateTime` parameter, while `SetMaxAge` takes a `TimeSpan` parameter.

The `Response.Cache` object also allows you to set sliding expiration times (see "Caching Objects" earlier today). To enable sliding expiration, you simply set the method to true:

```
Response.Cache.SetSlidingExpiration(true)
```

The cache will expire on a sliding time span that's updated with each new request.

Note that if you set sliding expiration to true, you must set the expiration date to some time *relative to the current time*. For instance, the following code snippet would not result in a sliding expiration date:

```
Response.Cache.SetExpires(DateTime.Parse("11/21/01 3:00:00PM"))
Response.Cache.SetSlidingExpiration(true)
```

ASP.NET cannot figure out how to slide the expiration from an exact time. However, the following snippet will work:

```
Response.Cache.SetExpires(DateTime.Now.AddSeconds(30))
Response.Cache.SetSlidingExpiration(true)
```

The sliding expiration will be 30 seconds from the last request.

You can also control if and where the cache is stored. The `SetCacheability` method allows you to specify who is allowed to cache your pages. Table 14.3 lists the types of cacheability.

TABLE 14.3 Types of Cacheability

Type	*Description*
`NoCache`	Allows no one to cache items. The client must revalidate the items with the server.

TABLE 14.3 continued

Type	*Description*
`Private`	Specifies that clients can cache the response, but not shared (proxy) servers. This is the default value.
`Public`	Specifies that both clients and proxy servers can cache the response.
`Server`	Specifies that the response is cached only at the server that generated the response.

Setting this property is useful when you know where your response is going and how you want it to be treated. For example, if your response is going to a network via a proxy server, you can prevent the proxy server from caching your response so the clients aren't dealing with a "middleman" cache:

```
Response.Cache.SetCacheability(HttpCacheability.Private)
```

In a similar vein, the `SetNoServerCaching` method stops the server from caching a document altogether. All future requests to that document will be processed fully—not retrieved from a cache. For example:

```
Response.Cache.SetNoServerCaching()
```

You may be wondering where you can place all these commands to the `Response.Cache` object. You have a lot of freedom—any method of your code declaration block will do. However, usually you'll want to place such commands at the beginning of your `Page Load` event handler to ensure that all of your output is handled correctly.

Varying Cache Mechanisms

Recall what you learned earlier today about caching and its examinations of querystrings using the `VaryByParam` attribute? The default behavior is for ASP.NET to store each different variation of the querystring as a separate item in cache. You can control this behavior very easily, however.

The `VaryByParams` property (note the "s" on the end) of the `Response.Cache` object tells how to cache objects based on parameters specified by the page, either through querystrings or through form variables. It works exactly the same as with page output caching. Listing 14.7 shows an example.

LISTING 14.7 Varying Caching by Parameters

```
1:     <%@ Page Language="VB" %>
2:     <%@ OutputCache Duration="60" %>
3:
4:     <script runat="server">
5:        sub Page_Load(Sender as Object, e as EventArgs)
6:           lblMessage.Text = "Welcome " & Request.Params("first") & _
7:              "! The time is now " & DateTime.Now.ToString("T")
8:
9:           lblMessage.Text += "<br>" & Response.Cache. _
10:              VaryByParams.Item("first").ToString
11:           lblMessage.Text += "<br>" & Response.Cache. _
12:              VaryByParams.Item("last").ToString
13:       end sub
14:    </script>
15:
16:    <html><body>
17:       <font size="5">Using the Output Cache</font><hr>
18:       <form runat="server">
19:          <asp:Label id="lblMessage" runat="server"/><p>
20:       </form>
21:    </body></html>
```

ANALYSIS Listing 14.7 is similar to Listing 14.2, with the addition of the `VaryByParams` properties on lines 9–12. When you request this page, you'll supply two parameters, `first` and `last`, which represent the first and last names of the user. On first viewing, the page looks like Figure 14.10.

The items `first` and `last` in the `VaryByParams` property (which evaluate to the `first` and `last` querystring parameters) both evaluate to false, as shown in Figure 14.9. This means that a separate version of this document is available in cache *for each* different parameter. The version varies depending on the parameter's value.

This is the default behavior, and you witnessed it earlier today in "Caching Page Output." Specifying different `first` and `last` values will result in a different page being stored in cache. Specifying the same parameters will retrieve the item already stored in cache.

This is where it gets interesting. Let's add the following line to Listing 14.7 as the first line in the `Page Load` event:

```
Response.Cache.VaryByParams.Item("first") = true
```

Now try changing the querystring parameters. Changing `first` will result in a new page being cached. Changing `last`, although it keeps `first` the same, won't result in a new cached page. It will return an old one, as evidenced by the time stamp. Figure 14.11 shows this difference.

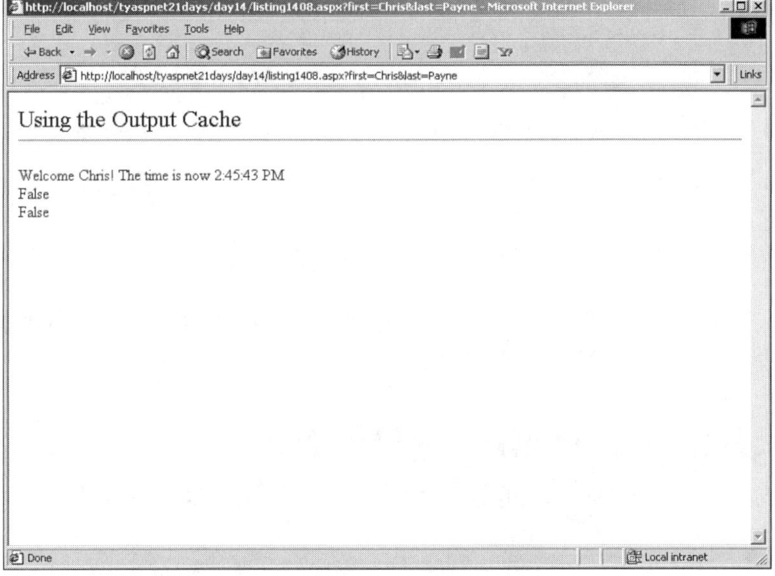

FIGURE 14.10
Showing the `VaryByParams` *items.*

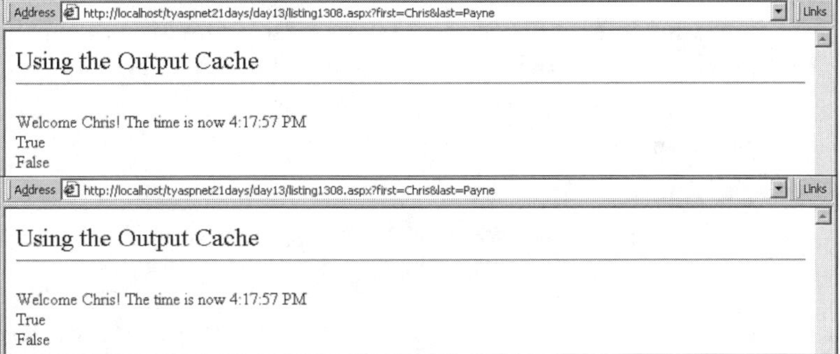

FIGURE 14.11
Varying the `last` *parameter does not cache a new page.*

By changing the `VaryByParams` value to true, you're telling ASP.NET to cache a new page *only* when the `first` parameter changes. Likewise, setting the following will cause ASP.NET to cache pages only when the `last` value changes:

```
Response.Cache.VaryByParams.Item("last") = true
```

This is a very useful property. Imagine, for instance, that you're caching pages for a site that determines a person's tax status by state. You pass the state abbreviation and her name in the querystring. However, all that matters for tax purposes is the state she lives

14

in, so you don't need to cache by her name. You could set the following to only update the cache when a new state is requested:

```
Response.Cache.VaryByParams.Item("state") = true
```

This can provide a large performance benefit if used correctly.

There's also a method to vary caching by HTTP headers called `VaryByHeaders`, which again works similarly to the attribute discussed in the section on page output caching. This book hasn't discussed the various HTTP headers in depth, so we'll leave it up to you to explore this topic. The `VaryByCustom` attribute is missing from the `Response.Cache` object, but the `SetVaryByCustom` method in its place works similarly. (See the .NET Framework SDK documentation for more information.)

Using Caching Effectively

Caching can greatly enhance the performance of your ASP.NET applications. In high-volume situations, even caching items for as little as one minute can help tremendously. If you save one second for each item cached, imagine the benefits when you receive a hundred requests a minute.

Retrieving information from memory is incredibly faster than retrieving the same information from a database or hard drive. As long as you have memory on your server to spare, throw things into cache! With memory caching, your Web site will be able to spit out Web pages faster than ever before.

Generally, there's a lot of information that can be cached safely. This includes data retrieved from a database or a file, complex calculations, and application settings.

However, there are times when it isn't a good idea to use caching. Imagine an online broker that must deliver up-to-the-second stock quotes. Caching here would be a bad idea unless you had adequate dependencies set. Even then, it might not be worth it.

Do	Don't
Do cache commonly accessed data that might not change often. **Do** cache settings or objects that will be used for your entire application, but that won't vary throughout its lifetime.	**Don't** cache pages with time-based values. Users may not understand why their clocks are behind. **Don't** cache objects that the user can modify at any time, such as a shopping cart, unless you build in ways to update the cache at appropriate intervals.

That's Not ASP!

Classic ASP only allowed caching control on the client side with `Response.Expires` and `Response.ExpiresAbsolute`. ASP.NET, however, allows you to control how caching is performed on both the server and client side. This is one of ASP.NET's greatest improvements over classic ASP: You now have a robust caching mechanism that can be controlled easily (and programmatically) in a number of ways. Such robust caching capabilities can provide impressive performance gains.

Summary

Today you learned about ASP.NET's extensive caching features, many of which are performed automatically. For example, ASP.NET automatically caches application settings and your compiled ASP.NET Web pages.

You also looked at caching the output of an ASP.NET Web page on the Web server. Part of the power of ASP.NET is the easy output caching. Simply use the `<%@ OutputCache %>` directive and specify a duration.

In addition to full-page output caching, you can implement fragment caching, which is the caching of specific user controls within an ASP.NET Web page.

The `Cache` object allows easy storage and retrieval of objects from the cache. The `Add` and `Insert` methods allow you to specify a cache's priority, the expiration time, and any dependencies. Dependencies allow a cache to base the validity of its contents on other items, such as files, directories, or other items in cache.

The `HttpCachePolicy` class, available through the `Response.Cache` object, allows further control of the caching mechanism. You can use the `VaryByHeaders` property to specify how pages should be cached when additional data is available, such as from querystrings or form submissions.

You've reached the end of another week! Next week will cover advanced ASP.NET application concepts, including Web services and configuration. These concepts will round out your ASP.NET skills, enabling you to tackle any ASP.NET situation. Be sure to check out the bonus project first!

Q&A

Q How is ASP.NET able to store cached data on computers other than the server?

A ASP.NET does this by taking advantage of HTTP caching headers. These headers are standardized by the World Wide Web Consortium (W3C) and used to set cache instructions that browsers must follow. These instructions specify how and where to store data, as well as additional information such as expiration times and cache vary parameters. The various caching mechanisms described today all use these headers in one way or another.

For more information on HTTP cache headers, check out the W3C's Web site at `www.w3c.org`. The document *RFC 2616: Hypertext Transfer Protocol - HTTP/1.1* provides detailed technical information on the HTTP headers used for caching.

Workshop

This workshop will help reinforce the concepts you've learned in today's lesson. Answers can be found in Appendix A.

Quiz

1. What's the difference between server-side and client-side caching?
2. Which caching mechanism stores cached data on the computer's hard drive?
3. What are the pros and cons of using the `Cache` class instead of output caching?
4. What's the difference between the `SetExpires` method and the `SetMaxAge` method of the `Response.Cache` object?
5. What's the full signature of the `Cache.Add` method?
6. Suppose you have a page that accepts the following querystring parameters: `userid`, `searchstring`, `pagenumber`, and `orderby`. Using `VaryByParams`, which items should you cache by, and what's the required code?

Exercises

Using Listing 14.5 as the basis for your testing, measure the performance benefit of retrieving the `DataView` from the cache instead of creating it explicitly. (Hint: use the `Ticks` property of the `DateTime` instance to return a small measure of time—100-nanosecond blocks, or 1-ten-millionth of a second.) Discuss the difference in time.

WEEK 2

In Review

You're moving along quite nicely! In the past week, you added all types of data access capabilities to your tool belt, transforming you from a beginner to an advanced ASP.NET developer! You now know how to use all types of controls in your pages, collect information from users, set up your applications, interact with databases, read and write files, and handle the cache. That's quite a list of accomplishments in only 14 days.

You should feel comfortable now learning new ASP.NET techniques, and be able to look at any ASP.NET page and figure out most of what's going on. However, there are a few topics I haven't yet covered that are essential for rounding out your skills. These include advanced programming skills such as debugging and security, as well as ASP.NET topics such as Web services. You'll tackle all of these next week.

Your Banking Application

Hold on a minute, you can't move on so easily! First, to ensure that you have a firm grip on your ASP.NET techniques, you're going to enhance the online banking program you started developing in the first bonus project.

This time, you're going to add data capabilities to your banking application. Specifically, you'll add the capability to record and display banking transactions. This should be very easy for you now that you've completed Week 2, and will make your application much more powerful.

Don't forget that you can enhance this project on your own. Feel free to explore other topics or add some existing features to this application. The more you play with the project, the stronger your skills will be.

Adding Data Capability

To add this capability to your application, you need to do two things: update your database (add new tables, modify existing ones, and create a few stored procedures) and build the capability into your ASP.NET pages.

You already have a table in the database to hold user information, but your banking application requires a bit more than that. Specifically, you'll need to add a table to hold data for online transactions and one for account information. Next you'll add stored procedures to handle interactions with the database, giving you better performance than if you didn't use stored procedures. Finally, you'll update the `.aspx` files you created in Bonus Project 1, adding data capabilities to all three main pages (the user controls will stay the same).

The Database

The first thing you need to do is to build the database tables. You already have one, the users table, started in Day 8, "Beginning to Build Databases." You'll have to modify that one slightly, and then build a few new tables.

Open the `Banking` database in Microsoft Access and open the `tblUsers` table in design mode. You need to add a password column so that users' identities can be verified when they try to log in to the application. You also need to add a username column so that users can have their own unique username when logging in—this value must be unique. Add the two new columns to the Design view grid, and assign `Text` data types to both.

> Creating these two new columns will append a new field to any existing records with the value of `Null`. You'll have to manually enter values for each row; otherwise, those users would never be able to log in!

Next, you need to add two more vital tables to the database: one to keep track of transactions and one to keep track of account information (that is, balances). Create the first table in Design view and add the following columns:

- `TransactionID`—An `autonumber` data type column to uniquely identify each transaction. Make this the primary key by right-clicking on this column and selecting Primary Key.
- `DatePosted`—A date/time value to hold dates.
- `Amount`—A `currency` data type to hold transaction amounts (can be negative).
- `Payee`—A `text` column representing who the payment was made to.
- `CheckNumber`—An optional `number` data type column to hold check numbers.
- `UserID`—A `number` column used to link transactions with users.

Save this table as `tblTransactions`. You now have to create a relationship between the `UserID` field in this table with the `UserID` in `tblUsers`. Select the Relationships item under the Tools menu. You'll see a box asking which tables you want to relate. Add both tables and you should see something similar to Figure BP2.1. Close the dialog box.

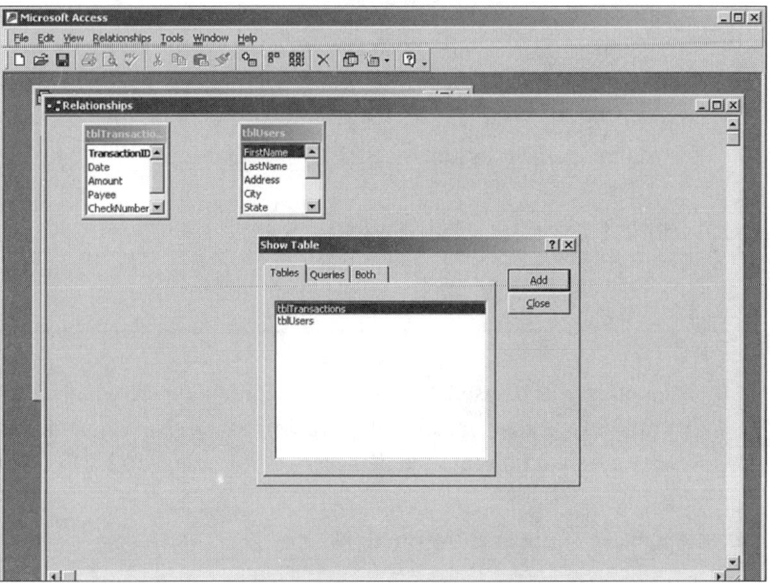

FIGURE BP2.1
Adding relationships between tables.

Scroll through the table windows until you can see the `UserID` field in both. Now click on one, drag the mouse cursor to the other, and release. You should see another dialog box confirming the field names to relate. If you don't see `UserID` in both columns, change them so you do. Click Create. You should now see a line between the two table windows, linking the `UserID` fields. Close the Relationships window and save it. One table down, one to go.

Create a new table in Design view with the following columns:

- `AccountID`—An `autonumber` data type to uniquely identify each account. Make this the primary key.
- `Balance`—A `currency` value to hold amount of money in the account.
- `UserID`—A `number` column used to link transactions with users.

Save this table as `tblAccounts`, and create a relationship with the `tblUsers` table just as you did with the `tblTransactions` table. Link the `UserID` columns.

> Make sure that you link the `tblAccounts` table with the `tblUsers` table, and not the `tblTransactions` table. The application will work either way, but you want to create a true relational database by relating the correct fields. The database will be much easier to follow as well.

Next, you need to create a few simple stored procedures. Recall that stored procedures are called *queries* in Access. Move to the query tab and create a new procedure in the manner described in Day 14, "Using ASP.NET's Improved Caching Capabilities." Place the SQL statement in Listing BP2.1 in the query.

Listing BP2.1 Returning Account Balances

```
SELECT Balance FROM tblAccounts WHERE
UserID = @UserID
```

This query will be used to return the account balance when supplied with a valid `UserID`. Save this query as `spRetrieveBalance`. Next, you need to create a query that inserts a transaction into the database. Use Listing BP2.2 to do so.

Listing BP2.2 Inserting Transactions

```
INSERT INTO tblTransactions (DatePosted, Amount, Payee,
   UserID)
VALUES
   (@Date, @Amount, @Payee, @UserID)
```

Save this procedure as `spInsertTransaction`. Note that the check number field is left out of this statement. Because the procedure is used for online transactions, a check number is not applicable; therefore, it is left out of the procedure. Access will insert the check number automatically as its default value (which should be an empty string). You need to add a stored procedure that will validate a user's identity when supplied with the correct user name and password. Listing BP2.3 shows the code for this query.

LISTING BP2.3 Validating a User

```
SELECT UserID FROM tblUsers
WHERE UserName = @UserName
AND Password = @Password
```

Save this as `spValidateUser`. You need another procedure that updates the account balance (when a transaction is made online). Listing BP2.4 shows this code. Save it as `spUpdateBalance`.

LISTING BP2.4 Gathering Transactions

```
UPDATE tblAccounts SET Balance = @NewBalance
WHERE UserID = @UserID
```

Finally, you need one more procedure that returns all the transactions for a given user. Listing BP2.5 shows this code.

LISTING BP2.5 Gathering Transactions

```
SELECT TransactionID, DatePosted, Amount, Payee,
   CheckNumber, UserID
FROM tblTransactions
WHERE UserID = @UserID
```

Save this procedure as `spGetTransactions`. That's all you need, so move on to the ASP.NET pages.

The ASP.NET Pages

You should still have the `account.aspx`, `bills.aspx`, and `login.aspx` pages, as well as the various user controls you created in the previous bonus project. You're going to have to do a few things with these pages.

First, you need to modify the login page so that users will be identified by the entries in the database, rather than by the hard-coded values you used last time. Then you need to update the account summary page to pull the account balance and transactions from the database. Both these values are read-only, so the users can't modify them here. Finally, update the bill payment page to allow users to enter transactions. This page will update the database in two ways: update the account balance and add a new transaction into the database. All the database operations described here will be handled with the stored procedures you created earlier. Figure BP2.2 shows a diagram of what your final application should look like.

FIGURE BP2.2

The banking application site diagram.

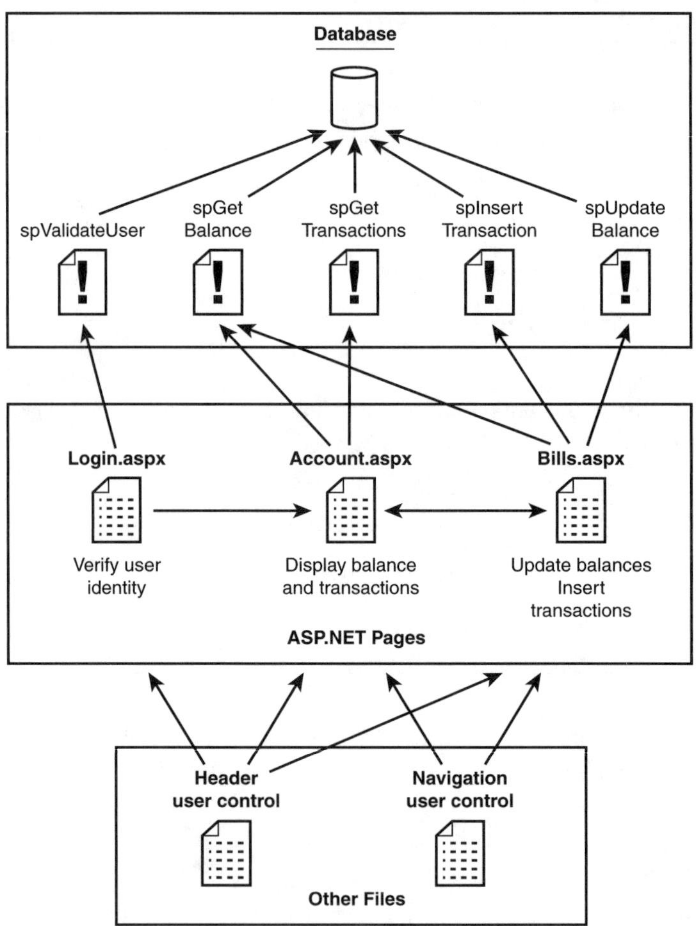

First, modify `login.aspx` to allow user authentication. This page will handle everything in one method—the event handler for the Submit button. Retrieving the values from the username and password text boxes, it will execute the `spValidateUser` stored procedure to determine whether you have a valid user, and then redirect or advise accordingly.

Because the HTML portion of this page remains the same as the last bonus project, Listing BP2.6 only shows the code declaration block.

LISTING BP2.6 The Login Method

```
<%@ Page Language="VB" %>
<%@ Register TagPrefix="ASPNETBank" TagName="Header"
➥src="header.ascx" %>
<%@ Import Namespace="System.Data" %>
<%@ Import Namespace="System.Data.OleDb" %>

<script runat="server">
   '*****************************************************
   '
   ' Login.aspx: Logs users in
   '
   '*****************************************************

   '*****************************************************
   ' When user clicks submit button, verify that they are a
   ' valid user. If they are, log them in, and set a cookie
   ' with their user name, and redirect to account.aspx.
   ' Otherwise display error message
   '*****************************************************
   sub Login(Sender as Object, e as EventArgs)
      dim intId as integer = 0
      dim Conn as new OleDbConnection("Provider=" & _
            "Microsoft.Jet.OLEDB.4.0;" & _
            "Data Source=c:\ASPNET\data\banking.mdb")

      dim objCmd as OleDbCommand = new OleDbCommand _
         ("spValidateUser", Conn)
      objCmd.CommandType = CommandType.StoredProcedure

      'set parameters for stored procedure
      dim objParam as OleDbParameter
      objParam = objCmd.Parameters.Add("@UserName", _
         OleDbType.BSTR)
      objParam.Value = tbUserName.Text

      objParam = objCmd.Parameters.Add("@Password", _
         OleDbType.BSTR)
      objParam.Value = tbPassword.Text

      try
         objCmd.Connection.Open
         intID = CType(objCmd.ExecuteScalar, Integer)
         objCmd.Connection.Close
      catch ex as OleDbException
```

LISTING BP2.6 continued

```
44:          lblMessage.Text = ex.Message
45:       end try
46:
47:       if intID <> 0 then
48:          Response.Cookies("Account").Value = intID
49:          Response.redirect("account.aspx")
50:       else
51:          lblMessage.Text = "<font color=red>Sorry, " & _
52:             "invalid username or password!</font><p>"
53:       end if
54:    end sub
55: </script>
```

ANALYSIS The first few lines are straightforward. You register your header user control, which displays a common header for all pages, on line 2, and then import a few namespaces on lines 3 and 4. The `Login` method performs all necessary functions. You instantiate `OleDbConnection`, `OleDbCommand`, and `OleDbParameters` on lines 21–30. You then set the parameter values to the values entered in the username and password text boxes (not shown here).

In the `try` block, you open and execute your query. If the user is valid, you'll be able to retrieve her user ID from the data reader with the `ExecuteScalar` method. Otherwise, `intId` will remain at its initial value, `0`.

The last bit of code on lines 47–53 performs the actual validation of the user's identity. If the variable `intId` has a value, this user is valid; you use the `Request.Cookie` object to store the account ID, and redirect to the account page. If `intId` is `0`, the credentials were invalid, so an error message is displayed.

Next, you need to update `account.aspx` to display the dynamic data from the database. First, you want to replace the static account balance from the old project with the actual value from the database. Then you need to display the transactions for the current user in a `DataGrid`. There is nothing really new here—you should be familiar with all these techniques.

> **Note** Before this page will display any data, you must enter values—such as account balances and any transactions—directly in the database.

Again, because the UI hasn't changed much, Listing BP2.7 displays only the code declaration block.

LISTING BP2.7 Account.aspx—Displaying Account Balances and Transactions

```
<%@ Page language="VB" %>
<%@ Register TagPrefix="ASPNETBank" TagName="Header"
➥src="header.ascx" %>
<%@ Register TagPrefix="ASPNETBank" TagName="Menu"
➥src="nav.ascx" %>
<%@ Import Namespace="System.Data" %>
<%@ Import Namespace="System.Data.OleDb" %>

<script runat="server">

   '******************************************************
   '
   ' Account.aspx: lists account summaries and current
   ' balances for the current user
   '
   '******************************************************

   'declare connection object
   dim Conn as new OleDbConnection("Provider=" & _
      "Microsoft.Jet.OLEDB.4.0;" & _
      "Data Source=C:\ASPNET\data\banking.mdb")

   '******************************************************
   ' When the page loads, display a welcome message in the
   ' and the current balance of the account, as well as
   ' any transactions
   '******************************************************
   sub Page_Load(Sender as Object, e as EventArgs)
      GetBalance()
      GetTransactions()
   end sub

   '******************************************************
   ' This function returns the balance of the account with
   ' the specified user ID (stored in the cookie created
   ' by forms authentication) and displays the value
   ' in a label
   '******************************************************
   sub GetBalance()
      dim decBalance as decimal
      dim objCmd as OleDbCommand = new OleDbCommand _
         ("spRetrieveBalance", Conn)
      objCmd.CommandType = CommandType.StoredProcedure

      'set parameters for stored procedure
      dim objParam as OleDbParameter
      objParam = objCmd.Parameters.Add("@UserID", _
         OleDbType.BSTR)
```

LISTING BP2.7 continued

```
47:         objParam.Direction = ParameterDirection.Input
48:         objParam.Value = Request.Cookies("Account").Value
49:
50:         try
51:            objCmd.Connection.Open()
52:            decBalance = CType(objCmd.ExecuteScalar, Decimal)
53:            objCmd.Connection.Close
54:         catch ex as OleDbException
55:            lblMessage.Text = ex.Message
56:         end try
57:
58:         lblBalance.Text = "<b>$" & decBalance.ToString & _
59:            "</b>"
60:      end sub61:
62:      '*****************************************************
63:      ' Returns all transactions for a given user id (stored
64:      ' in the cookie created by forms authentication), and
65:      ' displays them in a datagrid
66:      '*****************************************************
67:      sub GetTransactions()
68:         dim objCmd as OleDbCommand = new OleDbCommand _
69:            ("spGetTransactions", Conn)
70:         objCmd.CommandType = CommandType.StoredProcedure
71:         dim objReader as OleDbDataReader
72:
73:         'set parameters for stored procedure
74:         dim objParam as OleDbParameter
75:         objParam = objCmd.Parameters.Add("@UserID", _
76:            OleDbType.BSTR)
77:         objParam.Direction = ParameterDirection.Input
78:         objParam.Value = Request.Cookies("Account").Value
79:
80:         try
81:            objCmd.Connection.Open()
82:            objReader = objCmd.ExecuteReader
83:
84:            dgTransactions.DataSource = objReader
85:            dgTransactions.DataBind()
86:         catch ex as OleDbException
87:            lblMessage.Text = ex.Message
88:         end try
89:      end sub
90:   </script>
```

ANALYSIS That's quite a bit of code! Luckily, most of it is simple and easy to write. The `Page Load` event on line 26 simply calls the two other methods in this listing, `GetBalance` and `GetTransactions`.

`GetBalance`, beginning on line 37, executes the `spRetrieveBalance` stored procedure, passing in the `UserID` parameter you stored in a cookie when authenticating the user. This is specified on line 48 by `Request.Cookies("Account").Value`. On line 52, you execute the query and retrieve the balance as a `decimal` data type. The balance is displayed on line 58.

The `GetTransactions` method is similar, except that the `spGetTransactions` stored procedure is executed, which returns all the transactions for a given user. Again, the code uses the ID stored in your authentication cookie, as shown on line 78. After you execute the procedure on line 82, the data is bound to a `DataGrid`.

There wasn't much new with this listing. You've already learned how to execute stored procedures and pass in parameters, so you should feel comfortable doing this. Figure BP2.3 shows an example output from this listing.

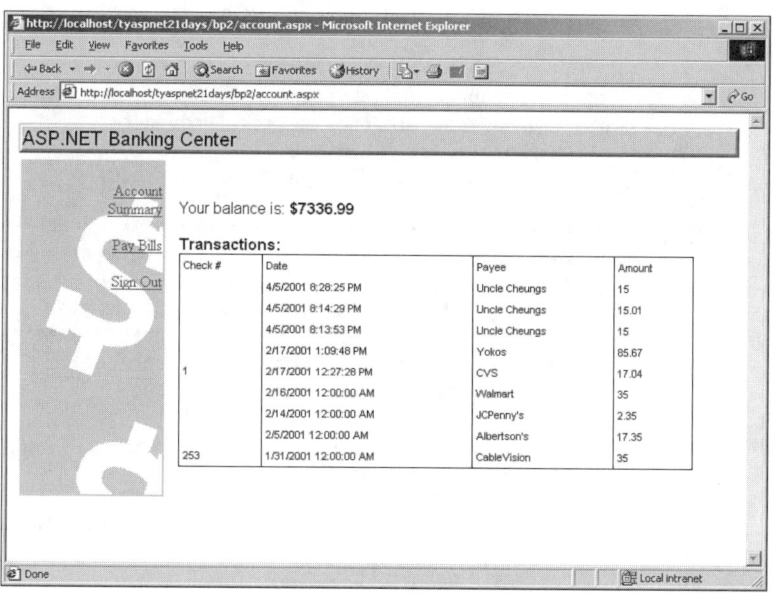

Check #	Date	Payee	Amount
	4/5/2001 8:28:25 PM	Uncle Cheungs	15
	4/5/2001 8:14:29 PM	Uncle Cheungs	15.01
	4/5/2001 8:13:53 PM	Uncle Cheungs	15
	2/17/2001 1:09:48 PM	Yokos	85.67
1	2/17/2001 12:27:28 PM	CVS	17.04
	2/16/2001 12:00:00 AM	Walmart	35
	2/14/2001 12:00:00 AM	JCPenny's	2.35
	2/5/2001 12:00:00 AM	Albertson's	17.35
253	1/31/2001 12:00:00 AM	CableVision	35

FIGURE BP2.3

The account balance and transactions are displayed for the current user.

Finally, you must update the `bills.aspx` page to allow users to enter new transactions (in other words, to pay bills online). When a user enters a transaction, you'll check whether he has sufficient funds, subtract the amount from his balance if he does, and update the transactions table. Note that you're allowing only *payments* and not *credits*. Banking hasn't evolved to the point yet where they trust us to specify our own deposits online!

This page should be fairly simple—executing stored procedures and supplying parameters as you're used to. You do have to perform a few additional checks to make sure that the amount the user enters is valid. Listing BP2.8 shows the code from this page.

LISTING BP2.8 `bills.aspx`—Entering Transactions

```
<%@ Page language="Vb" %>
<%@ Register TagPrefix="ASPNETBank" TagName="Header" src="header.ascx" %>
<%@ Register TagPrefix="ASPNETBank" TagName="Menu" src="nav.ascx" %>
<%@ Import Namespace="System.Data" %>
<%@ Import Namespace="System.Data.OleDb" %>

<script runat="server">

   '*******************************************************
   '
   ' Bills.aspx: Allows user to pay bills online
   '
   '*******************************************************
   'declare connection object
   dim Conn as new OleDbConnection("Provider=" & _
      "Microsoft.Jet.OLEDB.4.0;" & _
      "Data Source=C:\ASPNET\data\banking.mdb")

   '*******************************************************
   ' Event hander for submit button. Determines if amount
   ' is valid, and if so, calls necessary functions to
   ' update balance and add transaction
   '*******************************************************
   sub PayBill(Sender as Object, e as EventArgs)
      dim decBalance as Decimal = GetBalance
      dim decAmount as Decimal = tbAmount.Text

      if decAmount < 0 then
         lblMessage.Text = "<font color=red>The " & _
            "transaction amount cannot be negative!" & _
            "</font>"
         exit sub
      end if

      if decAmount <= decBalance then
         UpdateBalance(decBalance - decAmount)
         AddTransaction(tbPayee.Text, decAmount)

         lblMessage.Text = "<font color=red>Transaction " & _
            "added.</font>"
         tbAmount.Text = ""
         tbPayee.Text = ""
      else
```

LISTING BP2.8 continued

```
      lblMessage.Text = "<font color=red>You do not " & _
         "have enough funds to complete this " & _
         "transaction!</font>"
   end if
end sub

'*****************************************************
' This function returns the balance of the account with
' the specified user ID (stored in the cookie created
' by forms authentication)
'*****************************************************
function GetBalance as Decimal
   dim decBalance as decimal
   dim objCmd as OleDbCommand = new OleDbCommand _
      ("spRetrieveBalance", Conn)
   objCmd.CommandType = CommandType.StoredProcedure
   dim objReader as OleDbDataReader

   'set parameters for stored procedure
   dim objParam as OleDbParameter
   objParam = objCmd.Parameters.Add("@UserID", _
      OleDbType.BSTR)
   objParam.Direction = ParameterDirection.Input
   objParam.Value = Request.Cookies("Account").Value

   try
      objCmd.Connection.Open()
      decBalance = CType(objCmd.ExecuteScalar, Decimal)
      objCmd.Connection.Close()
   catch ex as OleDbException
      lblMessage.Text = ex.Message
   end try

   return decBalance
end function

'*****************************************************
' Adds a transaction into the database, calling
' spInsertTransaction and specifying amount, payee, and
' user id
'*****************************************************
sub AddTransaction(strPayee as string, decAmount _
   as Decimal)
   dim objCmd as OleDbCommand = new OleDbCommand _
      ("spInsertTransaction", Conn)
   objCmd.CommandType = CommandType.StoredProcedure

   'set parameters for stored procedure
```

LISTING BP2.8 continued

```
   dim objParam as OleDbParameter
   objParam = objCmd.Parameters.Add("@Date", _
      OleDbType.Date)
   objParam.Direction = ParameterDirection.Input
   objParam.Value = Datetime.Now

   objParam = objCmd.Parameters.Add("@Amount", _
      OleDbType.Decimal)
   objParam.Direction = ParameterDirection.Input
   objParam.Value = decAmount

   objParam = objCmd.Parameters.Add("@Payee", _
      OleDbType.BSTR)
   objParam.Direction = ParameterDirection.Input
   objParam.Value = strPayee

   objParam = objCmd.Parameters.Add("@UserID", _
      OleDbType.BSTR)
   objParam.Direction = ParameterDirection.Input
   objParam.Value = Request.Cookies("Account").Value

   try
      objCmd.Connection.Open()
      objCmd.ExecuteNonQuery
   catch ex as OleDbException
      lblMessage.Text = ex.Message
   finally
      objCmd.Connection.Close()
   end try
end sub

'*******************************************************
' Updates the account balance
' calls spUpdateBalance
'*******************************************************
sub UpdateBalance(decNewAmount as Decimal)
   dim objCmd as OleDbCommand = new OleDbCommand _
      ("spUpdateBalance", Conn)
   objCmd.CommandType = CommandType.StoredProcedure

   'set parameters for stored procedure
   dim objParam as OleDbParameter
   objParam = objCmd.Parameters.Add("@NewBalance", _
      OleDbType.Decimal)
   objParam.Direction = ParameterDirection.Input
   objParam.Value = decNewAmount

   objParam = objCmd.Parameters.Add("@UserID", _
```

LISTING BP2.8 continued

```
140:            OleDbType.BSTR)
141:         objParam.Direction = ParameterDirection.Input
142:         objParam.Value = Request.Cookies("Account").Value
143:
144:         try
145:            objCmd.Connection.Open()
146:            objCmd.ExecuteNonQuery
147:         catch ex as OleDbException
148:            lblMessage.Text = ex.Message
149:         finally
150:            objCmd.Connection.Close()
151:         end try
152:      end sub
153:   </script>
```

ANALYSIS The `PayBill` method on line 24 is the event handler for the click event of the Submit button. It grabs the information from the text boxes, verifies that the amount is not negative and is not greater than the balance, and calls the appropriate methods to update the balance and add the transaction to the database.

Following that is the `GetBalance` function on line 55, which is the same as the one for `account.aspx`, except that instead of printing the balance to the page, it returns the balance as a decimal value.

The `AddTransaction` method on line 85 executes the `spInsertTransaction` stored procedure and supplies the appropriate values as parameters. Finally, the `UpdateBalance` method executes the `spUpdateBalance` stored procedure.

Enter a transaction in this page, and then go back to the account summary page. You should now see a new transaction in the `DataGrid`, as well as a new balance.

Summary

That's all the changes you need to make. Your application is now a fully functional banking application, complete with online bill payment and transaction viewing. It is very helpful to lay out, in the beginning, the functions that you'll need to perform with your application. When you started, you first built all the stored procedures that would be necessary. Although this might have seemed tedious, it is a necessary step to ensure that your application has a strong design.

Although it works fully now, there is quite a bit you can do to enhance this application. You could add Validation controls to check that the payee and amount that the user enters on the bills page are valid. You could also add a filter to the transactions `DataGrid` to allow the user to view only those transactions within a specified time period.

Right now, all the money is stored in a single checking account. You could add another account type to the application, such as a savings account. You could store the account information in the same `tblAccounts` table, and add a new field for the type of account.

You also might have noticed that there is a lot of duplicate code in the listings, and that it is scattered throughout several pages. Next week, you'll learn about componentizing ASP.NET pages to overcome these problems by encapsulating commonly used code in modules.

WEEK 3

At a Glance

15

16

17

18

19

20

21

You've finally made it to the last week—only seven more days to go! In the first week, you covered the basics of ASP.NET—how to interact with users and how to set up ASP.NET. In the second week, you looked at data access and ASP.NET. You also examined databases, data binding, ADO.NET, XML, and file I/O. This week, you'll take a look at how to build complete Web applications.

It's true that you have already been building Web applications. But your applications so far have consisted of only ASP.NET pages and databases. To build a complete ASP.NET Web application, you need to explore components and services.

The first day of this week, "Using Business Objects," will be spent learning how to build and use components in ASP.NET. These allow you to add another layer of abstraction to your ASP.NET pages, encapsulating classes and objects to provide additional functionality and performance.

From there, you'll move on to Web services in "Creating Web Services" and "Consuming and Securing XML Web Services." A *Web service* is basically an application that is delivered over the Internet, rather than residing on a user's computer. You'll learn how to build and work with Web services, an integral part of ASP.NET.

Day 18, "Configuring and Deploying ASP.NET Applications," will examine how to control your ASP.NET application as a whole (rather than through individual pages) with the `global.asax` and `web.config` files. These two files provide programmatic access to control and customize your application.

After that, you'll spend a few days examining some advanced programming topics and how they apply to ASP.NET. First, you'll look at debugging mechanisms available for ASP.NET, including the tracing feature. Finally, you'll look at security and how to implement a secure ASP.NET application.

By the end of this week, you'll have all the parts of ASP.NET development under your belt. You'll be able to build an application from scratch, starting from the simplest pages moving all the way to the most complex applications and services.

Don't forget to check out the bonus days at the end of this book —they provide further examples to help you gain experience and become more proficient in ASP.NET!

Without further ado, let's begin!

WEEK 3

DAY 15

Using Business Objects

Today's lesson is moving into new ASP.NET development territory. In the past two weeks, you've learned about the basics of ASP.NET, as well as the data accessing mechanisms. Now you're going to start learning about advanced topics that will allow you to build complete ASP.NET applications.

Today's lesson will examine *business objects,* components that you can use in your ASP.NET applications. The difference between these components and the ones you've been using so far (such ADO.NET or XML objects) is that you're building these from scratch for your own uses. Today you're going to look at what business objects are for, how to build them, and how to use them.

Today's lesson will cover the following:

- What components and business objects are
- How ASP.NET uses components
- Why we use components
- How to create and use business objects
- How to use components that weren't created in a .NET environment

Introduction to Components

Components are objects that can be used over and over again in different applications. They usually characterize a real-world object. Let's go back to the clock factory analogy from Day 3, "Using Visual Basic.NET and C#." To build a clock, you take a bunch of components, such as springs, hinges, glass, wood, and pendulums, and put them together. ASP.NET applications, as well as regular applications, are exactly the same—they consist of bunches of parts that are assembled to build a cohesive whole.

Imagine that the clocks you're building consist of one component—each clock is one piece of wood. These clocks don't work very well—the hands don't move, the pendulum doesn't swing, and so on. However, once you split the clock into separate pieces—the second, minute, and hour hands; the pendulum; the face—it's much easier to construct the clock and make it work flawlessly. Also, when you have many pieces, switching them out becomes easier. If the minute hand breaks, for instance, you can easily take it out and add a new one. Or if a more advanced pendulum is developed, you can simply upgrade the old one, saving both time and money.

There is a counter argument to this, however. Having *too* many components defeats the purpose by introducing unnecessary complexity. Why would you need to divide the pendulum further? You're left with parts that work just as well in one piece.

In terms of ASP.NET, components are pieces of reusable code that enhance your application or give it new functionality. The user controls that you developed on Day 5, "Beginning Web Forms." are components. Code-behind forms can be thought of as components. Even Web controls are components that you can plug into your pages. A component is used to describe a real object, such as a calendar or a book. In an ASP.NET page, a text box or a database result set would be considered a component.

What Are Business Objects?

NEW TERM Business objects are components that encapsulate code that's applicable to your application. Writing code that's used to provide non-UI functionality is known as *business logic* or *business rules*. Hence, components that implement business logic are known as *business objects*.

For example, if you followed the last bonus project in "Week 2 in Review," all the code you developed for interacting with the database was business logic. It was the code that communicated between the UI and the database. Ideally, this logic should be separated from the ASP.NET pages into a business object. The ASP.NET page should only be used for UI purposes and processing that belongs on the client side of the application.

A common example of a business object is found in an e-commerce site, which has to retrieve shipping charges from different shipping companies. A developer can build this logic into an ASP.NET page, but then it would be difficult to modify if shipping rate calculations change in the future (not to mention that it's not very reusable). A smart developer can then come along and create a shipping component that can be used by any ASP.NET application. This component retrieves information from shippers' databases and provides the e-commerce application with everything it needs. The component is reusable, and any changes can be made in one place without disrupting the ASP.NET pages.

Why Use Components?

You may have heard of the three-tiered application model, which divides applications into three (sometimes not very distinct) layers: a UI or presentation layer, a business logic/object layer, and the data layer. This model is a good one for developing Web applications, and it's not very difficult to implement. Figure 15.1 illustrates this model.

FIGURE 15.1

The three-tier model consists of UI, business logic, and data layers.

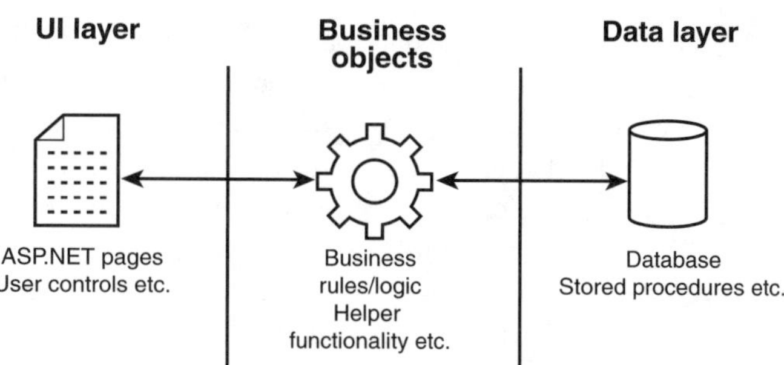

It's kind of like a theater production. The first layer is the performers on stage. They provide the "UI" for the audience, engaging their attention, giving them an experience, and so on. This is the level that the audience interacts with.

The second level consists of the people who provide the direction and cues: the orchestra, the stagehands, cue directors, and so on. All these people interact with the stage performers but aren't seen directly by the audience. They provide direction and give material to the actors.

Finally, the third level is the people responsible for the scenes and material: writers, artists, set designers, and so on. All of these people work together to provide the substance of the production. They're not seen by the audience except through what they produce.

This model of putting on performances is very well defined and fine-tuned. Imagine if a single layer was missing. Without the performers, the production couldn't be put on. Without the writers and artists, there would be no show to perform. Without the middle layer of stagehands and such, the performers would have a difficult time doing their job and one of the other layers would have to take up the slack.

The same model applies to developing Web applications. The absence of a layer makes the application that much more difficult to produce. In an e-commerce site, the first layer consists of the UI (forms, shopping cart, graphics, and so on). The middle business layer consists of logic to control pricing, shipping costs, and so on. The third layer, the data layer, consists of the inventory stored in a database. If any layer is missing, another layer must take up the slack.

In more concrete terms, using business objects in a middle tier allows you to better separate and define your application. Your ASP.NET pages no longer have long, obtuse code that doesn't deal with UI. ASP.NET pages are used to provide a visual focus for the user, so why crowd any code that doesn't deal with UI into those pages?

Granted, you've been doing just that for several days now. Functionality such as data access logic could be pushed into business objects in a middle tier. In many of the examples, though, the functionality was so simple that it wasn't necessary to introduce a third layer and the increased complexity that goes with it. Business objects are excellent for encapsulating non-UI logic, but you need to figure out whether or not an application is complex enough to warrant a third tier. Components also provide a more efficient mechanism for executing functionality. For instance, recall the calendar control from Day 5. With just a few lines of UI code, you can display a fully interactive calendar that's tailored to your design scheme. You don't have to worry about rendering the calendar, filling the weeks, figuring out the number of days in a month, and so on. All that is handled for you.

Likewise, you should develop a component so that the people who use it don't need to worry about how things work behind the scenes. They can just use it. Even if the developers and users happen to be the same people (you, in this case), this still provides an easy mechanism for implementing functionality.

Of course, don't forget the obvious benefits. The reuse of code is increased, making for a smaller and tighter application. Compiling code separately from ASP.NET pages improves performance. And maintenance is easier—change the business logic once and it affects the whole application. Also, as part of the .NET Framework, any objects you create can be inherited from and extended if needed.

Sometimes, though, the distinction between the layers isn't very apparent. Where exactly do you draw the line between UI functionality and business logic? This is a question that developers have been asking for quite some time. Today's examples will try to make the distinction as clear as possible, but sometimes it's a matter of judgment.

How ASP.NET Uses Components

ASP.NET uses the `/bin` directory, known as the *assembly cache*, for its compiled objects. After you develop your business objects later today, you'll compile them and place them in this directory. Any objects in `/bin` are automatically loaded by your ASP.NET application when it's started. This allows you to use the components you develop in your pages.

You can also manually load objects that aren't in this directory into your pages through the `web.config` file, but that's beyond the scope of this book. In most cases, you'll have no reason not to place your objects in `/bin`.

Once the objects are loaded, you use them in your pages just as you use built-in objects. For example, the `System` namespace and all its classes are compiled in a single object file, stored in the global assembly cache. When you use these in your pages, you can either import the `System` namespace or reference objects by their full names—`System.Integer`, for instance. You can use objects in the same way, as you'll learn later today.

Creating Business Objects

Objects are simply classes developed in VB.NET or C# (or whatever language you're most comfortable with), organized into logical groups.

Let's get right into development. Listing 15.1 shows the framework for a simple object in VB.NET, and Listing 15.2 shows the same object in C#.

LISTING 15.1 A Sample Framework for a Business Object in VB.NET

```
Imports System
Imports System.Data
Imports System.Data.OleDb

Namespace TYASPNET

   Public Class Database
   End Class

End Namespace
```

LISTING 15.2 A Sample Framework for a Business Object in C#

```
1:     using System;
2:     using System.Data;
3:     using System.Data.OleDb;
4:
5:     namespace TYASPNET {
6:
7:        public class Database {
8:        }
9:
10:    }
```

ANALYSIS Save this file as `Database.vb` or (`Database.cs` for Listing 15.2). This object will be used to provide abstract database functionality for your pages, such as connecting to, querying, and returning data. In other words, it represents a real-world database and should have all the properties and methods that define a database.

First, you import the namespaces you'll be using in your object. In this case, you'll need `System`, `System.Data`, and `System.Data.OleDb` (lines 1, 2, and 3, respectively). On line 5, you declare the namespace that this current object belongs to. Where did the namespace `TYASPNET` come from? Nowhere—you created it just now. It's that easy to extend the .NET Framework—simply declaring that you're using a new namespace creates it automatically. When you develop more objects for your applications, you can insert them into this namespace as well. Thus, it serves as a logical group for all your business logic.

For example, the `System.Data.OleDb` namespace has many classes, including `OleDbCommand`, `OleDbConnection`, and `OleDbDataAdapter`. Namespaces are simply used to group classes logically.

If you wanted to, you could have specified an existing namespace, such as `System.Web`. Your object would be added to that namespace. Remember, though, that namespaces are for logical grouping of objects. The object you're developing doesn't belong in any existing namespace, so you create your own. You can have a different namespace for every ASP.NET application you develop!

Do	Don't
Do create unique namespaces for objects in your applications.	**Don't** use existing namespaces for your objects. It will end up confusing you and could create problems.

Finally, you declare your class, which currently is empty, on line 7. You'll be adding to it shortly. Don't forget to write the closing class and namespace tags.

Let's compile this object so you can use it in your ASP.NET pages. To do this, you'll be using the VB.NET compiler that comes with the .NET Framework SDK. Open a command prompt window by clicking Start, Run and then typing `cmd.exe`. First, navigate to the root directory of your application (`c:\inetpub\wwwroot\`) and create a new `bin` directory with the following command:

```
mkdir bin
```

You'll place your business objects here in a moment. Next, navigate to the directory you saved this file in for instance, `c:\inetpub\wwwroot\tyaspnet21days\day15`.

Type the following command and press Enter:

```
vbc /t:library /out:..\..\bin\TYASPNET21Days.dll /r:System.dll
   /r:System.Data.dll Database.vb
```

Or for the C# version:

```
csc /t:library /out:..\..\bin\TYASPNET21Days.dll /r:System.dll
   /r:System.Data.dll Database.cs
```

The VB.NET and C# compilers have a lot of options and are very complex, so this section will only examine the options used with this particular command. (Most likely, these will be all you ever need for ASP.NET development.)

`vbc.exe` is the name of the VB.NET compiler. `csc.exe` is the name of the C# compiler. You use these program to compile your file into a DLL (also known as an assembly) for use with your application. `/t` specifies the type of file you want to compile to. `library` means an object that will be used by other applications—it can't be used by itself. The `/t` option can also be `exe` or `winexe`, which creates an executable file.

`/out` specifies the directory and filename where you want to send the compiled output. You need to place this in your `/bin` directory, so you specify the path relative to the current directory. The `/r` option means reference. In Listing 15.1, you referenced the

System, System.Data, and System.Data.OleDb namespaces. These namespaces are stored in the System.dll and System.Data.dll files, so you add references to both of them when compiling.

Caution

Remember to use references in your compilation command, and not just in the Import command in your code. Without these references, the Import commands would do nothing and you would receive errors when you tried to compile your object.

Finally, you specify the file that you want to compile, Database.vb. This class file will be compiled and loaded into your assembly cache, for use with your pages. You should see something similar to Figure 15.2.

FIGURE 15.2
Using the VB.NET compiler to build your objects.

Note

Don't worry if you're not very comfortable using the VB.NET compiler. You can usually use the same command over and over again, and where the syntax is different, it will be pointed out. For more information, see the .NET Framework SDK documentation.

Listing 15.3 shows a simple ASP.NET page that implements this object.

LISTING 15.3 Using the Business Object

```
<%@ Page Language="VB" %>

<script runat="server">
   sub Page_Load(Sender as Object, e as EventArgs)
      dim objDatabase as new TYASPNET.Database
```

LISTING 15.3 continued

```
6:          lblMessage.Text = "Object created"
7:       end sub
8:    </script>
9:
10:    <html><body>
11:       <asp:Label id="lblMessage" runat="server" />
12:    </body></html>
```

ANALYSIS On line 5, you declare a new object based on the business object you just created. You can't do anything with this object yet because you didn't implement any methods for it. You'll add some methods later today in "Developing Business Objects."

Note that you use the full name `TYASPNET.Database` for your object. You could simply use the object name (without the namespace name) by importing your custom namespace, just as you've done for other namespaces. For example, let's say you add the following code to line 2:

```
<%@ Import Namespace="TYASPNET" %>
```

This would allow you to use the following on line 5:

```
dim objDatabase as new Database
```

Developing Business Objects

Let's go back and implement some functionality for your business object that you created in Listing 15.1. Since your object represents a database, the first thing you need is a connection string property. You'll create this property inside your `Database` class, as shown in Listing 15.4.

LISTING 15.4 The Connection String Property

```
Imports System
Imports System.Data
Imports System.Data.OleDb

Namespace TYASPNET

   Public Class Database
      public ConnectionString as String
      private objConn as OleDbConnection
      private objCmd as OleDbCommand
       ...
```

Any page that uses this business object will be able to set and retrieve the connection string for the current database at any time. You also added two private variables that represent database objects. Because these two variables are private, they will be accessible to the methods in this class, but not to outside methods. In other words, the ASP.NET page that uses this business object won't be able to access these variables, but it will be able to access the public `ConnectionString` variable.

> Think of a class as a car engine. Everything that's private is inside and cannot be seen by anything on the outside. You may know that the pistons are inside the engine, but you can't see or access them (unless you take apart the engine, which is another story). Public items, however, reveal themselves to those on the outside. These include things such as the dipstick, spark plugs, and air filter.

Next, you need a method to retrieve information from the database. You'll create a function that will execute a specified SQL statement and return the data as an `OleDbDataReader`. You also need a function that performs database operations but doesn't return any data—for `Insert` and `Update` statements, for example. Listing 15.5 shows two methods for accessing data: one that returns information, and one that doesn't.

LISTING 15.5 Executing a Select Query

```
      public function SelectSQL(strSelect as string) as _
         OleDbDataReader
         try
            objConn = new OleDbConnection(ConnectionString)
            objCmd = new OleDbCommand(strSelect, objConn)
            objCmd.Connection.Open
            return objCmd.ExecuteReader
            objCmd.Connection.Close()
         catch ex as OleDbException
            return nothing
         end try
      end function

      public function ExecuteNonQuery(strQuery as string) _
         as Boolean
         try
            objConn = new OleDbConnection(ConnectionString)
            objCmd = new OleDbCommand(strQuery, objConn)
            objCmd.Connection.Open()
            objCmd.ExecuteNonQuery
            objCmd.Connection.Close()
```

LISTING 15.5 continued

```
33:            return true
34:         catch ex as OleDbException
35:            return false
36:         end try
37:      end function
38:
39:   End Class
40:
41: End Namespace
```

The `SelectSQL` function is standard. It opens a connection with an `OleDbCommand` object, executes the query, and returns a `DataReader`, as shown on line 18. You then close your connection on line 19. If anything goes wrong, the `try` block will catch the error and return `nothing`.

The `ExecuteNonQuery` method is similar, but it doesn't return a `DataReader`. Instead, it returns true or false depending on whether the command executed successfully.

Recompile this object with the same command that you used previously:

```
vbc /t:library /out:..\bin\TYASPNET21Days.dll /r:System.dll
   /r:System.Data.dll Database.vb
```

Now let's modify your ASP.NET page. Listing 15.6 shows a modified version of Listing 15.3. It sets properties of your new database object and displays data in a `DataGrid`.

LISTING 15.6 Using Your Object's Methods

```
<%@ Page Language="VB" %>
<%@ Import Namespace="System.Data" %>
<%@ Import Namespace="System.Data.OleDb" %>

<script runat="server">
   sub Page_Load(Sender as Object, e as EventArgs)
      dim objDatabase as new TYASPNET.Database

      objDatabase.ConnectionString = "Provider=" & _
         "Microsoft.Jet.OLEDB.4.0;" & _
         "Data Source=c:\ASPNET\data\banking.mdb"

       dim objReader as OleDbDataReader
       objReader = objDatabase.SelectSQL _
          ("Select * from tblUsers")

       if not objReader is nothing then
          DataGrid1.DataSource = objReader
```

LISTING 15.6 continued

```
19:             DataGrid1.DataBind()
20:             objReader.Close
21:          end if
22:       end sub
23:
24:    </script>
25:
26:    <html><body>
27:       <asp:Label id="lblMessage" runat="server" />
28:
29:       <asp:DataGrid id="DataGrid1"
30:          runat="server" BorderColor="black"
31:          GridLines="Vertical" cellpadding="4"
32:          cellspacing="0" width="100%"
33:          Font-Name="Arial" Font-Size="8pt"
34:          HeaderStyle-BackColor="#cccc99"
35:          ItemStyle-BackColor="#ffffff"
36:          AlternatingItemStyle-Backcolor="#cccccc" />
37:    </body></html>
```

ANALYSIS You declare your database object on line 7 and set the `ConnectionString` property on line 9. On line 14, you execute the `SelectSQL` statement that you built in Listing 15.5. You then grab the results and place them in an `OleDbDataReader`.

Remember that if an error occurs, the `SelectSQL` function returns `nothing`. Before you do anything with the data reader, on line 17 you verify that you actually have results. If you do, you bind the data to a `DataGrid` on line 19 and close your reader on line 20. This listing, when viewed through a browser, generates the output shown in Figure 15.3.

> The `Username` and `Password` columns were added during "Week 2 in Review." Check out the bonus project in that section to see how and why it was done.

Using your custom `Database` object is the same as using any other object you've used up to this point. You create an instance of the object, set some properties, and execute some methods.

You may be wondering why you did all that work just to save a few lines of code in your ASP.NET page. For a simple example such as this, it wasn't necessary to build a business object for your database query. However, when your applications start getting significantly larger, your business object can become much more complex. In those cases, this method can save you a lot of time writing ASP.NET pages.

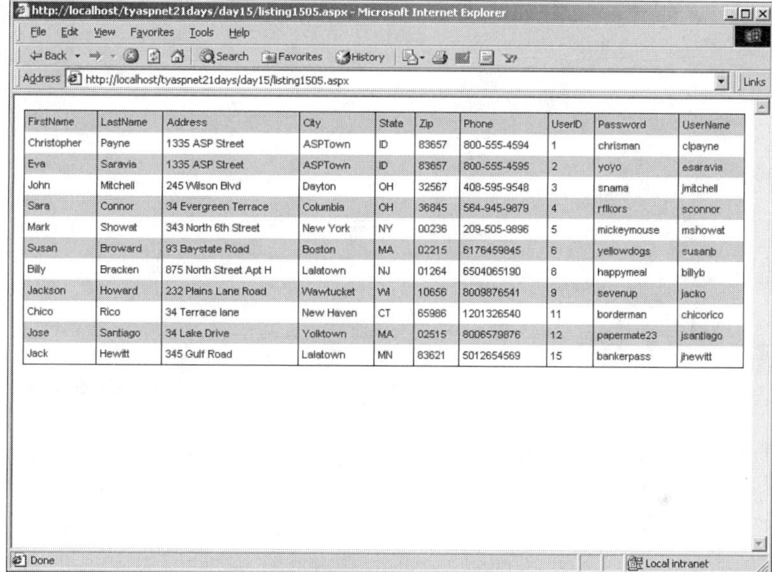

FirstName	LastName	Address	City	State	Zip	Phone	UserID	Password	UserName
Christopher	Payne	1335 ASP Street	ASPTown	ID	83657	800-555-4594	1	chrisman	clpayne
Eva	Saravia	1335 ASP Street	ASPTown	ID	83657	800-555-4595	2	yoyo	esaravia
John	Mitchell	245 Wilson Blvd	Dayton	OH	32567	408-595-9548	3	snama	jmitchell
Sara	Connor	34 Evergreen Terrace	Columbia	OH	36845	564-945-9879	4	rflkors	sconnor
Mark	Showat	343 North 6th Street	New York	NY	00236	209-505-9896	5	mickeymouse	mshowat
Susan	Broward	93 Baystate Road	Boston	MA	02215	6176459845	6	yellowdogs	susanb
Billy	Bracken	875 North Street Apt H	Lalatown	NJ	01264	6504065190	8	happymeal	billyb
Jackson	Howard	232 Plains Lane Road	Wawtucket	WI	10656	8009876541	9	sevenup	jacko
Chico	Rico	34 Terrace lane	New Haven	CT	65986	1201326540	11	borderman	chicorico
Jose	Santiago	34 Lake Drive	Yolktown	MA	02515	8006579876	12	papermate23	jsantiago
Jack	Hewitt	345 Gulf Road	Lalatown	MN	83621	5012654569	15	bankerpass	jhewitt

FIGURE 15.3

Your business object returns data that you can use in an ASP.NET page.

Also, you can now use this object in any ASP.NET page and get results. You can change the connection string to connect to another database and specify a different SQL statement to return different data. Although you saved yourself just 10–15 lines in this ASP.NET page, imagine how many lines you'll save when you have 10 or 20 ASP.NET pages that can all use this one object.

Another question you may be asking is "Why build a database business object when I can simply use the OleDb data classes directly from the ASP.NET pages? Why not build something more useful?" Your business object is very useful, actually. Not only does it allow the user to retrieve data with a single line of code, but it hides all the complexity of working with the data objects. The user (in this case, another programmer) need not worry about `OleDbCommands` or connections. He doesn't have to worry about wrapping things in a `try` block or catching errors. Your class handles all that for the user of your object. Figure 15.4 illustrates the difference between what the user sees and what he doesn't.

FIGURE 15.4

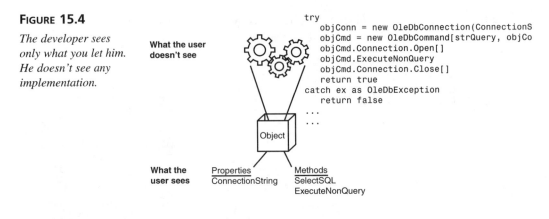

The developer sees only what you let him. He doesn't see any implementation.

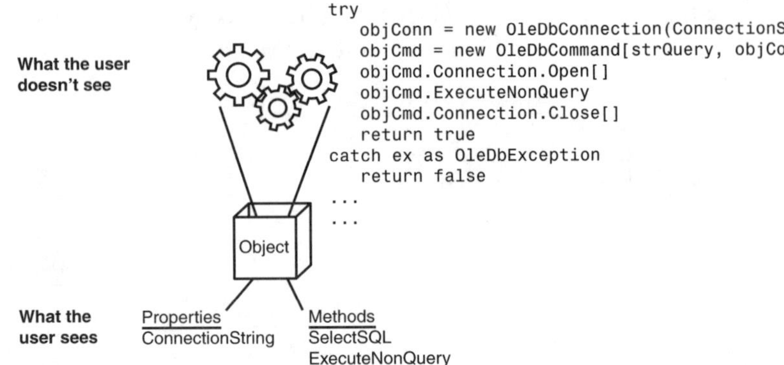
What the user doesn't see
try
objConn = new OleDbConnection(ConnectionS
objCmd = new OleDbCommand[strQuery, objCo
objCmd.Connection.Open[]
objCmd.ExecuteNonQuery
objCmd.Connection.Close[]
return true
catch ex as OleDbException
return false
...
...
Object
What the user sees
Properties
ConnectionString
Methods
SelectSQL
ExecuteNonQuery

A Working Example

Now that you've learned how to build and use a simple business object, let's use one to build something more useful. Many Web sites have areas that only registered users can access, or that offer personalized content for those users. In these Web sites, it may be useful to encapsulate the complexity of representing a registered user. All functions associated with a user, such as logging them on and off, updating their profile information, and so on, can be easily packaged into a business object.

In essence, this object will represent a generic user, and it should contain methods and properties that completely describe that user. It should also contain methods to perform actions on users, such as adding new users, deleting old ones, and validating. Specifically, you want the following properties:

- An object to represent a user's identity, including her full name, username, ID, and so on.
- Methods to add, remove, and update users.
- Methods to validate users.

This functionality will be implemented as two separate classes. One will be used to represent all the user's details, and another will perform the methods described previously. This allows you to treat the user's details as a group—a separate entity—that you can manipulate. Figure 15.5 depicts the relationship between your two objects.

You'll be using the user database you created on Day 8, "Beginning to Build Databases." The beginning of your file is shown in Listing 15.7.

FIGURE 15.5

The `UserDetail` *object will hold details, while the* `User` *object will hold functionality.*

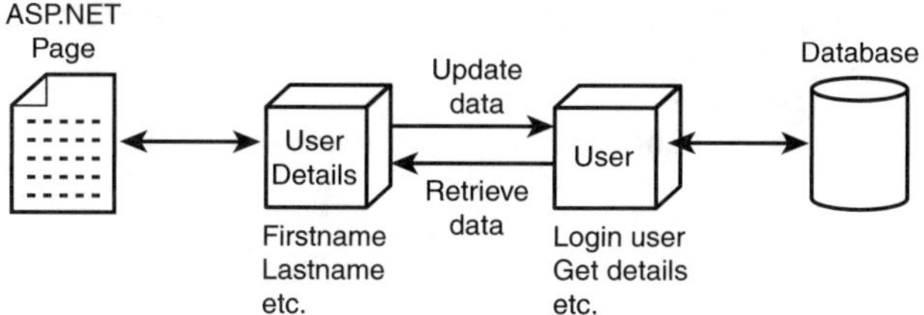

LISTING 15.7 The `UserDetails` Class

```
1:     Imports System
2:     Imports System.Data
3:     Imports System.Data.OleDb
4:
5:     Namespace TYASPNET
6:
7:        Public Class UserDetails
8:           public FirstName as string
9:           public LastName as string
10:           public UserName as string
11:           public Password as string
12:           public UserID as string
13:        End Class
```

ANALYSIS Save this file as `user.vb`. This file starts out the same way as the previous object. You import the necessary namespaces (lines 1 through 3) and declare your namespace (line 5). Your `UserDetails` class, beginning on line 7, contains all the properties that you'll need to represent your user. (These aren't all the properties in the database. Some have been left out for simplicity's sake. You can add more if you want.)

Note that if you are building this object using C#, you'll need to initialize these public properties to empty strings:

```
public string FirstName = "";
public string LastName = "";
...
```

This is because we'll be comparing these string values later on, and if they are not initialized, the comparison won't work properly.

Next you have your `User` class, which contains the functions you need. This class is shown in Listing 15.8.

LISTING 15.8 The User Class

```
   Public Class User
      public function Login(UserName as string, Password as _
         string) as string
         dim intId as string = "0"
         dim Conn as new OleDbConnection("Provider=" & _
            "Microsoft.Jet.OLEDB.4.0;" & _
            "Data Source=c:\ASPNET\data\banking.mdb")

         dim objCmd as OleDbCommand = new OleDbCommand _
            ("SELECT UserID FROM tblUsers WHERE " & _
            "UserName = '" & UserName & "' AND " & _
            "Password = '" & Password & "'", Conn)
         dim objReader as OleDbDataReader

         try
            objCmd.Connection.Open()
            objReader = objCmd.ExecuteReader

            do while objReader.Read
               intId = objReader.GetInt32(0).ToString
            loop
         catch ex as OleDbException
            throw ex
         end try

         return intID
      end function

      public function GetDetails(UserID as integer) as _
         UserDetails
         dim Conn as new OleDbConnection("Provider=" & _
            "Microsoft.Jet.OLEDB.4.0;" & _
            "Data Source=c:\ASPNET\data\banking.mdb")

         dim objCmd as OleDbCommand = new OleDbCommand _
            ("SELECT FirstName, LastName, UserName, " & _
            "Password FROM tblUsers WHERE UserID = " & _
            UserID, Conn)
         dim objReader as OleDbDataReader

         try
            objCmd.Connection.Open()
            objReader = objCmd.ExecuteReader
         catch ex as OleDbException
            throw ex
         end try

         dim objDetails as new UserDetails
```

LISTING 15.8 continued

```

         while objReader.Read()
            objDetails.FirstName = objReader.GetString(0)
            objDetails.LastName = objReader.GetString(1)
            objDetails.UserName = objReader.GetString(2)
            objDetails.Password = objReader.GetString(3)
            objDetails.UserID = UserID.ToString
         end while
         objReader.Close

         return objDetails
      end function

      public function Update(objDetails as UserDetails, _
         intUserID as integer) as boolean
         dim objOldDetails as new UserDetails
         objOldDetails = GetDetails(intUserID)

         with objDetails
            if .FirstName = "" then
               .FirstName = objOldDetails.FirstName
            end if
            if .LastName = "" then
               .LastName = objOldDetails.LastName
            end if
            if .Username = "" then
               .UserName = objOldDetails.UserName
            end if
            if .Password = "" then
               .Password = objOldDetails.Password
            end if
         end with

         dim Conn as new OleDbConnection("Provider=" & _
            "Microsoft.Jet.OLEDB.4.0;" & _
            "Data Source=c:\ASPNET\data\banking.mdb")

         dim strSQL as string = "UPDATE tblUsers SET " & _
             "FirstName = '" & objDetails.FirstName & _
                 "', " & _
             "LastName = '" & objDetails.LastName & "', " & _
             "UserName = '" & objDetails.UserName & "', " & _
             "[Password] = '" & objDetails.Password & _
              "' " & "WHERE UserID = " & intUserID
          dim objCmd as OleDbCommand = new OleDbCommand _
             (strSQL, Conn)

             objCmd.Connection.Open()
```

LISTING 15.8 continued

```
111:             objCmd.ExecuteNonQuery
112:          catch ex as OleDbException
113:             throw ex
114:          finally
115:             objCmd.Connection.Close
116:          end try
117:
118:          return true
119:       end function
120:    End Class
121:
122: End Namespace
```

ANALYSIS That's quite a large class, and you haven't even added all the methods yet. Luckily, it should be easy for you to understand and you can move through it quickly.

The `Login` function on line 15 takes a username and password and verifies it against the database. If they represent a valid user, you return the corresponding `UserID`.

The `GetDetails` function on line 42 takes a `UserID` value and retrieves the values from the database. On line 61, you create a new instance of the `UserDetails` class defined earlier. You set its properties to the values returned from the database and return that `UserDetails` object to the user. By storing all the values in this `UserDetails` object, you're providing an easy mechanism for the user to access the values.

The `Update` function updates a row in the user database. It takes a `UserDetails` object with the updated values for each property. What if the user only needs to change one value, though? You don't want to require the user to specify all the values if most of them haven't changed. Therefore, you allow the user to specify only the values that are changed in the `UserDetails` object, and this function automatically fills the others with the original values. This functionality is implemented on lines 77–93.

The *`objOldDetails`* variable on line 77 holds the original user property values, which are retrieved from the database using the `GetDetails` function. The subsequent series of `if` statements checks for the user detail values that haven't been specified by the user and sets them to the original values. Now you can build a SQL statement using the `UserDetails` object without worrying that you'll lose original data.

Tip

The `With` *`object`* keyword on line 80 means that all subsequent variables preceded by a period belong to *`object`*. For instance:

```
objDetails.FirstName = ""
objDetials.LastName = ""
```

That's the same as this:

```
With objDetails
   .FirstName = ""
   .LastName = ""
end with
```

The latter method saves you some typing when there are a lot of properties for the object.

The `with` keyword does not exist in C#, so you're stuck with using the long version.

You build your `update` SQL statement on line 99 and execute your query in the `try` block. If the update was successful, you return true.

Save this file as `User.vb`, navigate to the appropriate directory, and compile it with the following command:

```
vbc /t:library /out:..\bin\User.dll /r:System.dll
/r:System.Data.Dll User.vb
```

Tip

You can compile multiple files into a single DLL if you like. For example:

```
vbc /t:library /out:..\bin\TYASPNET.dll /r:System.dll
/r:System.Data.Dll User.vb Database.vb
```

This compiles both the user objects and the database object you created earlier into one file. This is easier to keep track of than multiple DLLs. In fact, instead of specifying each filename that you want to add into the single DLL, you can use wildcards. For example, the following line concatenates all files that end in `.vb` in the current directory into a single DLL:

```
vbc /t:library /out:..\bin\TYASPNET.dll /r:System.dll
/r:System.Data.Dll *.vb
```

Just be sure that you want all such files in the current directory to be compiled together.

Listing 15.9 shows a simple ASP.NET page that uses these objects (`UserDetails` and `User`).

LISTING 15.9 Using Your User Objects

```
<%@ Page Language="VB" %>

<script runat="server">
   sub Page_Load(Sender as Object, e as EventArgs)
      if Not Page.IsPostBack then
         dim objUser as new TYASPNET.User
         dim objDetails as new TYASPNET.UserDetails

         objDetails = objUser.GetDetails(1)
          lblMessage.Text = "Hello " & _
             objDetails.FirstName & "!"
       end if

    end sub

    sub Update(Sender as Object, e as EventArgs)
       dim objUser as new TYASPNET.User
       dim objDetails as new TYASPNET.UserDetails

       objDetails.FirstName = tbName.Text
       if objUser.Update(objDetails, 1) then
          objDetails = objUser.GetDetails(1)
          lblMessage.Text = "Hello " & _
             objDetails.FirstName & "!"
       else
          lblMessage.Text = "Update failed!"
       end if
    end sub
 </script>

 <html><body>
    <form runat="server">
       <asp:Label id="lblMessage" runat="server" /><p>
       Change your name?<br>
       <asp:Textbox id="tbName" runat="server"/><br>
       <asp:Button id="btSubmit" runat="server"
          OnClick="Update" Text="Submit" />
    </form>
 </body></html>
```

When the user first comes to this page, she will see a welcome message with the `UserID` 1. In the `Page Load` event, you instantiate your two new objects and use the `GetDetails` method to return a `UserDetails` object. You then display a simple welcome message.

When the user enters a new name in the box and clicks Submit, the `Update` method takes control. It sets the name property of a new `UserDetails` object to the new value and calls the `User.Update` method. If the update is successful, this method returns true and displays a welcome message with the new name. Figure 15.6 shows the output after entering a new name.

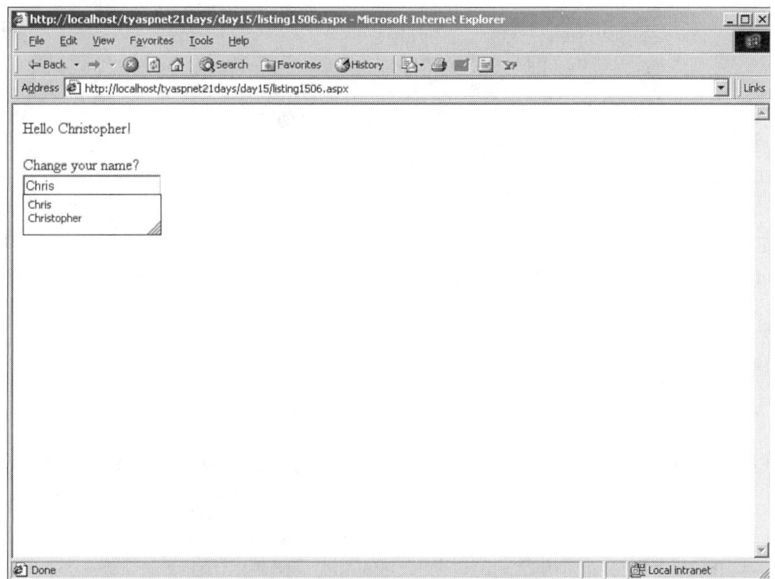

FIGURE 15.6
Your user objects manipulate user information with only a few lines of code in the ASP.NET page.

Your ASP.NET page is now very short. The equivalent page without the business objects would be much longer. Now, it only contains code that interfaces directly with the UI. Likewise, any other page that needs to implement this functionality is also spared the trouble of dealing with the database objects directly.

Imagine if you needed to add another function to the `User` object, or if the database structure changed. If you had implemented these individual functions on every ASP.NET page that required it, you'd have to make a lot of changes to reflect the database change. With the `User` object, you can just make one change in the `.vb` file and recompile. You're off and running again without having to dig through all the ASP.NET pages involved.

Another benefit of business objects is that they can be used on other Web servers. You could sell this `User` object for developers to use on their own sites. (Of course, you may want to add more functionality first.)

Instead of creating all the database commands and objects from scratch in the `User` class, you could just as easily use the `Database` class you created earlier today in "Developing Business Objects." When you compile the `User` objects, you have to modify the command as follows:

```
vbc /t:library /out:..\bin\User.dll /r:System.dll
/r:System.Data.Dll /r:TYASPNET.dll User.vb
```

Specifically, you need to add a reference to your database object in `TYASPNET.dll`.

A Few Considerations

Notice that you hard-coded a few values into your `user.vb` file, such as the connection string. This type of variable doesn't belong in the business object, but rather should be placed in a separate configuration file, such as `web.config` (we'll get to that in Day 18, "Configuring and Deploying ASP.NET Applications"). The business object could easily retrieve this string using the `GetConfig` method of the `HttpContext` object (see Day 18). This promotes a much more flexible application—you don't have to recompile every time the database changes.

Just because the business object shouldn't be dependent on which database you use, that doesn't mean the object should have no awareness of the database. Placing SQL statements that are specific to a particular database is fine, and it's done that way very often. A business object should depend on a format for the database, but not the actual location of it.

Of course, all SQL statements can be moved into stored procedures as well. The object can then pass parameters to the stored procedures. As long as the names of the procedures stay the same, you can easily add more functionality to them without having to modify the source code of the business objects and recompiling.

When you develop business objects, always try to think of the logical separations of functionality. The previous objects represented a user. They shouldn't contain any code that displays data to the user or any SQL statements that return data. They should only contain user-specific methods and properties. This will help you when designing your applications.

Also, don't try to stuff too much functionality into one object. For instance, you saw that the user information is easily and logically separated from the user methods. Rather than having one object perform all the functionality, you can have two that can rely on each other.

Working with Non-.NET Components

Recall that when you compile these objects in the .NET Framework, the objects must emit metadata describing themselves. The Common Language Runtime (CLR) uses this data to load the objects without any developer intervention. Simply place the objects in the `/bin` directory and you're off and running.

However, older objects that weren't developed in the .NET Framework (often known as Component Object Model, or COM, objects) did not provide that capability. There was no CLR to automatically manage and load these objects, and no metadata to tell the CLR about them. Developers had to register the components manually using `REGSVR32.exe`, which placed information into the Windows Registry (a location that contains information about all the applications and components installed on the machine).

COM objects are called "older" because the technology used to create them is older than the .NET technology—not because the objects themselves are older.

These COM objects were built in a non-.NET environment, so they're not managed by the CLR and are known as *unmanaged code*. Because of this, ASP.NET has a slightly harder time figuring out how to use these objects. For one thing, you cannot set COM objects' properties at design time.

ASP.NET still supports using these objects with the `CreateObject` method of the `HttpServerUtility` class. This method takes a string that describes the object's location in the Registry, and uses that to set the object's properties. This string is known as the *`progId`*. The syntax is

```
Server.CreateObject(progId)
```

For example, in classic ASP pages, I/O operations were performed with the `FileSystemObject` from the Scripting library. This object provided some of the same functionality as the classes you learned about on Day 13, "Reading and Writing Files on the Web Server." To use this object in your pages, you would have to use the following code:

```
dim objFSO as object
objFSO = Server.CreateObject("Scripting.FileSystemObject")
```

For example, Listing 15.10 demonstrates how to display the path of a given file.

LISTING 15.10 Using COM Objects

```
 1:   <%@ Page Language="VB" %>
 2:
 3:   <script runat="server">
 4:      sub Page_Load(Sender as Object, e as EventArgs)
 5:         dim objFSO, objFile
 6:         objFSO = Server.CreateObject _
 7:            ("Scripting.FileSystemObject")
 8:         objFile = objFSO.GetFile _
 9:            (Server.MapPath("../day13/log.txt"))
10:
11:          lblMessage.Text = objFile.Path
12:       end sub
13:    </script>
14:
15:    <html><body>
16:       <asp:Label id="lblMessage" runat="server"/>
17:    </body></html>
```

ANALYSIS This creates a `Scripting.FileSystemObject` and `Scripting.File` object on lines 6 and 8. You can then use these objects to perform some I/O functionality, such as displaying the full pathname of the file. Figure 15.7 shows the output of this listing.

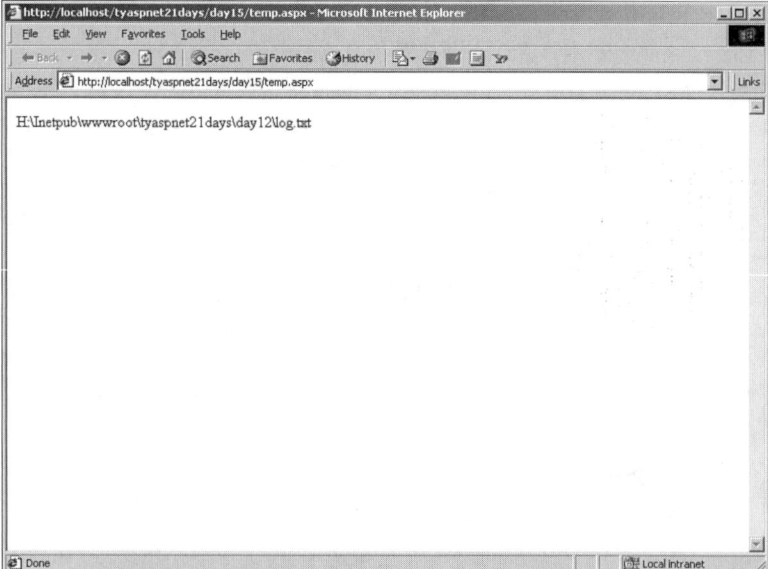

FIGURE 15.7

ASP.NET supports using older, unmanaged COM objects.

However, using `FileSystemObject` isn't very interesting because you already have better objects in the .NET Framework, such as `TextReaders` and `TextWriters`, which are fully object-oriented. The real benefit of .NET's capability to use COM objects is for developers who have already created many custom COM objects. Many businesses that have Web sites often use several COM objects to do the same types of operations that you used business objects to do earlier today. Having to rewrite all those COM objects would be a tremendous hassle.

Many other applications also expose their functionality through COM objects. For instance, you can create and manipulate Microsoft Word documents in your ASP.NET pages through the COM methods that Word exposes. All of Word's COM objects are unmanaged code, but that doesn't stop you from using them in the .NET Framework.

NEW TERM There's a drawback to using COM objects, however. Because there's no metadata associated with these objects, ASP.NET has a hard time determining what kind of data an object takes and returns, and often it has to convert data types. This process is known as *marshalling*. It impairs performance due to increased processing overhead, so you should avoid it if possible.

Luckily, the .NET Framework comes with a program that can convert unmanaged COM objects into managed .NET objects. This program, known as the Type Library Importer, examines the COM object and creates the appropriate metadata so that you can use it in your ASP.NET applications. This application is executed with the `tlbimp.exe` file.

For example, let's assume that you want to use the `FileSystemObject` in your ASP.NET pages, without the costs of marshalling. This object is stored in the `scrrun.dll` file, usually located in the `c:\winnt\system32` directory. Open up a command prompt and navigate to that directory. Type the following command into the window:

```
tlbimp scrrun.dll /out:scrrun_net.dll
```

This creates a new file called `scrrun_net.dll` from the `scrrun.dll` COM file, with the appropriate metadata. You should see something similar to the output in Figure 15.8.

Copy this new file into your assembly cache (`c:\inetpub\wwwroot\bin`). Now you can modify the previous listing to use the new, managed `FileSystemObject`. Listing 15.11 shows an example of using the new `FileSystemObject`.

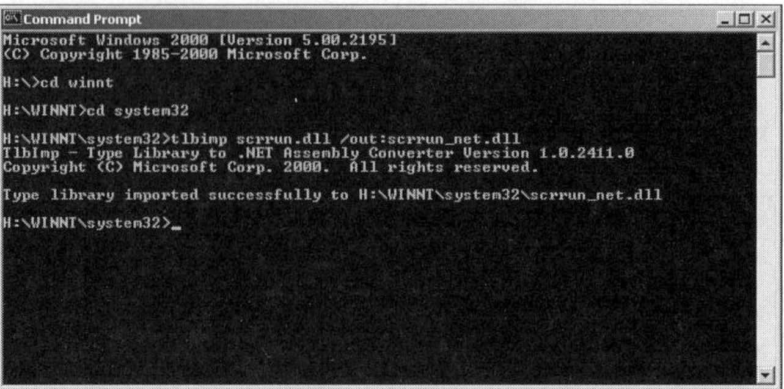

FIGURE 15.8

`tlbimp.exe` *imports older COM objects into the .NET Framework.*

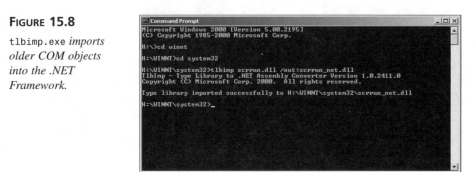

LISTING 15.11 Using Imported COM Objects

```
<%@ Page Language="VB" %>

<script runat="server">
   sub Page_Load(Sender as Object, e as EventArgs)
      dim objFSO as new Scrrun_net.FileSystemObject
      dim objFile as Scrrun_net.File
      objFile = objFSO.GetFile(Server.MapPath _
         ("../day12/log.txt"))

       lblMessage.Text = objFile.Path
    end sub
 </script>

 <html><body>
    <asp:Label id="lblMessage" runat="server"/>
 </body></html>
```

Now you're back to the familiar way of instantiating objects. Notice that the `FileSystemObject` now belongs to the `Scrrun_net` namespace, which is exactly the new filename you've created. This provides a large performance boost over the previous listing, and it allows you to use these older COM objects just as you would use any .NET object.

The .NET Framework doesn't actually convert the COM objects into .NET objects. Instead, it provides a wrapper that emits the necessary metadata—the existing object isn't changed. Thus, COM objects still lack the full support of the CLR.

That's Not ASP!

Traditional ASP developers may be in shock right about now. The greatest benefits of ASP.NET include being able to create DLLs without restarting the Web server, worrying about version conflicts, or registering the DLLs with `REGSVR32.exe`.

Previously, all COM objects needed to be registered manually, and the server needed to be restarted for changes to take effect. The first time you executed an ASP file that used a COM object, IIS would lock the DLL, meaning it was impossible to update it without restarting IIS. In effect, this prevented most types of remote administration of the server. The developer or an administrator had to be located at the machine to make changes. With ASP.NET, this is no longer necessary.

ASP.NET comes with a new configuration system that you'll learn about in Day 18 that can be modified easily by anyone with the proper permissions. The files placed in the `/bin` directory are loaded by the runtime automatically, and it's easy to make changes to these files because they're not locked by the server. Rather, ASP.NET makes shadow copies of these DLLs to execute, and leaves the original to be modified by you. You can just keep overwriting them without any worries. Changes are automatically picked up because the code is managed by the CLR.

This also means that Web application deployment is a simple process. Just copy the necessary files to the proper directories and the latest version is up and running. You don't need to restart the server or guide someone through the process if you're not on the premises.

Developing these DLLs in the .NET Framework is similar to the way you developed them previously. There are a few differences, such as the addition of namespaces and the new VB.NET compiler. However, much of the procedure for designing and writing the code remains unchanged.

If you're an ASP developer, you'll also be thankful that your libraries of COM objects aren't obsolete. ASP.NET can use these objects with the familiar `Server.CreateObject` method. This creates late-bound objects, just as in ASP. You can also use the Type Library Importer to provide these COM objects with some support for the CLR and early binding. However, in most cases you'll want to convert existing objects to take advantage of the many features of the .NET Framework.

Many of the concepts behind developing and using business objects remain the same in ASP.NET. It's the environment around the objects that has changed the most, which has caused a few welcome changes in the way you implement the objects.

Summary

Today you learned a lot about advanced Web development. Using and creating business objects is a big step toward becoming an expert ASP.NET developer. And as you learned today, using them with ASP.NET is simple!

Components are reusable programming elements that can provide additional functionality to your ASP.NET pages. They usually represent some form of real-world object, although they're not required to. Business objects are components that implement code that's applicable to your application in the middle layer of a three-tier application.

Building business objects is similar to building code-behind forms. You start with a class in VB.NET or C# and add the necessary functionality to describe your objects. You can compile them from the command line with the VB.NET or C# compiler. You then use them from your ASP.NET pages just as you would use any other object—declare a variable with the type of your new object, instantiate it with the `new` keyword, and use its properties and methods.

COM objects are older components developed in a non-.NET environment. These objects don't support the CLR and don't contain metadata. You can use them from your ASP.NET pages with the `Server.CreateObject` method by supplying a valid *`progId`*.

You can bring these COM objects into compliance with the CLR by using the Type Library Importer (`tlbimp.exe`) to produce the appropriate metadata. The Type Library Importer doesn't actually change the existing COM object, but rather creates an interpretation layer between the COM object and the CLR. This avoids the costs of marshalling the objects and lets you use them in your ASP.NET just as you use .NET objects.

Tomorrow you'll start looking at Web services, a new way to deliver applications over the Internet through ASP.NET.

Q&A

Q When should I consider moving common ASP.NET functionality into a business object?

A This is a highly subjective question. Many developers would say that all non-UI functionality should be moved into business objects, regardless of the application. However, this depends on the size of your application. When it only consists of a few pages, you might not need to add the complexity of a business object. Once you can logically see the tier divisions in your application, it may be a good idea to consider using business objects.

Q Can I create an object that expects parameters when instantiated?

A Absolutely. VB.NET and C# provide methods called *constructors* that allow you to specify how an object can be instantiated. This method is called `new` in VB.NET. In C#, it's simply the name of the class. For example:

```
'VB.NET
Class MyObject
   Public overloads Sub New()
      'do something
   End Sub

   Public overloads Sub New(strString as string)
      'do something
      ...
   end sub
End Class

//C#
class MyObject {
   public MyObject() {
      'do something
   }

   public MyObject(string strString) {
      //do something
      ...
   }
}
```

This class has two constructors—a default one that doesn't take any parameters, and one that takes a single `string` parameter. Inside the second constructor, you can perform any operation you want that uses that string. You could use the following line from an ASP.NET page:

```
dim objMyObject as new MyObject("hello!")
```

There are just a few things you need to know. Also be aware that you can only instantiate objects with the constructors you build. If you don't provide a constructor that doesn't take any parameters, you cannot do the following:

```
dim objMyObject as new MyObject
```

If you don't provide any constructors at all, VB.NET and C# automatically create one for you that doesn't take any parameters. Also, if you provide multiple constructors, be sure to use the `overloads` keyword in VB.NET to avoid errors that arise from having two methods with the same name.

For more information, see the VB.NET and C# documentation included with the .NET Framework SDK.

Q Is there any way to make managed .NET objects backward compatible with COM objects?

A You bet. The Assembly Registry tool (`regasm.exe`) will take the metadata from your .NET assemblies, export what is known as a type-library file, and register it, just like a COM object. You can then use your .NET objects just like older COM objects.

If you update the .NET object, you'll have to rerun `regasm.exe` for COM to notice the changes. This may require restarting IIS, depending on your situation.

Q How do I find out the filenames for COM objects? Or how do I find out the *`progId`* values?

A This can be rather difficult sometimes. The easiest way is to use a programming environment, such as Visual Studio.NET. These applications allow you to look through class libraries of available COM objects and find the filenames.

Or, you can go into the Windows Registry and search for the object you need. You can often find both the *`prodId`* and the filenames there.

Finally, you can use an application called the OLE/COM Object Viewer, usually bundled with MS Visual Studio, to determine the necessary strings.

For .NET objects, the methods are much easier. Usually, all of the .NET Framework classes are in files named after the namespaces. For example, the `System` namespace objects are in `System.dll`, and the `DataGrid` object is in `System.Data.dll`.

Workshop

This workshop will help reinforce the concepts you've learned in today's lesson. Answers can be found in Appendix A.

Quiz

1. What are the three levels of the three-tier application model?
2. True or false: You compile objects manually because they're specific to one page.
3. Write the command-line command to compile the object file `MyObject.vb`, referencing the `System` and `System.Web` namespaces in a subdirectory named `bin`.

4. Which of the following should be placed in a business object: a class implementing a `DataGrid`, a method that retrieves a connection string from a configuration file, a method that writes to the browser, or a property that describes the number of instances of this object?
5. True or false: You use `Server.CreateObject` to create business objects created in the .NET Framework.

Exercises

Modify the `User` object you created today to use the `Database` object you created earlier.

WEEK 3

DAY 16

Creating XML Web Services

Yesterday you learned about building components for your ASP.NET applications. These components can be used over the Internet to provide functionality for your ASP.NET pages. What happens, though, when you want these components to be available without having to use ASP.NET pages?

XML Web services are a new way to deploy applications. Using XML and other standard technologies, Web services enable applications and components to talk to other applications no matter where they're located, whether it's on the same machine or across the globe.

Today will be spent learning all about building Web services. They're a revolutionary way to think about Web applications and are an essential topic for ASP.NET developers. Tomorrow, you'll learn how use these services in your ASP.NET applications.

Today's lesson will cover the following:

- What Web services are
- How Web services work
- When to use Web services
- How to build Web services
- How to create Web services from existing business objects

The Way the Web Works—Revisited

When you began your journey through ASP.NET 15 days ago, you examined the fundamental operations of the Web—namely, the request/response model of operation. A client (such as a browser) requests a page from a Web server, and the server sends the page back to the client through a response.

Then you learned about the programmable Web. ASP.NET and other technologies allow you to perform tasks when the pages are requested. You can serve data to clients dynamically by providing programmatic capabilities on the server. Although ASP.NET extends this model by placing an event-driven mechanism on top, the fundamental mechanism of the Web is still the same: request/response.

ASP.NET pages provide a front end that allows users to interact with a Web site. Behind the UI, possibly in business objects, there may be some powerful application logic. What if the functionality in one Web site is so useful that other programmers want to include it in their sites? Or what if people want to use the functionality but can't use the UI, such as if they're working from a command prompt? How do you take advantage of the request/response model in these situations?

It's easy. Think of the way ASP.NET pages interact with business objects. They use methods and properties provided by the objects to perform some functionality, and the object may or may not return some information. In essence, you're sending a request to perform some function and waiting for a response.

Why can't any other application interact with the objects the same way? Just send a command over the Internet and wait for a response. Figure 16.1 illustrates this concept. The idea is very simple, but until now the technology to make it happen didn't exist.

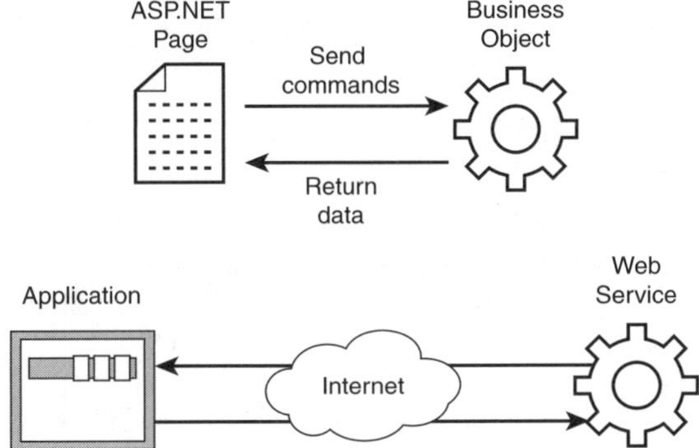

FIGURE 16.1
Applications should be able to interact with Web services just as ASP.NET pages interact with business objects.

In a more real-world example, one Web site should be able to make a request of a second Web site and wait for a response. The first Web site could interact with methods and properties available at that second. Figure 16.2 illustrates this concept with a stock price service. The user makes a request from a Web site, which in turn makes a request from a stock exchange site. The second Web site returns the data to the first, which can display the data to the user in any way it wants.

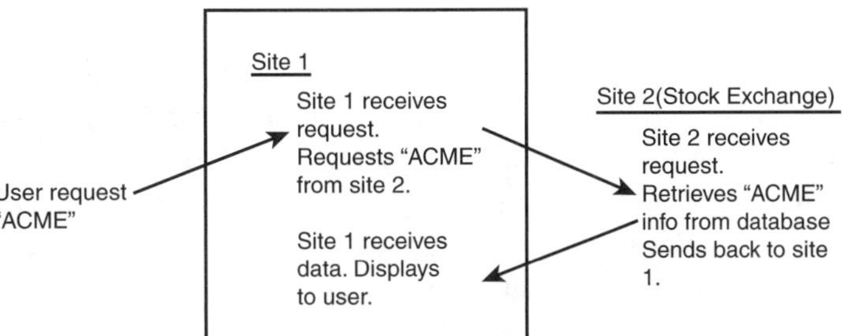

FIGURE 16.2
Web services allow Web sites to use functionality available on other sites.

Introduction to XML Web Services

NEW TERM Before you learn about Web services, it's a good idea to examine what a regular service is. When someone does a task for you, he's providing you a *service*. For example, you can go to a gas station and fill up your gas tank, or receive a tune-up. These are services provided to you by the gas station so that you don't have to do it yourself. Imagine if everyone had to have their own gas pump. Not an ideal situation. You also go to restaurants to receive food service. This is the type of task you can do yourself, but it requires work that you may not be willing to do. So a *service* is a value-added task provided by a person (or company) that frees you from having to do it yourself.

A Web service is the same thing. Web sites can provide a service that visitors, or even other Web sites, can take advantage of. Imagine a Web portal that presents information such as local and national news, weather information, sports scores, and other personalized content. It provides a service to visitors by compiling information from many different sources into one place. However, unless the portal has a very large budget and a huge staff, it's nearly impossible to keep writing up-to-date content for all these different sections. Instead, the portal can rely on content from other sites and simply provide the display mechanism. The portal still provides a service to users, but it relies on services provided by other sites.

This is already widespread in news reporting. The Associated Press provides a news service that newspapers can tap into. Next time you're reading a newspaper, look for articles written by the Associated Press. They've been pulled from a news service.

This type of system hasn't been widely used on the Internet because of complications involving how services should communicate. Many companies have attempted to build proprietary communication systems that allow services to be exchanged, but these are often too complex and expensive to be adopted by the general community. Also, problems have arisen due to the structure of security systems on the Internet. Many of these proprietary systems have difficulty transferring data across firewalls, which are designed to stop unauthorized traffic.

Web services, provided by the .NET Framework, are a solution to these and other problems. A Web service is a programmable object (just like a business object) that provides functionality that's accessible to any number of systems over the Internet. The reason Web services work is that they rely on standardized technologies for objects to communicate. Customized systems and proprietary mechanisms aren't necessary for Web services to work. All you need is an Internet connection.

XML Web services rely on the fact that any type of system or application can use HTTP, the standard protocol for Internet communication, and can use and convert XML, a standard for delivering data over the Web. XML Web services use XML to send commands and move data to and from objects residing on one server. The applications that use the data and send the commands can be written in any language, for any computer architecture, and they can be simple or complex. All the applications need to know is the Web service's location (basically, its Internet address).

Web services provide a new level of computing. In much the same way that you can assemble various objects and components to build an application, developers can assemble a group of Web services from completely different locations and use them in their own applications. Completely different platforms can now communicate easily, enabling disparate systems around the world to be tied together.

Web Service Scenarios

Imagine that you've built a component that performs simple calculation functions, like the calculator you built on Day 2, "Building ASP.NET Pages." Recall that the calculator performed simple arithmetic operations. Another Web site somewhere has built a component that can place orders to a home improvement store. Assuming these two components are Web services, a savvy developer could link them to create an application that allows a user to design her home. When the user needs to determine measurements and calculations, she uses your Web service's calculation functions. Then she places an order to the home improvement store through the other Web service. All this is accomplished from within one application, and the user doesn't need to know where the pieces of functionality came from. Figure 16.3 illustrates this example.

FIGURE 16.3

A single application can tie together many Web services.

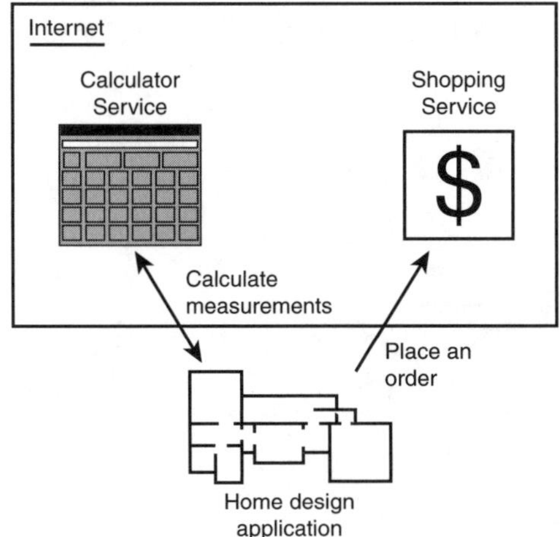

Web services can even be used by Internet applications. Imagine an e-commerce site that must calculate shipping charges for customers ordering supplies. Normally, this site would have to maintain an up-to-date table for calculating shipping costs based on the shipper, the shipping location, the priority, and so on. With Web services, the site can place a "call" to the shipping company directly, using a brief XML command, and receive the quotes instantly. Web services easily tie together applications that were once very difficult to assemble.

The Web Service Programming Model

As mentioned earlier, Web services use XML to communicate. But what exactly is being communicated?

NEW TERM The first messages that are sent usually involve a process known as *discovery*, which is how a client application finds and examines a Web service. The discovery process involves messages sent to and from the service that describe what the service can do. The client needs to know this before it tries to use the service. The service also tells the client what other kinds of messages it will accept.

The discovery process is not a necessary one. For instance, if a service doesn't want anyone to know about it, it can disable the discovery process. This is a protective measure so that not just anyone can use a particular Web service you've created.

Following discovery, the service must tell the client what it expects to receive (that is, which commands it will accept) and what it will send back. This is a necessary step so that both service and client know how to communicate with each other. This data is known as a Web service *description*. In a business object, the developer typically knows ahead of time which commands the object will support (through the documentation provided, for instance). The service description is essentially the documentation for the service in XML format.

Finally, messages are sent back and forth with commands to the service and data for the client, again in XML. Figure 16.4 illustrates the entire process.

FIGURE 16.4

Interaction with a Web service involves discovery, description, and commands.

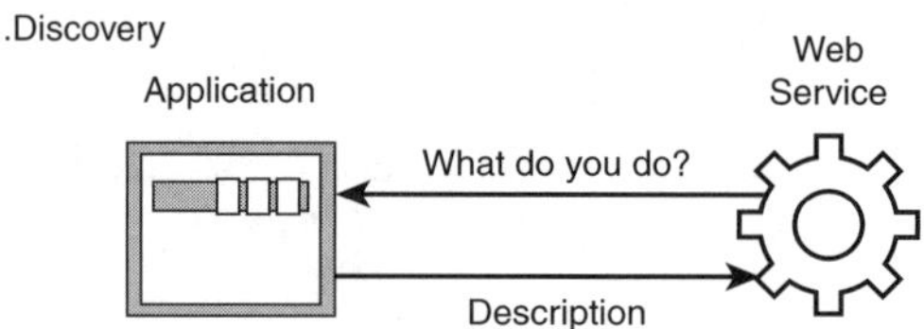

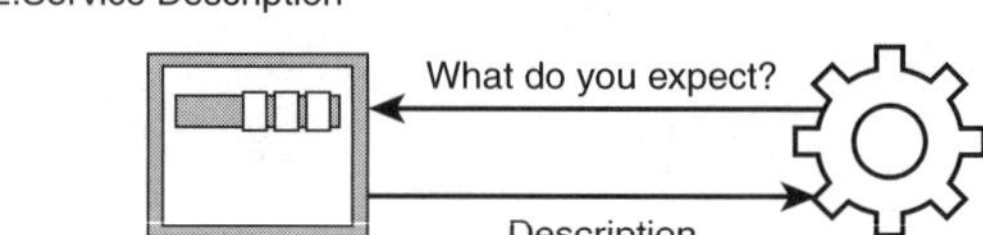

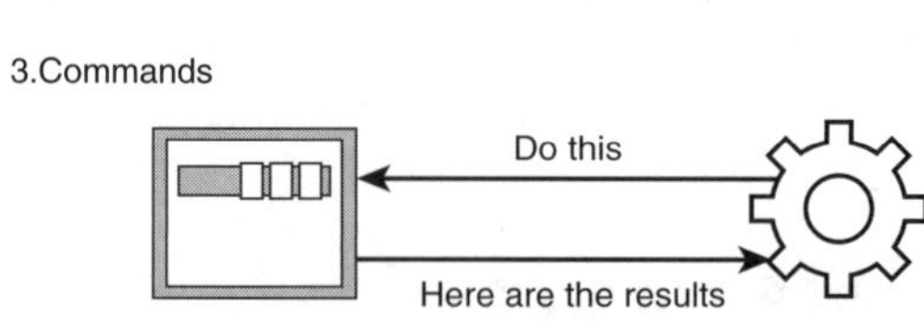

Luckily, ASP.NET provides most of the infrastructure needed to perform all these operations. After all, it can handle requests and responses, translate XML, and use business objects, making it ideal for Web service development. You just need to decide what your Web service will do and then build it.

Protocols for Accessing Web Services

You know that XML Web services rely on XML-formatted messages to send data and receive commands. Specifically, they use XML in the discovery process and service description. The messages containing commands aren't required to use XML, however. They can be sent in two additional methods, Http-Get and Http-Post, which are used in ASP.NET pages in querystrings and forms, respectively.

Web services support three protocols for interacting with clients: Http-Post, Http-Get, and the Simple Object Access Protocol (SOAP). Discussing these protocols in any depth is beyond the scope of this book, but you should have a basic understanding of them and how they affect Web services.

Http-Get

Http-Get is a standard protocol that enables clients to communicate with servers via HTTP. Http-Get is the way that you typically request Web pages. Think of the Http-Get operation as a client getting a Web page from a Web server. In essence, a client sends an HTTP request to the URL of the Web site, which responds with the appropriate HTML. Any parameters that are needed to process the request are attached via the querystring. For example:

```
http://www.myserver.com/default.aspx?id=Chris&sex=male
```

The parameters `id` and `sex` are passed as inputs to the Web server, attached to the end of the URL. An ASP.NET page could then retrieve these values with this code:

```
Request.Querystring("id")
Request.Querystring("sex")
```

Web services can use Http-Get and the querystring to pass commands and parameters, instead of XML messages. Note that information sent with Http-Get is part of the URL. Http-Get has limited functionality, however, because it can only send name/value pairs.

Http-Post

This protocol is similar to Http-Get, but instead of appending parameters onto the URL, it places them directly in the HTTP request message. When a client requests a page via Http-Post, it sends an HTTP request message with additional information that contains parameters and values. The server must then read and parse the request to figure out the parameters and their values. The most common use of Http-Post is in HTML forms.

For example, imagine an HTML form with the fields `id` and `sex`, as shown in the following code snippet:

```
<form method="post">
   <input type="Text" id="id">
   <input type="Text" id="sex">
```

```
    <input type="Submit" id="btSubmit" Value="Submit" />
</form>
```

When you submit this form, your browser takes the values entered in the text boxes and adds them to HTTP request message to the server. The server can retrieve these values with this syntax:

```
Request.Form("id")
Request.Form("sex")
```

This protocol, like the Http-Get protocol, is limited to sending name/value pairs.

Note that you can also send information via Http-Get with forms. In the form method, simply specify `"Get"` and the form will add the information to the querystring instead of the HTTP request header. For instance:

```
<form method="Get">
```

SOAP

The Simple Object Access Protocol is a relatively new standard that allows clients to send data to servers and vice versa. Unlike Http-Get and Http-Post, SOAP relies on XML to relay its information instead of an HTTP request message. This means that SOAP can send not only name/value pairs, but more complex objects as well, such as various rich data types, classes, objects, and others.

Sending SOAP messages is a bit different than what we're used to. With Http-Get, we send information via the querystring, and with Http-Post, we send it via form submissions. Both methods rely on the request/response model of operation. SOAP information is also transported via HTTP, but isn't limited to the request/response model. It can be used to send any types of messages, whether a client has requested them or not. Thus, SOAP is a very flexible medium to send data.

Many people get confused when comparing SOAP and XML. If SOAP is such a great way to send messages, why not use it instead of XML? The difference is that XML defines a data format, while SOAP defines a protocol for exchanging that data. SOAP relies on XML to send its messages. Plain XML is ideal for transporting most types of data. It's only when you want to transfer things such as commands and instructions that SOAP applies.

Because SOAP is based on XML, you can use it to transport data around the Web. XML is simply pure text, so it can be sent anywhere HTML pages can, including through firewalls. This is the default protocol that Web services use to communicate with clients.

Why Web Services?

Now that you know what Web services are, why should you use them?

Try to remember the world 10–15 years ago, before the rise of the Internet. Computer systems were usually standalone entities with no access to other systems. Applications were designed for use on one machine, with no sharing of data in any way. There was very little communication via computer within or between companies. Even interpersonal messages often had to be delivered by hand.

The Internet has changed the way the world communicates. It's also transformed the way applications are built. There are very few applications that don't take advantage of the Internet somehow. Many applications, such as instant messaging, rely on the Internet to provide users with data.

The next step in connecting users over the Internet is to deliver applications this way. Already, corporations are trying to tie traditional applications together into a single composite entity. When you consider the number of legacy applications still in use, this is a daunting task.

Web services provide a very simple mechanism for applications to communicate with each other. They allow components to be shared and functionality to be delivered to anyone, anywhere. Imagine never having to install another program on your computer again—simply connect to the Web and access the service.

All this may be great, but how do Web services make Web development better? One of the ways is through code reuse. Recall that one of the reasons for using business objects is that you can reuse the same code over and over again without having to create it each time. Even branching logic such as functions and subroutines promotes code reuse (see Day 3, "Using Visual Basic.NET and C#."). With Web services, you can now reuse code that other people have developed without having to download, copy, or install anything. This saves you time and energy, enabling you to easily add functionality to your ASP.NET applications.

Another benefit of Web services is ease of deployment and maintenance. No longer will you have to install custom objects or applications on many different systems. Instead, users will have a standard framework for accessing your application—directly over the Internet. Also, when changes need to be made, you won't have to issue a new release or an update. Simply make the changes in your Web service in one place, and all clients will benefit from it automatically. (Unless, of course, the change removes functionality that clients depend on, in which case they have to adjust. Either way, the process is easier for the developer.)

Building a Web Service

There are several steps to building a Web service, including building the actual functionality and the service description. The following sections will take you through each step with a simple Web service.

Building the Functionality

Web service files are essentially VB.NET or C# source files that end in an `.asmx` extension. A Web service, then, is represented by a class that derives from the `WebService` class. Listings 16.1 and 16.2 show a very simple Web service.

LISTING 16.1 A Simple Web Service in VB.NET

```
<%@ WebService Language="VB" Class="Calculator" %>

Imports System.Web.Services

public Class Calculator : Inherits WebService
   <WebMethod()> Public Function Add(intA As Integer, _
      intB As Integer) As Integer
       Return(intA + intB)
   End Function
 End Class
```

LISTING 16.2 A Simple Web Service in C#

```
<%@ WebService Language="C#" Class="Calculator" %>

using System.Web.Services;

public class Calculator : WebService {
   [WebMethod] public int Add(int intA,
      int intB) {
       return intA + intB;
   }
 }
```

ANALYSIS Save this file as `c:\inetpub\wwwroot\tyaspnet21days\day16\Calculator.asmx` (or `calculator.cs.asmx`). On line 1 you see the `@ WebService` directive, which is similar to the `@ Page` directive and declares that this file represents a Web service. This directive supports the familiar `Language` attribute, which you set to `VB` or `C#`. The directive also supports one other attribute, `Class`. This is the name of the Web service class that you're developing. In fact, on line 5 you see that the class name is indeed `Calculator`. A bit later, you'll learn about a neat feature of this attribute.

Next, you import the `System.Web.Services` namespace on line 3. This allows you to use all the necessary methods and classes of Web services. The class that you define on line 5 must inherit from the `WebService` class in this namespace.

> **Note** You can have many classes in one `.asmx` file, but only one may be used for the Web service—the one declared with the `WebService` directive at the top of the page.

Next, let's examine the only function in this class. The declaration for the `Add` method is pretty standard, with two notable items. The first is that the method must be declared `public`, meaning any other class or object can use it. If not, clients couldn't access this method of the Web service.

The second is the `<WebMethod()>` attribute, which tells ASP.NET that this method is available as a service to other applications. This is a very important attribute that must be present in order for clients to access methods, and you'll examine it a bit further later today in "The `WebMethod` Attribute."

Thus, methods that you want a client to access must be declared with `Public` and must contain the `<WebMethod()>` attribute.

Let's view this page in a browser. Figure 16.5 shows the output.

This is very interesting. What happened to the code? And where did the UI portion come from?

Like ASP.NET pages, `.asmx` files are compiled upon the first request. ASP.NET then serves up the service description whenever the page is requested. Figure 16.5, though in XML form, is what a client would see when he tries to access your service. The response tells the client the class name, `Calculator`, and the methods and properties that are publicly available for use. Click on Service Description on the right side of the page. This directs you to the same page with a querystring appended:

```
http://localhost/tyaspnet21days/day16/Calculator.asmx?WSDL
```

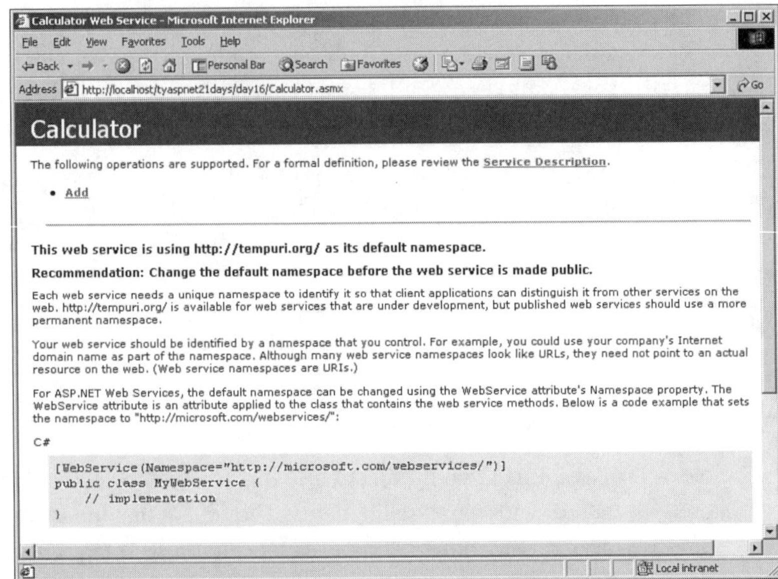

FIGURE 16.5
Viewing an `.asmx` file in a Web browser.

The WSDL tells ASP.NET that you want to see the service description in XML form. Figure 16.6 shows the XML for this service.

That's quite a bit of XML for one small Web service. This XML file uses a standard format called the Service Description Language (SDL) to tell clients what can be done with this service. We won't delve into this XML in any depth, but you should notice some familiar items. For instance, there's the following near the top of the output:

```
<s:element name="Add">
   <s:complexType>
      <s:sequence>
         <s:element name="intA" type="s:int"/>
         <s:element name="intB" type="s:int"/>
      </s:sequence>
   </s:complexType>
</s:element>
<s:element name="AddResponse">
    <s:complexType>
       <s:sequence>
```

```
            <s:element name="AddResult" type="s:int"/>
         </s:sequence>
      </s:complexType>
   </s:element>
```


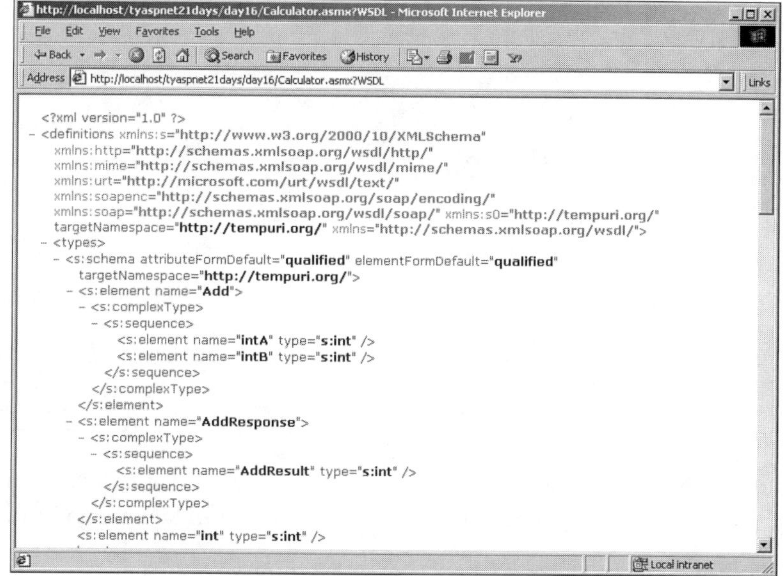

FIGURE 16.6

The XML service description for your Web service.

ANALYSIS The first element describes your method, `Add`, and the parameters it takes. The second element describes the response from your method, aptly named `AddResponse`. The rest of the file describes how the Http-Get, Http-Post, and SOAP protocols should access this service.

Let's go back to the regular view of the `.asmx` file. Click the `Add` method and find out what else ASP.NET has in store for you. Figure 16.7 shows this page.

It's clear that there are a lot of parts to Web services. This page, known as the *HTML description page*, details a lot of interesting items and even lets you test out the method. Enter two values in the text boxes and click the Invoke button. A new window opens up with the XML-formatted answer. This is exactly the response a client would receive after calling this Web method. The next three sections of the page, SOAP, HTTP GET, and HTTP POST, show examples of the different methods that these protocols must use to access this `Add` method.

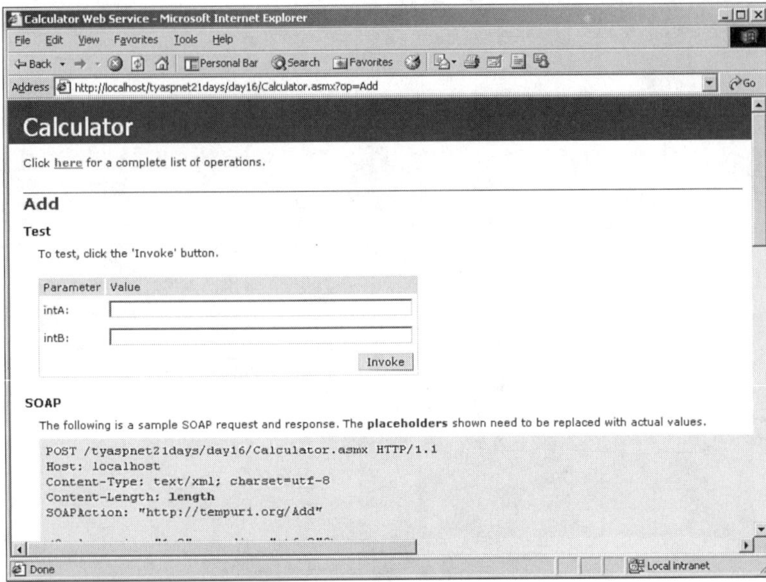

FIGURE 16.7

A detailed description of the `Add` *method.*

This page allows you to test your services. Note that because you're using a form to submit the data, you're using the Http-Post protocol to communicate with the service.

Enabling Discovery

Discovery is the process by which a client application finds a Web service and determines what it can do. This information is supplied by the service description, but most clients won't know (and *shouldn't* know) the filename of this description. Therefore, enabling discovery means giving clients links to these descriptions.

Discovery is enabled through `.disco` files for the Web service. These files are XML documents that contain links to descriptions of the service. Clients can access this file to figure out more about the available Web services.

Creating `.disco` files is simple. Listing 16.3 contains a sample discovery file for your calculator service.

LISTING 16.3 The Discovery File for Your Calculator Service

```
<?xml version="1.0"?>
<disco:discovery
   xmlns:disco="http://schemas.xmlsoap.org/disco/"
   xmlns:scl="http://schemas.xmlsoap.org/disco/scl">
   <scl:contractRef ref="Calculator.asmx?WSDL"/>
</disco:discovery>
```

ANALYSIS Save this file as `calculator.disco`. As you can see, this file is very simple because it only contains a link to the description of your service, shown on line 5. The additional namespaces provided by the `xmlns` tags specify the URLs (or namespaces) that define which valid names the `scl` and `disco` tags can use. In other words, the `xmlns` tags provide links to standard definitions of the `scl` and `disco` tags. Without these namespaces, your application won't know what to do with these extra tags.

The `disco:discovery` tag provides the links for a client to follow if he wants to find out about a Web service. These links can be to other `.disco` documents or to service descriptions. Service description links are provided with the `scl` tags, as shown on line 5. To provide a link to another `.disco` file, use the following syntax:

```
<disco:discoveryRef ref="link" />
```

Request this file from your browser and you should see the same XML file.

> The discovery file isn't necessary for clients to access Web services. If they know the proper URL, they can simply access the service description itself. Discovery documents only help anonymous clients find Web services that you want to make publicly available.

The `WebMethod` Attribute

Web services have methods just as regular classes and business objects do. However, only the methods marked with the `WebMethod` attribute (as shown on line 6 of Listing 16.1) are viewable to clients of the Web service. Recall from yesterday that only public variables are accessible to ASP.NET pages using a business object, while private methods are only viewable by the object itself. In the same way, `WebMethod` restricts access to clients.

Web methods act like regular class methods. They can interact with the ASP.NET `Session` or `Cache` objects (see Days 4, "Using ASP.NET Objects with C# and VB.NET," and 14, "Using ASP.NET's Improved Caching Capabilities"), they provide buffered responses just as ASP.NET pages do (Day 4), and they can interact with databases and data sources. In essence, they are exactly the same as regular class methods, with one, large, exception: They can be accessed over the Internet.

This is a very important concept. After all, the methods of a class are one of the most important parts; they represent how a user will interact with the class. Methods with the `WebMethod` attribute treat all callers as if they were local. In other words, there is no difference if you call a Web method from an ASP.NET page in the same directory as the

.asmx file, or from another server halfway across the world. This attribute is the key that allows Web services to be usable by clients; let's examine it further. The WebMethod attribute has a lot of interesting features. It's represented by the WebMethodAttribute class, which operates just like any other .NET class, with properties and methods. Thus, when you insert the attribute as follows, you're actually creating a new instance of the WebMethodAttribute class:

```
<WebMethod()> Public Function Add(intA As Integer)
```

Assigning values for the properties of this class is a bit different from what you're used to. For example:

```
'VB.NET_
<WebMethod(Description:="Adds two numbers")>
➥Public Function Add(intA As Integer, intB As Integer)

//C#
[WebMethod(Description="Adds two numbers")]
➥public int Add(int intA, int intB) {
```

You specify the property and value in the parentheses directly in the function declaration. Notice the colon before the equal sign in the VB.NET version—this means that you're initializing a property, and not supplying parameters. If you simply used:

```
<WebMethod(Description="Adds two numbers")>
```

ASP.NET would think that Description="Adds two numbers" is the name of a variable that should be used to construct the WebMethod. This makes for an odd-looking function declaration, but it lets you set properties for this WebMethod. Multiple properties are separated by commas:

```
<WebMethod(Description:="Adds two numbers", EnableSession:=False)>_
➥Public Function Add(intA As Integer, intB As Integer)
```

Table 16.1 describes the properties you can set.

TABLE 16.1 WebMethod Properties

Property	*Description*
BufferResponse	Specifies whether or not to buffer the output from the Web service. The default value is true, which specifies that any generated response is buffered on the server before being sent to the client. The data is sent back in chunks. If you're returning large amounts of data, it may be beneficial to set this property to false. This causes the data to stream to the client, providing slightly better performance. Otherwise, this property should always be true.

TABLE 16.1 continued

Property	*Description*
`CacheDuration`	Web methods are cacheable, just as ASP.NET pages are. This property gives the number of seconds the response should be cached. The default is 0, meaning caching is disabled. When this property is set to anything other than 0, the response is cached for that number of seconds and all subsequent calls to this method from the client will retrieve the data from the cache, rather than executing the method again. When you're sending large amounts of data, this property should be enabled. See Day 14 for more caching suggestions.
`Description`	This property provides a description of the Web method for clients. This description is viewable in the service description. The default value is `String.Empty`.
`EnableSession`	Specifies whether or not session state is enabled for the current method. If this is enabled (which it is by default), you can use the `Session` object to store data. If you don't need to store any data in session variables, you may want to turn this option off. You'll receive an increase in performance.
`MessageName`	This parameter is the name by which the Web method is called within the data that's sent to and from the service. By default, it's the same as the Web method's name. This parameter is most often used to make method names unique. For instance, if you had two overloaded `Add` methods that each took different parameters, you could use `MessageName` to distinguish the methods. This property must be unique to the service description.
`TransactionOption`	Like databases, Web services can also participate in transactions. Within a transaction, all code will be treated as a do-or-die situation. If one line fails, they all fail, and any changes that were made are rolled back. See Day 12, "Employing Advanced Data Techniques," for more information on transactions. The possible values for this property are `Disabled`—Method runs without a transaction. `NotSupported`—No transaction support. `Supported`—Transactions are supported, but the method isn't run within one.

16

Table 16.1 continued

Property	Description
	`Required`—A transaction is required; creates a new transaction. `RequiresNew`—A transaction is required; creates a new transaction.
`TypeID`	A unique ID to identify this attribute. Used to distinguish between two attributes that are of the same type.

Deploying Web Services

Deploying Web services is a simple matter. Since the Common Language Runtime handles all management of ASP.NET applications, just copy the appropriate `.asmx` files, `.disco` files, and custom business objects to the proper directories. Deploying applications has never been easier!

It's a common practice to include a `web.config` file for the directory containing the services (Day 18, "Configuring and Deploying ASP.NET Applications," will discuss this file in more detail). Often you'll want to implement security mechanisms for these services so that anonymous users don't come along and take advantage of your work. For example, if you develop a Web service for a company, it will most likely be used to generate revenue. If anyone could come along and use the service, the company would never make any money. Securing the Web service (as we'll learn about tomorrow) prevents this situation, and allows you to control who has access to your services.

The directory that you're deploying to must be flagged as an Internet Information Server (IIS) application directory. Otherwise, these services won't be executed and won't be exposed to clients.

Any directory you've created that allows ASP.NET pages to function is an IIS application directory.

Creating a Web Service from an Existing Business Object

You can also create a Web service from an existing business object so that you don't need to rewrite all the functionality. However, you must modify the existing object slightly to enable service support.

Let's modify the database business object you created in yesterday's lesson, "Using Business Objects." You need to do three things to turn this into a Web service: inherit from the `System.Web.Services.WebService` class, add the `WebMethod` attribute for the methods you want to expose, and change the `OleDbDataReader` into a `DataSet` because the former isn't transferable via XML (more on that later). Listing 16.4 shows this modified class, which is renamed `DatabaseService`.

You can leave the database class as-is and simply create a copy of the class in the same file with a slightly different name. (For instance, append the word "service" to the end.) Only the class that inherits from `WebService` will be exposed as a service. This allows you to create multiple versions of an object in one file!

LISTING 16.4 Modifying Your Database Business Object for Use as a Service

```
Imports System
Imports System.Data
Imports System.Data.OleDb
Imports System.Web.Services

Namespace TYASPNET

   Public Class DatabaseService : Inherits WebService
      private objConn as OleDbConnection
       private objCmd as OleDbCommand

       <WebMethod()> public function SelectSQL(strSelect as _
          string) as DataSet
          try
             objConn = new OleDbConnection("Provider=" & _
                "Microsoft.Jet.OLEDB.4.0;" & _
                "Data Source=c:\ASPNET\data\banking.mdb")
             dim objDataCmd as OleDbDataAdapter = new _
                OleDbDataAdapter(strSelect, objConn)

             Dim objDS as new DataSet
             objDataCmd.Fill(objDS, "tblUsers")
             return objDS
          catch ex as OleDbException
             return nothing
          end try
       end function

       <WebMethod()> public function ExecuteNonQuery _
```

LISTING 16.4 continued

```
30:            (strQuery as string) as Boolean
31:            try
32:               objConn = new OleDbConnection("Provider=" & _
33:                  "Microsoft.Jet.OLEDB.4.0;" & _
34:                  "Data Source=c:\ASPNET\data\banking.mdb")
35:               objCmd = new OleDbCommand(strQuery, objConn)
36:               objCmd.Connection.Open()
37:               objCmd.ExecuteNonQuery
38:               objCmd.Connection.Close()
39:               return true
40:            catch ex as OleDbException
41:               return false
42:            end try
43:         end function
44:
45:      End Class
46:
47:   End Namespace
```

ANALYSIS Save this file as `DatabaseService.vb`. On line 4, you import the additional namespace, `System.Web.Services`. In your class declaration on line 8, you inherit from the `WebService` class in that namespace. Next, you add `<WebMethod()>` to the functions you want to expose as services. Finally, in `SelectSQL`, you change the `OleDbDataReader` to a `DataSet` and change the `OleDbCommand` object into an `OleDbDataAdapter`. That's all there is to it. Recompile this file with the following command:

```
vbc /t:library /out:..\..\bin\TYASPNET.dll /r:System.dll
/r:System.Data.Dll /r:System.Web.Services.dll
/r:System.Xml.dll DatabaseService.vb ..\day15\User.vb
```

This command compiles the new `DatabaseService.vb` file and `User.vb` from yesterday's lesson into the library file `TYASPNET.dll`. You also reference two new DLLs: `System.Web.Services.dll` and `System.Xml.dll`. The reason for referencing the first file is obvious; the second reference is included because it contains necessary methods to send the `DataSet` via XML. For more information on the VB.NET compiler, see yesterday's lesson, "Using Business Objects."

The new objects should now be saved in the assembly cache and loaded from it. Let's create the `.asmx` file that will allow clients to access this object. See Listing 16.5.

Listing 16.5 The `.asmx` File That Exposes Your Database Service

```
<%@ WebService Class="TYASPNET.DatabaseService" %>
```

That's all there is to it. You only have to change the class name to reference the database service you just compiled. Save this file as `Database.asmx` and request it from the browser. You should see the two exposed methods, `SelectSQL` and `ExecuteNonQuery`.

If you use a precompiled object for your Web service, it must be located in the assembly cache in order for ASP.NET to locate and use it.

Click on the `SelectSQL` method and enter a SQL query in the test portion of the page: `Select * FROM tblUsers`. Then click the Invoke button. You should see something similar to Figure 16.8.

Figure 16.8

The data returned from your database service.


```
<?xml version="1.0" ?>
- <DataSet xmlns="http://tempuri.org/">
 - <xsd:schema id="NewDataSet" targetNamespace="" xmlns=""
     xmlns:xsd="http://www.w3.org/2000/10/XMLSchema" xmlns:msdata="urn:schemas-
     microsoft-com:xml-msdata">
   - <xsd:element name="tblUsers">
     - <xsd:complexType>
       - <xsd:all>
           <xsd:element name="FirstName" minOccurs="0" type="xsd:string" />
           <xsd:element name="LastName" minOccurs="0" type="xsd:string" />
           <xsd:element name="Address" minOccurs="0" type="xsd:string" />
           <xsd:element name="City" minOccurs="0" type="xsd:string" />
           <xsd:element name="State" minOccurs="0" type="xsd:string" />
           <xsd:element name="Zip" minOccurs="0" type="xsd:string" />
           <xsd:element name="Phone" minOccurs="0" type="xsd:string" />
           <xsd:element name="UserID" minOccurs="0" type="xsd:int" />
           <xsd:element name="Password" minOccurs="0" type="xsd:string" />
           <xsd:element name="UserName" minOccurs="0" type="xsd:string" />
         </xsd:all>
       </xsd:complexType>
     </xsd:element>
   - <xsd:element name="NewDataSet" msdata:IsDataSet="true">
     - <xsd:complexType>
       - <xsd:choice maxOccurs="unbounded">
           <xsd:element ref="tblUsers" />
         </xsd:choice>
       </xsd:complexType>
```


This XML document defines the structure of the `DataSet` your service returned. As you scroll down, you'll see the actual data values from the table. The client that receives this XML document can easily transform this object back into a `DataSet` if necessary.

Returning Data from Services

As demonstrated, Web services can return many types of data. This is because Web services are built on top of XML, which is very powerful for representing data. Even though XML is text-based, it uses a type naming system that allows other applications to determine data types easily.

For example, you know that `DataSets` are fundamentally represented as XML data in a computer's memory, so it's easy to extrapolate that a `DataSet` can be sent via XML. XML also has representations for strings, integers, arrays, and `DateTimes`, among other things. Table 16.2 lists the various data types that Web services can transmit.

TABLE 16.2 Supported Web Service Data Types

Type	*Description*
Arrays	Web services can send arrays of any of the types described below, including `DataSets`, primitive types, classes, and `XmlNodes`.
Classes	Classes with public properties.
`DataSets`	The `DataSet` is internally represented as XML by ADO.NET, so it can be transferred by Web services. Note that `DataSets` are the only ADO.NET data stores that are transferable. `DataReaders` and such are not.
Primitives	Primitives include `byte`, `Boolean`, `char`, `DateTime`, `Decimal`, `Double`, `GUID`, `int32`, `int16`, `int64`, `single`, `uint16`, `uint32`, `uint64`, and `XmlQualifiedName`.
`XmlNodes`	The .NET `XmlNode` class, an in-memory representation of XML data. See Day 11, "Using XML in ASP.NET."

A Web service can return all the types described in Table 16.2, but it's more restrictive about which types it will accept as parameters.

When you use SOAP to pass commands and parameters from the client to the service, you can use any of the previously described data types because SOAP is based on XML.

If you use either Http-Get or Http-Post, however, you're restricted to the types that these protocols can handle. That is, you can use a subset of the primitive types and arrays of primitives. Http-Get and Http-Post are also restricted to sending only name/value pairs, which excludes more complex types of data such as classes or `DataSets`.

That's Not ASP!

Web services are completely new to ASP.NET, so you've been treated to something new today if you're a traditional ASP developer. However, the ideas behind Web services, such as intercommunication of various disparate systems, are similar to COM objects. (See yesterday's lesson for more information on COM objects.)

The goal of COM was to allow developers to build applications composed of various components. Because these components relied on the COM protocol to communicate, they could be developed in different programming languages. COM suffered from being confined to a specific platform, though—Windows.

Web services go beyond COM because they don't adopt any proprietary protocols or binary formats of communication between objects. Instead, Web services are completely based on the open standards XML and HTTP, which means they truly allow interoperability between any disparate systems.

The concept of deploying applications over the Internet as services isn't completely new either. Previous attempts, similar to COM, have relied on complex proprietary standards, which limited their usefulness. It's the simplicity of XML and HTTP that makes Web services so effective.

Summary

Today you learned about a new way to deliver applications: over the Internet as Web services. Web services are an integral part of ASP.NET, and they use the XML and HTTP standards to allow components to talk to each other over the Web.

Web services work in three stages: discovery, a description of services, and command communication. Discovery is an optional process that allows clients to find out about a Web service; specifically, where it's located. The service description, provided in an XML-based standard called the Service Description Language, tells clients which methods are available to use remotely and which types of data are expected and returned. Finally, the service and client use these descriptions to send commands to the server and data back to the client.

Three protocols are used for Web service communication: Http-Get, Http-Post, and the Simple Object Access Protocol (SOAP). The first two allow the communication of simple name/value pairs of data. The last one, based on XML, is able to deliver much wider-ranging types of data.

You build Web services in `.asmx` files, just as you do with business objects. The difference is that you inherit from the `WebService` class, and all methods that will be exposed as services must use the `WebMethods` attribute. At a minimum, the `.asmx` file must contain the following:

```
<%@ WebService Class="class" %>
```

The `WebService` directive tells ASP.NET that this file contains or references a class that should be exposed as a Web service. The *`class`* attribute is the name of the class to expose. This class can be either contained within the `.asmx` file or separately compiled as a business object.

You enable discovery by using `.disco` files, which are XML documents that contain links to Web service descriptions. These files can be built manually, to define a specific service, or dynamically, to define a group of services available on a server.

Finally, you can view the `.asmx` files through the browser to see an HTML description page, which describes the methods available and allows you to test the functionality directly through Http-Post. You also can see the service description as XML from the `.asmx` page.

After today, you should be comfortable developing Web services and deploying them on your servers. Tomorrow's lesson will continue the discussion of Web services, and you'll learn how to use them from the client's side.

Q&A

Q How will Web services affect the average home user?

A Chances are that everyday home users won't see them in action for quite some time. Web services often require a high-bandwidth connection to the Web, such as DSL or cable modem. Right now, there aren't enough people connected to the Web this way to warrant full-scale use of Web services.

The most likely place you'll see Web services is within businesses that maintain large and strong networks. Information technology groups will find it much cheaper and easier to manage user workstations because they won't have to install and maintain applications on every single computer.

Q Is there any way to test a Web service with an Http-Get method? How about with SOAP?

A Absolutely. Simply append the function you want to test with any parameters to the address of the `.asmx` file. For example, you could use the following URL to test the calculator service's `add` method:

```
http://localhost/tyaspnet21days/day16/
Calculator.asmx/Add?intA=1&intB=2
```

Separate the function name from the URL with a forward slash, and append the parameters as you would with a querystring. This tests the service via the Http-Get protocol, and the returned XML data will be displayed in the same window.

You'll learn about using SOAP to test the service tomorrow when you examine using Web services from the client side.

Q Do my `.disco` files need to be named the same way as the Web service files?

A No, but it's conventional to do so.

Workshop

This workshop will help reinforce the concepts you've learned in today's lesson. The answers can be found in Appendix A.

Quiz

1. What's a Web service?
2. What does SOAP stand for, and what does it do?
3. What's a service description?
4. What class (including namespace) must a Web service inherit from?
5. Write an arbitrary Web method that enables caching and disables session state.
6. True or false: A Web method can take advantage of intrinsic ASP.NET objects, such as `Session` and cache.
7. True or false: A Web method can return a `DataSet`.

Exercises

1. Examine the XML service description for the database service you created earlier today. Try to understand each of the tags, recalling the discussions on XML and XML schemas. Note that much of the file describes how the different protocols (Http-Get, SOAP, and so on) are to send and receive data.

2. Create a Web service that converts one unit of measurement into another. This method should take three parameters: a value, a unit to convert from, and a unit to convert to. Allow the user to convert to and from the following: millimeters, centimeters, inches, feet, meters, yards, miles, and kilometers. Don't forget to test it with the HTML description page!

   (Don't worry if you don't know the exact conversions between units of measurement. Just make something up.)

WEEK 3

DAY 17

Consuming and Securing XML Web Services

Yesterday you learned all about creating Web Services: what they are, why we use them, and how to build them. Today's lesson will continue this examination of XML Web Services, looking at how to use a Web service through an ASP.NET page.

Today's lesson will cover the following:

- How to use discovery to find out about an existing Web Service
- How to generate proxy classes that access the service
- How to implement those proxy classes from your ASP.NET pages
- How to secure your services using SOAP headers

Consuming XML Web Services

Yesterday you learned how to use Web Services to build services that can be accessed over the Internet. For example, a site might want to offer a set of financial calculation functions. Once this Web service is designed and deployed on the site's Web server, anyone can come along and benefit from its functionality.

NEW TERM Suppose the developer of a banking Web site wants to use one of these financial calculator services to do interest calculations for CDs. His banking application must *consume* your service—in other words, access and use its methods. *Consumption* simply means that a client uses the methods available from a Web Service. The site's visitors can use the calculator without ever knowing where it came from.

When you go to a gas station, the attendants are providing you a service. Therefore, you're the consumer of the service. You can take advantage of any resources the gas station has to offer, such as a gas pump, the attendants' time and service, and any other convenience items they sell. (Naturally, you have to pay for these services, but that's irrelevant at this point.) This saves you the trouble of building your own gas pump or servicing your own car.

The consumer of a Web Service can do the exact same thing. It visits a service and consumes any resources that are available. Your computer could access a word processing service, for example. All the features of that service would be available to you, and you wouldn't have to buy and install a word processor yourself.

A Web service consumer can be nearly any application: a desktop computer, an ASP.NET page, or even a mobile device such as a cell phone! Today's lesson focuses on using ASP.NET pages as the consumers for Web services.

There are three stages in consuming a Web service:

1. Gathering information about the service, a process known as *discovery*.
2. Generating a proxy of the service.
3. Using the proxy to invoke the available services.

Caution

> Don't confuse a Web Service client with an Internet client. The former is an application or Web site that consumes a Web Service. The latter is an application that is used to browse the Web, such as a browser. A Web Service client accesses services, whereas a Web client accesses Web sites. The two are distinct, and you should fully understand the difference before attempting to build service clients.

Recall from yesterday that discovery is the process by which a client finds out about a Web Service. When you go to a new restaurant, first you read the menu to see what they serve. Consumers do the same for Web Services. They need to know what a service does before they use it.

This information is provided by the service description of the Web Service (see yesterday's lesson). Recall that this description is an XML file generated by the service. The client accesses this file to find out about the service; in other words, it reads the menu of features. The client then creates its own copy of the menu for use later.

Recall the `.disco` files from yesterday. These files are intended solely to aid clients. They provide links to the service descriptions available on a server that the client can use to find its way around. Note that a client can skip these `.disco` files if it already knows the exact URL of the service description.

Generating a proxy of the service is an interesting step. Here's an analogy: You want to go to a restaurant, but you can't because you don't have a valid driver's license. However, you convince your mother to take you in her car. She's acting on your behalf by taking you somewhere you can't go on your own. In other words, she's a *proxy* between you and the restaurant.

Web Service consumers are very similar. They know there's a service out there to consume, but they can't get to it themselves. They need a proxy to assist them. This proxy provides the mechanisms that transport information back and forth from the service to the client.

When you access a service from your ASP.NET page, you want it to be easily available. You don't want to have to worry about how to send XML messages, or transform your commands into the proper formats, or retrieve the returned data. Ideally, you want to be able to access the service as though it were a business object on your own computer, which means you only have to create an instance of the object.

Thus, you generate a proxy of the service. This is a class that resides on your computer and encapsulates all the complex functionality needed to communicate with the service. It allows you to interact with the service just as you would with any other object. In fact, the proxy will contain methods and properties that correspond to the ones provided by the service, and they will be named identically. Thus, if you know which methods the service offers, you can call the proxy with the same names. Figure 17.1 illustrates the process of using a proxy.

The proxy is generated from information in the service description. This tells the proxy everything it needs to know about how to send commands and what to expect in return. You'll learn more about this later today, in "Consuming a Web Service Through an ASP.NET Page."

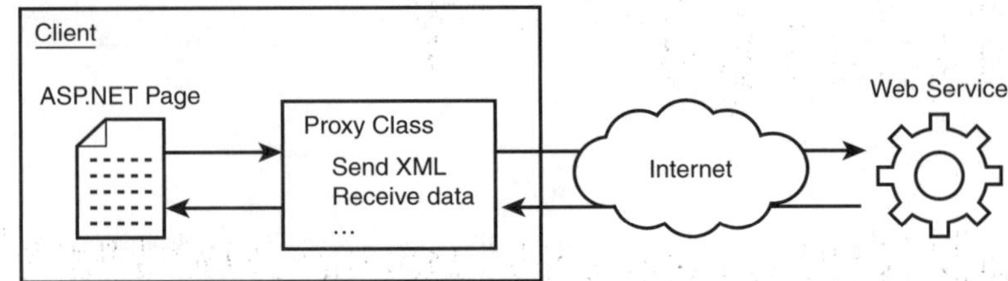

FIGURE 17.1
The proxy acts as an intermediary between a client and a service.

Finally, the consumer can use the Web Service's methods through the proxy class, just as it would any other object. All of this is transparent to an end user, and it isn't difficult for a developer to implement. Figure 17.2 illustrates the steps involved from the consumer's side.

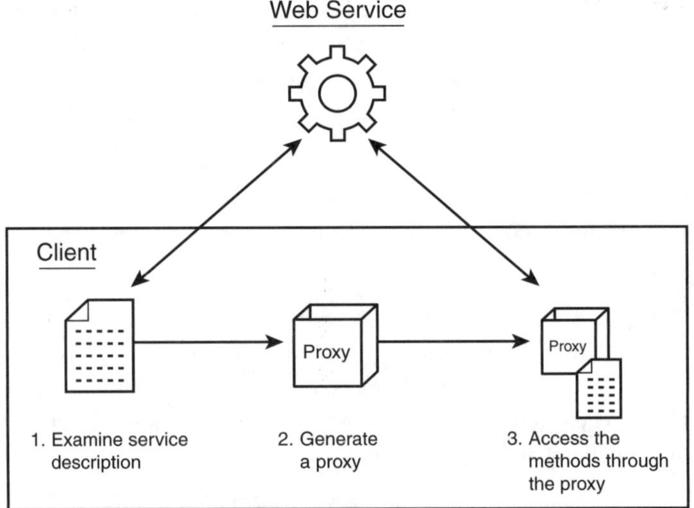

FIGURE 17.2
Consuming a Web Service involves three steps.

Note

> The most common consumers for Web Services are Web pages and other Web Services, although it's not uncommon for regular, desktop-based applications to access services as well.

Consuming a Web Service Through an ASP.NET Page

You've acted as a Web Service consumer already. By viewing the service description and HTML description pages, as you did yesterday, you performed the same methods a client would perform, except that you were interfacing directly with the service instead of through a proxy.

The following sections will describe how to perform the three steps of discovery, proxy, and implementation through ASP.NET pages, using SOAP as the communication mechanism. The first two steps require command-line tools, but luckily they don't require much other work on your part. The third step, implementation, is exactly the same as using business objects in your ASP.NET pages, thanks to the proxy class.

Discovery

You can perform discovery for a Web site by using the Web Services Discovery tool, `disco.exe`. This tool examines a Web site and returns a copy of the `.disco` files located on the server. You can then use this local copy to help generate your proxy.

Let's try an example. Open a command prompt and navigate to the `c:\inetpub\wwwroot\tyaspnet21days\day17` directory. Assuming you've created a discovery file called `calculator.disco` (as described yesterday) and placed it in the `tyaspnet21days/day16` directory, type the following command into the command window:

```
disco http://localhost/tyaspnet21days/day16/calculator.disco
```

(You'll examine the syntax for this utility in greater detail later today.) The `disco.exe` utility prints the URLs of the `.disco` files available on the specified server, as shown in Figure 17.3.

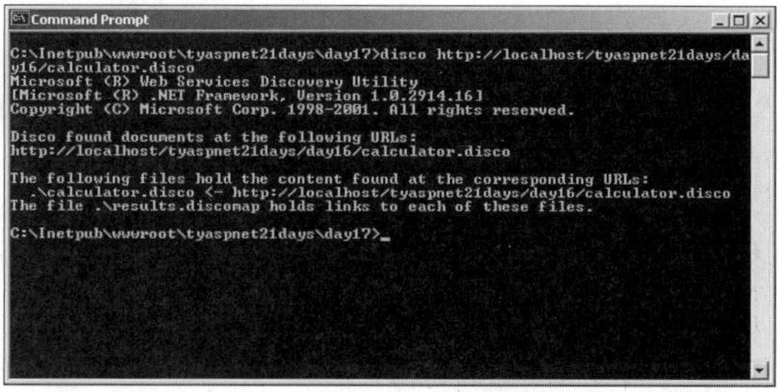

```
C:\Inetpub\wwwroot\tyaspnet21days\day17>disco http://localhost/tyaspnet21days/da
y16/calculator.disco
Microsoft (R) Web Services Discovery Utility
[Microsoft (R) .NET Framework, Version 1.0.2914.16]
Copyright (C) Microsoft Corp. 1998-2001. All rights reserved.

Disco found documents at the following URLs:
http://localhost/tyaspnet21days/day16/calculator.disco

The following files hold the content found at the corresponding URLs:
  .\calculator.disco <- http://localhost/tyaspnet21days/day16/calculator.disco
The file .\results.discomap holds links to each of these files.

C:\Inetpub\wwwroot\tyaspnet21days\day17>_
```

FIGURE 17.3

The results from using the `disco.exe` *tool.*

The utility also outputs a couple of files named `results.discomap` and `calculatorcau.disco` by default. `results.discomap` tells you the output of running `disco.exe`. It tells you which `.disco` files were found on the server, and where it saved the copies of those files. `calculator.disco` contains contents describing the `.disco` file on the server. These are both XML files, so they're easy to read. Figure 17.4 shows a typical `calculator.disco` file.

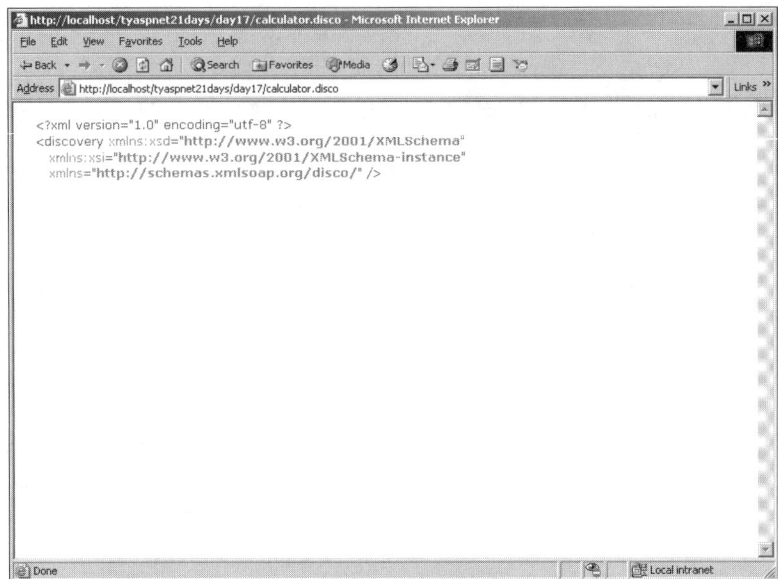

FIGURE 17.4
The `calculator.disco` *XML file displayed in the browser.*

Listing 17.1 shows the contents of `results.discomap`, which details the results of the discovery process.

LISTING 17.1 The Contents of `results.discomap`

```
<?xml version="1.0" encoding="utf-8"?>
<DiscoveryClientResultsFile
➥xmlns:xsd="http://www.w3.org/2001/XMLSchema"
➥xmlns:xsi="http://www.w3.org/2001/XMLSchema-instance">
  <Results>
    <DiscoveryClientResult referenceType="System.Web.
➥Services.Discovery.DiscoveryDocumentReference"
➥url="http://localhost/tyaspnet21days/day16/calculator.disco"
➥filename="calculator.disco" />
  </Results>
</DiscoveryClientResultsFile>
```

ANALYSIS This file contains the result of using discovery on your server. The portion you're interested in is contained within the `Results` tags. On line 4, the `referenceType` attribute specifies what kind of file you just examined—that is, a discovery document. The `url` attribute specifies where the `.disco` file was located—in other words, what URL is used to access it. The `filename` attribute specifies the location on your computer where the copy of the `.disco` file was made. You can use the `results.discomap` file later during the proxy building process.

The `disco.exe` tool has six command-line options, shown in Table 17.1.

TABLE 17.1 The `disco.exe` Tool Options

Option	*Description*
`/nologo`	Suppresses the proprietary Microsoft message displayed when using this tool.
`/nosave`	Specifies that the results of the discovery process shouldn't be saved to a file.
`/out`	Specifies the directory that you should save the results to. The default value is the current directory.
`/username`	Specifies the username needed to access the server.
`/password`	The password needed to access the server.
`/domain`	The domain needed to access the server.

For example, the following command suppresses the Microsoft logo and saves the results in the `c:\temp\disco` folder:

```
disco /nologo /out:c:\temp\disco http://localhost/
➥tyaspnet21days/services.disco
```

Building the Proxy Class

As mentioned earlier, the proxy class acts as a go-between for the Web Service and the consumer. It contains all the functionality needed to transport data over the Internet so that you don't have to build it yourself. As you'll see in a moment, this proxy looks remarkably similar to the `.asmx` file on the Web Service's server, but it makes a few different method calls.

You build the proxy class with another utility: the Web Services Description Language tool, `wsdl.exe`. The tool looks at either a `.discomap` or `.disco` file or the XML service description on the server and constructs a class with identical methods and properties as the Web service. This is to make the proxy as invisible as possible. You can build your

ASP.NET consumer as though you were interacting with the service directly. In addition, this tool creates methods and adds attributes that allow the proxy to send information over the Internet.

You could create a proxy yourself, of course, but why bother when `wsdl.exe` does it for you? (If you're determined to do it yourself, you'll see all the requirements when you look at an actual proxy later today.)

> Note that the `wsdl.exe` tool can examine the service description of a Web Service. This means that you don't need to use the `disco.exe` tool first if you know the service description URL.

Let's look at an example. Execute the following command from the command line:

```
wsdl /language:VB http://localhost/tyaspnet21days/day16/
➥Calculator.asmx?WSDL
```

You'll examine the syntax further later today. Right now, all you need to know is that the first parameter, the `/language` attribute, sets the programming language that the proxy class should be generated in (VB.NET in this case). The second parameter specifies the URL of the service description. (You discovered that URL in yesterday's lesson, "Creating Web Services.")

After running `wsdl.exe` with the parameters specified in the preceding code, you'll see a confirmation message like the following:

```
c:\Inetpub\wwwroot\tyaspnet21days\day17\Calculator.vb
Writing file
'c:\Inetpub\wwwroot\tyaspnet21days\day17\Calculator.vb'.
```

Note that the `wsdl.exe` utility has created a VB.NET class file, `calculator.vb`. This is your proxy class. Take a moment to examine the contents of this file. (It should be located in the same directory that you executed the command from.) Listing 17.2 shows the output of this file.

LISTING 17.2 The Generated `Calculator.vb` File

```
'------------------------------------------------------------
' <autogenerated>
'     This code was generated by a tool.
'     Runtime Version: 1.0.3705.0
'
'     Changes to this file may cause incorrect behavior and
```

LISTING 17.2 continued

```
'     will be lost if the code is regenerated.
' </autogenerated>
'------------------------------------------------------------

Option Strict Off
Option Explicit On

Imports System
Imports System.ComponentModel
Imports System.Diagnostics
Imports System.Web.Services
Imports System.Web.Services.Protocols
Imports System.Xml.Serialization

'
'This source code was auto-generated by wsdl, Version=1.0.3705.0.
'

'<remarks/>
<System.Diagnostics.DebuggerStepThroughAttribute(),  _
 System.ComponentModel.DesignerCategoryAttribute("code"),  _
 System.Web.Services.WebServiceBindingAttribute
➥(Name:="CalculatorSoap", [Namespace]:="http://tempuri.org/")>  _
Public Class Calculator
    Inherits System.Web.Services.Protocols.SoapHttpClientProtocol

    '<remarks/>
    Public Sub New()
        MyBase.New
        Me.Url =
➥"http://localhost/tyaspnet21days/day16/Calculator.asmx"
    End Sub

    '<remarks/>
    <System.Web.Services.Protocols.SoapDocumentMethodAttribute
➥("http://tempuri.org/Add", RequestNamespace:=
➥"http://tempuri.org/", ResponseNamespace:=
➥"http://tempuri.org/", Use:=System.Web.Services.
➥Description.SoapBindingUse.Literal,
➥ParameterStyle:=System.Web.Services.Protocols.
➥SoapParameterStyle.Wrapped)>  _
    Public Function Add(ByVal intA As Integer, ByVal intB
➥As Integer) As Integer
        Dim results() As Object = Me.Invoke("Add",
➥New Object() {intA, intB})
        Return CType(results(0),Integer)
    End Function

```

17

LISTING 17.2 continued

```
45:         '<remarks/>
46:         Public Function BeginAdd(ByVal intA As Integer,
➥ByVal intB As Integer, ByVal callback As System.AsyncCallback,
➥ByVal asyncState As Object) As System.IAsyncResult
47:             Return Me.BeginInvoke("Add", New Object()
➥{intA, intB}, callback, asyncState)
48:         End Function
49:
50:         '<remarks/>
51:         Public Function EndAdd(ByVal asyncResult As
➥System.IAsyncResult) As Integer
52:             Dim results() As Object = Me.EndInvoke(asyncResult)
53:             Return CType(results(0),Integer)
54:         End Function
55:     End Class
```

ANALYSIS This class was created by `wsdl.exe` to ease the process you have to go through to consume a Web Service. Note that it contains two methods in addition to the one provided by the service, as well as numerous attributes and properties that, among other things, make this code hard to read! Don't worry if you don't follow it completely. You needn't delve into the exact syntax of it.

Line 29 declares a class named `Calculator`, which has a `WebServiceBindingAttribute` attribute from the `System.Web.Services` namespace. This attribute defines the interface this class must use—that is, a predefined set of functions and properties. You really don't need to know much more about this attribute for the purposes of today's lesson. (See the .NET Framework SDK documentation for more information.) Note that this attribute isn't required for proxy classes, but one is generated automatically.

This class also inherits the `SoapHttpClientProtocol` class, as shown on line 30. This class provides the methods to talk to the Calculator service remotely via Simple Object Access Protocol (SOAP).

On line 33, the proxy contains a *constructor*, a method that's used to initialize the class (see the Q&A on Day 15, "Using Business Objects"). This constructor sets the URL for your Web Service.

Starting on line 39, you see something similar to the `Add` method you created yesterday. This function has the attribute `SoapDocumentMethodAttribute`, which provides parameters for use when the service talks to it via SOAP. On line 41, this function calls the `Invoke` method, which places a call to the service. This method takes two parameters: the name of the method in the service to invoke, and the parameters to send to the service. The results are stored in an array named `results` and are then returned on line 42.

The next two functions define asynchronous methods for communication with the service. See Day 13, "Reading and Writing Files on the Web Server," for more information on asynchronous method calls. Essentially, these methods allow you to perform other functions while they're executing. Regular methods, also known as *synchronous* methods, don't allow any other operations to be performed while they're executing.

This proxy class effectively wraps up the functionality needed to place calls over the Internet using different transport protocols, such as SOAP or Http-Get. You can use this proxy to interact with the service just as you'd use a business object. Thankfully, you don't have to create this proxy yourself.

The `wsdl.exe` utility has a few more options that you can specify to generate different types of proxies. It supports all the options in Table 17.1 (with the exception of `/nosave`), in addition to those shown in Table 17.2.

TABLE 17.2 `wsdl.exe` Options

Option	*Description*
`/language`	The language used to generate the proxy class. The default is C#.
`/namespace`	The namespace to use for the generated proxy. The default is the global namespace.
`/protocol`	The protocol to use for communication with the service. Can be SOAP, Http-Get, or Http-Post. The default is SOAP.

Many of the options for `wsdl.exe` and `disco.exe` have shortcuts. For instance, instead of typing `/language:`, you can use `/l:`. For more information, type `wsdl.exe /?` or `disco.exe /?` at the command line.

The following line creates a proxy class in VB.NET, using a custom namespace and the SOAP protocol:

```
wsdl /l:VB /namespace:MyWebServiceConsumer /protocol:SOAP
➥http://localhost/tyaspnet21days/day16/Calculator.asmx?WSDL
```

Implementing the Proxy Class

You're nearly ready to use the Web Service from an ASP.NET page. You now have your proxy class to interact with the service, but you can't use it just yet. First, you must compile it into an assembly (a DLL file), just as you did for business objects. This is accomplished with the VB.NET compiler (which you should be pretty familiar with by now). From the command prompt, enter the following command:

```
vbc /t:library /out:..\..\bin\CalculatorServiceClient.dll
➥/r:System.dll /r:System.XML.dll
➥/r:System.Web.Services.dll Calculator.vb
```

When you require long, multiple steps on the command line, such as using `disco.exe` followed by `wsdl.exe` and then `vbc.exe`, it's often helpful to use a batch file (`.bat`). This saves you from having to retype things over and over again.

Create a text file, change the extension to `.bat`, and copy the necessary commands in the file, separated by line breaks. Simply run this file and all the steps will be performed automatically.

This command will compile the proxy class into the DLL file and place it in the `/bin` directory, your assembly cache. Then you can use the component through an ASP.NET page to call a Web service. Listing 17.3 presents a simple ASP.NET page that consumes the calculator Web Service.

LISTING 17.3 Invoking a Web Service from an ASP.NET Page

```
1:    <%@ Page Language="VB" %>
2:
3:    <script runat="server">
4:       sub Page_Load(Sender as Object, e as EventArgs)
5:          dim objCalc as new Calculator
6:
7:          lblMessage.Text = objCalc.Add(1,5)
8:       end sub
9:    </script>
10:
11:    <html><body>
12:     The answer to 1 + 5 is:
13:       <asp:Label id="lblMessage" runat="server"/>
14:    </body></html>
```

ANALYSIS This ASP.NET page is pretty simple. In the `Page_Load` event on line 5, you create an instance of the `Calculator` proxy you just compiled. This object represents the calculator Web service. You can use it just as if you were interacting directly with the service. In other words, if you gave this compiled proxy to another developer, she wouldn't have any idea that it interacted with a Web service. She could use the proxy just as if it contained the service's methods itself.

On line 7, you call the `Add` method and store the result in the label on line 13. This method takes two integers, sums them, and returns the result. What actually happens here is that you're calling the proxy's `Add` method, which takes the two integers and sends them across the Internet to the service's `Add` method, which performs the actual calculation. The proxy then receives the answer in XML format, converts it into the proper format (an integer, in this case), and gives you the result. From the developer's point of view, the proxy simply takes the parameters, performs the calculations, and returns the result.

When viewed from the browser, this page will produce the screen in Figure 17.5.

FIGURE 17.5
The result of calling your Web Service.

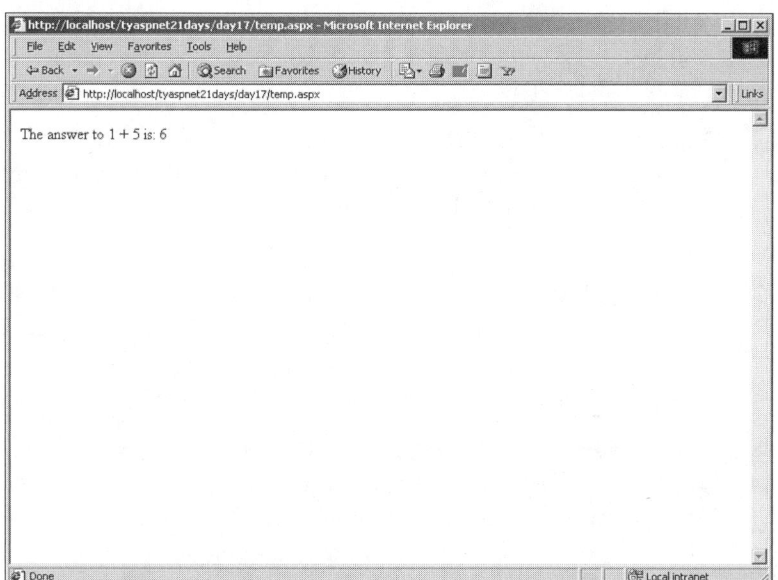

This example shows the beauty of using a proxy class—you don't need to perform any special tasks to communicate with the calculator Web service. All you have to do is call the Web service's method whose functionality you're interested in. This may seem like a lot of work just to get this simple output, but all you really need to do is perform three steps: Use the `wsdl.exe` tool to generate the proxy, compile it and place it in the assembly cache, and build the ASP.NET page to access its methods. (And if someone does the first two steps for you, you only need to provide the implementation.) You don't need to know the output generated by the discovery and proxy generation steps—it's irrelevant unless you want to create your own proxies manually. Thus, the proxy hides all the complex functionality. With just a few lines in your ASP.NET page, you're doing a lot of powerful work.

Note that you didn't have to import any additional namespaces to use this proxy class. Recall from Day 15 that an object is automatically loaded by ASP.NET when it's placed in the assembly cache (the `/bin` directory). You can access it as though it were part of your page.

Another Web Service Consumption Example

So far, you've accomplished quite a bit. Calling an object's methods from across the Internet is no small feat. Web Services open up a lot of possibilities for distributed computing. However, the previous example was a fairly simple exercise. It performed a calculation that could have been performed in an ASP.NET page and didn't require any complex data types.

Let's go through another example. Recall that you can also send database results through Web Services, thanks to XML. Yesterday, you built a database service that could take a SQL statement and retrieve the appropriate data. Let's consume this service from an ASP.NET page.

Let's skip discovery and move directly to generating the proxy. Execute the following command:

```
wsdl /language:VB /namespace:TYASPNET.Clients
➥http://localhost/tyaspnet21days/day16/Database.asmx?WSDL
```

You've already used the `wsdl.exe` tool, so this should look familiar. This command creates a proxy class of the database service and places it in the current directory. Because of the extensive functionality of the database service, this proxy is rather large and complex. Luckily, you don't need to worry about it at all. You only need to compile and implement it. Notice that you place the generated proxy in the `TYASPNET.Clients` namespace. Recall that we put the database service itself in the `TYASPNET` namespace—the new `TYASPNET.Clients` namespace is so we don't get confused between the database service and the proxy. This should produce a listing similar to Figure 17.6.

Next, you need to compile this service on the client. Use the following command:

```
vbc /t:library /out:..\..\bin\DatabaseService.dll /r:System.dll
➥/r:System.XML.dll /r:System.Web.Services.dll
➥/r:System.Data.dll DatabaseService.vb
```

Don't forget to reference the `System.Data` namespace! The proxy uses the objects in this namespace to convert the returned XML data into a `DataSet` that you can use in your ASP.NET page. Finally, let's build the ASP.NET page to use the Web Service, shown in Listing 17.4.

FIGURE 17.6

The generated proxy from the database service.

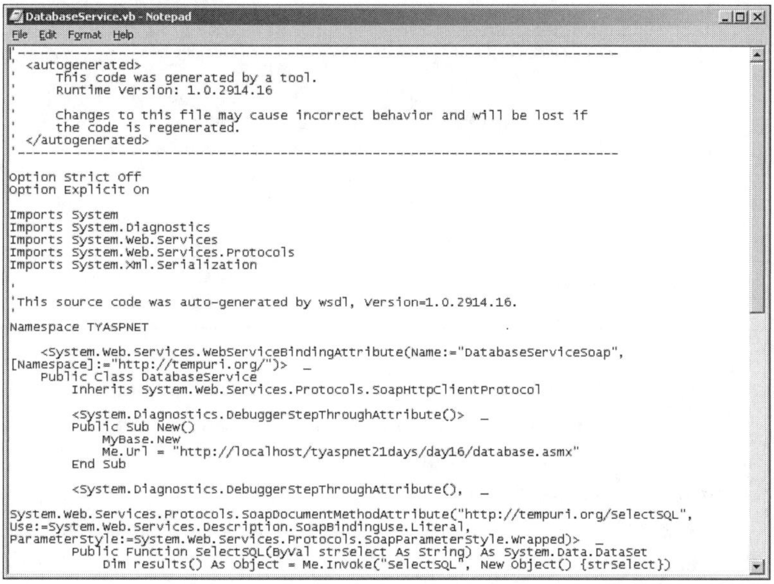

```
DatabaseService.vb - Notepad
File  Edit  Format  Help
'------------------------------------------------------------------------------
' <autogenerated>
'     This code was generated by a tool.
'     Runtime Version: 1.0.2914.16
'
'     Changes to this file may cause incorrect behavior and will be lost if
'     the code is regenerated.
' </autogenerated>
'------------------------------------------------------------------------------

Option Strict Off
Option Explicit On

Imports System
Imports System.Diagnostics
Imports System.Web.Services
Imports System.Web.Services.Protocols
Imports System.Xml.Serialization

'
'This source code was auto-generated by wsdl, Version=1.0.2914.16.
'

Namespace TYASPNET

    <System.Web.Services.WebServiceBindingAttribute(Name:="DatabaseServiceSoap",
[Namespace]:="http://tempuri.org/")>  _
    Public Class DatabaseService
        Inherits System.Web.Services.Protocols.SoapHttpClientProtocol

        <System.Diagnostics.DebuggerStepThroughAttribute()>  _
        Public Sub New()
            MyBase.New
            Me.Url = "http://localhost/tyaspnet21days/day16/database.asmx"
        End Sub

        <System.Diagnostics.DebuggerStepThroughAttribute(),  _

System.Web.Services.Protocols.SoapDocumentMethodAttribute("http://tempuri.org/SelectSQL",
Use:=System.Web.Services.Description.SoapBindingUse.Literal,
ParameterStyle:=System.Web.Services.Protocols.SoapParameterStyle.Wrapped)>  _
        Public Function SelectSQL(ByVal strSelect As String) As System.Data.DataSet
            Dim results() As Object = Me.Invoke("SelectSQL", New Object() {strSelect})
```

17

LISTING 17.4 Accessing Your Database Service

```
<%@ Page Language="VB" %>
<%@ Import Namespace="System.Data" %>

<script runat="server">
   sub Submit(Sender as Object, e as EventArgs)
      dim objService as new TYASPNET.Clients.DatabaseService
      dim objDS as new DataSet

      objDS = objService.SelectSQL(tbQuery.Text)
       DataGrid1.DataSource = objDS
       DataGrid1.DataMember = "tblUsers"

       DataGrid1.Databind()
    end sub
 </script>

 <html><body>
    <form runat="server">
       Enter a query:
       <asp:Textbox id="tbQuery" runat="server"/>
       <asp:Button id="btSubmit" runat="server"
          text="Submit"
          OnClick="Submit" />
       <p>
       <asp:DataGrid id="DataGrid1"
```

LISTING 17.4 continued

```
26:             runat="server" BorderColor="black"
27:             GridLines="Vertical" cellpadding="4"
28:             cellspacing="0" width="100%"
29:             Font-Name="Arial" Font-Size="8pt"
30:             HeaderStyle-BackColor="#cccc99"
31:             ItemStyle-BackColor="#ffffff"
32:             AlternatingItemStyle-Backcolor="#cccccc" />
33:
34:       </form>
35:    </body></html>
```

ANALYSIS This is a very simple page. The `Submit` method is its only function. When the user enters a query into the text box and clicks Submit, it creates a new instance of your newly compiled proxy class, as shown on line 6. Recall that you placed this proxy in the `TYASPNET.Clients` namespace, so you use its full name to declare the variable. (The calculator example earlier today wasn't placed in a specific namespace, so you didn't have to use a namespace name.)

Line 9 calls the `SelectSQL` method, which should return a `DataSet`. You then simply bind the returned data to the `DataGrid`, beginning on line 25. Figure 17.7 shows the returned page.

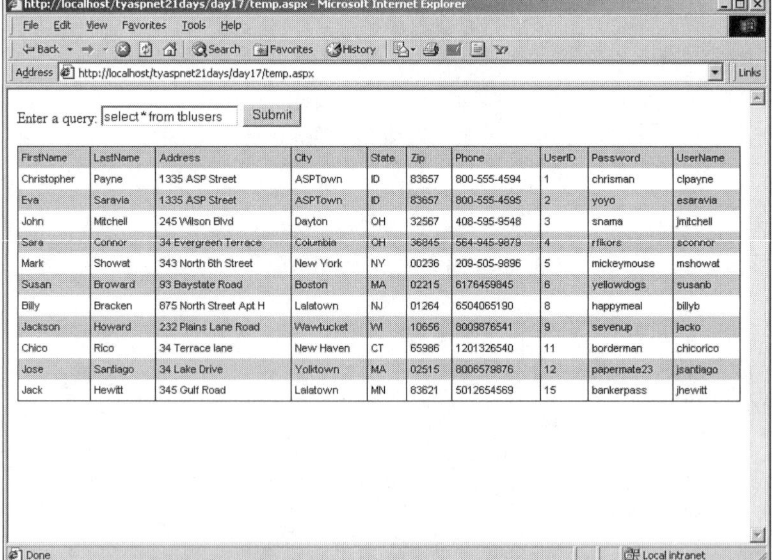

FirstName	LastName	Address	City	State	Zip	Phone	UserID	Password	UserName
Christopher	Payne	1335 ASP Street	ASPTown	ID	83657	800-555-4594	1	chrisman	clpayne
Eva	Saravia	1335 ASP Street	ASPTown	ID	83657	800-555-4595	2	yoyo	esaravia
John	Mitchell	245 Wilson Blvd	Dayton	OH	32567	408-595-9548	3	snama	jmitchell
Sara	Connor	34 Evergreen Terrace	Columbia	OH	36845	564-945-9879	4	rflkors	sconnor
Mark	Showat	343 North 6th Street	New York	NY	00236	209-505-9896	5	mickeymouse	mshowat
Susan	Broward	93 Baystate Road	Boston	MA	02215	6176459845	6	yellowdogs	susanb
Billy	Bracken	875 North Street Apt H	Lalatown	NJ	01264	6504065190	8	happymeal	billyb
Jackson	Howard	232 Plains Lane Road	Wawtucket	WI	10656	8009876541	9	sevenup	jacko
Chico	Rico	34 Terrace lane	New Haven	CT	65986	1201326540	11	borderman	chicorico
Jose	Santiago	34 Lake Drive	Yolktown	MA	02515	8006579876	12	papermate23	jsantiago
Jack	Hewitt	345 Gulf Road	Lalatown	MN	83621	5012654569	15	bankerpass	jhewitt

FIGURE 17.7
The data returned from the service.

This ASP.NET page can be located anywhere in the world in relation to the Web Service, and you can still receive the same results. In other words, your ASP.NET page can be located on your home computer in New York, while the service resides on a server in Tokyo! The service can receive commands from anywhere because they're transferred via XML, which is simply plain text, and typically the security measures in place on the Internet are designed to allow transmission of plain text.

Web Services allow developers to implement your custom functionality however they see fit. (This is unlike ASP.NET pages, where clients are stuck using the interface you build.) For example, using this database service and the data it returns, one developer could build an online address book application. Another developer could use the data to determine demographic information. Your service simply returns data. It doesn't care how that data is used or displayed.

These examples show the similarities between business objects and Web services. Both require compiled objects that are implemented on an ASP.NET page. The only difference is that with Web services, the compiled object can reside anywhere on the Internet. A proxy then ties the implementation and service together.

Web Service Consumption Recommendations

How you consume a Web Service depends on your situation. Recall from yesterday that you can access Web Services with three different protocols: Http-Get, Http-Post, and SOAP. The first two are the easiest to implement because they only require the URL of the Web Service. All of today's examples have used SOAP, which provides the richest methods for consuming services.

There's one drawback to using SOAP, however. As you may have noticed, encoding the commands and data in SOAP messages is rather complex (although creating the proxies that contain the methods to do so is not). The messages sent back and forth are quite large because SOAP must send XML schema information. Depending on the type of connection you or your clients have to the Internet, this can affect performance.

Another method of consuming a Web Service is Http-Get. If you know the URL of the service and the method(s) and parameter(s) it expects, you can invoke the service's methods. For example, you can access the following URL to consume the Add method from the Calculator service you created yesterday:

```
http://localhost/tyaspnet21days/day16/Calculator.asmx/
➥Add?intA=1&intB=2
```

Put a forward slash and the method name after the URL, followed with the parameters in a querystring. For example, the URL of the service is

```
http://localhost/tyaspnet21days/day16/Calculator.asmx
```

The suffix, containing the method name and parameters, is

```
/Add?intA=1&intB=2
```

When requested, this URL outputs the XML containing the output from the method. In this case, you see the following:

```
<?xml version="1.0"?>
<int xmlns="http://tempuri.org/">3</int>
```

You can also consume a service via an Http-Post operation. Simply set the `action` attribute of an HTML form to the `Add` method:

```
<form action="http://localhost/tyaspnet21days/day16/Calculator.asmx/Add">
```

This is the URL followed by a slash and the method name. When you submit the form, any parameters will be posted to the service and the appropriate XML output will be generated. Just remember that the form parameters must have the same names as the parameters expected by the service.

So which of these methods should you use? The choice is simple, really. When you require complex data to be sent back from the service, such as a `DataSet` or a class, use SOAP. The other two methods can't send this type of data.

If you don't require complex data, and your application or clients may be bandwidth-sensitive, use the Http-Get or Http-Post method. They send less data back and forth, resulting in better performance.

Do	Don't
Do use SOAP when you think you'll need complex data or rich programmatic access to your service.	**Don't** use SOAP when bandwidth is a critical factor. Use Http-Get or Http-Post instead.

Securing Web Services

Often you want to secure your Web Services. After all, even in the Internet age where everything is shared, you must protect *some* things. Imagine you've developed a Web Service in which the user types a stock ticker symbol and gets the stock's real-time quote. Typically, free stock quotes are delayed 20 minutes or more, so your service is something that people would be willing to pay for. You'd want to keep out any freeloaders.

So far, you've looked at how to create Web Services that are publicly available. Anyone who knows of the service can consume it (either through the `.disco` file or the direct URL). Fortunately, you can take steps to secure your Web Services so that only authorized parties may use them.

This security measure involves using SOAP (and thus XML) to send authentication information as part of the service commands. Because information is sent directly to the Web Service, the service is free to implement authentication however necessary. For example, you could access a database to determine the proper credentials for a user.

Before examining the technical details, let's look at an analogy. Imagine that you want to go to a very exclusive restaurant. They require identification at the door before they'll even let you in. To gain entrance and receive service, you must bring along some form of identification, such as a driver's license.

To pass along identification information when trying to consume a Web service, you'll use a SOAP header. This is an additional XML message attached to the regular communication of the service that provides custom information. It works similarly to a driver's license. Although it's transported with the SOAP messages, it's a separate entity. Your SOAP header will be used to pass username and password information so that only the users you choose can access the service.

To pass a SOAP header, you simply create a class that inherits the `System.Web.Services.Protocols.SoapHeader` class. Your Web Service class can then use this class to gather the authentication information. For example, Listing 17.5 shows a simple SOAP header class that accepts a username and password.

LISTING 17.5 A Simple SOAP Header Class

```
Imports System.Web.Services
Imports System.Web.Services.Protocols

Namespace TYASPNET

```

LISTING 17.5 continued

```
    Public Class Authenticator : Inherits SoapHeader
       Public Username as string
       Public Password as string
    End Class

  End Namespace
```

ANALYSIS This class, named `Authenticator`, can be used in the same file as your Web Service class. It contains two public string variables, `Username` and `Password`, that will contain the authentication information from the client.

Each class that you want to protect should declare an instance of this `Authenticator` class. You'll use this instance to restrict access to your Web methods. Each Web method, then, must use the `<SoapHeader>` attribute in addition to the `<WebMethod>` attribute:

```
Public Class DataBaseService
   dim sHeader as Authenticator
   ...
   <WebMethod(), SoapHeader("sHeader")>
   Public Function MyMethod()
      as String
      ...
   End Function
End Class
```

On the second line, you create the instance of the `Authenticator` class, stored in the variable `sHeader`. Then, in the function declaration, you add the `<SoapHeader>` attribute with the name of your `Authenticator` instance. This tells ASP.NET that it should expect a SOAP header in addition to the regular communications. Without this header, any messages from the client will be rejected.

Let's build a real-world example using the database service you created yesterday. First, let's modify your Web Service class to take advantage of custom SOAP headers. Listing 17.6 shows your modified class.

LISTING 17.6 A Secure Database Service Class

```
Imports System
Imports System.Data
Imports System.Data.OleDb
Imports System.Web.Services
Imports System.Web.Services.Protocols

Namespace TYASPNET
```

LISTING 17.6 continued

```
Public Class Authenticator : Inherits SoapHeader
    Public Username as string
    Public Password as string
 End Class

 Public Class SecureDatabaseService : Inherits WebService
    private objConn as OleDbConnection
    private objCmd as OleDbCommand
    public sHeader as Authenticator

    <WebMethod(), SoapHeader("sHeader")> public function _
       SelectSQL(strSelect as string) as DataSet

       if sHeader is Nothing then
          throw new Exception("Error: Invalid login!")
       end if

       if Authenticate(sHeader.UserName, _
          sHeader.Password) then
          try
             objConn = new OleDbConnection("Provider=" & _
                "Microsoft.Jet.OLEDB.4.0;" & _
                "Data Source=c:\ASPNET\data\banking.mdb")
             dim objDataCmd as OleDbDataAdapter = new _
                OleDbDataAdapter(strSelect, objConn)

             Dim objDS as new DataSet
             objDataCmd.Fill(objDS, "tblUsers")
             return objDS
          catch ex as OleDbException
             return nothing
          end try
       else
          return nothing
       end if
    end function

    private function Authenticate(strUser as string, _
       strPass as string) as boolean
       try
          dim intID as integer = 0
          objConn = new OleDbConnection("Provider=" & _
             "Microsoft.Jet.OLEDB.4.0;" & _
             "Data Source=c:\ASPNET\data\banking.mdb")

          dim strSelect as string = "SELECT UserID " & _
             "FROM tblUsers WHERE Username = '" & _
             strUser & "' AND Password = '" & _
```

LISTING 17.6 continued

```
57:                     strPass & "'"
58:                  objCmd = new OleDbCommand(strSelect, objConn)
59:                  objCmd.Connection.Open()
60:
61:                  Dim objReader as OleDbDataReader
62:                  objReader = objCmd.ExecuteReader
63:                  do while objReader.Read
64:                     intID = objReader.GetInt32(0)
65:                  loop
66:                  objReader.Close
67:
68:                  if intID <> 0 then
69:                     return true
70:                  else
71:                     return false
72:                  end if
73:               catch ex as OleDbException
74:                  return false
75:               end try
76:            end function
77:         End Class
78:
79:      End Namespace
```

ANALYSIS Save this file as `Database.vb` in the `day17` folder. Beginning on line 9 is the authentication class you build that inherits from `SoapHeader`. This class will be sent along as extra baggage during trips to and from the service. It has only two variables, `UserName` and `Password`, which you'll use to authenticate users.

On line 17, you create a new instance of the SOAP header class named `sHeader`. This instance will contain the authentication information passed from the client, which will be used by your methods to determine if the user has the correct permissions.

The new database service class is called `SecureDatabaseService`, just so you can keep the services you develop straight in your mind. Your `SelectSQL` function begins on line 19, but it's different from what you may remember from yesterday. First of all, in the declaration you include the `SoapHeader` attribute, set to the instance of the SOAP header class, `sHeader`. The rest of the declaration is the same as normal.

The first thing you do inside this function is determine if a username and password were supplied with the call from the client. If these parameters are missing, `sHeader` will equal `nothing` and you want to exit your function. You throw a custom `Exception` error on line 23, which is used to tell the client that he's forgotten to supply something.

It's not necessary to throw a specific error because ASP.NET will alert the user if the proper header isn't passed along. This error is shown in Figure 17.8.

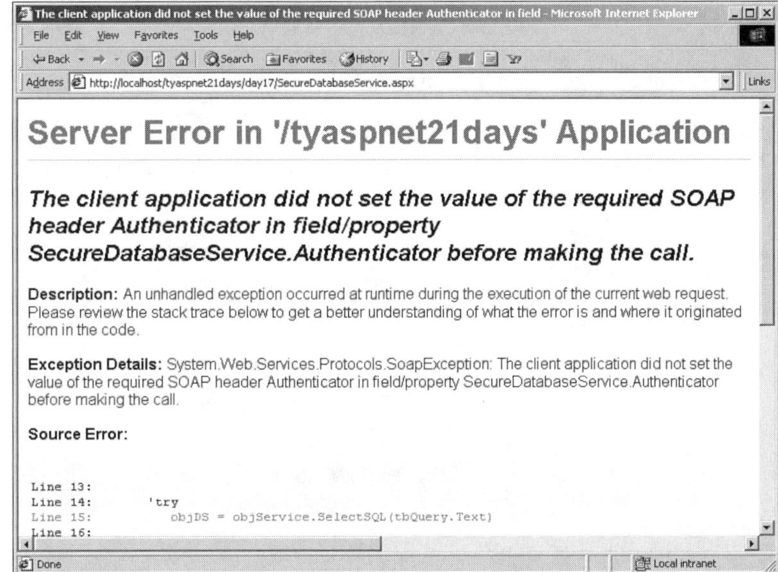

The client application did not set the value of the required SOAP header Authenticator in field - Microsoft Internet Explorer
File Edit View Favorites Tools Help
Back Search Favorites History
Address http://localhost/tyaspnet21days/day17/SecureDatabaseService.aspx
Links
Server Error in '/tyaspnet21days' Application
The client application did not set the value of the required SOAP header Authenticator in field/property SecureDatabaseService.Authenticator before making the call.
Description: An unhandled exception occurred at runtime during the execution of the current web request. Please review the stack trace below to get a better understanding of what the error is and where it originated from in the code.
Exception Details: System.Web.Services.Protocols.SoapException: The client application did not set the value of the required SOAP header Authenticator in field/property SecureDatabaseService.Authenticator before making the call.
Source Error:
Line 13:
Line 14: 'try
Line 15: objDS = objService.SelectSQL(tbQuery.Text)
Line 16:
Done
Local intranet

FIGURE 17.8

An error is generated if you forget to supply the SOAP header.

On line 26, you call your custom `Authenticate` method, which performs a database lookup to determine if the specified user is allowed to access this function. If the credentials are valid, `Authenticate` returns true and you move into the actual body of the function, beginning on line 28. This part should look familiar. It hasn't changed from the last version of this class. It executes the supplied query and returns a `DataSet` object.

The `Authenticate` function on line 44 performs the validation check. This function checks the database to see if the username and password supplied by the SOAP header describe an actual user. If so, it returns true. Otherwise, it returns false, and if so, you'll want to return `nothing` from your service, as done on line 42.

Compile this service with the following command:

```
vbc /t:library /out:..\..\bin\TYASPNET.dll /r:System.dll
➥/r:System.data.dll /r:System.xml.dll /r:System.Web.dll
➥/r:System.Web.Services.dll Database.vb ..\day15\user.vb
```

Build an `.asmx` file on the server that simply specifies the class name, as follows:

```
<%@ WebService Class="TYASPNET.SecureDatabaseService" %>
```

Save this file as `SecureDatabaseService.asmx`. Next, you need to build the proxy class from the client (in this case, the client and server are the same computer). Use the following command to generate the proxy:

```
wsdl /language:VB /namespace:TYASPNET.Clients
➥http://localhost/tyaspnet21days/day17/
➥SecureDatabaseService.asmx?WSDL
```

Again notice that you place this proxy in a new namespace, `TYASPNET.Clients`. Since all your work is being done on the same machine, this is to prevent class names from overlapping in one namespace.

The generated proxy class will be called `SecureDatabaseService.vb` by default. If you take a look at the generated code, you'll notice that the proxy has retrieved two things from the service: the authenticator and the secure database class. You'll need to use both of these in your client application to access the service.

Finally, compile this proxy with the following command:

```
vbc /t:library /out:..\..\bin\TYASPNET.Clients.dll /r:System.dll
➥/r:System.data.dll /r:System.XML.dll /r:System.Web.dll
➥/r:System.Web.Services.dll SecureDatabaseService.vb
```

All that's left is to build the ASP.NET page that will access this service. This page should allow the user to enter a username and password, as well as the query she wants to execute. Listing 17.7 contains the code for this page.

LISTING 17.7 The ASP.NET Page to Access Your Service

```
<%@ Page Language="VB" %>
<%@ Import Namespace="System.Data" %>

<script runat="server">
   sub Submit(Sender as Object, e as EventArgs)
      dim objService as new TYASPNET.Clients.SecureDatabaseService_
      dim sHeader as new TYASPNET.Clients.Authenticator
      dim objDS as new DataSet

       sHeader.Username = tbUser.Text
       sHeader.Password = tbPass.Text
       objService.Authenticator = sHeader

       try
          objDS = objService.SelectSQL(tbQuery.Text)
```

Listing 17.7 continued

```
16:
17:          if objDS is nothing then
18:             Response.Write("Invalid username or password")
19:          else
20:             DataGrid1.DataSource = objDS
21:             DataGrid1.DataMember = "tblUsers"
22:             DataGrid1.Databind()
23:          end if
24:       catch ex as exception
25:          Response.Write("Invalid username or password")
26:       end try
27:    end sub
28: </script>
29:
30: <html><body>
31:    <form runat="server">
32:       Username:
33:       <asp:Textbox id="tbUser" runat="server"/><br>
34:       Password:
35:       <asp:Textbox id="tbPass" runat="server"
36:          TextMode="password" /><p>
37:       Enter a query:
38:       <asp:Textbox id="tbQuery" runat="server"/>
39:       <asp:Button id="btSubmit" runat="server"
40:          text="Submit"
41:          OnClick="Submit" />
42:       <p>
43:       <asp:DataGrid id="DataGrid1"
44:          runat="server" BorderColor="black"
45:          GridLines="Vertical" cellpadding="4"
46:          cellspacing="0" width="100%"
47:          Font-Name="Arial" Font-Size="8pt"
48:          HeaderStyle-BackColor="#cccc99"
49:          ItemStyle-BackColor="#ffffff"
50:          AlternatingItemStyle-Backcolor="#cccccc" />
51:
52:    </form>
53: </body></html>
```


Analysis The only method in this page is `Submit`, the event handler for the Submit button. When this method is fired, it creates two new objects from your proxy class: the authenticator and the secure database class. You set the username and password properties of the authenticator to the values entered in the text boxes on lines 11 and 12. You then set this instance of the authenticator to the secure database's `Authenticator` property. The proxy now knows what to send along with the commands.

Finally, wrapped in the `try` block, you execute the service's method and bind the data to a `DataGrid`. Load this page in the browser and enter some user credentials and a SQL query. If the credentials are valid (that is, if they represent an actual user in the `tblUsers` table), you'll see the returned data, as shown in Figure 17.9.

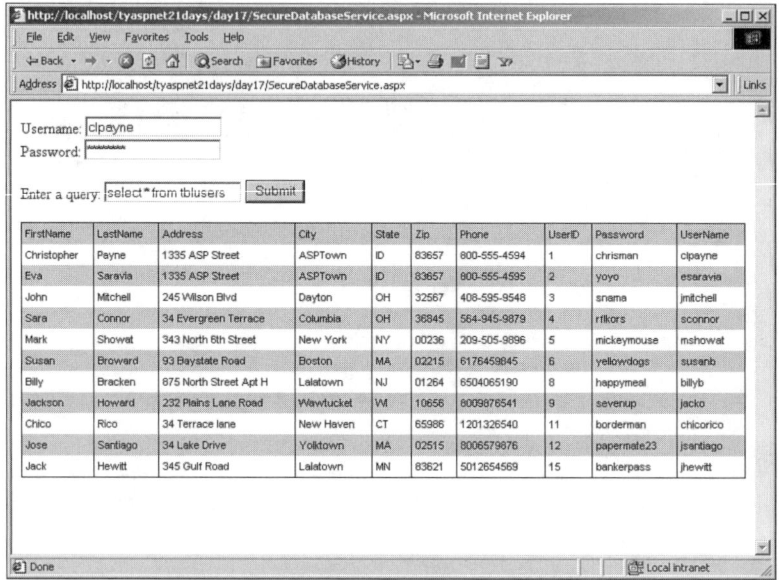

FirstName	LastName	Address	City	State	Zip	Phone	UserID	Password	UserName
Christopher	Payne	1335 ASP Street	ASPTown	ID	83657	800-555-4594	1	chrisman	clpayne
Eva	Saravia	1335 ASP Street	ASPTown	ID	83657	800-555-4595	2	yoyo	esaravia
John	Mitchell	245 Wilson Blvd	Dayton	OH	32567	408-595-9548	3	snama	jmitchell
Sara	Connor	34 Evergreen Terrace	Columbia	OH	36845	564-945-9879	4	rflkors	sconnor
Mark	Showat	343 North 6th Street	New York	NY	00236	209-505-9896	5	mickeymouse	mshowat
Susan	Broward	93 Baystate Road	Boston	MA	02215	6176459845	6	yellowdogs	susanb
Billy	Bracken	875 North Street Apt H	Lalatown	NJ	01264	6504065190	8	happymeal	billyb
Jackson	Howard	232 Plains Lane Road	Wawtucket	VM	10656	8009876541	9	sevenup	jacko
Chico	Rico	34 Terrace lane	New Haven	CT	65986	1201326540	11	borderman	chicorico
Jose	Santiago	34 Lake Drive	Yolktown	MA	02515	8006579876	12	papermate23	jsantiago
Jack	Hewitt	345 Gulf Road	Lalatown	MN	83621	5012654569	15	bankerpass	jhewitt

FIGURE 17.9

The results of a successful query to the secure service.

If you enter invalid credentials, however, you should see an error message stating "Invalid Username or Password." This is the reason for the `if` statement on line 17. Without it, supplying invalid credentials would result in returning an empty `DataSet`. Figure 17.10 shows an unsuccessful attempt.

SOAP headers are a common and effective tool for implementing secure Web Services. Although you pulled your authentication information from a database here, you can verify the supplied information any way you like.

There is a drawback to using SOAP headers, however. When you send user credentials across the Internet via SOAP headers, they're sent as plain text in XML format. This means that they're vulnerable to prying eyes. One method to get around this is to encrypt the user credentials prior to sending them and provide an equivalent decryption algorithm in your Web Service. Encryption is beyond the scope of this book, however. For other ways to secure your application, see Day 21, "Securing Your ASP.NET Application."

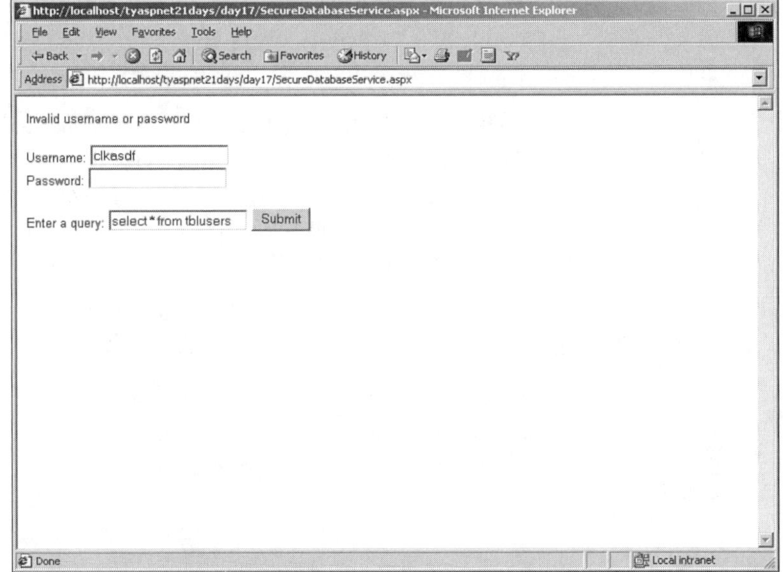

FIGURE 17.10
The results of an unsuccessful query to the secure service.

That's Not ASP!

For ASP developers, allowing clients to access Web applications isn't a new concept. Classic ASP let developers move applications online, allowing clients to access them. It's accessing *components* of applications over the Internet and using them for other programs that's completely new.

Allowing two separate pieces of an application to communicate with each other remotely is a new concept. Previously, business logic and ASP pages had to be on the same computer (or at least computers on the same network). With ASP.NET, these pieces can be located anywhere, giving rise to truly distributed applications.

Using SOAP to send commands and data via a standard language such as XML is a key factor in the success of Web Services. These SOAP instructions can be sent anywhere, even through firewalls, because they rely on pure text messages.

Summary

Today you learned how to access Web Services from client ASP.NET pages. Consuming Web Services is just as important to ASP.NET developers as building them.

Consuming Web Services from a client involves three stages: discovery, proxy class generation, and implementation of the proxy.

The `disco` tool is used to perform discovery on a service. It produces two files as output: one that describes the results of the discovery (typically called `results.discomap`), and another that contains the same contents as the discovery file residing on the server.

The Web Services Description Language tool, `wsdl.exe`, is used to generate a proxy class. This class has methods to execute the Web service commands remotely by providing built-in support for sending and receiving XML messages using SOAP. Once the class has been generated, you compile it just like any other business object. Then you can execute the service's methods through the proxy class from within your application.

You also looked at securing Web Services with custom SOAP headers. These headers are sent in addition to any messages sent to the service.

Tomorrow you'll look at configuring your ASP.NET applications. Throughout this book, you've seen examples of using the `web.config` or `global.asax` files, and you'll learn exactly what they do and how to use them to your advantage.

Q&A

Q Will non-Web method functions be seen in the proxy class as well?

A No, the proxy only sees the methods that contain the `<WebMethod()>` attribute. Recall that methods without this attribute cannot be seen at all over the Web.

Q Can SOAP headers be used for functions other than security?

A Absolutely! SOAP headers can contain any custom information you want. Any Web method that uses the `<SoapHeader()>` attribute will require the header to be sent along with any communication. Thus, this is a convenient way to send information that doesn't necessarily belong in the parameter list of a method.

Workshop

This workshop will help reinforce the concepts covered in today's lesson. Answers can be found in Appendix A.

Quiz

1. What is a proxy class?
2. Write an example of a typical use of the `disco.exe` tool.
3. Write an example of a typical use of the `wsdl.exe` tool.
4. True or false: Discovery must be performed before proxy generation.

5. Which two namespaces are required for using SOAP headers to access services?
6. Create a simple SOAP header class. What do you do with this class in a Web method? On the client?

Exercises

Generate a proxy class for the `ConvertUnits` service you created in exercise 2 on Day 16. Build an interface to allow users to enter values.

WEEK 3

DAY 18

Configuring and Deploying ASP.NET Applications

Through the past 17 days, you've learned how to build most of the parts of an application. However, you haven't yet examined how to control the application as a whole. Your applications prior to today have consisted mostly of single pages, occasionally interacting with a few supplemental files. Today, you'll learn how to tie those pages together into a single cohesive application, where all settings and events can be controlled from a single location.

`global.asax` and `web.config` are two important files for ASP.NET. The former file controls application events, allowing you to execute code the first time *any* page in your application is requested, or even every time a page is requested. The latter file contains settings for your application, such as how session state should behave or where to apply security. You'll learn to take advantage of these files today.

Finally, you'll learn just how easy it is to deploy your application to another server. Many times developers build an application on a test machine and transfer it to a production machine when it is complete and bug free. ASP.NET makes this process as easy as it can possibly be.

Today you will cover the following topics:

- An deeper look at ASP.NET applications
- What `global.asax` is and how to use it
- How to configure ASP.NET using `web.config`
- How to use some of the most common configuration settings
- How to create your own custom settings in ASP.NET
- How to deploy an ASP.NET application

Introduction to ASP.NET Applications

So far, you've explored most of the concepts in ASP.NET, from the basics of Web forms to building complex business objects. Using these components, you can build very powerful pages to perform just about any task. The next step is bringing everything together to form a single application, and configuring and deploying that application.

You can simply group a bunch of ASP.NET pages together and call it an application, but the formal definition extends a bit further. An ASP.NET application is defined as follows: the sum of all files, pages, event handlers, modules, and executable code that is invoked or run within the scope of a given virtual directory (and its subdirectories) on a Web application server. That's quite a mouthful.

Recall from Day 1, "Getting Started with ASP.NET," that a virtual directory is any directory that is not contained in your home directory, but that appears to Web clients as though it were. For example, if you have the default setup for IIS, `c:\inetpub\wwwroot` is one virtual directory (your home directory), and it is viewable from a Web client on your machine as `http://localhost`. Another virtual directory could be at `c:\myweb\mysite`, but still might be viewable as `http://localhost/mysite`. The second directory is not in your home directory, but Web clients wouldn't know the difference. You can create a virtual directory through the Internet Service Manager easily (see Day 1 for a refresher).

Subfolders within these virtual directory folders are not necessarily virtual directories, but can be if you set them up as such. Figure 18.1 shows a typical list of virtual directories on a Windows 2000 machine.

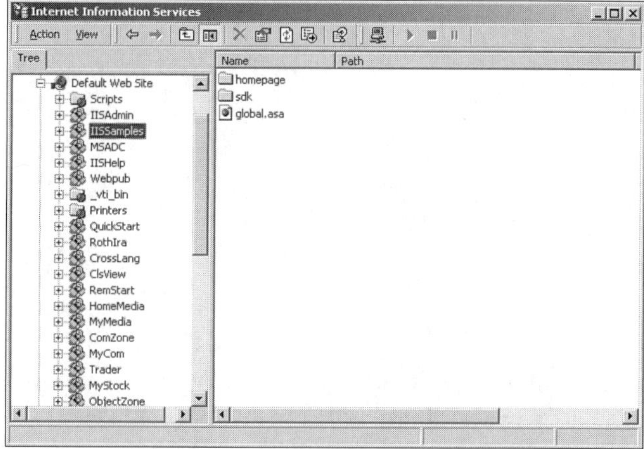

FIGURE 18.1

A typical virtual directory listing in IIS 5.0 on Windows 2000, shown through the Internet Services Manager.

ASP.NET applications are completely separate entities. Each ASP.NET application is handled in its own .NET runtime Application Domain (refer to the "Processing" section of Day 2, "Building ASP.NET Pages"), which means that each application can maintain its own set of configuration values and properties. So, given two virtual directories—`http://localhost/MyASP` and `http://localhost/MyASP/App2`—the latter virtual directory is a completely separate application, and is not contained or embedded within the first.

An ASP.NET application is created the first time a user makes a request from the server (more on this later). After this happens, you are able to use various application events to control execution of your program via the `global.asax` file, which I'll cover in depth later today.

The `/bin` Directory

NEW TERM ASP.NET introduces a new special directory for its applications: the `/bin` directory, also known as the *assembly cache*. As you learned from your lessons in business objects, this directory holds compiled binary files used by your applications (for example, DLLs). Each application has its own assembly cache, but can inherit one from its parent.

This directory is very important for ASP.NET applications. It provides an easily accessible store for objects used by your application. Assemblies placed here are automatically available to your `.aspx` files, so you don't have to worry about complex creation or registration procedures. For more information on using this directory, see Day 15, "Using Business Objects."

`global.asax`

You might not have thought of your ASP.NET pages as an actual application. It is an easy assumption to make because the pages are loosely connected groups of text files. We typically think of traditional applications as an executable (`.exe`) file, potentially with other supporting files, such as DLLs or `.inf` files. An ASP.NET application is different because a user can enter it from any page—there's no fixed starting point—and most associated files are readable by humans.

In reality, every virtual directory in IIS is very much an application. Regardless of which page is requested, the application starts the first time a page is requested. While users move from page to page, processing occurs in the background to handle the application. It can crash and be restarted just as any traditional application. The difference is that while a traditional application is started and run on a desktop computer allowing the user direct interaction, an ASP.NET application is started and run on a Web server, and a user must use a browser to access it.

Note

IIS allows you to specify which virtual directories are applications. By default, IIS does not automatically make virtual directories applications. To do so, go into the Internet Service Manager, right-click on a virtual directory, and select Properties. In the Directory tab, under Application Settings, note the application that the virtual directory belongs to. To create an application from this directory, click on Create.

Remember that everything in the .NET Framework is an object. That includes ASP.NET applications. The `HttpApplication` object provides methods, properties, and events, just as ASP.NET pages and server controls do. Revisiting the previous paragraph, you can now infer that whenever a page in your virtual directory is requested for the first time, an `HttpApplication` object is instantiated.

Note

Note that the application starts only the first time any page in your virtual directory is requested for the first time. This does *not* mean the first time a new page is requested. For example, if your application consisted of two files—`default.aspx` and `exit.aspx`—the application would start the first time either of these files is requested, not the first time each of the pages is requested. The former implies the application starts once, whereas the latter implies that the application starts every time a new page is requested.

So, how do you control the `HttpApplication` object (and thus your ASP.NET application)? The processing that occurs in each individual page accomplishes a certain task or tasks, but doesn't really control the application as a whole. One page cannot directly affect another. There must be a central location that controls the execution of the application. Enter `global.asax`.

The `global.asax` file is known as the *ASP.NET application file*. This file allows you to program against the `HttpApplication` object—you can control the ASP.NET application as you do any other object through its methods and events (you'll examine how to do this after some more background discussion).

> **Note**
>
> Note that the `global.asax` file is completely optional. If you do not create one for your application, the program operates in the default manner, with just enough processing to get things done. If you want to perform any additional functionality, however, you'll need this file.

The `global.asax` file is placed in the root directory of your ASP.NET application. For example, if you've been following the examples in this book, you should have created the virtual directory `http://localhost/tyaspnet21days`, which corresponds to the physical directory `c:\inetpub\wwwroot\tyaspnet21days`. This directory, by default, is not an application in itself; rather, the parent application is the `c:\inetpub\wwwroot` directory. The `global.asax` file then goes into this `\wwwroot` directory, and controls the application operation. Placing your `global.asax` file in the `\tyaspnet21days` directory will do no good unless this directory is marked as an application in the Internet Service Manager (see the note a few paragraphs back on how to do this).

ASP.NET configures this file so that it is not accessible from a browser. That way hackers cannot break in and modify your application. If someone tries to type `www.yoursite.com/global.asax` into his browser, he'll receive an error shown in Figure 18.2.

As mentioned earlier, `global.asax` is managed by the .NET Framework. Whenever this file has been modified, the CLR detects it and causes the application to restart so that the new settings can take effect. This can be a hassle for users, so modify this file sparingly.

The `HttpApplication` Class

You already know that the `HttpApplication` object allows you to control your ASP.NET application, but how does `global.asax` fit in? At runtime, `global.asax` is compiled into a dynamic class which is derived from the `HttpApplication` class. Thus, you can use the `global.asax` file to access objects and events that are available to the parent `HttpApplication` object.

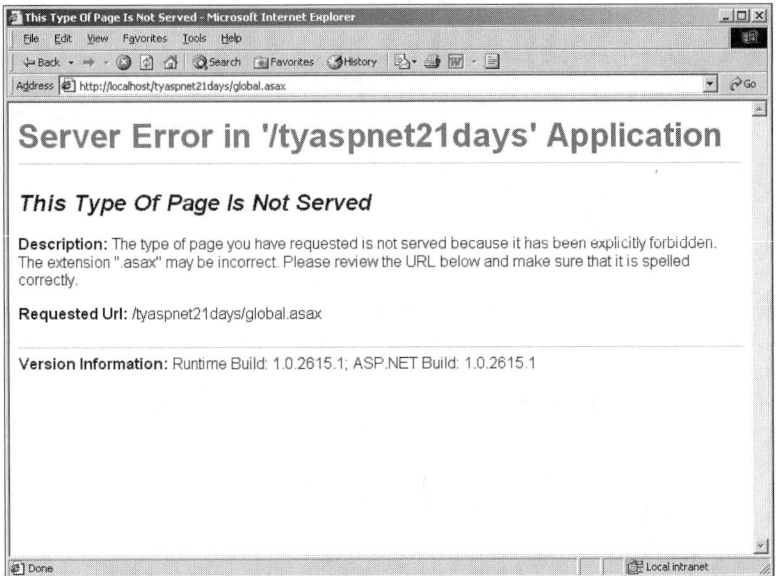

FIGURE 18.2 *Requesting* `global.asax` *from the browser produces an error.*

During application initialization, a number of `HttpApplication` instances are created, and each instance handles one particular HTTP request at a time. It handles all processing of that request, and after it finishes, it can then be assigned another request. That instance is responsible for managing that particular request throughout its lifetime.

Imagine that you own an exclusive upscale restaurant, with waiters who serve only one table at a time. When a new customer comes in, one waiter is in charge of meeting all the customer's needs, such as seating, informing about the specials, and meal delivery (even though your meal might actually be delivered by someone else, the waiter is in charge of when that happens). In the same way, an `HttpApplication` instance handles the "welcoming" of the HTTP request, taking note of any request variables, and rendering the page (note that the actual rendering is done by an `HttpHandler`, but the `HttpApplication` instance tells it when to go).

Because the `global.asax` class is derived from the `HttpApplication` class, it inherits many of the latter's methods and events. Those methods and events provide the programmatic access for your ASP.NET application. In `global.asax`, then, you define the handlers that take care of the events raised by the `HttpApplication` instance, which all have to deal with the application processing. These methods must conform to standard event handler naming scheme: `Application_EventName(event arguments)`. For example, `Application_Start(Sender as Object, e as EventArgs)`.

Programming `global.asax`

The `global.asax` file operates in many ways similar to `.aspx` files. You can use page directives (`@ Imports`, `@ Application`, and `@ Assembly`), server-side includes (see tomorrow's lesson, "Separating Code from Content"), and code declaration blocks. You use `global.asax` to sync any event exposed by the `HttpApplication` class, as listed in Table 18.1 (you'll see many of these again in Day 20, "Debugging ASP.NET Pages").

TABLE 18.1 `HttpApplication` Class Events

Event	*Description*
`AcquireRequestState`	Fired when the application obtains the cache for the request.
`AuthenticateRequest`	Fired when the application tries to authenticate the HTTP request.
`AuthorizeRequest`	Fired when the application tries to authorize the HTTP request.
`BeginRequest`	Fired when the HTTP request starts.
`EndRequest`	Fired when the HTTP request ends.
`Error`	Fired when an error is raised.
`PostRequestHandlerExecute`	Fired immediately after the HTTP handler processes the request.
`PreRequestHandlerExecute`	Fired immediately before the HTTP handler processes the request.
`PreSendRequestContent`	If the request contains additional content (querystring, form variables, and so on), this event is fired immediately before that content is received.
`PreSendRequestHeaders`	Fired immediately before the request headers are received.
`ReleaseRequestState`	Fired when the application releases the session state for the request.
`ResolveRequestCache`	Fired when the application resolves the cache for the request.
`UpdateRequestCache`	Fired when the application updates and releases the cache for the request.

Take a look at a sample process. Listing 18.1 is your `global.asax`.

LISTING 18.1 A Sample `global.asax`

```
<script language="VB" runat="server">

   Sub Application_Start(Sender as Object, e as EventArgs)
      Application("Time") = System.DateTime.Now
   End Sub

   Sub Application_AcquireRequestState(Sender as Object,
➥e as EventArgs)
      Response.Write("Acquiring request session state
➥...<br>")
   End Sub

   Sub Application_AuthenticateRequest(Sender as Object,
➥e as EventArgs)
      Response.Write("Authenticating request...<br>")
   End Sub

   Sub Application_AuthorizeRequest(Sender as Object,
➥e as EventArgs)
      Response.Write("Authorizing request...<br>")
   End Sub

   Sub Application_PostRequestHandlerExecute(Sender as Object,
➥e as EventArgs)
      Response.Write("Request handler executed...<br>")
   End Sub

   Sub Application_PreRequestHandlerExecute(Sender as Object,
➥e as EventArgs)
      Response.Write("Request handler executed...<br>")
   End Sub

   Sub Application_PreSendRequestContent(Sender as Object,
➥e as EventArgs)
      Response.Write("Receiving request content...<br>")
   End Sub

   Sub Application_PreSendRequestHeaders(Sender as Object,
➥e as EventArgs)
      Response.Write("Receiving request headers...<br>")
   End Sub

   Sub Application_ReleaseRequestState(Sender as Object,
➥e as EventArgs)
      Response.Write("Releasing request state...<br>")
   End Sub

   Sub Application_ResolveRequestCache(Sender as Object,
```

LISTING 18.1 continued

```
➥e as EventArgs)
40:          Response.Write("Resolving request cache...<br>")
41:       End Sub
42:
43:       Sub Application_UpdateRequestCache(Sender as Object,
➥e as EventArgs)
44:          Response.Write("Updating request cache...<br>")
45:       End Sub
46:
47:       Sub Application_Error(Sender as Object, e as EventArgs)
48:          Response.Write(Sender.Request.isAuthenticated &
➥" is authenticating request...<br>")
49:       End Sub
50:
51:       Sub Session_Start(Sender as Object, e as EventArgs)
52:          Response.Write("Session is starting...<br>")
53:       End Sub
54:
55:       Sub Application_BeginRequest(Sender as Object,
➥e as EventArgs)
56:          Response.Write("<b>Process</b><p>")
57:          Response.Write("Request is starting...<br>")
58:       End Sub
59:
60:       Sub Application_EndRequest(Sender as Object,
➥e as EventArgs)
61:          Response.Write("Request is ending...<br>")
62:       End Sub
63:
64:    </script>
```


ANALYSIS In this file, you provide functionality for most of the events listed in Table 18.1. In line 3, you use the `HttpApplication` object to record the application's start time for reference later (see Day 4, "Using ASP.NET Objects with C# and VB.NET," for more information on saving state). Each event then simply writes out a string to the page that tells you what it is doing—this allows you to see the order in which the request is processed.

Save this file in the root folder—`c:\inetpub\wwwroot`—unless you've created an application out of your `tyaspnet21days` directory, in which case you can put the `global.asax` file there.

With the `global.asax` file presented in Listing 18.2, a short message will be output when each of the application-level events fires. Note that some of these events fire every single time an ASP.NET page is reviewed. To illustrate this, create the ASP.NET page shown in Listing 18.2.

LISTING 18.2 Testing the `global.asax` Event Handlers

```
1:  <%@ Page Language="VB" %>
2:
3:  <script language="VB" runat="server">
4:     Sub Page_Load(Sender As Object, e As EventArgs)
5:        lblOutput.text = "Page loading...<p>" & _
6:           "Application started at: " & Application("Time") & "...<br>" & _
7:           "Current time: " & DateTime.Now & "...<br>"
8:     End Sub
9:
10:     Sub Click(obj As Object, E As EventArgs)
11:        Session.Abandon()
12:     End Sub
13:  </script>
14:
15:  <html><body>
16:     <form runat="server">
17:        <table align="center">
18:        <tr>
19:           <td valign="top" width="300"><b>Output</b></td>
20:        </tr>
21:        <tr>
22:           <td valign="top">
23:              <asp:label id="lblOutput" runat="server"/><p>
24:              <asp:Button id="btSubmit" runat="server"
25:                 OnClick="Click" Text="End This Session"/>
26:           </td>
27:        </tr>
28:        </table>
29:     </form>
30:  </body></html>
```

ANALYSIS Save this file as `Listing1802.aspx`. This page, when requested, displays a few messages to the user, including the time the application started and the current time (shown on lines 5–7). Line 25 contains a button control that, when clicked, abandons the current session. This will be useful to see how session is handled by the `HttpApplication` object. Figure 18.3 shows the output of the request.

When the page is first requested, several `HttpApplication` events fire, and the `global.asax` file handles them by outputting text. You can see the process of execution of the `HttpApplication` object on the left side of Figure 18.2, and the output from the `Listing1802.aspx` file on the right side. Notice how the output starts midway down the page; the application file processes the request and resolves the cache and session states, and then the HTTP request handler (I'll discuss those in the next section) takes over and produces the page output. Finally, the application file performs some additional functionality before the request is over. In other words, the methods execute in the following order:

1. `Application_OnStart`
2. `Application_BeginRequest`
3. `Application_AuthenticateRequest`
4. `Application_AuthorizeRequest`
5. `Application_ResolveRequestCache`
6. `Session_Start`
7. `Application_AcquireRequestState`
8. `Application_PreRequestHandlerExecute`
9. The `Page_Load` event inside the `.aspx` file, followed by any other page outputs
10. `Application_PostRequestHandlerExecute`
11. `Application_ReleaseRequestState`
12. `Application_UpdateRequestCache`
13. `Application_EndRequest`
14. `Application_PreSendRequestHeaders`

OUTPUT

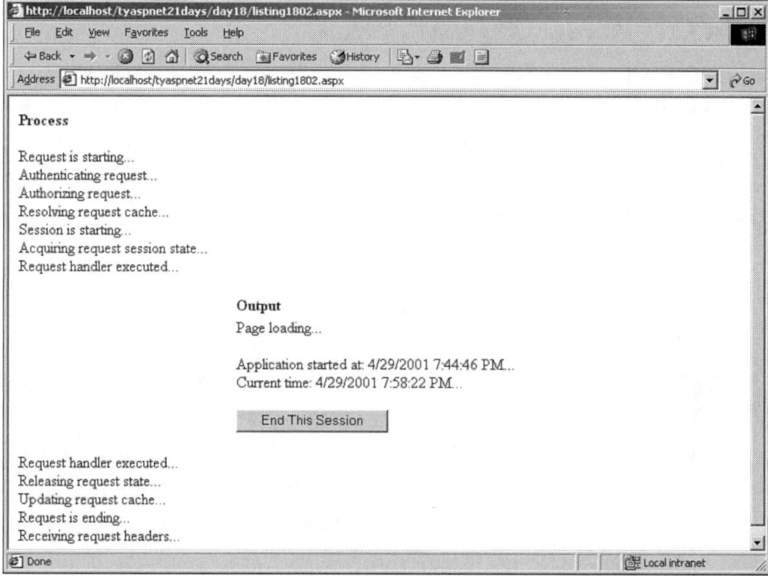

FIGURE 18.3
The page produced by Listing 18.3.

Note that the exact events that execute might depend on the circumstances of the request to your page. For instance, if you request the page a second time, the `Session_Start` method won't execute, and consequently, you won't see `Session is starting...` as in Figure 18.3.

Notice the time discrepancy from the start of the application (as specified by the `Application_Start` method) to the actual rendering of the page (the actual time difference is dependent on your machine configuration). Subsequent requests won't take as long because the application is already started and the pages are compiled. Changing `global.asax` in any way will restart the application.

The End This Session button in Figure 18.3 uses the `Abandon` method of the `Session` object to restart the session and, consequently, causes `Session is starting...` to reappear.

Therefore, the `global.asax` file allows you to control nearly every aspect of the processing of an ASP.NET page. You can use `HttpApplication` object events to perform actions that are invisible to the user, such as authentication or other personalization—the choices are yours.

Configuring ASP.NET

Just as it is necessary to control your application's processing, it is necessary to configure your application's settings. This includes handling how pages are displayed, how they are compiled, controlling access to the parts of your application, and so on. As you'll see in a moment, ASP.NET contains a lot of configurable parts, and it takes an elegant system to manage all those settings gracefully.

ASP.NET provides a hierarchical configuration system that is very extensible and, best of all, text-based, meaning that developers can access and modify the configuration remotely.

New Term With *hierarchical configuration*, the application configuration information is applied according to the virtual directory structure of your Web site. Subdirectories can inherit or override configuration options from their parent directories. In fact, all directories inherit from a default system configuration file, `machine.config`, typically located in the `WinNT\Microsoft.NET\Framework\`*`<version>`*`\CONFIG` directory. This provides you a lot of flexibility when designing your applications.

This robust system is implemented with the `web.config` file, an XML text-based file. Let's examine it further.

web.config

I've mentioned the `web.config` file quite a few times throughout this book. So far, you know that it holds information used by the application to control its behavior. There is nothing special about this file; it simply holds keys and values recognized by ASP.NET. These values are easily modifiable, and, in fact, you can add your own custom keys and values to control other settings that ASP.NET doesn't handle for you (more on that later).

As you learned earlier, the ASP.NET configuration system is hierarchical. In terms of the `web.config` file, this means that the settings you supply in each `web.config` file apply only to the directory that contains the file, and those below it. So, if you want to provide settings for your entire application, simply place this file in your root application folder. If a subdirectory has special application needs (such as disallowing unauthorized users), simply create another `web.config` with the new settings. The subdirectory will inherit its parent's settings, overriding those that are duplicated.

However, the hierarchical system is based on the virtual directory path, and not the actual physical path. To grasp this concept, imagine a Web site with the directory structure shown in Figure 18.4.

FIGURE 18.4

A sample directory structure.

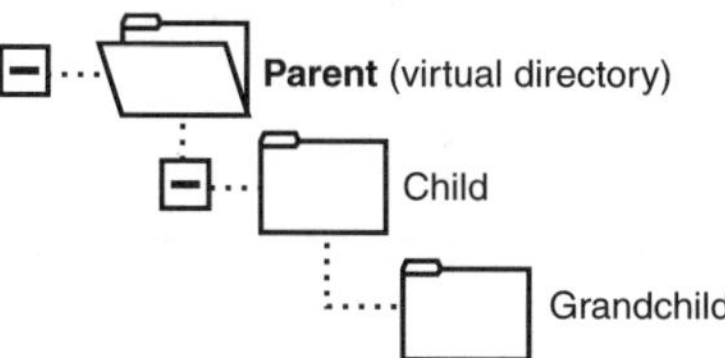

Let's assume that `Parent` is the only virtual directory. `Parent`, `Child`, and `Grandchild` all inherit the system-level `web.config` settings. The `Parent` directory can override or add settings with its own local `web.config` file. If a browser accesses `Child` with the URL `http://localhost/Parent/Child`, that directory will also inherit `Parent`'s settings, as will `Grandchild`. The two subdirectories are also able to override any of `Parent`'s settings with their own `web.config` files.

Now let's assume that `Child` is also a virtual directory, and can be accessed as `http://localhost/Child`. Because `web.config` settings are processed according to virtual directories (and not physical paths), it will *not* inherit any of `Parent`'s settings. `Grandchild` will now inherit different settings depending on how it is accessed. `http://localhost/Parent/Child/Grandchild` might produce different settings than `http://localhost/Child/Grandchild`, so be careful how you structure your virtual directories!

Like the `global.asax` file, ASP.NET also prevents the `web.config` file from being accessed via a Web client. If you try to get at this file, the browser will return the same error shown in Figure 18.2. This is quite helpful for stopping prying eyes from breaking into your application.

Changes to this file are automatically detected and, like the `global.asax` file, the application is automatically restarted for the new settings to take effect.

Enough theory, let's take a look at this file! The basic format of the `web.config` file is simple:

```
<configuration>
   <configSections>
      <!-- Handlers declared here -->
   </configSections>
   <system.web>
      <!-- ASP.NET Configuration Settings Would Go Here -->
   </system.web>
   <system.net>
      <!-- .NET Runtime Configuration Settings Would Go Here -->
   </system.net>
</configuration>
```

No script blocks or HTML code, just pure XML. Inside the `<configuration>` tags are typically two different elements: configuration section handlers and configuration section settings. The first section declares the types of data in the `web.config` file, and the second contains the actual key/value pairs of settings.

Configuration section handlers, denoted by the `<configSections>` element, process the XML data contained in `web.config` and return an appropriate object based on this data; you must specify these handlers so that ASP.NET knows what type of configuration data you have. For example, if a setting named "XmlFiles" contained a list of XML files, you would have a corresponding configuration section handler named "XmlFiles" that would return, for instance, an `XmlTextReader` object to your ASP.NET page when called. Luckily, ASP.NET already provides quite a few section handlers in the default `machine.config` file, so you don't have to declare these yourself.

For example, Listing 18.3 shows a portion of the default configuration section for the `system.web` section and its subsections.

LISTING 18.3 Sample Configuration Section Handlers

```
<configuration>
    <configSections>
        <sectionGroup name="system.web">
            <section name="browserCaps"
```

LISTING 18.3 continued

```
➥ type="System.Web.Configuration.
➥HttpCapabilitiesSectionHandler,System.Web" />
              <section name="clientTarget"
➥type="System.Web.Configuration.
➥ClientTargetSectionHandler,System.Web" />
              <section name="compilation"
➥type="System.Web.UI.CompilationConfigurationHandler,
➥System.Web" />
              <section name="pages"
➥type="System.Web.UI.PagesConfigurationHandler,
➥System.Web" />
          </sectionGroup>
     </configSections>
  </configuration>
```

As you can see, this file becomes quite complex, so I won't go into depth here. Just know that each section defined by the name elements contains settings used by ASP.NET (you'll examine these settings in the next section). Refer to the .NET Framework SDK documentation for more information.

> **Note** Note the format of each element in this web.config file. In elements consisting of multiple words, for example, sectionGroup, the first letter of the first word is lowercase, whereas all subsequent first letters are capitalized. This is known as *camel casing*, and is standard for the web.config file. The web.config file is case sensitive, and without the proper casing, your application will generate errors.

Configuration settings are the actual data that configure your application; the key/value pairs of information. There are, in turn, two types of these sections: system.net and system.web. The first section is for configuring the .NET runtime itself, so you won't bother much with that. The second is for controlling ASP.NET. All settings (with two exceptions, which I'll discuss in a moment) for your applications will be placed within the <system.web> tags. For example, Listing 18.4 shows a sample configuration file.

LISTING 18.4 Sample Configuration File

```
<configuration>
   <system.web>
        <trace
            enabled="false"
```

LISTING 18.4 continued

```
5:              requestLimit="10"
6:              pageOutput="false"
7:              traceMode="SortByTime"
8:              localOnly="true"
9:          />
10:          <globalization
11:                  requestEncoding="iso-8859-1"
12:                  responseEncoding="iso-8859-1"
13:          />
14:          <customErrors mode="RemoteOnly" />
➥<!-- Possible values for mode: On, Off, RemoteOnly -->
15:      </system.web>
16:  </configuration>
```

ANALYSIS This listing contains three different settings for ASP.NET. The first, `trace`, on line 3, contains settings for the trace service of ASP.NET (you'll learn about that in Day 20. The second setting, on line 10, controls how your application sends output to the browser; you'll examine that tomorrow. The final section, `customErrors`, controls how errors are displayed in your application.

> Again, note the camel casing of each element.

Table 18.2 lists all the configuration settings available for use in `web.config`. I won't cover all of them in this book because some are used only rarely, but this table will provide a good reference.

TABLE 18.2 `web.config` Configuration Settings

Section Name	*Description*
`<appSettings>`	Used to store your own custom application settings.
`<authentication>`	Configures how ASP.NET authenticates users (see Day 21, "Securing Your ASP.NET Applications").
`<authorization>`	Configures authorization of resources in ASP.NET (again, see Day 21).
`<browserCaps>`	Responsible for controlling the settings of the browser capabilities component.
`<clientTarget>`	Adds aliases for browser versions and names.

TABLE 18.2 continued

Section Name	*Description*
`<compilation>`	Responsible for all compilation settings used by ASP.NET. See Day 20 for more information.
`<customErrors>`	Tells ASP.NET how to display errors in the browser.
`<globalization>`	Responsible for configuring the globalization settings of an application (see Day 20).
`<httpHandlers>`	Responsible for mapping incoming URLs to `IHttpHandler` classes. Subdirectories do not inherit these settings. Also responsible for mapping incoming URLs to `IHttpHandlerFactory` classes. Data represented in `<httpHandlerFactories>` sections are hierarchically inherited by subdirectories.
`<httpModules>`	Responsible for configuring Http modules within an application. Http modules participate in the processing of every request into an application, and common uses include security and logging.
`<httpRuntime>`	Configures how your application runs—for example, how many requests it can take and the maximum time a request is allowed to execute before it is shut down.
`<identity>`	Controls how ASP.NET accesses its resources (which identity it uses to access those resources). See Day 21.
`<location>`	A special tag that controls how settings apply to a directory in your application.
`<machineKey>`	Keys to use for encryption and decryption of cookie data.
`<pages>`	Controls page-specific configuration settings.
`<processModel>`	Configures the ASP.NET process model settings on IIS Web server systems.
`<securityPolicy>`	Maps security levels to policy files.
`<sessionState>`	Responsible for configuring session state.
`<trace>`	Responsible for configuring the ASP.NET trace service.
`<trust>`	The code access security level for an application.
`<webServices>`	Controls settings for Web services (see Days 16, "Creating Web Services," and 17, "Consuming and Securing XML Web Services").

18

Configuration Sections

Although you can define any configuration sections you choose, ASP.NET comes built in with several that might already serve your purposes. The following sections provide examples and syntax for the most commonly used configuration settings.

Each section can support subelements, attributes, or both. *Subelements* are separate tags that are "below" the current tag, and can have their own subelements and attributes. Attributes define properties of the tag, such as the `id` attribute for server controls.

Remember that each of these settings must be placed in the `<system.web>` configuration section, with two exceptions that we'll discuss when we come across them.

<appSettings>

This section allows you to define your own custom attributes for your ASP.NET application, such as database connection strings (see Day 8, "Beginning to Build Databases," for more information on those). It contains one subelement: `add`, which contains two attributes, `key` and `value`.

This section is specifically designed to contain custom values; ASP.NET itself doesn't use the values here at all (unless, of course, you tell it to). The syntax is simple:

```
<appSettings>
   <add key="ApplicationName" value="MyApp" />
   <add key="DSN" value="Provider=Microsoft.Jet.OLEDB.4.0;
➥"Data Source=c:\ASPNET\data\banking.mdb"/>
</appSettings>
```

Accessing the values stored in `<appSettings>` is a bit different from accessing other configuration values; ASP.NET makes it easier to get these values. First, this tag does not have to be placed in the `<system.web>` section; it can reside directly under the `<configuration>` element. This is so that both ASP.NET applications and regular .NET applications can access the same values.

Next, you don't have to use the `GetConfig` method, which we'll examine later today, to access these values. ASP.NET provides an easy property for this section, `ConfigurationSettings.AppSettings`. For example, using the previous `<appSettings>` section, the following `Page_Load` method would write "MyApp" to the browser:

```
sub Page_Load(Sender as Object, e as EventArgs)
   Response.write(ConfigurationSettings.AppSettings _
      ("ApplicationName"))
end sub
```

Simply supply the key name in parentheses (or brackets in C#) and you can easily retrieve the appropriate value.

<browserCaps>

This section contains many different elements and settings. It represents all the capabilities of the client browser, such as whether it is JavaScript capable, its browser version, and so on. We won't cover them all here. The syntax for this element is as follows:

```
<configuration>
   <system.web>
      <browserCaps>
         browser="Unknown"
         version=0.0
         majorver=0
         minorver=0
         frames=false
         tables=false
         ...
      </browserCaps>
   </system.web>
</configuration>
```

Refer to the .NET Framework SDK documentation to examine each property in more detail.

`<customErrors>`

This section allows you to define custom errors for your application or override built-in ASP.NET errors. For example, when a user tries to access a page that doesn't exist, he'll see a page similar to the one shown in Figure 18.5.

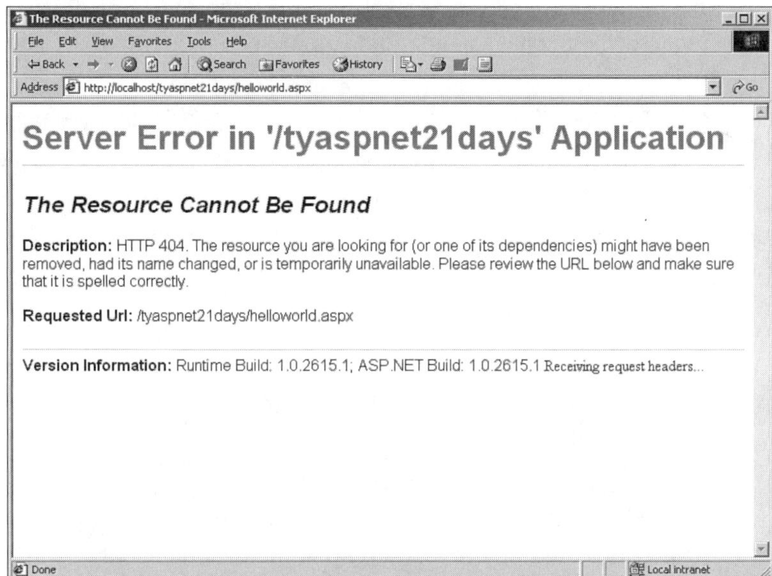

FIGURE 18.5
A typical error page displayed when a user tries to request `helloworld.aspx`, *which doesn't exist on the server.*

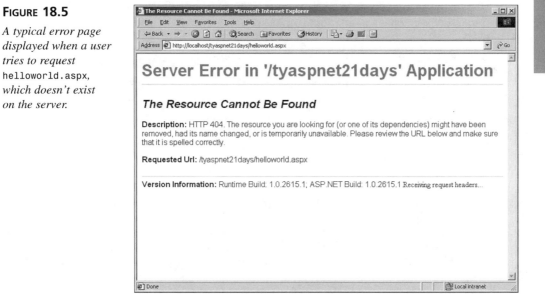

Although this page adequately informs the user of the error he has made, it might not fit into the design scheme of your site. Therefore, the `<customErrors>` element allows you to specify an alternative error page for this, and other errors.

<customErrors> has two attributes: defaultRedirect, which specifies the URL the browser should go to if any error occurs; and mode, which specifies whether custom errors are enabled (On), disabled (Off), or shown only to remote clients (RemoteOnly). In other words, you won't see the custom errors when developing the application, but your end users will.

This section also supports one subelement, error, which allows you to tailor handling for individual errors. For example, take a look at the following code:

```
<customErrors defaultRedirect="error.htm" mode="On">
   <error statusCode="404" redirect="error404.htm" />
</customerrors>
```

This specifies that if a 404 error occurs (Resource Cannot Be Found, as shown in Figure 18.5), ASP.NET should redirect users to error404.htm. This file could contain a customized error message that fits in with your design scheme. If any other error occurs, this code tells ASP.NET to go to error.htm, which, again, could contain another more general error message.

When custom error handling is on, and an error occurs, ASP.NET will pass a querystring parameter to the redirection page, aspxerrorpath, that contains the virtual path of the file that generated the error. For example, in the situation described earlier, when the user requests the file helloworld.aspx, the user would be redirected to the URL:

```
http://localhost/tyaspnet21days/error404.htm?
➥aspxerrorpath=/tyaspnet21days/helloworld.aspx
```

This value can be used for a number of different reasons: You can inform the user of the invalid URL and instruct him to check the address or update his bookmarks, or even log this error to a database, which is useful for analyzing problems in your site later.

<location>

This is the second configuration section that does not require placement in the <system.web> section. Its purpose is to allow you to apply other settings to only a specific location on your Web server. It is most commonly used for security settings, so I'll discuss it more in depth in Day 21.

Let's imagine a simple scenario. You have two pages in your site: default.aspx and members.aspx. The first is, obviously, the default page of your site, and anyone should be able to access it. The second should be accessible only by users who have registered and logged in to your site. Therefore, you want to apply security settings to only this one file. The code to do so would read as follows:

```
<configuration>
   <location path="members.aspx">
```

```
      <system.web>
         <authorization>
            <deny users="?"/>
         </authorization>
      </system.web>
   </location>
</configuration>
```

On the second line, you see the `<location>` tag with the path of the file to which the subsequent settings should apply; in this case, `members.aspx` (you can also specify directory names with this attribute). Don't worry about the `<authorization>` and `<deny>` tags—you'll get to those in Day 21. Notice that inside the `<location>` tags, you must specify `<system.web>`; `<location>` itself isn't specific to ASP.NET or .NET, but any tags within usually are.

Don't forget that the `web.config` file is hierarchical, so the `<location>` tag must also obey these rules. For example, take a look at the following code:

```
<configuration>
   <location path="subdirectory1">
      <system.web>
         <authorization>
            <deny users="?"/>
         </authorization>
      </system.web>
   </location>
</configuration>
```

18

The security settings would apply not only to the directory `subdirectory1`, but also to any subdirectories of that directory, and so on.

<pages>

This section allows you to control the page options that you would normally specify in page directives such as `@ Page`. The difference is that the settings in `<pages>` apply to all pages on the site, and not just one particular page. Let's look at the syntax:

```
<configuration>
   <system.web>
      <pages
         buffer="true"
         enableSessionState="true"
         enableViewState="true"
         enableViewStateMac="true"
         autoEventWireup="true"
         smartNavigation="true"
         pageBaseType="TYASPNET, TYASPNET.dll"
         userControlBaseType="TYASPNET"
   </system.web>
</configuration>
```

This particular code snippet contains all the `<pages>` element's properties. It turns on buffering for all pages, turns on session state and viewstate for Macs as well as other machines (see Day 4, "Using ASP.NET Objects with C# and VB.NET," for information on buffering, session state, and viewstate), and turns on page events. Smart navigation enhances the user experience by persisting element focus and scroll bar position between pages, among other things. `pageBaseType` indicates which code-behind every ASP.NET page should inherit from by default (I'll explain code-behinds tomorrow). `userControlBaseType` specifies which code behind every user control should inherit from by default.

This section is very useful if you need to make all your pages behave similarly. Be careful, however, because the default settings are usually sufficient; modifying these values for every single page could result in some repercussions in performance or possibly errors. You'll usually modify these settings on a per-page basis.

<sessionState>

ASP.NET provides many ways to customize session state. For instance, you can store session variables on a completely separate machine, in case the server crashes or needs to be replaced. This ensures that your session data is never lost. You can also store the session state in another process on the same system, which does something similar to what we just described. This section contains the following attributes:

- `mode`—This attribute specifies where session information should be stored. Valid options are `Off`, which disables session state; `InProc`, which specifies that session information is stored locally (default); `StateServer`, session information is stored on another machine; and `SQLServer`, which stores information in a SQL Server database.
- `cookieless`—Indicates whether cookieless session should be used (see Day 4 for more information on this topic and cookie munging).
- `timeout`—The number of minutes of idle time before a session is abandoned by ASP.NET (default is 20 minutes).
- `stateConnectionString`—The server name and port to store session information, when `mode` is set to `StateServer`; for example, `"tcpip=127.0.0.1:42424"`.
- `sqlConnectionString`—The connection string used to connect to the SQL server to store session information, when `mode` is set to `SQLServer`. See Day 10 for information on connection strings.

The syntax is

```
<configuration>
   <system.web>
```

```
      <sessionstate
         mode="InProc"
         cookieless="false"
         timeout="10" />
   </system.web>
</configuration>
```

It might seem like a good idea to always store session information on another server, for safety reasons. However, when you use another server, performance suffers; ASP.NET must make connections over the network and communicate with a remote machine, which introduces serious lag times. Storing information `InProc` or on the same machine might not be as safe, but it is tremendously faster.

Custom Configuration

`web.config` is not limited to only the sections listed in Table 18.2—you can add any type of information you want to this file.

What about the `<appSettings>` section? Doesn't that hold all the custom configuration information? You could, technically, put all custom information here, but you're limited to only key/value pairs here. When you use the `ConfigurationSettings.AppSettings` property (see the section on `<appSettings>` earlier today), ASP.NET creates a `NameValueCollection` object and populates it with the values from `<appSettings>`. This collection can easily be used to reference key/value pairs in this section.

18

However, sometimes a `NameValueCollection` isn't suitable for your needs. For example, suppose that your application relies on an XML file that contains information on a library of books. It's easy enough to add this filename to the `<appSettings>` section like so:

```
<appSettings>
   <add key="Library" value="c:\inetpub\wwwroot\tyaspnet21days\
➥day18\books.xml"/>
</appSettings>
```

When you retrieve this section from `web.config`, however, you'd rather receive an `XmlTextReader`, rather than a key/value pair describing the filename. ASP.NET allows you to build your own configuration sections, as well as their corresponding section handlers, which can return whatever type of object you want. Let's explore this situation a bit further. First, let's create a section handler that processes the input accordingly, and then build the section in `web.config` as well as an ASP.NET page to utilize it.

Custom Section Handlers

As described in the previous section, sometimes the built-in `web.config` section handlers aren't enough; they might not provide the functionality you need for your application.

When this happens, you can easily create your own handlers to perform whatever actions are necessary. Let's take a look at an example, shown in Listings 18.5 and 18.6.

LISTING 18.5 A Custom `web.config` Section Handler Class in VB.NET

```
Imports System
Imports System.Configuration
Imports System.Xml

Namespace TYASPNET.Handlers
   Public Class LibrarySectionHandler : Implements
➥IConfigurationSectionHandler
      Public Function Create(parent as Object,
➥configContext as Object, section as XmlNode) as Object
➥Implements IConfigurationSectionHandler.Create
         dim strFileName as String
         strFileName = section.Attributes.Item(0).Value

          dim objReader as new XmlTextReader(strFileName)
          return objReader
       End Function
    End Class

 End Namespace
```

LISTING 18.6 A Custom `web.config` Section Handler Class in C#

```
using System;
using System.Configuration;
using System.Xml;

namespace TYASPNET.Handlers {
   public class LibrarySectionHandler:
➥IConfigurationSectionHandler {
      object IConfigurationSectionHandler.Create
➥(Object parent, Object configContext, XmlNode section) {
         string strFileName;
         strFileName = section.Attributes.Item(0).Value;

          XmlTextReader objReader = new XmlTextReader
➥(strFileName);
          return objReader;
       }
    }
 }
```

ANALYSIS Save this file as `LibrarySectionHandler.vb` or `LibrarySectionHandler.cs`. Before you examine the code, let's take a brief overview of this class. A `web.config` file can declare this class as the handler for a configuration section, similar to Listing 18.3. Whenever ASP.NET accesses that section, typically through some code you've written, this class is created to handle the data contained in the section. In this case, the class reads a file path from `web.config`, creates an `XmlTextReader` from the path, and passes it to whoever requested it. The requester can then use this `XmlTextReader` directly.

As you can see, a custom section handler starts off as a VB.NET or C# class, just as a business object does. The difference is that this class must implement the `IConfigurationSectionHandler` interface, shown on line 6. An interface is a class that describes what methods and properties other classes should have; the `IConfigurationSectionHandler` tells you that your `LibrarySectionHandler` class must contain a `Create` method. Don't worry too much about interfaces; think of them simply as templates for other classes (see the .NET Framework SDK Documentation for more information). Also note the namespace to which this class belongs: `TYASPNET.Handlers`.

On line 6, you declare your section handler class, `LibrarySectionHandler` (recall that the `Implements` keyword is omitted for C#). This class will be responsible for retrieving the aforementioned XML library filename from the `web.config` file, and sending the appropriate output to the ASP.NET page.

18

Next, on line 7, you declare your `Create` method. Remember that `IConfigurationSectionHandler` already provided the template for this method, so you only have to follow it. You do this in VB.NET by again using the `Implements` keyword, and in C# by preceding the method name with the name of the interface and a period. The `IConfigurationSectionHandler` interface tells you that you need three parameters. The first is an `Object` that contains information about the parent of this `web.config` section. In other words, if this section inherited information from another `web.config` file, this first parameter would provide a link to the appropriate section in the other `web.config` file. You won't use this parameter here. The second parameter, `configContext`, is another `Object` that contains some contextual information; this parameter typically will never be used, so you'll ignore it also. The last parameter, `section`, is the most important. It contains the actual XML data from the `web.config` file. You'll use this parameter to parse the necessary information and spit out the appropriate data.

The next part of the listing should be simple because you've already covered XML in ASP.NET in Day 11. Lines 8 and 9 retrieve the sole attribute from the custom section in `web.config` (I'll show that in a moment). This attribute will contain the path to the XML file. Lines 11 and 12 create an `XmlTextReader` from this file path, and return it to the calling application.

It seems like an awful lot of work, but in reality, it's very simple. This listing was boilerplate, so you can cut-and-paste it over and over again, changing only the implementation of the `Create` method to suit your needs. With this listing, you can create an army of custom section handlers!

Before you are through here, you need to do one more thing: Compile this class and place it in your assembly cache. Again, you should be very familiar with this process. Enter the following command from the command prompt:

```
vbc /t:library /out:..\..\bin\TYASPNET.Handlers.dll /r:System.dll
➥/r:System.xml.dll /r:System.web.dll
➥LibrarySectionHandler.vb
```

or:

```
csc /t:library /out:..\..\bin\TYASPNET.Handlers.dll /r:System.dll
➥/r:System.xml.dll /r:System.web.dll
➥LibrarySectionHandler.cs
```

This command assumes that your assembly cache (the `/bin` directory) is two below the current directory (where the `LibrarySectionHandler.vb` file resides). It creates a new assembly called `TYASPNET.Handlers.dll` that contains your new handler class. Now let's look at how to use this new handler.

Creating and Retrieving Custom web.config Sections

This first step to use our custom handler is to declare the appropriate section in the `web.config` file. This is very simple, as shown in Listing 18.7.

Listing 18.7 The Custom `web.config`

```
<configuration>
   <configSections>
      <sectionGroup name="system.web">
         <section name="Library" type="TYASPNET.Handlers.
➥LibrarySectionHandler,TYASPNET.Handlers" />
      </sectionGroup>
   </configSections>

   <system.web>
      <Library file="c:\inetpub\wwwroot\tyaspnet21days\
➥day11\books.xml" />
   </system.web>
</configuration>
```

ANALYSIS Save this file as `web.config`, and place it in the same directory as the `LibrarySectionHandler.vb` file. Recall that there are two parts of the `web.config` file: the configuration handler section and the configuration settings. The first is denoted by the `<configSections>` element, shown on line 2. Line 3 tells you that the handler applies to the `<system.web>` section; you could just have easily specified `system.net` or even left this element out. It simply serves as a way to group settings.

On line 4, you declare a new section named `Library`. The `type` attribute specifies what handler will be associated with this section. In this case, you're using the `LibrarySectionHandler` you just created. You must specify its full namespace name, followed by the assembly it belongs to (`TYASPNET.Handlers.dll`).

Now you can create the actual settings for your application. On line 9, you have the `Library` section (declared on line 4) and an attribute `file` that specifies the path of the XML file (note that you're using an XML file from Day 11). You're done with the `web.config` file, so let's build the ASP.NET page, shown in Listing 18.8.

LISTING 18.8 Retrieving the Custom Configuration Settings

```
<%@ Page Language="VB" %>
<%@ Import Namespace="System.Xml" %>

<script runat="server">
   sub Page_Load(Sender as Object, e as EventArgs)
      'retrieve information
      dim i as integer

      dim objLibrary as XmlTextReader = _
         ConfigurationSettings.GetConfig
➥("system.web/Library")

       'display information
       While objLibrary.Read()
          Select Case objLibrary.NodeType
             Case XmlNodeType.Element
                if objLibrary.HasAttributes then
                   for i = 0 to objLibrary.AttributeCount
➥ - 1
                      lblLibrary.Text += objLibrary. _
                         GetAttribute(i) & " "
                   next
                   lblLibrary.Text += ", "
                end if
             Case XmlNodeType.Text
               lblLibrary.Text += objLibrary.Value & "<br>"
          End Select
       End While
```

LISTING 18.8 continued

```
27:
28:        objLibrary.Close
29:     end sub
30:  </script>
31:
32:  <html><body>
33:     <asp:Label id="lblLibrary" runat="server"/>
34:  </body></html>
```

ANALYSIS The only new part of this listing is on lines 9–10, so let's analyze those first. You retrieve the `Library` section from your `web.config` file with the `GetConfig` method. This method returns whatever object is specified by your custom handler. Recall from Listing 18.5 that your handler returned an `XmlTextReader`. Note that the `GetConfig` method must specify the path of the section to retrieve. Because your `Library` section was embedded in the `<system.web>` element, you must call the method appropriately:

```
GetConfig("system.web/Library")
```

Remember that `web.config` is case sensitive, so make sure that your capitalization is correct!

Lines 12–28 simply parse the returned `XmlTextReader` and display the data in the label on line 33. Refer to Day 11 for more information on this process. This listing will produce the output shown in Figure 18.6.

Let's summarize. You could have placed the XML file path in the `<appSettings>` section of `web.config`, and then retrieved it from your ASP.NET page using the `ConfigurationSettings.AppSettings` property. Then, the ASP.NET page would have to create an `XmlTextReader` itself, and finally display the data.

However, by building a custom section handler, your ASP.NET pages do not need to worry about parsing the data in `web.config` and creating an `XmlTextReader`; the custom handler does that for you when you call the `GetConfig` method. All that is left for the ASP.NET pages to do is to display the data. Depending on how many ASP.NET pages use this XML file, you might have saved yourself quite a bit of extra work.

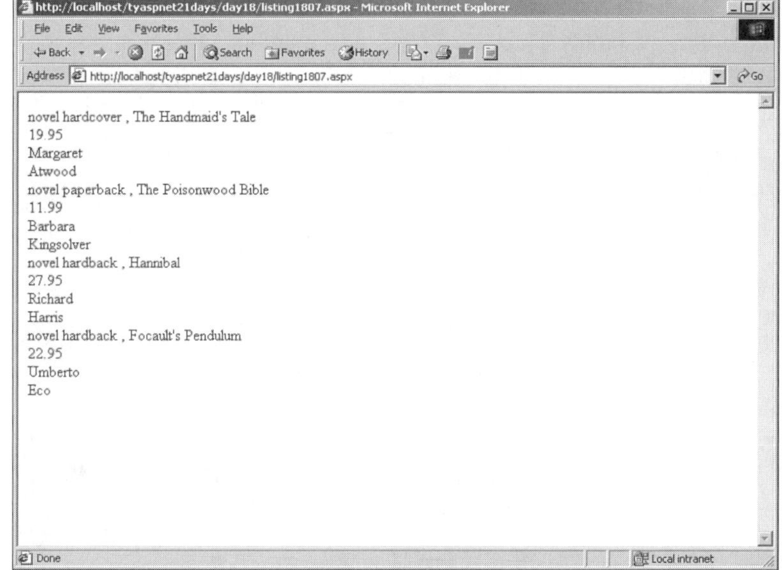

FIGURE 18.6
The `web.config` *Information is parsed and returned to you as an* `XmlTextReader`.

Deploying Your Application

Deploying Web applications was once one of the most tedious and difficult parts of ASP development. You had to configure the application settings "in person" at the server, and had to register components manually (using `REGSVR32.exe`) or via Microsoft Transaction Server. This often introduced many versioning problems, such as DLL hell, in which conflicting library versions would cause the application to function improperly, or not to function at all.

With ASP.NET, all that is required to deploy applications is simply to copy the needed files (ASP.NET Web pages, the `web.config` file, and necessary DLLs) to the deployment Web server—no more registering components or tweaking Web server settings! Let's take a deeper look at this marvelous mechanism.

Assembly Caches

Recall from Day 2, "Building ASP.NET Pages," that assemblies are the basic unit of sharing and reuse in the Common Language Runtime—a named unit for class deployment. Typically an assembly is a single DLL file, but may span multiple files (and even file types).

Assemblies are used by ASP.NET applications by placing them into either a global or local assembly cache. Global caches hold code that is accessed by all applications on an ASP.NET server. This cache, by default, is located in your `\WinNT\Assembly` directory.

Tip

You can use the global cache utility (`gacutil.exe`) from the command line to view, add, and remove assemblies from the global cache. The syntax is

```
Usage: Gacutil <option> [<parameters>]
 Options:
  -i
    Installs an assembly to the global assembly cache.
    Include the name of the file containing the manifest as a
    parameter.
    Example:  -i myDll.dll

  -u
    Uninstalls an assembly from the global assembly cache.
    Include the name of the assembly to remove as a parameter.
    Examples:.
      -u myDll
      -u myDll,Ver=1.1.0.0,Loc=en,PK=874e23ab874e23ab

  -l
    Lists the contents of the global assembly cache
  -?
    Displays this help screen
```

Beware, though, that specifying *`gacutil -u myDLL`* will remove all versions of *`myDLL`*, so be sure to specify as much information as necessary.

Local caches are accessible only by a particular application; the default cache is the `/bin` subdirectory in your application root. This directory is configured to deny access to any client requests—a helpful feature so that no one can steal your code. Let's take a look at a sample Web server directory structure as shown in Table 18.3.

TABLE 18.3 A Sample Web Server Directory Structure

Application URL	*Physical Path*
`http://www.site.com`	`c:\inetpub\wwwroot`
`http://www.site.com:85`	`c:\inetpub\wwwroot\port85`
`http://www.site.com/games`	`d:\www\games`
`http://www.site.com/games/users`	`d:\www\users`

Each of the physical directories in Table 18.3 is a virtual directory in IIS and a separate ASP.NET application. Each application can have its own local assembly cache in its `/bin` subdirectory; `c:\inetpub\wwwroot\bin` for `www.site.com`, for instance. Each `/bin` directory is applicable only to its local application. This allows you to deploy multiple versions of the same assembly on one site!

Shadowed Assemblies

Typically, when the CLR loads an assembly DLL into memory, it locks access to the file so that no other applications can access or corrupt it. The file is unlocked when the application domain referencing it is destroyed. This is great to ensure stability, but it results in high costs to replace those files. For example, with traditional ASP, these DLLs would remain locked until the server was restarted—a pain for administrators and site visitors.

ASP.NET solves this problem by not loading the actual assemblies into memory. Instead, shadow copies of the assemblies are created immediately before their use, and it is these that are locked and loaded into memory. Because the actual files are no longer locked, developers are free to replace them as they want—no restarts are necessary.

ASP.NET monitors and detects any changes to the actual files. If it discovers that the file has changed, it creates a shadow copy of the new file, loads it into memory, and gradually siphons off requests from the old version. After all requests reference the new version, the old version is destroyed. This is largely transparent to the end user. How's that for saving headaches!

That's Not ASP!

Today's lesson presents a number of large changes from classic ASP. Configuration and deployment in ASP.NET are much more refined and easy to implement than ASP, so developers may take some time getting used to the new system.

One thing that hasn't changed, at least in implementation, is the use of a file to control application events. In classic ASP, this was `global.asa`, and in ASP.NET, `global.asax`. Both files are fully compatible. If migrating your application from ASP to ASP.NET, you can simply copy the contents of `global.asa` to the new file, and be assured that your application will still function. There are differences behind the scenes, however. For example, in ASP.NET, `global.asax` is compiled to a .NET class. In classic ASP, the code in `global.asa` was interpreted, just as `.asp` pages were.

The configuration system is very different. With ASP, all settings had to be configured through IIS or other system applications. This typically required someone to be physically located at the server. Additionally, it was difficult to set up different settings for different applications or pieces within an application.

With ASP.NET, all settings that were modifiable in ASP (and then some) are now contained in XML files, which means that they are easy to modify. A text editor is all you need to change settings, and you can simply upload them to the server to apply them.

Additionally, the hierarchical ASP.NET configuration system allows much more granular control over the application than did classic ASP. You can limit settings to only a certain file or directory, control exactly how the ASP.NET process behaves, and even where to store session information. The `web.config` files are fully extensible, so you can add your own settings as well.

Finally, the new deployment paradigm might be an ASP developer's dream. No installation is necessary, registering components is now eliminated, and configuration settings are easily transferred from server to server. All that is required is copying the appropriate files. Never has application installation been so easy!

Summary

After today's lesson, you should be able to control every aspect of your application, from the UI to the behavior of session state. You learned a lot today, but much of it centers around two main concepts: the `global.asax` and `web.config` files.

You learned today that an ASP.NET application consists of all files contained in a virtual directory. This includes assemblies (DLL files), `.aspx` pages, images, and more. This application is represented on the server at runtime by the `HttpApplication` object, which contains the properties and methods needed to control the application.

You can take advantage of these properties and methods from the `global.asax` file. Table 18.1 listed the events of the application that you can build handlers for. These handler methods must use the syntax:

```
Application_EventName(Sender as Object, e as EventArgs)
```

Next, you learned about the `web.config` file. This XML file contains a number of sections that you can use to control how your application behaves. When these predefined sections aren't enough, you know how to build your own, as well as handlers to parse them and generate appropriate output.

Finally, you learned just how easy it is to deploy your application. I didn't spend too much time on this topic simply because it is a very easy one to learn. After all, the only thing you need to know is where to copy the files!

Tomorrow you'll learn how to manipulate your content (the output of your pages) without modifying any code at all! This includes topics such as localization and code-behind forms. See you then!

Q&A

Q Can I retrieve the predefined sections from `web.config` using the `GetConfig` method? Such as `<sessionState>`?

A This task is, unfortunately, a very difficult one. The handlers that ASP.NET uses to parse most of the predefined sections don't return objects that you can easily use. Most of them are declared as `private`, which means that they are inaccessible from your ASP.NET pages. This prevents most attempts at accessing them.

See the .NET SDK documentation for further details.

Q Will `web.config` security settings protect all resources?

A No, it will protect only resources that are processed by ASP.NET. Therefore, `.gif`, `.jpg`, `.txt`, and other files would all still be accessible by users. I'll discuss this topic more in Day 21.

Workshop

This workshop will help reinforce the concepts I've covered in today's lesson. It is very helpful to understand fully the answers before moving on. Answers can be found in Appendix A.

Quiz

1. True or False: You can access the `<appSettings>` section with the `ConfigurationSection.AppSettings` property.
2. Is it possible to view the `global.asax` file from your browser?
3. What interface must a custom handler implement?

The following questions deal with the directory structure shown in Table 18.4.

TABLE 18.4 A Web Server Directory Structure Exercise

Application URL	*Physical Path*
`http://www.site.com`	`c:\www\site`
`http://www.site.com/sales`	`c:\www\site\sales`
`http://www.site.com/hr`	`c:\www\site\sales\hr`
`http://www.site.com/users`	`d:\www\misc\users`

4. The `sales` virtual directory has a `web.config` with the following setting:

```
<httphandlers>
   <add verb="PUT, POST" path="index.aspx" type="System.Web.
      UI.PageHandlerFactory" />
</httphandlers>
```

   If the `hr` directory is accessed as follows, will it inherit this setting?

   `http://www.site.com/hr`

5. If the `hr` directory is accessed as follows, will it inherit this setting?

   `http://www.site.com/sales/hr`

6. Suppose that the `web.config` in `sales` also has the following setting:

```
<location path="hr/*.aspx">

   <authorization>
         <deny users="?" />
   </authorization>

</location>
```

   Is this an adequate security measure against entry into `hr`? Explain.

7. Describe a better use of `web.config` to address the preceding question.

Exercises

Set up a `web.config` file for a sample application that does the following:

- Turns on debug mode for the application.
- Sets custom errors to display an `errors.aspx` page.
- Declares a section called `authors` with a `PrimaryAuthor` key with the value of your name. This section should use the `DictionarySectionHandler` handler.

WEEK 3

DAY 19

Separating Code from Content

Throughout the last 18 lessons, you've examined several ways to separate the user interface elements from the programmatic code (the VB.NET and C# code). For example, you looked at moving non-UI functionality into business objects, leaving the ASP.NET pages with only UI code. Additionally, as we examined in Day 12, "Employing Advanced Data Techniques," you can move database commands into stored procedures to keep them out of your ASP.NET pages. You can even store settings and variables in configuration files such as `web.config`.

Today you're going to explore a few more advanced methods for separating the source code from the content. In other words, separating the code that controls your application from presentation code (such as the HTML and Web controls). This separation is one that ASP.NET developers often strive for to reduce clutter and group code more logically. After all, an ASP.NET page is used to present a user interface, so why should it contain any other type of code?

You're also going to look at methods to customize your ASP.NET pages based on the location of your users. These methods allow you to modify the page content separately from your separated page code.

You'll be looking at a lot of code today, so let's get started!

Today's lesson will cover the following:

- What code-behind forms are
- How to make your ASP.NET pages use code-behinds
- How to make your user controls use code-behinds
- How to determine where your users are located (by the language they speak)
- How to examine culture and region information for your users
- How to extract commonly used strings from your ASP.NET pages and store them separately in resource files

The Drive for Separation

Recall from way back in Day 2, "Building ASP.NET Pages," that ASP.NET strives to simplify code writing for developers by allowing them to group ASP.NET code and HTML code separately. For instance, most, if not all, ASP.NET code should be written in SCRIPT blocks, at the top of an `.aspx` file, separated from the HTML code. Figure 19.1 illustrates this.

Writing code this way is beneficial for a number of reasons: It's easier to modify the code and HTML; it presents a more logical view of the page; you don't have to search for code render blocks throughout your pages. ASP.NET allows you to do more than just this, however. You can separate the code from the page content completely with code-behind forms and resource files. The first approach allows you to move code into separate files, whereas the second allows you to place commonly used values (such as custom error descriptions) in one location, apart from your pages.

FIGURE 19.1

The ideal way to structure ASP.NET pages.

```
<VB Page Language = "VB" V>
<VB Import namespace="System.Drawing" V>

<HTML>
<HEAD>

<script language="VB" runat="server">
   ' This procedure handles the Change event of the
   Sub tbMessage_Change(Sender As Object, I As Even
      lblMessage.Text = "Hello " & tbMessage.Text :
   End Sub
</script>

</HEAD>
<BODY logocolor="sffffff">

   <font size="5">Sam's Teach Yourself ASP.NET im i

   <V Response.Write("Hello" & |
      "World'") V>

   <form runat="server">

      Please enter your name: <asp:textbox id="tbx
      <asp:button id="lotSubmit" Text="Submit" runat
      <asp:label id="lblMessage" font-size="10pt"  :
      <V--
      <asp:label id="lblMessage1" font=size="10pt"
      --V>

</form>
```


Code-Behind Forms

Looking back at Figure 19.1, you can see the benefits of separating code from content. What if you could move the top ASP.NET code portion of the page out of the `.aspx` file altogether? This would represent a true separation of code from content. ASP.NET allows you to do just that with code-behind forms. Code-behind forms serve as a method to separate any and all ASP.NET code from the user interface. Now, instead of one file as shown in Figure 19.1, you have two, as shown in Figure 19.2.

Let's take a look at the way ASP.NET works one more time so that we can better understand the code-behind model.

When a client requests an ASP.NET page (an `.aspx` file) for the first time, ASP.NET parses the page and examines all components on it, for instance, server controls. ASP.NET then creates a new class dynamically based on your `.aspx` file. It is this class that is compiled and executed to return HTML to the client. This class must derive from the `System.Web.UI.Page` class, which provides the definition for all ASP.NET pages. This all happens invisibly once a page is requested.

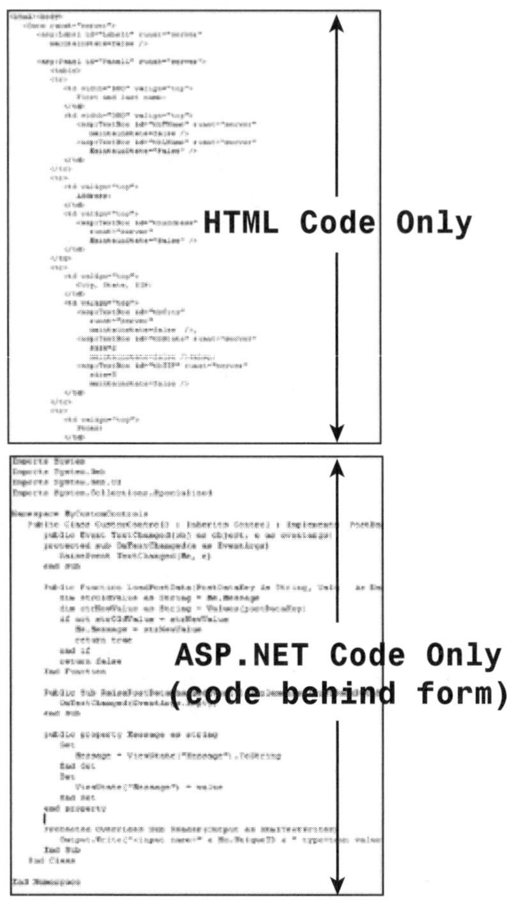

FIGURE 19.2

ASP.NET allows you to completely separate the UI from the logic with code-behind forms.

However, an `.aspx` file does not have to derive from the `Page` class directly; as long as it derives *somehow* from that class, everything will be fine. Thus, you can create an intermediary class that derives from the `Page` class, and make the `.aspx` file derive from it instead. This new class can contain any functionality that you want, and it will be available to the `.aspx` file. Figure 19.3 illustrates the relationships among all these classes.

This new intermediary class is your code-behind form. It defines functionality that your ASP.NET page can use. With so many classes floating around, it might quickly become confusing. Essentially, it all boils down to the fact that an ASP.NET page must derive from the `Page` class, and it's up to you to determine how.

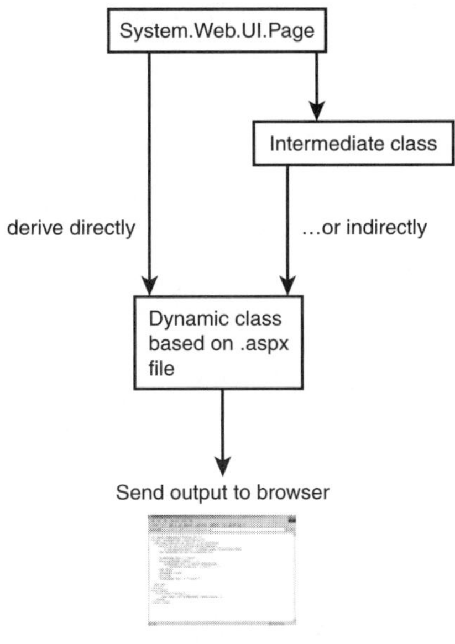

FIGURE 19.3
An ASP.NET page must derive directly or indirectly from the `System.Web.UI.Page` *class.*

Adding the code-behind class doesn't provide any obvious benefits. The code-behind page doesn't contain any inherent functionality, so your ASP.NET page isn't gaining anything new. It doesn't aid the execution of the ASP.NET page either. However, using a code-behind page does allow you to move your code into an intermediary class, leaving only UI-rendering HTML in a much-simplified ASP.NET page.

As you move into advanced levels of ASP.NET development, you'll use code-behind forms more and more. They are an advanced tool, but one that every ASP.NET developer should learn.

Using Code-Behind in ASP.NET Pages

Creating a code-behind form is very simple; it is similar to creating a business object, except that compiling isn't necessary. You must take some extra precautions, however, to ensure that it all works correctly. Listing 19.1 shows a typical ASP.NET page that displays information from a database. You'll use this listing to generate your code-behind form in a moment.

LISTING 19.1 A Typical ASP.NET Page Contains Code and HTML

```
<%@ Page Language="VB" %>
<%@ Import Namespace="System.Data" %>
<%@ Import Namespace="System.Data.OleDb" %>

```

LISTING 19.1 continued

```
<script runat="server">
   'declare connection
   dim strConnString as string = "Provider=" & _
      "Microsoft.Jet.OLEDB.4.0;" & _
      "Data Source=c:\ASPNET\data\banking.mdb"
   dim objConn as new OleDbConnection(strConnString)

   sub Page_Load(Sender as Object, e as EventArgs)
      FillDataGrid()
   end sub

   sub FillDataGrid
      'open connection
      dim objCmd as OleDbCommand = new OleDbCommand _
         ("select * from tblUsers", objConn)
      dim objReader as OleDbDataReader

      try
         objCmd.Connection.Open()
         objReader = objCmd.ExecuteReader
      catch ex as OleDbException
         lblMessage.Text = "Error retrieving from the " & _
            "database."
      end try

      DataGrid1.DataSource = objReader
      DataGrid1.DataBind()

      objReader.Close
      objCmd.Connection.Close()
   end sub
</script>

<html><body>
   <form runat="server">
      <asp:Label id="lblMessage" runat="server" />

      <asp:DataGrid id="DataGrid1" runat="server"
         BorderColor="black" GridLines="Vertical"
         cellpadding="4" cellspacing="0"
         width="100%" Font-Name="Arial"
         Font-Size="8pt"
         HeaderStyle-BackColor="#cccc99"
         ItemStyle-BackColor="#ffffff"
         AlternatingItemStyle-Backcolor="#cccccc" />
      </asp:DataGrid><p>
   </form>
</body></html>
```

ANALYSIS This listing connects to the user database we created on Day 8, "Beginning to Build Databases" (and modified in Week 2 in Review, "Bonus Project 2"). On lines 7 and 10, you create your connection string and `OleDbConnection` object. In the `Page_Load` event, you call the `FillDataGrid` method, which pulls information from the database and binds it to the `DataGrid` on lines 42–50. This listing produces the output shown in Figure 19.4 when viewed from the browser.

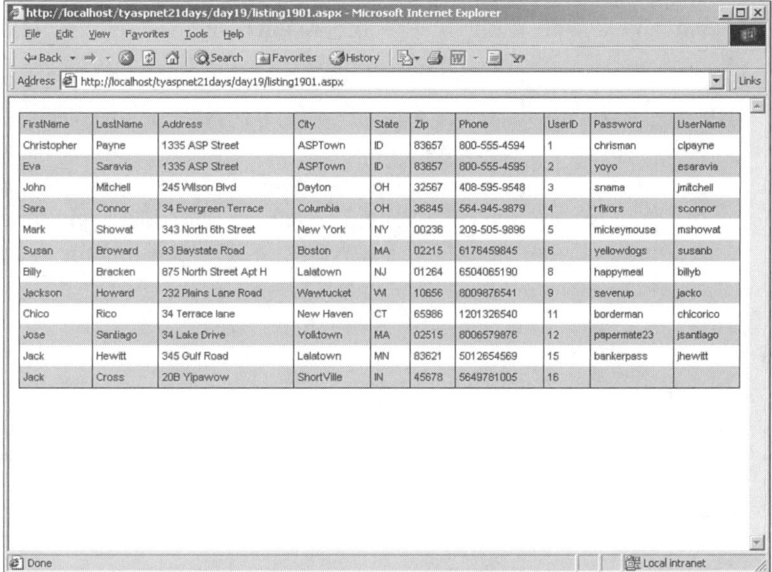

FirstName	LastName	Address	City	State	Zip	Phone	UserID	Password	UserName
Christopher	Payne	1335 ASP Street	ASPTown	ID	83657	800-555-4594	1	chrisman	clpayne
Eva	Saravia	1335 ASP Street	ASPTown	ID	83657	800-555-4595	2	yoyo	esaravia
John	Mitchell	245 Wilson Blvd	Dayton	OH	32567	408-595-9548	3	snama	jmitchell
Sara	Connor	34 Evergreen Terrace	Columbia	OH	36845	564-945-9879	4	rflkors	sconnor
Mark	Showat	343 North 6th Street	New York	NY	00236	209-505-9896	5	mickeymouse	mshowat
Susan	Broward	93 Baystate Road	Boston	MA	02215	6176459845	6	yellowdogs	susanb
Billy	Bracken	875 North Street Apt H	Lalatown	NJ	01264	6504065190	8	happymeal	billyb
Jackson	Howard	232 Plains Lane Road	Wawtucket	WI	10656	8009876541	9	sevenup	jacko
Chico	Rico	34 Terrace lane	New Haven	CT	65986	1201326540	11	borderman	chicorico
Jose	Santiago	34 Lake Drive	Yolktown	MA	02515	8006579876	12	papermate23	jsantiago
Jack	Hewitt	345 Gulf Road	Lalatown	MN	83621	5012654569	15	bankerpass	jhewitt
Jack	Cross	20B Yipawow	ShortVille	IN	45678	5649781005	16		

FIGURE 19.4
A simple data-driven ASP.NET page.

19

Now let's build your code-behind form using Listing 19.1 as a starting point. First, you need to create a VB.NET (or C#) class that derives from the `System.Web.UI.Page` class, as shown in the following code snippet:

```
Imports System
Imports System.Web
Imports System.Web.UI
Imports System.Web.UI.WebControls
Imports System.Data
Imports System.Data.OleDb

Public Class CodeBehind1 : Inherits Page
   'insert code here
End Class
```

This will be the basis for moving the code within the script block out of Listing 19.1. Recall that in VB.NET and C# classes, you have to manually import all the namespaces that were automatically imported by ASP.NET. You also have to import the `System.Data` and `System.Data.OleDb` namespaces because your ASP.NET page uses them to display data.

The next step is to create all the public variables you need. Because of the nature of code-behind forms, this process is a bit different than what you're used to. Let's examine it further. The code-behind class will be used to control the UI (that is, the Web form); it contains the logic that handles UI events. However, the code-behind class doesn't contain any UI elements itself—the UI is contained in the `.aspx` file. This leaves you with a problem. The code-behind form must control a UI that is located in a separate file. How can you accomplish this?

Now you see the reason that the ASP.NET file derives from the code-behind class: If you declare all the appropriate UI elements in the code-behind, the `.aspx` file can inherit them. In essence, the code-behind creates and provides logic for all the UI elements, but it doesn't display them. The ASP.NET file is responsible for that part. Figure 19.5 illustrates this concept.

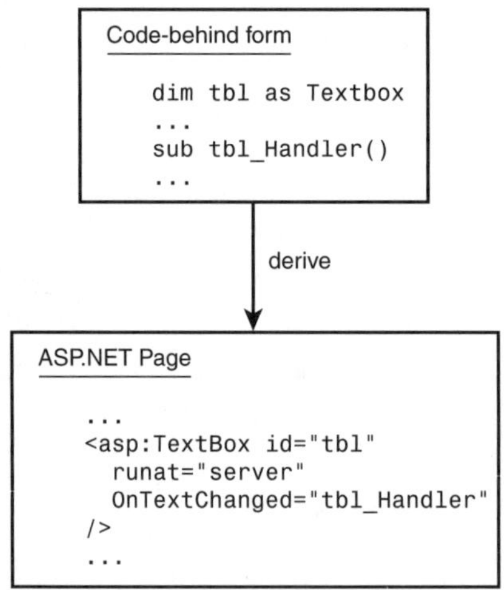

FIGURE 19.5
The code-behind declares UI elements and their logic, whereas the ASP.NET page simply displays them.

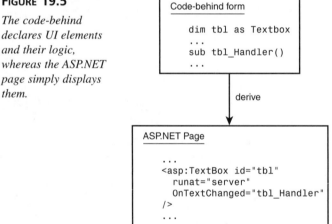

Let's move the code from Listing 19.1 into a code-behind form, as shown in Listings 19.2 and 19.3.

LISTING 19.2 The Code-Behind Containing All UI Functionality

```
Imports System
Imports System.Web
Imports System.Web.UI
```

LISTING 19.2 continued

```
Imports System.Web.UI.WebControls
Imports System.Data
Imports System.Data.OleDb

Public Class Listing1903 : Inherits Page
   'declare public variables for .aspx file to inherit
    public lblMessage as Label
    public DataGrid1 as DataGrid

    'declare connection
    private strConnString as string = "Provider=" & _
       "Microsoft.Jet.OLEDB.4.0;" & _
       "Data Source=c:\ASPNET\data\banking.mdb"
    private objConn as new OleDbConnection(strConnString)

    sub Page_Load(Sender as Object, e as EventArgs)
       if Not Page.IsPostBack then
          FillDataGrid()
       end if
    end sub

    private sub FillDataGrid
       'open connection
       dim objCmd as OleDbCommand = new OleDbCommand _
          ("select * from tblUsers", objConn)
       dim objReader as OleDbDataReader

       try
          objCmd.Connection.Open()
          objReader = objCmd.ExecuteReader
       catch ex as OleDbException
          lblMessage.Text = "Error retrieving from the " & _
             "database."
       end try

       DataGrid1.DataSource = objReader
       DataGrid1.DataBind()

       objReader.Close
       objCmd.Connection.Close()
    end sub

End Class
```

LISTING 19.2.CS The Code-Behind Containing All UI Functionality in C#

```
using System;
using System.Web;
using System.Web.UI;
using System.Web.UI.WebControls;
using System.Data;
using System.Data.OleDb;

public class Listing1903 : Page {
   //declare public variables for .aspx file to inherit
    public Label lblMessage;
    public DataGrid DataGrid1;

    //declare connection
    private OleDbConnection objConn = new OleDbConnection
➥("Provider=Microsoft.Jet.OLEDB.4.0;Data Source=
➥C:\\ASPNET\\data\\banking.mdb");

    void Page_Load(Object Sender, EventArgs e) {
       if (!Page.IsPostBack) {
          FillDataGrid();
       }
    }

    private void FillDataGrid() {
       FillDataGrid(-1);
    }

    private void FillDataGrid(int EditIndex) {
       //open connection
       OleDbCommand objCmd = new OleDbCommand
➥ ("select * from tblUsers", objConn);
       OleDbDataReader objReader;

       try {
          objCmd.Connection.Open();
          objReader = objCmd.ExecuteReader();

          DataGrid1.DataSource = objReader;
          DataGrid1.DataBind();

          objReader.Close();
       } catch (OleDbException ex) {
          lblMessage.Text = "Error retrieving
➥from the database.";
       }
```

LISTING 19.2.CS continued

```
43:            objCmd.Connection.Close();
44:        }
45:
46:    }s
```

ANALYSIS Save this file as `listing1903.vb` or `listing1903.cs`. On lines 1–6, you import the necessary namespaces, and on line 8 you declare your code-behind class. Note that its name is `Listing1903` and that it derives (that is, inherits) from the `Page` class. We use this name because this code-behind will be inherited by `listing1903.aspx` in a moment. Naming your code-behind the same name (minus, of course, the extension) as the ASP.NET page that inherits from it is a good coding convention that will help you keep things straight.

Remember from Listing 19.1 that you used two server controls: a label named `lblMessage` and a `DataGrid` named `DataGrid1`. These controls are declared as variables on lines 10 and 11 here. Now your ASP.NET page can inherit these controls, as well as any functionality that goes along with them. The rest of the file is the same as Listing 19.1, except that there is no HTML here. Let's look at the `.aspx` file that will inherit from this code-behind, shown in Listing 19.3.

LISTING 19.3 Inheriting from the Code-Behind Class

```
<%@ Page Inherits="Listing1903" src="Listing1903.vb" %>

<html><body>
   <form runat="server">
      <asp:Label id="lblMessage" runat="server" />

      <asp:DataGrid id="DataGrid1" runat="server"
         BorderColor="black" GridLines="Vertical"
         cellpadding="4" cellspacing="0"
          width="100%" Font-Name="Arial"
          Font-Size="8pt"
          HeaderStyle-BackColor="#cccc99"
          ItemStyle-BackColor="#ffffff"
          AlternatingItemStyle-Backcolor="#cccccc"
          AutoGenerateColumns="True" />
       </asp:DataGrid><p>
    </form>
 </body></html>
```

Save this listing as `listing1903.aspx` in the same directory as your code-behind file.

ANALYSIS With the exception of line 1, this listing is the same as the HTML portion of Listing 19.1. Line 1 has something new: The `@ Page` directive now has the attributes `Inherits` and `src`. `Inherits` specifies the class from which this page derives. In this case, you want to derive from the code-behind class you just created, `Listing1903`. The `src` attribute specifies the path of the file containing the code-behind class (which means that you aren't required to place the code-behind and the `.aspx` file in the same directory). That's all there is to it! Request this listing from the browser, and you should see the same output shown in Figure 19.4. Note that you can replace the `src` attribute on line 1 with `Listing1903.cs` and the page will work exactly the same way, without needing to convert your code to C#.

The `DataGrid` and `Label` server controls in Listing 19.3 are instances of the `Listing1903` class variables declared in Listing 19.2. Thus, although it's not shown here, any code in the code-behind that refers to these variables will have full access to the properties of the control instances on the Web form, such as the text contained in the label. Let's look at an example that handles form events. This time, you'll create both files from scratch. Listing 19.4 shows the ASP.NET page that holds the UI.

> You can still create UI elements and logic within your ASP.NET page; there's no requirement that all the code must be in a code-behind form, and code-behind doesn't disallow inclusion of UI elements. You can also add code in an `.aspx` file to control a UI element declared in your code-behind. However, why add code to your ASP.NET page if you already have a code-behind?

LISTING 19.4 An `.aspx` File Without Any ASP.NET Code

```
<%@ Page Inherits="Listing1904" src="Listing1904.vb" %>

<html><body>
   <form runat="server">
      <asp:Calendar id="Calendar1" runat="server"
         OnSelectionChanged="DateChanged"
         Cellpadding="5" Cellspacing="5"
         DayHeaderStyle-Font-Bold="True"
         DayNameFormat="Short"
          Font-Name="Arial" Font-Size="12px"
          height="250px"
          NextPrevFormat="ShortMonth"
          NextPrevStyle-ForeColor="white"
          SelectedDayStyle-BackColor="#ffcc66"
          SelectedDayStyle-Font-Bold="True"
```

Listing 19.4 continued

```
16:             SelectionMode="DayWeekMonth"
17:             SelectorStyle-BackColor="#99ccff"
18:             SelectorStyle-ForeColor="navy"
19:             SelectorStyle-Font-Size="9px"
20:             ShowTitle="true"
21:             TitleStyle-BackColor="#ddaa66"
22:             TitleStyle-ForeColor="white"
23:             TitleStyle-Font-Bold="True"
24:             TodayDayStyle-Font-Bold="True" />
25:       </form>
26:       You selected:
27:       <asp:Label id="lblMessage" runat="server"/>
28:    </body></html>
```

This listing contains a calendar server control and a label. Although you haven't created the code-behind file yet, line 1 already specifies a class and filename, so you'll know ahead of time what to create. On line 6, you provide a handler for the `SelectionChanged` event of the calendar. Also note the names of the two controls: `Calendar1` and `lblMessage`.

If you try to request this page by itself, it will result in an error for two reasons. The first is that ASP.NET will look for the code-behind specified in the `Inherits` attribute of the `@ Page` directive, but won't find it. The second reason is that the `SelectionChanged` event handler is specified as `DateChanged`, but there isn't a `DateChanged` method in this file. Let's create the code-behind to remedy these problems, as shown in Listings 19.5 and Listing 19.5.cs.

Listing 19.5 Controlling the Calendar's Events

```
Imports System
Imports System.Web
Imports System.Web.UI
Imports System.Web.UI.WebControls

Public Class Listing1904 : Inherits Page
   public lblMessage as Label
   public Calendar1 as Calendar

    Public sub Page_Load(Sender as Object, e as EventArgs)
       if not Page.IsPostBack then
          Calendar1.SelectedDate = DateTime.Now
          lblMessage.Text = Calendar1.SelectedDate. _
             ToString("dddd, MMMM dd yyyy")
       end if
```

LISTING 19.5 continued

```
      End Sub

      Public sub DateChanged(Sender as Object, e as EventArgs)
         if Calendar1.SelectedDates.Count > 1 then
            lblMessage.Text = Calendar1.SelectedDates(0). _
               ToString("dddd, MMMM dd yyyy") & " through " & _
               Calendar1.SelectedDates(Calendar1. _
               SelectedDates.Count - 1). _
               ToString("dddd, MMMM dd yyyy")
         else
            lblMessage.Text = Calendar1.SelectedDate. _
               ToString("dddd, MMMM dd yyyy")
         end if
      End Sub
   End Class
```

LISTING 19.5.CS Controlling the Calendar's Events in C#

```
   using System;
   using System.Web;
   using System.Web.UI;
   using System.Web.UI.WebControls;

   public class Listing1904 : Page {
      public Label lblMessage;
      public Calendar Calendar1;

      public void Page_Load(Object Sender, EventArgs e) {
         if (!Page.IsPostBack) {
            Calendar1.SelectedDate = DateTime.Now;
            lblMessage.Text = Calendar1.SelectedDate.
➥ToString("dddd, MMMM dd yyyy");
         }
      }

      public void DateChanged(Object Sender, EventArgs e) {
         if (Calendar1.SelectedDates.Count > 1) {
            lblMessage.Text = Calendar1.SelectedDates[0].
➥ToString("dddd, MMMM dd yyyy") + " through " +
➥Calendar1.SelectedDates[Calendar1.SelectedDates.Count - 1].
➥ToString("dddd, MMMM dd yyyy");
         } else {
            lblMessage.Text = Calendar1.SelectedDate.
➥ToString("dddd, MMMM dd yyyy");
         }
      }
   }s
```

ANALYSIS Save this file as `Listing1904.vb` and `Listing1904.cs`. On line 6, you declare this code-behind class as `Listing1904`, which was specified earlier by the ASP.NET page. On lines 7 and 8, you create two public variables, `lblMessage` and `Calendar1`. Recall that these are the same names used for the controls in the `.aspx` file. On lines 10–16, the `Page_Load` event sets the calendar's selected date to today, and displays a message to the user in the label. Finally, the `DateChanged` method on line 18 is the event handler for the calendar's `SelectionChanged` event, as specified on line 6 of Listing 19.4. This method displays the date in long format to the user. If more than one day is selected (as specified by the `SelectedDates.Count` property), you want to alert the user that he's selected a range of dates (lines 19–24). Otherwise, you simply display the selected date (line 26). Viewing Listing 19.4 now produces the output shown in Figure 19.6.

FIGURE 19.6

The code-behind form handles the events of the ASP.NET page.

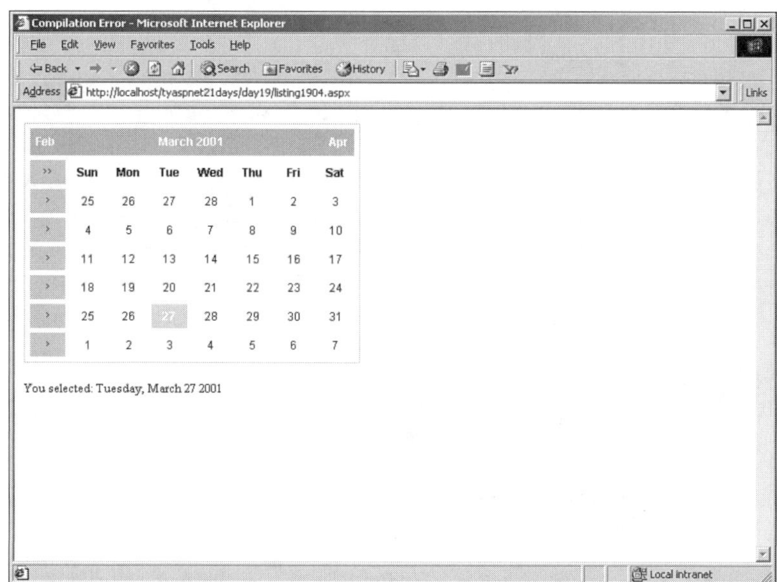

Now you can completely separate your Web form's code from its presentation layer!

Using Code-Behind in User Controls

Using code-behind forms with user controls differs from using them with ASP.NET pages. Specifically, you must derive from the `System.Web.UI.UserControl` class instead of the `Page` class (see Day 6, "Learning More About Web Forms," for more information on user controls). Listings 19.6 through 19.8 show a modification of the calculator you developed in Day 2 as a user control with a code-behind form.

19

LISTING 19.6 The User Control

```
1:    <%@ Control Inherits="CalculatorControl"
➥src="Calculator.vb" %>
2:
3:    Number 1: <asp:textbox id="tbNumber1" runat="server"/><br>
4:    Number 2: <asp:textbox id="tbNumber2" runat="server"/><p>
5:    <asp:button id="btAdd" runat="server" Text="+"
6:       OnClick="btOperator_Click" />
7:    <asp:button id="btSubtract" runat="server" Text="-"
8:       OnClick="btOperator_Click"/>
9:    <asp:button id="btMultiply" runat="server" Text="*"
10:      OnClick="btOperator_Click"/>
11:   <asp:button id="btDivide" runat="server" Text="/"
12:      OnClick="btOperator_Click"/><p>
13:   The answer is:
14:   <asp:label id="lblMessage" runat="server"/>
```

ANALYSIS Save this listing as `Calculator.ascx`. This is a straightforward user control. It simply provides the HTML to display a couple text boxes for users to enter values, four buttons to perform arithmetic operations, and a label to display the answer. You use the `@ Control` directive on line 1 instead of the `@ Page` directive you used with ASP.NET pages, but the syntax is still the same: You use the `Inherits` and `src` attributes to specify your code-behind file. Take note of the names of each control because you'll have to use them in your code-behind form. Listing 19.7 shows the code-behind file for this user control.

LISTING 19.7 The Code-Behind Class

```
Imports System
Imports System.Web
Imports System.Web.UI
Imports System.Web.UI.WebControls

Public Class CalculatorControl : Inherits UserControl
   public lblMessage as Label
   public btAdd as Button
   public btSubtract as Button
   public btMultiply as Button
   public btDivide as Button
   public tbNumber1 as TextBox
   public tbNumber2 as TextBox

   Sub btOperator_Click(Sender as Object, e as EventArgs)
      lblMessage.Text = Operate(CType(Sender, Button).Text, _
         tbNumber1.Text, tbNumber2.Text).ToString
```

LISTING 19.7 continued

```
18:        End Sub
19:
20:        private function Operate(operator as string, number1 as
➥string, optional number2 as string = "1") as double
21:           select case operator
22:              case "+"
23:                 Operate = CDbl(number1) + CDbl(number2)
24:              case "-"
25:                 Operate = CDbl(number1) - CDbl(number2)
26:              case "*"
27:                 Operate = CDbl(number1) * CDbl(number2)
28:              case "/"
29:                 Operate = CDbl(number1) / CDbl(number2)
30:           end select
31:        end function
32:     End Class
```

ANALYSIS Save this listing as `Calculator.vb`. The functionality here is a bit more complex than in Listing 19.5, but the format is the same. You import the necessary namespaces on lines 1–4. On line 6, you declare your class, `CalculatorControl`, which inherits from the `UserControl` class (not the `Page` class). Then on lines 7–13, you declare public variables that correspond to the server controls in your user control.

When a user clicks one of the buttons in the user control, the `btOperator_Click` event handler is executed. It calls the `Operate` method, which takes three parameters: the operation to perform, and the two numbers to perform the operation on. The button that caused the event will be represented by the `obj` variable in line 15 when the page is requested. Take a look at the first parameter of the `Operate` method, shown on line 16:

```
CType(Sender, Button).Text
```

This parameter retrieves the `Text` property from the button that fired the event (for example, if the user clicked the Add button, this value would be `+`). If this were in an ASP.NET page, you could simply use `Sender.Text` to retrieve this value. However, VB.NET and C# classes act a bit differently than ASP.NET pages. Specifically, they don't allow late binding.

NEW TERM *Late binding* means that variables that are of type `Object` (as `Sender` is) are not processed until runtime. Until then, you can use them to represent any type of object you want, which is why you can use `Sender.Text` even though the `Object` data type doesn't have a `Text` property. ASP.NET won't balk at this because it knows that when the page is requested, the `Sender` variable might become a `Button` (if it doesn't, you might have problems).

Without late binding, the `Object` data type is processed immediately, and the compiler will throw an error when it realizes that you've tried to access a property that isn't there (`Object` does not have a `Text` property). Therefore, you have to make VB.NET or C# believe that `Sender` is indeed a button, even before the page is requested, so that you can access the `Text` property with your code. The `CType` method casts one data type into another, and on line 16, you cast a variable of type `Object` into one of type `Button`. This seems like a rather convoluted solution, but after you develop more examples and learn about late binding, it'll all become clearer.

The `Operate` method, on lines 20–31, analyzes the operator passed to it by the `btOperator_Click` method with a `select case` statement. Depending on the operator, a different operation is performed on the two numbers. The value is then returned to `btOperator_Click` and displayed to the user.

Finally, let's take a look at the short ASP.NET page that implements this user control, shown in Listing 19.8.

LISTING 19.8 The ASP.NET Page That Implements the User Control and Code-Behind Form

```
1:    <%@ Register TagPrefix="TYASPNET"
➥TagName="Calculator" src="Calculator.ascx" %>
2:
3:    <html><body>
4:       <form runat="server">
5:          <TYASPNET:Calculator id="Calc1" runat="server"/>
6:       </form>
7:    </body></html>
```

ANALYSIS This page is straightforward. Recall from Day 6 that you must use the `@ Register` directive to register a user control on your pages. Then you may use the control just as any other server control, as is done on line 5. View this page from the browser, and try entering some values and performing some operations. You should see something similar to Figure 19.7.

Code-Behind Recommendations

Once you understand the process model behind code-behind forms, they become easy to use. They just require a bit more planning up front to build your pages—which can be a good thing.

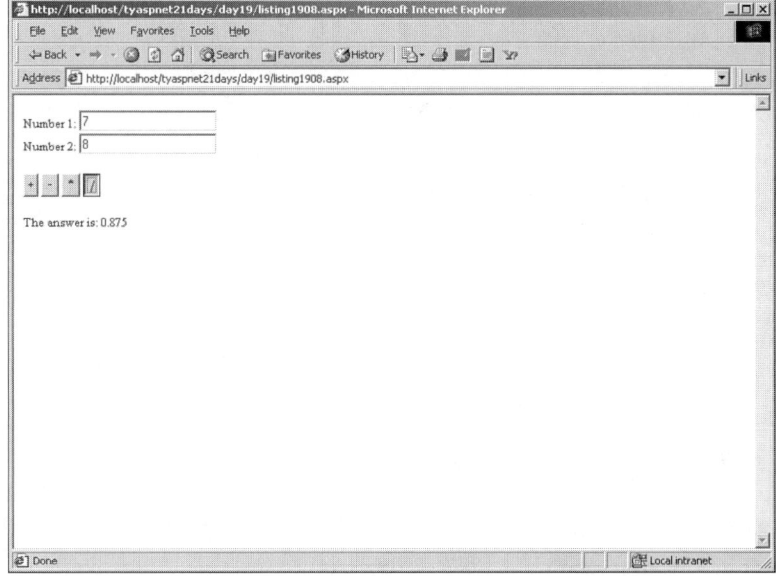

FIGURE 19.7

The code-behind form handles the events of the user control on the ASP.NET page.

In general, if your pages are at all complex, you'll want to move into code-behind forms. This by no means is required, but it will help you down the road by keeping complex code separate from HTML content; the final choice on whether or not to use code-behind is a personal choice.

Code-behind forms become more important as you have more and more people working on a single site—especially those who have different areas of expertise. You can let your HTML people build the UI for your pages, while you build the actual functionality. Even better, if the layout of the page needs to change, but the functionality stays the same, no one else has to look at your ASP.NET code.

19

We've avoided code-behind forms throughout this book because it's easier to present code that resides in a single file. In real life, however, code-behind forms are your friend.s

Resource Files and Localization

When you go on a vacation, you pack a suitcase with clothes, toiletries, and other personal belongings. You *could* carry the stuff with you as opposed to using your suitcase, but it would be very awkward (not to mention the fact that you only have limited number of pockets!). This suitcase serves as an invaluable resource for your trip; without it, your vacation would be a disaster.

ASP.NET allows you to "pack a suitcase" for your application, so to speak. Any custom information (such as variables, messages, text blurbs, images, and so on) can be packed away in a resource file. Your pages can then easily access the resources in these files whenever they are needed.

NEW TERM Resource files are typically used for localizing your applications. *Localization* is the process of modifying the output of your applications so that they are compatible with different cultures and languages. You can create a resource file for each different culture that will be using your application. For instance, you can store a welcome message in your resource file. If an English-speaking person accesses the page, you would display "Hello!" If a French person views it, you would display "Bonjour!" By storing each language's messages in a different resource file, you don't have to worry about creating a new ASP.NET page for every new language. It's much easier simply to create a new resource file.

ASP.NET makes localization and resource grouping a simple process. These processes allow you to modify your content output without having to change any code, thus separating code from content again. In the next couple of sections, you'll take a look at determining who's accessing your pages and how to adjust for them, and then how to pack your resources into files.

Localizing Your Application

Ideally, when localizing your Web application, you want to be able to automatically detect the locations of your users so that you can set the appropriate output languages and other culture-related info. Unfortunately, due to the nature of the Web, there is no standard way to easily determine the geographical location of a Web surfer.

Luckily, there are a few ways around this. You can determine the primary language the visitor is using in his Web browser. Typically, although not always, this indicates the language and culture the user is most comfortable with, and you can adjust accordingly. This information is provided by the `Request.UserLanguages` object, which gathers the languages used from the browser, and sorts them according to the priority the user has set. Listing 19.9 shows an example of detecting the primary user language.

LISTING 19.9 Using the `Request` Object to Determine User Language Preferences

```
<%@ Page Language="VB" %>
<%@ Import Namespace="System.Globalization" %>

<script runat="server">
```

LISTING 19.9 continued

```
5:      sub Page_Load(Sender as Object, e as EventArgs)
6:         lblMessage.Text = Request.UserLanguages(0).ToString
7:      end sub
8:   </script>
9:
10:   <html><body>
11:      Your primary language is:
12:      <asp:Label id="lblMessage" runat="server"/>
13:   </body></html>
```

ANALYSIS On line 2, you import a new namespace, `System.Globalization`. This namespace contains many of the objects you'll need to alter your output for different cultures. Note that none of the objects in this namespace is used in this listing, but you'll be using them soon! On line 6, you retrieve and display the user's primary language. The `UserLanguages` property returns an array of the languages that a visitor uses (as specified by his browser), sorted by priority (common languages and their codes are shown in Table 19.1). `UserLanguages(0)` returns the default language, or the one with the highest priority. Listing 19.9 produces Figure 19.8 when viewed from the browser.

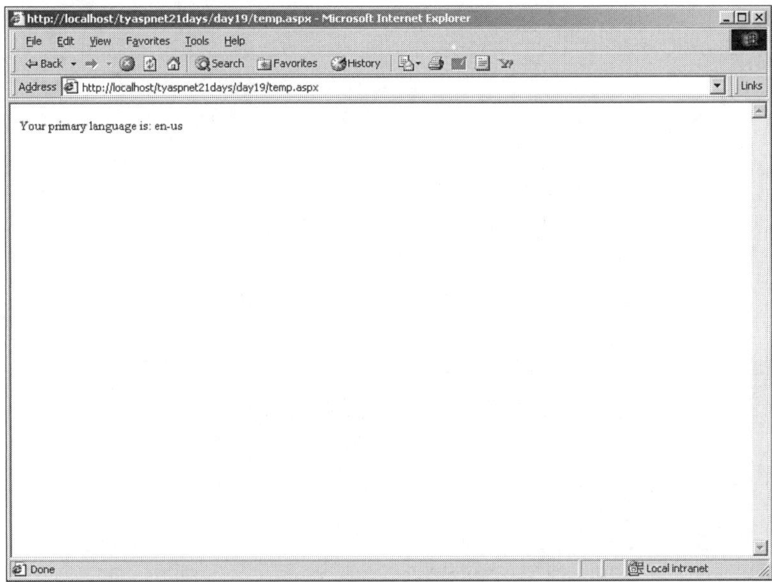

FIGURE 19.8
The `Request` *object can be used to determine a user's primary language.*

TABLE 19.1 Commonly Used Languages and Abbreviations

Language	*Code*
Arabic (Egypt)	ar-eg
Chinese (Hong Kong)	zh-hk
Dutch (Belgium)	nl-be
English (Australia)	en-au
English (Canada)	en-ca
English (United Kingdom)	en-gb
English (United States)	en-us
French	fr
German	de
Italian	it
Japanese	ja
Korean	ko
Portuguese	pt
Russian	ru
Spanish (Mexico)	es-mx
Spanish (Traditional)	es

Now that you've got the user's primary language, you can use it to set the culture information for your ASP.NET page. This will be done using the `System.Globalization.CultureInfo` object. This object contains information that completely represents the culture indicated by the language used, such as the calendar used, the country names, the date and time format, and so on. Listing 19.10 shows an example of using this object.

LISTING 19.10 Using the `CultureInfo` Object

```
<%@ Page Language="VB" %>
<%@ Import Namespace="System.Globalization" %>

<script runat="server">
   sub Page_Load(Sender as Object, e as EventArgs)
      dim strLanguage as string = Request. _
         UserLanguages(0).ToString

      lblMessage.Text = "Primary language: " & _
         strLanguage & "<br>"
```

Listing 19.10 continued

```
11:
12:          dim objCulture as new CultureInfo(strLanguage)
13:          lblMessage.Text += "Full name: " & objCulture. _
14:             EnglishName & "<br>"
15:          lblMessage.Text += "Native name: " & objCulture. _
16:             NativeName & "<br>"
17:          lblMessage.Text += "Abbreviation: " & objCulture. _
18:             ThreeLetterISOLanguageName & "<br>"
19:          lblMessage.Text += "Current Time: " & DateTime.Now. _
20:             ToString("D", objCulture)
21:       end sub
22:    </script>
23:
24:    <html><body>
25:       <b>Your user information:</b> <p>
26:       <asp:Label id="lblMessage" runat="server"/>
27:    </body></html>
```

Analysis This listing is a modification of the previous one. On line 2, you again import the `System.Globalization` namespace. On lines 6 and 7, you retrieve the primary language used by the visitor, as you did in Listing 19.9. This is displayed in the label on line 26. On line 12, you create a new `CultureInfo` object based on the primary language retrieved from line 6. Lines 13–20 display various properties of this culture, including its name, abbreviation, and date, formatted appropriately for the culture. To format the date properly, you use the `ToString` method with two parameters: the first indicates how the date should be displayed, and the second is the `CultureInfo` object that provides customization info. Figure 19.9 shows the output from this listing when the primary language is French.

The `CultureInfo` object has a lot of properties that allow you to determine more detailed information. Table 19.1 lists the most common of these properties.

Table 19.1 `CultureInfo` Properties

Property	*Description*
`Calendar`	The calendar used by the culture (that is, Gregorian, Korean, and so on).
`CurrentCulture`	Retrieves the culture used by the server (not by your user's browser). Returns a `CultureInfo` object. This property is read-only.
`CurrentUICulture`	Retrieves the culture used by the server. This property is used to specify the culture of resource files. See "Packing Resources into Files" later today. This property is read-only.

TABLE 19.1 continued

Property	Description
`DateTimeFormat`	Returns a `DateTimeFormatInfo` object that specifies how to format date and time information for the culture. See the .NET SDK Documentation for more details.
`DisplayName`	The full name of the `CultureInfo` object in the language used by the UI.
`EnglishName`	The full name of the `CultureInfo` object in English.
`Name`	Same as `DisplayName`, but read-only.
`NativeName`	The full name of the `CultureInfo` object, in its native language.
`NumberFormat`	Describes how to display numbers (that is, where to place commas, decimal points, and so on). Returns a `NumberFormatInfo` object.
`ThreeLetterISOLanguageName`	The ISO 3166 standard three-letter code for the culture.
`ThreeLetterWindowsLanguageName`	The Windows version of the three-letter code for the culture.
`TwoLetterISOLanguageName`	The ISO 3166 standard two-letter code for the culture.

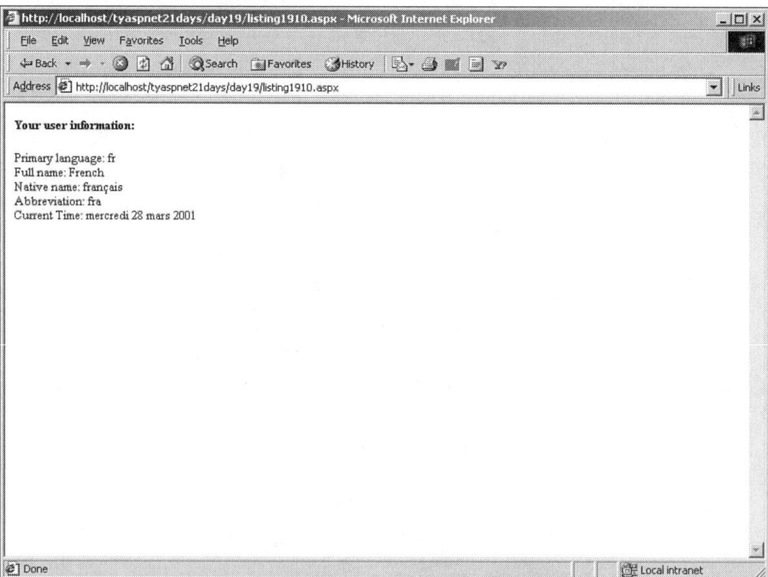

FIGURE 19.9

The output of the page is customized to the culture of the user, without any code modifications.

You can also set the culture information for a page with the `Culture` attribute of the `@ Page` directive. The following line sets the culture to German (`de`):

```
<%@ Page Language="VB" Culture="de" %>
```

Whenever you use culture-specific objects in your ASP.NET page, they will use this value as the default instead of what is specified by the server. For example, when the culture is set to German, the code `DateTime.Now.ToString("D")` produces the output:

```
Mittwoch, 28. März 2001
```

When the culture is set to `en-us`, the same code generates the output:

```
Wednesday, March 28, 2001
```

This is an easy way to set the culture at the page level if you know ahead of time what you'll be using.

> **Note**
>
> The `CultureInfo.CurrentCulture` property is actually a shortcut to the `System.Threading.CurrentThread.CurrentCulture` object. Both return a `CultureInfo` object that can be used as you have done here. The difference is that the former is read-only, whereas the latter is not. Therefore, when you want to change the current culture, use the latter object.
>
> Culture is a property of the currently running thread (in other words, the currently running piece of the current application). When setting the culture information, ASP.NET does so for the entire application. Thus, you can access the culture information for current thread, as well as for the current `CultureInfo` object. (You'll use the `System.Threading.CurrentThread` object later today.)

In addition to the `CultureInfo` object, you can use `RegionInfo`, which provides information such as currency symbol and whether or not the region uses the metric system. The syntax for this object is similar to the `CultureInfo` object, but it doesn't use languages to present customized information. Rather, it uses country abbreviations. For instance, `US` for the United States and `FR` for France. Listing 19.11 shows an example.

LISTING 19.11 Displaying Information About a User's Region

```
<%@ Page Language="VB" %>
<%@ Import Namespace="System.Globalization" %>

<script runat="server">
   sub Page_Load(Sender as Object, e as EventArgs)
```

LISTING 19.11 continued

```
6:           dim objRegion as RegionInfo
7:
8:           if Page.IsPostBack then
9:              objRegion = new RegionInfo(btRegion.Text)
10:           else
11:               objRegion = RegionInfo.CurrentRegion
12:           end if
13:
14:           lblMessage.Text = "Region: " & objRegion.Name & "<br>"
15:           lblMessage.Text += "Full name: " & objRegion. _
16:               EnglishName & "<br>"
17:           lblMessage.Text += "Currency: " & objRegion. _
18:               CurrencySymbol & "<br>"
19:           lblMessage.Text += "Abbreviation: " & objRegion. _
20:               ThreeLetterISORegionName & "<br>"
21:           lblMessage.Text += "Metric system: " & objRegion. _
22:               IsMetric
23:      end sub
24:   </script>
25:
26:   <html><body>
27:      <form runat="server">
28:         <b>Your information:</b> <p>
29:         <asp:Label id="lblMessage" runat="server"/><p>
30:         Change to (i.e. 'US', 'FR', 'JP', etc):
31:         <asp:TextBox id="btRegion" runat="server"
32:            AutoPostBack=true />
33:      </form>
34:   </body></html>
```

ANALYSIS When this page loads for the first time, the default region is loaded into a `RegionInfo` object, as shown on line 11 with the `CurrentRegion` property. Lines 14–22 display properties of the region, such as the currency symbol and abbreviation. When a user enters information into the text box on line 31, the page is automatically posted because the `AutoPostBack` property is set to `true`. The region code entered by the user is then used to create a new `RegionInfo` object, as shown on line 9. Figure 19.10 shows the output for the region `JP`, or Japan.

Table 19.2 lists the common properties of the `RegionInfo` object.

TABLE 19.2 `RegionInfo` Properties

Property	*Description*
`CurrencySymbol`	The symbol used to represent monetary values in the specified region.

TABLE 19.2 continued

Property	Description
`CurrentRegion`	Retrieves the region used by the server (not by your users). Returns a `RegionInfo` object.
`DisplayName`	The full name of the `RegionInfo` object in the language used by the UI.
`EnglishName`	The full name of the `RegionInfo` object in English.
`IsMetric`	A Boolean value specifying whether the current region uses the metric system.
`ISOCurrencySymbol`	The ISO code that represents `CurrencySymbol`. For example, `USD` is the ISO code for `$`.
`Name`	Same as `DisplayName`, but read-only.
`ThreeLetterISORegionName`	The ISO 3166 standard three-letter code for the region.
`ThreeLetterWindowsRegionName`	The Windows version of the three-letter code for the region.
`TwoLetterISORegionName`	The ISO 3166 standard two-letter code for the region.

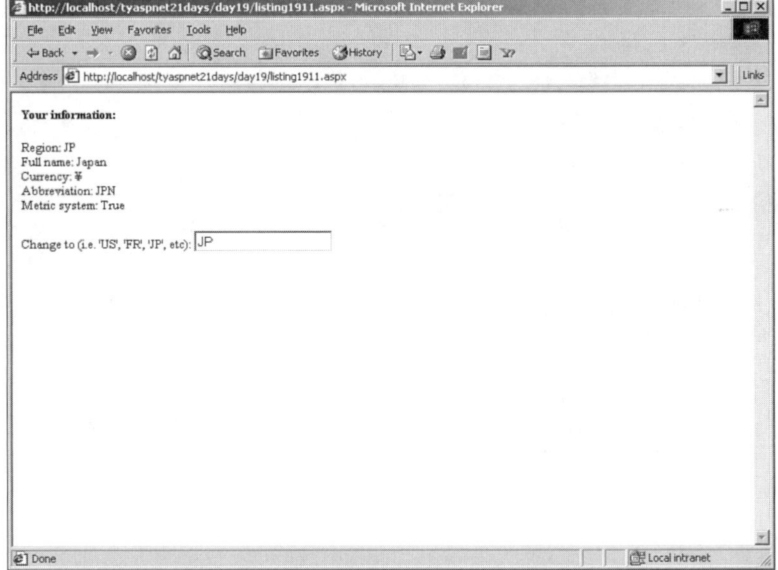

FIGURE 19.10
The information is displayed for the specified region.

19

NEW TERM Finally, you can specify the *encoding* of the output of your ASP.NET pages. Encoding represents how characters are represented by the computer; for instance,

Unicode or ASCII. ASP.NET, by default, uses Unicode, but encoding varies from region to region.

There are two different ways to specify the encoding for your application: directly in the ASP.NET page or in the `web.config` file. In the ASP.NET page, simply specify the encoding in the `@ Page` directive with the `ResponseEncoding` attribute:

```
<%@ Page Language="VB" ResponseEncoding="UTF-8" %>
```

In the `web.config` file, use the following syntax:

```
<configuration>
   <system.web>
      <globalization fileEncoding="utf-8" />
   </system.web>
</configuration>
```

So far, you've examined how to change the output of culture-specific objects, such as the `DateTime` object. What about plain text? How can you convert plain text into culture-specific languages? Unfortunately, there's no easy way to do so; you have to translate the text manually. When you have multiple languages in your site's audience, this usually means you have to create multiple versions of each page. Fortunately, you don't have to resort to that in ASP.NET; resource files are the answer.

Packing Resources into Files

Resource files are used to store application data apart from an application. You can have multiple versions of a resource file, so that your ASP.NET pages can present different information without requiring any changes in code. Using localization as an example, you can have multiple resource files—one for each culture that will view your pages. Each resource file contains the same information, but translated into different languages.

Let's examine a simple ASP.NET page with content that can be extracted into resource files, shown in Listing 19.12.

LISTING 19.12 An ASP.NET Page Used for Resource Extraction

```
<%@ Page Language="VB" %>

<script runat="server">
   sub Page_Load(Sender as Object, e as EventArgs)
      lblMessage.Text = DateTime.Now.ToString("t")
   end sub
</script>

<html><body>
    <b>Welcome!</b> The time is now:
```

LISTING 19.12 continued

```
11:       <asp:Label id="lblMessage" runat="server"/><p>
12:
13:       This page demonstrates using resource files with
14:       ASP.NET.<p>
15:
16:       <font size=1>Don't forget to try this at home!</font>
17:    </body></html>
```

This listing is uncomplicated. It displays some static text as HTML, and the current time in the label on line 11. Figure 19.11 shows the output of this page.

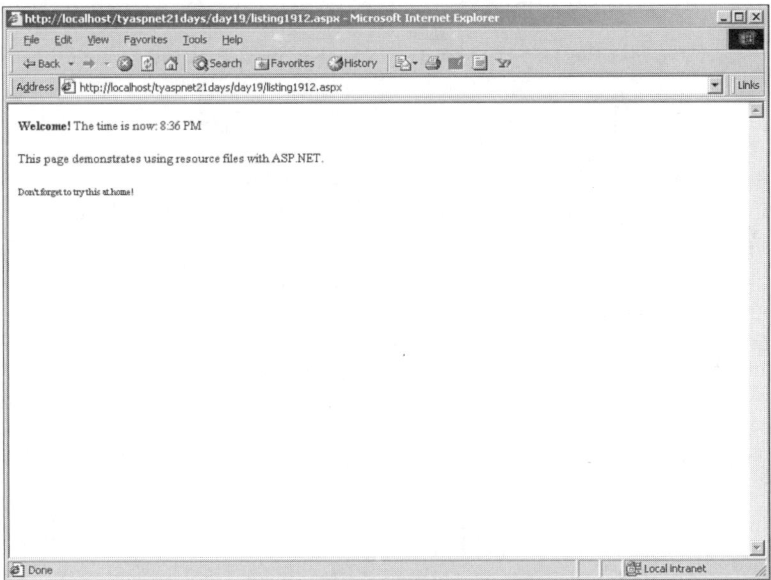

FIGURE 19.11
A simple ASP.NET page ready for a resource file.

Suppose that you wanted to translate this page into French. You could create a new file with the same format but different text, but why bother? You could create two separate resource files instead. These are pure text files, and can be created with any text editor. Let's make the English version first. Type the following code into your text editor:

```
Greeting=Welcome!
Time=The time is now:
Blurb=This page demonstrates using resource files with ASP.NET
Disclaimer=<font size=1>Don't forget to try this at home!
</font>
```

Save this file as `data.en-us.txt` (I'll get to the reason behind the filename in a moment). This file contains one section that contains all your string values. The information is organized into key/value pairs. In the line

```
Greeting=Welcome!
```

`Greeting` is the name of the resource you'll refer to in your ASP.NET page, whereas `Welcome!` is the actual value that will be displayed to the user. The French version is as follows:

```
Greeting=Bonjour!
Time=L'heure maintenent est:
Blurb=Cette page démonste comment utiliser les files de resource à
ASP.NET
Disclaimer=<font size=1>N'oublie pas essayez de faire ceci chez soi!</font>
```

Save this file as `data.fr-fr.txt`. (Keep each string value on one line! You'll receive an error if there are line breaks in the string.) Notice that the key names haven't changed. They must stay the same or your ASP.NET page won't be able to find the resources.

ASP.NET, however, can't use these text files as they are. You must convert them into a format that ASP.NET understands, using the Resource Generator tool (`resgen.exe`). This tool converts the format and spits out `.resources` files. Open a command prompt and navigate to the directory you saved these `.txt` files in. Type the following commands into the window (don't forget to press Enter after each command):

```
resgen data.en-us.txt

resgen data.fr-fr.txt
```

After each command, you will see something like the following:

```
Read in 4 resources from 'data.en-us.txt'
Writing resource file...  Done.
```

You will now see two additional files in your directory: `data.en-us.resources` and `data.fr-fr.resources`. These files are readable by ASP.NET's resource manager, so let's use them in your pages!

The `System.Resources.ResourceManager` object is responsible for handling all resource files for ASP.NET. This object finds the resource file that corresponds to the user's culture, and loads all resources within that file. Listing 19.13 shows this object in action.

LISTING 19.13 Using the `ResourceManager` to Load Resource Files

```
<%@ Page Language="VB" %>
<%@ Import Namespace="System.Globalization" %>
<%@ Import namespace="System.Resources" %>
```

LISTING 19.13 continued

```
4:  <%@ Import namespace="System.Threading" %>
5:
6:  <script runat="server">
7:     sub Page_Load(Sender as Object, e as EventArgs)
8:        dim objRM as ResourceManager
9:        dim strLanguage as string = Request.UserLanguages(0). _
10:           ToString
11:        dim objCulture as new CultureInfo(strLanguage)
12:        Thread.CurrentThread.CurrentCulture = new _
13:           CultureInfo(strLanguage)
14:        Thread.CurrentThread.CurrentUICulture = new _
15:           CultureInfo(strLanguage)
16:
17:        objRM = ResourceManager. _
18:           CreateFileBasedResourceManager("data", _
19:           Server.MapPath("."), Nothing)
20:
21:        lblGreeting.Text = objRM.GetString("Greeting")
22:        lblTime.Text = objRM.GetString("Time") & " " & _
23:           DateTime.Now.ToString("t")
24:        lblBlurb.Text = objRM.GetString("Blurb")
25:        lblDisclaimer.Text = objRM.GetString("Disclaimer")
26:
27:        objRM.ReleaseAllResources
28:     end sub
29:  </script>
30:
31:  <html><body>
32:     <b><asp:Label id="lblGreeting" runat="server"/></b>
33:     <asp:Label id="lblTime" runat="server"/><p>
34:
35:     <asp:Label id="lblBlurb" runat="server"/><p>
36:
37:     <asp:Label id="lblDisclaimer" runat="server"/>
38:  </body></html>
```


ANALYSIS First, note the additional namespaces on lines 3 and 4. `System.Resources` is needed to use the `ResourceManager` object; the `System.Threading` namespace is needed, too (its purpose will be explained in a moment). On line 8, you declare a new `ResourceManager` just as with any other object. On lines 9 and 10, you retrieve your visitor's primary language from the browser, as you did in Listing 19.9.

Lines 12–15 set the culture information for this page based on the primary language. Recall from the "Localizing Your Application" section earlier today that you can set the culture with the `System.Threading.CurrentThread.CurrentCulture` property, which takes and returns a `CultureInfo` object. On line 12, you use the primary language to set the `CurrentCulture` property to the proper culture. All localizable objects will now use the new culture you've specified (for example, the time, in the French culture, will display 22:06 instead of 10:06 PM).

However, just changing the culture won't cause ASP.NET to retrieve resources from a different resource file. You must set the `System.Threading.CurrentThread.CurrentUICulture` property to the new culture as well, as shown on lines 14–15. It is this property that ASP.NET uses to determine which resource files to load.

On lines 17–19, you do the actual loading of the resource file with the `CreateFileBasedResourceManager` method. This method takes three parameters: a prefix to use for your resource files, the path of the resource files, and an optional object used to parse your resources. In the second parameter, you use the `Server.MapPath` method to return the physical path of the directory where your resource files are stored. (Refer to "The `HttpServerUtility` Object" in Day 4, "Using ASP.NET Objects with C# and VB.NET," for more information on the `MapPath` method.) You don't need another object to parse your resource files, so the third parameter is `Nothing`.

Recall that you named each of your resource files in the format: `data.`*`culture`*`.resources`. The `CreateFileBasedResourceManager` method searches for files with the format *`prefix.culture`*`.resources`. Thus, the prefix you specify in the first parameter of this method must be the prefix you used for your resource files' names. In this case, when the culture is `en-us` (English, United States), this method searches for the file `data.en-us.resources`. Likewise, if the culture were `fr-fr` (French), this method would look for the `data.fr-fr.resources` file. The prefix serves as a logical way to group your resource files.

Finally, on lines 21–25, you use the `GetString` method of the `ResourceManager` to retrieve the key/value pairs stored in the resource files. Each of these values is displayed in label controls shown in lines 30–35. When the resource manager opens the resource files, it places a lock on them so that no other application can alter them while they are in use. Call `ReleaseAllResources` to release the lock on these files, as shown on line 27. Figures 19.12 and 19.13 show the output of this listing when the culture is `en-us` and `fr-fr`, respectively.

Note

Recall that you can set the culture from the `@ Page` directive as well:

```
<%@ Page Language="VB" Culture="fr" %>
```

If you do this, the code in Listing 19.13 will not pull from the proper resource file. This is because line 9 set the culture from the value retrieved from the user's browser, and not the value in the `@ Page` directive. To fix this, change lines 9–11 to the following line:

```
dim strLanguage as string = CultureInfo.CurrentCulture.ToString
```

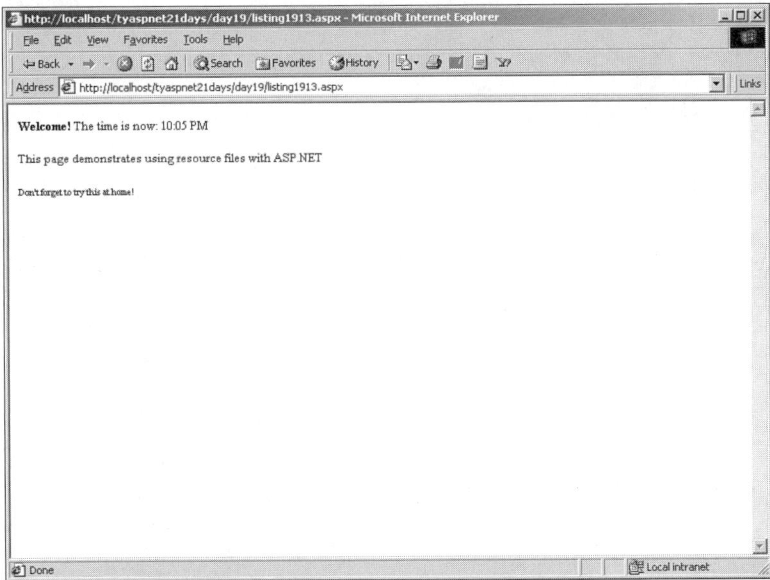
http://localhost/tyaspnet21days/day19/listing1913.aspx - Microsoft Internet Explorer
File Edit View Favorites Tools Help
Address http://localhost/tyaspnet21days/day19/listing1913.aspx
Welcome! The time is now: 10:05 PM
This page demonstrates using resource files with ASP.NET
Don't forget to try this at home!
Done
Local intranet

FIGURE 19.12
When the culture is set to `en-us`*, ASP.NET uses the* `data.en-us.resources` *resource file.*

No code changes are needed at all. Depending on the user's culture, he will see a different page. Using resource files is akin to storing customized information in a database and retrieving specific data depending on the user's preferences.

Tip

Because the culture information should be constant throughout your application, you might consider setting the culture in the `Application_BeginRequest` method of the `global.asax` file. This way, the culture is properly set automatically upon every new request to the server.

Also, you could create the `ResourceManager` object and store it as an application-level variable in the `Application_OnStart` event to avoid having to re-create it with every new request. For example, the following code could be added to the `Application OnStart` event in `global.asax`:

```
Application("RM") = New ResourceManager("data", _
   Server.MapPath("."), Nothing)
```

You now have one `ResourceManager` available to your entire application, which can be accessed through the `Application("RM")` variable.

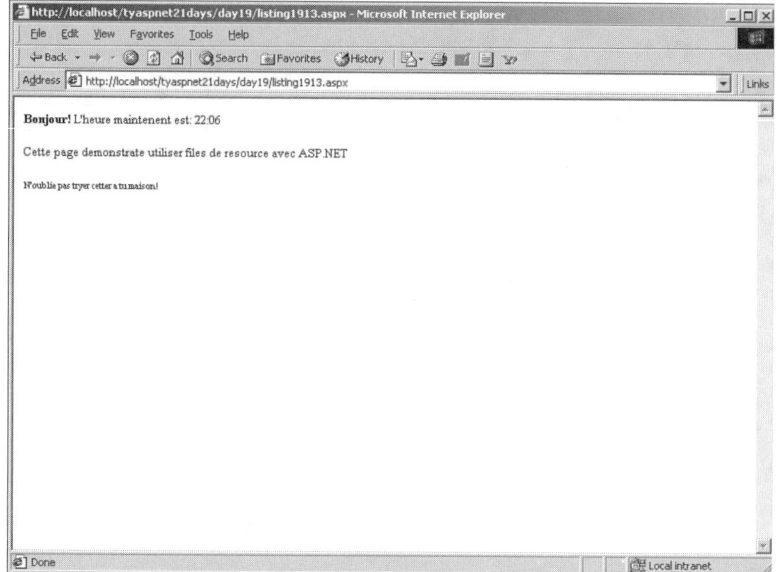

FIGURE 19.13
When the culture is set to `fr-fr`*, ASP.NET uses the* `data.fr-fr.resources` *resource file.*

That's Not ASP!

The desire to separate code from content and to receive the benefits received from such separation is not new to ASP.NET. In fact, developers have been striving to do this for some time, especially with classic ASP, which relied on code render blocks instead of code declaration blocks. This caused a problem known as "spaghetti code," where code was intermingled with HTML throughout a page. This made it very difficult to debug and modify the pages because developers had to search through an entire page to find errors. With code declaration blocks, this problem is mostly solved because all code is in one location: at the top of the page.

With classic ASP, developers relied on server-side includes to separate their code from their content. These files could contain any type of code, including HTML, so they were often used to hold common UI functionality. Server-side includes, although still available for use, are typically replaced with user controls or code-behind forms in ASP.NET. Both user controls and code-behind forms offer greater programmatic control than server-side includes, which technically offered none.

Resource files are new to ASP.NET. Developers familiar with compiled languages such as VB and C++ might recognize these files. They were commonly used in those languages for the same reasons you learned about today: simply to separate code from content. Classic ASP has no built-in way to store localizable information separate from the page, so multiple versions of entire sites often had to be created. In addition, classic ASP didn't allow modification of culture and region information.

All these new capabilities make ASP.NET much more versatile than classic ASP. Developers now have many more options when designing the code layout on their pages.

Summary

Today you learned about a few new methods to maintain the content of your pages separately from the code. With the Web forms framework, you can use code-behind forms, which separate code from content by placing them in separate files. You can use localization and resource files to display different content to your users without modifying your code.

To create a code-behind form, you need to create a class that derives from the `System.Web.UI.Page` class (or the `System.Web.UI.UserControl` class if the code-behind is for a user control). Move all ASP.NET code from the `.aspx` file into the new class, and declare public versions of the server controls used in your page. For example, if you have a label named `lblMessage` in your `.aspx` file, add the following to your code-behind:


```
public lblMessage as Label
```

This ensures that you are able to handle the properties and events generated by the server controls. Then add the `Inherits` and `src` attributes to your `.aspx` file, specifying the name of the code-behind class and the location of the file, respectively. Your code-behind and ASP.NET combination should work the same as it did prior to building the code-behind.

You can use the `Request.UserLanguages` property to retrieve a user's primary language from the browser. You can use this language to set culture information with the `CultureInfo` object. This object provides numerous methods to retrieve culture information such as date and time formats. The `RegionInfo` object is similar to `CultureInfo`, but provides information about a specified region or country, such as the currency symbol and country abbreviation.

Use the `resgen.exe` tool to generate `.resources` files from your resource text files. Be sure to name these latter files in the format: *`prefix.culture`*`.txt`. Create a new resource file for every language that you want your pages to be displayed in. These files store information in name/value pairs. You can then use the `ResourceManager` object to load these resource files and display the localized strings.

Tomorrow you'll look at another very important part of developing ASP.NET pages: debugging them. No one's perfect, so chances are that you've made mistakes when building your pages. Tomorrow's lesson will examine quite a few ways to track down and correct these errors.

Q&A

Q Can I change my default primary language for my browser?

A You bet! Go to Start, Settings, Control Panel, Internet Options. On the window that pops up, you should see a Languages button. Click it to modify the primary language for your browser. With the new window that pops up, you can add new languages, remove old ones, and change the priority for each.

Q Can I use resource files with compiled code, such as business objects? Can I compile my resource files?

A Absolutely on both counts! Using resource files with business objects can be accomplished in two ways: compile the resource files along with the business object, or leave them as separate `.resources` files. In the latter case, you can use them exactly as you have done today. In the former case, you'll have to change your code slightly.

The `CreateFileBasedResourceManager` method won't work when the resource files are compiled. Instead, you have to specify the assembly that contains the compiled resource files, with the following `ResourceManager` constructor:

```
dim objRM as New ResourceManager("prefix", System.Reflection. _
   Assembly.GetExecutingAssembly(), Nothing)
```

The first and third parameters are the same as for the `CreateFileBasedResourceManager` method. The second parameter, `System.Reflection.Assembly.GetExecutingAssembly`, returns an `Assembly` object that represents the assembly that the code is executing from. ASP.NET then knows where to look for the resource files, and you can retrieve values from them the same way as before.

Resource files can be compiled the same way as VB.NET or C# files, with the `vbc.exe` or `csc.exe` program. Compiled files that contain only resource files are known as *satellite assemblies*. Refer to the .NET Framework SDK documentation for more information, or check out *Sams Teach Yourself .NET Windows Forms in 21 Days* for information on localizing non-Web applications.

Workshop

This workshop will help reinforce the concepts you've covered in today's lesson. It is very helpful to understand fully the answers before moving on. Answers can be found in Appendix A.

Quiz

1. True or false: A code-behind file must derive from the `System.Web.UI.Page` class.
2. Why must you declare public variables in a code-behind for the server controls you use on an ASP.NET page?
3. Create an `@ Page` directive that uses a code-behind class named `MyControl`, in a `.vb` file with the same name.
4. What is a resource file?
5. What does the following line do?

   ```
   dim strVar as string = Request.UserLanguages(0)
   ```
6. What does the `resgen.exe` tool do?
7. What is the difference between `CurrentCulture` and `CurrentUICulture`?
8. True or false: The `CultureInfo.CurrentCulture` is a shortcut for the `System.Threading.CurrentThread.CurrentCulture` object.

Exercises

Create a currency exchange calculator for several different countries. Allow the user to enter a monetary value in one region's units, and convert to another by selecting a value from a select box. Use a resource file to store the exchange values. (Don't worry if you don't know the exchange rates, just make something up!) Use code-behind techniques!

WEEK 3

DAY 20

Debugging ASP.NET Pages

Today you're going to learn about a very important topic: debugging. No matter how strong a programmer you may be, we all make mistakes and debugging applications is a fact of life. The more code you write, the more bugs you'll create.

Chances are that you've come across many bugs in computer applications. Imagine all the times you've received messages, whether from a desktop application or a Web site, describing some error that you can't understand. Most of the time, those errors caused the application to crash; other times a bug caused the application to produce an output that you weren't expecting. Either way, you were not able to get done what you set out to do. Ideally, we could write code once and be done with it, but that's often not the case.

ASP.NET provides two great tools for debugging your applications: the Microsoft Common Language Runtime Debugger and the Trace Service. You'll learn about both of these today, as well as the `try` and `catch` blocks.

Today's lesson will cover the following:

- How to use `try` and `catch` statements to debug
- How to debug using `Response.Write`

- How to create and throw your own custom errors
- What the trace tool is and how to use it
- How to perform runtime debugging with the CLR debuggers

Introduction to Debugging

You've probably stumbled upon errors while developing your ASP.NET pages, ranging from forgetting the `runat='server'` attribute to more complex errors that take days to track down. Getting errors is frustrating, and seeing a screen like Figure 20.1 can make you want to pull your hair out.

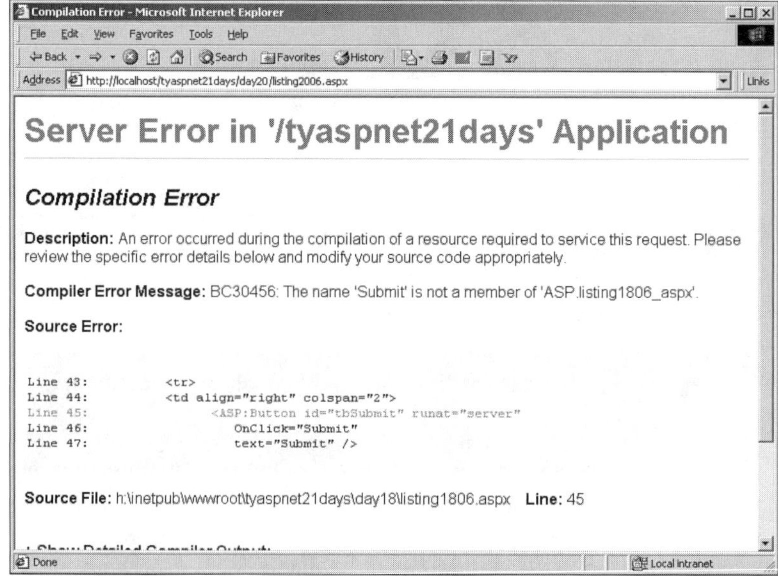

FIGURE 20.1
A typical error in ASP.NET.

As applications get more and more complex, it becomes harder and harder to prevent potential bugs and to track and fix existing ones. Let's look at a typical example, shown in Listing 20.1.

LISTING 20.1 Finding Bugs

```
<%@ Page Language="VB" %>
<%@ Import Namespace="System.Data" %>
<%@ Import Namespace="System.Data.OleDB" %>

<script runat="server">
```

LISTING 20.1 continued

```
sub Page_Load(Sender as Object, e as EventArgs)
   'set up connection
   dim objConn as new OleDbConnection _
      ("Provider=Microsoft.Jet.OLEDB.4.0;" & _
       "Data Source=c:\ASPNET\data\banking.mdb")

    'open connection
    dim objCmd as new OleDbDataAdapter _
       ("select * from tblUsers", myConnection)

    'fill dataset
     dim ds as DataSet = new DataSet()
     objComm.Fill(ds, "tblUsers")
  end sub
</script>

<html><body>
 <form runat="server">

 </form>
</body></html>
```

Try viewing this listing from the browser (don't forget to turn debug mode on in your `web.config` file). You'll see something similar to Figure 20.2.

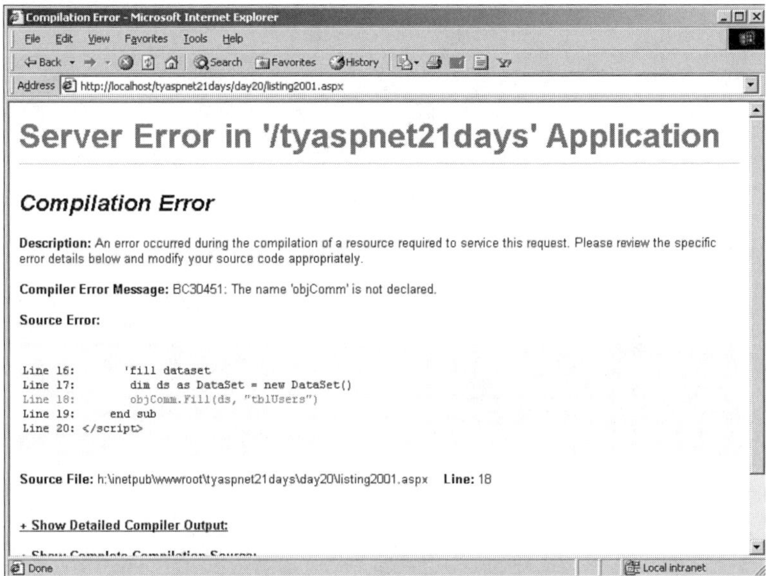

FIGURE 20.2
Uh oh, something's wrong with your code.

20

There's obviously something wrong with the code in Listing 20.1, and if you haven't spotted it already, the page in Figure 20.2 will help. Notice that Figure 20.2 highlights the exact line where the error occurred, and describes the file and line number as well. It looks like you simply have a typo on line 18: You used `objComm` instead of `objCmd`. This is an easy problem to fix, thanks to this detailed error page, and after the error is corrected, your code will work correctly.

Let's explore this error page. You'll notice that it provides quite a bit of additional information about the source of the error. For example, if you scroll down in this error page, you see two links: Show Detailed Compiler Output and Show Complete Compilation Source. Expanding these links produces what's shown in Figure 20.3.

FIGURE 20.3

More detailed error information.

Note

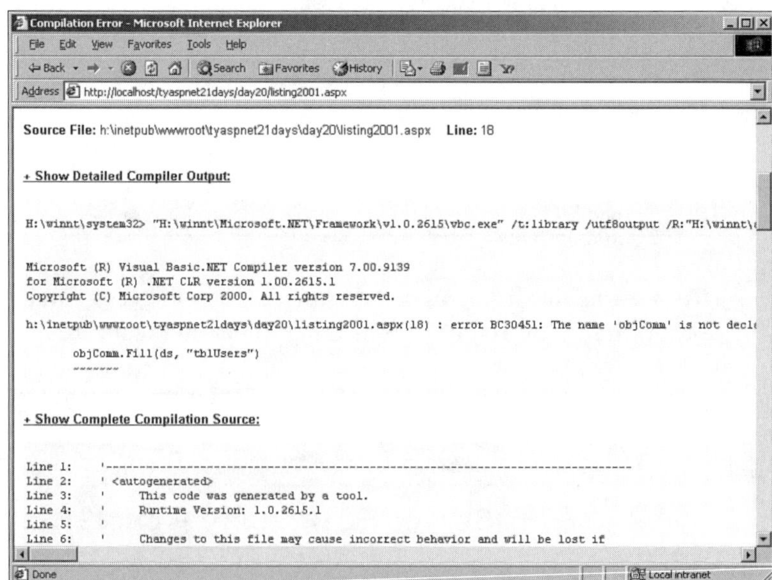

If you don't have debug mode enabled, you might not see the links to this additional information. Refer to Day 18, "Configuring and Deploying ASP.NET Applications," for more information.

In the first section, Show Detailed Compiler Output, ASP.NET shows you what it tried to do and what prevented it from happening. The first line in Figure 20.2 shows the command that ASP.NET used to compile the ASP.NET source code. (As you can see, it uses `vbc.exe`, the Visual Basic.NET compiler.) After examining the compiler and business objects, everything in this line should be familiar.

The compiler then produces output that helps you determine the cause of the error. This message is also shown in Figure 20.2. In the second section of Figure 20.3, under Show Complete Compilation Source, you see the complete source of the file that ASP.NET is trying to compile, including all compiler commands and CLR functions.

In general, this is *not* a good thing to show users. First of all, most users don't want to see error messages in their applications. Second, a clever user can use this source code against you. Thus, it's imperative to use all the debugging mechanisms you have available during development to prevent errors.

Fortunately, ASP.NET provides a few mechanisms to help you out. You've already seen the first one: the `try` and `catch` statements in various places, such as in yesterday's Listing 19.1. These help catch possible errors in your application. The tracing tool also helps in this manner, as well as providing additional information. Finally, the Common Language Runtime debugger is a powerful method of discovering and fixing bugs once they've occurred.

try and catch

Normally, when a piece of code causes an error, it stops your application and displays an error message, as shown when you tried to execute Listing 20.1. If it's at all possible to stop this error, you want to do so (after all, ideally, you should never see an error).

When you use a `try` statement, you tell ASP.NET that you want it to tentatively execute a block of code. If any of the code inside the `try` statement causes an error, instead of your application crashing and displaying the error, the execution continues and allows you to try to deal with the problem. For example, if you wrapped line 18 of Listing 20.1 in a `try` statement, you could have potentially stopped the error from crashing your application, and continued on with the rest of the code.

The `try` statement is used to guard a section of code that may cause errors. In traditional application development, this is a must because certain actions are *expected* to produce errors. For instance, although you may not know it, clicking the Cancel button on a dialog box typically causes an error, which the application must handle somehow. The `try` statement and its associated statements are known as *structured exception handling*.

As you've seen in a few examples throughout this book, the syntax for this statement is simple. It consists of a `try` statement, followed by the code to be guarded and a `catch` or `finally` statement. For example:

```
'VB.NET
1:  'create OleDbCommand object here
2:  try
3:     objCmd.Connection.Open
4:     ...
5:  catch
6:     hander error
7:  end try

//C#
1:  //create OleDbCommand object here
2:  try {
3:     objCmd.Connection.Open();
4:     ...
5:  } catch {
6:     hander error
7:  }
```

In this case, you guard the code between lines 2 and 5 because it can cause an error. If no errors occur inside the `try` block, the execution of code transfers to line 7 and the code continues as normal. If an error does occur, the execution of code moves to the `catch` statement on line 5, which will contain code to handle the error.

New Term Let's examine the technical details more closely. When an error occurs in an ASP.NET application, an *exception* is *thrown*. This means that something has occurred that shouldn't have, and VB.NET or C# tosses an error in the air for someone to see. If you don't do anything about the exception, the error comes crashing down, along with your application, and the person who sees the error will be the end user.

Throwing exceptions allows you to intercept the error before it crashes the application and the user sees it. If you intercept it in time, you can prevent a crash and fix the problem.

Enter the `try` statement. When an error occurs, the `try` statement will alert its companion statement, `catch`, which will catch the exception and handle it. Listing 20.2 shows an example.

LISTING 20.2 A Debugging Example

```
<%@ Page Language="VB" %>
<%@ Import Namespace="System.Data" %>
<%@ Import Namespace="System.Data.OleDb" %>

<script runat="server">
   dim Conn as new OleDbConnection("Provider=" & _
            "Microsoft.Jet.OLEDB.4.0;" & _
            "Data Source=c:\ASPNET\data\banking.mdb")

    sub GetData(Sender as Object, e as EventArgs)
       dim objCmd as OleDbCommand = new OleDbCommand _
          ("select * from tblUsers where UserID = " & _
          tbID.Text, Conn)
       dim objReader as OleDbDataReader

       objCmd.Connection.Open()
       objReader = objCmd.ExecuteReader

       dgData.DataSource = objReader
       dgData.DataBind()

       objReader.Close
       objCmd.Connection.Close()
    end sub
 </script>

 <html><body>
    <form runat="server">
       <asp:Label id="lblMessage" runat="server"
          maintainstate=false /><br>
       Enter an ID: <asp:TextBox id="tbID" runat="server"
          AutoPostBack=True
          OnTextChanged=GetData /><p>
       <asp:DataGrid id="dgData" runat="server"
          BorderColor="black"
          GridLines="Vertical"
          width="100%"
          Font-Name="Arial"
          Font-Size="8pt"
          HeaderStyle-BackColor="#cccc99"
          ItemStyle-BackColor="#ffffff"
          AlternatingItemStyle-Backcolor="#cccccc"
          AutoGenerateColumns="true" />
    </form>
 </body></html>
```

ANALYSIS This is a simple page that returns user information based on the user ID. When you enter a number in the text box, the database commands are executed and bind the returned data to the `DataGrid`. However, what happens when you accidentally enter a letter instead? Figure 20.4 shows this situation.

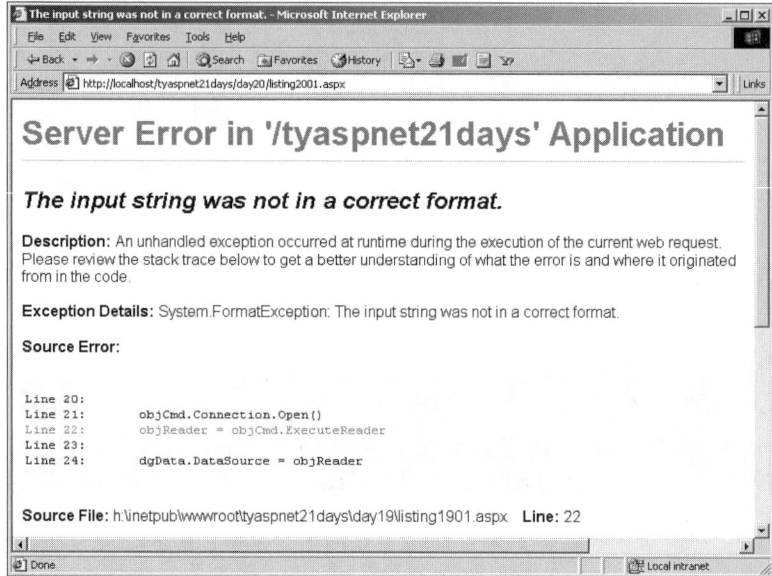
The input string was not in a correct format. - Microsoft Internet Explorer
File Edit View Favorites Tools Help
Back Search Favorites History
Address http://localhost/tyaspnet21days/day20/listing2001.aspx
Links
Server Error in '/tyaspnet21days' Application.
The input string was not in a correct format.
Description: An unhandled exception occurred at runtime during the execution of the current web request. Please review the stack trace below to get a better understanding of what the error is and where it originated from in the code.
Exception Details: System.FormatException: The input string was not in a correct format.
Source Error:
Line 20:
Line 21: objCmd.Connection.Open()
Line 22: objReader = objCmd.ExecuteReader
Line 23:
Line 24: dgData.DataSource = objReader
Source File: h:\inetpub\wwwroot\tyaspnet21days\day19\listing1901.aspx Line: 22
Done
Local intranet

FIGURE 20.4
The wrong user input causes an error.

This isn't a good thing to show users. Let's add a `try` statement to the listing to handle the error gracefully. Replace lines 16–23 with Listing 20.3.

LISTING 20.3 Using a `try` Block with Listing 20.2

```
16:  try
17:     objCmd.Connection.Open()
18:     objReader = objCmd.ExecuteReader
19:
20:     dgData.DataSource = objReader
21:     dgData.DataBind()
22:
23:     objReader.Close
24:     objCmd.Connection.Close()
25:  catch
26:     lblMessage.Text = "Invalid input!"
27:  end try
```

Now request the page again. You should see what's shown in Figure 20.5.

FIGURE 20.5
Handling the error gracefully.

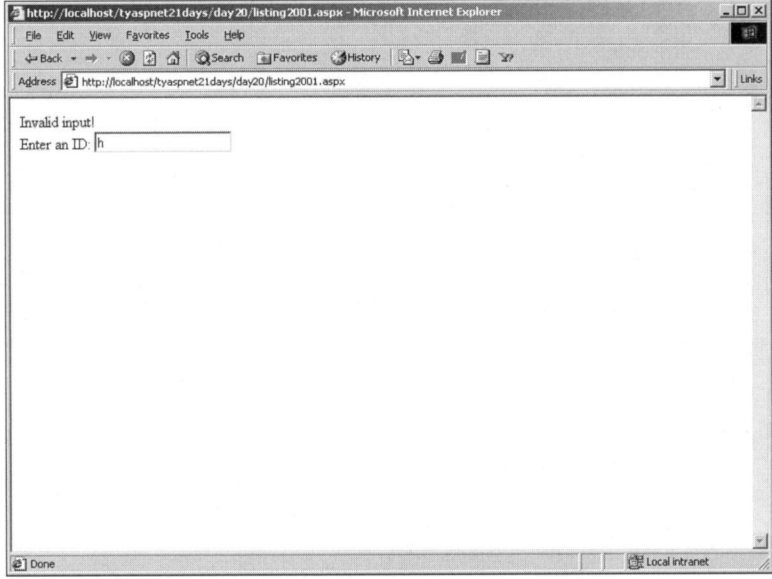

The `try` block caught the error before it caused problems and displayed an error message, as shown on line 26 of the previous code snippet. The execution then picked up after line 27 and was completed normally.

Exceptions are grouped hierarchically. The `System.Exception` class is the base exception and contains all other exceptions. Directly under `Exception` is `SystemException`, and under that are various others, such as `OleDbException` and `FormatException`. As you move down the hierarchy, the errors become more and more specific. For example, `SystemException` covers all built-in exceptions, but `FormatException` only covers the error caused by invalid user input. All these exceptions are .NET classes, just as the other objects we've been dealing with so far have been. Figure 20.6 shows an example of the exception hierarchy.

Note that although `SystemException` falls below `Exception` in the exception hierarchy, it still belongs to the `System` namespace. That is, you use `System.SystemException` and not `System.Exception.SystemException`.

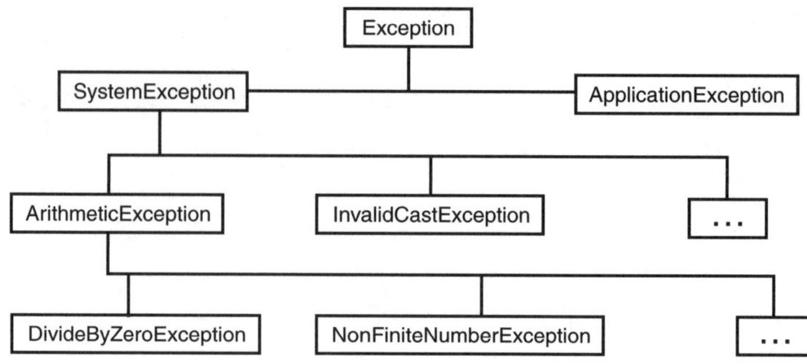

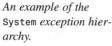

FIGURE 20.6
An example of the `System` *exception hierarchy.*

Using a generic `catch` statement, as you did previously, catches all errors of every type. In other words, it catches any exception under the base `Exception` class. However, you can specify the types of errors you want to handle with this syntax:

```
catch VariableName as ExceptionType
```

For example, you could replace the previous listing with Listing 20.4.

LISTING 20.4 A Revised `try` Block

```
16:  try
17:     objCmd.Connection.Open()
18:     objReader = objCmd.ExecuteReader
19:
20:     dgData.DataSource = objReader
21:     dgData.DataBind()
22:
23:     objReader.Close
24:     objCmd.Connection.Close()
25:  catch objEx as FormatException
26:     lblMessage.Text = objEx.Message
27:  catch objEx as OleDbException
28:     lblMessage.Text = "Database error!"
29:  catch objEx as Exception
30:     lblMessage.Text = "Unknown error!"
31:  end try
```

On line 25, you catch an exception of the type `FormatException` (as well as those below it). Don't worry about the `Message` property on line 26; you'll get to that soon. On line 27, you catch an `OleDbException`. And on line 29, you catch all exceptions. Because exceptions are hierarchical, a `catch` statement will handle the exception it declares, as well as all of the more-specific exceptions. Therefore, you should write `catch` statements in order of specificity, putting the less-specific exceptions last. When using `catch` statements, be aware of the following:

- Derived exception classes (such as `FormatException` or `OLEDBException`) represent specific error scenarios that you are testing for due to the possibility that they could occur or that specific action might be required in those cases.
- The `try...catch` structure stops evaluating exceptions after it encounters a `catch` block that applies.
- `Exception` is the catch-all in this scenario, similar to `case else` in an `if` statement.

This listing produces what's shown in Figure 20.7.

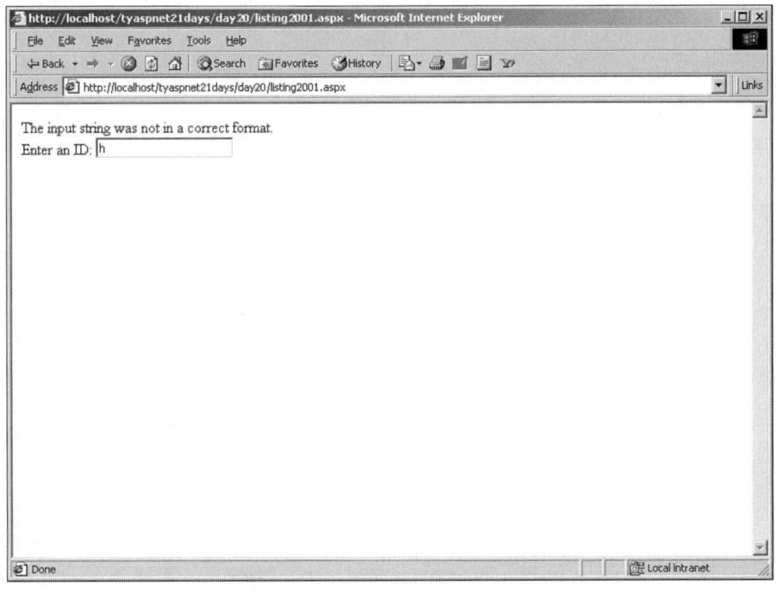

FIGURE 20.7
Multiple `catch` *statements catch more specific errors. Use the exception* `Message` *property to display the error text associated with the exception.*

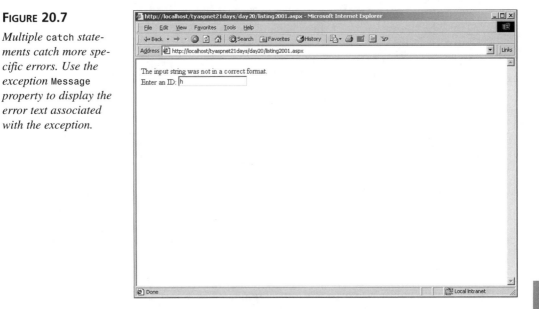

There's one more statement associated with the `try` statement: the `finally` statement. You can use this block to execute some clean-up code or other end processing, whether or not an exception occurs. You could insert the code in Listing 20.5 into Listing 20.2 to close your database connection no matter what happens.

Listing 20.5 Using the `finally` Statement

```
objCmd.Connection.Open()
try
   objReader = objCmd.ExecuteReader

   dgData.DataSource = objReader
   dgData.DataBind()

   objReader.Close
catch objEx as Exception
   lblMessage.Text = "Unknown error!"
finally
   objCmd.Connection.Close()
end try
```

Figure 20.8 illustrates the process when using a `try` block.

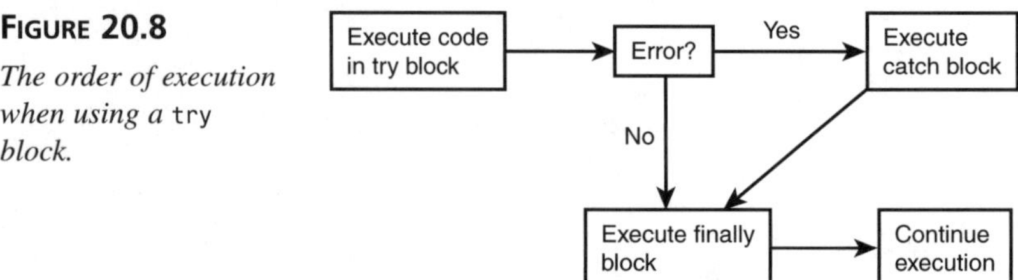

Figure 20.8
The order of execution when using a `try` *block.*

Every exception class has a few properties that you can use to determine the cause of the error:

- `HelpLink`—A link to a file containing more information about the error (note that you must create the link and file yourself).
- `InnerException`—A reference to an inner exception. If another exception was caught and passed to another exception handler, this returns the reference to the first exception.
- `Message`—The message describing the exception.
- `Source`—A string containing the name of the object that caused the error.

- `StackTrace`—Returns a stack trace that specifies the cause of the error. (More about that in "Tracing" later today.)
- `TargetSite`—The method that caused the error.

Throwing Exceptions

Exceptions are very useful, and they aren't only used for catching errors. In fact, there may be times when you want to throw your own custom exceptions.

For example, recall the Web Services you built on Days 16 ("Creating Web Services") and 17 ("Consuming and Securing XML Web Services"). Suppose that you're verifying information against a database and the validation fails. You could throw a custom exception in your service for the client application to handle with a `try` and `catch`.

To throw an exception, simply use the `throw` keyword:

```
throw new Exception("I'm taking exception to that!")
```

(The syntax is the same in C#.) This statement creates a new custom exception based on the `Exception` class. The string inside the parentheses is the error message. When you add this line to the beginning of the `GetData` method in Listing 20.1, you'll receive the page displayed in Figure 20.9 after you submit the form.

FIGURE 20.9

Using `throw` *to cause a custom exception.*

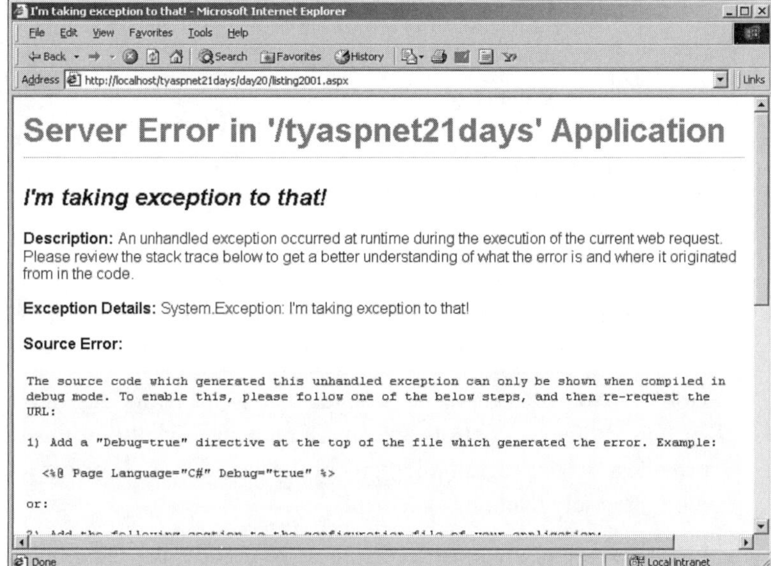

20

Throwing a custom exception can be very useful if you don't want to handle the exception yourself. As long as the function that called the code that produced the error can handle the exception, you don't have to worry about it.

For example, one case in which throwing a custom exception might be useful is when a user is entering input into a form. After the form has been posted, your post handler code calls a validation method that determines whether one of the entries is invalid (for instance, the user has entered a number instead of his name). The validation routine could throw a custom error to alert the calling method that an error has occurred. The calling method could then handle it as needed.

Note that you don't have to throw a custom exception—you can throw an exception of any available type. For instance, the following throws an error specifying that a required parameter was missing:

```
throw new ArgumentNullException()
```

This is useful when you're building business objects, and it allows implementers to handle the errors as they see fit.

When to Use a `try` Statement

`try` statements are useful for debugging code, allowing you to discover errors without breaking execution. There are a few general rules you should follow when using `try` statements.

First, you should always use `try` when you're accessing systems outside of the ASP.NET environment—when you're accessing databases or files, for instance. There are many factors you have no control over that can go wrong—the file may not exist, the user may not have proper permissions to access the file, the database might be offline, the database table you're trying to access may have been deleted, and so on. Because of this, `try` statements are a must.

Use `try` blocks when you're unsure of code, especially for testing and debugging. For example, there may be times when you create code that depends highly on other factors in your application (binding to `DataGrids` is a perfect example).

Don't rely on `try` statements to catch user input errors. Instead, use another method, such as Validation controls, which are built specifically for this purpose. These controls provide a richer programming model for handling these errors and can pinpoint errors more precisely than `try` statements.

Finally, don't use `try` blocks for all of your code; use them only as necessary. The processing overhead that this statement introduces may be small, but it isn't always worth the expenditure.

Tracing

You may have already found a way to debug your applications through clever use of comments and `Response.Write`. If you suspect that a piece of code is causing errors, you can comment it out and use well-placed `Response.Write` methods to see if your guess was correct. For example, take a look at Listing 20.6.

LISTING 20.6 Testing Portions of Code

```
1:  <%@ Page Language="VB" %>
2:  <%@ Import Namespace="System.Data" %>
3:  <%@ Import Namespace="System.Data.OleDb" %>
4:
5:  <script runat="server">
6:     sub Submit(Sender as Object, e as EventArgs)
7:        dim strSQL as string = _
8:           "SELECT UserID FROM tblUsers WHERE " & _
9:           "UserName = '" & tbUserName.Text & "' AND " & _
10:           "Password = '" & tbPassword.Text & "'"
11:
12:        'do database stuff here
13:     end sub
14:  </script>
15:
16:  <html><body>
17:     <form runat="server">
18:        <asp:Label id="lblMessage" runat="server" />
19:        Username:
20:        <asp:Textbox id="tbUserName" runat="server" /><p>
21:        Password:
22:        <asp:Textbox id="tbPassword" runat="server"
23:           TextMode="password" /><p>
24:        <ASP:Button id="tbSubmit" runat="server"
25:           OnClick="Submit"
26:           Text="Submit" />
27:     </form>
28:  </body></html>
```


ANALYSIS This form accepts a username and password to query a database. Although this is a very simple example, suppose that you're receiving errors—perhaps the correct information isn't being returned from the database. In a situation like this, it's common to verify that the SQL statement is correct.

You can add the following line after line 10 to verify that your SQL statement is in the correct format:

```
Response.Write(strSQL)
```

Then comment out any lines that are suspect to prevent the error from happening again. Figure 20.10 shows the output.

FIGURE 20.10

`Response.Write` *allows you to test the value of variables.*

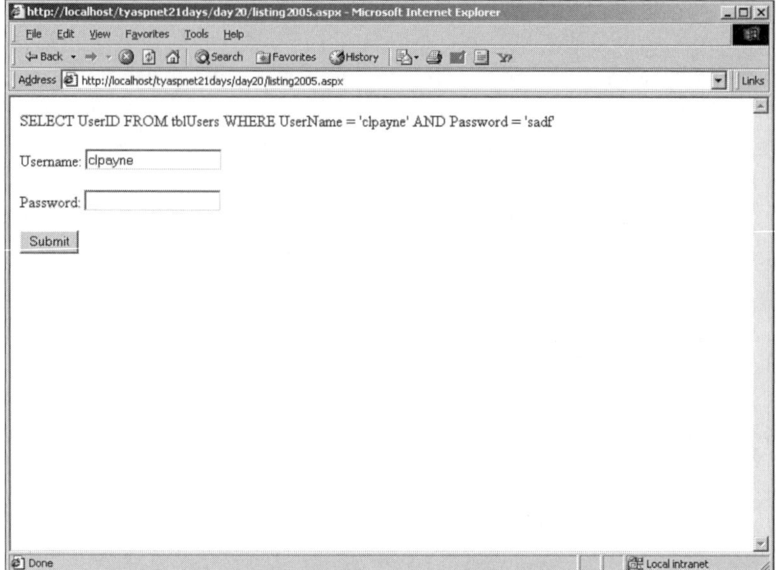

`Response.Write` is a very helpful tool for following variables and checking their values. Unfortunately, this method doesn't offer much information other than a value, and it can be a pain to keep adding and removing these statements in different places.

ASP.NET tracing solves this problem, allowing you to output debugging statements and follow the execution of your code. Tracing tells you which methods have been executed, how much time each method took to execute, what the values of variables are, and so on, all in an easy-to-read format.

Also, you don't have to remove any trace debugging statements when you're through debugging. You can disable all of them with one command. Tracing can be enabled for a single page or for all pages across an application. Either way, these debugging statements don't affect your application at all when they're disabled, nor do they send any output to the client.

There are two levels of tracing in ASP.NET: page level and application level. Let's cover page-level tracing first because application-level tracing is simply an extension of it.

Page-Level Tracing

You can see tracing in action easily. Add the `Trace="True"` directive to line 1 in Listing 20.6, like so:

```
<%@ Page Language="VB" Trace="true" %>
```

This turns tracing on for that page. Figures 20.11 and 20.12 show what the page should look like on your browser.

FIGURE 20.11
Tracing provides a great deal of debugging information.

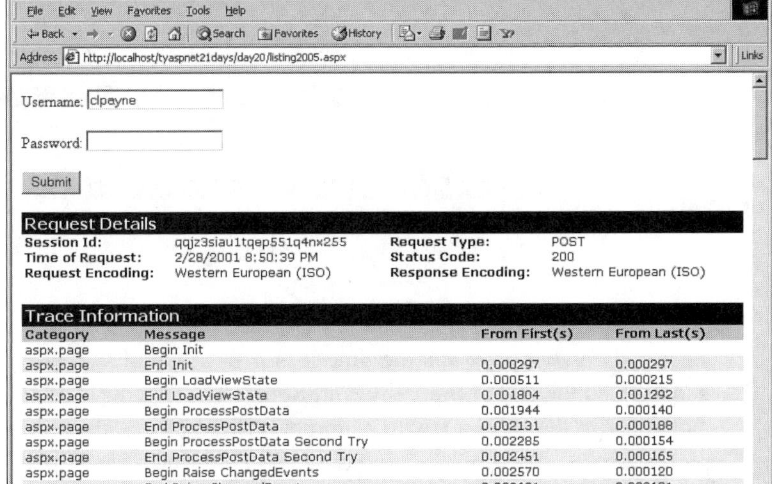

Whoa, what happened? All of a sudden, your page is filled with new information. Scroll through the output and examine each item. This trace information provides just about all the information there is on your page! Let's look at each section, one at a time.

At the top of the page, you still see your page from Listing 20.6. You can interact with it as though none of the information below it were there. ASP.NET adds these tables of information to your pages automatically when you enable tracing. They're simply for debugging and performance information. Obviously, you wouldn't want to let an end user see this information.

The next section, Request Details, tells how the client requested the page. It contains the unique session ID for the current user, the time of the request, the request verb (POST or GET, typically), the status code, and the encoding information. There's not much you can do with this information in this case, but it can be useful nonetheless.

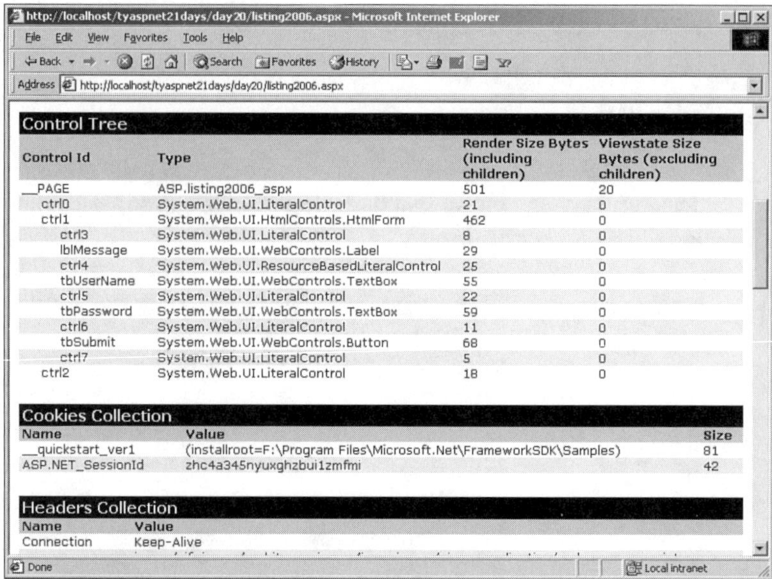

FIGURE 20.12

Further down the tracing output.

The Trace Information section shows the execution of your page. It lists each event that occurred on your page and the time it took to accomplish, both from the start of the request and the end of the last event. Some of the events in Figure 20.11 should look familiar, but there are a few that are new. The category shows where each trace occurred. In the next section, you'll learn how to add your own categories.

The next section, Control Tree, shows all the server controls used in your page, in hierarchical order. Notice that it even shows `LiteralControls` (see Day 2, "Building ASP.NET Pages," for a description of these objects). This section displays the size (in bytes) of each control and the number of bytes required to maintain the viewstate information. Here you can clearly see how much memory is required to maintain state in your form and decide whether to disable viewstate maintenance.

The Cookies Collection section shows any cookies in use and their values. This may or may not contain any information, depending on the nature of your application.

Headers Collection shows the information stored in the HTTP header. This information includes the host server, browser version and type, referring URL, content type, and so on.

The optional Form Collection section shows any data that was sent via a POST operation. If you just submitted the input form on this page, you should see the values you entered here, as well as the viewstate information.

Finally, the Server Variables section displays information such as HTTP headers, the server name and port, the type of HTTP connection, and so on. This is the information used by the server to set up your application.

You can also sort all the tracing information on this page by the times that the events occurred, or by the category they belong to in the `TraceMode` property. For example:

```
<%@ Page Language="VB" Trace="true" TraceMode="SortByTime" %>
```

This is the default sort order. `SortByCategory` organizes the output differently, but you won't see any difference yet because you only have one category in Figure 20.11.

This page provides a lot of performance information for your application. You can see exactly how long each stage of processing takes and determine if adjustments need to be made. For example, note that the time between `Begin Render` and `End Render`—that is, the time it takes to display the page in the browser—consistently is one of the largest time values.

You can use the `Trace` object to write custom debugging information to your ASP.NET page. This class has two methods of its own: `Write` and `Warn`. These methods are nearly identical. The first simply outputs debug information, whereas the second outputs the same information in red.

Let's try an example. Add the following code to line 11 of Listing 20.6 (replacing `Response.Write` if you still have it there):

```
Trace.Write("Custom category", strSQL)
```

The first parameter is the category you want your output to belong to, and the second is the string to display. Submit the form and you should see what's shown in Figure 20.13.

Notice the new category midway through the Trace Information section. This event occurred between the `Begin Raise PostBack` and `End Raise PostBack` events, which handle the form submission events. This new item contains the value in `strSQL`. Note that no new text appeared in the actual page because `Trace.Write` and `Trace.Warn` only write to the trace log, not to the client output.

Let's examine a slightly more complex example. Listing 20.7 is similar to Exercise 1 from Day 14, "Using ASP.NET's Improved Caching Capabilities." You create a `DataSet`, store it in cache, and bind the data to a `DataGrid`. The data is retrieved from the cache instead of the database on subsequent requests, saving processing time. There's also a button that allows the user to render the cache invalid, causing the retrieval process to start over.

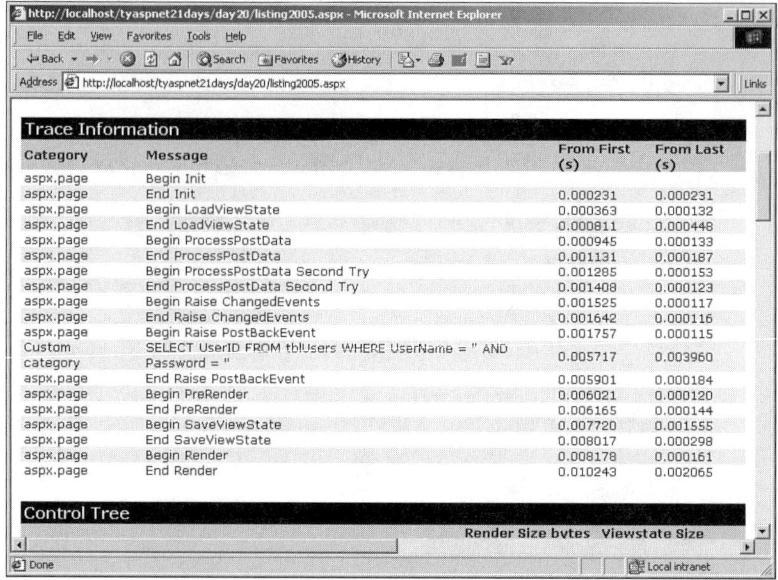

FIGURE 20.13 *Adding custom debugging information.*

LISTING 20.7 Tracing with a More Complex Example

```
<%@ Page Language="VB" Trace="true" %>
<%@ Import Namespace="System.Data" %>
<%@ Import Namespace="System.Data.OleDb" %>

<script language="VB" runat="server">
sub Page_Load(Sender as Object, e as EventArgs)
    Trace.Warn("Custom", "Page loading...")
  if not Page.IsPostBack then
     Trace.Warn("Custom", _
         "No post, calling CreateData...")
      CreateData()
   end if
end sub

sub CreateData
   dim source as DataView
     source = Cache("DataView")

     if source is nothing then
        dim strConnString as string = "Provider=" & _
           "Microsoft.Jet.OLEDB.4.0;" & _
           "Data Source=c:\ASPNET\data\banking.mdb"

        Trace.Warn("Custom", _
           "Creating OleDbDataAdapter...")
```

LISTING 20.7 continued

```
       dim objCmd as OleDbDataAdapter = new _
          OleDbDataAdapter("select * from tblUsers", _
          strConnString)
       Trace.Warn("Custom", "SQL value: " & _
          objCmd.SelectCommand.CommandText)

       dim ds as DataSet = new DataSet()
       objCmd.Fill(ds, "tblUsers")

       source = new DataView(ds.Tables(0))
       Trace.Warn("Custom", "Inserting into cache...")
       Cache.Insert("DataView", source)

       lblMessage.Text = "Data set created explicitly"
    else
       lblMessage.Text = "Data set retrieved from " & _
          "cache<br>"
    end if

    Trace.Warn("Custom", "Binding data...")
    dgData.DataSource = source
    dgData.DataBind()
 end sub

 sub ExpireCache(Sender as Object, e as EventArgs)
    Trace.Warn("Custom", _
       "Removing from cache, call CreateData")
    dim dv as dataview = Cache.Remove("DataView")
    CreateData()
 end sub
</script>

<html><body>
 <form runat="server">
    <asp:Label id="lblMessage" runat="server"
       maintainState=false/><p>
    <asp:Button id="btSubmit" runat="server"
       text="Expire Cache"
       OnClick="ExpireCache"/><p>
    <asp:DataGrid id="dgData" runat="server"
       BorderColor="black" GridLines="Vertical"
       cellpadding="4" cellspacing="0"
       width="450" Font-Name="Arial"
       Font-Size="8pt"
       HeaderStyle-BackColor="#cccc99"
       ItemStyle-BackColor="#ffffff"
       AlternatingItemStyle-Backcolor="#cccccc" />
 </form>
 </body></html>
```

ANALYSIS First, notice that you've enabled tracing on line 1 with the `Trace="true"` directive. Your page will now display tracing information, and all the `Trace.Write` and `Trace.Warn` statements in your code will print debug information.

You've strategically placed `Trace.Warn` statements on lines 7, 9, 24, 29, 36, 45, and 51 to tell you when specific events are occurring. After viewing this page once and clicking the Expire Cache button, you should see the trace information displayed in Figure 20.14.

FIGURE 20.14

Viewing custom debug information.

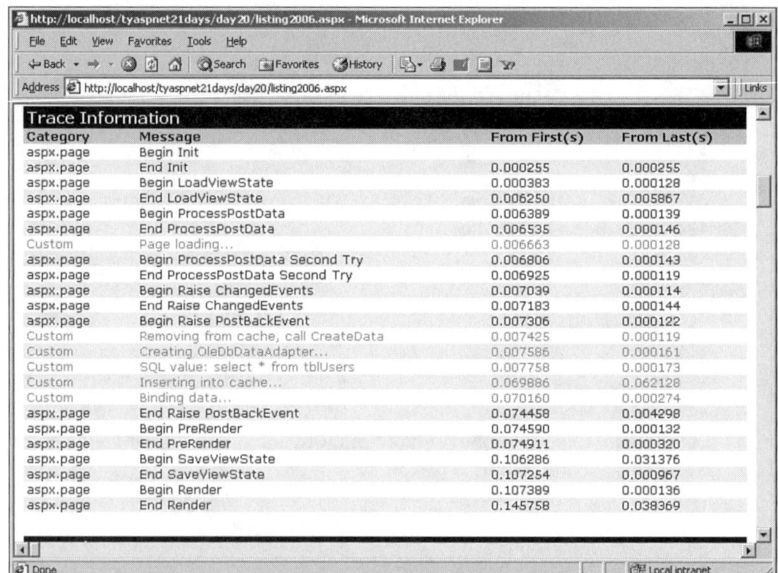

Trace Information

Category	Message	From First(s)	From Last(s)
aspx.page	Begin Init		
aspx.page	End Init	0.000255	0.000255
aspx.page	Begin LoadViewState	0.000383	0.000128
aspx.page	End LoadViewState	0.006250	0.005867
aspx.page	Begin ProcessPostData	0.006389	0.000139
aspx.page	End ProcessPostData	0.006535	0.000146
Custom	Page loading...	0.006663	0.000128
aspx.page	Begin ProcessPostData Second Try	0.006806	0.000143
aspx.page	End ProcessPostData Second Try	0.006925	0.000119
aspx.page	Begin Raise ChangedEvents	0.007039	0.000114
aspx.page	End Raise ChangedEvents	0.007183	0.000144
aspx.page	Begin Raise PostBackEvent	0.007306	0.000122
Custom	Removing from cache, call CreateData	0.007425	0.000119
Custom	Creating OleDbDataAdapter...	0.007586	0.000161
Custom	SQL value: select * from tblUsers	0.007758	0.000173
Custom	Inserting into cache...	0.069886	0.062128
Custom	Binding data...	0.070160	0.000274
aspx.page	End Raise PostBackEvent	0.074458	0.004298
aspx.page	Begin PreRender	0.074590	0.000132
aspx.page	End PreRender	0.074911	0.000320
aspx.page	Begin SaveViewState	0.106286	0.031376
aspx.page	End SaveViewState	0.107254	0.000967
aspx.page	Begin Render	0.107389	0.000136
aspx.page	End Render	0.145758	0.038369

This page tells you quite a bit of information. First, you see the order of occurrence of events. Specifically, you see that the `Page_Load` event happens much earlier than any Web form event processing. Failing to take note of this while developing pages is a common mistake.

Second, this page shows you the value of the SQL statement you're executing. The statement in this example is static, so this doesn't help you much. However, it's very useful when you have to assemble a SQL statement dynamically.

Next, notice the time difference between the `"Inserting into cache..."` and `"SQL Value: ..."` events. This time span represents the time it takes to retrieve the information from the database. It's over 300 times greater than the time spans of any of the other custom events, and it's almost more than all the other events combined. Thus, you can see that the cost of retrieving information from a database is high.

Refresh the page (without reposting the form data) and take a look at the trace information once again. Note that the total time is nearly cut in half.

Finally, scroll down further to the Control Tree section and notice the amount of memory that is required to maintain the viewstate (see Day 2), as indicated by the Viewstate Size Bytes (excluding children) column. After summing the values in this column, you'll see that this page requires approximately 6KB, nearly 40% of the memory needed to render the page completely (shown by the Render Size Bytes column). If you don't need to maintain the viewstate, it will pay to disable it through the `EnableViewState="false"` page directive.

Page-level tracing is a powerful tool for debugging and improving the performance of your pages. When you don't need to display this information any more, you can simply disable tracing with `Trace="false"` in the page directive and leave the `Trace.Warn` statements in. They don't alter execution in any way, nor do they affect performance.

There may be times when you want to execute a portion of code only if tracing is enabled. For instance, you may want to display custom debugging information that you create yourself. In this case, you can simply check the `Trace.IsEnabled` property:

```
If Trace.IsEnabled then
   For I = 0 to ds.Tables("tblUsers").Rows.Count - 1
      Trace.Write("User Info", ds.Tables("tblUsers"). _
         Rows(i)(0).ToString)
   next
end if
```

This code writes values from the returned data to the trace log, but only if the `Trace` directive is set equal to true. Thus, you can also use `Trace` to stop code from executing, which is another common necessity during debugging, and provides you more options than simply using `Trace.Write` and `Trace.Warn`.

Application-Level Tracing

Tracing is a very useful tool, but it can be a pain to go through every page on your site enabling and disabling it. Also, page-level tracing provides you with statistics only for the page in question—it doesn't tell you about any other pages in your site. With application-level tracing, you can easily turn tracing on and off for every page, as well as view the trace output in one location.

You can enable tracing for all pages across the site by adding a directive to your `web.config` file:

```
<configuration>
   <system.web>
      <trace enabled="true" />
```

```
    </system.web>
</configuration>
```

The `web.config` file with this attribute must be at the root folder of your application for this to work. (In our case, it will be `c:\inetpub\wwwroot`, unless you explicitly changed it from IIS.) This turns on tracing for the entire site, which means that every page in your site (unless it explicitly turns tracing off) now outputs trace information. By default, application-level tracing doesn't display the tracing information on every page. Rather, you view the cumulative information via a special file on your server: `trace.axd`. (You don't have to create this file. ASP.NET handles it for you automatically; in fact, you won't even be able to see it through Windows Explorer or IIS—ASP.NET creates it dynamically.) View this file from any directory in your site with the URL:

```
http://localhost /trace.axd
```

This page will show something similar to Figure 20.15, depending on what pages are being requested on your site.

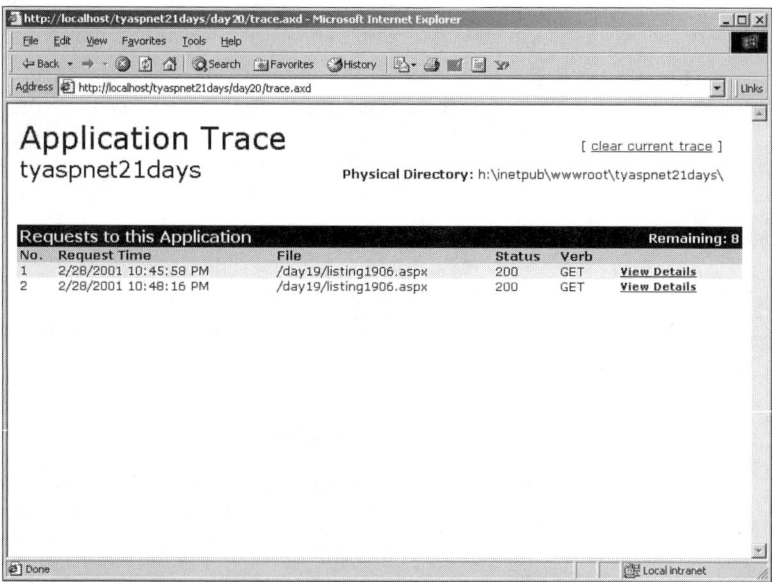

FIGURE 20.15

Application-level tracing via the `trace.axd` file.

Note

Make sure you add the `<trace enabled="true">` line to your `web.config` file first or you won't see any information at `trace.axd`!

By default, this page shows the information for the last 10 requests to your site, including the time of the request, the particular file requested, how it was requested (the HTTP verb), and the status of the request. The view details link brings up a window similar to Figure 20.11 (but without the UI portion). The clear current trace link clears the application log of all the trace data. Since trace information uses up a lot of memory, clearing this data may increase performance slightly. (Just beware that the requests may add up again very quickly!)

Open a new browser window, request any page in your application, and click Refresh a few times. Go back to `trace.axd` and click the Refresh button. You should see a few more requests here. Also note that Remaining decreases with each request. When you request more than the limit, the older requests are pushed off the stack.

`trace.axd` is highly configurable. You can alter the number of requests to store, the method of trace display, and where to display the output. The complete syntax for the `web.config` section is as follows:

```
<trace enabled="boolean" pageOutput="boolean"
   requestLimit="number" traceMode="mode" />
```

The `traceMode` attribute is exactly the same as it is for page-level tracing; it tells ASP.NET how tracing should behave. `pageOutput` specifies whether you want the trace information to be displayed on every page in addition to `trace.axd`; the default value is false. `requestLimit` specifies the number of requests to keep in memory; the default is 10.

If you specify `Trace="false"` on a particular page, it overrides the application-level tracing for that page. This means that `trace.axd` won't display any information for that particular page.

Application-level tracing provides an easy way to view statistics on all pages on your site quickly. You can use this tool to detect any bottlenecks in your application when it's under stress from many Web visitors.

The CLR Debugger

Debugging compiled applications can require special consideration; sometimes they are not able to produce output directly for the developer to see (for example, compiled business objects generally don't display any data). Normally, the executing code has been translated to machine language or MSIL, which makes it harder to follow along. These types of application require a different kind of debugger—one that can attach to a running process.

New Term When you run an application, compiled code is executed by the computer. This code executes instructions, creates variables along the way, assigns values to those variables, and destroys them as well. Recall that all of these variables are stored in memory. *Attaching a debugger* means that another application, a debugger, is watching the memory used by the first application. The debugger can interpret the instructions and memory used by the application and tell the developer know what's going on, in readable terms.

The previous methods you've seen today involve altering the code before execution and watching the output after execution is through. Attaching a debugger is very helpful when you need to watch and alter commands *during* execution. Figure 20.16 illustrates the difference.

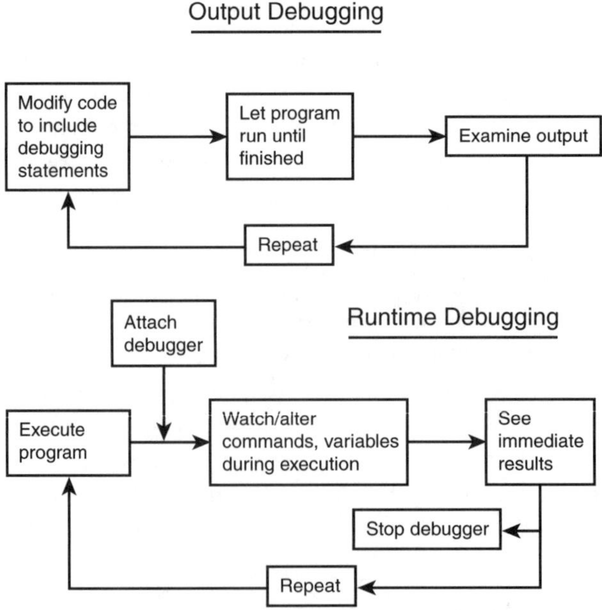

Figure 20.16
Attaching a debugger allows you to watch the execution step by step.

Note that you can also run an application from the debugger, so you don't have to attach it after the program is already running.

Because ASP.NET pages are compiled, you can use debugging tools similar to those used for traditional application debugging. Specifically, you'll be using the Common Language Runtime Debugger included with the .NET Framework SDK.

Using the CLR Debugger

Before you use the debugger, you need to enable debugging in your application in the `web.config` file. Add the following lines to `web.config` in your root directory:

```
<configuration>
   <system.web>
      <compilation debug="true" />
   </system.web>
</configuration>
```

NEW TERM This line generates a *symbol file (.pdb)* for your application. This file tells the debugger how to map the machine instructions that must be interpreted to the code in the source file. This allows you to track the execution by looking at the code you've written instead of cryptic machine code.

This line also shows you some rudimentary debugging information in your ASP.NET pages when you receive an error, as you learned about earlier today in "Introduction to Debugging."

Note that you should disable the `debug` option in your `web.config` file as soon as you're done debugging. Compiling with `debug` enabled really slows down your applications.

Let's start the CLR debugger. The file is called `DbgCLR.exe`, and it's located at `c:\Program Files\Microsoft.NET\FrameworkSDK\GuiDebug` by default. Double-click on this file, and you should see what's shown in Figure 20.17.

Once you've opened the debugger, debugging your applications is a four-step process:

1. Open the file you want to debug.
2. Attach the debugger to the ASP.NET process.
3. Set breakpoints.
4. Use the debugger's tools to manipulate your application.

FIGURE 20.17

The Common Language Runtime Debugger Interface.

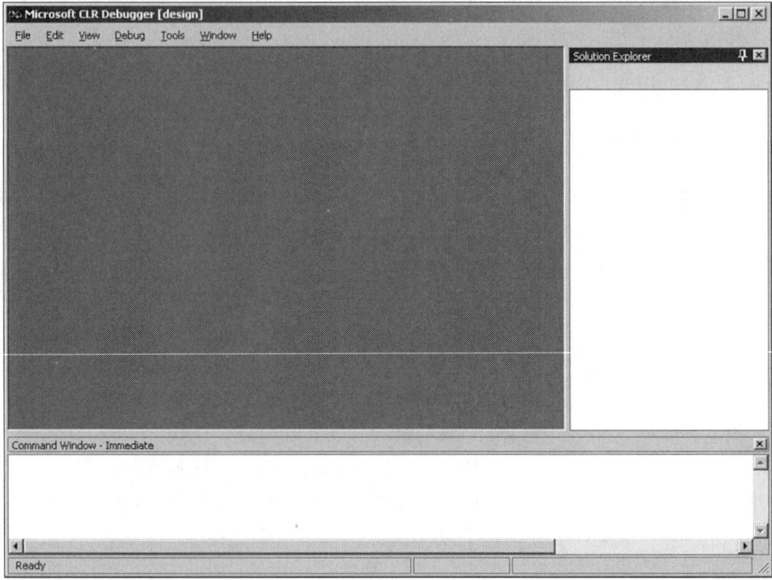

Assuming that you've saved Listing 20.7 as `listing2007.aspx`, open it from your browser and allow it to execute normally. This will start the ASP.NET process and your application—if they aren't already running. Open this file in the CLR debugger as well by clicking on File, Open, File, and then selecting the appropriate source file. You should see the source code in the CLR debugger, and the file will appear in the Solution Explorer window on the right side of the debugger.

To attach the debugger to the ASP.NET process, click Tools, Debug Processes. You should see the window shown in Figure 20.18.

Click Show System Processes (if you haven't already) and find the `aspnet_wp.exe` process. Select this process and click the Attach button. In the window that pops up, check Common Language Runtime. At the bottom of the window, you should see the name of your application (`tyaspnet21days`). Click OK and close the processes window.

A new window is now available in the CLR debugger, called Disassembly. This window shows the interpreted instructions as seen by the computer.

Caution

> When you attach to any process with a debugger, that application is usually frozen (unusable) and any unsaved information may be lost. ASP.NET is no different. When you attach to the process, make sure that you're not blocking any production applications.

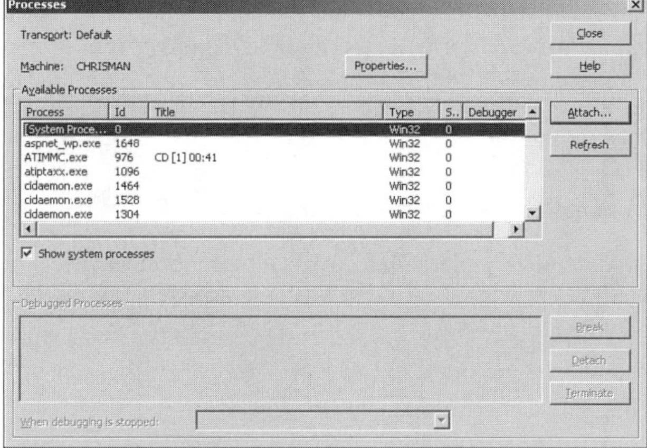

FIGURE 20.18

Attaching the debugger to the ASP.NET process.

NEW TERM A *breakpoint* is a place in the code where execution is paused. Breakpoints are very useful for debugging specific lines in your code. For example, if you know a line is causing errors in your page, you can set a breakpoint immediately before it and use the debugger to analyze the instructions and variables.

To set a breakpoint, click the left-hand column next to the source code of your file. A red dot should appear, meaning the execution will halt at this line. (If a question mark appears in the red dot, you may not have enabled debugging in `web.config`.) Hold your mouse cursor over the breakpoint and you'll see exactly where it will occur, as shown in Figure 20.19.

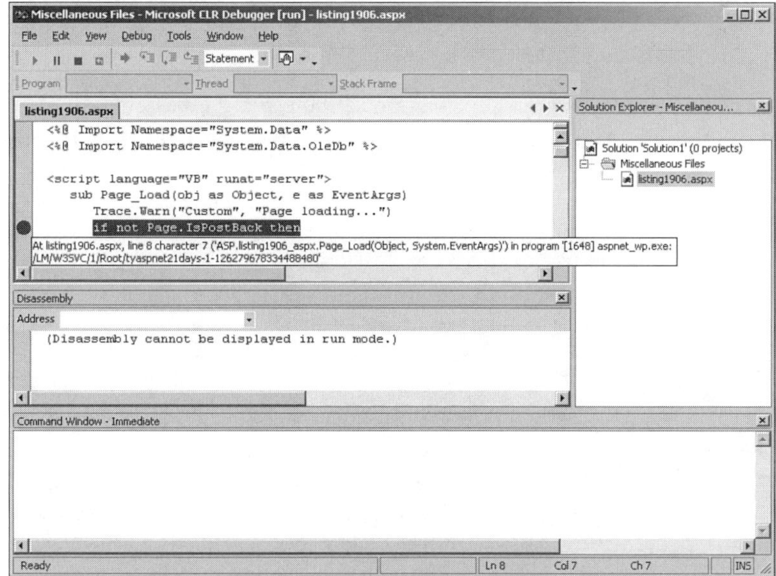

FIGURE 20.19

Setting a breakpoint in your code causes execution to halt temporarily at the specified line.

Now request `listing2007.aspx` from the browser again. When the execution reaches the breakpoint, the application will stop and the debugger will take control.

At the top of the CLR debugger window are controls that allow you to control the execution, such as moving to the next line of execution or stopping debugging altogether. The debugger is a very complex tool, and you can do a lot with it. For more information, see the .NET Framework SDK Documentation.

Debugging compiled applications can be a pain because you cannot stop execution without losing information, nor can you watch variables in real-time. This makes it difficult to track down where an error is occurring, especially if your application is very complex. The CLR debugger provides all the preceding capabilities for ASP.NET pages, which makes debugging a snap.

ASP.NET applications aren't all the CLR debugger can attach to. It can attach to and debug any .NET Framework application that you have running. (In other words, it must have been developed under the .NET Framework; you couldn't, for instance, debug Windows 95 with this debugger.) Just remember that the application must be enabled for debugging, meaning it must have symbol files.

Debugging Recommendations

ASP.NET provides a few different methods for debugging applications. So which should you use, and where?

If you're unsure of the location of the error, the best, and often easiest, method to use is tracing. Add `Trace.Write` and `Trace.Warn` throughout your code, and take note of which ones are executed and which aren't. Usually, this will lead you directly to the error, and from there you can handle it accordingly.

You should use `try` and `catch` whenever you're unsure of the code you've written, especially when you don't want users to see an error. Catch the error and handle it gracefully so users aren't caught by surprise.

Finally, use the CLR debugger when you want to follow the execution of your program in real-time. You can step through each line of code, watching variables to make sure they're assigned properly. This is a very powerful method of locating and correcting errors, but it can cause side effects such as loss of data and additional overhead. When you attach to a process (such as ASP.NET), all execution is frozen—meaning it won't be able to function correctly—which can cause problems for your application and users.

You'll generally only want to use the CLR debugger when the other methods have failed in solving your problems.

That's Not ASP!

ASP.NET definitely has more debugging capabilities than traditional ASP. Many classic ASP developers will be familiar with the `Response.Write` method of debugging, and it's still fully supported in ASP.NET.

However, now there are better methods of debugging applications. The trace tool provides a lot of information that you can use to debug and analyze the performance of your application. In classic ASP, the closest thing to this was using `Response.Writes` to output the information used by your pages.

Also, since ASP.NET pages are compiled, you can use a runtime debugger such as the Common Language Runtime Debugger. This tool provides methods for watching the state of your application. Again, classic ASP had nothing of the sort.

Debugging support in ASP.NET is greatly improved over traditional ASP. You can now use actual debugging tools instead of coping with the limited information that `Response.Write` provides. This will allow you to build stronger, more bug-free applications.

Summary

You covered a lot of material today. Debugging in ASP.NET is complex, but the available tools will help you find and squash any ugly bugs quickly and easily.

One method of debugging involves using the `Response.Write` method to output debugging information when you execute your pages. This method can help you follow the execution of the program and locate errors. Unfortunately, you have to add and remove these statements manually so they don't display private information to end users.

You can use `try` and `catch` statements to catch errors and handle them gracefully, allowing execution to continue without problems. You can also use the `throw` keyword to bring up your own errors.

The trace tool provides a much better method for debugging than using `Response.Write`. This tool provides detailed statistical information on your page, including execution times, objects used in your pages, form and HTTP header information, and server variables. You enable the trace tool by adding `Trace="true"` to your page directive.

You can use `Trace.Write` and `Trace.Warn` to display custom debugging information in the trace log. These statements are similar to `Response.Write`, except that they don't produce any client output, so you don't need to remove them when you're finished debugging your pages. The output from these methods only affects the trace log, and even then only when tracing is enabled. Otherwise, they don't affect your application at all.

You can also enable tracing for your entire application at once by placing `<trace enabled="true"/>` in the `web.config` file. You can then view overall statistics and trace output for each page by requesting the `trace.axd` file on your server.

Finally, you examined the Common Language Runtime Debugger, a useful tool for watching execution while it's happening. Using this tool requires attaching it to the ASP.NET application in question, which can cause some serious side effects. To use the CLR debugger, you must first add `<compilation debug="true"/>` to your `web.config` file.

Once the debugger is attached, you can set breakpoints and step through your code line by line, watching over any variables and their values.

Tomorrow you're going to take a look at ASP.NET security. This has always been a very serious issue for developers. ASP.NET provides a number of different ways to secure your applications, and you'll examine them all tomorrow.

Q&A

Q Will changes made in a `try` block before an error be kept or rolled back?

A Because execution continues after the `try` block, any changes are kept. To be able to roll back changes made within `try` blocks, use transactions.

Q Is there a way to write trace information to a persisted log?

A Unfortunately, not directly. However, using the file I/O methods you learned on Day 13, "Reading and Writing Files on the Web Server," capturing custom trace information shouldn't be a problem. You can simply save the output HTML file to capture all the trace information.

Workshop

This workshop will help reinforce the concepts covered in today's lesson. The answers can be found in Appendix A.

Quiz

1. Will the following code snippet work?

```
try
   objCmd.Connection.Open
   objReader = objCmd.ExecuteReader
end try
```

2. True or False: The `finally` statement is required in a `try...catch` block.
3. What is the trace tool, and how do you enable it at the page level? At the application level?
4. What's the difference between `Trace.Write` and `Trace.Warn`?
5. True or False: `Trace.Write` and `Trace.Warn` print information in the client display.
6. What are symbol files?
7. True or False: Attaching a debugger to an application is a perfectly safe procedure and doesn't interrupt program usage.
8. What's a breakpoint, and what is it used for?

Exercises

1. Use the trace tool to compare performance times in your application. Determine if disabling viewstate results in faster execution times, what the difference is between using an `OleDbDataReader` versus a `DataSet`, and if comments affect execution times at all.
2. Explore the CLR debugger and step through the execution of several pages. Use the Watch window to watch your variables as your application progresses. Try purposely introducing some errors and see what happens in the debugger.

WEEK 3

DAY 21

Securing Your ASP.NET Applications

Web security is a complex topic that's often confusing to both developers and end users, but it's a necessary one in today's Internet. Security involves validating user credentials (authentication) and determining access to resources (authorization). There are many ways to accomplish these steps with ASP.NET, and fortunately none of them are very complex to implement.

ASP.NET makes securing your applications easy. Once you've got a grip on the fundamentals of security, implementing the necessary security measures with ASP.NET is a snap.

Today's lesson will cover the following:

- What Web security is
- How Windows handles security
- What the three different forms of authentication are and how to implement them

- How to control access to server resources
- What impersonation is and how to use it

Security Basics

By default, most Web sites allow anonymous access. That is, anyone with an Internet connection can come along and view the pages on your site. Users don't need to be authenticated or have their identity validated; they can access any files available on your server. Imagine that you run a site in which members have to pay a subscription fee to view the content—perhaps an insider stock picking service. Without some form of security, anyone could view the pages where you post your expert stock tips. That would be horrible for your business—why should users pay for access when they don't need to? Web security is designed to restrict access to certain files to only a certain group of users.

Let's say you work at a top-secret government agency. Anyone is allowed in the lobby of the building, but only people with the proper authorization can move past the lobby. Every time you need to open a door in the secret complex, you need to provide proper authorization again by submitting to a retinal scan.

NEW TERM This process demonstrates the basics of a Web security transaction. The first step is *authentication*, which is the process of identifying the user who's requesting the information. The user is identified by his *credentials*, which can come in many forms (most commonly a username and password). Authentication ensures that a person is who he says he is. If the security system cannot identify the user based on his credentials, authentication fails and the unknown user is denied access. If the credentials are valid, the user is allowed into the system and is given a valid, known identity.

NEW TERM Once a user is given an identity, the system determines which resources he has access to. This process is known as *authorization*. In the secret government-complex scenario, for example, you must be authorized to enter certain doors. The system authorizes you depending on the permissions assigned to your identity. You might be allowed through some doors but not others. On the Web, certain users may have access to certain files while other users have access to different ones.

NEW TERM Finally, the last step is *impersonation*. Imagine the security system of the government building as the guardian of the complex. It has access to every room in the building and can open any door it chooses, easily bypassing the retinal scans. Now imagine that a clever spy breaks into the security system. That spy has access to every room, and the security system fails.

As an additional security measure, the designers of the security system added an impersonation feature. When a person tries to enter the building or access the computers, the guardian impersonates that person, thereby restricting its own access privileges. In other words, the guardian willingly gives up its own power so that hackers can't use it. It is similar to a general in the army taking a magical pill to make himself forget top-secret files, in case an enemy captures and interrogates him. This concept is a bit abstract, but it will make more sense as you apply it to ASP.NET pages. Figure 21.1 illustrates the process a user goes through to gain access to a secure resource.

FIGURE 21.1
The typical security protocol.

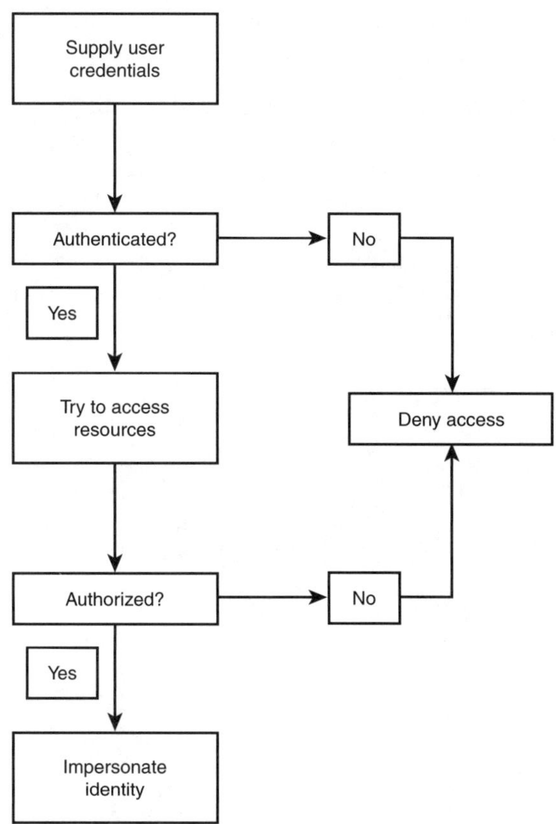

Essentially, security in ASP.NET is implemented with two different methods. You can authenticate and authorize credentials by comparing them to the operating system's identities (through IIS), or you can compare them to permissions in a data source (such as through `web.config`). The first method requires very little coding or modification to your ASP.NET pages, but it provides less control over authentication. The second, inversely, requires more coding, but gives more flexibility. We'll discuss these methods in the security sections later today.

Security in Windows

NEW TERM The Windows operating system supports *role-based security*. A *role* defines a type of identity. For instance, if you're in charge of maintaining a computer system and installing hardware and software, you're in the administrator's role. If someone simply wants to type a term paper or browse the Internet, she's in the guest role (that is, a guest to the computer's resources). Roles define how much control someone has over the computer and which permissions are available.

Typically, roles have several identities associated with them. You could have several people maintaining your computer, which could mean that there are several administrators. Chances are that you're also in an administrative role. In Windows, these identities are known as *users*.

Let's take a look at the users available on your computer. In Windows 2000, select Start, Settings, Control Panel, Users and Passwords. You should see a window similar to Figure 21.2.

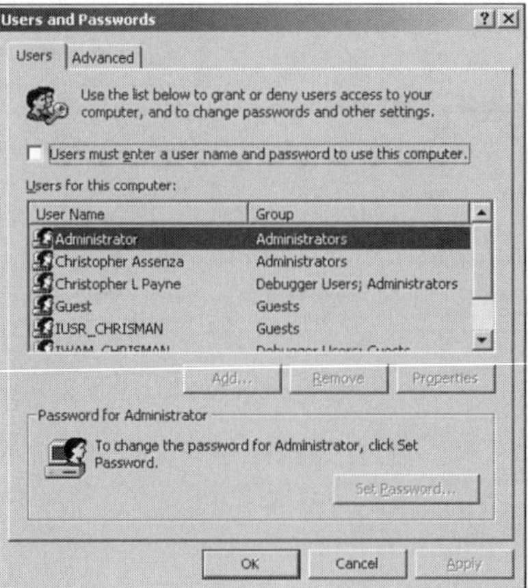

FIGURE 21.2
A list of users and groups in Windows.

In the User Name column, you see various users who can log on to your computer. There are probably a few in there that you didn't know about! The Group column lists the roles that each user belongs to.

One common and easy-to-implement security measure is simply to remove many of the users that you are not familiar with listed in Figure 21.2. Be careful not to eliminate your own identity or the system's, though!

Scroll down until you see the `IUSR_MachineName` user. This is the default identity that a client uses when it accesses your machine through its local Web server. It's an anonymous account, which means that no password is required to access your machine when using this identity. As such, the permissions granted to this identity are very minimal by default.

Note that you can't set any permissions here. You'll look at how to accomplish that later today in "Authorization."

Authentication

Authentication in ASP.NET is implemented through authentication providers—modules that contain the code for authenticating requests from Web clients. These providers are controlled through the `web.config` file, with the `authentication` tags. The basic syntax is as follows:

```
<configuration>
   <system.web>
      <authentication mode="Mode">
      </authentication>
   </system.web>
</configuration>
```

Additionally, within the `authentication` tags, you may specify `form` and `credentials` elements. You'll learn about these later today in "Forms Authentication."

The `authentication` tag can be used only at the root `web.config` file. Attempting to use it in `web.config` files in any subdirectories will result in an error.

ASP.NET provides three methods, or modes, for authenticating users, each implemented through a separate authentication provider: Windows, Passport, and Forms. Windows authentication is performed with IIS, requiring little or no modification to your pages. Passport and Forms authentication are similar: The latter is implemented on your own server; the former through a subscription service from Microsoft. Each of these methods is detailed in the following sections.

Windows Authentication

When clients make requests to ASP.NET pages, they first encounter Microsoft's Web server, Internet Information Server (IIS). At this point, IIS can authenticate the user, or hand off the authentication duties to the ASP.NET application. When IIS handles authentication, it can talk directly to the operating system (Windows NT, 2000, or XP) to validate the user's credentials. Figure 21.3 illustrates the IIS Web application architecture.

FIGURE 21.3

The ASP.NET security architecture.

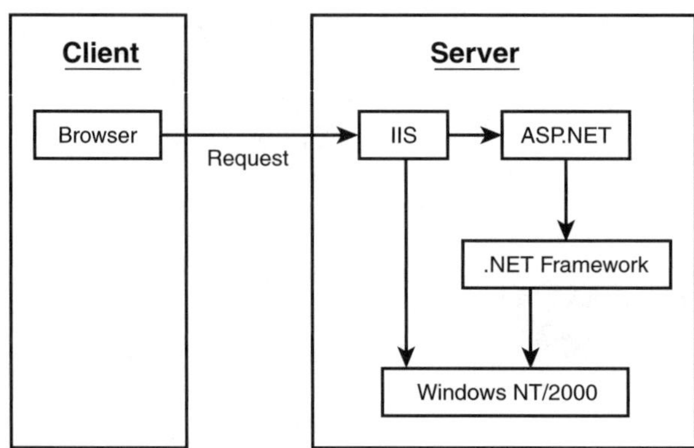

> **Note**
>
> Authentication is not *required* by IIS. IIS can let users into the application without authentication, relying on the ASP.NET pages to provide any authentication. Any users who IIS lets by without valid credentials are known as *anonymous users*.

The identities that IIS assigns are defined by Windows user accounts, hence the name *Windows authentication*. These user accounts are similar to the roles you saw in Figure 21.2. The Web clients are restricted to the same permissions that Windows users and roles are restricted to. For example, if a Web client accesses an administrative role, she has permissions to modify the filesystem in any way she chooses, such as deleting and moving files.

You enable this method of authentication by using the following line in `web.config`:

```
<authentication mode="Windows" />
```

IIS uses three different types of Windows authentication: Basic, Digest, and NTLM (also known as *integrated windows authentication*). Let's examine each of these methods and how to implement them.

Basic authentication is the simplest form of authentication next to no authentication at all. Chances are you've already seen this one used on Web sites. It's an industry-standard way of collecting user credentials, and it's part of the HTTP specification from the World Wide Web Consortium. The process of basic authentication is as follows:

1. The client requests a restricted resource from the server.
2. The Web server responds with `"401 Unauthorized"`.
3. The Web browser receives this message and asks for the user's credentials, usually a username and a password.
4. The Web browser then tries to access the server resources using these credentials.
5. If the credentials fail, the process starts over at step 2.
6. When authentication succeeds, the browser has access to the requested resource(s).

Now let's secure something! Open the Internet Services Manager (ISM) by selecting Start, Settings, Control Panel, Administrative Tools, Internet Service Manager. Expand the Default Web site node in the window that pops up. Choose a directory to secure (you'll use `/tyaspnet21days/day21` for this example, create it in the `c:\inetpub\wwwroot` folder if necessary). Right-click the directory and select Properties, as shown in Figure 21.4.

FIGURE 21.4
Accessing directory properties in Internet Services Manager.

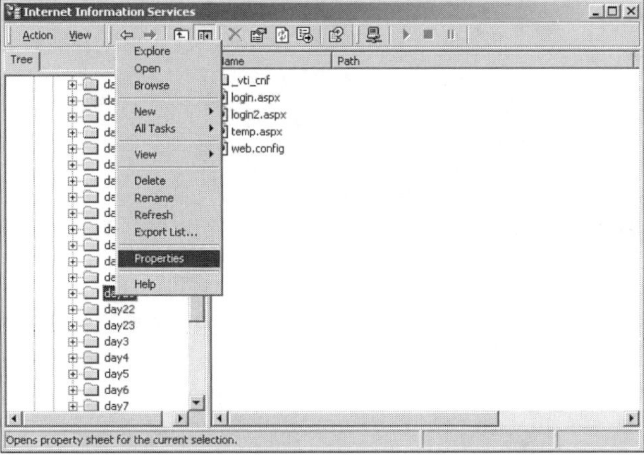

Select Directory browsing on the Directory tab so you know when your authentication is successful. Find the Directory Security tab and edit the Anonymous access and authentication control. You should see the window shown in Figure 21.5.

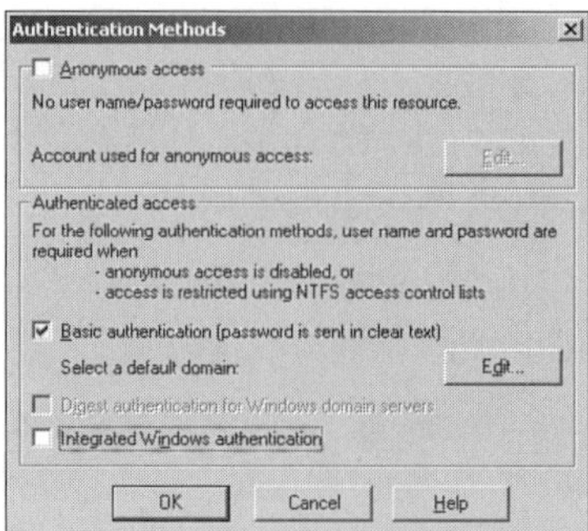

FIGURE 21.5

Setting authentication properties.

Deselect Anonymous access if it's checked. Anonymous access allows any user to access the directory via the Web site, which you don't want for your application. Check Basic authentication instead (deselect Integrated Windows authentication if it's checked).

Click OK twice to get back to the ISM window. Now enter the following URL into your browser:

```
http://localhost/tyaspnet21days/day21
```

You should see the dialog box in Figure 21.6, which asks for your credentials.

FIGURE 21.6

When basic authentication is enabled, the browser asks for credentials.

Enter the credentials for an account on your computer (for instance, the username and password you use to log on to your machine). IIS will compare these values to the operating system's list of users, and will authenticate or deny your request. If it's successful, you should see something similar to Figure 21.7.

If authentication succeeds and you want to try again with another username and password, you'll have to close all windows of your browser and try again. The browser will remember the supplied credentials for as long as it's running, so opening a new browser window while one is still open won't work.

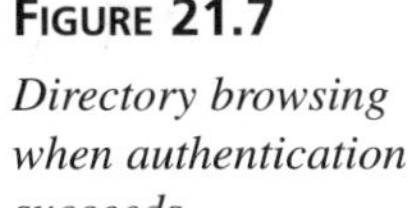

FIGURE 21.7

Directory browsing when authentication succeeds.

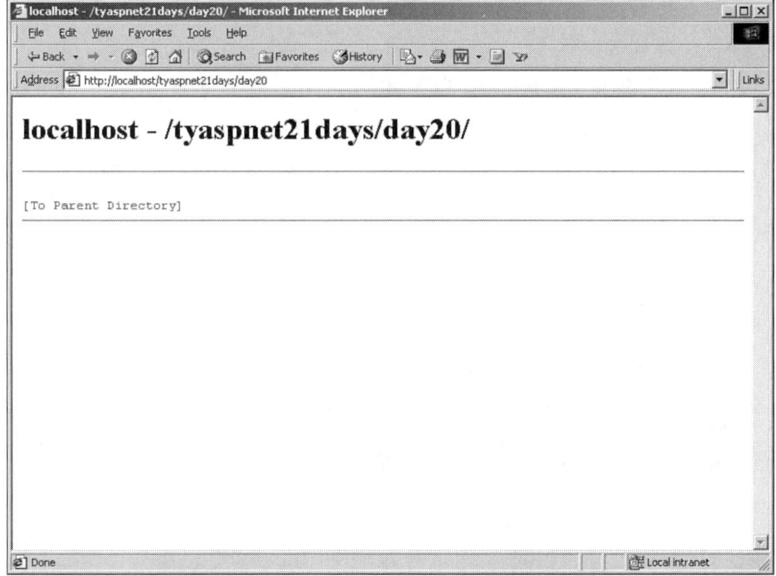

With basic authentication, the username and password you entered in the dialog box in Figure 21.6 is sent across the network to the server as plain text. This is an effective mechanism for authentication, but it's not very secure. A clever hacker can intercept the message before it arrives at the server, and then can use the username and password information to break into your system.

Digest authentication works similarly to basic authentication, but the username and password are encrypted first before they're sent across the network. This encryption mechanism, known as *hashing*, alters the information so it's not possible to decrypt it. It's truly a one-way process:

1. The client requests a restricted resource from the server, and the server sends a request for authentication.
2. The Web server responds with `"401 Unauthorized"`.
3. The Web browser receives this message and asks for the user's credentials. The browser adds some unique information to the supplied data and encrypts it. This unique data ensures that no one will be able to copy the hashing and gain access later.
4. The Web browser sends the encrypted credentials and an additional copy of the unique information, unencrypted, to the server. The server then uses the additional information to encrypt its own copy of the credentials (that is, the credentials stored in the Windows user account information).

5. The server compares the newly encrypted credentials with the values sent by the browser.
6. If the credentials fail—that is, the two encrypted versions don't match—the process starts over at step 3.
7. When authentication succeeds, the browser gains access to the resources.

To enable digest authentication, check Digest authentication for Windows domain servers from the Authentication Methods dialog (shown in Figure 21.5) (note that this option might be disabled if you are not connected to a domain). Make sure Anonymous access is *not* selected!

Finally, with NTLM authentication, the user never sees a prompt for credentials. Instead, once the browser contacts the server, it sends the encrypted username and password information that the user used to log on to your computer. The server evaluates this information to determine if the user should have access. This is all invisible to the user.

You can also enable this method from the Authentication Methods dialog shown in Figure 21.5. However, be aware that this method only works when both the server and client machines are using the Windows operating system. Note that if you have more than one method selected, the more restrictive method takes precedence (for instance, Windows authentication overrides anonymous access).

Normally, Windows authentication is used when you want an easy-to-implement method that doesn't require any ASP.NET coding. All you have to do is set properties in IIS and you're done.

Both digest mode and Windows authentication require that your users are running Internet Explorer, so confirm your target audience for implementing these methods. Additionally, Digest mode works only on a special type of server. See the following article for more information:

`http://support.microsoft.com/support/kb/articles/q222/0/28.asp`

Forms Authentication

With ASP.NET, you can opt to authenticate not through IIS but through your ASP.NET application via a process known as *Forms authentication*. This gives you more control over your site's authentication scenarios. For example, you can store your users' credentials in a database or XML file instead of through Windows.

With this method, users are directed to a login form on your Web site, where they supply their credentials. If your application accepts the credentials based on the custom scenario you've built, ASP.NET creates an authorization cookie on the browser's computer (see

Day 4, "Using ASP.NET Objects with VB.NET and C#," for information on cookies). This cookie contains either the credentials, in some form, or a string that can be used to acquire the credentials. This cookie is then used throughout your application for authorization. The process is as follows:

1. A client requests a secure page from your site.
2. If the request doesn't contain a valid authentication cookie, your Web server redirects the user to the URL specified in the `loginURL` attribute of the `Authentication` tag in your `web.config` file. This URL should contain a login form for the user.
3. Credentials are entered into the form and submitted via a form post.
4. If the credentials are valid (this is determined in several different methods; we'll discuss it in more detail later today), ASP.NET creates an authentication cookie on the client.
5. The user can then be redirected back to the originally requested page.

Figure 21.8 illustrates the Forms authentication process.

Once the authorization cookie is set, all subsequent requests will be authenticated automatically until the user closes the browser or the session ends. At that point, the user will have to log in again. Or, you can specify that the cookie never expires and the user is always authenticated, as you'll see in a moment.

Let's take a look at the necessary settings for Forms authentication in `web.config`:

```
<configuration>
   <system.web>
      <authentication mode="Forms">
         <forms name="name" loginUrl="loginForm" />
      </authentication>
      <authorization>
         <deny users="?" />
      </authorization>   </system.web>
</configuration>
```

The third line specifies that you're using Forms authentication. The fourth line tells ASP.NET the name of the cookie to use for authentication and the URL of the login page. When you turn on Forms authentication, you'll typically want to deny access to non-authorized users (otherwise, why turn authentication on?), so you must also supply the `<authorization>` element. We'll cover this element more later today. For now, just know that lines 6–8 deny access to anonymous users.

21

FIGURE 21.8

The Forms authentication workflow.

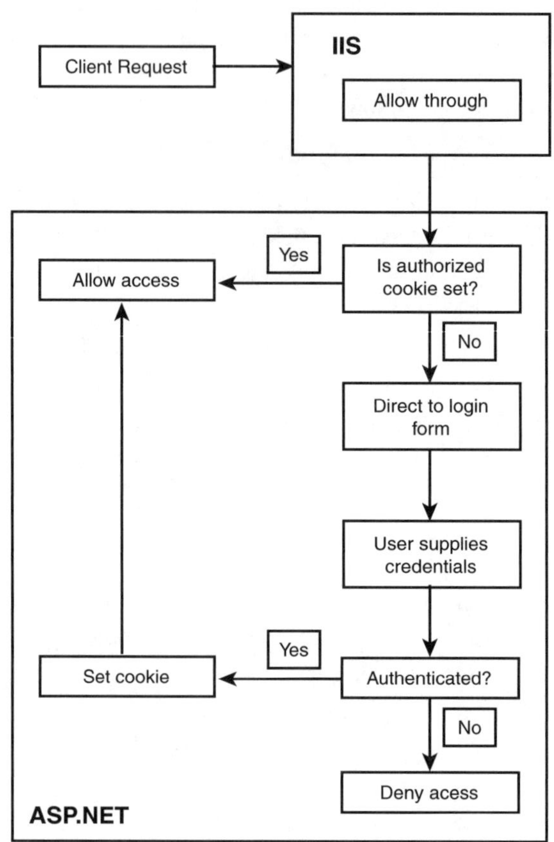

Let's look at an example. Enable anonymous access again and disable other forms of IIS authentication in the `/tyaspnet21days/day21` folder, as shown in "Windows Authentication" earlier today. Now edit the `web.config` file in your root directory (`c:\inetpub\wwwroot`), adding the following code in the location specified in the previous code snippet:

```
<authentication mode="Forms">
   <forms name="AuthCookie" loginUrl="/tyaspnet21days/day21/login.aspx" />
</authentication>
<authorization>
   <deny users="?" />
</authorization>
```

When a user is authenticated, a cookie named `AuthCookie` is created. If this cookie is not present, the user is redirected to `/tyaspnet21days/day21/login.aspx`, which should contain a form that allows a user to enter his credentials. Next, create a simple login form named `login.aspx` in the `/day21` directory, as shown in Listing 21.1.

LISTING 21.1 A Simple Login Form

```
1:  <%@ Page Language="VB" %>
2:
3:  <script runat="server">
4:     sub Login(Sender as Object, e as EventArgs)
5:        if tbUserName.Text = "clpayne" and _
6:           tbPassword.Text = "hello" then
7:           FormsAuthentication.SetAuthCookie(tbUserName.Text, false)
8:
9:           Response.redirect("account.aspx")
10:        else
11:           lblMessage.Text = "<font color=red>Sorry, " & _
12:              "invalid username or password!</font><p>"
13:        end if
14:     end sub
15:  </script>
16:
17:  <html><body>
18:     Please enter your username and password.<p>
19:
20:     <form runat="server">
21:        <asp:Label id="lblMessage" runat="server" />
22:
23:        Username:
24:        <asp:Textbox id="tbUserName" runat="server" /><br>
25:        Password:
26:        <asp:Textbox id="tbPassword" TextMode="password"
27:           runat="server" /><p>
28:        <asp:Button id="Submit" runat="server"
29:           OnClick="Login"
30:           Text="Submit" />
31:     </form>
32:  </body></html>
```

ANALYSIS This form allows the user to enter her username and password into the text boxes on lines 24 and 26. When the form is submitted, the `Login` method examines the supplied credentials and determines if the user is valid. This is just a simple authentication test, so on line 5 you hard-code the valid username and password. If the values entered by the user match these hard-coded values, you'll authenticate that user. On line 7, you call the `SetAuthCookie` method of the `FormsAuthentication` object, which creates a cookie with the user ID supplied by the first parameter. The second parameter specifies whether or not the cookie should persist after the user closes her browser. Using

True here will cause the cookie to be persisted even across browser restarts, meaning that the user won't have to log in again on her next visit to the site. Finally, on line 9, you redirect the user to an account page (make sure this page exists, otherwise you'll receive an error after authentication passes).

If the supplied credentials are invalid, the `else` statement on line 10 prints out an error message. Figure 21.9 shows the output after invalid credentials have been entered.

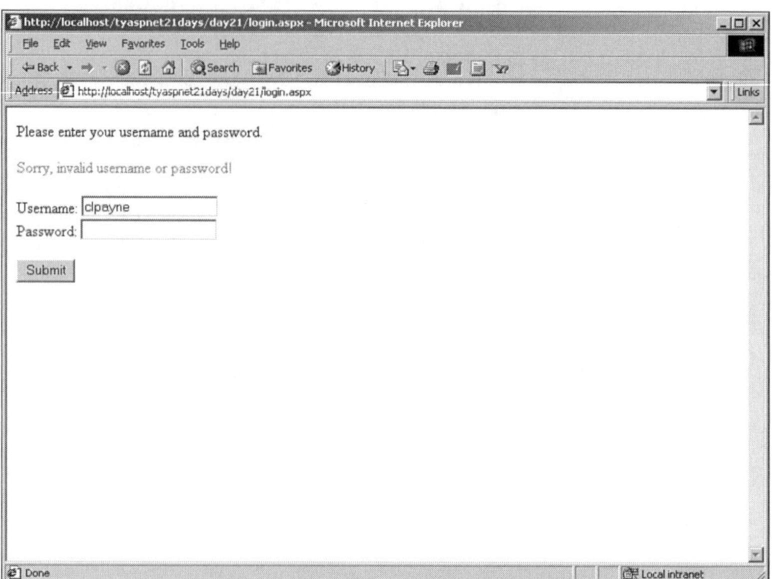

FIGURE 21.9

The output after Forms authentication fails.

> **Note**
>
> You don't have to validate against hard-coded values. In the `Login` method, you can build any validation mechanism you want, including connecting to and comparing values against a database.

In addition to the `forms` attribute, you can specify a `credentials` attribute that provides username and password definitions to be used with authentication. This allows you to validate the user's credentials against `web.config`, as shown in Listing 21.1, instead of checking them manually.

Modify your `web.config` file to read as follows:

```
<configuration>
   <system.web>
      <authentication mode="Forms">
```

```
         <forms name="AuthCookie" loginUrl="day21/login.aspx" >
            <credentials passwordFormat="Clear">
               <user name="clpayne" password="helloworld" />
            </credentials>
         </forms>
      </authentication>
      <authorization>
         <deny users="?" />
      </authorization>
   </system.web>
</configuration>
```

The `credentials` section contains valid user identities that should be used by ASP.NET when authenticating. The `passwordFormat` specifies the encryption method that should be used when sending credentials to the server. This attribute can have these values: `Clear`, which specifies no encryption, or `MD5` or `SHA1`, which are both well-known encryption algorithms. Any of the values will work in most modern Web browsers.

Inside the `credentials` section, you add the `user` element. It contains two attributes, `name` and `password`, which specify valid user credentials. Note that you can have as many `user` elements here as you want. Listing 21.2 is a login form that uses the `credentials` section.

LISTING 21.2 Validating User Credentials Against the `credentials` `web.config` Section

```
<%@ Page Language="VB" %>

<script runat="server">
   sub Login(Sender as Object, e as EventArgs)
      if FormsAuthentication.Authenticate(tbUserName.Text, _
         tbPassword.Text) then
         FormsAuthentication.SetAuthCookie(tbUserName.Text, false)

         lblMessage.Text = "<font color=red>Success!</font>
➥<p>"
      else
         lblMessage.Text = "<font color=red>Sorry, " & _
            "invalid username or password!</font><p>"
      end if
   end sub
</script>

<html><body>
   Please enter your username and password.<p>

   <form runat="server">
      <asp:Label id="lblMessage" runat="server" />

      Username:
```

LISTING 21.2 continued

```
24:          <asp:Textbox id="tbUserName" runat="server" /><br>
25:          Password:
26:          <asp:Textbox id="tbPassword" TextMode="password"
27:             runat="server" /><p>
28:          <asp:Button id="Submit" runat="server"
29:             OnClick="Login"
30:             Text="Submit" />
31:       </form>
32:    </body></html>
```

ANALYSIS Save this listing as `login2.aspx`. This form is very similar to Listing 21.1. It contains the same UI elements and event handlers. The only major difference is on line 5. Instead of comparing the supplied user credentials against hard-coded values, you call the `Authenticate` method of the `FormsAuthentication` object. This method takes two parameters—the supplied username and password—and validates them against the information contained in the `credentials` section of `web.config`. If the supplied credentials match any of the `user` elements, `Authenticate` returns true and you can set the authentication cookie, as shown on line 7. Thus, the `web.config` file provides an easy way to define valid users.

The `FormsAuthentication` object, used in Listings 21.1 and 21.2, provides many helper methods used for authenticating users and controlling authentication tickets. You've already seen a few of these methods, such as `Authenticate` and `SetAuthCookie`.

When a user requests a page that's restricted, ASP.NET automatically sends him to the URL specified in the `loginUrl` attribute of the `forms` configuration element. The URL that was originally requested is then stored in the querystring, for use later. So far you've been ignoring this value, but you can use it to redirect users back to the original URL upon successful authentication.

The `FormsAuthentication.RedirectFromLoginPage` method sets the authentication cookie exactly like the `SetAuthCookie` method, but it also causes a redirect back to the original URL. If there's no original URL in the querystring, this method redirects to `default.aspx` in the root directory. For example, you could change the `Login` method of Listing 21.2 to read as follows:

```
4:       sub Login(Sender as Object, e as EventArgs)
5:          if FormsAuthentication.Authenticate(tbUserName.Text, _
6:             tbPassword.Text) then
7:             FormsAuthentication.RedirectFromLoginPage
➥(tbUserName.Text, false)
8:          else
9:             lblMessage.Text = "<font color=red>Sorry, " & _
```

```
                  "invalid username or password!</font><p>"
            end if
         end sub
```

If you request this listing directly, upon successful authentication ASP.NET will redirect you to `default.aspx`. So, be sure that you have one available! This method is useful for sending the users back where they came from, but it doesn't allow you to perform any functionality after setting the authentication cookie. If you simply want to set the authentication cookie and retrieve the original URL from the querystring *without* redirecting, you can use the `GetRedirectURL` method:

```
dim strURL as string = FormsAuthentication.GetRedirectURL
➥("username", false)
```

Another helpful method of the `FormsAuthentication` object is the `GetAuthCookie` method. This method creates an `HttpCookie` object with the authentication information. (For more information on the `HttpCookie` object, refer back to Day 4.) It doesn't set the cookie on the user's computer, however. This method allows you to perform additional functionality after the authentication cookie is created, but *before* the cookie is set. For example, you could add additional information to the authentication cookie. Just remember to set the cookie when you're finished, or the user won't be authenticated! Listing 21.3 shows an example.

LISTING 21.3 Using `GetAuthCookie` to Enhance Your Authentication Cookie

```
<%@ Page Language="VB" %>

<script runat="server">
   sub Login(Sender as Object, e as EventArgs)
      if FormsAuthentication.Authenticate(tbUserName.Text, _
         tbPassword.Text) then

         dim cookie as HttpCookie

         cookie = FormsAuthentication.GetAuthCookie
➥("clpayne", false)
         cookie.Expires = DateTime.Now.AddMinutes(2)

         Response.Cookies.Add(cookie)

         lblMessage.Text = "<font color=red>Success!</font>
➥<p>"
      else
         lblMessage.Text = "<font color=red>Sorry, " & _
            "invalid username or password!</font><p>"
      end if
   end sub
</script>
```

ANALYSIS This listing is very similar to Listings 21.1 and 21.2, so the UI portion of the page has been left out. On line 8, you create a new `HttpCookie` object named `cookie` to hold your authentication cookie. On line 10, you create this cookie using the `GetAuthCookie` method, with the same parameters used in the `SetAuthCookie` method, and store it in your `cookie` variable. Now you're free to manipulate the authentication cookie however you want before authenticating the user. On line 11, you change the expiration time to two minutes from the current time. You then set the authentication cookie on line 13 by adding it to the `Response.Cookies` collection.

The `FormsAuthentication` object also contains `SignOut`, a method to log the user out. It removes the authentication cookie and forces users to log in again if they want to access restricted resources again. Many sites that require a user to log in also provide a method to log out, for additional security. This ensures that two users sharing one computer do not use the same account. To log out a user, simply have him visit an ASP.NET page that calls the `SignOut` method:

```
FormsAuthentication.SignOut
```

Forms authentication is very powerful and gives developers a lot of flexibility when implementing authentication. Additionally, because the settings are contained in the `web.config` file, this method of authentication is easy to implement. All you need to do is build a login page. Recall that you don't have to put the user information in `web.config`. You can put the information in a database and build your own custom routines to authenticate users but, of course, doing so disallows you from using the `Authenticate` method to validate the users.

Passport Authentication

Passport authentication is a centralized authentication service (*not* a Web Service) provided by Microsoft. It works very similarly to Forms authentication, except that you don't need to build any custom functionality yourself. Both create authentication cookies that reside on the client, and are used for authorization. When a user encounters passport authentication on your site, he's redirected to the Passport login page (see `http://www.passport.com` for details on that), which provides a very simple form to fill out. This form then checks the user's credentials against Microsoft's Passport service and determines if the user is valid. Then it sets an authentication cookie, similarly to Forms authentication. The exact steps are as follows:

1. A client requests a secure page from your site.
2. If the request doesn't contain a valid Passport authentication cookie, your Web server will redirect the user to the Passport login service. The Web server also passes some encrypted information about the request to the Passport service.

3. The user is presented with a login form on the Passport login site. Credentials are entered and submitted via a form post (using SSL encryption).
4. If the credentials are valid, the Passport service creates an authentication ticket and places it in the querystring. The user is then redirected back to the original site.
5. When the server sees that an authentication ticket is present in the querystring, it creates the authentication cookie for the user.

Thus, the Passport authentication service doesn't actually create the authentication cookies. That's left to the originating Web server.

You won't examine this service much further because your site must be a member of Microsoft's Passport service to use this authentication method. Additionally, you need to pay a fee to become a member. For more information, check out the Passport documentation at `http://www.passport.com/business`. Once you've become a member, you'll need to download the Passport SDK and configure your application accordingly.

The final step in setting up Passport authentication is to set up your `web.config` file properly. The syntax is simple:

```
<configuration>
   <system.web>
      <authentication mode="Passport">
      </authentication>
   </system.web>
</configuration>
```

The Passport service is a very useful and easy way to implement security you can trust on your site. Many existing Web sites, including nearly all of Microsoft's sites, use the Passport service. After a user has a valid passport identity, he can log in to any and all the Passport sites with the same username and password. Thus, if you ever plan to team up with other sites, or to build a family of different sites, the Passport service might be a good security measure to look into.

Authorization

Recall that any security system serves two functions: authentication and authorization. Authentication, which you just examined, is the process of identifying a user based on his credentials. The purpose of authorization is to determine which resources an authenticated user can access. Authorization in ASP.NET works in two ways. It can rely on Windows to tell it which resources an authenticated user has access to, which is known as *file authorization*. Or it can rely on the URL of the requested resource, which is known as *URL authorization*. It's easy to set up both methods.

Before you examine how file authorization works, let's take a quick look at how the operating system handles security. Open Windows explorer, right-click on a file or folder (for example, `c:\winnt`), and select Properties. Next, select the Security tab. You should see something similar to Figure 21.10.

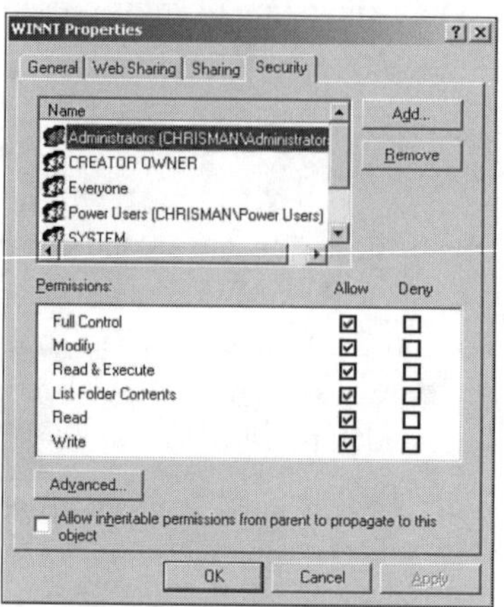

FIGURE 21.10
Operating system security options.

NEW TERM Assuming you're running Windows NT, 2000, or XP and your hard drive is formatted with NTFS (see your operating system help documentation for more information), Windows can set security options for every single file and folder on your computer. These options include allowing users to read or write files, execute applications, and view contents of folders, as shown in the Permissions window in Figure 21.10. These file and folder permissions are stored in Access Control Lists (ACLs) on the Windows operating system. It's easy to modify these lists by checking and unchecking boxes for each user on the Security tab.

With file authorization, ASP.NET interacts with Windows to correlate user identities with the ACLs. When an authenticated user tries to access a file on your Web server, Windows checks the ACL to determine if that role or identity is allowed to view that file. This all happens automatically and invisibly, and it's an easy way to implement security. File authorization works with impersonation to determine ACL permissions. (See "Impersonation" later today for more information.)

However, sometimes ACLs can be a chore to manage. If you have a Web site with 50 different directories, each with several files, setting the ACLs can be a huge headache. Thus, ASP.NET also allows URL authorization, which maps user identities to the directories specified in the requested URLs. (You've already used URL authentication in the bonus projects, so it should look familiar.)

To enable URL authorization, you have to set a few properties in the `web.config` file. Let's look at the syntax of the `authorization` tag:

```
<authorization>
   <allow users="comma-separated list of users"
          roles="comma-separated list of roles" />
   <deny users="comma-separated list of users"
         roles="comma-separated list of roles" />
</authorization>
```

The `allow` and `deny` attributes specify lists of identities that should be allowed or denied access to resources. If you place the following `web.config` file in the root of your directory, and assuming no other `web.config` files override these settings, the user `clpayne` will have access to all resources and `john` won't:

```
<authorization>
   <allow users="clpayne" />
   <deny users="john" />
</authorization>
```

These tags can specify authorization for both user identities and roles. Thus, you can deny a whole group of users simply by specifying the role that they belong to.

Note

> Note that permissions specified with the `allow` and `deny` tags apply to the directory containing the corresponding `web.config` and those below it. In other words, it follows the hierarchical configuration system like the rest of the `web.config` file.

There are two special identities in ASP.NET that allow further grouping of users. A question mark in the `users` attribute signifies anonymous users—those that haven't been authenticated otherwise. An asterisk indicates all users, regardless of their authentication status. For example, a resource that's restricted to valid users could use the following to deny anyone who isn't authenticated:

```
<authorization>
   <deny users="?" />
</authorization>
```

On the other hand, the following code snippet could be used to allow anyone into a certain directory:

```
<authorization>
   <allow users="*" />
</authorization>
```

This is the default behavior of ASP.NET when no other authentication or authorization methods are specified.

In addition to specifying users and roles, ASP.NET allows you to specify authorization information based on *how* those users access resources. The `verb` attribute specifies the HTTP action that can be taken to access a resource: either `GET` or `POST`. For example, the following snippet allows all users to get pages, but only `clpayne` can post:

```
<authorization>
   <allow verb="GET" users="*" />
   <allow verb="POST" users="clpayne" />
   <deny verb="POST" users="?" />
</authorization>
```

Why would you ever need to implement this scenario? Imagine you've built a very useful piece of functionality in ASP.NET, such as a mortgage calculator. You want to allow anyone to view the calculator and interact with it in basic ways, but you only want to allow registered users to use the calculator because it requires posting data to the server. In essence, all users are allowed a "sneak peek" at the functionality, which should entice them to register at your site and gain full access to your calculator.

Although this hierarchical configuration system is very handy, it doesn't provide much fine-grained control. For example, the settings in `web.config` will apply to the directory this file resides in as well as any subdirectories. If you want to override the security settings, you need to build new `web.config` files in each directory that requires it. This is a lot like the headaches you experienced with ACLs.

The `web.config` file allows you to control the resources that users are authorized to access through the `location` tag, with more granularity. This tag can be implemented in any `web.config` file, and it specifies which resources are restricted according to the directory structure of the site. For example, you can use the `web.config` file described in Listing 21.3 in the root directory, and it will control authorization for several directories below it. See Listing 21.4.

LISTING 21.4 Controlling Authorization for Several Directories from One `web.config` File

```
<configuration>
   <location path="day21/account.aspx">
      <system.web>
         <authorization>
            <deny users="?"/>
         </authorization>
      </system.web>
   </location>
   <location path="day21/subdir2/">
```

LISTING 21.4 continued

```
10:          <system.web>
11:             <authorization>
12:                <deny users="?"/>
13:             </authorization>
14:          </system.web>
15:       </location>
16:    </configuration>
```

ANALYSIS On line 2, you set security information for the `day21/account.aspx` file. In the `authorization` tag on line 4, you prevent all anonymous users from accessing this file. On line 9, you set authorization properties for the `day21/subdir2` directory, again keeping out all anonymous users. You can specify as many directories as you want here, regardless of their depth in the file hierarchy.

Notice that the `location` tags are *outside* of the `authorization` tags. A common beginner's mistake is to place them inside the tags. Also note that you need a separate `location` tag for each directory for which you want to specify authorization information.

Impersonation

Impersonation allows ASP.NET to execute pages with the identity of the client on whose behalf it's operating. In other words, if a user is authenticated with the identity `clpayne`, ASP.NET will restrict or deny access based on that user's permissions.

Wait a minute. Isn't that what normally happens anyway? Let's take a look at Figure 21.11 to make more sense of this.

By default, impersonation is disabled. As the user moves from IIS authentication to the ASP.NET application, ASP.NET itself takes on the identity that IIS is configured to use (by default, this is the "Local Machine" identity). Typically, this identity has permission to access all files and folders. Other security measures must be used to handle access, such as URL authorization.

When impersonation is enabled, ASP.NET takes on the role of the identity that IIS passes to it, rather than the one IIS is using for itself. If the user is unauthenticated, ASP.NET will impersonate the anonymous user, and if the user is authenticated, ASP.NET will take on that identity. Now that ASP.NET is impersonating another user, Windows can restrict access to the application as a whole by using ACLs.

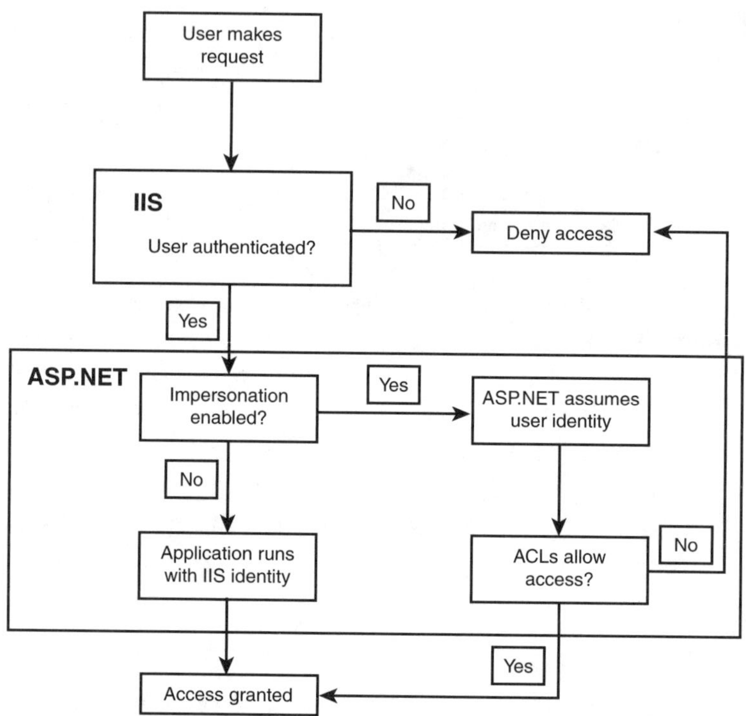

FIGURE 21.11

The process flow when impersonation is enabled.

An ASP.NET application is a user of the system's resources. It accesses files and folders, memory, and so on. By default, the ASP.NET application process has fairly liberal permissions, and generally can access everything the system has to offer. This is necessary because ASP.NET must use these resources to operate correctly. However, you may want to restrict access to certain resources, depending on the person who's using the ASP.NET application. For example, an anonymous user shouldn't be able to take advantage of the application's permissions and access all of the system's resources. Thus, an ASP.NET application can impersonate its users in order to restrict access.

When ASP.NET impersonates a user, it acts like that user in every way. In fact, the operating system will believe that ASP.NET *is* that particular user accessing the resources. The access control lists now apply and can restrict access to both ASP.NET and the user.

Let's imagine a typical scenario with impersonation enabled. A registered but non-administrative user named JoeSchmoe visits your site. As soon as JoeSchmoe is authenticated, ASP.NET assumes his identity, and all code is executed under his account.

One page on your site, `files.aspx`, lists all the files on the server computer for administrative purposes. Naturally, only administrative users should be able to access this page. If JoeSchmoe tries to access this page, ASP.NET (now impersonating JoeSchmoe) won't be able to execute the code because it doesn't have permission to read every file on the server under JoeSchmoe's account. Thus, impersonation stops users from accessing files to which they aren't allowed access. Shouldn't ASP.NET *automatically* provide this capability, however? The answer is no. By default, ASP.NET assumes that other authentication and authorization methods are used, and impersonation isn't necessary. For example, using Windows authentication, you would stop users from accessing resources before they could even reach the page in question. Impersonation isn't necessary here because the user never gets to try to execute the code. If there is a chance, however, that a user could access a file that she shouldn't be able to, impersonation is very helpful.

Note

> Even with impersonation, ASP.NET still uses its regular identity to access configuration information. Otherwise, the application wouldn't function properly. For example, most users don't have access to files such as the machine-level `machine.config` file, which contains information on configuring all ASP.NET applications.

So, why wouldn't you want to use impersonation, if it offers a convenient way to control access? Recall that managing permissions with ACLs can be troublesome. Often you'll want to implement another method of authorization, such as URL authorization. Also, to use impersonation, you need to use IIS to authenticate your users, which is a necessity some would rather not deal with.

Do	Don't
Do use impersonation if you don't want to spend time writing ASP.NET code. With impersonation, you only need to set IIS authentication and manage the ACLs.	**Don't** use impersonation if you'd rather build the authentication system yourself.

Enabling impersonation is very simple. You just need to add a single line to the `web.config` file:

```
<configuration>
   <system.web>
```

```
        <identity impersonate="true" username="user"
➥password="pw" />
    </system.web>
</configuration>
```

The only required attribute is `impersonate`. Set it to True to enable impersonation, or False otherwise. The optional `username` and `password` attributes specify that ASP.NET should always impersonate a certain user, rather than the IIS-authenticated user. This is useful if all users should have a defined set of permissions—that is, if no one user will have more permissions than another.

For example, suppose that you have many Windows identities, all of which should have the same permissions. Due to the time required to manage the ACLs for each file and user, you've set the correct permissions for only one user. Now, any of these users can be authenticated through IIS, and they all can impersonate the one user that has the correct permissions, thus saving you quite a bit of time.

Another example would be if a user identity resides on another computer on the network domain. After a user is authenticated on the server machine, ASP.NET could impersonate an account on a separate machine, which might have different permissions than the authenticated user. This simple setting will allow ASP.NET to impersonate an incoming user and use the Windows ACLs to restrict access.

Dealing with Secured Users

Now that you've authenticated users who access your site, what can you do with them? Authorization and impersonation happen automatically without your intervention, but what if you need to access information about the user explicitly? For example, imagine you built a forms authentication page where the user enters her username and password. Assuming authentication is successful, the user moves into the site, the first page of which needs to display a welcome message with the user's username.

This sounds like a simple task, but may be more involved than you think. If you didn't store the user's information from the login page manually, you won't have access to it on any other page, unless you ask the user for it again.

Luckily, ASP.NET has got you covered. When you implement security in your Web site, ASP.NET attaches what is known as a Windows principal (represented by the `WindowsPrincipal` class). The `WindowsPrincipal` class allows your applications to check information about the currently authenticated user.

Unfortunately, though, dealing with Windows principals and such is not a fun task. There is a whole slew of advanced security topics that deal with principals. ASP.NET has simplified the process for you so the Windows principal objects are behind the scenes and out-of-mind (but they are there if you need to use them).

The `Page` object has a `User` property that represents the currently authenticated user; it returns a `WindowsPrincipal` object. This object has only one property that we're interested in: `Identity`. The `Identity` property returns a `WindowsIdentity` object that contains the actual user information. (It's not as complex as it sounds—you'll see once we get into an example.) The `WindowsIdentity` class has the properties listed in Table 21.1.

TABLE 21.1 `WindowsIdentity` Properties

Property	*Description*
`AuthenticationType`	The type of authentication used to authenticate the user.
`IsAnonymous`	Indicates if the user is anonymous.
`IsAuthenticated`	Indicates if the user is authenticated.
`IsGuest`	Indicates if the user is using the system Guest account.
`IsSystem`	Indicates if the user is using the System account.
`Name`	The user's logon name.
`Token`	The Windows token for the user.

The following code snippet shows how to display the current user's logon name:

```
sub Page_Load(Sender as Object, e as EventArgs)
   lblName.Text = User.Identity.Name
end sub
...
<asp:Label id="lblName" runat="server"/>
```

That's all there is to it. All you really need to know about Windows principals here is the `User.Identity` property. This will allow you access to the user's information.

That's Not ASP!

Basic methods of authentication were available in classic ASP as well. For example, IIS could be used to authenticate users with basic, digest, or integrated Windows methods. Developers could even use the Passport SDK to build custom authentication methods, although it was often a time-consuming task. Many sites also used some type of Forms authentication, although each mechanism had to be built from scratch.

The real change is in ASP.NET's ease of implementation. Forms authentication is built into ASP.NET, and it requires very little work by the developer. The groundwork is already laid, and all you need to do is decide where user credentials should be validated against.

Authorization is also easier to implement. File authorization was used in classic ASP, but URL authorization is a big step forward in access control. And the `web.config` file provides an easy, powerful method for controlling URL authorization.

Impersonation should be a familiar concept if you're comfortable with classic ASP security. For compatibility, ASP.NET supports the same type of impersonation as classic ASP did. The only change is in the way it's enabled.

Implementing security in classic ASP often required an administrator to be present at the server to configure IIS and the operating system. With ASP.NET and its `web.config` file, this is no longer necessary. A developer can modify settings and apply them to remote applications without leaving her desk.

ASP.NET security was designed to make developer's lives easier while maintaining tight security measures. All the classic methods are still available, and new methods provide easy-to-use security.

Summary

You learned about a lot of security topics today. In ASP.NET, security is implemented in three stages. First there's authentication, which ensures that users are who they say they are. Authorization controls access to resources. And impersonation allows ASP.NET to use Windows access control lists (ACLs) to control access.

Authentication is implemented in three different ways: Windows, Forms, and Passport. Windows authentication relies on IIS to authenticate users, and it can be accomplished using three separate methods: basic, digest, and integrated Windows (also known as NTLM). The basic method simply sends user credentials across the network unencrypted, whereas the digest method encrypts the credentials first. Integrated Windows authentication relies on both server and client containing the Windows operating system, and sends Windows logon information across the network, without asking for credentials from the user.

Forms authentication allows developers to build custom authentication mechanisms, with help from the built-in `FormsAuthentication` object. Passport authentication is a centralized authentication service provided by Microsoft that requires subscription and a fee.

Authorization is implemented in two different ways: via files, and via URLs. The former relies on Windows access control lists to determine user permissions on a per-file and directory level. URL authorization maps users and roles to directories specified in the requested URL. The `deny` and `allow` elements in `web.config` control which users have access to which resources. The `location` element provides additional granularity in controlling access.

Impersonation allows ASP.NET to take on the identity of its users. This allows it to use Windows ACLs to control access, thereby letting you implement security with a minimal amount of coding.

Q&A

Q How can I encode and decode data?

A Encoding and decoding data is part of *cryptography*, which is beyond the scope of this book. However, ASP.NET does support cryptographic operations and more, including digital signature creation, hashing, and message authentication. The `System.Security.Cryptography` namespace provides all the methods and objects you'll need for these mechanisms. See the .NET Framework SDK documentation for more information.

Q Does the ASP.NET security system protect non-ASP.NET resources?

A Unfortunately, no. Resources such as `.txt`, `.htm`, `.jpg`, `.gif`, and so on, which aren't associated with ASP.NET, aren't protected by security settings in the `web.config` file. Even though `.aspx` files or directories may be protected by `web.config`, users can view these other files freely (assuming they know the exact filenames, of course).

You can force ASP.NET to protect these files by mapping them to the ASP.NET process (`aspnet_wp.exe`) through the IIS Admin tool. This will cause security settings to be applied to these files, but it may result in a performance decrease.

Workshop

This workshop will help reinforce the concepts covered in today's lesson. The answers can be found in Appendix A.

Quiz

1. What's the difference between authentication and authorization?
2. What's the difference between basic and digest authentication?
3. What's the anonymous user account's name in Windows?
4. Write some code to set an authorization cookie and redirect to an originating URL.

5. What does the second parameter in the `SetAuthCookie` method do?
6. Will the following code work?

```
<configuration>
       <authentication mode="Forms">
          <forms name="AuthCookie" loginUrl="day21/login.aspx">
          </forms>
       </authentication>
</configuration>
```

7. What do the wildcard characters `*` and `?` mean to ASP.NET within the authorization section of `web.config`?
8. True or False: When impersonation is enabled, ASP.NET can operate on behalf of the operating system.

Exercise

Create a login page that validates user credentials against a database. Create a `web.config` file that uses forms authentication and directs all anonymous users to this login page.

WEEK 3

In Review

Congratulations on making it all the way through 21 days! You've covered the most important topics that make up ASP.NET. You learned about the Web forms framework and the basics of building ASP.NET Web pages in Week 1; all about data access and data binding in Week 2; and how to complete your application with business objects and Web services in Week 3. There shouldn't be much that you'll come across in your further journeys through ASP.NET that you haven't at least been exposed to here.

You'll come away from this book with a strong understanding of the way ASP.NET works, and an appreciation of the way it allows you to build powerful Web applications easily. If you are familiar with classic ASP, you've also learned how ASP.NET has been improved over its predecessor, making your life as a developer easier. For example, configuration and deployment are now simple to implement, while still increasing the power available to the developer.

So, where do you go from here? As always, be sure to practice, practice, practice! Feel free to return to earlier examples and build on them. Don't be afraid to delve into a previous topic that you've been curious about. The .NET Framework SDK Documentation provides a lot of technical details on all the concepts you've covered, so it should be an invaluable resource. Also, don't forget the bonus project in the next section, and the bonus days (Days 22 and 23) following this review. These lessons explore topics that will make you an even stronger ASP.NET developer!

Bonus Project 3

When you left your banking application last time (see "Week 2 in Review"), you had just added the database functionality. Users could now log in and have their credentials validated against the database, they could view their account information, and they could even pay bills online. As you might recall, there was a lot of code in the ASP.NET pages you built.

This time, you're going to move much of the functionality into business objects, and you've already done much of the hard work! This will decrease the sizes of your ASP.NET pages tremendously by reducing the amount of duplicated code, and making it easier for you to make changes later on.

You're also going to build a Web Service that allows retailers to post transactions to your application remotely—for example, when a customer makes ATM or debit purchases.

Adding the Business Objects

Recall from Day 15, "Using Business Objects," that business objects often represent a real-world object; they contain properties and methods to completely represent that object. For example, a business object that represents a car would contain properties such as color, make, and model, and methods such as start, brake, and open door.

In the banking application, a customer's account is easily represented in this manner. Your business object will contain methods to retrieve and update a user's account, and perform other general functions.

Luckily, you've already written all the code that will go into your business object; it is interspersed throughout your ASP.NET pages. All you need to do is collect the code you have already written and place it in the appropriate methods of the business object. After you've compiled the business object, your ASP.NET page will require a slight modification to take advantage of it. Listing BP3.1 shows the entire VB.NET source file for your account object.

LISTING BP3.1 Representing an Account with a Business Object

```
Imports System
Imports System.Data
Imports System.Data.OleDb

Namespace ASPNETBank

   Public Class Account
```

Listing BP3.1 continued

```
   'declare connection object
   private objConn as new OleDbConnection("Provider=" & _
      "Microsoft.Jet.OLEDB.4.0;" & _
      "Data Source=c:\ASPNET\data\banking.mdb")
   private strUsername as string

   public sub New(Username as string)
      strUsername = Username
   end sub

   '*****************************************************
   ' This function returns the balance of the account
   ' with the specified user ID
   '*****************************************************
   public function GetBalance() as Decimal
      dim decBalance as decimal
      dim objCmd as new OleDbCommand( _
         "spRetrieveBalance", objConn)
      objCmd.CommandType = CommandType.StoredProcedure
      dim objReader as OleDbDataReader

      'set parameters for stored procedure
      dim objParam as OleDbParameter
      objParam = objCmd.Parameters.Add("@UserID", _
         OleDbType.BSTR)
      objParam.Direction = ParameterDirection.Input
      objParam.Value = strUsername

      try
         objConn.Open()
         decBalance = CType(objCmd.ExecuteScalar, _
            Decimal)
         objConn.Close
      catch ex as OleDbException
         throw ex
      end try

      return decBalance
   end function

   '*****************************************************
   ' Returns all transactions for a given user id
   '*****************************************************
   public function GetTransactions() as OleDbDataReader
      dim objCmd as new OleDbCommand( _
         "spGetTransactions", objConn)
      objCmd.CommandType = CommandType.StoredProcedure
      dim objReader as OleDbDataReader
```

LISTING BP3.1 continued

```

         'set parameters for stored procedure
         dim objParam as OleDbParameter
         objParam = objCmd.Parameters.Add("@UserID", _
            OleDbType.BSTR)
         objParam.Direction = ParameterDirection.Input
         objParam.Value = strUsername

         try
            objConn.Open()
            return objCmd.ExecuteReader
         catch ex as OleDbException
            throw ex
         end try
      end function

      '****************************************************
      ' Adds a transaction into the database, calling
      ' spInsertTransaction and specifying amount, payee,
      ' and user id
      '****************************************************
      public sub AddTransaction(strPayee as string,
➥decAmount as Decimal)
         dim objCmd as OleDbCommand = new OleDbCommand _
            ("spInsertTransaction", objConn)
         objCmd.CommandType = CommandType.StoredProcedure

         'set parameters for stored procedure
         dim objParam as OleDbParameter
         objParam = objCmd.Parameters.Add("@Date", _
            OleDbType.Date)
         objParam.Direction = ParameterDirection.Input
         objParam.Value = Datetime.Now

         objParam = objCmd.Parameters.Add("@Amount", _
            OleDbType.Decimal)
         objParam.Direction = ParameterDirection.Input
         objParam.Value = decAmount

         objParam = objCmd.Parameters.Add("@Payee", _
            OleDbType.BSTR)
         objParam.Direction = ParameterDirection.Input
         objParam.Value = strPayee

         objParam = objCmd.Parameters.Add("@UserID", _
            OleDbType.BSTR)
         objParam.Direction = ParameterDirection.Input
         objParam.Value = strUsername
```

LISTING BP3.1 continued

```
103:
104:          try
105:             objConn.Open()
106:             objCmd.ExecuteNonQuery
107:             objConn.Close
108:          catch ex as OleDbException
109:             throw ex
110:          end try
111:       end sub
112:
113:       '*****************************************************
114:       ' Updates the account balance
115:       ' calls spUpdateBalance
116:       '*****************************************************
117:       public sub UpdateBalance(decNewAmount as Decimal)
118:          dim objCmd as OleDbCommand = new OleDbCommand _
119:             ("spUpdateBalance", objConn)
120:          objCmd.CommandType = CommandType.StoredProcedure
121:
122:          'set parameters for stored procedure
123:          dim objParam as OleDbParameter
124:          objParam = objCmd.Parameters.Add("@NewBalance", _
125:             OleDbType.Decimal)
126:          objParam.Direction = ParameterDirection.Input
127:          objParam.Value = decNewAmount
128:
129:          objParam = objCmd.Parameters.Add("@UserID", _
130:             OleDbType.BSTR)
131:          objParam.Direction = ParameterDirection.Input
132:          objParam.Value = strUsername
133:
134:          try
135:             objConn.Open()
136:             objCmd.ExecuteNonQuery
137:             objConn.Close
138:          catch ex as OleDbException
139:             throw ex
140:          end try
141:       end sub
142:    End Class
143: End Namespace
```

ANALYSIS Save this file as `Account.vb`. Much of this code should look familiar. The `GetBalance` function on line 22 was pulled from the `account.aspx` and `bills.aspx` files; the `GetTransactions` function (line 51) was pulled from `account.aspx`; both `AddTransaction` on line 77 and `UpdateBalance` on line 117 were pulled from `bills.aspx`. Much of the code has remained the same since the last time you looked at these methods, so I won't go into detail here (see "Week 2 in Review" for details on each method). However, there are some vital changes that you should know about.

On line 9, you declare an `OleDbConnection` object for use with your methods; it's easier to create it once here than it is to create it in every single method. Line 12 creates a private variable to hold a user's account name; you'll return to this in a moment.

Line 14 declares the `New` method. This method is a constructor for the `Account` class; it executes whenever you instantiate the class (recall that in C#, the constructor shares the same name as the class—`Account`, in this case). For example, the `New` method is executed when you use the following code:

```
dim objAccount as New Account
```

or in C#:

```
Account objAccount = new Account()
```

This method takes a string parameter, `Username`, and stores it in the private `strUsername` variable you created on line 12. Now users of this class can use the following code to instantiate this class:

```
dim objAccount as New Account("clpayne")
```

This value will be used to retrieve the correct account from the database—it will be supplied from the authentication cookie created when the user logs on (more on this later).

Caution

Because you've created a constructor that takes a parameter, your user *must* supply a value for that parameter whenever the class is instantiated. The following line will now generate an error:

```
dim objAccount as New Account
```

If you want users to still be able to use the preceding code, create another `New` method that doesn't accept any parameters and add the `Overloads` keyword to both methods:

```
sub Overloads New Account(Username as String)
...
sub Overloads New Account()
...
```

This creates an overloaded method. Recall that overloaded methods are methods that have the same name, but take different parameters (and possibly execute different code). Thus, overloaded methods make it possible for your class to be instantiated in multiple ways. See Day 15 for more information, including how to do this in C#.

Next, the first two methods have been changed from a `sub` to a `function`. The original methods didn't need to return any values; they assigned any calculated values to labels or text boxes. However, the object can't do this. So, it instead returns the calculated data to the calling page, which will then assign it to the proper display element. Notice that each function also returns an appropriate type. For example, beginning on line 22, the `GetBalance` function returns a `Decimal`:

```
public function GetBalance() as Decimal
   dim decBalance as decimal
   ...
   return decBalance
end function
```

Likewise, `GetTransactions` returns an `OleDbDataReader`.

Each of the methods in Listing BP3.1 uses `OleDbParameters` to retrieve data from the database, one of which is the `@UserID` parameter, which ensures that you are retrieving the correct account information.

The code uses the value from the `strUsername` variable that is created on line 12, and instantiated on line 15, in the class's constructor. This variable will contain the account name supplied from the code that instantiates this class.

Now, compile this object for use in your pages. From the command prompt, in the same directory that this listing was saved in, issue the following command:

```
vbc /t:library /out:..\..\bin\ASPNETBank.dll /r:System.dll
➥/r:System.data.dll Account.vb
```

With that done, it's time to examine that changes to each of the ASP.NET pages. None of the UI has changed, so this discussion looks only at the code declaration blocks. Listing BP3.2 shows the changes to `account.aspx`.

LISTING BP3.2 Implementing the `Account` Object in `account.aspx`

```
<script runat="server">
   sub Page_Load(Sender as Object, e as EventArgs)
      dim objAccount as New ASPNETBank.Account( _
         User.Identity.Name)
      lblBalance.Text = "<b>$" & objAccount.GetBalance() & _
         "</b>"
      dgTransactions.DataSource = objAccount.GetTransactions
      DataBind
   end sub
</script>
```

ANALYSIS Quite a change from last time! On line 3, you instantiate your newly created `Account` object, supplying the user's account name. (The `User` object contains information about the authenticated user; `Identity.Name` specifies the value stored in the authentication cookie. This means that this page won't work unless you have some form of authentication enabled—we'll create a `web.config` file to do so in a moment.) On line 5, you use the `GetBalance` function to retrieve a `Decimal` variable that contains the account balance, and display it in a label named `lblBalance` (not shown here).

Next, on line 7, the `GetTransactions` method returns an `OleDbDataReader` object which you bind to a `DataGrid` named `dgTransactions` (again, not shown here). Call the `DataBind` method on line 8, and that's it! Viewing this page from the browser should produce the same image as last time, shown in Figure BP3.1.

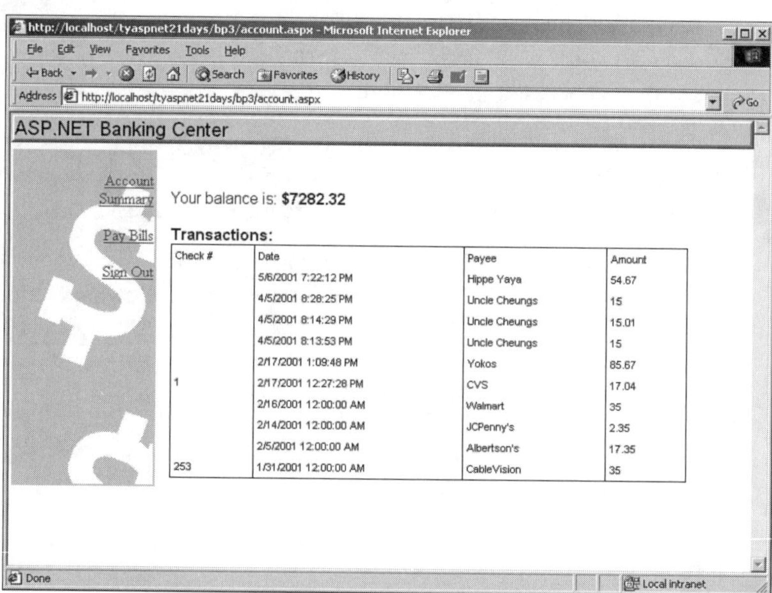

FIGURE BP3.1
Viewing the account information with a new `Account` *object.*

Let's look at the changes for `bills.aspx`, shown in Listing BP3.3.

LISTING BP3.3 Implementing the `Account` Object in `bills.aspx`

```
<script runat="server">
   sub PayBill(Sender as Object, e as EventArgs)
      dim objAccount as new ASPNETBank.Account( _
         User.Identity.Name)
      dim decBalance as Decimal = objAccount.GetBalance()
      dim decAmount as Decimal = tbAmount.Text
```

Listing BP3.3 continued

```
 7:
 8:       if decAmount < 0 then
 9:          lblMessage.Text = "<font color=red>The " & _
10:              "transaction amount cannot be negative!" & _
11:              "</font>"
12:           exit sub
13:        end if
14:
15:        if decAmount <= decBalance then
16:           objAccount.UpdateBalance(decBalance - decAmount)
17:           objAccount.AddTransaction(tbPayee.Text, decAmount)
18:
19:           lblMessage.Text = "<font color=red>" & _
20:              "Transaction added.</font>"
21:           tbAmount.Text = ""
22:           tbPayee.Text = ""
23:        else
24:           lblMessage.Text = "<font color=red>You do not " & _
25:              "have enough funds to complete this " & _
26:              "transaction!</font>"
27:        end if
28:     end sub
29:  </script>
```

Analysis This page contains only one method, `PayBill`, which is the event handler for a submit button click. Essentially, this page compares the current balance of the account to the value specified by the user (to pay a bill). If the former is greater than the latter, the transaction is added to the database, and the value is subtracted from the account. Otherwise, the user is alerted of the error.

On line 3, you create a new `Account` object just as you did for Listing BP3.2. Again, because we haven't yet implemented authentication, this page won't work. Line 5 retrieves the balance of the account, and line 6 retrieves the value specified by the user. Line 8 simply ensures that the amount specified by the user isn't negative, and alerts the user if it is. Line 15 performs the check to ensure that the current balance is greater than the bill amount. Lines 16 and 17 are responsible for calling methods in the `Account` object that subtract the value from the account and add the transaction to the database, respectively. Finally, a message is displayed to the user on lines 19–22. This page is shown in Figure BP3.2.

`login.aspx` changes only slightly. Because you now know how to use forms authentication, you can take advantage of it to log in the users properly. Previously, all you did was set a cookie and redirect the user. Now, you can set a valid authentication cookie. In `login.aspx`, change the following line (line 48 of Listing BP2.6):

```
Response.Cookies("Account").Value = intID
```

to read as follows:

```
FormsAuthentication.SetAuthCookie(intID, false)
```

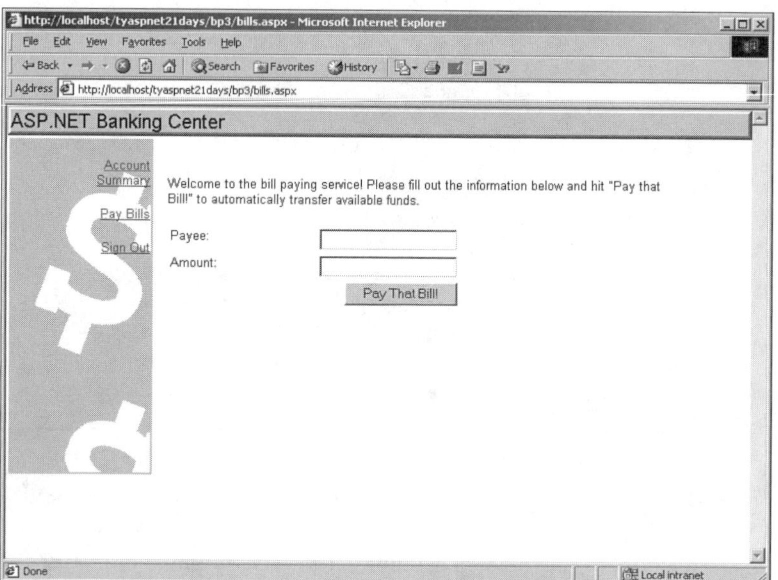

FIGURE BP3.2
The updated `bills.aspx` *page.*

That's all there is to it! Additionally, because you now log users in properly, you'll want to allow them to log out as well. Listing BP3.4 shows `logout.aspx`, which removes the authentication cookie.

LISTING BP3.4 Logging Users Out Is a Simple Process

```
<%@ Page Language="VB" %>
<%@ Register TagPrefix="ASPNETBank" TagName="Header"
➥src="header.ascx" %>

<script runat="server">

   '*******************************************************
   '
   ' Logout.aspx: Logs users out
   '
```

LISTING BP3.4 continued

```
10:     '*******************************************************
11:
12:     '*******************************************************
13:     ' We need to log users out as soon as they hit this page
14:     ' so use Page_Load and CookieAuthentication.Signout
15:     '*******************************************************
16:     sub Page_Load(Sender as Object, e as EventArgs)
17:        FormsAuthentication.SignOut
18:     end sub
19:  </script>
20:
21:  <html><body topmargin="0" leftmargin="0">
22:     <ASPNETBank:Header runat="server" />
23:     <font face="arial">
24:     <p>
25:     Thank you for using the ASP.NET Banking Center. Please
26:     come again!.<p>
27:
28:     <a href="login.aspx">Login again?</a><p>
29:     </font>
30:  </body></html>
```

As you can see, the only code in this page is in the `Page_Load` method on line 16. `FormsAuthentication.SignOut` removes the authentication cookie you set when the user logged in, which effectively logs the user out. If she wants to access your application again, she must log in again.

You also know how to implement security in your application through `web.config`. You'll need to protect the pages in this application so that unauthorized users aren't able to see account information. Specifically, you'll have to secure `account.aspx` and `bills.aspx`. Listing BP3.5 shows the `web.config` file that implements these changes.

LISTING BP3.5 Implementing Security with `web.config`

```
<configuration>
   <system.web>
      <authentication mode="Forms">
         <forms name="AuthCookie"
➥loginUrl="tyaspnet21days/bp3/login.aspx"/>
      </authentication>
   </system.web>
   <location path="tyaspnet21days/BP3/account.aspx">
      <system.web>
         <authorization>
               <deny users="?"/>
```

LISTING BP3.5 continued

```
11:          </authorization>
12:       </system.web>
13:    </location>
14:    <location path="tyaspnet21days/BP3/bills.aspx">
15:       <system.web>
16:          <authorization>
17:             <deny users="?"/>
18:          </authorization>
19:       </system.web>
20:    </location>
21: </configuration>
```

After your lesson in security in Day 21, this listing should be easy to understand. Line 3 turns on forms authentication. Line 4 provides the name of the authentication cookie and the URL to which unauthenticated users should be directed, `login.aspx`. The `<location>` elements on lines 7 and 14 use the `<authorization>` tags to deny access to `account.aspx` and `bills.aspx` to anonymous users. Note that this `web.config` must reside in the root directory of your application. The `<location>` tags throw an error when used in subdirectories.

The files `header.ascx` and `nav.ascx` stay the same. These two were static user controls, and didn't contain any code to modify.

You might be wondering why you haven't created a `User` object to represent the current user and log him in, sign him out, and so on. Currently, the only method that applies to users is the submit event handler for `login.aspx`, which validates credentials against the database. Because there's only one method here and it won't be used anywhere else, there's no need to spend the energy to move it into a business object. (Don't let that stop you, however, if you feel the urge to create more business objects!)

The Web Service

This Web Service will allow payees to remotely post transactions to your account. For example, if you use a debit card at a restaurant, the restaurant could access this Web Service and determine immediately whether you could pay.

Thanks to the `Account` business object, this Web Service is fairly easy to create. Listing BP3.6 shows the code.

LISTING BP3.6 The Web Service Uses the Existing `Account` Object

```
1:  <%@ WebService Language="VB" Class="Bills" %>
2:
3:  Imports System
4:  Imports System.Data
5:  Imports System.Data.OleDb
6:  Imports System.Web.Services
7:
8:  public Class Bills : Inherits WebService
9:     private objConn As New OleDbConnection("Provider=" & _
10:        "Microsoft.Jet.OLEDB.4.0;" & _
11:        "Data Source=c:\ASPNET\data\banking.mdb")
12:
13:    <WebMethod()> Public function PostBill(UserID as
➥Integer, strPayee as string, decAmount as Decimal)
➥as String
14:       dim objAccount as New ASPNETBank.Account( _
15:          UserID.ToString)
16:       dim decBalance as Decimal = objAccount.GetBalance
17:
18:       if decAmount <= decBalance then
19:          objAccount.UpdateBalance(decBalance - decAmount)
20:          objAccount.AddTransaction(strPayee, decAmount)
21:          return "Success"
22:       else
23:          return "Insufficient funds"
24:       end if
25:    end function
26: End Class
```

ANALYSIS Save this file as `PostTransaction.asmx`. Line 1 declares that this file is a Web Service, and that the Web Service class is `Bills`, which is declared on line 8. Note that it inherits from the `WebService` class. Line 9 declares an `OleDbConnection` object for use with your only method, `PostBill`, on line 13.

The rest of the code should look very similar to the `PayBill` method from Listing BP3.3. The `PostBill` method, however, takes a few more parameters; specifically, parameters that declare the `UserID` (and consequently the account ID), the merchant who is posting the bill, and the amount of the bill. Note that it also returns a string—you'll get to that in a moment. Line 14 creates a new `Account` object with the specified user ID, and line 16 retrieves the current balance from the account.

Line 18 determines whether the amount of the posted bill is less than the current balance. If so, the account is updated with the new balance and transaction. If the transaction is successful, you return the string `"Success"` to the merchant. That way, the merchant has a definite confirmation from you. If the transaction fails, you return a reason why—this is why returning a string from this method is helpful. Rather than the service simply saying that the transaction failed, you can give detailed information on why it failed, using the returned string.

That's all there is to it! Figures BP3.3 and BP3.4 show a test of this Web Service and the results generated.

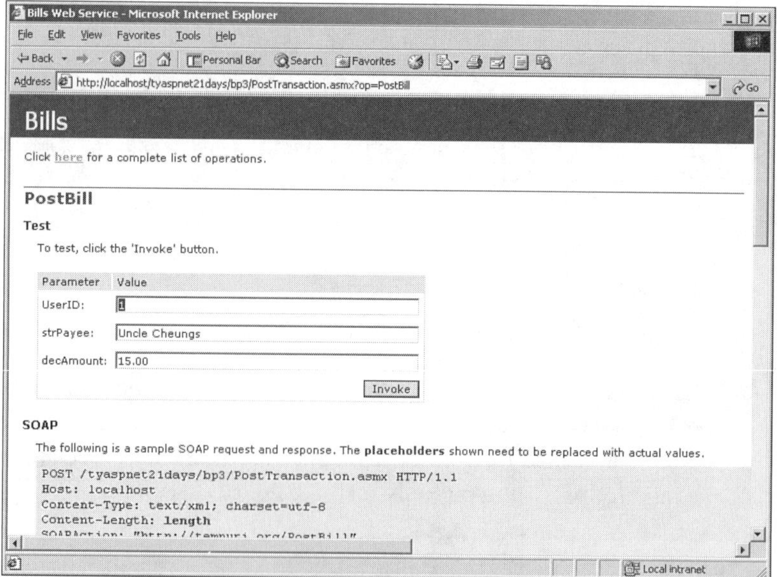

FIGURE BP3.3

Testing the Web Service with Http-Post.

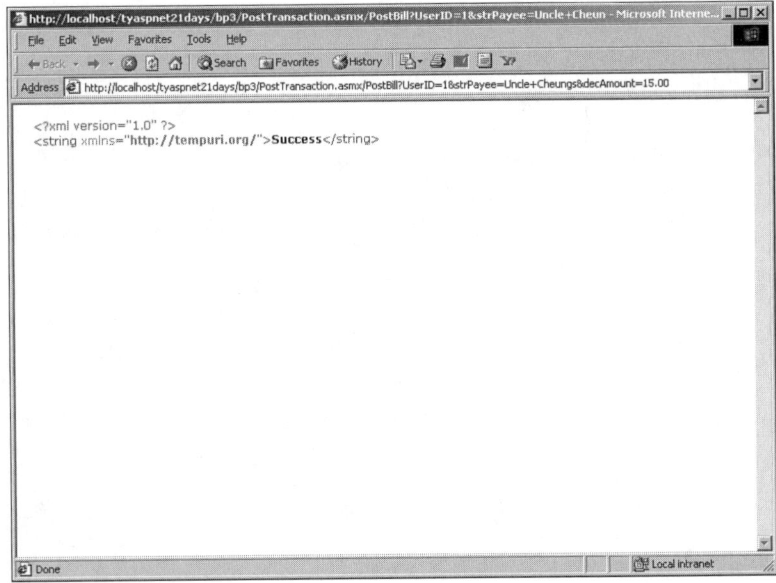

FIGURE BP3.4

The XML results generated from the text.

Summary

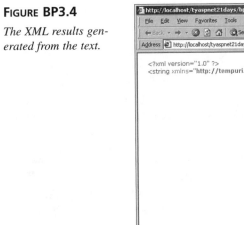

We are now through with the banking application. You built this fully fledged program starting in Bonus Project 1, piece-by- piece, adding as you learned. The application implements quite a few of the technologies covered in this book, such as security, business objects, and Web Services, Web forms, user controls, and databases. Quite a menagerie of concepts!

Let's take a brief overview of the process thus far. At the end of Week 1, you built the foundation for the application—the basic user interface—with ASP.NET server controls. At the end of Week 2, you turned the application into a data-driven one by creating a database and interacting with it to store user and account information. Users could view transactions stored in the database, and add new ones through the bill payment page. Finally, in this lesson, you completed the application by adding business objects and providing security for your pages through `web.config`. You also added a Web service for payees to post debit information.

There is, of course, more you can do with this application. For example, currently, the Web Service allows anyone to post transactions to the database. This could result in some unscrupulous individuals artificially lowering the balance of a user's account. One suggestion is to secure this service, using the techniques from Day 17, "Consuming and Securing XML Web Services."

Additionally, many improvements can be made in performance. Caching the transactions from a user's account might greatly increase performance, but don't overdo it! You don't want one user seeing the cached transactions of another user; make sure to empty the cache if necessary, such as when a user logs off the system. Also, validation controls could be added to validate user input on the client-side, resulting in less time-consuming traffic traveling across the Internet. Finally, you can disable state management for the controls that don't require it using `EnableViewState="false"`. Depending on the size of the controls, this can also increase performance.

Don't be hesitant to modify the code as you see fit. The more modifications you make, the better a programmer you will become. Try adding new features, and enhancing older ones. This application is typical of something you may be asked to develop one day in the real world. The more familiar you are with it and its technologies and paradigms, the better suited you'll be in the future. Happy programming!

BONUS DAY

DAY 22

Building a Complete Application

Now that you've successfully traversed the landscape of ASP.NET, you should be fairly comfortable building your own applications and dissecting those that others have built. Today's lesson concentrates on building a complete application from scratch to take you through the entire process.

You will design the application around a fictional company's business model. In this lesson, you will examine this fictional company's requirements, and then you will build the Web application accordingly. Today's discussion recaps many of the lessons you've completed during these past three weeks, but concentrates on the design and development part of the application. You won't spend much time re-learning things that you've already gone over.

There will be a lot of coding in this chapter because you'll have to build everything from stored procedures to ASP.NET pages to business objects and Web Services. Let's get started!

Today's lesson covers the following:

- How to properly set up a design for an application's requirements
- How to accomplish tasks in a logical manner
- Building databases and stored procedures from given requirements
- Building business objects that interact with your databases
- Determining what UI functionality you need and building it

The Scenario: BananaMobiles

You've been approached by BananaMobile, Inc., which wants to take its business online. Specifically, the company wants a complete application that will allow visitors to build and customize their own BananaMobiles online (see Figure 22.1), and then place an order for their specially designed vehicle. You will be supplied with all the necessary specifications so that users have choices of BananaMobile parts.

In addition, all BananaMobiles have built-in wireless Internet access from the vehicles. The access uses a proprietary mechanism, known as BananaConnect, that implements its own Web browser. The company wants you to build a Web service that BananaConnect can access to allow users to post information about their vehicles to a central database. This information includes mileage, top speeds, and max throttle generated (yes, BananaMobiles are used competitively for sport, in addition to transporting bananas).

FIGURE 22.1 *The legendary BananaMobile.*

Now that you've examined the requirements, let's start building the ASP.NET application!

Designing the Application

The most important step in developing an application is design. Without a proper design, things can get very hairy later down the line. Spending one minute at this stage saves you ten minutes during development. Therefore, before you start development, you must lay down a solid foundation in design schemes and have a plan of attack.

The BananaMobile application will use a three-tier approach (see the "Why Use Components" section of Day 15, "Using Business Objects"). You'll have the data stores in the back end, a layer of business objects to interact with data and perform operations will be in the middle tier, and of course, the user interface will be developed in ASP.NET in the front end. The next few sections examine each of these tiers, and lay out what needs to be accomplished in each.

Banana Data

First, let's analyze the back end and data stores required for the site. Obviously, this application is going to require a database. Specifically, you'll need to keep track of four things: customers and their information, orders, BananaMobile parts and information, and data posted from the BananaConnect system.

The information that BananaMobile, Inc. keeps for customers is fairly standard, so you can simply use a version of the user database developed in Day 8, "Beginning to Build Databases." This database includes information such as names, contact information, site username, and password.

When keeping track of customer orders, you'll need to store information on who ordered items and what exactly was ordered. Because the site allows users to completely customize their BananaMobile configuration, each order can be different. You'll need to make sure that this information is accurately tracked. Therefore, you'll have one field for each of the customizable types, as well as a price field that contains the running sum of the parts ordered.

The BananaMobile parts and information data will be fairly straightforward. After consulting with BananaMobile, Inc., you've determined that there are six different customizable parts: wheels, color of the banana, engine, the patented BananaThrowing system (the BTS, used for competitions), the type of base frame of the vehicle, and interior carpet. Each customizable item will have an associated price and description. You'll build one large table that will hold all the items, making sure to group each by category.

The data posted from the BananaConnect system contains only mileage, throttle, and max speed information, so this can be kept in a simple table.

Finally, the shopping cart information (see "The Banana Front End" section later today) will be stored in the database, so you'll need a table to hold temporary information while users are browsing. This table simply holds the customer ID and a part ID for each of the customizable parts; everything else can be pulled from one of the other tables. This table will be a temporary version of the orders table; when a user places the order, you'll move the information from this temporary table to the orders table.

You'll also create a variety of stored procedures. However, until you know the functionality needed by the front and middle layers, you won't know for sure what procedures to create. From analyzing the data so far, you know that you'll need procedures to accomplish the following tasks:

- Validate a user's credentials
- Add users to the customers table
- Retrieve and add information to the shopping cart table
- Retrieve information from the customizable parts table
- Move information from the temporary shopping cart table to the permanent orders table
- Add information to the BananaConnect table

You'll get back to this later.

After analyzing the data requirements, you'll end up with something similar to Figure 22.2. There will be four tables holding the different categories of data discussed earlier—orders, parts, shopping carts, and BananaConnect information—and a user table. In addition, the orders and user tables will be related (each order needs to be linked to a particular user). Also, the shopping cart table will be linked to the user table. The BananaConnect table will need to be related to the user table, so only registered users are allowed to post information.

Note that this diagram isn't the end-all of the design. In fact, it leaves out many of the fields that you'll require for your application (I'll discuss those later today). This diagram is merely meant to provide a simple illustration to get you started building. It can be changed easily, but it presents you with a very good vantage point when you start development.

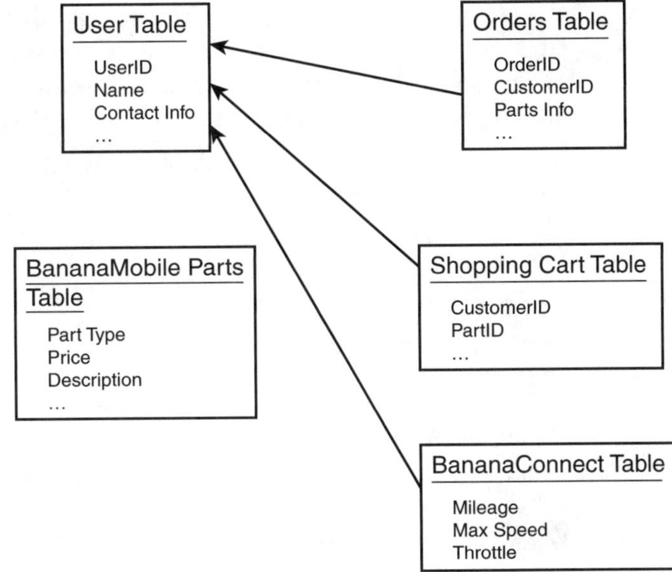

FIGURE 22.2
The data relationship diagram.

The Banana Front End

The requirements for the UI are derived directly from the requirements given you by BananaMobile, Inc. You'll need a shopping-type interface, so that users can browse through BananaMobile parts and add selected items to their shopping cart. The difference between this functionality and shopping carts on other sites is that yours will be used to assemble a BananaMobile, rather than holding a collection of unrelated items. Therefore, users should be allowed to add only one of each item; subsequent additions will replace existing components. Additionally, only registered users should be able to purchase or add items to their shopping cart, so you'll need a login page and a registration page to add users to your database.

You'll also need a page for users to check out and actually purchase their completed BananaMobile. Note that you're not going to build a place for collecting payment information such as credit card numbers—just assume that customers have valid account information.

You'll also have to build a Web service that allows data about the BananaMobile's automotive performance to be posted. This service will take the automotive performance data and insert it into the database. Naturally, you'll want only registered BananaMobile users to post information, so you'll have to secure the service as well.

You'll incorporate several user controls into the application, which will display common pieces of the UI, such as headers and footers. The use of user controls will make development go faster and more smoothly. Also, user controls will be invaluable because you want to present a consistent user interface across all pages in your site.

Let's recap the pages you'll need:

- Login page
- Registration page
- Product browsing page
- Shopping cart page (allows users to view and remove items in their cart)
- Checkout or purchase page
- A default or home page (every site needs one of these)
- At least two user controls: a common header and a common menu/navigation bar

Banana Business Objects

Recall from Day 15 that business objects are reusable pieces of code that can be plugged into your applications. They often represent real-world objects and encapsulate commonly used code so that you don't have to worry about the additional complexity or extra code. You'll be using two business objects in the BananaMobile application.

As you are probably already aware, a BananaMobile is an ideal candidate for representation as a business object. The BananaMobile business object will contain the functionality to add and remove parts, as well as keeping track of which parts a BananaMobile-in-progress contains. Because all this data will be stored in the database, this object's methods will utilize stored procedures.

You'll also build a business object used to represent a customer. This site will require a secure logon to purchase a BananaMobile, and this object will provide the methods to validate users and retrieve their information.

Building the BananaMobile Site

Now that you've got the design of the site nailed down, it's time to start building the functionality. Divide the development into four stages: building the databases, the business objects, the ASP.NET pages, and finally, the Web service. This progression will allow you to easily move through development; each step will set the stage for the next step.

Creating the Database

The BananaMobile database will be created in Access, so create a new database as you did in Day 8, and save it as `banana.mdb`. Next create the database tables you will need. Starting with the `tblUsers` table, which stores information about your registered BananaMobile users, create a new table in design view, as shown in Figure 22.3, and add the following fields. Unless otherwise noted, all fields are `Text` data types.

- `UserID` (`Autonumber`)
- `Username`
- `Password`
- `FirstName`
- `LastName`
- `Address`
- `City`
- `State`
- `Zip`
- `Phone`
- `Email`

Note that we're using Access here because it is easier to use and is more readily available to developers. If you are building a site that is expecting heavy traffic or lots of database functionality, it might be wise to move your database to SQL Server, which is better capable of handling large loads.

These are all the fields you'll need to store user information. Don't forget to set the primary key on the `UserID` field. Close this table and save it as `tblUsers`. Following the same process, create three more tables. Table 22.1 shows the fields and data types for each database table (to change a numeric field type to `Double`, use the Field Size drop-down list on the General property sheet for the table).

TABLE 22.1 The Banana Database Structure

Table	*Fields*
`tblParts`	`PartID*` (`Autonumber`)
	`Name` (`Text`)
	`Category` (`Text`)

TABLE 22.1 continued

Table	*Fields*
	`Price` (`Currency`)
	`Description` (`Memo`)
`tblOrders`	`OrderID*` (`Autonumber`)
	`UserID` (`Number`)
	`BTS` (`Number`)
	`Carpet` (`Number`)
	`Color` (`Number`)
	`Engine` (`Number`)
	`Frame` (`Number`)
	`Wheels` (`Number`)
	`SubTotal` (`Currency`)
`tblShoppingCart`	`UserID*` (`Number`)
	`BTS` (`Number`)
	`Carpet` (`Number`)
	`Color` (`Number`)
	`Engine` (`Number`)
	`Frame` (`Number`)
	`Wheels` (`Number`)
`tblBananaConnect`	`RecordID*` (`Autonumber`)
	`UserID` (`Number`)
	`Mileage` (`Number, Double`)
	`MaxSpeed` (`Number, Double`)
	`Throttle` (`Number, Double`)
	`Date` (`Date/Time`)

An asterisk indicates column is a primary key

Next, create the relationships between the tables in Access, according to the diagram in Figure 22.2. Under the Tools menu, select Relationships, and add each table to the view. Simply click and drag to form relationships; you should end up with something similar to Figure 22.4. Note that you didn't relate each customizable part in the `tblOrders` table to the `tblParts` table; multiple relationships with the same two tables are difficult to work with, so they are left out. However, this relationship should still be enforced in your code.

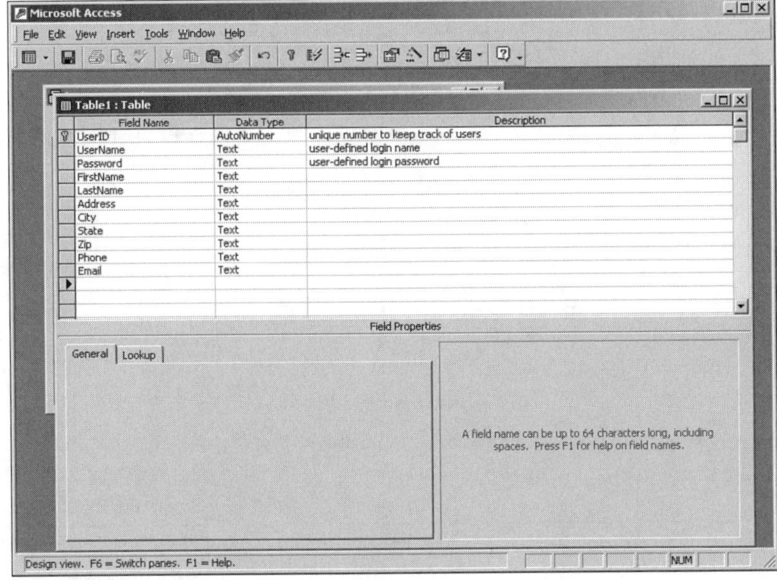

FIGURE 22.3
Creating the user table.

Note

Relationships like these are helpful to maintain your database properly, but beware of using them too often; they can slow down performance if used improperly (this is true in SQL Server as well). When possible, maintain relationships through other mechanisms, such as validation procedures in your code.

Now that you've got the tables set up, it's time to insert the data. Table 22.2 lists some of the various items that BananaMobile, Inc. offers as customizable parts. Insert this data into the `tblParts` table, and don't be afraid to add your own!

TABLE 22.2 BananaMobile Inc.'s Customizable Parts List

Name	*Category*	*Price*	*Description*
Catapult	BTS	$150	The Catapult upgrade offers tremendous power, shotgunning bananas at 50 km/hr.
Shag	Carpet	$100	Get that groovy feeling with our thick shag carpet.
Plush	Carpet	$125	Our beautiful plush carpet provides comfort for the entire family.
Standard	Color	$20	Our standard banana yellow color is the most popular choice.

TABLE 22.2 continued

Name	*Category*	*Price*	*Description*
Standard	Engine	$400	Our standard engine provides plenty of power with the purr of a small kitten. Perfect for family vehicles!
BananaSplit	Engine	$1400	The top of the line banana engine. The BananaSplit provides a screaming 2,000 bananas of power, perfect for tearing up asphalt.
Sedan	Frame	$400	This five-seater provides plenty of leg room for the whole family. Our stylish design will make your neighbors jealous.
Wheels	Chrome	$400	For the person who wants to be the scene, our chrome wheels will bring the spotlight to your BananaMobile.

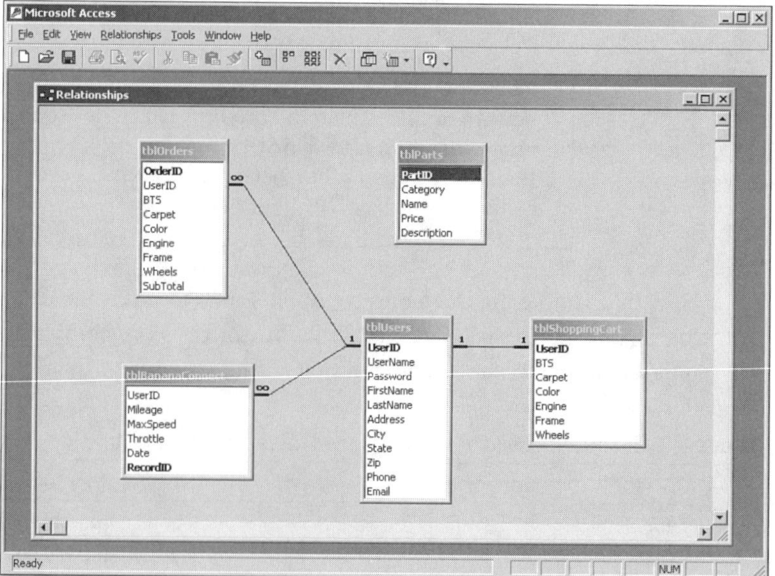

FIGURE 22.4
The relationship diagram in Access.

Also add a user or two to your `tblUsers` table. You don't need to enter information into the other tables because the users will do that for you. After you've entered this information into the `tblParts` and `tblUsers` tables, you're ready to create your stored procedures. Recall from Day 12, "Employing Advanced Data Techniques," that stored procedures are called *queries* in Access; I'll use the terms interchangeably here. These stored procedures will allow you to use parameters to retrieve data from your ASP.NET pages.

First, you'll need to create a query that validates a user's identity; that is, one that checks whether the supplied username and password are correct. Listing 22.1 shows this query.

LISTING 22.1 Validating a User

```
SELECT UserID FROM tblUsers
WHERE Username = @Username
   AND Password = @Password
```

Save this query as `spLoginUser`. This is a simple SQL statement that uses two parameters, `@Username` and `@Password`, both of which will be supplied by the user during login. Next, create a query that adds users to the database when they register. This is a simple parameterized `INSERT` query, shown in Listing 22.2.

LISTING 22.2 Adding New Users

```
INSERT INTO tblUsers (Username, Password, FirstName,
   LastName, Address, City, State, ZIP, Phone, Email)
VALUES (@Username, @Password, @FirstName, @LastName,
   @Address, @City, @State, @ZIP, @Phone, @Email)
```

Save this procedure as `spAddUser`. When a user adds items to his shopping cart, which usually follows immediately after the login, you first need to verify that he has a shopping cart; that is, whether there is an entry in the `tblShoppingCart` table with his user ID. If not, you need to add a new entry. Listing 22.3 accomplishes this.

LISTING 22.3 Adding a New Cart

```
INSERT INTO tblShoppingCart (UserID)
VALUES @UserID
```

Save this listing as `spAddCart`. This statement simply inserts a new row in `tblShoppingCart` with the value specified by `@UserID` for the `UserID` field. All the other fields (such as `BTS`, `Color`, and so on) are left at default values.

After you've created a shopping cart, you'll need a way to retrieve its ID. This is useful when you need to verify that a cart exists for a specific user. Listing 22.4 shows this query.

LISTING 22.4 Retrieving a Shopping Cart ID

```
SELECT UserID
FROM tblShoppingCart
WHERE UserID=@UserID
```

Save this listing as `spGetCart`.

Next, you'll need to create a set of queries that update each part in the `tblShoppingCart` table; for instance, one query to update the frame part number, one for the wheels part number, and so on. Luckily, these queries will all follow the same syntax, with the exception of the field name to update. Listings 22.5–22.10 show each of these `UPDATE` queries.

LISTING 22.5 Updating the BTS Part ID

```
1: UPDATE tblShoppingCart SET tblShoppingCart.BTS = @PartID
2: WHERE tblShoppingCart.UserID=@UserID
```

Save this code as `spAddBTS`. This SQL statement updates the `BTS` value in the shopping cart table with a value that the user has selected from the site (`@PartID`). Because shopping carts are linked to user IDs, update the correct cart by specifying the `@UserID` parameter on line 2. Listings 22.5–22.10 follow the same pattern, but substitute different part categories in place of `BTS`.

LISTING 22.6 Updating the Carpet Part ID

```
UPDATE tblShoppingCart SET tblShoppingCart.Carpet = @PartID
WHERE tblShoppingCart.UserID=@UserID
```

LISTING 22.7 Updating the Color Part ID

```
UPDATE tblShoppingCart SET tblShoppingCart.Color = @PartID
WHERE tblShoppingCart.UserID=@UserID
```

LISTING 22.8 Updating the Engine Part ID

```
UPDATE tblShoppingCart SET tblShoppingCart.Engine = @PartID
WHERE tblShoppingCart.UserID=@UserID
```

LISTING 22.9 Updating the Frame Part ID

```
UPDATE tblShoppingCart SET tblShoppingCart.Frame = @PartID
WHERE tblShoppingCart.UserID=@UserID
```

LISTING 22.10 Updating the Wheels Part ID

```
UPDATE tblShoppingCart SET tblShoppingCart.Wheels = @PartID
WHERE tblShoppingCart.UserID=@UserID
```

Save these as `spAddCarpet`, `spAddColor`, `spAddEngine`, `spAddFrame`, and `spAddWheels`, respectively. An interesting feature of these queries is that they can also be used to remove items from the cart. Setting the `@PartID` parameter to `0` when calling the query effectively removes the existing part.

You have six queries left to write (including one for the BananaConnect system), three of which are a bit more complex than the ones you've seen so far. The first one, `spGetSubTotal`, examines each item in a specific shopping cart, retrieves the price for each, and sums them at the end. Let's look at the code, shown in Listing 22.11.

LISTING 22.11 Retrieving Price Information

```
1:  SELECT SUM(Price)
2:  FROM tblParts, tblShoppingCart
3:  WHERE (tblParts.PartID=tblShoppingCart.BTS
4:     OR tblParts.PartID=tblShoppingCart.Carpet
5:     OR tblParts.PartID=tblShoppingCart.Color
6:     OR tblParts.PartID=tblShoppingCart.Engine
7:     OR tblParts.PartID=tblShoppingCart.Frame
8:     OR tblParts.PartID=tblShoppingCart.Wheels)
9:     AND tblShoppingCart.UserID=@UserID
```

This statement has a few different parts, so let's step through it slowly. Ignore the `SUM` command on line 1 for now, and imagine that it says `SELECT Price`. In plain English, this statement means, "Retrieve the prices for all items in `tblShoppingCart` from `tblParts`, given a specific user ID."

This query pulls information from two different tables: `tblParts` and `tblShoppingCart`. This makes sense because you're trying to find the prices (stored in `tblParts`) for each of the items in `tblShoppingCart`. Lines 3–8 relate each of the six different categories in `tblShoppingCart` to a `PartID` in `tblParts`. For example, if the `BTS` field in tblShoppingCart had the value 2, line 3 would match it to the corresponding item in tblParts. Likewise, if the Carpet field had a value of 7, line 4 would match it to the item in tblParts that has the same value. That way, you are assured that you are retrieving the correct price.

Each field in tblShoppingCart can potentially have the value 0 (if the user hasn't added that part yet). However, there isn't a PartID in tblParts with the value 0. Therefore, this query will return data from the tblParts table without a matching item from the tblShoppingCart table. For example, if the Color field is 0, you won't get a corresponding price from tblParts. Use the keyword OR on lines 4–8 to ignore these mismatches, and return prices for only the ones that do match; any returned data that has a PartID of 0 will be ignored. If you replace all the ORs with ANDs, chances are this query won't return anything, because of the zeroes in tblShoppingCart.

On line 9, you make sure that you are retrieving information from the correct shopping cart by supplying the UserID. Finally, after you have the prices for each item in tblShoppingCart, you use the SUM function to add them all up. The result is one aggregate value instead of six separate ones.

Next, you'll need a stored procedure that retrieves all information about a specific shopping cart. This query, as shown in Listing 22.12, is very similar to Listing 22.11.

LISTING 22.12 Retrieving Cart Information

```
1:  SELECT tblParts.PartID, Name, Category, Price
2:  FROM tblParts, tblShoppingCart
3:  WHERE tblParts.PartID=tblShoppingCart.BTS
4:     OR tblParts.PartID=tblShoppingCart.Carpet
5:     OR tblParts.PartID=tblShoppingCart.Color
6:     OR tblParts.PartID=tblShoppingCart.Engine
7:     OR tblParts.PartID=tblShoppingCart.Frame
8:     OR tblParts.PartID=tblShoppingCart.Wheels
9:     AND tblShoppingCart.UserID=@UserID
```

Save this listing as spViewMobile. The syntax is nearly identical to spGetSubTotal except that you're not performing an aggregate function. Rather, you are simply retrieving several fields from the database. This query returns the PartID, Name, Category, and Price information for the items in a specific shopping cart, by linking the tblParts and tblShoppingCart tables.

The next query is similarly complex. Listing 22.13 shows the code.

LISTING 22.13 Moving Items from `tblShoppingCart` to `tblOrders`

```
1:  INSERT INTO tblOrders (UserID, BTS, Carpet, Color,
2:     Engine, Frame, Wheels, SubTotal)
3:     SELECT tblShoppingCart.UserID, tblShoppingCart.BTS,
4:        tblShoppingCart.Carpet, tblShoppingCart.Color,
5:        tblShoppingCart.Engine, tblShoppingCart.Frame,
6:        tblShoppingCart.Wheels, @SubTotal AS Expr1
7:     FROM tblShoppingCart
8:     WHERE tblShoppingCart.UserID=@UserID
```

Save this listing as `spPurchase`. This query will be executed when the user decides to purchase the items in his shopping cart. Essentially, it moves all information stored in the temporary `tblShoppingCart` table to the permanent `tblOrders` table.

Again, it often helps to examine the statement's meaning in plain English first. This one reads, "Insert all fields from `tblShoppingCart` with the specific user ID into `tblOrders`." On lines 1 and 2, you notice the familiar beginnings of a normal `INSERT` statement. All the fields (except `OrderID`) are included in this update. On line 3, however, you see a `SELECT` statement. What's going on?

Lines 3–8 contain a *subquery*, that is, a SQL query inside another query. In this case, it's a `SELECT` query inside an `INSERT` query. The inner query serves to supply data for the outside query. Immediately after line 2, the `INSERT` statement expects values for the eight fields specified in between the parentheses on lines 1 and 2. The `SELECT` statement supplies just those values. In fact, if you examine the `SELECT` statement, you'll notice that it is fairly standard. The only differences between this and what you're used to are the addition of the table names in front of each field (that is, `tblShoppingCart.Carpet` instead of just `Carpet`) and the snippet `@SubTotal AS Expr1` on line 6. The addition of table names is necessary because the `tblOrders` and `tblShoppingCart` tables have fields with the same name. Without additional clarification, the application would get confused; it wouldn't know where to retrieve data from.

The `SELECT` statement returns only seven values, however, and you need eight for the `INSERT` statement. The line `@SubTotal AS Expr1` means that in addition to the values returned by the `SELECT` statement, you're adding a field named `Expr1`. The value for this field doesn't come from a table or a `SELECT` statement; rather, it comes from the `@SubTotal` parameter, which you'll specify in the application. Thus, you now have all the values you need for the `INSERT` statement, effectively transferring all data from the shopping cart table to `tblOrders`.

You'll also need a query to retrieve all the parts in a specified category. This will help in building "browsing" pages for your customers. Listing 22.14 shows this query.

LISTING 22.14 Correlating Part Category and ID Information

```
SELECT PartID, Name, Price, Description, Category
FROM tblParts
WHERE Category=@Category
```

Save this query as `spGetCategory`. Finally, after you've transferred the data from the shopping cart to `tblOrders`, you need to remove it from `tblShoppingCart`. This is easily done with the statement shown in Listing 22.15.

LISTING 22.15 Deleting Old Shopping Cart Information

```
DELETE *
FROM tblShoppingCart
WHERE UserID=@UserID
```

Save this query as `spRemoveCart`. So far, you've got 15 stored procedures, as shown in Figure 22.5.

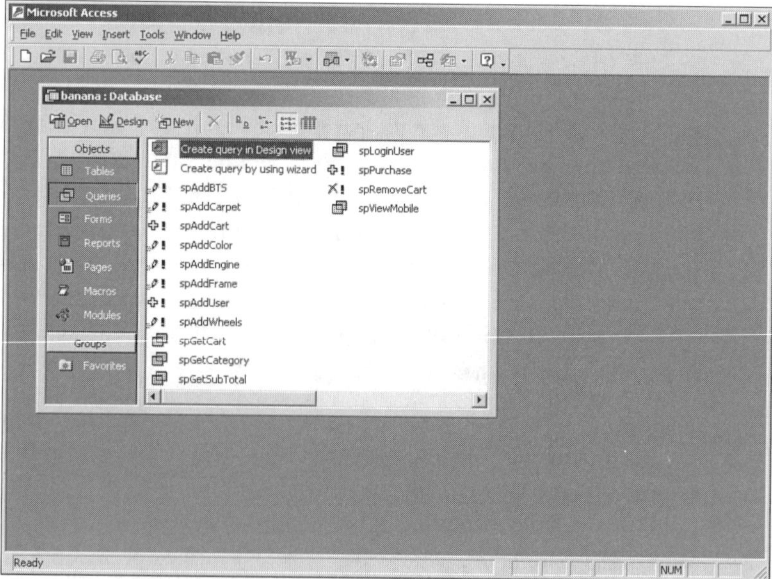

FIGURE 22.5
The Banana queries in Access.

You've got one more to go: the `BananaConnect` procedure. This query takes parameters from each BananaMobile and adds them to the database. You want to allow each

BananaMobile owner to have as many records in the database as he wants, so this query will simply be an `INSERT` statement. This query is shown in Listing 22.16.

LISTING 22.16 Adding Data from the BananaConnect System

```
1:  INSERT INTO  tblBananaConnect
2:     (UserID, Mileage, MaxSpeed, Throttle, [Date])
3:  VALUES (@UserID, @Mileage, @MaxSpeed, @Throttle, @Date)
```

Save this query as `spBananaConnect`. Note that on line 2 you had to enclose the field `Date` in brackets. That's because the word `Date` has special meaning in Access, and will cause an error if you use it here by itself. To let Access know that you're referring to a field and not a special keyword, surround the field with brackets. That's it for the database! Let's move on to the business objects.

Tip

> You can optionally surround each of the column names with brackets. In fact, if your column names contain spaces, brackets are required!

The Business Objects

Now that you've created all your stored procedures, you can build the business objects that will use them. From the design stage you stepped through earlier in this chapter, you know that you need two different objects: one to represent a user and one to represent a BananaMobile.

The user object will contain only two methods: one to validate a user's identity and one to add a new user to the database. This user class is similar to the one you built in Day 15. It utilizes a `UserDetails` class that simply holds identity values for a user. Listing 22.17 shows both these classes.

LISTING 22.17 `User.vb`, the `User` and `UserDetails` Classes

```
Imports System
Imports System.Data
Imports System.Data.OleDb

Namespace BananaMobile

   Public Class UserDetails
      public UserID as Integer
      public Username as string
```

LISTING 22.17 continued

```
   public Password as string
   public FirstName as string
   public LastName as string
   public City as string
   public State as string
   public ZIP as string
   public Address as string
   public Phone as string
   public Email as string
End Class

Public Class User
   private objConn As New OleDbConnection("Provider=" & _
         "Microsoft.Jet.OLEDB.4.0;" & _
         "Data Source=c:\ASPNET\data\banana.mdb")

   public function Login(strUsername as String, _
      strPassword as String) as Integer
      dim intId as Integer

      Dim objCmd As New OleDbCommand("spLoginUser", _
         objConn)
      objCmd.CommandType = CommandType.StoredProcedure

      Dim objParam As New OleDbParameter("@Username", _
         OleDbType.Char)
      objParam.Value = strUsername
      objCmd.Parameters.Add(objParam)

      objParam = New OleDbParameter("@Password", _
         OleDbType.Char)
      objParam.Value = strPassword
      objCmd.Parameters.Add(objParam)

      Try
         objConn.Open
         intID = CType(objCmd.ExecuteScalar, Integer)
         objConn.Close
      Catch e As Exception
         throw e
      End Try

      if intID.ToString = "" then
         return 0
      end if
      return intID
   end function

```

LISTING 22.17 continued

```
public sub AddUser(objUser as UserDetails)
   Dim intID as Integer
   Dim objReader as OleDbDataReader
   Dim objCmdID As New OleDbCommand( _
      "SELECT MAX(UserID) FROM tblUsers", objConn)
   Dim objCmd As New OleDbCommand("spAddUser", _
      objConn)
   objCmd.CommandType = CommandType.StoredProcedure

   Dim objParam As New OleDbParameter("@Username", _
      OleDbType.Char)
   objParam.Value = objUser.Username
   objCmd.Parameters.Add(objParam)

   objParam = New OleDbParameter("@Password", _
      OleDbType.Char)
   objParam.Value = objUser.Password
   objCmd.Parameters.Add(objParam)

   objParam = New OleDbParameter("@FirstName", _
      OleDbType.Char)
   objParam.Value = objUser.FirstName
   objCmd.Parameters.Add(objParam)

   objParam = New OleDbParameter("@LastName", _
      OleDbType.Char)
   objParam.Value = objUser.LastName
   objCmd.Parameters.Add(objParam)

   objParam = New OleDbParameter("@Address", _
      OleDbType.Char)
   objParam.Value = objUser.Address
   objCmd.Parameters.Add(objParam)

   objParam = New OleDbParameter("@City", _
      OleDbType.Char)
   objParam.Value = objUser.City
   objCmd.Parameters.Add(objParam)

   objParam = New OleDbParameter("@State", _
      OleDbType.Char)
   objParam.Value = objUser.State
   objCmd.Parameters.Add(objParam)

   objParam = New OleDbParameter("@ZIP", _
      OleDbType.Char)
   objParam.Value = objUser.ZIP
   objCmd.Parameters.Add(objParam)
```

LISTING 22.17 continued

```
106:
107:         objParam = New OleDbParameter("@Phone", _
108:            OleDbType.Char)
109:         objParam.Value = objUser.Phone
110:         objCmd.Parameters.Add(objParam)
111:
112:         objParam = New OleDbParameter("@Email", _
113:            OleDbType.Char)
114:         objParam.Value = objUser.Email
115:         objCmd.Parameters.Add(objParam)
116:
117:         Try
118:            objConn.Open
119:            objCmd.ExecuteNonQuery
120:            objUser.UserID = CType(objCmdID. _
121:               ExecuteScalar, Integer)
122:            objConn.Close
123:         Catch e As Exception
124:            throw e
125:         End Try
126:
127:         if objUser.UserID.ToString = "" then
128:            objUser.UserID = 0
129:         end if
130:      end sub
131:   End Class
132: End Namespace
```

ANALYSIS Whew, that's a lot of code! Luckily though, much of it is easy to follow and redundant. Save this listing as `User.vb` in your `c:\inetpub\wwwroot\tyaspnet21days\day22` directory.

On lines 7–19, you define the `UserDetails` class. This class contains properties that correspond to each of the fields in the user database. This class will be helpful when you need to present a user's complete information, such as during registration.

On line 26, you declare the `Login` function, which takes a username and password, and calls the `spLoginUser` stored procedure to verify a user's credentials. If successful, this method returns the user's ID. On line 31, you create a new `OleDbCommand` object to execute the query, and you tell ASP.NET that you're executing a stored procedure on line 33. Lines 35–43 add parameters used for the query (see Day 12 for information on parameters). The values for these parameters are taken from the parameters supplied to the function.

Caution

> Be sure to add the parameters to your command object in the order that the SQL query expects them! For example, the `spLoginUser` query reads as follows:
>
> ```
> SELECT UserID FROM tblUsers
> WHERE Username=@Username And Password=@Password
> ```
>
> The `@Username` parameter is declared before `@Password`. Therefore, in Listing 22.17, you create the `@Username` parameter first, followed by `@Password`.

On line 45, you open the `OleDbConnection` object declared on line 22; on line 46, you retrieve the first value returned by the query (which should be the user's ID) with the `ExecuteScalar` method; and on line 46, you close the connection. `ExecuteScalar` returns an `Object` data type, so you must cast it to an integer. On lines 52–55, you check to make sure that the query did indeed return a value. (If the parameters were incorrect or the query did not find any valid data, it would return an empty string.) If it didn't, you return zero, signaling to the ASP.NET page that the user credentials are invalid.

The `AddUser` method, beginning on line 58, is responsible for adding new users to the database. It takes a `UserDetails` object as a parameter, and executes the `spAddUser` stored procedure. Much of this method (lines 67–115) simply adds parameters obtained from the `UserDetails` object to the query, so it won't be discussed here.

There is, however, a peculiar situation in this function. After the `spAddUser` query has executed, you need to return the `UserID` of the user you just added, so that you can log the user in correctly. Because of Access's inability to handle output parameters, you have to execute another query to do this (SQL Server could do so easily within one stored procedure). On line 62, you create the query `SELECT MAX(UserID) FROM tblUsers`, which returns the highest `UserID` value from `tblUsers`. Presumably, after the `spAddUser` query has executed, the newest user will have the highest ID because `UserID` is an automatically incrementing field. Therefore, on line 120, after `spAddUser` has been executed, you retrieve the highest `UserID` value, and return it to the calling ASP.NET page. Figure 22.6 illustrates this procedure.

Caution

> Beware that this method of retrieving the last-inserted ID is iffy at best. Especially on higher trafficked sites, there is no guarantee that you will retrieve the correct ID. This method is used simply for illustration purposes.
>
> Instead, you should employ a more secure method. There are quite a few methods available. For example, you could add a date field to your `tblUsers`

table. Before you insert the user, retrieve the date and time from ASP.NET (for example, with `DateTime.Now.ToString`) and insert that value into the database. That way, your ASP.NET page knows accurately when the user was created, and thus, can easily access his or her ID.

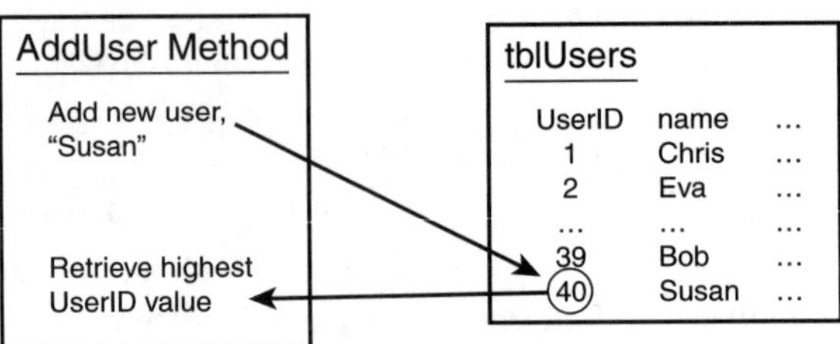

FIGURE 22.6
Retrieving the `UserID` *in a separate step.*

Next, you have the `BananaMobile` object. This object contains methods that add and remove parts from a BananaMobile-in-progress, purchase a specified BananaMobile, and display information about a particular BananaMobile. The code is quite long, so it will be broken up into several listings. Luckily, much of this code is also redundant. Listing 22.18 shows the class declaration and the first method, `AddPart`.

LISTING 22.18 Adding Parts to a BananaMobile

```
Imports System
Imports System.Data
Imports System.Data.OleDb

Namespace BananaMobile

   Public Class BananaMobile
      private objConn As New OleDbConnection("Provider=" & _
            "Microsoft.Jet.OLEDB.4.0;" & _
             "Data Source=c:\ASPNET\data\banana.mdb")

       public Sub AddPart(UserID as Integer, PartID as
➥Integer, Category as String)
          dim strSPName as string

          select case Category
             case "BTS"
                strSPName = "spAddBTS"
             case "Carpet"
                strSPName = "spAddCarpet"
             case "Color"
                strSPName = "spAddColor"
```

LISTING 22.18 continued

```
22:          case "Engine"
23:             strSPName = "spAddEngine"
24:          case "Frame"
25:             strSPName = "spAddFrame"
26:          case "Wheels"
27:             strSPName = "spAddWheels"
28:       end select
29:
30:       Dim objCmd As New OleDbCommand(strSPName, objConn)
31:       objCmd.CommandType = CommandType.StoredProcedure
32:
33:       Dim objParam As New OleDbParameter("@PartID", _
34:          OleDbType.Integer)
35:       objParam.Value = PartID
36:       objCmd.Parameters.Add(objParam)
37:
38:       objParam = New OleDbParameter("@UserID", _
39:          OleDbType.Integer)
40:       objParam.Value = UserID
41:       objCmd.Parameters.Add(objParam)
42:
43:       Try
44:          objConn.Open
45:          objCmd.ExecuteNonQuery
46:          objConn.Close
47:       Catch e As Exception
48:          throw e
49:       End Try
50:    End Sub
51:
```

ANALYSIS The class declaration is standard. On line 8, you create an `OleDbConnection` for use with your methods. Beginning on line 12, the `AddPart` method takes three parameters: the `UserID` of the current user (which corresponds to the shopping cart ID), the part ID to add, and the category to which the new part belongs. Depending on the category, you'll need to execute a different stored procedure, as shown in the `select case` statement on lines 15–28. This `select case` block stores the name of the stored procedure to execute in the variable `strSPName`, and the `OleDbCommand` object on line 30 uses this variable to execute the procedure.

Lines 33–41 simply add parameters to the `OleDbCommand` object, as you did with the `User` object in Listing 22.17. Finally, in the `try` block on lines 43–49, you execute the query with the `ExecuteNonQuery` method, which doesn't return any results. The effect is that when a user adds a part to his BananaMobile, this method executes and uses one of the spAdd*Category* stored procedures to enter the information in the database.

The next five methods in the `BananaMobile` class are fairly simple. They are shown in Listing 22.19.

LISTING 22.19 Various Methods to Control a `BananaMobile` Object

```
      public sub AddCart(UserID as Integer)
         Dim objCmd As New OleDbCommand("spAddCart", _
            objConn)
         objCmd.CommandType = CommandType.StoredProcedure

         Dim objParam As New OleDbParameter("@UserID", _
            OleDbType.Integer)
         objParam.Value = UserID
         objCmd.Parameters.Add(objParam)

         Try
            objConn.Open
            objCmd.ExecuteNonQuery
            objConn.Close
         Catch e As Exception
            throw e
         End Try
      End sub

      public function CartExists(UserID as Integer) as _
         Boolean
         Dim blnEmpty as Boolean = false

         Dim objCmd As New OleDbCommand("spGetCart", _
            objConn)
         objCmd.CommandType = CommandType.StoredProcedure

         Dim objParam As New OleDbParameter("@UserID", _
            OleDbType.Integer)
         objParam.Value = UserID
         objCmd.Parameters.Add(objParam)

         Try
            objConn.Open
            if not objCmd.ExecuteScalar = "" then
               blnEmpty = True
            end if
            objConn.Close
         Catch e As Exception
            throw e
         End Try

         return blnEmpty
      End function
```

LISTING 22.19 continued

```

      public function GetSubTotal(UserID as Integer) as _
         Double
         Dim objSubTotal as Object
          Dim objReader as OleDbDataReader

          Dim objCmd As New OleDbCommand("spGetSubTotal", _
             objConn)
          objCmd.CommandType = CommandType.StoredProcedure

          Dim objParam As New OleDbParameter("@UserID", _
             OleDbType.Integer)
          objParam.Value = UserID
          objCmd.Parameters.Add(objParam)

          Try
             objConn.Open
             objSubTotal = objCmd.ExecuteScalar
             objConn.Close
          Catch e As Exception
             throw e
          End Try

          if objSubTotal.GetType is GetType(DBNull) then
             return 0
          end if
          return CType(objSubTotal, Double)
       End function

       public function GetCategory(Category as String) as _
          OleDbDataReader
          Dim objReader as OleDbDataReader

          Dim objCmd As New OleDbCommand("spGetCategory", _
             objConn)
          objCmd.CommandType = CommandType.StoredProcedure

          Dim objParam As New OleDbParameter("@Category", _
             OleDbType.Char)
          objParam.Value = Category
          objCmd.Parameters.Add(objParam)

          Try
             objConn.Open
             objReader = objCmd.ExecuteReader
          Catch e As Exception
             throw e
          End Try
```

LISTING 22.19 continued

```
144:
145:            return objReader
146:         End function
147:
148:         public Function ViewMobile(UserID as Integer) as _
149:            OleDbDataReader
150:            Dim objReader as OleDbDataReader
151:
152:            Dim objCmd As New OleDbCommand("spViewMobile", _
153:               objConn)
154:            objCmd.CommandType = CommandType.StoredProcedure
155:
156:            Dim objParam As New OleDbParameter("@UserID", _
157:               OleDbType.Integer)
158:            objParam.Value = UserID
159:            objCmd.Parameters.Add(objParam)
160:
161:            Try
162:               objConn.Open
163:               objReader = objCmd.ExecuteReader
164:            Catch e As Exception
165:               throw e
166:            End Try
167:
168:            return objReader
169:         End Function
```

ANALYSIS Each of these methods performs a very similar function: executing a stored procedure. This is a standard procedure—it creates an `OleDbCommand` object and adds parameters—therefore, we won't go into the details of each.

The `AddCart` method on line 52 executes the `spAddCart` stored procedure. When a user first logs in to the site, you'll use this method to create an entry in the `tblShoppingCart` table to store parts that the user adds. It takes a `UserID` parameter, and doesn't return anything.

The `CartExists` function on line 71 executes the `spGetCart` procedure. This function determines whether the user has an associated shopping cart, and returns a Boolean value indicating the answer. This function will be used in conjunction with the previous method, `AddCart`, to first determine whether a user has a cart before adding a new one.

On line 97, the `GetSubTotal` method retrieves the value from the `spGetSubTotal` query; that is, it returns the total price of all items currently in a specified shopping cart. This method is a bit different than the others. If no shopping cart exists for the specified user, the `OleDbCommand.ExecuteScalar` method on line 113 returns an object of type `DBNull`, which is the database's way of saying there was no data. You have to compare the type of the returned data to determine whether an answer or `DBNull` was returned. Use the `GetType` method to compare the results, as shown on line 119.

The `GetCategory` method returns an `OleDbDataReader` that contains all the products in a specified category. This method will be used to display products to users of the site.

Finally, the `ViewMobile` function on line 148 returns all the information about a specified shopping cart. As you can see, you have quite a bit of code here, but not much complex functionality.

The final method for your `BananaMobile` class is the `Purchase` method. It executes the stored procedure `spPurchase`, which transfers information from the `tblShoppingCart` table to the `tblOrders` table. This code, as well as the end of the `BananaMobile` class, is shown in Listing 22.20.

LISTING 22.20 The `Purchase` Method Places an Order from a User

```
      public Sub Purchase(UserID as Integer)
         Dim objReader as OleDbDataReader
         Dim dblSubTotal as Double = 0

         dblSubTotal = GetSubTotal(UserID)

         Dim objCmdPurchase As New OleDbCommand( _
➥"spPurchase", objConn)
         objCmdPurchase.CommandType = CommandType. _
➥StoredProcedure

         Dim objCmdRemove As New OleDbCommand(
➥"spRemoveCart", objConn)
         objCmdRemove.CommandType = CommandType. _
➥StoredProcedure

         Dim objParam As New OleDbParameter("@SubTotal", _
➥OleDbType.Double)
         objParam.Value = dblSubTotal
         objCmdPurchase.Parameters.Add(objParam)

         objParam = New OleDbParameter("@UserID",
➥OleDbType.Integer)
         objParam.Value = UserID
         objCmdPurchase.Parameters.Add(objParam)

         objParam = New OleDbParameter("@UserID",
➥OleDbType.Integer)
```

LISTING 22.20 continued

```
191:            objParam.Value = UserID
192:            objCmdRemove.Parameters.Add(objParam)
193:
194:            Try
195:               objConn.Open
196:               objCmdPurchase.ExecuteNonQuery
197:               objCmdRemove.ExecuteNonQuery
198:               objConn.Close
199:            Catch e As Exception
200:               throw e
201:            End Try
202:         End Sub
203:
204:      End Class
205:   End Namespace
```

ANALYSIS There are three different things that go on in this method. First, on line 175, you retrieve the total price for all items in the shopping cart, which you'll use in the next step. Next, you execute the `spPurchase` stored procedure. This procedure, in addition to the items in the `tblShoppingCart` table, inserts the price into the `tblOrders` table (see Listing 22.13 for details). Finally, you remove the information in `tblShoppingCart` after it has been transferred.

Save Listings 22.18–22.20 in `BananaMobile.vb`. Now both of your business objects are complete. Before you can use them, however, you must compile them. Do so from the command line with the following command:

```
vbc /t:library /out:..\..\bin\BananaMobile.dll /r:System.dll
➥/r:System.data.dll BananaMobile.vb User.vb
```

Note that this command assumes that your `/bin` directory is two levels above the current directory. If it isn't, adjust the command accordingly or simply copy the generated file, `BananaMobile.dll`, into the `/bin` directory.

The ASP.NET Pages

In the previous two sections, you created the data stores and business objects for your BananaMobile application. The only thing left to do is build your ASP.NET pages, and with so much of the functionality already encapsulated in stored procedures and business objects, this step will be a snap.

Before building the pages, let's first examine the user controls you'll need. For this site, you'll use three user controls: a header, a menu sidebar that presents static links for the user, and a control to display current news. The header will contain the logo and links to move around the site, allowing the users to log in, return to the default page, or log out. The menu control will display links to each of the customizable item categories. The news control, which will be used only on the default page (`default.aspx`), will contain links to news items (for this exercise, you'll simply create dead links; that is, links that don't go anywhere).

Listing 22.21 shows the code for the header control.

LISTING 22.21 The Header Control Displays a Common Header for Every Page in the Site

```
<tr>
   <td colspan="2" nowrap>
      <table cellspacing=0 cellpadding=0 width="100%">
         <tr>
            <td><img src="images/bm_sm.gif"></td>
            <td align="right" nowrap>
               <font size="6">
               <b><i>BananaMobiles, Inc</i></b>
               </font>
            </td>
            <td width="10"> </td>
         </tr>
      </table>
   </td>
</tr>
<tr>
   <td colspan="2" nowrap>
      <table cellspacing=0 cellpadding=0 width="100%">
         <tr bgcolor="#AACC88">
            <td align="right">
               <font color="white">
               <a href="/tyaspnet21days/day22/default.aspx">
                  Home</a> |
               <a href="/tyaspnet21days/day22/login.aspx">
                  Login</a> |
               <a href="/tyaspnet21days/day22/
➥MyMobile.aspx">My BananaMobile</a> |
               <a href="/tyaspnet21days/day22/Signout.aspx">
                  Sign Out</a>
               </font>
            </td>
         </tr>
      </table>
   </td>
</tr>
```

Save this file as header.ascx. Recall that user controls don't contain any <html>, <body>, or <form> tags; they present only the UI and any associated logic. This control displays an image on line 5, a logo on line 8, and four links, shown on lines 22, 24, 26, and 28. This is all wrapped in table rows. However, note that the table definition, <table>, is not included. These tags will be placed in the ASP.NET pages. In other words, you'll create "slots" in your pages for your user controls to fit in. When you look at an actual ASP.NET page, this will make more sense.

Note that you might have to replace the images specified in this and subsequent listings with your own. The images here are designed for the examples in this book.

Listing 22.22 shows the menu control, menu.ascx.

LISTING 22.22 The Standard Menu Bar for the Application

```
1:  <td valign="top" width="125">
2:     <table valign="top" height="100%" cellspacing=0
3:        cellpadding=0 width="125">
4:        <tr height="100%">
5:           <td valign="top">
6:               <br>
7:              Personalize your:<p>
8:              <a href="products.aspx?cat=BTS">BTS</a><br>
9:              <a href="products.aspx?cat=Carpet">Carpet</a><br>
10:              <a href="products.aspx?cat=Color">Color</a><br>
11:              <a href="products.aspx?cat=Engine">Engine</a>
12:              <br>
13:              <a href="products.aspx?cat=Frame">Frame</a><br>
14:              <a href="products.aspx?cat=Wheels">Wheels</a>
15:           </td>
16:        </tr>
17:     </table>
18:  </td>
```

This user control also presents static HTML; specifically, six links on lines 8–14. This control also is only part of a table definition; the rest will be in the ASP.NET page. Notice that each of the links goes to the same place: products.aspx. You'll get to the details in a moment, but this one page will be responsible for displaying the different categories, with the aid of a querystring variable.

Listing 22.23 shows the final user control.

LISTING 22.23 Displaying News Headlines

```
1:   <br>
2:  <table width="250">
3:     <tr>
4:        <td valign="top"><b>Banana Headlines</b></td>
5:     </tr>
6:     <tr>
7:        <td valign="top">
8:           <li><a href="somewhere.aspx">Banana shortage
9:              reported in Bolivia</a><br>
10:           <li><a href="somewhere.aspx">United Nations
11:              promises no more banana slaughterings</a><br>
12:           <li><a href="somewhere.aspx">73rd Banana Cup
13:              begins in Spain</a><br>
14:           <li><a href="somewhere.aspx">Don't forget the
15:              April 16th Banana tax deadline!</a><br>
16:           <li><a href="somewhere.aspx">New use found for
17:              bananas, brings total to 13,456</a><br>
18:        </td>
19:     </tr>
20: </table>
```

Save this listing as `news.ascx`. On lines 8–17, you display five imaginary headlines with links that lead nowhere. In the future, these headlines and their links could be pulled from a database or XML file, but for now, static HTML will suffice.

Now on to the ASP.NET pages! (Note that we'll build all the `.aspx` files first, and then build the `web.config` file to implement security.) The default or home page for an application is typically named `default.aspx`, so let's start with this page. The `default.aspx` page will simply welcome the user to the BananaMobiles site, and will implement all three user controls. Listing 22.24 shows the code for `default.aspx`.

LISTING 22.24 The Home Page Doesn't Display Any Dynamic Content

```
<%@ Page Language="VB" %>
<%@ Register TagPrefix="Banana" TagName="Header"
➥Src="header.ascx" %>
<%@ Register TagPrefix="Banana" TagName="Menu"
➥Src="menu.ascx" %>
<%@ Register TagPrefix="Banana" TagName="News"
➥Src="news.ascx" %>

<html><body background="images/banana_bg.gif">
   <table height="100%" cellspacing=0 cellpadding=0 width="100%">
   <Banana:Header runat="server"/>
   <tr height="100%">
```

LISTING 22.24 continued

```
10:        <Banana:Menu runat="server"/>
11:
12:        <td align=left valign="top" width=100% nowrap>
13:           <table height="100%" valign="top" align="left"
14:              cellspacing=0 cellpadding=0 width="100%">
15:           <tr height="100%" valign="top">
16:              <td nowrap>
17:                 <table cellspacing=0 cellpadding=0
18:                    width="100%">
19:                 <tr>
20:                    <td valign="top">
21:                        <br>
22:                       <b>Welcome to BananaMobiles!</b>
23:                       <p>
24:                       With this site, you can build your own
25:                       customized BananaMobile and order it
26:                       online! Choose from the options on the
27:                       left to select parts to build your
28:                       BananaMobile!
29:                       <p>
30:                       Each BananaMobile comes built-in with
31:                       BananaConnect technology, to connect
32:                       you to the Internet without leaving
33:                       your banana. Our proprietary software
34:                       allows you to post track records to
35:                       compete online!
36:                    </td>
37:                    <td valign="top">
38:                       <Banana:News runat="server"/>
39:                    </td>
40:                 </tr>
41:                 </table>
42:              </td>
43:           </tr>
44:           </table>
45:        </td>
46:     </tr>
47:     </table>
48:  </body></html>
```

ANALYSIS This page contains no ASP.NET code; it is all plain HTML and Web control tags. The code is rather long, but most of the length is due to the HTML tables that are used for page layout. On line 8, you implement the header user control. Recall from Listing 22.21 that this control started and ended with `<tr>` tags—now you see how they fit into the ASP.NET page. You could simply copy the code from the user control and paste it in on line 8, but the user control makes things easier to follow.

The menu user control is on line 10. It presents a column on the left side of the page. Finally, the news control is on line 38, which displays on the right side of the page. Note that the section in lines 21–38 is the main area of the page, where much of the information will be presented to the user. Therefore, this listing serves as a template for all other pages in the site. Each page will simply replace lines 21–38 with its own information. Therefore, not all the presentation code for the ASP.NET pages will be shown—only the information particular to each page.

22

Figure 22.7 shows this page from the browser.

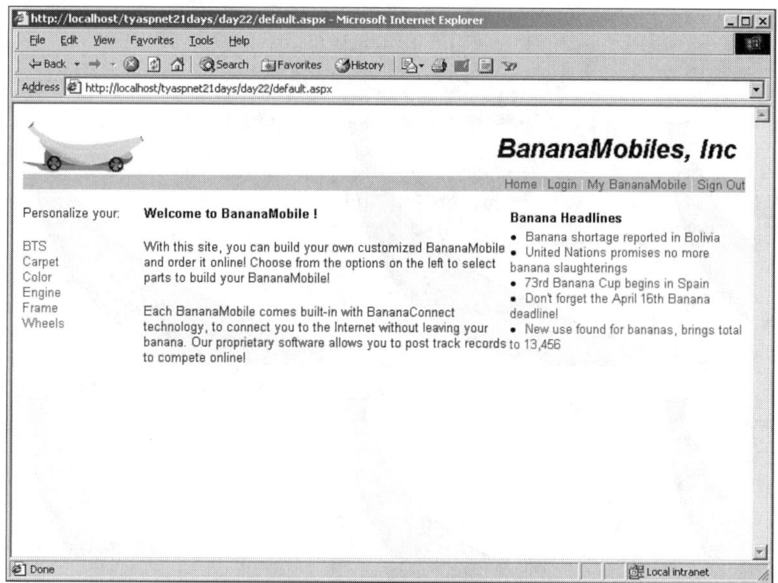

FIGURE 22.7
The BananaMobiles home page.

All the necessary links are displayed on the home page, allowing easy movement from page to page.

The next most important pages are the ones that allow users to log in and register to the site. You've built quite a few of these types of pages throughout this book, so this should be familiar to you. Listing 22.25 shows the login page.

LISTING 22.25 Using Forms Authentication to Validate Users

```
<%@ Page Language="VB" %>
<%@ Register TagPrefix="Banana" TagName="Header"
➥Src="header.ascx" %>
```

LISTING 22.25 continued

```
<%@ Register TagPrefix="Banana" TagName="Menu"
➥Src="menu.ascx" %>
<%@ Import Namespace="System.Data" %>
<%@ Import Namespace="System.Data.OleDb" %>

<script runat="server">
   Sub Login(Sender As Object, e As EventArgs)
      dim objUser as New BananaMobile.User
      dim objBM as New BananaMobile.BananaMobile
      dim intID as integer

      intID = objUser.Login(tbUsername.Text, _
         tbPassword.Text)
      if intID <> 0 then
         Session("UserID") = intID

         'check if user has a cart
         if not objBM.CartExists(intID) then
            objBM.AddCart(intID)
         end if

         FormsAuthentication.RedirectFromLoginPage(intID, _
            false)
      else
         lblMessage.Text = "<font color=red>That is not a
➥valid login or password</font>"
      end if
   End Sub
</script>
<html><body background="images/banana_bg.gif">
   <table height="100%" cellspacing=0 cellpadding=0
      width="100%">
      <Banana:Header runat="server"/>
      <tr height="100%">
         <Banana:Menu runat="server"/>

         <td align=left valign="top" width=100% nowrap>
            <table height="100%" align="left" cellspacing=0
               cellpadding=0 width="100%">
               <tr height="100%" valign="top">
                  <td nowrap>
                     <table cellspacing=0 cellpadding=0
                        width="100%">
                        <tr>
                           <td valign="top">
                               <br>
                              Please enter your username and
                              password to gain access to
```

LISTING 22.25 continued

```
these secure features.
<p>
Or, if you are a new user,
click <a href="register.aspx">
here</a> to register and gain
access to our site!<p>

<asp:Label id="lblMessage"
   runat="server" />
<form runat="server">
   <table>
   <tr>
      <td width="75"
         rowspan="3"> 
      </td>
      <td width="50"
         valign="top">
         <font face="arial">
         Username:
         </font>
      </td>
      <td width="50"
         valign="top">
         <font face="arial">
         <asp:Textbox
            id="tbUsername"
            runat="server" />
         </font>
      </td>
   </tr>
   <tr>
      <td valign="top">
         <font face="arial">
         Password:
         </font>
      </td>
      <td valign="top">
         <font face="arial">
         <asp:Textbox
            id="tbPassword"
            runat="server"
            TextMode="password"/>
         </font>
      </td>
   </tr>
   <tr>
      <td align="right"
         colspan="2">
```

LISTING 22.25 continued

```
 97:                                      <font face="arial">
 98:                                      <asp:Button
 99:                                         id="btSubmit"
100:                                          runat="server"
101:                                          OnClick="Login"
102:                                          Text="Submit" />
103:                                       </font>
104:                                    </td>
105:                                 </tr>
106:                                 </table>
107:                              </form>
108:                           </td>
109:                        </tr>
110:                     </table>
111:                 </td>
112:              </tr>
113:           </table>
114:        </td>
115:     </tr>
116:   </table>
117: </body></html>
```

Save this page as `login.aspx`. There is one method on this page, `Login`, which is executed when the user clicks a submit button (not shown). This method creates instances of both of your business objects, `User` and `BananaMobile`, on lines 9 and 10. Then, on line 13, you use the `Login` method of the `User` object to determine whether the credentials supplied by the user are valid. If they are (and consequently `intID` is a nonzero value), you store the user's ID in a session variable on line 16. You'll use this variable throughout your pages to gather information about a particular shopping cart.

On lines 19–21, you check whether the current user has a shopping cart. That is, if he has a row in the `tblShoppingCart` table that matches his user ID. This is accomplished with the `CartExists` method. If one doesn't exist, you create one on line 20 with the `AddCart` method. Recall that both these methods take a user ID as a parameter.

Finally, the user is authenticated and directed back to the page he came from on line 23 (see yesterday's lesson for more information on security and forms authentication). This page is shown in Figure 22.8.

22

FIGURE 22.8
The login page.

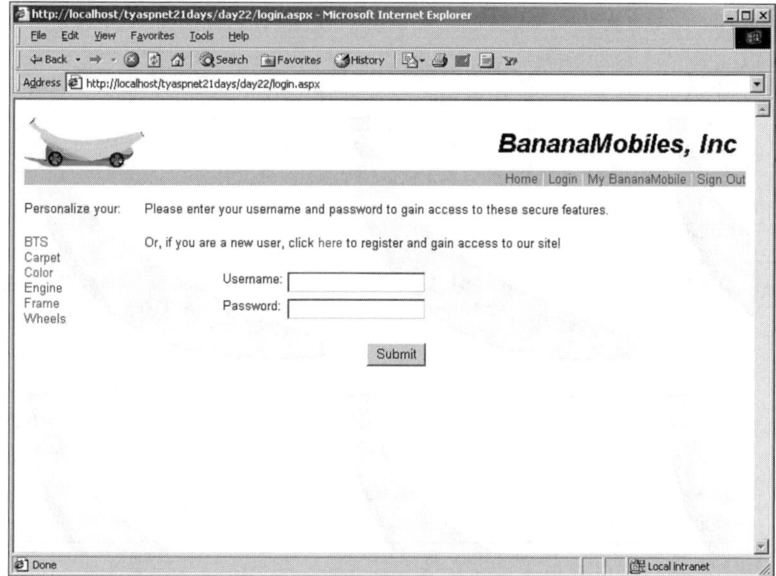

The registration page, thanks to your `User` business object, is fairly simple. It needs only to gather information from a user, and call the `User.AddUser` method with the appropriate parameters. Listing 22.26 shows the code for this page. Because the HTML portion of this page is standard, and follows the same pattern as the previous two pages, I won't include it here (besides, the HTML code would run on for pages!).

LISTING 22.26 Gathering User Information

```
<%@ Page Language="VB" %>
<%@ Register TagPrefix="Banana" TagName="Header"
➥Src="header.ascx" %>
<%@ Register TagPrefix="Banana" TagName="Menu"
➥Src="menu.ascx" %>

<script runat="server">
   Sub Submit(Sender As Object, e As EventArgs)
      if Page.IsValid then
         dim objUserDetails as New BananaMobile.UserDetails
         dim objUser as New BananaMobile.User

         objUserDetails.Username = tbUName.Text
         objUserDetails.Password = tbPword.Text
         objUserDetails.Firstname = tbFName.Text
         objUserDetails.Lastname = tbLName.Text
         objUserDetails.Address = tbAddress.Text
```

LISTING 22.26 continued

```
16:            objUserDetails.City = tbCity.Text
17:            objUserDetails.State = tbState.Text
18:            objUserDetails.ZIP = tbZIP.Text
19:            objUserDetails.Phone = tbPhone.Text
20:            objUserDetails.Email = tbEmail.Text
21:
22:            objUser.AddUser(objUserDetails)
23:
24:            Session("UserID") = objUserDetails.UserID
25:            FormsAuthentication.SetAuthCookie(objUserDetails. _
26:               UserID, false)
27:            Response.Redirect("default.aspx")
28:         else
29:            lblMessage.Text = "Some information is invalid.
➥User not added to database."
30:         end if
31:      End Sub
32:   </script>
```

ANALYSIS Save this listing as `register.aspx`. Similar to the login page, this listing only has one method, `Submit`, which executes when the user submits the form. In our case, we've used Validation controls to ensure the user doesn't leave out information. The `Page.IsValid` check on line 7 ensures that all the information has been entered correctly. On lines 8 and 9, you create a `UserDetails` object to hold the information collected in the form, and a `User` object. On lines 11–20, you set values for the properties of the `UserDetails` object from text boxes the user has filled out (not shown here). You then pass this data-filled `UserDetails` object to the `User.AddUser` method on line 22.

Finally, after the user information has been added, the `AddUser` method assigns the new user ID to the `UserDetails`' `UserID` property. You store this in a session variable on line 24, and authenticate the user on line 25. Essentially, you are logging the user in to your site; after all, there's no reason to have him fill out this form and then have to log in again. This page produces something similar to the screenshot in Figure 22.9.

Now that you've got the basic functionality for your site, you can allow users to browse the products you have to offer. This will be accomplished via one ASP.NET page. You'll customize the page depending on what category of items a user wants to see. Let's take a look at the code first, shown in Listing 22.27.

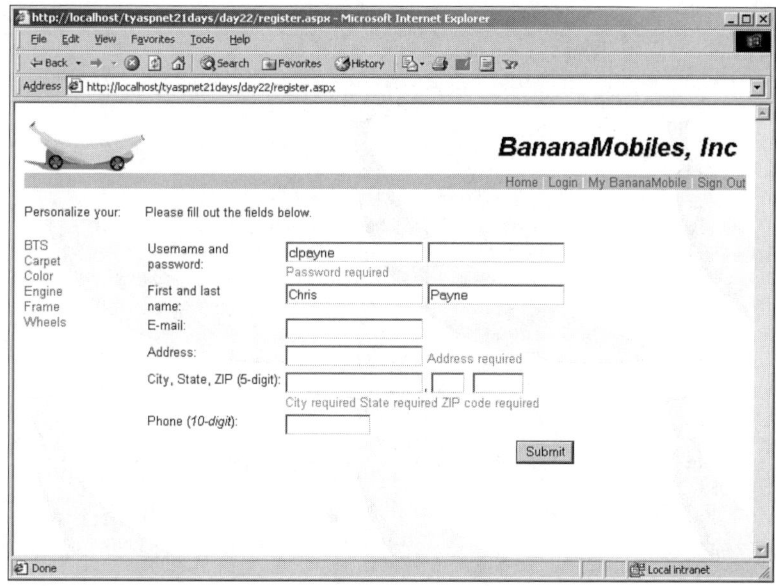

FIGURE 22.9
The registration page.

LISTING 22.27 Browsing Product Categories

```
<%@ Page Language="VB" %>
<%@ Register TagPrefix="Banana" TagName="Header"
➥Src="header.ascx" %>
<%@ Register TagPrefix="Banana" TagName="Menu"
➥Src="menu.ascx" %>
<%@ Import Namespace="System.Data" %>
<%@ Import Namespace="System.Data.OleDb" %>

<script runat="server">
   Sub Page_Load(Sender As Object, e As EventArgs)

      ' Obtain CategoryID from QueryString
      Dim CategoryID As String = CStr(Request.Params("cat"))

      'set image and label
      imgCategory.ImageURL = "images/" & CategoryID & ".gif"
      lblCategory.Text = "<b>" & CategoryID & "</b>"

      ' Populate List with Category Products
      Dim objBanana As New BananaMobile.BananaMobile
      Dim objReader As OleDbDataReader = objBanana. _
         GetCategory(CategoryId)
      dlItems.DataSource = objReader
      dlItems.DataBind()
      objReader.Close()
```

LISTING 22.27 continued

```
24:
25:     End Sub
26:  </script>
27:  ...
28:  ...
29:     <td valign="top" width="110">
30:        <asp:Image id="imgCategory" runat="server"
31:           Border="1" Align="TextTop"/><br>
32:        <asp:Label id="lblCategory" runat="server"/>
33:     </td>
34:     <td valign="top">
35:        <form runat="server">
36:           <asp:DataList id="dlItems" RepeatColumns="2"
37:              runat="server">
38:              <ItemTemplate>
39:                 <table border=0 width="200">
40:                 <tr>
41:                    <td width="200" valign="center">
42:                       <b><%# Container.DataItem("Name")
➥%></b><br>
43:                       <%# Container.DataItem("Description")
➥%><br>
44:
45:                       <b>Price: </b><%# System.String.
➥Format("{0:c}", Container.DataItem("Price")) %><br>
46:
47:                       <a href="AddToCart.aspx?PartID=<%#
➥Container.DataItem("PartID") %>&cat=<%#
➥Container.DataItem("Category") %>">
48:                          <font color="#9D0000"><b>Add To
49:                          Cart<b></font>
50:                       </a>
51:                    </td>
52:                 </tr>
53:                 </table>
54:              </ItemTemplate>
55:           </asp:DataList>
56:        </form>
57:     </td>
```

ANALYSIS Save this listing as `products.aspx`. In a nutshell, this page displays all items in a specified category in a `DataList` control. The `DataList` contains links that allow users to add an item to the shopping cart. Let's take a look at the code declaration block on lines 7–26 first.

All of this page's functionality occurs in the `Page_Load` event. On line 12, you retrieve the category to be displayed from the querystring. For example, the string `"Engine"` would cause this page to display all the items belonging to the engine category (see Listing 22.22 for details on where these querystring values came from).

You've created an image for each category of items. These images are stored in an `images` subdirectory, and are named following their categories. For example, the image for the frame category is `frame.gif`. Thus, line 14 causes the image control on line 30 to display the image appropriate for the selected category. Line 15 simply displays the category name to the user in the label on line 32.

On lines 18 and 19, you instantiate a new `BananaMobile` object and retrieve all items for the specified category using the `GetCategory` method, which returns an `OleDbDataReader`. Then on lines 22–23, you bind the data to the `DataList` on line 36 and close the data reader.

Let's next move down to the `DataList`. Using the `ItemTemplate` tag on line 38, you define a custom layout to display the products. Specifically, you use a table to present the names and descriptions for each product. Line 42 binds the name, and line 43 binds the description for each item (see Day 9, "Using Databases with ASP.NET," for more information on binding data). Line 45 binds the price data to the page, but uses the `Format` method of the `String` class to format it first. Let's examine this method in more detail.

The `Format` method takes two parameters: one that specifies how to format the string and another that specifies what string to format. The first parameter uses special characters to denote the formatting (similar to regular expressions). It follows the following format:

```
{ N [, M ][: formatString ]}
```

where *`N`* is an integer representing the argument to be formatted, *`M`* is an optional integer indicating the width of the region that contains the formatted string, and *`formatString`* is an optional string of formatting code. For example, if you called:

```
Format("You get {0:####} dollars!.", 3453)
```

thc output would be

```
"You get 3453 dollars!"
```

The string `{0:####}` means format the first parameter as four numeric digits. If you are familiar with C or C#, this syntax will look familiar to you. In this case, line 45, `Format("{0:c}", Container.DataItem("Price"))`, tells ASP.NET to format the price of each item as currency, which means it automatically adds a currency symbol, such as $, to the value.

Finally, line 47 binds the `PartID` and `Category` to a link in the page. This link points to `AddToCart.aspx`, which is responsible for adding the item to the database (you'll get to that in a moment). Depending on the category selected and the data you entered into the `tblParts` table, this page produces pages similar to Figures 22.10 and 22.11.

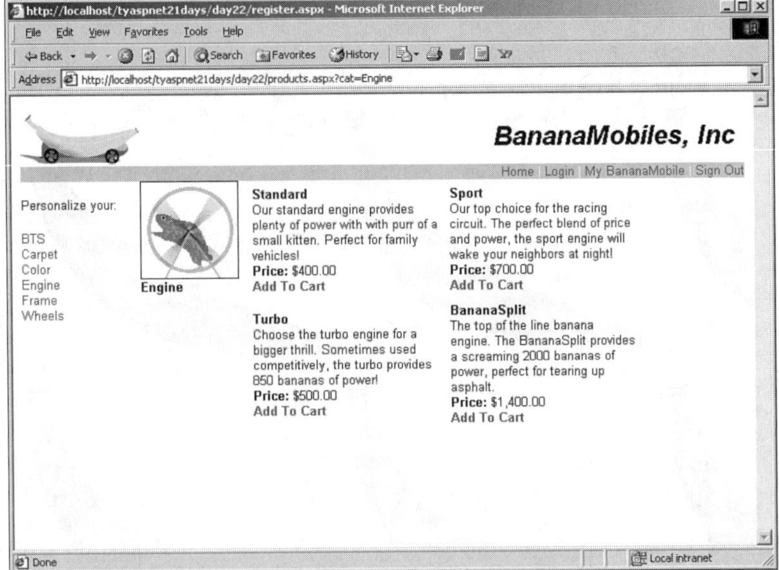

FIGURE 22.10
Displaying the Engine category.

Now that users can browse and select items, you need to be able to add the items to the database (specifically, the user's shopping cart). Listing 22.28 shows `AddToCart.aspx`, which accomplishes just that.

LISTING 22.28 Adding Selected Items to the Database

```
<%@ Page Language="VB" %>
<%@ Import Namespace="System.Data" %>
<%@ Import Namespace="System.Data.OleDb" %>

<script runat="server">
   private objConn As New OleDbConnection("Provider=" & _
            "Microsoft.Jet.OLEDB.4.0;" & _
            "Data Source=c:\ASPNET\data\banana.mdb")

   Sub Page_Load(Sender As Object, e As EventArgs)
      If not Request.Params("PartID") is Nothing Then
         Dim intUserID as integer = Session("UserID")
         Dim objBM As New BananaMobile.BananaMobile

```

```
15:            ' Add Product Item to Cart
16:            objBM.AddPart(intUserID, CInt(Request.Params(
➥"PartID")), Request.Params("cat").ToString)
17:         End If
18:         Response.Redirect("MyMobile.aspx")
19:      End Sub
20:   </script>
```

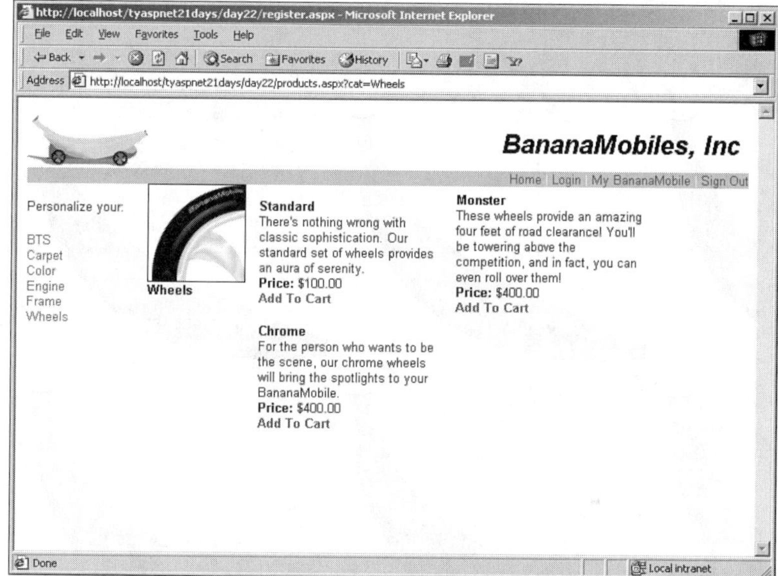

FIGURE 22.11
Displaying the Wheels category.

ANALYSIS This page doesn't contain any UI—it simply adds the item to the `tblShoppingCart` table in the database and immediately redirects the visitor to another page, `MyMobile.aspx`, which you'll look at in a moment. When this page loads, you first check whether a part ID is available in the querystring, as shown on line 11. If so, you call the `BananaMobile.AddPart` method on line 18, which takes three parameters: the `UserID` of the cart to add the part to, the `PartID` to add to the database, and the category to which the part belongs.

Recall that the `AddPart` method examines the category to determine which stored procedure to execute. Using the data that you bound to the link in the `DataList` in `products.aspx`, `PartID`, and `Category`, and the user ID stored in the session variable, this page can add whatever item you want, to the cart you specify.

`MyMobile.aspx`, shown in Listing 22.29, displays the status of the current shopping cart to the user. It also allows them to remove items from their cart. Let's look at the code.

LISTING 22.29 Viewing BananaMobile Information

```
<%@ Page Language="VB" %>
<%@ Register TagPrefix="Banana" TagName="Header"
➥Src="header.ascx" %>
<%@ Register TagPrefix="Banana" TagName="Menu"
➥Src="menu.ascx" %>
<%@ Import Namespace="System.Data" %>
<%@ Import Namespace="System.Data.OleDb" %>

<script runat="server">
   Sub Page_Load(Sender As Object, e As EventArgs)
      dim intUserID as Integer = Session("UserID")
      dim objBM as new BananaMobile.BananaMobile

      lblSubTotal.Text = objBM.GetSubTotal(intUserID)

      if lblSubTotal.Text = "0" then
         btPurchase.Visible = False
      end if

      ' Populate List with Category Products
      Dim objReader As OleDbDataReader = objBM.
➥ViewMobile(intUserID)
      dlItems.DataSource = objReader
      dlItems.DataBind()
      objReader.Close()
   End Sub

   Sub BuyIt(Sender As Object, e As EventArgs)
      dim objBM as new BananaMobile.BananaMobile

      objBM.Purchase(Session("UserID"))

      Response.Redirect("thanks.aspx")
   End Sub
</script>

   <td valign="top">
       <br>
      <b>Your BananaMobile:</b><p>
      <asp:DataList id="dlItems" runat="server" Width=100%>
         <ItemTemplate>
            <table width="100%">
            <tr>
               <td width="25%">
                  <%# Container.DataItem("Category") %>
               </td>
               <td width="25%">
                  <%# Container.DataItem("Name") %>
               </td>
```

LISTING 22.29 continued

```
47:                 <td width="25%">
48:                    <b>Price: </b><%# System.String.
➥Format("{0:c}", Container.DataItem("Price")) %>
49:                 </td>
50:                 <td width="25%">
51:                    <a href="RemoveItem.aspx?PartID=<%#
➥Container.DataItem("PartID") %>&cat=<%#
➥Container.DataItem("Category") %>">Remove</a>
52:                 </td>
53:              </tr>
54:              </table>
55:           </ItemTemplate>
56:        </asp:DataList>
57:        <br>
58:        <form runat="server">
59:           <b>SubTotal: $<asp:Label id="lblSubTotal"
60:              runat="server"/></b>
61:           <p>
62:           <center>
63:           <asp:Button id="btPurchase" runat="server"
64:              Text="Buy It!"
65:              OnClick="BuyIt"/>
66:           </center>
67:        </form>
68:     </td>
```

ANALYSIS This page is very similar to `products.aspx`, except that it uses a `DataList` control to display all the items in the specified shopping cart instead of category. Even the formatting of the data is the same, such as the price on line 51. This page has a button that allows the user to purchase the displayed BananaMobile.

When the page loads, you retrieve the subtotal and display it in the label on line 59. If this subtotal is zero, it means that there are no items in the shopping cart. If there are no items in the shopping cart, you don't want to allow the user to click the Purchase button on line 63. Line 14 checks this condition, and sets the button to be invisible to the user if the subtotal is zero, effectively preventing him from submitting the form.

On lines 19–22, you simply retrieve the BananaMobile information with the `BananaMobile.ViewMobile` method, and bind it to the `DataList`.

The `BuyIt` method, beginning on line 25, executes when the user submits the form. This method simply calls the `Purchase` method of the `BananaMobile` object, and redirects to a static thank-you page, thanking the user for purchasing with BananaMobile, Inc. This is left for you to develop. Figure 22.12 shows the `MyMobile.aspx` page when viewed from the browser, after adding some items to the cart.

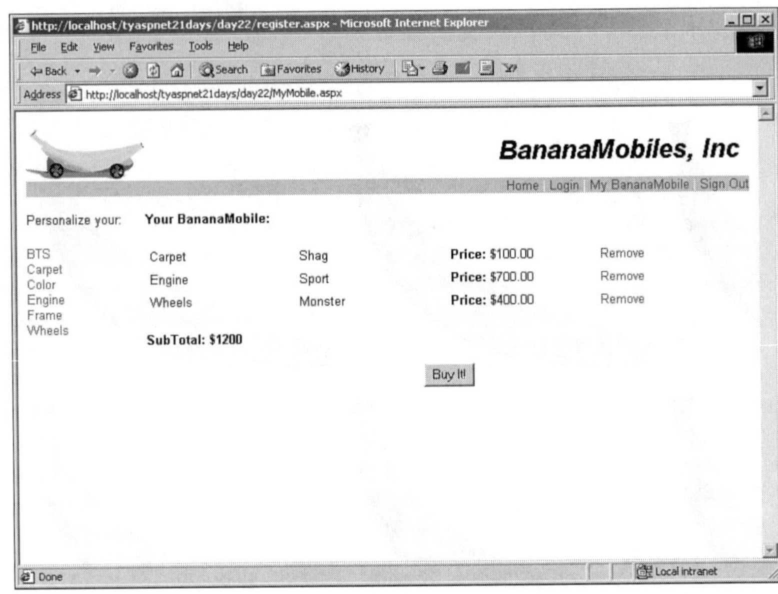

FIGURE 22.12
Viewing the information for the current BananaMobile.

The link on line 51 allows users to remove certain items from their BananaMobile. This page, `RemoveItem.aspx`, is nearly identical to the `AddToCart.aspx` page. Let's take a quick look at it in Listing 22.30.

LISTING 22.30 Removing Items from the Shopping Cart

```
<%@ Page Language="VB" %>
<%@ Import Namespace="System.Data" %>
<%@ Import Namespace="System.Data.OleDb" %>

<script runat="server">
   private objConn As New OleDbConnection("Provider=" & _
            "Microsoft.Jet.OLEDB.4.0;" & _
            "Data Source=c:\ASPNET\data\banana.mdb")

    Sub Page_Load(Sender As Object, e As EventArgs)
       If not Request.Params("PartID") is Nothing Then
          Dim objBM As New BananaMobile.BananaMobile

          ' Add Product Item to Cart
          objBM.AddPart(CInt(Session("UserID")), 0,
➥Request.Params("cat").ToString)
       End If
       Response.Redirect("MyMobile.aspx")
    End Sub
</script>
```

The only difference between this page and `AddToCart.aspx` is the second parameter of the `AddPart` method on line 15. This parameter normally specifies which part to add to the database. However, the user is removing this category of item from his BananaMobile altogether, so you can simply set this parameter to `0`.

There's only one more page to go: `signout.aspx`, which allows users to log off from your application. This page is shown in Listing 22.31.

LISTING 22.31 Logging Users Off

```
<%@ Page Language="VB" %>
<%@ Register TagPrefix="Banana" TagName="Header"
➥Src="header.ascx" %>
<%@ Register TagPrefix="Banana" TagName="Menu"
➥Src="menu.ascx" %>

<script runat="server">
   sub Page_Load(Sender as object, e as eventargs)
      FormsAuthentication.SignOut
   end sub
</script>
<html><body background="images/banana_bg.gif">
   <table height="100%" cellspacing=0 cellpadding=0
      width="100%">
      <Banana:Header runat="server"/>
      <tr height="100%">
         <Banana:Menu runat="server"/>

         <td align=left valign="top" width=100% nowrap>
            <table height="100%" valign="top" align="left"
               cellspacing=0 cellpadding=0 width="100%">
               <tr height="100%" valign="top">
                  <td nowrap>
                     <table cellspacing=0 cellpadding=0
                        width="100%">
                        <tr>
                           <td valign="top">
                               <br>
                              You have been logged off.
                              Thanks for visiting!
                           </td>
                        </tr>
                     </table>
                  </td>
               </tr>
            </table>
```

Listing 22.31 continued

```
            </td>
         </tr>
      </table>
   </body></html>
```

As you can see, this page only does one thing: call the `FormsAuthentication.SignOut` method to delete the authentication cookie and log users off the site.

So far, I've discussed every page in the site, but I've neglected to mention how to implement security. Because you're using forms authentication, this can be accomplished with only a few lines in the `web.config` file, as shown in Listing 22.32.

Listing 22.32 Using `web.config` to Provide Security

```
1:  <configuration>
2:     <system.web>
3:        <authentication mode="Forms">
4:           <forms name="AuthCookie" loginUrl="
➥day22/login.aspx" />
5:        </authentication>
6:     </system.web>
7:     <location path="day22/AddToCart.aspx">
8:        <system.web>
9:           <authorization>
10:              <deny users="?"/>
11:           </authorization>
12:        </system.web>
13:     </location>
14:     <location path="day22/MyMobile.aspx">
15:        <system.web>
16:           <authorization>
17:              <deny users="?"/>
18:           </authorization>
19:        </system.web>
20:     </location>
21:  </configuration>
```

Save this file in the root directory of your application (for example, `c:\inetpub\wwwroot`). If you already have an existing `web.config` file, you can simply merge the settings of this one with the existing one. This file does three things. First, it sets the authentication mode to `Forms` on line 3. Line 4 tells ASP.NET that if an unauthenticated user accesses resources that aren't available to him, it should redirect him to the `login.aspx` page of the application. The `name` attribute specifies that the authentication cookie generated should be named `AuthCookie`.

The `location` tags on lines 7 and 14 restrict access to specific files, namely the `AddToCart.aspx` and `MyMobile.aspx` pages. The reason these two pages are used is simple. You want to allow users to browse the site, but only registered users can add items to their shopping cart, which is accomplished with `AddToCart.aspx`. Therefore, this file is restricted to non-anonymous users. Also, unauthenticated users should not be able to see information about their BananaMobile; if they are unauthenticated, you have no idea who they are, and thus you don't know which shopping cart belongs to them. If they try to access `MyMobile.aspx` without logging on first, they'll receive an error because the application doesn't know who they are.

That's all there is to it! You examined quite a few files, but many of them perform similar functionality. After you've built the default page, you can follow its template to rapidly produce the other pages in the site. And because all the functionality can be accomplished with one or two calls to your business objects, none of these ASP.NET pages has complex functionality; they have only code that deals directly with the UI.

This process went fairly smoothly because you spent a bit of time designing the application beforehand. By developing the application in the order you did (database items and logic, followed by business objects, and then ASP.NET pages), the process went quickly, and you didn't have to switch development gears by moving to different tiers of the application before one tier was finished.

However, you're not quite done yet! There's still the matter of the BananaConnect system and the Web Service.

The Web Service

The BananaConnect system needs to be able to post information about each BananaMobile easily from a remote system. BananaMobile, Inc. has told you that it only wants the functionality to add this information, but that the company itself will build the interface. Thus, you've decided to create a Web Service; the functionality will be there, and BananaMobile, Inc. will be free to implement it as the company sees fit.

Additionally, only registered BananaMobile owners can post information to the service. This means that the Web Service must implement some form of security to control access. SOAP headers are a logical choice to add this functionality (see Day 17, "Consuming and Securing XML Web Services," for more information on using these custom headers to implement secure Web Services). Let's take a look at the code, shown in Listing 22.33.

LISTING 22.33 The Secure BananaConnect Web Service

```
<%@ WebService Language="VB" Class="BananaConnect" %>

Imports System
Imports System.Data
Imports System.Data.OleDb
Imports System.Web.Services
Imports System.Web.Services.Protocols

Public Class Authenticator : Inherits SoapHeader
    Public Username as string
    Public Password as string
 End Class

 public Class BananaConnect : Inherits WebService
    public sHeader as Authenticator
    private objConn As New OleDbConnection("Provider=" & _
       "Microsoft.Jet.OLEDB.4.0;" & _
       "Data Source=c:\ASPNET\data\banana.mdb")

    <WebMethod(), SoapHeader("sHeader")> Public sub
➥UpdateData(UserID as Integer, Mileage as Double,
➥MaxSpeed as Double, Throttle as Double)
       if sHeader is Nothing then
          throw new ArgumentNullException()
       end if

       if Authenticate(sHeader.UserName, sHeader.Password) then
          Dim objCmd As New OleDbCommand("spBananaConnect", _
             objConn)
          objCmd.CommandType = CommandType.StoredProcedure

          Dim objParam As New OleDbParameter("@UserID", _
             OleDbType.Integer)
          objParam.Value = UserID
          objCmd.Parameters.Add(objParam)

          objParam = New OleDbParameter("@Mileage", _
             OleDbType.Double)
          objParam.Value = Mileage
          objCmd.Parameters.Add(objParam)

          objParam = New OleDbParameter("@MaxSpeed", _
             OleDbType.Double)
          objParam.Value = MaxSpeed
          objCmd.Parameters.Add(objParam)

          objParam = New OleDbParameter("@Throttle", _
             OleDbType.Double)
```

LISTING 22.33 continued

```
         objParam.Value = Throttle
         objCmd.Parameters.Add(objParam)

         objParam = New OleDbParameter("@Date", _
            OleDbType.Date)
         objParam.Value = DateTime.Now.ToString
         objCmd.Parameters.Add(objParam)

         Try
            objConn.Open
            objCmd.ExecuteNonQuery
            objConn.Close
         Catch e As Exception
            throw e
         End Try
      end if
   End sub

   private function Authenticate(strUser as string, strPass as string) as boolean
      try
         dim intID as integer = 0
         dim objCmd as new OleDbCommand("spLoginUser", _
            objConn)

         Dim objParam As New OleDbParameter("@Username", _
            OleDbType.Integer)
         objParam.Value = strUser
         objCmd.Parameters.Add(objParam)

         objParam = New OleDbParameter("@Password", _
            OleDbType.Integer)
         objParam.Value = strPass
         objCmd.Parameters.Add(objParam)

         objConn.Open
         intID = CType(objCmd.ExecuteScalar, Integer)
         objConn.Close

         if intID.ToString = "" then
            return false
         end if
         return true
      catch ex as OleDbException
         return false
      end try
   end function
End Class
```

ANALYSIS Save this file as `BananaConnect.asmx`. This Web Service has two classes. The first, `Authenticator`, shown on lines 9–12, contains two properties that will be used to authenticate users. This class inherits from the `SoapHeader` class, so you know that it will be sent along as extra baggage with the regular communication from the consumer of this service.

The second class, `BananaConnect`, beginning on line 14, is the actual Web Service. This is indicated on line 1 with the `Class` attribute of the `@ WebService` directive. This class must inherit from the `WebService` class. On line 15, you declare an instance of the `Authenticator` class, and on line 16, you declare an `OleDbConnection` object—both of which will be used in your methods.

The only method available to consumers, `UpdateDate`, begins on line 20. Notice the use of the `<WebMethod>` and `<SoapHeader>` attributes in the function declaration. The first attribute is necessary for clients to be able to access this method over the Internet. The second attribute specifies that this method will require a SOAP header to be sent along in addition to the regular communication. On lines 21–23, you check whether a SOAP header was indeed sent, and if not, you throw an exception (see Day 20, "Debugging ASP.NET Pages," for details on exceptions).

Line 25 calls the `Authenticate` method to validate the credentials supplied in the SOAP header. You'll get to this method in a moment. If the credentials are valid, you insert the supplied data into the database. Lines 26–61 should look familiar: You create an `OleDbCommand` object, build parameters, and execute the `spBananaConnect` query.

Finally, the `Authenticate` method on line 65 is very similar to the `Login` method shown in Listing 22.17. It takes a username and password as parameters, and executes the `spLoginUser` stored procedure to determine whether the credentials match a registered user. This is the heart of the validation mechanism for this Web Service.

Naturally, you want to test this service before you let BananaMobile have it. Let's do so using ASP.NET and Http-Post. Unfortunately, when you try to access this service through the browser with the URL `http://localhost/tyaspnet21days/day22/BananaConnect.asmx?op=UpdateData`, you won't be able to input any parameters to test the method. This is because your SOAP headers can't be sent via Http-Post; therefore, your method won't allow you to access it.

To get around this, you can either build a proxy and use the Web service from another ASP.NET page that supplies the SOAP header, or you can simply disable the SOAP headers for now, and put them back in when necessary. Let's go with the latter method. Change line 20 of Listing 22.33 to read:

```
<WebMethod()> Public sub UpdateData(UserID as Integer,
➥Mileage as Double, MaxSpeed as Double,
➥Throttle as Double)
```

The only change is the removal of the `<SoapHeader>` attribute. Also comment out lines 21–23, 25, and 62. These lines are responsible for the validation routines using the SOAP header, so you don't need them for now. Now request this page from the browser again, and you should see Figure 22.13.

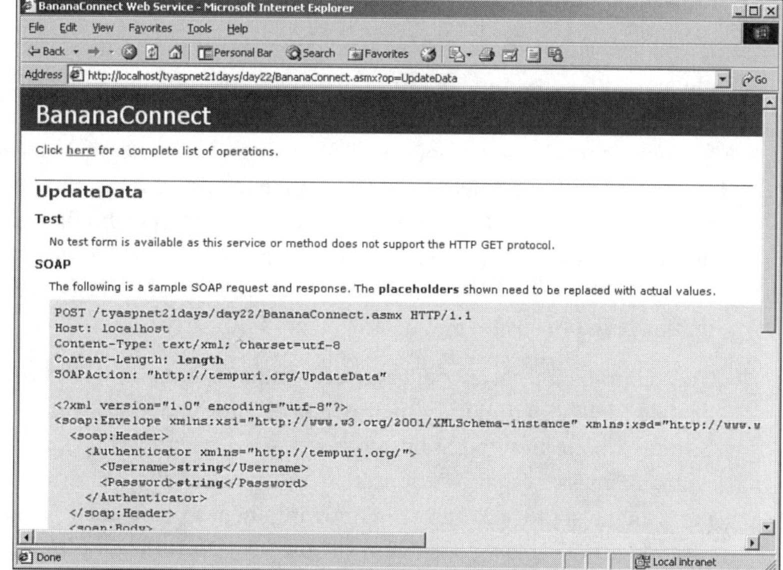

FIGURE 22.13
Testing the Web Service using Http-Post.

Enter some information into the `UserID`, `Mileage`, `MaxSpeed`, and `Throttle` fields and click the Invoke button. If all goes well, another browser window should open and display any returned data. Remember that this Web method didn't return any data, so you shouldn't see anything in the new window. You can make a quick check to the `tblBananaConnect` table in your database to be sure that the data was entered properly. If so, you can uncomment lines 21–23, 25, and 62, add the `<SoapHeader>` attribute back, and you're ready to roll!

Where to Go from Here

You now have a complete application. Feel free to browse through, adding items to your cart, registering, removing items, and eventually purchasing a BananaMobile. You'll be amazed at how well the site works after assembling it in only one lesson.

However, there is also a lot of room for improvement. For example, the news user control should pull its headlines from a data store or other news feed. This can easily be accomplished in the user control itself, but requires appropriate data resources.

You might eventually want to allow users to build more than one BananaMobile at a time, or allow them to purchase individual parts for their existing BananaMobiles. These two features would require changes in all three tiers of the application, such as modifying the shopping cart table and its stored procedures, and redesigning the UI to display the data in new ways.

If you are familiar with database design, you know that the system used here is very simple and not in an optimized form. Changes could be made, for example, to move the `Category` field of the `tblParts` table into another table. `tblParts` would then refer to a foreign key in the new category table. This is a more normalized approach to the data, and would make maintenance easier in the long run. Also, further changes could be made to streamline the `tblOrders` and `tblShoppingCart` tables. Rather than maintaining six different fields (one for each customizable part), you could create one `ProductID` field, which would link to the `tblOrders` table. Additional security measures would have to be implemented to ensure that data is entered properly.

The shopping interface could use a few new features as well. For instance, users should be able to view and modify their personal information, as well as their order histories. Site personalization might be another desired feature. This includes using customized welcome messages, allowing users to rearrange the layout of the page or to decide what parts they want to see, and even allowing them to view their BananaMobile as it is assembled! (This last part requires some very clever use of images and data.)

There is a lot of additional functionality that can be placed in the Web Service. Users, through the BananaConnect system, should also be allowed to download all their statistical information at once. You could even set up a system to compare different users' statistics to enable a competitive online environment!

Your work is never done, and there will always be new features and technologies to add to the site.

That's Not ASP!

Regardless of the programming paradigm you use, designing an application always follows similar steps: analyze the requirements, examine what you have to work with, and lay out the functionality in the most logical way possible.

Building the application, however, is a different story. As you worked through this application, you were able to rely on (or even take for granted!) ASP.NET features that made your life much easier. With classic ASP, many of these features were simply not available, or had to be built manually. This includes the forms authentication mechanism and the `DataList` objects used to display products. Each of these would have to have been manually built in classic ASP, requiring much more development time and energy. Indeed, using ASP.NET can easily cut your development time in half when compared to classic ASP.

Hopefully, this lesson showed you how, in many ways, ASP.NET and classic ASP application scenarios are similar. Good design techniques are universal among all programming technologies and languages. This chapter also showed you how much of an advantage ASP.NET has over classic ASP, in terms of available functionality and ease of development.

Summary

Today was a recap of many of the central concepts you've covered throughout this book. The most important part of today's lesson was that you learned how to assemble the various parts of ASP.NET to build a complete application. Another important concept you examined today was using good design skills before even beginning development. This is an essential step that makes future development much easier.

Initially, you took the requirements from BananaMobile, Inc. and transferred them into technology requirements. Just from the knowledge that the company wanted an e-commerce site, you knew you needed several database tables, a registered user base, several different business objects, and the ASP.NET pages to control it all. You laid out each of the three tiers of the application, starting with the database back end and ending with the business objects in the middle tier. This logical process allowed you to see what functionality was required, with a minimum of backtracking.

This method, certainly, is not the best method all the time. Certain situations might demand other processes, but the method demonstrated today is good for general use.

Next you started developing the site. Again, you started with the database back end, and assembled all the tables and stored procedures required by your application. You already knew much of what needed to be accomplished from the design phase. When this tier was done, it was an easy process to build the business objects that interacted with the databases and executed stored procedures. Many of the business objects' method executed only stored procedures, although some required a few more advanced steps.

Developing the ASP.NET pages was also an easy step because of what you had already built. The UI often takes the longest to build, but with the aid of templates, user controls, and server controls, it went by rather quickly. Much of the ASP.NET code you developed called on the business objects to do the grunt work, so coding these pages was easy.

Finally, you looked at building a secure Web Service. Although the functionality inside the service was rather simple, the addition of SOAP headers and authentication methods made it more complex. Even so, the development of the service was not overly complex or difficult.

Tomorrow, your last day in your adventures in ASP.NET, studies mobile forms. These are part of the Web forms framework, but allow your pages to be displayed on any Web-enabled mobile device, such as cell phones or PDAs. You have to build only one page, and it will work with all these devices. See you then!

Q&A

Q There seemed to be a few stored procedures that were used only once. Couldn't I put them in the ASP.NET page or business object itself?

A Yes, but remember the advantages of stored procedures: speed, readability, and reusability. The first two benefits are easily used here, but the latter isn't so much. Regardless, using stored procedure names in your business objects instead of actual queries allows you to copy and paste much of the functionality when building new methods, and to change only one word, the name of the stored procedure.

Q How could I enhance the performance of this application?

A There are several ways. The first is to find which pages and controls don't need to have their viewstate maintained, and disable them using `EnableViewState=false`. Additionally, you could disable session state for those pages that didn't need it. Caching the data returned from the database, as well as the page outputs, would also help increase functionality.

Don't forget to use the trace functionality (described in Day 20) to help locate trouble spots. When you know what parts of the application are causing the most slowdowns, you can address them specifically.

Workshop

This workshop will help reinforce the concepts covered in today's lesson. It is very helpful to understand the answers fully before moving on. Answers can be found in Appendix A.

Quiz

1. Presented with the knowledge that you must build an e-commerce site, what generic database tables do you know will be required?
2. True or false: ASP.NET pages should be built before the other tiers.
3. What do the `MAX` and `SUM` SQL commands do?
4. What does the `Format` method do? What is the syntax?
5. What are three things needed to secure a database service using SOAP headers?

BONUS DAY

DAY 23

Creating Mobile Web Forms

Mobile devices are everywhere. These days, it seems everyone walking (or driving) down the street is using a cellular phone. Those who aren't are using personal digital assistants (PDAs) or pagers. There are numerous ways to stay connected to one another with wireless devices.

Also increasingly popular is the ability to access the Internet from these wireless devices. Cell phones are able to browse the Web; you can buy stocks through your Pocket PC; you can even check your e-mail from your PDA. These mobile devices allow you to connect to the World Wide Web in all the ways that traditional land lines allow.

It is only logical, then, that as Web developers, we start taking advantage of this new territory. ASP.NET provides (optionally) a mobile component that allows you to easily build applications for any of these devices, using familiar ASP.NET concepts, without much hard work or fuss. Today you'll focus on building ASP.NET pages for your mobile device and look at how the building process differs from building regular ASP.NET pages.

Today's lesson will cover the following:

- What are mobile Web forms?
- How to install the Mobile Web SDK
- How mobile pages work, and how they differ from ASP.NET pages
- How to develop mobile pages
- How to learn about mobile device capabilities

What Are Mobile Web Forms?

Imagine that you're a stock day trader. Because of the quick-paced economy, you must keep track of the markets at all times: when you're away from your computer, waiting to pick up your kids at school, cooking dinner, or even when going to the bathroom! You never know when a grand opportunity to buy the next big thing will come along. But as anyone who's dealt with the stock market knows, to play in the market, you need data: prices for stocks, company news, and other financial information.

You can get all this information, displayed as you want it, from your computer. If you're away from your keyboard, though, things start to get problematic. Stock prices are difficult to get on small devices such as cell phones, and you can forget about receiving charts and historical data. Those small, typically monochromatic screens can't hold very much data at once, and don't lend themselves well to interesting presentations. Executing a buy or sell is also difficult (unless you use the phone to call your broker, but that's a different story—we're talking Web here).

Mobile Web forms are ASP.NET's answer to this problem. Their programming model is nearly identical to that of ASP.NET pages; similar syntax is used, and they even have an `.aspx` file extension. Their power comes from the fact that mobile Web forms use specialized server controls that are designed especially for use with mobile devices. These controls produce rich displays on any mobile device, and automatically adapt themselves to the type of device used. Thus, you can build one version of a page and everything from Nokia cell phones to Pocket PCs can access and utilize your application. In fact, mobile Web forms work even in normal browsers, just as ASP.NET pages.

Prior to ASP.NET and mobile Web forms, programming mobile Web applications was difficult. Wireless devices, unfortunately, don't provide a common set of features or capabilities for developers to rely on. Thus, each application had to be rewritten for each new device that would access it (for instance, a cell phone would require different code than a PDA). The mobile Web forms framework does away with this difficulty by automatically adjusting the pages for each particular device. I'll get into this in much more depth later today; first, let's examine mobile Web forms a bit more.

How Are Mobile Web Forms Different from ASP.NET Web Forms?

If mobile Web forms work in browsers as well, and they function similarly to ASP.NET pages, why do we need ASP.NET Web forms? Why can't we just use mobile forms all the time?

Because mobile forms are designed specifically for mobile devices, they function slightly differently from normal Web forms. An ASP.NET `Label` control and a mobile `Label` control both produce text to display on the browser, but their internal mechanics are different. For example, an ASP.NET label need concern itself only with rendering HTML to the browser; it doesn't care how much text is rendered or how it is rendered. A mobile label, however, needs to take into account the small screen size of mobile devices, and provide the proper paging mechanisms if the text to be displayed is very long. Also, a mobile label spits out different content depending on what type of device is used: HTML for browsers and WML (Wireless Modeling Language) for most cell phones (more on that in the next section).

Also, taking into account the various types of displays on mobile devices, mobile controls typically do not provide as much rendering control or style capabilities as ASP.NET server controls. Thus, they are not as appropriate for display in desktop browsers.

Throughout today's lesson, you'll see more examples of how mobile forms differ from ASP.NET Web forms. You'll also learn the many similarities between the two. All your ASP.NET skills still apply when working with mobile devices, so you're already ahead of the game!

What Do I Need to Use Mobile Web Forms?

Thankfully, you don't need a mobile device or phone service to work with mobile forms. They are completely compatible with your normal Web browser, so as long as you have that, you are all set.

However, if you do not have a mobile device but prefer working in that type of environment, there are quite a few simulators available that work with your PC, such as Microsoft's Mobile Explorer. The UP.SDK simulation package from `http://developer.phone.com` is another very popular simulation toolkit that is often used by Microsoft developers. Each of these simulators works differently, so I won't cover them here. All examples in today's lesson are shown using a normal Web browser.

Specifically, you'll need the same things required to develop ASP.NET pages: Windows 2000 or XP with IIS, the .NET Framework SDK, and additionally, the Microsoft Mobile Internet Toolkit (MMIT) (more in the next section). Any device you have that supports the WML or HTML is capable of displaying mobile forms, although some devices might differ in presentation (just as some Web browsers present things differently). WML is a markup language—similar to HTML—that is designed to specify user interfaces on wireless phones. HTML, obviously, is a markup language used to present UIs in a Web browser.

Because the .NET Framework SDK and the Mobile Web SDK are two different products that ship separately, make sure that you are using compatible versions! An older version of the MMIT might not work correctly with newer versions of the .NET Framework SDK.

Installing the Mobile Internet Toolkit

As with the .NET Framework SDK, you can download the mobile Web SDK from Microsoft at `http://msdn.microsoft.com/downloads/default.asp?url=/downloads/sample.asp?url=/msdn-files/027/000/976/msdncompositedoc.xml&frame=true` (don't worry, it's a small download at just over 3.5MB). This SDK contains all the files, assemblies, and namespaces that you need to get started building mobile applications, as well as documentation and examples.

After you have a copy of the SDK file, `oblieit.exe`, double-click it to begin the installation process. You should see the image in Figure 23.1.

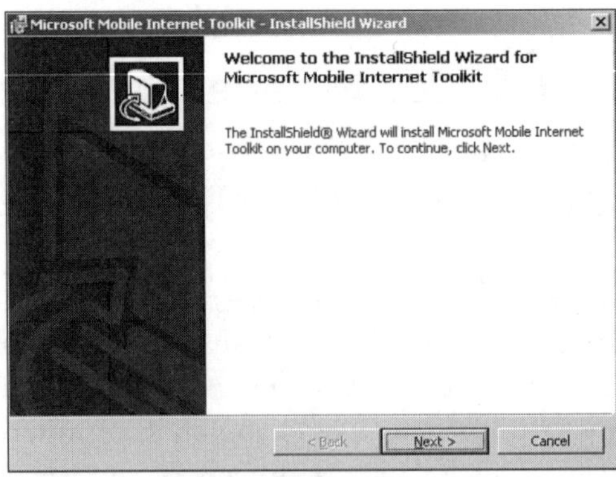

FIGURE 23.1
Installing the mobile Web SDK is a breeze.

Click the Next button, accept the license agreement, and then click Next again to begin the installation. Follow the directions to the end; the process is very simple, consisting of only five or so steps. After the steps are completed, you should see the screen in Figure 23.2.

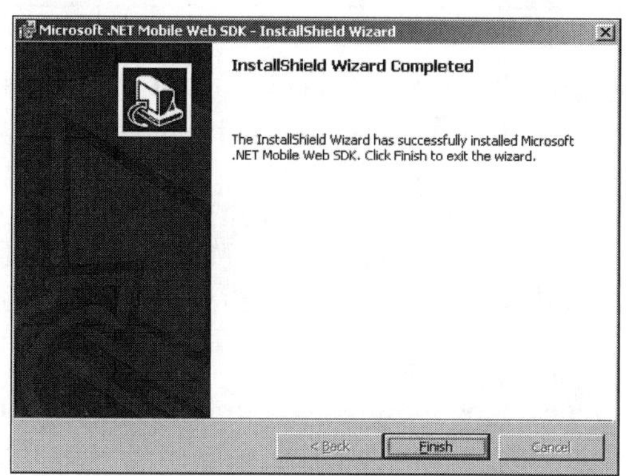

FIGURE 23.2
The final screen for the Mobile Web SDK installation.

You should now see a shortcut to an HTML document titled .NET Mobile Internet Toolkit Overview in your Start menu. Open this file in your browser and explore the documentation. This HTML page contains links to release notes, up-to-date development issues, as well as the official documentation and examples.

Now you're ready to get underway developing mobile applications!

Getting Started with Mobile Web Forms

Just as with ASP.NET pages, mobile pages consist of Web forms and server controls. Recall that ASP.NET pages can have server controls, script blocks, and HTML. In a mobile Web page, however, only server controls and script blocks are allowed; they cannot contain any HTML.

Let's take a quick look at a short example, shown in Listing 23.1.

LISTING 23.1 Your First Mobile Page

```
<%@ Page Inherits="System.Web.UI.MobileControls.MobilePage"
➥Language="VB" %>
<%@ Register TagPrefix="Mobile"
➥Namespace="System.Web.UI.MobileControls" Assembly="System.Web.Mobile" %>
```

LISTING 23.1 continued

```
4:  <Mobile:Form BackColor="#ccddcc" runat="server"
5:     FontName="Times" FontSize="3">
6:      <Mobile:Label runat="server" Text="Hello World!"/>
7:  </Mobile:Form>
```

ANALYSIS Save this listing as `listing2301.aspx`. At first glance, this looks like any other ASP.NET page that inherits from a code-behind (Day 19, "Separating Code from Content") and implements a user control (Day 6, "Learning More About Web Forms"). Recall that the `Inherits` attribute on line 1 specifies a class that this page should inherit from (instead of the usual `System.Web.UI.Page` class). All mobile pages must inherit from this class so that ASP.NET knows that you're building a special type of ASP.NET page.

Line 2 looks like the registration for a user control. In essence, that's what it is. The namespace `System.Web.UI.MobileControls` contains all the mobile server controls that you'll be using in your mobile pages—it resides in a file named `System.Web.Mobile.dll`. This means that mobile server controls are not directly part of ASP.NET; you have to register them explicitly. Note the `TagPrefix` set to `Mobile`; I'll touch on this next.

> **Note**
>
> Lines 1 and 2 highlight the two lines of code that *must* be in every mobile Web page:
>
> ```
> <%@ Page Inherits="System.Web.UI.MobileControls.MobilePage"
> Language="VB"%>
> <%@ Register TagPrefix="Mobile"
> Namespace="System.Web.UI.MobileControls" %>
> ```
>
> Don't forget these lines in your pages!

On line 4, you start a mobile Web form, which is similar to an ASP.NET Web form, except that instead of using the tag prefix `ASP`, you use `Mobile`, as declared on line 2. Note that this form also must have the `runat="server"` attribute, which gives it the same capabilities as regular Web forms. In the declaration of this form, you specify a few additional properties, such as `BackColor` and `FontName` (the values chosen here are used to reflect what a cell phone user would see on her LCD screen).

On line 6, you declare a mobile `Label` control, which works just like a regular `Label` control. Note that it also uses the `Mobile` tag prefix, and contains the `runat="server"` attribute.

Finally, on line 7, you close the mobile Web form. When viewed from the browser, this listing produces Figure 23.3.

FIGURE 23.3

The page as shown from a cell phone...sort of.

You'll examine more of the mobile server controls later today, but they are typically very similar to their counterparts in ASP.NET. Table 23.1 shows all the controls available to mobile Web forms.

TABLE 23.1 The Mobile Web Server Controls

Control	*Description*
`AdRotator`	Displays ads specified from an XML advertisement file.
`Calendar`	Displays an interactive calendar.
`Command`	Provides a way to invoke event handlers; similar to a button in ASP.NET.
`CompareValidator`	Compares the value in one control to a constant value or another control.
`CustomValidator`	Allows you to provide your own custom validation routines.
`DeviceSpecific`	Used for templates on mobile Web forms.
`Form`	A container for controls in a mobile page.
`Image`	Displays an image.

TABLE 23.1 continued

Control	*Description*
`Label`	Displays noninteractive text.
`Link`	Creates a hyperlink to another form or page.
`List`	Renders a list of items.
`MobilePage`	The base class for all mobile ASP.NET pages.
`ObjectList`	Similar to a `List` control, but lists data types.
`Panel`	A container for other mobile controls.
`PhoneCall`	Displays a device-dependent user interface for automatically calling or displaying telephone numbers.
`RangeValidator`	Validates the value in a control against a specified range of values.
`RegularExpressionValidator`	Validates the value in a control against a regular expression string.
`RequiredFieldValidator`	Ensures that a value is entered into a control (that is, ensures that the control is not left blank).
`SelectionList`	Similar to the ASP.NET `CheckBox`, `ListBox`, and `RadioButton` controls.
`StyleSheet`	Used to organize styles for controls; does not provide a visual display.
`TextBox`	Displays a single-line text box for user entry. Use the `Type` property to determine which kind of box to display: `Text` (works normally), `Password` (hides input with asterisks), or `Numeric` (restricts input to numeric values, useful for cell phones).
`TextView`	Displays a large amount of noneditable text. Similar to the `Label` control.
`ValidationSummary`	Displays a summary of all validation errors that have occurred on the page.

Note that many of the properties of these controls are dependent on the viewing device. For example, setting the `Type` property on a `TextBox` to `Numeric` should theoretically allow only numbers to be entered as input. In a Web browser, this restriction is not enforceable without complex client-side scripting. It *is* enforceable, however, in cell phones. Take note of your viewing audience (see "Device-Specific Output and Template Sets," later today).

The Way Mobile Forms Work

Aside from a few small changes, Listing 23.1 looks and works just as an ASP.NET page does. Mobile forms can, however, get a bit more complex.

Let's examine the design of mobile devices a bit further. If you've ever used a cell phone or similar device, you know that interacting with one is not exactly the same as interacting with a PC. Due to the small size of the screen and the form of the input devices, applications must present information in a different way. Specifically, information is gathered into small chunks that can be displayed on a few "pages" of the device. There isn't a lot of text to display, there are hardly any complex images, and users make choices by selecting from a menu. Compare this to Web pages, where text is a very prominent feature, images are abundant, and most user interaction is accomplished by clicking on links or buttons, and you can see why a different paradigm is needed.

Also, navigation in mobile devices isn't as easy as in a browser; users can't simply type in the URL to a new page, and loading new pages often takes a very long time due to the limited bandwidth of these devices.

To address this, mobile Web forms have several differences from ASP.NET Web forms. The first, and probably largest, is that mobile pages can contain as many server-side forms as necessary, whereas ASP.NET pages can only contain one. Each form can contain different information and controls to display; this minimizes the need to load new pages into the device. A single page can post back onto itself, and depending on the criteria, the page can choose to display a different form. Thus, a mobile Web form and a mobile page are two highly distinguishable entities. A single mobile page can contain an entire application's worth of mobile forms. Figure 23.4 illustrates the use of multiple forms on one mobile page.

Mobile Web forms also focus more on presenting information to the user as menus and lists, rather than long paragraphs of text and links. Menus and lists are the easiest elements for users to interact with in the mediocre input controller world of wireless devices, so it is only logical that emphasis would be placed on these constructs.

There are other minor differences that you'll come across as you're developing your pages. There are numerous similarities as well, such as event handling and user input validation, which work the same as with ASP.NET pages. Let's build some more examples.

FIGURE 23.4

An entire application can be contained in one mobile page, but several mobile forms.

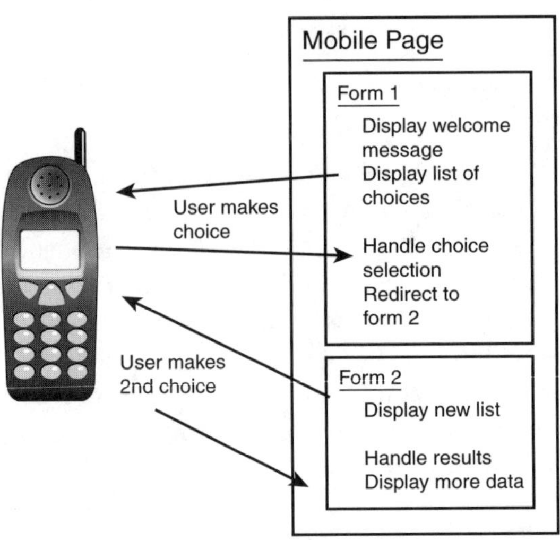

Building a More Apropos Interface

Before I go into more examples, though, you might have noticed that Figure 23.3 isn't exactly the ideal interface for developing mobile applications. The screen might be too large to show developers what their pages will actually look like. Therefore, let's develop a different interface, one that better reflects the target audience.

Listing 23.2 shows a page that presents your mobile pages in an Iframe—a type of HTML frame that can contain different URLs within the containing page.

LISTING 23.2 Developing a Better Suited Interface

```
<script Language="VB" runat="server">
   sub Page_Load(Sender as Object, e as EventArgs)
      frmScreen.Attributes("src") = Request.Params("page")
   end sub
</script>
<html><body>
   <p> <p>
   <center>
   <table border=1 width=100 height=100>
    <tr>
       <td valign="top">
          <iframe id="frmScreen" width="125" height="100"
             marginwidth="2" marginheight="2"
             runat="server"></iframe>
       </td>
    </tr>
```

LISTING 23.2 continued

```
17:     </table>
18:     </center>
19: </body></html>
```


Save this listing as `Frame.aspx`. This page is mostly plain HTML that displays an IFrame, shown on line 12. The IFrame does not map to a predefined ASP.NET server control, but that doesn't stop you from making it into a generic control (represented by the `HtmlGenericControl`; see Appendix C, "ASP.NET Controls: Properties and Methods," for more information). Notice that the `src` property, which determines which page to display in the IFrame, is set to the value returned from a `Request` parameter on line 3. This code retrieves a variable named `page` from the querystring—this variable holds the actual mobile page you want to display.

Now request this page from your browser with the following URL:

```
http://localhost/tyaspnet21days/day23/Frame.aspx?page=
➥listing2301.aspx
```

Note that the querystring contains the mobile page you developed earlier. This URL should produce the display shown in Figure 23.5.

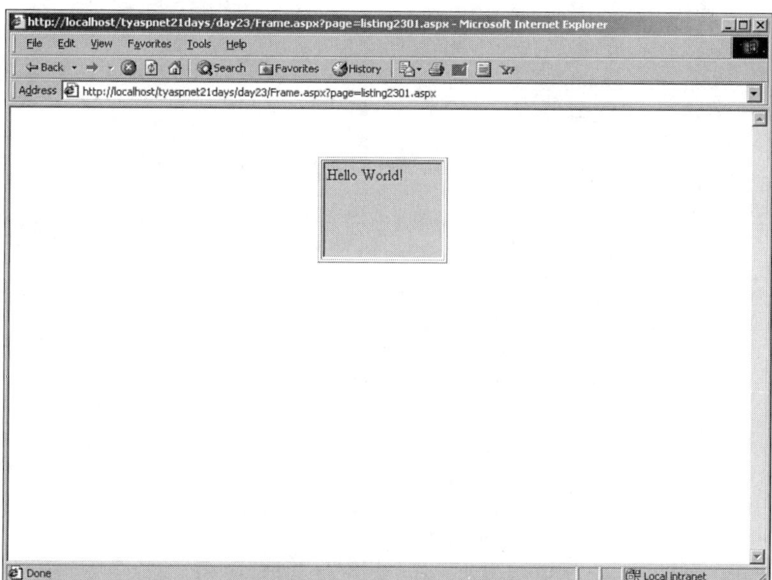

FIGURE 23.5

The IFrame allows you to display a mobile page in a way more representative of your target audience.

Now that looks more like it! It's not exactly a representation of a cell phone, but this will allow you to better see how your pages will look in smaller devices. The rest of the examples in this chapter use `Frame.aspx` with a particular querystring to display the output.

Developing Mobile Pages

Let's examine a more complex example, employing a list and event handlers. Listing 23.3 demonstrates a stock price application, utilizing multiple mobile Web forms in a single page. This listing highlights many of the most common features found in mobile Web applications. You'll see just how easy it is to build mobile pages, especially with your existing knowledge of ASP.NET pages.

LISTING 23.3 Handling User Events

```
<%@ Page Inherits="System.Web.UI.MobileControls.MobilePage"
➥Language="VB" %>
<%@ Register TagPrefix="Mobile"
➥Namespace="System.Web.UI.MobileControls" Assembly="System.Web.Mobile" %>

<script runat="server">
   sub StockPick(Sender as Object, e as ListCommandEventArgs)
      lblName.Text = "Price for " + e.ListItem.Text
      lblPrice.Text = e.ListItem.Value
      ActiveForm = frmPrice
   end Sub
</script>

<Mobile:Form id="frmMenu" BackColor="#ccddcc"
   runat="server"
   FontName="Times" FontSize="3">
   <Mobile:Label runat="server" StyleReference="title"
      Text="Companies"/>
   <Mobile:List runat="server" OnItemCommand="StockPick">
      <Item Text="Microsoft" Value="56.10" />
      <Item Text="Cisco" Value="32.45" />
      <Item Text="AMD" Value="132.34" />
      <Item Text="Agilent" Value="132.33" />
   </Mobile:List>
</Mobile:Form>

<Mobile:Form id="frmPrice" BackColor="#ccddcc"
   runat="server"
   FontName="Times" FontSize="3">
    <Mobile:Label id="lblName" runat="server"/>
    <Mobile:Label id="lblPrice" runat="server"/>
</Mobile:Form>
```

Save this listing as `Listing2303.aspx`, and view it through your browser with the URL:

```
http://localhost/tyaspnet21days/day23/Frame.aspx?page=listing2303.aspx
```

You should initially see Figure 23.6, and Figure 23.7 after clicking one of the list items.

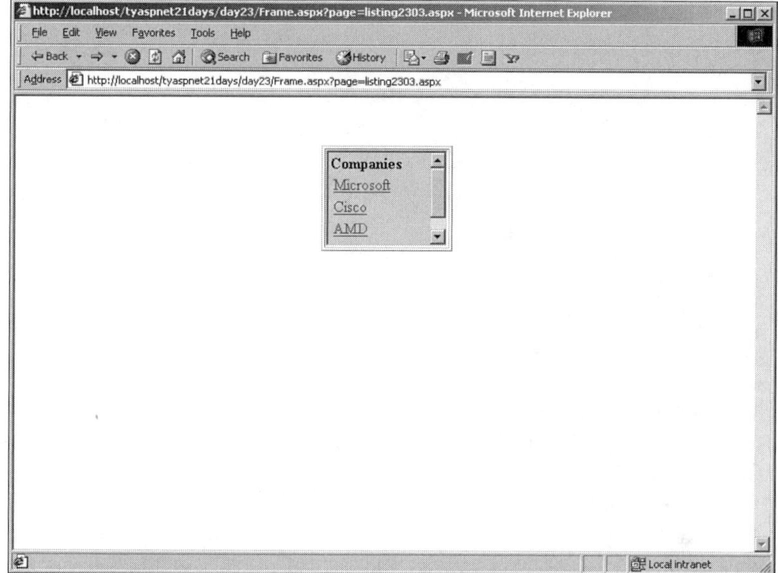

FIGURE 23.6

Menus make it easy to make selections in mobile devices.

Listing 23.3 creates two mobile forms, beginning on lines 12 and 25. Yet Figure 23.6 only shows one. What gives?

ASP.NET displays only the first form in a mobile Web page at any time; unless otherwise specified, it is the first form in the page. You can control this by setting the `ActiveForm` property to the form to display, as shown on line 8. When a user clicks on one of the items in the list, the second form is displayed. Let's examine the rest of the code.

Lines 1 and 2 show the standard header required by all mobile pages. Moving down to line 12, you see a typical mobile Web form declaration. Inside this form, you have two controls: a `Label`, which has already been discussed, and a `List` control, which is very similar to the `ListBox` control in ASP.NET. The `Label` has a property you haven't seen before: `StyleReference`. Although you can build your own styles for each control, this property refers to a built-in style provided by ASP.NET. These built-in styles ensure that your control will be rendered correctly for each different mobile device. `StyleReference` can have one of two values: `Title` (causes the control to render in bold with emphasis) or `Error` (renders the control in a red, italicized text).

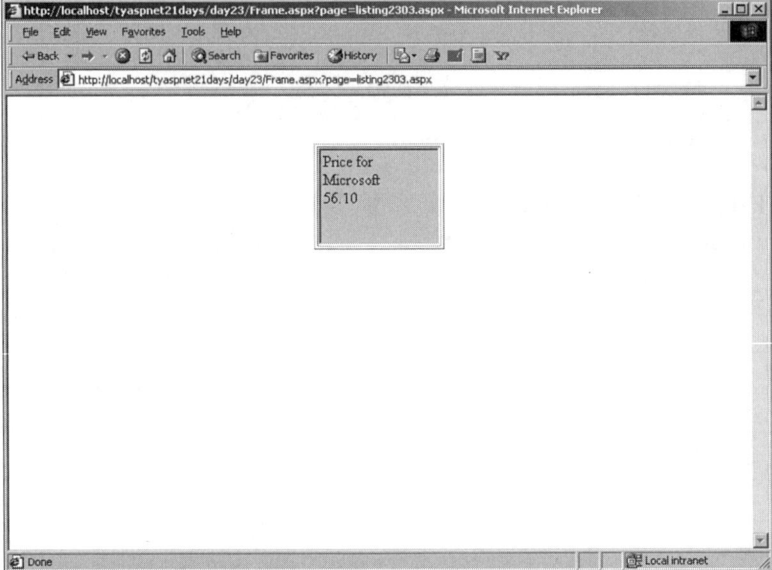

FIGURE 23.7
The second mobile form is displayed when a menu item is clicked.

The `List` control provides many different properties and methods, similar to the ASP.NET `ListBox` control; they are not all covered here. The `List` control uses `Item` controls to display individual items in the list, as shown on lines 18–21. When a user selects one of these items, the `ItemCommand` event fires. On line 17, you set the event handler for this method to the `StockPick` method, shown on line 5 (more on that in a moment). You can set the `SelectType` property of the `ListBox` to alter its behavior on the devices that support it. This property can be `DropDown`, `ListBox`, or `Radio`; each of these values is self-explanatory. You can also change the `Decoration` property to alter its appearance; this property can be `None`, `Bulleted`, or `Numbered`.

The second mobile form, named `frmPrice`, begins on line 25. This form simply contains two `Label` controls, which will display stock prices after a user has clicked on an item in the first Web form.

In the `StockPick` method, on lines 6 and 7, you simply display the details of the chosen selection in the labels on lines 28 and 29, in the second Web form. This is done with syntax very similar to ASP.NET. On line 8, you set the `ActiveForm` property to `frmPrice`, which causes the second form to be displayed instead of the first. Because you already set the values for the labels in the second form, the user is shown the proper data. In this way, it is easy to present user interfaces across different mobile devices.

Mobile server controls also support the full data binding behavior of ASP.NET server controls. This means you can retrieve information from a database by storing it in a `DataSet`, and binding that `DataSet` to the control. The `List` control will automatically loop through and display the records in the data, just as regular server controls would do. Listing 23.4 shows an example using the database created in Day 8, “Beginning to Build Databases.” This example creates an address book, similar to the ones in many cell phones.

LISTING 23.4 Mobile Controls Support Data Binding

```
<%@ Page Inherits="System.Web.UI.MobileControls.MobilePage" Language="VB" %>
<%@ Register TagPrefix="Mobile" Namespace="System.Web.UI.MobileControls"
➥Assembly="System.Web.Mobile" %>
<%@ Import Namespace="System.Data" %>
<%@ Import Namespace="System.Data.OleDb" %>

<script runat="server">
   sub Page_Load(Sender as Object, e as EventArgs)
      dim objConn as new OleDbConnection _
         ("Provider=Microsoft.Jet.OLEDB.4.0;" & _
          "Data Source=c:\ASPNET\data\banking.mdb")

       dim objCmd as new OleDbDataAdapter _
          ("select * from tblUsers", objConn)

       dim ds as DataSet = new DataSet()
       objCmd.Fill(ds, "tblUsers")

       lNames.DataSource = ds.Tables("tblUsers").DefaultView
     lNames.DataBind()
    end sub

    sub NamePick(Sender as Object, e as ListCommandEventArgs)
       lblName.Text = e.ListItem.Text
       lblPhone.Text = e.ListItem.Value
       ActiveForm = frmPrice
    end Sub
 </script>

 <Mobile:Form id="frmMenu" BackColor="#ccddcc"
    runat="server">
    <Mobile:Label runat="server" StyleReference="title"
       Text="Names" />
    <Mobile:List id="lNames" runat="server"
       OnItemCommand="NamePick"
       DataTextField="FirstName"
       DataValueField="Phone" />
 </Mobile:Form>
```

LISTING 23.4 continued

```
38:
39:  <Mobile:Form id="frmPrice" BackColor="#ccddcc"
40:     runat="server">
41:      <Mobile:Label id="lblName" runat="server"/>
42:      <Mobile:Label id="lblPhone" runat="server"/>
43:  </Mobile:Form>
```

ANALYSIS Save this file as `Listing2304.aspx`. Lines 7–19 should be nothing new. You create an `OleDbConnection` object on line 8, and an `OleDbDataAdapter` object on line 12 that retrieves all rows from the `tblUsers` table. You create a `DataSet` and fill it on lines 15 and 16, and finally set the `DataSource` and bind the `List` control on lines 18–19.

The `NamePick` method beginning on line 22 is the same as the `StockPick` method from Listing 23.3, except for the name change. The UI portion of the page, lines 29–43, is also nearly identical to the previous listing, except that the `Item` elements are removed from the `List` control, and two new properties are added to the `List`: `DataTextField` and `DataValueField`. Recall that these properties are used to determine which fields from the database will be used to populate, respectively, the text and value portions of the list. These properties were also available on the `ListBox` ASP.NET server control. Therefore, this entire listing should be familiar.

Viewing this listing with the URL `http://localhost/tyaspnet21days/day23/Frame.aspx?page=listing2304.aspx` produces the image shown in Figure 23.8. Figure 23.9 shows the output when a name is clicked.

When a user clicks on one of the links in Figure 23.8, the `NamePick` method executes, which sets the `Text` properties of the labels in the second form, and then displays the second form with `ActiveForm`. The chosen name and phone number is then displayed to the user.

Adding Paging Capabilities

Obviously, because cell phones don't use Web browsers such as Internet Explorer or Netscape, you won't see the scroll bar shown in Figure 23.8. Those tiny screens display one set of data at a time, chunked into pages; you don't scroll through a long list on one page, but rather move to different pages that each contain a few list items.

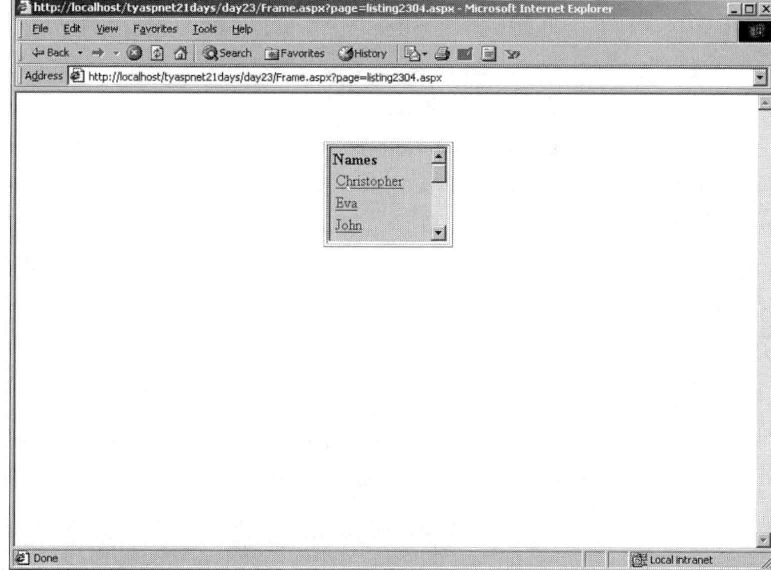

FIGURE 23.8

Listing 23.4 produces an address book type display.

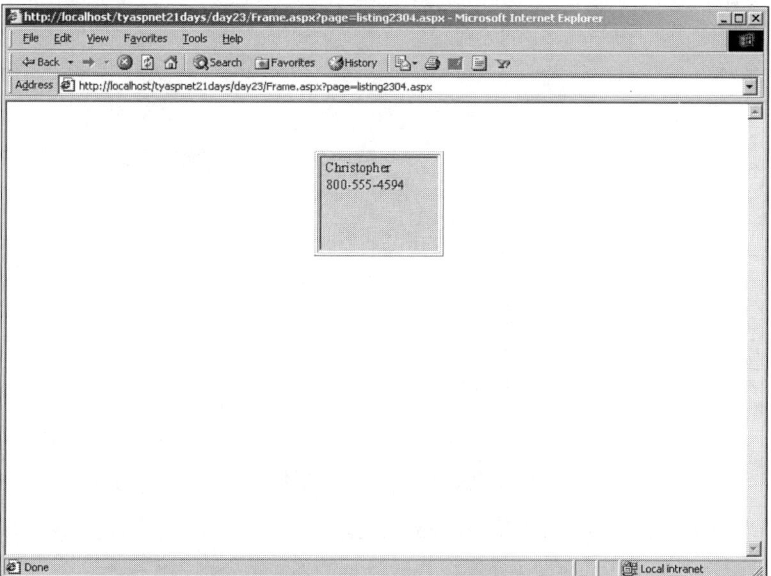

FIGURE 23.9

The information displayed in the second mobile form.

The mobile server controls all provide automatic-paging features that present an appropriate display depending on the device being used; this is known as *internal pagination*. By default, internal pagination is turned off, but you can easily turn it on using the `AllowPaging` property. For example, change the `List` control on line 33 of Listing 23.4 to read as follows:

```
33: <Mobile:List id="lNames" runat="server"
34:    OnItemCommand="NamePick"
35:    DataTextField="FirstName"
36:    DataValueField="Phone"
37:    AllowPaging="true" />
```

The `List` control will now automatically add Next and Previous menu items to navigate through the list. Depending on the device, these items will appear differently. Add the following code before line 19:

```
lNames.PageSize = 2
```

ASP.NET will automatically determine how many items should be displayed on each page depending on the viewing device's screen size. However, you can modify this using the `PageSize` property. `PageSize` tells ASP.NET how many items should be shown per page. If you set this value to something higher than the number of items that one page on the device can display at once, ASP.NET generates the necessary navigation (such as a Next menu item) for the device. This listing should now produce the image in Figure 23.10.

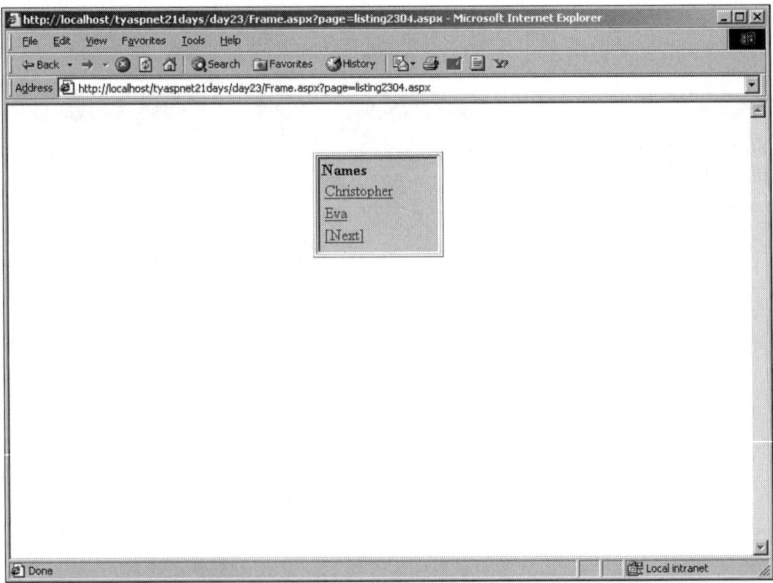

FIGURE 23.10
Internal pagination causes Next and Previous menu items to appear.

With internal pagination, ASP.NET will look at how many items are in your data source and automatically create the appropriate number of pages. You can also define a custom routine for handling pagination by setting the `AllowCustomPaging` property to true and setting a number for the `VirtualItemCount` property, which specifies how many items *should* be in the list in total. The purpose of custom pagination is to allow you to fetch data as needed; normal pagination retrieves all records at once, and renders only a few at a time. Custom pagination, however, retrieves only a few records at a time and it is up to you to retrieve the next set when necessary. The `PageIndexChanged` event is typically where you would handle this.

For example, the following code snippet provides a method to handle the `PageIndexChanged` event, and checks to see whether the Next or Previous button was clicked:

```
sub GetNewData(Sender as Object, e as PageChangedEventArgs)
   if e.NewPageIndex > e.OldPageIndex then
      'user clicked next, grab next set of data
   else
      'user clicked previous, grab previous set of data
   end if
end sub
...
<Mobile:List runat="server"
   ...
   OnPageIndexChanged="GetNewData"/>
```

You can then define the code to actually retrieve the data in question.

Device-Specific Output and Template Sets

Even though ASP.NET automatically handles the rendering of each mobile control depending on the device being used, there might be times where its capabilities don't suit your needs. You might want to display one control when viewed from a cell phone, or another, different control when viewed from a browser.

For example, when someone using a device with a color screen comes to your site, you might want to show an image of a logo. However, this image won't come across very well in monochromatic devices such as certain cell phones, so for these you'd simply display the text version of the logo.

For this, ASP.NET introduces the `<DeviceSelect>` and `<Choice>` elements. These allow you to render different items depending on the parameters specified by the device in question (you'll learn about these parameters in the next section). Let's take a look at some code to familiarize you with these two elements, shown in Listing 23.5.

LISTING 23.5 Modifying User Interfaces for Different Devices

```
<%@ Page Inherits="System.Web.UI.MobileControls.MobilePage"
➥Language="VB" %>
<%@ Register TagPrefix="Mobile"
➥Namespace="System.Web.UI.MobileControls" Assembly="System.Web.Mobile" %>

<Mobile:Form runat="server">
   <DeviceSelect>
      <Choice Capability="PreferredRenderingType"
➥Argument="html32">
         <template name="HeaderTemplate">
```

LISTING 23.5 continued

```
8:             <table width="100%" height="100%">
9:             <tr>
10:                <td bgcolor="#cccc99">
11:                   <img src="header.gif" height="26"
12:                      width="100">
13:                </td>
14:             </tr>
15:             <tr>
16:                <td bgcolor="#ffffff" valign="top">
17:          </template>
18:          <template name="FooterTemplate">
19:             </td></tr>
20:             <tr><td bgcolor="#cccc99" height="4"></td></tr>
21:             </table>
22:          </template>
23:       </Choice>
24:       <Choice>
25:          <template name="HeaderTemplate">
26:             <Mobile:Label runat="server"
27:                StyleReference="Title"
28:                Text="MySite.com" />
29:          </template>
30:       </Choice>
31:    </DeviceSelect>
32:    <Mobile:Label FontSize="Small" FontName="Arial"
33:       Text="Welcome to my site!" />
34: </Mobile:Form>
```

ANALYSIS Lines 1–4 should look familiar—it's the same header we've been using for all the mobile pages so far. Line 5 begins something new with the `<DeviceSelect>` element, which acts as a container for `<Choice>` elements, shown on lines 6 and 24. The first `<Choice>` examines a capability of the calling device called `PreferredRenderingType`, which indicates what type of display the device has. If the device renders HTML version 3.2, the `Argument` property on line 6 tells ASP.NET to display the UI on lines 7–22 (the code contained within the first `<Choice>` element). If the device doesn't support HTML 3.2 (most cell phones don't), display the content contained in the second `<Choice>` element. Because the second `<Choice>` doesn't contain an `Argument` property, it will be used as the default choice.

You can have as many `<Choice>` elements in a `<DeviceSelect>` container as you want—one for every different type of display you expect, if necessary. Only one of these elements will be rendered: the one that best matches the capabilities of the device. If two match identically, the one that appears first in the source code is chosen. If, however, none of them matches, ASP.NET will display the UI as it would normally, according to the device used.

There are a few more elements which will be familiar in this listing; specifically, the templates on lines 7, 18, and 25. Recall that you used these same templates in the `Repeater`, `DataList`, and `DataGrid` ASP.NET server controls (refer to Day 9, "Using Databases with ASP.NET"). They function identically here, providing a portion of a user interface to display. Figures 23.11 and 23.12 show the output of this listing from a browser when the different choices are selected.

Note

Template controls are not necessary in `<Choice>` elements; if you don't need much layout control, you can specify the content to render in the `<Choice>` element itself with the `value` property:

```
<Choice Capability="PreferredRenderingType" Argument="html32"
   value="header.gif"
```

The preceding code causes the `header.gif` image to be displayed if the capability and argument match.

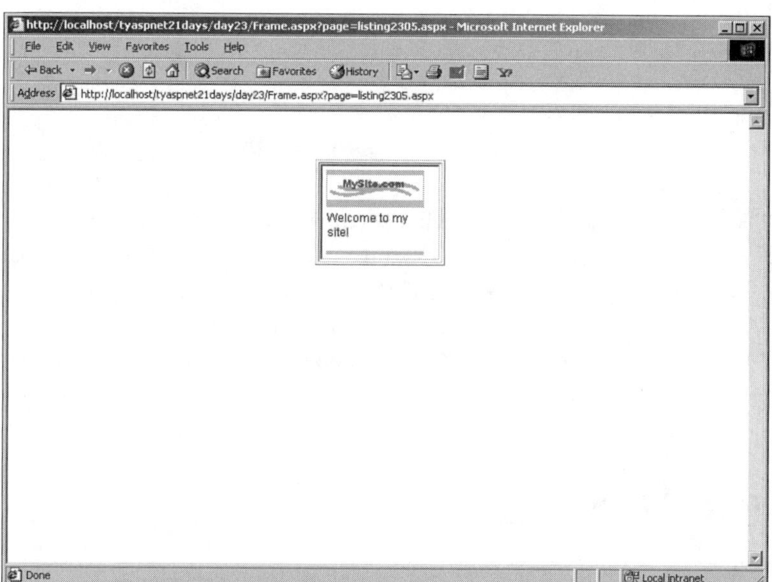

FIGURE 23.11
When the device is capable of displaying HTML 3.2, the first `<Choice>` *is selected.*

Using Mobile Device Capabilities

When a Web browser requests a Web page, it passes along certain information to the Web server. This information identifies the browser, letting the server determine the browser's capabilities, such as whether it can support Java applets, JavaScript, and so on.

Mobile devices pass along such identifying information as well, and the mobile forms framework can use this identification information to determine the device's features and functionalities.

FIGURE 23.12

The second `<Choice>` *is selected if the device isn't capable of HTML 3.2.*

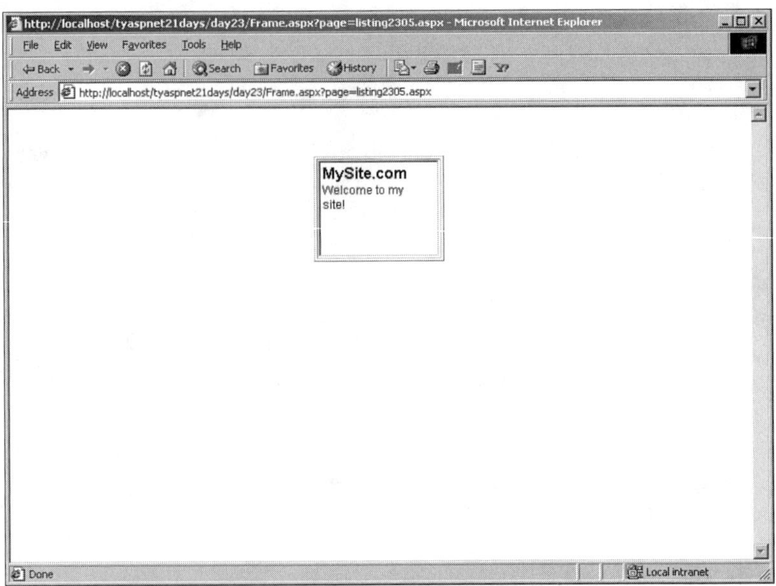

Because each mobile device potentially provides a different display mechanism, ascertaining its capabilities is essential. All the content that you output must be tailored for each specific mobile device accessing the mobile Web page, and luckily, ASP.NET handles much of this for you. As shown in the previous section, you can use the `<DeviceSelect>` and `<Choice>` elements to alter your display depending on the capabilities of the viewing devices. Table 23.2 lists all the capabilities specific to mobile devices. (Note that not all devices support all of these capabilities, but this is the general set.)

TABLE 23.2 Mobile Device Capabilities

Property	*Default*	*Description*
`Browser`	"Unknown"	The brand of browser being used.
`CanCombineFormsInDeck`	true	Indicates if the particular device can have multiple mobile Web forms on one page.

TABLE 23.2 continued

Property	*Default*	*Description*
`CanInitiateVoiceCall`	false	Indicates whether the device can make a voice phone call.
`CanRenderEmptySelects`	true	Indicates if the device will render empty <select> elements.
`CanRenderInputAndSelectElementsTogether`	true	Indicates if the device can render `<input>` and `<select>` elements together.
`CanRenderMixedSelects`	true	Indicates if the device can handle `<select>` tags with `<option>` elements that include both `onpick` and `value` attributes.
`CanRenderOneventAndPrevElementsTogether`	true	Indicates if the device can handle the elements `<Onevent>` and `<do type="prev" label="Back"></prev></do>` when they are put together.
`CanRenderPostBackCards`	true	Indicates if a device can use postback cards.
`CanRenderSetvarZeroWithMultiSelectionList`	true	Indicates if the device can accepts the `<setvar>` element with `value` set to zero.
`CanSendMail`	true	Indicates if the device can send mail.
`GatewayMajorVersion`	0	Major version number of the current gateway (that is, 4.*x*).
`GatewayMinorVersion`	0	Minor version number of the gateway (that is, *x*.5).
`GatewayVersion`	"None"	Version string of gateway.
`HasBackButton`	true	Indicates if the device browser has a dedicated back button.
`HidesRightAlignedMultiselectScrollbars`	false	Indicates if the scroll bar for a `<select multiple>` element is hidden by the scroll bar for the page.

23

TABLE 23.2 continued

Property	*Default*	*Description*
InputType	" "	Type of input device (that is, VirtualKeyPad, telephoneKeypad).
IsColor	false	Indicates whether the device's display is color.
IsMobileDevice	true	Indicates if the device is mobile.
Item	N/A	The default indexer used to retrieve mobile capabilities.
MaximumRenderedPageSize	2000	The max length of the page in bytes the device can display.
MaximumSoftKeyLabelLength	8	Max length of labels for soft-keys in characters.
MobileDeviceManufacturerer	"Unknown Mobile Device Manufacturer"	Manufacturer of the device.
MobileDeviceModel	"Unknown Mobile Device Model"	The model of the device.
NumberOfSoftKeys	0	The number of softkeys.
PreferredImageMime	image/gif	The MIME type of the image content preferred by the device.
PreferredRenderingMime	"text/html"	MIME type for rendering content.
PreferredRenderingType	"html32"	MIME type for rendering text.
RendersBreaksBeforeWmlSelectAndInput	false	Indicates if the device renders a line break before a <select> or <input> element.
RendersBreaksAfterHtmlLists	true	Indicates if the device renders breaks after HTML list tags.
RendersBreaksAfterWmlAnchor	false	Indicates if a break is rendered after a standalone anchor.
RendersBreaksAfterWmlInput	false	Indicates if a break is rendered after input elements have been received.

TABLE 23.2 continued

Property	Default	Description
`RendersWmlDoAcceptsInline`	true	Indicates if `<do>` is rendered as an inline button or softkey.
`RendersWmlSelectsAsMenuCards`	false	Indicates if `<select>` elements are rendered as menu cards instead of combo boxes.
`RequiredMetaTagNameValue`	" "	Returns a meta tag value required by some devices.
`RequiresContentTypeMetaTag`	false	Indicates if the browser is Pocket Internet Explorer.
`RequiresAttributeColonSubstitution`	false	Indicates if colons in tag names need to be substituted with a different character on rendering.
`RequiresHtmlAdaptiveErrorReporting`	false	Indicates if the device should get the default ASP.NET error message, or an adaptive one.
`RequiresLeadingPageBreak`	false	Indicates if the device should render an extra break at the beginning of a page.
`RequiresNoBreakInFormatting`	false	Indicates if formatting tags must not contain ` ` tags.
`RequiresOutputOptimization`	false	Indicates if the adapter will try to generate minimal output to reduce page size.
`RequiresPhoneNumbersAsPlainText`	false	Indicates if the device only supports phone dialing based on plain text instead of special markup.
`RequiresSpecialViewStateEncoding`	false	Indicates if the device requires special encoding on view state information.
`RequiresUniqueFilePathSuffix`	false	Indicates if unique file suffixes are needed to stop gateways and devices from caching pages.

TABLE 23.2 continued

Property	*Default*	*Description*
RequiresUniqueHtmlCheckboxNames	false	Indicates if `<input>` tags require unique attribute values.
RequiresUrlEncodedPostfieldValues	false	Indicates if the device encodes text from a form post.
ScreenBitDepth	8	The depth of the display in pixels.
ScreenCharactersHeight	40	The height of the screen in characters.
ScreenCharacterWidth	80	The width of the screen in characters.
ScreenPixelsHeight	480	The height of the screen in pixels.
ScreenPixelWidth	640	The width of the screen in pixels.
SupportsAccessKeyAttribute	false	Indicates if the device can handle the `AccessKey` attribute for `<a>` and `<input>` elements.
SupportsBodyColor	true	Except where noted, all of the following properties indicate if the device supports a particular HTML element. `SupportsBodyColor`, for instance, indicates if the device supports the `bgcolor` attribute in the `<body>` tag.
SupportsBold	false	
SupportsCacheControlMetaTag	true	Indicates if the device supports the meta tag `Cache-Control: max-age-0`.
SupportsCss	false	
SupportsDivAlign	true	
SupportsDivNoWrap	false	
SupportsFontColor	true	
SupportsFontName	false	
SupportsFontSize	false	

Table 23.2 continued

Property	Default	Description
`SupportsImageSubmit`	false	
`SupportsIModeSymbols`	false	Indicates if the device supports i-mode symbols.
`SupportsInputIStyle`	false	Indicates if the device supports the `IStyle` attribute in `<input>` elements.
`SupportsInputMode`	false	
`SupportsItalic`	false	
`SupportsJPhoneMultiMediaAttributes`	false	Indicates if the device supports J-Phone multimedia attributes.
`SupportsJPhoneSymbols`	false	Indicates if the device supports J-Phone specific picture symbols.
`SupportsQueryStringInFormAction`	true	
`SupportsUncheck`	true	

Let's take a look at these properties in an example. Listing 23.6 shows an example of iterating through these capabilities.

Listing 23.6 Retrieving and Displaying the Capabilities of the Viewing Device

```
<%@ Page Inherits="System.Web.UI.MobileControls.MobilePage"
➥Language="VB" %>
<%@ Register TagPrefix="Mobile"
➥Namespace="System.Web.UI.MobileControls" Assembly="System.Web.Mobile" %>
<%@ Import Namespace="System.ComponentModel" %>

<script runat="server">
   sub Page_Load(Sender as Object, e as EventArgs)
      if not Page.IsPostBack then
         dim objProp as PropertyDescriptorCollection = _
            TypeDescriptor.GetProperties(Request.Browser)
          if not objProp is nothing then
            lCapabilities.DataSource = objProp
            lCapabilities.DataBind()
          end if
       end if
    end sub

    sub ShowProperty(Sender as Object, e as
```

LISTING 23.6 continued

```
➥ListCommandEventArgs)
19:         dim strName as String  = e.ListItem.Text
20:         lblName.Text = strName
21:         lblValue.Text = DataBinder.Eval(Request.Browser, _
22:            strName, "{0}")
23:
24:         ActiveForm = frmProperty
25:      end sub
26:   </script>
27:
28:   <Mobile:Form runat="server">
29:      <Mobile:Label runat="server" StyleReference="title"
30:         Text="Mobile Capabilities" />
31:      <Mobile:List runat="server" id="lCapabilities"
32:         DataTextField="Name" OnItemCommand="ShowProperty"
33:         AllowPaging="true" />
34:   </Mobile:Form>
35:
36:   <Mobile:Form runat="server" id="frmProperty">
37:      <Mobile:Label runat="server" id="lblName"
38:         StyleReference="title" />
39:      <Mobile:Label runat="server" id="lblValue" />
40:   </Mobile:Form>
```

ANALYSIS This page retrieves all the capabilities of the viewing device and displays them in a `List` control on line 31. When one of the items is clicked, the second form (shown on line 36) is populated with the value of the capability and then displayed. Let's analyze the code.

The `Page_Load` event retrieves all the capabilities and binds them to the list control. Line 9 declares a new `PropertyDescriptorCollection` object (which is very useful for storing this type of information), and populates it with the capabilities of the browser, shown on line 10. The `TypeDescriptor.GetProperties` method retrieves the properties for a component—the `Browser` object in this case (which you retrieve by calling `Request.Browser`). The variable `objProp` now contains a list of all the properties and capabilities of the device and browser, so you simply bind it to the `List` control on lines 12 and 13.

The `ShowProperty` method on line 18 executes when an item in the list is clicked. It sets values for the labels in the second form on the page. The `DataBinder.Eval` method formats the data to be displayed in the label as text. On line 24, the second form is set to active.

The UI portion of this listing is fairly standard; all these elements and properties were covered earlier today. Now take a look at this listing from the browser. Note that `Frame.aspx` is not used here because we simply want to display the capabilities. This isn't part of a mobile application. Figure 23.13 shows the output.

FIGURE 23.13

Click on an item to see the value for that particular capability.

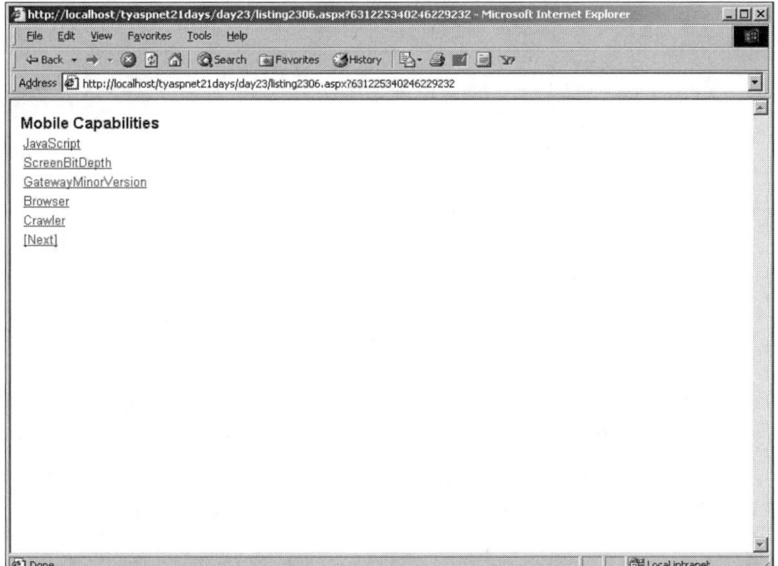

That's Not ASP!

The mobile Web component for ASP.NET is unlike anything available in classic ASP. The mobile Web forms offer easy-to-build mobile applications, the mobile server controls render adaptively to their viewing environment, and these pages support many of the same features as their counterparts in ASP.NET, such as caching, input validation, and error control.

Prior to the mobile Web component, developers had to build multiple versions of a page to support mobile devices, requiring long and complex development stages. In addition, developing for this arena often required the developer to learn different programming languages, such as WML and the WAP protocol, neither of which is very intuitive.

ASP.NET makes mobile application development much easier. Using the familiar ASP.NET syntax and concepts, you can easily create complex user interfaces, as well as the logic to control them. In fact, ASP.NET makes development so easy, there's no excuse for not having a wireless device–capable site!

Summary

Today you took a quick overview of developing pages for mobile devices. Because much of today's topic is so similar to the concepts you've covered in ASP.NET, the discussion breezed through this topic rather quickly.

The first thing you must do is download the Mobile Web SDK from Microsoft at `http://msdn.microsoft.com/downloads/default.asp?url=/downloads/sample.asp?url=/msdn-files/027/000/976/msdncompositedoc.xml&frame=true`. After you have it correctly installed, developing pages is a snap because you are already familiar with ASP.NET.

Each mobile page can consist of one or more mobile Web forms, which in turn consists of mobile server controls. All these elements are similar to their counterparts in ASP.NET, with many of the same properties and methods. A notable exception is that there can be many mobile forms to one mobile page, which allows you to creatively present different output to clients depending on their interactions.

There are quite a few mobile server controls, including the `List` and `Label` controls that were examined today. Many of these controls take into account the fact that mobile devices have smaller screens and less power than PCs, and render output accordingly, by providing features such as internal pagination.

Finally, you can use the `<DeviceSelect>` and `<Choice>` elements to selectively render different output depending on the device being used. These elements make use of the mobile capabilities supplied by the mobile devices to display content. You can specify the content to render in the `<Choice>` element itself using the `value` property, or you can use templates to provide more fine-tuned layout capabilities.

Q&A

Q Where can I find out more about WML and WAP?

A There are quite a few resources online for you to learn more about these two technologies. For a discussion of what exactly those resources are, check out these links:

WAP—`http://www.allnetdevices.com/faq/?pair=01.001`

WML—`http://www.allnetdevices.com/faq/?pair=01.002`

For a central repository of links, check out this great resource:

`http://www.4guysfromrolla.com/webtech/LearnMore/WAP.asp`

Q Is a card the same thing as a mobile page?

A In wireless communications technology, a *card* is a unit that can be displayed on a single screen. Therefore, a card is analogous to a mobile Web form. A *deck*, or set of cards, is analogous to a mobile page.

Q Are there compatibility issues between ASP.NET and mobile Web forms?

A Unfortunately, yes, although there are only a few. The first is that mobile pages do not support user controls—files with the `.ascx` extension. The second is the use of error pages. With ASP.NET, if an error occurs in the application, the user receives a fairly detailed error page along with a description of the error. Mobile devices often aren't able to display such a complex UI, although they do try. You might want to set up your own custom error pages by using the `customErrors` element in your `web.config` file:

```
<customErrors defaultredirect="errors.aspx" mode="on" />
```

Use mobile server controls in this custom error page to ensure that the message is properly displayed on the device.

Similarly, the page-level tracing feature, which causes additional HTML to be tacked on the end of your ASP.NET pages when viewed, might cause problems in a mobile device. Use application-level tracing instead if necessary.

Finally, keep in mind that many mobile devices do not support cookies. Try not to rely too much on cookies in your mobile applications, and if you're using session state, configure your application to use cookieless sessions.

Workshop

This workshop will help reinforce the concepts covered in today's lesson. It is very helpful to understand fully the answers before moving on. Answers can be found in Appendix A.

Quiz

1. What are the two headers required for every mobile page?
2. True or false: Mobile server controls don't require the `runat="server"` attribute.
3. What does the `Call` server control do?
4. What are the two values for the `StyleReference` property?
5. How do you explicitly display a mobile Web form programmatically?

6. True or false: You can respond to mobile server control events the same as ASP.NET server control events.
7. What does the `<DeviceSelect>` element do, and what does it represent on the page?

Exercises

Create a mobile application that will allow users to make credit card payments through their cell phones. Users should be allowed to enter a credit card number and a value for the amount to be paid (don't forget to supply a way to submit the input). Don't worry about recording or applying the payment to something. Simply display a thank-you message to the user when the submission is complete.

APPENDIX A

Answers to Quiz Questions

Answers for Day 1

Quiz

1. What must ASP.NET do before it sends anything to the browser?

   Convert the output to HTML so the browser can understand it.

2. What does CLR stand for?

   Common Language Runtime.

3. What is metadata?

   Information produced by an application to describe its properties. The Common Language Runtime uses metadata to load and run applications.

4. What are three programmatic improvements of ASP.NET over ASP?

   Ease of deployment, improved session state, and the use of code declaration blocks.

5. How does ASP.NET work with the client and server machines?

   ASP.NET uses client-side code to send messages back to the server. Thus, the server can be aware of what's happening on the client.

6. Why can't you simply double-click on an ASP.NET file to run it?

   An ASP.NET page must be processed by a Web server. If you double-click on it, you're trying to open the file without using that process.

7. What is a virtual directory?

   A folder on your computer that can be accessed from a browser as though it were in your root directory (typically, `c:\inetpub\wwwroot`).

8. If you created a file called `hello.aspx` and placed it in the `c:\inetpub\wwwroot\tyaspnet21days\MyApplication` directory, how could you access it from the Web browser?

   At the following URL:

   `http://localhost/tyaspnet21days/MyApplication/hello.aspx`

9. What's the difference between code declaration blocks and render blocks?

   Code render blocks are inline code, denoted by `<%` and `%>` tags, and aren't compiled. Code declaration blocks define a page's methods and members, are denoted by script tags, and are compiled.

Exercises

What will be the output of the following ASP.NET page? Where would you save this file so users could access it?

```
<%@ Page Language="VB" %>

<script runat="server">
   sub Page_Load(Sender as Object, e as EventArgs)
      lblMessage.Text = "This is my first exercise!"
   end sub
</script>

<html><body>
     <asp:Label id="lblMessage" runat="server"/>
 </body></html>
```

This page would display "This is my first exercise!" You could save this file in the `c:\inetpub\wwwroot\tyaspnet21days\day1` folder as `exercise1.aspx` and view it through the browser with `http://localhost/tyaspnet21days/day1/exercise1.aspx`.

Answers for Day 2

Quiz

1. How does ASP.NET maintain the state of server controls?

   By placing hidden HTML tags in the ASP.NET page that remember the values entered.

2. What namespace do the ASP.NET `Page` and `LiteralControl` classes belong to?

   `System.Web.UI`

3. What are the seven namespaces automatically imported into every ASP.NET page?

   `System`, `System.Collections`, `System.IO`, `System.Web`, `System.Web.UI`, `System.Web.UI.WebControls`, and `System.Web.UI.HTMLControls`.

4. What does "type-safe" mean?

   This ensures that an object only references memory locations that it's allowed to, preventing data corruption. Essentially, it means that one type of object cannot be used as another type accidentally.

5. What is the Common Language Specification (CLS)?

   It's the basic subset of features provided by the CLR that are found in every modern object-oriented programming language. The CLS ensures that cross-language objects can interact with each other.

Exercises

1. Create a simple ASP.NET page that accepts two number inputs from the user and displays their product when the Submit button is clicked. Use two text box controls, a label control, and a Submit button control. Also use the standard event handler code defined in the "Code Declaration Blocks" section of today's lesson. Try using the `Cint()` function to convert the text in the text boxes to integers for multiplication, such as `Cint(tbNumber1.Text)`.

   Follow Listing 2.1 for guidance.

   The code for the ASP.NET page is as follows:

```
<%@ Page Language="VB" %>
<script language="VB" runat="server">
   Sub btSubmit_Click(Sender As Object, E As EventArgs)
      lblMessage.Text = Cint(tbNumber1.Text) * _
         Cint(tbNumber2.Text)
   End Sub
</script>
<html>
```

```
<body>
    <font size="5">Sam's Teach Yourself ASP.NET in 21 Days:
    Day 2, Exercise 1</font><hr><p>

    <form runat="server">

       Number 1: <asp:textbox id="tbNumber1" runat=server/>
       Number 2: <asp:textbox id="tbNumber2" runat=server/>
       <asp:button id="btSubmit" Text="Submit"
          OnClick="btSubmit_Click" runat=server/><p>
       <asp:label id="lblMessage" font-size="20pt"
          runat=server/>
    </form>

 </body></html>
```

2. Build upon the previous exercise by providing multiple Submit buttons that perform the basic arithmetic operations, essentially creating a calculator.

   The code for the ASP.NET page is as follows:

```
<%@ Page Language="VB" %>
<script runat="server">
   Sub btAdd_Click(Sender As Object, E As EventArgs)
      lblMessage.Text = "The answer is: " & _
         Cint(tbNumber1.Text) + Cint(tbNumber2.Text)
   End Sub

   Sub btSubtract_Click(Sender As Object, E As EventArgs)
      lblMessage.Text = "The answer is: " & _
          Cint(tbNumber1.Text) - Cint(tbNumber2.Text)
    End Sub

    Sub btMultiply_Click(Sender As Object, E As EventArgs)
       lblMessage.Text = "The answer is: " & _
          Cint(tbNumber1.Text) * Cint(tbNumber2.Text)
    End Sub

    Sub btDivide_Click(Sender As Object, E As EventArgs)
       lblMessage.Text = "The answer is: " & _
          Cint(tbNumber1.Text) / Cint(tbNumber2.Text)
    End Sub
 </script>
 </html><body>

    <font size="5">Sam's Teach Yourself ASP.NET in 21 Days:
    Day 2, Exercise 2</font><hr><p>

    <form runat="server">

       Number 1: <asp:textbox id="tbNumber1" runat=server/>
```

```
            <br>
            Number 2: <asp:textbox id="tbNumber2" runat=server/>
            <p>
            <asp:button id="btAdd" Text="   +   "
               OnClick="btAdd_Click" runat=server/>
            <asp:button id="btSubtract" Text="   -   "
               OnClick="btSubtract_Click" runat=server/>
            <asp:button id="btMultiply" Text="   *   "
               OnClick="btMultiply_Click" runat=server/>
            <asp:button id="btDivide" Text="   /   "
               OnClick="btDivide_Click" runat=server/><p>
            <asp:label id="lblMessage" font-size="20pt"
               runat=server/>

         </form>
      </body>
      </html>
```


Answers for Day 3

Quiz

1. When should you use a `for` loop? A `while` loop?

   Use a `for` loop when you know the number of times the code should execute. Use a `while` loop when you don't know this.

2. What is the output of the following code snippet?

   ```
   Dim I as integer = 5
   Do
      Response.Write(I & " ")
      I = I + 2
   Loop Until I > 10
   ```

   The output is

   ```
   5 7 9
   ```

3. What is the output of the following code snippet?

   ```
   Dim I as integer = 5
   Do
      I = I + 2
    Response.Write(I & " ")
   Loop Until I > 10
   ```

   The output is

   ```
   7 9 11
   ```

4. What are the standard event handler parameters for ASP.NET pages?

   The standard parameter list is `(Sender as Object, e as EventArgs)`.

Exercise

Create an ASP.NET page with a class that represents you, with properties that describe your hair color, eye color, and birth date. Use the `dayofweek` property of the `datetime` data type to determine the day of the week of your birthday. The `dayofweek` property returns an integer—convert this into the day of the week. Call this method whenever a user clicks the Submit button, and print the output to the browser.

Here's the code:

```
<%@ Page Language="VB" %>

<script runat="server">
   Class Chris
      public dtBirthDay as DateTime = #6/27/78#
      public strHairColor as string = "Brown"
      public strEyeColor as string = "Brown"

      function GetDayOfWeek()
          dim strDay as string

          select case dtBirthDay.DayOfWeek
             case 0
                return "Sunday"
             case 1
                return "Monday"
             case 2
                return "Tuesday"
             case 3
                return "Wednesday"
             case 4
                return "Thursday"
             case 5
                return "Friday"
             case 6
                return "Saturday"
          end select
       end function

    End Class

    sub Button_Click(Sender as Object, e as EventArgs)
       dim objChris as new Chris
       Response.write(objChris.GetDayOfWeek)
    end sub

 </script>
```

```
<html><body>
   <form runat="server">
      <asp:button id="btSubmit" Text="Submit"
         runat=server
         OnClick="Button_Click"/><p>
   </form>
</body></html>
```

Answers for Day 4

Quiz

1. What are static members?

   Static members are members of an object that don't belong to any specific instance of the object, such as a counter. These can be accessed by the following:

   `Object.member`

2. Will the following code snippet work?

   ```
   <html><body>
      Hi there!
      <% Response.Redirect("page2.aspx") %>
   </body></html>
   ```

   No. `Response.Redirect` must be called before any output is sent to the browser.

3. What language is the following code snippet written in?

   ```
   Response.Write("Hello there!")
   ```

   This is VB.NET. Often the only giveaway between the languages is the semicolon at the end of the statement.

Exercises

1. Create an ASP.NET page in C# that acts as a secure login page. Allow the user to enter a username and password in a text box. If they match a string you specify, redirect the user to a "success" page. Otherwise, display an error. If the user is valid, save her username in a `Session` variable.

   The code for `example1.aspx` is as follows:

   ```
   <%@ Page Language="C#" %>

   <script runat="server">
      void Submit_Click(Object Sender, EventArgs e) {
         if (tbPass.Value == "mypass") {
            Session["UserName"] = tbUser.Value;
            Response.Redirect("exercise2.aspx");
         } else {
   ```

```
            Label1.Text = "<font color=red>That " +
                "is the wrong password!</font>";
        }
    }
</script>

<html><body>
    <form runat="server">

        Please enter your username and password:<p>
        <input type="text" id="tbUser"
            runat="server"/><br>
        <input type="password" id="tbPass"
            runat="server"/>

        <p>
        <asp:Button id="btSubmit"
            text="Submit"
            runat="server"
            OnClick="Submit_Click" /><p>

        <asp:Label id="Label1" runat="server"/>
    </form>
</body></html>
```

2. Write the success page in VB.NET. Display a personalized Welcome message using the `Load` event of the `Page` object and a `label` control. Also inform the user of the current time and his Session ID. Check the `IsPostback` property of the `Page` object to ensure that this message is only displayed the first time he arrives at the page. Provide a button for him to log out, with a confirmation message.

   The source for `exercise2.aspx` is as follows:

```
<%@ Page Language="VB" %>

<script runat="server">
    sub Page_Load(Sender as Object, e as EventArgs)
        if not Page.IsPostBack then
            Label1.Text = "Welcome " & Session("Username") & _
                "!<p>"

            Label1.Text = Label1.Text & "The current time " & _
                "is: " & DateTime.Now.ToString("T") & "<p>"

             Label1.Text = Label1.Text & "Your session id " & _
                "is: " & Session.SessionID & "<p>"
        end if
    end sub

    sub Submit_Click(Sender as Object, e as EventArgs)
```

```
            Session.Abandon
            Label1.Text = "Your session has ended."
            btSubmit.Visible = false
        end sub
    </script>

    <html><body>
        <form runat="server">
            <asp:Label id="Label1" runat="server"/>

            <asp:Button id="btSubmit"
                text="Submit"
                runat="server"
                OnClick="Submit_Click" /><p>
        </form>
    </body></html>
```


Answers for Day 5

Quiz

1. How do Web forms keep track of viewstate?

   Through hidden form variables.

2. What does the state bag do, and how do you access it?

   The state bag allows you to store custom values (values that aren't entered in controls) between form posts. You can access it through the `ViewState` variable:

   `ViewState("MyItem") = MyValue`

3. True or false: Events in Web forms are processed before the `Page_Load` event.

   False. The `Page_Load` event is always processed first, followed by the events, in no particular order.

4. What is the standard event parameter list?

   `(Sender as Object, e as EventArgs)`

5. What is the importance of the `runat="server"` tag?

   This tag converts an HTML element to a server control. Without it, the server couldn't keep track of controls, the viewstate wouldn't be maintained, and you couldn't have programmatic access to the control on the server. This is a key element of Web forms.

6. Why should you use HTML server controls?

   To convert existing HTML elements into server controls that you can manipulate through code.

7. What's wrong with the following code snippet?

   ```
   <asp:Button id="btSubmit"
      Click="HandleThis" >
   ```

   It's missing the `runat="server"` attribute. The event declaration should read `OnClick="HandleThis"`. And there's no closing tag: `</asp:Button>`.

8. Which property can be used to make a control post immediately to the server upon an event?

   `AutoPostBack`

9. When should you use Web controls instead of HTML server controls?

   Anytime you create new Web forms (that is, when you're not converting old pages).

Exercises

1. Build an application for choosing a baby's name. The user will select the sex of the baby, and then a `ListBox` will display a few possible names. When the user selects a name, a message is displayed using the selected name.

   The code is as follows:

```
<%@ Page Language="VB" %>

<script runat="server">
   sub ChangeNames(Sender as Object, e as EventArgs)
      if rlSex.SelectedIndex = 0 then
         'female
         lbNames.Items(0).Text = "Sally"
         lbNames.Items(1).Text = "Sara"
         lbNames.Items(2).Text = "Hope"
         lbNames.Items(3).Text = "Kaylee"
      else
         'male
         lbNames.Items(0).Text = "John"
         lbNames.Items(1).Text = "Chris"
         lbNames.Items(2).Text = "Daniel"
         lbNames.Items(3).Text = "Walter"
      end if
   end sub

   sub DisplayMessage(Sender as Object, e as EventArgs)
      lblMessage.Text = Sender.SelectedItem.Text & _
         " is a wonderful name!"
   end sub

</script>

```

```
<html><body>
   <form runat="server">
      <asp:Label id="lblMessage" runat="server"/><p>

      Choose the sex of your baby:
      <asp:RadioButtonList id="rlSex" runat="server"
         OnSelectedIndexChanged="ChangeNames"
         AutoPostBack="true" >
         <asp:ListItem>Female</asp:ListItem>
         <asp:ListItem>Male</asp:ListItem>
      </asp:RadioButtonList><p>

      Possible names:<br>
      <asp:ListBox id="lbNames" runat="server"
         OnSelectedIndexChanged="DisplayMessage"
         AutoPostBack="true" >
         <asp:ListItem></asp:ListItem>
         <asp:ListItem></asp:ListItem>
         <asp:ListItem></asp:ListItem>
         <asp:ListItem></asp:ListItem>
      </asp:ListBox><p>

   </form>
</body></html>
```


2. Build a standard user registration page with the following fields: name (required), address, phone (required), fax, and e-mail address (required). If any of the required values are missing, display an error message to the user.

   The code is as follows:

```
<%@ Page Language="VB" %>

<script runat="server">
   sub Submit(Sender as Object, e as EventArgs)
      if tbName.Text = "" then
         lblMessage.Text = "You forgot your name!<br>"
      end if
      if tbPhone.Text = "" then
         lblMessage.Text += "You forgot your phone!<br>"
       end if
       if tbEmail.Text = "" then
          lblMessage.Text += "You forgot your email!<br>"
       end if

       if lblMessage.Text = "" then
          lblMessage.Text = "Your information has been " & _
             "submitted!"
       end if
```

```
    end sub
</script>

<html><body>
    Please enter the following information.<p>

    <asp:Label id="lblMessage" runat="server"/>
    <form runat="server">
        <table cellpadding="2" cellspacing="2" border="1">
        <tr>
            <td width="250">Name* </td>
            <td width="150">
                <asp:TextBox id="tbName" runat="server"/>
            </td>
        </tr>
        <tr>
            <td>Address</td>
            <td>
                <asp:TextBox id="tbAddress" runat="server"/>
            </td>
        </tr>
        <tr>
            <td>Phone* (area code first)</td>
            <td>
                <asp:TextBox id="tbPhone" runat="server"/>
            </td>
        </tr>
        <tr>
            <td>Fax (area code first)</td>
            <td>
                <asp:TextBox id="tbFax" runat="server"/>
            </td>
        </tr>
        <tr>
            <td>Email*</td>
            <td>
                <asp:TextBox id="tbEmail" runat="server"/>
            </td>
        </tr>
        <tr>
            <td colspan="2">
                <asp:Button id="btSubmit" runat="server"
                    Text="Submit"
                    OnClick="Submit" />
            </td>
        </tr>
        </table>
        <p>
        <i>An asterisk (*) indicates a required field.</i>
    </form>
</body></html>
```

Answers for Day 6

Quiz

1. True or False: A user control can be used on its own.

   False. It needs to be embedded in an ASP.NET page.

2. What are the three requirements to turn an `.aspx` file into a user control?

   Remove all `<html>`, `<form>`, and `<body>` tags; change `@ Page` directives to `@ Control` directives; and rename your file to include an `.ascx` extension.

3. Build a `@ Register` directive for a user control with the tag prefix and the names `ACMEVBCustomControls` and `TextWriter`, located in the `shared.ascx` file in a subdirectory named `ucontrols`.

   The proper syntax is

```
<%@ Register TagPrefix="ACMEVBCustomControls" TagName="TextWriter"
➥src="ucontrols/shared.ascx " %>
```

4. True or False: A custom control must be compiled to be used on an ASP.NET page.

   True.

5. True or False: A custom control must be derived from the `Object` class, directly or indirectly.

   False. It must inherit from the `System.Web.UI.Control` class.

6. Using VB.NET's property element syntax, create a simple property for a custom control called `Color` that stores information in viewstate.

```
public property Color as string
   Get
      Color = ViewState("Color").ToString
   End Get
   Set
      ViewState("Color") = value
   End Set
end property
```

7. True or False: The `LoadControl` method can be used to load a custom control dynamically.

   False. `LoadControl` can load user controls dynamically.

Exercises

1. Enhance the calculator exercise from Day 2 so that it resembles the Windows calculator. Include memory functions (using Session variables), clear and backspace buttons, and the additional operator buttons. Encapsulate it as a user control. This

exercise can get fairly complex, but don't worry! You've learned all of the techniques you need to build it.

The code for the user control, `Calculator.ascx`, is as follows:

```
<script language="VB" runat="server">
   private answer as double

   Sub btOperator_Click(Sender as Object, e as EventArgs)
      if (hiddenvalue.value <> "" and hiddenvalue.value <> "0")
         tbNumber.Text = Operate(Sender.Text, hiddenvalue.value,
➥ tbNumber.Text)
         hiddenvalue.value = ""
         hiddenoperator.value = ""
      else
         'save old number as hidden input field
         ' and clear text box
         hiddenvalue.value = tbNumber.Text
         hiddenoperator.value = Sender.Text
         tbNumber.Text = "0"
      end if
   End Sub

   Sub btSpecOperator_Click(Sender as Object, e as EventArgs)
      tbNumber.Text = Operate(Sender.Text, hiddenvalue.value,
➥tbNumber.Text)
      hiddenvalue.value = ""
      hiddenoperator.value = ""
   End Sub

   Sub btNumber_Click(Sender as Object, e as EventArgs)
      response.write(answer.ToString)
      if tbNumber.Text <> "0" then
         tbNumber.Text = tbNumber.Text & Sender.Text
      else
         tbNumber.Text = Sender.Text
         answer = nothing
      end if
   end sub

   Sub btClear_Click(Sender as Object, e as EventArgs)
      tbNumber.Text = "0"
      hiddenoperator.value = ""
      hiddenvalue.value = ""
   end sub

   Sub btBS_Click(Sender as Object, e as EventArgs)
      if tbNumber.Text <> "0" then
         tbNumber.Text = Left(tbNumber.Text,
➥len(tbNumber.Text)-1)
      end if
```

```
    end sub

    Sub btMemory_Click(Sender as Object, e as EventArgs)
       select case Sender.text
          case "MC"
             Session("memory") = ""
             Indicator.Text = ""
          case "MS"
             Session("memory") = tbNumber.Text
             Indicator.Text = "M"
          case "MR"
             tbNumber.Text = Session("Memory")
          case "M+"

       end select
    end sub

    Sub btEqual_Click(Sender as Object, e as EventArgs)
       if hiddenvalue.value <> "" then
          if hiddenoperator.value <> "" then
             'operate numbers
             tbNumber.Text = Operate(hiddenoperator.value,
➥hiddenvalue.value, tbNumber.Text)
             hiddenvalue.value = ""
             hiddenoperator.value = ""
             answer = tbNumber.Text
          else
             'do nothing
          end if
       else
          'do nothing
       end if
    end sub

    private function Operate(operator as string, number1 as
➥string, optional number2 as string = "1") as double
       select case operator
          case "+"
             Operate = CDbl(number1) + CDbl(number2)
          case "-"
             Operate = CDbl(number1) - CDbl(number2)
          case "*"
             Operate = CDbl(number1) * CDbl(number2)
          case "/"
             Operate = CDbl(number1) / CDbl(number2)
          case "sqrt"
             Operate = CDbl(Math.sqrt(number2))
          case "1/x"
             Operate = CDbl(1 / cdbl(number2))
          case "+/-"
             Operate = CDbl(-cdbl(number2))
```

```
            end select
        end function
    </script>

    <asp:Panel id="Frame" runat="server">
        <table width="250">
        <tr>
            <td width="100%" colspan="7">
                <asp:textbox id="tbNumber" runat=server
                    text="0"
                    enabled="false"
                    width="100%" />
            </td>
        </tr>
        <tr>
            <td align="right" width="100%" colspan="7">
                <asp:Label id="Indicator" text=""
➥runat="server" />
                <asp:button id="btBS" Text="Backspace"
                    OnClick="btBS_Click" runat=server width="75"/>
                <asp:button id="btClear" Text="C"
                    OnClick="btClear_Click" runat=server
➥width="35"/>
            </td>
        </tr>
        <tr>
            <td width="32" valign="top">
                <asp:button id="btMC" Text="MC"
                    OnClick="btMemory_Click" runat=server
                    width="35"/>
            </td>
            <td width="58"></td>
            <td width="32">
                <asp:button id="bt7" Text="7"
                    OnClick="btNumber_Click" runat=server
                    width="35"/><p>
            </td>
            <td width="32">
                <asp:button id="bt8" Text="8"
                    OnClick="btNumber_Click" runat=server
                    width="35"/><p>
            </td>
            <td width="32">
                <asp:button id="bt9" Text="9"
                    OnClick="btNumber_Click" runat=server
                    width="35"/><p>
            </td>
            <td width="32">
                <asp:button id="btDivide" Text="/"
                    OnClick="btOperator_Click" runat=server
                    width="35"/><p>
```

```
        </td>
        <td width="32">
           <asp:button id="btSqrt" Text="sqrt"
              OnClick="btSpecOperator_Click" runat=server
              width="35"/><p>
        </td>
     </tr>
     <tr>
        <td width="32" valign="top">
           <asp:button id="btMR" Text="MR"
              OnClick="btMemory_Click" runat=server
              width="35"/>
        </td>
        <td width="8"></td>
        <td width="32">
           <asp:button id="bt4" Text="4"
              OnClick="btNumber_Click"
              runat=server width="35"/><p>
        </td>
        <td width="32">
           <asp:button id="bt5" Text="5"
              OnClick="btNumber_Click" runat=server
              width="35"/><p>
        </td>
        <td width="32">
           <asp:button id="bt6" Text="6"
              OnClick="btNumber_Click" runat=server
              width="35"/><p>
        </td>
        <td width="32">
           <asp:button id="btMultiply" Text="*"
              OnClick="btOperator_Click" runat=server
              width="35"/><p>
        </td>
        <td width="32">
           <asp:button id="btPercent" Text="%"
              OnClick="btOperator_Click" runat=server
              width="35"/><p>
        </td>
     </tr>
     <tr>
        <td width="32" valign="top">
           <asp:button id="btMS" Text="MS"
              OnClick="btMemory_Click" runat=server
              width="35"/>
        </td>
        <td width="8"></td>
        <td width="32">
           <asp:button id="bt1" Text="1"
              OnClick="btNumber_Click" runat=server
              width="35"/><p>
```

```
         </td>
         <td width="32">
            <asp:button id="bt2" Text="2"
               OnClick="btNumber_Click" runat=server
               width="35"/><p>
         </td>
         <td width="32">
            <asp:button id="bt3" Text="3"
               OnClick="btNumber_Click" runat=server
               width="35"/><p>
         </td>
         <td width="32">
            <asp:button id="btSubtract" Text="-"
               OnClick="btOperator_Click" runat=server
               width="35"/><p>
         </td>
         <td width="32">
            <asp:button id="btOneOver" Text="1/x"
               OnClick="btSpecOperator_Click" runat=server
               width="35"/><p>
         </td>
      </tr>
      <tr>
         <td width="32" valign="top">
            <asp:button id="btMP" Text="M+"
               OnClick="btMemory_Click" runat=server
               width="35"/>
         </td>
         <td width="8"></td>
         <td width="32">
            <asp:button id="bt0" Text="0"
               OnClick="btNumber_Click" runat=server
               width="35"/><p>
         </td>
         <td width="32">
            <asp:button id="btNegate" Text="+/-"
               OnClick="btSpecOperator_Click" runat=server
               width="35"/><p>
         </td>
         <td width="32">
            <asp:button id="btDot" Text="."
               OnClick="btNumber_Click" runat=server
               width="35"/><p>
         </td>
         <td width="32">
            <asp:button id="btAdd" Text="+"
               OnClick="btOperator_Click" runat=server
               width="35"/><p>
         </td>
         <td width="32">
            <asp:button id="btEqual" Text="="
```

```
                OnClick="btEqual_Click" runat=server
                width="35"/><p>
          </td>
       </tr>
       </table>
    </asp:Panel>
    <input type="hidden" id="hiddenvalue" value=""
       runat="server" >
    <input type="hidden" id="hiddenoperator" value=""
    runat="server" >
```

The code for the ASP.NET page is as follows:

```
<%@ Page language="VB" %>
<%@ Register TagPrefix="TYASPNET" TagName="Calculator"
➥src="Calculator.ascx" %>

<html><body>
   <form runat="server">
      <TYASPNET:Calculator id="Calc1" runat="server"/>
   </form>
</body></html>
```


2. Create a meeting planner. It should include a calendar, a text box for user entries, and a label to display the current data. Use `AutoPostBack` and the `TextChanged` event when the user enters something in the text box to add notes. Store them in session variables so that the user may return to them at a later time. When a note is added, create a label dynamically to provide feedback. Use Appendix C to learn about the Calendar control's events and methods.

   The code for the user control, `planner.ascx` is as follows:

```
<script language="VB" runat="server">
   Public sub Page_Load(Sender as Object, e as EventArgs)
      if not Page.IsPostBack then
         Session.Clear
         Calendar1.SelectedDate = DateTime.Now
         DayLabel.Text = Calendar1.SelectedDate. _
            ToString("dddd, MMMM dd yyyy")
      end if
   End Sub

    Public sub SelectionChanged(Sender as Object, e as
➥EventArgs)
       DayLabel.Text = Calendar1.SelectedDate. _
          ToString("dddd, MMMM dd yyyy")

       if not (Session(Calendar1.SelectedDate.ToString) is _
          nothing)
          dim l as Label = new label
          l.Text = Session(Calendar1.SelectedDate.ToString)
```

```
         DayPanel.Controls.Add(l)
      end if
   End Sub

   Public sub NoteChanged(Sender as Object, e as EventArgs)
      if obj.text <> "" then
         dim l as Label = New Label
         l.text = "<li>" & Sender.Text & "</li>"

         DayPanel.Controls.Add(l)
         Session(Calendar1.SelectedDate.ToString) = l.text
         NoteBox.Text = ""
      end if
   End Sub
</script>

<table width="100%">
<tr>
   <td width="50%" valign="top">
      <font face="arial">
         <asp:Label id="DayLabel" runat="server"
            Height="25px" Width="100%"
            BackColor="#ddaa66" ForeColor="white"
            Font-Bold="true" BorderStyle="groove" />
         <br>
         <asp:Panel id="DayPanel" runat="server"
            backcolor="#ffffff" borderStyle="groove"
            Height="225px" >

            <asp:Textbox id="NoteBox" runat="server"
               OnTextChanged="NoteChanged"
               TextMode="Multiline"
               Rows=5 Width="100%"
               AutoPostBack="true" /><p>
         </asp:Panel>
      </font>
   </td>
   <td width="50%" rowspan="2" valign="top">
      <asp:Calendar id="Calendar1" runat="server"
         OnSelectionChanged="SelectionChanged"
         Cellpadding="5" Cellspacing="5"
         DayHeaderStyle-Font-Bold="True"
         DayNameFormat="Short"
         Font-Name="Arial" Font-Size="12px"
         height="250px"
         NextPrevFormat="ShortMonth"
         NextPrevStyle-ForeColor="white"
         SelectedDayStyle-BackColor="#ffcc66"
         SelectedDayStyle-Font-Bold="True"
         SelectionMode="DayWeekMonth"
         SelectorStyle-BackColor="#99ccff"
```

```
                SelectorStyle-ForeColor="navy"
                SelectorStyle-Font-Size="9px"
                ShowTitle="true"
                TitleStyle-BackColor="#ddaa66"
                TitleStyle-ForeColor="white"
                TitleStyle-Font-Bold="True"
                TodayDayStyle-Font-Bold="True" />
          </td>
       </tr>
       </table>
```

The code for the ASP.NET page is as follows:

```
<%@ Page Language="VB" debug="true" %>
<%@ Register TagPrefix="TYASPNET" TagName="Planner"
➥src="planner.ascx" %>

<html><body>
   <form runat="server">
      <TYASPNET:Planner id="Planner" runat="server" />
   </form>
</body></html>
```


Answers for Day 7

Quiz

1. What are the five Validation controls?

   `RequiredFieldValidator`, `CompareValidator`, `RangeValidator`, `RegularExpressionValidator`, and `CustomValidator`.

2. True or false: Validation controls are created on the client side.

   False. Validation controls are created server-side, just like all other server controls.

3. What two properties should every Validation control have?

   `ControlToValidate` and `ErrorMessage`.

4. What does the `clienttarget=downlevel` parameter do?

   It makes ASP.NET believe you're developing for an older browser, disabling all DHTML events (including Validation controls).

5. Assuming you have two server controls, `tbName` and `tbAge`, will the following validator work?

```
<asp:CompareValidator runat="server"
   ControlToValidate="tbName"
   ValueToCompare="tbAge"
   ErrorMessage="Error!"/>
```

No, you should use `ControlToCompare` instead of `ValueToCompare`.

6. What's the property you need to set for the `CustomValidator` control that specifies the event handler?

   `OnServerValidate`.

Exercise

Build a login page similar to Listing 7.6, but build it into a user control. Handle all validation inside the user control, as opposed to the containing ASP.NET page.

```
<script runat="server">
   sub Submit(Sender as Object, e as EventArgs)
      if Page.IsValid then
         'do something
      end if
   end sub

   sub ValidateThis(Sender as Object, args as _
   ServerValidateEventArgs)
       if len(args.Value) < 8 then
          args.IsValid = false
       else
          args.IsValid = true
       end if
    end sub
 </script>

       <asp:Label id="lblMessage" runat="server" />
       <table>
       <tr>
          <td valign="top">Username:</td>
          <td valign="top">
             <asp:Textbox id="tbUserName" runat="server"
                /><br>
             <asp:CustomValidator runat="server"
                OnServerValidate="ValidateThis"
                OnClientValiate="validateLength"
                Display="Dynamic"
                ControlToValidate="tbUserName"
                ErrorMessage="The username must be 8
➥characters or longer"/>
          </td>
       </tr>
       <tr>
          <td valign="top">Password:</td>
          <td valign="top">
             <asp:Textbox id="tbPassword" runat="server"
                TextMode="password" />
          </td>
```

```
        </tr>
        <tr>
           <td align="right" colspan="2">
              <ASP:Button id="tbSubmit" runat="server"
                 OnClick="Submit"
                 text="Submit" />
           </td>
        </tr>
  </table>
```

Answers for Day 8

Quiz

1. What is a relational database?

   It's a database in which multiple tables are related to each other using foreign key relationships. This methodology is used to minimize redundant information, and for efficiency.

2. What does SQL stand for, and what does it do?

   SQL is the Structured Query Language and is used to communicate with databases.

3. What does ODBC stand for?

   Open Database Connectivity.

4. True or False: You can access any ODBC-compliant database through ASP.NET.

   True.

5. What are the five steps to accessing a database from ASP.NET?

   1. Set up a database connection.
   2. Open the database connection.
   3. Fill a `Dataset` with the desired data.
   4. Set up a `Dataview` to display data.
   5. Bind a server control to the `Dataview`.

Exercise

Create your own database from scratch and use it to store information on pets that you've owned. (If you've never owned any, make some up!) What fields do you need?

Possible fields include pet name, pet type (dog, cat, and so on), years owned, and last vet visit. Don't forget to set a primary key. You can query the data using the SQL statements you've learned today.

Answers for Day 9

Quiz

1. What namespaces must you import to use data mechanisms in your ASP.NET pages?

   System.Data, and optionally either System.Data.OleDb or System.Data.SQL. These provide additional methods and objects that allow you to work with databases.

2. True or False: The DataSet can contain multiple tables.

   True.

3. What are the three collections of the DataSet, and what do they do?

   Tables—Holds all DataTable objects.

   ExtendedProperties—Holds additional information about a data store, such as usernames and passwords.

   Relations—Holds information on relations defined between DataTables.

4. What is the syntax for data-binding expressions?

   <%# *property or collection* %>

5. Does the DataList control support paging?

   No, it doesn't inherently support paging.

6. What are the two properties of a DataGrid that you must specify to turn on sorting and paging, respectively?

   AllowSorting="true"

   AllowPaging="true"

Exercise

Enhance the planner application from exercise 2 in Day 6 to use data binding. Bind the DayLabel to the Calendar's selectedDate, and format it properly.

The code is the same as before, with the following changes:

In planner.ascx—Add a method call to DataBind in the Page_Load event, inside the postback check, and also to the end of the SelectionChanged method, after the if statement.

Remove the lines DayLabel.Text = (Calendar1.SelectedDate).Format("dddd, MMMM dd yyyy", nothing) and DayLabel.Text = (obj.SelectedDate).Format("dddd, MMMM dd yyyy", nothing) from the Page_Load and SelectionChanged events, respectively.

Add the line `Text='<%# Calendar1.SelectedDate.Format("dddd, MMMM dd yyyy", nothing ) %>'` to the declaration of `DayLabel`.

Be sure to import the `System.Data` namespace!

Answers for Day 10

Quiz

1. What are the two parts of ADO.NET?

   The `DataSet` object and the managed providers.

2. What do the managed providers do?

   They provide the interface for communication between data stores and `DataSets`. The two managed providers for ADO.NET are SQL and ADO.

3. What is disconnected data?

   A data representation, such a `DataSet`, that doesn't require a continuous database connection.

4. Which of the following constructors isn't valid for the `OleDbCommand` object (line 4, 5, 6, 8, or 9)?

   ```
   dim strSQL as string = "SELECT * FROM tblUsers"dim Conn as new
   ➥OleDbConnection("DSN=21DaysBanking")

   dim objCmd as new OleDbCommand()
   dim objCmd as new OleDbCommand(strSQL)
   dim objCmd as new OleDbCommand(strSQL, _
      Conn)
   dim objCmd as new OleDbCommand(Conn)
   dim objCmd as new OleDbCommand(strSQL, _
      "DSN=21DaysBanking")
   ```

   Line 8 is an invalid constructor.

5. What type of data model does an `OleDbCommand` object fill?

   An `ADODataReader` object.

6. Does an `OleDbCommand` object need to be closed?

   No, only the `OleDbDataReader` and `OleDbConnection` object need to be closed explicitly.

7. What are the five members of the `OleDbDataAdapter` object?

   `UpdateCommand`, `InsertCommand`, `DeleteCommand`, `SelectCommand`, and `TableMappings`.

8. Which of the following constructors isn't valid for the `OleDbDataAdapter` object (line 5, 6, 7, 9, or 10)?

```
dim strSQL as string = "SELECT * FROM tblUsers")
dim Conn as new OleDbConnection("DSN=21DaysBanking")
dim objADOCmd as new OleDbCommand(strSQL, Conn)

dim objCmd as new OleDbDataAdapter()
dim objCmd as new OleDbDataAdapter(objADOCmd)
dim objCmd as new OleDbDataAdapter(strSQL, _
   Conn)
dim objCmd as new OleDbDataAdapter(Conn)
dim objCmd as new OleDbDataAdapter(strSQL, _
   "DSN=21DaysBanking")
```

Line 9 is the invalid constructor.

Exercise

Modify the example application you built today to use the `OleDbDataAdapter` and `DataSet` objects, instead of the `OleDbCommand` and `OleDbDataReader`.

The new code declaration block should read as follows:

```
<%@ Page Language="VB" %>
<%@ Import Namespace="System.Data" %>
<%@ Import Namespace="System.Data.OleDb" %>

<script runat="server">
   'declare connection
   dim Conn as new OleDbConnection( _
      "Provider=Microsoft.Jet.OLEDB.4.0;" & _
      "Data Source=C:\ASPNET\data\banking.mdb")
    dim ds as new DataSet("tblUsers")

    sub Page_Load(Sender as Object, e as EventArgs)
       if Not Page.IsPostBack then
          FillDataGrid()
       end if
    end sub

    sub GetData()
       'open connection
       dim objCmd as new OleDbDataAdapter _
          ("select * from tblUsers", Conn)
       'fill dataset
       objCmd.Fill(ds, "tblUsers")

       'define primary key
       dim keys() as DataColumn = {ds.Tables("tblUsers"). _
          Columns("UserID")}
       ds.Tables("tblUsers").PrimaryKey = keys
```

```
         ds.Tables("tblUsers").Columns("UserID").AutoIncrement = true
      end sub

      sub Submit(Sender as Object, e as eventargs)
         'insert new data
         dim i, j as integer
         dim params(7) as string
         dim strText, strSQL as string
         dim blnGo as boolean = true

         j = 0
         GetData()

         dim dr as DataRow = ds.Tables("tblUsers").NewRow()
         for i = 0 to AddPanel.Controls.Count - 1
            if AddPanel.controls(i).GetType Is GetType(TextBox) then
               strText = Ctype(AddPanel.Controls(i), TextBox).Text
               if strText <> "" then
                  dr(j) = strText
                  Ctype(AddPanel.Controls(i), TextBox).Text = ""
               else
                  blnGo = false
               lblMessage.Text = lblMessage.Text & "You forgot to " & _
                     "enter a value for " &
➥AddPanel.Controls(i).ID & "<p>"
                  lblMessage.Style("ForeColor") = "Red"
               end if
               j = j + 1
            end if
         next

         if not blnGo then
            exit sub
         end if

         ds.Tables("tblUsers").Rows.Add(dr)

         ExecuteStatement()

         FillDataGrid()
      end sub

      sub dgData_Edit(Sender as Object, e as DataGridCommandEventArgs)
         FillDataGrid(e.Item.ItemIndex)
      end sub

      sub dgData_Delete(Sender as Object, e as
➥DataGridCommandEventArgs)
         GetData()

```

```
            ds.Tables("tblUsers").Rows(e.Item.ItemIndex).Delete

            ExecuteStatement()

            FillDataGrid()
        end sub

        sub dgData_Update(Sender as Object, e as
DataGridCommandEventArgs)
            if UpdateDataStore then
               FillDataGrid(-1)
            end if
        end sub

        sub dgData_Cancel(Sender as Object, e as
DataGridCommandEventArgs)
            FillDataGrid(-1)
        end sub

        sub dgData_PageIndexChanged(Sender as Object, e as
➥DataGridPageChangedEventArgs)
            dgData.DataBind()
        end sub

        function UpdateDataStore(e as DataGridCommandEventArgs) _
            as boolean

            dim i,j as integer
            dim params(7) as string
            dim strText as string
            dim blnGo as boolean = true

            j = 0
            GetData()

            for i = 1 to e.Item.Cells.Count - 3
               strText = Ctype(e.Item.Cells(i).Controls(0),
➥TextBox).Text
               if strText <> "" then
                  ds.Tables("tblUsers").Rows(e.Item.ItemIndex)(j)
➥= strText
                  j = j + 1
               else
                  blnGo = false
                  lblMessage.Text = lblMessage.Text & "You forgot to " &
_
                     "enter a value<p>"
               end if
            next

            if not blnGo then
```

```
         return false
         exit function
      end if

      ExecuteStatement()
      return blnGo
   end function

   sub FillDataGrid(Optional EditIndex as integer=-1)
      GetData()

      if not EditIndex.Equals(Nothing) then
         dgData.EditItemIndex = EditIndex
      end if

      'select data view and bind to server control
      dgData.DataSource = ds
      dgData.DataMember = "tblUsers"
      dgData.DataBind()
   end sub

   function ExecuteStatement()
      'open connection
      dim objCmd as new OleDbDataAdapter _
         ("select UserID, FirstName, LastName, Address, City,
➥State, Zip, Phone from tblUsers", Conn)
      dim objAutoGen as New OleDbCommandBuilder(objCmd)

      try
         objCmd.Update(ds, "tblUsers")
      catch ex as Exception
         lblMessage.Text = ex.Message
      end try

      ds.Clear
   end function
</script>
```


Answers for Day 11

Quiz

1. When should you use an `XmlTextReader` versus an `XmlDocument`?

   An `XmlTextReader` should be used when you only need to view data and don't need any higher-level functionality. The `XmlDocument` provides more functionality using the XML Document Object Model, but it introduces additional overhead.

2. What does XML DOM stand for?

   Extensible Markup Language Document Object Model.

3. What's the difference between a node and an element?

   An element is represented by a single tag in an XML file. A node is an entire branch of data, consisting of start and end tags, children elements, and any attributes.

4. Will the following code snippet work?

   ```
   dim xmldoc as new XMLDataDocument()

   xmldoc.DataSet.ReadXml("books.xml")
   ```

   No, the `ReadXml` requires the full path to the XML data file. The last line should read as follows:

   ```
   xmldoc.DataSet.ReadXml(Server.MapPath("books.xml"))
   ```

Exercises

1. Create a new XML file that uses the `books-schema.xml` schema. Make sure your format is correct by using ASP.NET to validate it.

2. Build an interface that allows users to edit XML data from a `DataGrid`. Be sure to write the changes back to the file!

   Here's the code for the solution:

   ```
   <%@ Page Language="VB" %>
   <%@ Import Namespace="System.Xml" %>
   <%@ Import Namespace="System.Data" %>
   <%@ Import Namespace="System.Data.OleDb" %>

   <script runat=server>
      private i, j as integer
      private strOutput as string = ""
      public xmldoc as new XMLDataDocument()

       sub Page_Load(Sender as Object, e as EventArgs)
          if not Page.IsPostBack then
             GetData()
             BindControl()
          end if
       end sub

       sub UpdateBtn_Click(Sender as Object, e as EventArgs)
          dim Title as TextBox
          dim Genre as TextBox
          dim Style as TextBox
          dim Price as TextBox
   ```

```
      GetData()

      'update data
      For i = 0 To DataGrid1.Items.Count-1
         Title = DataGrid1.Items(i).FindControl("Title")
         Genre = DataGrid1.Items(i).FindControl("Genre")
         Style = DataGrid1.Items(i).FindControl("Style")
         Price = DataGrid1.Items(i).FindControl("Price")

         xmldoc.DataSet.Tables(0).Rows(i)("title") = _
            Title.Text
         xmldoc.DataSet.Tables(0).Rows(i)("genre") = _
            Genre.Text
         xmldoc.DataSet.Tables(0).Rows(i)("style") = _
            Style.Text
         xmldoc.DataSet.Tables(0).Rows(i)("price") = _
            Price.Text
      Next

      try
         xmldoc.Save(Server.MapPath("books.xml"))
      catch
         output.Text = "Error updating data"
      end try

      BindControl()
   end sub

   sub GetData()
      try
         xmldoc.DataSet.ReadXml(Server.MapPath("books.xml"))
      catch ex as Exception
         output.Text = "Error accessing XML file"
      end try
   end sub

   sub BindControl()
      DataGrid1.DataSource = xmldoc.DataSet
      DataGrid1.DataMember = xmldoc.DataSet.Tables(0). _
         TableName
      DataGrid1.DataBind()
   end sub
</script>

<html><body>
   <asp:Label id="output" runat="server" />

   <form runat="server">

   <asp:DataGrid id="DataGrid1"
```

```
      BorderColor="black"
      GridLines="Vertical"
      width="450"
      Font-Name="Arial"
      Font-Size="10pt"
      HeaderStyle-BackColor="#cccc99"
      ItemStyle-BackColor="#ffffff"
      AlternatingItemStyle-Backcolor="#cccccc"
      AutogenerateColumns="false" runat="server" >

      <Columns>

         <asp:TemplateColumn HeaderText="Title">
            <ItemTemplate>
               <asp:TextBox id="Title" runat="server"
                  Text='<%# Container.DataItem("title") %>'
                /> 
            </ItemTemplate>
         </asp:TemplateColumn>

         <asp:TemplateColumn HeaderText="Genre">
            <ItemTemplate>
               <asp:TextBox id="Genre" runat="server"
                  Text='<%# Container.DataItem("genre") %>'
                  width="75px" />
            </ItemTemplate>
         </asp:TemplateColumn>

         <asp:TemplateColumn HeaderText="style">
            <ItemTemplate>
               <asp:TextBox id="Style" runat="server"
                  Text='<%# Container.DataItem("style") %>'
                  width="75px" />
            </ItemTemplate>
         </asp:TemplateColumn>

         <asp:TemplateColumn HeaderText="Price">
            <ItemTemplate>
               <asp:TextBox id="Price" runat="server"
                  Text='<%# Container.DataItem("price") %>'
                  width="50px" />
            </ItemTemplate>
         </asp:TemplateColumn>

     </Columns>
   </asp:DataGrid>
   <p>
   <center>
   <asp:Button id="update" runat="server"
```

```
            OnClick="UpdateBtn_Click"
            text="Update!" />
        </center>
        </form>
    </body></html>
```

Answers for Day 12

Quiz

1. Specify a SQL statement to create an empty stored procedure (one that doesn't execute any SQL statement) that accepts one input parameter and one output parameter of your choice.

   ```
   CREATE PROCEDURE SelectIDFromName
   @Input varchar,
   @Output int OUTPUT
   AS
   ```


2. What are the four parameter directions?

   `Input`, `Output`, `InputOutput`, and `ReturnValue`.

3. True or false: You use output parameters if you want to return multiple rows of data.

   False. Generally, output parameters are used for queries that return single values.

4. Will the following code work?

   ```
   Response.Write("ID = " & objCmd.Parameters("@ID"). _
      Value.ToString())
   objReader.Close()
   ```

   No, because output parameters aren't returned until `DataReader` is closed.

5. What's the difference between `XPathNavigator` and `XmlDocument`?

   `XPathNavigator` provides dynamic node loading and supports XPath queries and XSL transforms. The `XmlDocument` loads an entire node tree upon opening an XML file, and it doesn't support XPath queries or XSL Transforms.

6. What is an XSL stylesheet used for, and how is it related to XPath queries?

   An XSL stylesheet is used to format XML data into a new structured document. It specifies nodes in an XML document to be formatted, which are retrieved by dynamically generated XPath queries.

7. How do you return data from an XSL Transform with `XmlReader`? With `XmlTextWriter`?

   With `XmlReader`:

   ```
   objReader = objXslT.Transform(objNav, nothing)
   ```

   With `XmlTextWriter`:

   ```
   objXslT.Transform(objNav, nothing, objWriter)
   ```

Exercise

Create a stored procedure that inserts a new row into your `tblUsers` table using parameters. Build an ASP.NET page that allows users to enter this data, and execute this procedure with parameters.

The code for the stored procedure (in Access) is as follows:

```
INSERT INTO tblUsers ( FirstName, LastName, Address,
   City, State, Zip, Phone )
VALUES (@FirstName, @LastName, @Address,
   @City, @state, @Zip, @Phone)
```

The code for the ASP.NET page is as follows:

```
<%@ Page Language="VB" %>
<%@ Import Namespace="System.Data" %>
<%@ Import Namespace="System.Data.OleDb" %>

<script runat="server">
   'declare connection
   dim Conn as new OleDbConnection("Provider=" & _
            "Microsoft.Jet.OLEDB.4.0;" & _
            "Data Source=c:\ASPNET\data\banking.mdb")

    sub InsertData(Sender as Object, e as EventArgs)
       dim objCmd as OleDbCommand = new OleDbCommand _
          ("InsertUser", Conn)
       objCmd.CommandType = CommandType.StoredProcedure

       dim objParam as OleDbParameter
       objParam = objCmd.Parameters.Add("@FirstName", _
          OleDbType.BSTR)
       objParam.Direction = ParameterDirection.Input
       objParam.Value = tbFName.Text

       objParam = objCmd.Parameters.Add("@LastName", _
          OleDbType.BSTR)
       objParam.Direction = ParameterDirection.Input
       objParam.Value = tbLName.Text
```

```
         objParam = objCmd.Parameters.Add("@Address", _
            OleDbType.BSTR)
         objParam.Direction = ParameterDirection.Input
         objParam.Value = tbAddress.Text

         objParam = objCmd.Parameters.Add("@City", _
            OleDbType.BSTR)
         objParam.Direction = ParameterDirection.Input
         objParam.Value = tbCity.Text

         objParam = objCmd.Parameters.Add("@State", _
            OleDbType.BSTR)
         objParam.Direction = ParameterDirection.Input
         objParam.Value = tbState.Text

         objParam = objCmd.Parameters.Add("@Zip", _
            OleDbType.BSTR)
         objParam.Direction = ParameterDirection.Input
         objParam.Value = tbZip.Text

         objParam = objCmd.Parameters.Add("@Phone", _
            OleDbType.BSTR)
         objParam.Direction = ParameterDirection.Input
         objParam.Value = tbPhone.Text

         try
            objCmd.Connection.Open()
            objCmd.ExecuteNonQuery
         catch ex as OleDbException
            lblMessage.Text = ex.Message
         end try

         objCmd.Connection.Close()
         lblMessage.Text = "User successfully added."
      end sub
   </script>

   <html><body>
      <form runat="server">
         <asp:Label id="lblMessage" runat="server"
            maintainstate=false /><br>
         <asp:Panel id="Panel1" runat="server">
            <table>
            <tr>
               <td width="100" valign="top">
                  First and last name:
               </td>
               <td width="300" valign="top">
```

```
               <asp:TextBox id="tbFName" runat="server" />
               <asp:TextBox id="tbLName" runat="server" />
            </td>
         </tr>
         <tr>
            <td valign="top">
               Address:
            </td>
            <td valign="top">
               <asp:TextBox id="tbAddress"
                  runat="server" />
            </td>
         </tr>
         <tr>
            <td valign="top">
               City, State, ZIP:
            </td>
            <td valign="top">
               <asp:TextBox id="tbCity"
                  runat="server" />,
               <asp:TextBox id="tbState" runat="server"
                  size=2 /> 
               <asp:TextBox id="tbZIP" runat="server"
                  size=5 />
            </td>
         </tr>
         <tr>
            <td valign="top">
               Phone:
            </td>
            <td valign="top">
               <asp:TextBox id="tbPhone" runat="server"
                  size=11 /><p>
            </td>
         </tr>
         <tr>
            <td colspan="2" valign="top" align="right">
               <asp:Button id="Submit" runat="server"
                  text="Add"
                  OnClick="InsertData" />
            </td>
         </tr>
         </table>
      </asp:Panel>
   </form>
</body></html>
```

Answers for Day 13

Quiz

1. What is the difference between a file and a stream?

   A file is a physical collection of data residing on a computer. A stream is a way to access data from different locations, such as a file, memory, or over the network.

2. What are the six `FileMode` values?

   `Append`, `Open`, `OpenOrCreate`, `Create`, `CreateNew`, and `Truncate`

3. What does the `Peek` method do, and why is it helpful?

   The `Peek` method reads the next character from a stream, but doesn't actually return the character. It is useful for determining when you're at the end of a stream.

4. How do you verify the existence of a file or directory on a server?

   The `FileExists` or `DirectoryExists` methods from the `File` and `Directory` classes, respectively.

5. Use the `File` object to open a file called `userdata.txt` in the root directory of your `c:` drive, for appending. If this file doesn't exist, use the `File` object to create it, and make sure that no other applications can access this file while you are using it.

```
dim f as new File("c:\userdata.txt")
f.Open(FileMode.Append, FileAccess.ReadWrite, FileShare.None)
```


Exercises

1. Create an ASP.NET page that will open a file specified by a user in a text box, and display the contents in a label. Make sure to check whether the file exists. Note that the user must be required to enter the full path to the file as well.

   The code for the answer is as follows:

```
<%@ Page Language="VB" %>
<%@ Import namespace="System.IO" %>

<script runat="server">
   sub DisplayFile(Sender as Object, e as EventArgs)
      dim strFile as string = tbFile.Text
      dim objReader as StreamReader

      if strFile <> "" then
         if File.Exists(strFile) then
            objReader = new StreamReader(strFile)
```

```
            lblMessage.Text = "<pre>"
            while objReader.Peek > -1
               lblMessage.Text += Server.HTMLEncode _
                  (objReader.ReadLine) & "<br>"
            end while
            lblMessage.Text += "</pre>"

            objReader.Close
         end if
      end if
   end sub
</script>

<html><body>
   <form runat="server">
      <asp:TextBox id="tbFile" runat="server"
         OnTextChanged="DisplayFile"
         AutoPostBack=true /><p>

      <asp:Label id="lblMessage" runat="server"
         MaintainState=false/>
   </form>
</body></html>
```

2. Modify exercise 1 so that the content of the file is displayed in an editable text box. Allow the user to make changes, and when the user clicks a submit button, write the changes back to the file.

```
<%@ Page Language="VB" %>
<%@ Import namespace="System.IO" %>

<script runat="server">
   sub Page_Load(Sender as Object, e as EventArgs)
      if not Page.IsPostBack then
         tbContents.Visible = false
      end if
   end sub

    sub DisplayFile(Sender as Object, e as EventArgs)
       dim strFile as string = tbFile.Text
       dim objReader as StreamReader

       if strFile <> "" then
          if File.Exists(strFile) then
             if not tbContents.Visible then
                tbContents.Visible = true
             else
```

```
               tbContents.Text = ""
            end if

            objReader = new StreamReader(strFile)

            tbContents.Text = Server.HTMLEncode _
                  (objReader.ReadToEnd)
            objReader.Close
         else
            tbContents.Text = "Invalid file"
         end if
      end if
   end sub

   sub WriteFile(Sender as Object, e as EventArgs)
      dim strContents as string = tbContents.Text
      dim strFile as string = tbFile.Text
      dim objWriter as StreamWriter

      if File.Exists(strFIle) then
         objWriter = new StreamWriter(strFile, false)

         objWriter.Write(strContents)

         objWriter.Close
      end if

   end sub
</script>

<html><body>
   <form runat="server">
      <asp:TextBox id="tbFile" runat="server"
         OnTextChanged="DisplayFile"
         AutoPostBack=true /><p>

      <asp:TextBox id="tbContents" runat="server"
         visible=true
         TextMode="Multiline"
         Columns="50"
         rows="20" /><p>

      <asp:Button id="btSubmit" runat="server"
         OnClick="WriteFile"
         Text="Submit"/>
   </form>
</body></html>
```

Answers for Day 14

Quiz

1. What's the difference between server-side and client-side caching?

   Server-side caching caches output before it's sent to the browser. Subsequent requests to that data will retrieve from the cache. Client-side caching stores data (such as pages accessed over the Internet) on a user's hard drive so that it doesn't need to be downloaded again.

2. Which caching mechanism stores cached data on the computer's hard drive?

   Output caching. (This includes the `HttpCachePolicy` object.)

3. What are the pros and cons of using the `Cache` class instead of output caching?

   It allows you to use sliding expiration, provides more granularity for caching individual items, and allows you to set dependencies on cached items.

   The `Cache` class stores data in memory as opposed to on disk, meaning it uses more valuable resources than page output caching.

4. What's the difference between the `SetExpires` method and the `SetMaxAge` method of the `Response.Cache` object?

   The `SetExpires` method sets the exact time that the content should expire, in terms of a `DateTime` object. The `SetMaxAge` function sets the time limit before the content expires in terms of a `TimeSpan` object.

5. What's the full signature of the `Cache.Add` method?

   ```
   Cache.Add(key, source, dependencies, AbsoluteExpiration,
   ➥SlidingExpiration, Priority, OnRemoveCallBack)
   ```

6. Suppose you have a page that accepts the following querystring parameters: `userid`, `searchstring`, `pagenumber`, and `orderby`. Using `VaryByParams`, what items should you cache by, and what's the required code?

   You should cache by `searchstring` and `orderby`. These are the only two parameters that wouldn't necessarily change each request and aren't personal information.

   The code is as follows:

   ```
   Response.Cache.VaryByParams.Item("searchstring") = true
   Response.Cache.VaryByParams.Item("orderby") = true
   ```

Exercise

Using Listing 14.5 as a test bed, measure the performance benefit of retrieving the DataView from the cache instead of creating it explicitly. (Hint: use the `Ticks` property of the `DateTime` instance to return a small measure of time—100-nanosecond blocks.) Discuss the difference.

The code is as follows:

```
<%@ Page Language="VB" %>
<%@ Import Namespace="System.Data" %>
<%@ Import Namespace="System.Data.OleDb" %>
<%@ Import Namespace="System.IO" %>

<script language="VB" runat="server">
   private timStart as long
   private timEnd as long

    sub Page_Load(Sender as Object, e as EventArgs)
       if not Page.IsPostBack then
          CreateData()
       end if
    end sub

    sub CreateData
       dim source as DataView
       timStart = DateTime.Now.Ticks

       source = Cache("DataView")

       if source is nothing then
          dim strConnString as string = "Provider=" & _
             "Microsoft.Jet.OLEDB.4.0;" & _
             "Data Source=c:\ASPNET\data\banking.mdb"

          dim objCmd as OleDbDataAdapter = new _
             OleDbDataAdapter("select * from tblUsers", _
             strConnString)

          dim ds as DataSet = new DataSet()
          objCmd.Fill(ds, "tblUsers")

          source = new DataView(ds.Tables(0))
          Cache.Insert("DataView", source)

          timEnd = Datetime.Now.Ticks
          lblMessage.Text = "Data set created explicitly" & _
             "<br>" & timEnd - timStart
       else
          timEnd = Datetime.Now.Ticks

          lblMessage.Text = "Data set retrieved from " & _
             "cache<br>" & timEnd - timStart
       end if

```

```
      dgData.DataSource = source
      dgData.DataBind()
   end sub

   sub ExpireCache(Sender as Object, e as EventArgs)
      dim dv as dataview = Cache.Remove("DataView")
      CreateData()
   end sub
</script>

<html><body>
   <form runat="server">
      <asp:Label id="lblMessage" runat="server"
         maintainState=false/><p>
      <asp:Button id="btSubmit" runat="server"
         text="Expire Cache"
         OnClick="ExpireCache"/><p>
      <asp:DataGrid id="dgData" runat="server"
         BorderColor="black"
         GridLines="Vertical"
         cellpadding="4"
         cellspacing="0"
         width="450"
         Font-Name="Arial"
         Font-Size="8pt"
         HeaderStyle-BackColor="#cccc99"
         ItemStyle-BackColor="#ffffff"
         AlternatingItemStyle-Backcolor="#cccccc" />
   </form>
</body></html>
```

The average time to create the data explicitly on your machine is 580,835 100-nanosecond blocks (.058 seconds). The average time to retrieve the data from the cache is 0 100-nanosecond blocks. (This doesn't mean it was instantaneous; just that the amount of time was too small for ASP.NET to measure this way.)

The difference is only six-hundredths of a second for nine records from the database. Imagine returning 1,000 records for 100 different simultaneous users. Caching would be very useful.

Answers for Day 15

Quiz

1. What are the three levels of the three-tier application model?

   A UI layer, a business objects layer, and a database layer.

2. True or false: You compile objects manually because they're specific to one page.

   False. They're compiled because multiple pages will use them.

3. Write the command-line command to compile the object file `MyObject.vb`, referencing the `System` and `System.Web` namespaces in a subdirectory named bin.

   The command is

   ```
   vbc /t:library /out:bin\MyObject.dll /r:System.dll
   /r:System.Web.dll MyObject.vb
   ```

4. Which of the following should be placed in a business object: a class implementing a `DataGrid`, a method that retrieves a connection string from a configuration file, a method that writes to the browser, or a property that describes the number of instances of this object?

   The second and fourth items belong in a business object. The others do not.

5. True or false: You use `Server.CreateObject` to create business objects created in the .NET Framework.

   False. `Server.CreateObject` is for unmanaged COM objects *not* created in the .NET Framework.

Exercise

Modify the `User` object you created today to use the `Database` object you created earlier.

Save the following code as `User2.vb`:

```
Imports System
Imports System.Data
Imports System.Data.OleDb

Namespace TYASPNET

   Public Class UserDetails
      public FirstName as string
      public LastName as string
       public UserName as string
       public Password as string
       public UserID as string
    End Class

    Public Class User
       public function Login(UserName as string, Password _
          as string) as string
          dim intId as string = "0"

          dim objDatabase as new Database
```

```
      objDatabase.ConnectionString = "Provider=" & _
         "Microsoft.Jet.OLEDB.4.0;" & _
         "Data Source=C:\ASPNET\data\banking.mdb"

      dim objReader as OleDbDataReader
      objReader = objDatabase.SelectSQL _
         ("SELECT UserID FROM tblUsers WHERE " & _
         "UserName = '" & UserName & "' AND " & _
         "Password = '" & Password & "'")

      do while objReader.Read
         return objReader.GetInt32(0).ToString
      loop
   end function

   public function GetDetails(UserID as integer) as _
      UserDetails

      dim objDatabase as new Database
      objDatabase.ConnectionString = "Provider=" & _
         "Microsoft.Jet.OLEDB.4.0;" & _
         "Data Source=H:\ASPNET\data\banking.mdb"

      dim objReader as OleDbDataReader
      objReader = objDatabase.SelectSQL _
         ("SELECT FirstName, LastName, UserName, " & _
         "Password FROM tblUsers WHERE UserID = " & _
         UserID)

      dim objDetails as new UserDetails

      while objReader.Read()
         objDetails.FirstName = objReader.GetString(0)
         objDetails.LastName = objReader.GetString(1)
         objDetails.UserName = objReader.GetString(2)
         objDetails.Password = objReader.GetString(3)
         objDetails.UserID = UserID.ToString
      end while
      objReader.Close

      return objDetails
   end function

   public function Update(objDetails as UserDetails, _
      intUserID as integer) as boolean
      dim objOldDetails as new UserDetails
      objOldDetails = GetDetails(intUserID)

      with objDetails
         if .FirstName = "" then
            .FirstName = objOldDetails.FirstName
```

```
                end if
                if .LastName = "" then
                   .LastName = objOldDetails.LastName
                end if
                if .Username = "" then
                   .UserName = objOldDetails.UserName
                end if
                if .Password = "" then
                   .Password = objOldDetails.Password
                end if
             end with

             dim objDatabase as new Database
             objDatabase.ConnectionString = "Provider=" & _
                "Microsoft.Jet.OLEDB.4.0;" & _
                "Data Source=C:\ASPNET\data\banking.mdb"

             objDatabase.ExecuteNonQuery("UPDATE tblUsers " & _
                "SET FirstName = '" & objDetails.FirstName & _
                "', LastName = '" & objDetails.LastName & _
                "', UserName = '" & objDetails.UserName & _
                "', [Password] = '" & objDetails.Password & _
                "' WHERE UserID = " & intUserID)

             return true
          end function
       End Class

    End Namespace
```

Compile this with the following command:

```
vbc /t:library /out:TYASPNET.dll /r:System.dll
/r:System.Data.Dll User2.vb Database.vb
```

The same ASP.NET pages can be used with this new object.

Answers for Day 16

Quiz

1. What's a Web service?

   It's a piece of functionality that's accessible over the Internet via standard protocols such as XML and HTTP.

2. What does SOAP stand for, and what does it do?

   The Simple Object Access Protocol is a way for Web services to communicate with clients. It's based on XML.

3. What's a service description?

   It's an XML file that tells clients what a Web service does and what types of data it expects and returns.

4. What class (including namespace) must a Web service inherit from?

   `System.Web.Services.WebService`

5. Write an arbitrary Web method that enables caching and disables session state.

```
<WebMethod(CacheDuration=60, EnableSession=False)> public function
➥ HelloWorld() as String
   Return "Hello World!"
end function
```

6. True or false: A Web method can take advantage of intrinsic ASP.NET objects, such as `Session` and cache.

   True.

7. True or false: A Web method can return a `DataSet`.

   True. A `DataSet` is internally represented by ADO.NET as XML, so it's easy to transport the data to a client as XML.

Exercises

1. Examine the XML service description for the database service you created earlier today. Try to understand each of the tags, recalling the discussions on XML and XML schemas. Note that much of the file describes how the different protocols (Http-Get, SOAP, and so on) are to send and receive data.

2. Create a Web service that converts one unit of measurement into another. This method should take three parameters: a value, a unit to convert from, and a unit to convert to. Allow the user to convert to and from the following: millimeters, centimeters, inches, feet, meters, yards, miles, and kilometers. Don't forget to test it with the HTML Description page!

   (Don't worry if you don't know the exact conversions between units of measurement. Just make something up.)

```
<%@ WebService Language="VB" Class="ConvertUnits" %>

Imports System
Imports System.Web.Services

public Class ConvertUnits : Inherits WebService

   '********************************************************
   ' Convert: Assumes that the incoming value is of unit
    ' millimeter, and converts to strTo.
```

```
    ' Then passes converted value to ConvertTo function,
    ' which corrects for the unit that was actually passed in
    ' ie dblValue=10, strFrom=yd, strTo=in,
    ' answer = 10mm=>inches = 10/25.4 = .394 inches
    '*******************************************************
    <WebMethod(Description:="Converts " & _
       "values to and from a specified unit of measure", _
 EnableSession:=false)> Public Function Convert(dblValue As Double, _
       strFrom as String, strTo as String) As Double

       select case strTo
          case "mm"
             Return ConvertTo(dblValue/1, strFrom)
          case "cm"
             Return ConvertTo(dblValue/10, strFrom)
          case "in"
             Return ConvertTo(dblValue/25.4, strFrom)
          case "ft"
             Return ConvertTo(dblValue/304.8, strFrom)
          case "m"
             Return ConvertTo(dblValue/1000, strFrom)
          case "yd"
             Return ConvertTo(dblValue/914.4, strFrom)
          case "mi"
             Return ConvertTo(dblValue/1609344, strFrom)
          case "km"
             Return ConvertTo(dblValue/1000000, strFrom)
          case else
             return 0.0
      end select
    End Function

    '*******************************************************
    ' ConvertTo: Receives a value from Convert, and adjusts
    ' for strFrom.
    ' We can do this because Convert assumed that incoming
    ' value was millimeter, so we can just alter the value
    ' depending on what the incoming unit actually was
    ' ie dblValue=26.7, strFrom=cm,
    ' answer = cm=>mm = 26.7*10 = 267
    ' try it, it really does work!
    '*******************************************************
    Private Function ConvertTo(dblValue as double, _
       strFrom as string) as double

       Select case strFrom
          case "mm"
             return dblValue * 1
          case "cm"
             return dblValue * 10
```

```
            case "in"
               return dblValue * 25.4
            case "ft"
               return dblValue * 304.8
            case "m"
               return dblValue * 1000
            case "yd"
               return dblValue * 914.4
            case "mi"
               return dblValue * 1609344
            case "km"
               return dblValue * 1000000
            case else
               return 0.0
         End Select
      End Function
   End Class
```

Answers for Day 17

Quiz

1. What is a proxy class?

   A class that provides methods for a client application to access a Web Service's methods. You use the proxy class because it provides built-in support for sending and receiving XML messages.

2. Write an example of a typical use of the `disco.exe` tool.

   `disco http://localhost/tyaspnet21days/services.disco`

3. Write an example of a typical use of the `wsdl.exe` tool.

   ```
   wsdl /language:VB
   http://localhost/tyaspnet21days/day16/Calculator.asmx?WSDL
   ```

4. True or false: Discovery must be performed before proxy generation.

   False. Discovery isn't a necessary step.

5. Which two namespaces are required for using SOAP headers to access services?

   `System.Web.Services` and `System.Web.Services.Protocols`.

6. Create a simple SOAP header class. What do you do with this class in a Web method? On the client?

   ```
   Public Class SOAPHeader : Inherits SoapHeader
      Public Username as string
      Public Password as string
   End Class
   ```

You need to create an instance of this class in any class that you want to expose as a service. The Web methods that use this class must specify the attribute `<SoapHeader()>`.

The client must create an instance of the class as well (through the proxy), and set its properties.

Exercise

Generate a proxy class for the ConvertUnits service you created in exercise 2 from Day 16. Build an interface to allow users to enter values.

First create a proxy with the following command:

```
wsdl /l:VB /namespace:TYASPNET.Clients
http://localhost/tyaspnet21days/day16/ConvertUnits.asmx?WSDL
```

Compile the proxy with the following command:

```
vbc /t:library /out:..\..\bin\TYASPNET.Clients.ConvertUnits.dll
/r:System.dll /r:System.Data.dll /r:System.Web.dll
/r:System.Web.Services.dll /r:System.Xml.dll ConvertUnits.vb
```

Then build the ASP.NET page:

```
<%@ Page Language="VB" %>

<script runat="server">
   sub Submit(Sender as Object, e as EventArgs)
      dim objService as new TYASPNET.Clients.ConvertUnits
      dim dblResult as double

      dblResult = objService.Convert(tbValue.Text, _
         lbUnitsFrom.SelectedItem.Text, _
          lbUnitsTo.SelectedItem.Text)

       lblMessage.Text = tbValue.Text & " " & _
          lbUnitsFrom.SelectedItem.Text & " = " & _
          dblResult & " " & lbUnitsTo.SelectedItem.Text
   end sub
</script>

<html><body>
   <form runat="server">
      Convert:
      <asp:TextBox id="tbValue" runat="server" />
      <asp:ListBox id="lbUnitsFrom" runat="server"
         Size="1">
         <asp:ListItem>mm</asp:ListItem>
         <asp:ListItem>cm</asp:ListItem>
         <asp:ListItem>m</asp:ListItem>
         <asp:ListItem>km</asp:ListItem>
```

```
            <asp:ListItem>in</asp:ListItem>
            <asp:ListItem>ft</asp:ListItem>
            <asp:ListItem>yd</asp:ListItem>
            <asp:ListItem>mi</asp:ListItem>
         </asp:ListBox>
         to:
         <asp:ListBox id="lbUnitsTo" runat="server"
            Size="1">
            <asp:ListItem>mm</asp:ListItem>
            <asp:ListItem>cm</asp:ListItem>
            <asp:ListItem>m</asp:ListItem>
            <asp:ListItem>km</asp:ListItem>
            <asp:ListItem>in</asp:ListItem>
            <asp:ListItem>ft</asp:ListItem>
            <asp:ListItem>yd</asp:ListItem>
            <asp:ListItem>mi</asp:ListItem>
         </asp:ListBox><p>

         <asp:Button id="btSumit" runat="server"
            Text="Submit"
            OnClick="Submit" /><p>
         <asp:Label id="lblMessage" runat="server" />
      </form>
   </body></html>
```

Answers for Day 18

Quiz

1. True or False: You can access the `<appSettings>` section with the `ConfigurationSection.AppSettings` property.

   True.

2. Is it possible to view the `global.asax` file from your browser?

   No, ASP.NET protects this file so that outside viewers cannot view it at all.

3. What interface must a custom handler implement?

   `IConfigurationSectionHandler`

The following questions deal with the directory structure shown in Table 18.4.

TABLE 18.4 A Web Server Directory Structure Exercise

Application URL	*Physical Path*
`http://www.site.com`	`c:\www\site`
`http://www.site.com/sales`	`c:\www\site\sales`

TABLE 18.4 continued

Application URL	*Physical Path*
`http://www.site.com/hr`	`c:\www\site\sales\hr`
`http://www.site.com/users`	`d:\www\misc\users`

4. The `sales` virtual directory has a `web.config` with the following setting:

```
<httphandlers>
   <add verb="PUT, POST" path="index.aspx" type="System.Web.
      UI.PageHandlerFactory" />
</httphandlers>
```

If the `hr` directory is accessed as follows, will it inherit this setting?

`http://www.site.com/hr`

No, the `hr` directory will not inherit the setting because configuration information is processed by virtual directories, not physical path.

5. If the `hr` directory is accessed as follows, will it inherit this setting?

`http://www.site.com/sales/hr`

No, the `hr` directory will not inherit the setting because the `<httpHandlers>` setting is not inherited by subdirectories.

6. Suppose that the `web.config` in `sales` also has the following setting:

```
<location path="hr/*.aspx">

   <authorization>
         <deny users="?" />
   </authorization>

</location>
```

Is this an adequate security measure against entry into `hr`? Explain.

No, anonymous users could still access this directory through the `hr` virtual directory, `www.site.com/hr`, without having to supply valid credentials.

7. Describe a better use of `web.config` to address the preceding question.

A better measure would be to place a `web.config` in the `hr` directory, with the necessary security measures. This would ensure that no matter how this directory was accessed, only valid users would be able to see the content. For example, place the following in `c:\www\site\sales\hr\web.config`:

```
<authorization>
   <deny users="?" />
</authorization>
```

Exercise

Set up a `web.config` file for a sample application that does the following:

- Turns on debug mode for the application.
- Sets custom errors to display an `errors.aspx` page.
- Declares a section called `authors` with a `PrimaryAuthor` key with the value

of your name. This section should use the `System.Web.Configuration.DictionarySectionHandler` handler.

The `web.config` should follow the following format:

```
<configuration>
   <configSections>
      <section name="authors" type="System.Web.
➥Configuration.DictionarySectionHandler, System.Web"/>
   </configSections>

   <system.web>
      <compilation debugMode="true" />

      <customErrors defaultRedirect="error.htmaspx"
➥mode="off">
         <error statusCode="404" redirect="error.htmaspx"/>
      </customerrors>

      <authors>
         <add key="PrimaryAuthor" value="Chris Payne">
      </authors>
   </system.web>
</configuration>
```

Answers for Day 19

Quiz

1. True or false: A code-behind file must derive from the `System.Web.UI.Page` class.

   True, unless the code-behind is for a user control, in which case it should derive from the `System.Web.UI.UserControl` class.

2. Why must you declare public variables in a code-behind for the server controls you use on an ASP.NET page?

   A code-behind file must programmatically control server controls that are located on a separate page; normally, this would be impossible. However, if you declare the controls in the code-behind and provide event handlers for them, ASP.NET can provide implementations for those controls. The ASP.NET page can use the controls declared in the code-behind because it derives from the code-behind. A code-behind declares and provides event handlers for server controls, whereas the ASP.NET page simply displays them.

3. Create an `@ Page` directive that uses a code-behind class named `MyControl`, in a `.vb` file with the same name.

   ```
   <%@ Page Inherits="MyControl" src="MyControl.vb" %>
   ```

4. What is a resource file?

   It is a file that contains localizable values for an ASP.NET application.

5. What does the following line do?

   ```
   dim strVar as string = Request.UserLanguages(0)
   ```

   It retrieves the primary language of a user as indicated by her browser, and stores it in a string variable named `strVar`.

6. What does the `resgen.exe` tool do?

   It converts your text resource files into `.resources` files, which can be read by ASP.NET's resource manager.

7. What is the difference between `CurrentCulture` and `CurrentUICulture`?

   Both represent the culture used by an application, but the latter is used by ASP.NET to load resource files. The former is used by localizable objects, such as `DateTime`.

8. True or false: The `CultureInfo.CurrentCulture` is a shortcut for the `System.Threading.CurrentThread.CurrentCulture` object.

   True. The former is read-only, whereas the latter can be used to set culture information.

Exercise

Create a currency exchange calculator for several different countries. Allow the user to enter a monetary value in one region's units, and convert to another by selecting a value from a select box. Use a resource file to store the exchange values (don't worry if you don't know the exchange rates, just make something up!). Use code-behind techniques!

This solution uses `en-US`, `fr`, `de`, and `jp` for the culture encodings. The resource files contain the conversion units for each culture. The file `exchange.en-US.txt` is as follows:

```
Toen-US=1
Tofr=.7
Tode=1.67
Tojp=1098.45
```

The file `exchange.fr-fr.txt` is as follows:

```
Toen-US=1.43
Tofr=1
Tode=2.34
Tojp=1569.21
```

The file `exchange.jp-ja.txt` is as follows:

```
Toen-US=.0009
Tofr=.00064
Tode=.0015
Tojp=1
```

The file `exchange.de-ge.txt` is as follows:

```
Toen-US=.59
Tofr=.42
Tode=1
Tojp=657.7
```

Don't forget to use `resgen.exe` to place these files in `.resource` files.

The user interface, `exercise1.aspx`, is as follows:

```
<%@ Page Inherits="ExchangeCalculator" src="exercise1.vb" %>

<html><body>
   <font size="5">Currency Calculator</font><hr>
   <form runat="server">
      <asp:Label id="lblCurrency" runat="server"/>
      <asp:TextBox id="tbValue" runat="server"/> to
      <asp:ListBox id="lbRegion" runat="server"
         Size=1
          AutoPostBack=true>
          <asp:ListItem>en-US</asp:ListItem>
          <asp:ListItem>fr-FR</asp:ListItem>
          <asp:ListItem>de-ge</asp:ListItem>
          <asp:ListItem>jp-ja</asp:ListItem>
        </asp:ListBox>
    </form>
    <asp:Label id="lblAnswer" runat="server"/>
 </body></html>
```

The code-behind, `exercise1.vb`, uses the conversions in the resource files to convert monetary values. It needs to retrieve the currency symbols, so it converts from culture to region by using a `case` statement; the user selects a culture, which is transferred to a region, which is used to retrieve the currency symbol. The code is as follows:

```
Imports System
Imports System.Web
Imports System.Web.UI
```

```
Imports System.Web.UI.WebControls
Imports System.Globalization
Imports System.Resources
Imports System.Threading

Public Class ExchangeCalculator : Inherits Page
    public lblAnswer as Label
    public lblCurrency as Label
    public tbValue as TextBox
    public lbRegion as ListBox

    sub Page_Load(Sender as Object, e as EventArgs)
       dim objRM as ResourceManager
       dim strLanguage as string = Request.UserLanguages(0).
➥ToString

       dim objCulture as new CultureInfo(strLanguage)
       Thread.CurrentThread.CurrentCulture = new
➥CultureInfo(strLanguage)
       Thread.CurrentThread.CurrentUICulture = new
➥CultureInfo(strLanguage)

       dim objRegion as new RegionInfo(GetRegionFromCulture
➥ (objCulture.Name))
       lblCurrency.Text = objRegion.CurrencySymbol.ToString

       if Page.IsPostBack then
          objRM = ResourceManager.
➥CreateFileBasedResourceManager("exchange", _
             Server.MapPath("."), Nothing)
          objRegion = new RegionInfo(GetRegionFromCulture
➥ (lbRegion.SelectedItem.Text))
          dim dblAnswer as double
          dblAnswer = Ctype(tbValue.Text, Double) *
➥CType(objRM.GetString("To" & lbRegion.SelectedItem.Text),
➥Double)
          lblAnswer.Text = objRegion.CurrencySymbol.
➥ToString & dblAnswer.ToString

          objRM.ReleaseAllResources
       end if
    end sub

    private function GetRegionFromCulture
➥ (strCulture as string) as string
       select case strCulture
          case "en-US"
             Return "us"
          case "ja-ja"
             Return "jp"
          case "de-ge"
```

```
                Return "de"
            case "fr-FR"
                Return "fr"
        end select
    end function
End Class
```

Answers for Day 20

Quiz

1. Will the following code snippet work?

   ```
   try
      objCmd.Connection.Open
      objReader = objCmd.ExecuteReader
   end try
   ```

   No. There's no `catch` statement.

2. True or False: The `finally` statement is required in a `try...catch` block.

   False.

3. What's the trace tool, and how do you enable it at the page level? At the application level?

   The trace tool gives your applications statistical and debugging capabilities by printing information to a log.

   To enable it at the page level, add `Trace="true"` to the page directive. To enable it at the application level, add `<trace enabled="true"/>` to `web.config`.

4. What's the difference between `Trace.Write` and `Trace.Warn`?

   They're exactly the same, except that `Trace.Warn` outputs information in red.

5. True or False: `Trace.Write` and `Trace.Warn` print information in the client display.

   False. They only print to the trace log.

6. What are symbol files?

   Symbol files tell a debugger how to map executing instructions to lines in an uncompiled source file.

7. True or False: Attaching a debugger to an application is a perfectly safe procedure and doesn't interrupt program usage.

   False. The debugger incurs a lot of overhead and blocks users from the debugged application.

8. What's a breakpoint, and what is it used for?

A breakpoint is a point in your application where execution is halted. You can use breakpoints to determine where errors occur in your code.

Exercises

1. Use the trace tool to compare performance times in your application. Determine if disabling viewstate results in faster execution times, what the difference is between using an `OleDbDataReader` versus a `DataSet`, and if comments affect execution times at all.

   Viewstate test:

   Average total execution time when using an `OleDbDataReader`, returning 12 rows, viewstate enabled (5 tries): .1236036 seconds

   Average total execution time when using an `OleDbDataReader`, returning 12 rows, viewstate disabled (5 tries): .0931142 seconds

   Result: ~33% increase in execution times with viewstate enabled

   Data test:

   Average total execution time when using an `OleDbDataReader`, returning 12 rows (5 tries): .1295954 seconds

   Average total execution time when using a `DataSet`, returning 12 rows (5 tries): .15766 seconds

   Result: ~22% increase in execution times when using a `DataSet`.

   Comments test:

   Average total execution time when using 20 lines of comments, 80 characters each (5 tries): .1004834 seconds

   Average total execution time when using 0 lines of comments (5 tries): .1082878 seconds

   Result: ~.08% increase in execution times without using comments. Not statistically significant!

2. Explore the CLR debugger and step through the execution of several pages. Use the Watch window to watch your variables as your application progresses. Try introducing some errors purposely and see what happens in the debugger.

   Try exploring the Tools, Options menu. The Debugging tab allows you to customize the way the debugger works. The Debug menu provides several different ways to execute your application, such as different stepping methods, running to cursors, and executing without debugging. Try debugging some compiled business objects created in earlier lessons. Run them from within ASP.NET pages, and watch the output in the debugger.

A

Answers for Day 21

Quiz

1. What's the difference between authentication and authorization?

   Authentication is the first step in security. It requires the user to supply valid credentials to access an application. Authorization occurs after the user has been authenticated, and it tests user permissions against those set on resources to restrict access.

2. What's the difference between basic and digest authentication?

   Digest authentication encrypts user credentials before sending them across the network, using a one-way encoding technique known as *hashing*. Basic sends credentials across the network without any encryption.

3. What's the anonymous user account's name in Windows?

   `IUSR_MachineName`, where `MachineName` is the name of your Web server.

4. Write some code to set an authorization cookie and redirect to an originating URL.

   ```
   FormsAuthentication.RedirectFromLoginPage("username", false)
   ```

5. What does the second parameter in the `SetAuthCookie` method do?

   Specifies whether or not a cookie should be persisted across browser restarts, allowing a user to return to the Web site without having to log in again.

6. Will the following code work?

   ```
   <configuration>
         <authentication mode="Forms">
            <forms name="AuthCookie" loginUrl="day21/login.aspx">
            </forms>
         </authentication>
   </configuration>
   ```

   No, because the `authentication` element isn't wrapped in `system.web` tags. Also, even though the `<authentication>` tag is present, all users will still be able to access the files in question because there is no `<authorization>` tag to stop them.

7. What do the wildcard characters * and ? mean to ASP.NET within the authorization section of `web.config`?

   `*` means all users, and `?` means the anonymous user.

8. True or False: When impersonation is enabled, ASP.NET can operate on behalf of the operating system.

   False. ASP.NET will operate on behalf of the user it impersonates.

Exercise

Create a login page that validates user credentials against a database. Create a `web.config` file that uses forms authentication and directs all anonymous users to this login page.

You'll use the existing banking database you created earlier in the book. The code for the `web.config` file is as follows (put this in the `TYASPNET21Days` root folder):

```
<configuration>
   <system.web>
      <authentication mode="Forms">
         <forms name="AuthCookie" loginUrl="login.aspx" />
      </authentication>
      <authorization>
         <deny users="?" />
      </authorization>
   </system.web>
 </configuration>
```

The code for the login page, `login.aspx`, is as follows:

```
<%@ Page Language="VB" %>
<%@ Import Namespace="System.Data" %>
<%@ Import Namespace="System.Data.OleDb" %>

<script runat="server">
   sub Login(Sender as Object, e as EventArgs)
      dim intId as integer = 0
      dim Conn as new OleDbConnection("Provider=" & _
            "Microsoft.Jet.OLEDB.4.0;" & _
             "Data Source=c:\ASPNET\data\banking.mdb")

       dim objCmd as OleDbCommand = new OleDbCommand _
          ("SELECT UserID from tblUsers WHERE " & _
          "Username = '" & tbUserName.Text & "' " & _
          "AND Password = '" & tbPassword.Text & "'", Conn)
       dim objReader as OleDbDataReader

       try
          objCmd.Connection.Open()
          objReader = objCmd.ExecuteReader

          do while objReader.Read
             intId = objReader.GetInt32(0).ToString
          loop
       catch ex as OleDbException
          lblMessage.Text = ex.Message
       finally
          objReader.Close
          objCmd.Connection.Close()
```

```
         end try

         if intID <> 0 then
            FormsAuthentication.SetAuthCookie(intID, false)
            lblMessage.Text = "<font color=red>Success!
➥</font><p>"
         else
            lblMessage.Text = "<font color=red>Sorry,
➥invalid username or password!</font><p>"
         end if
      end sub
   </script>

   <html><body>
      <form runat="server">

         <asp:Label id="lblMessage" runat="server" />

         Username:
         <asp:Textbox id="tbUserName" runat="server" />
         Password:
         <asp:Textbox id="tbPassword" TextMode="password"
            runat="server" /><p>
         <asp:Button id="Submit" runat="server"
            onClick="Login" text="Submit" />
      </form>
   </body></html>
```

Answers for Day 22

Quiz

1. Presented with the knowledge that you must build an e-commerce site, what generic database tables do you know will be required?

   At a minimum, you'll typically need a user or customer table, one or more tables to hold products and their information, and a table to hold orders.

2. True or false: ASP.NET pages should be built before the other tiers.

   Generally, this is false, but it depends on your personal preferences. From a design standpoint, building the ASP.NET pages after the database is set up will make development much easier.

3. What do the `MAX` and `SUM` SQL commands do?

   `MAX` examines a set of database rows and returns the highest value in the field specified. `SUM` sums all the values in a set of data rows and returns the result.

4. What does the `Format` method do? What is the syntax?

   It formats data in a specified format. The syntax is

   ```
   Format( {N[,M ][: formatString ]}, Data)
   ```

5. What are three things needed to secure a database service using SOAP headers?

   You need a class that inherits from the `SoapHeader` class, the `<SoapHeader>` attribute placed in the Web method declaration, and a custom authentication function. Additionally, you might need to check whether a SOAP header is supplied to the Web method, and whether your authentication method certifies valid credentials.

Answers for Day 23

A

Quiz

1. What are the two headers required for every mobile page?

   The standard header is as follows:

   ```
   <%@ Page Inherits="System.Web.UI.MobileControls.MobilePage"
   ➥Language="VB" %>
   <%@ Register TagPrefix="Mobile"
   ➥Namespace="System.Web.UI.MobileControls" %>
   ```

2. True or false: Mobile server controls don't require the `runat="server"` attribute.

   False. Mobile server controls are still server controls, and therefore are required to be created on the server.

3. What does the `Call` server control do?

   It presents UI to enable the user to dial a phone number.

4. What are the two values for the `StyleReference` property?

   `Title`, which causes text to be displayed in bold, and `Error`, which causes text to be rendered in italicized red.

5. How do you explicitly display a mobile Web form programmatically?

   Set the `ActiveForm` property to the form's name.

6. True or false: You can respond to mobile server control events the same as ASP.NET server control events.

   True.

7. What does the `<DeviceSelect>` element do, and what does it represent on the page?

   The `<DeviceSelect>` provides a means to display different content depending on the viewing device. It is used as a container on the page for `<Choice>` elements.

Exercise

Create a mobile application that will allow users to make credit card payments through their cell phones. Users should be allowed to enter a credit card number and a value for the amount to be paid (don't forget to supply a way to submit the input). Don't worry about recording or applying the payment to something. Simply display a thank-you message to the user when the submission is complete.

The code for the exercise is as follows:

```
<%@ Page Inherits="System.Web.UI.MobileControls.MobilePage"
➥Language="VB" %>
<%@ Register TagPrefix="Mobile"
➥Namespace="System.Web.UI.Mobile.Controls" %>

<script runat="server">
   sub PayBill(Sender as Object, e as EventArgs)
      lblMessage.Text = "Thank you for using the " & _
         "Mobile Payment service. The details of " & _
         "your transaction are:"
      lblNumber.Text = tbNumber.Text
      lblAmount.Text = tbAmount.Text

      ActiveForm = frmThanks
   end sub
</script>

<Mobile:Form runat="server">
   <Mobile:Label runat="server" StyleReference="title"
      Text="Pay Bill" />
   <Mobile:Label runat="server" Text="CC #" />
   <Mobile:TextBox runat="server" id="tbNumber"
      Type="Numeric" />
   <Mobile:Label runat="server" Text="Amount $" />
   <Mobile:TextBox runat="server" id="tbAmount"
      Type="Numeric" />
   <Mobile:Command runat="server" id="btSubmit"
      OnClick="PayBill"
      Text="Pay Bill!" />
</Mobile:Form>

<Mobile:Form runat="server" id="frmThanks">
   <Mobile:Label runat="server" id="lblMessage" />
   <Mobile:Label runat="server" id="lblNumber" />
   <Mobile:Label runat="server" id="lblAmount" />
</Mobile:Form>
```

APPENDIX B

Common ASP.NET Mistakes

This appendix covers a lot of the common mistakes that developers will make with ASP.NET whether they are new to server programming or have a background in classic ASP. There are many simple errors that will leave developers scratching their heads trying to figure out what is wrong with their code. Often, these mistakes are very simple to fix. This appendix is designed as a quick reference to these common mistakes so that developers can easily find a solution and learn techniques to tackle the problem in future.

This appendix is divided into two sections. The first section describes mistakes specific to ASP.NET that are often overlooked. The second section covers changes that must be observed when moving from classic ASP to ASP.NET. These include breaking syntactical changes from VBScript to VB.NET.

ASP.NET Conundrums

ASP.NET has many peculiarities that can easily cause development woes. Each of the following sections lists the error message typically encountered with a problem, a detailed description, and a possible solution(s). (Note that italicized words in the error messages can be substituted for specific names.)

Problems with Web Forms

Problem: `Unexpected end of file looking for </asp:`*`Control`*`> tag`

Description: You've forgotten to add the closing tag for an ASP.NET server control.

Solution: All server controls must have corresponding closing tags. Add a closing tag using one of the following sample syntaxes:

```
<asp:Label id="lblMessage" runat="server" />

<asp:Label id="lblMessage" runat="server">  </asp:Label>
```

Problem: `Literal content ("`*`html`*`") is not allowed within a '`*`control`*`'`

Description: You've tried to use a server control without a closing tag.

Solution: This problem typically occurs with `DataList` or `DataGrid` controls because you forgot to include the closing server tag. Without this tag, ASP.NET considers all following HTML code as part of the server control and throws an error. Simply add the closing tag for this control.

Problem: Server control does not display or act as it should.

Description: ASP.NET is not properly interacting with the server control; form data isn't being recognized, display properties are not being displayed, and so on.

Solution: The most likely reason for this problem is the lack of the `runat="server"` attribute on the server control. Add this attribute to the server control in question.

Problem: Data is not being displayed in a server control as it should.

Description: ASP.NET does not seem to display the data at all or it isn't updating as it should.

Solution: You've forgotten to call the `DataBind` method.

Problem: `An exception has been thrown by the class constructor for System.Drawing.Internal.SystemColorTracker`

Description: ASP.NET isn't able to draw the specified control properly (typically a `DataGrid`).

Solution: Restart the application. This can be done in any of the following ways:

- Call `iisreset` from the command prompt.
- Modify and save either the `global.asax` or the `web.config` file.
- Recompile a business object in the application's `\bin` directory.

Problem: Your event handling routines are not producing the expected results.

Description: Using Web forms and server controls, you are trying to produce a desired output, but it isn't working as expected. For example, you are trying to modify the value contained in a text box or label, but the value isn't changing or isn't changing to what you intended.

Solution: Recall that the `Page_Load` event *always* executes before any event handlers, and that the event handlers execute in no particular order. Your `Page_Load` event might be modifying or resetting the target value before your event handler has an opportunity to use it. For example, the following code snippet demonstrates this situation:

```
sub Page_Load(Sender as Object, e as EventArgs)
   tbMessage.Text = "Hello world!"
end sub

sub HandleSubmit(Sender as Object, e as EventArgs)
   Response.Write(tbMessage.Text)
end sub
...
...
<asp:TextBox id="tbMessage" runat="server"
   OnTextChanged="HandleSubmit"
   AutoPostBack=true />
...
```

When the text in the text box changes, the form is posted. However, the `Page_Load` method executes first and resets the value in the text box to "Hello World!" no matter what else occurs. Then your event handler displays "Hello World!" rather than the new text.

One solution is to check the `Page.IsPostBack` property in the `Page_Load` event to determine whether or not the form was just submitted, and therefore the value should not be reset:

```
sub Page_Load(Sender as Object, e as EventArgs)
   if not Page.IsPostBack then
```

```
      tbMessage.Text = "Hello World!"
   end if
end sub
...
```

Another solution is simply to restructure your routines.

Other Problems

Problem: `MissingMethodException: Member not found.`

Description: You've tried to reference a method or property of an object, typically when it is passed from a method.

Solution: Although there are many potential causes to this problem, a very common one has to do with data type casting. For example, look at the following event handler:

```
sub MyHandler(Sender as Object, e as EventArgs)
   Response.Write(obj.Text)
end sub
```

Assuming that an event from a label causes this method to execute, the variable `Sender` should represent that label, and you should be able to access its `Text` property. However, you should never rely on what you expect a variable to represent; never assume that an object is what it should be. Instead, you should cast the object accordingly:

```
Response.Write(CType(Sender, Label).Text)
```

Often, variables of type `Object` in ASP.NET are early-bound, meaning they are evaluated when the page is compiled (versus when the page is requested). Because of this, ASP.NET balks at your call to the `Text` property—an `Object` does not have a `Text` property. When the page is requested, however, the appropriate reference will be set and you will be able to call `Text`, but by then, it's too late. Always cast your variables accordingly.

Problem: `The type` *`object`* `in Assembly` *`name`*`, Version=`*`version`*`, Culture=`*`culture`*`, PublicKeyToken=`*`token`* `is not marked as serializable.`

Description: You've tried to persist an object in session or application state.

Solution: Some objects, such as `DataSets`, are not able to be persisted automatically in a state variable. Try using the `ShouldSerialize`*`Object`* method of the object in question (see Appendixes C and D).

Problem: `Type not defined:` *`type`*

Description: You try to declare an instance of a known object.

Solution: Make sure that you've spelled the type correctly. Also, be sure that the necessary namespaces are imported. Remember that VB.NET classes (such as code-behind forms and business objects) do not automatically import namespaces as do ASP.NET pages.

Changes from Classic ASP

When moving from classic ASP and VBScript to ASP.NET and VB.NET, developers will often run into syntactical errors or other problems due to the migration. The following sections describe these errors and their solutions.

Problems with VBScript

Error: `Wend is no longer supported; use End While instead.`

Description: You've tried to close a `while` statement with the keyword `wend`.

Solution: In VB.NET, the `wend` keyword is not supported. Simply use `End While` instead.

Error: `The syntax <lower bound> To <upper bound> is no longer supported for specifying array bounds.`

Description: Your array is trying to declare a fixed size.

Solution: In VBScript, you are able to use `dim MyArray(0 to 5)` to declare a fixed-size array. This is not supported in VB.NET.

Error: `The name 'myArray' is not declared.` where *`myArray`* is an array variable.

Description: You haven't yet declared the array variable.

Solution: You are trying to declare an array using the `ReDim` keyword. In VB.NET, you must declare an array using the `Dim` keyword *before* using `ReDim`, unlike VBScript.

Error: `A value of type 'type' cannot be converted to 'object'.`

Description: This typically means that you are trying to assign a property to an object without specifying the property name.

Solution: In VBScript, objects supported default properties. In other words, you weren't required to specify the name of a property to set it. For example, given a `Label` control, the following would be possible in VBScript:

```
dim Label as Label
Label = "Hello World"
```

B

This would set the `Text` property to the string `"Hello World"`. In VB.NET, default properties are no longer supported unless they take parameters. You must instead use the following:

```
Label.Text = "Hello World"
```

Problem: `Let and Set are no longer supported on assignment statements.`

Description: You are using the `Let` or `Set` keyword to assign something to an object.

Solution: These keywords are not supported in VB.NET. Simply remove them and your code should work.

Problem: `The name 'N' is not declared.` even though you have declared it.

Description: The declaration for a variable in one part of your page is not accessible by another part of your page.

Solution: In VBScript, variables declared within blocks (any set of statements terminated with `End`, `Next`, or `Loop`) are viewable outside the block. For example, the following code will write `11` to the browser:

```
dim I as integer
For I = 1 To 10
   Dim N As Double
   N = N + I
Next
Response.write(N)
```

In VB.NET, the variable `N` in the preceding code has block scope, meaning it is not accessible outside the code block (the `for` loop, in this case). Thus, this code will produce an error. Instead, declare your variable outside the loop.

Problem: `Optional parameters must always specify a default value.`

Description: You've declared a function with the `optional` keyword, specifying that a parameter is optional.

Solution: In VB.NET, optional parameters must specify a default value. For instance, change the following VBScript code:

```
sub MySub(Optional MyParam as String)
```

to

```
sub MySub(Optional MyParam as String = "HI")
```

Also, the `IsMissing` function, used to detect whether an optional parameter was specified in VBScript, is not supported in VB.NET.

Problem: `Argument lists in all call statements must now be enclosed in parentheses.`

Description: You tried to call a function or sub without using parentheses. For example:

```
Response.Write "Hello World"
```

Solution: In VB.NET, all function and sub calls must enclose any parameters in parentheses, whether or not they return values. Instead of the preceding code, use the following:

```
Response.Write("Hello World")
```

Problem: `Type-declaration character & does not match declared data type` *`type`*`.`

Description: You are trying to use the ampersand to concatenate strings.

Solution: In VBScript, it was possible to concatenate strings using the ampersand, without any spaces between variable names. For example, the following code in VBScript would write `HI there everyone` to the browser:

```
dim a as string = "HI "
dim b as string = "there "
dim c as string = "everyone"
Response.Write(a&b&c)
```

This will cause an error in ASP.NET. Instead, use

```
Response.Write(a & b & c)
```

B

Problems with Classic ASP

Problem: `Syntax Error` or `Expected variable, constant, Enum, Type, or procedural declaration.`

Description: Method and global variable declarations don't work properly. You are trying to declare a method or variable within a code render block. For example:

```
<%
   dim I as Integer
   sub HelloWorld
      ...
   end sub
%>
```

Solution: In VB.NET, all method and global variable declarations must be contained within code declaration blocks (within `<script>` tags). Also, any non-assignment statements must be placed within another method, such as `Page_Load`.

Problem: `Request` doesn't return what you expect it to.

Description: You are using the `Request` object to return data from the HTTP request; for example, `Request.Form` or `Request.QueryString`.

Solution: In classic ASP, the `Request` object would return strings containing the entire collection of variables. For example, given the URL `http://localhost/test/Test.asp?values=45&values=600` and the following code:

```
Response.Write(Request.Querystring(values)
```

classic ASP would display a single string, `45, 600`, in the browser. In ASP.NET, the `Request` object returns arrays of strings instead of one concatenated string. For example, with the earlier URL and the code

```
Response.Write(Request.Querystring(values)(0)
```

ASP.NET would display `45`, and the following:

```
Response.Write(Request.Querystring(values)(1)
```

would display `600`. This functionality is the same for `Request`, `Request.Querystring`, and `Request.Form`.

APPENDIX C

ASP.NET Controls: Properties and Methods

This appendix covers the properties and methods for every ASP.NET server control, including HTML server controls, Web server controls, and validation controls. Also refer to the .NET Framework SDK Documentation for further reference.

All of the following controls inherit the properties described in Table C.1 from the `System.Web.UI.Control` class.

TABLE C.1 Properties of the `Control` Class Inherited by All Server Controls

Property	*Description*
`ClientID`	The ID generated for the control by ASP.NET.
`Controls`	Returns a `ControlCollection` object that represents all the child controls for the specified control.
`EnableViewState`	Specifies whether the control should maintain its view-state and the viewstate of any child controls.

TABLE C.1 continued

Property	*Description*
`ID`	Specifies the identifier for the control. This property must be present to enable programmatic control and event handling.
`NamingContainer`	Retrieves a reference to the control's naming container.
`Page`	Gets the `Page` object that contains the control.
`Parent`	Gets the control's parent in the UI hierarchy.
`Site`	Specifies the site information for the control.
`TemplateSourceDirectory`	Specifies the virtual directory of the page that contains the control.
`UniqueID`	Specifies the unique, hierarchically qualified identity for the control. This differs from `ID` because it includes the full object hierarchy of the control.
`Visible`	Specifies whether the control should render on the page.

Table C.2 lists the methods shared by all server controls, inherited from the `Control` object.

TABLE C.2 Methods of the `Control` Class Inherited by All Server Controls

Method	*Description*
`DataBind`	Binds data to the specified control.
`Dispose`	Performs any final cleanup before the control is destroyed.
`FindControl`	Searches the current container control for a control specified by *`string`*. Returns a `Control` object.
`HasControls`	Indicates whether the control has any children.
`RenderControl`	Outputs control content to an `HtmlTextWriter` object specified by *`writer`*.
`ResolveUrl`	Resolves a relative URL to an absolute URL based on the value passed to the `TemplateSourceDirectory` property.

Table C.3 lists the events shared by all server controls, inherited from the `Control` object.

TABLE C.3 Events of the `Control` Class Inherited by All Server Controls

Event	*Description*
`DataBinding`	Occurs when data is bound to the control.
`Disposed`	Occurs when the control is released from memory.

TABLE C.3 continued

Event	*Description*
`Init`	Occurs when the control is initialized (this is the first step).
`Load`	Occurs when the control is loaded to the `Page` object.
`PreRender`	Occurs immediately before the control is rendered.
`Unload`	Occurs when the control is unloaded from memory.

HTML Server Controls

This section lists the details for each HTML server control in the Web forms framework. Recall that any HTML element can be turned into an HTML server control simply by adding the `runat="server"` attribute. All the predefined HTML server controls are documented here, and those that aren't predefined all inherit the same common properties, shown in the next section.

Common HTML Server Control Properties

Table C.4 lists the properties shared by all HTML server controls inherited from the `System.Web.UI.HtmlControls.HtmlControl` class.

TABLE C.4 Shared HTML Server Control Properties

Property	*Description*
`Attributes`	Retrieves all attribute name and value pairs.
`Disabled`	Specifies whether a control is read-only in the Web page.
`Style`	Retrieves all cascading style sheet (CSS) properties.
`TagName`	Retrieves the name of the control.

Table C.5 lists the properties shared by all HTML server input controls (such as `HtmlInputText`, `HtmlInputCheckBox`, and so on) inherited from the `System.Web.UI.HtmlControls.HtmlInputControl` class.

TABLE C.5 Shared HTML Server Input Control Properties

Property	*Description*
`Name`	Specifies a unique name for the control.
`Type`	Retrieves the type of the control.
`Value`	Specifies the contents of a control.

Table C.6 lists the properties shared by all HTML server container controls (such as `HtmlTable`, `HtmlForm`, and so on) inherited from the `System.Web.UI.HtmlControls.HtmlContainerControl` class.

TABLE C.6 Shared HTML Server Control Container Properties

Property	*Description*
`InnerHtml`	Specifies the content between the opening and closing tags of the control.
`InnerText`	Same as `InnerHtml`, but provides HTML encoding and decoding.

The HTML Server Controls

This section lists all properties and methods for the predefined HTML server controls. Note that additional properties are inherited from other objects (refer to previous two sections).

`HtmlAnchor`

This control represents an anchor or link in a Web page. Table C.7 lists the properties and events of the `HtmlAnchor` server control. The syntax is

```
<a href="..." ... runat="server">...</a>
```

TABLE C.7 Properties and Events of the `HtmlAnchor` Control

Property	*Description*
`Href`	Specifies the URL target.
`Name`	Specifies the bookmark name for the control.
`Target`	Specifies the target window to load the URL.
`Title`	Specifies the title displayed by the browser for a Web page.
Event	*Description*
`ServerClick`	Occurs when the user clicks the control.

`HtmlButton`

Represents a button (available only on browsers that support HTML 4.0). Table C.8 lists the property and event of the `HtmlButton` server control. The syntax is

```
<button ... runat="server">
```

TABLE C.8 Property and Event of the `HtmlButton` Control

Property	Description
`CausesValidation`	Indicates if the `HtmlButton` should perform validation when clicked.
Event	*Description*
`ServerClick`	Occurs when the user clicks the control.

`HtmlForm`

Represents an HTML form. Table C.9 lists the properties of the `HtmlForm` server control. The syntax is

```
<form ... runat="server">
```

TABLE C.9 Properties of the `HtmlForm` Control

Property	Description
`Action`	Specifies the URL of the page that handles and processes the form's submission.
`EncType`	The encoding used by browsers to post the form's data, such as `"text/plain"` or `"image/jpeg"`.
`Method`	Specifies how the form posts data to the server, such as `"Get"` or `"Post"`.
`Name`	Specifies the identity of the form.
`Target`	Specifies the target window to load the URL.

C

`HtmlImage`

Represents an image in a Web page. Table C.10 lists the properties of the `HtmlImage` server control. The syntax is

```
<img ... runat="server">
```

TABLE C.10 Properties of the `HtmlImage` Control

Property	Description
`Align`	The alignment of the image with respect to other items on the page.
`Alt`	The alternative text caption for the image.
`Border`	The width of the frame containing the image.

TABLE C.10 continued

Property	*Description*
`Height`	The height of the image.
`Src`	The source of the image file.
`Width`	The width of the image.

`HtmlInputButton`

Represents an input button control in an HTML form. Table C.11 lists the events of the `HtmlInputButton` server control. The syntax is

```
<input type="button" ... runat="server">
```

TABLE C.11 Events of the `HtmlInputButton` Control

Property	*Description*
`ServerClick`	Occurs when the user clicks the control.

`HtmlInputCheckBox`

Represents a check box. Table C.12 lists the properties and events of the `HtmlInputCheckBox` server control. The syntax is

```
<input type="checkbox" ... runat="server">
```

TABLE C.12 Properties and Events of the `HtmlInputCheckBox` Control

Property	*Description*
`Checked`	Indicates whether the control is checked.
Event	*Description*
`ServerChange`	Occurs when the form is posted and the state of the control is different from the previous post.

`HtmlInputControl`

Represents a generic input control used with HTML forms. Table C.13 lists the properties of the `HtmlInputControl` server control. The syntax is

```
<input ... runat="server">
```

TABLE C.13 Properties of the `HtmlInputControl` Control

Property	Description
`Name`	The unique name for the control.
`Type`	Retrieves the type of the control. Value could be `"text"`, `"password"`, `"checkbox"`, `"radio"`, `"button"`, `"submit"`, `"reset"`, `"file"`, `"hidden"`, or `"image"`. This property is read-only.
`Value`	The contents of the control.

`HtmlInputFile`

Represents a form element that allows users to upload files to the server. Table C.14 lists the properties of the `HtmlInputFile` server control. The syntax is

```
<input type="file" ... runat="server">
```

TABLE C.14 Properties of the `HtmlInputFile` Control

Property	Description
`Accept`	Specifies a list of MIME types of files to accept.
`MaxLength`	The maximum length of file to accept.
`PostedFile`	Gets access to the posted file. Returns an `HttpPostedFile` object.
`Size`	The width of the text box in which the file path is entered.

`HtmlInputHidden`

Represents a hidden form field. Table C.15 lists the events of the `HtmlInputHidden` server control. The syntax is

```
<input type="hidden" ... runat="server">
```

TABLE C.15 Events of the `HtmlInputHidden` Control

Event	Description
`ServerChange`	Occurs when the posted content is different than the previous post.

`HtmlInputImage`

Represents an input button using an image instead of a push-style button. Table C.16 lists the properties and events of the `HtmlInputImage` server control. The syntax is

```
<input type="image" ... runat="server">
```

TABLE C.16 Properties and Events of the `HtmlInputImage` Control

Property	Description
`Align`	The alignment of the image with respect to other elements on the page.
`Alt`	The alternative text displayed for the image.
`Border`	The width of the frame containing the image.
`Src`	The location of the image file.
Event	*Description*
`ServerClick`	Occurs when the user clicks the control.

HtmlInputRadio

Represents a radio form element. Table C.17 lists the properties of the `HtmlInputRadio` server control. The syntax is

```
<input type="radio" ... runat="server">
```

TABLE C.17 Properties of the `HtmlInputRadio` Control

Property	Description
`Checked`	Indicates whether the control is selected.

HtmlInputText

Represents a text box form element. Table C.18 lists the properties of the `HtmlInputText` server control. The syntax is

```
<input type="text" ... runat="server">
```

TABLE C.18 Properties of the `HtmlInputText` Control

Property	Description
`MaxLength`	The maximum number of characters that can be entered into this element.
`Size`	The visible width of the element in characters.
`Value`	The content of the control.

HtmlSelect

Represents a drop-down box of selectable items. Table C.19 lists the properties and events of the `HtmlSelect` server control. The syntax is

```
<select ... runat="server">
```

TABLE C.19 Properties and Events of the `HtmlSelect` Control

Property	*Description*
`DataMember`	The name of a data table or view to use (used when the `DataSource` property is assigned a `DataSet`).
`DataSource`	The data source to populate this control with.
`DataTextField`	A field in the data source that is displayed in the drop-down box.
`DataValueField`	A field in the data source that specifies the value for each selectable item.
`InnerHtml`	The HTML code contained within the opening and closing tags of this control.
`InnerText`	The text-only portion of the content contained within the opening and closing tags of this control.
`Items`	Gets the list of items in the select box. Returns a `ListItemCollection` object.
`Multiple`	Specifies whether multiple values can be selected at once (using the Shift key or Control key).
`SelectedIndex`	The index number of the currently selected item in the list. If multiple items are selected, this value represents the first item.
`Size`	The number of list items to display at once.
`Value`	The value of the currently selected item.
Event	*Description*
`ServerChange`	Occurs when the posted selected item is different than in the previous post.

C

HtmlTable, HtmlTableCell, and HtmlTableRow

These controls represent a table and its cells and rows. Table C.20 lists the properties common to all these server controls.

Table C.20 Properties Shared by the `HtmlTable`, `HtmlTableCell`, and `HtmlTableRow` Controls

Property	*Description*
`Align`	The alignment of the control as opposed to other elements on the page.
`BGColor`	The background color of the control.
`BorderColor`	The color of the border around the control.
`Height`	The height of the control.

Table C.21 lists the properties of the `HtmlTable` server control. The syntax is

```
<table ... runat="server">
```

Table C.21 Properties of the `HtmlTable` Control

Property	*Description*
`Border`	The width of the border around the table and in between cells.
`CellPadding`	The padding within cells.
`CellSpacing`	The spacing between cells.
`InnerHtml`	The HTML code contained within the opening and closing tags of this control.
`InnerText`	The text-only portion of the content contained within the opening and closing tags of this control.
`Rows`	Returns an `HtmlRowCollection` object representing all rows in the table.

Table C.22 lists the properties of the `HtmlTableCell` server control. The syntax is

```
<td ... runat="server">
```

Table C.22 Properties of the `HtmlTableCell` Control

Property	*Description*
`ColSpan`	The number of columns this cell spans.
`NoWrap`	Indicates whether the text within this cell should be allowed to wrap.
`RowSpan`	The number of rows this cell spans.
`VAlign`	The vertical alignment of text within this cell.
`Width`	The width of the table cell.

Table C.23 lists the properties of the `HtmlTableRow` server control. The syntax is

```
<tr ... runat="server">
```

TABLE C.23 Properties of the `HtmlTableRow` Control

Property	*Description*
`Cells`	Returns an `HtmlTableCellCollection` representing the cells contained in this row.
`InnerHtml`	The HTML code contained within the opening and closing tags of this control.
`InnerText`	The text-only portion of the content contained within the opening and closing tags of this control.
`VAlign`	The vertical alignment of the cells within this row.

`HtmlTextArea`

This control represents an HTML textarea element. Table C.24 lists the properties and events of the `HtmlTextArea` server control. The syntax is

```
<textarea ... runat="server">
```

TABLE C.24 Properties and Events of the `HtmlTextArea` Control

Property	*Description*
`Cols`	The number of columns (in characters) of this element.
`Name`	Specifies the unique name for the control.
`Rows`	The number of visible rows.
`Value`	The content contained within this control.
Event	*Description*
`ServerChange`	Occurs when the content of this control has changed from one post to another.

Web Server Controls

Web server controls are objects that reside on the server, but render HTML that provides a familiar display to the browser. This section details each of these controls.

Common Web Server Control Properties

Table C.25 describes properties and methods that are available to all ASP.NET Web server controls inherited from the `System.Web.UI.WebControls.WebControl` class.

TABLE C.25 Properties and Methods Common to All Web Server Controls

Property	*Description*
`AccessKey`	Specifies a character that, when combined with the Alt key, represents a keyboard shortcut to the control. Supported only in Internet Explorer 4.0 and higher.
`Attributes`	Returns an `AttributeCollection` object that represents the attributes for each control (this does not included defined properties).
`BackColor`	The background color of the control.
`BorderColor`	The border color of the control.
`BorderStyle`	A border style. Possible values are `Dashed`, `Dotted`, `Double`, `Inset`, `Groove`, `None`, `NotSet`, `Outset`, `Ridged`, and `Solid`.
`BorderWidth`	The width of the border around the control.
`ControlStyle`	The style of the control (used when developing custom controls).
`ControlStyleCreated`	Indicates whether the style associated with the control has been created.
`CssClass`	The Cascading Style Sheets class to assign to the control.
`Enabled`	Makes the control read-only if false.
`Font`	The style attributes for the font displayed in the control.
`ForeColor`	The color of the foreground of the control (the foreground is generally text).
`Height`	The height of the control.
`Style`	A `CSSStyleCollection` of attributes that are displayed for the control.
`TabIndex`	The control's position in the tab order.
`ToolTip`	Text that is displayed when the mouse cursor rests over the control.
`Width`	The width of the control.
Method	***Description***
`ApplyStyle`	Applies any non-blank elements of the specified `Style` object to the control, overwriting existing styles.

TABLE C.25 Properties and Methods Common to All Web Server Controls

Method	*Description*
`CopyBaseAttributes`	Copies the `AccessKey`, `Enabled`, `ToolTip`, `TabIndex`, and `Attributes` properties from a specified server control to this control.
`MergeStyle`	Applies any non-blank elements of the specified `Style` object to the control, without overwriting existing styles.
`RenderBeginTag`	Renders the opening tag of the corresponding HTML output to the browser.
`RenderEndTag`	Renders the closing tag of the corresponding HTML output to the browser.

Table C.26 describes properties and events that are available to all ASP.NET Web server list controls (`CheckBoxList`, `DropDownList`, `ListBox`, `RadioButtonList`) inherited from the `System.Web.UI.WebControls.ListControl` class.

TABLE C.26 Properties and Events Common to All Web Server List Controls

Property	*Description*
`AutoPostBack`	Indicates whether the form should be posted immediately upon the control's event.
`DataMember`	The table name of a data source to use to fill the list control (used when `DataSource` is set to a `DataSet`).
`DataSource`	The data source to use to fill the list control.
`DataTextField`	The field in the data source used to provide the text content of the list control.
`DataTextFormatString`	The format of the text in `DataTextField`.
`DataValueField`	The field in the data source used to provide the value content of the list control.
`Items`	A `ListItemCollection` of items of the list control.
`SelectedIndex`	The index of the selected item. If multiple items are selected, this specifies the first one.
`SelectedItem`	A `ListItem` representing the current selected item. If multiple items are selected, returns the first one.
Event	*Description*
`SelectedIndexChanged`	Occurs when the selected item has changed and the form is posted to the server.

Table C.27 describes properties, methods, and events that are available to all ASP.NET Web server datalist controls (`DataList`, `DataGrid`) inherited from the `System.Web.UI.WebControls.BaseDataList` class.

TABLE C.27 Properties, Methods, and Events Common to All Web Server Datalist Controls

Property	*Description*
`CellPadding`	The padding within the data cells.
`CellSpacing`	The spacing between data cells.
`DataKeyField`	The primary key field in the data source.
`DataKeys`	A `DataKeyCollection` of the key fields in a data source.
`DataMember`	The table name in the data source to use to fill the control with data (used when `DataSource` is set to a `DataSet`).
`DataSource`	The data source with which to populate the datalist control.
`GridLines`	The grid line style. Can be `Both`, `Horizontal`, `None`, or `Vertical`.
`HorizontalAlign`	Specifies the alignment of rows with respect to the surrounding elements.
Method	***Description***
`DataBind`	Specifies whether a data type is bindable to the datalist control.
Event	***Description***
`SelectedIndexChanged`	Occurs when the selected item has changed and the form is posted to the server.

The ASP.NET Web Server Controls

The following sections detail all the available ASP.NET Web server controls. The syntax for all Web controls is as follows:

```
<asp:controlName properties runat="server"/>
```

For example, for the `AdRotator` control in the next section, a sample declaration would be

```
<asp:AdRotator Target="blank" runat="server"/>
```

AdRotator

This control displays a set of rotating advertisements, defined by an XML file. Table C.28 lists the properties and events of this server control.

TABLE C.28 Properties and Events of the `AdRotator` Control

Property	*Description*
`AdvertisementFile`	The path to an XML file containing advertisement information.
`KeywordFilter`	A category filter that limits the ads displayed, according to categories in the XML advertisement file.
`Target`	Specifies the target window to load the URL linked by an advertisement.
Event	*Description*
`AdCreated`	Occurs after the creation of the control, before page rendering. Uses an `AdCreateEventArgs` object for the event parameter. This object contains the following properties:
	`AdProperties`—The properties for the current ad.
	`AlternateText`—The alternative text displayed for the image.
	`ImageUrl`—The URL of the image to display for the ad.
	`NavigateUrl`—The URL to which the ad directs users.

BoundColumn

Represents a column in a `DataGrid` that is bound with a field in a data source. Table C.29 lists the properties and methods of this server control.

TABLE C.29 Properties and Methods of the `BoundColumn` Control

Property	*Description*
`DataField`	The name of the data field bound to this column.
`DataFormatString`	The format to display the data in this column.
`ReadOnly`	Indicates whether the data in the column is read-only (often used in conjunction with `EditCommandColumns`).
Method	*Description*
`Initialize`	Initializes the column.
`InitializeCell`	Initializes a cell in the column.

Button

Displays a simple HTML button. Table C.30 lists the properties and events of this server control.

TABLE C.30 Properties and Events of the `Button` Control

Property	*Description*
`CommandArgument`	The value propagated in the `Command` event with the associated `CommandName` property.
`CommandName`	The command associated with the `Command` event.
`Text`	The content of the control.
Event	***Description***
`Click`	Occurs when the button is clicked.
`Command`	Same as `Click`.

`ButtonColumn`

Represents a column in a `DataGrid` control that displays a column with a set of buttons. Table C.31 lists the properties of this server control.

TABLE C.31 Properties of the `ButtonColumn` Control

Property	*Description*
`ButtonType`	Specifies the type of button to display. Can be `LinkButton` or `PushButton`.
`CommandName`	A string that represents the command to perform when a button is clicked.
`DataTextField`	The field name of the data source that is displayed in this column.
`DataTextFormatString`	Indicates how the content from `DataTextField` should be formatted.
`Text`	The caption displayed by the button.

`Calendar`

This control displays a fully customizable and interactive calendar in the browser. Table C.32 lists the properties and events of this server control.

TABLE C.32 Properties and Events of the `Calendar` Control

Property	*Description*
`CellPadding`	The padding within a day cell in the calendar.
`CellSpacing`	The spacing between days cells in the calendar.
`DayHeaderStyle`	The style for displaying the names of the days of the week.

TABLE C.32 continued

Property	*Description*
`DayNameFormat`	The format for displaying the names of the days of the week. Can be `FirstLetter`, `FirstTwoLetters`, `Full`, or `Short`.
`DayStyle`	The style for displaying days.
`FirstDayOfWeek`	The first day of the week to display in the calendar. Can be `Default` (as specified by the server) or any of the days `Sunday` through `Saturday`.
`NextMonthText`	The text displayed for the next month navigation (for example, `"Next"` or `">"`).
`NextPrevFormat`	The format of the next and previous month navigation links. Can be `CustomText` (default; use with `NextMonthText` and `PrevMonthText`), `FullMonth`, or `ShortMonth`.
`NextPrevStyle`	The style for displaying next and previous month navigation links.
`OtherMonthDayStyle`	The style for days displayed that are not in the current month.
`PrevMonthText`	The text displayed for the previous month navigation link (for example, `"Previous"` or `"<"`).
`SelectedDate`	The selected date.
`SelectedDates`	A collection of `DateTime` objects that represent the selected dates in the calendar.
`SelectedDayStyle`	The style for selected days.
`SelectionMode`	Specifies how a user is allowed to select dates (that is, only select individual days, select weeks at a time, and so on). Can be `Day`, `DayWeek`, `DayWeekMonth`, or `None`.
`SelectMonthText`	The text displayed for the month selection link.
`SelectorStyle`	The styles for the month and week selection links.
`SelectWeekText`	The text displayed for the week selection link.
`ShowDayHeader`	Specifies whether the days of the week header should be shown.
`ShowGridLines`	Specifies whether grid lines between calendar days should be shown.
`ShowNextPrevMonth`	Specifies whether the next and previous month navigation links are shown.
`ShowTitle`	Specifies whether the title of the calendar should be shown.
`TitleFormat`	The format for the title of the calendar. Can be `Month` or `MonthYear`.
`TitleStyle`	The style of the title of the calendar.

TABLE C.32 continued

Property	*Description*
TodayDayStyle	The style for today's date on the calendar.
TodaysDate	Specifies today's date.
VisibleDate	The date that specifies the month that is currently visible in the calendar. (Note that the selected date and visible date do not have to coincide.)
WeekendDayStyle	The style for weekends in the calendar.
Event	***Description***
DayRender	Occurs when each day cell is created in the calendar. Uses a DayRenderEventArgs object for the event parameter. This object contains the following properties: Cell—A TableCell object that represents the cell being rendered in the calendar. Day—A CalendarDay that represents the day being rendered in the calendar.
SelectionChanged	Occurs when the user selects a day, week, or month.
VisibleMonthChanged	Occurs when the user navigates to a different month. Uses a MonthChangedEventArgs object for the event parameter. This object contains the following properties: NewDate—The date that determines the currently visible month. PreviousDate—The date that determines the previously visible month.

CheckBox

This control represents an HTML form check box. Table C.33 lists the properties and events of this server control.

TABLE C.33 Properties and Events of the CheckBox Control

Property	*Description*
AutoPostBack	Indicates whether the form should be posted immediately upon the CheckedChanged event.
Checked	Indicates whether the control is checked.
Text	The text to display next to the check box.
TextAlign	The alignment of the text associated with this control.
Event	***Description***
CheckedChanged	Occurs when the Checked property changes.

CheckBoxList

This control displays a list of checkboxes in the browser that describe related information. Table C.34 lists the properties of this server control.

TABLE C.34 Properties of the CheckBoxList Control

Property	Description
CellPadding	The padding within the cells containing the CheckBox controls.
CellSpacing	The distance between the cells containing the CheckBox controls.
RepeatColumns	The number of columns to use to display the CheckBox controls.
RepeatDirection	Specifies whether the CheckBox controls should be repeated horizontally (Horizontal) or vertically (Vertical).
RepeatLayout	The layout of the CheckBox list. Can be Table (to display the controls in a table) or Flow (without a table).
TextAlign	The alignment for the text associated with each CheckBox.

DataGrid

This control displays a complex table from a supplied data source. Table C.35 lists the properties, and events of this server control.

TABLE C.35 Properties, and Events of the DataGrid Control

Property	Description
AllowCustomPaging	Indicates whether custom paging is enabled.
AllowPaging	Indicates whether paging is enabled.
AllowSorting	Indicates whether sorting is enabled.
AlternatingItemStyle	Style properties for alternating items in the DataGrid.
AutoGenerateColumns	Indicates whether the DataGrid should automatically generate BoundColumn columns using the data supplied in a data source (the DataGrid will use all fields in the data source to do so).
BackImageUrl	The URL of an image to display in the background of the control.
Columns	A collection of objects that represent the columns in the DataGrid.
CurrentPageIndex	The index of the current page.
EditItemIndex	The index of the item in the DataGrid to edit (this causes BoundColumn column to become editable, unless specified as read-only).

TABLE C.35 continued

Property	*Description*
`EditItemStyle`	The style for items that are in edit mode.
`FooterStyle`	The style of the footer in the `DataGrid`.
`HeaderStyle`	The style of the header in the `DataGrid`.
`Items`	A collection of `DataGridItems` that represent the individual items in the `DataGrid`.
`ItemStyle`	The style of the items in the `DataGrid`.
`PageCount`	The total number of pages used to completely display the data in the `DataGrid`.
`PagerStyle`	The style of the paging links.
`PageSize`	Specifies the number of items to display on a single page.
`SelectedIndex`	The index of the currently selected item.
`SelectedItem`	The selected item.
`SelectedItemStyle`	The style of the selected item.
`ShowFooter`	Indicates whether the footer should be shown.
`ShowHeader`	Indicates whether the header should be shown.
`VirtualItemCount`	Indicates the number of total items to be displayed by the `DataGrid`. Used only when `AllowCustomPaging` is set to `true`.
Event	***Description***
`CancelCommand`	Occurs when button is clicked with the `CommandName` property set to `"Cancel"`. Uses a `DataGridCommandEventArgs` object for the event parameter. This object contains the following properties: `CommandArgument`—The argument for the command. `CommandName`—The name of the command. `CommandSource`—The object that raised the command. `Item`—The selected item in the list.
`DeleteCommand`	Occurs when button is clicked with the `CommandName` property set to `"Delete"`. Uses a `DataGridCommandEventArgs` object.
`EditCommand`	Occurs when button is clicked with the `CommandName` property set to `"Edit"`. Uses a `DataGridCommandEventArgs` object.
`ItemCommand`	Occurs when button is clicked. Uses a `DataGridCommandEventArgs` object.
`ItemCreated`	Occurs immediately before an item is created in the `DataGrid`. Uses the `DataGridItemEventArgs` object for the event parameter. This object contains the following property:

Table C.35 continued

Event	Description
	Item—The currently selected item.
ItemDataBound	Occurs when data is bound to an item in the DataGrid. Uses the DataGridItemEventArgs object.
PageIndexChanged	Occurs when one of the pager links is clicked. Uses the DataGridPageChangedEventArgs object for the event parameter. This object contains the following properties:
	CommandSource—The object that generated the command.
	NewPageIndex—The index of the newly selected page.
SortCommand	Occurs when a column is sorted. Uses the DataGridSortCommandEventArgs object for the event parameter. This object contains the following properties:
	CommandSource—The object that generated the command.
	SortExpression—The expression used to sort the DataGrid.
UpdateCommand	Occurs when button is clicked with the CommandName property set to "Update". Uses a DataGridCommandEventArgs object.

DataList

This control renders a customized display from a supplied data source, using templates. Table C.36 lists the fields, properties, and events of this server control.

Table C.36 Fields, Properties, and Events of the DataList Control

Field	Description
CancelCommandName	The name of the Cancel command.
DeleteCommandName	The name of the Delete command.
EditCommandName	The name of the Edit command.
SelectCommandName	The name of the Select command.
UpdateCommandName	The name of the Update command.
Property	*Description*
AlternatingItemStyle	Style properties for alternating items in the DataList.
AlternatingItemTemplate	The template to use for alternating items in the DataList.
EditItemIndex	The index of the item in the DataList to edit.
EditItemStyle	The style for items that are in edit mode.
EditItemTemplate	The template to use for items that are in edit mode.

TABLE C.36 continued

Property	*Description*
`ExtractTemplateRows`	Indicates whether template rows should be extracted.
`FooterStyle`	The style of the footer in the `DataList`.
`FooterTemplate`	The template to use for the footer.
`GridLines`	Indicates the type of grid lines to use. Can be `Both`, `Horizontal`, `None`, or `Vertical`.
`HeaderStyle`	The style of the header in the `DataList`.
`HeaderTemplate`	The template to use for the header.
`Items`	A collection of `DataListItems` that represent the individual items in the `DataList`.
`ItemStyle`	The style of the items in the `DataList`.
`ItemTemplate`	The template to use for generic items in the `DataList`.
`RepeatColumns`	The number of columns to use to display the data.
`RepeatDirection`	The direction to repeat the data items. Can be `Horizontal` or `Vertical`.
`RepeatLayout`	The layout for items to be displayed. Can be `Table` or `Flow`.
`SelectedIndex`	The index of the currently selected item.
`SelectedItem`	The selected item.
`SelectedItemStyle`	The style of the selected item.
`SelectedItemTemplate`	The template to use to display to currently selected item.
`SeparatorStyle`	The style of the separator between items.
`SeparatorTemplate`	The template to use to display separators between items in the `DataList`.
`ShowFooter`	Indicates whether the footer should be shown.
`ShowHeader`	Indicates whether the header should be shown.
Event	*Description*
`CancelCommand`	Occurs when an event is raised with the `Command` property set to `"Cancel"`. Uses a `DataListCommandEventArgs` object for the event parameter. This object contains the following properties: `CommandArgument`—The argument for the command. `CommandName`—The name of the command. `CommandSource`—The object that raised the command. `Item`—The selected item in the list.

TABLE C.36 continued

Event	*Description*
DeleteCommand	Occurs when an event is raised with the Command property set to "Delete". Uses the DataListCommandEventArgs object.
EditCommand	Occurs when an event is raised with the Command property set to "Edit". Uses the DataListCommandEventArgs object.
ItemCommand	Occurs when an event is raised. Uses the DataListCommandEventArgs object.
ItemCreated	Occurs immediately before an item is created in the DataGrid. Uses the DataListItemEventArgs object for the event parameter. This object contains the following property: Item—The currently selected item.
ItemDataBound	Occurs when data is bound to an item in the DataGrid. Uses the DataListItemEventArgs object.
UpdateCommand	Occurs when an event is raised with the Command property set to "Update". Uses the DataListCommandEventArgs object.

DropDownList

This control represents a dropdown list of selectable items. Table C.37 lists the properties of this server control.

TABLE C.37 Properties of the DropDownList Control

Property	*Description*
BorderColor	The color of the border surrounding the list box.
BorderStyle	The style of the border surrounding the list box.
BorderWidth	The width of the border surrounding the list box.
SelectedIndex	The index of the currently selected item.

EditCommandColumn

This control represents a column in a DataGrid that displays links allowing users to edit fields. Table C.38 lists the properties of this server control.

TABLE C.38 Properties of the `EditCommandColumn` Control

Property	*Description*
`ButtonType`	The type of buttons to display. Can be `LinkButton` or `PushButton`.
`CancelText`	The text to display for the cancel button.
`EditText`	The text to display for the edit button.
`UpdateText`	The text to display for the update button.

`HyperLink`

This control represents an HTML hyperlink. Note that it does not generate any events; it simply redirects users. To generate events that can be handled, use the `LinkButton` control. Table C.39 lists the properties of this server control.

TABLE C.39 Properties of the `HyperLink` Control

Property	*Description*
`ImageUrl`	The URL of an image to display for the link.
`NavigateUrl`	The URL that this link directs users to.
`Target`	The target window to display the linked content in.
`Text`	The text to display for the link.

`HyperLinkColumn`

Represents a column in a `DataGrid` that is bound with a field in a data source. These fields will become navigable hyperlinks. Table C.40 lists the properties and methods of this server control.

TABLE C.40 Properties and Methods of the `HyperLinkColumn` Control

Property	*Description*
`DataNavigateUrlField`	The name of the data field that provides the link for this column.
`DataNavigateUrlFormatString`	The format to display the data field that provides the link in this column.
`DataTextField`	The name of the data field that contains the text to display for the link.
`DataTextFormatString`	The format to display the data containing the text to display links.
`NavigatUrl`	The URL to navigate to when a link is clicked.
`Target`	The window to display the page loaded by the URL.
`Text`	The text to display for the link.

TABLE C.40 continued

Method	*Description*
`Initialize`	Initializes the column.
`InitializeCell`	Initializes a cell in the column.

Image

This control represents an image displayed in the browser. Table C.41 lists the properties of this server control.

TABLE C.41 Properties of the `Image` Control

Property	*Description*
`AlternateText`	The text to display in place of the image.
`Enabled`	Indicates whether the control is enabled.
`Font`	The font properties for the alternative text.
`ImageAlign`	The alignment of the image on the page with respect to other UI elements.
`ImageUrl`	The URL of the image to display.

ImageButton

This control represents an HTML form button with an image instead of a push-style button. Table C.42 lists the properties and events of this server control.

TABLE C.42 Properties and Events of the `ImageButton` Control

Property	*Description*
`CommandArgument`	An argument that provides additional information about the `CommandName` property.
`CommandName`	The name of the command to execute when this image is clicked.
Event	*Description*
`Click`	Occurs when the image is clicked.
`Command`	Occurs when the image is clicked.

Label

This control displays text in the browser. Table C.43 lists its only property.

C

TABLE C.43 Properties of the `Label` Control

Property	*Description*
`Text`	The text to display in the browser.

`LinkButton`

This control represents an HTML form button with a link instead of a push-style button. Table C.44 lists the properties and events of this server control.

TABLE C.44 Properties and Events of the `LinkButton` Control

Property	*Description*
`CommandArgument`	An argument that provides additional information about the `CommandName` property.
`CommandName`	The name of the command to execute when this image is clicked.
`Text`	The text to display for the link.
Event	***Description***
`Click`	Occurs when the image is clicked.
`Command`	Occurs when the image is clicked.

`ListBox`

This control represents a dropdown list of selectable items. Table C.45 lists the properties of this server control.

TABLE C.45 Properties of the `ListBox` Control

Property	*Description*
`BorderColor`	The color of the border surrounding the list box.
`BorderStyle`	The style of the border surrounding the list box.
`BorderWidth`	The width of the border surrounding the list box.
`Rows`	The number of rows to display in the list box.
`SelectionMode`	Allows single (`Single`) or multiple (`Multiple`) selections in the list box.

`Panel`

This control represents a container for other controls. Table C.46 lists the properties of this server control.

TABLE C.46 Properties of the `Panel` Control

Property	*Description*
`BackImageUrl`	The image to display in the background of this control.
`HorizontalAlign`	The horizontal alignment for the content within this control.
`Wrap`	Indicates whether the control's contents should wrap.

RadioButton

This control represents an HTML radio button. It inherits from the `CheckBox` control, so all of the `CheckBox`'s events and properties are available to it as well. Table C.47 lists the only unique property of this server control.

TABLE C.47 Properties of the `RadioButton` Control

Property	*Description*
`GroupName`	The name of the group to which this radio button belongs.

RadioButtonList

This control displays a list of radio buttons in the browser that describe related information. Table C.48 lists the properties of this server control.

TABLE C.48 Properties of the `RadioButtonList` Control

Property	*Description*
`CellPadding`	The padding within the cells containing the `RadioButton` controls.
`CellSpacing`	The distance between the cells containing the `RadioButton` controls.
`RepeatColumns`	The number of columns to use to display the `RadioButton` controls.
`RepeatDirection`	Specifies whether the `RadioButton` controls should be repeated horizontally (`Horizontal`) or vertically (`Vertical`).
`RepeatLayout`	The layout of the `RadioButton` list. Can be `Table` (to display the controls in a table) or `Flow` (without a table).
`TextAlign`	The alignment for the text associated with each `RadioButton`.

Repeater

This control renders a customized display from a supplied data source, using templates. Table C.49 lists the properties and events of this server control.

TABLE C.49 Properties and Events of the `Repeater` Control

Property	Description
`AlternatingItemTemplate`	The template to use for alternating items in the `Repeater`.
`DataMember`	The specific table to use for data binding (used when `DataSource` is set to a `DataSet`).
`DataSource`	The data source to use for data binding.
`FooterTemplate`	The template to use for the footer.
`HeaderTemplate`	The template to use for the header.
`Items`	A collection of `RepeaterItems` that represent the individual items in the `Repeater`.
`ItemTemplate`	The template to use for generic items in the `Repeater`.
`SeparatorTemplate`	The template to use to display separators between items in the `Repeater`.
Event	*Description*
`ItemCommand`	Occurs when an event is raised. Uses the `RepeaterCommandEventArgs` object for the event parameter. This object contains the following properties: `CommandArgument`—The argument for the command. `CommandName`—The name of the command. `CommandSource`—The object that raised the command. `Item`—The `RepeaterItem` associated with the event.
`ItemCreated`	Occurs immediately before an item is created in the `DataGrid`. Uses the `RepeaterItemEventArgs` object for the event parameter. This object contains the following property: `Item`—The currently selected item.
`ItemDataBound`	Occurs when data is bound to an item in the `Repeater`. Uses the `RepeaterItemEventArgs` object.

`Table, TableCell, TableRow`

These controls represent all the elements of an HTML table. Table C.50 lists the properties of the `Table` control.

TABLE C.50 Properties of the `Table` Server Control

Property	Description
`BackImageUrl`	The URL of the image to display in the background of the table.
`CellPadding`	The padding within cells.

TABLE C.50 continued

Property	Description
`CellSpacing`	The spacing between cells.
`GridLines`	The style of gridlines in the table. Can be `Both`, `Horizontal`, `None`, or `Vertical`.
`HorizontalAlign`	The horizontal alignment of the table in the page.
`Rows`	Returns a `TableRowCollection` object representing all rows in the table.

Table C.51 lists the properties of the `TableCell` server control. Note that there also is a `TableHeaderCell` object that derives from the `TableCell` object and contains the same properties.

TABLE C.51 Properties of the `TableCell` Control

Property	Description
`ColumnSpan`	The number of columns this cell spans.
`HorizontalAlign`	The horizontal alignment of the content within the cell.
`RowSpan`	The number of rows this cell spans.
`Text`	The text contained in the cell.
`VerticalAlign`	The vertical alignment of text within this cell.
`Wrap`	Indicates whether the cell's contents should wrap.

Table C.52 lists the properties of the `TableRow` server control.

TABLE C.52 Properties of the `TableRow` Control

Property	Description
`Cells`	Returns a `TableCellCollection` representing the cells contained in this row.
`HorizontalAlign`	The horizontal alignment of the content within the cells.
`VerticalAlign`	The vertical alignment of the cells within this row.

`TemplateColumn`

This control represents a column in a `DataGrid`. Table C.53 lists the properties of this server control.

TABLE C.53 Properties of the `TemplateColumn` Control

Property	*Description*
`EditItemTemplate`	Gets the template that defines how items in edit mode are displayed.
`FooterTemplate`	Gets the template that defines how footers are displayed.
`HeaderTemplate`	Gets the template that defines how headers are displayed.
`ItemTemplate`	Gets the template that defines how generic items are displayed.

TextBox

This control represents an HTML text box. Table C.54 lists the properties and events of this server control.

TABLE C.54 Properties and Events of the `TextBox` Control

Property	*Description*
`AutoPostBack`	Indicates whether the form should be posted immediately upon the `TextChanged` event.
`Columns`	The display width of the control, in characters.
`MaxLength`	The maximum number of characters allowable in the text box.
`ReadOnly`	Indicates whether the content in the text box is editable.
`Rows`	The number of rows to display for a multiline text box.
`Text`	The text to display.
`TextMode`	The behavior of the text box. Can be `MultiLine`, `Password`, or `SingleLine` (default).
`Wrap`	Indicates whether text should wrap in a multiline text box.
Event	*Description*
`TextChanged`	Occurs when the form is submitted and the `Text` property is different than the previous post.

Validation Server Controls

This section lists the detailed properties for each of the ASP.NET validation server controls. These controls are used to provide user input validation for other server controls.

Common Validation Server Control Properties

Table C.55 lists properties and methods that are common to all validation controls inherited from the `System.Web.UI.WebControls.BaseValidator` class except the `ValidationSummary` control.

TABLE C.55 Properties and Methods of the `BaseValidator` Class

Property	*Description*
`ControlToValidate`	Specifies the control that should be validated.
`Display`	The display behavior for the validation control. Can be one of the following: `None`—The error message is not displayed. `Static`—If validation fails, the control's error message is displayed where the control resides in the page layout. The control will take up space in the layout even if the error message is not visible. `Dynamic`—Error messages are displayed when validation fails, and the control doesn't take up any space in the page layout if a message is not displayed.
`EnableClientScript`	Specifies whether client-side script will be generated to handle validation client-side via DHTML. Note that client-side script must be created manually.
`Enabled`	Indicates if the validation control is enabled.
`ErrorMessage`	The message to display if the input is not valid.
`ForeColor`	Sets the font color of the error message.
`IsValid`	Specifies whether the input in the control specified by `ControlToValidate` is valid.
Method	*Description*
`GetValidationProperty`	Retrieves the validation property of a control.
`Validate`	Determines whether the watched over server control's content is valid, and updates the `IsValid` property.

The Validation Server Controls

The following section lists the details of each validation control. Note that the `ControlToValidate` property must be set to a valid server control for these controls to function properly.

C

`CompareValidator`

This control compares values in a control to another value, or another control. Table C.56 lists the properties of this server control.

TABLE C.56 Properties of the `CompareValidator` Control

Property	*Description*
`ControlToCompare`	The ID of the control to compare values with.
`Operator`	The comparison to make. Can be `DataTypeCheck`, `Equal`, `GreaterThan`, `GreaterThanEqual`, `LessThan`, `LessThanEqual`, or `NotEqual`.
`ValueToCompare`	A constant value to compare against.

`CustomValidator`

This control validates controls' contents via a server-side or client-side validation routine, created by you. Table C.57 lists the properties and events of this server control.

TABLE C.57 Properties and Events of the `CustomValidator` Control

Property	*Description*
`ClientValidationFunction`	The client-side function that should be used to validate the specified control.
Event	*Description*
`ServerValidate`	Occurs during a form post; indicates which server-side method will be used to validate the control.

`RangeValidator`

This control compares values in a control against a possible range of values. Table C.58 lists the properties of this server control.

TABLE C.58 Properties of the `RangeValidator` Control

Property	*Description*
`MaximumValue`	The maximum allowed value for the watched over control's input. Can be a string or number.
`MinimumValue`	The minimum allowed value for the watched over control's input. Can be a string or number.

`RegularExpressionValidator`

This control compares values in a control to a regular expression. Table C.59 lists the properties of this server control.

TABLE C.59 Properties of the `RegularExpressionValidator` Control

Property	*Description*
`ValidationExpression`	A regular expression to validate the watched-over control's content against.

`RequiredFieldValidator`

This control ensures that content is entered into a server control; it is not left blank. Table C.60 lists the properties of this server control.

TABLE C.60 Properties of the `RequiredFieldValidator` Control

Property	*Description*
`InitialValue`	The initial value associated with the watched-over control.

`ValidationSummary`

This control provides a central location for all other validation controls to display their error messages. It can be used in conjunction with the control's in-line error messages. Table C.61 lists the properties of this server control.

TABLE C.61 Properties of the `ValidationSummary` Control

Property	*Description*
`DisplayMode`	The display behavior of this control. Can be `BulletList`, `List`, or `SingleParagraph`.
`EnableClientScript`	Indicates whether client-side validation should be used.
`ForeColor`	The font color to display the error messages.
`HeaderText`	The header displayed at the top of this control.
`ShowMessageBox`	Indicates whether the error messages should be shown in a pop-up message box.
`ShowSummary`	Indicates whether the validation summary is displayed inline.

APPENDIX D

ADO.NET Controls: Properties and Methods

ADO.NET consists of two main parts: the `DataSet` and its related classes, and the managed providers that facilitate communication with data sources. This appendix describes the classes in each of these parts. The tables here list only non-inherited members of each class.

The `DataSet` and Related Classes

The following are the details for the `DataSet` and related items, such as `DataRelation`, `DataTable`, and so on.

`Constraint` and `ConstraintCollection`

This `Constraint` class represents a rule on a table that limits the data that can be modified. Table C.1 lists the properties of the `Constraint` class.

TABLE C.1 Properties of the `Constraint` Class

Property	*Description*
`ConstraintName`	The name of this constraint.
`ExtendedProperties`	Retrieves a collection of user-defined properties.
`Table`	Returns `DataTable` to which this constraint applies.

Table C.2 lists the property, methods, and event of the `ConstraintCollection` class.

TABLE C.2 Property, Methods, and Event of the `ConstraintCollection` Class

Property	*Description*
`Item`	Gets a constraint in the collection with either the name of the constraint or its index in the collection.
Method	*Description*
`Add`	Adds a constraint to the collection. This method is overloaded. See the .NET Framework SDK documentation for more information.
`AddRange`	Copies the elements from another `ConstraintCollection` object into the current one.
`CanRemove`	Indicates if a constraint specified by *`Constraint`* can be removed from the `DataTable`.
`Clear`	Clears the collection of all `Constraint` objects.
`Contains`	Indicates if the `Constraint` with the name *`name`* exists in the collection.
`IndexOf`	Retrieves the index of the specified constraint. This method is overloaded. See the .NET Framework SDK documentation for more information.
`Remove`	Removes the specified constraint from the collection. This method is overloaded. See the .NET Framework SDK documentation for more information.
`RemoveAt`	Removes the `Constraint` at the specified index.
Event	*Description*
`CollectionChanged`	Occurs when the collection is changed through additions or removals. Uses a `CollectionChangeEventArgs` object for the event parameter. This object contains the following properties: `Action`—Returns a value (`Add`, `Remove`, `Refresh`) indicating how the collection has changed. `Element`—Returns the instance of the collection that changed.

DataColumn and DataColumnCollection

A DataColumn represents a column of information in a DataTable. Table C.3 lists the properties and method of the DataColumn class.

TABLE C.3 Properties and Method of the DataColumn Class

Property	*Description*
AllowDBNull	Indicates if null values are allowed in this column.
AutoIncrement	Indicates if the value of the column automatically increments with the addition of a new row.
AutoIncrementSeed	The starting value for AutoIncrement
AutoIncrementStep	The increment value used by AutoIncrement.
Caption	The caption for this column.
ColumnMapping	Returns a MappingType object indicating how the column is mapped when written as XML.
ColumnName	The name of the column.
DataType	The type of data stored in this column.
DefaultValue	The default value for this column when creating new rows.
Expression	A string expression used to filter rows, calculate the column's value, or create an aggregate column.
ExtendedProperties	Returns a PropertyCollection of custom user information.
MaxLength	The maximum length of a text column.
Namespace	The XML namespace containing the elements used in this column.
Ordinal	The position of this column in the DataColumnCollection.
Prefix	The prefix used for this column when represented as XML.
ReadOnly	Indicates if the column allows changes.
Table	Returns DataTable to which this column belongs.
Unique	Indicates if each value in the column must be unique.
Method	*Description*
ToString	Returns the Expression of this column, if one exists.

Table C.4 lists the property, methods, and event of the DataColumnCollection class.

TABLE C.4 Property, Methods, and Event of the `DataColumnCollection` Class

Property	*Description*
`Item`	Gets a `DataColumn` in the collection with either the name of the column or its index in the collection.
Method	*Description*
`Add`	Adds a column to the collection. This method is overloaded. See the .NET Framework SDK documentation for more information.
`AddRange`	Adds an array of `DataColumn` objects to the collection.
`CanRemove`	Indicates if a column specified by *`Column`* can be removed from the collection.
`Clear`	Clears the collection of all `DataColumn` objects.
`Contains`	Indicates if the `DataColumn` with the name *`name`* exists in the collection.
`IndexOf`	Retrieves the index of the specified column. This method is overloaded. See the .NET Framework SDK documentation for more information.
`Remove`	Removes the specified column from the collection. This method is overloaded. See the .NET Framework SDK documentation for more information.
`RemoveAt`	Removes the `DataColumn` at the specified index.
Event	*Description*
`CollectionChanged`	Occurs when the collection is changed through additions or removals. Uses a `CollectionChangeEventArgs` object for the event parameter. This object contains the following properties: `Action`—Returns a value (`Add`, `Remove`, `Refresh`) indicating how the collection has changed. `Element`—Returns the instance of the collection that changed.

`DataRelation` and `DataRelationCollection`

A `DataRelation` class represents the relationship between multiple tables in the `DataSet`. Table C.5 lists the properties of the `DataRelation` class.

TABLE C.5 Properties of the `DataRelation` Class

Property	*Description*
`ChildColumns`	Returns an array of `DataColumn` objects that represent the child columns of this relation.
`ChildKeyConstraint`	A `ForeignKeyConstraint` object for this relation.

TABLE C.5 continued

Property	*Description*
`ChildTable`	Returns a `DataTable` representing the child table of this relation.
`DataSet`	Returns the `DataSet` to which this relation belongs to.
`ExtendedProperties`	Returns a `PropertyCollection` of custom user information.
`Nested`	Indicates if relations are nested.
`ParentColumns`	An array of `DataColumn` objects that represent the parent columns of this relation.
`ParentKeyConstraint`	A `UniqueConstraint` object for this relation.
`ParentTable`	Returns the `DataTable` representing the parent table of this relation.
`RelationName`	The name of this relation.

Table C.6 lists the property, methods, and event of the `DataRelationCollection` class.

TABLE C.6 Property, Methods, and Event of the `DataRelationCollection` Class

Property	*Description*
`Item`	Gets a `DataRelation` in the collection with either the name of the relation or its index in the collection.
Method	***Description***
`Add`	Adds a relation to the collection. This method is overloaded. See the .NET Framework SDK Documentation for more information.
`AddRange`	Adds an array of `DataRelation` objects to the collection.
`CanRemove`	Verifies whether the specified `DataRelation` can be removed from the collection.
`Clear`	Clears the collection of all `DataRelation`objects.
`Contains`	Indicates if the `DataRelation` with the name *`name`* exists in the collection.
`IndexOf`	Returns the index of the specified `DataRelation`.
`Remove`	Removes the specified relation from the collection. This method is overloaded. See the .NET Framework SDK Documentation for more information.
`RemoveAt`	Removes the `DataRelation` at the specified index.

TABLE C.6 continued

Event	*Description*
`CollectionChanged`	Occurs when the collection is changed through additions or removals. Uses a `CollectionChangeEventArgs` object for the event parameter. This object contains the following properties: `Action`—Returns a value (`Add`, `Remove`, `Refresh`) indicating how the collection has changed. `Element`—Returns the instance of the collection that changed.

`DataRow` and `DataRowCollection`

A `DataRow` represents a row of information in a `DataTable`, that is, an individual record of data. Table C.7 lists the properties and methods of the `DataRow` class.

TABLE C.7 Properties and Methods of the `DataRow` Class

Property	*Description*
`HasErrors`	Indicates if the data in the row contains any errors.
`Item`	Specifies the data contained in the specified column. The method is overloaded. See the .NET Framework SDK documentation for more details.
`ItemArray`	Specifies the data contained in the entire row, through an array.
`RowError`	The custom error description for the row.
`RowState`	The state of the row. Can be `Detached`, `Unchanged`, `New`, `Deleted`, or `Modified`.
`Table`	Returns `DataTable` to which this row belongs.
Method	***Description***
`AcceptChanges`	Commits all changes made to the row.
`BeginEdit`	Begins an edit operation on the row.
`CancelEdit`	Cancels an edit operation, repealing edits.
`ClearErrors`	Clears all errors for the row.
`Delete`	Deletes the row.
`EndEdit`	Ends the edit operation on the row.
`GetChildRows`	Returns an array of `DataRow` objects representing the child rows of this row, when using the specified `DataRelation`.

TABLE C.7 continued

Method	Description
GetColumnError	Gets the error for a specified column in the row. This method is overloaded. See the .NET Framework SDK documentation for more information.
GetColumnsInError	Gets an array of DataColumn objects that have errors.
GetParentRow	Returns a DataRow representing the parent of this row. This method is overloaded. See the .NET Framework SDK documentation for more details.
GetParentRows	Returns an array of DataRow objects representing the parent of this row using the specified DataRelation. This method is overloaded. See the .NET Framework SDK documentation for more details.
HasVersion	Indicates if a specified version of the row exists.
IsNull	Indicates if the specified column in the row contains a null value. This method is overloaded. See the .NET Framework SDK documentation for more details.
RejectChanges	Rolls back all changes made to the row.
SetColumnError	Sets the error description for the column. This method is overloaded.
SetParentRow	Sets the parent row of a given child row. This method is overloaded.

Table C.8 lists the property and methods of the DataRowCollection class.

TABLE C.8 Property and Methods of the DataRowCollection Class

Property	Description
Item	Gets a DataRow in the collection with either the name of the row or its index in the collection.
Method	*Description*
Add	Adds a row to the collection. This method is overloaded.
Clear	Clears the collection of all DataRow objects.
Contains	Indicates if the DataRow with the name *name* exists in the collection.
Find	Gets a specified DataRow. This method is overloaded.
InsertAt	Inserts a new DataRow at the specified location.
Remove	Removes the specified row from the collection. This method is overloaded.
RemoveAt	Removes the DataRow at the specified index.

DataSet

Table C.9 lists the properties, methods, and event of the DataSet class, which represents a disconnected data source.

TABLE C.9 Properties, Methods, and Event of the DataSet Class

Property	*Description*
CaseSensitive	Indicates if string comparisons in a DataTable are case-sensitive.
DataSetName	The name of this DataSet.
DefaultViewManager	Returns a DataViewManager that contains a customized view of the data in the DataSet.
EnforceConstraints	Indicates if constraint rules are followed when updating the data.
ExtendedProperties	A PropertyCollection object containing custom user information.
HasErrors	Indicates if the data in any of the rows of this DataSet contain errors.
Locale	The locale information used to compare strings. Returns a CultureInfo object.
Namespace	Indicates the namespace of the DataSet.
Prefix	An XML alias for the namespace of the DataSet.
Relations	A DataRelationCollection object that represents all relations between tables in the DataSet.
Site	Returns an ISite interface for the DataSet (used to bind components to containers).
Tables	A DataTableCollection object representing all tables in the DataSet.
Method	*Description*
AcceptChanges	Commits all changes made to the DataSet.
Clear	Removes all rows in all tables in the DataSet.
Clone	Produces a DataSet identical to the current DataSet, without data.
Copy	Produces a DataSet identical to the current DataSet, with data.
GetChanges	Produces a DataSet that contains only the data that has changed.
GetXml	Returns the data in the DataSet in XML format.
GetXmlSchema	Returns the XML schema for the data in the DataSet.
HasChanges	Indicates if the data in the DataSet has changed at all.

TABLE C.9 continued

Method	*Description*
`InferXmlSchema`	Builds the data structure from an XML data source. This function is overloaded; see the .NET SDK documentation for more details.
`Merge`	Merges the specified `DataSet` with the one specified.
`ReadXml`	Inserts data and schema information from an XML file in a `DataSet`.
`ReadXmlSchema`	Builds the data structure from an XML schema. This function is overloaded; see the .NET SDK documentation for more details.
`RejectChanges`	Undoes all changes that have been made to this `DataSet`.
`Reset`	Resets the `DataSet` to its default properties.
`WriteXml`	Writes the content of the `DataSet` in XML format. This function is overloaded; see the .NET SDK documentation for more details.
`WriteXmlSchema`	Writes the structure of the `DataSet` in XML format. This function is overloaded; see the .NET SDK Documentation for more details.
Event	*Description*
`MergeFailed`	Occurs when a target and source `DataRow` have the same primary key value, and `EnforceConstraints` is `true`.

`DataTable` and `DataTableCollection`

A `DataTable` represents a table of information in a `DataSet`. Table C.10 lists the properties, methods, and events of the `DataTable` class.

TABLE C.10 Properties, Methods, and Events of the `DataTable` Class

Property	*Description*
`CaseSensitive`	Indicates if string comparisons in the table are case-sensitive.
`ChildRelations`	Returns a `DataRelationCollection` of the child relations of this table.
`Columns`	Returns a `DataColumnCollection` object representing the column in this table.
`Constraints`	Returns a `DataRelationCollection` object representing the data relations in this table.
`DataSet`	Returns the `DataSet` this table belongs to.
`DefaultView`	Returns a `DataView` representing a customized view of the data in this table.

TABLE C.10 continued

Property	*Description*
`DisplayExpression`	A string expression that returns a value indicating how to display this table in the UI.
`ExtendedProperties`	Returns a `PropertyCollection` of custom user information.
`HasErrors`	Indicates if there are any errors in any of the rows of this table.
`Locale`	A `CultureInfo` object used to determine how strings are compared.
`MinimumCapacity`	The initial starting size for this table.
`Namespace`	The XML namespace containing the elements used in this table.
`ParentRelations`	A `DataRelationCollection` of the parent relations of this table.
`Prefix`	The prefix used for this table when represented as XML.
`PrimaryKey`	An array of `DataColumn` objects that serve as the primary keys of the table.
`Rows`	A `DataRowCollection` object representing the rows belonging to this table.
`Site`	Returns an `ISite` interface for the `DataTable` (used to bind components to containers).
`TableName`	The name of the table.
Method	***Description***
`AcceptChanges`	Commits all changes made to this table.
`BeginInit`	Begins the initialization of this table.
`BeginLoadData`	Begins the data loading process.
`Clear`	Clears the table of all data.
`Clone`	Makes a copy of the `DataTable`'s structure, including all its relations.
`Compute`	Computes the expression specified in the first parameter on the rows that pass the specified filter.
`Copy`	Copies both the structure and data contained in the `DataTable`.
`EndInit`	Ends the initialization process.
`EndLoadData`	Ends the data loading process.
`GetChanges`	Gets a copy of the `DataTable` that contains only the changes made to it since it was first created, or since `AcceptChanges` was called.
`GetErrors`	An array of `DataRow` objects that contain errors.
`ImportRow`	Copies a `DataRow` object into the `DataTable`.

TABLE C.10 continued

Method	*Description*
`LoadDataRow`	Finds and updates a `DataRow` with the specified values. If a row is not found, a new one is created.
`NewRow`	Returns a blank `DataRow` with the same schema as the table.
`RejectChanges`	Rolls back all changes made to the table since it was first loaded or since `AcceptChanges` was last called.
`Reset`	Resets the `DataTable` to its default properties.
`Select`	Returns an array of `DataRow` objects. This method is overloaded.
`ToString`	Returns the `TableName` and `DisplayExpression` of this table.
Event	*Description*
`ColumnChanged`	Occurs when a column has changed. Uses a `DataColumnChangedEventArgs` object for the event parameter. This object contains the following properties:
	`Column`—The column that changed. `ProposedValue`—The value to change to column to.
	`Row`—The `DataRow` to change.
`ColumnChanging`	Occurs when changes have been submitted for this column. Uses a `DataColumnChangedEventArgs` object.
`RowChanged`	Occurs when a row has changed. Uses a `DataRowChangedEventArgs` object for the event parameter. This object contains the following properties:
	`Action`—The action that occurred on the `DataRow`.
	`Row`—The `DataRow` to change.
`RowChanging`	Occurs when changes have been submitted for this column. Uses a `DataRowChangedEventArgs` object.
`RowDeleted`	Occurs after a row is deleted. Uses a `DataRowChangedEventArgs` object.
`RowDeleting`	Occurs before a row is deleted. Uses a `DataRowChangedEventArgs` object.

Table C.11 lists the property, methods, and events of the `DataTableCollection` class.

TABLE C.11 Property, Methods, and Events of the `DataTableCollection` Class

Property	Description
`Item`	Gets a `DataTable` in the collection with either the name of the table or its index in the collection.
Methods	***Description***
`Add`	Adds a table to the collection. This method is overloaded.
`AddRange`	Adds an array of `DataTable` objects to the collection.
`CanRemove`	Indicates if the table specified can be removed from the collection.
`Clear`	Clears the collection of all `DataTable` objects.
`Contains`	Indicates if the `DataTable` with the specified name exists in the collection.
`IndexOf`	Retrieves the index of the specified table. This method is overloaded.
`Remove`	Removes the specified table from the collection. This method is overloaded.
`RemoveAt`	Removes the `DataTable` at the specified index.
Event	***Description***
`CollectionChanged`	Occurs when the collection is changed through additions or removals. Uses a `CollectionChangeEventArgs` object for the event parameter. This object contains the following properties: `Action`—Returns a value (`Add`, `Remove`, `Refresh`) indicating how the collection has changed. `Element`—Returns the instance of the collection that changed.
`CollectionChanging`	Occurs before the collection is changed. Uses a `CollectionChangeEventArgs` object.

DataView

A `DataView` class represents a customized view of the data in a `DataSet`. Table C.12 lists the properties, methods, and event of the `DataView` class.

TABLE C.12 Properties, Methods, and Event of the `DataView` Class

Property	Description
`AllowDelete`	Indicates if deletes are allowed in this view.
`AllowEdit`	Indicates if edit are allowed in this view.

TABLE C.12 continued

Property	*Description*
AllowNew	Indicates if new rows can be added in this view.
ApplyDefaultSort	Indicates if the default sort should be used.
Count	Returns the number of records in the DataView.
DataViewManager	The DataView that created this view (a pointer to the DataSetView that owns the corresponding DataSet).
Item	Gets a specified row of data from a table.
RowFilter	An expression used to filter which rows are added to the DataView.
RowStateFilter	Specifies which version of rows is added to the DataView. Can be None, Unchanged, New, Deleted, ModifiedCurrent, ModifiedOriginal, OriginalRows, and CurrentRows (default).
Sort	The columns to sort by.
Table	The source DataTable from which to pull data.
Methods	***Description***
AddNew	Adds a new row to the DataView.
BeginInit	Begins the initialization of this DataView.
CopyTo	Copies items into an array.
Delete	Deletes a row at the specified index.
EndInit	Ends the initialization process.
Find	Finds a specified row in the DataView. This method is overloaded.
FindRows	Returns an array of DataRowView objects that match the specified criteria.
GetEnumerator	Returns an IEnumerator that can be used to iterate through this DataView.
Event	***Description***
ListChanged	Occurs when the list managed by the DataView changes. Uses a ListChangedEventArgs object for the event parameter. This object contains the following properties: ListChangedType—The way the list changed. NewIndex—The new index of the item that changed. OldIndex—The old index of the item that changed.

The Managed Providers

Managed providers allow ADO.NET to interact with any type of OleDB-compliant data source. These providers are used to move data into the `DataSet` and its related classes, and can be used independently to modify data as well.

There are two managed providers: `OleDB` and `SQL`. The former deals with all OleDB-compliant data stores, whereas the latter deals only with SQL Server. In nearly all cases, classes in one provider correspond exactly to classes in the other; the only difference is the use of a prefix: `OleDb` and `Sql`. For instance, both providers have an class that provides lightweight access to data, respectively named `OleDbDataReader` and `SqlDataReader`.

Because of the similarities of these two providers, only the `OleDb` managed provider is covered here. Where there are differences in the two, a note is made.

OleDbCommand

The `OleDbCommand` class represents a SQL statement to be made to a data source. Table C.13 lists the properties and methods of this class.

TABLE C.13 Properties and Methods of the `OleDbCommand` Class

Property	*Description*
`CommandText`	The SQL statement to execute.
`CommandTimeout`	The time limit in which the command must execute before termination.
`CommandType`	Specifies how the `CommandText` property is interpreted. Can be `StoredProcedure`, `TableDirect`, or `Text` (default).
`Connection`	Specifies an `OleDbConnection` used by this object.
`DesignTimeVisible`	Indicates if the command object should be visible in a custom Windows Forms designer control.
`Parameters`	Gets an `OleDbParameterCollection` object representing the parameters for use with this command.
`Transaction`	The `OleDbTransaction` used by the command.
`UpdatedRowSource`	The number of records affected by the command. Typically one if the command succeeds, and less than one otherwise.
Method	*Description*
`Cancel`	Cancels the execution of the command.
`CreateParameter`	Creates an `OleDbParameter` for use with this command.

TABLE C.13 continued

Property	*Description*
`ExecuteNonQuery`	Executes a SQL statement that doesn't return any data.
`ExecuteReader`	Returns an `OleDbDataReader` filled with the data returned from the command.
`ExecuteScalar`	Executes the query, and returns value in the first column and first row of the returned results.
`Prepare`	Creates a compiled version of the command.
`ResetCommandTimeout`	Resets the `CommandTimeout` property to the default value.

`OleDbCommandBuilder`

The `OleDbCommandBuilder` class represents an easy way to generate commands for use against a data source. Table C.14 lists the properties and methods of this class.

TABLE C.14 Properties and Methods of the `OleDbCommandBuilder` Class

Property	*Description*
`DataAdapter`	The name of an `OleDbDataAdapter` for which the commands are generated.
`QuotePrefix`	Specifies a prefix to use when specifying data source object names (such as `tbl` for tables, `sp` for stored procedures, and so forth).
`QuoteSuffix`	Specifies a suffix to use when specifying data source object names.
Method	*Description*
`DeriveParameters`	Fills the `OleDbCommand`'s `Parameters` collection with values specified in the stored procedure.
`GetDeleteCommand`	Gets the automatically generated SQL statement to delete rows from the data source.
`GetInsertCommand`	Gets the automatically generated SQL statement to insert rows into the data source.
`GetUpdateCommand`	Gets the automatically generated SQL statement to update rows in the data source.
`RefreshSchema`	Retrieves the schema of the data source.

OleDbConnection

The `OleDbConnection` class represents a connection to a data source. Table C.15 lists the properties, methods, and events of this class.

TABLE C.15 Properties, Methods, and Events of the `OleDbConnection` Class

Property	*Description*
`ConnectionString`	The string used to open a database.
`ConnectionTimeout`	The time limit for establishing a connection to the database, after which an error will be generated.
`Database`	The name of the database to use once the connection is established.
`DataSource`	The name of the database to connect to.
`Provider`	The name of the database provider.
`ServerVersion`	A string containing the version of the server to which the client is connected.
`State`	The current state of the connection.
Method	***Description***
`BeginTransaction`	Begins a database transaction. This method is overloaded.
`ChangeDatabase`	Changes the current database to another specified value.
`Close`	Closes the database connection.
`CreateCommand`	Returns an `OleDbCommand` object to execute commands against the database.
`GetOleDbSchemaTable`	Returns schema information from a data source specified by a GUID. (This method does not exist in the corresponding `SqlConnection` class.)
`Open`	Attempts to open the connection to the database.
`ReleaseObjectPool`	Indicates that the `OleDbConnection` object pooling can be cleared when the last underlying OLE DB provider is released.
Event	***Description***
`InfoMessage`	Occurs when the provider sends a message. Uses an `OleDbInfoMessageEventArgs` object for the event parameter. This object contains the following properties: `ErrorCode`—An `HRESULT` value indicating the standard error. `Errors`—An `OleDbErrorCollection` of warnings sent by the provider.

TABLE C.15 continued

Event	Description
	Message—The full text of the error message sent from the provider.
	Source—The name of the object that generated the error.
StateChange	Occurs when the state of the connection changes. Uses a StateChangeEventArgs for the event parameter. This object contains the following properties:
	CurrentState—The new state of the connection.
	OriginalState—The original state of the connection.

OleDbDataAdapter

The OleDbDataAdapter class represents a set of data commands and a database connection that are used to fill a DataSet. Table C.16 lists the properties, methods, and events of this class.

TABLE C.16 Properties, Methods, and Events of the OleDbDataAdapter Class

Property	Description
DeleteCommand	Returns an OleDbCommand object that contains a SQL statement for deleting data from the DataSet.
InsertCommand	Returns an OleDbCommand object that contains a SQL statement for inserting data into the DataSet.
SelectCommand	Returns an OleDbCommand object that contains a SQL statement for selecting data from the DataSet.
UpdateCommand	Returns an OleDbCommand object that contains a SQL statement for updating data in the DataSet.
Method	*Description*
Fill	Adds or changes rows in a DataSet to match the data source. This method is overloaded.
FillSchema	Adds a DataTable to the specified DataSet and configures the schema of the table. This method is overloaded.
GetFillParameters	Returns an array of IDataParameter objects that are used with the SELECT command.
Update	Updates the data source with the information in the DataSet using the Delete, Insert, and UpdateCommand properties. This method is overloaded.

D

TABLE C.16 continued

Event	Description
FillError	Occurs when an error is returned during a Fill operation. Uses a FillErrorEventArgs object for the event parameter. This object contains the following properties: Continue—Indicates if the operation should continue. DataTable—The DataTable being updated when the error occurred. Errors—Returns an Exception object representing the errors being handled. Values—Returns an object representing the values for the row being updated when the error occurred.
RowUpdated	Occurs after an Update command has executed. Uses an OleDbRowUpdatedEventArgs object for the event parameter. This object contains the following properties: Command—Returns the OleDbCommand executed when Update is called. Errors—Returns an Exception object representing the errors that occurred. RecordsAffected—The number of records affected. Row—Gets the DataRow used by Update. StatementType—The type of SQL statement being executed. Status—An UpdateStatus object representing the status of the command. TableMapping—Gets the DataTableMapping sent with the Update command.
RowUpdating	Occurs before an Update command has executed. Uses an OleDbRowUpdatingEventArgs object for the event parameter. This object contains the following properties: Command—Returns the OleDbCommand to execute when Update is called. Errors—Returns an Exception object representing the errors that occurred. Row—Gets the DataRow used by Update. StatementType—The type of SQL statement to execute.

TABLE C.16 continued

Event	*Description*
	`Status`—An `UpdateStatus` object representing the status of the command.
	`TableMapping`—Gets the `DataTableMapping` sent with the `Update` command.

`OleDbDataReader`

The `OleDbDataReader` class represents a lightweight, streaming method for retrieving data from a data source. It is similar to a `DataSet`, but provides less functionality with increased performance. Table C.17 lists the properties and methods of this class.

TABLE C.17 Properties and Methods of the `OleDbDataReader` Class

Property	*Description*
`Depth`	The depth of the reader.
`FieldCount`	The number of fields within the current record.
`IsClosed`	Indicates if the data reader is closed.
`Item`	The value at the specified column in its native format. This method is overloaded.
`RecordsAffected`	The number of records affected by the command. Typically, this is one if successful, less than one otherwise.
Method	***Description***
`Close`	Closes the `OleDbDataReader` object.
`GetBoolean`	Returns the value at the column specified as a `Boolean` value.
`GetByte`	Returns the value at the column specified as a `Byte` value.
`GetBytes`	Returns the value at the column specified as a `Byte` array.
`GetChar`	Returns the value at the column specified as a `Char` value.
`GetChars`	Returns the value at the column specified as a `Char` array.
`GetDataTypeName`	Returns the data type of the column specified.
`GetDateTime`	Returns the value at the column specified as a `DateTime` value.
`GetDecimal`	Returns the value at the column specified as a `Decimal` value.
`GetDouble`	Returns the value at the column specified as a `Double` value.
`GetFieldType`	Gets the `Type` that is the data type of the object.
`GetFloat`	Returns the value at the column specified as a `Float` value.

TABLE C.17 continued

Method	Description
`GetGuid`	Returns the value at the column specified as a globally unique identifier value.
`GetInt16`	Returns the value at the column specified as a 16-bit signed integer.
`GetInt32`	Returns the value at the column specified as a 32-bit signed integer.
`GetInt64`	Returns the value at the column specified as a 64-bit signed integer.
`GetName`	Returns the name of the column specified.
`GetOrdinal`	Gets the column's index, given the column name.
`GetSchemaTable`	Returns a `DataTable` object that describes the column metadata for this object.
`GetString`	Returns the value at the column specified as a `String` value.
`GetTimeSpan`	Returns the value at the column specified as a `TimeSpan` value.
`GetValue`	Returns the value at the column specified in its native format.
`GetValues`	Returns all of the attributes for the current record, and places them in a specified array.
`IsDBNull`	Used to indicate nonexistent values.
`NextResult`	Advances the reader to the next result, when reading from the results of batch SQL statements.
`Read`	Moves the reader to the next record.

`OleDbError` and `OleDbErrorCollection`

The `OleDbError` class collects information about a warning supplied from the data source. Table C.18 lists the properties of this class.

TABLE C.18 Properties of the `OleDbError` Class

Property	Description
`Message`	A short description of the error.
`NativeError`	The database-specific error information.
`Source`	Gets the object that generated the error.
`SQLState`	Retrieves the five-character standard error code for the database.

Table C.19 lists the properties and method of the `OleDbErrorCollection` class, which represents a collection of `OleDbError` objects.

TABLE C.19 Properties and Method of the `OleDbErrorCollection` OClass

Property	*Description*
`Count`	The number of errors in the collection.
`Item`	Gets an `OleDbError` in the collection with the specified index.
Method	***Description***
`CopyTo`	Copies the entire collection to an array, starting at the specified index.

`OleDbParameter` and `OleDbParameterCollection`

The `OleDbParameter` class represents a value that is passed along with a database command to provide additional information or options. Table C.20 lists the properties and method of this class.

TABLE C.20 Properties and Method of the `OleDbParameter` Class

Property	*Description*
`DbType`	The data type of the data source.
`Direction`	Indicates how the parameter will be used. Can be: `Input`, `InputOutput`, `Output`, or `ReturnValue`.
`IsNullable`	Indicates if the parameter is allowed to contain a null value.
`OleDbType`	Specifies the `Type` of this parameter. (This property does not exist in the corresponding `SqlParameter` class.)
`Offset`	The offset to the `Value` property. (This property only exists in the `SqlParameter` class.)
`ParameterName`	The name of the parameter.
`Precision`	The maximum number of digits used to represent the parameter.
`Scale`	The number of decimal places used to represent the parameter.
`Size`	The maximum size of this parameter.
`SourceColumn`	The name of the column in the data source mapped to the `DataSet` used for returning `Value`.
`SourceVersion`	Specifies the row version to use when loading data.
`Value`	The value of the parameter.
Method	***Description***
`ToString`	Returns the `ParameterName`.

Table C.21 lists the properties and methods of the `OleDbParameterCollection` class, which represents a collection of `OleDbParameter` objects.

D

TABLE C.21 Properties and Methods of the `OleDbParameterCollection` Class

Property	*Description*
`Count`	The number of `OleDbParameter` objects in the collection.
`Item`	Gets an `OleDbParameter` in the collection with either the name of the parameter or its index in the collection.
Method	***Description***
`Add`	Adds a parameter to the collection. This method is overloaded.
`Clear`	Clears the collection of all `OleDbParameter` objects.
`Contains`	Indicates if the `OleDbParameter` with the specified name exists in the collection.
`CopyTo`	Copies the entire collection to a specified array, starting at the specified index.
`IndexOf`	Retrieves the index of the specified parameter. This method is overloaded.
`Insert`	Inserts an `OleDbParameter` object at the specified index.
`Remove`	Removes the specified parameter from the collection. This method is overloaded.
`RemoveAt`	Removes the `OleDbParameter` at the specified index.

`OleDbTransaction`

The `OleDbTransaction` class represents a transaction that occurs at the data source. Table C.22 lists the properties and methods of this class.

TABLE C.22 Properties and Methods of the `OleDbTransaction` Class

Property	*Description*
`Connection`	The `OleDbConnection` object associated with this transaction.
`IsoloationLevel`	The isolation level for this transaction. Can be `Chaos`, `ReadCommitted` (default), `ReadUncommitted`, `RepeatableRead`, `Serializable`, or `Unspecified`.
Methods	***Description***
`Begin`	Starts the transaction. Subsequent commands and changes will all be stored in a transaction log pending committal, and can be rolled back at any time.
`Commit`	Commits all changes since calling `Begin`.
`RollBack`	Rolls back all changes that have been made to the data source since the `Begin` or `Commit` methods were called.

INDEX

Symbols

A

D

E

F

G

J-K

N

O

P

Q

R

S

T

W

X-Z